UNDERSTANDING
INSIDER
MOVEMENTS

Following Jesus is not a matter of one culture or nomenclature. This enlightening book presents a range of approaches and perspectives concerning indigenous Jesus movements around the world. Ultimately this crucial work encourages us to critically embrace what God is doing beyond our historic boundaries, just as God helped his people to do in Acts.

—CRAIG S. KEENER
professor of New Testament, Asbury Theological Seminary;
author of *The IVP Bible Background Commentary: New Testament*

The Cape Town Commitment has this to say about the phenomenon known as insider movements:

> This is a complex phenomenon and there is much disagreement over how to respond to it. Some commend such movements. Others warn of the danger of syncretism. Syncretism, however, is a danger found among Christians everywhere as we express our faith within our own cultures. We should avoid the tendency, when we see God at work in unexpected or unfamiliar ways, either (i) hastily to classify it and promote it as a new mission strategy, or (ii) hastily to condemn it without sensitive contextual listening.
>
> In the spirit of Barnabas who, on arrival in Antioch, "saw the evidence of the grace of God" and "was glad and encouraged them all to remain true to the Lord," we would appeal to all those who are concerned with this issue to: (1) Take as their primary guiding principle the apostolic decision and practice: "We should not make it difficult for the Gentiles who are turning to God." (2) Exercise humility, patience and graciousness in recognizing the diversity of viewpoints, and conduct conversations without stridency and mutual condemnation. (IIC.4)

This amazing and unprecedented anthology reflects that opening statement about complexity, and allows us to hear multiple voices, from those who commend and those who warn. It is a treasure chest of biblical and theological reflection and critique, along with diverse lived experience from many cultural and religious backgrounds. We hear facts through objective description and subjective testimony, and both are immensely valuable.

But what encourages me most about this volume is that its editors and contributors embody the spirit of Barnabas referred to in the second paragraph from that Cape Town Commitment section. The book as a whole and in its parts is a magnificent model of the "humility, patience and graciousness" that does its work "without stridency and mutual condemnation." For that reason, and because it fills a major gap in missiological reflection, it is to be warmly welcomed and commended.

—CHRISTOPHER J. H. WRIGHT
international ministries director for the Langham Partnership;
author of *The Mission of God* and *The Mission of God's People*

Today hundreds of thousands of Hindu, Buddhist, and Muslim people claim that they have been born again through faith in Jesus and follow the Bible as authoritative. Yet they still consider themselves members of their original religious communities. While their beliefs and spiritual experiences have changed radically, they remain loyal to their ancestral heritages. These identities are cultural more than religious, they feel. Certainly, as the Holy Spirit works in ways that we would not imagine, and human beings from all kinds of backgrounds are drawn to Jesus, their journeys transcend our categories. This volume explores that movement.

—MIRIAM ADENEY
associate professor of world Christian studies, Seattle Pacific University;
author of *Kingdom without Borders* and *Daughters of Islam*

God is doing a new thing in our days, as he did in the "insider movement" in the early gatherings of believers (church) within the synagogues and Jewish society at large. Given the present widespread understanding of "church planting" and reproducing stereotypical "churches," this compilation of articles makes the reader rethink our methodology for effective ways of influencing communities from within. I am very pleased that these articles have been written by friends who have actually experienced and worked with insider movements for years and who do not just rely on theories. I have known a few of them personally for many years, becoming familiar with their work, and interacted with many of them at different times over the years.

These bold experiments and results are a breath of fresh air in the midst of replanting denominational churches. Mission leaders tend to reproduce the forms and practices of the churches they have come from, such as priestly cassocks, styles, songs, hymns, and liturgies, which make no sense to many peoples of the countries where they earnestly labor.

I am grateful for the authors from across the world who are talking about the theme of insider movements. These writings should be treated as a manual and taught in the circles of new movements of missionaries from *ethne* to *ethne* in our globalized world. These principles must be put into practice, for the sake of both local peoples and the growing diasporas of professionals, refugees, students, and family migrants. The world is at our doorstep, and we need to recognize and initiate insider movements in every region of the world. I highly recommend this book as a rethinking of how we must take the good news of Christ to the ends of the earth.

—K. RAJENDRAN
World Evangelical Alliance Mission Commission, Bangalore, India

Regardless of one's position on insider movements, this volume represents an important contribution to missiological understanding.

—DAVID GARRISON
missionary and author of *A Wind in the House of Islam*

Understanding Insider Movements takes the traditional Christian on an illuminating journey through the eye of the needle and into grassroots, Jesus-following, but not Christian, religious movements. This is essential reading for American Christian leaders to comprehend how God is transforming people within their religious culture. Christians should not be watching these developments on the sidelines, but rather actively engaging these Jesus followers to learn from them and share in discipleship. The authors are honest in addressing the controversy and opportunity within insider movements, which are on the growth edge of the global body of Christ. Readers will be delighted with the comprehensive scope of this book.

—TIM MORGAN
senior editor of global journalism, *Christianity Today*

This book is like a swath of light slicing through the many murky issues surrounding Jesus movements in Muslim countries. It also holds up before us the difficulties posed by our historical moment: a reprise of the Jew-Gentile social crisis of the first century.

In the same way that early Jewish followers were faced with new and strange wineskins emerging from Greek customs and habits of thought, today's "Christian West" is now being made nervous by a gospel making its way within religious traditions that rival Christianity in social and philosophical depth. The book squarely puts before us the challenge of contextualization within Muslim cultures, framing it within the larger work of God in discipling the "nations." It goads us to once for all step out of the shadows of the old wineskins of "Christendom" and discern the fresh outbreak of the Spirit within the structures of other human cultures, which at bottom are all religiously based at any rate.

I heartily recommend this book to all who wish to catch the fresh wind of the Spirit that is now at work among their own peoples.

—MELBA PADILLA MAGGAY
president of the Institute for Studies in Asian Church and Culture

Imagine having about fifty authors from more than ten nations, with cross-cultural experience from every corner of the globe, sharing a conversation about what it takes to be a follower of Christ among various living faiths. Furthermore, allow for a diversity of opinions all the way from strong support to ambivalence to friendly critique, all of them supported by a careful and hospitable biblical-theological and practical argumentation. What kind of book would you have? This is exactly what you are holding in hand right now! And the topic is one of the most burning ones in Christian mission, often titled "insider movements." Take up and read!

—VELI-MATTI KÄRKKÄINEN
professor of systematic theology, Fuller Theological Seminary;
docent of ecumenics on the Faculty of Theology, University of Helsinki

Harley Talman and John Jay Travis's massive collection of essays on insider movements has been for me a true revelation. It provides a powerful way of understanding the real essence of New Testament faith as the following of Jesus of Nazareth, as well as an equally powerful way of understanding what contextualizing our faith might really mean. Most of all, reading the essays in this collection gave me a glimpse into how the Jerusalem community in Acts 15 might have viewed the Gentile Christian community in Antioch, and how radical was the community's decision in the same chapter as they and the Holy Spirit decided to impose "no further burden" but the essentials.

—STEPHEN B. BEVANS
Louis J. Luzbetak, SVD, Professor Emeritus of Mission and Culture,
Catholic Theological Union;
author of *Models of Contextual Theology*

God is obviously doing something among people within the major religions that we have not seen before, as thousands are submitting to Jesus Christ. It often gets messy as his new followers pick their way out of the old dominions and into his kingdom of light. The route is so uncharted and perilous that many of us who are watching are skeptical that it can even be done. Consequently, controversy rules at a time when we should, instead, be praising God and interceding for these new family members.

This anthology, *Understanding Insider Movements*, is an essential read for anyone who is seriously interested in the growth of the gospel in our world. You probably won't agree with everything you read; some of it might even set you off. But this is a serious work, done by over fifty authors, most of whom have devoted decades of their lives to this enterprise. They have been there and speak out of firsthand experience. But there is something else they have in common that makes this book so valuable: the message they communicate can be summarized in one person, Jesus Christ. And they are unwavering in their commitment to Scripture and in their confidence that the Holy Spirit will do his part.

—JIM PETERSEN
missionary and author of *Church without Walls*

I am impressed. Talman and Travis have given us not simply a large book, but a veritable library of source material to help grasp the significance and nature of a growing phenomenon that is changing the way ministry is done among adherents to the major world religions. The fundamental premise should not be strange to a Christian—namely, that institutional religious adherence, whether to Christianity or another religion, is secondary to grasping the life-changing dynamic of Jesus Christ. The book incorporates the thinking of both Western and non-Western (i.e., Majority World) writers, explaining how they view the reality of Jesus followers who remain within the context of their social, cultural, and religious communities. Can this really happen? Is it really happening? Should this affect the way I minister the good news? This volume goes a long way toward answering these questions. It should be a part of missionary preparation in general, contextualization courses, and specific preparation for particular religious settings.

—MICHAEL POCOCK
senior professor emeritus at Dallas Theological Seminary

We would prefer our life to consist of easy answers of right and wrong, as in the digital world. But already at the interfaces between the digital and the real world it becomes very clear that an application is quite difficult. In intercultural cooperation, especially, we become aware pretty fast that thinking in those categories prevents any progress. Life is much more complicated and diverse. Our perception is tainted by our culture of origin; everything we see and perceive we assess through our cultural lenses, which influence our understanding. Every reader of this book reads it in the light of his or her previous experiences and automatically applies this to his or her understanding of insider movements.

Our situation in Europe clearly shows the difficulties of developing a common understanding for Europe. Languages and cultures are quite different, and individual European nations have already been marked by cultural diversity through migration. Similarly, among Christians there are quite different views on mission and contextualization, so it was to be expected that the topic of insider movements would raise further issues.

After many discussions about insider movements and the question of what it is all about anyway, you now hold in your hands a book that finally shows their diversity and different forms. I highly recommend making the effort and getting involved in the broadening of your horizon. Only a few will have the opportunity to get in contact with insider movements, but we should have confidence in those who engage themselves that they will make every effort to contextualize the gospel in a good way.

Culture is not static but needs to be seen as a changing process, and so every insider movement is changing and different. God as God the Creator is still changing us and this world. "Therefore, if anyone is in Christ, he is a new creation; old things have passed away; behold, all things have become new" (2 Cor 5:17).

—Wolfgang Büsing
chairman of the European Evangelical Mission Association

One of the biggest obstacles to the gospel in non-Christian religious communities has been the idea that they must leave family and society to come to Christ. Insider movements open a way for them to remain. This is probably the best book to date to help understand this methodology and theology.

—Patrick Cate
president emeritus of Christar

As it was in the beginning, is now, and always will be—the good news of Jesus Christ is being received into the lives of people in worshiping communities around the world in transformative ways. In testimony after testimony, this wise and careful anthology leads the inquiring reader into the lives of people who find in Jesus Christ the love and hope for which they hunger and thirst. What happens to their worshiping lives when people receive the transforming grace of Jesus Christ? This volume tells us. Seekers, life-long Christians, new followers of Jesus Christ, Muslims, Hindus, Daoists, comparative historians, and more will find in this volume deep insight into the manifesting of God's kingdom now, here in this world, in ways that carry us beyond the modern stumbling block of "religions" into new vistas of understanding God's intentions for healing and transformation.

—Diane B. Obenchain
professor of religion, Fuller Theological Seminary;
former professor of religious studies, Calvin College (2005–14)

The God of the universe lived among us as a contextualized, parochial human being. We who by the Spirit's guidance follow that risen Galilean do so in a vast array of ever-changing parochial socioreligious contexts. In order to be faithful and prophetic witnesses in our contexts, to be in the world but not of it, we all need the friendship and input of others who are contextually different. These carefully compiled essays, through their attention to "insider movements," give biblical, historical, missiological, and practical insights for all of Jesus' followers to live faithfully and prophetically—whether our socioreligious contexts have been partially shaped by one of the many Christian traditions or by one of the many other religious traditions. In the shifting, kaleidoscopic religious landscape of the early twenty-first century, including a North American landscape marked by the unraveling for many of an assumed and settled Christian way of life, these essays provide a welcome stimulus to hear afresh through the Scriptures and through others how God works in people's lives, as well as how people in turn seek to follow their Savior and Master, Jesus of Nazareth.

—Rev. J. Nelson Jennings
former executive director of the Overseas Ministries Study Center
and editor of the *International Bulletin of Missionary Research*

The global expansion and maturation of the church have proved to be fertile soil for renewing our theology and practice, if we're willing to listen to one another. Establishing gospel presence and witness in new contexts forces us to more nuanced hermeneutics and theologizing than some are comfortable with. And that's good. Both the push to innovate and the pull to conserve are valuable forces in the church. This book gives voice and an opportunity to view from many perspectives what many consider the most intriguing challenge of contextualization that the church has faced in recent years. What a blessing for us all.

—Mark Young
president of Denver Seminary

Understanding Insider Movements is a must-read for those concerned with the progress of God's kingdom in today's world. However, it is not a volume to be digested in a single evening. *Understanding Insider Movements* is a monumental work—a collection of sixty articles by fifty contributors—some six hundred pages. Harley Talman and John Jay Travis, as both editors and contributors, have produced a truly historic publication. Articles are well written and carefully reasoned, inviting reflection and thoughtful discussion, while challenging a number of traditional understandings of God's actions in history. In the process *Understanding Insider Movements* accomplishes its purposes with a spirit of grace, humility, and openness. A magnificent work.

—Robert C. Douglas
former director of the Zwemer Institute for Muslim Studies

I have heard so many things said about insider movements that were not true. We need to find the right way to deal with this issue in light of the Bible. This book should assist us toward that end.

—Moussa Bongoyok
assistant professor of intercultural studies, Biola University;
founder of the Francophone University of International Development

The scope and scholarship of this book are impressive in that it seeks to answer questions not only about insider movements among Muslims but also about those among Hindus, Buddhists, Sikhs, and Jews. The material by some fifty contributing authors covers biblical, theological, and historical material, plus case studies from around the globe. Given the significant number of polemical works on such movements in recent years and the ongoing controversy, this was waiting to be written, and every one of the sixty-four chapters is worth reading. Because of the risk of syncretism and concern for the purity of the gospel, not all questions are answered, but there is little doubt that God is doing a new thing among the major religions of the world.

—Warren Larson
professor emeritus at the Zwemer Center for Muslim Studies, Columbia International University

Understanding Insider Movements moves beyond being just a collection of previous articles to include fresh contributions to the subject. What results is a valuable collection of articles from over forty practitioners and writers covering the major issues regarding insider movements. Regardless of one's particular understanding of these movements to Jesus in diverse cultures and faith traditions, this volume serves as a valuable reference tool to clarify misunderstandings and wrestle with theological, missiological, cultural, and ethical issues raised. While other works have brought to wider attention the reality of the movement of God's Spirit across the Muslim world, this work will serve those wishing to delve deeper into understanding the various ways God's mission is being "leaven in the lump" across various religious communities. Therefore, it is a must-have reference for anyone seriously concerned with God's mission in today's divided world. It serves as a benchmark in the discussion of mission. I would hope that it will encourage an increasing flow of research, direct accounts, and testimonies from within insider movements so that both etic and emic practitioners will be enabled to cooperate with God's purposes for all peoples.

—Jerald Whitehouse
former director of the Global Center for Adventist-Muslim Relations

That the insider movement phenomenon has in the last few decades attracted a lot of attention and debate within missiological circles is a given fact. Some of the conversations and debates have been very productive and enlightening. Unfortunately, others have been acrimonious and divisive. Part of the confusion, though, is due to the fact that the phenomenon—or rather the ways it has hitherto been articulated—appeared new, fluid, and controversial to many. The range of chapters in this volume, mostly written by scholar-missionaries with firsthand experience of insider movements, and by Muslim believers in Jesus, sheds fresh light and helpful insights that will move the conversation forward. This volume will certainly not satisfactorily answer all the critics. Nevertheless, the spirit and scholarship contained here are highly commendable to those who are genuinely seeking to understand and engage with what God may be doing in the Muslim world in our generation.

—JOHN AZUMAH
professor of world Christianity and Islam, Columbia Theological Seminary

Beating the same drum the same way only produces the same sound. People long for the sound of the orchestra, a harmony of notes that satisfies the soul. The blending of the sound of instruments tells a story that fulfills longing. *Insider* is the sound of a symphony waiting to be played. *Insider* is the message of grace from a God of grace who conducts the orchestra. The orchestra, composed of a wide range of instruments and mutually dependent musicians, delivers the redemptive song through a new sound. *Understanding Insider Movements* is worth the listen.

—WARREN REEVE
vice president of the National Evangelical Church of Kuwait;
founder of the Missional International Church Network

UNDERSTANDING
INSIDER
MOVEMENTS

DISCIPLES OF JESUS
WITHIN DIVERSE
RELIGIOUS COMMUNITIES

HARLEY
TALMAN

JOHN JAY
TRAVIS

EDITORS

WILLIAM CAREY
LIBRARY

Published by William Carey Library
1605 E. Elizabeth Street
Pasadena, CA 91104 | www.missionbooks.org

Brad Koenig, copyeditor
Josie Leung, graphic design
Rose Lee-Norman, indexer

Cover concept by Dawn High

William Carey Library is a ministry of
Frontier Ventures | www.frontierventures.org

Printed in the United States of America

19 18 17 16 15   5 4 3 2 1 BP1000

Library of Congress Cataloging-in-Publication Data

Understanding insider movements: disciples of Jesus within diverse religious cultures / Harley Talman and John Jay Travis, editors.

    pages cm

Includes bibliographical references and index.

ISBN 978-0-87808-041-0 -- ISBN 0-87808-041-4 1. Insider movements. I. Talman, Harley, editor of compilation.

BR128.I57U53 2014

280--dc23

                    2014016579

To the many thousands of disciples of Jesus
who bear witness to him as insiders

CONTENTS

SIDEBARS

Ahmad Abdul-Rashid was born and raised in a Muslim family in Asia. Jesus Christ has been his Lord and Savior for more than twenty years, and his wife and three children are following Jesus with him. He is working on a PhD in comparative religions from an Islamic university.

Martin Accad directs the Institute of Middle East Studies at the Arab Baptist Theological Seminary in Lebanon. Accad is currently writing a book, through the Langham Writer's Grant, on moving beyond conflict in Christian-Muslim dialogue. He holds a PhD from Oxford University.

Eric Adams and his family led a pioneering team to an unreached people in Asia for many years. More recently they have been involved in mentoring and training initiatives while residing in Britain, investing in the next generation of workers.

Jens Barnett lived for eighteen years with his family in the Middle East, heavily involved in the discipleship and training of believers coming from a Muslim religiocultural background. He holds a master's degree in global issues in contemporary mission from Redcliffe College, United Kingdom.

Leonard N. (Len) Bartlotti is an ethnographic folklorist, educator, strategist, and consultant to humanitarian organizations. He served for fourteen years among a large Muslim tribal people, and earned his PhD from the Oxford Centre for Mission Studies, University of Wales.

Paul-Gordon Chandler is the rector of the Anglican/Episcopal Church of St. John the Baptist in Cairo, Egypt. He grew up in French-speaking West Africa and has visited over one hundred countries working with ministries such as the International Bible Society, SPCK, and the Anglican Church. From 1999 to 2003 he was president and CEO of Partners International, a Christian relief and development ministry that serves Christian minorities.

O. Kandaswami Chetti (1867–1943) was a Hindu follower of Christ whose vision embodied the insider paradigm. He had fellowship with others in the body of Christ, but did not join the existing Indian churches or change his identity to "Christian," as he sought to prepare the way for a movement to Christ from within Hindu society.

Virginia Cobb (1927–70) was a Southern Baptist missionary to Lebanon. Her groundbreaking paper to the Tehran Conference of June 1969 on missionary approaches among Muslims emphasized witness to the person of Jesus rather than specific religious affiliations or doctrine.

Joseph Cumming and his family lived for fifteen years in a Muslim community in North Africa. He has served as director of the Reconciliation Program at the Yale Center for Faith and Culture, Yale University, and meets regularly with senior Muslim leaders around the world. (For more information, visit www.josephcumming.com.)

Frank Decker has worked in cross-cultural disciple-making ministry through The Mission Society since 1986. He served in Ghana until moving to Atlanta in 1994 to focus on the training and development of cross-cultural workers. His formal education includes a BA from West Virginia Wesleyan College and an MDiv from Emory University. He has written over sixty columns and articles on missions.

Darren Duerksen is currently the director and assistant professor of intercultural studies at Fresno Pacific University. He has worked in India in various capacities for the past ten years, focusing on researching and resourcing those working among Hindu and Sikh communities. He has published this and other work based on his PhD research at Fuller Theological Seminary.

Gavriel Gefen is an observant Jewish follower of Jesus. He is the founding director of Keren HaShlichut (www.shlichut.com), Israel's first mission sending agency. Gefen has served among more than five hundred different tribal peoples in more than 130 countries.

Tim Green has enjoyed the friendship of Christ's followers from Muslim background since 1979. He worked in South Asia (1988–2003) and in the Middle East (2003–2005) with in-context training programs for national Christians. He currently assists indigenous programs in different parts of Asia that equip and empower believers through local mentoring groups.

Bradford Greer has worked to facilitate a church-planting movement among a Muslim unreached people group in South Asia for twenty-five years. He has been a contributing author to the *International Journal of Frontier Missiology, St. Francis Magazine,* and *Evangelical Missions Quarterly.* He holds a PhD in intercultural studies from Fuller Theological Seminary.

Archbishop Gregoire Haddad is Metropolitan Archbishop emeritus of Beirut–Gibail of the Greek-Melkites (Greek Catholic Church) in Lebanon and Titular Archbishop of Adana. He is the founder of several social and cultural organizations and a journal. He was awarded an honorary doctorate in social sciences by the Lebanese University, and his lifetime achievements in civic activism were honored by the American University of Beirut.

Kevin Higgins has lived in several Muslim countries and is currently involved in Bible translation, training men and women from a variety of countries for more sensitive and effective cross-cultural communication, and encouraging believers in Jesus to follow him in the context of their cultures and communities. He is recognized by many for his writings on these issues. He holds a PhD in intercultural studies from Fuller Theological Seminary.

Herbert Hoefer served for fifteen years as a missionary of the Lutheran Church–Missouri Synod (LCMS) to India. He is currently professor of theology at Concordia University, Portland, Oregon, and LCMS area director for India and Sri Lanka. He is also the chairman of the Rethinking Hindu Ministry Forum. His writings have been primarily on the subject of faith and culture, most notably in the book *Churchless Christianity* (William Carey Library, 2001), about the non-baptized believers in Christ in India.

Kyle Holton worked for nine years in northern Mozambique among the Yao, helping initiate grassroots community initiatives based upon natural resources, sustainability, and group cooperation. With an MA in intercultural studies from Wheaton Graduate School and an MS in environmental science from Johns Hopkins University, Holton has interests in development theory, interreligious dialogue, orality, and cultural ecology.

Joshua Iyadurai (PhD, University of Madras) is director of the Mylapore Institute for Indigenous Studies in Chennai. He is a guest faculty member at the University of Madras in Chennai and on the faculty of the Center for Advanced Theological Studies, SHIATS, in Allahabad, India. He can be reached at jiyadurai@gmail.com.

Richard Jameson (ThM, Dallas Theological Seminary) taught New Testament at a seminary in East Asia, where he assisted national Christians in planting more contextually appropriate churches in the Muslim community. He has been walking alongside new communities of Muslim-background followers of Jesus in various Asian countries for over twenty-five years and currently oversees international ministries of a mission agency.

Abu Jaz started following Jesus the Messiah as the Savior about twenty years ago. He is a key leader in a movement of several thousand Muslims in eastern Africa who have come to faith in Christ but remained socially and culturally a part of their Muslim communities. He is married and has three children.

Eli Stanley Jones (1884–1973), a Methodist missionary, has been called the "Billy Graham of India," having delivered a host of religious lectures to the country's educated classes. His friendship with Mahatma Gandhi and India's foremost thinkers and leaders prompted him to reflect on the growing attraction to the person of Jesus within Hindu society, something he described in *The Christ of the Indian Road*, which sold over a million copies globally. Jones was also the founder of the Christian Ashram movement.

Charles H. Kraft served as a missionary in Nigeria with his wife, Marguerite. He retired after forty years as professor of anthropology and intercultural communication at Fuller Theological Seminary's School of Intercultural Studies. He teaches and writes in the areas of anthropology, worldview, contextualization, cross-cultural communication, inner healing, and spiritual warfare.

Rebecca Lewis and her husband, Tim, live with three generations of their family in Muslim Asia, having realized that God's plan has always been to covenant with godly families and through them to bless all the families of the earth.

Samuel Livingway and his family live in the Muslim world. He has worked full-time with Muslims for the past twelve years and has been in ministry for twenty-three. He holds an MDiv from Fuller Theological Seminary and a ThM from Princeton Theological Seminary, and is currently pursuing a doctorate investigating what the Qur'an says specifically about the Bible.

Mazhar Mallouhi identifies himself as a "Sufi Muslim follower of Christ." He founded and directs Al-Kalima, which produces and distributes books and new Arabic translations of Scripture that are understandable to Muslim readers. Author of the first Arabic Christian novel, Mazhar currently has five in print. His story is told in *Pilgrims of Christ on the Muslim Road: Exploring a New Path between Two Faiths* by Paul-Gordon Chandler (Rowman and Littlefield, 2008).

Paul McKaughan and his wife ministered in Brazil for fourteen years. He served as coordinator of the missions entity of the Presbyterian Church in America, was COO for the Lausanne Congress on World Evangelization, and coordinated the Second Lausanne Congress. His last assignment was as president of the Evangelical Fellowship of Mission Agencies for fifteen years. McKaughan has been granted honorary doctorates by Denver Seminary and Belhaven College.

Ben Naja has served among unreached Muslim people groups in different countries in Africa for the last twenty years. In partnership with local ministries, he has trained, facilitated, and coached numerous church-planting tentmakers for cross-cultural pioneer ministry in several African and Asian countries. He is also involved in training disciples and developing leaders in two emerging movements from Muslim background. Together with his spouse and children, he currently lives and ministers in eastern Africa.

Phil Parshall served with SIM (Serving in Mission) for forty-four years in Bangladesh and the Philippines. He earned a DMiss from Fuller Theological Seminary and has authored numerous articles in missions journals and nine books on Islam, including the groundbreaking *New Paths in Muslim Evangelism: Evangelical Approaches to Contextualization* (Baker, 1980).

Tom Payne moved into one of the world's largest unengaged Muslim people groups in 1996, and since then has seen God do amazing miracles as Muslims who follow Jesus witness to and pray for other Muslims in Jesus' name. Payne is very active in peace and reconciliation efforts between Muslims and Christians through education and interfaith prayer, while facilitating peace-promoting events at both a local and national level.

Sheila Pritchard is a New Zealander, spiritual director and supervisor of spiritual directors, retreat and workshop leader, and writer. She taught spiritual formation for twenty years at the Bible College of New Zealand. She has a blog at www.sheilapritchard.blogspot.com.

H. L. Richard was involved in grassroots Christian ministry in India for ten years before devoting another ten years to the study of Hinduism and Christian work among Hindus, with a focus on what have been called insider movements. He has published a number of books and many articles related to the gospel of Christ in the Hindu world.

Kurt Anders Richardson (DTh in historical and contemporary theology, University of Basel) is professor of Abrahamic studies at the Graduate Institute of Applied Linguistics in Dallas, Texas. He previously served on the theological faculties of the University of Toronto, McMaster University, and Gordon-Conwell and Southeastern Baptist seminaries. He is co-founder of the Society for Scriptural Reasoning and Comparative Theology research groups in the American Academy of Religion and is regularly invited to lecture and publish internationally.

John Ridgway has taught as a professor and worked as a multinational consultant in Asia for twenty-seven years and coached missionary teams for over forty. He has seen responses in the Hindu, Muslim, Buddhist, Shinto, and secular mainstreams of Asia, with these families in turn influencing their natural relational networks. Ridgway has contributed related articles to the *International Journal of Frontier Missiology* and *Mission Frontiers*. He holds a PhD in physics.

Henry H. Riggs (1875–1943) was born in Sivas, Turkey, to a family of missionaries stationed in the Ottoman Empire. He traveled to the United States to attend Carleton College in Minnesota and Auburn Seminary. Riggs served as president of Euphrates College in Harpoot, Turkey, from 1903 to 1910, and continued to do missionary work there (1912–17). He worked as a teacher and evangelist among Armenian refugees in Beirut from 1923 to 1940 and died in Jerusalem.

Michael Roberts has been involved with Muslims in the Middle East since 1976, living there with his family for twenty-two years. He has an MA in applied linguistics, is a certified Arabic translator, and has studied the Bible and Qur'an in the original languages and translated them.

Taweeporn Sarun, born in 1963, has been a Buddhist follower of Christ for only a few years. Saved and serving by grace, she lives in a Buddhist community, ministering to Buddhist people. She has almost no firsthand experience of Western Christian culture, only a fourth-grade education, and no competency in English.

Hanna Shahin is a Palestinian who was raised in the old city of Jerusalem. Transformed by the grace of God, he became a Christian broadcaster and for many years headed the Arabic Ministry of Trans World Radio, impacting millions of listeners from Iraq to Morocco. In 2005 he and his wife, Evelyn, founded a church-planting ministry, Endure International. Shahin holds degrees in theology, philosophy, psychology, biblical counseling, and missiology.

Alex G. Smith is minister-at-large for OMF International. He travels extensively across the globe for training and speaking. He was northwest director for OMF International (US) from 1984 to 2002. Prior to that he spent twenty years as a pioneer church planter in central Thailand.

Wilbur Stone (PhD, intercultural studies, Asbury Theological Seminary) has served as professor of global evangelization and contextual ministry, and as program director of the MA in global and contextual studies at Bethel Seminary, St. Paul, Minnesota. Prior to that he served as a missionary in Hong Kong and Malaysia, spending twelve years overseas and fifteen years in pastoral ministry.

Harley Talman lived for almost two decades in the Arab world and Africa, culminating in God using him to help dozens of Muslim village chiefs become followers of Christ. Having served in church planting, field leadership, theological education, and humanitarian aid, he now directs a center for Islamic studies, writes, and teaches internationally on ministry among Muslims. His education includes a ThM (Dallas Theological Seminary) and a PhD in Islamic studies.

Anthony Taylor has worked in the Muslim world for over two decades and currently serves as president of a mission agency. He has a PhD in intercultural studies.

David Taylor is a research director, strategy coordinator, and mobilizer for frontier missions. He is currently engaged in research on twenty-five insider movements taking place in the Muslim world. David's field experience includes ten years serving among Muslims in the Philippines.

Anna Travis, along with her family, has lived most of her adult life in Muslim communities. Her ministry involvement has included outreach, discipleship, community development, healing prayer, and intercessory prayer. Anna has authored and coauthored journal articles and chapters in books as well as a training manual on inner healing and deliverance. She holds an MA in intercultural studies from Fuller Theological Seminary.

John Jay Travis has lived extensively in Muslim communities, twice with Muslim families. With experience in church planting, community development projects, and Bible translation, he has written on the topics of cross-cultural ministry, contextualization, and healing prayer. Presently he and his wife, Anna, train and teach throughout the Muslim world. John holds a PhD in intercultural studies and is an affiliate faculty member at Fuller Theological Seminary's School of Intercultural Studies.

K. Venkatesh is an international scientist with experience in both the United States and India. He is an aeronautical engineer by training and is also a very committed believer who follows Jesus.

Andrew Walls is one of the leading missiologists and historians of Christian mission. He is an honorary professor at Edinburgh University, where he was founder and director of the Centre for the Study of Christianity in the Non-Western World.

Banpote Wetchgama describes himself as a servant of God who wants to see Christ born again in other cultures. He was instrumental in the movement of thousands of people to Christ in the Isaan region of Thailand and in articulating the theology of the movement.

Jesse S. Wheeler is the central administrator and projects manager for the Institute of Middle East Studies (IMES), Lebanon. He is managing editor of the IMES blog (www.imeslebanon.wordpress.com), directs the Middle East Immersion summer practicum program, is the programs support faculty member for the Master of Religion in Middle Eastern and North African Studies degree, and provides logistical support for the annual Middle East Consultation.

Ralph D. Winter (1924–2009) served for ten years as a missionary among Mayan Indians in the highlands of Guatemala. He was then called to be a professor at Fuller Theological Seminary's School of World Mission. Ten years later, he and his wife, Roberta (1930–2001), founded the Frontier Mission Fellowship in Pasadena, California, and he became the general director, also birthing the U.S. Center for World Mission and William Carey International University.

J. Dudley Woodberry is dean emeritus and senior professor of missions at Fuller Theological Seminary's School of Intercultural Studies, specializing in Islamic studies. His major ministry experience has been in Pakistan, Afghanistan, and Saudi Arabia. Woodberry's most recent edited book is *From Seed to Fruit: Global Trends, Fruitful Practices, and Emerging Issues among Muslims* (William Carey Library, 2011). He holds a PhD in Islamic studies from Harvard University.

Mark Young (ThM, Dallas Theological Seminary; PhD in educational studies, Trinity Evangelical Divinity School) is president of Denver Seminary. He was founding academic dean of the Evangelical Theological Seminary in Wroclaw, Poland, and served as professor of missions at Dallas Theological Seminary. He has written and spoken on issues in theological education and mission for numerous international symposia and conferences.

Brother Yusuf is one of the spiritual leaders of the insider movements in his country. He and his colleagues have often endured persecution instigated by religious clerics, both Muslim and Christian.

ABBREVIATIONS

BMB   believer from a Muslim background

CT   *Christianity Today*

EMQ   *Evangelical Missions Quarterly*

HYB   Hindu Yeshu bhakta

IBMR   *International Bulletin of Missionary Research*

IJFM   *International Journal of Frontier Missiology*
(formerly *International Journal of Frontier Missions*)

IM   insider movement

JMW   Jesus movement within

MBB   Muslim-background believer

MF   *Mission Frontiers*

MFC   Muslim follower of Christ

NBBC   non-baptized believer in Christ

UIM   *Understanding Insider Movements*

FOREWORD
Toward Mutual Understanding, Edification, and Cooperation

Recently I sat at a table with colleagues who were involved with new movements of followers of Jesus from Muslim families. We had different perspectives on insider movements (IMs), but we had common concerns: we all wanted to see these new followers of Jesus grow in their faith and witness through Bible study and fellowship with other believers and develop a second generation of mature followers of Christ. This led us first to seek to understand each other, correct our misunderstandings where necessary, and then cooperate to the extent possible.

The current volume is intended as a step in this direction. Much has been written on the topic of IMs by those who have never seen one and hence must rely on hearsay and conjecture. The editors of the current collection of essays have had years of experience both with traditional churches and missions and with IMs in Asia and Africa. For example, John Travis and his wife, Anna, after eighteen years of praying and sharing with Muslims in Asia, saw a small IM begin in their own neighborhood while they were temporarily out of the country. This IM began with the witness of a respected middle-aged Muslim woman who had studied the Bible for years and had just recently begun praying with Anna (see chap. 16). Harley Talman, in turn, discipled Muslim tribal sheikhs in a war-torn African country. They were drawn to the stories of the prophets that point to Jesus—who came not to establish a new religion, but to bring the kingdom of God. Dozens of sheikhs decided together to become his followers so that the gospel could transform their communities.

My own exposure to IMs resulted from my being asked to oversee a three-year study of new movements to Christ in Asia and Africa that included an IM in South Asia. Those in the latter group said that they felt closer to God when reading the Gospel than when reading the Qur'an and were studying the Gospel on a regular basis. When surveyed again five years later, these believers had grown considerably in their understanding of the Bible and in spiritual maturity.

The importance of IMs was found in the most comprehensive recent research on fruitful practices of field workers among Muslims, including both nationals as well as expatriates. The study showed that the more the newly planted fellowships were contextualized to the Muslim community, the more they began to spread spontaneously.[1] A major reason for this was that the IM believers remained within their social networks.[2] While this certainly is not the most important factor, it is significant.

---

1   See Rick Brown, Bob Fish, John Travis, Eric Adams, and Don Allen, "Movements and Contextualization: Is There Really a Correlation?" *IJFM* 26, no. 1 (2009): 21–23. Teams that planted three or more churches/fellowships had all been involved in contextualized plants—6 percent used mother tongue and cultural but not "Muslim" forms; 22 percent used mother tongue and biblically acceptable "Muslim" forms; and 39 percent were Christ- and Bible-centered but at the same time culturally and officially Muslim (i.e., IMs).

2   Andrea and Leith Gray, "Transforming Social Networks by Planting the Gospel" and "Attractional and Transformational Models of Planting," in *From Seed to Fruit: Global Trends, Fruitful Practices, and Emerging Issues*

One problem is what to call these movements. This book uses "insider movements," since this is the most common term; however, I like the contrast of the "attractional model" of the traditional church and the "transformational model" of the IMs. Both are biblical concepts. The traditional churches seek to use the "attractional model" (see Matt 5:14–16), but often cultural, ethnic, and historical factors hinder this approach both from the Muslim and Christian sides. On the other hand, the "transformational model" (see Rom 12:2) of planting the gospel in social networks allows the inquirers to be transformed in their context through group Bible study conducted under the enabling of the Holy Spirit.[3]

The present book is an anthology of articles on IMs. As such it represents a variety of views. As Kevin Higgins observes (chap. 5), everything that you have heard about China is true in some part of China. The same might be said about IMs. Here, however, the emphasis is on what is typically true of these movements. Therefore he deals with certain misconceptions of IMs, such as that they are primarily the result of pressure from expatriates, or are watering down the gospel, or are attempts to avoid persecution.

Others, such as Tim Green (sidebar, chap. 58), Eric Adams (chap. 61), and Jens Barnett (chap. 62) note that people in transition tend to have dual or even multiple identities—core, social, and collective. Though not focusing on IMs specifically, their findings are helpful to us in understanding them. The core identity of Jesus followers in IMs is their relationship with God through Jesus. Their social identity with their family and coworkers and their collective identity in their society place them within the broader Muslim community of which they are a part. John and Anna Travis (chap. 63) note the factors that influence the identity that Jesus followers choose—such as whether the national church (if any) is culturally and ethnically compatible with the Muslim community, or is welcoming or defensive. IMs are seen as valid to bring the gospel to communities that in many cases the traditional church can barely reach at all. Their identities evolve as the new Jesus followers study God's word in fellowship together.

God is working across the spectrum of Jesus followers as never before. If we from different perspectives can sit around a table as a group of us did recently, we can seek to understand each other, change our perspectives if needed, and cooperate where we can. If we do, that table can be a foretaste of the table that Jesus is preparing for all his followers in his kingdom (Mark 14:25).

J. Dudley Woodberry
dean emeritus and senior professor of Islamic studies
School of Intercultural Studies, Fuller Theological Seminary

---

among Muslims, 2nd ed., ed. J. Dudley Woodberry (Pasadena, CA: William Carey Library, 2011), 275–308.

3   See Gray, "Transforming Social Networks" and "Attractional and Transformational Models," in Woodberry, *From Seed to Fruit.*

ACKNOWLEDGMENTS

"One hand can't clap" is a proverbial truth shared by many cultures. This book is truly the result of many pairs of hands. From start to finish it has been a marvelous team effort.

Before acknowledging the many people who in some way were a part of this team, we begin by giving thanks and praise to God, from whom all blessings flow, the one who holds our very lives in his hands. Without his constant care and inspiration, this project would never have happened.

The backbone of this anthology is the combined writings of over fifty authors hailing from more than a dozen nations, some of whom are now with the Lord in glory. Collectively they have lived and worked in every corner of the world and in many different religious communities. Not all of them are necessarily proponents of insider movements; however, in each case something they have written or some tool they have developed is very helpful in bringing clarity to this field of study, and they were gracious enough to allow their thoughts to appear here. To all contributors to this book, we express our heartfelt thanks.

Thanks are also in order to the many publishing houses and journals that granted us permission to reprint articles that they had previously published.

As is the case with many writing projects, we originally conceived of a much shorter volume. However, as we sought input from colleagues around the world, the number of articles and breadth of issues to address increased. To accommodate the larger number of chapters and sections, a team of graduate students from Fuller Theological Seminary's School of Intercultural Studies volunteered many hours to give us input on new articles and invaluable assistance in assembling this large manuscript. Special thanks go to Amanda, who coordinated this effort, and to her fellow graduate students Katharina, Hannah, and Mark.

How we appreciate the team of publishers at William Carey Library! Jeff Minard, the manager of WCL, was a joy to work with during all phases of the project. We also give our special thanks to the team of amazing editors—Suzanne, Melissa, Aidan, Mel, and Brad.

We also extend special thanks to David Taylor, author of one of the chapters in the book and associate editor of the anthology. His extensive efforts, keen insight, and experience as an author of several other books were of great help. We are indebted to others, particularly Jeff and Pat Feinberg and Anthony Taylor, who volunteered their expertise in editing several articles, as well as to Anna Travis and Gavriel Gefen for their review of many chapters.

Finally, we thank our loving families for their constant prayers, encouragement, and input over the three years that we worked on this book.

The Editors

God is doing a new thing . . . again! Large numbers of people from the world's major religious traditions are choosing to follow Jesus of Nazareth. In following Christ, some of these are joining traditional Christian churches and leaving the religious communities of their birth. Others, however, are following Jesus in different ways. The Center for the Study of Global Christianity at Gordon-Conwell Theological Seminary calculates,

> As of 2010 approximately 5.9 million non-Christians were following Christ from within the context of their own religious and cultural traditions. These include insider movements as well as hidden and secret believers. The Center's estimate for the year 2000 for these types of believers was 4.6 million, which means that they grew at 2.5% per year from 2000–2010 or twice as fast as Christianity as a whole. 85% of these individuals are either Hindus or Muslims. Given current trends, these are expected to grow to 6.5 million by mid-2014.[1]

Similar to how discipleship to Jesus in the first century moved beyond the confines of the Jewish community, opening a way for Gentiles to follow Jesus, we are now witnessing the growth of discipleship movements to Jesus *within* non-Christian religious traditions. This phenomenon, often referred to as "insider movements" (IMs) or "Jesus movements within" (JMWs), has caught the attention of many people.

Numerous articles have appeared over the past fifteen years on the topic of insider movements. There has been confusion and controversy as well as misunderstanding and misrepresentation. Newcomers to the conversation are often bewildered, scarcely knowing where to start reading. Moreover, even those who are heavily engaged in this issue find it difficult to keep abreast of all that has been written. Until now, no book has been published that seeks to present this phenomenon in a comprehensive fashion. *Understanding Insider Movements: Disciples of Jesus within Diverse Religious Communities* is a response to the many voices that have been calling for such a publication.

As the title indicates, we describe these discipleship movements as occurring within diverse *religious communities* rather than *religions*, as the latter might connote a mixing of biblical faith with

---

1 Todd M. Johnson and Gina A. Zurlo, eds., *World Christian Database* (Leiden/Boston: Brill, accessed July 2013).

unbiblical theological beliefs and practices.[2] However, neither do we describe these movements as merely being within "diverse communities" or "diverse cultures," as if the discipleship were being expressed through neutral, non-religious forms. These are *religious* communities with *religious* cultures, replete with their own holidays, histories, customs, foods, vocabularies, and ways of life.

Western readers must understand that the way religions function in much of the world is very different from how they function in most secular or Western countries, especially where a separation of church and state exists. Religious forms, symbols, and culture for much of the world are often fused so that religions function like cultures. While those who follow Christ in insider movements undergo transformation of their spiritual lives and theological beliefs, they retain much of their religious culture.

Our initial intent was to compile an anthology of existing articles. We sifted through the many published articles, seeking to select those seminal, influential, or representative writings that get to the heart of this subject. However, as we surveyed these articles, it became evident that there were some gaps in the literature. As a result, a substantial number of articles have been written and included as fresh contributions to this subject. Due to space limitations, we have sometimes given priority to succinct treatments over lengthier ones or used relevant excerpts instead of full articles. We have also taken the liberty of standardizing the transliteration of Arabic and foreign-language words and names for the convenience of readers, as well as making many minor changes for accuracy and consistency in mechanics, spelling, source documentation style, etc.—changes that aid understanding without altering style or meaning.

We rejoice over all the ways that God is moving in the world today. Much has already been written elsewhere about more traditional approaches. It is not our purpose in this book to give equal time to all opinions on the subject of insider movements—space alone precludes this. But we do aim to clarify common misunderstandings, offer answers to oft-heard objections, and address areas of legitimate concern so that the reader may more accurately understand insider movements (as promised by this book's title). Our hope is that readers will understand the nature and significance of these movements and acquire an even deeper appreciation of the great variety that exists worldwide within the body of Christ.[3]

Our primary intended audience is those committed to seeing the good news of Jesus Christ cross social, cultural, and religious barriers. Educators might choose this volume as a textbook for students in religious studies and cross-cultural training programs. Those positively disposed toward insider movements may find it useful in helping explain the complex issues of these movements to their constituencies. This book may also be useful as a reference guide for those interested or engaged in cross-cultural witness among those of non-Christian religious traditions.

We trust that our aim of bringing greater understanding of insider movements will be achieved by the arrangement of our presentation into the following seven parts:

---

2   However, see chap. 39; Kurt Anders Richardson explains that it is actually proper to state that these movements occur within other "religions."

3   One topic not addressed in this book is Bible translation; there are two reasons for this. First, there is no inherent link between insider movements and Bible translation. A number of movements are thriving while using existing and quite traditional translations. There are insider leaders who prefer more literal translation approaches and Christian leaders who support more dynamic and Muslim- or Hindu-friendly ones. Second, the topic of what constitutes good translation is a large and complex field. To do justice to it would require a book of its own.

1. Setting the Stage
2. Examples, Testimonies, and Analysis
3. Biblical and Theological Perspectives
4. Contextualization, Religion, and Syncretism
5. Approaches in Witness
6. Concerns and Misunderstandings
7. Identity

Some readers may be from non-Christian religious communities. Perhaps you have only caught glimpses of a Jesus clothed exclusively in culturally Christian forms or, worse, one who is tied to foreign political systems and civilizations. We hope you will discover in these pages that we, as followers of Jesus, deeply regret how the impression has often been given that Jesus is for some but not for others—as though one group had a monopoly on Jesus. In fact the opposite is true: we believe that the love of God in Jesus is for every community, family, and person on earth regardless of culture, religious community, or nationality. We as his followers are called to share this message and do all we can to remove barriers that might separate anyone from him. We support the right of all people to know and follow the risen Jesus regardless of their religious community or label. Our heart's desire, dear reader, is that all would experience the life about which Jesus spoke: "Now this is eternal life: that they know you, the only true God, and Jesus Christ, whom you have sent" (John 17:3).

This anthology is long, intended to serve as a reference guide. We recommend, however, reading all of part 1, "Setting the Stage," before delving into other sections. We pray for God's blessing in your life as you read this book.

The Editors

PART 1

SETTING THE STAGE

INTRODUCTION TO PART 1

Our goal must not be to populate the Christian religion but to bring people into a genuine relationship with God. We must make a clear distinction between the religion of Christianity and the revolution that Jesus began 2000 years ago.

—Erwin McManus[*]

"Isaac" was a holy man, a Sufi master. He lived in a remote and traditional region of the country, where he had a large following. Several thousand people were looking to him for spiritual guidance, for blessings for their crops, for prayers for health, and most of all for intercession for their eternal salvation. Master Isaac, however, was worried about his own salvation, and it troubled him that his thousands of followers believed that he himself could save them on the day of judgment. So he began to pray in earnest that God would show him the *sirat mustaqim*, the true path to salvation.

One night in 2002, while Isaac was praying to be shown the way of salvation, the Lord Jesus appeared to him in radiant white clothing. Jesus told him to travel to such-and-such a town and consult a holy man from such-and-such a village whose father was named so-and-so and whose grandfather was so-and-so. Jesus showed him in a vision the way to the house. Isaac realized that this man's grandfather had been his very own Sufi master, and this excited him.

Although it was still very early in the morning and there was a terrible rainstorm outside, Isaac vowed not to eat or drink until he met the man of God to whom Jesus had directed him and had discovered from him the way of salvation. So he walked through the storm to a bus station, boarded an early bus, and traveled some forty miles to the town.

It was about six o'clock in the morning when Isaac reached the place that Jesus had revealed to him in the vision. When he knocked on the door, he was surprised to see a man wearing ordinary clothes rather than the robes of a Sufi master. It was Brother Jacob, who was the leader of an "insider movement" of Muslim followers of Jesus. When Isaac asked Jacob about his father, his grandfather, and the village he came from, he realized that this was the very man Jesus had told him to consult. So he told Jacob about the vision and asked him to reveal the way of salvation.

---

[*] *Unleashed: Release the Untamed Faith Within* (Nashville: Thomas Nelson, 2011), 91.

Citing passages from both the Qur'an and the Bible, Brother Jacob told Isaac the story of God creating the world as a good place, about Adam and Eve and the temptation of Satan, and about their disobedience of God. He declared that as a consequence of their sin, Adam and Eve became alienated from the presence of God and enslaved to darkness, sin, and death. So how could their relationship with God be restored? How could they return to the garden of Eden?

Brother Jacob went on to talk about Cain and Abel, the descent of the world into evil, and the rescue of Noah and his family. He noted that God called Abraham from Babylon to follow him and gave him eight sons. He talked about the descendants of Abraham, about David, about the disobedience of his son Solomon and his descendants, until it came to the true son of David, the true heir of Abraham's promises, the second Adam, Jesus, who was the first human being in history to completely submit himself to the will of God. He said that it was the will of God that Jesus the Messiah should suffer death on the Cross to save humanity, and that God raised him back to life. God exalted Jesus to sit at his own right hand as Lord and Savior of the world.

Brother Jacob said that the Lord Jesus had appeared to him as well, in 1969, and had shown him that he was the way of salvation. He read in the Gospel where Jesus said, "I am the way and the truth and the life. No one comes to the Father except through me" (John 14:6). Jesus, he said, was himself the *sirat mustaqim*. Master Isaac said he believed in Jesus and was ready to serve him and wanted to be baptized right then and there. Brother Jacob, however, counseled him to wait. He said, "God has made you a great leader, and he wants all of your followers to know that Jesus the Messiah, and he alone, is the way of salvation. Go home and tell your wives and children first that Jesus is the Lord and Savior, and then tell your closest disciples." Isaac agreed, and they set a date for Jacob to come and share the good news.

About two weeks later, at the appointed time, Jacob arrived to find a gathering of two hundred or more of Isaac's leading disciples. The Sufi master began by telling them all the story of his prayer and the vision he was given by God. He described traveling during a storm to get to Brother Jacob's house to ask him the secret of salvation. He then asked Brother Jacob to tell them all the way.

So Brother Jacob told the story again, starting with the Qur'an and then moving to the Bible. He told the story of Creation, the Fall, and the descendants of Adam down to Jesus the Messiah. He called them to put their faith in Jesus as their Lord and Savior. All of the leaders agreed, but they said they must first share this news with their wives and children.

A few weeks later Master Isaac sent word to Brother Jacob to come back. Brother Jacob arrived to find that the Sufi master and 250 of his leading disciples were ready to be baptized. So Brother Jacob baptized Isaac and his wives and son. Then he told Isaac's wives to baptize their daughters. He then instructed Isaac to baptize the 250 senior leaders of his movement and to send them home to baptize their own wives and children, share the word with others, and baptize those who believed. On that day several thousand people were baptized, thus beginning a movement to Christ within a culturally Muslim community.

Brother Jacob had brought along three cases of New Testaments, and he gave these to Master Isaac for distribution to his leaders. But three days later Isaac returned the cases, saying they were obviously not for his people, as they were not in his language—at least not the way they used it. There were too many foreign and ecclesiastical terms, and too many occurrences of words that pertained to a different ethnic group. Brother Jacob, however, had a poetic paraphrase of the gospel story that he had prepared, using familiar and acceptable language, and he offered that. Master Isaac thought this book was wonderful, and he took a large quantity back with him for his flock. At that point Brother Jacob realized that these new disciples of Christ needed a Bible in familiar and intelligible language, and so he initiated a Bible translation project for them, starting with the Gospel of Mark.

These two movements continue as culturally sensitive house-church movements, in spite of various forms of persecution—both from some church people who do not like this approach and from those Muslims who are not happy to see people following Christ. Master Isaac has died, but the movement he led continues under the pastoral care of his sons. They are confident that since it was the Lord Jesus himself who directed them to Brother Jacob and his insider approach, the Lord will also guide and protect them and through them bless the Muslim community to which they belong.[1]

The preceding story describes a Jesus movement within a Muslim community—but there is more to it than that. These Muslims became disciples of Jesus in what we could call a "house-church movement," but which remained part of the Muslim community. Following the guidance of God's Spirit, they were not integrated into the existing national church, as most Christians would expect.

What happened with Brother Jacob and Master Isaac may be unusual, but it is not unique. Similar stories have emerged, at times causing controversy or conflict within the Christian community (both local and global), not to mention their own non-Christian communities. Within the Christian missions community, this kind of discipleship-to-Jesus movement has often been referred to as an "insider movement" (IM).

As the title indicates, the aim of this book is to aid the reader in "understanding insider movements." Part 1 sets the stage. Six articles orient the reader to these "disciples of Jesus within diverse religious communities" by providing definition, historical background, conceptual perspective, answers to common questions and objections, and critical reflection on our assessment criteria.

Chapter 1, "Insider Movements: Coming to Terms with Terms" by John Jay Travis, offers a working definition of IMs based on a description of their fundamental characteristics.

In chapter 2, "Historical Development of the Insider Paradigm," Harley Talman notes that IMs resemble what took place in first-century movements, where original socioreligious identity was retained, but that they differ from the traditional paradigm of Protestant missions. Nevertheless, we can trace the emergence of IM ideas in the modern era back to the late nineteenth century.

Chapter 3, "Muslim Followers of Jesus?" by Joseph Cumming, gives a balanced presentation of two opposing viewpoints, along with a response by an Arab Christian, Martin Accad.

Chapter 4, "When God's Kingdom Grows like Yeast: Frequently Asked Questions about Jesus Movements within Muslim Communities," comes from the pens of John Jay Travis and J. Dudley Woodberry, two recognized authorities on IMs in Islamic contexts. (Please keep in mind that IMs occur within communities of other religious traditions as well.)

Chapter 5, "Myths and Misunderstandings about Insider Movements" by Kevin Higgins, Richard Jameson, and Harley Talman, addresses concerns commonly raised by critics.

Chapter 6, "Seeing Inside Insider Missiology" by Len Bartlotti, examines the "lenses" through which we analyze and assess insider movements. It may be that some of our core convictions and theological standards reflect assumptions and personal preferences rather than biblical mandates.

---

1   This account is based on the testimony of Brother Jacob and a foreign worker. Investigated and verified by several Christian leaders in that country, it was then published in a slightly different form in Rick Brown, "How One Insider Movement Began," in *Perspectives on the World Christian Movement: A Reader*, 4th ed., ed. Ralph D. Winter and Steven C. Hawthorne (Pasadena, CA: William Carey Library, 2009), 706–7. Reprinted by permission.

Insider Movements
Coming to Terms with Terms
John Jay Travis

Both Scripture and church history indicate that when people discover Jesus, they want to tell others about it. Similar to the woman at the well, who joyfully shared with fellow Samaritans,[1] many others over the centuries have told their families and friends about Jesus in ways that have led to movements. This present volume explores *insider movements*, whereby people of non-Christian religions follow Jesus as Lord and Savior while remaining integrally part of the family and socioreligious community of their birth. This first chapter focuses on the meaning and usage of a number of key terms and important related concepts found throughout the book.[2]

"Socioreligious" and "Religiocultural"

The terms "socioreligious" and "religiocultural" are used to describe the close relationship that is often observed between religion and culture. Millions worldwide understand their religion or religious identity as something inseparably bound to their ethnic, national, social, or family identity. It is instructive that many people with little or no belief in God or interest in spiritual matters still view themselves as members of a religion. This phenomenon might help explain why in the United States, for instance, a recent poll indicates that 77 percent of the population self-identify as "Christian"[3] even though it is hard to imagine that this many Americans are actual followers of Jesus. Similar statistics involving religious identity are found in other countries as well, causing some to speak of "cultural Jews," "cultural Muslims," or "cultural Christians" (note: while observers may use this terminology, members of these religions do not usually add the word "cultural" when referring to themselves). By using the terms "socioreligious" and "religiocultural," we remind ourselves that for most of the world, a change of religions is not simply a shift in personal beliefs; it means separation from family, community, and society.

"Christian," "Christianity," and "Follower of Jesus"

The way the terms "Christian" and "Christianity" are generally used in this book differs from the narrower meaning that evangelicals typically give them (i.e., denoting true saving faith in Jesus; being

---

1   John 4:39–42 states that through the woman's testimony and the visit of Jesus, many Samaritans came to believe that Jesus was the Savior of the world.

2   Because *UIM* contains writings from more than fifty authors who do not all use the same vocabulary, we cannot guarantee uniformity of terms among the various chapters. Thus in this chapter we will point out terms that have roughly equivalent meanings. Please refer to the glossary for other terms not mentioned here.

3   Frank Newport, "In U.S., 77% Identify as Christian," Gallup, December 2012, http://www.gallup.com/poll/159548/identify-christian.aspx.

"born again"). Rather, most of the authors, having spent much of their lives in cross-cultural ministry, use the terms "Christian" or "Christianity" to designate socioreligious categories, as do many cultures of the world. Thus these terms are applied to both committed and nominal "Christians," be they Catholic, Protestant, Orthodox, or other. The terms "follower/disciple of Jesus" or "follower/disciple of Christ" are more commonly used in this book to refer to those with true faith and heart allegiance to Jesus—what most evangelicals mean when they use the term "Christian." The initially strange-sounding phrase "non-Christian followers of Christ," therefore, would indicate people who are socioreligiously not "Christian"—they identify as Jewish, Muslim, Buddhist, etc.—yet are spiritually, morally, and biblically true followers or disciples of Jesus.

"Insider," "Insider Movements," and Related Terms

Although the term "insider" can be used in a variety of ways, here we mean "a person from a non-Christian background who has accepted Jesus as Lord and Savior but retained the socioreligious identity of his or her birth." This means that in following Jesus, insiders have not left the religious community in which they were raised, nor have they joined a denomination or branch of Christianity.

Several good definitions of "insider movements" have been published and widely used since 2004.[4] In the following section is a working definition of this term based on key characteristics of these movements. First, though, we look at two other, related expressions: "Jesus movements within" and "the Insider Movement."

The term "Jesus movements within" (JMW) is often used in place of "insider movements."[5] Many prefer this term because of the clear focus on Jesus and the ability to indicate the religious community in which the movement is occurring: "a Jesus movement within the Hindu community," or "within a Muslim community," and so forth.

At times we read the term "the Insider Movement." Many consider this a misnomer, however, because there is no singular movement, organization, institution, or group that could rightly be called "*the* Insider Movement." The majority of insider movements worldwide are localized, organic, and largely unaware of each other. Hence most people who understand them speak of "insider movements" in the plural rather than "the Insider Movement."[6]

A Working Definition of Insider Movements

Throughout this book we only refer to movements as *insider* movements if they contain each of the five following dynamics or characteristics:[7]

1. *Following Jesus and the Bible:* following Jesus as the risen Lord and Savior and the Bible as the word of God.

---

4   See Kevin Higgins, "The Key to Insider Movements: The 'Devoted's' of Acts," *IJFM* 21, no. 4 (2004): 155–65 (*UIM*, chap. 25); Rebecca Lewis, "Promoting Movements to Christ within Natural Communities," *IJFM* 24, no. 2 (2007): 75–76.

5   However, this term has other uses as well, so we will not use it here exclusively as a synonym for IMs.

6   Use of the singular by a few authors in this volume has been preserved when what they are referring to, albeit informally, is the insider paradigm.

7   This does not mean that the life of every individual in a given movement perfectly reflects these characteristics any more than members of any other spiritual community or church perfectly attain its ideals.

2. *Fellowships with indigenous leadership:* gatherings occurring in culturally appropriate ways for prayer, Bible study, and fellowship (i.e., biblical *ekklesiae*) within families and social networks, led by fellow insiders whom God has raised up for leadership.

3. *Spiritual transformation:* spiritual transformation occurring through the leading of the Spirit and the study of Scripture, resulting in certain cultural and religious beliefs and practices being retained, others reinterpreted, and still others rejected.

4. *Remaining as witnesses:* disciples remaining integral members of their families and socioreligious communities, as witnesses for Jesus.

5. *Multiplication:* ongoing witnessing and prayer leading to the multiplication of new followers of Jesus, new insider leaders, and reproducing insider fellowships.

A useful working definition of insider movements, therefore, is the following: *Multiplying networks of Jesus followers in insider-led fellowships where the Bible is obeyed as the word of God, spiritual transformation occurs, and insiders remain part of the families and socioreligious communities of their birth, bearing witness to Jesus, their risen Lord and Savior.*

Related Concepts

The following concepts are explored in greater depth throughout the book. They are mentioned briefly here, however, because they bring greater immediate clarity to the working definition of insider movements given above.

1. While insider believers have some different beliefs from fellow Hindus, Sikhs, Buddhists, Muslims, or Jews who do not yet follow Jesus, they intentionally look for ways to find common ground with their people. But they do this while staying true to the Bible and the daily leading of the Spirit in their lives. They retain anything from their socioreligious community that is helpful, praiseworthy, and not contrary to Scripture.

2. This dynamic of remaining within one's religious community while having some different beliefs causes both continuity and discontinuity with the past. This means that while much is retained, some beliefs and practices are reinterpreted or rejected. For instance, Hindu followers of Jesus reject the worship of multiple gods and goddesses (polytheism). Instead they worship only the one true God, the maker of heaven and earth, whom they know through Jesus Christ. They would, however, as God leads them, be part of the life of the local Hindu community as much as is biblically possible, not taking steps to adopt another socioreligious membership or identity.

3. In other contexts, Jewish followers of Jesus reject the standard Jewish teachings that Yeshua (Jesus) is not the Messiah and that the New Testament is not true Scripture, yet they still live traditionally Jewish lives as respectful members of the Jewish community. Muslim followers of Jesus whom we know reject the commonly disseminated teachings that Jesus did not die and rise again and that the New Testament has been corrupted; however, they continue to live as part of their Muslim community, respecting it and participating in its traditions and practices insofar as conscience and the Bible allow. Similar patterns of retaining, rejecting, and reinterpreting aspects of religious life and culture in light of the word of God and the leading of the Spirit are seen in insider movements among Buddhists and Sikhs as well (see chaps. 11 and 19). Even as Jews in the first century eventually pressured Jews who followed Jesus to leave, so it may happen with some insider movements. The point is that even if insiders

are one day rejected or feel the need to leave, they are not the ones initiating the separation from their families and communities.[8]

4. It is crucial to point out, however, that even though those in insider movements follow Jesus as their Lord and Savior and obey the Bible as God's revealed word, *they should not be viewed as simply Christians by another name.* These are fresh expressions of faith in Jesus where he was not known before. Insider leaders are involved in the same process of self-discovery and self-theologizing that countless others have gone through since the gospel broke out of the Jewish context and entered Gentile contexts two thousand years ago. The reality of insider movements raises the question of who is really a part of the kingdom of God and the body of Christ, and of who has the right to interpret Scripture.

5. Finally, a key feature in describing the fellowships in these movements is that (depending on the local situation) they are open and inviting to those who do not yet know Jesus. In addition, these groups, which are generally family centered and home based, are relationally linked with numerous similar groups, fostering momentum and movement.

Bibliography

Higgins, Kevin. "The Key to Insider Movements: The 'Devoted's' of Acts." *International Journal of Frontier Missions* 21, no. 4 (2004): 155–65.

Lewis, Rebecca. "Promoting Movements to Christ within Natural Communities." *International Journal of Frontier Missiology* 24, no. 2 (2007): 75–76.

---

8 There are many accounts of Jesus followers who, under threat of physical harm and even death, have felt forced to leave their family and community. Jesus predicted this would at times happen (e.g., Matt 10:21–23), and our prayers are with those who for the sake of Jesus have suffered separation from loved ones. However, insider movements are occurring where, for a variety of reasons explored in *UIM,* groups of insiders have found ways to remain within their natural social networks and still not compromise their faith in Jesus.

CHAPTER 2

Historical Development of the Insider Paradigm

Harley Talman

First men say that it is not true, then that it is against religion, and, in the third stage, that it has long been known.

—LOUIS AGASSIZ ON NEW THEORIES[*]

Insider Movements: Old or New?

Ever since the Jewish roots of the gospel first produced Gentile fruit, there have been varied viewpoints among God's people regarding the interrelations of faith in Christ, religious tradition, and sociocultural-political identity. Therefore, differing perspectives on insider movements should not surprise us.

One of the current points of discussion is whether insider movements have historical precedent or if they are an entirely new phenomenon and represent a new paradigm of mission. In support of the former are those who find precursors and principles foundational to insider movements in the Old Testament.[1] Others note, additionally, that Jesus never advocated a proselyte model of conversion: Jewish converts remained socioreligious Jews, Samaritans did not become Jewish to follow Jesus, and various groups of Gentiles followed Jesus as Gentiles.[2] Furthermore, the Apostle Paul insisted in his letters to the Romans and Galatians that faith in Christ should not carry its religious trappings into a new socioreligious context, and the Jerusalem Council confirmed this missionary principle and practice.[3] Hence many do not view insider movements as something new at all, but as similar to the movements that took place in the first century.

Others, however, describe insider phenomena from the vantage point of modern history. They observe that insider movements are strikingly different from the typical fruit of modern Protestant

---

[*] Stephen Jay Gould cites Karl Ernst von Baer as ascribing these words to Agassiz. See Gould, *Ontogeny and Phylogeny* (Cambridge, MA: Belknap Press of Harvard University Press, 1977), 184.

1 See Talman, chap. 21.

2 See Roberts and Jameson, chap. 22; Ridgway, chap. 23; Higgins, chap. 24; and Lewis, chap. 28. In each of these contexts, whether Jew, Samaritan, or Gentile, new believers were expected to change what was not in keeping with the way of Christ but retain those things that were acceptable—for instance, Gentile disciples would renounce pagan idolatry.

3 See also Woodberry, chap. 26; Talman, chap. 27; and Lewis, chap. 28.

mission, where both tribal peoples and those few from the world's major religious traditions who came to faith in Jesus joined some branch of Christianity to express their faith.[4]

Therefore we can say that the insider paradigm is both old and new: it is old in that it resembles what took place in first-century movements, where original socioreligious identity was retained, and it is new in that it differs from the traditional paradigm of Protestant missions. Insider movements are new expressions of an ancient pattern. As we read of this "new" paradigm, we should remember that it accords with ways God has been working that are as old as the gospel itself.

This chapter identifies examples of insiders in the modern era and discussions in the literature that envisioned or described such an approach, emphasizing the newness of the paradigm in contrast to traditional Protestant mission.

In the process we will observe another "old/new" phenomenon: the fact that God's elect have often displayed negative or even hostile attitudes toward those of other religious traditions. Just as Jesus' Jewish disciples were allergic to Samaritans and Gentiles, so modern Christians frequently have an aversion to non-Christian religions. Yet new disciples of Jesus from the major religious traditions have often sought to integrate their life in Christ with the thought and practices of their social and religious heritage. This chapter will trace early attempts at such indigenization and contextualization in the modern era, which have contributed to the development of the insider paradigm. We shall see that then, as now, such endeavors have often met with resistance from traditional Christians.

Early Advocates of the Insider Paradigm

Brahmabandhab Upadhyay (1861–1907) was an Indian nationalist who, after deciding to follow Jesus, sought to indigenize his faith in Christ by integrating Hindu and Catholic identities. He utilized Hindu philosophy to express gospel truth (akin to Hellenistic Christians exploiting Greek philosophy).[5] His dream of a Hindu-friendly Catholic monastery was rejected by the church as being too radical. He was thwarted by the top clerics in the Indian church, and his writings were eventually banned by Rome.[6] His later life was marked by disillusionment with the West and its influence, and he determined that political engagement was essential for the evangelization of his homeland.[7]

But we find a happier engagement between a Hindu follower of Christ and the Christian church in the life of Kandaswami Chetti (1867–1943). He more authentically embodies the insider paradigm. While affirming his membership in the body of Christ, he did not join the existing Indian churches or change his identity to "Christian." His motivation was to "prepare the way for a movement from within Hindu society towards a Christ who shall fulfill India's highest aspirations and impart that life of freedom for which she has been panting for ages."[8]

At the same time, but with no apparent connection to the likes of Upadhyay and Chetti, a radically different conception of mission to Hindus began to appear among Christian workers. The year

---

4   However, the father of the modern Protestant mission movement, William Carey, used the term "Hindu Christians," allowing these believers to retain some measure of original religious identity.

5   See the superb study by Julius J. Lipner, *Brahmabandhab Upadhyay: The Life and Thought of a Revolutionary* (New Delhi: Oxford University Press, 1999). Lipner deems Upadhyay's theology to be essentially "neo-Thomism in Sanskritic disguise" (387). I am indebted to H. L. Richard for sources on early Hindu insider developments.

6   Ibid., 274–76.

7   Ibid., 222–24.

8   "'Why I Am Not a Christian': A Personal Statement" was read at the Madras Missionary Conference in 1915, and the paper subsequently appeared as chap. 5 in the *Madras Christian College Magazine* (*UIM*, chap. 10).

1893 records the voice of an obscure member of the Wesleyan Missionary Society from Mysore City (in South India), the Reverend H. Haigh. Without providing us with details of his vision, Haigh argues for a drastically different approach to mission that corresponds with the insider mentality:

> The principle I contend for, then, is this: *that the books which we publish should be carefully related to Hindu thought, expressed in its terms, done in its style, adopting where it can its positions, and leading on, still in Hindu fashion and in its terminology, from points of agreement to essential points of difference.* In this way we may, perhaps, be able to furnish an effectual exhibition of legitimately "Hinduized Christianity."[9]

N. V. Tilak (1861–1919) was also a zealous Indian nationalist and talented poet. This Brahmin was challenged to read the Bible and was soon converted and baptized in 1895. As a Protestant missionary, he pioneered use of Hindu forms to express biblical faith, especially his devotional songs and poetry.[10] After more than twenty years of service, he resigned and entered the fourth and final stage of high-caste Hindu life, *sannyasa* (renunciation), but contextualizing it with seven biblical requirements. At age fifty-five, he launched "God's *darbar*" ("the royal court of God"). Through this fraternity of baptized as well as unbaptized Christ followers (for whom, among the latter, baptism represented antipatriotism),[11] Tilak sought to offer to India a de-Westernized Jesus as its ultimate guru. However, Tilak died within two years, and the *darbar* with him. But he left a legacy of a radical attempt at indigenized discipleship—seeking to be fully biblical and fully Hindu.[12]

In subsequent years, kingdom yeast silently penetrated the dough of Hindu society.[13] Decades later (c. 1980), Lutheran missionary Herbert Hoefer stumbled upon some Hindu Christ followers in South India, whom he labeled "non-baptized believers in Christ." *Churchless Christianity* presented the astounding conclusion of his research—that there were more of these Hindu followers of Christ in Chennai than there were Indian Christians.[14] But his description of their theological thinking and practice was troubling to outside observers. However, since that time, these believers have defined themselves as "Jesu *bhaktas*" (devotees of Jesus), an accepted category within Hindu piety. Moreover, these Hindu disciples of Christ complained to Hoefer about the title of his book on two counts. First of all, they insisted that they were not "churchless," even though the structure of their faith community differed from that of the West. Secondly, they were not "Christianity," because their biblical faith was expressed through Hindu religious forms and identity.[15]

---

9 H. Haigh, "Vernacular Literature," in *Report of the Third Decennial Missionary Conference Held at Bombay, 1892–93,* vol. 2, ed. Alfred Mainwaring (Bombay: Education Society's Steam Press, 1893), 667; emphasis in the original.

10 H. L. Richard, *Following Jesus in the Hindu Context: The Intriguing Implications of N. V. Tilak's Life and Thought* (Pasadena, CA: William Carey Library, 1998), viii.

11 Baptism not only put a convert into a new religion, but also into a new legal and social community under Indian law; see Richard in *UIM,* chap. 17.

12 Richard, *Following Jesus,* 95–107.

13 Many see the description in Luke 13:20,21 as a characteristic dynamic of the kingdom of God.

14 Herbert Hoefer, *Churchless Christianity* (Pasadena, CA: William Carey Library, 2001); see also Hoefer in *UIM,* chap. 30, and the review by Richard, chap. 18.

15 See Hoefer, "Church In Context," *EMQ* 43, no. 2 (2007): 200–208 (*UIM,* chap. 30).

Shifting to the Muslim world, we find early expression of insider paradigm thinking in Rev. Henry Riggs' 1938 "Report Written on Behalf of the Near East Council on Muslim Evangelism." Veteran missions thinkers felt that decades of "missionary work among Moslems has not produced the results that ought to be expected from so much sacrifice and labor." So the Near East Christian Council conducted a two-year investigation to explore the reasons for this "sterility." The council found two fundamental causes. The first was that "Christian teaching does not mean the same to the Moslem that it does to the Christian" (this highlighted the need for what was later termed "contextualization"). The second was that "in the thought of the Moslem a change of religion is primarily a change of group-connection and group-loyalty." The report concluded,

> In the thought of the Moslem a change of religion is primarily a change of group-connection and group-loyalty. "Every convert to Christianity is a dead loss to the community." "The Moslem Community is a noble and sacred thing, a social-political-religious fellowship for which the believer is willing to give his life." "The greatest handicap against which the Christian missionary has to strive is the power of Moslem solidarity." "There are thousands of men and women who believe in Christ and are trying to follow him, but they cannot bring themselves to face the break with their own community."
>
> The great fact pointed out in these statements is very evident. But is this unwillingness to break with their own community due only to lack of courage or conviction? Not always. Many cases have been reported of true believers in Christ who have refused to break with the Moslem community because they wish to live among their own people, to make Christ known to them. . . .
>
> It is the conviction of a large number of workers among Moslems that the ultimate hope of bringing Christ to the Moslems is to be attained by the development of groups of followers of Jesus who are active in making him known to others while remaining loyally a part of the social and political groups to which they belong in Islam. . . .
>
> The aspiration here expressed is that the church of Christ might take root within the social-political body called Islam, and not as an alien body encroaching from without."[16]

It was recognized that the report's findings would demand "*radical* changes in the attitudes, methods and thinking" of Christian workers among Muslims, but Riggs and his colleagues were realists who recognized that most of their fellow missionaries felt "duty bound to follow the traditional lines of

---

16 Henry H. Riggs, "Near East Christian Council Inquiry on the Evangelization of Moslems" (paper, Library of the Near East School of Theology, Beirut, November 1938), available at http://www.scribd.com/doc/110704319/NEAR-EAST-CHRISTIAN-COUNCIL-INQUIRY-ON-THE-EVANGELIZATION-OF-MOSLEMS-November-1938-by-H-Riggs-and-the-Near-East-Christian-Council. Most of this inquiry was later published in Riggs, "Shall We Try Unbeaten Paths in Working for Muslims?" *The Moslem World* 31, no. 2 (1941): 116–26 (*UIM*, chap. 43). Thanks are due to John Travis for sharing his knowledge of Riggs and early insider thinkers.

presentation."[17] This in fact was the reaction of the majority at Delhi and Tambaram (Madras) conferences in December 1938. Riggs later reported that at both places "discussion was almost entirely devoted to a few of the suggestions, mainly regarding unbaptized believers. Objections to the encouragement of such believers were so urgent as to crowd out almost entirely any real consideration of the underlying principles quoted above."[18]

In 1941 the *Moslem World* featured the Near East Council's report sandwiched between responses by two critics. Samuel Zwemer's editorial cited a resolution of a group from the Madras conference and the preconference gathering in Delhi that rejected the report due to "the vital necessity of open witness to Christ within the fellowship of the Christian Church" and the need for the Moslem "to break with his past to accept a new way of life in Christ."[19] Zwemer rightly rejected the ecumenical agenda of Harvard professor William Hocking (who advocated a "new World Faith with elements of value taken from all the living religions of humanity").[20] Zwemer likewise opposed those who sought to replace evangelism with social action. In nearly the same breath, Zwemer rejected proposed changes in missionary method. Although he acknowledged that the Riggs report had "much to commend it," he viewed its prospects as having even less impact than even a "merely social gospel."[21] Similarly, J. Christy Wilson understood the report as advocating secret belief and cried out for "open confession."[22]

However, the following year the *Moslem World* published the response of one who had attended both the Delhi and Madras deliberations. He asserted that the objections of Zwemer and Wilson to the Near East Council's report were based on a grave misunderstanding of two of its central tenets. First, it was arguing against extraction evangelism:

> The very terminology ["convert from Islam"] puts before the reader
> the idea of controversy, of struggle to take out of one group, and put
> into another group, which the Near East survey sought to obviate.
> The idea of that survey was rather to permit the follower of Jesus
> to stay within Islam, to claim his right as a "Muslim," one sur-

---

17 Riggs, "Inquiry," foreword.

18 Riggs, "Unbeaten Paths," 118.

19 Samuel M. Zwemer, "The Dynamic of Evangelism," *The Moslem World* 31, no. 2 (1941): 112.

20 Ibid., 109.

21 Citing Hugh Thomson Kerr, Zwemer remonstrated that we are "not to preach sociology but salvation; not economics but evangelism; not reform but redemption; not culture but conversion; not progress but pardon; not the new social order but the new birth; not revolution but regeneration; not renovation but revival; not resuscitation but resurrection; not a new organization but a new creation; not democracy but the Gospel; not civilization but Christ" (ibid., 115). Lyle L. Vander Werff views the response to the Riggs report through the eyes of the majority at the Delhi gathering and Tambaram—who unfortunately presumed that the report was part of Hocking's agenda of theological syncretism: "The majority at Tambaram rejected the ideas set forth by Hocking and Riggs because the basic presupposition that 'theological tenets are discoverable by human experience' was no longer tenable." Vander Werff, *Christian Mission to Muslims: The Record* (Pasadena: William Carey Library, 1977), 263. But liberal theology had nothing to do with the Riggs report. However, Vander Werff correctly observes that the "disillusionment following World War I, the renewed emphasis upon the 'theology of the Word,' and conviction that the church's mission involved proclamation had had far-reaching consequences" (ibid.). This forceful reaction to liberalism was trumpeted by Hendrik Kraemer's book *The Christian Message in a Non-Christian World*. Both Zwemer and Kraemer "agreed that evangelism, the proclamation of the Christian message, was the essence of mission. *They were wary of novel methods*." Vander Werff, *Christian Mission to Muslims*, 264; emphasis added.

22 J. Christy Wilson, "Public Confession and the Church," *The Moslem World* 31, no. 2 (1941): 127, 137.

rendered and dedicated to God—to investigate the prophet Jesus and his Revelation and to follow all the way in obedience to Jesus, considering himself all the while not one who has left Islam but one who, taking Muhammad at his word as to Jesus and the Gospel, has discovered what that really means and has gone on to the more advanced position of utter surrender to the revelation of God in Jesus. This should be the inalienable right of every Moslem. No one ought to have to think that this necessarily involves the proclamation to the world of consequent separation from Islam.[23]

The second misunderstanding was that "such a follower of Jesus will not witness by words as well as by life."[24] This defender of the Riggs report insisted that Zwemer, Wilson, and other critics had drawn a false dichotomy.

The contrast between the "unbeaten path" suggested by Mr. Riggs and the long-trodden path of the last century is not between "dynamic Christians" and "secret believers," but between 100-percent followers of Jesus who are trying to be both "wise as serpents and harmless as doves" and ill-advised followers who, like foolish farmers, are scattering their precious seed broadcast on soil that is dry and hardened into something like rock by long exposure to the sun. The first group are not less loyal to Jesus. They simply take more thoughtfully his repeated teaching that fruit will be born only from seed cast on prepared ground and that it is foolish to offer precious gifts to those whose training and preparation can only make them trample these underfoot.[25]

In 1944, after an obituary that eulogized Riggs, who had recently died, an article by S. A. Morrison expressed his view that the issues raised by the Riggs report had not been sufficiently discussed. While agreeing with the Near East Council's diagnosis, he proposed that the solution to the problem of corporate solidarity in Islam was "promotion of religious freedom in Moslem lands."[26] But this offered little hope for the near term (as in the seventy years since). More realistically, he acknowledged a growing consensus against "controversy" in evangelism, and the need to win the family or group, delaying individual baptisms if necessary to do so.[27]

---

23 X, "A Letter from the Near East," *The Moslem World* 32, no. 1 (1942): 76.
24 Ibid.
25 Ibid., 77.
26 S. A. Morrison, "Thoughts on Moslem Evangelism," *The Moslem World* 32 (1944): 204.
27 Ibid., 203, 206.

Many Religions, One Gospel[*]

I do not conceive of the gospel of Christ as a religion at all. Jesus never used the word. It was foreign to his conception. He was not coming to set one religion over against another. He came to set the gospel over against human need, whether that need be in the Jewish faith, the Gentile religions, or among Jesus' own followers. "There are many religions; there is but one gospel." For religions are man's search for God; the gospel is God's search for man. One is from man up to God, and the other is from God down to man.

I know, when I say that, it sounds presumptuous, for a religion was built up around Jesus ... but the gospel confronts that man-made and fallible system with the same demand and offer as it does the other religions. We do not preach this system built up around Jesus; we preach to it just as we would preach to any other human need. Our message is not the system, but the Savior.

He is the gospel. The gospel lies in his Person. He himself is the good news. He didn't come to bring the good news. He is the good news. We therefore bring him to East and West and say: The issue is simple. Christ and his kingdom is the issue. Take him direct. . . . Go straight to the Gospels to discover Jesus anew.

—*E. Stanley Jones*

* Excerpt from E. Stanley Jones, *Mahatma Gandhi: An Interpretation* (Nashville: Abingdon-Cokesbury Press, 1948), 63–64.

It was not until 1947 that the *Moslem World* resumed its discussion of the Near East Council's report with A. R. Stevenson's "Whoever Shall Confess Me Before Men. . . ."[28] He acknowledged that there were good reasons to support the report's position, but he would present only the case against it: "Christian converts drawn from the Moslem community should be urged to make public profession of their faith."[29] His article emphasized the example of apostolic witness and the utter absence of NT teaching supporting "secret belief." Methodologically, Stevenson could not see how a vital, growing church could ever materialize following the latter alternative. Thus the erroneous understanding of what the Near East Council report had advocated persisted. Critics could only conceive of two options: aggressive, outspoken public witness or secret belief—despite the 1942 clarification that the unbeaten path being proposed was a third way: that of faithful disciples of Christ who were wise-as-serpent witnesses and did not "cast their pearls before swine." Perhaps if the critics lived another generation and witnessed the spectacular growth of the underground church in Communist China, they might have responded differently; for under repressive totalitarian communism, the underground church did not follow an "open, public confession" methodology, but instead that of discreet and opportune witness similar to the "unbeaten path" envisioned by the Riggs report.

Thereafter, discussion of these ideas disappeared from the pages of the *Moslem World*, but they did not die. In 1969, veteran Southern Baptist missionary Virginia Cobb was weakened by disease and soon to be in the presence of the Lord, but her paper was read at the Tehran Conference, greatly impacting the conferees:

28 "Whoever Shall Confess Me Before Men . . . ," *The Moslem World* 37, no. 2 (1947): 99–106.
29 Ibid., 99.

> We are not trying to change anyone's religion. Religion consists of
> affiliation with a group . . . [a] dogma, and structure of authority.
> . . . The New Testament is quite clear that none of these saves. It
> is possible to change all of them without knowing God. . . . Our
> message is a Person we've experienced, not a doctrine, system, [or]
> religion.[30]

A few years later, in 1976, Martin Goldsmith reiterated the social impediment to conversion, hinting at the difference between personal piety and religious identity in Islamic society:

> Islam is within the whole warp and woof of society—in the fam-
> ily, in politics, in social relationships. To leave the Muslim faith
> is to break with one's whole society. . . . Many a modern educated
> Muslim is not all that religiously minded; but he must, neverthe-
> less, remain a Muslim for social reasons. . . . This makes it almost
> unthinkable for most Muslims even to consider the possibility of
> becoming a follower of some other religion.[31]

For this reason, it has been observed that the conversion of a Muslim to Christianity has usually trig-gered a mechanism similar to the "transplant rejection" phenomenon in medicine. Converts are cut off from the family and society, and if the traditional sanction against "apostasy" (i.e., death) is not applied, they are forced to return to Islam, to join one of the isolated minority communities, or to emigrate to the West.[32]

The following year John D. C. Anderson proposed the concept of a "Jesus Muslim":

> Is it possible for a man to be a child of God, a worshipper of Christ,
> and yet still to fall under the broad national and cultural category
> of being a Muslim? . . . There are many experienced Christians who
> would regard it as blatant compromise, or as a form of religious
> syncretism. But our need is to differentiate between the traditional
> concept of making a Muslim into a Christian, with all the trans-
> fer of his loyalties to an imported Christian subculture that this
> involves, and, in contrast, that of making him into a disciple of
> Jesus Christ, with a primary loyalty to him as Saviour and lord
> from amidst his nationalities. His headlong confrontation with
> conservative Muslim theology will come sooner or later. But may
> he have enough time to demonstrate to his family and friends that
> the servant of Christ is neither a blasphemer of Allah, nor a traitor
> to the best interests of his country, but in the highest possible sense
> one who submits himself to the will of God (which is what Islam
> means)? *Thus the emphasis we are trying to make is upon the Muslim*

---

30 Virginia Cobb, "An Approach to Witness," *The Commission* 32, no. 9 (September 1970): 5–9 (*UIM*, chap. 44), available at http://archives.imb.org/solomon.asp.

31 Martin Goldsmith, "Community and Controversy: Key Causes of Muslim Resistance," *Missiology: An International Review* 4, no. 3 (July 1976): 318.

32 Samuel Schlorff, "Contextualization in Islamic Society: Issues and Positions," *Seedbed* 3, no. 1 (1988): 3–4.

and his culture being changed from within. It was just in such a way that our Western culture has been changed from within, when once the transforming gospel made its entree. This approach is not currently accepted by the Western church. It is contended here, however, that its implications need much closer study. In any case, what are we to say to the fact that our traditional approach to the Muslim has been so singularly unproductive? In the past, a convert from Islam has only been seen by his fellow countrymen in a negative light as one who throws out Islam in toto. Whereas in fact, there is much in Islam that appeals to the conscience of good men.

The issue is really *where the ultimate spiritual battle is to be fought.* Is it to be *inside Islam, or outside?* In the one case a few expelled converts try, if they have the courage, to persuade their erstwhile Muslim friends to leave Islam and to join the Christians. In the other, a thousand earnest disciples, with varying depths of spiritual perception, are asking questions within Islam, which may ultimately shake it to its foundations.[33]

Also in 1977, John Wilder wrote optimistically of Muslim people movements to Christ taking place along these lines.[34] At the Glen Eyrie conference that same year, Harvie Conn outlined key concepts that laid foundations for later insider movement thinking.[35] Conn emphasized the need to move beyond the traditional apologetic approach that set Christianity against Islam as monolithic ideologies. Moreover, essentialist views of religion failed to account for the sociological diversity found in Muslim cultures and precluded attempts to "transform or possess Islamic culture for Christ."[36] Conn also argued for conversion as a process of discipleship and for group decisions in an effort to remove unnecessary social, cultural, and communal obstacles to Muslims coming to Christ. The only barrier must be Christ alone. Conn's attitude toward the notion of "Jesus Muslims" or a "Muslimun 'Issawiyun (submission to Jesus) movement"[37] was indicated by his conclusion: "We must look for a verbal equivalent similar to the Jews for Jesus movement who speak instead of being 'completed in Christ.'"[38] Meanwhile Charles Kraft called for "dynamic equivalence" churches that focused on true "faith-allegiance" versus Christianity as a religious system.[39] These writings, all published prior to 1980, were followed by a seminal article

---

33 John D. C. Anderson, "The Missionary Approach to Islam: Christian or 'Cultic,'" *Muslim World Pulse* 6, no. 1 (1977): 4–5; emphasis added.

34 John W. Wilder, "Some Reflections on Possibilities for People Movements among Muslims," *Missiology: An International Review* 5, no. 3 (1977): 301–20. See John Travis' discussion of Wilder in *UIM,* chap. 16.

35 Harvie M. Conn, "The Muslim Convert and His Culture," in *The Gospel and Islam: A 1978 Compendium,* ed. Don M. McCurry (Monrovia, CA: MARC, 1979): 97–113.

36 Ibid., 99.

37 Ibid., 97.

38 Ibid., 108.

39 Charles H. Kraft, "Dynamic Equivalence Churches in Muslim Society," in *The Gospel and Islam: A 1978 Compendium,* ed. Don M. McCurry (Monrovia, CA: MARC, 1979), 114–24. See also Kraft in *UIM,* chap. 36.

by J. Dudley Woodberry in 1989 that provided one of the first case studies of the birth and growth of an IM.[40]

Meanwhile, outside the arena of these missiological discussions, new practices were quietly being pioneered on the ground. For example, beginning in the 1930s, Rev. Fouad Accad, chairman of the Bible Society of the Middle East for forty-two years, had a fruitful evangelistic ministry among Muslims in the Arab world that embodied insider paradigm principles.[41] By the 1970s, he was mentoring several missionaries and nationals in his approach (a number of whom are still active in insider ministry). Accad pored over the Qur'an along with Muslim commentaries and literature, searching for stepping stones to Jesus. He then developed and wrote *The Seven Muslim Christian Principles*, supporting each principle with verses from the *Tawrah* (OT), *Zabur* (Psalms), *Injil* (NT), and Qur'an.[42] The team he was mentoring field-tested the book and saw it bear fruit. Accad's mentoring ministry spread internationally, helping movements develop in other parts of the globe.[43]

Contemporary Developments Regarding Insider Movements

During the past two millennia, millions of adherents of the world's "minor religious traditions" (e.g., animistic, tribal, and ethnic belief systems) have accepted Jesus and embraced an entirely new religion, Christianity. However, those from the world's present-day "major religious traditions" of Islam, Hinduism, Judaism, and Buddhism have shown far less openness to the gospel, especially when it has been presented as available only within the religion of Christianity.[44] The same factors cited above as impeding the gospel in Muslim contexts are at work among these other major religious traditions. Two decades ago, H. L. Richard asked, "Is extraction evangelism still the way to go?"[45] He noted the dichotomous dealings of missions of the church in India between tribal works, where missionaries are expected as much as possible to develop churches as an integral part of tribal society, and high-caste Hindu and Muslim outreaches, where individuals are called to profess Christ and join the Christian denominations and churches, extracting them from home and society and destroying bridges for the gospel. Not surprisingly, tribal outreach has been much more successful, as opposed to the lack of effectiveness in winning high-caste Hindus and Muslims. Richard acknowledged that we must be concerned about avoiding compromise with Hindu and Muslim cultures, but that we should take note of the elasticity of these cultures to oftentimes tolerate renegade religious elements:

---

40 J. Dudley Woodberry, "Contextualization among Muslims: Reusing Common Pillars," in *The Word Among Us: Contextualizing Theology for Mission Today*, ed. Dean S. Gilliland (Dallas: Word Books, 1989), 282–312 (*UIM*, chap. 45).

41 See also the testimony of his grandson, Martin Accad, in his response to Joseph Cumming in *UIM*, chap. 3.

42 Fouad Elias Accad, *The Seven Muslim Christian Principles* (Limassol, Cyprus: Al-Rabitah, n.d.). The book was later retitled *Theological Principles from the Tawrah, Zabur, Injil, and Qur'an*. It was subsequently included in Accad's book *Building Bridges: Christianity and Islam* (Colorado Springs, CO: NavPress, 1997), published posthumously.

43 Spending a weekend with Accad and continued association with some of those he mentored have been significant influences in the development of my missiological thinking.

44 The exceptions occur in cases of oppression and severe disillusionment, desperation, or trauma. Oppressed minorities, like the once-Christian Berbers reacting to Arab discrimination in North Africa, or the outcaste Dalits among Hindus, are rejecting their religion in favor of another. Iranians disillusioned with radical Islam are either rejecting religion completely or choosing Christianity.

45 H. L. Richard, "Is Extraction Evangelism Still the Way to Go?" *EMQ* 30, no. 2 (1994): 170–74.

> The presence of anti-idolatry movements within Hinduism should make us pause. Why can an educated Hindu reject idol worship and stay in his home (usually not without problems), while those who under Christian influence reject idolatry are expelled? The same applies to caste, which many modern Hindus are defying to various extents.[46]

By tracing the preceding historical developments, we can see how missiological thinking was making room for IMs. The question of linkage has not been adequately studied, but it is only since the 1980s that we have witnessed the birth of such movements in the modern era. Just as the new non-Jewish form of faith that emerged as Gentile Christianity created conflict in the body of Christ in the first century, so these Jesus movements outside our Christian religious traditions have caused controversy in our own time. By the same token, the seminal articles that we surveyed—and the far-reaching ideas they proposed—seem to have been largely confined to the towers of academic missiology. It was the 1998 publication of John Travis' "C1–C6 Spectrum," together with Phil Parshall's grave concerns,[47] that seems to have put these ideas on the radar of the missions community at large, eventually leading to the current controversy.

In an attempt to address the growing tension, the International Society of Frontier Missiology invited both proponents and critics of IMs to Atlanta in 2006 in hopes of bringing insight and clarification in a respectful and scholarly environment. The conference papers were then published in the *International Journal of Frontier Missions* (*IJFM*) to facilitate a process of enlightened interaction, signaling a step toward rapprochement.

In 2009 *Christianity Today* (*CT*) attempted to reduce the rhetoric with Joseph Cumming's "Muslim Followers of Jesus?"[48] and soon after John Jay Travis and J. Dudley Woodberry brought clarification in "When God's Kingdom Grows Like Yeast."[49] Because the phrase "insider movements" had become so misrepresented and distorted, they wrote in terms of "Jesus movements within Muslim communities." Publications on the topic proliferated, and churches in North America and abroad entered the discussion.

In 2011 concerned missiologists initiated "Bridging the Divide" (BtD) consultations, bringing together workers among Muslims with diverse views on IMs annually to discuss their differences and agreements face to face.[50] The *Evangelical Review of Theology* performed a notable service by devoting its October 2013 issue to dialogues between the BtD participants over important IM issues. Influential publications have attempted to educate the Christian public.[51]

---

46 Ibid., 172.

47 See Travis, "The C1–C6 Spectrum: A Practical Tool for Defining Six Types of 'Christ-Centered Communities' ('C') Found in the Muslim Context," *EMQ* 34, no. 4 (1998): 411–15; Parshall, "DANGER! New Directions in Contextualization," *EMQ* 34, no. 4 (1998): 404–10; and Travis in *UIM*, chap. 51.

48 Cumming, "Muslim Followers of Jesus?," *CT*, December 2009 (*UIM*, chap. 3).

49 Travis and Woodberry, "When God's Kingdom Grows like Yeast: Frequently Asked Questions about Jesus Movements within Muslim Communities," *MF*, July–August 2010 (*UIM*, chap. 4).

50 The first three BtD gatherings met at Houghton College, NY, in 2011, 2012, and 2013. See Roberts' assessment in *UIM*, chap. 57.

51 For instance, *CT* cast favorable light on IMs in an interview between Gene Daniels and a Muslim follower of Jesus. See Daniels, "Worshiping Jesus in the Mosque," *Christianity Today*, January 2013.

A significant event in 2014 was the publication of Southern Baptist David Garrison's in-depth research on the momentous surge of Jesus movements in the Muslim world.[52] Garrison cautiously revealed that a number of them were IMs. He had previously viewed the notion somewhat negatively due to deficiencies he presumed to be inherent in IMs, but his investigations showed that his concerns were unfounded, and he was amazed by what God was doing among insiders.

The controversy shows little sign of abating soon, but the ratio of heat to light may be diminishing. Recently, scholars have suggested that the chief causes of the controversy may not actually be theological, but rather differences in personal preferences, mission paradigms, cultural patterns, and worldview (e.g., the confusion caused by the Western construction and reification of the concept of "religion").[53] Without question, the relevant issues are many and complex. It is the aim of this volume to tackle the most significant of them. So having set the historical background, let us begin.

Bibliography

Accad, Fouad Elias. *Building Bridges: Christianity and Islam.* Colorado Springs, CO: NavPress, 1997.

———. *The Seven Muslim Christian Principles.* Limassol, Cyprus: Al-Rabitah, n.d. Subsequently retitled *Theological Principles from the Tawrah, Zabur, Injil, and Qur'an.*

Anderson, John D. C. "The Missionary Approach to Islam: Christian or 'Cultic.'" *Muslim World Pulse* 6, no. 1 (1977): 4–5.

Chetti, Kandaswami. "'Why I Am Not a Christian': A Personal Statement." *Madras Christian College Magazine*, 1915.

Cobb, Virginia. "An Approach to Witness." *The Commission* 32, no. 2 (1970): 5–9. Available at https://solomon.3e2a.org/public/ws/perdl/www2/documentp/Record?parenttreeid=3956693&sessiondepth=2&parenttreeid=3956693&sessiondepth=2&w=NATIVE%28%27PUBLICATION+%3D+%27%27The+Commission%27%27+and+YEAR+%3D+%27%271970%27%27%27%29&upp=0&order=native%28%27YEAR%27%29&rpp=10&r=1&m=9.

Conn, Harvie M. "The Muslim Convert and His Culture." In *The Gospel and Islam: A 1978 Compendium,* edited by Don M. McCurry, 97–113. Monrovia, CA: MARC, 1979.

Daniels, Gene. "Worshiping Jesus in the Mosque." *Christianity Today,* January 2013.

Garrison, David. *A Wind in the House of Islam: How God Is Drawing Muslims around the World to Faith in Jesus Christ.* Monument, CO: WIGTake, 2014.

Goldsmith, Martin. "Community and Controversy: Key Causes of Muslim Resistance." *Missiology: An International Review* 4, no. 3 (1976): 317–23.

Haigh, H. "Vernacular Literature." In *Report of the Third Decennial Missionary Conference Held at Bombay, 1892–93,* vol. 2, edited by Alfred Mainwaring. Bombay: Education Society's Steam Press, 1893.

Hoefer, Herbert. "Church In Context." *Evangelical Missions Quarterly* 43, no. 2 (2007): 200–208.

———. *Churchless Christianity.* Pasadena, CA: William Carey Library, 2001.

Kraft, Charles. "Dynamic Equivalence Churches in Muslim Society." In *The Gospel and Islam: A 1978 Compendium,* edited by Don M. McCurry, 114–24. Monrovia, CA: MARC, 1979.

---

52 David Garrison, *A Wind in the House of Islam: How God Is Drawing Muslims around the World to Faith in Jesus Christ* (Monument, CO: WIGTake, 2014).

53 See Bartlotti, chap. 6; Holton, chap. 38; Richard, chap. 40; and Iyadurai, chap. 60.

Lipner, Julius J. *Brahmabandhab Upadhyay: The Life and Thought of a Revolutionary*. New Delhi: Oxford University Press, 1999.

Morrison, S. A. "Thoughts on Moslem Evangelism." *The Moslem World* 32 (1944): 203–6.

Parshall, Phil. "DANGER! New Directions in Contextualization." *Evangelical Missions Quarterly* 34, no. 4 (1998): 404–10.

Richard, H. L. *Following Jesus in the Hindu Context*. Pasadena, CA: William Carey Library, 1998.

———. "Is Extraction Evangelism Still the Way to Go?" *Evangelical Missions Quarterly* 30, no. 2 (1994): 170–74.

Riggs, Henry H. "Near East Christian Council Inquiry on the Evangelization of Moslems." Paper, Library of the Near East School of Theology, Beirut, November 1938. Available at http://www.scribd.com/doc/110704319/NEAR-EAST-CHRISTIAN-COUNCIL-INQUIRY-ON-THE-EVANGELIZATION-OF-MOSLEMS-November-1938-by-H-Riggs-and-the-Near-East-Christian-Council.

———. "Shall We Try Unbeaten Paths in Working for Muslims?" *The Moslem World* 31, no. 2 (1941): 116–26.

Schlorff, Samuel. "Contextualization in Islamic Society: Issues and Positions." *Seedbed* 3, no. 1 (1988): 3–4.

Stevenson, A. R. "Whoever Shall Confess Me Before Men . . ." *The Moslem World* 37, no. 2 (1947): 99–106.

Travis, John. "The C1–C6 Spectrum: A Practical Tool for Defining Six Types of 'Christ-Centered Communities' ('C') Found in the Muslim Context." *Evangelical Missions Quarterly* 34, no. 4 (1998): 411–15.

Vander Werff, Lyle L. *Christian Mission to Muslims: The Record*. Pasadena, CA: William Carey Library, 1977.

Wilder, John W. "Some Reflections on Possibilities for People Movements among Muslims." *Missiology: An International Review* 5, no. 3 (1977): 302–20.

Wilson, J. Christy. "Public Confession and the Church." *The Moslem World* 31, no. 2 (1941): 127–39.

Woodberry, J. Dudley. "Contextualization among Muslims: Reusing Common Pillars." In *The Word among Us*, edited by Dean S. Gilliland, 303–6. Dallas: Word Publishing, 1989.

X. "A Letter from the Near East." *The Moslem World* 32, no. 1 (1942): 76.

Zwemer, Samuel M. "The Dynamic of Evangelism." *The Moslem World* 31, no. 2 (1941): 109–15.

CHAPTER 3

Muslim Followers of Jesus?[*]

Joseph Cumming

In 1979 my best friend decided he saw himself not as a "Christian" but as a "Messianic Jew." John had come from a secular Jewish background and was actually a practicing Hindu before he met Jesus. Then for three years he was active in a Bible-believing Christian church. But now John felt called to reconnect with his Jewish roots, join a Messianic synagogue, keep a kosher home, and raise his children Jewish. He saw no contradiction between following Jesus as Messiah and identifying—ethnically and religiously—as Jewish.

Like most Christians in the 1970s, I initially reacted with skepticism, quoting biblical texts I thought rejected *kashrut* (the Jewish dietary laws) as contrary to our liberty in Christ. I gradually learned that those texts could be understood differently, and came to respect the legitimacy of the fledgling Messianic movement—but not before I hurt my friend by my hostility to his effort to explore his identity as a Jewish follower of Jesus.

The wider Jewish community also reacted negatively. Most saw Messianic Judaism as simply repackaging centuries-old efforts to convert Jews, destroying Jewish identity. To them Messianic Jews were not Jews at all. Recently, however, some Jewish scholars have cautiously suggested that Messianic Jews who faithfully observe Torah and *halakha*, who participate constructively in the life of the Jewish community, and who pass on Jewish traditions to their children are in error but must be recognized as fellow Jews.

In the 1980s a similar movement began among Muslims who had come to faith in Christ. These were Muslims who trusted Jesus as Lord and divine Savior, believed Jesus died for their sins and rose again, and insisted this did not make them ex-Muslims or converts to the Christian religion. They wanted to remain within their Muslim community, honoring Jesus in that context.

Reactions from both Muslim and Christian communities have varied widely. On the Muslim side, some have persecuted these believers, while others cautiously accept them within their communities. On the Christian side, defenders see them as "Messianic Muslims" whom we should accept—just as we accept Messianic Jews—as authentic disciples of Jesus. Critics argue that Islam and Judaism are different, that Muslim identity cannot be reconciled with biblical faith.

Mixed Faiths, Mixed Reactions

When Nabil had a life-transforming encounter with Jesus, he remained within the Muslim community, participating in Muslim prayers. As his love for Jesus became known to family and friends, some followed his example, but others actually attempted to murder him. After being imprisoned for his

---

[*] Originally published in a slightly different form in *Christianity Today*, December 2009. Reprinted by permission.

beliefs, he decided he no longer considered himself a Muslim. He saw Islam as the system responsible for persecuting him. Today Nabil considers himself a Christian. But some who followed him in faith still see themselves as Muslims.

Ibrahim was a well-respected scholar of the Qur'an, a *hafiz*. When he decided to follow Jesus, he closely examined the qur'anic verses commonly understood as denying the Trinity, denying Jesus' divine Sonship, denying Jesus' atoning death, and denying the textual integrity of the Bible. He concluded that each of these verses was open to alternate interpretations, and that he could therefore follow Jesus as a Muslim. Soon members of his family and community came to share his faith in Jesus as Lord and Savior. Ibrahim was also imprisoned for his faith, but unlike Nabil, Ibrahim still wanted to follow Jesus as a Muslim. Nonetheless, some whom he led to Jesus no longer see themselves as Muslims. Ibrahim and Nabil are friends and respect each other as brothers, though they disagree about their identity.

As Christians from other cultures meet believers like Nabil and Ibrahim, they have mixed reactions. Phil Parshall and John Travis have, between them, worked for more than sixty years among Muslims, and they respectfully disagree with each other. They have published a series of articles in missiological journals, setting forth points on which they differ. Numerous articles by others have followed.

In technical terms this is known as the "C4/C5 debate," drawing on a scale designed by Travis to describe various Christ-centered communities (Cs) with which Muslim-background believers in Jesus (MBBs) identify, and the ways they understand their identity:

- C1: MBBs in churches radically different from their own culture, where worship is in a language other than their mother tongue.
- C2: Same as C1, but worship is in the MBBs' mother tongue.
- C3: MBBs in culturally indigenous Christian churches that avoid cultural forms seen as "Islamic."
- C4: MBBs in culturally indigenous congregations that retain biblically permissible Islamic forms (e.g., prostrating in prayer), investing these with biblical meaning. They may call themselves something other than Christians (e.g., "followers of Jesus"), but do not see themselves as Muslims.
- C5: Muslims who follow Jesus as Lord and Savior in fellowships of like-minded believers within the Muslim community, continuing to identify culturally and officially as Muslims.
- C6: Secret/underground believers.

The most vigorous disagreement is between C4 and C5 advocates. To help readers understand the issues, I'll set forth concerns expressed by C1–C4 advocates troubled by C5. Then I'll summarize responses from C5 defenders. These concerns and responses are in quotation marks to make clear that these are others' views, not necessarily my own. Then I'll add my own comments.

C4 concern: "Scripture (e.g., 1 Kgs 18:21; 2 Kgs 17:27–41) condemns syncretism. Trying to be both Muslims and followers of Jesus is syncretistic."

C5 response: "This is not the syncretism Scripture condemns. C5 believers live under the authority of the Bible (e.g., Acts 16:1–3; 21:20–40; 1 Cor 9:19–23), reinterpreting or rejecting anything contrary to Scripture."

Comment: Both sides of this discussion have done serious exegetical work in Scripture, which they believe supports their view. It is impossible to do justice to either side in this article. Readers would do well to examine articles in *Evangelical Missions Quarterly* and the *International Journal of Frontier Missions,* where the biblical issues are set forth.

C4 concern: "Islam and Judaism are different: one cannot compare 'Messianic Islam' with Messianic Judaism. The Hebrew Scriptures are recognized by Christians as inspired; the Qur'an is not. The mosque is pregnant with Islamic theology that explicitly denies biblical truths."

C5 response: "Islam and Judaism are different, but both are monotheistic. Islam recognizes the Torah and New Testament as Scripture alongside the Qur'an. Rabbinic Judaism sees as authoritative not just the Hebrew Scriptures (*Tanakh*) but also the Talmud, which, like the Qur'an, contains a mixture of material compatible and incompatible with the New Testament. Traditional synagogue liturgy also seems to repudiate New Testament teachings, but both liturgies can be reinterpreted, and attendance at prayers does not necessarily mean affirming every word of liturgy."

Comment: The term "Messianic Islam" is unhelpful. For Jews the messiahship of Jesus is a watershed issue, whereas Muslims recognize Jesus as Messiah but raise other objections to Christian beliefs about Jesus. Most Muslims believe the text of the Bible has been corrupted, but some Muslim scholars disagree. C5 believers affirm the Bible as God's word. Sacred texts must be examined closely, considering whether proposed interpretations are legitimate and honest.

C4 concern: "The C5 approach is deceitful. How would you feel if Muslims showed up at your church claiming to be Christians, then tried to convert your people to Islam?"

C5 response: "It is not deceitful if C5 believers are transparent with the Muslim community about who they are and what they believe. C5 believers honestly see themselves as Muslims, not as Christians pretending to be Muslims. They are *not* seeking to convert Muslims to Christianity."

Comment: Remember, Travis' scale describes how believers born and raised as Muslims understand their identity, *not* how people raised as Christians describe themselves.

C4 concern: "The Muslim community won't tolerate such aberrant Muslims within their ranks."

C5 response: "It's too soon to be certain of that."

Comment: The Muslim community can speak for itself. When I have discussed this with Muslim leaders, their primary concern has been whether these people continue to *practice* the moral and ritual requirements of the Muslim community with which they identify (i.e., what *madhhab* they follow). They also assert that all Muslims follow Jesus as prophet and Messiah, just not in the terms Christians draw from the New Testament.

C4 concern: "To call oneself Muslim is to affirm Muhammad as a true prophet of God. That is incompatible with the Bible."

C5 response: "Actually, 'Muslim' means different things to different Muslims. C5 believers have a variety of views about Muhammad, including: (1) one can be culturally Muslim without any theological affirmation about Muhammad; (2) Muhammad was a prophet, but not always infallible (cf. Caiaphas in John 11:51; 1 Thess 5:20,21); (3) Muhammad was a prophet for Arabs, but not for other peoples; (4) Muhammad was a true prophet whose words have been misinterpreted; (5) this question is unimportant either way."

Comment: For the overwhelming majority of Muslims, the prophethood of Muhammad is nonnegotiably essential to Muslim identity. But the word *"Muslim"* (literal Arabic meaning: "submitted to God") does mean different things in different contexts. The Qur'an calls Jesus' first disciples "Muslims" (Q3:52). In some societies, "Muslim" and "Christian" refer more to ethnicity than to religious beliefs.

C4 concern: "C5 MBBs retain Muslim identity to avoid persecution for the cross of Christ."

C5 response: "That's an unfair judging of motives. The issue is religiocultural identity, not the cross of Christ, which C5 believers affirm."

Comment: If C5 believers are trying to avoid persecution, it isn't working. Many have been terribly persecuted, suffering imprisonment and worse for their convictions.

C4 concern: "What about the church? Do C5 believers see themselves as part of Christ's body?"

C5 response: "C5 believers form Christ-centered fellowships in which they study the Bible, pray, and celebrate baptism and the Lord's Supper. These are *ekklesiae* in the New Testament sense, though they may look very different from what Christians usually call 'churches.'"

Comment: Studying and obeying Scripture helps local fellowships be holy and apostolic. But Scripture also calls fellowships to recognize the unity and universality of the worldwide body of Christ. Some C5 fellowships, and some workers partnering with them, have very negative views of or broken relationships with non-MBB churches. Other C5 fellowships have healthy attitudes toward the wider church.

C4 concern: "I have heard some C5 groups have sloppy Christology. This alarms me."

C5 response: "Some C5 believers do have fuzzy Christology, but so do many ordinary Christians everywhere. What matters is C5 believers' direction of movement: toward Jesus Christ. They pray in his name, worship him as Lord, and experience his supernatural working in their lives. Their Christology keeps moving higher."

Comment: That seems reasonable for new believers. But as this movement grows and its leaders mature, one hopes those leaders will understand sound Christology and articulate it in terms intelligible to their flock. Sensitivity to direction of movement is right, but only with clarity about the ultimate destination of that movement—toward Jesus Christ, not only as Savior and sin-bearing Lamb, but also as eternal, uncreated *Logos,* God manifest in human flesh.

Thoughts Regarding Identity

C5 believers like Ibrahim challenge assumptions about what it means to be Muslim or Christian. We all have more than one identity and community. For example, most American Christians assume one can be both a patriotic American (loyal to that community) and a faithful Christian, though they may disagree with some things their fellow Americans do or teach. Believers like Ibrahim seek to be both authentic Muslims (loyal to the community of their birth) and faithful disciples of Jesus, critically evaluating what their fellow Muslims do and teach in light of the teachings of Christ—sometimes accepting, sometimes reinterpreting, sometimes disagreeing. Do such disagreements require American believers to repudiate American identity and community, or require C5 believers to repudiate the Muslim community and their Muslim identity? How can believers best be "critically loyal" to the community of their birth and to their family heritage, respectfully critiquing what is unscriptural, while upholding God's commandment to "honor your father and mother"?

Ever since the Wesleyan revival and the Great Awakening of the eighteenth century, evangelicals have insisted that what matters most to God is not one's identity as "being a Christian," but rather whether one has a life-transforming relationship with Jesus Christ. David Brainerd was expelled from Yale University in 1742 for remarking that a certain faculty member (a loyal "Christian") had "no more grace than this chair" because he did not have a personal relationship with Jesus.

Does it follow that it is totally unimportant for believers to call themselves Christians? With Messianic Jews, the evangelical community mostly accepts that the label "Christian" is not essential. Is the same true for C5 believers, or is Islam too radically different? If the latter, then what specific differences between the Jewish and Muslim communities prompt us to accept one and reject the other?

Let me close with a plea from my heart. In recent months this debate has grown acrimonious. Muslim-background believers like Nabil and Ibrahim are mostly unable to participate directly in the discussion, because doing so would expose them to further persecution. Instead, Christians from non-Muslim backgrounds are holding a debate without them, anathematizing first Ibrahim, then Nabil. But Nabil and Ibrahim themselves respect each other as brothers and are able to disagree in love.

As for me, remembering how I hurt my Jewish friend in 1979, I want to be very careful not to hurtfully reject brothers who have already suffered rejection and prison for Jesus. Jesus said, "Whoever comes to me I will never drive away" (John 6:37).

As Nabil and Ibrahim understand their position in the universal body of Christ, they must listen to counsel from others around the world. But if we understand our position in that same body, then we must respect their fundamental human right to sort out—under the authority of Scripture—how they express their identity as followers of Christ. It is they whose lives are quite literally on the line. If they can respect each other after suffering prison for Jesus, then surely we can treat them both with respect.

Response to Joseph Cumming by Martin Accad: Away with the Sterile Debates!

As a follower of Jesus with a Christian family background, as a Lebanese having grown up and currently living on the Muslim-majority side of Beirut, as the grandson and son of grandparents and parents who have loved and served the Muslim community with the gospel of Jesus throughout their lives, I am often alarmed at how sterile and decontextualized much of the whole debate over so-called "contextualization" has often become in churches, seminaries, and missionary circles. The irony is that most of those directly affected on a day-to-day basis by the issue, the "Nabils" and "Ibrahims" in the Muslim world, whose lives are on the line yet for whom the victory of one side of the debate over the other is virtually meaningless, are not even aware this debate is raging. Did members of the Gentile churches of the New Testament await the outcome of the debate within the Jerusalem church about their legitimacy before they became and called themselves Christ followers (*Christianoi*)? Thank God they did not!

Joseph Cumming has served us well in his article by distilling this tiresome debate for us in around two thousand words. He puts faces and names to the controversial phenomenon: "Nabil" and "Ibrahim" summarize the main issues of the debate dialectically in eight concise points. Cumming helpfully recasts the debate in the comparative context of Messianic Judaism. I say "helpfully" because today, unlike in the 1970s, most American Christians have become sympathetic to the cause of Messianic Jews. Conversely, due to the widespread attitude of suspicion of all things Muslim since 9/11, a substantial number of American Christians find it hard to believe there is anything legitimate or even redeemable in a Muslim's religion and culture. Never mind the fact that, as an Arab Christian, I share much more with the culture of Arab Muslims than with that of American Christians.

I remember sitting half-amused some time ago at an international missions conference lunch table, while two gentlemen debated whether my grandfather, Fouad Accad (author of *Building Bridges: Christianity and Islam*), would have sat more comfortably with the C4 or the C5 side of the "contextualization" debate. My grandfather was an Arab Christian, a friend of Muslims, conversant in the Qur'an and Muslim traditions and practices. He lived and died in the Arab world, was there as friend and mentor at the side of many high-profile Muslim leaders as they embarked on the path of Christ and remained respected leaders in their communities. He did not engage them in a debate on whether they should proclaim their break with Islam, pack their bags and travel "West," or simply await persecution and death. He did not give them a list of items they could legitimately keep in their religious bag and others they should do away with. Nor would he have awaited the decision of mission and church leaders on whether he should proceed with his calling using the C4 or C5 model of ministry. Thank God he did not!

Those like my grandfather and father, who are engaged in living and modeling Christ in the Muslim world (be they cultural insiders or outsiders), should not, and indeed do not, await a green light from some mission-theory gurus sitting in the West in order to pursue Christ's calling. Joseph Cumming and his family are an excellent example of that. They lived the way of Christ and shared his love in the context of real-life friendships in North Africa, and they practiced responsible and wise discipleship several years before the C1–C6 debate began to rage. This kind of discipleship continues to ask two simple, time-tested questions: (1) How will you make sense of your social identity, with full respect for your context and avoiding the loss of your social influence, in the light of your experience of the living Christ and in obedience to his word? And (2) how will you live your life in the path of Christ in a way that is compelling and can serve as a model for your family, relatives, and broader community? These are the two great questions of *relevance* and *continuity* that no effective servant of the good news can afford to ignore.

When certain key figures of the Jerusalem synagogue (Paul in Acts 9) and of the Jerusalem church (Peter in Acts 10) came to terms with the fact that their primary accountability was to God and to the living Christ, rather than to Judaism and its precepts,[1] they were released for effective ministry to the Gentiles, for whom, they realized, Jesus had died as well. When we, in our churches, come to terms with the fact that our primary accountability is to God and the living Christ, rather than to Christianity and its institutional boundaries, we will be released for effective ministry to Muslims, for whom Jesus has indeed died. Cumming has mastered the art of marrying relational transparency with gospel clarity, on the one hand, with the ability, on the other, to explain clearly some complex and sensitive issues of missiology to the internal audience of the church. Let me be clear. It is not the classification of a phenomenon on a scale that is the problem. On the contrary, when Travis developed his C1–C6 Spectrum in 1998, he provided an important framework to understand what God had been doing across the world.[2] It is the ensuing discourse, which turned an interpretive framework into a missional methodology, that misses the forest for the trees.

Bibliography

Travis, John. "Must All Muslims Leave Islam to Follow Jesus?" *Evangelical Missions Quarterly* 34, no. 4 (1998): 411–15.

---

1 As interpreted by the Jewish religious establishment of that time.—Ed.
2 See Travis, "Must All Muslims Leave Islam to Follow Jesus?" *EMQ* 34, no. 4 (1998): 411–15.

CHAPTER 4

When God's Kingdom Grows like Yeast

*Frequently Asked Questions about Jesus
Movements within Muslim Communities**

John Jay Travis and J. Dudley Woodberry

In Matthew 13:33 and Luke 13:20 Jesus likens the kingdom of God to yeast, a substance that transforms from the inside out. In the days surrounding his death and resurrection, Jesus instructed his followers to proclaim the good news of the kingdom to all peoples of the world. Today numbers of Muslims have accepted this good news, allowing the yeast of the kingdom to transform their lives and their families, while remaining part of their own Muslim communities. Since there is a variety of perspectives on this phenomenon, even among the Islamic Studies faculty where we teach, we here seek to address some frequently asked questions about it.

1. *What are some examples of this type of movement to Jesus within Muslim communities?*[1] In one such movement, a middle-aged Muslim woman read the New Testament with a Christian friend for a number of years. During that time, her son was dramatically healed of a serious disease after receiving prayer by her friend's husband. A year later she came to faith in Jesus as a Muslim. Soon thereafter she felt God calling her to take the message of Jesus to her Muslim family and friends. She was known as a devout woman with true concern for her community. Due to the empowering of the Holy Spirit and her gifts as a communicator and community organizer, she led dozens to faith and began many small Jesus fellowships, primarily through her own extended family, neighborhood, and work associates. The message of Jesus and the kingdom continues to multiply like yeast, Muslim follower of Jesus to Muslim, through a number of social networks.

Another such movement began with a high-ranking Muslim leader who had a dream that involved Jesus. He sent some of his followers to a group of local Christians to see if someone could help him understand the dream. Over time this Muslim leader felt God was calling him to follow Jesus. He did not believe, however, that God was calling him to change his religious community. He shared the dream and his subsequent experiences with a number of people under his spiritual care. Many of them became followers of Jesus as well. The yeast of the kingdom continues to permeate this large Muslim network.

In another Jesus movement, a young Muslim man boarded with a Christian family, and came to faith as he joined them in their daily reading of the Bible. He came from an influential family and, once saved, committed himself to sharing the gospel with family members in a way they would understand, Muslim follower of Jesus to Muslim. The entire family accepted Jesus as Lord and Savior, and through them the gospel spread to in-laws and distant family members. These Jesus-following Muslims gather

---

*   Originally published in a slightly different form in *MF*, July–August 2010. Reprinted by permission.

1   The authors are acquainted with the following examples, along with others, but actual names and locations have been omitted.

regularly in their homes to study the New Testament. Due to natural networks created through marriage and careers, this Jesus movement has spread to a number of nearby ethnic groups.

In yet another case, the scholars running a qur'anic academy began studying the Bible, and God confirmed his word to them through dreams, visions, and answers to prayer. They believed in Jesus as Lord and Savior and began offering Bible instruction in their academy, in addition to instruction in the Qur'an. They also encouraged the formation of home groups for study and prayer. This launched a movement that has grown quite rapidly.

A very different example is the movement that began when a Muslim Sufi master was praying earnestly to be shown the way of salvation. He was told in a vision to travel to a particular town, to a specific house, where he would meet a man of such-and-such ancestry, who would show him the way of salvation. In the end, the man's Sufi movement became a Jesus movement.[2]

Another movement was started by a convert from Islam who, after years of rejection by both the traditional church of a different ethnicity and by his community of birth, apologized to his father for shaming the family and unnecessarily cutting himself off from them. He began witnessing within his original community, and a large movement has resulted.[3]

2. *If Muslims confess Jesus as Savior and Lord, why would they not simply want to join the Christian religion?*
In some cases, they do. Numbers of Muslims accepting Christ leave Islam and take on a Christian religious identity. For many, however, religious identity is strongly linked with all other aspects of life, so that a change of identity would make it nearly impossible to remain a part of their own family and community. Martin Goldsmith expresses this well:

> Islam is within the whole warp and woof of society—in the family,
> in politics, in social relationships. To leave the Muslim faith is to
> break with one's whole society. Many a modern educated Muslim
> is not all that religiously minded; but he must, nevertheless, remain
> a Muslim for social reasons. . . . This makes it almost unthinkable
> for most Muslims even to consider the possibility of becoming a
> follower of some other religion.[4]

It is because of this strong fusion of family, community, and socioreligious identity that some Muslims who have received the gospel, in an effort to keep their family and social networks intact, choose to remain Muslim, so long as they can be true to Jesus, the Bible, and the leading of the Spirit. The dynamics of witness then become Muslim follower of Jesus to fellow Muslim. Where Muslims find a way to do this, Jesus movements within their communities become viable.

3. *Why is the phenomenon of Jesus movements within Muslim communities only being observed in recent years?*
Much of church history since the advent of Islam has been the story of reaching *peoples from animistic*

---

2   See Rick Brown, "Brother Jacob and Master Isaac: How One Insider Movement Began," *IJFM* 24, no. 1 (2007): 41–42.

3   For another such case study, see Woodberry, chap. 45.

4   Goldsmith, "Community and Controversy: Key Causes of Muslim Resistance," *Missiology: An International Review* 4, no. 3 (1976): 318.

or pagan backgrounds,[5] devotees of what are called minor religious traditions.[6] As for those in the major religious traditions such as Islam and Judaism, few have ever embraced the good news of Jesus.

Today, however, numbers of adherents of the world's major religions are turning to Jesus, some of them sensing no call of God to leave the religious community of their birth.[7] For example, some Jews have accepted Jesus as Messiah while retaining their Jewish socioreligious identity.[8] A similar trend is happening among some Muslims who have become sincere followers of Jesus, obey the Bible, and have remained within their own religious community without joining a branch of the traditional Christian community.

4. It is an interesting idea that the kingdom could move like yeast within a person's original religious community. However, are there not risks or concerns associated with Jesus movements remaining inside such communities? Yes, it would be naive to suggest there are no risks or reasons for concern. At least four areas of particular concern exist for Jesus movements within Muslim communities.

The first is that folk or popular Islamic practices (the use of charms, amulets, divination, numerology, or occult rituals to obtain spiritual power) are deeply ingrained in many Muslim societies, though largely forbidden by formal Islam. These must be renounced by followers of Jesus in order to experience spiritual freedom. If still practiced, Jesus movements would become syncretistic. (*Syncretism,* as often understood in Christian circles, refers to the incorporation of values, beliefs, and practices contrary to the Scriptures, resulting in a sub-biblical faith and a compromised message.) All movements, including those that take place in Christian denominations, have the potential to become sub-biblical or syncretistic if they do not adhere closely to God's word and the leading of his Spirit.

The second concern is that although many Muslim beliefs are compatible with biblical revelation, some commonly held Muslim teachings and interpretations of the Qur'an contradict the gospel. If these are retained, the gospel message would be compromised. (See question 5 below.)

The third is that the presence of strong family and community solidarity may interfere with ultimate allegiance to God through Christ. This solidarity is a strength for Jesus movements when extended families embrace the good news together. On the other hand, community pressure can overwhelm new followers of Jesus, making discipleship difficult and witness tenuous. It follows that they must walk in both wisdom and boldness, with great sensitivity to the Holy Spirit.

The fourth is that in some Islamic communities, violence may await any who deviate from locally established norms and teachings. In these situations, the lives of Jesus followers are sometimes at risk.

5. How do movements remain faithful to Jesus and the Bible when Islam contains teachings that are not compatible with biblical revelation? Among groups of Muslims who follow Jesus, a threefold pattern is observed: they reject certain traditional beliefs and practices that are contrary to the Bible, they reinterpret others in accordance with the Bible, and they minimize others. To understand this, it may be helpful to look at a similar phenomenon within Judaism, another monotheistic Abrahamic faith. Judaism traditionally

---

5   Peoples of tribal or animistic backgrounds who have turned to Christ since the coming of Islam would include some peoples of Northern Europe (e.g., Vikings), Africa, and Asia, and indigenous peoples of North and South America.

6   Typically these new believers linked themselves with various branches of Christianity. This has meant moving from a minor to a major tradition—from a locally known religion to the global religion of Christianity.

7   Various terms have been used to describe these types of Jesus movements, such as "insider movements," "Messianic movements," or "Christ-centered movements"; see Travis, chap. 1.

8   Some of these Jews are quite integrated into the traditional Jewish community and synagogue life; others maintain a more nominal Jewish identity.

holds, for example, that Jesus is not the Messiah, that forgiveness of sins is not granted through his sacrificial death, and that the New Testament is not the word of God. Jews who follow Jesus, however, affirm that Yeshua[9] is the Messiah and Savior of the world and that the New Testament is the word of God. They interpret the traditional Jewish prayers in ways compatible with their belief that Jesus is the Messiah, fast on Yom Kippur, and observe other Jewish traditions in light of new covenant understanding.

A similar process is happening among Jesus-following Muslims. Most Muslims interpret the Qur'an to say that Jesus did not die on the Cross and that the biblical text has been corrupted. However, the meaning of certain qur'anic verses is unclear, and historically Muslim commentators have given interpretations of the Qur'an that affirm the authenticity and reliability of the Bible and point the way toward believing in the literal death of Christ.[10] Born-again Muslims fully believe in the bodily death and resurrection of Jesus ('Isa)[11] and affirm the authority of the Bible[12] as the word of God. They reject the pursuit of spiritual power through mystical or magic-oriented practices that are common in many Muslim contexts. Similar to Yeshua-following Jews who fast during Yom Kippur (the Day of Atonement), many Isa-following Muslims keep the Ramadan fast and daily prayers yet interpret their meaning in a way compatible with their faith in Jesus. They do not view the fast and daily prayers as a means of salvation and forgiveness of sin, but as a means to draw near to God. Just as with all followers of Jesus, as wholehearted allegiance to God is realized in obedient lives, the relative importance of some components of their background is minimized.

6. *By not calling oneself a Christian, could not this be viewed as a form of denying Christ, the very thing Jesus warned of in Mark 8:38 and in Matthew 10:32,33?* The answer depends on what is meant by the word "Christian." In many, perhaps most, parts of the Muslim world, "Christian" does not mean what it does to Western evangelicals. For evangelicals, it has a spiritual meaning: one has experienced new birth in Christ and follows him as Lord. In most of the Muslim world, however, "Christian" has an almost exclusively cultural, ethnic, or political meaning: Christians are either Westerners (often seen as immoral) or members of local non-Muslim ethnic minorities. They have their own calendar, rituals, holidays, clergy, terminology, diet, and dress. Historic animosity for nearly a thousand years (since the time of the Crusades) taints the word "Christian."

If asked whether they are Christians, Jesus-following Muslims rightly say no: they are Muslims, not Christians. If asked, however, whether they follow Jesus as Lord and Savior, they say yes, and give

---

9 Many Jews who follow Jesus refer to him by his Hebrew name, Yeshua.

10 For major Muslim qur'anic commentators who allow for a real crucifixion, see Joseph Cumming, "Did Jesus Die on the Cross? Reflections in Muslim Commentaries," in *Muslim and Christian Reflections on Peace: Divine and Human Dimensions*, ed. J. Dudley Woodberry, O. Zumrut, and M. Koylu (Lanham, MD: University Press of America, 2005), 32–50.

11 Many Jesus-following Muslims refer to Jesus by his qur'anic name, 'Isa, which is commonly understood to be an Arabized form of the name Syriac-speaking Christians used. See Alphonse Mingana, "Syriac Influence on the Style of the Koran," *Bulletin of the John Rylands Library* 11 (1927): 84.

12 Many Jesus-following Muslims refer to the Bible using the terms *Tawrat, Zabur,* and *Injil.* The *Tawrat* (literally the first five books of the Old Testament, but often interpreted as referring to the entire Old Testament), *Zabur* (Psalms), and *Injil* (Gospel, although often used for the Gospels or the entire New Testament) are understood to be the word of God in the Qur'an. Muslim scholar Abdullah Saeed's article "The Charge of Distortion of the Jewish and Christian Scriptures" (*The Moslem World* 92 [2002]: 419–36) shows how both the Qur'an and Islamic tradition support the view that the texts of the *Tawrat, Zabur,* and *Injil* have not been corrupted and are still to be regarded as holy books by Muslims.

an appropriate explanation. Though they retain an official, social, and/or cultural identity as Muslims and do not identify with "Christianity" as a socioreligious institution, they do identify with Jesus, and this is the very point of the Mark 8 and Matthew 10 passages. They are not ashamed of Christ, and many are bold evangelists.

7. *What does it mean to retain an official, social, and/or cultural Muslim identity?* Retaining official Muslim identity means that Jesus followers have not legally or publically taken steps to remove themselves from Islam. In some Muslim countries, one's religious identity is determined by law, and often laws specify that people born of Muslim parents are legally Muslims and cannot change their religious identity. In other Muslim countries, religious identity is determined only at the community level.

Retaining a social and/or cultural Muslim identity means that followers of Jesus see themselves, and are seen by others in society, as Muslim.[13] However, like genuine disciples of Jesus in all societies, they clearly hold a variety of new values and beliefs that would likely not be shared by the majority of their coreligionists.

There is already great variance throughout the Muslim world in beliefs and practices. Many Muslims lean toward belief systems technically incompatible with Islam, such as secularism, communism, occultism, or even agnosticism. Yet they identify with the Muslim community and are considered full members of it. A well-known Muslim follower of Jesus notes that Muslims do not have to perform all practices or believe all doctrines of Islam to be Muslims. But the day they choose to renounce their identity as Muslims is the day they are no longer seen as part of the Muslim community (see Mallouhi, chap. 12).

8. *Are Jesus movements within Muslim communities the only type of movement among Muslims today?* No; numerous types of movements large and small exist, and different movements consist of different types of fellowships. The C1–C6 Spectrum (fig. 4.1 below) is one means of identifying six of these different fellowship types.

9. *What is the C1–C6 Spectrum?* The C1–C6 Spectrum describes six types of fellowships (or "Christ-centered communities," represented by the letter *C*) that Muslims either join or form when they follow Jesus. The six types are differentiated in terms of language, culture, religious forms, and religious identity. An individual Christ-centered community or church may or may not be part of a movement; movements are comprised of multiplying, interrelated fellowships. Recent movements to Jesus are most often of the C3, C4, or C5 type. Points along the Spectrum are meant to be descriptive rather than prescriptive, and dynamic rather than static. A given Jesus fellowship or movement may take on different expressions over time.[14]

---

13 The particulars of retaining Muslim identity vary according to the given Muslim context.

14 The Spectrum is explained in greater detail in chap. 51.

• • • C1 • • •	• • • • • C2 • • •	• • • • • C3 • • •	• • • • • C4 • • •	• • • • • C5 • • •	• • • • • C6 • • •
Traditional fellowship where worship is not in the language of the local Muslim community (e.g., Coptic churches in Egypt, English-speaking congregations in the Middle East); worship forms feel foreign to Muslims; believers refer to themselves as Christians.	Traditional fellowship where worship is in the language of the local Muslim community (e.g., Arabic-speaking congregations in the Middle East); worship forms and religious terminology, however, still feel foreign to Muslims; believers refer to themselves as Christians.	Fellowship of MBBs using their own language and any non-Islamic cultural expressions (e.g., certain types of folk music, dress, or artwork); fellowship feels somewhat less foreign to Muslims; believers refer to themselves as Christians.	Fellowship of MBBs using their own language and cultural expressions as well as biblically acceptable Muslim forms (in dress, diet, Muslim terminology, prayer forms, etc.); feels less foreign to Muslims; believers refer to themselves as followers of Isa or something similar.	Fellowship of Muslims who follow Jesus yet remain part of the socioreligious community of their birth; their commitment to the risen Messiah and the Bible makes them a unique type of Muslim; believers refer to themselves simply as Muslims or Muslim followers of Isa (or something similar).	Underground or isolated gathering of Muslim followers of Jesus who have little fellowship with others and often survive in a very dangerous environment; believers most often refer to themselves simply as Muslims.

Fig. 4.1 The C1–C6 Spectrum: Six types of Christ-centered communities (ekklesiae) *in the Muslim world*

10. *How do these movements start?* Individuals become followers of Jesus in a variety of ways, with the most common factors being (1) reading or hearing about Jesus in the Gospel narratives; (2) hearing the experiences of fellow Muslims who are disciples of Jesus; (3) seeing the message of Jesus confirmed through answered prayer; and (4) dreams and visions given directly by God, often following the personal witness of friends. For example, a Muslim hears the story of a friend at work who has just become a Jesus follower; he then has a dream about Jesus; he finds a Bible and reads it, and then takes the message directly to his family and friends. It should be noted that outsiders have often been instrumental in leading the first few Muslims to faith, and have also been heavily involved in Bible translation, translating the "JESUS" film, and protracted intercessory prayer. Jesus movements launch, however, when Muslims themselves become convinced that this good news of Jesus is for their family and friends and begin sharing the message throughout their own networks.

11. *Scripture teaches that in Christ we are "one body" (Eph 4:4–6). Even though Jesus-following Muslims do not join traditional Christian churches or denominations, do they see themselves as part of the body of Christ?* Based on comments from Muslim followers of Jesus as well as colleagues who know these believers well, we can affirm that the great majority of Jesus-following Muslims view all people who are truly submitted to God through Christ, whether Christian, Muslim, or Jewish, as brothers and sisters in Christ and part of God's kingdom. The presence of the Spirit of God in both born-again Christians and born-again Muslims points to realities—the body of Christ and the kingdom of God—that go beyond socioreligious labels and categories. This reality was apparent in the Acts 10 account of Peter's visit to Cornelius' Gentile home, and it later prompted his magnificent declaration in Acts 15:11, "We believe it is through the grace of our Lord Jesus Christ that we [Jews] are saved just as they [Gentiles] are." Jesus-following Muslims are saved today by the same grace that saves those Jesus followers who identify themselves as Christians.

12. *Fellowship and commitment in a local expression of the body of Christ is central to life in Christ. Do Muslim followers of Jesus gather together, or are they simply individuals who have believed in Jesus?* Normally they meet in their homes for prayer, fellowship, and the study of God's word, and are highly committed to one another. They become an expression of the body of Christ in that locale. Having said this, however, they must be discreet and wise in how and where they meet. In some cases they meet like the underground church of China; in other locations they are more open. In some contexts the interpersonal or social skills of Jesus-following Muslims significantly impact neighborhood reaction and freedom to meet.

13. *Some have said that Jesus movements within Islam exist so that Muslims can avoid persecution and suffering for their faith in Christ. Is this true?* By far the most common reason Jesus-following Muslims give for staying inside their original religious community is their burden and desire to see their loved ones experience the good news of Jesus. Their hope is that Jesus movements among Muslims would be like the earliest Jesus movement, described in Acts 2:46–47: "Every day they continued to meet together in the temple courts. They broke bread in their homes and ate together with glad and sincere hearts, praising God and enjoying the favor of all the people. And the Lord added to their number daily those who were being saved."

While we rejoice whenever the Lord is daily adding to the number of Jesus followers and whenever Jesus movements are experiencing the favor of the Muslim community, we realize that movements are not static. As the biblical record of the first Jesus movement shows, seasons can change. While not hoping that any movement would move out of a season of favor, we pray earnestly for these believers to be prepared for any suffering that may come.[15]

While a certain stigma of "changing religious communities" is avoided in these movements, in many Muslim contexts pressure is still exerted (from either family or religious leaders) on members of the community who have different spiritual ideas. In some cases this pressure increases to full-blown persecution. A tragic case occurred in August 2009, when a leader in one Jesus movement died as a martyr, poisoned by his own family. Villagers said this leader was killed because he would not stop talking about Jesus, and this was an embarrassment to the family. Other Jesus movements have similar stories.

14. *It has been said that some Christians have assumed a Muslim identity in order to relate to and have an audience with Muslims. Does the existence of Jesus movements within Muslim communities suggest that Christians should take on a Muslim identity in order to reach Muslims with the gospel?* No—not at all. These are two separate issues. The movements we are discussing here involve Muslims who were born inside those communities.

There have been rare instances where Christians have assumed varying degrees of Muslim identity in an effort to "become all things to all men" to "win as many as possible" (1 Cor 9:19–23). Though the decision of a Christian to *change* socioreligious identity is entirely different from the decision of a Muslim to *retain* socioreligious identity, some critics of the type of Jesus movements discussed here have attempted to link the two. In short, "insider movement" refers to how Muslims respond to the gospel and not what Christians do to share it.

---

15 The very movement described in Acts 2–4 moved into a season of persecution a number of years later, as recorded in Acts 5 onward, especially noted in Acts 8:1–3.

15. *What about the traditional Christian sacraments of baptism and communion? Are these followed in Jesus movements within Muslim communities?* In some movements it seems to be a common practice to remember the sacrifice of Jesus for the forgiveness of sins during a meal shared together.

Most Jesus-following Muslims practice some form of water baptism as well, not to indicate a change of religious affiliation, but as a sign of identifying with Jesus, who has opened the way for the cleansing of sin and for new life through him. Some Muslim disciples of Jesus who do not yet practice outward water baptism consider themselves to have been baptized spiritually because of their relationship with Christ, who baptizes with the Holy Spirit.[16]

16. *Do Jesus-following Muslims still repeat the confession "There is no god but God, and Muhammad is God's Messenger"?* We are unsure if any outsider has a definitive answer to this question (although it is discussed at length in chap. 53). We have heard the following explanations given by some Jesus-following Muslims who do continue to recite the confession: Muhammad called his people to turn from polytheism to the God of Abraham; he commended to them the holy books of the Jews and Christians, and he warned of an impending day of God's judgment, for which all people must be prepared. For these reasons, he is honored. In one large movement some Jesus followers explained that they do not repeat the second part of the Islamic confession, choosing instead to substitute something that is both biblically and qur'anically correct, such as "Jesus is the Word of God."[17] It should be noted, however, that in the Jesus movements with which we are familiar, Muhammad is not viewed as a mediator, intercessor, or savior.

17. *Do Jesus-following Muslims still refer to God as* Allah? Yes. Not only do Jesus-following Muslims use the term *Allah*, but all *Arab Christians* use *Allah* as their term for God, as do many thousands of Christians in other parts of the world.[18] Even before the rise of Islam, Arabic-speaking Christians called God *Allah*, since the name *Allah* predates Islam.[19] Jews later used the term *Allah* in their Arabic translation of the Old Testament.[20] Following in the tradition of Arab and Christian use of the term *Allah,* the Qur'an uses *Allah* to refer to God, the creator of heaven and earth, the God who revealed himself to Abraham, the God of the Bible—indeed, the God of the Jews, Christians, and Muslims. A person's understanding of God is a separate issue from the term used for God.[21]

18. *How do Muslims who follow Jesus communicate with fellow Muslims about Jesus and the Bible?* Jesus-following Muslims who share their experience of Jesus with other Muslims are convinced that Jesus is

---

16 This is similar to the position on baptism held by Quakers and the Salvation Army.

17 It is worth noting that Abu Hamid al-Ghazali (d. 1111), Islam's most celebrated theologian, on two occasions gave a confession that both Christians and Muslims can affirm: "Jesus is the Apostle of God." See Ghazali, *Al-Qustas al-Mustaqim,* ed. Victor Chelhot, 68, cited in Chelhot, "La Balance Juste," *Bulletin d'Etudes Orientales* 15 (1958); Ghazali, *Al-Munqidh min al-dalal (The Deliverer from Error),* 3rd ed., ed. Jamil Saliba and Kamal 'Ayyad (Damascus: Matba'at al-Jami'a al-Suriya, 1939), 101; and Ghazali, *The Faith and Practice of al-Ghazali,* trans. W. Montgomery Watt (London: Allen and Unwin, 1953), 39.

18 In Indonesia alone, the entire Christian population of over thirty million uses the term *Allah* for God.

19 See P. K. Hitti, *History of the Arabs,* 6th ed. (London: Macmillan, 1956), 101.

20 Sa'adiah Gaon bin Joseph, a ninth- and tenth-century Jewish scholar, translated the Jewish Scriptures from Hebrew into Arabic, using *Allah* for God. See Kenneth J. Thomas, "Allah in Translations of the Bible," *The Bible Translator: Technical Papers* 52, no. 3 (2001): 301–5.

21 See J. Dudley Woodberry, "Do Christians and Muslims Worship the Same God?" *Christian Century,* May 18, 2004.

for them—he died for them and is on their side. They know that Jesus is not only the Savior of Christians, but that he is the Savior of every person who calls on his name. They believe that salvation truly is through the sacrifice of Jesus alone and is not dependent upon a particular religious affiliation. They are also convinced that salvation is only through Christ, and are therefore determined to find a way to explain this to family and friends. It is this Muslim-to-Muslim communication of the good news and personal testimony, with divine confirmation, that fuels the growth of Jesus movements.

Muslims know that the Qur'an affirms the holy books that came beforehand to the Jews and Christians,[22] and this is one of the six basic articles of Islamic faith. So when Jesus-following Muslims talk about their reading of the "neglected" holy books of Islam, some of their friends become interested in joining them. Once seekers begin to ingest the word of God, especially the accounts of the life of Jesus, and see it confirmed in the lives of their friends, the power of God is released in their lives, often resulting in their coming to Christ in faith (see Isa 55:10,11; Heb 4:12).

While miracles of healing and provision draw Muslims to the gospel, the greatest attraction is the changed lives of Muslim followers of Jesus, who are growing in love and holiness, within the religious communities of their birth.

Bibliography

Brown, Rick. "Brother Jacob and Master Isaac: How One Insider Movement Began," *International Journal of Frontier Missiology* 24, no. 1 (2007): 41–42.

Cumming, Joseph. "Did Jesus Die on the Cross? Reflections in Muslim Commentaries." In *Muslim and Christian Reflections on Peace: Divine and Human Dimensions*, edited by J. D. Woodberry, O. Zumrut, and M. Koylu, 32–50. Lanham, MD: University Press of America, 2005.

Ghazali, Abu Hamid, al-. *Al-Munqidh min al-dalal (The Deliverer from Error)*. 3rd ed. Edited by Jamil Saliba and Kamal 'Ayyad. Damascus: Matba'at al-Jami'a al-Suriya, 1939.

———. *Al-Qustas al-Mustaqim*. Edited by V. Chelhot. In V. Chelhot, "La Balance Juste." *Bulletin d'Etudes Orientales* 15 (1958).

Goldsmith, Martin. "Community and Controversy: Key Causes of Muslim Resistance." *Missiology: An International Review* 4, no. 3 (1976): 317–23.

Hitti, P. K. *History of the Arabs*. 6th ed. London: Macmillan, 1956.

Mingana, Alphonse. "Syriac Influence on the Style of the Koran." *Bulletin of the John Rylands Library* 11 (1927): 77–98.

Saeed, Abdullah. "The Charge of Distortion of the Jewish and Christian Scriptures." *The Moslem World* 92 (2002): 419–36.

Thomas, Kenneth J. "Allah in Translations of the Bible." *The Bible Translator: Technical Papers* 52, no. 3 (2001): 301–5.

Watt, W. Montgomery, trans. *The Faith and Practice of al-Ghazali*. London: Allen and Unwin, 1953.

Woodberry, J. Dudley. "Contextualization among Muslims: Reusing Common Pillars." In *The Word among Us*, edited by Dean S. Gilliland, 303–6. Dallas: Word Publishing, 1989.

———. "Do Christians and Muslims Worship the Same God?" *Christian Century*, May 18, 2004.

---

22 Over forty times the Qur'an refers to the books of the Bible (*Tawrat, Zabur, or Injil*—the books that came beforehand) as holy books.

CHAPTER 5

Myths and Misunderstandings about Insider Movements

Kevin Higgins, Richard Jameson, and Harley Talman

Our heavenly Father is creative. He reaches people with the gospel in a wide variety of ways. There is no "one-size-fits-all" approach for evangelism or discipleship. The Holy Spirit draws people to Jesus through a wide variety of means. We find this diversity even among people of the same ethnic group and the same religious background living in the same city.

One problem that confronts us as we think about ministry is ethnocentrism. No matter how hard we try to get around it, there seems to be an inbuilt tendency to think that "our experience" with Christ is normative. We see this tendency even among Muslims, Hindus, Buddhists, and Jews who have come to Christ. Yet the longer we have been involved in ministry, the more we have come to expect the unexpected in ministry. Those who reflect on current and vastly different approaches in ministry in contexts of these world religions are wise to be self-reflective on the impact of ethnocentrism on their assumptions, perceptions, and assessments of these differing approaches.

In this light, the present chapter looks at one paradigm of ministry called insider movements (IMs). We will limit our discussion of these movements to those that are occurring among Muslim peoples—because we, the authors, know some true followers of Christ who have retained their Muslim identities. These people were born into Muslim families and cultures, and they along with others like them became a significant evangelistic force that God has used to draw other Muslims to himself. These followers of Christ from Muslim backgrounds consider themselves and are seen by their friends, family, and communities as Muslims. These disciples of Jesus have embraced their Muslim identity and are using it for the glory of God and the expansion of Christ's kingdom, enabling other Muslims to enter into a life-transforming relationship with Jesus Christ.

This phenomenon has been discussed in missiological journals over the last fifteen years. However, in the last few years some have attempted to systematically discredit these followers of Christ. Much of the literature that criticizes this approach appears to construct and then condemn a "straw man." We contend that what has been attacked is largely a fabrication created in the imaginations of the critics. We would like to describe and respond to eight popular myths about Muslim followers of Christ (MFCs) and then several misunderstandings about the Scriptures and theology related to IMs.

Myths about Insider Movements

There is a Chinese proverb that says, "Whatever you have heard about China is true *somewhere* in China." We acknowledge that some of the assertions of critics that we mention may be true of some of the work and workers in some places. However, the proposition that these assertions accurately characterize IMs is a myth.

Let us take a moment to define what we mean by "myth." In popular usage the term "myth" can refer to a story that may have its origins in some actual person or event, but the resulting story itself is not true. Likewise, someone may have seen a certain worker or believer who can be justly criticized for a certain practice. Then they surmise that this practice must be widespread. Therefore they create a myth about this practice. The myth is not that the practice occurred; rather, the myth is that this practice characterizes the whole.

In our discussion of these myths, the perspectives we share are based not only on our personal experiences but also on what we know from a broad range of people and organizations working in a variety of contexts across the globe. Hence our views reflect what the mainstream of missiologists, writers, and field workers supportive of insider movements are saying and seeing in the field.

1. The "Naive Worker" Myth

Those who advocate for "Muslim followers of Christ" do not realize what every Muslim believes about Jesus. These naive workers get all excited when they encounter Muslims who say, "We love Jesus." When they hear this they assume that they have found a hidden church.

These naive workers do not know Islam and do not understand the Qur'an. They do not realize that one cannot be considered a Muslim unless one holds to a traditional, orthodox interpretation of the Qur'an. They do not know that either the correct interpretation of every "friendly" verse in the Qur'an insulates Muslims from the gospel or that those verses have been abrogated by later verses. In addition, since deception is acceptable within Islam, it is acceptable for Muslims to pretend to agree with these workers' strange new interpretations of the Qur'an in order to further the cause of global Islamic jihad. These "Muslim followers of Christ" are taking advantage of the workers' naiveté, and these workers have no idea that they are being duped.

These naive workers are also unaware of the power of the demonic world and do not understand that religious forms have inherent spiritual meaning and hold people in bondage. Pro-insider workers and IM leaders fail to adequately address the dark side of Islam. By not demanding a clean break from all the old religious forms, true discipleship is made impossible. Documented cases of Muslim followers of Christ who have fallen into sin prove the point.

The Reality

Most expatriate workers walking alongside these movements hold graduate degrees in theology, Islamics, or intercultural studies. The workers and the MFC leaders realize that they are engaged in intense spiritual warfare. Deliverance from demonization is a major component of these ministries. Kevin Higgins has indicated that those he works with are regularly engaged in deliverance ministries. The leaders he knows speak of the evil bondage Islam exerts over people. John Travis and his wife have developed an extensive ministry of inner healing and deliverance for Muslim contexts (see chap. 55). So spiritual warfare is not theory for expatriate workers. In addition, some expatriate workers have known the MFC leaders for more than twenty years and are close friends with them. The expatriates have witnessed the life-transforming work of the Holy Spirit in the MFC leaders' lives. Due to their long-term engagement with these leaders, the accusation that these expatriate workers are naive is simply a fabrication, a myth.

2. The "Compulsion" Myth

Muslims who truly come to faith in Christ want to get as far away from Islam as they can. However, due to pressure from a Western friend they feel compelled to keep their Muslim identity. Most insider movements are the result of Western workers pushing Muslims to remain in Islam, the mosque, and the practice of Islamic rituals.

A variation on this myth: *John Travis described and thus created a mythical C5 movement. Even though it doesn't really exist, misled workers keep trying to force it into existence.*

In the most nefarious version of this myth, it has been stated that *Western missionaries seduce people from a Muslim background to maintain their Muslim identity with promises of money, employment, or other tangible rewards.*

The Reality

It is true that many Muslims come to Christ and want to get as far from Islam as they can. Freedom from the many religious regulations within Islam is very attractive to them. However, MFC movements are being led by mature followers of Christ who, motivated by love, have chosen to stay in their old environment for the sake of seeing family and friends discover the Jesus of the New Testament and the transforming work of the Holy Spirit. Traditional discipleship has involved compelling converts to disconnect from their socioreligious communities and offered very little freedom to stay aligned with one's socioreligious community. In contrast, the expatriate workers who have been walking alongside these movements have pleaded with other Christians to recognize that freedom in Christ can mean freedom to remain as well as freedom to leave.

As in the case of Brother Jacob and Master Isaac, whose story was narrated at the beginning of this book, some IMs have been divinely initiated and arose with little or no influence from outside Christians. One movement began when a Muslim convert who had totally rejected his Muslim identity was introduced to seven young Muslims by a Western missionary. The Western missionary had shared the gospel with these seven young men, and he was hoping this convert would study with these young men and eventually bring them to Christ and into the church. The convert studied the Bible with them but told them, "Don't do what I did, or else you will not be able to tell your families and friends the gospel. Instead, go home. Don't call yourselves 'Christians,' but instead just share with them what you are learning from the Bible. See what happens." This was the idea and initiative of the convert. The missionary he knew was sorely disappointed. Several weeks later the young men returned with elders from their homes. The elders wanted to learn the gospel too. A movement began that included house churches and ongoing Bible teaching. This movement is still growing.

In other cases, "alongsiders" (see chap. 47) have made direct or indirect contributions that supported or facilitated the emergence of a movement. While there may have been instances where a Muslim was compelled to keep his or her identity as a Muslim, no mainstream supporter of IMs that we know of approves of pressing people to not become Christians when they desire to do so. In contrast, the reverse has historically been the norm. Christian workers have pushed Muslims to reject their religious culture and community. New believers who would have preferred to remain within their communities in order to win them for Christ have been challenged to join existing Christian churches (which were often comprised of a different social, cultural, or ethnic group). At the very least, this was expected and no alternative to following Christ was offered. The tragic result has often been isolation or extraction from the community.

The IM that John Travis describes in chapter 16 actually began while the Travises were out of the country for several months. The movement was begun through the testimony of a woman follower of Isa from that neighborhood who often prayed with Anna Travis, but the movement was entirely the initiative of this woman insider. Some critics, though they acknowledge that there was no direct action of the Travises in this case, still attribute the movement to the strong influence of the expatriate workers.

Richard, coauthor of this chapter, describes what he saw happen in one movement:

> There were a few of us who were standing like rocks in the stream, asking the question, "Is it possible that some of these forms could be redeemed and filled with new meaning?" As workers used vocabulary and some religious forms common to the surrounding Muslim community, the Muslims who came to Christ quite naturally used the same language and forms. What I observed was that where the ethnic and religious identity were so closely tied, when they continued to use the same religious vocabulary and religious forms that they had used before coming to Christ, their surrounding community continued to view them as Muslim. It was at this juncture that foreigners had the greatest influence. They could have taught the young believers that they needed to repudiate their Muslim identity. Instead they focused on repudiating and renouncing everything demonic, allowing the believers to continue to think of themselves as Muslim. This grew to active encouragement, as they saw the speed at which the gospel was flowing from the "in Christ" Muslims to "lost Muslims," as opposed to from "Christian" to "Muslim."

The woman referenced above had interacted with a number of "in Christ" Muslims before she came to faith. The primary influence on the identity that she took for herself was that of the first generation of MFCs. It was not due to the influence of the foreigners with whom she had interacted. If foreigners had any influence, it was that they accepted these MFCs and treated them as part of their spiritual family. The woman in question repeatedly saw this.

The claim that Muslims have only kept their Muslim identity because they were pushed in that direction by foreigners is a myth. Nonetheless, it is fair to say that without foreigners affirming the legitimacy of retaining socioreligious identity, the movement probably would not have happened to the same extent.

3. The "Fear of Persecution" Myth

Due to the fear of persecution, "Muslim followers of Christ" are continuing to pretend to be Muslim when they know they really are not. Pro-insider Western workers are encouraging insiders to stay inside to avoid persecution.

The Reality

There are Muslims who keep their Muslim identity out of fear of persecution. Some of these would be called "secret believers." They keep their faith hidden from their family and friends, though they may sometimes be found secretly attending a meeting of believers or a Christian church. However, MFC movements are led by people who are very active and vocal in their witness for Jesus as Lord and Savior. They try to be as wise as serpents so that they don't get crushed. However, they do not hide their faith in Christ out of fear. If they were hiding their faith, then these movements would not have happened. In our experience, "insiders" stay inside in order to share the gospel. They want others to hear the message and believe. They are not secret. They speak. They meet in small house churches for fellowship and prayer and worship and Bible study. Kevin, coauthor of this chapter, states that in a one-year period in his work, four were arrested for their faith: one was beaten to death in jail; the other three were finally released.

On September 1, 2011, a brother Kevin has known for nineteen years was kidnapped because of his faith and his evangelistic activities. Until his release on January 13, 2012, he was repeatedly beaten, given electric shocks, hung upside down by his feet, questioned, kept awake, had a wooden stick thrust up into his lower intestines, and forced to watch several men have their throats cut. He was finally released because tribal leaders from his area put pressure on the local police to release him. The police in turn put pressure on the kidnappers.

Today he is healed and has returned to gathering leaders of the movement to train and equip them. His family wanted him to leave the country for his safety. In response to their concerns, he prayed and fasted for three days. However, after this time of prayer he felt he heard the Lord say to him, "I am your protector and guardian." So he decided he needed to stay and continue the work.

There are similar stories in other movements. In the movements we know, secrecy and safety are not the reason for "remaining within." Instead people remain within their communities for the purpose of sharing the gospel—in close quarters with those who can oppose and retaliate.

4. The "Syncretistic Cult" Myth

Muslim followers of Christ are picking and choosing from two religions and creating a new hybrid religion that is neither biblical nor qur'anic. Muslim followers of Christ hold onto traditional Muslim theology and try to harmonize this with some Christian teaching. Thus "most of those involved in insider movements hold high views of Islam, the Qur'an, and Muhammad."

The Reality

Two cults referred to as "Chrislam" do exist. Both come from Nigeria. One, called Ifeoluwa, was founded by Tela Tella in the 1980s, and a second one known as Oke-Tude was founded by Prophet Saka. In these, an exclusive emphasis on external forms has generally led to syncretism. As Roman Catholicism and Islam spread, the way these religions were adapted to local contexts provides classic examples of syncretism. MFC movements, in contrast, are grounded in intensive discipleship. The focus of the work is on heart transformation.

It is a valid observation that beliefs change gradually within MFC movements. However, this is not syncretism. There is real change taking place, not adaptation. IM defenders have seen that the closer people get to Jesus, the less important Muhammad and the Qur'an become in their lives. This happens because of the hours spent weekly in intensive study of the Bible. Due to consistent Bible study, MFCs become fully evangelical in their theology. The problem is that the majority of critics have not personally taken the time to get to know MFCs.

In one country, two brothers were raised in the same Muslim home and went to the same madrasa. On the day their family was baptized in the late 1990s, one brother described his Islamic heritage like this: "I do not like Islam, Muhammad is not a prophet, and the Qur'an is not a holy book." The other said after his baptism, "All my life Islam has been my house. It is a good house. Today my house is complete."

The first brother had been a believer for some time, and had been exposed to several approaches, including the local existing church community in his country. The second brother had memorized much of the Qur'an and was in training as an imam. He had been a jihadist as well. However, as part of the discipleship process he had abandoned his jihadist involvement before he turned to Jesus.

Nonetheless, both brothers agreed on this point: "If we are going to reach our families and the rest of our people, we need to stay in the community and even go to religious events and practices as much as possible." And they both continued to identify themselves as Muslim. The second brother, after more Bible study, has a very different view of Islam today, but he still identifies himself as a Muslim.

MFCs hold to a wide range of views on Islam, the Qur'an, and Muhammad (see chaps. 11 and 50). However, empirical research has shown that as MFCs study the Bible together and apply its truths to their lives and community, progressive transformation of character happens and biblical perspectives and behaviors develop (see the case study in chap. 15).

5. The "Separatistic Cult" Myth

Insider believers reject the established national church and break up the unity of the body of Christ. In addition, "pro-insider workers encourage MFCs to avoid all contact with the broader body of Christ because such exposure would shine light on their heresies."

The Reality

Harley: Disunity in the body of Christ is often caused by attitude. Many Christian denominations fail to cooperate and fellowship together. Some churches will not fellowship with churches that do not use the King James translation of the Bible. Many mission agencies will not accept as members those Christians who are Catholic, mainline Protestant, or charismatic, and some will not partner on projects with them. Where there is disunity, it is usually rooted in an exclusivist attitude that rejects those who are different. These differences appear to be differences in perspective rather than differences in fundamentals of the faith, such as the bodily death and resurrection of Christ, the authority of the Scriptures, and the virgin birth. Such denominational and organizational disunity occurs even among local Christians in the Muslim world. Some of these local Christians have not accepted their fellow countrypersons who are Muslim, Hindu, or Buddhist in background and who are followers of Christ, while they have accepted expatriate believers (see "Letter from a Jesus Muslim to Christians," sidebar, chap. 16).

Richard: Every MFC I have met has embraced me as a brother in Christ even though I am from a Christian background. However, MFCs get rather defensive when they are attacked and branded as heretics. They also get a little defensive when well-meaning Christians attack them for the way they dress, the vocabulary they use, the way they worship, for keeping Muslim dietary laws, etc. I stated in a recent trip report,

> I've had some wonderful meetings with MFCs in the last couple
> of weeks. It has been fun to see how their eyes light up when they
> are meeting with other true followers of Jesus, even those who
> don't share a common religion with them. There is an immediate

recognition that we comprise a higher community that surpasses our religions. Paul's "no dividing line" (Eph 2:11–22) is alive and well. We could easily add that *in Christ* there is no dividing line between Jews and Muslims, between Muslims and Christians, or between Christians and Jews.

Kevin: In the two movements I know best, all the leaders say clearly that Christians are their brothers in Christ. And in both movements, MFCs have reached out to those in local churches. There are cases of cooperation as well as mutual and respectful decisions to bless each other to proceed in their own ways of ministry. I go into more depth on this issue in terms of possible processes and means by which relationships between MFC movements and local churches can be fostered elsewhere.[1] If, however, critics are demanding that the only sign of unity is to meet and worship in one place and in one way, then these people must demonstrate that they themselves abide by this standard. It is likely that they themselves are not part of churches where this standard is practiced, whether Western or other.

6. The "Truncated Discipleship" Myth

Pro-insider workers and insider leaders sometimes water down the gospel to make it easy. It will be difficult for people who stay within their previous socioreligious community of birth to grow to maturity in Christ. This was the problem being addressed by the book of Hebrews. The best solution is clear separation from the religious practices of the previous community.

The Reality

The goal in IMs is not to make the gospel easy, but to make it clear. No one advocates watering down the gospel. However, we do want to keep the gospel free from any extra additions that are sometimes added. Therefore the convictions guiding IMs may be compared to those of the Reformers who articulated the famous *sola*'s (*sola* means "only" or "alone"). The gospel is about grace alone, through Christ alone, by faith alone. And the Scriptures alone are sufficient for life and doctrine, and sufficiently clear in what they teach about the essentials of the faith.

Muslim followers of Christ study the Bible. They are living out community as followers of Christ, practicing the "one another" commands of the New Testament. The MFCs who we know personally are evidencing the fruit of the Spirit in their daily communal lives.

7. The "Postmodern Relativism" Myth

Muslim followers of Christ are the result of postmodern relativism, believing that any religious system sincerely followed is as valid as any other.

The Reality

Postmodern relativism may exist among liberal Christians. However, neither the MFCs nor the alongsiders working with them are postmodern relativists. All fully believe what Jesus said:

> Enter through the narrow gate. For wide is the gate and broad is
> the road that leads to destruction, and many enter through it. But

---

1 See Kevin Higgins, "Acts 15 and Insider Movements among Muslims: Questions, Process, and Conclusions," *IJFM* 24, no. 1 (2007): 29–40.

> small is the gate and narrow the road that leads to life, and only a few find it. . . . Many will say to me on that day, "Lord, Lord, did we not prophesy in your name, and in your name drive out demons and in your name perform many miracles?" Then I will tell them plainly, "I never knew you. Away from me, you evildoers!" (Matt 7:13,14,22,23)

8. The "Deception" Myth

There are true followers of Christ who are intentionally keeping their Muslim identity. However, they must knowingly deceive their community in order to maintain this identity. Western workers are encouraging this deceptive behavior.

The Reality

The accusation of deception does not necessarily mean a person is being deceptive. Jesus was accused of being deceptive (Matt 27:63; John 7:12,47), as was Paul (2 Cor 6:8). Living out 1 Corinthians 9:19–23 can open one up to an accusation of being deceptive without those accusations having merit. As we have sat with these MFCs, their love for Jesus who died so that their sins could be forgiven shines in their eyes. Every one of these MFCs could readily echo Paul's word: "Rather, we have renounced secret and shameful ways; we do not use deception, nor do we distort the word of God. On the contrary, by setting forth the truth plainly we commend ourselves to everyone's conscience in the sight of God" (2 Cor 4:2). MFCs are setting forth to their communities the truth of the gospel and their allegiance to Christ.

An Example

Imagine that you were born into a Muslim family in an ethnic group that is virtually 100 percent Muslim. For you, being Muslim is not just a set of beliefs or religious practices. Rather every aspect of your life, family, customs, and culture is integrated into that title that you proudly wear. To be Muslim is synonymous with your cultural heritage and invokes the same kind of cultural pride that we might feel when we say, "We are Americans."

You become aware of a growing group of Muslims in your community who are always talking about Jesus the Messiah. Even though they are always talking about the prophet Jesus—something quite strange from your experience—these Muslims seem to be filled with peace and joy. This is particularly evident when one of their members dies. Because of their love for one another and for those in the community in need, they are generally well thought of by most and tolerated by the religious elite. Most consider them to be a different type of Muslim.

Although they don't make a big deal about the need to keep the pillars of the faith, they seem to be faithful in the prayers and in fasting. They are thought of as pious Muslims, even if a little strange in their beliefs about Jesus.

One day your son becomes quite ill. Many in your city have died of the same illness, and you are quite concerned. A couple of members of the Jesus group show up at your door and ask if you would allow them to pray for your son. Although you don't know the Qur'an well, you remember that Jesus did great healing miracles. So when members of the Jesus group lay hands on your son and pray in the name of Jesus, you're more curious than disturbed. When the fever apparently miraculously disappears and your son, who moments before seemed on the point of death, sits up and says, "I'm hungry!" you are shocked. You have never seen spiritual power like this and are desperate to know more.

You invite members of the Jesus group to begin to study with your family. You quickly recognize that they are studying the holy books that God sent to Jesus and the prophets before him, which you have never seen. You learn they are studying the Gospel. You learn that this Jesus group believes that the Qur'an was only intended to be a road sign, pointing people back to the books that came before, and to Jesus.

Confused, you begin to read the Qur'an diligently to see if what your friends are saying to you is true. Their interpretation of the Qur'an is radically different than what you have heard from the imam. Then someone dressed in brilliant white appears to you in a dream and confirms what your Jesus group friends have been telling you. Convinced that Jesus has appeared to you, you engage in the study of the *Injil* (New Testament) with great enthusiasm. As you study you realize that Jesus is far more than just a prophet. He is the eternal Word of God that entered the womb of the Virgin Mary. Because in his very nature he is the eternal, uncreated Word of God through whom everything that has been created was created, he was bold to say that whoever had seen him had seen God (John 14:9). Although rejected by the Jews and delivered to the Romans for crucifixion, God raised him from the dead and exalted him as King over all kings and Lord over all lords. You learn from the *Injil* that whoever puts their full trust in Jesus need never fear death, for he will bring that person safely into the presence of God when they die.

You and your family transfer your allegiance from a religious system to the person of Jesus Christ. The joy that you have seen in the lives of the Jesus group members overwhelms you. You begin to recognize a new inner power to live in ways pleasing to God. You recognize that this must be the Holy Spirit described in the *Injil*, the Gospel entrusted to us through Jesus. Religious duties that previously seemed onerous now become joyous ways of expressing your love for the God who sent Jesus on your behalf.

No one from the Jesus group ever says anything negative about Muhammad or the Qur'an. In fact, had it not been for their positive attitude towards the testimony of the Qur'an received through the Prophet Muhammad, you would have probably never been willing to begin your study of the Bible. However, you find as you go deeper in your faith in Jesus that everything else fades into insignificance in comparison to him.

As you grow in your faith, you are surprised to learn that there are Christians who have this same faith in Jesus. You had always thought that all Christians were greedy, uncaring, drunkards, and sexually immoral. You actually meet some of these Christians who love Jesus and are striving to obey him just as you are. You quickly decide these must be the Christians described in the Qur'an who are closest in love to the Muslims. You rejoice that although of different religions, you share a common faith in Christ with these Christians. There is an instant bond of unity.

Your passion for seeing Muslims around the world discover the same truth about Jesus that you have discovered only increases. You dream of the day when this Jesus group, of which you are now firmly a member, will spread throughout the Muslim world, drawing millions of Muslims into a saving knowledge of Jesus Christ.[2]

---

2 The above story is a composite of dozens of personal testimonies from Muslim followers of Christ whom Richard Jameson has met.

Misunderstandings of Scripture and Theology Related to Insider Movements

In addition to the above myths, there are several common misunderstandings or misapplications of the Scriptures and theology in regard to IMs. We have grouped them into three topics.

Misunderstanding #1

Muslims, Hindus, and others are saved by faith in Jesus alone, but they cannot grow to maturity without joining a Christian church and adopting the mature theology and practice that we have developed.

This assertion is not well founded in Scripture or reality. House gatherings are called churches (*ekklesiae*) in the NT. Insider believers typically meet in this way, fulfilling the same biblical functions. Moreover, the spiritual commitment, Christlike character, and practice of Bible study of insider believers is often higher than that of believers in the Christian churches. Furthermore, this misconception betrays a fundamental principle of the Protestant Reformation, that of the perspicuity of Scripture (i.e., that the Bible does not demand an official interpreter outside of itself). The Bible alone is the transcultural and timeless authority for all theology. To be sure, in order for the body of Christ around the world to come to full maturity (as in Eph 4), local theology must be done in global conversation. But this does not require institutional assimilation or ecclesiastical uniformity.

Misunderstanding #2

The IM paradigm is based on just a few debatable passages, such as Naaman (1 Kgs 19), the Samaritan woman (John 4), "remaining" (1 Cor 7), and the Jerusalem Council (Acts 15).

On the contrary, hundreds of other passages in the Scripture support IMs. The message preached by Billy Graham supports it, especially the multitude of passages he quotes that insist that salvation is by grace through faith alone. The NT never speaks of salvation as adopting a new religion or changing one's socioreligious affiliation. The central message of the Scripture is not about a religion but about the kingdom of God. The theology of the Old Testament endorses retaining religious beliefs and practices that are compatible with Scripture while reinterpreting or reforming those that are not. To reject IMs is to add unnecessary regulations to the gospel. The fundamental principles of the Protestant Reformation undergird IMs, as does the theology of esteemed theologians like J. H. Bavinck (see chap. 31).

The better question to ask is, what Scripture does not support IMs? The few that are most often cited against IMs are addressed below.

Misunderstanding #3

Insider movements disregard biblical commands for holiness and separation from the world.

a. *"Come out from them and be separate" (Isa 52; 2 Cor 6:17).* Isaiah exhorted the exiles of Israel to depart from Babylon and return to Palestine and live holy lives, free of sin: "Depart, depart, go out from there! Touch no unclean thing! Come out from it and be pure, you who carry the articles of the LORD's house" (Isa 52:11). The Apostle Paul cites this in 2 Corinthians 6:17 to warn against participating in idol worship with unbelievers. This admonition is clearly relevant to followers of Christ in Hindu and Buddhist contexts as they seek to live among idol worshipers without compromising their dedication to Christ. First Corinthians provides guidance for them: eating meat offered to idols may be permissible (1 Cor 8), but eating it as part of an idol-worshiping ceremony is not (1 Cor 10), because such ceremonies involve the worship of demons (10:18–20). Muslims reject the worship of idols—Muhammad condemned and removed them. However, folk Islamic practices are a form of allegiance to the demonic and must be renounced (see chap. 55). Followers of Christ wherever they live face the danger of idolatry. Christians in the materialistic West face it in the form of greed and covetousness (Col 3:5). Biblical sanctification must include forsaking any idol that defiles.

Second Corinthians 6:17 is sometimes cited by critics of IMs to argue that insider believers should leave their non-Christian socioreligious communities. But we should not equate associating with unbelievers with participating in evil. The Apostle Paul's instructions to the Corinthians in regard to nonassociation with immoral people meant that they should separate from immoral *believers*, not from immoral unbelievers, for "in that case you would have to leave this world" (1 Cor 5:11). This lends support to insiders living godly lives while remaining amidst unbelievers in their socioreligious communities. In this Paul followed the teaching of the Lord Jesus, who did not seek his followers' withdrawal from the world but their protection from evil/the evil one (John 17:15). This being in the world but not of the world reflects the tension between what Andrew Walls calls the "pilgrim principle" and the "indigenizing principle" of the gospel (see chap. 33). This tension seems to underlie some of the fears and opposition of IM critics. The biblical support for the pilgrim paradigm is so prevalent in their minds that they fail to the see the necessity for the indigenizing principle of the gospel in non-Christian socioreligious contexts. On the other hand, some IM proponents could be pulled toward the opposite imbalance. We must strive to hold these two principles in Spirit-controlled tension.

b. The root meaning of "church" (ekklesia) *is "called out"; therefore we must separate from the world.* This popular idea that *ekklesia* means "called out of the world" is based on the "root meaning fallacy" and lacks any basis in linguistic history.[3] The word refers to an assembly of citizens who are called out of their homes to attend it. The assembly at Ephesus in Acts 19 is an example, where the word is used three times—twice for the impromptu assembly, and once for a regularly scheduled assembly that would meet later. As believers we are called out of the dominion of darkness and sin to the kingdom of Christ, to whom we give our whole allegiance. We are called to be in the world, but not part of its sinful ideas and practices. Some have misinterpreted this as requiring withdrawal from unbelievers in the world, whereas the Lord Jesus prayed "not that you take them out of the world but that you protect them from the evil one. . . . As you sent me into the world, I have sent them into the world" (John 17:15,18).

c. "Let us, then, go to him outside the camp, bearing the disgrace he bore" (Heb 13:13). Must insiders become outsiders? The Jewish believers addressed in this epistle were in danger of forsaking their identity in Christ and corporate fellowship. According to Carson and Moo, they were succumbing to the temptation to return to a "reliance on the cultic structures of the old covenant" in order to avoid persecution. "Christ, his sacrifice, and his priestly work are so relativized that they are effectively denied, and apostasy is only a whisker away. It is to prevent just such a calamity that the author writes this epistle."[4] To abandon Christ and rely once again upon these structures was a serious danger for early Jewish believers. Similarly, for insiders to abandon their identity in Christ and to abandon corporate fellowship with other insider believers in order to avoid persecution would be wrong (just as it would be for any other

---

3   Rodney J. Decker, "Some Notes on Semantics, Illustrated with *ekklesia*," *NT Resources* (blog), accessed May 23, 2013, http://ntresources.com/blog/documents/ekklhsia3G.pdf.

4   D. A. Carson and Douglas J. Moo, *An Introduction to the New Testament*, 2nd ed. (Grand Rapids, MI: Zondervan, 2005), 612.

Christ follower). Insider believers must be willing to bear the shame that results from moving outside the camp of traditions that stand against the person and work of Christ (be they cultural or religious) as they fully embrace Jesus and all that he has done for us.

Nonetheless it is presumptuous to assume that believers are compromising their commitment to Christ if they remain within their socioreligious communities, because this is not what we typically find happening. Rather than giving up the hope of their confession and withdrawing from assembly with other believers (Heb 10:23–25), insider believers regularly meet in homes for Bible study, prayer, fellowship, and worship. While some Muslim Christ followers also go to the mosque, they seek to maintain or develop relationships within their communities in order to talk about Jesus, not to hide their faith.[5]

A major theme in Hebrews is the superiority of Jesus over traditional religion (especially the OT prophets and sacrifices) and the need to embrace him. Embracing Christ did not require that his followers abandon their Jewish religious practices, especially since we know that Jewish Christians continued to practice them in the early centuries. Yet it does entail relying on Christ, his covenant, his lordship, and his sacrifice, rather than on traditional rituals, whether practiced or not. This is what we are seeing in IMs: Christ's followers are relying on Christ rather than on traditional rules and rituals. Yet they do this without abandoning all the traditions in the community.

The Apostle Paul said he was willing to abstain from various foods and days if this helped him relate to his brothers in the Lord, even though such rituals and taboos do not make one acceptable to God. The author of Hebrews would have agreed. He repeatedly asserts that Christ is greater than the old covenant prophets, priests, and practices, and fulfills them, but he does not say that Christ is opposed to these things. He does not tell his Hebrew readers that they should eat pork, work on the Sabbath, abstain from religious rituals, etc. They may be free to do these things, but they are also free to conform to community expectations that are not contrary to discipleship to Christ.

Members of the Jewish community believed that membership in the covenant community was essential for salvation. In the same way, some Muslims believe that salvation is found only in the *ummah*.[6] A crucial discipleship issue for IMs is helping new believers realize that their salvation comes only through the person and work of Jesus, not through their good standing in the *ummah*. Nevertheless, following Jesus does not require that they abandon their community—just as the early Jews were not required to abandon theirs. While we are concerned that Muslims understand that salvation does not depend upon membership in the *ummah*, we do not believe that Scripture requires new believers to forsake their birth communities. Obedience-based discipleship is the appropriate way to address any area in their lives and in their beliefs, assumptions, and values that is contradictory to following Christ. This is similar to the message of the epistle to the Hebrews, in which the author emphasizes the sufficiency of the work of Christ and the deficiency of the ritual sacrificial system to save.

---

5   Though they were formerly like the Samaritans of John 4, to whom Jesus said, "You worship that which you do not know," MFCs believe that true worship is not a matter of praying in the right house of worship but worshiping God "in spirit and truth" as he is revealed in Jesus. See Rick Brown, "Who was 'Allah' Before Islam? Evidence that the Term 'Allah' Originated with Jewish and Christian Arabs," in *Toward Respectful Understanding and Witness Among Muslims: Essays in Honor of J. Dudley Woodberry*, ed. Evelyne A. Reisacher (Pasadena, CA: William Carey Library, 2012), 147–78.

6   *Ummah* is derived from an Arabic word meaning "mother." It refers to the worldwide community of Muslims.

Conclusion

We give thanks to God that so many Muslims are coming to faith in Jesus in our generation. What an amazing time to be alive! We enthusiastically rejoice in the various means that God is using as he draws Muslims, Hindus, Buddhists, and Jews to himself in Jesus Christ. IMs represent just one of the ways God is using. May he continue to favor every organization, team, worker, church, and believer with his grace and power. Amen.

Bibliography

Brown, Rick. "Who was 'Allah' Before Islam? Evidence that the Term 'Allah' Originated with Jewish and Christian Arabs." In *Toward Respectful Understanding and Witness Among Muslims*, edited by Evelyne A. Reisacher, 147–78. Pasadena, CA: William Carey Library, 2012.

Carson, D. A., and Douglas J. Moo. *An Introduction to the New Testament*. 2nd ed. Grand Rapids, MI: Zondervan, 2005.

Decker, Rodney J. "Some Notes on Semantics, Illustrated with *ekklesia*." *NT Resources* (blog). Accessed May 23, 2013. http://ntresources.com/blog/documents/ekklhsia3G.pdf.

Higgins, Kevin. "Acts 15 and Insider Movements among Muslims: Questions, Process, and Conclusions." *International Journal of Frontier Missiology* 24, no. 1 (2007): 29–40.

CHAPTER 6

Seeing Inside Insider Missiology
Exploring Our Theological Lenses and Presuppositions*
Leonard N. Bartlotti

As a scholar-practitioner, when I hear reports of movements of "Muslim followers of Christ" who retain their socioreligious identity "inside" the Muslim community, I find myself rejoicing within a zone of ambiguity. Annoying questions sometimes pop the effervescent bubbles of excitement over Muslims "following Jesus." The cacophony of voices exuberantly affirming or stridently objecting to this "new thing" in the Islamic world suggests that I am not alone in my intellectual quandary.[1]

Part of my caution is based on my experience that some reports of insider movements appear to slide from the "descriptive" (what is, which appears to be, or what is said to be happening among Muslims as a sort of *deus ex machina*, so-called "Jesus movements" attributable to sovereign acts of God) to the "prescriptive" (what could or should be modeled or allowed to happen elsewhere). Biblical, cultural, and historical rationales are then marshaled to defend, affirm, encourage, or endorse the rights and pioneering (some would say, aberrant, heterodox) practices and understandings of local believers and/or their defenders, promoters, and "alongsiders."[2]

Counterbalancing these doubts is the fact that this is truly great news! New communities of faith are springing up within a religiocultural sphere that historically has seemed impervious to biblical faith. Innovative expressions of what it means to follow Jesus are being forged on the edges of the kingdom of God.

I began to ask myself, "Why, then, am I reacting to these reports?" "Why is it so hard to accept some of the legitimizing arguments and missiological rationale for insider movements?" "What is really going on here—in their thinking, and in mine?"

I am no stranger to the challenges of gospel contextualization and theologizing in a global context. My family and I served fourteen years in a sensitive Islamic context. I strove to overcome barriers and explored bridges to communication. I have seen firsthand the challenges and dangers Muslims face in "following Jesus" in communities of faith (fellowships, house churches) that aspire to both biblical *faithfulness* and cultural *fit*. I empathize with the desire to remain "inside" preexisting social networks, and appreciate the gospel potential of what McGavran famously called the "bridges of God."[3]

---

* Published in a slightly different form in *IJFM* 30, no. 4 (2013): 137–53. Reprinted by permission.

1 For a discussion of current issues related to insider missiology and movements, see "Insider Movements: Bridging the Divide," ed. Rob Haskell and Don Little, a special issue of the *Evangelical Review of Theology* 37, no. 4 (2013).

2 Regarding "alongsiders," see John and Anna Travis, chap. 47.

3 Donald McGavran, *The Bridges of God: A Study in the Strategy of Missions* (Eugene, OR: Wipf & Stock, 2005 [1955]).

Nevertheless, the way insider missiology has been framed and promoted raised unsettling questions in my mind. Finally, I realized that I was not reacting to one thing, but to many things.

This is because, on closer examination, insider missiology itself is not saying one thing; it is saying many things. Like a fiberoptic cable, multiple theological "strands" have been bundled together to present what appears to be a singular case for biblical faith and Jesus community "inside" Muslim identity, networks, and community. This complicates theological assessment.

Similarly, for observers, one's own presuppositions function like ocular lenses, or visual and photographic filters. These, too, affect the intensity, color, and clarity of the light and the resulting image.

Thus, for proponents and critics alike, our presuppositions or background beliefs affect what they *say* and what we *see* when we assess insider movements or evaluate similar attempts to apply the biblical text to new contexts.

I realized that if we can identify these presuppositions—the background understandings on which insider missiology appears to be grounded, or by which it is being judged—we may be in a better position to examine each assumption from a biblical, theological, and missiological perspective. Rather than accepting, or rejecting, insider missiology outright or *in toto,* we can explore a range of possible understandings of each associated concept. Then, in a spirit of biblical truth seeking and evangelical collegiality, we may discern truth and error, explore alternative understandings, and advance the theory and praxis of frontier mission.

What are some of the lenses, filters, and theological presuppositions that affect what we see when we look inside and evaluate insider movements?

This paper proposes that there are at least nine alternative lenses by which we can see inside insider movements and assess insider missiology and its nexus of associated theories and praxis. The beliefs and assumptions associated with each concept raise questions, highlight issues and problems, and provide an opportunity for biblical and missiological reflection and evangelical dialogue. The nine lenses are (1) ecclesiology, (2) authority, (3) culture, (4) pneumatology, (5) history, (6) doing theology, (7) other religions, (8) Islam, and (9) conversion-initiation.

Admittedly, the nine subject areas are broad, and entire books have been written about each one of them. It will not be possible to explore these themes in any detail. We shall touch upon only those dimensions that shed light on diverse approaches to Muslim contextualization, and that suggest some additional lines of inquiry and dialogue to advance our understanding of insider missiology and insider movements.

Sincere Christians hold a range of views on each concept, and each functions as an evaluative criterion. Thus, viewed singly or taken together, the lenses or filters help us evaluate insider missiology along a spectrum—a decidedly biblical and evangelical (rather than deviant or heterodox) spectrum of faith and practice.

At the first Bridging the Divide Consultation (Houghton, New York, June 2011), participants were encouraged to reflect on their own position along the spectrum of understandings for each issue. They then discussed how their own position, ecclesiastical tradition, views, or presuppositions on each issue affected their critique, positive or negative, of insider movements. The presentation (humorously dubbed "Len's Lenses") drew an enthusiastic response and, more importantly, facilitated robust interaction.

The utility of this conceptual approach is itself based on three interrelated assumptions:

Assumption 1: There are boundaries of orthodox biblical truth, and sincere Christians can and do hold differing positions within these explicit or implicit endpoint boundaries.

Assumption 2: Believers and groups may be described as holding positions weighted to the right or left of a presumed midpoint on each issue. That is, the scale is not so much "1–10" (from least to most extreme) as "plus 1–5" or "minus 1–5" around a near-consensual midpoint: -5 -4 -3 -2 -1 0 +1 +2 +3 +4 +5.

Assumption 3: Positioning oneself on the broad spectrum is first a reflective and descriptive exercise, not an evaluative one. The suggested starting point is not to judge oneself or another as right or wrong, but to understand how a given position affects how and what one might "see."

As you look at insider movements through each of the following lenses or filters, consider how these lenses—your underlying beliefs about each issue—affect how you *see* insider movements and assess insider missiology: "Where am I on the evangelical spectrum of faith and practice?"

Lens 1: Ecclesiology

Word / sacraments / discipline / order / leadership / Pauline emphasis

or

Word / Spirit / "two or three gathered" / Synoptic Jesus emphasis

A major theological presupposition of insider theory and praxis involves ecclesiology. Certain understandings of what it means to be and do "church" are used to promote or defend developing faith communities in Islamic contexts.

At the minimalist end of the ecclesiological spectrum, insider advocates emphasize the spiritual and ecclesial DNA within even the smallest communal structure: "For where two or three gather in my name, there am I with them" (Matt 18:20). In this view of church, believers who gather around the Word and the Spirit of Christ have essentially all they need to grow and develop in faith, practice, Christlikeness, and witness.

This side of the spectrum values simplicity, freedom, informality, and a synoptic "Jesus style" somewhat removed from Pauline theologizing and complexities, but not removed from Pauline dynamics. Similar to the Radical Reformation as described by Haight,[4] the emphasis to carry the movement forward is on small, voluntary groups, meetings in houses, diverse low-level leaders, and vibrant inner faith—rather than on superimposed concepts, structures, and organization. They share the vision of Roland Allen's *Spontaneous Expansion of the Church* and raise similar questions: *Missionary Methods: St. Paul's or Ours?*[5]

At the other end of the spectrum, traditional Reformation ecclesiology and its evangelical derivatives value the Word rightly preached and the sacraments, or ordinances (Lord's Supper and baptism), rightly administered. Additional criteria include church order, discipline, and approved leadership (official, trained, certified, or ordained), within the more textured ecclesiology usually associated with Paul (e.g., 1 Corinthians, Ephesians, Colossians). Moving toward the pole, the "eucharistic ecclesiology" of Lutheran, Catholic, and Orthodox theology positions the Lord's Supper at the heart of the church; the Eucharist is the center of the Spirit's action for the transformation of both the elements and the people.[6]

---

4   Roger Haight, *Christian Community in History,* vol. 2 (New York: Continuum International, 2005), 218–22.

5   See Allen, *The Spontaneous Expansion of the Church: And the Causes Which Hinder It* (Eugene, OR: Wipf & Stock, 1997 [1927]); and Allen, *Missionary Methods: St. Paul's or Ours?* (Grand Rapids, MI: Eerdmans, 1962 [1912]).

6   Paul McPartlan, *Sacrament of Salvation: An Introduction to Eucharistic Ecclesiology* (Edinburgh: T&T Clark, 1995), 8–9.

There are many historical precedents linking gospel breakthrough with ecclesial tensions. The religious energy of the sixteenth-century Reformation resulted in new ecclesial structures, with their own views of church polity, doctrine, spirituality, practice, and engagement with society. According to Littell, for dissenting Anabaptists, the real issue was not the act of baptism but "a bitter and irreducible struggle between two mutually exclusive concepts of the church."[7]

At the heart of the Wesleyan movement was a desire to experience true spiritual transformation in Christ. Importantly, "perfect love" for God and others was to be worked out in community, leading to the classes, bands, or societies of early Methodism. The early nineteenth-century Restoration Movement advocated abandoning formal denominationalism, creeds, and traditions altogether, in favor of practices modeled solely on the pattern of the New Testament church.

As Benjamin Hegeman observes, *ekklesia* is used in six different ways in the New Testament; various models of church may be associated with differences in governance, models of worship, and "ligaments and sinews" (Col 2:19) to hold it together: universal (Matt 16:18), global (Eph 3:10), national (Gal 1:2), regional (Acts 9:31), urban (Acts 8:1), and household (Rom 16:5).[8] Hegeman notes that liturgical churches (following a "Temple worship" model) are least attractive to Muslim followers of Christ, but "ironically, new African initiated churches find that model most attractive."[9] Yet churches in Iran and Algeria follow patterns of worship, buildings, and home groups that Western and Middle Eastern churches would recognize.

Whichever side we lean toward, our heritage, understanding, and experience of "church" may affect our assessment of "insider" communities of faith.

Lens 2: Authority

Scripture / apostolic teaching and ministries / outside resourcing

or

Scripture / local believers / local decisions

A second lens through which to view and assess insider missiology and movements involves the related concept of authority. By this I mean the processes and influences by which decisions are made in a pioneer context. "Who decides?" and how are decisions made related to biblical faithfulness and cultural fit?

Theoretically, the answer is local believers. However, one need simply revisit the missiological discussions surrounding the words "contextualization," "indigenization," and "inculturation" to appreciate the nuances involved. Early literature on contextualization was faulted for overemphasizing the role of the missionary in the contextualization process. Today, there is welcome sensitivity to issues of *power* and *process*.

The current emphasis on insider dynamics and movements represents a pendulum swing in the opposite direction: the processes of biblical decision making and local theologizing lie in the local community. Local believers make local decisions based on their own understanding, however limited at the time: "Give them the Bible and the Spirit, and leave them alone—they'll work it out!"

---

7   Franklin H. Littell, *The Origins of Sectarian Protestantism: A Study of the Anabaptist View of the Church* (New York: Macmillan, 1964), 14, quoted in Haight, *Christian Community in History*, 223.

8   Email message to author, May 22, 2012.

9   Ibid.

Those on the other side do not deny this as a goal, or diminish this expression of the "priesthood of all believers." All would recognize that local assemblies are in *process* toward maturation. But the *relationship* with missionaries, teachers, and other representatives of the wider body of Christ, while not essential, is validated as biblical and "apostolic."

Similarly, Scripture is the final authority on both sides of the spectrum. But one side tends to emphasize the local *discovery and application* of biblical truth, and the other, the *discernment and impartation* of biblical truth by those who embody the teaching ministry of the church.

This is not a matter of mere pedagogy, for both approaches utilize discovery methods of teaching. In reality, the underlying presuppositions involve understandings of the degree to which, and the manner by which, the church in this generation, through its apostolate to the nations, functions as a faithful "steward of the mysteries of God" (1 Cor 4:1 NASB) and "contend[s] for the faith that was once for all entrusted to God's holy people" (Jude 3).

The other side of the spectrum draws its energy and very identity from apostolic mandates to "command and teach these things" (1 Tim 4:11), "preach the word; . . . correct, rebuke and encourage. . . . Discharge all the duties of your ministry" (2 Tim 4:2,5). "He is the one we proclaim, admonishing and teaching everyone with all wisdom, so that we may present every one fully mature in Christ. To this end I strenuously contend with all the energy Christ so powerfully works in me" (Col 1:28,29).

Interestingly, in one Asian context, local believers responded indignantly to what they considered a condescending notion: that they did *not* need outside teaching and resources (e.g., books and teaching on the Ancient Near East, social background of the NT, church history, councils, doctrinal disputes, etc.). Outside resources were considered assets for growth and local decision making about contextual issues.

In another context, a leader who works extensively with Muslim-background believers described his experience at a recent meeting:

> As we discussed I began with the Apostles Creed. One leader said "this is wonderful, someone has already done this for us. When was this written?" I was overjoyed by his embrace but saddened that after so many years working with other expats and western agencies that this basic biblical and historical creed was not a foundation stone to his faith! He had never heard of it. We googled it together so he could understand its value and the importance of being tied to the historic faith.[10]

As we affirm Scripture as the final authority for faith and practice, to what degree does the local decision-making process involve elders in the faith as teachers-cum-advisers, and welcome the wisdom of the historic and global church?

Lens 3: Culture

Christ *against* / Christ *over* or *in paradox with*

or

Christ *of* / Christ *transforming*

---

10 Email message to author, January 28, 2014.

A third lens by which to view insider missiology involves understandings of the relationship between the gospel and culture. Richard Niebuhr's seminal typology, *Christ and Culture*,[11] sets out five positions: Christ "against" culture, "over" or "in paradox with" culture, "of" culture, or "transforming" culture. He enriches the discussion with a range of historical examples from every period of Christian history.

While there are clear weaknesses in Niebuhr's schema,[12] for the purposes of this paper, the typology provides another useful way to view insider missiology. Insider followers of Christ—who talk or pray (in Jesus' name) in mosques and wear a Muslim cultural identity—follow the Christ "of" culture, who eats with "tax collectors and sinners" and who sparks what some advocates consider an "insider" messianic movement when conversing with a woman at the well in Samaria. Insider proponents emphasize the *continuity* of socioreligious identity as one follows Christ and lives out biblical faith in a given context.

These kinds of "Jesus movements" are viewed hopefully as "salt and light" transforming culture—*including* the constituent socioreligious structures and/or social networks—from *within*. Gospel meaning can be ascribed to and coexist within virtually any form, including religious forms, except those that specifically contradict Scripture. Meaning is negotiated by the local believer in his or her context.

The objective is for believers to remain in the social role and networks in which they were called and to transform this context from within. Using Acts 15 as a hermeneutical guide and paradigm, Gentiles do not have to be circumcised and become Jews. Rather, "Each person should remain in the situation they were in when God called them" (1 Cor 7:20), sacrificially serving family and community. All become the best possible fathers and mothers, sons and daughters, brothers, sisters, and citizens of their community, embodying not only biblical ideals, but also the highest social and spiritual aspirations of their people and culture—in Jesus' name.

Critics of insider movements and missiology propose an alternative view of culture. They would not say that they are against transformation; nor are they unengaged with Muslims as people. Rather, their critiques emphasize the extent to which "false" understandings permeate every dimension of Islamic religion and Muslim culture. Sin and Satan have defiled and distorted the hearts and minds, understandings of God, social relationships, practices, and structures of Islam—and every other sociocultural and religious expression of humankind—at the deepest level. Properly understood on their own terms, Islam and biblical faith are simply incompatible.

Following Christ, then, involves a *radical break* with the past; regeneration and sanctification through the sacrifice and Spirit of Christ inevitably rescue us "from the dominion of darkness" and bring us "into the kingdom of the Son he loves, in whom we have redemption, the forgiveness of sins" (Col 1:13,14).

Importantly, this "rescue" has visible and dramatic *social* consequences beyond an inner conversion of heart and worldview or an ethical change; namely, a *new social identity*. As universally understood by social scientists, identities by definition are constructed, reconstituted, negotiated, and contested vis-à-vis the "Other." For insider critics, following Christ means a rejection, not retention, of Islam as embedded within Muslim cultures. Most markers of "Islamic" identity are eschewed in favor of a new identity in Christ and with his people that is visible, if not always socially viable without persecution. "However, if you suffer as a Christian"—the word is a term of derision used as a sociolinguistic marker—"do not be ashamed, but praise God that you bear that name" (1 Pet 4:16).

---

11 H. Richard Niebuhr, *Christ and Culture* (New York: Harper and Row, 1956).

12 For a current critique of Niebuhr, see D. A. Carson, *Christ and Culture Revisited* (Grand Rapids, MI: Eerdmans, 2008).

Fortunately, we do not have to choose one or another of Niebuhr's types. The way forward is far more complex than either proponents or critics of insider missiology have acknowledged. According to contemporary critiques, Niebuhr's construction of "culture" (as in "Christ against culture") lacks an appreciation of the multiple issues, dynamics, and groups operating within cultural settings, and of the way individuals negotiate their own multiple identities and contest them within social groups.

Thus, D. A. Carson emphasizes, our understanding of the relation between Christ and culture is contextually shaped; and it depends, in part, on "the concrete historical circumstances in which Christians find themselves."[13] There is no single model. Christians shaped by Scripture, "who are taking their cue (and thus their worldview) from outside the dominant culture, not only shape and form a Christian culture recognizably different from that in which it is embedded but also become deeply committed to enhancing the whole."[14]

Therefore, one agenda for insiders, observers, and alongsiders of "Jesus movements" in Islamic contexts is a thoroughgoing exploration of biblical and historical models of the relation between the gospel and culture.

Lens 4: Pneumatology

Spirit-appointed leadership / sacraments and channels of
grace / wisdom tradition / disciplined growth / "wind"
or
Spirit-anointed leadership / sovereignty of Spirit /
spontaneous expansion / "mighty rushing wind"

A fourth theological presupposition of insider missiology involves an understanding of pneumatology, the work of the Holy Spirit. Advocates defend insider movements as a unique work of the Holy Spirit in our day. Sometimes Christian witness and teaching is not present. The Spirit is sovereignly using a variety of means to lead Muslims to Christ—from signs, wonders, dreams, and visions, to references to *Isa al-Masih* (Jesus Christ) in the Qur'an.

What we are witnessing, then, is a Spirit-inspired movement to Christ, the "rushing mighty wind" of the book of Acts, resulting in the spontaneous expansion of the church. Yes, it's messy and may appear chaotic to outsiders, but give it time. Trust the irrepressible lordship of the Spirit, and surely things will eventually work out. "The Advocate, the Holy Spirit, whom the Father will send in my name, will teach you all things and will remind you of everything I have said to you" (John 14:26). "But when he, the Spirit of truth, comes, he will guide you into all the truth" (John 16:13).

In this, as with early champions of the charismatic movement in Roman Catholic and Conciliar denominations in the 1960s and 1970s, we hear echoes of the compulsion that took the Apostle Peter across cultural frontiers: "The Spirit told me to go with them" (Acts 11:12 NASB). Indeed, one of the contributions of insider missiology is a strong, prophetic call for the church to discern, embrace, and rejoice in the "out of the box" and "out of the temple" work of the Spirit of God in the hearts and lives of tens of thousands of our Muslim cousins in Abrahamic faith.

---

13 Ibid., 65.
14 Ibid., 143–44.

Confronted with indicators of true faith in Isa al-Masih in the lives of Muslims,[15] detractors or questioners unfortunately can be judged as opposing the work of God himself! Likened to Judaizers in the book of Acts, these doubters are said to be hindering Gentiles from coming to Christ "by faith alone," apart from the religious accoutrements associated with "Christianity" as we know it.

The argument is that, if God is doing a new thing, then of course "we" (usually meaning anyone not directly familiar with the persons or situation involved) do not understand it and do not know "them." Thus we do not have the right to criticize what is happening. Neither the "home base" nor any outsider should hamper field initiatives or innovation. Nor do we have the right to "impose" (the verb is pejorative, backed by sensitivities to and resentment of power dynamics) "our views" on "them" (who must remain anonymous for security reasons, and whom we must protect from outside interference).

Leaving aside the hints of independence and dysfunctional social dynamics in church-mission relations, other theological assumptions are at work.

Concerned observers at the opposite end rightly emphasize that Spirit-appointed leaders are also "gifts" to the body of Christ: "And He gave some as apostles, and some as prophets, and some as evangelists, and some as pastors and teachers, for the equipping of the saints for the work of service, to the building up of the body of Christ" (Eph 4:11,12 NASB). Leadership and ministry are spiritual gifts given by God.

In this broad view of the Spirit's work, gifted leaders, sacraments (ordinances), and the variegated wisdom of the church through the ages, including the rich spiritual insights of non-Western churches, are channels of grace to every part of the body of Christ.

Thus insider advocates must also recognize that to minimize these potential avenues of spiritual growth is to risk "quenching" the Holy Spirit, the voices of prophets and teachers, and the "word of wisdom" through his people. The disciplines of 1 and 2 Corinthians and the "wind" blowing through the Pastoral Epistles are no less "spiritual" than the "mighty rushing wind" and rapid growth in the book of Acts. "All Scripture is inspired by God and profitable for teaching, for reproof, for correction, for training in righteousness; so that the man of God may be adequate, equipped for every good work" (2 Tim 3:16,17 NASB).

At all points along the spectrum, believers are more or less comfortable with certain aspects of the workings of the Spirit. The challenge for everyone is to have ears to "hear what the Spirit says to the churches" (Rev 2:7).

Lens 5: History

> Spirit active throughout history / church's wisdom, tradition (creeds,
> councils, theologies) / faithfulness / "faith once delivered"
>
> or
>
> Spirit active now in local context / contemporary insights,
> expressions / "a new thing" / freedom / faith newly understood

One's understanding of culture and the work of the Spirit are interrelated with Lens 5, presuppositions involving history. As suggested in Lens 4, insider proponents have an optimistic, open-ended view of God at work in human history by his Spirit.

---

15 Some evidence is anecdotal; other evidence is based on surveys and a growing body of field-based research in progress.

The emphasis, however, is on the activity of the Spirit in the "now," in our day. Insider movements are thought to represent a *kairos* moment in two ways: (1) at the *macro* level, in the history of the Muslim-Christian encounter (usually contrasted with polemical, hostile, or hopeful but largely ineffective evangelistic endeavors of the past); and (2) at the *micro* level, gospel breakthroughs in specific local Muslim contexts (sometimes in contrast with decades or centuries of perceived unfruitfulness or resistance). New expressions of the faith are springing up in what was rocky ground.

Appealing again to the historic Jerusalem Council, advocates report insider movements as a breakthrough on par with the gospel breaking out from its Jewish soil into the Hellenistic cultural sphere. Here, too, Acts 15 is used as a template and "globalizing hermeneutic"[16] to argue that Muslim followers of Jesus should have the same freedom as Gentiles to retain their socioreligious identity and live out their faith with minimal cultural imposition from other "Christians" (Judaizers?). "It is my judgment, therefore, that we should not make it difficult for the Gentiles who are turning to God" (Acts 15:19).

But history is a two-edged sword. Without imputing authority to tradition, cautious observers argue that the Spirit has been active throughout the history of the church, as represented for example in the historic creeds, confessions, and traditions of the Christian faith. Thus, even notoriously independent evangelicals retain the Nicene Creed as a plumb line of orthodoxy, while affirming with the Westminster Confession that Scripture is "the only infallible rule of faith and practice." Faithfulness to the "faith once delivered to the saints" is the primary evaluative criterion.

What is important to recognize is that both sides use history, but in different ways. One side of the spectrum uses history to argue that diversity, heterodoxy, and the danger of syncretism are *normal*—a natural consequence of the messy but mighty expansion of the Christian faith across cultural boundaries. The *fact* of theological heterodoxy, and its *cultural* roots, are justification for tolerance today. The other side uses history to defend orthodoxy (as represented in the Western theological tradition) as *normative*—in the face of the slippery slope of syncretism, cultural relativism, and the dreaded *H* word (heresy) perceived in some of the principles and practices of the insider approach.

Bosch summons us to humility:

> Humility also means showing respect for our forebears in the faith, for what they have handed down to us, even if we have reason to be acutely embarrassed by their racist, sexist, and imperialist bias. The point is that we have no guarantees that we shall do any better than they did. . . . We delude ourselves if we believe that we can be respectful to other faiths only if we disparage our own.[17]

Lens 6: Doing Theology

universal truths / Western theological tradition / "pilgrim principle"

or

local (contextual) theologies / theologies from Majority
World church / "indigenizing principle"

---

16 David K. Strong and Cynthia A. Strong, "The Globalizing Hermeneutic of the Jerusalem Council," in *Globalizing Theology: Belief and Practice in an Era of World Christianity*, ed. Craig Ott and Harold A. Netland (Grand Rapids, MI: Baker Academic, 2006), 127–39.

17 David J. Bosch, *Transforming Mission: Paradigm Shifts in Theology of Mission* (Maryknoll, NY: Orbis, 1991), 485.

A sixth lens for viewing insider movements is suggested by my earlier comments on the use of history, and perhaps is best encapsulated in the title of Timothy Tennent's book *Theology in the Context of World Christianity: How the Global Church Is Influencing the Way We Think About and Discuss Theology*.[18] Christianity is a global movement. Secularization, the decline of Christendom in the West, and the concurrent growth of the church in the non-Western world have led to a shift in the center of gravity of Christian faith to the Global South, where the majority of today's Christians now live.

This demographic shift has theological implications. No longer do Westerners sit alone at the theological table or dominate the discussion. But as Tennent observes, "The Western church has not yet fully absorbed how the dramatic shifts in global Christianity are influencing what constitutes normative Christianity."[19] "The universal truths of the Gospel are being revisited and retold in new, global contexts."[20] Tennent calls this process "theological translatability," which he defines as "the ability of the kerygmatic essentials of the Christian faith to be discovered and restated within an infinite number of new global contexts."[21]

Accordingly, some of the difficulty in discussing matters of Muslim contextualization appears to arise from tensions in the way various parties conceive of "doing theology" in the twenty-first century. In the well-known words of Andrew Walls, the missionary movement in history involves a tension between two principles: the "pilgrim principle" and the "indigenizing principle."[22] The pilgrim principle is the "universalizing force of the gospel," which provides a common "adoptive past" and identity that transcends the particularities of the local, associating them with people and things outside their cultural sphere. The indigenizing principle is the particular force of the gospel as it impacts and takes root within specific cultures, enabling followers of Christ to be at home with their group and context.[23]

Those who lean toward the insider side of the spectrum seem more comfortable with the move toward "local (or contextual) theologies" as one aspect of the inculturation of the gospel in particular contexts.[24] Schreiter describes this shift from traditional theological reflection: "Rather than trying, in the first instance, to apply a received theology to a local context, this new kind of theology began with an examination of the context itself" and "a realization that all theologies have contexts, interests, relationships of power, special concerns—and to pretend that this is not the case is to be blind."[25]

Here's how one respected practitioner in the Middle East described the process, in the context of discussing the translation of key terms:

> If we start with our denomination's theology, or a creed, etc. instead
> of the NT, we may be guilty of imposing our theology on people,
> instead of giving them the meaning of the NT words and allow-
> ing the Holy Spirit to show them how it applies to their culture.
> Theologies are developed to answer the issues of a certain culture

---

18 Timothy Tennent, *Theology in the Context of World Christianity: How the Global Church Is Influencing the Way We Think About and Discuss Theology* (Grand Rapids, MI: Zondervan, 2007).

19 Ibid., xviii.

20 Ibid., 2.

21 Ibid., 16.

22 Walls, *The Missionary Movement in Christian History: Studies in the Transmission of Faith* (Maryknoll, NY: Orbis, 1996), 7–9. See *UIM*, chap. 33.

23 Ibid.; see also Tennent, *Theology in the Context of World Christianity*, 1–24.

24 See Robert J. Schreiter, *Constructing Local Theologies* (Maryknoll, NY: Orbis, 1985), 1–21.

25 Ibid., 4.

> in a certain time and are not necessarily relevant to other times and places. For instance, how many American seminaries teach courses on idolatry or witchcraft? It is not a major issue in our culture, so we don't develop detailed theologies to deal with it.[26]

This description—beginning with context, rather than the text—tends to make those schooled in Western seminaries very nervous, with their traditional curriculum of systematic theology, historical theology, etc. The latter have learned to contend for universal biblical "Truth" in the face of "tolerance," cultural relativism, and the declining influence of Christianity in government, education, and the public square. Voices raised against the relativistic tide decry a kind of "anthropological captivity of missiology," and reaffirm the importance of doctrine, propositional truth, and the "transcendent message" of the gospel.[27]

For example, in a 2008 conference address, Dr. John MacArthur famously decried contextualization as "zip-code ministry":

> The apostles went out with an absolute disdain for contextualization. The modern drive for cultural contextualization is a curse, because people are wasting their time trying to figure out clever ways to draw in the elect. Contextualization is "zip-code ministry." The message of Jesus Christ, on the other hand, is transcendent. It goes beyond its immediate culture or sub-culture. It crosses the world, and ignores the nuances of culture. It never descends to clothing or musical style, as if that had anything to do with the message of the gospel.[28]

But as some respondents wryly noted, MacArthur's ministry is itself culture-shaped and zip-code based. All truth is expressed in cultural forms, from the language and literary structures of Scripture (Hebrew, Aramaic, Greek; proverbs, poetry, epistles, law, treaties, genealogies, stories, parables, laments, curses, blessings, etc.) to the supreme paradigm of the Incarnation itself, when "the Word became flesh." The Son of God did not clock "hang-time" somewhere between heaven and earth, like a demigod or jumping athlete. He taught and ate and left his footprints in Nazareth, Galilee, and the rural routes of Palestine. He suffered, died on a cross, and rose from a tomb left empty in the urban "zip-code" of Jerusalem. In the process, he dignified space and time, culture and creation.

As a final note here, one detects in Schreiter's comments above, as well as MacArthur's, the nuance that local theologizing is taking place—must, should, will take place—in apposition to the real or imagined imposition of a "received theology" from the outside. The identity of local theologies is being constructed, contested, negotiated; local/contextual theologizing takes place vis-à-vis critique of (or by) the *perceived "Other,"* a universal, usually Westernized church and theology. In the words of

---

26 Email message to author, May 18, 2012.

27 See the website BiblicalMissiology.com for representative samples of vocal opposition to Muslim contextualization, including the debate over Bible translation principles for Muslim audiences. See also *St. Francis Magazine,* published online at http://www.stfrancismagazine.info/ja/.

28 This text is from a detailed "summarized paraphrase" of MacArthur's message by Nathan Busenitz published in *Pulpit Magazine: A Ministry of Shepherds' Fellowship,* March 5, 2008, http://www.sfpulpit.com/2008/03/05/opening-session-%e2%80%93-wednesday-morning/.

Kwame Bediako, "Western theology was for so long presented in all its particulars as *the* theology of the Church, when, in fact, it was geographically localized and culturally limited, European and Western, and not universal."[29]

This helps us situate insider missiology and movements within the vestiges of the post-colonial project, as part of the Majority World church and the trend toward global theologizing, with all the attendant challenges and sensitivities involved.

Thus the development of local theologies in Islamic contexts (represented by insider missiology—with more or less input from outsider "alongsiders") is taking place in an environment sensitized to issues of power, injustice, oppression, economic inequities, etc., as well as the troubled history of Islam and the West. If we add the post-9/11 steroids of prejudice, bigotry, hate, fear, mistrust, and misunderstanding in relation to Islam and Muslims, we end up with a toxic brew that threatens to distort our visual acuity and poison our discussion of theological issues and the process of theological reflection.

As Tennent advises, we must find a "proper balance" between the universal and the particular, or (as Walls puts it) between the pilgrim principle and the indigenizing principle—affirming the universal truths of the gospel for all peoples in all places and times, while remaining open to new insights into gospel truth as the Word takes root and bears fruit in the soil of new hearts and minds and cultures.[30]

Lens 7: Other Religions

discontinuity / exclusivism / radical disjunction

or

continuity / fulfillment / *praeparatio evangelica* / "Christ
does not arrive as a stranger to any culture"

The seventh and eighth lenses are closely related: the seventh involves our philosophical approach to other religions, while the eighth lens looks at approaches to *Islam* and Muslims in particular.

The New Testament clearly affirms the uniqueness and exclusivity of Christ as the only way to God and salvation (John 14:6; Acts 4:12). There are different understandings, however, of the notion of religion itself, and different Christian attitudes and approaches toward non-Christian religions and faith communities.[31] These are usually classified as three broad positions generally known as exclusivism, inclusivism, and pluralism,[32] or exclusivism, fulfillment, and relativism.[33] Bosch contends that "the two largest unsolved problems for the Christian church" today are "its relationship (1) to *world views which offer this worldly salvation,* and (2) to *other faiths.*"[34]

In the debate over insider missiology, one issue is the continuity or discontinuity between religions and religious worldviews. On one end of the spectrum, Christian faith comes as the fulfillment of the aspirations of other religious traditions, and becomes what Scottish missionary J. N. Farquhar (1861–

---

29 Quoted in Kevin J. Vanhoozer, "'One Rule to Rule Them All?' Theological Method in an Era of World Christianity," in Ott and Netland, *Globalizing Theology*, 88.

30 Tennent, *Theology in the Context of World Christianity*, 13.

31 Bosch, *Transforming Mission*, 474–89.

32 Christopher J. H. Wright, "Theology of Religions," in *Evangelical Dictionary of World Missions*, ed. A. Scott Moreau (Grand Rapids, MI: Baker, 2000), 951–53.

33 Bosch, *Transforming Mission*, 478–83.

34 Ibid., 276–77; emphasis in the original.

1929) called the "crown" (of Hinduism).[35] Insider missiology is clearly sympathetic to this perspective in relation to Islam. Elements of culture and other religions function as *praeparatio evangelica*; these prepare the way for the gospel.[36]

Thus Lamin Sanneh argues that divine preparation for the gospel preceded the arrival of missionaries in Africa.[37] The coming of gospel light "rekindles" the sparks "entrusted to all living cultures" into a "living flame" of faith. This provides a theological basis for translating the Scriptures into all vernacular cultures. He notes further that the response to Christian faith in Africa is linked to those societies where the indigenous name for God was used; thus the notion that "Christ does not arrive as a stranger to any culture."

The contrasting side is aligned with Kraemer's position,[38] rejecting continuity and compatibility between Christianity and other religions and instead asserting radical discontinuity and a clear line of distinction.[39] The differences, then as now, involve intense dispute.

In a separate but related argument, some insider advocates, following post-Enlightenment and contemporary Western critiques of religion,[40] use the terms "religion," "church," and "Christianity" in a pejorative sense, in juxtaposition to their preferred terms "kingdom" and "Jesus-centered new movements." Analysis of their argumentation exhibits a method of defending insider missiology and movements by painting their critics as historically and culturally rooted defenders of the (Western) faith, whose now reduced place in the global Christian movement serves to undermine the legitimacy of their claims to superior wisdom and insight.

The net effect is to allow for an escape from the burden of Christian history and the "common adoptive past" affirmed by Walls: who wants to be left "holding the bag" in defense of "Christianity" and two thousand years of real or imagined Christian sins?

As E. Stanley Jones argued in 1925, perhaps more hopefully than presciently, "India can now take from Christ because she is able to disassociate him from the West. . . . The centering of everything upon the person of Jesus clears the issue and has given us a new vitalizing of our work."[41] In a similar vein for Sundar Singh and N. V. Tilak, "the direct experience of Jesus" was foundational to their faith and led them to walk outside the boundaries of the organized church.[42]

Granted, insider proponents argue that insider believers do, in fact, identify with the larger body of Christ. But this identity would appear to be largely in their hearts, in the meeting room, and with select individuals who, in effect, mediate that relationship. For *security* reasons, for *social* reasons, and

---

35 J. N. Farquhar, *The Crown of Hinduism* (London: H. Milford, 1913). See Harold Netland, *Encountering Religious Pluralism: The Challenge to Christian Faith and Mission* (Downers Grove, IL: InterVarsity Press, 2001), 33ff.

36 For the discussion related to Islam, see David Emmanuel Singh, "Hundred Years of Christian-Muslim Relations," *Transformation: An International Journal of Holistic Mission Studies* 27 (2010): 225–38.

37 Lamin O. Sanneh, *Whose Religion is Christianity? The Gospel Beyond the West* (Grand Rapids, MI: Eerdmans, 2003); and Sanneh, *Translating the Message: The Missionary Impact on Culture* (Maryknoll, NY: Orbis, 2009).

38 Hendrik Kraemer, *The Christian Message in a Non-Christian World* (Grand Rapids, MI: Kregel / International Missionary Council, 1947).

39 Cf. Singh, "Hundred Years," 234.

40 See Bosch, *Transforming Mission*, 474–76.

41 E. Stanley Jones, *The Christ of the Indian Road* (New York: Abingdon Press, 1925), 109–10.

42 David Emmanuel Singh, "Sunder Singh and N. V. Tilak: Lessons for Missiology from 20th Century India" (papers presented at the Seoul Consultation, March 22–24, 2009), http://www.edinburgh2010.org/en/study-themes/9-mission-spirituality-and-authentic-discipleship/seoul-consultation.html.

now for *theological* reasons, Christian identity is not assumed or marked in public, or in the now global-ized public square.

One major question, therefore, involves our understanding of identity, one of the most complex and well-researched concepts in every branch of the social sciences today. To what degree is public identi-fication with the heritage and adoptive past of a religious community—as it is commonly understood, even by the Muslim *ummah*—relevant to following Jesus?

There are pragmatic reasons for saying it is not. Certainly anyone with experience sharing the good news with Muslims wants to maintain distance from exterior religion, false or nominal Christians, and the historical and highly charged stereotypes associated with Christianity. The focus is on the person of Jesus himself as embodying "the gospel."

But some insider theorists and practitioners are saying more than this. "Religious identity" is contrasted with "following Jesus." The former is reified as a negative category, an idol of human fabri-cation.[43] It is reduced to historically conditioned human efforts, ethics, and cultic observances; and it is associated with identity in a largely Western, bounded social group.[44]

The boundaries associated with faith communities are also rejected. This reductionist generaliza-tion about "religion" is contrasted with a "kingdom" ideal based on the New Testament, to promote and defend the emergence of Restoration-type movements to (and communities of) Jesus that retain and/or reframe their former "religious" identity within their faith movement. In this view, according to Bosch, "what is really called for, however, is not just in*cultur*ation but in*religion*ization,"[45] the implanting of a new faith and spiritual center within an existing religious tradition, community, and system.

Note in passing that in insider missiology, public identification with one faith community's socio-religious identity (Christian) is rejected, while the other (Muslim) is affirmed as necessary, or at very least acceptable, for the sake of a larger *telos* (e.g., rapid evangelization, church-planting movements, cultural transformation from within).

But really, this is nothing new. One again hears echoes from the past—for example, E. Stanley Jones' *Christ of the Indian Road:*

> Christianity is actually breaking out beyond the borders of the Christian Church and is being seen in the most unexpected plac-es. If those who have not the spirit of Jesus are none of his, no matter what outward symbols they possess, then conversely those who have the spirit of Jesus are his, no matter what outward sym-bols they may lack. In a spiritual movement like that of Jesus it is difficult and impossible to mark its frontiers. Statistics and classifi-cations lose their meaning and are impotent to tell who are in and who are not.[46]

For Jones, "Jesus told us it would be so" by describing kingdom growth in two ways: (1) "outwardly," like a mustard seed growing into a tree, that is, "men coming into the organized expression of the King-dom, namely, the Christian Church"; and (2) "silently," like leaven permeating the whole: "This tells of

---

43 Cf. the discussion of Calvin and Barth in Bosch, *Transforming Mission*, 478–79.

44 See, for example, Carl Medearis, *Speaking of Jesus: The Art of Not-Evangelism* (Colorado Springs, CO: David C. Cook, 2011).

45 Bosch, *Transforming Mission*, 477.

46 Jones, *Christ of the Indian Road*, 59.

the *silent permeation of the minds and hearts of men by Christian truth and thought* until, from within, but scarcely knowing what is happening, *the spirit and outlook of men would be silently leavened by the spirit of Jesus*—they would be *Christianized from within*. We see these two things taking place with the impact of Christ upon the soul of the East."[47]

Few descriptions capture better the Christocentric passions and dreams of insider practitioners. Jones' prediction is certainly true in the Muslim world—that Christianity is actually "breaking out beyond the borders" of the church and is "being seen in the most unexpected places." Jones raises a probing parallel question: "Will the Christian Church be Christ-like enough to be the moral and spiritual center of this overflowing Christianity?"[48]

This suggests that the way Muslim followers of Christ understand and work out their new identity in Christ in a given context is not merely a local affair. How does this "overflowing Christianity" relate to the "moral and spiritual center" represented by the Christian church? The manner by which new identities are constructed, negotiated, or contested by others—in the national/regional/global Christian community, as well as in the Muslim *ummah*—is critical.

The reality is that the Christian faith is a historical religion like any other, with characteristics common to all. This enables us to speak of and understand other religions and their adherents without judgment,[49] even as we invite them, with love and respect, to follow Christ.

To inform the ongoing discussion, we need to draw not only on mission field surveys, but also analyses from the fields of psychology, sociology, religious studies, church history, the history of religions, conversion studies, and other disciplines, including historical studies (e.g., the heated controversy over the theology of religions in the 1920s and 1930s). An appreciation for the church's diverse and "shifting perspectives" on other religions[50] can broaden our frame of reference and foster much-needed patience, intellectual humility, and understanding in the contemporary dispute over engagement with other religions such as Islam.

Lens 8: Islam

"Islam" / historically essentialized / "Muslims" / Islamic tradition

or

"islams" / culturally embedded / "muslims" /
"Which Islam?" "Whose Islam?"

Approaches to Islam (and Muslims) appear to move us to the heart of the divide. "The Nature of Islam" was chosen as one of three major topics at the Bridging the Divide Consultation 2012. This lens is influenced by the other lenses or filters, as well as by one's academic-cum- disciplinary perspective, each of which has its own favored methodologies, aims, scopes, and agendas.[51]

---

47 Ibid., 59–60; emphasis added. See also Jeff Morton, review of *Christ of the Indian Road,* by E. Stanley Jones, http://biblicalmissiology.org/2012/11/19/book-review-christ-of-the-indian-road/.

48 Jones, *Christ of the Indian Road,* 69.

49 Singh, "Hundred Years," 230; cf. Ninian Smart, *The World's Religions* (Cambridge: Cambridge University Press, 1998).

50 See, for example, Netland, *Encountering Religious Pluralism,* 23–54.

51 Gabriele Marranci, *The Anthropology of Islam* (Oxford, UK: Berg, 2008), 3.

One primary dichotomy here is represented by the contrast between Islam viewed as (1) a unifying *essence* across disparate social, cultural, intellectual, and historical realities; and (2) a *social* phenomenon variously embedded in local contexts.

The traditional approach of oriental studies tends to be textual (Qur'an, Hadith), focused on Arabic, philosophy, theology, history, and related literatures (Persian, Turkish, Urdu). Islam is also viewed developmentally as an historical tradition and phenomenon. Dominated by Western scholars, orientalism has suffered well-known criticisms for perpetuating stereotyped representations of Islam and Muslims.

In contrast, the social and anthropological approach to Islam emerged in the 1970s and 1980s utilizing social science methodologies (e.g., participant observation). The focus is not on an essentialized Islam, but on the anthropology of Islam and its unique regional and local expressions.

Geertz's seminal *Islam Observed*, followed by el-Zein, Gellner, and Gilsenen, influenced a generation of anthropologists.[52] Eickelman, Caton, and Abu-Lughod carried forward the study of "Islam in local contexts," albeit primarily in the Middle East/North Africa.[53]

In 1977, El-Zein proposed that there is not one "Islam" but many "islams" (lowercase, plural). Esposito emphasizes that diversity in Islam is also affected by leadership, authority, and global forces.[54] Thus we need to ask two major questions: "Whose Islam?"—that is, "Who decides, interprets, leads, and implements" reform in a given context (rulers, military, clergy, activists, intellectuals, etc.)?; and "Which Islam?"—that is, is Islam envisioned as "a restoration of past doctrines and laws, or is it a reformation through reinterpretation and reformulation of Islam to meet the demands of modern life?"[55]

Textured ethnographic studies of everyday Islam ("lived Islam") among Muslim people groups have enormous value; they are greatly needed if servants of Christ are to move beyond stereotypes, sterile generalizations, and surface understandings of Islam as a lived religion. This challenge, and the studies cited above, inspired my own ethnographic research into Pashtun identity and folklore in Afghanistan and northwest Pakistan.[56]

Anthropologist Marranci succinctly summarizes the shift: "We should start from Muslims, rather than Islam," and make the former our object of study.[57] The emphasis is on understanding Muslims as people, what being a Muslim means to them, how Muslim identity is marked, and the distinct self-understandings, values, and emotions of Muslims in diverse contexts. The knowledge base is textured ethnographic studies.

---

52 Clifford Geertz, *Islam Observed: Religious Development in Morocco and Indonesia* (New Haven: Yale University Press, 1968); Abdul Hamid el-Zein, "Beyond Ideology and Theology: The Search for the Anthropology of Islam," *Annual Review of Anthropology* 6 (1977): 227–54; Ernest Gellner, *Muslim Society* (Cambridge: Cambridge University Press, 1981); Michael Gilsenen, *Recognizing Islam: Religion and Society in the Modern Middle East* (London: I.B. Tauris, 1990 [1982]).

53 Dale F. Eickelman, "The Study of Islam in Local Contexts," *Contributions to Asian Studies* 17 (1982):1–16; Eickelman, *The Middle East and Central Asia: An Anthropological Approach*, 3rd ed. (Englewood Cliffs, NJ: Prentice-Hall, 1997 [1981]); Steven C. Caton, *Peaks of Yemen I Summon: Poetry as Cultural Practice in a North Yemeni Tribe* (Berkeley, CA: University of California Press, 1990); Lila Abu-Lughod, *Veiled Sentiments: Honor and Poetry in a Bedouin Society* (Berkeley, CA: University of California Press, 1986); and Abu-Lughod, *Writing Women's Worlds: Bedouin Stories* (Berkeley, CA: University of California Press, 1993).

54 John L. Esposito, *What Everyone Needs to Know About Islam* (Oxford: Oxford University Press, 2002).

55 Ibid., 70–71.

56 Leonard N. Bartlotti, "Negotiating Pakhto: Proverbs, Islam and the Construction of Identity among Pashtuns" (PhD thesis, Oxford Centre for Mission Studies/University of Wales, UK, 2000).

57 Marranci, *Anthropology of Islam*, 7.

Putting it another way, the dichotomy is between (1) "Muslims" understood as having a common way of believing, thinking, behaving, etc., despite disparities of culture, and (2) "muslims" (lowercase) understood as cultural muslims, whose sense of religious identity is locally, ethnically, and culturally constructed. In a critical corollary for insider advocates, this leaves room for idiosyncratic expressions and constructions of Muslimness (namely, as "Muslim followers of Christ").

The essentialism of the traditional approach tends to smooth out ethnographic particularities, leading to what Marranci calls "the fallacy of the 'Muslim mind theory.'"[58] Generally, insider practitioners and advocates lean toward the other side of the spectrum.

The insider emphasis on particularities, however, risks overlooking historical influences, downplaying connectivities, and oversimplifying notions of causality. The local is sacralized.

In a globalized world, flattened lines of authority, multiple networks, transnational identities, economic migration, and social media add complexity to our understanding of identity and ethnicity[59] and the often exoticized "local."

Whether the focus is on the macro or the micro, the state or local-regional dynamics, Eickelman reminds us that the "universalistic and particularistic strains" of Islam are "in dynamic tension with each other,"[60] and they have come to constitute an important area for study. Scholar-practitioners across the divide must learn to appreciate the "dynamic tension" and drill down into new pools of knowledge, while drawing upon a wide range of resources and insights available via multiple disciplinary perspectives.

Lens 9: Conversion-initiation

event / believing, behaving, belonging / people of God
/ "bounded set" / in-out markers of identity
or
process / belonging, behaving, believing / kingdom of
God / "centered set" / moving toward Christ

A final lens through which to view insider movements is a subset of frontier missiology that may be called "conversion studies." In this case, I have chosen a broader heading based on the classic study by New Testament scholar James D. G. Dunn[61] on the baptism in the Holy Spirit in the book of Acts. In the social sciences, the term "conversion" can refer to the complex of cognitive/emotional/religious meanings associated with personal change; "initiation" involves elements and behaviors related to recruitment, participation, and belonging to a new social group or movement.

Dunn shows that water baptism is one element in a "conversion-initiation" process. (In the phenomenology of Lukan theology, Luke is concerned not with the *ordo salutis*, but with visible markers of the age of the Spirit inaugurated by the Messiah.) Conversion-initiation in Acts involves five elements: repentance, faith, water baptism, Spirit baptism or the gift of the Spirit, and incorporation into the community of faith.

---

58 Ibid., 6.

59 See Marcus Banks, *Ethnicity: Anthropological Constructions* (New York: Routledge, 1996).

60 Dale F. Eickelman, "Popular Religion in the Middle East and North Africa," in *The Oxford Encyclopedia of the Modern Islamic World*, ed. John Esposito (Oxford: Oxford University Press, 1995), 342.

61 James D. G. Dunn, *Baptism in the Holy Spirit: A Re-examination of the New Testament Teaching on the Gift of the Spirit in Relation to Pentecostalism Today* (Philadelphia: Westminster Press, 1970).

At issue, then, is the process of *how* people (Muslims) come to faith and begin to follow Christ as members of his people, and the biblical *markers* of change.

Traditionally, the truth encounter is in the foreground. Crisis conversion is followed by a discipleship process, leading to life change and incorporation into a (generally heterogeneous) group or church. There are clear markers of faith and new life; namely, public confession of faith, identification with the Christian community, water baptism, open witness, etc. Believers are to be bold in witness and renounce their former way of life. People know who is "in" or "out" of the family of faith.

On the other side of the spectrum, closer to the insider view, the notion of *process* and the concept of faith as a *journey* are central. This is expressed in the now familiar "belonging-behaving-believing" schema popular in the "emerging church" model in the West. Faith emerges in the context of an "Emmaus Road" journey to faith with others, involving a gradual discovery of the person of Christ, his truth and way of salvation.

Hiebert introduced an analogy from set theory that is used to undergird this approach.[62] He proposed viewing the church in terms of "bounded sets" versus "centered sets." In the former, the focus tends to be on who is "in" or "out," and there are clear boundaries to the faith community. In a centered set, the focus is not on the boundaries but on the center, Jesus Christ; and the critical issue is one's movement toward, or away, from him.

The "process" side of the spectrum is comfortable with conversion-initiation as a long road without clear mile markers or what most people consider "religious distinctives" associated with a particular faith community. The length of journey, timing of regeneration, and boundary lines are fuzzy, as are the progress markers; the direction, however, is not.

Centered-set theory is nearly unchallengeable truth in some circles, and appears to be one assumption of insider advocates. Moving "toward" Christ approximates "following" Christ and his teaching. Movement in turn is equated with "true" faith = follower of Jesus = a real "Christian" (though not publicly so named). This contrasts with those who are so in name only, who are made to bear the weight of that maligned historical identity. The "distance" between various people and Jesus is reduced to a matter of personal contact or experience or degree of perceived obedience (not confession, regeneration, or baptism). The key issue is the direction of the arrow toward or away from Jesus—not the distance or relation to a boundary.

The conversion-initiation lens also focuses our attention on the theological issue of the *social* implications of spiritual *reconciliation* in Christ (e.g., between Jew and Gentile). As Constantineanu demonstrates in his study of Pauline theology, reconciliation is an essential aspect of salvation and contains "an intrinsic, social, horizontal dimension" that cannot be separated from vertical reconciliation with God: the two are "inseparable," "two dimensions of the same reality."[63] The new identity believers share as reconciled people in Christ is "the basis for their sharing in, or living out, a reconciled life with others."[64]

Can one argue for the liberty of Muslim followers of Christ (cf. Acts 15:7–11) to continue to identify with Muslims but find it inconvenient for them to identify publicly with "Christian" brothers and

---

62 Paul Hiebert, *Anthropological Reflections on Missiological Issues* (Grand Rapids, MI: Baker, 1994).

63 Corneliu Constantineanu, *The Social Significance of Reconciliation in Paul's Theology: Narrative Readings in Romans* (New York: Continuum, 2010), 209.

64 Ibid.

sisters—due to the consequences or *social* stigma in the eyes of their own people? Peter tried it (Gal 2:11–16) and was rebuked by Paul.

Relationships potentially *veil or reveal the reality of a redeemed humanity.* "The shared table was the acid test."[65]

A concerted study of the complexity of conversion can shed light on critical issues. This includes field studies of conversion to Christ (on the order of Syrjänen),[66] as well as Christian conversion to Islam, in various cultural contexts in the West and Global South. Manger's study of the Lafofa of Sudan, for example, shows that Muslim identity is a dynamic process; "being a Muslim" is contested through the manipulation of the meaning(s) of a changing set of diacritical markers (individual customs and traits) that become symbols of Muslim identity.[67]

It is well known that conversion is a multifaceted process involving personal, cultural, social, and religious dimensions. Thus studies are needed that include, but go beyond, surveys and interviews with converts and assumptions about causality. Buckser and Glazier suggest studies of the "contextual matrix of conversion" (e.g., the role of the family and others in the individual intrapsychic process); the processes of conversion, including the subtleties of "first contact"; longitudinal versus synchronic studies, to explore the long-term consequences of religious change; the definition of "conversion" itself (what exactly is changed?); differences between outsider and insider points of view (epistemologically, phenomenologically); and the role of theology in the way the process is understood and framed.[68]

The disciplines of theology, biblical studies, anthropology, sociology, psychology, and historical studies—all offer possible perspectives through which to understand the multifaceted processes involved in Muslims coming to faith in Christ in diverse contexts around the world. There is no single way to understand conversion. There are multiple theoretical approaches, multiple "lenses." This brings us full circle.

Conclusion

This paper has argued that *multiple theological presuppositions* lie at the heart of insider missiology. These presuppositions consciously or unconsciously affect the way proponents have presented, and concerned observers have critiqued, insider movements and insider missiology. The nine interrelated assumptions, or background beliefs, discussed above—ecclesiology, authority, culture, pneumatology, history, doing theology, other religions, Islam, and conversion-initiation—comprise an array of "talking points" for further dialogue and critique.

The question, "Are you for or against insider movements?" has been shown to be simplistic in the extreme. An individual observer—whether an advocate, insider, or alongsider, or a critic, concerned Christian, or scholar-activist—may deem one of these theological/missiological lenses more significant than others in assessing insider movements.

---

65 Walls, *The Missionary Movement*, 78.

66 Seppo Syrjänen, *In Search of Meaning and Identity: Conversion to Christianity in Pakistani Muslim Culture* (Helsinki: Finnish Society for Missiology and Ecumenics, 1984).

67 Leif O. Manger, "On Becoming Muslim: The Construction of Identities among the Lafofa of the Sudan," in *Muslim Diversity: Local Islam in Global Contexts*, ed. Leif Manger (London: Curzon, 1999).

68 Andrew Buckser and Stephen D. Glazier, *The Anthropology of Religious Conversion* (Lanham, MD: Rowman and Littlefield, 2003), 212ff.; see also Kathryn A. Kraft, *Searching for Heaven in the Real World: A Sociological Discussion of Conversion in the Arab World* (Eugene, OR: Wipf & Stock, 2013).

| 5 | 4 | 3 | 2 | 1 | 0 | 1 | 2 | 3 | 4 | 5 |

	Theological Lens	**Insider Missiology**
Word sacraments discipline/order leadership Pauline emphasis	**ecclesiology/church**	Word Spirit two or three gathered simple church emphasis on Synoptic Jesus
Scripture apostolic teaching & ministries outside resourcing	**authority**	Scripture local believers local decisions
Christ *against* Christ *over/in paradox with*	**culture**	Christ *of* Christ *transforming*
Spirit-appointed leadership sacraments & channels of grace wisdom tradition disciplined growth "wind"	**pneumatology/Holy Spirit**	Spirit-anointed leadership sovereignty of Spirit prophetic tradition spontaneous expansion "mighty rushing wind"
Spirit active throughout history wisdom, tradition (creeds, councils, theologies) faithfulness "faith once delivered"	**history**	Spirit active now in local context new insights and expressions freedom "a new thing"
universal truths Western theological tradition "pilgrim principle"	**doing theology**	local (contextual) theologies theologies from majority world church "indigenizing principle"
discontinuity exclusivism, radical disjunction	**other religions**	continuity fulfillment *praeparatio evangelica*
"Islam" historically essentialized "Muslims" Islamic tradition	**Islam**	"islams" culturally embedded "muslims" "Which Islam?" "Whose Islam?"
event believing, behaving, belonging bounded set people of God clear in/out markers of identity	**conversion-initiation**	process belonging, behaving, believing centered set kingdom of God moving towards Christ

Table 6.1: Theological presuppositions of insider missiology and the evangelical spectrum

The righthand column of table 6.1 summarizes the primary theological presuppositions associated with insider missiology. To date, most discussions of insider missiology have been complicated by the fact that advocates have braided these notions into one tight, multi-strand argument legitimizing or promoting insider approaches and movements. Likewise some critics have adopted a "zero-sum" approach that reduces the debate to winners and losers.

This analysis has shown that insider missiology is multivocal, not univocal: insider advocates are saying many things, not one thing. Thus insider missiology must be assessed—and must be willing to be judged, and adjusted—accordingly. Each element involves critical theological issues.

How we view any single element in this set of interrelated issues influences what we "see" when we look "inside" insider movements, and affects our judgment of what is true, right, fair, and biblical in relation to one of the most contentious subjects on the current mission scene.

Throughout this paper, my aim is not to defend or criticize a particular position, nor to argue for one approach over the other. I have taken the risk of oversimplifying and dichotomizing a set of immensely complex concepts in order to underline the point that there is a *spectrum of defensible and contested biblical positions* on each issue.

The doyen of Islamic studies, Bernard Lewis, was recently described as someone who has always been "unusually alert to nuance and ambiguity; he is wary of his sources and tests them against other evidence."[69] Alertness to nuance, tolerance for ambiguity, and a willingness to test sources against other evidence are difficult qualities to cultivate in the high-octane world of missions, where pragmatics ("What works?") can trump diagnostics ("What's really going on here?") and biblical hermeneutics can become the handmaiden of our own cherished presumptions.

Thus, in addition to suggestions for dialogue and further study interlaced with analysis throughout this paper, I would like to offer a few closing recommendations:

1. *Understand insider missiology and movements from within,* by talking with and listening to the voices of Muslim followers of Christ. In this, the emerging research and data from the field will play an important role in helping us move toward a "thick description"[70] of what following Christ means for these new believers and groups.

2. *Balance empathy with a sanctified hermeneutic of questioning.* Other voices must be heard as well. This recommendation applies particularly to sympathetic local workers, alongsiders, and researchers. In most insider contexts, we are dealing with cultures where interpersonal and intercultural communication are influenced by notions of honor and shame, patron-client relationships, economics, and power dynamics. Suspicion and intrigue are in the air. One mark of wisdom, understanding, and spirituality is the ability to distinguish the *outside* dimension (Arabic *zahir,* "exterior, apparent meaning") from that which is on the *inside* (Arabic *batin,* "hidden, inner, spiritual dimension"). This applies not only to understanding the holy books and to spirituality, but also, importantly, to relationships. In the latter

---

69 Eric Ormsby, "The Tale of the Dragoman," review of *Notes on a Century: Reflections of a Middle East Historian,* by Bernard Lewis, *Wall Street Journal Online,* May 11, 2012, http://online.wsj.com/article/SB100014240527 02304743704577380390207004120.html/.

70 A key term in the anthropology of Clifford Geertz, "thick description" of a culture goes beyond factual description to analyze the conceptual structures and complex layers of meaning and interpretation ascribed to specific contextual happenings. See Geertz, "Thick Description: Toward an Interpretive Theory of Culture," in *The Interpretation of Cultures* (New York: Basic Books, 1973).

case, failure to question or discern inner intentions can be, in local eyes, both a sign of foolishness and patently dangerous.

3. *Listen with discernment.* Alongsiders, analysts, and observers need to discern the full range of cultural, relational, economic, linguistic, and other dynamics at work in a given situation. The reality is that insider voices are generally mediated voices, due to security issues, language, and other factors. Sympathizers and critics alike bear a special responsibility to discern their own biases; to exercise discernment of spirits; to acknowledge the role of their own theological and missiological presuppositions; to recognize the line between description and prescription; and to speak with love and respect, boldness and humility. As a faculty at the Oxford Centre for Mission Studies, we used to challenge our PhD scholars to dig deeper into field realities by raising this one important question: "What's really going on when what's going on is going on?"[71]

4. *Ask the hard questions.* "Facts are friendly," one of my former colleagues used to say, quoting his doctoral supervisor. Let's not be afraid to ask critical questions, especially questions related to biblical exegesis and hermeneutics. The word of God is our final authority. Notwithstanding the desire to be culturally sensitive and contextually relevant, we must discipline ourselves to think biblically and deeply about these matters. In this process, scholar-practitioners must resist the temptation to prooftext their case or make hermeneutical leaps. This is a call for a deeper immersion in the Scriptures.

5. *Explore multiperspectival views.* The same situation can be interpreted in different ways. A multidisciplinary and multiple-lens approach to insider missiology should be welcomed. This does not minimize or discredit more narrow disciplinary analyses. We must welcome expertise derived from biblical studies, theology, missiology, Islamic studies, anthropology, linguistics, and other disciplines, and not dismiss the insights of those who may lack "field" experience. What is required is a Jesus style of scholarship that (1) allows others to sit at the table and have a voice, even if we disagree, and (2) raises one's own voice with both courage and humility.

6. *Engage the ongoing process of "globalizing theology."* We need to hear again Hiebert's call for "metatheology," for local Christian communities to "do theology within their own local contexts but *in conversation with other Christians globally.*"[72] Netland defines "globalizing theology" as "theological reflection rooted in God's self-revelation in Scripture and informed by the historical legacy of the Christian community through the ages, the current realities in the world, and the diverse perspectives of Christian communities throughout the world, with a view to greater holiness in living and faithfulness in fulfilling God's mission in all the world through the church."[73] Insider advocates in local settings bear a special responsibility to engage in both deeper theological reflection and a broader global conversation.

7. *Bridge the divide.* The divide on matters of Muslim contextualization is both ideological and relational. Bridging the divide involves content and process, biblical interpretation and biblical fidelity, boldness of conviction and mutual respect, purity of heart and a Christ-like tone of voice. In the ongoing process, we must embrace the tensions and ambiguities and persevere in love, listening, speaking,

---

71 I am grateful to Dr. Bernard Farr, Senior Residentiary Research Fellow at the Oxford Centre for Mission Studies, for this insight.

72 Paul Hiebert, "Metatheology: The Step beyond Contextualization," in *Anthropological Reflections on Missiological Issues* (Grand Rapids, MI: Baker, 1994), 102–3; emphasis added.

73 Netland, "Introduction," in Ott and Netland, *Globalizing Theology*, 30.

and learning with others in the worldwide church. Let us affirm evangelical unity, delight in (or at least tolerate) evangelical ambiguity, and create space for evangelical diversity.

Joyfully we can affirm that this process of seeking spiritual wisdom and insight from the word of God now includes new brothers and sisters with a Muslim heritage. These communities of faith in Jesus Christ are singing praises to the Lamb of God, who reigns on high and in thousands of hearts within the heart of the Islamic world.

Bibliography

Abu-Lughod, Lila. *Veiled Sentiments: Honor and Poetry in a Bedouin Society.* Berkeley, CA: University of California Press, 1986.

———. *Writing Women's Worlds: Bedouin Stories.* Berkeley, CA: University of California Press, 1993.

Allen, Roland. *The Spontaneous Expansion of the Church: And the Causes Which Hinder It.* Eugene, OR: Wipf & Stock, 1997 [1927].

———. *Missionary Methods: St. Paul's or Ours?* Grand Rapids, MI: Eerdmans, 1962 [1912].

Banks, Marcus. *Ethnicity: Anthropological Constructions.* New York: Routledge, 1996.

Bartlotti, Leonard N. "Negotiating Pakhto: Proverbs, Islam and the Construction of Identity among Pashtuns." PhD thesis, Oxford Centre for Mission Studies/University of Wales, UK, 2000.

Bosch, David J. *Transforming Mission: Paradigm Shifts in Theology of Mission.* Maryknoll, NY: Orbis, 1991.

Buckser, Andrew, and Stephen D. Glazier. *The Anthropology of Religious Conversion.* Lanham, MD: Rowman and Littlefield, 2003.

Carson, D. A. *Christ and Culture Revisited.* Grand Rapids, MI: Eerdmans, 2008.

Caton, Steven C. *Peaks of Yemen I Summon: Poetry as Cultural Practice in a North Yemeni Tribe.* Berkeley, CA: University of California Press, 1990.

Constantineanu, Corneliu. *The Social Significance of Reconciliation in Paul's Theology: Narrative Readings in Romans.* New York: Continuum, 2010.

Dunn, James D. G. *Baptism in the Holy Spirit: A Re-examination of the New Testament Teaching on the Gift of the Spirit in Relation to Pentecostalism Today.* Philadelphia: Westminster Press, 1970.

Eickelman, Dale F. "The Study of Islam in Local Contexts." *Contributions to Asian Studies* 17 (1982):1–16.

———. "Popular Religion in the Middle East and North Africa." In *The Oxford Encyclopedia of the Modern Islamic World,* edited by John L. Esposito, 339–43. Oxford: Oxford University Press, 1995.

———. *The Middle East and Central Asia: An Anthropological Approach.* 3rd ed. Englewood Cliffs, NJ: Prentice-Hall, 1998.

Esposito, John L. *What Everyone Needs to Know about Islam.* Oxford: Oxford University Press, 2002.

Farquhar, J. N. *The Crown of Hinduism.* London: H. Milford, 1913.

Geertz, Clifford. *Islam Observed: Religious Development in Morocco and Indonesia.* New Haven, CT: Yale University Press, 1968.

———. "Thick Description: Toward an Interpretive Theory of Culture." Chap. 1 in *The Interpretation of Cultures.* New York: Basic Books, 1973.

Gellner, Ernest. *Muslim Society.* Cambridge: Cambridge University Press, 1981.

Gilsenan, Michael. *Recognizing Islam: Religion and Society in the Modern Middle East.* London: I.B. Tauris, 1990.

Haight, Roger. *Christian Community in History: Comparative Ecclesiology.* Vol. 2. New York: Continuum, 2005.

Haskell, Rob, and Don Little, eds. "Insider Movements: Bridging the Divide." Special Issue of the *Evangelical Review of Theology* 37 (2013).

Hiebert, Paul. *Anthropological Reflections on Missiological Issues.* Grand Rapids, MI: Baker, 1994.

Jones, E. Stanley. *The Christ of the Indian Road.* New York: Abingdon Press, 1925.

Kraemer, Hendrik. *The Christian Message in a Non-Christian World.* Grand Rapids, MI: Kregel / International Missionary Council, 1947.

Kraft, Kathryn A. *Searching for Heaven in the Real World: A Sociological Discussion of Conversion in the Arab World.* Eugene, OR: Wipf & Stock, 2013.

Littell, Franklin H. *The Origins of Sectarian Protestantism: A Study of the Anabaptist View of the Church.* New York: Macmillan, 1964.

Manger, Leif O. "On Becoming Muslim: The Construction of Identities among the Lafofa of the Sudan." In *Muslim Diversity: Local Islam in Global Contexts,* edited by Leif Manger, 224–43. London: Curzon, 1999.

Marranci, Gabriele. *The Anthropology of Islam.* Oxford, UK: Berg, 2008.

McGavran, Donald. *The Bridges of God: A Study in the Strategy of Missions.* Eugene, OR: Wipf & Stock, 2005 [1955].

McPartlan, Paul. *Sacrament of Salvation: An Introduction to Eucharistic Ecclesiology.* Edinburgh: T&T Clark, 1995.

Medearis, Carl. *Speaking of Jesus: The Art of Not-Evangelism.* Colorado Springs, CO: David C. Cook, 2011.

Morton, Jeff. Review of *Christ of the Indian Road,* by E. Stanley Jones, November 19, 2012, www.biblicalmissiology.org/2012/11/19/book-review-christ-of-the-indian-road/.

Netland, Harold. *Encountering Religious Pluralism: The Challenge to Christian Faith and Mission.* Downers Grover, IL: InterVarsity Press, 2001.

Niebuhr, H. Richard. *Christ and Culture.* New York: Harper and Row, 1956.

Ormsby, Eric. "The Tale of the Dragoman." Review of *Notes on a Century,* by Bernard Lewis. *Wall Street Journal Online,* May 11, 2012, http://online.wsj.com/article/SB100014240527023047437045773803902 07004120.html/.

Ott, Craig, and Harold A. Netland. *Globalizing Theology: Belief and Practice in an Era of World Christianity.* Grand Rapids, MI: Baker Academic, 2006.

Sanneh, Lamin O. *Whose Religion Is Christianity? The Gospel beyond the West.* Grand Rapids, MI: Eerdmans, 2003.

———. *Translating the Message: The Missionary Impact on Culture.* Maryknoll, NY: Orbis, 2009.

Schreiter, Robert J. *Constructing Local Theologies.* Maryknoll, NY: Orbis, 1985.

Singh, David Emmanuel. "Hundred Years of Christian-Muslim Relations." *Transformation: An International Journal of Holistic Mission Studies* 27 (2010): 225–38. http://trn.sagepub.com/content/27/4/225.

———. "Sunder Singh and N. V. Tilak: Lessons for Missiology from 20th Century India." Papers presented at the Seoul Consultation, March 22–24, 2009. Available at http://www.edinburgh2010.org/en/study-themes/9-mission-spirituality-and-authentic-discipleship/seoul-consultation.html.

Smart, Ninian. *The World's Religions*. Cambridge: Cambridge University Press, 1998.

Strong, David K., and Cynthia A. Strong. "The Globalizing Hermeneutic of the Jerusalem Council." In Ott and Netland, *Globalizing Theology,* 127–39.

Syrjänen, Seppo. *In Search of Meaning and Identity: Conversion to Christianity in Pakistani Muslim Culture.* Helsinki: Finnish Society for Missiology and Ecumenics, 1984.

Tennent, Timothy C. *Theology in the Context of World Christianity: How the Global Church Is Influencing the Way We Think About and Discuss Theology.* Grand Rapids, MI: Zondervan, 2007.

Vanhoozer, Kevin J. "'One Rule to Rule Them All?' Theological Method in an Era of World Christianity." In Ott and Netland, *Globalizing Theology,* 85–126. Grand Rapids, MI: Baker Academic, 2006.

Walls, Andrew. *The Missionary Movement in Christian History: Studies in the Transmission of Faith.* Maryknoll, NY: Orbis, 1996.

Wright, Christopher J. H. "Theology of Religions." In *Evangelical Dictionary of World Missions,* edited by A. Scott Moreau, 951–53. Grand Rapids, MI: Baker, 2000.

Zein, Abdul Hamid el-. "Beyond Ideology and Theology: The Search for the Anthropology of Islam." *Annual Review of Anthropology* 6 (1977): 227–54.

1. What is most challenging or encouraging to you about Travis' definition of IMs (chap. 1)? As you continue to read through this anthology, note how your impressions change or develop.

2. What in IM history (chap. 2) surprises you? What insights led to people changing their understanding of what God might be doing or wanting them to do? How does this history provide a clearer view of what an insider movement is and is not?

3. Can you identify your own position in Cumming's overview of the C4/C5 debate (chap. 3)? What experiences have shaped your response to this debate? Do you agree with Accad's response? Why or why not?

4. Which questions listed by Travis and Woodberry (chap. 4) were most helpful for better understanding IMs? Which questions about IMs did you find most important to ask and answer? Did any questions or answers stand out to you? What questions about IMs do you have that were not asked? Which responses require further explanation?

5. Does chapter 5, "Myths and Misunderstandings," address any concerns or hesitations you have about IMs? If so, which ones, and how?

6. Have you identified your own "theological lenses" (chap. 6)? If so, what are they, and how have they challenged or influenced your perspective on insider movements?

EXAMPLES, TESTIMONIES, AND ANALYSIS

INTRODUCTION TO PART 2

> All roads do not lead to God, but God can be found walking on all
> of those roads.
>
> —WILBUR STONE*

One of the earliest recorded church controversies arose over the question of circumcision: did the new followers of Jesus from non-Jewish backgrounds need to be circumcised in accordance with the teaching and tradition of the Old Testament or not? Acts 15 records how early church leaders, including James, Peter, Paul, and Barnabas, met in Jerusalem to resolve this issue. It is instructive for us to note the process the early church went through in resolving this theological and socioreligious issue. They chose first to hear testimony from the lips of Paul and Barnabas of the miraculous "signs and wonders God had done among the Gentiles through them" (v. 12). Verses 4 and 7–14 describe this. It appears that these case studies and testimonies from trusted men informed the way in which James, the brother of Jesus, helped bring resolution to the question and apply Amos 9:11,12 to their first-century situation. In the following pages we find the testimonies of trusted men and women who likewise describe what the Spirit has done through or around them.

Part 2, section 1, "Examples and Testimonies," consists of eight articles.

Chapter 7 is by Gavriel Gefen. As a Jewish follower of Jesus who ministers not only to fellow Jews but to peoples of diverse ethnicities and religious traditions, he orients us to the nature of some Jesus movements he has witnessed in different settings.

Frank Decker illuminates in chapter 8, "When 'Christian' Does Not Translate," through brief accounts of insider believers in Buddhist and Muslim settings.

This is followed by the testimony of Dr. K. Venkatesh, who comes from a high-caste Hindu family, in chapter 9. Today he is a committed follower of Jesus who describes himself as being still "very much part of our Hindu community." He now has quite a few Hindu friends who also follow Jesus and meet regularly to pray, study Scripture, and encourage each other.

To see historical precedent for such Hindu discipleship to Jesus, we travel back to the early twentieth century to read the testimony of an early insider. In 1915 Hindu Christ follower Kandaswami

---

* "Islamic Studies—The Insider's Approach" (unpublished paper), 1. A version of this paper was later published as chap. 24 in *World Mission in the Wesleyan Spirit*, ed. Darrell L. Whiteman and Gerald H. Anderson (Franklin, TN: Providence House, 2009).

Chetti was invited to a Christian conference to speak on the topic "Why I Am Not a Christian"; chapter 10 is the transcript of his response.

As in many places, strongly negative cultural meanings are attached to the term "Christian" in Thailand, giving rise to alternative terms like "New Buddhists." In chapter 11, Banpote Wetchgama explains how the gospel is expressed using Buddhist thought forms so that Buddhists can follow Christ.

In chapter 12, Mazhar Mallouhi, Arab author and Muslim follower of Jesus, presents an insider's view of IMs.

In chapter 13, highly respected Arab Christian radio broadcaster Hanna Shahin shares the jarring paradigm shift he underwent, relating poignant personal experiences of Muslim enemies becoming his Muslim brothers in Christ.

In chapter 14, Tom Payne provides remarkable testimony from his field journal of an insider movement he and his wife have witnessed in the country where they have worked for sixteen years. This chapter involves the miraculous work of the Spirit in giving tongues, healings, and other signs and wonders to this movement.

Part 2, section 2, "Case Study Analysis," features an additional five articles.

In chapter 15, Ben Naja presents data from research on an East African movement of Muslims who follow Jesus. The data reveals the group's strong activity in evangelism, regular meeting as home fellowships, and high rates of Bible reading; at the same time, they maintain strong ties to the wider Muslim community, and over 90 percent of those in the movement refer to themselves as "Muslim followers of Isa" or simply as Muslims.

In chapter 16, John Jay Travis reflects on several IMs among Muslims in Asia, drawing on insights from John Wilder and J. Dudley Woodberry.

In chapter 17, H. L. Richard tells the story of the conversion of a famous nineteenth-century Indian social reformer, Pandita Ramabai. The case study illustrates the complex religious, social, legal, and cultural dynamics of "conversion" in India, subsequently factors in the emergence of insider expressions of faith in that country.

In chapter 18, Richard insightfully analyzes a study of "non-baptized" Hindu and Muslim followers of Jesus carried out in Madras by Herbert Hoefer.

We conclude this section with first-hand research by Darren Duerksen in chapter 19. He presents a thorough case study describing new patterns of Jesus-centered congregational life inside Hindu and Sikh communities in North India.

As is common with testimonies and case studies from areas where new believers may be in harm's way, many names and locations have deliberately not been mentioned. As we read these testimonies, let us pray for the people involved and give thanks to God for his grace and Spirit being so powerful and active among us.

SECTION 1

Examples and Testimonies

CHAPTER 7

Jesus Movements
Discovering Biblical Faith in the Most Unexpected Places*
Gavriel Gefen

There is a growing phenomenon taking place concurrently within at least every sizable region of the world today. People within numerous different tribal cultures and also people within the cultures of each of the major world religions are increasingly accepting Jesus without converting to Christianity and without joining churches. They are encountering Jesus in ways that change their lives forever, without their leaving one group for another. They are learning to discover for themselves what it means to be faithful to Jesus within their own cultures and within their own birth communities. Conversion for them is believed to be a matter of the heart and not one of joining a different, competing cultural community.

It is usually the case that after a number of these individuals within the same community are following Jesus, they begin meeting regularly as a small group. Over time this expands into multiple small groups among the same people group or within the same country. Eventually, it becomes established as a full-fledged movement of believers in Jesus that is outside of Christendom. It becomes a Jesus movement within another tradition. Does this mean they are living their lives outside the boundaries of biblical faith? Or are they merely living beyond the boundaries of Christendom as a competing community?

How did Jesus live as a son of Israel? Did he create a separate and competing community from the one that was already there? Did he tell people to leave their synagogues? Did he start his own synagogues? Didn't he seek to bring transformation and new life to the community that was already there?

The first followers of Jesus did not leave their synagogues. They began meeting regularly in small groups for fellowship, study, and prayer centered on Jesus while remaining part of the synagogues they were already in. These small group meetings were not under the auspices of the wider community, yet the people within them remained relationally and culturally loyal to their wider community. Some new customs and expressions of prayer and music developed among the followers of Jesus, but these were practiced in addition to, not in place of, established Jewish traditions. There were a number of circumstances that led to the above dynamics changing, but this was the original model.

Jewish believers in the first century faced the Roman occupation, the acceleration of Jewish exile, the increasing threat of assimilation of Jews among the Gentiles, and growing numbers of non-Jews embracing new covenant faith. These circumstances led to Jewish followers of Jesus being both pushed out and pulled out of the traditional Jewish community. Two thousand years later, Jews in Israel today finally have the conditions necessary to be able once again to confidently and wholeheartedly accept Jesus as Israel's Messiah while remaining firmly within the traditional synagogue community.

---

* Excerpt from Gavriel Gefen, "Discovering Biblical Faith in the Most Unexpected Places," *MF*, May–June 2011, with minor revisions. Reprinted by permission.

This is not a reference to what is called the Messianic Jewish movement. This is referring to a growing phenomenon of Jews following Jesus within Judaism. Increasing numbers of Jews are learning to follow Jesus faithfully within their traditional synagogue communities. Upon accepting Jesus, they begin meeting regularly in small groups for fellowship centered on Jesus while remaining loyal members of their synagogue communities.

The meetings of these small groups usually take place midweek, as each family already prays in their respective synagogue on the Sabbath. When they come together as devotees of Jesus, they seek to avoid duplicating or replacing activities or traditions that they are already upholding in the synagogue. With each of them engaged congregationally in synagogues, most of the dimensions of congregational life are already fulfilled there. Some of the midweek small group meetings are separate for men and women, as this has been found to be more intimate and more helpful in their lives. These meetings often operate similar to a talking circle, which is more like a support group than a formal congregation. There is an intimate time of discussion and prayer explicitly centered on Jesus, and everyone in the circle participates.

Involvement in these small groups connects each of these believers to the worldwide community of new covenant faith, which Christians call the church or the body of Christ. Yet members of these groups have neither converted to Christianity nor joined a church, nor even joined the Messianic Jewish movement, which has its own structures and organizational agendas. Also, being spiritually connected to the much larger worldwide community of believers in Jesus does not replace their membership or service in their local synagogue community. They simultaneously have larger and smaller group relationships that obligate them to overlapping responsibilities and also to other responsibilities that are unique and different to each group.

Relational faithfulness within this dynamic is not a zero-sum game of all or nothing on one side or the other. These believers are faithful to Jesus and are also faithful in their relationships within their birth community of faith. They are not undermining the preexisting community and especially not creating a new separate and competing community. They seek to bring transformation and new life to what is already there, serving from within.

Movements to Jesus like this are springing up among Muslims, Hindus, Buddhists, and many other cultures of the world. When these peoples come to understand the fullness of who Jesus is and then learn to faithfully follow him within their own heritage, they do a similar thing to what Jewish followers of Jesus are beginning to do in Israel once again. It is not exactly the same, but it is similar. Most of the dynamics at play and the issues that they encounter in creating Jesus movements among their peoples are the same dynamics and issues that are encountered by Jews following Jesus within the traditional Jewish community.

When a movement to Jesus like this is born within yet another culture, the believers there will go through their own process of confronting their culture with the message of Jesus. There will be some cultural expressions and traditions in which they can rightly continue only by redirecting the focus and giving them new meaning. In this process of renewing their culture, they may discover that there are some cultural expressions in which they can no longer engage as followers of Jesus.

I believe that the message of Jesus was never intended to be spread by means of cultural conquest. I am convinced that Jesus' message will increasingly spread among peoples of other faith traditions only as God's kingdom grows like yeast from within. By the grace of God and the discernment of his Spirit, growing numbers of Jesus followers within various Christian traditions are increasingly coming to recognize the work of God through Jesus within other cultures.

CHAPTER 8

When "Christian" Does Not Translate*

Frank Decker

"I grew up as a Muslim, and when I gave my life to Jesus I became a Christian. Then I felt the Lord saying, 'Go back to your family and tell them what the Lord has done for you.'" Such was the beginning of the testimony of a sweet sister in Christ named Salima.[1] As she stood before the microphone at a conference held recently in Asia, I thought about how her story would have been applauded by my Christian friends back home.

But then she said something that would have probably shocked most American Christians. She told us that in order to share Christ with her family, she now identifies herself as a Muslim rather than a Christian. "But," she added, "I could never go back to Islam without Jesus, whom I love as my Lord."

Like this woman, countless people, primarily in Asia, who live in Muslim, Buddhist, and Hindu contexts are saying yes to Jesus, but no to Christianity. As Westerners, we assume that the word "Christian" ipso facto refers to someone who has given his or her life to Jesus, and a "non-Christian" is an unbeliever. However, in the words of one Asian attendee, "The word 'Christian' means something different here in the East."

Consider the story of Chai, a Buddhist from Thailand. "Thailand has not become a Christian country, because in the eyes of the Thai, to become a Christian means you can no longer be Thai. That's because in Thailand 'Christian' equals 'foreigner.'" So when Chai gave his life to Jesus, he began referring to himself as a "child of God" and a "new Buddhist." He then related a subsequent incident in which he had a conversation with a Buddhist monk on a train. "After I listened to his story, I told him that he was missing one thing in life. He asked me what that was and I told him it was Jesus."

Chai continued to tell us the story in which the monk not only gave his life to Christ, but also invited Chai to come to his Buddhist temple to share about Jesus. Then Chai said, "At the beginning of our conversation the monk asked me, 'Are you a Christian?' and I said no. I explained that Christianity and Jesus are two different things. Salvation is in Jesus, not in Christianity. If I had said I was a 'Christian,' the conversation would have ended at that point." But it didn't end. And the monk now walks with Jesus.

Indeed, an American missionary who has been working in Asia for about two decades said, "For the first five or seven years of our ministry in [a Muslim country] we were frustrated because we were trying to get people to change their religion." He went on to say how in evangelical circles we talk a lot

* Excerpt from Frank Decker, "When 'Christian' Does Not Translate," *Good News Magazine*, May–June 2005. *Good News Magazine* is a renewal ministry within the United Methodist Church. Reprinted by permission.

1 The names in this story have been changed.

about how it is not our religion that saves us; it is Jesus. "If we really believe that, why do we insist that people change their religion?"

Asif is a brother in Christ with whom I have spent time in his village in a country that is 90 percent Muslim. Traditional Christian organizations in that country have only had a significant impact on the other 10 percent that has never been Muslim. Make no mistake—Asif is sold out to Jesus, as are the other members of this Muslim-background believer movement. I will never forget seeing the tears stream down Asif's face as he told me how he and his brother, also a believer in Jesus, were beaten in an attack that his brother did not survive. These are Muslims who walk with Jesus and openly share with their Muslim friends about the Lord, who in Arabic is referred to as *Isa al-Masih* (Jesus the Messiah).

These "insider movements" are not intended to hide a believer's spiritual identity, but rather to enable those within the movement to go deeper into the cultural community—be it Islamic, Hindu, or Buddhist—and be witnesses for Jesus within the context of that culture. In some countries, such movements are just getting started. In other places, estimates of adherents are in the hundreds of thousands.[2]

As the body of Christ, we should be very careful that the things we uphold as sacred are not post-biblical accoutrements, but are indeed transcendent. If we are not open to "new wineskins," we may unwittingly find ourselves attached to traditions, as were the Pharisees in the day of Jesus.

---

2   See *UIM*, chap. 30, first paragraph.

CHAPTER 9

Living and Discipling in the Hindu World*

K. Venkatesh

My name is Venkatesh and my home is India. I was brought up in a strict, high-caste Hindu family, and we had our own *pooja* room where we had daily prayers to the Hindu gods. We maintained all the Hindu festivals and were very diligent to fulfill all the requirements of our Hindu faith and religion.

My father was a highly placed government official and very orthodox in all his practices. He treated with disdain the religion of the Christians because of their habits of smoking, drinking, and dancing. He viewed them as unclean. His overall impression of the Christianity of the West was molded by what he saw in the Western movies, especially from America.

Because my father occasionally had to travel to America on behalf of the Indian government, he observed the values and practices of the Americans directly. He was very impressed with the technological advances of the West but felt they were quite inferior when it came to their lifestyle and personal values. He did meet one man who was very kind to him, and he explained that he was a Christian. But generally my father was very skeptical of Christianity.

After I completed my undergraduate studies in one of the top Institutes of Technology in India, I got a scholarship to study in America. My father was reluctant, but he agreed that I could go on the basis that I stay away from religious cults and weird groups. I was happy with that arrangement and proceeded to start my postgraduate studies.

Upon my arrival at the university, I met a group of Christians who were very nice to me. They helped me to get furniture for my new apartment and introduced me to many of the facilities on campus. I appreciated this very much. Then they invited me to a discussion group where they talked a lot from the Bible. I felt they were trying to convert me. But I continually argued with them, and that got tiresome for everyone.

Then I went on to my PhD studies in aeronautical engineering, hoping to work in one of the top research labs when I returned to India. However, at the beginning of my PhD program, tragedy struck my family. My sister's marriage had been arranged to a young man, and it was all going well for a few months. Then the young man became abusive towards my sister and began to beat her. Then he became very demanding about money, as my family was quite well off. My sister wrote to me that she was very unhappy and did not know what to do. My parents were distraught and began to visit many temples and made many prayers to the Hindu gods. I also did the same in the Hindu temple in Atlanta and prayed every day to many of the Hindu gods. But things got worse. Then my parents came to find out that the family of the young man had lied about him and his credentials and that they were really after

---

* Originally published in a slightly different form in *MF*, May–June 2011. Reprinted by permission.

our family wealth. My parents were distraught and could only think of divorce. But that is a very slow process in India, and the other party has to agree, which seemed very unlikely.

Several of my Christian friends had continued to have discussions with me. Now I told them of my family problem and explained that I would have to go back to India, as divorce would be a huge family embarrassment and my family had spent so much money on the wedding. They were humiliated and did not have very many financial resources left, as they were hoping that I would get a good salary when I graduated. My Christian friends said that they would pray for me, and they continued to inquire about our family situation. Although I had not been particularly impressed with their arguments for Christianity, I was overwhelmed by their love and interest in me with my family crisis.

I went back to India to help with the divorce proceedings of my sister, hoping to expedite the process. But it did not look very hopeful, and all the family members were very depressed, especially my mother, who wept all the time.

I decided one day to look at the New Testament that my Christian friends had given me in America and began to read through the story. It was a bit hard to follow, as I had no idea about the actual story of Jesus. But I got to Matthew 7:7 and read Jesus' words, "Ask and it will be given you." I decided to try praying to Jesus. The Hindu gods had given no answers, and I thought, *At least I can try praying to Jesus. What could I lose?* So I prayed to Jesus that he would make the divorce proceed quickly.

The next day, we heard from the other party that they were ready to agree to a divorce. The following day we were able to proceed with the legalities, and before long the matter had been settled. I could not believe that my simple prayer was answered so quickly. Then I began to read the New Testament with great eagerness. This person Jesus never spoke about the Christian religion but only spoke about following him.

When I returned to the United States, I met another Hindu man who told me that he also followed Jesus. He was not a practicing Christian who went to church, but he maintained his own Hindu culture and social habits, and he loved Jesus and read the Bible, and he knew it very well. He explained to me that he was a Hindu by his first birth and was proud of this heritage, which was from God, and showed me Acts 17:26, where God is explained as the one who determines where and when we are born. Then he explained how he had experienced a second birth, when he became one of God's children and a member of his kingdom. This second birth was not a physical birth but a spiritual birth, and as God's Spirit lived in us we would gradually become very attractive people who cared for others and helped them in their troubles. He showed me John 1:12, and so I decided to believe in Jesus. As a result I became one of his children and knew that my past was forgiven and that I had a great hope after I died.

Immediately I Skyped my sister in India and told her what was happening to me. She was also very interested, as she had witnessed the answers to all the prayers that I had made to Jesus regarding her divorce and how Jesus had answered every prayer. She too has now experienced Jesus in her life and no longer prays to the Hindu gods. The changes in her attitude have touched my mother and father, who are now showing a lot of interest.

I have since returned to India, and I am very much part of our Hindu community. I am engaged in all the activities of our family and extended family. There are many discussions about Jesus, and I am sharing the Bible with many people in our community. Because of my academic qualifications and the good job I now have, I have a very good standing in our community, and so people listen to me. I continually explain to them that I am not trying to "convert" them to Christianity but to "convert" them to Jesus as they live out their lives in the Hindu community. Now I have quite a few friends who are also following Jesus, and we meet regularly to pray together and share the Scriptures and to encourage each other. We sense that God is going to cause many people in our community to know and love him. We are claiming the verse Isaiah 60:22, that a little one shall become a thousand and a small one will become a mighty nation, and that God will hasten all this in his time. This is already beginning to happen.

CHAPTER 10

"Why I Am Not a Christian"
A Personal Statement*
O. Kandaswami Chetti

The secretary of this conference, acting under instructions from the committee, has thought fit to ask me to say why I remain outside the Christian church. Concerning my religious position, he justifies putting to me a question which he would not, I take it, think of addressing to almost any other whom he regards as outside the Christian church. He probably thinks that I am what one calls a Christian at heart. Now what does this description mean? It means one who believes in Christ as the Saviour of men, but who would not show to the world that Christ is the God in whom he believes, to whom he prays, from whom he seeks enlightenment and strength, and whose will he would earnestly study and endeavour to carry out in his life. This is a description, however, I must confess I accept only partially when applied to me.

It is true that I believe in Christ as the Saviour of men. When I say this, I do not mean that he is one of *many* saviours whom God is said to have sent down into the world from time to time. I know only too well that one attempt to defeat and counteract Christian teaching in this country is not to contradict it—for that would "go against the grain" of the highest in every man. Rather, an effort to rob it of its distinctiveness, and the potency that comes from that recognition, represents Christ as one of many avatars or manifestations or messengers of God, whom as such the Hindus should have no objection to receive. But any claim for a special or unique place in the economy of the universe should be resisted as being nothing short of treason against the country and its peculiar civilization. To my mind, the idea of "many" spoils the peculiar beauty and efficacy of God becoming incarnate. Does not God reveal himself every moment of our lives in nature, in his sustaining providence, in the great men whom he raises as leaders, in the accidents that determine the course of the future for individuals as well as for communities, and in the great movements of history? Why then should he break through the screen behind which he acts so continuously and so powerfully if it were not for the purpose of revealing himself, not to the intellect of man but to his wayward heart? And does not a repetition of the process bring it within the sphere of normal manifestations, which, though appealing to the intellect, fail to convert the heart?

There is a vital difference between a king appearing in flesh and blood before his subjects and living and moving among them so that they feel the charm and force of his personality and get a glimpse of his loving heart, and a king acting from behind a constitutional system of well-balanced forces. His incarnate appearance speaks with an authority which could not be commanded by any middle agency, which could only half-reveal and half-conceal the soul within. Moreover, he establishes with his subjects a channel of communication and a method of interpretation, which would have been impossible

---

* "'Why I Am a Christian': A Personal Statement" was read at the Madras Missionary Conference in 1915 and subsequently appeared as chapter 5 in the *Madras Christian College Magazine*. Public domain.

but for the priceless advantage of a face-to-face contact and acquaintance. Such a king need not come more than once. Once come, he is come forever. Every act of his, even from behind the veil of nature and of history, becomes fraught with new meaning and alive with new significance. His personality, once revealed, acts in the mind and in the heart of his loyal subjects. Every fresh message from the great King-Emperor, whether in prosperity or in distress, in peace or in war, comes charged with the remembrance of his loving visit to his far-off subjects, and acts with an electric moral force which would have been impossible but for that majestic though informal visit.

For my part I believe that there are in this universe two planes of manifestation—one plane addressed to the natural instincts and faculties of man, with all their tendencies for good and for evil; the other plane addressed to the heart, which would fain see its God and having once seen him follow him whithersoever he leadeth. It is on the latter plane that God has drawn near to man in Christ.

> The very God! Think, Abib; dost thou think?
> So, the All-Great were the All-Loving too—
> So, through the thunder comes a human voice
> Saying, "O heart I made, a heart beats here!
> Face my hands fashioned, see it in myself!
> Thou hast no power nor mayest conceive of mine,
> But love I gave thee, with myself to love,
> And thou must love me who have died for thee!"
> The madman saith He said so: it is strange.[1]

It is strange, but it is *true*. To my mind, the divinity of Christ is, however, not a truth that can be communicated from man to man, nor established by arguments that would satisfy a purely scientific mind. It comes as an answer to a soul which, conscious of its weakness and thirsting after a righteousness it does not find in itself nor anywhere else, sees it in One who suffered as no man ever suffered, all because he was sinless while others were sinful. The desire for the vision of God comes to be established in the heart of a man—a desire not for a physical vision which would bring no satisfaction to a heart hungering for righteousness, but a moral vision which alone could purify and elevate and energise. Once this desire has been created in the heart of a man—a desire rendered all the keener by a spiritual apprehension of the life of Christ culminating as it did on the Cross—the truth dawns upon the mind and the soul, or rather flashes upon it like lightning as it did upon Peter. To him Christ said, "Blessed art thou, Simon Barjona: for flesh and blood hath not revealed it unto thee, but my Father which is in heaven" (Matt 16:17 KJV). This truth reveals that the Creator, at all events the Increaser of this desire, is also its Fulfiller. Instead of preaching Christ's divinity, or rather his divine personality, to those who would not recognize it, disinterested efforts could be directed to creating a desire for knowledge of a holy God. A spiritual vision of him would purge the heart of man and strengthen it for all the works of love and the problems of social fellowship which wait upon man's energies. Then men would naturally turn towards Christ as the Revealer of God and their Saviour from the thralldom of sin and their Reconciler with God. I speak from experience. This, at all events, is the road along which I have come, to what measure I have attained of a consciousness of the interpretation in human terms of God's inmost nature to be found in Christ. Holding this view, it has always seemed to me an invidious, thankless,

---

1 Chetti is quoting the narrator in Robert Browning's poem "An Epistle Containing the Strange Medical Experience of Karshish, the Arab Physician."—Ed.

and sometimes mischievous task—I would even go further and say it is very often a man-imposed and not a God-inspired task—to go and tell people who believe they have seen God in one or another of the saints and religious heroes of history and mythology that they can see God in Christ and no other. If that is their belief and this is yours, your duty is plain—to deepen and enlarge their sense of need until they are enabled to realize that Christ and not another will answer their purpose and meet their case.

If such a spiritual hunger and thirst is created in man, and if before such a man you place the great religious leaders of the world and among them the Christ of history, I have no fear as to whom the choice will fall upon, the choice of the thirsty soul which panteth after the waters of the brook. A choice too which will be heartily hailed by the masters of the religious world themselves who, I fondly believe, will exclaim with the just and devout prophet Simeon:

Lord, now lettest thou thy servant depart in peace,
   according to thy word:
For mine eyes have seen thy salvation,
Which thou hast prepared before the face of all people;
A light to lighten the Gentiles, and the glory of thy people Israel.
(Luke 2:29–32)

On the other hand, any iteration and reiteration on your part of Christ's claims on the human heart and on human homage with people in whom a desire for a moral comprehension of God's nature has not been sufficiently awakened, may give you the satisfaction of feeling that you have done what you deem your duty. But this will not advance the cause of the kingdom in the same way as would an intelligent adaptation which springs from a desire to cooperate with God in his own endeavours to get man to realize his loving purpose towards him.

I have said that the description of "a Christian at heart" applies to me only partially, so far as I can understand myself: there is only One who knows me and you as we truly are. I repudiate that description in its negative significance of one who would not let the world know the faith that is in him.

I am conscious that belief in Jesus as the Saviour of the world carries with it a duty and a privilege—namely, that of communicating it to our fellow men. I do not speak of the command which Christ gave to his immediate disciples, to spread the truth over the then-known world and preserve it for all ages and create a human vehicle through which the Spirit of God works for the highest good of mankind. I am thinking rather of the dynamic force of the truth itself, which urges men to go forth, facing danger, disease, and death in strange climes and among strange peoples. I am aware also that Christ is not a mere moral philosopher who has come to inculcate a system of principles of conduct. He came to found an ever-present society of which he is the head, and all who believe on him are the members, receiving wisdom, guidance, and inspiration through communion with him. I realize the immense blessing to them and to the world, which comes from fellow believers congregating for the worship of their common Master and encouraging one another in their attachment and obedience to their common Lord.

Nothing would give me a deeper satisfaction than to feel that I belong to his body. I am not altogether sure that I remain outside the Christian church. The wording of the subject is not mine: it is Mr. Leith's and his committee's. The fact that I have consented to speak on it does not, I believe, commit me to an admission that the statement implied in it is true. It is not unlike trying to answer the question of why I beat my mother last night. It does not mean I suppose an admission on my part that I beat my mother or even that she is alive (I lost my mother when I was seven or eight years old—I have a picture impressed on my mind of a short, smiling, bustling lady). All I can say is that I count myself a follower of Christ and would fall at his feet and like Mary Magdalene wash them with my tears. I would proclaim him as my Saviour:

> Sun of my soul, Thou Saviour dear,
> It is not night, if Thou be near,
> O may no earthborn cloud arise
> To hide Thee from Thy servant's eyes.

I am not sure *he* would repudiate me; *you* may, and some of you have done so, but I have no grievance against you. My feelings on the other hand are those of endless gratitude to those who have led me to his feet. But for them, humanly speaking, I should not have known him. And how can I best return their services to me but by making known in my turn him whom they and I acknowledge as

> the true Light, which lighteth every man that cometh into the world. He was in the world, and the world was made by him, and the world knew him not. He came unto his own, and his own received him not. But as many as received him, to them gave he power to become the sons of God, even to them that believe on His name: which were born, not of blood, nor of the will of the flesh, nor of the will of man, but of God. And the Word was made flesh, and dwelt among us, (and we beheld his glory, the glory as of the only begotten of the Father,) full of grace and truth. (John 1:9–14)

This is the central truth which I have learnt from my teachers in Madras Christian College, and I feel the responsibility of communicating it to my countrymen at large, but not by mere words. Too often, words spring from no experience on the part of the speaker, unrelated to the experience of the world at large. Words convey no meaning such as thrills and throbs through a man's being—words, words, words serve as shibboleths in the war of organized religions and serve rather to alienate than to enlighten. I feel the responsibility of communicating the truth of Christ crucified for you and me to live, of communicating it through the testimony, very often silent but nonetheless powerful or compelling on the account, of a life and a lifework inspired by it, but which when expressed in words at all is best expressed in words which spring naturally and spontaneously out of that life and that life work.

I speak with all the humility and shame arising from a consciousness of failure, however incomplete, and I speak without any claim of merit—I am not altogether sure that I have not endeavoured to communicate the truth, in however remote a form. For suggestions which are sometimes more potent and thought-compelling and hence more fruitful of spiritual results than bare, bold statements, have to be more or less remote to those with whom it has pleased God to bring me into contact. This is a matter at which one can only delicately and tremblingly hint; to do anything else would be to adopt the style of the Pharisee's prayer, if prayer it could be called.

It is true that I have never felt any inward call such as I could recognise as divine in its inspiration to join the Christian church in the narrow sense in which some evidently use the term. For I believe such a step as this can be justified on not less an authority than the constraining power of God such as compelled Abraham to leave his people and found a family in which all the nations of the world were blessed. I have no feeling but one of reverence towards those, and they are many, who shift their tents under orders from above. I look upon them as more blessed than myself. But I have nothing but contempt for those, and they also are many, who, yielding to very human influences and to a call from unworthy quarters, cut themselves off from those with whom it is their duty to be in touch, if for nothing else, at least in the interests of the Lord whom they profess to follow. Nor do I believe that while every believer is called upon to let his light shine before all the world, he is also called upon to join the Christian church in the narrower sense of the term. There is nothing essentially sinful in Hindu society any more than there is anything essentially pure in Christian society—for that is what this Christian church amounts to—such that one should hasten from the one to the other like the Pilgrim from the City of Destruction to the Heavenly City. The City of Destruction is unfortunately so overspread as to include within its borders tracts belonging to both civilizations, while the Heavenly City requires for its realization the working of the Spirit of Christ in one society as well as in the other. The servants of Christ have work to do in both societies, and they should recognize their brotherhood and devise ways of strengthening and stimulating one another through their common Lord. If the testimony of a Christian believer in Hindu society for their Lord and Master is weak and timid, it is very often the fault of believers within the Christian church who boycott him for his imputed cowardice so that in course of time he either becomes ashamed of his Lord or is frightened into the Christian church. Instead of trimming the lamp within the magic lantern of his soul so that an increasingly steady and bright picture of the Lord may be cast upon the canvas of Hindu society, they either put out the lamp or remove the whole lantern for repair elsewhere.

In this connection there is one point on which I should touch, in justice to myself if not in fairness to you: what about the customs and social practices of a Christian believer in Hindu society? So long as the believer's testimony for Christ is open, and as long as the believer's attitude towards Hindu society in general is critical (and willing to protest all those social and religious practices which are inconsistent with the spirit of Christ), I would allow him to struggle his way to the light, with failure here and there perhaps but with progress and success on the whole. Assuredly, the spirit of Christ is against all appeasement with error and sin. If you cooperate with that spirit, your Christian believer in Hindu society will come out all right in the end.[2] He may not join your church, but he will prepare the way for a movement from within Hindu society towards a Christ who shall fulfill India's highest aspirations and impart that life of freedom for which she has been panting for ages. Is this not a consummation for which you would give your lives?

---

2 This and the previous two sentences have been reworded to try to capture Chetti's meaning. The original states, "So long as the believer's testimony for Christ is open, and as long as his attitude towards Hindu society in general is critical and, towards social and religious practices inconsistent with the spirit of Christ in particular, is protestant and practically protestant, I would allow him to struggle his way to the light, with failure here and there perhaps but with progress and success on the whole. The spirit of Christ is a peace-destroying spirit, I may assure you. If you co-operate with that spirit, your Christian believer in Hindu Society will come out all right in the end." The point of the "peace-destroying" phrase seems to be that Christ will destroy a believer's personal peace if he or she is involved in sin, injustice, error, corruption, etc. "If you cooperate with that spirit" may well mean "If the believer cooperates with that spirit."—Ed.

CHAPTER 11

The New Buddhists
*How Buddhists Can Follow Christ**

Banpote Wetchgama

The Word "Christian": Biblical Background

It is inevitable. As soon as a person has converted and believes in Jesus Christ, he or she will be labeled a Christian. This person has suddenly embraced Christianity. Yet we see the word "Christian" appear only a few times in the New Testament. It was an insult from nonbelievers. Within the community of faith the believers referred to themselves as saints[1] or children of God.[2] Only later did they refer to themselves and other followers as Christians. When the term was first adopted by believers they interpreted the meaning to be "those belonging to Jesus Christ," but when people from other languages and cultures started adopting this term, the meaning continued to change.

The Word "Christian": Multiple Meanings in Thailand

When the Roman Catholics arrived in what is now Thailand, they were called *Khittang*. Later, Protestants were called *Khris-tee-yen*, understood to be different from *Khittang*. Both terms referred to what the foreigners called "Christian." Regardless of the term applied, *Khris-tee-yen* or *Khittang*, if they follow only the outward forms, they are merely following cultural expressions of the Western church. For example, someone who attends church each Sunday and doesn't depend upon the grace of God isn't really a child of God.

Khris-tee-yen (Christian): Negative Meanings in Thailand

In Thailand today, particularly in the northeastern region, *Khris-tee-yen* brings the following meanings to the hearts and minds of Thai people:
1. A person who follows a foreign religion.
2. A person who works for foreigners.
3. A person who has sold out his or her nationality to foreigners. Thai people like to say, "Our religion is fine. Why do you need to follow the ways of foreigners?" When we follow another religion it is felt that we have sold out our nationality to others.

---

* Originally published in a slightly different form in *MF*, November–December 2014. Reprinted by permission.

1 See Acts 9:13 and Rev 19:8 (KJV) as examples. The term "saint" in the Thai Bible refers to the followers of the truth and referred to all believers. It was not limited only to those of special merit as in the definition from the Roman Catholic Church.

2 The phrase "children of God" appears thirteen times from Matt 5:9 to 1 John 5:19 (NIV).

4. A person who has leprosy. The first Thai people who came to believe in Jesus were lepers. Protestant missionaries in those days had projects to help lepers, who then responded to Jesus and entered into Christianity.

5. A person who has descended from evil spirits. They were expelled from their villages and established new villages, later to become Christians.

6. A person who did not get a proper funeral attended by a Buddhist monk. To a Buddhist this means there was no honor given to the deceased and that they will not be able to go to heaven.[3] This perception about the death of Christians prevents many Buddhists from becoming Christians.

Removing Cultural Barriers

Because the word *Khris-tee-yen* is a barrier that keeps many Thai people from believing in God, some believers in Isaan (Eastern Thailand) no longer use the term. They remove cultural barriers by using one of two alternatives: *Luk Phra Chao* (child of God) and *Puttasasanikachon mai* (New Buddhist).

Luk Phra Chao (Child of God)

We have a model of the term *Luk Phra Chao* (child of God) in the actions of God himself when he allowed his Son, Jesus, to be incarnated in human flesh in the Jewish culture. He did not bring a new religion as a set of new external forms from outside (John 1:14–18). Instead, God brought the Word (*Logos*; see John 1:1) into the world, born as a Jew, using the cultural forms and rituals of the Jews that were in accordance with Scripture. The cultural forms and rituals the Jewish religious leaders (Pharisees) and their ancestors created that were not in accordance with the word of God Jesus objected to completely and denied the use of. This can be a model for keeping what is in accordance with the word of God within Buddhism.

Following God's approach, when the Apostle Paul began his mission to the Gentiles he did not bring the culture of the Jews

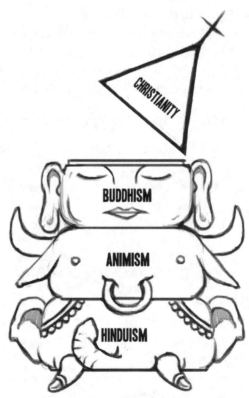

Illustration by Katie Koch

with him in his message to the Gentiles (Acts 15:1–21). He did not force Gentiles to be circumcised. The ritual of circumcision had nothing to do with salvation from sin and therefore was not required of the Gentiles.

---

3 Many Buddhists believe in many heavens and even hells.

Thai people believe they are born as followers of the Buddhist religion. They are Buddhists, as were their ancestors, a view that mirrors the way Jews saw themselves as Jewish along with their ancestors. However, only a few Thai people truly follow the heart of Buddha's teachings. Buddhists in Thailand actually follow an amalgamation of beliefs, including animism, Hinduism, and Buddhism, which blend together into one set of beliefs. None of the three are denied. When Christianity enters into society, Thais attempt to add it to the other three. Rev. Dr. Nantachai Mejudhon has portrayed it as on the opposite page.

But Christianity, with its roots in Western culture and rituals, cannot be added on top of other Thai beliefs, because Thais revere their own traditions and see it as a foreign religion. They believe their own religion is fine. To change is to insult one's ancestors and society.

Puttasasanikachon Mai (A New Buddhist)

The way Thai people can be freed from their sins through Jesus—without building barriers—depends on making a change in the way evangelism is done. Instead of presenting the externals of Christianity, Western church forms, the presenter should follow what is suggested in Scripture and allow the Word (*Logos*) to be the main focus. The message of the gospel must be reborn or repackaged in the best forms from Thai culture that are in accordance with the gospel. Thai people will believe in Jesus without a need to change religions or believe in Christianity (the external forms). They can still be Thai Buddhists as before, and follow the traditions of their people that are in accordance with the gospel. Thai people who follow Jesus in this way can be called New Buddhists, not *Khris-tee-yen*.

There are two reasons for using the term "New Buddhist": (1) Buddhism is incomplete. Those who are followers of Buddhism have not received salvation from their sins. Buddhism teaches that we must depend upon ourselves for everything and that life is suffering; the only way to be released from suffering is to follow the Noble Eightfold Path. (2) Buddhists know they cannot keep the teachings of Buddha. They attempt to do it, understanding that attempting a little is better than doing nothing. My mother once said, "The monks told me that if I did as little good as an elephant wiggling his ear or a snake flashing his tongue, I will go to heaven." Very few Buddhists would be willing to say that they have done enough to reach that stage of enlightenment known as *nibbana*.[4]

The certainty of attaining *nibbana* is missing in Buddhism, but for a New Buddhist, Jesus brought *nibbana* to them.

Christ in the Heart of Buddhists

When we understand this issue we can bring the heart message of the gospel to Buddhists. The Bible teaches that all have sinned and Buddhism teaches that all life is suffering. Both have a common origin, the desire for possession (in Genesis 3, the possession of the knowledge of good and evil).

A Thai proverb warns, "What is mine is mine, the source of suffering." This means that the desire for possession is where suffering comes from. It is important to release all desires for possession, which will allow a person to be released from suffering. The problem with people is that in their own power they are unable to disconnect. The root of sin is to cling to everything "mine." The Bible does not just

---

4   *Nibbana* is a Pali term used by Buddhists. (*Nirvana* is the Sanskrit equivalent used in Hindu tradition; the meanings are not the same but have similarities.) In a nutshell, *nibbana* is the goal of Buddhism, a cessation of suffering and death. It is not a place or a thing; neither is it nothingness. It is attained through enlightenment. Literally it means "blowing out."

teach that doing wrong is sin but that doing wrong is the result of the sinful nature. Buddhists are not willing to accept that we are born with a sinful nature. However, if we give reasons and examples, we can show that humans are sinful from birth. There is an inborn tendency towards sin because people are inherently self-centric and desire to be great. This is why humans are the enemy of God and ultimately encounter death. Death, therefore, is suffering, as in accordance with the teachings of the Buddha.

Release from Suffering and Sin: Savior Jesus

Buddhism teaches that through our own efforts we must follow and obey the teachings. Within Buddhism there is no messiah figure. The Buddha taught that he brought the word of enlightenment to others because he himself experienced enlightenment. Whoever desires to be released from sin/suffering must follow his teachings personally. Unlike the Messiah, the Buddha cannot assist anyone in the process.

The problem is, no person has the individual potential to do enough to escape death and suffering. Therefore humans must rely on God to assist us, since we are unable to do it ourselves. Jesus died and paid the debt of sin and suffering to God because "the wages of sin is death, but the gift of God is eternal life in Christ Jesus" (Rom 6:23 NIV). Jesus was victorious over death in the place of all humans. Anyone who believes in this will be released from sin and suffering. There is no need to change the external forms or religions. This completes what is unfulfilled in Buddhism. These believers are still Thai people according to rituals and customs as they were before.

Teachings of the Buddha that are incomplete must be replaced with Scripture. For example, the teaching of the dependence upon self in order to reach *nibbana* will be replaced with the scriptural teaching that says that humans are not able to depend upon themselves; humans are sinful, and therefore human life is suffering. Effort for doing good is insufficient for *nibbana*. To use Christian terms, the good deeds of humans are insufficient to reach God. Therefore it is necessary to find a new way. The new way to reach *nibbana* or God himself is Jesus Christ. He is the way, the truth, and the life.

Christ, not a cultural form, saves Thai believers. Therefore those who believe in Jesus in Eastern societies, particularly Thai society, do not need to change the external forms of their religion or replace them with Western external religious forms. Christianity in and of itself cannot save. Jesus is the only one who can do this. He is the way. He can be in any cultural form or expression, because all cultural forms come from the Creator.

The Good News Reborn in Eastern Expression

For Eastern people, to understand and accept the true heart of the gospel without any barriers, we must allow the good news, or the *thamma*,[5] to be reborn in the forms and cultural expressions of Eastern people. In the Thai Buddhist context, we can easily explain the meaning of the release from sin and suffering using the teachings of Buddha himself. This is another reason why these followers of Christ can be called New Buddhists.

I have never told someone who did not know beforehand that I was a Christian or that I followed Christianity. Instead, I have told people that I am a New Buddhist. I do this because if I were to say to

---

5   *Thamma* is the truth taught by Buddha. In its meaning *thamma* comes very close to *Logos*. Because *thamma* is understood in the sense of ultimate truth, truth that leads to *nibbana*, some use it in the sense of "the word of truth." The apostle John used *Logos* (John 1:1) in a way it was never used before, basically meaning Christ, in the same manner some are using *thamma*. Inasmuch as Jesus is the good news, *thamma* is the good news.

people that I am a Christian, people would have no further interest in pursuing a friendship with me or spending time with me. Opportunities to share what it means to be released from the result of sin and suffering would no longer be available. However, if I say that I am a New Buddhist, people ask, "How does this differ from the old Buddhism?" I then have an opportunity to explain what the difference is between the old and the New Buddhism. In the old Buddhism I had to depend completely upon myself. New Buddhism means complete dependence upon God and his grace as expressed through his Son, Jesus Christ. If we depend upon the grace of God, we will receive salvation from our sins. We will be released from our suffering to reach *nibbana*, which is equivalent to "being with God" in Christian terms.

Therefore, the person who is a New Buddhist is a person who knows that the source of life is God himself and that he will see God in the end, free from suffering. Aside from this, the person is awakened and conscious of what is happening to him. The "person being awakened" refers to one who does not fool himself with any animistic practices. Blind belief or belief without any foundation of reason is an animistic form of belief that was also rejected by Buddha himself.[6]

The term "enlightened one" means the one who is pleased to gain this knowledge, not one who receives it as a burden. The person is happy, joyful, even if life is full of difficulties. There is still a happiness from inside because of the knowledge that the person is no longer in debt to sin. He is released from suffering. When this life is over, that individual knows that he will go and be with God (*nibbana*).

---

6   See *Anguttara Nikaya* 3:65.

CHAPTER 12

Comments on the Insider Movement*

Mazhar Mallouhi

A recent book, which is essentially a biographical account of my spiritual journey, characterizes me as a "Muslim follower of Jesus," a term which I have often used to describe myself. I am certainly not the first or the only person to describe himself this way, but because of the high profile of the book, the high profile of the Bible translation projects I am involved with, and my long-term involvement with missions, I am among those targeted by detractors of the insider movement. Since I have never actually publicly commented on this movement (and just realized I am part of it!), I thought it would be appropriate to do so.

An "insider" is someone, like me, who comes from a family and country that is Muslim and chooses to maintain their culture after being irretrievably changed by the transforming power of our Lord. Admittedly, my description of an insider is overly simplistic, and it is not my intention to assert that all those who don't claim to be insiders have abandoned all aspects of their culture. Nevertheless, I would like to describe some of what I have seen among believers in Christ who come from a Muslim background.

I don't think that most armchair practitioners (that is, interested people who don't actually live in the Muslim world) realize how many unnecessary and harmful changes can be prescribed when Muslims become Christians. It is more severe than in any other context. These changes have nothing to do with the requirements of kingdom living, but are simply cultural. The well-known evangelical saying "Being born in a garage doesn't make you a car, and being born in a Christian family/country doesn't make you a Christian" is not something Muslim people agree with. Being born in a Muslim family *does* automatically make you a Muslim and part of the Muslim community. I am born a Muslim, not a Hindu nor a Christian nor a Jew. Muslims need never publicly or personally appropriate faith as is expected in the Christian tradition of baptism or confirmation, but on the contrary must take decisive action if they want to remove themselves from the community.

What defines a Muslim follower of Jesus has nothing to do with whether they read the Qur'an, where or how they pray, or what they think of Muhammad. Insiders can be defined as those who affirm that the circumstances into which they were born were ordained by God and played a part in their personal salvation story. They do not see that faith in Jesus as Lord requires them to automatically renounce all they previously learnt about God, or to denounce their culture, community, and family as evil. There are actually very few ways to publicly reject my community, but one sure way is to publically embrace Western anti-Muslim politics, polytheism, and idolatry, which in Muslim understanding is what people do when they convert to Christianity.

---

* Originally published in a slightly different form in *St. Francis Magazine* 5, no. 5 (2009): 3–14. Reprinted by permission.

Westerners typically have inherited dualistic Greek thinking about religious and secular life, whereas Muslims do not usually think in this way. So for Muslims all of life is spiritual, including family relationships and matters from daily life, ranging from eating meals together to worshiping together. So to attempt to differentiate between religious and secular culture is from the beginning a non-Muslim way of thinking. More importantly, it is a nonbiblical way of thinking. In a biblical world-view, life is viewed more holistically. In this particular issue, it is the Muslim outlook, not the dualistic Western outlook, that is closer to the biblical model.

Being an insider does not mean that I am free to do or believe whatever I want; it doesn't mean that I am not obligated to refrain from evil or immoral facets of my culture. This is the same for someone born an insider in Western Christian or post-Christian cultures. However, many Muslims are still taught that they must leave behind all vestiges of Islam, including language, dress, hospitality customs, and prayer language. Basically this amounts to designating everything in their culture as evil! I took up this issue with a group of Arab Christian theology students who were initially hostile to the idea of Muslims remaining as believers in their own community. I asked, "Which practices in a Muslim's life may need to be changed once he or she follows Christ?" We filled a blackboard with all that denotes belonging to a Muslim community. The students listed practices of dress, food, language, marriage, worship, religious practices such as fasting, etc. After much debate, the group arrived at the conclusion (to their surprise) that only two practices were contra-indicated by the gospel: the pilgrimage to Mecca and the testimony (*shahadah*).

Vocabulary is a big issue in this debate. One such argument commonly brought to my attention is "Christians shouldn't call God 'Allah.'" Anyone who knows better can tell you that the only true word for God in Arabic is "Allah." "Allah" is the normal and usual word used by Christian Arabs for God. Even Arab evangelicals who oppose the insider movement use this term for God. It is the word for the one and only God, and shares a Semitic root with Hebrew words for God—*el, eloah,* and *elohim.* This is just one example of how weak some of the arguments are. Yet I have known Muslim-background Christians who abandon their native tongue and talk to their children exclusively in English because it's more "Christian."

Many people from a Muslim background who become Christians move to the West and seldom return. Often Muslim-background believers who study theology abroad never return to their home to live as a witness. It is as if they have come to believe that being in a Christian garage makes you a Christian car. They want their children to be Christians, so they must be born in a so-called Christian culture.

Many of those from Muslim backgrounds who become (cultural) Christians are people who are already disillusioned with their country/culture/religion and come to the faith already hating Islam. I myself at one time hated my own culture and resented my background, not because of doctrine or theology or belief, but because somehow I was led to believe that it was ugly, and that only things Western and thus *Christian* were beautiful.

Those who criticize followers of Jesus who want to remain in their largely Muslim culture don't understand the severity of the alternative. My heart breaks for young believers who receive subtle (and perhaps unintentional) messages from Christians that the way of life handed down to them is ugly. They are given the impression that God cannot be in their culture.

For me and others like me, being an insider is not primarily about doctrine and it is not about belief, but rather about attitude. Some Christian friends have called on me to declare my beliefs or answer for myself in theological terms. "Prove to me that you are orthodox!" or "Show me that you are evangelical!" My burden, however, is to cry, "Show me that you love Muslims! Show me that your attitude is like that of our Lord! Demonstrate to me that your actions are rooted in the heart of God and not something else! Show me that you are acting out of love and not out of the emotions that surface when two civilizations collide!"

I have spent the greater part of a long life engaged with the church in the West and involved in the global missions movement, and it pains me to say that if more people exhibited different attitudes to Islam, then there would be no need for myself and others like me to distinguish ourselves as insiders. It is attitude, not belief, which causes this distinction.

I am perplexed by the unfair treatment that Muslim people are given by the Protestant missions movement. There is nothing new about being an insider, but Muslim insiders are unfairly singled out. If I were a Jewish believer continuing to call myself a Jew and remaining inside my Jewish community, I would be lauded by most of the Christian West. My experience is that most Jewish ideology rejects the entirety of the New Testament and often reviles our Lord; yet even with those obstacles, believers that remain inside Judaism do not undergo the same scrutiny by Christians. My experience in America has made me aware of groups such as Christian motorcycle gangs and Christian hippies, all of whom remain outside traditional church circles and inside their (sometimes questionable) former communities. These groups don't seem to undergo the same scrutiny either. The unfair and unbalanced scrutiny given to Muslim insiders over other types of insiders suggests to me that this is not so much a missiological issue as it is one of attitude.

Some people are unhappy that I am unwilling to engage in polemics or criticism of Islam. Here is something that most people in the West don't understand: I was born into a confessional home. Islam is the blanket with which my mother wrapped me when she nursed me and sang to me and prayed over me. I imbibed aspects of Islam with my mother's milk. I inherited Islam from my parents, and it was the cradle which held me until I found Christ. Islam is my mother. You don't engage a man by telling him his mother is ugly. No matter how hideous your friend's mother may be, you don't say to him, "Your mother is ugly." Even if he knows she is, his initial reaction will certainly be to fight you. For me being an insider means that I have an emotional attachment to my culture which I imbibed along with my mother's milk. Islam is *my* mother too.

However, although I am born a Muslim, I am not obligated to practice it, nor am I obligated to believe all of it. But the day I reject it outright, I disavow myself of my family, my community, and my people. There are many ways to bring the gospel into this confessional home, and the words I use to describe a life-changing relationship with God through Christ will determine how the community understands and reacts to my journey.

I realize that as Christians engaging Muslims, some may want to act in a way that makes them feel like St. Boniface triumphantly cutting down a tree in defiance of paganism, but we do not need to crush the other to share our light and truth.

I travel all over the Arab world, and when I do I ask the same question: "Where are the second-generation communities among Muslim-background believers?" There are a few, but then I am forced to ask the question, "Are there any that are not tied to Western money?" How can there be second-generation churches when believers are removing themselves from their communities? Our Lord taught by example and command that we should be witnesses within our context. I have received honors and awards from Muslim institutions (not necessarily religious institutions, but those in which members are professing Muslims) that are not allowed to recognize non-Muslims. I have been invited and embraced by Muslim groups that would have nothing to do with Muslims who have been extracted from their culture and have become Christians. Were I not an insider, I would not have access to these groups, and I would be unable to testify about my Lord in these places. And the only thing that is required of me to stay inside is to not be against my Islamic heritage.

I don't mean to imply that the issues involved are simple. Nor do I mean to suggest that all insiders will necessarily receive favor, or that none of them will be disowned by their families or experience persecution. Following our Lord is never easy. What I do mean to say is that the kind of witness that will birth productive communities doesn't require us to compromise our beliefs, but only change our attitudes.

Staying inside a Muslim context has not pressured me towards bad doctrine. I have received no temptation as an insider to minimize the deity of my Lord Jesus Christ (his peace be upon us). I experience no enticement to deny the Trinity or elevate the Qur'an above the Bible. This isn't to say that

Presenting Christ as a Middle Easterner

Heightened interest in Islam has recently been evident among Christians, with many sincerely and open-mindedly seeking to understand Muslims. Nevertheless, a quickly growing discord between the two has also been evident. Some Western Christians have sought to demonize Islam, portraying it as the last great enemy to be conquered. Rather than create further alienation between Muslims and Christians, Mallouhi advocates a non-confrontational approach to Muslims and demonstrates the importance of building on commonalities between Islam and Christianity. Christ's followers today need to be involved in an all-out effort to help Muslims, not to conquer them, embodying goodwill, appreciation, and sympathy in the spirit of Christ.

By offering respect and reciprocity, Mallouhi has found an amazing openness among Muslims toward his faith in Christ. For example, Muslim students, studying in the prestigious Islamic intellectual and missionary center of Al-Azhar Mosque in Cairo, have sat around him in the courtyard of the mosque as he taught them of Christ, opening the Scriptures to them.

Perhaps Mallouhi's most significant spiritual contribution is that of stripping Christ of his Western trappings and introducing him to Muslims as one who was born, lived, and died in the Middle East. This Christ, one that Muslims can understand, is the Christ that Mallouhi met, which explains why he calls himself simply a Syrian Arab follower of Christ, avoiding the label "Christian."

Muslims generally perceive Christianity as part of a Western political agenda and see Christ as a Westerner with no relationship to Eastern culture. Christianity, however, is Middle Eastern in origin, not a Western faith. Christ, a Middle Easterner, was culturally more like today's Arab than a Western Christian.

Mallouhi effectively bridges this gap because of his own personal experience. When he became a follower of Christ, he was told by Christians that he needed to leave his cultural past behind, change his name (take a "Christian" name), stop socializing in coffee shops (the primary meeting place of Arab men), not attend his family's religious celebrations, keep his distance from mosques and Muslims, cease to fast, begin to pray in a different posture (not bowing or prostrate), and begin to eat pork (to prove he was converted!). As a result, he quickly became alienated from his family and all his former friends, whom he was advised by Christians to reject. Ironically, no matter there are no temptations in the predominantly Muslim community in which I live, but I can say with certainty that I find far more temptation and negative influence in the materialistic, secular culture of Australia. Furthermore, I can't say that I am doctrinally infallible. One day when I am in paradise, my Lord may show me long lists of errors, but they will be the result of the limits of my mind and the weakness of my character, not because of my unwillingness to reject my heritage.

Muslim insiders are being transformed by the same Holy Spirit that transforms all of us. We read the same Holy Bible that all Christians throughout the centuries have read. Our respect for and familiarity with God's word varies, but it varies in the exact same way that it varies in other parts of the church. Shouldn't we leave it to the Holy Spirit to show us if we need to relearn how to pray or change our forms and customs and not be forced to new, external forms of worship that have special meaning to others but not us? How can an outsider know the impact of our customs and forms on our hearts?

what he did, Mallouhi still was not fully accepted by the local Christian community, because of his coming from a Muslim background.

Over time, however, Mallouhi realized that following Christ does not mean denying his loyalty to Middle Eastern culture and becoming part of an alien "Christian" culture. Although he worships Christ, he continues to embrace his Middle Eastern roots, the very roots of the one he serves. He came to understand that his family's rejection of him was not because he was following Christ but rather because of the way Christians had told him to act and to explain his new life. It was not good news to his family. In their eyes he was turning his back on family and community values in favor of Western individualism, rejecting a monotheistic faith for polytheism, and abandoning strong moral traditions for morally lax Western styles of behavior. They saw him as rebelling against all the best values they had taught him; any decent family would have been similarly and rightly concerned.

Today, Mallouhi enjoys praying and meditating in the quiet, reverent atmosphere of a mosque, where he sits on the carpeted floor and reads his Bible. While there, he often visits the sheikhs and imams, who are his friends. Mallouhi says, "Islam is my heritage and Christ is my inheritance," and as a result he has kept his Islamic and Arab culture while being a follower of Christ for four decades. Mallouhi's official Syrian identity papers still list him as a Muslim, as the government does not allow a change in one's religious identity. And he encourages new followers of Christ from Muslim backgrounds not to leave their family, people, or culture. He emphasizes that following Christ does not require taking a Christian name, wearing a different type of clothing, using the symbol of the cross (not used by the early church), changing the day of public worship (Sunday instead of Friday), adhering to a different style of worship within a church building, eating different foods, drinking alcohol (Muslims do not drink alcohol, whereas many Christians do), using pictures of Christ (most illustrate a Jesus of European descent), or ceasing to fast. He works to help them become disciples of Christ without having to join the "Christian" West.

—*Paul-Gordon Chandler*

* Excerpt from Paul-Gordon Chandler, "Mazhar Mallouhi: Gandhi's Living Christian Legacy in the Muslim World," *IBMR* 27, no. 2 (2003): 54–59. Reprinted by permission. The *International Bulletin of Missionary Research* is a publication of the Overseas Ministries Study Center, New Haven, Connecticut; see www.omsc.org for more information.

If Muslim followers of Jesus say their religious customs do not negate what is in their hearts, then how can others negate their faith?

I will not naively assume that my description of what it means for me to be an insider fully addresses the controversial aspects of the subject. In particular, I do not have much to say about the issues surrounding "insider proponents." These are the mostly Western cross-cultural workers who advocate more contextualized methods of evangelism. It is difficult for me to comment on insider proponents because the controversy surrounding them is largely doctrinal, and my concern is mostly about attitudes. On the other hand, I believe this controversy is also raging because of attitude rather than doctrine.

I appreciate the attitudes of insider proponents, who seek to export as little of their own culture as possible to Muslims who choose to follow our Lord. They go to great lengths to make sure that Muslims who choose to follow the way of our Lord don't feel pressured to reject their heritage. Furthermore, they make significant efforts to rise above the clashes between Christianity and Islam, or Western and Eastern civilization, clashes which encourage many of the church's negative attitudes towards Muslims. I can empathize with insider proponents as well, because as I observe their opponents attacking them, I notice some of the same unfairness applied to them that I have described above. For example, some of the notions advocated by insider proponents are very similar to decades-old ideas put forward by missionaries working among animist peoples. Insider proponents, however, experience far greater scrutiny than their predecessors. It seems to me that the controversy surrounding them also springs largely from attitude, not doctrine.

I don't share the fear of some that somehow insider proponents are advocating a form of postmodern relativism that threatens the fabric of orthodox belief. I don't understand why such an approach should warrant such a strong reaction. For one hundred years, Protestant missionaries have been pushing the envelope, and we have largely left them alone because they are willing to go where the rest of us aren't, but as soon as they apply their creativity to the Islamic world the rules change. That is how I see it, anyway.

Insider proponents receive a great deal of criticism for their views of Muhammad. Often the criticism is about the issue of whether or not he can be considered a prophet. This is a good example of how insider proponents and their detractors talk past each other. Insider proponents are not suggesting that *we* need to declare Muhammad to be a prophet. Rather, this issue relates to people from Muslim backgrounds who have come to love our Lord because of what is written about him in the Qur'an. Insider proponents argue that if something written by Muhammad leads some people ultimately to *the truth*, then why shouldn't these insiders have a positive view of Muhammad as the one who led them to Christ? I have not heard any insider proponents speaking of Muhammad as a prophet equal to Christ. But insider proponents are actually being judged because of what they will *not* say about Muhammad rather than what they are saying. Many insider proponents will not denounce Muhammad nor criticize aspects of Islam simply because they do not want to be "anti-Islam" but would rather be "for Christ." Unfortunately, detractors of insider proponents insist on making the assumption that their silence means they believe the opposite. The point is that insider proponents (along with myself) want the emphasis placed on what Christ is, and not what Muhammad is not.

I notice in some of my Christian brothers and sisters almost a sense of betrayal if anyone says something positive about Muhammad. Many insider proponents have a high view of Muhammad. This is not to say that they speak of him as a prophet, but from a historical point of view they often can comfortably cite the positive aspects of his life and consider him a reformer. This tends to make many Christians very uncomfortable. They usually argue something like, "We also have to be honest about the negative aspects of Muhammad's life." Why is this so important? I am allowed to say good things about Oliver Cromwell without being reminded that he chopped off the king's head. I am allowed to speak positively about Thomas Jefferson without incessant interruptions that he impregnated his slave. Do people think that we are somehow admitting defeat, or dishonoring Christ, if we focus on the positive aspects of Muhammad or the religion that he founded? I have no particular affection for Muhammad, but neither do I think that an opinion about a man who lived long ago can somehow damage the good news of our Lord. If I have to choose between honoring someone whom I disagree with, on the one hand, and dishonoring him, thereby showing an attitude that is not from our Lord, on the other, then the choice for me is easy.

I am an insider because I was born into a Muslim context and I don't wish to reject my heritage. Islam is my heritage and Christ is my inheritance. I am not an insider proponent, because it seems to me to be a mostly Western thing, and because it strikes me as being about ideas and strategy, while I am mostly interested in attitudes and people. I am not a "C5" advocate, because I think that the Incarnation needs to be our model for church planting, not the "C-scale." And I optimistically (and perhaps naively) believe that all of us who follow the ways of our Lord and Messiah Jesus (his peace be upon us) are capable of agreeing on a common goal of seeing the emergence of groups of Jesus followers in Muslim communities, groups that are authentic, indigenous, reproducible, and not dependent on Western money.

Additionally, I long for the day when we can go about our work while erring on the side of preferring one another and respecting one another, while resisting the temptation to search out heresy every time someone disagrees with us or challenges the status quo.

Furthermore, I am convinced that Christians aren't required to dislike Islam in order to engage it. Finally, I would like to encourage my friends, acquaintances, and fellow laborers from the West to earnestly and honestly ask themselves how much of their attitude towards Muslims is a result of political opinions, xenophobia, a post–Cold War clash of civilizations, or being caught in the trap of dueling religions. Even as my brothers and sisters commit to this sort of introspection, I also pledge to search out the planks in my own eye. May the peace of our Lord be upon us all.

1. *A monkey passed by a pond and found a fellow monkey pulling fish out and hanging them in a nearby tree. He asked, "What are you doing?" The monkey replied, "They were drowning and I saved them."*
2. *Would anyone consider transplanting banana tree shoots to Alaska, expecting they will thrive there?*

CHAPTER 13

My Enemy . . . My Brother
A Palestinian Christian Meets His Muslim Brothers*
Hanna Shahin

Christian or Follower of Christ?

The day was Sunday; I had finished preaching at the only Baptist church in that town and was headed back home to Amman. A little further down the road, there was one soldier standing alone. I stopped my vehicle. Without hesitation he jumped in and sat next to me in the front seat. He was young, about my age or a little younger. I looked at the badge he had pinned on his chest: against a dark background, the name Mustapha popped up in bold white letters.

For the next few minutes I spoke and he listened. I told him my name and where I was from, which explained my differing accent. I told him that I had been invited to speak at a church in that region. I even gave him a brief outline of the message I had preached that morning. I paused for a few seconds, allowing the little I had said to sink in. I wanted to get a general reading of his reaction and interest, or possibly the lack of it. Mustapha was interested—very interested. His questions kept coming. He wondered what led me to become a preacher.

I spoke about my religious upbringing and the false security that gave me. I did not hide behind my sinful past, nor did I blow it up for him. I said it as it was. I finally explained to him that neither the church nor my religion could pull away my mask of religiosity. In fact, they provided the mask for me. I went on to speak of the eventful experience I had had at the Jerusalem Baptist Church during the revival meetings where his Jordanian compatriot Rev. Zomot preached twelve years before. Christ had transformed my life. There was no reason to be ashamed of him.

I had spoken for about ten minutes. This was not a message I was preaching at some church. This was a friendly interaction. Or at least I hoped it would be. I paused again. I needed to hear Mustapha. Most of what I shared was completely new to him. His religious background and tradition as a Muslim presented huge doctrinal obstacles. And while I was not discussing doctrines or religions with him, his mind might easily wander into such territory. That would be a minefield. Doctrinal differences between the two faiths are irreconcilable.

A couple of minutes passed in complete silence. "What was it you prayed that evening?" he asked suddenly, referring to that eventful revival service back in Jerusalem. Rather than explain it, I offered to pray the prayer out loud—and I did, right then and there.

---

* This chapter consists of excerpts from Hanna Shahin, *My Enemy . . . My Brother: God's Grace in the Life of a Palestinian* (Fort Washington, PA: CLC, 2009), 106–12, 115–58, 173–78, 183–84. Reprinted by permission. Section headings are not in the original.

A minute or two passed without a word. He asked to get off. I hoped that my act of service would help cover any misgivings that I may have created by presenting Christ to him. I had avoided any reference to religions or doctrines. Such a discussion was irrelevant, immaterial. I was a sinner whose life was transformed by Christ. He was just the same, also a sinner. Christ was just as able to transform his life like he did mine.

There was no guarantee I would see him again, and I wanted to leave something with him just in case he was sympathetic to what I had said. I had several copies of the New Testament in the glove compartment. I reached out, took one, and asked him if he cared to take it. I explained that this book presented more truths about the life-changing Christ than I had time to share with him. Mustapha was now standing outside the car with the door open. He stretched his hand to shake mine, thanked me for the ride, took the New Testament, and said, "Brother Hanna, I will see you in heaven."

Glued to my seat, I saw him walk away. I was still parked on the side of the road. My eyes welled up. I could not control my feelings. I had never seen anything like that before. He called me his brother. Mustapha and Hanna—brothers! This cannot be the work of humans. I knew I did not do it. I could not possibly have done it. He did not do it either. Something, somebody, was at work here. Without further hesitation, and oblivious to the traffic that was coming on my left side, I opened my door, jumped out, ran after him, and hugged him.

As I drove off, I laughed and cried. I had one more brother—Mustapha! He did not know anything about my Muslim nursing mother; that is not why he called me "brother." He did so because Christ had made us both part of his family. Only Christ works across national, ethnic, cultural, and religious divides. To him, these are futile human inventions that have only caused problems within the human race. To him, there is no Jew, Christian, or Muslim. There is no Arab or Israeli. There is no black or white. We all lose our differences in him.

I have never forgotten my brother Mustapha. I have no idea of his whereabouts, whether he is still in the army, or if he is still alive! But one thing I know: Christ had done a miracle in his life. Mustapha had joined me in that prayer, confessing his sins and receiving the forgiveness that only Christ can give and the promise of eternal life that comes with it. Mustapha had become a follower of Christ. But he was not a "Christian"! He was a Muslim, with a Muslim name. But he was a follower of Jesus nonetheless.[1]

It is not my intention to change anyone from one religion to another. I know that religions are different in many aspects. I also know that they are similar in many aspects. Religions are systems: ethical, and sometimes moral, regulatory systems of right and wrong. Religions are systems of approaching deity, and sometimes of defining and regulating human relationships. In this way, any religion is as good as another.

I will not push one religion over another, not even Christianity over Judaism or Islam. I have serious doubts that Christianity can do more for someone than another religion can. Religions have caused many wars in the history of mankind, and under their guise much blood has been shed. Yet regrettably, this is not the way most people see and understand religions. Their religions become the answer to everything. Their religions become so sacred in their eyes that they are willing to die and kill defending them.

---

1   Based on Mustapha's parting words, Shahin concluded that he must have joined him in the prayer he prayed.—Ed.

My experience with Mustapha, and with scores of others after that, has often haunted me. Here I was, seeking to repay my debt to my Muslim nursing mother, and choosing to do so by directly, and indirectly, inviting my Muslim brothers and friends to allow Christ to invade their lives. I want them also to experience the power of Christ to meet their every need, in the same way he met and continues to meet mine.

A Changed Theology or a Transformed Life?

In seeking to reach out to my Muslim brothers and friends, I had learned a very important lesson about how they prioritize their belief systems and their practices. As a Christian, my belief system comes first and my practices are always secondary. This influences my approach to ministry in general. One of the first things I learned to do, as was done with me, was cover the basics. My theology had to be right.

Going back to my Christian journey of thirty-some years ago, this is how it all started. The challenge I faced with my Catholic catechism was about a belief system. It was not about Christian practices. The Catholic nuns at the orphanage in Bethany lived a sacrificial and exemplary life. My Catholic teachers, the monks that ran the day school, lived an impeccable life. They were completely above reproach. But I got fixated on the theological side of things. I wanted to have a solid biblical foundation. I was interested in what I could learn in class.

My Muslim brothers and friends have since taught me a great deal about how and why they do what they do. To them practice comes first. It is their practice that carries their faith. This is not to say that they do not have their theology. They definitely do. However, their practices are the foundation. To be a Muslim, you have to exercise a certain number of duties. Prayer is one, fasting during the month of Ramadan is another, and there are others.

In Christianity, at least in evangelical Christianity, it seems like the most important part is to have your theology correct. What you do after that seems to make some, but not much, difference. I am always amazed when I attend a baptismal service for adults. The baptizer seems always hung up on issues of theology. His questions to the person being baptized mostly revolve around such issues.

I am watching and waiting to find out how it is that the life of the person being baptized has changed. What has his newfound faith changed in his lifestyle? How has it changed his values? Was he a moneymonger and now gives his money to the poor? Where are the changes that look like the ones that happened to Matthew the tax collector, or to Zacchaeus, or many others in Scripture?

For one reason or another, we have shifted the emphasis from a changed life to a changed theology. We do this either in total ignorance of what the Gospels present to us, or in total defiance of it. In his encounters with everyday people, Jesus did not ask about their theology. What he did was give them new life: "Go and sin no more" (John 8:11 NLT).

How has this shift in emphasis affected Christianity? Is there any room for self-criticism? Could it be that our permissive societies, our liberal views, and our moral laxity were born out of our emphasis on theological correctness rather than the testimony of a changed life?

Christology or Christ?

It was over ten minutes before a taxi stopped. Under his rearview mirror hung a small, transparent plastic folder containing his driver's license. His photo and name were clearly visible: Ahmad. Nothing unique about that name—it is shared by millions of individuals in the world of Islam. It was one of the names of the prophet of Islam.

With a smile on my face, I greeted him, addressing him by his first name. He said, "What is your name?" I expected him to ask something about me, possibly where I was from, since my accent betrayed me. (I spoke Arabic, but not his dialect.)

"Hanna," I answered. "My name is Hanna." He did not seem too concerned about my family name. As it was, my first name proved to be more than enough for the next projectile. This guy was really prepared.

"How come you Christians worship three gods?" he fanatically asked. That obviously was not a question. It was not meant to be. It was an accusation. He pressed on. "This is idolatry."

For the next five or ten minutes, I kept stressing and pressing the case that we should not be fixed on our names. Names are only means of identifying one person from another, not of identifying whether this one is a Muslim, and that one a Christian, or anything else. In the hot religious climate of the Middle East, names are always loaded. Names, like religions, have divided people.

One thing I have learned, and learned well, is never to argue with someone from another faith. Christ is not about religions; I am convinced he could not care less. Christ is not about safeguarding Christianity as a religious system. What Christ is all about is giving new life to people, regardless of their religion, faith, or denomination.

I was not concerned about defending Christianity as an organized religion. I was concerned about the person of Christ. Christianity cannot change people. Religion can only create religious people, and that is not Christ's purpose. He is concerned about changing human nature to be as best an imitation of him as possible.

Ahmad and I had been in his car for about two-thirds of the way by now. Ten more minutes and I would arrive at my destination. At the start of this taxi ride, I wished I had not even taken this man's cab; now I found myself wishing we had a longer distance to travel. The discussion was taking on a new dimension. I did not want him to go before I had a chance to tell him about what Christ meant to me and what he could mean to him.

I know full well that presenting Christ to someone who follows another religious system, faith, or prophet can be as challenging and as ensnaring as discussing doctrine. This is why I hasten to say that by asking for a chance to tell Ahmad about what Christ meant to me, I did not intend to go into the field of Christology. This had nothing to do with Christ's virgin birth, or with him being one with God, or any of the doctrinal statements or theology about Christ. This was about the power and influence that Christ had had in my life. This was about his power to forgive, to heal, and to give new meaning to life. If he could do that for me, he could do it for anybody. The understanding of who *Jesus* really is should come later.

Inside Our Christian Box or Out?

I do not know if anyone ever reached Om Ahmad, my Muslim foster mother. I say that with a lump in my throat. Oh how I wish I had known the power of Christ in my life when I met her! But I was only full of myself, full of religion, as dead as could be! I do not know if anyone cared enough to follow Christ before her, and thereby invite her to do likewise. I am not privy to that information. How wonderful the world would be if we ceased being simply Christians—dare I say, bigots—and learned to follow our master: to imitate his life and love and forgiveness!

Muslims have no need for another religion. They are full to overflowing with religion. Muslims, like the rest of us, have needs the same way we do. Christ is their answer, just like Christ is our answer.

I have been asked, "Why is it that Christ appears to Muslims in visions and dreams, and not to Christians? Why is it that Christ seems to answer the prayers lifted by Muslims, and we do not hear of such among ourselves? How is it that when a Muslim sees Christ in a dream, or when Christ answers his prayers, he immediately becomes a follower of him?"

I have said it before, but it bears repeating: Christ is *not* for Christians alone. Christ is universal. In our prejudices, we have tended to take ownership of him, to monopolize him. We want him for us and us alone. He just will not do that, to the dismay of many.

So why do we shake our heads in shock when he acts outside our Christian box? Why do we shake our heads in disbelief when he acts outside our denominational box? It is about time we learned that Christ will not be boxed in. He shocked his generation. He will continue to shock ours.

Earlier I spoke of the huge percentage of illiterates in some Middle Eastern and North African countries. I gave an example of a radio program that caters to this segment of the Arab society.[2] That program had to be made. It had to be different, because the illiterate society thinks differently. They compute differently. They do not necessarily follow the Greek methodology that we have been taught to use in our educational systems.

We can think of Christ's appearances to Muslims in the same way. To us who are literate, Christ will speak through a book—through *the* Book, the Bible—and not necessarily through a dream! If Christ were to appear to me in a dream, I would not even recognize him. Why would he therefore speak to me in that way?

There is another element. Muslims are predisposed to dreams. They are predisposed to the influence of dreams and visions, whereas many of us are not. That should be ample explanation. Because our Muslim friends are predisposed to dreams, they will act on what they see and interpret, much more than we would through the influence of a good book or any other means. Their dreams take on the size of life itself. It is visual and not virtual. It becomes part of their spiritual reality. Many simply act on it, waking up to say, to our amazement and their own, that they have become followers of Christ. They may not be Christian, but they are followers of Christ. Here they have a lot to teach us, and we have a lot to learn.

---

2   See Shahin, *My Enemy . . . My Brother*, 179.—Ed.

CHAPTER 14

And the Spirit Fell upon Them

Testimonies of the Holy Spirit's Activity in One Insider Movement

Tom Payne

We have been privileged to work among a nearly 100-percent Muslim people group now for sixteen years. In that time, we've seen many Muslims who have come to faith in Christ. Some have changed their identity to "Christian" and joined a local church of another ethnic group. Most of those have paid for their decision with threats made on their lives by their own families, or they have had to move far away from their families and communities to practice their new religion safely. But many have chosen to remain in their own sociocultural Muslim identity in hopes that their families and communities can experience a Jesus who wears their traditional clothes. Some of these have also been persecuted, but none that we know of have been killed, and most maintain close relationships with their families. In fact, the gospel is spreading rapidly along their family and community lines, and the Holy Spirit is bearing witness with manifestations, signs, and wonders.

Our particular movement is centered on a young woman whom we call "Mary." Mary is an insider; that is, she is a committed follower of Jesus but still maintains the Muslim identity of her birth, family, and community. Mary has started several groups of Muslims who gather to read the *Injil* (New Testament), ask the Holy Spirit how to understand and obey it, and help one another follow Jesus in their Muslim community. A man whom we call "Life" was a leader in the neighborhood mosque and came to faith through this group. Life then became Mary's husband. We are privileged to "shadow pastor" Mary and Life, meaning that we don't attend their meetings, but meet with the leaders privately. Most of the new believers don't know who we are. Almost none of the Muslims Mary ministers to or who gather to read the Scriptures have ever been inside a church. Their whole concept of a life of following Jesus is founded solely upon what they read in the Gospels and Acts (not on man's religious traditions) and what the Holy Spirit leads them to do. Thus the testimonies you are about to read have nothing to do with influence from local Christians or foreign workers; they are the direct result of a faith community that knows only the *Injil* and the guidance of the Holy Spirit.

The original *Injil*-reading group has now multiplied many times over, with new insider groups starting in several other places around the country. Over the past five years we have journaled about forty pages of the work of the Holy Spirit in Mary's life and in this insider movement she is catalyzing. We have numerous accounts of extraordinary miracles of healing, deliverance, supernatural provision, prophetic revelations, dreams and visions, and even a small number of personal visitations of Jesus. The evidence of the Spirit's work in these disciples' lives is amazing and undeniable. But for the sake of this chapter, we have chosen to present just four journal entries that relate specifically to the Holy Spirit manifesting among the insiders (and in two of the cases, upon near-proximity unbelievers) as they prayed for the Spirit to come. This reminds us of Peter's explanation to the Jerusalem Council in Acts

15:8,9: "God, who knows the heart, showed that he accepted them by giving the Holy Spirit to them, just as he did to us. He did not discriminate between us and them, for he purified their hearts by faith."

It should be noted that although we were not present at these events, Mary is our spiritual daughter and we trust her completely. She lived in our home for eighteen months before all these events took place, so she does not need to gain our affection. She also has resisted receiving financial support from Christians. She does not visit churches or individuals to tell her stories and thus gain support. She lives in her Muslim community with the money she makes selling food from her roadside stall. We have also met some of the members of her group who can bear witness to the truth of her stories because they were present, or because they were the ones healed. Mary frequently gets calls requesting prayer from Muslims all over our city because of the many notable miracles God has done through her prayers in Jesus' name.

Journal Entry 1—Manifestations of the Spirit

In early July 2007, on a typical morning when Mary and her newlywed husband, Life, were praying at 3 a.m. as usual, they both felt God's presence come into the room. Mary was given the gift of speaking in tongues, and her hands started shaking. Life went face down on the floor, weeping, and couldn't get up until 8 a.m. The family members in the next room decided from the noise that they must be having their first marriage fight! Mary testified later that they both felt like they died and were resurrected, and as Life took Mary to her workplace (late), they laughed the whole way there, experiencing a fresh anointing of the joy of the Lord.

Journal Entry 2—A Baptism of Tongues

One day Mary told my wife that what she really wanted for her group was a greater ministry of the Holy Spirit, like what the group had been reading about recently in the book of Acts. So they prayed together for the Spirit to fall upon the group. The answer wasn't long in coming.

On May 1, 2008, Mary's group gathered on Jesus' Ascension Day, and they felt they needed to cry out for more of the Holy Spirit. So they met in one of the members' homes to pray. As they prayed, the Holy Spirit visited them and they all started speaking loudly in tongues for the first time, just as Life and Mary had experienced. Some were also vomiting blood as deliverance was happening without any-one even praying for them. (Many of these Muslims come to Christ still carrying the influence of their past syncretistic, shamanistic practices, which opened the door to demonic oppression.) It was loud, and the neighbors gathered around, peeking in the windows to find out what was going on. Everyone was oblivious to the onlookers until Mary noticed the staring faces and suggested that the group quiet down. But it was no use; they were completely focused on what the Holy Spirit was doing in their midst. Later they testified that they felt different and were more confident to go out and share about Jesus.

Mary got to talk to one of the upset neighbors afterwards. "That doesn't look Muslim to me!" she said. Mary answered, "We're just experiencing God. His Spirit is here." "Muslims don't experience God, and we don't have his Spirit. We're just supposed to say the prayers and experience nothing," the woman answered. "Then why don't you come and join us and experience him too?" Mary asked. The woman refused.

Other neighbors have protested too, and the group discussed stopping their meetings because of the opposition. Instead they decided to stop focusing on the persecution and to pray for the protesters as they keep sharing with them that they too can experience God.

Journal Entry 3—And the Spirit Fell upon the . . . Mosque!

In mid-July 2008, one of the ex-prostitutes whom we now call one of "God's lovers" (several Muslim prostitutes had already come to faith in Jesus by this time) came bursting into Mary's house. "God told me to pray at your mosque today! Will you go with me? And bring your friends too!"

So Mary invited a few of the other women from her *Injil*-reading group, and they all went over to her neighborhood mosque, where a big women's meeting was already going on, celebrating an event in Muhammad's life. The women slipped in, and in the midst of songs about Muhammad and various Arabic prayers, they just started praying to God and inviting his presence.

Suddenly the Holy Spirit fell! People started shaking, some were throwing up in what looked like spontaneous deliverances, and people were coming under conviction of sin. The whole group of Muslim women experienced this, not just Mary's friends who are believers. When it was over people were buzzing: "We've never experienced a meeting like that before!" "Does our teacher have some special power we didn't know about?" "I haven't been very nice to my husband lately—I'm going home right now to apologize to him!"

Mary herself was surprised and had to ask my wife if this could really be God—the Spirit falling in a mosque, even on people chanting Muhammad's name? But my wife reminded her that there is power in the prayers of her little group to change the atmosphere wherever they are, and the fruit was clearly good. Is this a glimpse of what is coming?

Some of the women in the mosque recognized that Mary's group was praying in the national language, not in Arabic, and they thought that might have had something to do with the strange phenomenon. In the weeks to follow, three different Muslim women who had been at the mosque that day came to Mary on their own asking to learn more about how to pray, or about Jesus. One woman from the mosque even borrowed an *Injil*!

Journal Entry 4—The Spirit Falls in a Hospital Room

Mary and Life's roadside food stall is visible from several windows of a prostitute's hotel. Recently one of the prostitutes we will call "Tammy" experienced a strange illness of paralysis down her left side and part of her face, with her skin on that side turning a bluish hue. She looked so strange that people began saying she was half ghost!

Several of her relatives were gathered at the hospital, presumably to witness her death, on October 1, 2010, the day that several prostitutes and Mary went to visit her. Since she was a poverty-stricken patient, the nurses didn't do much for her, and Mary found that she was bleeding profusely in large clots from her uterus. None of the family would do anything to clean her up, so Mary took it on herself to serve Tammy. When she finished, she asked, "Do you want to be healed? Let's pray through Isa for a miracle."

One of the relatives asked, "Why Isa? Why not Muhammad?"

Mary responded, "I like Muhammad too, but if you want a healing miracle, you need to pray through Isa! Do you want that, Tammy?"

Tammy replied, "Yes!" She didn't care what it took to get healed.

So Mary began, "We invite the Holy Spirit to fill this place in the name of Isa." Immediately several people started weeping; others started shaking and exhibiting other manifestations. One of the women hugged Mary, exclaiming, "This is amazing! God is here!" Everyone was so moved at how God was touching them personally that at first they didn't notice Tammy. She started waving her previously paralyzed left arm at them. "I'm healed! I'm healed!"

The blue color didn't disappear right away, but the paralysis healing greatly impacted the family and the prostitutes, who knew Mary wasn't a witchdoctor because she didn't use any witchcraft items like holy water. Most of the prostitutes are becoming good friends with Mary and Life. Since several other prostitutes have already joined the *Injil*-reading group, we hope these new friends will also be interested in visiting the group.

Conclusion

Among the many signs of regenerated life that we look for in those who profess faith in Jesus (such as submission to Scripture, growth in godly character, and so on), we have been blessed to observe in this particular insider movement the fruit of the Spirit, the gifts of the Spirit, and clear manifestations of the Holy Spirit's presence, including signs and wonders. These Muslims are sharing their faith in Christ boldly and experiencing Hebrews 2:4: "All the while God was validating it [the message of salvation] with gifts through the Holy Spirit, all sorts of signs and miracles, as he saw fit" (MSG). Never in our lives have we seen an expression of God's kingdom here on earth that so closely resembles what we read of in the Gospels and Acts as does this amazing insider movement.

SECTION 2
Case Study Analysis

CHAPTER 15

Jesus Movement
A Case Study from Eastern Africa[*]
Ben Naja

Around thirty years ago, Sheikh Ali heard a voice: "You are in darkness and you lead all your people into darkness. I am *Ruhullah*, follow me." He looked around him. Where did this voice come from? It was not a human voice. And where did this light come from? It was Friday afternoon. He was gathered with many of his disciples in the mosque. Sheikh Ali was a respected leader throughout the region in a very remote rural area of eastern Africa. According to the Qur'an, the book he was teaching to his disciples, *Ruhullah* (Spirit of God) was one of the titles for Jesus. Was Jesus calling him to become his disciple?

Over the next twenty-five years and to his best knowledge, Ali taught about Isa al-Masih. However, he did not have a Bible, he had never met a Christian, and he had never seen a church. After around twenty-five years, Jesus came to him a second time and said the exact same thing: "You are in darkness and you lead all your people into darkness. I am *Ruhullah*, follow me." However, this time, the voice continued and said, "Send some of your disciples to the Christians so that you learn the full truth about me." After this vision, he sent seven of his disciples to an evangelical church in a nearby town to ask for teaching.

Ted was the general secretary of that church's denomination. He had just started to serve in this role at about that time. Ted had received a call to work with Muslims in the mid-seventies. For almost thirty years, he had been "pregnant" with this vision, praying and waiting for God to open the door for him to fulfill this calling. The sheikh's seven disciples were led to a local church of the denomination, whose general secretary was Ted. The local church leaders called him and said, "Some Muslims came and knocked at our door." Ted asked, "Did they come for trouble or for salvation?" "For salvation," they said. Ted recognized that this was God's answer to his thirty years of prayer, jumped in his car, and rushed to that town in order to meet the seven disciples.

This was in 2006. Ted then started to give these seven disciples biblical teaching about Isa al-Masih. Later the sheikh chose ten of his disciples, and several expatriate workers partnered with Ted to regularly gather these ten disciples over a period of two years for discipleship. After this first training round, more than forty other disciples were trained over another two-year period. And in 2010 a similar training took place with fifty additional disciples. Many of these trainees are currently leaders of believers' groups in their respective villages.

Over the last several years many have come to faith, several hundred have been baptized, dozens of home-based fellowships have been started, and in two instances Jesus mosques have been built and are used for the gatherings of the Jesus disciples. This movement is still growing. The trainees of the discipleship gatherings take the gospel back to their villages, where people are coming to Jesus and new fellowships are being formed.

---

[*] Originally published in a slightly different form in *IJFM* 30, no. 1 (2013): 27–29. Reprinted by permission.

Ted is my closest friend and partner. I meet regularly with him and the leaders from the movement for mutual learning, coaching, discipling, teaching, training, and leadership development.

In December 2011 we conducted in-depth research in order to know more about the disciples in the rural areas. I present some initial findings in the subsequent paragraphs. A more thorough analysis will be forthcoming later. The data is based on 322 interviews with believers from a Muslim background who are from 64 different villages and *ekklesiae* in several districts. I intentionally show the data with minimal commentary.

How long have you followed Jesus?
- 82 percent: less than 5 years
- 15 percent: between 5 and 10 years
- 3 percent: more than 10 years
- Are you the only one in your family who follows Jesus?
- 65 percent: no
- 35 percent: yes

Comment: Although the movement started around thirty years ago with a sovereign act of God, it is still growing. Most disciples have been following Jesus for less than five years. The gospel is mainly moving through family lines.

Why did you decide to follow Jesus?
- 64 percent: verses about Jesus in the Qur'an
- 57 percent: love and witness of other followers of Jesus
- 41 percent: supernatural experience (dream, vision, healing, deliverance)
- 30 percent: the Bible

Comment: Most disciples decided to follow Jesus through a combination of different factors. The most important factor was Jesus verses in the Qur'an.

Beliefs
- 95 percent believe Jesus died on the Cross.
- 96 percent believe Jesus is the Son of God.
- 96 percent believe God forgives people through faith in Jesus the Messiah and his atoning death.
- 98 percent believe that it is important to know the Bible.
- 99 percent turn to Jesus for forgiveness of their sins.
- 7 percent believe that they are saved because of Muhammad's intercession for them.

Comment: The data shows that the believers have a clear understanding that their salvation is in Jesus alone. Although they primarily came to faith through Qur'an verses, they have now clearly reached a biblical understanding of Jesus and salvation. Only a tiny minority still hold to the folk Islamic belief that Muhammad's intercession can save them.

Identity
When Muslims ask me, I identify myself as a . . .
- 80 percent: Muslim who follows Isa al-Masih
- 13 percent: Muslim
- 4 percent: Christian
- 3 percent: other

Although I follow Isa al-Masih, I feel that I am still part of the Muslim community.

- 59 percent: true
- 41 percent: not true

Comment: Although 95 percent or more of the disciples hold beliefs not generally accepted by the Muslim community, almost two-thirds still feel that they are part of the ummah. When asked, most disciples would maintain that they are Muslims, but in a qualified sense—namely, Muslims who follow Isa al-Masih.

Practices

- 93 percent participate in *ekklesia* meetings.
- 88 percent read or listen to the *Injil* at least once a week.
- 85 percent of the leaders read or listen to the *Injil* every day.
- 12 percent read or listen to the Qur'an every day.
- 81 percent are baptized.

Comment: Compared to the Qur'an, the Bible plays a prominent role in their lives. Almost all members of the movement are part of ekklesia *gatherings, and most are baptized.*

Where does your fellowship meet?

- 78 percent: in houses
- 11 percent: in a church building
- 11 percent: other (outside in nature, at the mosque, etc.)

How many meet in your fellowship?

- 63 percent: fewer than 10 adults
- 28.5 percent: between 10 and 20 adults
- 8.5 percent: more than 20 adults

Comment: This is clearly a home-based movement of relatively small fellowships with generally less than twenty members per group.

Have you suffered persecution for your faith?

- 53 percent: no
- 47 percent: yes

Comment: Although they are inside the Muslim community, about half of the disciples have suffered for their faith. Being part of the Muslim community has not eliminated persecution.

How do you share your faith with fellow Muslims?

- 77 percent: using verses from the Qur'an
- 46 percent: using the Bible
- 30 percent: giving my personal testimony
- 27 percent: praying for healing for the sick
- 7 percent have not shared

Comment: Most disciples share their faith within their Muslim community. The Bible, the Qur'an, healing prayer, and the witness of other Jesus followers have been key elements in the growth of this movement. In most cases, a combination of several approaches is used in evangelism.

Summary comment: The research findings of these ten areas give a glimpse of key aspects in this movement. Most striking are the high fidelity to biblical beliefs and practices and the high percentage of members who regularly meet in *ekklesia* gatherings and who share their faith. Remarkable is the high percentage of people in the movement who see themselves in their context as a type of Muslim, and that almost two-thirds of the members feel that they are accepted as full members within the Muslim community despite the fact that they hold non-Islamic beliefs.

Sheikh Ali and many of these believers are perceived by their wider community as Muslims; however, they joined us in the wider family of God by truly trusting in Jesus for their salvation and following him as their Lord.

CHAPTER 16

Insider Movements among Muslims
*A Focus on Asia**
John Jay Travis

In the 1970s Presbyterian John Wilder, a long-term field worker in South Asia, wrote a thought-provoking article entitled "Some Reflections on Possibilities for People Movements among Muslims."[1] In this largely theoretical work, Wilder drew upon the ideas of Donald McGavran,[2] mission executive John Anderson,[3] the recent experience of the Messianic Jewish movement, and his own long-term observations in the Muslim world. Movements strikingly similar to what he suggested then as possibilities have since taken place.

In this chapter I first discuss Wilder's article and some of what has occurred since its publication. I then turn to the writings of J. Dudley Woodberry, showing how his work has contributed to our understanding of movements to Christ among Muslims. I close with a recent case study from Asia and a description of some dynamics observed in several other Asian movements.

Wilder's Article and the Following Decades

In 1977 Wilder postulated that if a movement were to occur in a particular Muslim context, it would most likely take one of two forms: "a people movement to Christ which remains within Islam" or "a people movement constituting a new church of Muslim cultural orientation."[4] In terms of the C1–C6 Spectrum,[5] Wilder was describing what I have referred to elsewhere as C4 and C5 types of movements. Wilder made it clear that he would prefer "a people movement constituting a new church of Muslim

---

  * Originally published in a slightly different form in Evelyne A. Reisacher, ed., *Toward Respectful Understanding and Witness among Muslims: Essays in Honor of J. Dudley Woodberry* (Pasadena, CA: William Carey Library, 2012): 233–44. Reprinted by permission.

  1 John W. Wilder, "Some Reflections on Possibilities for People Movements among Muslims," *Missiology: An International Review* 5, no. 3 (1977): 302–20.

  2 Donald McGavran was the founding dean of the School of World Mission, Fuller Theological Seminary. He was one of the mission world's leading thinkers on the subject of people movements. *The Bridges of God* (London: World Dominion, 1955) is considered one of his seminal works on the dynamics of people movements.

  3 John D. C. Anderson, a medical missionary working among Muslims, authored a seminal article in 1976 suggesting an insider approach and new ways of thinking for missionaries entitled "The Missionary Approach to Islam: Christian or 'Cultic,'" *Missiology: An International Review* 4, no. 3 (1976): 258–99.

  4 Wilder, "Possibilities for People Movements," 310.

  5 I developed this continuum to show a range of types of biblical *ekklesiae*, which I refer to as "Christ-centered communities," that exist in the Muslim world today. See John Travis, "The C1–C6 Spectrum," *EMQ* 34, no. 3 (1998), 411–15. C4 is an *ekklesia* that is Islamic in its forms but seen as existing outside of Islam. C5 movements have also been called "*insider movements*" or "*Jesus movements within Muslim communities*" due to the fact that believers stay socioreligiously within Islam. The two terms are often used interchangeably, as I use them in this writing.

orientation" (i.e., C4), but also felt a movement to Jesus that remained within Islam (i.e., C5) would be valid and might occur quite naturally as the gospel moves through a Muslim community. He astutely pointed out that a genuine movement, settling either within Islam (C5) or outside of it (C4), would likely not be led by outsiders (e.g., missionaries or non-Muslim-background church leaders).

Regarding movements to Christ within Islam, Wilder stated that those coming to faith would differ in many ways from Muslims who do not yet follow Jesus. However, by remaining a part of the community, hopefully, they would be considered neither traitors to their people nor "apostates" (*murtaddūn*).[6] He postulated four other features of movements to Christ within Islam: (1) they would engage in self-theologizing,[7] (2) they might have different views of the sacraments,[8] (3) they might emphasize different parts of the Bible from what Christians traditionally have emphasized,[9] and (4) they would likely have very little contact, if any, with existing non-Muslim-background churches. Wilder stated, however, that "missionaries and concerned nationals might have opportunities through personal contacts, of forming links of fellowship, understanding and dialogue," thus keeping this portion of the body of Christ linked in some ways to other parts of Christ's body.[10]

Regarding movements that settle outside of Islam, Wilder believed that they would likely retain a strong Islamic cultural flavor. He also felt that they might need the broader perspective of cross-cultural workers to assist them in thinking through different issues. Examples were whether to retain circumcision, on which day of the week to worship, the role of clergy, the use of Muslim wedding customs, the need for and/or method of baptism, the place of women in the faith community, and how the fellowships are to be governed. Whatever the case, Wilder believed that for a movement to occur, a Bible translation for Muslim readers that used familiar Islamic terms such as *'Isa* for Jesus and *Allah* for God would be essential.[11]

Since the publication of Wilder's article, tens of thousands of Muslims worldwide have come to faith in Jesus. Among some Muslim people groups, these are the first known Jesus followers. The new fellowships being formed are not only C4 and C5 in nature (as Wilder predicted) but C2 and C3 as well.[12] We now turn to the contributions of J. Dudley Woodberry to better understand some of the dynamics of these movements.

For further explanations on insider movements among Muslims / Jesus movements within Muslim communities, see Travis and Woodberry in *UIM*, chap. 4.

6   There are many sects and spiritual streams within Islam, including millions of Sufis, numerous Asian mystical orders, and Alevis in Turkey. They are seen as different, but are not rejected, because they remain a part of the Muslim community.

7   While creative theologizing is characteristic of many of the movements I have learned about or observed, the basic gospel message, including the death and resurrection of Jesus Christ, is the foundation of them all.

8   They may not emphasize communion or baptism. It is interesting to note that at least two Christian groups, the Salvation Army and the Quakers, do not practice these two sacraments as outwardly celebrated rites.

9   Wilder stated that, due to the Islamic belief in the *Tawrat* (Pentateuch), *Zabur* (Psalms), and *Injil* (the Gospels), it was possible that Jesus movements inside Muslim communities would emphasize only those parts of the Bible.

10   Wilder, "Possibilities for People Movements," 315.

11   Ibid.

12   I have not seen evidence of C1 movements (where, by definition, the new believers would not be using their own language) or C6 movements (which by definition refer to only small, isolated, or secret groups of believers).

Woodberry's Contributions toward Understanding Movements among Muslims

J. Dudley Woodberry's writings show a deep love and understanding of Muslim peoples and their cultures, flowing out of his many years spent in the Muslim world, including significant time in South Asia. Five of Woodberry's works in particular are helpful in this discussion of movements among Muslims, one of which (2006) involves 650 interviews Woodberry has collected of Muslims who have come to faith in Christ.[13] I will first mention five circumstances Woodberry has identified that are impacting movements among Muslims today. Next I will share six ways that Jesus followers can be involved in helping facilitate movements, based upon my own ministry experience and the findings of Woodberry's 650 interviews. I will then turn to share a key finding from field research that Woodberry, Higgins, and others conducted in a large insider movement in Asia.[14]

Movements to Christ and the Hand of God in the Glove of Current Events

Woodberry has described five circumstances present in the Muslim world today that God is using to draw Muslims to himself. He speaks of these circumstances as "the hand of God in the glove of current events."[15] The first finger in the glove is political factors; in particular, resurgent Islam, a situation causing many Muslims to reject extremism and search for other spiritual options. The second and third fingers are natural catastrophes and mass migration of refugees due to war and famine, met with the sacrificial love shown by Christ's people in response. The fourth is the desire for blessing (*baraka*) or power, a very real issue for vast numbers of Muslims worldwide. The fifth is ethnic and cultural resurgence, sometimes expressing itself in a rejection of an oppressive Muslim regime or a dominant Islamic people group.

Ways that Followers of Jesus Can Facilitate Movements to Christ

Movements to Christ involve the hand of God and the actions of his people. The following six factors can help facilitate movements to Christ among Muslims by properly responding both to world events and spiritual conditions (e.g., dreams, visions, personal spiritual hunger).[16]

---

13 See Woodberry, "Contextualization among Muslims: Reusing Common Pillars," *IJFM* 13, no. 4 (1996): 171–86 (*UIM*, chap. 45); Woodberry, *Muslims and Christians on the Emmaus Road: Crucial Issues in Witness among Muslims* (Monrovia, CA: MARC, 1989); Woodberry, "The Relevance of Power Ministries for Folk Muslims," in *Wrestling with Dark Angels*, ed. C. Peter Wagner and F. Douglas Pennoyer (Ventura, CA: Regal, 1990), 313–31; Woodberry, "A Global Perspective on Muslims Coming to Faith in Christ," in *From the Straight Path to the Narrow Way: Journeys of Faith*, ed. David H. Greenlee (Downers Grove, IL: InterVarsity Press, 2006): 11–22; and Woodberry, "To the Muslim I Became a Muslim?" *IJFM* 24, no. 1 (2007): 23–28.

14 Information based on the author's personal conversations with Higgins and Woodberry regarding their research.

15 Woodberry, "A Global Perspective," 11–13.

16 I am not mentioning general dynamics of movements (e.g., the gospel moving through community networks, the need for group decisions, minimal outsider involvement, etc.), but rather data that pertains more specifically to Muslim contexts.

1. Prayer with and for Muslims

This factor is placed first to emphasize the strong correlation between prayer and movements to Christ.[17] In a movement in one Muslim country, the number of followers of Jesus increased tenfold during the year that hundreds of people worldwide joined together to intercede for that nation. Woodberry states that answered prayer in the name of Jesus was one of the most important factors mentioned regarding people coming to Christ in his survey.[18]

2. An Appropriately Contextualized Message

A key aspect of contextualization is developing appropriate ways to express the gospel message for specific audiences.[19] When Jesus and his followers proclaimed the gospel to Jews, Samaritans, and Gentiles, people in all three groups received the message as one of hope for them—it spoke to their hearts and met their needs.[20] When sharing the gospel with Muslims, our message must convey, and they must understand, that Jesus really is for them and not just for others (like Westerners and Christians).[21] He is the healing prophet and Savior who is on the side of all peoples. In addition, for the gospel to take root and spread through an unreached people group, following Jesus must be understood as a viable or feasible life option for them right now, just as they are. Jesus and his followers not only preached truth but also shared the next appropriate step that people could take to demonstrate allegiance to Christ.[22]

3. An Appropriate Messenger

For movements to take place, it is important to consider not only what is shared and how it is shared, but also who shares it. In Woodberry's survey regarding why Muslims came to Christ, the lifestyle and life message of a follower of Jesus whom the respondent had known personally ranked highest.[23] Who that appropriate messenger of the gospel might be, in order to see movements begin in a given context, depends upon a cluster of political, historical, religious, and social factors in that context. Generally, however, people tend to come to faith and the message tends to spread more readily when the people

---

17 Of course prayer is essential in any move of God, but perhaps even greater prayer—"extraordinary prayer"—is needed where resistance to the gospel is particularly great. David Garrison has identified "extraordinary prayer" as the most significant factor in seeing church planting movements happen. See Garrison, *Church Planting Movements: How God Is Redeeming a Lost World* (Monument, CO: WIGTake, 2004), 172.

18 Woodberry, "A Global Perspective," 15.

19 On the contextualization of the gospel message, see Rick Love, *Muslims, Magic, and the Kingdom of God: Church Planting among Folk Muslims*; Phil Parshall, *Beyond the Mosque: Christians in Muslim Community* (Grand Rapids, MI: Baker, 1985); and Woodberry in *UIM*, chap. 45.

20 The good news of the kingdom has many facets. Jesus and his followers ministered differently in their words and actions depending upon the ethnicity, felt needs, and social standing of the audience (see Matt 4:23–25; 8:5–13; Mark 1:21–27; John 4:7–42).

21 In the movement that I describe in the case study below, a key dynamic has been a clear sense that Jesus *loves* Muslims and is *for* them.

22 For some examples of steps given to show allegiance, see Mark 1:17; 5:19; Luke 19:5; John 8:11; Acts 2:38; 26:29.

23 J. Dudley Woodberry, Russell G. Shubin, and G. Marks, "Why Muslims Follow Jesus: The Results of a Recent Survey of Converts from Islam," *CT*, October 2007.

see the messenger as being one of them. Sinclair points out that the spiritual gifting of the messenger is also a major factor in seeing people respond to the gospel.[24]

4. Contextualized Bible Translations

In order for a movement to occur, it is crucial to have an appropriately contextualized Bible (or Bible portions) that a Muslim will read and then want to pass on to fellow Muslims. Both Woodberry and Wilder note that relevant religious terminology is a vital part of an appropriate translation.[25] Even when a Bible is in use by an existing Christian population, it is likely that another translation will be necessary that intentionally uses affectively and cognitively meaningful vocabulary for Muslim readers.[26]

5. The Use of "Power Ministries"

Woodberry points out that today "the major movements to Christ in the Muslim world are among folk Muslims," with "power ministries" (e.g., prayer for healing, inner healing, deliverance) being an important part of these movements.[27] Woodberry states that cross-cultural workers can pray more effectively for Muslims by understanding first the effect that power objects, power rituals, power times, power places, and power people exert over many Islamic people groups. Woodberry's survey indicates that prayer for healing and deliverance was highly ranked as a reason associated with people coming to faith.[28]

6. Compassionate Responses to Natural, Economic, and Political Crisis

Woodberry states that from the Sahara to South Asia, a "cup of cold water or milk in Christ's name" has met people's physical needs and helped open the way for the meeting of spiritual needs as well.[29] While assistance from Christians has at times aroused suspicion on the part of Muslims, the sincerity and selflessness of many Christian relief and development workers, especially those living in close proximity to the community, has afforded many opportunities to share and exemplify the good news of the kingdom.

A Key Finding from Research Done on a Movement in South Asia

An important finding in understanding movements came out of research that Higgins, Woodberry, and others carried out in the 1990s on a large insider movement in South Asia.[30] Research questions

---

24 Daniel Sinclair, *A Vision of the Possible: Pioneer Church Planting in Teams* (Waynesboro, GA: Authentic, 2006), 1–13, 251–59.

25 Woodberry, chap. 45; Wilder, "Possibilities for People Movements," passim; and Travis, "Producing and Using Meaningful Translations of the Taurat, Zabur and Injil," *IJFM* 23, no. 2 (2006): 73–77.

26 At the very least, the words *Tawrat, Zabur,* and *Injil,* and personal names such as *Isa al-Masih, Yahya* (John), and *Maryam* (Mary) should be used; *Allah* should be considered for YHWH, *Elohim,* or both; and culturally appropriate ways to translate "Holy Spirit," "Son of God," "Lord," "Christian," and "church" need to be discovered.

27 Woodberry, "Relevance of Power Ministries," 321.

28 Woodberry, Russell, and Marks, "Why Muslims Follow Jesus." For a model integrating power ministries and evangelism, see Charles H. Kraft, "What Kind of Encounters Do We Need in Our Christian Witness?" *EMQ* 27, no. 3 (1991): 258–65. For a model of inner healing and deliverance that has been used among Muslims, see Anna Travis in *UIM*, chap. 55.

29 Woodberry, "A Global Perspective," 12–13.

30 Information based on the author's personal conversations with Higgins and Woodberry regarding their research.

Letter from a Jesus Muslim to Christians[*]

Warm greetings to you, my brothers and sisters who have made Isa your Lord.

Brothers and sisters, I am a Muslim who has made *Isa Alaihi Salam* [Jesus, peace be upon him] my personal Lord and Savior. I know that some of you may find it strange to hear that I, a Muslim, confess Isa as my Lord and Savior. I called on Isa to save me for two reasons: The first was a realization that I am a sinner and that I am incapable of making it to heaven based upon my own merit and effort. The second is that I believe that the *Tawrat, Zabur,* and *Injil* are truly the word of Allah.

I realize that between us there are differences in ethnic background, the color of our skin, the way we worship, or even in some points of theology; however, let us strive for unity in our diversity, a unity that is based on our common place as members of the body of al-Masih. Isa has made us of one faith (Eph 2:11–22), even if we are a part of two different religious communities and cultures.

Brothers and sisters, my hope is that you can receive me as a brother as I have received you as mine. Perhaps we will never meet here before we meet in heaven, but let us remember each other in prayer. My prayer is that *Allah Subhana Wa Ta'ala* [God, may he be glorified and exalted] will pour out his grace on us so that we will never become tired of showing love toward those who do not yet know Allah or know Isa as their personal Savior and Lord. *Amin* [Amen].

—*Ahmad Abdul-Rashid*

---

[*] This letter was presented in a plenary session of the Global Trends and Fruitful Practices Consultation, Thailand, 2007. The author, Ahmad Abdul-Rashid, is a Muslim follower of Jesus from Southeast Asia. Translated by John Travis and printed here by permission of the author.

---

in this study were grouped into three categories—affective, cognitive, and behavioral—in order to reflect these three dimensions of the new believers' faith in Christ. In response to questions dealing with the affective (feeling/emotions) and behavioral (actions/habits) dimensions, the Muslim followers of Christ reflected a very biblical, Jesus-centered life. In response to some of the cognitive (propositional) dimension questions, however, some of those interviewed gave answers differing from typical Christian understandings. Higgins points out that in this movement, behaviors and allegiance to Jesus have preceded the ability to express some aspects of belief in the cognitive, propositional categories that theologians often emphasize. Three important points are brought out by this study. First, the allegiance of one's heart and subsequent demonstrated behavior may be a very valid way to understand the direction and maturity of a movement to Christ. Second, in Christward movements, people may come to faith and wholeheartedly follow Jesus with only a minimal amount of biblical knowledge at first. Third, the ability to state propositional, theological truths may not be a good indicator of a movement's true spiritual condition. We now turn to one such emerging Asian movement among Muslims.

A Recent Case Study of an Emerging Insider Movement in Asia

For more than twenty years my family and I have had the privilege of living in two different Asian Muslim neighborhoods. In the last number of years we have watched the emergence of a small yet growing insider movement that began in the community where we lived and has spread to several sur-rounding towns and villages.

This movement began with just a handful of men and women. The human agent most active in the initial stages is a jovial Muslim woman whom we will call "Anisa." Previously, over a ten-year period of time, she read the New Testament weekly with a Christian and privately on her own. During this time, God miraculously healed one of her relatives when Christians prayed for him. She felt drawn to Jesus but thought this was improper for her as a Muslim. One day a Christian she happened to meet told her that salvation comes through faith in Jesus alone and not through religious affiliation. That very day, as a Muslim, she felt free to pledge her allegiance to Christ without an added requirement of leaving the religious community of her birth.[31] During the five years following her decision, she regularly at-tended a small gathering of Muslims who also had found Christ (the group was started by an expatriate Asian). Then came a change in jobs and a new circle of acquaintances; Anisa sensed God was going to do something new. In a matter of months, her new acquaintances became dear friends and fellow Muslim followers of Christ. Shortly thereafter, her husband, children, extended family, and finally some neighbors came to faith. Simple fellowships like the one Anisa had attended were started, and the gospel spread to several outlying areas, continuing on to other towns.

The home fellowships in this small movement include men, women, and children. Most are from a lower middle-class background. The gospel is spreading through family networks, similar to what Mc-Gavran referred to as "bridges." Some members of these groups had been previously witnessed to and prayed for by Christians, but it seems their final decision to make Jesus their Lord and join an *ekklesia*[32] came about only after a fellow Muslim shared the gospel with them. The group meetings, which I do not attend but hear about regularly, are quite simple. They meet weekly at a set time and are led by a group leader. They pray for the guidance of the Holy Spirit to help them understand the Scriptures, then study at least one chapter from the *Injil*. They use a translation produced specifically for Muslim readers. After the passage is read and discussed, they decide as a group how to apply it in their lives. They then pray for each other, have a simple snack, and go home. Among the believers that my wife and I know personally, we observe that they admit sin to each other and turn from it, forgive each other, pray for the sick in Jesus' name, read Scripture regularly with their families, and routinely share Christ with their neighbors and relatives. Out of their own meager salaries, they help each other and the poor in their neighborhoods as well. As new groups develop, they are led by the believer who started the group, who then later appoints an assistant. The evidence of the grace of God is obvious.

Not many years after the movement began, Anisa's husband shared his new faith in Jesus with a Muslim teacher who works in their neighborhood. That teacher is now sharing Christ with his stu-dents in his small Islamic boarding school, and gives copies of the *Injil* to his older students. They, in turn, have started to share what they are learning with families in their hometowns. A second Muslim teacher has come to faith as well.

---

31 For Anisa, her ethnicity, culture, and religion are fused, reflecting what Martin Goldsmith observed while working in Muslim lands: "Islam is within the whole warp and woof of society—in the family, in politics, in social relationships. To leave the Muslim faith is to break with one's society. Many a modern, educated Muslim is not all that religiously minded; but he must, nevertheless, remain a Muslim for social reasons. . . . This makes it almost unthinkable for most Muslims even to consider the possibility of becoming a follower of some other religion." Goldsmith, "Community and Controversy: Key Causes of Muslim Resistance," *Missiology* 4, no. 3 (1976): 318.

32 When I use the word *ekklesia* I am referring to a local body of believers in Christ. I refrain from using the word "church" because of the foreign or Western traditions often associated with this term.

The Muslim followers of Christ in these groups are bold in their witness. Most witnessing and forming of new groups occurs through family networks, yet many neighbors and other acquaintances are also hearing the good news. The new followers of Jesus, like Jesus followers anywhere, experience the normal challenges of living out their new faith in Jesus—forgiving enemies, dealing with the flesh, taking on the disciplines of Bible study and personal prayer—yet up to this point, this emerging movement has not faced any serious threat to its existence. A major challenge, however, has been in seeing members set free from some entrenched occult folk practices. In spite of challenges, by the grace of God this movement is consistently growing in size and spiritual maturity.

Dynamics Observed in Several Asian Insider Movements

Movements similar to the one I have just described are happening in a number of Asian settings. I have studied the dynamics of several of these insider movements. Dynamics vary from place to place, depending upon nationality, ethnicity, and culture. Some movements involve primarily men, others primarily women; some are rural, others urban; some have good leaders, while others have suffered through poor leadership. Some have gone through times of intense persecution from fellow Muslims, while others have faced interference from local Christians. In spite of the differences, however, I have observed a number of dynamics that seem to be true in the lives of most of the Asian Muslim followers of Jesus in these movements:

- Having a strong desire to share Jesus with family and other fellow Muslims who do not yet know Christ.
- Seeing themselves as a unique type of Muslim due to their relationship with Jesus as Lord and Savior. (However, this does not mean they necessarily refer to themselves as anything other than "Muslim.")
- Remaining within their family and social networks, they regularly gather to pray, study the Bible, and have fellowship as biblical *ekklesiae* in culturally appropriate ways.
- Developing a biblical worldview and theology based on the leading of the Spirit and group Bible study, causing them to retain, reject, or reinterpret various beliefs and practices,[33] opening the way for participation in the cultural and socioreligious life of their Muslim community in ways that do not violate their conscience, contradict the Bible, or displease God.[34]
- Creating ways to explain their biblical faith to fellow Muslims through the use of Islamic categories, forms, and themes.[35]

---

33 For example, these Muslims who follow Jesus *reject* the Muslim teaching that Isa did not die on the cross. They *retain* the Ramadan fast yet also *reinterpret* it in some ways. We have heard comments like "I used to fast during Ramadan in hopes of having my sins forgiven. But now that Isa has forgiven my sins, I keep the fast to draw near to God and pray for my family and community who do not yet know Isa."

34 Woodberry and others have pointed out that a myriad of Islamic practices, such as fasting, giving alms, regular daily prayers, prayer forms, head coverings for women, and religious terminology, were borrowed from the observed practices of the Jews and Christians in the Middle East in the time of Muhammad; see Woodberry in *UIM,* chap. 45. If seen through the lens of the Bible, much of the cultural and socioreligious life of Muslims has biblical or historical precedent and could potentially be maintained.

35 In the Asian movement described above involving Anisa, Jesus followers often ask their friends and neighbors how many of the four holy books (*Tawrat, Zabur, Injil,* and Qur'an) they have read. They also ask how many lives of the prophets they have studied. The notion of four holy books and numerous prophets of God is firmly

- Among the first few Jesus followers, being discipled by believers from outside the community, with subsequent generations of believers discipled by the insiders themselves.
- Experiencing the grace of God through transformed lives, restored relationships, and a deep inner peace, as well divine dreams, healing, and deliverance from demons.
- Understanding they have a spiritual unity with all others who call on God through the Lord Jesus, regardless of race, ethnicity, or religious affiliation.

Summary

Over the past few decades the Lord has ushered many tens of thousands of Muslims into his kingdom, not just in Asia, but throughout the Muslim world. In some places, these believers represent the first known followers of Jesus in history from their particular people group. These movements have happened in a variety of ways involving divine intervention, the actions of God's people, and certain world events. There is no one single ministry or methodology that can account for these breakthroughs.

This chapter has focused on Jesus movements, or insider movements, with special emphasis on movements in Asia. We rejoice that many Muslims are finding salvation and new life in Jesus, oftentimes with very little socioreligious dislocation. Yet we must keep in mind the big picture: the task of sharing the love and message of Isa al-Masih both in Asia and the entire Muslim world is only beginning. May God guide us in our prayers and actions for the millions of Muslims who do not yet know the risen Jesus.

Bibliography

Anderson, John D. C. "The Missionary Approach to Islam: Christian or 'Cultic.'" *Missiology: An International Review* 4, no. 3 (1976): 258–99.

Garrison, David. *Church Planting Movements: How God Is Redeeming a Lost World.* Monument, CO: WIGTake, 2004.

Goldsmith, Martin. "Community and Controversy: Key Causes of Muslim Resistance." *Missiology: An International Review* 4, no. 3 (1976): 317–23.

Kraft, Charles H. "What Kind of Encounters Do We Need in Our Christian Witness?" *Evangelical Missions Quarterly* 27, no. 3 (1991): 258–65.

Love, Rick. *Muslims, Magic and the Kingdom of God: Church Planting among Folk Muslims.* Pasadena, CA: William Carey Library, 2003.

McGavran, Donald. *The Bridges of God.* London: World Dominion, 1955.

Parshall, Phil. *Beyond the Mosque: Christians in Muslim Community.* Grand Rapids, MI: Baker, 1985.

Sinclair, Daniel. *A Vision of the Possible: Pioneer Church Planting in Teams.* Waynesboro, GA: Authentic, 2006.

Travis, John. "Producing and Using Meaningful Translations of the Taurat, Zabur and Injil." *International Journal of Frontier Missions* 23, no. 2 (2006): 73–77.

———. "The C1–C6 Spectrum: A Practical Tool for Defining Six Types of 'Christ-Centered Communities' ('C') Found in the Muslim Context." *Evangelical Missions Quarterly* 34, no. 3 (1998), 411–15.

---

rooted in Muslim theology. By asking these two questions, they are able to invite those who are open to study Scripture with them.

Travis, John, and Anna Travis. "Deep-level Healing Prayer in Cross-cultural Ministry: Models, Examples, and Lessons." In *Paradigm Shifts in Christian Witness: Insights from Anthropology, Communication, and Spiritual Power,* edited by Charles Van Engen, Darrell Whiteman, and J. Dudley Woodberry, 106–15. Maryknoll, NY: Orbis, 2008.

———, with contributions by Phil Parshall. "Factors Affecting the Identity That Jesus-followers Choose." In *From Seed to Fruit: Global Trends, Fruitful Practices, and Emerging Issues among Muslims,* edited by J. Dudley Woodberry, 193–205. Pasadena, CA: William Carey Library, 2008.

Wilder, John W. "Some Reflections on Possibilities for People Movements among Muslims." *Missiology: An International Review* 5, no. 3 (1977): 302–20.

Woodberry, J. Dudley. "A Global Perspective on Muslims Coming to Faith in Christ." In *From the Straight Path to the Narrow Way: Journeys of Faith,* edited by David H. Greenlee, 11–22. Downers Grove, IL: InterVarsity Press, 2006.

———. "Contextualization among Muslims: Reusing Common Pillars." *International Journal of Frontier Missions* 13, no. 4 (1996): 171–86.

———. *Muslims and Christians on the Emmaus Road: Crucial Issues in Witness among Muslims.* Monrovia, CA: MARC, 1989.

———. "The Relevance of Power Ministries for Folk Muslims." In *Wrestling with Dark Angels,* edited by C. Peter Wagner and F. Douglas Pennoyer, 313–31. Ventura, CA: Regal, 1990.

———. "To the Muslim I Became a Muslim?" *International Journal of Frontier Missiology* 24, no. 1 (2007): 23–28.

Woodberry, J. Dudley, Russell G. Shubin, and G. Marks. "Why Muslims Follow Jesus: The Results of a Recent Survey of Converts from Islam." *Christianity Today,* October 2007.

CHAPTER 17

Pandita Ramabai and the Meanings of Conversion*

H. L. Richard

Pandita Ramabai (1868–1922) was one of the first modern women to learn Sanskrit. She was also a renowned social reformer whose conversion to Christianity shook late colonial India. Her testimony, especially as she herself wrote and published it (originally in 1907), is one of the most famous conversion stories from India. This chapter will briefly tell Ramabai's story and then consider some of the theological, missiological, and legal complexities related to her conversion and to conversion in India in general.

Ramabai's father, Anant Shastri Dongre, was a Brahman who defied convention by teaching the Sanskrit language to his wife and daughter. From her parents Ramabai learned only the later Hindu texts, the Puranas, as the sacred Vedas were not made accessible to women—even by her father. Thorough knowledge of the Bhagavata Purana earned Ramabai the titles of *Pandita* ("learned woman") and *Saraswati* (name of the goddess of learning) from the pandits of Calcutta in 1878.

Ramabai's father went out on pilgrimage with his family and served as a reciter of sacred texts, especially the Puranas. But itinerant life was hard, and Ramabai's father refused to beg. In the great South Indian famine of 1874 Ramabai lost both her parents and a sister, and her surviving brother and she lost much faith in the Hindu gods. Ramabai was thus prepared for the reformist version of Hinduism, the Brahmo Samaj of Calcutta, which encouraged her to study the Vedas and supported her marriage to a non-Brahman man.

From the Brahmo Samaj the Pandita adopted a rationalistic faith that would later complicate her conversion to Christianity. From her husband's library she first read a Gospel of Luke, and she also got to know a Baptist missionary friend of his. But Ramabai's life in Calcutta fell apart with the deaths of her brother and husband, leaving her with only her daughter, Manoramabai.

In the turmoil of life as a widow, Ramabai returned to her home language area and began a home for child widows in Pune.[1] Here Ramabai began a more serious study of the Bible and befriended both

---

* This chapter and the next were written by H. L. Richard. The central character in this first case study, Pandita Ramabai, does not completely typify an insider believer as discussed elsewhere in this volume, yet her case illustrates the complex aspects of "conversion" underlying insider movements, including the interrelations between changes of religion, culture, church as an institution, church as a community of believers, sociological community, and the soul. Initially Ramabai converted to the Christian religion and the Christian social community but not to Christ. Later, after having gained Christ, she rejected many religious and cultural elements of what we deem to be Hinduism, yet she could still be regarded as authentically Hindu. This introduction to the complexity of conversion dynamics in India prepares us for Richard's second article, which shows why insider phenomena are so abundant in India.—Ed.

1 Girls were generally married before puberty—another area where Ramabai's father defied tradition. Often marriages were between children five years old or younger, and when the child husband died the child widow was forbidden to remarry and became a burden on her parental household.

reformist Hindus and Christians. She decided to go to England and train to be a medical doctor, a vision that failed to come to fulfilment due to a hearing impediment that worsened during her time in England.

The Community of St. Mary the Virgin, an Anglo-Catholic sisterhood, welcomed Ramabai into their midst in England. Under their auspices she became acquainted with relief work aimed at destitute women, and became convinced that Christianity as a religion had a nobler perspective on women than anything she had found in Hinduism. She was baptized as a Christian on September 29, 1883, just five months after arriving in England.

Ramabai herself later described what she considered to be the difference between this conversion to Christianity and a later conversion of heart: "I came to know after eight years from the time of my baptism that I had found the Christian *religion*, which was good enough for me; *but I had not found Christ, Who is the Life of the religion*, and '. . . the true Light which lighteth every man that cometh into the world.' 1 John 1:9."[2]

Tensions arose between Ramabai and her Anglican mentors. The rationalistic faith she had imbibed from the Brahmo Samaj caused her to struggle with the doctrine of the Trinity. Another struggle related to controversy over the suitability of Ramabai to teach Sanskrit in England; she was certainly capable, but was forbidden by church authorities who deemed it unsuitable for a young Indian woman to teach Englishmen. As Susanne Glover writes in her excellent study of Ramabai's conversions, "Ramabai's failure to accept the authority of the Church in all matters of faith and doctrine appeared to the Community [of St. Mary the Virgin] to be an act of rebellion against God and a denial of her baptismal vows."[3]

Ramabai interpreted her baptism in a broad sense, not as a joining of the Anglican Church, and she parted ways with the Anglicans in favor of Free Church teachings on the freedom of the conscience and the priesthood of all believers. Disputes among various factions of Christians troubled Ramabai, and after returning to India and renewing her work among widows she faced strong opposition, even from some who had previously supported her. It was related to this context in 1891 that she later declared, "One thing I knew by this time was that I needed Christ and not merely His religion."[4]

Ramabai had come across a Holiness book by William Haslam entitled *From Death unto Life,* and saw in the author's journey from Anglicanism to deeply experiential faith in the Holiness tradition a picture of her own situation and need. Later, hearing teaching from George Pentecost, she entered into a deeper Christian experience on November 11, 1891. Ramabai later "disputed Pentecost's claim that she had been 'sensationally' converted under his ministry."[5] But this was part of her finding Christ and not merely the religion of Christ.

Related to this new experience of Christ, Ramabai became an evangelist. She changed her ministry from its prior social emphasis to a particularly Christian focus. Ramabai also embraced the doctrines of evangelical Christianity, and wrote that "the most precious truth which I have learned since my conver-

---

2   Pandita Ramabai, *A Testimony of Our Inexhaustible Treasure,* 11th ed. (Kedgaon, Maharashtra, India: Pandita Ramabai Mukti Mission, 1992 [1907]), 27–28; emphasis in the original.

3   Susanne Lae Glover, "Of Water and of the Spirit: The Baptism of Pandita Ramabai Saraswati; A Study in Religious Conversion" (PhD diss., University of Sydney, 1995), 127.

4   Ramabai, *A Testimony,* 29.

5   Glover, "Of Water," 296.

sion is the second coming of the Lord Jesus Christ."[6] The story of Hudson Taylor and the China Inland Mission inspired her to run her ministry as a faith mission, making no public appeals for funds. During another great Indian famine in 1896–97, Ramabai expanded her work to take in hundreds of orphans.

Ramabai's new faith mission was called Mukti, which means "salvation," and it continues to this day. In 1905 revival broke out at Mukti Mission, with Pentecostal manifestations being the most controversial aspect of a controversial spiritual awakening. Ramabai never embraced or promoted any of the particular schools of Holiness or Pentecostal thought. She clearly supported the revival at Mukti and saw much fruit from it. In her own words, "The results of this have been most satisfactory. Many hundreds of our girls and some of our boys have been gloriously saved, and many of them are serving God and witnessing for Christ at home and in other places."[7]

Related to her newfound spirituality and theology, Ramabai decided that a better Marathi Bible translation was needed. She proceeded to learn Greek and Hebrew and produce her own translation. This work dominated the final two decades of her life. Sadly, her Bible translation principles were faulty. Ramabai had become reactionary against her Sanskrit heritage, even forbidding her daughter Manoramabai from learning the language.[8] Thus she wanted to remove Sanskritic terms from her translation, which could only impoverish her work.[9]

Related to her Holiness experiences, Ramabai embraced divine healing and downplayed medicine. She refused medical treatment for a prolonged struggle with influenza from 1918 and for the septic bronchitis that led to her death in 1922.[10] Yet Ramabai had not become a fundamentalist. She retained a lifestyle in continuity with her Hindu heritage, including strict vegetarianism. She was unhappy with Westernization in Indian Christianity and published a book of contextual songs (*bhajans*).

In a paper looking at the religiocultural rapprochement developed by five Hindus who became followers of Jesus, I consider Ramabai to have been "living with the tension of conflicting heritages."[11] Susanne Glover sees great continuity between the Vaishnava devotionalism of Ramabai's childhood and the Holiness brand of Christianity that finally satisfied her spiritual quest,[12] and also suggests that Ramabai remained greatly respectful towards her father and sought to fulfill his life vision.[13]

Ramabai's story thus illustrates many complexities involved in conversion. Her initial conversion was later self-defined as primarily a change of religion. The encounter between India and Europe in the colonial era, and particularly the definitions of "religion" and "conversion" that developed, lie behind this interpretation. British colonial law initially favored the rights of a convert from Hinduism to Christianity to maintain his or her place in Hindu society, but later shifted to an emphasis on the discontinuity between Hinduism and Christianity. Chandra Mallampalli spells this out.

---

6   Ramabai, *A Testimony*, 43.

7   Ibid., 42.

8   Glover, "Of Water," 317.

9   See S. M. Adhav, *Pandita Ramabai*, Confessing the Faith in India 13 (Madras: Christian Literature Society, 1979), 196–215.

10   Glover, "Of Water," 321.

11   H. L. Richard, "The Church and the Hindu Heritage: Historical Case Studies in a Rocky Relationship," in *Rethinking Hindu Ministry: Papers from the Rethinking Forum*, ed. H. L. Richard (Pasadena, CA: William Carey Library, 2011), 72.

12   Glover, "Of Water," 301–13.

13   Ibid., 39, 48, 256, 302.

Officials of the British Raj adopted two policies toward "Native Christians." One policy sought to preserve the civil rights of converts by treating them, for all practical purposes, as if they still belonged to their Hindu families. The Caste Disabilities Removal Act (XXI of 1850), also known as the Lex Loci Act, was designed to protect the civil rights of persons who had changed their religion or, for any other reason, had "lost caste." The second policy comes later and was radically different. It sought to stabilize the "Christian community" by defining it in terms of personal laws that were distinct from Hindu and Muslim personal laws. Modeled on English laws, the Indian Succession Act (X of 1865) and the Indian Christian Marriage Act (XV of 1872) served to reify Indian Christians as an alien community.[14]

By this legislation "change of religion" also came to mean "change of sociological community." This remains a fundamental issue in India today. Hans Staffner points out that "there is also little doubt that the real reason why the Hindu community is so strongly opposed to conversion is not that they think it harmful if some of their members choose to live in the spirit of Christ, but because baptism involves a change of one's social community."[15] Staffner goes on to propose that Indian Christians should appeal to be brought under the Hindu Succession Act of 1956, citing the study *Christian Law in India* by E. D. Devadason, who considers this more modern law simply better than the 1865 Act.[16]

Conversion in India continues to be mainly understood in terms of "change of religion" and "change of community." Julian Saldanha has also written on this reality:

A Hindu who professes the Christian faith ceases generally to be a member of his social group and family. This fact is forcefully brought home to him through various provisions of Hindu personal laws. . . . He is faced with the dilemma of choosing between loyalty to Christ and to his family. In order to overcome this dilemma it is necessary to ensure that converts remain fully integrated within their traditional community, notwithstanding their open profession of faith in Christ.[17]

Ramabai's story points to a more biblical understanding of "conversion" as "change of heart." Her personal transformation happened many years after her change of religion and change of community, and really was not related to that formal "conversion." Different terminologies urgently need to be developed for these different aspects of "conversion."

---

14   Chandra Mallampalli, *Christians and Public Life in Colonial South India, 1863–1937: Contending with Marginality* (New York: RoutledgeCurzon, 2004), 196–97. Mallampalli seems to read a measure of malice in some later judicial application of this Succession Act, writing, "The [Madras] judiciary found in the Indian Succession Act of 1865 a means to further reify a 'Christian community' so that it was further removed from the inner workings of Hindu society" (50).

15   Staffner, *Jesus Christ and the Hindu Community: Is a Synthesis of Hinduism and Christianity Possible?* (Anand, Gujarat, India: Gujarat Sahitya Prakash, 1988), 242.

16   Ibid., 243.

17   Saldanha, *Conversion and Indian Civil Law* (Bangalore: Theological Publications in India, 1981), 138.

Cultural change, or cultural "conversion," is another important aspect of this discussion. Ramabai, as noted above, was conflicted in this area, maintaining her vegetarian diet while lambasting the Sanskrit language. Nicol Macnicol, in his biography of Ramabai, suggested that greater continuity with Hindu traditions was present in her life than even she recognized.

> The spirit of bhakti at its purest and highest is in no wise alien to the spirit of Christian loyalty and devotion, and Ramabai, we cannot doubt, took over more than she was aware of from the long line of Hindu saints and seekers, and carried it with her into the Christian faith that seemed to her so different and so new.[18]

In this light, Macnicol celebrated Ramabai as truly Hindu despite her devotion to Christ.

> In spite of the fact that she rejected peremptorily so much that we call Hindu, it was as what we must call a Hindu woman that she so charmed and subdued. Her soul was in its texture Indian and in her we see what such a soul may be under the control of Christ. The instinct of India, in spite of so much alienation and so much calumny, recognized with pride this kinship and, when she died, in many of the cities of the land people gathered to honour one who by her life had brought honour to her race. In Bombay at a public memorial meeting Mrs. Sarojini Naidu . . . laid claim to her in behalf of Hinduism as "the first Christian to be enrolled in the calendar of Hindu saints."[19]

From the postcolonial world of the twenty-first century it is easy to see the limitations of various constructs and definitions of the colonial era. Developing more adequate paradigms, and seeing those better constructs adopted and applied, remains a challenge. Understanding "conversion" is a vital case in point, and the story of Pandita Ramabai illustrates its complexity and importance.

Bibliography

Adhav, S. M. *Pandita Ramabai.* Confessing the Faith in India 13. Madras: Christian Literature Society, 1979.

Glover, Susanne Lae. "Of Water and of the Spirit: The Baptism of Pandita Ramabai Saraswati; A Study in Religious Conversion." PhD diss., University of Sydney, 1995. Available online at http://ses. library.usyd.edu.au/handle/2123/1954.

Macnicol, Nicol. *Pandita Ramabai.* Builders of Modern India. London: Student Christian Movement, 1926.

Mallampalli, Chandra. *Christians and Public Life in Colonial South India, 1863–1937: Contending with Marginality.* New York and London: RoutledgeCurzon, 2004.

Ramabai, Pandita. *A Testimony of Our Inexhaustible Treasure.* 11th ed. Kedgaon, Maharashtra, India: Pandita Ramabai Mukti Mission, 1992 [1907].

---

18 Nicol Macnicol, *Pandita Ramabai,* Builders of Modern India (London: Student Christian Movement, 1926), 4.

19 Ibid., 140.

Richard, H. L. "The Church and the Hindu Heritage: Historical Case Studies in a Rocky Relationship." In *Rethinking Hindu Ministry: Papers from the Rethinking Forum,* edited by H. L. Richard, 61–74. Pasadena, CA: William Carey Library, 2011.

Saldanha, Julian. *Conversion and Indian Civil Law.* Bangalore: Theological Publications in India, 1981.

Staffner, Hans. *Jesus Christ and the Hindu Community: Is a Synthesis of Hinduism and Christianity Possible?* Anand, Gujarat, India: Gujarat Sahitya Prakash, 1988.

CHAPTER 18

Christ Followers in India Flourishing— but Outside the Church

A Review of Herbert E. Hoefer's Churchless Christianity*

H. L. Richard

In striking research begun in 1980 and first published in 1991, Herbert E. Hoefer found that the people of Madras City are far closer to historic Christianity than the populace of any cities in the Western Christian world could ever claim to be. Yet these are not Christians, but rather Hindus and Muslims. In their midst is a significant number of true believers in Christ who openly confess to faith in fundamental biblical doctrines yet remain outside the institutional church. It was the locating and understanding of these that especially motivated Hoefer's research.

Fundamental questions on the nature of Christianity and the church are raised by this study. The colonial legacy of Christianity as a foreign religion is taken seriously, and steps toward transcending the constrictions of this heritage are suggested. Dr. Herbert Hoefer, author of *Churchless Christianity*, knows he is treading new ground, and so is careful to document his facts and conclusions while allowing that his views are far from definitive, but rather only exploratory.

A Brief Background

In October of 1980 Hoefer surveyed pastors in three Lutheran as well as five Church of South India dioceses regarding their knowledge of unbaptized believers in Christ. That study identified 246 believers, more than eighty of whom Hoefer proceeded to personally contact. Though these people were traditionally thought of as "secret believers," Hoefer notes that just 6 percent of the pastors queried indicated that they felt the people were denying Christ by not taking baptism. "In most cases the pastors also reported that the non-baptized believer welcomes him and other church workers to his/her home. Their faith in Christ is public, and their relation to the church is as close as possible."[1]

It is important to note that throughout his study Hoefer is careful to maintain a high definition of what constitutes a believer in Christ. He describes a meeting with some Hindu families who had a high view of Christ (as an *avatar*, but not sinless), and pride in their stand for religious harmony and learning from the best in all religions. He comments:

> Such people—who are, of course, very numerous—I do not classify as non-baptized believers in Christ. They have neither orthodox belief nor devoted practice which is expected of a follower of Christ. Jesus has no special place in their spiritual life, and they have made no break with their Hindu pattern of worship.[2]

---

* Originally published in a slightly different form in *MF*, December 2001. Reprinted by permission.

1 Herbert Hoefer, *Churchless Christianity* (Pasadena, CA: William Carey Library, 2001), xvi.

2 Ibid., 11.

It is demonstrated that low-caste unbaptized believers are often outside the church due to political and economic pressure. The church is composed, largely, of lower-caste people, and cultural change in joining the church is, for them, minimized. The largest problem in embracing Christianity and the church for these low-caste people is the loss of government benefits involved in any legal change from Hindu to Christian religion. For the high-caste non-baptized believer in Christ (NBBC), however, the issue is social. His family and social group are far removed culturally from "Christian" society, and cannot understand conversion in anything but sociological terms. Hoefer summarizes the impossible predicament of the high-caste NBBC by pointing out:

> We cannot ignore the *close association in Indian tradition between religion and culture.* The NBBC is caught in a predicament where he wants to distinguish between these two in his life, whereas neither most of his Hindu kinsmen nor most of his Christian co-believers are able to. The common Protestant reaction to the close association of Indian culture with Hindu religion has been to develop a separate culture for the new religion: differences in devotions, festivals, names, appearance, lifestyle, worship, gestures, etc. If you are to join this religion, you must get accustomed to its culture. . . . This is the basis for all the accusations about a "forsaking religion" and a forsaking of the family heritage. . . .
>
> The NBBC is *trying to change religion without changing culture,* even to the extent of asserting that he's not really changing religion at all. . . . Unfortunately, he suffers from suspicion and rejection on the part of *both Hindu kinsmen and Christian co-believers.* Even if one is baptized, but does not participate in the mores of the Christian "culture," he will not be accepted. Sometimes the only way he can assert his cultural identity is by keeping aloof from the Christian community—which doesn't really know what to do with him anyway. . . . The consequence of this strategic aloofness is that the Christian community can then self-righteously judge the genuineness of his faith, and the NBBC ends up even more isolated and deprived spiritually.[3]

Hoefer is rightly sympathetic to people in this situation, and demonstrates that their religious activity, while centered on Christ, often follows a Hindu rather than traditionally Christian pattern. That is, the church building is used like a temple for occasional visits when the need is felt; a picture of Christ is central to their devotion; they attend large Christian conventions rather on the pattern of taking a pilgrimage; and they follow an *ishta devata* theology of Jesus as a personal, chosen deity among many gods, if not in abstract theology, at least in practice in their highly pressurized situations. Interestingly, Hoefer comments that "these spiritual seekers are on the Indian quest for 'shanti' [peace], and they have found it in Christ. They are still Indians, they haven't yet become Protestants."[4] His highly appreciative closing summary must be quoted in full:

---

3   Ibid., 51–52; emphasis in the original.
4   Ibid., 61.

The general portrait of the non-baptized believer in Christ in rural Tamil Nadu, no matter from what background he may come, is an encouraging one. He is a thoughtful and sincere person who takes his spiritual life seriously. He responds with gratitude and faithfulness when he has reached conviction about the love and power of Christ. Most often this conviction comes in some experience of healing, but it also often derives from the experience in a Christian school. The strength of his relationship to the church depends on whether the local congregation is of his own caste background or not. He clearly needs this relationship because of the financial, social and spiritual problems he faces. In spite of all these problems, however, he/she presents us with a clear Indian experience of Christ as the fulfillment of the traditional spiritual quest for peace of mind and a clean heart. The non-baptized believer of rural Tamil Nadu is an admirable person. Thanks be to God.[5]

Having become convinced of the quality of faith of the NBBCs, Hoefer sought a way to gauge their quantity. A survey of Madras City was the simplest way to get solid data on this, and had the advantage of providing an urban counterpart to the less scientific rural study. As the Department of Statistics at Madras Christian College had previously done political surveys, it was equipped for a broad-based analysis. Hoefer explains:

We decided to broaden the Madras City study in order to give us an idea of the place of Jesus Christ in the faith and practice of the whole population, not only the NBBCs. For our theological understanding and practical planning it is important to know the general background of which the non-baptized believer is a particular phenomenon. The questionnaire was designed in order to give us a clear idea of how Hindus and Muslims are already related to Christ and how we might best reach them.[6]

No unbaptized believers were identified among the Muslim sample population. But "our primary problem seems to be lack of effort rather than lack of results. Once again, the sociological differences between the Christian and the Muslim community are the major barrier."[7] Among the Hindu population the results were striking indeed. "In Madras City our regular church ministries are reaching primarily twelve percent of the population, the Harijan community," he notes.[8] Yet Hoefer found the

---

5   Ibid., 63.

6   Ibid., 69.

7   Ibid., 97.

8   Ibid., 93. Terminology related to caste is almost as controversial as caste itself. Hoefer at one point is careful to point out that by speaking of "high" caste he is merely using traditional terminology and does not at all accept that there are higher and lower people. His chosen term for what are traditionally called "outcastes" (or Pariahs, *panchamas,* or Scheduled Castes) is the Gandhi-coined term *Harijan,* meaning "people of God." This is now for many as unacceptable a term as those previously mentioned, as it is considered condescending. The politically correct term of the hour is *Dalit,* which means "the oppressed."

number of high-caste Hindus who worship Christ equal to the entire Protestant population of Madras! It must be noted again that Hoefer employed a high definition for an NBBC. He points out that

> even if we take the "hard-core" figures of those who worship only Jesus, in terms of numbers the Hindu Harijan worshippers are only one-half of the total [NBBCs]. . . . There are as many Protestants wholly devoted to the worship of Christ as there are people of all castes outside the church. The "churchless Christianity" is a diverse group but certainly united in firm devotion to Christ under most difficult circumstances.[9]

Sorting It Out

"What does all this mean?" asks Hoefer as he begins his final section evaluating all the data. He again carefully warns against taking his suggestions as anything more than tentative. God has done an unexpected work, and we must continue to observe and learn from it. The primary point, without which all discussion of the subject will be misdirected, is to see that the "problem" of these believers staying outside the church has nothing to do with theology but rather with sociology. As Hoefer says, "The issue is the sociological distortion of theology in practice. . . . If baptism and the church were carried out in practice as our theology conceives them, there would be no problem and there would be no non-baptized believers."

> It is clear, furthermore, that the communalized nature of the church exists quite apart from baptism. Even among the non-sacramental churches where baptism is considered unnecessary (as among the Salvation Army) or merely symbolic (as among the Baptists) the church is just as exclusively communal as among those churches who emphasize the necessity of baptism. . . . The character of the church is formed by the structure of the society irrespective of the theology or practice of baptism.[10]
>
> Therefore, the primary questions raised for us by the phenomenon of non-baptized believers in Christ around us are not about their authenticity but about ours. The questions are about our recognition of sociological realities in ecclesiastical structures and mission planning. The questions are about developing a style of church fellowship and ministry which make the call of Christ and gift of His Spirit available to all in the fullest possible freedom and power.[11]

---

9   Ibid., 96.

10   It seems strange that in his long and helpful discussion of baptism Hoefer never refers to the complex legal issues involved therein, which most strikingly demonstrate that the baptism of non-Christians in India involves decidedly extrabiblical (if not antibiblical) elements. On this see Julian Saldanha, *Conversion and Indian Civil Law* (Bangalore: Theological Publications in India, 1981). Further, Hoefer makes no concrete suggestions on the line of reconceptualizing baptism in terms of the initiatory rites (often involving water) of numerous schools and sects of Hinduism. Omitting these rather obvious points is the only major flaw in his study.

11   Ibid., 146. Hoefer's study is deeply instructive for issues all across India, but is very Tamil specific in its findings. The "Churchless Christian" phenomena seem far stronger in the Tamil world than in the other major linguistic regions of India.

In the final chapter Hoefer considers implications for the future. New structures are needed as well as new missiological insight. This is especially imperative in light of the irrelevance of present Christian activity:

> It will be important for the church to share its inner experience and "mysteries" in a manner which is acceptable to those it seeks to reach. Most of the eighty percent of India around us feel no need for what we have to offer. They are quite proud of their own spiritual heritage, even if they have never drawn upon it seriously themselves. . . .[12]
>
> At issue there is really a matter of fundamental mentality, not merely a change of candles to oil lamps. . . .
>
> . . . Can Christianity really be absorbed into this totally different religio-cultural environment?
>
> Certainly, it cannot be done by the church, but it has already begun among the non-baptized believers as we have seen in our survey. . . . Christianity grew out of Judaism because Christ was incarnated there. However, when He is "grafted into" a totally new tree, we must only expect a new hybrid, a Church of Gentile customs and a theology of Gnostic and mystical ideas. Only then will Christ "of whom and to whom and through whom are all things," be "all in all" among the varying cultures of the world (Rom. 11:20–24, 36). . . .
>
> However, some might argue that this [the "smothering embrace of Hinduism"] is the danger with the "ishta devata" strategy I am proposing. It will lead not to an indigenous Christianity but to a Christianized Hinduism. Perhaps more accurately we should say a "Christ-ized Hinduism." I would suggest that really both are the same, and therefore we should not worry about it. We do not want to change the culture or the religious genius of India. We simply want to bring Christ and His Gospel into the center of it.
>
> . . . The real move toward an indigenous Christian faith can never come from the Christian community. It must grow out of the "churchless Christianity," with the help and encouragement of the church.[13]

One leaves Hoefer rather gasping for breath as his vision stretches so far beyond our normal parameters of thought. Our emotional ties to historic Christianity and its cultural forms inevitably give birth to feelings of uneasiness as we think of "Christ-ized Hinduism."[14] But Hoefer has wrestled with the

---

12 Ibid., 191.

13 Ibid., 200–202.

14 Hoefer does not seem to be careful enough in defining this striking terminology. At this point he is clearly viewing Hinduism as primarily cultural phenomena. On this point, see the striking analysis of Hans Staffner in *Jesus Christ and the Hindu Community* (Anand, Gujarat, India: Gujarat Sahitya Prakash, 1988). Staffner argues

complex and disturbing rise of what Robin Boyd called the "Latin captivity of the Indian church."[15] He confesses to having learned a great deal from Hindus and high-caste NBBCs regarding the fact that Christ is "captivated" within the Indian church. He says he writes on behalf of numerous Christian workers, of whom

> many are already bending and ignoring missiologically frustrating church practices in order that the call and nurture of the Gospel can readily go beyond the church walls. Their greatest frustration and anger is directed not against the non-baptized believers but against the rigid church rules and rigid congregational attitude which hinder the free flow of the Gospel into the community. They want to be servants of the Kingdom, rather than servants of the church.[16]

Nonetheless, one must question whether Hoefer in the end is either too traditionally attached to the church or just not careful enough to define what he means in saying that this churchless Christianity needs the church. Did Gentile Christianity need the Jerusalem church? Arguably, it needed to be protected from that church. It needed sensitive apostles from that church, and this seems the parallel to today. India's NBBCs need to be guarded against a great deal of trouble that Christians will cause them (clearly enough demonstrated in Hoefer's study), but they certainly need help. May all potential helpers be as careful and quick as the Apostle Paul to renounce oversight and insist on immediate leadership from within the local context!

Herbert Hoefer's study documenting the existence and vitality of faith in Christ outside the institutional church may well be the most significant missiological publication related to India to have appeared in the second half of the twentieth century. On the basis of experiential findings, followed up with careful research, Hoefer challenges the assumptions and practices of established church and mission structures. He calls for a paradigm shift in thinking about service for Christ in India, and for radical adjustment of ministry models to deal with a significant but ignored work of the Holy Spirit in our midst. In the years since the publication of *Churchless Christianity*, little notice seems to have been taken, debate has not been stirred, and, most tragically, ministry strategies that affirm and empower the NBBC have not been born.

Yet this is a book that demands debate and response. But where and by whom might this begin? Hoefer's is yet one more voice against the "captivated" Christ of the Indian church. What hope lies in his plea that "what we desperately need is that these mumblings of frustration become a rising chorus of objection which we can no longer ignore"?[17] After a century of refining its ability to ignore just such "mumblings of frustration" and "anger against church rules and rigid congregational attitudes," one wonders if even a "rising chorus of objection" would be greeted by institutional leaders with anything other than rebuke for lack of humility and ungodly impatience. Rather than vainly objecting to the church, the need is for pioneer ministries within Hindu contexts to be born, movements to empower NBBCs and help them forward in biblical and contextual discipleship. As a new reality in discipleship to Christ emerges, the existing churches will adapt or die. Thus it happened in the first century as the

---

that "Hinduism is a culture that has room for many religions" and "Christianity is a religion which can become incarnate in any culture."

15 Boyd, *India and the Latin Captivity of the Church* (London: Cambridge University Press, 1974).

16 Hoefer, *Churchless Christianity*, xvi–xvii.

17 Ibid., xviii.

Gentile churches overtook the Jewish; herein lies the hope of India in the twenty-first century. Herbert Hoefer has given a foundation for hope and a direction for planning; who now will take action?

Bibliography

Boyd, Robin H. *India and the Latin Captivity of the Church.* London: Cambridge University Press, 1974.

Hoefer, Herbert. *Churchless Christianity.* Pasadena, CA: William Carey Library, 2001.

Saldanha, Julian. *Conversion and Indian Civil Law.* Bangalore: Theological Publications in India, 1981.

Staffner, Hans. *Jesus Christ and the Hindu Community.* Anand, Gujarat, India: Gujarat Sahitya Prakash, 1988.

CHAPTER 19

Ecclesial Identities of Socioreligious "Insiders"

A Case Study of Fellowship among Hindu and Sikh Communities*

Darren Duerksen

One of the contentious issues surrounding "insider movements" regards the question of church. Is church important for those seeking to follow Jesus within their socioreligious community? If so, what does it look like in these settings? The issues are numerous and familiar to the myriad of missionaries and church leaders who have debated the degree to which churches should reflect local culture. The issues are made more complex, however, when the culture in question includes practices and identities closely related to a non-Christian religion. If, as I will assume for this article, churches are communities of Christ followers with practices and beliefs that are distinct from their surrounding communities, is it possible for such churches to also reside "inside" a Hindu, Sikh, Muslim, or Buddhist cultural and religious community? How and why should an ecclesial community, for example, identify with its Hindu socioreligious community?

This chapter is based on a field study of several groups of Christ followers in North India who are seeking to renegotiate their relationship with the wider Hindu and Sikh communities. Though relatively new in their formation, the experiences of these groups provide opportunity for fresh reflection on how Christ followers understand the nature of other religious communities and how to "be church" in these contexts.

Theoretical Background and Issues

The debate regarding how Christianity should relate to the socioreligious context of India has a long and rich history. The most recent iterations of this debate were ignited through Herbert Hoefer's *Churchless Christianity*.[1] In this study Hoefer and his colleagues identified people who professed faith in Christ but had not received baptism or joined a local church. Though Hoefer's findings provoked much discussion, it was perhaps the book's title that raised the most eyebrows. Was it possible, or acceptable, for people to be devoted to Christ but "churchless"? Hoefer's title was not so much a theological statement as an observation that some people are following Christ outside of the existing sociological and institutional structures known as the Christian church. Nevertheless, Hoefer's title highlighted what has sometimes been a weakness among those advocating close associations between Christ followers and their non-Christian socioreligious community—namely, if and how a group of Christ followers can cultivate both ecclesial and the socioreligious identities. Can both be maintained, or are these mutually exclusive?

Religious studies scholars have long maintained that a view of world religions as bounded (i.e., as mutually exclusive, or nonoverlapping) is a recent development that reflects modernity and that such a

---

* Originally published in a slightly different form in *IJFM* 29, no. 4 (2012): 161–67. Reprinted by permission.

1 Herbert Hoefer, *Churchless Christianity* (Pasadena, CA: William Carey Library, 2001).

view does not always agree with sociological realities.[2] Furthermore, numerous anthropological studies have demonstrated ways in which religious boundaries tend to blur in the face of local terminology and practices.[3] Such blurring and overlap becomes more apparent when researchers avoid imposing and reifying classic Western religious categories and identities, such as "Hindu," "Muslim," or "Sikh," and instead research religious practices and discourses as used by the communities themselves.

The critique of Western views of religions comes not only from the field of religious studies; in recent years evangelical leaders and theologians in various parts of Asia have begun to fault the ways in which Western evangelicals have characterized and interacted with other religions. For example, Japanese theologian Jin Arai discusses the difficulty some Japanese Christians have in reconciling their Christian and their Japanese identities, seeing their difficulty as stemming in part from Western perceptions of religions.

> For Western scholars, non-Christian religions are "other" religions, and never "their own" religions. As a result, they try to establish dialogues with different religious groups, to cooperate for social justice, and to participate in "other" religions in order to enhance mutual understanding. However, "other" religions are not "other" but rather "our" religions for Japanese people. This represents a distinct vantage point.

Arai further suggests that the Western understanding of non-Christian religions as "other" has had an impact on the practices and self-understanding of Japanese Christians: "Japanese Christian churches . . . have not provided their members adequate opportunities to reflect upon the relation between Christian tradition and non-Christian traditions. As a result, a fragmentation of our identity as both Christian and Japanese occurs."[4]

Such critiques suggest that groups of evangelical Christ followers ought to consider ways of understanding and interacting with non-Christian socioreligious communities that lead not to fragmentation of identities but toward integration. But how can the ecclesial identity of a group of Christ followers be both integrated with, and at the same time distinct from, the social identity of their wider socioreligious community?

---

2   See Jacqueline Suthren Hirst and John Zavos, "Riding a Tiger? South Asia and the Problem of 'Religion,'" *Contemporary South Asia* 14, no. 1 (2005): 3–20.

3   See Kathinka Froystad, ed., *Blended Boundaries: Caste, Class, and Shifting Faces of "Hinduness" in a North Indian City* (New Delhi: Oxford University Press, 2005); Peter Gottschalk, *Beyond Hindu and Muslim: Multiple Identity in Narratives from Village India* (New York: Oxford University Press, 2000); Dominique-Sila Khan, *Crossing the Threshold: Understanding Religious Identities in South Asia* (London: I.B. Tauris, 2004); Harjot Oberoi, ed., *The Construction of Religious Boundaries: Culture, Identity, and Diversity in the Sikh Tradition* (Delhi: Oxford University Press, 1994); and Margrit Pernau, "Multiple Identities and Communities: Re-Contextualizing Religion," in *Religious Pluralism in South Asia and Europe*, ed. Jamal Malik and Helmut Reifeld (New Delhi: Oxford University Press, 2005), 147–69.

4   Jin Arai, "Religious Education in Christ-with-Culture from a Japanese Perspective," *Religious Education* 91, no. 2 (1996): 222–23; see also Jonathan Y. Tan, "Rethinking the Relationship between Christianity and World Religions, and Exploring Its Implications for Doing Christian Mission in Asia," *Missiology: An International Review* 39, no. 4 (2011): 497–509.

Hindu and Sikh Yeshu Satsangs

To answer such questions, we consider a group of Yeshu Satsangs in northwest India. *Satsang* (literally, "truth gathering") refers to a religious gathering, often occurring in homes or meeting halls, whose purpose is to worship, pray, and listen to and embrace truth as revealed by scriptures and gurus. Such gatherings may include songs, discourses, and other worship rituals. This study focuses on several Yeshu Satsangs, or Jesus truth gatherings, located in Punjab, eastern Himachal Pradesh, and northern Haryana, all in northwest India.[5] Four of the Yeshu Satsang leaders live in predominantly Hindu communities, and four live in predominately Sikh communities. An experience common among all eight leaders is that they all came to faith in Jesus through, and were discipled in, churches and/or Christian parachurch organizations. Most led house churches for a time and, at various times since around 2000, came into contact with other leaders who were uncomfortable with the identity and practices of Christian churches. In particular, all of these leaders began to disagree with the ways in which Christian church identities and practices were viewed as distinctly "other" by their Hindu/Sikh friends and family, and which created barriers between them and others when sharing Christ.

Countering Christian "Otherness"

Christian pastors and churches in northwest India have often distinguished themselves, not only through their distinct beliefs, but also through the practices that they have embraced or rejected. For their part, the Yeshu Satsang leaders agree with Christian pastors that Christ followers should practice rituals and a lifestyle that focus on Christ. They disagree, however, regarding the types of rituals and lifestyles that Christ followers should and should not embrace. In particular, the Yeshu Satsang leaders argue that Christian pastors have often promoted practices and teachings that perpetuate the social "otherness" of Christian churches. For example, some Christian leaders and missionaries have at times requested converts to express their new faith by adopting new names, dress, and Christian ritual practices. Concurrently, believers have also been instructed to reject Hindu or Sikh burial practices, as well as to avoid participating in or attending prayers and other religious rituals. To counter this tendency, the Yeshu Satsang leaders have created several strategies to minimize the otherness that certain practices can produce.

First, these leaders *reframe and adapt current church practices* to minimize some of their Christian associations. An example of such a change involves the physical handling of the Bible. In order to symbolize the centrality of the Bible in satsang teaching, leaders often place it in a central position on a *rehal*, a traditional wooden stand, exactly where Hindu groups place an idol and Sikh groups put their sacred text, the Guru Granth Sahib. In addition, the Sikh Yeshu Satsangs refer to the Bible by the Sikh term *bani*, or "word," and at least one of the Hindu Yeshu Satsangs calls the Bible the *PranVeda*, or Life-Word/Knowledge. In these ways the Bible is honored and referenced in ways that would befit Scripture according to Hindus and Sikhs and that, more broadly, signal an association with the Hindu and Sikh communities. Similarly, the Yeshu Satsangs adapt the forms of the Lord's Supper and baptism in ways that allow Hindus and Sikhs to see them as somewhat related to their own socioreligious communities.

Another way in which Yeshu satsangis (or members of a satsang) and leaders seek to minimize their social otherness is to *de-emphasize the need for a change of social identity*, emphasizing instead the

---

5   I became acquainted with some of the leaders of these satsangs while living and working in North India from 2005 to 2008 and then conducted research among them for six months in 2010.

need for internal change. Hindu and Sikh relatives, when hearing a satsangi pray to or talk about Jesus, sometimes suspect that he or she has become a Christian. In response, satsangis commonly respond, "I have not changed my religion, but I have changed my heart." Here "religion" (*dharma* in Hindi) is used to refer to the duties and responsibility to a community and its culture, not necessarily to doctrines, philosophies, or spiritual beliefs. Some of the satsangis thus argue that they can stay within the Hindu/Sikh religious community while changing the focus of their personal devotion to Jesus.

A third strategy used by Yeshu Satsang leaders is to *give new followers of Christ more time to change practices and lifestyles* than what many Christian pastors advocate. Rather than insisting that Hindus and Sikhs quickly adopt a set of rules and changes when they begin following Jesus, they instead argue that leaders should be more patient and should place high emphasis on the gradual work of God to transform people. For example, while satsang leaders desire their satsangis to stop worshiping idols, they do not set a rigid timetable for this change but will give the satsangis more time to come to this decision on their own. Such an approach, the leaders assert, will bring about authentic changes in the person, perhaps also fewer disruptions between the believer and his or her socioreligious community. The Yeshu Satsang leaders thus attempt to emphasize a process of change that, they hope, will not result in the type of otherness or estrangement created by some Christian churches and practices.

A fourth strategy of Yeshu Satsang leaders is to *resist demonizing Hinduism and Sikhism*. Many Christians in northwest India object to Hindu and Sikh practices not only because of different ideologies, such as Hindu polytheism or devotion to the Sikh scriptures, but because of the belief that Hindu/Sikh practices are intrinsically demonic, and that any contact with them could allow evil power to enter the practitioners. Yeshu Satsang leaders do generally believe in the power of demons to possess or influence people. They do not agree, however, that Hindu and Sikh practices and scriptures are in themselves demonic. For example, Navdeep, a Sikh Yeshu Satsang leader, was told by a pastor to say, "Whatever Sikhs are doing, they are doing for Satan" (P).[6] However, after learning about a Yeshu Satsang from a friend, Navdeep came to believe that Sikh practices and scriptures were not inherently evil. In fact, such scriptures could contain "some truth" that agreed with the Bible. He thus rejects the sense that Sikh practices necessarily contain evil properties that affect people.

Padman, a leader of a Hindu Yeshu satsang for his family and parents, also resists the idea that his people and family follow and worship Satan. Having heard pastors criticize his own Yeshu Satsang, he says, "[We] are not taken into consideration generally by pastors. . . . And [my satsang] is, it is totally [labeled] as 'devil's workshop.' Openly! In churches it is opposed, and it is labeled as this. Not God's. It is totally devil's. . . . So, if somebody will say to my father that you are worshiping a devil, so what will be the reaction?" (E).

In contrast, Padman draws from Acts 17 the idea that his Hindu family and community are worshipers of "the unknown God." Just as Paul acknowledged that the Athenians' interest in God was valid but incomplete, so Padman affirms the overall questing spirit and sensitivity of his community. They are not, he asserts, under satanic influence, but they do need guidance toward a greater knowledge of God through Jesus.

---

6   In this study I indicate the language of the original quotation by (E), (H), or (P) (English, Hindi, or Punjabi). All quotations are from my research in 2010.

Use of Hindu/Sikh Practices

Though the Yeshu Satsangs retain and adapt certain practices that are shared with local and global Christ-following communities, they have also incorporated select Hindu/Sikh practices and in various ways are seeking to reidentify themselves with their Hindu/Sikh communities. Implicitly critiquing a bounded understanding of religion and religious community, they have chosen to follow various practices that involve language, *bhakti* (or devotion), and symbols.

Language

Many Yeshu Satsang leaders have made changes in the way they identify themselves in terms of their religious community, including their use of greetings. One self-ascription used among Hindus is "Hindu Yeshu bhakt" (Hindu Jesus devotee). Ravi, a Hindu Yeshu Satsang leader, reflects on this phrase: "I always say it like this, 'I am not a Christian, I am a Hindu Yeshu Bhakt.' Then I am ready for their questions, like, 'You believe in Jesus, then how are you a Hindu?' Then I say, 'On my [birth certificate] and my father's it is written "Hindu." And I live in Hindustan [India], and I speak Hindi. That is why I am a Hindu. And also Hindu is not a religion, it's a community'" (H). As this quotation indicates, many Hindus and Sikhs associate a Yeshu satsangi with the Christian community once the satsangi begins to pray or mention the name "Yeshu." In response, Ravi clearly distances himself from the Christian community and embraces a Hindu identity.

Just as some Hindu Yeshu satsangis call themselves Hindu, some of the Sikh Yeshu satsangis continue to call themselves Sikh. When I asked one satsangi about her Sikh identity, she responded that one of the literal meanings of "Sikh" is "learner." She went on to explain: "I am still Sikh. . . . People have said that 'you are now Christian.' And we have told them, 'We don't have any change in our clothes. So we change only our heart. We change only our life. So how you can say that we . . . are now Christian? We are still Sikh. We are learning'" (E).

In addition to self-ascriptions, the satsang leaders encourage the use of other local terms. While many Christians in Punjab often greet each other with "Jai Masih di" (Praise the Messiah), the Sikh Yeshu Satsang leaders encourage their satsangis to retain the Sikh greeting "Sat Sri Akal" (God is ultimate truth). Instead of "amen," the Sikh Yeshu Satsangs use the Punjabi word *satbachan* (true word), and the Hindu Yeshu Satsangs use *tathaastu* (so be it). Likewise, "Satguru Yeshu" (True-guru Jesus) often replaces "Prabhu Yeshu Masih" (Lord Jesus Christ/Messiah) as a title for Jesus. In each case the choice of language is designed to create association and identity with the Hindu/Sikh communities while also facilitating worship and teaching.

The Path and Worship Practices of Bhakti

Yeshu Satsang leaders generally shape worship gatherings to reflect the reverent and devotional gatherings of many Hindu bhakti groups or a Sikh *gurdwara* (temple). *Bhakti* refers to the tradition known as *bhakti marga*, which emphasizes the role of devotion and self-surrender in obtaining *moksha*, or salvation. Hindu bhakti sects and traditions are prevalent throughout India and vary in location and emphasis. In northwest India, bhakti teachings helped to shape and inspire various leaders and movements, including those who would eventually identify themselves as Sikhs. While Hindu and Sikh bhakti may be directed to various gods, the Yeshu Satsangs direct their bhakti to Jesus.

One practice through which the Yeshu Satsang leaders express and promote ideals of bhakti devotion is the use of *bhajans,* or *kirtans,* which are a particular genre of devotional music intimately tied to Hindu and Sikh bhakti traditions.[7] The use of bhajans shapes the ecclesial and social identity of the satsangs in two ways. First, since Hindus and Sikhs associate the sound and style of the bhajans with the Hindu/Sikh communities, the Yeshu Satsang leaders use bhajans to express their own Hindu/Sikh identities to their neighbors. One satsang leader, for example, refuses to use worship songs common among Christian churches of the area because they reflect "a Western style of worship." Instead he uses a book of bhajans compiled by other Yeshu Satsangs that sound more like the Bollywood bhakti bhajans that the Hindu people in his area like. Such an association is important for him, since he is conscious that his Hindu neighbors hear the music that his Yeshu Satsang sings. The Hindu associations of certain bhajans thus help foster a social connection between the Yeshu Satsang and the surrounding Hindu community.

Second, in addition to the connection to the Hindu/Sikh communities, bhajans help some satsangis feel close to God by evoking feelings of peace and the "right" atmosphere through which to approach and relate to the divine. For example, one satsangi, who enjoyed bhajans growing up, reflects on those that she now sings in the Yeshu Satsang. "When we sing bhajans, when we pray with the bhajans, then I feel very good at that time because we feel that we are not on the earth. It seems that we are flying in the heaven. I like this part [of the satsang] very much" (H).

Symbolism

Though Hindu sects of northwest India use symbols less than those of South India,[8] symbols still form an important part of most Hindu worship gatherings. For this reason the Hindu Yeshu Satsangs incorporate select Hindu symbols into their satsangs. For example, when preparing for Communion, some leaders use the *diya* (oil lamp), incense, and coconut. These objects, especially the coconut, are important symbols for some Hindus, creating an atmosphere that connotes worship of the divine.

In addition to using a coconut, satsang leaders always sit on the floor, use Indian instruments such as the *tabla* and *harmonium,* use a *rehal* for the Bible, and sometimes blow the *shankh* (shell horn), which is commonly blown in Hindu worship. When used, such Hindu symbols create a valued association with the Hindu community. One satsangi explains, "This is our Indian culture. That's why we are using this. [We] want to give the message to others that we can serve the Lord in an Indian style" (H). In these instances, Hindu symbols help to counter the contradictory message that followers of Jesus are not Indian, or are "other," having abandoned their Indian (Hindu) culture.

Achieving a New Ecclesial Identity

The Yeshu Satsangs of this study are still very new, and any analysis must be seen as provisional at best. Still, their use of practices and identity markers are consistent with some of the nonbounded, Asian definitions of religion highlighted by recent scholarship. In particular, Yeshu satsangis are seeking to

---

7   See Ashok Da. Ranade, *Music Contexts: A Concise Dictionary of Hindustani Music* (New Delhi: Promilla & Co., 2006); and John Stratton Hawley, "The Music in Faith and Morality," *Journal of the American Academy of Religion* 52, no. 2 (1984):243–62.

8   Sikhism has had a profound impact on worship practices in northwest India, particularly through its de-emphasis of symbols. As a result, many religious sects in the area use symbols much less than do groups in South India.

identify socially with their Hindu/Sikh socioreligious communities through various practices that they are selectively adapting to shape a distinct, Christ-focused ecclesial identity. In these ways they seek to transcend and mend identity fragmentation.

The types of identities that the Yeshu Satsangs attempt to forge are similar to what sociologists have called an "achieved identity."[9] These are identities that counter or modify the ascribed identities that they have received from their Hindu/Sikh and the Christian communities. To do so, they embrace what sociologist Margaret Archer has called "emergent properties."[10] According to Archer, a people and a community derive their identity from any number of practices and beliefs. People select from and engage certain practices that they feel are important for relationship within the community and for creating or sustaining a personal and corporate identity. These practices thus have emergent properties that can accomplish particular social and cultural goals. The practices make up one's cultural repertoire, or "cultural toolkit," as sociologist Ann Swidler describes them,[11] which helps them successfully navigate and shape their own roles and identities.

The Yeshu Satsangs have created practices that, they hope, will accomplish at least two goals. On the one hand, they accept practices of Hindu/Sikh culture in order to affirm an ascribed identity that they share with the larger Hindu/Sikh community. On the other hand, they modify or reframe these practices to forge an identity that expresses their devotion and commitment to Jesus. They have thus sought to enlarge their repertoire to achieve an ecclesial identity (focused on Christ) that also affirms a wider and socially ascribed identity.

Why are the Yeshu Satsang leaders so concerned with questions of identity? First of all, such identity negotiation is important for their *evangelism*. Yeshu satsangis talk about the desire to witness more effectively to their Hindu/Sikh friends and family by lowering what they see as unnecessary and unhelpful barriers put up by the Christian church. Evangelism is thus a major motivation. In addition, the attention to identity addresses many satsangis' *desire for cultural belonging*. Rather than accepting practices that place them in the "other" (Christian) socioreligious community, the Yeshu Satsang leaders seek to remain connected to the communities that gave them birth and social structure. I suggest that this latter reason provides rich material for theological reflection. Hindu/Sikh practices not only provide an opportunity to enhance evangelism, but they also in some sense express God's presence and activity within the larger culture. Rather than demonize these communities and their practices, the satsangis are open to considering how God has placed evidence of himself within these practices. Thus bhakti, for example, provides a helpful framework through which to pursue and express devotion to God. With such a sense, it is not a contradiction to embrace a Hindu/Sikh identity, and even celebrate it, while also embracing Christ as one's Savior.

---

9   Nancy T. Ammerman, "Religious Identities and Religious Institutions," in *Handbook of the Sociology of Religion,* ed. Michele Dillon (New York: Cambridge University Press, 2003), 207–27; Phillip E. Hammond, "Religion and the Persistence of Identity," *Journal for the Scientific Study of Religion* 27, no. 1 (1988): 1–11; Lori Peek, "Becoming Muslim: The Development of a Religious Identity," *Sociology of Religion* 66, no. 3 (2005): 215–42; R. Stephen Warner, "Work in Progress toward a New Paradigm for the Sociological Study of Religion in the United States," *American Journal of Sociology* 98, no. 5 (1993): 1044–93.

10   Margaret Scotford Archer, *Structure, Agency, and the Internal Conversation* (New York: Cambridge University Press, 2003), 5.

11   Ann Swidler, "Culture in Action: Symbols and Strategies," *American Sociological Review* 51 (April 1986): 273–86; and Swidler, *Talk of Love: How Culture Matters* (Chicago: University of Chicago Press, 2001).

In light of the attempt by Yeshu Satsang leaders to reembrace Hindu/Sikh practices while remaining committed to Jesus, we might question some of the more functional views of church practices that are common among Western evangelicals.[12] For many evangelicals, church practices and their accompanying symbols are important primarily because of their functional value. Also, because Western evangelicals have often emphasized countercultural ecclesiologies, cultural practices are used and "contextualized" so as to present a clear and Christ-focused alternative to the prevailing socioreligious culture.

Though such concerns are important and valid, the Yeshu Satsangs are perhaps more positive in the view they advance of Hindu/Sikh practices and communities. Rather than viewing them with skepticism, we can imagine that Hindu/Sikh practices may contain aspects of God's goodness that wait to be fully developed by the aid of the church. When a church sees itself in a positive relationship with its context, it would seek to present not only an alternative world but a better world.[13] In other words, the practices and identities of ecclesial communities represent the longing of people, not to counter their socioreligious context, *but to fulfill it*. In this respect there is perhaps merit in revisiting aspects of the classic fulfillment theology of Farquhar and others,[14] not as an apologetic seeking to convince Hindus to follow Christ, but as a theology of how Hindu (and other) socioreligious communities possess symbolic longings that reflect God's presence and handiwork.

Conclusion

The Yeshu Satsangs of northwest India, though relatively new and tentative in their formation, nonetheless help address an important question regarding insider movements, or people who in various ways follow Christ "inside" their non-Christian socioreligious community. Not only do the satsangs show that such Christ followers need not remain churchless, but they raise a needed critique of bounded understandings of religious practices and identities. In addition, the way in which they frame religion and religious identities creates space for a church to develop a distinct and Christ-focused ecclesial identity while at the same time affirming a Hindu/Sikh socioreligious identity. Finally, the trajectory of the Yeshu Satsangs opens up helpful and rich theological possibilities regarding the ways in which God might use a church not only to counter aspects of culture but also to activate elements that he himself has built into that culture. The development of relationships with the larger Hindu/Sikh culture needs to be seen as more than just a means to the end of evangelism. It is quite possible that practices that encourage a greater level of congruity between a church's ecclesial and social identities will lay a strong foundation for understanding more deeply why and how to be church in the midst of a variety of multifaith contexts.

---

12 In the following I draw on William Dyrness' recent discussion regarding practices of "poetic theology"; see Dyrness, *Poetic Theology: God and the Poetics of Everyday Life* (Grand Rapids, MI: Eerdmans, 2011).

13 Ibid., 245.

14 J. N. Farquhar, *The Crown of Hinduism* (London: Oxford University Press, 1913).

Bibliography

Ammerman, Nancy T. "Religious Identities and Religious Institutions." In *Handbook of the Sociology of Religion*, edited by Michele Dillon, 207–27. New York: Cambridge Univresity Press, 2003.

Arai, Jin. "Religious Education in Christ-with-Culture from a Japanese Perspective." *Religious Education* 91, no. 2 (1996): 222–23.

Archer, Margaret Scotford. *Structure, Agency, and the Internal Conversation*. New York: Cambridge University Press, 2003.

Dyrness, William. *Poetic Theology: God and the Poetics of Everyday Life*. Grand Rapids, MI: Eerdmans, 2011.

Farquhar, J. N. *The Crown of Hinduism*. London: Oxford University Press, 1913.

Froystad, Kathinka, ed. *Blended Boundaries: Caste, Class, and Shifting Faces of "Hinduness" in a North Indian City*. New Delhi: Oxford University Press, 2005.

Gottschalk, Peter. *Beyond Hindu and Muslim: Multiple Identity in Narratives from Village India*. New York: Oxford University Press, 2000.

Hammond, Phillip E. "Religion and the Persistence of Identity." *Journal for the Scientific Study of Religion* 27, no. 1 (1988): 1–11.

Hawley, John Stratton. "The Music in Faith and Morality." *Journal of the American Academy of Religion* 52, no. 2 (1984): 243–62.

Hirst, Jacqueline Suthren, and John Zavos. "Riding a Tiger? South Asia and the Problem of 'Religion.'" *Contemporary South Asia* 14, no. 1 (2005): 3–20.

Hoefer, Herbert. *Churchless Christianity*. Pasadena, CA: William Carey Library, 2001.

Khan, Dominique-Sila. *Crossing the Threshold: Understanding Religious Identities in South Asia*. London: I.B. Tauris, 2004.

Oberoi, Harjot, ed. *The Construction of Religious Boundaries: Culture, Identity, and Diversity in the Sikh Tradition*. Delhi: Oxford University Press, 1994.

Peek, Lori. "Becoming Muslim: The Development of a Religious Identity." *Sociology of Religion* 66, no. 3 (2005): 215–42.

Pernau, Margrit. "Multiple Identities and Communities: Re-Contextualizing Religion." In *Religious Pluralism in South Asia and Europe*, edited by Jamal Malik and Helmut Reifeld, 147–69. New Delhi: Oxford University Press, 2005.

Ranade, Ashok Da. *Music Contexts: A Concise Dictionary of Hindustani Music*. New Delhi: Promilla & Co., 2006.

Swidler, Ann. "Culture in Action: Symbols and Strategies." *American Sociological Review* 51 (April 1986): 273–86.

———. *Talk of Love: How Culture Matters*. Chicago: University of Chicago Press, 2001.

Tan, Jonathan Y. "Rethinking the Relationship between Christianity and World Religions, and Exploring Its Implications for Doing Christian Mission in Asia." *Missiology: An International Review* 39, no. 4 (2011): 497–509.

Warner, R. Stephen. "Work in Progress toward a New Paradigm for the Sociological Study of Religion in the United States." *American Journal of Sociology* 98, no. 5 (1993): 1044–93.

1. What are some specific ways in which Jewish, Hindu, Buddhist, and Muslim believers have approached their faiths so that they can remain within their preexisting communities and not create competing socioreligious communities?

2. It is important to recognize that the term "Christian" does not mean the same thing to all people. What do non-Christian religious communities often understand by the terms "become a Christian" or "Christianity" (or equivalent terms in their own languages)? Do the Scriptures require them to adopt the Christian religion? Explain. How does an essentialist view of religion(s) differ from a sociological/cultural/socioreligious one?

3. In the case studies and testimonies presented, which practices of Christians have helped others come closer to Christ? Which practices have been detrimental?

4. What can Mazhar Mallouhi's testimony (chap. 12) teach us about the relationship between cultural and spiritual identity? Do you agree with Mallouhi that an approach to insiders is often more about attitude than doctrine? How does this affect your perspective?

5. Hanna Shahin (chap. 13) points out that practices are the foundation of faith for Muslims, while theology, or "right belief," is generally more important among Christians. How might the initial emphasis on right theology be a stumbling block for Muslims who want to follow Christ? How can this inform gospel witness among Muslims?

6. How can we reevaluate traditional understandings of the church to avoid identity fragmentation in new Christ followers?

7. What does Travis' case study (chap. 16) reveal about the role of Christians among Muslim movements to Christ? Who are the primary agents for the spread of the gospel?

8. What interesting phenomena, new insights, or important lessons did you find in the case studies and analysis?

PART 3

BIBLICAL AND THEOLOGICAL PERSPECTIVES

By the time the creeds were written in the third century, what had happened to the conception of the kingdom of God? The Nicene Creed mentions it once, but only in reference to our life beyond the borders of this life, in heaven: "Thy kingdom is an everlasting kingdom." The Apostles' Creed and the Athanasian Creed don't mention it at all. The three great historic creeds summing up Christian doctrine, mention once what Jesus mentioned a hundred times. Something had dropped out. A vital, vital thing had dropped out. A crippled Christianity went across Europe, leaving a crippled result. . . . A vacuum was left in the soul of Western civilization.

—E. STANLEY JONES

Are insider movements biblical? Or are they merely a missiological strategy with scant theological legitimacy, as some critics assert? As we continue our study of these movements, our next endeavor will be to answer this question. Part 3 consists of a dozen biblical and theological studies that nourish the IM paradigm. Here we will find principles, concepts, examples, and arguments that provide scriptural validation of Jesus movements within diverse religious communities.

In chapter 20, Anthony Taylor presents the overarching theme of the Bible, the kingdom of God, as a biblical alternative to the "conflict of religions" paradigm for mission.

In chapter 21, Harley Talman brings new perspective to the IM discussion from the Old Testament. Its dual attitude of absorption and rejection of other religions, assessment criteria, sociological considerations, and sanction of non-proselyte conversion all have significant implications for how we should view insider movements.

Chapter 22, a study of the New Testament concept of conversion by Michael Roberts and Richard Jameson, reveals the New Testament's requirement for turning to God, not to a new religious system. The gospel calls people to follow Christ as Savior and Lord within their socioreligious communities, not as "proselytes" to a different one. The authors also posit a continuum of various kinds of nonbelieving socioreligious communities in the New Testament. Where a given context falls on this spectrum has implications for how we might expect the Holy Spirit to work.

In chapter 23, John Ridgway briefly surveys Jesus' ministry to Jews, Gentiles, and Samaritans, showing how the Messiah went to the lost where they were. By not extracting them from their messy situations, Jesus ensured that they could in turn impact their own communities.

In chapter 24, Kevin Higgins takes a more detailed look at Jesus' ministry in Samaria, which he offers as a church-planting paradigm among Muslims.

In chapter 25, Higgins presents a biblical basis for insider movements; he provides examples of vibrant Jesus movements and uncovers their scriptural dynamics of transformation, mirroring the pattern of Acts 2:42.

In chapter 26, J. Dudley Woodberry explores the pattern of incarnational ministry exemplified by Jesus, Paul, and the early church, showing its relevance to insider movements.

In chapter 27, Harley Talman argues that Acts 15 models a theological process and provides principles for approaching missiological phenomena like IMs. Just as Jewish Christ followers accept Western Christians whose practice of discipleship has departed from the divinely mandated practices of the OT (followed by Jesus and his disciples), so we must give the same liberty to believers from non-Christian religious traditions "to live a life that is determined by Christ and his Spirit."

In chapter 28, Rebecca Lewis contends that the issue at stake in insider movements is not missiological strategy but preserving the integrity of the gospel, in the tradition of the Apostle Paul, whose gospel penetrated radically different cultures and transformed them.

In chapter 29, Talman argues that the Bible alone, not the creeds, confessions, or theologies of the church in the West, is the measure of theological truth in new contexts. However, local theology should be done in global conversation.

In chapter 30, Herbert Hoefer examines the ecclesiology of Hindu devotees to Christ, which differs from the traditional Western model. He addresses the resulting criticisms by outlining several theological principles, primarily from the Protestant Reformation, that Western missiologists have often failed to embrace.

H. L. Richard in chapter 31 concludes this part with a look at the Apostle Paul's astonishing claim that "all things are yours" (1 Cor 3:21). He probes the theology of famous Dutch Reformed missiologist Johan Herman Bavinck in applying this Pauline principle to our topic.

CHAPTER 20

The Kingdom of God
A Biblical Paradigm for Mission
Anthony Taylor

When people turn to Christ, what are they supposed to do? What behaviors demonstrate that they have truly been born from above?

Answering this question is not as easy as it seems. For example, a German friend of mine told me that when people turn to Christ in Germany, if they had been members of the Landeskirche (popularly but erroneously referred to in English as the "state church"), they must leave it and join themselves to a "believing" church (in his mind, Baptist or Pentecostal). He asserted this because he is ecclesiologically a separatist. In his narrative world, no one who remains in the Landeskirche can do well in her or his faith. Therefore, new believers must separate themselves from the Landeskirche and join a church that is based upon regenerate church membership. Other non-Landeskirche German friends hold this same position. In contrast, I have another German acquaintance who is involved in the Landeskirche. His faith is vibrant and he knows and has meaningful fellowship with many others who are actively following Christ within the Landeskirche. They see themselves functioning like yeast, salt, and light, promoting spiritual growth in their communities.

So what is the German who has recently turned to Christ supposed to do? Separate from the Landeskirche or remain within it? It appears that the answer depends on the perspective of the one answering. The Scripture does not appear to give a definitive answer on this, because separatists and non-separatists offer biblical support for their position. If we allow the practices of those within the church to help guide us, it appears that either response is appropriate. Some believers have stayed within the Landeskirche (Dietrich Bonhoeffer being a notable example), while others have separated and joined "free churches." It appears that the rightness or wrongness of either position depends on the conscience and the context of the individuals who have turned to Christ.

Nonetheless, my German friend finds it difficult to accept this ambiguity, because he is a committed separatist. His separatist viewpoint assumes that people cannot grow in their faith if they stay within the Landeskirche.

My friend is not alone. Separatist thinking along with its assumptions is widespread, influencing not only evangelical ecclesiology but also evangelical missiology. This separatist ecclesiological paradigm has contributed to the formation of a "conflict of religions" paradigm in the church's approach to mission. Rather than build bridges with other groups (Christian or non-Christian) by using that which exists in these groups and which could be classified as helpful or neutral, the "conflict of religions" paradigm leads one to categorize much, if not all, of what exists in "other" groups as wrong or potentially harmful. Due to this, groups that use a "conflict of religions" approach are inclined to promote their distinctives (that is, their particular theological formulations, their church polity, their style of worship) in contrast to (and at times in opposition to) the distinctives of other groups. While each of these distinctives can be useful for nurturing God's people and for advancing God's purposes, they should not be viewed as necessary ends in themselves.

An alternative to the "conflict of religions" paradigm is the paradigm of the kingdom of God.[1] This paradigm assumes that what is most important is the quality of one's relationship to Christ and to a community of believers, and that such communities can have different practices and emphases, whether novel or traditional, foreign or indigenous, as long as they are compatible with the Bible. This kingdom paradigm does not seek to advance the distinctives of a particular denomination or religious tradition and instead focuses on that which fundamentally demonstrates that a person has been transferred from the domain of darkness to the kingdom of God's beloved Son (Col 1:13). It assumes that when the Spirit of Christ enters a person, he places the person inside his kingdom. Christ's entrance into the believer's life is manifested by a change in one's core identity[2] (being in Christ and in the body of Christ) and a commitment to obey the Word. Christ's placement is manifested by a growing change in worldview (beliefs) and lifestyle. The community of believers consequently lives in ways that reflect the presence and reign of Christ in their lives.[3]

This kingdom paradigm is biblical and missional. Referring to how this paradigm is biblical, Ralph Winter wrote, "The Bible consists of a single drama: the entrance of the kingdom, the power and the glory of the living God in this enemy-occupied territory."[4] Referring to it being missional, Mark Driscoll states, "At its simplest, the kingdom of God is the result of God's mission to rescue and renew his sin-marred creation."[5]

The redirected focus of the kingdom paradigm is well suited to help the church negotiate social, cultural, and religious barriers when interacting with individuals and communities from the world religions of Hinduism, Buddhism, Judaism, and Islam.

In this chapter we will demonstrate how this kingdom paradigm is biblical and missional and consider its implications for those in Christ who belong to communities from the world religions.

The idea of the kingdom of God originates with the commission of the first couple. Having been made in God's image, they were empowered to function as God's regal representatives on earth. God, in response to humanity's waywardness, formed the children of Israel into a nation to create a theocratic

---

1   See Rick Brown, "The Kingdom of God and the Mission of God: Part 1," *IJFM* 28, no. 1 (2011): 5–12; and Brown, "The Kingdom of God and the Mission of God: Part 2," *IJFM* 28, no. 2 (2011): 49–59.

2   Regarding this classification of core identity, along with other issues surrounding identity, see Tim Green, "Conversion in the Light of Identity Theories," in *Longing for Community: Church,* Ummah, *or Somewhere in Between?,* ed. David Greenlee (Pasadena, CA: William Carey Library, 2013), 41–51.

3   Max Turner, addressing this idea through the specific lens of Luke-Acts, writes, "At the center of gravity of Luke's multifaceted view of 'salvation' is God's invasive dynamic presence in strength (kingdom of God), powerfully transforming Israel into a community of radical filial obedience (sonship), joyful witness and worship." Turner, "The Spirit and Salvation in Luke-Acts," in *The Holy Spirit and Christian Origins: Essays in Honor of James D. G. Dunn,* ed. Graham N. Stanton, Bruce W. Longenecker, and Stephen C. Barton (Grand Rapids, MI: Eerdmans, 2004), 107.

4   Ralph D. Winter, "The Kingdom Strikes Back: Ten Epochs of Redemptive History," in *Perspectives on the World Christian Movement: A Reader,* 4th ed., ed. Ralph D. Winter (Pasadena, CA: William Carey Library, 2009), 210.

5   Mark Driscoll, *Doctrine: What Christians Should Believe* (Wheaton, IL: Crossway, 2010), 411.

kingdom, a kingdom that would reflect his redemptive purposes for the world (Deut 4:5–8).[6] When God had delivered the children of Israel from Egypt and had brought them to Mt. Sinai, he said to them, "You shall be to me a kingdom of priests and a holy nation" (Ex 19:6).[7] God was their King (Isa 44:6) and they were his people (Ex 6:7; Deut 7:6). When David and his descendants were appointed to be kings over God's people, they understood that they were subordinate to God, the "Great King." They ruled as his "sons" over his kingdom (1 Chr 17:13,14; 29:11; Ps 89:27). Abijah recognized this delegation of God's kingdom to the Davidic kings and referred to this understanding in his speech to Jeroboam, saying, "And now you think to withstand the kingdom of the LORD in the hand of the sons of David" (2 Chr 13:8).

In addition, God continued to use this kingdom concept as a vehicle to describe his redemptive purposes. Jeremiah revealed that in the future God would put a righteous son of David on the throne who would save God's people and rule his kingdom in righteousness (Jer 33:14–16; see also Isa 9:6,7; 11:1–10). Daniel also spoke of this messianic kingdom:

> And in the days of those kings the God of heaven will set up a kingdom that shall never be destroyed, nor shall the kingdom be left to another people. It shall break in pieces all these kingdoms and bring them to an end, and it shall stand forever. (Dan 2:44)
>
> I saw in the night visions, and behold, with the clouds of heaven there came one like a son of man, and he came to the Ancient of Days and was presented before him. And to him was given dominion and glory and a kingdom, that all peoples, nations, and languages should serve him; his dominion is an everlasting dominion, which shall not pass away, and his kingdom [is] one that shall not be destroyed. (Dan 7:13,14)

This Old Testament revelation of the kingdom provided the conceptual context for Jesus and his disciples. This is why, as Matthew tells us, when Jesus began his ministry, the initial content of his preaching was, "Repent, for the kingdom of heaven is at hand" (Matt 4:17). Jesus preached this way because he had come to establish his kingdom.[8] Matthew then tells us that Jesus went throughout all of Galilee, "proclaiming the gospel of the kingdom and healing every disease and every affliction among the

---

6   Christopher J. H. Wright asks us to read the Bible "from the assumption that the whole Bible renders to us the story of God's mission through God's people in their engagement with God's work for the sake of the whole of God's creation." Wright, *The Mission of God: Unlocking the Bible's Grand Narrative* (Downers Grove, IL: IVP Academic, 2006), 51. In this light, Timothy Tennent states, "Missions, therefore, arises not simply as a response of obedience to a command given to the church (although it is never less than that) but as a joyful invitation to *participate with God* in his redemptive work in the world." Tennent, *Invitation to World Missions: A Trinitarian Missiology for the Twenty-first Century* (Grand Rapids, MI: Kregel, 2010), 61; emphasis in the original. This provides the hermeneutical background for the kingdom paradigm.

7   Scripture quotations in this chapter are from the English Standard Version (ESV) unless otherwise noted.

8   "The gospels are not about 'how Jesus turned out to be God.' They are about how God became king on earth as in heaven." N. T. Wright, *Simply Jesus: A New Testament Vision of Who He Was, What He Did, and Why He Matters* (New York: HarperCollins, 2011), 149.

people" (Matt 4:23). Jesus' innumerable miracles of healing demonstrated that he was inaugurating the kingdom of God.[9]

Even though Jesus was inaugurating his kingdom, his kingdom was going to look vastly different from all the other kingdoms of this world. This difference is seen in its stages of development. When Jesus had completed the work of inaugurating his kingdom on earth, he ascended into heaven and sat down at the right hand of God. Prior to his ascension he told his disciples that all authority in heaven and on earth had been given to him (Matt 28:18). Having understood the significance of these words, Peter declared in his speech to Cornelius that Jesus Christ was "Lord of all" (Acts 10:36). Jesus' commission and Peter's words meant that Jesus' reign had begun. However, Jesus' reign is invisible. During this stage of Jesus' invisible reign, the kingdom continues to expand as the church engages in its commission to make disciples of all nations (Matt 28:19).[10] At the end of this age Jesus will physically return. When he returns he will judge all people, eliminate those who oppose his rule, remove evil, and visibly extend his kingdom over all the earth. Finally, John reveals to us that there will be a new heaven and new earth (Rev 21:1). In this era of newness, God, the Lamb, and the redeemed from the nations will reign together:

> The throne of God and of the Lamb will be in it, and his servants
> will worship him. They will see his face, and his name will be on
> their foreheads. And night will be no more. They will need no light
> of lamp or sun, for the Lord God will be their light, and they will
> reign forever and ever. (Rev 22:3–5)

From these stages we see that there is not only a future dimension to the kingdom of God but a very real present dimension as well. Paul refers to some characteristics of this present kingdom in Romans 14: "For the kingdom of God is not a matter of eating and drinking but of righteousness and peace and joy in the Holy Spirit" (v. 17). Paul does not say that the kingdom *will be* righteousness and peace and joy in the Holy Spirit at some point in time in the distant future, but that the kingdom *is* righteousness, peace, and joy in the Holy Spirit. The reality of its present form is also evident in Paul's declaration that believers have already been transferred into the kingdom of God's beloved Son (Col 1:13).

This present dimension to the kingdom indicates that, though the king reigns invisibly, his kingdom can be visibly seen. The context of Romans 14:17 gives us the clue as to how this can be. Paul wrote this section to help the Roman believers build a healthy community. The loving, thoughtful way that they treated one another would visibly demonstrate the presence and rule of Christ in their midst (see also John 13:35).

Building on this biblical foundation, the kingdom paradigm directs each person's attention toward developing relationally oriented character qualities that enhance one's relationship with Christ and with one another. Developing these qualities reflects the fact that one is living in the present kingdom of God. The Cape Town Commitment of the Lausanne Movement speaks about the importance of having these character qualities:

---

9   David Crump, *Knocking on Heaven's Door: A New Testament Theology of Petitionary Prayer* (Grand Rapids, MI: Baker Academic, 2006), 43.

10   Even though Jesus is reigning now (Eph 1:20,21), and even though we reign with him (Eph 2:6), we reign in weakness and in suffering (Eph 4:1; 6:10–20; see also Phil 3:10).

The Bible portrays a quality of life that should mark the believer and the community of believers. From Abraham, through Moses, the Psalmists, prophets and wisdom of Israel, and from Jesus and the apostles, we learn that such a biblical lifestyle includes justice, compassion, humility, integrity, truthfulness, sexual chastity, generosity, kindness, self-denial, hospitality, peacemaking, non-retaliation, doing good, forgiveness, joy, contentment and love—all combined in lives of worship, praise and faithfulness to God.[11]

These qualities should characterize members of the kingdom of God. Developing them in our own strength would be impossible. However, living "in the Spirit" enables these qualities to grow by God's grace (see also Rom 8:3–14; Gal 5:22–25; also Ezek 36:24–27). This is why an integral feature of the kingdom paradigm is emphasizing one's dependence on the continuous working of the Holy Spirit. The Spirit is the one who enables people to live the quality of life that is reflective of being in Christ and living in his kingdom community.

Godly character is not developed in a vacuum. The kingdom paradigm recognizes that God's plan is for his people to live in community—with him and with one another in the fellowship of the Holy Spirit (1 Cor 12:13; 2 Cor 13:14). Thus an integral aspect of the kingdom paradigm is the development of visible communities of followers of Christ who are living expressions of the kingdom of God.

Finally, the kingdom paradigm recognizes that God values the wonderful diversity he has created among the many peoples of humankind and that he intends to bring this diversity under Christ's lordship. Isaiah 2:1–4 indicates that the nations will come under his lordship while they maintain their distinctiveness (see also Isa 56:6–7; Rev 5:9; 7:9). Revelation 21 indicates that even in the world to come, diverse ethnic groups will continue to exist and will walk by the light of the Lamb (v. 24). Lamin Sanneh recognizes that this diversity within the body of Christ is a fundamental characteristic of our biblical faith. He says that embedded within the gospel is "a commitment to the pluralist merit of culture within God's universal purpose."[12]

Thus this kingdom paradigm is biblical and it is missional. It does not focus on such particulars as methods of prayer and worship, manners of dress and food, religious traditions, denominationalism, social identity—particulars that play a central role in the "conflict of religions" paradigm. Rather, the kingdom paradigm focuses on the transforming presence of Christ, the spiritual identity, and the godly relationships that the Spirit of Christ seeks to produce, which are to reflect the manifest presence and character of Christ's kingdom (see Col 3:1–17).

In the "conflict of religions" approach, people are persuaded to abandon their own religious traditions and adopt those of another culture. Thus, if one were to attend a Pentecostal worship service in Springfield, Missouri, and one in Peshawar, Pakistan, one would notice a remarkable degree of similarity in the ways worship is ritualized and the Word is taught. Though there is nothing "wrong"

---

11 The Lausanne Movement, "The Cape Town Commitment: A Confession of Faith and a Call to Action," 2011, I.6.D, http://www.lausanne.org/content/ctc/ctcommitment (accessed May 6, 2015).

12 Lamin Sanneh, *Translating the Message: The Missionary Impact on Culture*, 2nd ed. (Maryknoll, NY: Orbis, 2009), 1. Sanneh states, "Christianity identified itself with the need to translate out of Aramaic and Hebrew, and from that position came to exert a dual force in its historic development. One part of that was to resolve to relativize its Judaic roots, with the consequence that it promoted significant aspects of those roots. The other part was the destigmatization of the Gentile culture by adopting that culture as a natural extension of the new religion" (ibid.).

with conforming to other traditions, it has its limitations. While attending the service in Peshawar, one would observe how mono-ethnic the worshiping community was. Members from the two largest people groups in the area (Pashtun and Hindko) would be noticeably absent. It does appear that such expressions of the biblical faith can be so laden with outside culture, ethnicity, association, and identity that they are neither attractive nor viable.

Within the kingdom paradigm, people are not asked to align themselves with a particular religious tradition or a particular ethnic group. Conversion, therefore, does not require a rejection of one's socio-religious community. What it requires is aligning oneself to Christ and allowing Christ to work within one's community, transforming it from the inside (Mark 1:17; 5:19).

This paradigm reflects the way that Jesus worked. When Jesus proclaimed the kingdom of God among the Samaritans in Samaria (Luke 17:11–19; John 4:5–42), to Gentiles in Lebanon and the Decapolis (Mark 5:1–20; 7:24–8:10), and to Romans in Galilee (Matt 8:5–13), he did not command them to observe the Jewish religious practices that he and his disciples observed. Jesus directed them to the surpassing grace of the King and of his kingdom.[13] Jesus did not elevate one particular method of worship over another; yet he did advocate wholehearted love for the one true God (Mark 12:30), worshiping him "in spirit and truth" (John 4:23–24).

Through the history of the church, prayer and worship have been conducted by different groups and organizations in a great variety of forms and rituals. This shows that religious traditions and institutions are instruments of God's mission rather than the goal of God's mission. In this regard Mark Driscoll concludes,

> Therefore, while not imposing religion on anyone, the church of
> Jesus Christ is to constantly be proposing reconciliation with God
> to everyone . . . [using] timely biblical methods that are changing
> depending upon culture. This is the essence of what it means to be
> a missional church that contextualizes its ministry.[14]

E. Stanley Jones wrote about this relationship between the kingdom of God and religions, including the differing forms of "the Church," by which he meant institutional Christianity. He wrote,

> This kingdom is bound up with no culture, no nation, no race, and
> no religion. It is open to everybody, everywhere on equal terms.
> Jesus never used the word religion, for he was not founding a new
> religion to set over against other religions, for religion is [humani-
> ty's] search for God. The gospel is God's search for [human beings].
> So anything good in any race, religion, or culture, which is worth
> preserving, will not be lost in the kingdom. "I come not to destroy
> but to fulfill." Anything good that can be fitted into the kingdom
> in culture or religion will be fulfilled in the kingdom. "Into it the
> kings of earth bring their glories. . . . They shall bring to it the glo-
> ries and treasures of the nations" (Rev 21:24,25 Moffat).

---

13 Is not this what in part impacted John and inspired him to write, "For from his fullness we have all received, grace upon grace. For the law was given through Moses; grace and truth came through Jesus Christ" (John 1:16,17)?

14 Driscoll, *Doctrine*, 312.

> But the church is not the exclusive agency of the coming of the kingdom. Wherever [human beings] bring forth the fruits of the kingdom, there the kingdom is, to that degree, inside the church or outside the church.[15]

Jones observed people who belonged to diverse socioreligious groups and who were faithful followers of Jesus. In his view, these people belonged to the kingdom of God. Nowadays there are hundreds of thousands of born-again followers of Christ within non-Christian socioreligious groups, such as Jews, Hindus, Buddhists, and Muslims, and Christ is undeniably present among them.

However, this way of thinking is difficult to accept for some. Their perspective seems to be shaped by a "conflict of religions" paradigm. They themselves have been richly blessed by the distinctives of their socioreligious communities. Therefore they view their distinctives as normative. They encourage those who belong to other socioreligious groups to separate themselves from their communities and adopt their distinctives. This perspective persists even though what appears to be central in Scripture for spiritual growth is not adherence to any particular religious tradition but (1) being in Christ, (2) studying and obeying the Word, (3) living a quality of life that demonstrates one is a member of Christ's kingdom and puts it first in one's life, and (4) being joined with others who are active members of Christ's kingdom.

In conclusion, what is the new follower of Christ supposed to do? It appears that Christ and his kingdom should take priority in the lives of believers over loyalty to denominations and traditions, whether those of their own society or those of Christians who interact with them. This means they should seek Christ's leading on how to express their faith. If Christ leads his followers to separate themselves from their socioreligious communities and align themselves with a denomination and adopt its traditions, then they should obey. If, on the other hand, Christ leads his followers to remain within their socioreligious communities in order to be faithful witnesses to him, then they should obey him by doing this. Those who come alongside to help should support these believers to follow the leading of the Lord. Those who come alongside might also remember that Christ is leading the community of believers on a journey as well, and their future might look different from their present.

Bibliography

Brown, Rick. "The Kingdom of God and the Mission of God: Part 1." *International Journal of Frontier Missiology* 28, no. 1 (2011): 5–12.

———. "The Kingdom of God and the Mission of God: Part 2." *International Journal of Frontier Missiology* 28, no. 2 (2011): 49–59.

Crump, David. *Knocking on Heaven's Door: A New Testament Theology of Petitionary Prayer.* Grand Rapids, MI: Baker Academic, 2006.

Driscoll, Mark. *Doctrine: What Christians Should Believe.* Wheaton, IL: Crossway, 2010.

Green, Tim. "Conversion in the Light of Identity Theories." In *Longing for Community: Church, Ummah, or Somewhere in Between?*, edited by David Greenlee, 41–51. Pasadena, CA: William Carey Library, 2013.

Jones, E. Stanley. *The Unshakable Kingdom and the Unchanging Person.* Nashville, TN: Abingdon, 1972.

---

15   E. Stanley Jones, *The Unshakable Kingdom and the Unchanging Person* (Nashville, TN: Abingdon, 1972), 292–93.

Sanneh, Lamin. *Translating the Message: The Missionary Impact on Culture.* 2nd ed. Maryknoll, NY: Orbis, 2009.

Tennent, Timothy C. *Invitation to World Missions: A Trinitarian Missiology for the Twenty-first Century.* Grand Rapids, MI: Kregel, 2010.

Turner, Max. "The Spirit and Salvation in Luke-Acts." In *The Holy Spirit and Christian Origins: Essays in Honor of James D. G. Dunn,* edited by Graham N. Stanton, Bruce W. Longenecker, and Stephen C. Barton, 103–16. Grand Rapids, MI: Eerdmans, 2004.

Winter, Ralph. "The Kingdom Strikes Back: Ten Epochs of Redemptive History." In *Perspectives on the World Christian Movement: A Reader,* 4th ed., edited by Ralph D. Winter and Steven C. Hawthorne, 209–27. Pasadena, CA: William Carey Library, 2009.

Wright, Christopher, J. H. *The Mission of God: Unlocking the Bible's Grand Narrative.* Downers Grove, IL: IVP Academic, 2006.

Wright, N. T. *Simply Jesus: A New Testament Vision of Who He Was, What He Did, and Why He Matters.* HarperCollins, 2011.

CHAPTER 21

The Old Testament and Insider Movements*

Harley Talman

The past several years have witnessed a controversy over the issue of the growing indigenous disci-pleship-to-Jesus movements within the world's major religious traditions. Within Christian mission discussions, these have been most commonly referred to as "insider movements." This paper seeks to offer fresh perspective from an Old Testament theology of religions, so as to discover how theological foundations might inform our attitude toward these movements.

Before embarking on an exploration of biblical theology, we must remind ourselves that the Old Testament does not directly ask or answer the questions contemporary missiology is asking about the nature and validity of other religions. It does not even use a word for religion.[1] Nevertheless, biblical scholars have observed two contrasting elements in the OT's attitude toward the nations and their religions: particularism/exclusiveness/rejection versus universalism/acceptance/absorption. In our ex-amination of the OT perspective on religions of the nations we will first look at the positive attitude.

Attitude of Absorption toward Other Religions

The argument of this section is as follows: The image of God is still evident in humanity, despite the effects of the Fall. Thus human cultures and religions will reflect this reality in some measure. The Scriptures indicate that other cultures (which include their religions) do indeed provide many moral and spiritual insights and not just ignorance and error.[2] Evidences of religious influences on Israel's re-ligion are unmistakable, and often acceptable, beneficial, or useful as bridges to communication—even though they are not sufficient as sources of truth without the additional special revelation given directly by God through and to Israel. Allow me to elaborate.

Many aspects of openness to other religious influences are evident in the patriarchal period. First, elements of other religions are borrowed. While theologically liberal critics view this strictly as a human phenomenon of cultural borrowing, some conservatives may fear that this is suggesting syncre-tism. Instead, we are on more solid ground if we understand it to be God's intentional contextualization

---

* Originally published in a slightly different form in *IJFM* 30, no. 2 (2013): 49–58. Reprinted by permission.

1 Kwesi A. Dickson, *Uncompleted Mission: Christianity and Exclusivism* (Maryknoll, NY: Orbis, 1991), 7.

2 John Goldingay, "How Does the First Testament Look at Other Religions?," 2–3. This is an expansion and revision of a paper written for the Tyndale Fellowship Conference on Religious Pluralism in 1991, revised in light of comments by Christopher J. H. Wright as respondent, and published under both names as "'Yahweh Our God Yahweh One': The Old Testament and Religious Pluralism," in *One God, One Lord: Christianity in a World of Re-ligious Pluralism*, 2nd ed., ed. Andrew D. Clarke and Bruce W. Winter (Grand Rapids, MI: Baker, 1992), 43–62. Page numbers in the book differ from those in the paper I cite.

through Abraham and other patriarchs to present a culturally meaningful witness to the surrounding nations. Charles Van Engen maintains that God's covenant relationship with Israel was a contextualization aimed at bringing light to the nations.[3] The book of Genesis, as a whole, records God's promises and their fulfillment in order to more fully reveal him. As Goldingay explains, "The purpose of God's particular action in the history of Israel is ultimately that God, as the saving and covenantal God Yahweh, should be known fully and worshipped exclusively by those who as yet imperfectly know God as El."[4] At the same time, the Old Testament infers that there are some constructive things that Israel could appropriate or learn from these religions.[5]

For example, it has been noted that the patriarchs worshiped at or near traditional Canaanite sacred sites, such as at Shechem (Gen 12:6), Bethel (Gen 12:8), Hebron (Gen 13:18), and Beersheba (Gen 21:33).[6] In their early period, Israelites lived next to Canaanites in Shechem, even though the latter were Baal worshipers.[7] Despite being immigrants from the desert, the patriarchs and early Israelites assimilated into the agriculturalist culture of the Canaanites, adopting their "language, architecture, farming, legal system, and values."[8]

Furthermore, the high god of other religions is viewed in certain passages as referring to the God of Israel, although not yet fully known. The Canaanite name for the high God, El, was used for the

---

3   Charles Van Engen, *God's Missionary People: Rethinking the Purpose of the Local Church* (Grand Rapids, MI: Baker, 1991), 102–3.

4   Goldingay, "The First Testament," 4.

5   Ibid.

6   Gen 12:6 states, "Abram passed through the land as far as the site of Shechem, at the Terebinth of Moreh. The Canaanites were then in the land." Jewish commentator Nahum Sarna explains, "The Terebinth of Moreh, in Hebrew *'elon moreh,* was undoubtedly some mighty tree with sacred associations. *Moreh* must mean 'teacher, oracle giver.' This tree (or a cluster of such trees) was so conspicuous and so famous that it served as a landmark to identify other sites in the area. The phenomenon of a sacred tree, particularly one associated with a sacred site, is well known in a variety of cultures. A distinguished tree, especially one of great antiquity, might be looked upon as the 'tree of life' or as being 'cosmic,' its stump symbolizing the 'navel of the earth' and its top representing heaven. In this sense, it is a bridge between the human and the divine spheres, and it becomes an arena of divine-human encounter, an ideal medium of oracles and revelation." Sarna, *Genesis,* JPS Torah Commentary (Philadelphia: Jewish Publication Society of America, 1989), 91. The *Jewish Heritage Online Magazine* explains, "Because trees are rooted in the earth and reach toward the sky, many ancient religions worshiped them in sacred groves and imagined spirits inhabiting them." See "The Sacred Tree: Tree Worship in Ancient Israel," http://www.jhom.com/topics/trees/worship.htm. Accordingly, Gen 12:7 says that "the Lord appeared to" Abram at this Canaanite holy site and so he built an altar to the Lord there. According to OT scholar Homer Heater, "Just as Christians built churches on pagan sites, and Muslims build mosques on church sites . . . so the ancients followed their predecessors at sites." Whether worship was "at" or "near" these sacred places would not seem to be a significant distinction, since "the general area of the site was where they worshipped." The fact that "they built altars at the sites indicates the uniqueness of what they were doing at a previously existing sacred site, much as a church, using a Shriner's hall, would put up a pulpit and a cross" (email to author, December 17, 2014). Goldingay, in contrast, asserts that "the ancestors' words and deeds do not imply the belief that other peoples in Canaan have no knowledge of God, though the ancestors do seem to establish their own places of worship, near those of the Canaanites, rather than making use of Canaanite sanctuaries" ("The First Testament," 3).

7   Bruce Vawter, *On Genesis: A New Reading* (New York: Doubleday, 1977), 355, cited in Donald Senior and Carroll Stuhlmueller, *The Biblical Foundations for Mission* (Maryknoll, NY: Orbis, 1983), 17.

8   Senior and Stuhlmueller, *Biblical Foundations,* 18.

God of Israel.[9] (This does not mean that the Canaanite conception of God was the same as the Bible's. I would view this as a divinely inspired appropriation. The sub-biblical Canaanite conception of El was redeemed and sanctified by attributing to it all of the attributes and acts of the God of Israel that are recorded in the Hebrew Bible.) Evangelical scholar Gerald McDermott asserts that Abraham's identification of El Elyon with Yahweh indicates that he considered that the priest Melchizedek (I do not think he would say this of the Canaanites in general) worshiped the true God, but by a different name.[10] Goldingay states:

> Apparently Abram and Genesis itself recognize that Melchizedek . . . serves the true God but does not know all there is to know about that God. It is in keeping with this that Israel in due course takes over Melchizedek's city of Salem and locates Yahweh's own chief sanctuary there. . . . Joseph and Pharaoh, too, seem to work on the basis that the God they serve is the same God[11] (see Gen 41:16,39; and compare Pharaoh's giving and Joseph's accepting an Egyptian theophoric name and a wife who was a priest's daughter, 41:45).[12]

Goldingay describes other absorptions as well:

> The wilderness sanctuary of Exodus 25–40 follows Canaanite models for a dwelling of El, in its framework construction, its curtains embroidered with cherubim, and its throne flanked by cherubim. Such adapting continues with the building of the temple, the religion of the Psalter, and the ideology of kingship (divine and human). It continues in the oracles of the prophets, whose admission to the council of Yahweh is an admission to the council of El (cf. Ps 82) where they overhear El giving judgment, and in the visionary symbolism of the apocalypses. Occasional specific texts indicate concrete dependence (see Ps 104?). This is not to say that these institutions, ideas, or texts are unchanged when they feature within Yahwism, but that it was able to reach its own mature expression with their aid.[13]

---

9   Goldingay, "The First Testament," 7. The name *Baal* ("owner") might also have been appropriated, but it seems that his status as a lesser deity was a main cause for its being rejected, as worship of Baal implied worship of gods other than Yahweh.

10   Gerald McDermott, "What If Paul Had Been from China? Reflections on the Possibility of Revelation in Non-Christian Religions," in *No Other Gods before Me: Evangelicals and the Challenge of World Religions*, ed. John G. Stackhouse (Grand Rapids, MI: Baker, 2001), 18–19. Goldingay is of the same persuasion, as is Kärkkäinen; see Veli-Matti Kärkkäinen, *An Introduction to the Theology of Religions: Biblical, Historical and Contemporary Perspectives* (Downers Grove, IL: InterVarsity Press, 2003).

11   This could not be said of the Pharaoh of Moses' time.

12   Goldingay, "The First Testament," 3. He elaborates: "'Yahweh roars from Zion' (Amos 1:2); indeed, 'El, God, Yahweh' shines forth from Zion (Ps 50:1)" (ibid.). A similar implication emerges from Abraham's calling on God as Yahweh El Olam in Gen 18:33. El Olam appears only here as a designation of Yahweh, but comparable phrases come elsewhere to designate Canaanite deities. Such Canaanite texts also more broadly refer to El as one who blesses, promises offspring, heals, and guides in war, like Yahweh.

13   Goldingay, "The First Testament," 5.

Positive aspects in other religions also allowed for Jewish borrowing from them for law, literature, and wisdom. The OT refers positively to wise men of Egypt, Phoenicia, and Edom; the book of Proverbs reflects Israel's willingness to incorporate Egypt's wisdom literature (while rejecting its polytheism).[14]

Furthermore, the OT emphatically affirms the oneness of humanity and that all peoples are under his sovereign rule, even those under pagan viceroys. Thus Jeremiah attributed the Babylonian king's conquest of Jerusalem to Yahweh (32:26–28). Despite his eclecticism, Cyrus, the king of Persia who is called God's "anointed" (Isa 45:1), declared that "the God of Israel" moved him to allow the Jewish exiles to return (Ezra 1:1,2).[15] We frequently find the prophets proclaiming Yahweh's universal purposes and sovereignty over the nations. Sitting at the center of the chiastic structure of the book of Daniel is Nebuchadnezzar's proclamation, "I blessed the Most High, and praised and honored the one who lives forever" (Dan 4:34 NRSV), emphasizing it as the book's central point.[16] Likewise, Darius confessed Yahweh to be the living God and ordered all those in his kingdom to "tremble and fear before" him (Dan 6:26,27 NRSV). Large sections of the Prophets are aimed at non-Jewish people (e.g., Isa 13:1–23:18; Jer 46–51; Ezek 25–32; Amos 1:3–2:3; Obadiah; Jonah; and Nahum). Even the messages of severe judgment imply God's concern for these peoples.[17] However, the prophets did not only pronounce judgment on pagan nations, they heralded salvation, peace, and blessing to Egypt (Isaiah), Moab, Ammon, Elam (Jer 48–49), and other nations so that they would "know that I am the Lord" (Ezek 36:23 NRSV). The Psalms similarly emphasize that God's blessings and salvation are not intended just for Israel, but for all the nations of the earth (67:2).[18]

Noble and genuine faith is evident among Abraham's predecessors (such as Abel, Enoch, Noah, and Job), his contemporaries (Melchizedek, Lot, and Abimelech), his successors (Rahab and Ruth), and holy "pagans" outside of Israel (Jethro, Naaman, the queen of Sheba, and others). These men and women seem to have been in right relationship with God.[19]

Others see the contribution of "pagan" religions to God's call upon Abraham as natural and necessary, in order to build upon, correct, and purify it through further biblical revelation. Senior and Stuhlmueller elaborate:

> A message is being flashed to us that religion is never a pure creation by God but a synthesis of the best under a new inspiration from God. . . . A new religious experience took place without the creation of a new religion. Abraham remained within the Canaanite religious system. Despite this system's proclivity to sexual excess in the Baal worship, Abraham recognized a dignity and a genuineness about it, and through its instrumentality he acquired his own religious language, style of worship, and system of moral values. In fact the "God of the Ancestors" appeared to Abraham at Canaanite holy places. Religious practices and even the perception of

---

14 Dickson, *Uncompleted Mission*, 20.

15 Ibid., 16–17.

16 R. Torpin, "Lessons from a Study of Daniel" (unpublished paper, 2012).

17 Kärkkäinen, *Theology of Religions*, 40.

18 Ibid.

19 Clark H. Pinnock, *A Wideness in God's Mercy: The Finality of Jesus Christ in a World of Religions* (Grand Rapids, MI: Zondervan, 1992), 92. We cannot be sure that all of them obtained full knowledge of all revelation that had been given, but the latter ones may have been regarded as righteous under the terms of the Noahic covenant.

> God's special presence evolved *within* the geography and politics of
> a local area. Only by first accepting the worth and authenticity of
> preexistent religions were biblical people able to purify, challenge,
> and develop them.[20]

Thus we have seen much evidence of an OT attitude of appropriation of positive elements in pagan religions. This seems to reflect Yahweh's desire to communicate his message with maximum impact by using ideas, terms, forms, and elements that were already familiar to the audience. This should inform our view of insider movements as well.

Attitude of Rejection of Other Religions

In contrast to the OT's attitude of absorption is a strong exclusivist strand. Stuhlmueller refers to this dual process as "absorption and rejection."[21] In that vein, Goldingay declares,

> Gen 1–11 suggests that the religions, like all human activity, be-
> long in the context of a world that needs restoration to the destiny
> and the relationship with God that were intended for them, which
> God purposed to bring about through the covenant with Israel that
> culminated in the mission and accomplishment of Jesus.[22]

Thus we find in the OT an emphatic judgment on the dark, deceptive, destructive, and sometimes demonic character of the religions of the Canaanites and other neighbors of Israel. This included prohibitions on adopting pagan practices such as mourning rites, eating unclean creatures, the abominable acts associated with the pagan worship, and covenant breaking by pursuing other gods.[23] During the Mosaic period a distinct religion with its own rituals, priesthood, and teachings developed. And although outside influences continued, through the Mosaic law, Israel acquired the religious apparatus by which it could accept or reject these influences.[24]

Even where there was a positive influence from outside the Hebrew tradition, as in wisdom literature, it could not substitute for the knowledge of Yahweh that came through his unique dealing with Israel.[25] Other religions, observes Goldingay,

> are not inherently demonic or merely sinful human attempts to
> reach God. . . . Yet they are not equally valid insights into the truth
> about God. They may provide a starting point and certain areas
> of common ground, but not a finishing point. They cannot tell us

---

20 Senior and Stuhlmueller, *Biblical Foundations*, 18.

21 Ibid., 17.

22 Goldingay, "The First Testament," 2.

23 Dickson, *Uncompleted Mission*, 11–14. This last reason was the primary factor in the injunctions against intermarriage with non-Jews.

24 Senior and Stuhlmueller, *Biblical Foundations*, 18. In earlier times, the patriarchs' practices of worship more closely followed those of their neighbors. For instance, Abraham planted a tree and worshiped there (Gen 21:33). But as Canaanite worship degenerated such trees became idols. Hence, by the time of the Mosaic law, Israelites were prohibited from planting a tree near the altar of God (Deut 16:21) as a protection from these idolatrous associations. See I. E. Davidson, *The Tabernacle: Its Symbolism and Spiritual Significance* (Chislehurst, Kent, UK: Barbican Book Room, n.d.), 9–10.

25 Goldingay, "The First Testament," 2.

about the special and vital activity of God in Israel that came to a climax in Christ. . . . [26]

All human religion is not only inevitably tainted by our wayward life in this earth, but can be the very means we use to keep at arm's length the God we choose not to obey. Religion can express our rebellion as well as our response. . . . Religion always has this duality or ambiguity, a simultaneous seeking after God our creator and fleeing from God our judge.[27]

Kärkkäinen suggests that where we find the OT being critical of other religions, it "is not so much a general principle but rather a desire to purify religions and focus on their major task, that is, the worship of the true God of Israel."[28] When religion in Israel suffered from similar defects, the prophets were equally strong in their condemnation.

Consequently the OT's critical attitude toward religions cuts both ways. Biblical faith must not be seen as merely a matter of belonging to the "right" religion (though the full range of biblical truth is indispensable for true worship—John 4:23,24). God is not partial in his critique of religions. There is great danger when the people of God enjoy a false peace at having "arrived"[29] or forget the possibility that other religions may have something to teach them.

Old Testament Criteria for Judging a Religion or Religious Tradition

Two fundamental criteria for assessing other religions stand out in the OT. The first was whether its adherents feared God—even if they lacked the fuller revelation possessed by Israel. As stated earlier, Abraham inferred that Melchizedek and Abimelech feared God (albeit by a different name), and Moses similarly viewed Jethro.[30] Of course, God's ultimate purpose was always that all might know him more fully:

In dealing with the ancestors of Israel, the living God, later disclosed as Yahweh, made an accommodation to the names and forms of deity then known in their cultural setting. This does not thereby endorse every aspect of Canaanite El worship. The purpose of God's particular action in the history of Israel is ultimately that God, as the saving and covenantal God Yahweh, should be known fully and worshiped exclusively by those who as yet imperfectly know God as El.[31]

The second standard was the pursuit of righteous behavior—what kind of morality did religion result in? Goldingay asserts,

What Elijah (and Yahweh) so vehemently opposed was not merely the worship of the wrong God (or rather of a no-god), as focused on

---

26 Ibid.
27 Ibid., 3.
28 Kärkkäinen, *Theology of Religions*, 47.
29 Senior and Stuhlmueller, *Biblical Foundations*, 20.
30 Kärkkäinen, *Theology of Religions*, 49.
31 Goldingay, "The First Testament," 4.

Mount Carmel, but the hijacking of the whole social, economic and legal ethos of Israel by the religious vandalism of Jezebel's Phoenician Baalism, as focused in the Naboth incident (1 Kgs 21). The struggle was not simply over what was the right religion, but over what was a right and just society for Naboth to live in. Baal religion undergirded, or at least imposed no restraint on, the way Ahab and Jezebel treated Naboth. It could be argued, therefore, that the moral, social, and cultural effects of a major religious tradition do give us some grounds for a discriminating response to it, though this can be as uncomfortable an argument for Christianity as a cultural religion as for any other.[32]

These two criteria—fearing God and pursuing righteous living—were expressed in the OT by "conversion." There were two different forms of conversion: non-proselyte and proselyte.

Non-proselyte Conversion in the Old Testament

God's plan since the time of Abraham has been to bless all of the nations, peoples, and families of the earth (Gen 12:3). His redemptive program focused on Abraham's descendants—Isaac, Jacob, and the nation of Israel, who were to serve as a "light to the nations." There was no clear or specific command to engage in proselytism, and thus for many centuries the Jews did not send out many evangelists or missionaries. Yet even this attracting power and purpose of Israel's light did not necessarily have proselytism and religious cultural conformity in mind. For conspicuously absent from the Old Testament is a call for the nations to follow Israel in observing the Mosaic law.[33] Accordingly, the prophet Amos pronounces judgment on other nations on the basis of their treatment of human beings, but when the prophet condemns Judah and Israel, the covenant becomes a standard of judgment. A principal reason is because the Law was the covenantal expression of its national religion, the legal code of Israel's theocratic government. God's purpose for giving the Law was not to create a world religion, but to reveal his identity, character, and ways to the nations through his dealings with Israel as it lived in covenantal relationship with him through the Torah. Thus Israel would be a "light to the nations," showing them that they too could enjoy the presence and blessing of Yahweh by acknowledging him as supreme and treating people according to the moral standards reflected in the Torah (Isa 2:2–4).

As mentioned earlier, the OT affirms the faith of people of faith who were outside of the stream of Abrahamic revelation, such as Melchizedek, Abimelech, and the queen of Sheba. Jethro, the priest of Midian, rejoiced in God's great deeds through Moses, but returned home without joining Israel. The message of Israel's prophets pronounced judgment on the surrounding nations for their sins of idolatry, injustice, oppression, and wickedness, but nowhere do we see a call for them to adopt the Jewish way of life and system of worship prescribed in the law of Moses. A case in point is Yahweh-fearing Naomi, who exhorts Ruth to return to her own people and god; Ruth has to persuade her mother-in-law to allow her to go with her to join Naomi's people and worship her God.[34] Even the prophets sent to Israel's

---

32 Ibid., 8.

33 Note that in Amos 1 and 2 these nations are judged on the basis of treatment of humans, but when the prophet comes to Judah and Israel, the covenant becomes a standard of judgment.

34 Homer Heater, email to author, July 28, 2012.

enemies (Obadiah to Edom, Jonah to Nineveh, and Nahum to Assyria) do not call for adopting the religion of Israel or temple worship in Jerusalem. The Lord commissioned Jonah to preach repentance to the Ninevites lest they perish, but there is not a hint that proselyte conversion was required for them to be "saved." Repeatedly we hear that God's purpose for the nations was that they "know that I am the Lord" (Ezek 36:23), which demanded that they, like Israel, recognize his supremacy and do justice, love kindness, and walk humbly with God (Mic 6:8). The details of what this would look like in each nation were not spelled out,[35] but it may be implied that to the degree Israel showed its light to the nations, they were to abide by the ethical principles exemplified in the Torah. In the *eschaton,* Isaiah (2:2–9) pictures the nations coming to God's temple to learn "his ways" (the standards of morality that God requires of people).

A famous example of that purpose being fulfilled is found in the case of Naaman the Syrian. His healing from leprosy (2 Kgs 5) provides an example of non-proselyte conversion. The witness of a captured Israelite servant girl leads Naaman to the king of Israel and then to the house of Elisha. The prophet is determined to demonstrate the power and grace of God. The result is that Naaman declares his new faith that "there is no god in all the world except in Israel." He asks for two mule-loads of dirt so that he can build an altar to the Lord, in keeping with his vow that he will not offer a sacrifice or burnt offering to other than Yahweh. (While Yahweh can be worshiped anywhere, Scripture also supports the notion of sacred space. Exodus 20:24 legislates that altars be constructed of soil, *'adamah,* the same word that Naaman uses. Whether Naaman knew this is not important, for biblical characters often "know" more than they actually know.[36] "The petition to get earth of Israel indicates the clear intention to worship Yahweh alone," observes Daniel Baeq.[37]) This request indicates that Naaman had no intention of being a "secret believer." (It would have been well nigh impossible to keep his faith a secret, given the visible proof of his miraculous healing, his entourage's hearing of his vow, the mules carrying dirt, and then a constructed altar.) But neither does Naaman consider participating in Jewish religious rites in Jerusalem's temple. As Baeq suggests,

> More likely, he would have offered up sacrifices in the most reverent and worshipful way he knows. Certainly the likelihood of his generating syncretism was there, but more likely, because the material that made up the altar was from Israel, he would never forget that he is, in fact, worshiping God. That altar would represent no being other than YHWH, the God who searches the hearts of men, the God who would accept his sacrifices.[38]

However, returning to his country, people, and job will entail fulfilling his duties as the king's top general—one of which is to escort the king into the temple of Rimmon. With the king leaning on his

---

35 Perhaps the legal and religious life of the Gentiles would be analogous to a comparison of codes of law in two countries today; many of the moral demands of the law are the same (prohibiting murder, theft, etc.), but dissimilarities reflect their different contexts and cultural values. Some later Jews (as in the Talmud) viewed the Gentiles as being under the Noahic covenant.

36 Frank Anthony Spina, *The Faith of the Outsider: Exclusion and Inclusion in the Biblical Story* (Grand Rapid, MI: Eerdmans, 2005), 86.

37 Daniel Shinjong Baeq, "Contextualizing Religious Form and Meaning: A Missiological Interpretation of Naaman's Petitions (2 Kings 5:15–19)," *IJFM* 27, no. 4 (2010): 200.

38 Baeq, "Contextualizing Religious Form and Meaning," 203.

arm, Naaman must assist him in bowing in worship, and for this Naaman asks "forgiveness." Some, like Timothy Tennent, interpret this request for "forgiveness" as springing from Naaman's feelings of guilt for what both he and Elisha "knew was wrong." But Baeq shows how

> the symmetrical structure of his petition explicitly showed that his bowing did not have the same meaning as his master's bowing, which was described as "worshiping" . . . Rimmon. If he does not attach a pagan spiritual meaning to his form of bowing, it should not be interpreted as an act of idolatry.[39]

Naaman's confession makes clear his complete faith that only the Lord is God, as he swears full allegiance to and exclusive worship of him. So it appears to me that Naaman is not asking for permission to engage in an act of idolatrous syncretism. In assisting the king to bow, he must bow with him—but Naaman's bowing is not one of worship of the idol. As Baeq explains,

> Naaman knows that as the commander of the army and a notable and powerful official, he is unable to excuse himself from all the state functions, which usually entailed religious rituals. Thus, rather than trying to hide what he would be required to do, he is earnest and honest before Elisha, voluntarily informing Elisha of an unavoidable, inevitable activity in his home land. The fact that he even brought up this subject strongly indicates that Naaman had already considered the future and foreseen what serving YHWH would entail in his home country. In essence, Naaman is explaining to Elisha that even though he has to physically bow down before the idol, he is not worshiping the idol.[40]

Thus the best interpretation of Naaman's request for "forgiveness" is that he is seeking "understanding" from Elisha.[41] As Frank Spina concludes, "The new convert wants to make sure Elisha realizes that, appearances aside, under no circumstances are his actions to be taken as sincere acts of worship."[42] His request is not for advance pardon of actual sin, but for the potential for misunderstanding based on mere appearances. This explanation is more convincing to me than suggesting that Elisha gave tacit approval for syncretistic idolatry—for that was the one thing that the prophets of Israel did not permit. Yet Elisha's reply is, "Go in *shalom*."

But regardless of how one interprets the significance or meaning of this concession, many Christians today would have acted differently than Elisha, had they been in his place. Many of us[43] would have insisted that Naaman avoid even an appearance of syncretism by joining our community of faith, becoming a Jewish proselyte through covenantal circumcision, and living according to the true religion

---

39 Ibid., 204.

40 Ibid., 203.

41 Ibid., 204.

42 Spina, *Faith of the Outsider*, 86.

43 This surmise of mine may be due to my being the product of a Western individualistic culture. One colleague noted that most Christians are now from the collectivist South, and that those he knows are much more sympathetic to the pressures that lead other collectivists to continue going along with certain things as they go through a process of redefining them internally.

of God (the Mosaic law). That Elisha does not even suggest this option indicates to me divine sanction for God's saving deeds being made known to the nations by non-proselyte converts such as Naaman.

Was Naaman an Insider?

It is somewhat anachronistic to refer to Naaman as an "insider" as defined by insider movement proponents, since he preceded the church age and life under the lordship of Jesus Christ. According to Lewis, insider movements have two essential characteristics:

1. Preexisting families and social groupings develop into fellowships of believers as they become followers of Christ; so the preexisting community becomes the church, rather than a new social group being created or "planted" as a church.
2. The believing families in insider movements remain inside their socioreligious communities by retaining their God-given birth identity while living under the lordship of Jesus Christ and the authority of the Bible.[44]

Even though we lack sufficient information to be certain, Naaman might have illustrated these two key attributes of an insider:

1. By not becoming a Jewish proselyte and instead returning to Aram, he could have remained within his preexisting social network—his household—which could have become his "church." (In the ancient world, members of a household normally followed the faith of its head. Moreover, we know for sure that his wife's servant-girl was a believer in Yahweh, and it seems likely that Naaman's servants who encouraged and witnessed his healing would have also believed.)

2. By fulfilling his duty as the king's adjutant, it appears that he could retain his identity as a *member* of his socioreligious *community* (even though he did not retain some of the fundamental tenets of what we would call the "religion" of his socioreligious community). Remaining part of this community would not have been possible had he joined the socioreligious community of Israel.[45]

Socioreligious Community versus Religion

Differentiating between a "religion" and "socioreligious community" has proven difficult for some: "How can someone be a Hindu follower of Christ when Hindus are idolatrous polytheists and believe in reincarnation?" This response reflects an "essentialist" view of "world religions" that defines them and their adherents by a monolithic set of basic beliefs and practices in contradistinction to other religions.[46]

---

44 Rebecca Lewis, "Insider Movements: Honoring God-given Identity and Community," *IJFM* 26, no. 1 (2009): 16.

45 Homer Heater finds in 1 Kgs an ironic parallel in the case of Obadiah (email to author, July 28, 2012). Obadiah faithfully followed the Lord even while serving in the court of Ahab and Jezebel, the arch-promoters of idolatrous worship and persecutors of God's prophets. Yet he remained part of the same socioreligious community (Israel), while rejecting Ahab and Jezebel's form of "religion."

46 Jan-Erik Lane and Svante O. Errson elaborate: "In the essentialist approach to religion, the emphasis is placed on its core ideas. The core of a religion is a set of beliefs or values which are in some sense fundamental to the religion in question, at least in the eyes of its virtuosi. It may be a controversial task to specify this core, but often religions have key sources from which one may distil its core beliefs or values. However, one may have to be content with laying down a variety of core interpretations of a religion since these will have been interpreted differently at various times. For instance, Christianity received a number of authoritative interpretations when it was established as a state religion, but this did not prevent it from later splitting into several core sets of beliefs

While the essentialist view is often assumed, contemporary research in the field of religious studies seriously challenges it. For example, Heinrich Von Stietencron asks, "Why is 'Hinduism' so difficult to define? This is because we always try to see it as one 'religion.' Our problems would vanish if we took 'Hinduism' to denote a socio-cultural unit or civilization which contains a plurality of distinct religions."[47]

A nineteenth-century British census report from the Punjab testifies, "It would hardly be expected that any difficulty or uncertainty should be felt in classing the natives of the Province under their respective religions. Yet, with the single exception of caste, no other one of the details which we have recorded is so difficult to fix with exactness."[48]

Dietrich Jung expresses similar sentiments about Islam:

> I have asked myself why Islam is so frequently represented in the holistic terms of an all-encompassing socioreligious system. How is the persistence of this specific image of Islam to be explained against all empirical evidence? Having worked and lived in various Muslim countries in the Middle East and beyond, I have been confronted with so many different Islams. No scholarly erudition is required to see the enormous variety. . . . Why, so the mind-boggling question, do then so many Muslims and non-Muslims nevertheless retain this essentialist image of "true Islam" in their minds?[49]

This sociological or cultural perspective accounts for the diversity in the history, beliefs, practices, and customs in the various religious traditions. It calls for us to speak in the plural (Christian traditions, Hindu faith traditions, and Islams) or in particulars (Algerian Berber Tijaniyya Sufi Islam).

Contemporary NT scholars tell us that the same was true of first-century Judaism. J. Andrew Overman states,

> So varied was Jewish society in the land of Israel during this period, and so varied were the Jewish groups, that scholars no longer speak of Judaism in the singular when discussing this formative and fertile period in Jewish history. Instead we speak about Judaisms. In this time and place there existed a number of competing, even rival Judaisms.[50]

---

and values. The same process has taken place within Islam." Lane and Errson, *Culture and Politics: A Comparative Approach* (Burlington, VT: Ashgate, 2005), 147.

47 Heinrich Von Stietencron, *Hindu Myth, Hindu History: Religion, Art and Politics* (Delhi: Permanent Black, 2005), 228.

48 Denzil Ibbetson, *Report on the Census of the Panjáb Taken on the 17th of February 1881* (Calcutta: Superintendent of Government Printing, 1883), 101.

49 Dietrich Jung, *Orientalists, Islamists and the Global Public Sphere: A Genealogy of the Essentialist Image of Islam* (Sheffield, UK: Equinox, 2011), 1. For additional challenges facing essentialist approaches to describing Islam, see Ronald Lukens-Bull, "Between Text and Practice: Considerations in the Anthropological Study of Islam," *Marburg Journal of Religion* 4, no. 2 (1999): 1–10.

50 Andrew Overman, *Church and Community in Crisis: The Gospel according to Matthew,* New Testament in Context (Valley Forge, PA: Trinity Press International, 1996), 9, cited in Charles H. Talbert, *Reading the Sermon*

Matthew's Gospel writing reflects one of these Judaisms. He did not view confronting the synagogue as a break from Judaism, but more akin to the Qumran community's perception of itself as faithful Israel. Matthew's Judaism had a different center (Jesus as the actualization of Torah), a different view of the will of God (the kingdom of God over the nation), and new leadership (the apostles challenging the unfaithful among the synagogue establishment)—but he still perceived the followers of Jesus as within Judaism (whereas some may view them as Christians).[51]

A sociological perspective helps explain how Muslims, Hindus, Buddhists, Jews, or others outside of traditional "Christianity" may be regarded as members of their socioreligious communities, even though they do not adhere to certain beliefs or practices of a religion (as prescribed by textbook definitions). Often even atheists can be considered part of such a socioreligious community, as long as they do not forsake it by becoming proselytes to a different socioreligious community.

Hence, given the frequency of such diversity within a given religious tradition, it is quite feasible for a movement of Christ followers inside it to retain an affiliation within that tradition that is distinctively different from other groups (due to its biblical character). It needs to be mentioned that such diversity is also evident among various insider movements. Sometimes even within the same geographical area, they do not look, act, interrelate, or self-identify monolithically.

Proselyte Conversion in the Old Testament

Conversion in the OT was not essentially a change to another religion (i.e., proselytism), but rather the conversion of the person to faith in the God of Israel. Nevertheless, proselytism was one way in which faith in the God of Israel was expressed.

God's stated intent was for Egypt to know that he was the Lord and serve him. Some of the fruit of God's mission through Moses was the "mixed multitude" that joined Israel's exodus. These would become "proselytes," becoming members of the covenant nation (formalized with their participation in circumcision with the Israelites in the wilderness). Thus the proselyte model of conversion does have a valid place in redemptive history. But at least in the case of the Egyptians and Edomites, the Law stipulated that only in the third generation could children of foreigners integrate into the community of Israel, "the assembly of the Lord" (Deut 23:1–8). Moreover, the Midianites (Num 10:29ff.) joined Israel while retaining their identity, of whom the Kenites (Judges 1:16; 4:11) dwelled among the Israelites in Canaan. Non-Israelite aliens dwelling with Israel were to participate in feasts and Sabbath and abstain from drinking blood, but to participate in Passover they had to be circumcised (Ex 12:48,49). All of this points to a degree of religious inclusion without religious conversion (becoming a proselyte).[52] Thus it appears that non-Jews could affiliate with Israel either as "God fearers" (who were not required to abide

on the Mount: Character Formation and Ethical Decision Making in Matthew 5–7 (Grand Rapids, MI: Baker Academic, 2006), 5.

51　I have nuanced the view of NT scholar Anthony J. Saldarini, who asserts that the different center was Jesus *rather than* Torah, the different view of the will of God was the kingdom of God *rather than* the nation, and the new leadership was the apostles *in place of* the synagogue establishment. See Saldarini, "Delegitimation of Leaders in Matthew 23," *Catholic Biblical Quarterly* 54, no. 4 (1992): 668, cited in Talbert, *Reading the Sermon on the Mount,* 5–6.

52　Dickson, *Uncompleted Mission,* 25–26.

by the Law in its entirety) or as proselytes (who entered by circumcision, baptism, temple sacrifice, and Torah observance; yet even the latter could never regard Israel's patriarchs as their fathers).[53]

Two of the most notable proselytes were Rahab and Ruth, who made the God and people of Israel their own. In contrast to women, who were unaffected by it, circumcision was a major obstacle to proselyte conversion for men. Even so, sources outside of the OT testify to the fact of proselyte conversion, as it required Gentiles to become Jews through ritual baptism, as purification from their pagan past. However, there is scant evidence for significant numbers of conversions to the religion of Israel in its early period.

Later, in the Hellenistic period, Jewish missionaries actively pursued the proselytizing of Gentiles.[54] While such Jews sought to make God fearers into proselytes, Jesus did not. He never required anything of Gentiles beyond simple faith. In his method of mission, his Jewish disciples remained Jews (but did not adhere to the false teachings of the religious establishment); Samaritan believers remained Samaritans (but now offered true, spiritual worship to the Father through the Savior of the world—John 4); and Gentile followers remained Gentiles, as Jesus' witnesses to what great things God had done for them (Mark 5:19). As we all know, after an intense struggle, the church eventually followed the model of Jesus in not requiring Jewish proselytism of Gentiles (Acts 15). Noteworthy for this study is how the Apostle James validated what they saw happening on the ground by quoting from the OT (Amos 9:11,12 LXX): "So that the rest of mankind may seek the Lord, and all the Gentiles who are called by My name" (Acts 15:17,18 NASB). James concluded that if the Gentiles were bearing God's name, then they were necessarily included in the people of God as *Gentiles*. This provides NT substantiation for the non-proselyte conversion model that is followed in insider movements.

Implications of This Study for Insider Movements

There are several implications that the OT attitude of openness toward other religions has for insider movements among non-Christian religious communities. Factors supporting insider movements include the following:

1. The recognition that God created all peoples and that human diversity reflects the will of God. Moreover, religions do not save—not even Israel's (nor ours); only God does. This should temper our temptation to follow the paradigm of proselyte conversion, which requires the adoption of identity and forms belonging to our Christian religious tradition.

2. OT openness provides a counterbalance to the exclusivist approach that other peoples are excluded from a relationship with God and their identity should be eliminated. Although Yahweh chose a particular people to be participants in the story of his revelatory and saving acts, belonging to this socioreligious group was insufficient apart from a right response to him. Likewise, not belonging to this socioreligious group did not preclude others from making this story their own and becoming a chapter in it. In fact, religions may provide a "starting point for people on their way to recognizing that the definitive acts of God are found in the story of Israel that comes to a climax in Jesus."[55]

---

53 Emil Schürer, *The History of the Jewish People in the Age of Jesus Christ*, vol. 3 (Edinburgh: T&T Clark, 1986), 161, cited in Dickson, *Uncompleted Mission*, 27.

54 The zeal of the Pharisees in traveling "land and sea to make one convert [proselyte]" (Matt 23:15) may be a reference to this. But others see this as an attempt to convert Jews to the stricter Pharisaic traditions of *halakhah*. See Daniel Boyarin, *The Jewish Gospels: The Story of the Jewish Christ* (New York: The New Press, 2012), 115.

55 Goldingay, "The First Testament," 6.

3. The significance of religion in Israel was not as a set of beliefs and practices for all to follow, nor in the number of its distinctive features, nor as a comparison with other religions. Rather, it was its testimony to God and his acts. As Goldingay affirms:

> Israel's significance lay in its status as witness to the deeds of the living, active, saving God. This is the repeated thrust of Isa 40–55: written in the context of overbearing religious plurality, the prophet did not encourage Israel to compare its religion with the Babylonians' and feel superior, but directed their thoughts to the acts of Yahweh in its actual history and declared, "You are Yahweh's witnesses."[56]

Likewise, what validates insider believers is their bearing witness to their community of what God in Christ has done for them and for the world.

4. Furthermore, other religious traditions can even enrich our own spiritual life and worship.[57]

At the same time, OT exclusivist attitudes toward other religions call for an approach of duality:

1. The Old Testament's attitude toward other religions "apparently varies not only with the nature of the religion, but also with the nature of the power and the pressure exercised by its adherents, but both openness and guardedness seem to feature in all contexts"[58]—as they must in insider movements. Thus, where a socioreligious tradition exerts more negative pressure on the insider community, greater resistance and rejection toward it will be needed.

2. The OT's dual stance toward other religions provides a foundation for insider approaches today,[59] with negative features of other religions being rejected, and positive aspects emulated. "Alongsiders" testify that this is in fact what they observe happening as insider believers seek to remain within the socioreligious community of their birth. As they evaluate their religious heritage, they retain the good and reject, reinterpret, or relegate the bad. More specifically,

    a. They can *retain* anything that is compatible with the Bible.[60]

---

56 Ibid., 11. Although "the prophet did not encourage Israel to compare its religion with the Babylonians' and feel superior," Isaiah did exhort the exiles of Israel to depart from Babylon and return to the Palestine: "Depart, depart, go out from there; touch no unclean thing; go out from the midst of her; purify yourselves, you who bear the vessels of the Lord" (52:11). The Apostle Paul cited this in 2 Cor 6:17 to warn, as did Isaiah, against participation in idol worship; biblical sanctification should include forsaking anything that defiles. This verse is frequently cited by critics to argue that insiders should leave their non-Christian socioreligious community. However, associating with unbelievers should not be equated with participation in evil. Paul's instructions to the Corinthians in regard to nonassociation with immoral people meant that they should separate from immoral *believers*, not from immoral unbelievers, "for then you would have to go out of the world" (1 Cor 5:9–11). This lends support to insiders living godly lives while remaining amidst unbelievers in their communities. In this Paul followed the teaching of the Lord Jesus, who did not seek his followers' withdrawal from the world but their protection from evil/the evil one: "My prayer is not that you will take them out of the world, but that you will keep them from the Evil One" (John 17:15). This duality reflects the tension between what Andrew Walls calls the "pilgrim principle" and the "indigenizing principle" of the gospel. See Walls in *UIM*, chap. 33.

57 Dickson, *Uncompleted Mission*, 61–66.

58 Goldingay, "The First Testament," 9.

59 Ibid., 14.

60 This is not to say that all Jesus followers will arrive at the same understandings of what the Bible teaches; for example, Calvin allowed only what was explicitly permitted in the Bible to be used in worship; Luther and Zwingli rejected only what the Bible forbade.

    b. They *reject* those elements of religious teaching that contradict the Bible (such as that Jesus did not die on the Cross, the Bible has been corrupted, Jesus is not the Savior, or salvation is by works).

    c. They *reinterpret* aspects that can be redeemed. For example, Muslims might continue to fast during Ramadan, no longer to earn salvation but to intensify their intercession for the salvation of their community. Those who continue the practice of ritual prayer would do so according to Jesus' instructions (Matt 6:5–15), making whatever adjustments they deem necessary to "worship in spirit and in truth" (John 4: 23,24 NRSV).

    d. They *relegate* (diminish or marginalize) the role that any previous religious authorities or writings had over their lives.[61]

3. Furthermore, an approach of duality should be reflected in each insider movement's identity (i.e., they should have a dual identity). The first Jesus community retained their identity within Judaism, while adopting a second identity as members of a renewal movement (the Way) that was a subgroup of their corporate Jewish identity. Published evidence of the dual, hybrid, and multiple identities among Muslim followers of Christ living in Islamic communities is provided by Jens Barnett.[62] Dudley Woodberry, one of the leading authorities on insider movements, maintains that all insider movements do end up with some kind of dual identity.[63]

Conclusion

The purpose of this study was to investigate possible theological foundations that would support insider movements. After becoming acquainted with the historical origins and a definition of insider movements, an Old Testament theology of other religions revealed dual attitudes of acceptance and rejection. We also determined that the OT's two fundamental criteria for assessing religions was their promotion of the fear of God and the pursuit of righteous living and that these could be expressed in "conversion." Two types of conversion were found in the OT: non-proselyte and proselyte. Naaman fits the non-proselyte model and illustrates conversion in the insider paradigm.

Those who hold to an essentialist view of religion cannot reconcile the idea of followers of Christ remaining within a non-Christian socioreligious community with the possibility of authentic discipleship. But we saw that contemporary scholarship argues against the essentialist view in favor of the cultural view of religions. The diversity inherent in the cultural view of a socioreligious tradition makes feasible the existence of a subgroup of Christ followers within it who develop a dual identity: one is a socioreligious identity that reflects their affiliation with that socioreligious tradition; the second is a spiritual identity (as Christ followers) that is distinctively different from the larger group.

The second type of OT conversion was the proselyte pattern. Though it was uncommon in early Jewish history, it became prominent during the later Hellenistic period. But Jesus opposed the proselytizing of Gentiles (as well as Samaritans); his only requirement for them was simple faith. By Acts 15 the church opted for the model of Jesus in not requiring Jewish proselytism of Gentiles. This decision was rooted in the theology of the OT (Amos 9). Hence, the NT supports the non-proselyte conversion model that is followed in insider movements.

---

61 Adapted from John Jay Travis, who uses "reassess" in place of "relegate."

62 Jens Barnett, "Conversion's Consequences: Identity, Belonging, and Hybridity amongst Muslim Followers of Christ" (MA thesis, Redcliffe College, August 2008).

63 Woodberry has stated this on many occasions, as well as in an email to the author, February 29, 2012.

Lastly, implications of this study for insider movements were offered. The OT's attitude of acceptance sanctions the appropriation of prior cultural forms and identity that enrich spiritual life and worship. What truly matters is the Jesus community's witness to what God has done in Christ. But OT exclusivist attitudes call for an approach of duality: negative features of other religions must be rejected (or reinterpreted or relegated), but positive aspects can be retained. Duality should also be expressed in identity: in socioreligious identity as well as spiritual identity (being in Christ and his body).[64]

Bibliography

Baeq, Daniel Shinjong. "Contextualizing Religious Form and Meaning: A Missiological Interpretation of Naaman's Petitions (2 Kings 5:15–19)." *International Journal of Frontier Missiology* 27, no. 4 (2010): 197–207.

Barnett, Jens. "Conversion's Consequences: Identity, Belonging, and Hybridity amongst Muslim Followers of Christ." MA thesis, Redcliffe College, August 2008.

Dickson, Kwesi A. *Uncompleted Mission: Christianity and Exclusivism.* Maryknoll, NY: Orbis, 1991.

Goldingay, John, and Christopher J. H. Wright. "'Yahweh Our God Yahweh One': The Old Testament and Religious Pluralism." In *One God, One Lord: Christianity in a World of Religious Pluralism*, 2nd ed., edited by Andrew D. Clarke and Bruce W. Winter, 43–62. Grand Rapids, MI: Baker, 1992.

Ibbetson, Denzil. *Report on the Census of the Panjáb Taken on the 17th of February 1881.* Calcutta: Superintendent of Government Printing, 1883.

Jewish Heritage Online Magazine. "The Sacred Tree: Tree Worship in Ancient Israel." http://www.jhom .com/topics/trees/worship.htm (accessed December 17, 2014).

Jung, Dietrich. *Orientalists, Islamists and the Global Public Sphere: A Genealogy of the Essentialist Image of Islam.* Sheffield, UK: Equinox, 2011.

Kärkkäinen, Veli-Matti. *An Introduction to the Theology of Religions: Biblical, Historical and Contemporary Perspectives.* Downers Grove, IL: InterVarsity Press, 2003.

Lane, Jan-Erik, and Svante O. Errson. *Culture and Politics: A Comparative Approach.* Burlington, VT: Ashgate, 2005.

Lukens-Bull, Ronald. "Between Text and Practice: Considerations in the Anthropological Study of Islam." *Marburg Journal of Religion* 4, no. 2 (1999): 1–10.

McDermott, Gerald. "What If Paul Had Been from China? Reflections on the Possibility of Revelation in Non-Christian Religions." In *No Other Gods before Me: Evangelicals and the Challenge of World Religions*, edited by John G. Stackhouse, 17–35. Grand Rapids, MI: Baker, 2001.

---

64 This study has attempted to at least show that non-Israelites in the OT could be saved without becoming Jewish proselytes. It has not attempted to specify exactly what they had to believe or practice in order to be saved. For example, the OT is not entirely clear whether or not non-Israelites had to believe in/worship YHWH alone for salvation. Some theologians do not believe Nebuchadnezzar was saved, even though he recognized the supremacy of the God of Israel, because he did not offer exclusive worship to him. (Note that the same could be said of Solomon and Gideon.) Another question is whether they could in some sense be saved even if they did not know YHWH, a corollary to the contemporary issue of whether some who have not yet heard of Christ can be saved because of what he has done. But these issues are not central to insider movements, where disciples of Jesus proclaim salvation through Christ while remaining in their non-Christian socioreligious communities. The possibility of the salvation of those communities apart from the gospel of Christ is not in view.

Pinnock, Clark H. *A Wideness in God's Mercy: The Finality of Jesus Christ in a World of Religions*. Grand Rapids, MI: Zondervan, 1992.

Sarna, Nahum. *Genesis*. JPS Torah Commentary. Philadelphia: Jewish Publication Society of America, 1989.

Schürer, Emil. *The History of the Jewish People in the Age of Jesus Christ*. 4 vols. Edinburgh: T&T Clark, 1986.

Senior, Donald, and Carroll Stuhlmueller. *The Biblical Foundations for Mission*. Maryknoll, NY: Orbis, 1983.

Spina, Frank Anthony. *The Faith of the Outsider: Exclusion and Inclusion in the Biblical Story*. Grand Rapids, MI: Eerdmans, 2005.

Stietencron, Heinrich Von. *Hindu Myth, Hindu History: Religion, Art and Politics*. Delhi: Permanent Black, 2005.

Talbert, Charles H. *Reading the Sermon on the Mount: Character Formation and Ethical Decision Making in Matthew 5–7*. Grand Rapids, MI: Baker Academic, 2006.

Van Engen, Charles. *God's Missionary People: Rethinking the Purpose of the Local Church*. Grand Rapids, MI: Baker, 1991.

Vawter, Bruce. *On Genesis: A New Reading*. New York: Doubleday, 1977.

CHAPTER 22

Conversion in the New Testament
Michael Roberts and Richard Jameson

This chapter focuses on the ministries of Jesus and Paul as they pertain to conversion. Jesus and Paul were primarily concerned with moving people from the dominion of darkness into the kingdom of light. For both Jews and non-Jews this required turning away from sin and turning to Jesus as Savior and Lord. Early Jewish followers of Jesus could enter this new kingdom while continuing to remain in their socioreligious communities and using many of their traditional religious forms. This turning to Jesus for the Gentiles required a complete rejection of idolatry, while allowing these Gentiles to remain as Gentiles within their sociocultural communities. To demonstrate this we will look at (1) the meaning of the pertinent Greek words as they relate to conversion, (2) Jesus' ministry among Jews in Israel, (3) Jesus' Jewish followers in the book of Acts, (4) Jesus' ministry to Gentiles, (5) Jesus' ministry to Samaritans, and finally, (6) Paul's teaching and lifestyle.

The Concept of Conversion

The word "conversion" in common usage creates a sociolinguistic difficulty, because it carries the connotation of changing from one religious system to another.[1] There are myriad religious systems in today's world. As evangelicals, we hold that regeneration by the Holy Spirit is the experience that transfers people from the dominion of darkness into the kingdom of God's beloved Son (Col 1:13). It appears that the vast majority of adherents to these many religious systems, including nominal adherents to the Christian faith, currently live within the dominion of darkness. If "conversion" refers to moving from one religious system to another religious system, "converts" may be simply relocating themselves within this dominion.

Greek Words and Their Meanings[2]

A Greek word used in the New Testament for one who changes from one religious system to another is *proselytos* (proselyte, convert), and it is used four times (Matt 23:15; Acts 2:11; 6:5; 13:43). In every instance, it refers to Gentiles converting to Judaism. It is not used to refer to someone who has come to

---

1   Cf. the definition at *Merriam-Webster Online*, s.v. "conversion," accessed May 7, 2015, http://www.merriam-webster.com/dictionary/conversion.

2   This section is derived and adapted from Samuel Livingway, "Were There Any Converts in the New Testament?" (unpublished paper, presented at the Common Ground Consultation, 2003).

Christ, repented from sin, turned to God, found new life or transformation in Christ, or put his or her trust in Christ as Savior and Lord.[3]

A second Greek term, *epistrophe* (verb *epistrepho*, from the root *strepho*), is used once in the New Testament (Acts 15:3) and is sometimes translated "conversion." *Strepho* and its cognates, however, are used many times and are rarely translated "to convert." Half of the thirty-six occurrences of *epistrepho* refer to a physical turning, and the other half to turning to the Lord from all that stands opposed to Christ and his kingdom. In translation, *strepho* is typically rendered "to turn" or "return." *A Greek-English Lexicon of the New Testament and Other Early Christian Literature* (BAGD) provides five definitions, all of which deal with turning or bringing back something. BAGD goes on to say, "The English term 'conversion' could suggest a change from one religious persuasion to another, which is not the case in these passages."[4] The *New International Dictionary of New Testament Theology* states that *strepho* "is often synonymous with *metanoeo*,"[5] generally signifying repentance and transformation, and this brings us closer to its true meaning. Thus if *epistrophe* in Acts 15:3 were simply translated "turning (from sin to God)," it might help avoid some of the confusion created by the connotation of the word "conversion" in English.

The Contemporary English Version does just this: "The men who were sent by the church went through Phoenicia and Samaria, telling how the Gentiles had turned to God. This news made the Lord's followers very happy."[6] *Epistrophe* here clearly refers to the Gentiles having turned to God, not their embracing the Judaistic religious system through circumcision. Religious identity through circumcision was in fact what the conflict was about. Some of the believing Pharisees, the Judaizers, demanded that the Gentiles convert to Judaism. However, the decision of Acts 15 rejected their demand; Gentile followers of Christ were not required to adopt Judaism as a new religious system.[7]

In Acts 15 we hear of the Gentiles believing the word of God (v. 7). We hear of God making no distinction between them and the Jews (v. 8). The Gentile believers were saved by the grace of the Lord Jesus, just as the Jewish believers were (v. 11). They were now a people for his name (v. 14). James states his conclusion in verse 19: "It is my judgment, therefore, that we should not make it difficult for the Gentiles who are turning to God." The "turning" to God here is *epistrephousin*, another use of the root *strepho* and parallel to *epistrophe* in 15:3. These verbs envelop the Jerusalem Council, and none of the translations examined here translates this later usage with a form of the English word "conversion." A better translation would show the parallelism with like terms and use a form of "turning" in both cases.

---

3   For some of the implications of the word *kyrios* and its use with and without the definite article, see Rick Brown and Christopher Samuel, "The meanings of κυριος 'Lord' in the New Testament" (SIL Publications, 2002).

4   Walter Bauer, William F. Arndt, F. Wilbur Gingrich, and Frederick W. Danker, *A Greek-English Lexicon of the New Testament and Other Early Christian Literature*, 2nd ed. (Chicago: University of Chicago Press, 1979), s.v. "*epistrepho*." BAGD abbreviates the surnames of the authors and editors of this work.

5   F. Laubach, "*epistrepho*," in *The New International Dictionary of New Testament Theology*, ed. Colin Brown, vol. 1 (Grand Rapids, MI: Zondervan, 1982), 355.

6   See also the GWT, NCV, GNT, GNTD, GNB, ERV, OJB translations which move away from conversion language and employ a form of turning or movement to Christ.

7   The new Gentile believers were asked to abide by four prohibitions that related to the prohibitions for "the alien who sojourns among you" in Leviticus. For a thorough analysis of the relationship between Acts 15:20 and Lev 17–18 see Richard Bauckham, "James and the Gentiles (Acts 15:13–21)," in *History, Literature and Society in the Book of Acts*, ed. Ben Witherington III (Cambridge: Cambridge University Press, 1996), 165–69.

A popular memory verse that also contains *strepho* is Matthew 18:3. The KJV translates it as "Verily I say unto you, except ye be converted, and become as little children, ye shall not enter into the kingdom of heaven." However, the NLT, the ESV, and the NET more appropriately use the language of turning—"unless you turn from your sins," "unless you turn," and "unless you turn around," respectively.

Thus *strepho* can be understood as a technical word that is best translated with some form of "turning," especially when describing our relationship to God. This is what the majority of translations do with the verb, nearly univocally, and especially in Acts (see 3:19; 7:39; 9:35; 11:21; 14:15; 26:18; cf. 2 Cor 3:16; 1 Thess 1:9). "Converting" to a new religious system is not in view.

Another Greek term that is *sometimes* translated "convert" is *aparche*. This word is found in Paul's closing remarks in Romans and 1 Corinthians. The NRSV renders Romans 16:5 as "Greet my beloved Epaenetus, who was the first convert in Asia for Christ," while the KJV says, "Salute my well-beloved Epaenetus, who is the *firstfruits* of Asia unto Christ" (emphasis added). The NRSV translates 1 Corinthians 16:15, "You know that members of the household of Stephanas were the first converts in Achaia." The NASB, however, translates, "You know the household of Stephanas, that they were the *first fruits* of Achaia" (emphasis added). Each of these translations is making a choice about how to render the Greek word *aparche*.

BAGD defines *aparche* as "firstfruits" or "beginning of a sacrifice."[8] *First fruits* connects a life of sacrifice and giving with following Christ. It is a beautiful description of a powerful concept. It links the Old Testament concept of sacrifice, and offering first fruits, with our call to serve and obey Christ. We offer our best. But note also that this is not the only time *aparche* is used in Romans and 1 Corinthians. In Romans 8:23 we read, "Not only so, but we ourselves, who have the firstfruits of the Spirit, groan inwardly as we wait eagerly for our adoption to sonship, the redemption of our bodies"; and in Romans 11:16, "If the part of the dough offered as firstfruits is holy, then the whole batch is holy; if the root is holy, so are the branches." In 1 Corinthians 15:20,23 we read, "Christ has indeed been raised from the dead, the firstfruits of those who have fallen asleep. . . . But each in turn: Christ, the firstfruits; then, when he comes, those who belong to him."[9]

Aparche is the same word that is used in Romans 16:5 and 1 Corinthians 16:15 to describe new believers—rendered "convert(s)" by some translators! Why the lack of consistency? Can you imagine saying in 1 Corinthians 15:20 that Christ is "the first convert of those who have fallen asleep"? Yet it is the same Greek word. It would be better to translate consistently in these instances and say that Epaenetus and the household of Stephanas were the first fruits of the movement to Christ in those regions. This beautiful image expresses something that is organic and growing, and it is consistent with the entire biblical witness related to first fruits.

Jesus' Ministry among Jews in Israel

The Bible expects followers of Jesus to imitate Christ (e.g., Eph 5:1; 1 Cor 11:1; 1 Thess 1:6). Yet did Jesus assume that this imitation would require his Jewish followers to leave Judaism? What did Jesus expect from the Jewish people as they turned to follow him?

All of Jesus' apostles and most of his followers were Jews. Numerous times Jesus called people to repent and to turn to God, but Jesus did not tell his Jewish disciples to abandon their Jewish roots. It

---

8   Bauer et al., *A Greek-English Lexicon*, s.v. "*aparche*."

9   Quotations in this paragraph are taken from the NIV.

appears that changing religions was not a part of Jesus' message, because the earliest disciples and the earliest followers of Jesus remained as integral members in their Jewish socioreligious communities.

Jesus' Jewish Followers in the Book of Acts

As we read the book of Acts we see that the early disciples of Jesus remained within their Jewish religious communities. They not only remained within their communities, but they also felt comfortable performing Jewish religious rituals and celebrating Jewish religious festivals. In Acts 2:1 we discover that the disciples were celebrating Pentecost in Jerusalem: "Now when the day of Pentecost had come, they were all together in one place."[10]

Besides being at a Jewish feast at the time of Pentecost, the Jewish believers continued to go to the temple for prayer. In Acts 2:46 we read, "Every day they continued to gather together by common consent in the temple courts." This is reinforced by Peter and John's actions, as they regularly went to the temple for the Jewish ritual prayers: "Now Peter and John were going up to the temple at the time for prayer, at three o'clock in the afternoon" (Acts 3:1). Acts 5:12 demonstrates that the disciples continued in this habit: "They were all meeting together in Solomon's Portico." This verse also seems to indicate that the Jewish followers of Jesus gathered in a specific place within the temple.

Even though the believers remained as integral members within their socioreligious communities, this did not keep them from getting into trouble with other Jews and with the Jewish authorities. After Peter and John healed the lame man in Acts 3, they were arrested by the rulers. We read in Acts 4:5–7 of their trial:

> On the next day, their rulers, elders, and experts in the law came together in Jerusalem. Annas the high priest was there, and Caiaphas, John, Alexander, and others who were members of the high priest's family. After making Peter and John stand in their midst, they began to inquire, "By what power or by what name did you do this?"

In spite of this harassment and arrest, the apostles remained true to the Lord and proclaimed that Jesus was not only the source of the lame man's healing but also the only way of salvation:

> Be it known to you all, and to all the people of Israel, that by the name of Jesus Christ of Nazareth, whom you crucified, whom God raised from the dead, by him this man is standing before you well. This is the stone which was rejected by you builders, but which has become the head of the corner. And there is salvation in no one else, for there is no other name under heaven given among men by which we must be saved. (Acts 4:10–12 RSV)

The distinction Jesus' followers had was not that they had separated themselves from their socioreligious communities but that they had distinct beliefs and were different in character. We read in Acts 5:13 that people were afraid to join Jesus' followers after Ananias and Sapphira died, but that Jesus' followers were well respected: "None of the rest dared to join them, but the people held them in high

---

10   Scripture quotations in this chapter are taken from the NET Bible translation (NET) unless otherwise stated.

honor." The context indicates that the people's respect was based upon the believers' integrity and the presence of the Holy Spirit.

We see in Acts 5:42 that Jesus' Jewish followers continued to meet and teach at the temple, and this gave them a venue to faithfully proclaim Jesus as the promised Messiah: "And every day both in the temple courts and from house to house, they did not stop teaching and proclaiming the good news that Jesus was the Christ."

While these early Jewish followers of Jesus remained within their communities, their differences in beliefs continued to surface. Stephen, as a Jew of the Diaspora, was apparently one of the first to challenge traditional Jewish ideas about the land and the temple. In response to this threat, a group of Hellenistic Jews lured Stephen into a trap. In Acts 6:11,12 we read, "Then they secretly instigated some men to say, 'We have heard this man speaking blasphemous words against Moses and God.' They incited the people, the elders, and the experts in the law; then they approached Stephen, seized him, and brought him before the council."

Stephen was not charged with trying to create a new religion, but he was charged with challenging traditional and cherished understandings. In Acts 6:14 we read of the accusation against him: "For we have heard him saying that Jesus the Nazarene will destroy this place and change the customs that Moses handed down to us." In response, Stephen refers to his accusers and the ruling council as brothers. "So he replied, 'Brothers and fathers, listen to me. The God of glory appeared to our forefather Abraham when he was in Mesopotamia, before he settled in Haran'" (Acts 7:2). They were not brothers because of their shared faith in Jesus as Messiah; they were brothers because they were members of the same socioreligious community.

In Acts 9 we read of the persecution that arose after Stephen's death and of Saul's desire to broaden the persecution of believers to Damascus: "Meanwhile Saul, still breathing out threats to murder the Lord's disciples, went to the high priest and requested letters from him to the synagogues in Damascus, so that if he found any who belonged to the Way, either men or women, he could bring them as prisoners to Jerusalem" (vv. 1,2).

Letters from a Jewish high priest would only have validity within a Jewish community, since a Roman city like Damascus was not under the jurisdiction of the high priest. The Jewish disciples of Jesus in Damascus had remained within their socioreligious communities and were meeting in Jewish synagogues. They were still Jews, but they were considered a special group of Jews, members of "The Way."

Deviating from traditional religious-cultural boundaries caused trouble for Peter in Acts 10 and 11. In Acts 10 Peter went to Cornelius' house and ate with Cornelius and his household. We read of the response of the Jewish believers in Jerusalem to this act in Acts 11:2,3: "So when Peter went up to Jerusalem, the circumcised believers took issue with him, saying, 'You went to uncircumcised men and shared a meal with them.'" The prohibition to not eat with Gentiles would have been irrelevant if Peter had not kept his Jewish identity and left his Jewish socioreligious community. However, Peter was a Jew. What made him distinct even in his believing Jewish community was that he was governed by God's directions, not by traditional Jewish customs.

The fact that Gentiles had come to faith in Jesus but remained within their socioreligious communities was difficult for some Jewish followers of Jesus to accept. It raised quite the controversy. In Acts 15 Paul and Barnabas went to Jerusalem to try to resolve this issue. At this meeting of the church, "some from the religious party of the Pharisees who had believed stood up and said, 'It is necessary to circumcise the Gentiles and to order them to observe the law of Moses'" (Acts 15:5). What is significant is that these Jewish followers of Christ were not only Jewish in terms of their socioreligious identity, but they were also members of the party of the Pharisees. They saw no conflict in being Pharisees and followers of Jesus, and neither did anyone else at the meetings.

Paul exemplifies this "remaining in community" as well. Even though Paul knew that he was called to reach out to the Gentiles, it appears that he never lost his fundamental identity as a Jew. We see this in a number of his actions. In Acts 20 Paul wanted to get to Jerusalem so he could celebrate the Jewish feast of Pentecost. "For Paul had decided to sail past Ephesus so as not to spend time in the province of Asia, for he was hurrying to arrive in Jerusalem, if possible, by the day of Pentecost" (Acts 20:16). Then when Paul arrived in Jerusalem and contacted the believers there, we read that many of the believers were still zealous for the Mosaic law: "Then they said to him, 'You see, brother, how many thousands of Jews there are who have believed, and they are all ardent observers of the law'" (Acts 21:20). Due to their zeal for the Law, Paul agreed to not only ritually purify himself and worship in the temple but pay for four others to worship in the temple as well (Acts 21:23–26; see also Acts 24:11).

It was while Paul was worshiping in the temple that a commotion arose and he was arrested. In his defense to the crowd, Paul identified himself as a Jew: "Then Paul said, 'I am a Jew'" (Acts 22:2,3).

Paul did not only identify himself as a Jew, but he also identified himself as a Pharisee. In Acts 23:6 we read, "Paul . . . shouted out in the council, 'Brothers, I am a Pharisee, a son of Pharisees. I am on trial concerning the hope of the resurrection of the dead!'"

At the end of the book of Acts (28:17), Paul calls the local Jewish leaders together and refers to them as his "brothers." They do not believe in Jesus, but they are brothers to Paul. This is because he has remained as an integral member of his socioreligious community.

In conclusion, the early Jewish followers of Christ maintained their socioreligious identity as Jews even at the very end of the book of Acts. However, these Jewish followers were no longer "standard" Jews who merely believed and acted the same way as other Jews. The Jewish followers of Jesus also had distinctions in doctrine, belief, life, morals, and customs. Some of these were the natural result of increased fellowship shared with Gentiles. Due to these distinct differences, they were somewhat marginalized in their socioreligious communities because of their faith in and obedience to Jesus.[11]

Jesus' Ministry to Gentiles

This principle of remaining within one's community appears to surface in four of Jesus' encounters with Gentiles: with the Gerasene demoniac, the Syrophoenician woman, the four thousand whom he fed, and the Roman centurion.

---

11 The book of Hebrews may offer us some cautions in the application of these principles in a contemporary setting. We must warn in love any community of faith that (1) exalts spiritual beings (angels) as equal to or higher than Jesus; (2) exalts any person, living or dead, to the degree that it challenges Jesus' rightful and unique place as the King of kings and personal Lord of their lives; (3) holds to any book or tradition as having authority over the canonical Scriptures either as an inviolable interpretive base or as subsequent inspired revelation; (4) teaches salvation through any means other than faith in the work of Christ (e.g., through human constructs such as adherence to a religious system or the recitation of creeds); or (5) mitigates the cost of discipleship.

The Demoniac

Jesus' ministry to a Gentile with the most detail in the Gospels is his ministry to the Gerasene demoniac. Mark presents the demoniac as a Gentile based on location,[12] associations,[13] and family connections.[14] The demoniac, once healed, begged Jesus to allow him to remain with Jesus.[15] The healed Gentile wanted to leave his community and follow Jesus. To follow a Jewish rabbi around in Jewish territories would have necessitated full conversion to Judaism. Contrary to popular expectations at the time, Jesus did not allow this Gentile to travel with him. Instead Jesus told him, "Go to your home and to your people and tell them what the Lord has done for you, that he had mercy on you" (Mark 5:19). One might say that the healed demoniac was asking to "convert" in the modern sense, and Jesus refused his request. However, the text explicitly indicates that he was a changed man. He was clothed and in his right mind (5:15), and he was a witness to his family, relatives, and everyone in the Decapolis (5:20).

The Syrophoenician Woman

While in the area of Tyre and Sidon, Jesus encountered a Syrophoenician woman whose daughter was demonized. This woman was a Gentile, as she is called a Greek and a Syrian/Phoenician (Mark 7:26). It appears that Jesus initially spoke a bit harshly to her. Nonetheless, she demonstrated a unique trust in Jesus and a remarkable humility. It appears that the Spirit had been working upon her prior to her coming to Jesus. Jesus in response healed her daughter. Jesus did not ask her to convert to Judaism.

The Feeding of the Four Thousand

Jesus then traveled north to Sidon, east to the Decapolis (modern-day Syria), and then south through the Decapolis to the Sea of Galilee (Mark 7:31). All these were Gentile areas. When he arrived at the

---

12   Mark 5:1 mentions the location of the demoniac in the country of the Gerasenes, a Roman area.

13   Mark 5:11 mentions a large herd of swine, 5:14 the relationship the swineherds had with the people of the area, and 5:14–17 the relationships the people of the area had with the demoniac.

14   Mark 5:19,20 indicates that the demoniac's household and relatives were in the Decapolis, which was a Roman area.

15   In the words of Christopher Wright, he is "the first Gentile missionary to Gentiles, commissioned by Christ himself. Clearly his testimony bore fruit in the region, for on Jesus' next visit to the Decapolis (from which, remember, he had been begged to depart), people brought the man who was both deaf and dumb for healing." Christopher J. H. Wright, *The Mission of God: Unlocking the Bible's Grand Narrative* (Downers Grove, IL: IVP Academic, 2006), 508. We note but are unpersuaded by the contrasting view of Rikki Watts, who asserts that the demoniac was a Jew, symbolizing Jews in exile; see Watts, *Isaiah's New Exodus in Mark* (Grand Rapids, MI: Baker Academic, 2000), 163–69. However, Watts recognizes that the identity of the demoniac is ambiguous; and this ambiguity was likely intentional by Mark. Watts states, "[If] these events, although located in predominantly Gentile regions, are nevertheless concerned with 'exiled' Israelites . . . then Jesus can be seen as acting in harmony with a stricter INE [Isaianic New Exodus] agenda. So why then Mark's ambiguity? It may be that his Gospel represents a combination of both agendas: Mark's Jesus restricts his activity to Israel, but Mark, by means of his indeterminate identifications, foreshadows that Jesus' ministry will ultimately result in 'light to the Gentiles.'" Thus even the possibility of identifying the demoniac as Jewish does not negate the significance or character of Jesus' ministry in this Gentile-dominated area. This is because v. 20 says, "And he went away and began to proclaim in the Decapolis how much Jesus had done for him, and everyone marveled." So the demoniac proclaimed his deliverance to all. The result of his proclamation was that "everyone"—Jew and Gentile—"marveled." In Watts' view, the result of the demoniac's proclamation, combined with Jesus' ministry to others in this Gentile-dominated region, was the mixed Gentile and Jewish crowd at the feeding of the four thousand.

Sea of Galilee, he fed four thousand people. When we compare the feeding of the five thousand in Mark 6:30–44 and the feeding of the four thousand in Mark 8:1–10, there are textual indications that Gentiles were among those in the latter group. These indications include the geographical area (east of the Sea of Galilee), the number of baskets and the number of loaves (seven each), and that some of those in the crowd had "come from a great distance" (Mark 8:3).[16] Mark seems to be indicating that these Gentiles had been affected by the demoniac's witness and the healing of the Syrophoenician woman, since their regions of witness were those through which Jesus had just traveled. In the text Jesus does not require that these recipients of his grace become Jews.

The Roman Centurion

The Roman centurion is another Gentile to whom Jesus ministered (Matt 8:5–13). In their interaction Jesus commended him for his faith and said that he would share the banquet with Abraham, Isaac, and Jacob. This promise of eternal salvation by Jesus was not contingent upon the centurion's conversion to Judaism. However, it is significant that the centurion's beliefs were different from standard Roman beliefs. The centurion had great faith in Jesus, and he was a different man as a result.

In conclusion, in these encounters Jesus did not ask the Gentiles to convert to Judaism. Nonetheless, for the individual Gentiles who encountered Jesus, we see that they demonstrated a faith in Jesus that was unique and transformative.

Jesus' Ministry to the Samaritans[17]

Jesus considered the Samaritans to be foreigners, even though they believed in and worshiped one God, avoided images, and had a sense of being the chosen people with attachment to the land given to the fathers (Israel/the northern tribes).[18] They also were loyal to the Law given by Moses, observed the Sabbath, were circumcised, celebrated festivals, and expected a glorious destiny.[19]

Despite these similarities they had significant differences from the Jews. These differences included their own priesthood, their worship practices and rituals, and their religious teachings and writings. For instance, they believed that when God said, "Let there be light," that light was the Holy Spirit, which was the preexistent Moses.[20] Several scholars have affirmed that Samaritanism was a separate religion.[21]

---

16 Robert Guelich writes, "Mark's geographical and literary setting does imply that this Feeding involved Gentiles. . . . Following as it does the discussions of 7:1–23 with both the Pharisees and the disciples about purity laws regarding eating that had formed part of the social boundaries between Jews and Gentiles, this Feeding set in Gentile territory would certainly have included Gentiles. They, like the Syrophoenician woman and the deaf-mute, receive the benefit of Jesus' redemptive ministry in their territory." Robert A. Guelich, *Word Biblical Commentary*, ed. Ralph P. Martin, vol. 34A, *Mark 1–8:26* (Dallas: Word, 1989).

17 The authors are indebted to Samuel Livingway for the information in this section; see Livingway in *UIM*, appendix 1.

18 Luke 17:15–19; see also John 8:48; 2 Kgs 17:20.

19 Everett Ferguson, *Backgrounds of Early Christianity*, 3rd ed. (Grand Rapids, MI: Eerdmans, 2003), 534–35.

20 John Bowman, "Samaritan Studies," *Bulletin of the John Rylands Library* 40 (1957–58), 303. Available at https://www.escholar.manchester.ac.uk/api/datastream?publicationPid=uk-ac-man-scw:1m1946&datastreamId =POST-PEER-REVIEW-PUBLISHERS-DOCUMENT.PDF.

21 See Ida Glaser, "Facing Samaritan Religion," chap. 11 in *The Bible and Other Faiths: Christian Responsibility in a World of Religions* (Downers Grove, IL: IVP Academic, 2005); John Bowman, "The Religion of the Samaritans," chap. 1 in *The Samaritan Problem: Studies in the Relationships of Samaritanism, Judaism, and Early Christianity*

The Samaritan Woman

Jesus' principle of not requiring conversion to Judaism is seen in his discussion with the Samaritan woman (John 4:7–26). In 4:9,10 Jesus avoided discussing their differences in faith. It is written,

> So the Samaritan woman said to him, "How can you—a Jew—ask me, a Samaritan woman, for water to drink?" (For Jews use nothing in common with Samaritans.) Jesus answered her, "If you had known the gift of God and who it is who said to you, 'Give me some water to drink,' you would have asked him, and he would have given you living water."

If Jesus had gotten sidetracked into a discussion of religion (Jews are better than Samaritans; our religion is right and yours is wrong), the conversation likely would not have proceeded further.

In their discussion Jesus could have talked about "conversion" with this woman by telling her that Jerusalem was the rightfully ordained place for worship, not Mount Gerizim. Instead Jesus told the Samaritan woman that where one worshiped was not important. What was important was how one worshiped: in Spirit[22] and truth. Then Jesus directed the Samaritan woman's attention to himself. The focus of Jesus' message was himself, not the Jewish religious system.[23]

In John 4:20–26 we read this part of their discussion:

> "Our fathers worshiped on this mountain, and you people say that the place where people must worship is in Jerusalem." Jesus said to her, "Believe me, woman, a time is coming when you will worship the Father neither on this mountain nor in Jerusalem. You people worship what you do not know. We worship what we know, because salvation is from the Jews. But a time is coming—and now is here—when the true worshipers will worship the Father in spirit and truth, for the Father seeks such people to be his worshipers. God is spirit, and the people who worship him must worship in spirit and truth." The woman said to him, "I know that Messiah is coming" (the one called Christ); "whenever he comes, he will tell us everything." Jesus said to her, "I, the one speaking to you, am he."

The Samaritan Community

This principle is reinforced in Jesus' ministry to the Samaritan community. Since Jesus had focused his conversation with the Samaritan woman on himself and the issues in her life, the woman went back

---

(Pittsburgh: Pickwick Press, 1975); John MacDonald, *The Theology of the Samaritans,* New Testament Library (Philadelphia: Westminster Press, 1964); and Everett Ferguson, *Backgrounds of Early Christianity,* 3rd ed. (Grand Rapids, MI: Eerdmans, 2003), 534. Reinhard Pummer in *The Samaritans* (Leiden: Brill, 1987) shows how even to this day differences between the Samaritan religion and Judaism exist. For example, modern-day Samaritans wash their hands and feet before prayers, leave their shoes outside the prayer place, prostrate to the ground and hold hands open while standing in prayer, and pray in lines facing the front; see Plates XXI, XXII, and XXIII.

22   Or "in spirit."

23   Most of the details of Christian churches today do not come from the Bible, but are of cultural origin. See Frank Viola and George Barna, *Pagan Christianity? Exploring the Roots of Our Church Practices* (Carol Stream, IL: BarnaBooks, 2008).

to her community and had them come and encounter Jesus for themselves. The result of this encounter was that many believed (John 4:39). Their encounter with Jesus was so powerful that they entreated him to remain with them a bit longer, and many more believed (4:41). John seems to indicate that these Samaritans had become true believers. "We have heard for ourselves, and we know that this one really is the Savior of the world" (4:42).

The outcome of Jesus' ministry among the Samaritans and the Gentiles was that many believed in him. Thus "Jesus movements" had begun. John's use of the terms "many" and "many more" in 4:39–41 indicates that a movement among the Samaritans had begun. Since Gentiles were among the four thousand fed (Mark 8:1–10), it appears that a Jesus movement had begun in those Gentile areas as well. We read in Acts 21:20 that thousands of Jews believed, and they were all zealous for the Law. This demonstrates that a Jesus movement had swept through Jewish communities as well.

It is unlikely that these movements would have begun if Jesus had told the Samaritan woman she had to embrace Judaism, if he had directed the demoniac to convert to Judaism, or if the thousands of Jews who had believed had been told that they had to leave Judaism and convert to "Christianity."

Paul's Example and Teaching

Paul continued in Jesus' footsteps by not requiring conversion to Judaism. In Acts 15:2, Paul disagreed with those who sought to require Gentiles to be circumcised and convert to Judaism. In Galatians, he was even stronger in his disagreement. Paul wrote,

> I am astonished that you are so quickly deserting him who called you in the grace of Christ and turning to a different gospel—not that there is another gospel, but there are some who trouble you and want to pervert the gospel of Christ. But even if we, or an angel from heaven, should preach to you a gospel contrary to that which we preached to you, let him be accursed. As we have said before, so now I say again, If any one is preaching to you a gospel contrary to that which you received, let him be accursed. (Gal 1:6–9 RSV)

Paul later in this same letter restated this position:

> Now I, Paul, say to you that if you receive circumcision, Christ will be of no advantage to you. I testify again to every man who receives circumcision that he is bound to keep the whole law. You are severed from Christ, you who would be justified by the law; you have fallen away from grace. For through the Spirit, by faith, we wait for the hope of righteousness. For in Christ Jesus neither circumcision nor uncircumcision is of any avail, but faith working through love. You were running well; who hindered you from obeying the truth? This persuasion is not from him who calls you. A little leaven leavens the whole lump. I have confidence in the Lord that you will take no other view than mine; and he who is troubling you will bear his judgment, whoever he is. But if I, brethren, still preach circumcision, why am I still persecuted? In that case the stumbling block

> of the cross has been removed. I wish those who unsettle you would
> mutilate themselves! (Gal 5:2–12 RSV)

Paul likened the Gentiles' conversion to Judaism to "deserting" the faith and to "turning to a different gospel." He said it led to being cursed, severed from Christ, and falling away from grace. Circumcision was *not* just unnecessary—it was warned against with some very strong terms.[24]

Perhaps none of Paul's letters give better insight into his missiological principles than his two letters to the Corinthian church. This church was perhaps the most dysfunctional church referenced in the New Testament. Pride, factionalism, sexual sin, and participation in pagan temple worship apparently continued to be common among these young believers. Yet even to this church Paul could write,

> I always thank my God for you because of the grace of God that was
> given to you in Christ Jesus. For you were made rich in every way
> in him—in all your speech and in every kind of knowledge—just
> as the testimony about Christ has been confirmed among you—so
> that you do not lack any spiritual gift as you wait for the revelation
> of our Lord Jesus Christ. He will also strengthen you to the end, so
> that you will be blameless on the day of our Lord Jesus Christ. God
> is faithful, by whom you were called into fellowship with his son,
> Jesus Christ our Lord. (1 Cor 1:4–9)

Though Paul was firmly against the believers participating in temple worship, Paul encouraged Corinthian believers to stay involved in their communities (1 Cor 5:9,10; 9:19–23; 10:31; 11:1). When confronted with the question of whether or not it was proper to remain married to an unbeliever, Paul wrote that they should remain in that marriage for the sake of witness (1 Cor 7:12–16). Paul then expanded this principle into a variety of other relationships (7:17–24).

Concerning this passage, Terence Paige writes, "When Paul called on believers to remain in the condition in which they were called (1 Cor 7:24), he was stressing that spirituality was not tied to social status."[25] One should be a spiritual witness within the community where he or she was a member before trusting Christ. In this passage, the phrase "remain in the condition in which they were called" refers to being slave or free, married or single, and circumcised or uncircumcised (Jew or Gentile). Paul specifically commands the circumcised not to seek uncircumcision and vice versa (7:18). So spirituality is not tied to social status, marital status, or religious community. Furthermore, Paul implies that this is not a local application that applies only in certain circumstances, but says it is his "rule in all the churches" (7:17 RSV). Thus it was a universal rule.

In harmony with Paul's admonition "to remain within" for the sake of witness is Paul's admonition to separate oneself from everything that is not in harmony with Christ's kingdom. Instead of factionalism Paul calls for unity. Instead of pride Paul calls for love and humility. Instead of sexual immorality Paul calls for purity. Finally, instead of ongoing participation in temple prostitution and idolatry, Paul

---

24 Paige states the same idea when he says, "It is not to be disputed that the apostolic community eventually came to the agreement that Gentile converts were not under the Mosaic Covenant." Terence Paige, "Early Gentile Christianity, Conversion, and Culture-shift in the New Testament" (paper presented at the Bridging the Divide conference, Houghton College, Houghton, NY, June 20–24, 2011), 9.

25 Paige, "Early Gentile Christianity," 15.

calls for quick and decisive separation. He writes, "Therefore, my dear friends, flee from idolatry" (1 Cor 10:14).

Application to the Contemporary Context

In this light, we see in Jesus and Paul the same message: Conversion to or from Judaism is not the focus of the gospel. Moving from one religious system to another is neither required nor encouraged. The gospel calls people to follow Jesus as Savior and Lord within the context in which they were called.

One might conceptualize the New Testament models of socioreligious communities on a continuum. On one end were Jewish believers. They came from the covenant community of faith and remained firmly embedded within their socioreligious communities as followers of Jesus. On the other end of the spectrum were the Greeks. As opposed to the monotheism and high moral convictions of the Jewish community, the Greeks came from a background of polytheism and rampant sexual immorality. Sexual immorality was an aspect of Greek temple worship. With regard to immorality and idolatry, Paul commanded the Gentile followers of Jesus to "come out from their midst, and be separate" (2 Cor 6:17). Samaritans might be placed on this continuum closer to the Jewish end of the spectrum, even though they were not part of the covenant community. Likewise, the God-fearing Gentiles could be placed away from their pagan counterparts, closer to the Jewish end of the spectrum.

In shifting to contemporary contexts, one might ask if the nonbelieving socioreligious community in which one is working is more similar to the Jewish covenant community or more similar to the immoral, idolatrous Gentile communities. Where a nonbelieving socioreligious community fits on this continuum has implications for the way the Holy Spirit might work within this community.

Many of us who have been involved with so-called insider movements among Muslims have witnessed the Spirit of God working with believers in ways somewhat similar to the way he worked among the first-century Jewish community. This should not be surprising. Even though Muslim socioreligious communities are not the same as first-century Jewish, God-ordained covenant communities, many see a number of similarities between them. Consider the following similarities between first-century Judaism and contemporary Islam:

1. Uncompromising monotheism
2. Rejection of the deity of Christ
3. Salvation based on being a member of the community along with faith plus good works ("What good thing must I do to get eternal life?")
4. Rejection of any atoning meaning for the Cross
5. Belief in an eternal "Word" of God in heaven from which their holy book is drawn: for second-temple Judaism this was the *Logos* concept drawn from Greek thought; for Muslims it is the *Umm al-Kitab* (the "Mother of the Book")
6. Rejection of the "Christian" interpretation of their holy book
7. Religious practices that are drawn primarily from traditions (cf. Mark 7)
8. Many similar religious forms[26]
9. Religious system that is primarily in the kingdom of darkness
   a. "You belong to your father, the devil, and you want to carry out your father's desires" (Jesus to religious leaders, John 8:44)

---

26 See Merrill F. Unger, *The New Unger's Bible Dictionary* (Chicago: Moody, 1988), 1025–26.

    b. "You make him twice as much a child of hell as yourselves!" (Jesus concerning those who are propagating Judaism, Matt 23:15); "Synagogue of Satan" (Jesus concerning Jews who reject him as Messiah—according to Jesus they are not really Jews; see Rev 2:9; 3:9)

10. Religion fully integrated into every aspect of life
11. Religious community that is made up of
    a. religious police ensuring scrupulous obedience to the religious law
    b. fundamentalists
    c. secularists
    d. mystics
    e. those promoting violence (Zealots/Sicarii) (Matt 10:4; Acts 21:23)

In spite of these similarities, historically most Muslims when turning to Christ have left their socioreligious community of birth. They have "converted" to Christianity. However, in recent years, perhaps as a result of these similarities, we are witnessing new ways that the Spirit of God is working among some Muslim communities. In certain places in the Muslim world, we are witnessing a new type of Christ followers—those who think of themselves as being Muslim followers of Christ. There are striking similarities between these contemporary Muslim Christ followers and their first-century Jewish counterparts:

1. Although unique in belief and practice, continuing to identify as part of their socioreligious community of birth
2. Strong dependence upon the work of the Holy Spirit
3. Lots of miracles, dreams, visions, and power encounters
4. Reinterpretation of the religious community's "book" and using it as a bridge to proclaim Christ
5. Intensive discipleship taking place in the home as true believers gather for prayer and teaching
6. Believers continuing to participate with the not-yet-believing community in some religious rituals and continuing to identify as part of this community
7. Bold and fruitful witness for Christ within their socioreligious community of birth
8. Persecution for not holding to "orthodoxy" within their religion of birth

Conclusion

As we have seen in this article, turning to Christ (conversion) does not necessarily demand that one leave one's socioreligious community of birth. The degree to which a follower of Christ must separate oneself from the religious practice of one's birth community seems to depend upon where that practice might fall on a continuum with highly moral, monotheistic Judaism on one end and immoral, polytheistic Greek religious practice on the other.

    In recent years a growing number of Muslims are turning to Christ, yet following a pattern similar to that seen in the first-century Jewish community. They are forging a new identity for themselves as Christ followers, yet retaining their identity within their socioreligious community of birth. They don't think of themselves as being "converts," since they have not left one socioreligious community in order to embrace another. They still consider themselves Muslims. Yet they are turning to Christ in repentance, placing their faith in Jesus as King and Savior, and actively drawing others to Jesus through their personal witness within their socioreligious communities.

How should the broader body of Christ view these Muslim Christ followers? We would propose that we embrace them as brothers and sisters in the Lord, walk alongside them, and encourage them to grow in their faithful obedience to our King. Just as New Testament "movements" began among the Jews, the Samaritans, and the Gentiles, let us pray for movements among Muslim communities around the world.

Bibliography

Bauer, Walter, William F. Arndt, F. Wilbur Gingrich, and Frederick W. Danker. *A Greek-English Lexicon of the New Testament and Other Early Christian Literature*. Chicago: University of Chicago Press, 1979.

Bowman, John. *The Samaritan Problem: Studies in the Relationships of Samaritanism, Judaism, and Early Christianity*. Pittsburgh: Pickwick Press, 1975.

————. "Samaritan Studies." *Bulletin of the John Rylands Library* 40 (1957–58): 298–327. Available at https://www.escholar.manchester.ac.uk/api/datastream?publicationPid=uk-ac-man-scw:1m 1946&datastreamId=POST-PEER-REVIEW-PUBLISHERS-DOCUMENT.PDF.

Brown, Rick, and Christopher Samuel. "The meanings of κυριος 'Lord' in the New Testament." SIL Publications, 2002.

Ferguson, Everett. *Backgrounds of Early Christianity*. 3rd ed. Grand Rapids, MI: Eerdmans, 2003.

Glaser, Ida. *The Bible and Other Faiths: Christian Responsibility in a World of Religions*. Downers Grove, IL: IVP Academic, 2005.

Guelich, Robert A. *Mark 1–8:26*. Vol. 34A of *Word Biblical Commentary*. Edited by Ralph P. Martin. Dallas: Word, 1989.

MacDonald, John. *The Theology of the Samaritans*. New Testament Library. Philadelphia: Westminster Press, 1964.

Paige, Terence. "Early Gentile Christianity, Conversion, and Culture-shift in the New Testament." Paper presented at the Bridging the Divide conference, Houghton College, Houghton, NY, June 20–24, 2011.

Pummer, Reinhard. *The Samaritans*. Leiden: Brill, 1987. Plates XXI, XXII, and XXIII.

Unger, Merrill. *The New Unger's Bible Dictionary*. Chicago: Moody, 1988.

Viola, Frank, and George Barna. *Pagan Christianity? Exploring the Roots of Our Church Practices*. Carol Stream, IL: BarnaBooks, 2008.

Watts, Rikki. *Isaiah's New Exodus in Mark*. Grand Rapids, MI: Baker Academic, 2000.

Wright, Christopher J. H. *The Mission of God: Unlocking the Bible's Grand Narrative*. Downers Grove, IL: IVP Academic, 2006.

CHAPTER 23

Jesus Living and Discipling among the Lost[*]

John Ridgway

In the Gospels we have recorded for us four distinct breakthroughs of the gospel of the kingdom. Two of them were among the Jews. Matthew's Gospel gives the details of a breakthrough in Galilee involving at least five thousand men (Matt 14:21), and this did not include women and children. The other Jewish breakthrough, what could even be termed a movement, was in Judea. John's Gospel describes this movement by saying that many people were believing in Jesus (John 2:23; 8:30; 10:42; 11:45; 12:11; 12:42).

However, there were two other breakthroughs outside of the Jewish mainstream. One was among the Samaritans, and the other was among the Gentiles. Both of these breakthroughs offer guidance for us as we seek to bring the good news of the kingdom of God to the Hindu, Muslim, Buddhist, Shinto-Buddhist, secular, and other mainstreams of the world today.

Among the Jewish people, Jesus often taught in their synagogues, but in the case of these two breakthroughs among the Samaritans and the Gentiles, telling of the good news of the kingdom started through a significant personal encounter with an individual.

In the case of the Gentiles living in the Decapolis, a likely contributing factor was the healing by Jesus of a man who apparently had thousands of demons (a "legion" of them) living in him. In Mark 5:1 we are told that the disciples and Jesus crossed the lake to the region of the Gerasenes and that Jesus got out of the boat. This area was known as the Decapolis. Due to it being a Gentile area with high Greek culture, it was not a place that Jews would readily visit. Also, this specific spot was a place of pigs and a place of the dead. This may explain why there is no record of the twelve disciples getting out of the boat. Yet in the midst of this very uninviting context was a man in extreme need. Night and day he cried out and cut himself with stones. The internal pain was so great that relief came only when he cut himself externally. He was alive but not truly living, and his existence was only possible among the dead.

Jesus came to this distraught man and removed the huge burden in his life that he was never meant to carry. After this extraordinary encounter, the man wanted very much to go with Jesus. But Jesus said to him, "Go home to your own people and tell them how much the Lord has done for you, and how he has had mercy on you" (Mark 5:19).

We most likely would not have given Jesus' advice but would have rather suggested the course of action that the healed man wanted. We probably would have told him to join the team of disciples with Jesus and be trained and grounded in the faith in a "safe" and separate place before facing his family.

Jesus understood that it took a Gentile to reach the Gentiles and that immediate family and friends and relatives are the first priority. Indeed, many times in the New Testament we see the good news

---

[*] Originally published in a slightly different form in *MF*, May–June 2011. Reprinted by permission.

coming to an individual and his family. One primary example of this is Cornelius and his relatives and close friends, as mentioned in Acts 10:24.

However, our tendency has often been to draw individuals out of their family and community and ask them to join another community that professes Christianity, rather than to disciple them in their own contexts, where they can reach their own family members and relatives and friends and work colleagues.

In the case of the healed Gentile man, it seems that he not only went back to his own family but "began to tell in the Decapolis [literally, ten cities] how much Jesus had done for him." And his testimony had quite an impact—as the verse states, "And all the people were amazed" (Mark 5:20).

Several months later, when Jesus revisited the area of the Decapolis (Mark 7:31), it is recorded that now at least four thousand men were showing interest in what Jesus had to say (Mark 7:31–8:9). It seems reasonable to biblical scholars, like Christopher Wright,[1] to assume that a number of them were among those who had earlier been "amazed" (Mark 5:20) at the man's deliverance and testimony of Jesus.

In like manner Paul advised the Corinthians to remain in the situation they were in when God called them (1 Cor 7:20). He advised them not to change their context or place in life but to focus on their relationship to Jesus with a desire to obey him (1 Cor 7:17–24). Paul indicated that this was his practice in all the situations where he was ministering. By people remaining in their contexts, the good news of the kingdom could spread throughout their communities, and this would eventually lead to the nations being discipled (Matt 28:19).

In the case of the Samaritan community, Jesus again sought out a needy individual, who in this case was a woman with a history of immorality. The disciples were surprised that he would be talking to such a person, as in those days the two communities had no dealings with each other. Also, a religious leader did not normally talk with a woman in public. However, this woman had an encounter with Jesus that changed her life. She raced back from the well to the Samaritan town and caused many of the Samaritans to come and listen to Jesus.

The Samaritans then invited Jesus to come and stay in their town. There is no record of the twelve disciples going, as it may have been outside their comfort zone. But Jesus stayed with the Samaritans for two days. We do not read of him criticizing their lack of understanding of God's purposes or their temple at Mount Gerizim. He presumably ate their food, slept on their beds, and used their washing facilities in the midst of their particular context. He literally lived and discipled amongst the lost, and there was a great response (note John 4:39,41,42).

As they listened to Jesus, they responded, "We have heard for ourselves, and we know that this man really is the Savior of the world" (John 4:42). They discovered that he was not only a Jewish prophet but was someone who really loved them just as much as he did his own Jewish people.

Our tendency has often been to pull people out of their messy circumstances or what appear to be difficult contexts and disciple them in safe environments where we are comfortable. In contrast, Jesus chose to go to the lost in their own contexts and relate to them right where they were. Following his example, these people in turn impacted many of their relatives and friends in their own community. If the Samaritan woman had been extracted out of her own community, it is doubtful that such an impact would have occurred.

---

1   Christopher J. H. Wright, *The Mission of God: Unlocking the Bible's Grand Narrative* (Downers Grove, IL: IVP Academic, 2006), 508.

Today the great need of the mission workforce is that we die to our own plans and strategies. We need to listen to the voice of God leading us to needy people who want to respond to the good news of the kingdom of God. We need to help those people to influence their own families and relatives and friends and work colleagues in their own communities so that they in turn will disciple their own people. In this way we will see the fulfillment of the Great Commission taking place in our generation and the generations to come.

Bibliography

Wright, Christopher J. H. *The Mission of God: Unlocking the Bible's Grand Narrative.* Downers Grove, IL: IVP Academic, 2006.

CHAPTER 24

Jesus in Samaria

A Paradigm for Church Planting among Muslims[*]

Kevin Higgins

Jesus' encounter with the woman at the well has long been a gold mine for Christians seeking to follow his example as effective communicators of the gospel. But his ministry to the entire Samaritan village through the woman shows Jesus not only as an evangelist but also as a church planter. John 4 is, therefore, of supreme importance to church planters among Muslims, for it chronicles the way the Master himself approached the task of establishing his church among a "resistant" people. Consider the tremendous parallels between the obstacles Jesus faced when reaching Samaritans and the obstacles Christians face reaching Muslims.

Worship Location

Samaritans and Jews had separate centers for worship. Islamic worship revolves around the *qibla* (i.e., the direction one faces to worship God). One source of conflict between early Muslims and Jews was over the issue of whether the true worshiper should face Mecca or Jerusalem.

After acknowledging Jesus as a prophet, the Samaritan woman's first comment resembles Islamic regard for place in worship: "Must worship really be offered in Jerusalem to be acceptable, or is Mount Gerizim, where our fathers worshiped, sufficient?" As we seek to reach Muslims, this same issue of place for true worship emerges. How did the Master establish his church in this context?

Scripture

Samaritans and Jews shared a similar scriptural tradition, along with significant differences. Like Jews, Samaritans accepted the five books of the Pentateuch, but they disregarded all additional books in the Jewish canon. Furthermore, the Samaritan pentateuch differed from the Jewish Pentateuch at several important points. For example, the prophecy of "a prophet like [Moses]" (Deut 18:15–18 in the Jewish Pentateuch) has been displaced in the Samaritan pentateuch to Exodus 20:21ff. In fact, Edersheim states that it was by "impudent assertion and falsification of the text of the Pentateuch" that Samaritans claimed the superiority of Gerizim.[1]

One of many obstacles in evangelism among Muslims concerns our view of Scripture. Like Samaritans and Jews, Muslims believe we share a common scriptural heritage but disagree about who holds the "true Scripture" (i.e., the complete and uncorrupted version). Christians believe the Qur'an

---

[*] Originally published in a slightly different form in *IJFM* 17, no. 1 (2000): 25–31. Reprinted by permission.

[1] Alfred Edersheim, *The Life and Times of Jesus the Messiah* (Grand Rapids, MI: Eerdmans, 1971), 396.

distorts clear biblical revelation, and Jews surely felt similarly toward Samaritans. How did the Master establish his church in this context?

Religious Vocabulary

Samaritans and Jews shared many theological concepts and terms, but some had very different meanings. For example, all Jewish sects believed in some kind of Davidic Messiah. The Samaritans, however, did not share this messianic expectation in quite the same way. They expected the Taheb (Teacher) would come to restore true worship, assumed to be on Mt. Gerizim. There was no Davidic connection to the Taheb, which should not surprise us given the historical conflict between Judah and Samaria.

Like Jews and Samaritans, Christians and Muslims share a similar religious vocabulary and main theological concepts. Yet few would deny that we often use the same words to mean different things. How did the Master establish his church in this context?

Ritual Purity

While they were similar in many ways, Jews considered Samaritans so "unclean" that association with them resulted in defilement (John 4:9). Similar concerns for ritual purity arise between Muslims and Christians. After I entered a village mosque at the invitation of a Muslim friend, there was great anxiety about my presence as a foreigner. I soon learned that they were not worried about my faith, but about whether or not I was circumcised. If not, their mosque would be desecrated and their prayers nullified. They were much relieved to hear that I too bore the sign of God's covenant with Abraham, and I was much relieved that they did not demand proof! Similar issues of purity and pollution among Muslims involve eating pork, using the left hand, washing after intercourse, and numerous other examples—many of which were equally important to Jews and Samaritans. So how did Jesus establish his church among people with so many complex issues? Surely we have much to learn from his example.

Jesus' Approach to Place of Worship

As with Jews and Samaritans, we cannot overestimate the importance of place to Muslims during worship. While the woman may have been dodging Jesus' very personal remarks about her marital status (John 4:17,18), her response reveals a very pointed question: which religion is true? Notice how Jesus answered her—and how he did not. Jesus declared,

> Believe me, a time is coming when you will worship the Father
> neither on this mountain nor in Jerusalem. You Samaritans worship
> what you do not know; we worship what we do know, for salvation
> is from the Jews. Yet a time is coming and has now come when the
> true worshipers will worship the Father in the Spirit and truth, for
> they are the kind of worshipers the Father seeks. (John 4:21–23)

Jesus responded that the Father desires neither Jerusalem nor Gerizim to be central for worship. Did he thereby nullify worship both in the Jerusalem temple and on Mt. Gerizim as false and unacceptable to God? Did Jesus repudiate every physical *qibla* (direction for prayer) in favor of a spiritual *qibla*?

Given that the earliest Jerusalem church and the apostles continued meeting in the temple for prayer (Acts 3:1), we must conclude that Jesus' closest followers, though they were surely among those who "worshiped in the Spirit and truth," did not interpret Jesus' teaching in the strict literal sense.

Rather, they understood the real force of Jesus' teaching: regardless of "here" or "there," true worshipers will worship in the Spirit and truth. In other words, "place" is not the main issue—the heart is.

So Jesus initially answered the question of which religion was "true" by suggesting that neither religion's location of worship was "the place." Still, having heard him say "neither/nor," his disciples did not apply this in a literal sense. They continued worshiping at the temple. Considering they were Jews, this does not seem so odd. But what of the Samaritan followers of Jesus? Did they continue worshiping on Mt. Gerizim? What did Jesus teach about these matters to all the Samaritans who came from town to receive him as the promised Savior of the world (John 4:39–43)? Jesus spent two full days teaching these new Samaritan believers. Surely they must have been filled with questions similar to those of the woman at the well: How do we worship? Will Jerusalem become our place? Where is our *qibla* today?

Outside of Jesus' instructions to the woman at the well, Scripture is silent about what Jesus taught these Samaritans during those two days. However, his Jewish followers, having heard him say "neither in Jerusalem," continued to worship in Jerusalem since they understood the real meaning of his teaching. Therefore, it seems reasonable to assume that Samaritan believers also understood Jesus' teaching and continued to worship in the Spirit and truth on Gerizim. Just as the Jewish followers of Jesus continued to participate in the cultural and religious life of their Jewish community, we can safely assume Samaritan believers did likewise, with one major difference: they were now disciples of Jesus.

Historical evidence is scant to prove Samaritan believers continued to worship within the Samaritan religious system, but if they did not, there is a strange silence about this in Acts 8, where the apostles do not mention a "proper place" for worship or an alternative to Samaritan religion. We see instead a believing, Spirit-filled community, apparently within Samaritan society. Why don't we see the apostles extracting believers out of Samaritanism? Unlike Judaizers, the apostles were simply following the same approach they personally observed from Jesus when he ministered in Samaria.

In spite of Jesus' example in Samaria, many hesitate to do similarly in Islamic contexts. They explain that Islam is different from Samaritanism. Islam was founded by a false prophet, who may have borrowed from biblical revelation but nevertheless ended with incomplete and inaccurate conclusions about Scripture and the Messiah. However, this is precisely how Jews saw Samaritans in the first century. Jesus' ministry in Samaria is therefore highly applicable to our work among Muslims.

Jesus' Approach to the Samaritan Scriptures

Jesus handled the issue of different Scriptures in a way that was both simpler and more complicated than his response to place in worship. Jesus simply avoided direct confrontation about her concept of Scripture, though he alluded to the superiority of Jewish Scripture when saying, "Salvation is from the Jews" (John 4:22). Jesus addressed the matter in another way. This is where the issue becomes more complicated, partly because Jesus was, in a very real sense, "making Scripture" as he lived. Jesus gave Samaritan believers two days of "living Scripture" through his direct teaching and presence. Indeed, Jesus left this very living Scripture with his disciples, which eventually became the New Testament Gospels we so treasure today. Nevertheless, we have no evidence that denigration of Samaritan scripture was ever part of Jesus' ministry.

In a later mission to Samaritans (Acts 8), we see that the apostles followed Jesus' example. Peter and John taught Samaritan believers what Jesus taught. And once again, we hear no debate over whether use of the Samaritan pentateuch was to be discontinued or not. Based on Jesus' clear statement that salvation is from the Jews, who know what they worship, whereas the Samaritans do not, we know the

Samaritan version of the Pentateuch was unacceptable to Jesus. Nevertheless, Jesus' approach did not greatly emphasize or debate the errors of the Samaritan scripture.

Jesus' Approach to Contextualizing Language

Jesus uses Samaritan religious terminology freely. We might miss how contextualized his dialogue about "living water" really is, but Samaritan wisdom literature contains numerous references to "living water."[2] Jesus chooses to redirect the metaphor toward himself.

Jesus also uses Samaritan religious terminology critically. Samaritans, as mentioned above, expected a Taheb to appear and restore true worship, on Mt. Gerizim in particular. It is therefore no accident that Jesus addresses the theme of true worship—but note the context in which he does this. Samaritans believed the Taheb would be the prophet promised by Moses (Deut 18:15–19).[3] The woman's declaration that Jesus is a prophet therefore implies she may believe Jesus to be the Taheb (John 4:19). By following her declaration with a question about true worship—a subject about which the Taheb would know since he was expected to restore true worship[4]—she further reveals her hunch that she is standing before the Taheb himself. Jesus answers her question about true worship and, in effect, lets her believe he is the Taheb—the one come to restore true worship. However, Jesus does not affirm the Samaritan belief about Gerizim; he directly corrects and transforms it (John 4:21–24).

So we see that while Jesus freely uses and even assumes the religious vocabulary and concepts of Samaritanism, he does so critically. Every Samaritan belief is not accepted. There is correction and transformation as he ultimately brings the focus back to himself.

Jesus' Approach to Ritual Purity

In the Muslim-Christian encounter, the Muslim, whom we seek to reach, is very sensitive about ritual purity. The situation is reversed in John 4. In order to reach them, Jesus exposed himself to—from a Jewish perspective—an "unclean" Samaritan. He did not observe the cultural and ceremonial (i.e., religious) taboos that separated them.

But what might Jesus have done in the opposite situation? Would he have adopted ceremonial cleanliness in the eyes of those he was trying to reach to minimize barriers to the gospel? While we do not see Jesus doing this in the Gospels, Paul surely did and had Timothy do the same when being circumcised to gain Jewish acceptance (Acts 16:3; 1 Cor 9:19–23). In Paul's own words, he lived "like one under the law" among Jews and "like one not having the law" among Gentiles (1 Cor 9:20,21). And just as Paul urges us to follow his example as he follows the example of Christ (1 Cor 11:1), I have no doubt that Jesus would have adopted ceremonial cleanliness to reach people even as he set aside such ceremonial purity to reach Samaritans.

Following Jesus' Approach to Ministry

Let us summarize these lessons from Jesus' approach to ministry and apply them to our work among Muslims today.

---

2   Colin Brown, ed., *The New International Dictionary of New Testament Theology*, vol. 3 (Grand Rapids, MI: Zondervan, 1971), 459.

3   Raymond E. Brown, *The Gospel According to John*, vol. 1 (Garden City, NY: Doubleday, 1983), 171– 72.

4   Ibid.

Indigenous Worship in Community

At the time of Jesus, Samaritans represented a distinct religion with their own focus of worship. They were at best heretical in the eyes of Jews. More often, they were viewed by Jews as demonized. In reality, Jews felt about Samaritanism much the same way many Christians feel about Islam. In spite of this fact, we see no command from Jesus to leave Samaritan "religion."

Jesus, and later the apostles, apparently planted a community of believers within Samaritan society. This was to be a community that would worship in the Spirit and truth, following the teachings of Jesus. Application to an Islamic context seems clear: expect God will raise up a believing community of true worshipers who follow the teachings of Jesus within Islamic society.

We have seen how Jesus stayed with the Samaritans for two days and then left. No one was there to organize this new community of believers or make decisions for them. They put their faith in the truth Jesus revealed during his time with them and were left to develop "on their own." Answers to questions about worship practices and other matters were not in the hands of outsiders or "missionaries." Such answers could not even be found by observing the example of a "missionary," because none remained long enough to observe. The "missionary" (in this case, Jesus) was gone. In contrast to the uneasiness of mission leaders today to leave new believers to themselves after only two days of teaching, Jesus did not seem overly concerned about their propensity toward syncretism. I believe this was because Jesus trusted the "truth-impacting-lives" process enough to leave truth on its own, even in an environment that did not seem conducive to the flourishing of truth—i.e., a different religion, different scriptures, and a different content for similar theological concepts.

Giving Scripture without Polemics

Samaritan scripture differed from Jewish Scripture in both content and form. How did Jesus handle this extremely challenging issue? We don't find Jesus debating Samaritan leaders about the superiority of Jewish Scripture. Instead, he provides two full days of living Scripture, teaching truth and letting it do its own work in Samaritan hearts.

Although every believer is a temple for the Holy Spirit, we are surely in no place to duplicate "living Scripture." We are not Jesus, and our words will not be canonized as Scripture. Nevertheless, the principle we learn from Jesus remains: give what biblical truth we can (written, audio, video, verbal, etc.), then let his truth do its work in the hearts of Muslims. My repeated experience has been that when a new Muslim believer begins to drink in the Word, there is no need to argue about the Qur'an.

Adoption and Transformation of Religious Terminology

Samaritans and Jews had theological similarities akin to Christians and Muslims. We saw how Jesus assumed and used Samaritan terms both freely and critically, while correcting and transforming erroneous concepts. This is how Jesus established his church among Samaritans.

In our work with various Muslims, should we use Islamic terms? If so, what will it mean to use such terms both freely and critically? We may freely adopt, for example, terms for Jesus such as *Mahdi* (divinely guided one, Deliverer), or qur'anic titles for Jesus such as *Kalimatullah* (Word of God) and *Ruhullah* (Spirit of God). But to use these terms critically will mean that new biblical content must reshape and revise a Muslim's understanding of these terms. Just as Jesus assumed the role of the Samaritan Taheb and in the process transformed the word (John 4:21–23), so too we can freely and critically adopt Islamic terminology. Like Jesus' own example, the end result of our effort must always point to him.

Adjusting to Islamic Ritual Purity

Jews believed Samaritans were unclean. But to accomplish his mission, Jesus was willing to cross this line and accept water "polluted" by an unclean and adulterous Samaritan woman. These taboos were not merely cultural. The distinction between culture and religion may seem reasonable to our Western and disintegrated view of life, but such distinctions were and are meaningless and absurd to peoples whose worldview was and is more holistic, like the Jews of Jesus' day and Muslims today.

Adjusting to Islamic concepts of ritual purity may require low usage of our left hand, abstinence from pork, and women dressing according to Muslim views of modesty. But how will we pray? Should we do ablutions or prostrations, use a prayer liturgy, kiss our Bibles before reading them, or wrap the Bible with special cloth and keep it on the highest shelf?

Church Planting or Kingdom Sowing

Let us question an assumption that has rested quietly throughout this article. I stated that Jesus' mission in Samaria can rightly be seen as a model for church planting. But was Jesus really "church planting"? Our answer to this question depends greatly upon our understanding of the "church planting" metaphor, which in turn rests upon how we understand its component words "church" and "planting." In our minds these are shaped, I believe, not so much by the Bible as by our mental images of what "church" means and what we think it takes to "plant" one.

As a young boy, I used to spend summers riding motorcycles in the desert. One day I was sitting on the back while my cousin drove. I noticed an interesting rock and pointed it out to my cousin over the handlebars. Immediately our motorcycle veered in the direction of the rock, and we ended up picking cactus needles from our backsides. The point is that we tend to head for what we look at. Many church planters among Muslims are consciously or unconsciously looking at a "model" that may not be what Jesus had in mind at all.

Consider the idea of "church." Surely few missionaries head out today armed with the cultural imperialism of earlier times. We are prepared to think in terms of "dynamic equivalent" Bible translations and "planting indigenous churches." But I am convinced that hidden in the word "church" for many of us are concepts that are not entirely biblical, but are rather identified with our experience of church as independent, isolated, and self-contained congregations. We therefore run the risk of equating that experience with the essence of "church."

While Jesus mentioned "the church" (*ekklesia*) only three times, he spoke far more about "the kingdom" (*basileia*). However, Jesus' portrait of the kingdom is far removed from what most of us think of as "church," influenced as we often are in the West by a congregational polity. There certainly is a congregational element to the meaning of "church," especially in Paul's use of *ekklesia*. But I am convinced that we need to balance this with a recovery of Jesus' view of the kingdom. Although these two concepts (*ekklesia* and *basileia*) are certainly not identical, they nevertheless should not be held in isolation from each other. Let us look briefly at Jesus' teaching concerning the kingdom of God in Matthew 13.

1. *The kingdom is like seed sown in various types of soil.* Sowing seed requires letting go. It assumes a natural process of growth. How different from thinking of church as an organization to be built, struc-

tured, trained, coached, and coaxed! Sowing is also very different from "gathering" believers. Sowing puts seed "down and in," quite the opposite of gathering wheat at a harvest.

2. *The kingdom is like wheat growing in the presence of tares.* The owner hesitates to separate. Here the "gathering" or "harvesting" (i.e., what we often think of as "church planting") is something assumed to come at the end of the age. Until then, let the wheat (and notice it is good wheat from good seed) grow right there among the tares. There's no fear of syncretism. Why? Because wheat cannot become tares; it remains wheat. Good seed is sown, takes root, and grows—*among* the tares. In Jesus' day this occurred as his disciples continued worshiping God at the temple and synagogues with fellow Jews, including many who did not yet believe that Jesus was the Messiah. Their fellowship with other disciples occurred elsewhere (Acts 2:46,47), so Muslim followers of the Way may well do something similar today, as did Samaritan believers in their day.

3. *The kingdom is like a mustard seed.* It starts small—very small, according to Jesus. But it grows until birds can fill its branches. Thus the kingdom can be considered "planted" even when very small and insignificant. Some missionaries talk about not having "planted a church" because there are only two believers. This kind of thinking seems totally foreign to Jesus' view.

4. *The kingdom is like yeast in dough.* Again the imagery is something "down and in," which then permeates all throughout. The kingdom spreads and grows, transforming all it touches. In stark contrast, many of us who work among Muslims expect a church will form or be gathered by extracting members from a people rather than transforming members in a people.

The church, when understood from a kingdom perspective, is not so much a congregation as it is a movement, a life, an organism, a seed. According to Jesus' metaphors, the church lives and grows amidst all sorts of other things: weeds, rocks, and dough. To plant the church among Muslims we must recover the imagery Jesus used for the kingdom.

"Planting," the other word in the phrase "church planting," is by itself a good term and carries everything Jesus envisioned. However, when we couple it with the word "church," which we functionally understand as something structural and organizational, we seem to subtly distort the natural and organic element of the metaphor. When we use "planting" after "church," we usually refer to the building, organizing, gathering, and establishing of a church. These concepts are of course part of the overall mix of mission—we do seek to "gather" communities of faith. But overemphasis on the "gathering" imagery misses the full import of Jesus' vision of "planting."

Therefore I propose we use a new metaphor: "kingdom sowing." To plant something we focus on a single location and often on a single plant. But to sow, we scatter, broadcast, and spread seed widely and freely. Sowers trust that in many cases, though not all, their seeds will take root and grow. So perhaps it is time to return to the actual language of Jesus' parables and advocate the metaphor of "kingdom sowing" rather than "church planting."

A "kingdom sowing" metaphor is consistent with Jesus' actual practice in John 4. All that we saw in our study of John 4 flows perfectly from Jesus' teaching in Matthew 13 about how the kingdom spreads. Jesus not only envisioned a spreading, growing, organic movement that would be sown like seed, grow like wheat, and spread like yeast, but everything he did promoted that end. It is wise to ask ourselves whether or not there is such congruence between our own mission theory and practice.

Because metaphors have inherent power to guide and shape our destinations, it is crucial to use ones that actually describe where we want to go. For this reason, I believe "kingdom sowing" is more appropriate. At the very least, it seems necessary to refill the time-honored term "church planting" with fresh biblical content.

Conclusion

Jesus' example of kingdom sowing in Samaria provides us with several applications in an Islamic context. Kingdom sowing means we seek and expect a believing community to form and remain within the religiocultural world of the Muslim community, at least for some time. In the New Testament era, for quite some time the Jewish disciples of Jesus continued to live in and with their community. Eventually a time came in which other Jewish leaders began to push disciples of Jesus out from the temple and synagogues, and so too believers in Jesus among Muslims may in time be pushed out of their community by other Muslims, away from the Muslim religious community.

Forming a community of believers within the religiocultural world of Muslims will include Islamic places and patterns of worship. This is what happened in Samaria (John 4; Acts 8), and it seems to be what Jesus expected when he taught about kingdom sowing in parables, especially the parables of the yeast in the dough and the wheat and the tares.

Kingdom sowing in an Islamic context means that no confrontational effort to replace the Qur'an with the Bible is needed, at least not at the beginning. While Jesus must have believed the Samaritan scriptures were insufficient, he made little mention of their deficiencies. God's Spirit will lead his people into all truth. As Jesus trusted his truth to have its own power and sway, so too we can trust his truth to be like yeast that transforms the dough. Therefore we will be passionate about getting his truth to our Muslim friends in effective styles and forms they can access, whether in print, audio, video, or orally memorized, or even chanted.

Kingdom sowing means truth will be communicated in the language of Muslims, including their religious vocabulary. In so doing, concepts will be changed from the inside out. Though Jesus assumed the role of the Samaritan Taheb, he transformed the concept as well. We need not fear syncretism, for the heart of Jesus' truth will transform whatever vocabulary it encounters.

Kingdom sowing is incarnational, adopting the religious and cultural forms of our Muslim friends. A community of believers will remain in their world, though not of it. Many behaviors, customs, and values will be retained by a believing community and will need to be adopted by the cross-cultural missionary. But unbiblical values will also be challenged and changed from within, by believers under the guidance of the Holy Spirit (John 16:13).

I know that much of what I have proposed in this article has been addressed and debated elsewhere. Nevertheless, I humbly submit that the teaching and practice of Jesus, especially in Samaria, point us unmistakably in this direction. Obedience and faithfulness to him beckon us to walk in his steps toward the fulfillment of his vision for the kingdom in the Muslim world.

Bibliography

Brown, Colin, ed. *The New International Dictionary of New Testament Theology*, vol. 3. Grand Rapids, MI: Zondervan, 1971.

Brown, Raymond E. *The Gospel according to John*, vol. 1. Garden City, NY: Doubleday, 1983.

Edersheim, Alfred. *The Life and Times of Jesus the Messiah*. Grand Rapids, MI: Eerdmans, 1971.

CHAPTER 25

The Key to Insider Movements
The "Devoteds" of Acts[*]
Kevin Higgins

This chapter seeks to contribute to the ongoing conversation among cross-cultural workers about insider movements, movements to Jesus that remain to varying degrees inside the social fabric of Islamic, Buddhist, Hindu, or other people groups. I write as a "thinking practitioner" who has worked among Muslims in North America, East Africa, and South Asia. In South Asia I have been honored to be a part of an emerging movement to Jesus that is gaining significant momentum among four people groups. In my role I have made many mistakes and will continue to make more. But my mistakes have always driven me back to the Scriptures and prayer, to further reflection and readjustment.

So are insider movements just a missiological fad? Are our conversations about these movements simply about the appropriateness of certain pragmatic, tactical approaches to contextualizing the gospel? Or are they actually conversations about the nature of the gospel itself?

I believe that the debate about insider movements actually is a debate about the gospel, one potentially as earth-shaking as the Lutheran, Reformed, Anglican, and Anabaptist reform movements of the sixteenth century. Those movements were driven by the recovery of basic, foundational biblical truths such as justification by faith, a gospel of grace, the priesthood of all believers, and the place of the Bible in the life of the church and of the believer. And they forced church leaders to re-evaluate church practice and doctrine.

Similarly, I see insider movements as fueling (and being fueled by) a rediscovery of the Incarnation, of a thoroughly biblical approach to culture and religion, of the role of the Holy Spirit in leading God's people to "work out" the gospel in new ways, and of an understanding of how God works in the world within his covenant people, but also works in the world in contexts where there are no known believers. In the latter case I am referring to God's sovereign work of drawing men and women to himself and thereby into his covenant.

Scope and Approach

This chapter cannot address every facet of what I see as an emerging reformation. Nor is it my purpose here to defend or develop that thesis. Rather, I will focus on two basic issues that must be addressed in the discussion of whether catalyzing insider movements is an appropriate aim of mission effort in the first place. We will consider those questions from two perspectives:

1. Insider movements in the Bible—does Scripture provide any models and dynamics of healthy, vital movements to Jesus? This question forces us to articulate and address valid concerns about how such movements to Jesus develop on a foundation that is grounded in God's word.

---

[*] Originally published in a slightly different form in *IJFM* 21, no. 4 (2004): 155–65. Reprinted by permission.

2. Can a "movement to Jesus" be an insider movement? What is the relationship between the emerging Jesus movements (and their biblical worldview and discipleship) and the worldview, religious life, and cultural context inside of which these movements are "moving," so to speak? This question forces us to articulate and address valid concerns about how such movements to Jesus develop within the cultural and religious framework of their particular context. Here we need to continue to develop biblical perspectives regarding culture and God's involvement in culture.

Insider Movements: A Working Definition

Before addressing those two major questions, we need to be sure what it is we're talking about. I know of no generally accepted definition for an insider movement, so I will try to define how I use the term. Let us begin with some background.

The question of whether insider movements are an appropriate goal of mission effort is actually part of an older missiological conversation. In the second half of the twentieth century, thinkers such as Donald McGavran and Alan Tippett began to popularize the idea of "people movements." One assumption of the people movement concept was that people in many parts of the world made decisions together rather than as individuals, and that such "togetherness" included tribal, caste, and other types of unity.[1]

I find that the definition of insider movements offered by Rebecca Lewis adequately captures the main features of the descriptions of people movements referenced above, but adds "religion" to the list of attributes. Her definition includes two main points:

> An Insider Movement is any movement to faith in Christ where
> a) the Gospel flows through pre-existing communities and social
> networks, and where b) believing families, as valid expressions of
> the Body of Christ, remain inside their socioreligious communities,
> retaining their identity as members of that community while living
> under the Lordship of Jesus Christ and the authority of the Bible.[2]

Such a definition is intended to make clear that followers of Jesus can continue to embrace at least some of their people's religious life, history, and practice without compromising the gospel or falling into syncretism. Indeed, I will attempt to show from the Scriptures that, at least in some sense, the gospel can actually fulfill or complete certain aspects of the religion of a people group. The exact nature of such fulfillment will vary greatly from context to context, and more specifically from religion to religion.

Such movements to Jesus will develop "church" forms, leadership structures, and theological work. The specific forms of community, leadership, worship, and theological discourse that develop within such movements will emerge as leaders within the movement discover biblical functions and express them by *adopting* and *adapting* existing cultural forms from within their culture and religion.

---

1   A good introduction to the people movement conversation is found in David J. Hesselgrave, "People Movements," in *Evangelical Dictionary of World Missions,* A. Scott Moreau, ed. (Grand Rapids, MI: Baker, 2000), 743–44.

2   Rebecca Lewis, "Promoting Movements to Christ within Natural Communities," *IJFM* 24, no. 2 (2007): 75–76. See also Lewis in *UIM,* chap. 58.

Part 1: Jesus Movements in the Bible

Now, I want to begin to address our two major issues. First, what are the models and dynamics of a healthy, vital movement to Jesus?

Every movement to Jesus is in some way an insider movement. Every movement to Jesus is inside of some culture or some aspects of a culture. In addition, movements to Jesus, no matter what culture they are "inside," are movements that bring families, tribes, groups, and individuals into a saving relationship with Jesus and new experiences of community in him.

But what exactly would that look like? How do we know there is a movement? What biblical model or models can we discover that describe healthy movements? Can the dynamics of such a movement be described in such a way that we can use the model to assist us in our own ministries among the unreached—or to avoid "killing" such movements (by failing to develop them fully or by inadvertently squelching a key dynamic and thus not allowing an emerging movement to blossom)?

I believe the book of Acts provides such a model and gives us clear descriptions of the dynamics of such a movement. I refer to these dynamics as "keys" and see at least some of those keys in Luke's use of the Greek word *proskartereo*. Usually translated "devoted" in our English Bibles, this interesting word is used in a number of other ways. For example, in Acts 10:7, *proskartereo* refers to the devotion of one of Cornelius' servants to Cornelius and could be rendered "service." The word can also have the sense of "continuing with" or "staying with" someone or something, as in Acts 8:13, where Simon is said to "continue with Phillip" following his baptism.

Of the seven applications of the word in Acts, six seem to describe dynamics of the emerging Jesus movement, and I will focus on those.[3] The various things or practices to which the early church was "devoted" describe, in my view, the key dynamics of a vital and healthy movement.

The First "Devoted": Prayer

The word "devoted" first appears in Acts 1:14, where we find the 120 devoting themselves to united prayer as they wait for the promise referred to in Acts 1:8.

Indeed, in the movements to Jesus that we see exploding in Acts among the Jews of Jerusalem, Hellenized Jews, and Gentiles, devotion to prayer is a key dynamic. In fact it seems clear in Luke's overall design that devotion to prayer was a lesson first learned by the disciples in their walk with Jesus himself.

Biblically authentic insider movements are not primarily a missiological strategy or a program. They are a spiritual phenomenon driven by the Sovereign Lord through the prayers of his people. Prayer will be a major dynamic in authentic movements to Jesus.

In missions, we have increasingly and rightly emphasized intercession for movements to Jesus, but this "devoted" refers to passionate and consistent prayer by people within the movement as well. Prayer is both a sign of an authentic movement and a source of the spiritual vitality unleashed in such movements.

---

3   The reference in 10:17 might help us understand something of the range of usage, but it does not directly relate to a dynamic in the movement itself, so I do not include it as a seventh dynamic—as tempting as it might be to have seven keys!

The Second "Devoted": The Apostles' Teaching and Fellowship

The English text of Acts 2:42 might lead us to assume there are four "devoted's" in this one verse. However, in Greek the word *proskartereo* is used just once, in verse 42, and is referring to two sets of two closely linked actions. The early believers were devoted "to the apostles' teaching and to fellowship" (both actions are linked together in the text) *and* "to the breaking of bread and to prayer" (NASB) (also linked together closely in the text). Here we will deal with the first of those two combinations.

The early church in Acts was devoted to the teaching or doctrine of the apostles and to being in fellowship, or *koinonia*, with them. This not only refers to a commitment to apostolic truth but also points to a relational partnership with the company of the apostles. It refers to learning from the apostles, joining with the apostles, and receiving from and sharing with the apostles' ministry.

Authentic insider movements will be devoted to the apostolic witness to Christ as we find it in the New Testament. Insider movements will develop leaders and tools to facilitate the process of plumbing the depths of Scripture so as to apply it to new situations in keeping with the message and example of the apostles and their writings.[4]

This "devoted" includes a commitment not only to right apostolic doctrine, but also to right apostolic ministry. It is not only the message of the apostles that we are to learn and embrace but also their method of ministry. How did they communicate the gospel, plant churches, and build leaders? Being devoted to the apostles' teaching and fellowship means seeking to do apostolic work the apostolic way.

This also implies that insider movements will not be isolated from—or independent of—other movements to Jesus. Being in the apostles' fellowship would seem to imply some sort of connection to other apostolic movements. This is certainly the pattern we see in Acts: a connection between the emerging Jewish and Gentile movements flowing respectively from Jerusalem and Antioch.

The Third "Devoted": The Breaking of Bread and Prayer

The second coupling in Acts 2:42 refers to the closely linked "breaking of bread" and "prayer." The context seems to support the interpretation that the former term refers to early celebrations of the Lord's Supper, probably within the context of a real meal, rather than a separate and isolated religious ceremony apart from a meal (as is commonly practiced in Christian churches in both Western and Eastern expressions of Christianity around the world).[5]

That "breaking bread" is closely linked in the grammar of the Greek text with "prayer" shows us the importance already being placed upon the Lord's Supper in the early church. "The prayers" (plural in the Greek) are best understood not merely as a general reference to prayer as a spiritual discipline

---

4   I am suggesting here a radical departure from much of the theological education that is established in "the field." Instead of attempting to teach correct theology (based on whatever school or books the missionary has been influenced by), I am proposing a model in which emerging leaders within the movement are guided into a process of engaging Scripture and their culture in a "conversation" that leads to the long-term goal of a thoroughly biblical theology in culture.

5   This is certainly the background of the Lord's Supper as Paul describes it in 1 Cor 11. That this was a real meal is clear from the necessity Paul feels of reminding the Corinthians that they should not eat all the food before other members of the church arrive. Doing so, says Paul, means it is no longer the Lord's Supper. By separating the Lord's Supper from the context of a real meal, we eventually came to the logically absurd practice in the West of holding a "Lord's Supper" in the early morning and thus having a meal that is not a "supper" in any but a symbolic sense.

(private or corporate), but more specifically as prescribed prayers in the temple. The early believers were devoted to expressions of worship that included the Lord's Supper and temple prayers, though clearly not in the same event or ceremony.

There is an important point here that could easily be missed. On the one hand, proponents of insider movements might point to this devotion to "the prayers" as a biblical model of a community of disciples that remains within the religious forms that shaped its life prior to conversion to Christ. Whether that is a right application is a question to which we will return below. This question involves the complex issue of how far the model of a movement that emerged within Judaism can authentically be applied within other religious contexts, such as Islam or Hinduism.

However, the fact that Luke links "the prayers" with the Lord's Supper here shows us that even as the new community continued to embrace the temple prayers, it also added major new emphases and interpretations. The early church was devoted to "the prayers," but in the same breath reference is made to the radically reinterpreted Passover supper that had been inaugurated by Jesus himself. The practice of this meal by the early church transformed the Jewish rite in at least two ways. First, its meaning was dramatically altered. Second, the frequency of observance changed and eventually came to be a weekly event rather than an annual Passover celebration. We can draw an important conclusion from this: *Insider movements, even as they continue to embrace old forms and expressions, also bring in radically new meanings and truths.*

The Fourth "Devoted": Meeting in the Temple and House to House

This "devoted" continues a theme introduced in "devoted" three. Acts 2:46 says that the early church was devoted to meeting "in the temple" and "from house to house" (NASB).

What Marks a Movement as True to the Gospel?

Before considering insider movements, one thing we can do spiritually and theologically is to orient ourselves to the secret of the gospel. Five cardinal rules or truths that are to guide the movements as true to the gospel are:

1. Jesus' confession reveals his followers: "No one can say, 'Jesus is Lord,' except by the Holy Spirit" (1 Cor 12:3).

2. Jesus' command reveals his mandate: "The most important one," answered Jesus, "is this: 'Hear, O Israel: The Lord our God, the Lord is one. Love the Lord your God with all your heart and with all your soul and with all your mind and with all your strength.' The second is this: 'Love your neighbor as yourself.' There is no commandment greater than these" (Mark 12:29).

3. Jesus' prayer reveals his salvation: "This is eternal life, that they know you, the only true God, and Jesus Christ, whom you have sent" (John 17:3).

4. Jesus' presence reveals his church: "Where two or three gather in my name, there am I with them" (Matt 18:20).

5. Jesus' mission reveals his authority: "Make disciples of all nations.... I am with you always, to the very end of the age" (Matt 28:19,20).

—*Kurt Anders Richardson*

First, we will examine the issue of meeting in the temple. In light of Peter's habit of going to the temple at set times for prayer (Acts 3:1) and the believers' devotion to "the prayers," clearly the best reading of Acts 2:46 is that the early church not only continued in temple and synagogue worship, but they were "devoted" to this.

Proponents of insider movements, especially among Muslims, have pointed to possible parallels here. They have argued from this passage and others that a biblical precedent exists for new believers from Islam to remain in the mosque and continue to practice other religious expressions of Islamic life. Opponents of this position argue that the parallel is ill conceived because Islam (or, say, Hinduism) does not occupy the same position in salvation history as Judaism. This debate cannot really be settled on the basis of the Acts texts alone.

One might ask if there are any other biblical precedents for movements to Jesus that remain in some way inside of another religious "skin." Of particular interest will be examples in which new believers remained connected to a culture within a religious context that was not Jewish.

This discussion requires a slight excursus at this point to examine just two possible examples.

Naaman and the Temple of Rimmon

In 2 Kings 5 we read the fascinating story of Namaan and Elisha. Namaan is the commander of the armies of Israel's enemy. He is a pagan Assyrian whose king worships the god Rimmon.

Relevant to our discussion is the interaction between Namaan and Elisha following Namaan's healing. The miracle convinces Namaan that the God of Israel is the true God. He wants to reward the prophet, but upon being refused this honor he makes a twofold request instead.

First, he asks for two bags of dirt. Why Naaman makes this request is not clear from the text. It may be that Namaan still has a territorial understanding of the gods, and thus while he genuinely desires to honor Israel's God as the true God, he may see the dirt as a way of somehow "bringing God" with him to Assyria. If so, we have an example of a believer who is genuinely "converted" but is still undergoing the long process of having his worldview fully transformed by his new faith and experience.

Namaan's second request is even more directly related to our question about possible biblical precedents for insider movements. Namaan asks Elisha to forgive him, because when he returns to Assyria he will accompany his king into the temple of Rimmon to bow down in worship there. Elisha's response? "Go in peace" (2 Kgs 5:19).

Now Namaan is one "convert," not a movement. And Elisha's "Go in peace" is given in response to a request for forgiveness. But the text is an example of a follower of another religion who becomes a believer in the true God and yet continues to worship the true God within the religious life and practices of his prior religion. Not only is it a description, but the text also includes the clear blessing of the prophet upon the practice. In this text we find at least one case where God blesses "remaining inside."

The Samaritan Woman and the Two Mountains

John 4 describes the familiar story of the woman at the well. I have written in greater detail about this in another article[6] and will not repeat the details here. But this story makes at least two relevant points.

The first point concerns the woman's question about worship. Jesus' answer to her question is rather shocking if we put ourselves in Jewish shoes. He replies that true worship will not be found in Samaria

---

6   See chap. 24.

or in Jerusalem. Instead, he calls the woman (and us) to embrace the worship of the Father in the Spirit and truth.

But later in John we find Jesus himself in the temple. So what of his statement that true worship would not be in Samaria or in Jerusalem? Clearly his vision of "worship in the Spirit and truth" (that is, neither in Samaria or Jerusalem) did not preclude him from continuing to worship in Jerusalem, one of the locations he said would not be a place for true worship.

Thus it is fair to say that true worship is not limited by or defined by its location. True worship is determined by whether one worships in the Spirit and truth.

And it is logical to assume that the Samaritans did the same after Jesus left their village. After their conversion recorded in John 4, they worshiped in the Spirit and truth. But they did so in Samaria (in their prior place of worship), just as Jesus worshiped the Father in the Spirit and truth in Jerusalem, in the temple.

That this episode is an example of an insider movement is further suggested by a second feature of the passage. After Jesus spends two days in the Samaritan village, the villagers affirm that they now believe Jesus is the Savior of the world. Then Jesus leaves. What does he leave behind? A group of believers.[7]

It is impossible to question John's intention in making that point. In the drama of his Gospel, John compares the response of the Samaritans (and later of the Greeks who seek for Jesus at the festival in Jerusalem) with the responses to Jesus from among the Jews. The Samaritans are examples of people who believe and accept Jesus.

The believing but "young" community Jesus leaves behind after only two days will presumably continue in its prior Samaritan religious life with a major difference: Jesus' revelation of himself has changed them.

Back to Acts and the "Devoted's"

As we have seen, Acts 2:46 is not the only example in Scripture of people coming to authentic faith in the true God and yet remaining in some way connected to their prior religious practices and culture. So while I would grant that Judaism is in fact a different case than, say, Islam, the parallel still holds. When we consider that the worship in the temple was led by priests, many of whom did not follow Jesus (and in fact, many of them had likely voted to condemn Jesus to death), the opposition that the early believers would have encountered in the temple provides a strong parallel to Islamic contexts (more on that in the second half of this paper). Later we learn that in fact many priests did come to faith in Jesus (see Acts 6).

Not only did the insider movement of the early chapters of Acts meet in the temple (where worship was not led by believers and was not supportive of the new community's faith in Jesus as the Messiah

---

7   Since writing the article cited in the previous footnote (originally published in *IJFM* 17, no. 1 [Spring 2000]: 25–31), my thinking has progressed. I would now put more emphasis on the fact that Jesus clearly had thought long-term about the Samaritan "mission." For example, it can be argued from the context that Luke 10 represents an intentional and specifically Samaritan mission. I recognize the complex issues involved in dating events in the Synoptics and in John. But my assumption would be that John 4 took place before Luke 10, which could thus be said to be another step in the strategy of "church planting" or "kingdom sowing" in Samaria. Acts 1:8, when read in this context, shows that Jesus was still clearly intentional about further work in Samaria to follow up and "establish" what had begun in John 4 and expanded in Luke 10. However, I would still defend my basic thesis that Jesus' work in Samaria is a model and example of what we are referring to here as an insider movement.

and Lord), it was also devoted to meeting in homes. So a new structure for fellowship and community and nurture emerged to sustain the believers in the movement.

The Fifth "Devoted": Leaders Devoted to the Word and Prayer

In Acts 6, we find the apostles wrestling with the problems of growth within the emerging Jerusalem movement. Verse 4 shows that they clearly understood an important principle of their calling and of movements. They saw that for the movement to grow, *their* leadership would need to remain devoted to prayer and "the word."

In the context of Acts, "the word" refers not simply to the internal teaching of the Word to believers, but to the spreading of the Word to not-yet-believers. This is confirmed by Act 6:6, where the result of this "devotion" is that the word grew and spread (it is also worth noting that "a large number of priests became obedient to the faith").

Movements to Jesus will remain "movements" if they embrace this principle of keeping key leadership focused on the spread of the Word. If as we nurture a new movement we neglect this important dynamic, we risk cutting off the flow of new believers, thus choking the growth of the movement.[8]

The Sixth "Devoted": Relational Discipleship

In Acts 8, Simon, a new believer, is baptized. Philip, himself a fairly new believer, has evangelized him. This in and of itself is a key movement dynamic. Philip was appointed in Acts 6 to serve tables, then used by God to share with the Ethiopian, then whisked away, and then used of God in Simon's life. Philip has baptized Simon. And he has baptized him rather quickly.[9]

Note that this is a new believer baptizing another new believer. And the model of discipleship? Simon "continues with" Philip (Acts 8:13), showing that the movement has continued to follow Jesus' own highly relational model for making and multiplying disciples. New disciples make new disciples, including baptizing and mentoring them through a relational, "life-on-life" process.

So far we have identified six keys or dynamics of movements to Jesus in the book of Acts. These six keys can be described and measured; they're either happening in a movement or they're not. In our work it has become a regular part of ministry evaluation and planning to occasionally ask ourselves whether we're doing these things and whether we see others doing these things in the movement. To summarize, these six dynamics are (1) prayer, (2) the apostles' teaching and fellowship, (3) breaking bread and the prayers, (4) remaining "in the temple" and meeting "from house to house," (5) developing structures that keep key leadership focused on the spread of the word and prayer, and (6) relational discipleship.

In my own organization, Global Teams, we have been trying to find ways to describe movements and their dynamics in practical and tangible ways so that our work and prayers can be focused on doing the things that actually promote the kind of movement Acts describes. In several contexts, we have been working with the following four markers of healthy and vibrant movements to Jesus:

1. Self-propagating: leaders from within the movement are planning and doing evangelism, church multiplication, and cross-cultural mission sending.

---

8   Acts 6 is often used by proponents of various church "polities" to support their particular viewpoint. But Luke is not giving us a once and for all structure. His intention is to show how the community was led to adopt and adapt new forms as needs arose in order to stay focused on their purpose.

9   That this is a common practice in Acts seems clear from Acts 2; the accounts of the Ethiopian eunuch, Simon the Sorcerer, Cornelius, the Philippian jailer; and other examples.

2. Self-governing: the movement regularly and intentionally multiplies its own leadership, and is responsible before God for all decisions concerning the work.

3. Self-supporting: the movement, through the stewardship of its disciples and/or other enterprises governed by leaders in the movement, funds its own internal operations and ministries.

4. Self-theologizing: the movement is actively engaged in the ongoing process of doing thorough biblical theology "in culture."

The above four markers describe insiders (people from within the movement) from the point of view of their actions, as well as the dynamics of a movement. The first three "selves" (borrowed from Henry Venn and Rufus Anderson)[10] are an attempt to summarize the material from Acts, while the fourth marker, or "self-," describes critical contextualization carried on by insiders.

Drawing upon these four "selves," we have developed a tool with more detailed descriptions of these four dynamics, which we incorporate into an annual re-examination of the ministry of each pioneer team.[11]

Summary: Part 1

So far we have attempted to outline six dynamics, or keys, to healthy and vital movements to Jesus. We tried to show some of the biblical bases for such movements remaining, to some degree, within the religious context in which they are birthed and spread.

Now we need to examine the question of insider movements more closely from the perspective of the religious context inside of which we're arguing that they can take place. We need to engage the issue of how a biblical movement to Jesus can be in any sense also an insider movement.

Part 2: Insider Movements: The Relationship to Culture and Religion

Let's assume a healthy movement to Jesus is emerging among people Z. What is the relationship of the emerging Jesus movement (and its biblical worldview and discipleship) to the worldview, religious life, and cultural context inside of which the movement is "moving"? Can any of the culture (especially religious culture) be incorporated and kept? Beyond that, can any of the culture be seen as in any way preparatory for the gospel, and thus in some sense "fulfilled" when the gospel is embraced?

I would like to begin here by offering some introductory thoughts toward a biblical theology of God's work in cultures and religion. In view of space constraints, I will focus on one passage: Acts 17.

A Theology of Culture and Religion in Acts 17

First, let me attempt to dispel what I consider a "myth" about Paul's visit to Athens in Acts 17. A widespread opinion seems to be that Acts 17 represents a sort of anomaly for Paul; that is, Paul experimented in Athens with a "contextualized" approach to presenting the gospel. Disappointed in the results, he returned to a straight and simple proclamation of the Cross, according to his own testimony in the early chapters of 1 Corinthians.

However, this viewpoint founders on two counts. First, Acts 17 is not an anomaly; Paul had used almost the same method of presentation in Acts 14 as well. Luke presents this as a method Paul used

---

10 It is debated which of the two first wrote on this concept. See Wilbert R. Shenk, "Rufus Anderson and Henry Venn: A Special Relationship?" *IBMR* 5, no. 4 (1981): 168–72.

11 To obtain a copy of this tool, please contact the author at khiggins@global-teams.org.

regularly, depending upon his hearers and his context.[12] Second, the Corinthian correspondence itself contains the clearest and perhaps best known of Paul's statements on "contextualization." The famous "Jew to the Jew" and "Greek to the Greek" passage (1 Cor 9:19–22) is descriptive of Paul's ministry "habit." In today's Western church culture we might refer to this as Paul's vision and mission statement. His vision was to see all saved. His mission was to become all things to all men that by all means he might save some. Far from "rethinking" his approach in Athens, he seems to reaffirm it.

Now we turn to Acts 17. First, Paul is clearly disturbed by the religious worldview and life in Athens. Contextualization and the promotion of insider movements does not imply that the missionary or "insider" leader assumes everything in a culture is pleasing to God. Acts 17 forces us to wrestle with the issue of sin and darkness in other cultures and religions, including our own.

There is a personal challenge in the passage as well. Is my heart as sensitive as Paul's? Do I care at a deep and passionate level about the people I am called to reach? How easy it is for our missionary call to descend to the level of a job, and our passion to settle into an intellectual interest in "truth." Paul was deeply disturbed by what he saw, and it moved him to act.

Second, Paul takes this passion and inner turmoil and communicates it in a very focused way. Here is a summary of the main points:

1. Paul begins by affirming what he can truly and honestly affirm: "I see that in every way you are very religious. For . . . I even found an altar with this inscription: to an unknown god" (Acts 17:22,23).

2. But Paul goes beyond this. There is a sense in which he sees the altar to the unknown god as preparation for what he will say about the gospel. Whether this is mere pragmatism and opportunism remains to be seen. We will address that in a moment. For now we need to remind ourselves of what is really taking place. A Jewish monotheist (Paul) is using a pagan altar as a sign that the people he addresses are religious and that they have in fact been worshiping the true God without knowing it. This is not the same thing as saying that this "anonymous worship" is salvific. I am not arguing that, nor do I believe it. But Paul is assuming that they have been worshiping the true God without knowing him.

3. From the altar Paul moves to creation. Here again Paul's approach is not merely to affirm what he sees in the Athenians, but to point out areas that will need correction in the light of God's truth. So although he clearly sees the altar as preparing the Athenians for his message about the true God, he does not take that to mean that everything in their religion and culture is preparation that can be fulfilled. Some things will need to be corrected or discarded, polytheism being an obvious example.

4. To support his creation arguments, he cites sources and texts from the Athenians' literary background. One text is taken from a hymn dedicated to Zeus. But since it says something Paul knows is true about the true God, he uses it while changing its reference point.

5. It is interesting to note that while Paul never cites Scripture directly in this encounter, he does speak biblical truth, using poets and writers to support the biblical truths he proclaims.

6. Paul closes his argument by calling for a worldview change and repentance. In context this would mean accepting monotheism specifically and, minimally, accepting Paul's general argument about a day of judgment and a coming judge who has been raised from the dead (this person is unnamed in this sermon, though Paul may be assuming his hearers will connect the reference to Jesus, whom he had named

---

12 To counter this point, it could be argued that Paul does not use the same method again after Acts 17. However, Paul's letter to the believers in Rome, written after his ministry in Athens, lays a foundation in its opening chapter that is very much in keeping with the thought and assumptions in his sermon in Acts 17.

in Athens prior to being invited to the gathering of philosophers). It is almost like offering a "sample" to see if the Athenians want more. Some clearly did not, while others clearly did.

7. Finally, we return to the question raised (but not addressed) under point (b) above, as to whether Paul's use of the altar and the poets was merely a pragmatic move or was based instead on a deeper understanding of God's ways in the cultures and religions of mankind. In these verses Paul argues that God has created every nation, every culture, *pan ethnos*. And not only did he create them—he also determined the era of history in which they would live and the geographical area they would inhabit. This is very careful, sovereign planning on God's part, and encompasses, again, every nation and people. But there is a purpose for this careful planning and design; verse 27 makes this very clear. The purpose is so that they (the nations) should "seek him," "reach out for him," and indeed "*find* him," although in fact "he is not far from any one of us." This latter phrase includes the nations. Paul's use of the altar and the poets is a very logical outworking of his worldview, which can be summarized in this way: the true God has designed the cultures, seasons, and locations of the nations to further the process by which all peoples might seek after and actually find him.

Based upon this reading of Paul's message to the Athenians, it is biblical to speak of the gospel as a fulfillment of the "seeking, reaching out, and finding" process in every culture and religion. This is true not only in the Jewish religion (where we can point to direct Old Testament prophecies and "types" that are fulfilled in Christ) but also in a pagan religious culture such as that found in Athens.[13] Thus insider movements can be said to relate to their religious context from this perspective of fulfillment, as well as from the perspective that the gospel will correct and change the culture.

The preceding is a brief and incomplete attempt to outline a biblical theology of religion and culture. A fuller treatment would need to examine texts and themes such as

- the Bible's clear and steady stance against idolatry and polytheism as at least "empty" in some circumstances and as "demonic" in others[14]—this needs to be part of the discussion among those of us more disposed to approve of the idea of insider movements;
- God's jealousy for his people, which would need to be taken into account in any exposition of his work among other nations;
- the covenants or claims to "ownership" in relationship to non-Jewish people—Ishmael in Genesis, Edom and Moab and Philistia in Psalm 108, for example;
- the theology of "natural revelation" in Romans 1; and
- John 1:9 and the light that enlightens every human being.

There is much more that needs to be explored in this important area.

---

13   I am not in any sense equating the OT revelation with the work of God among the nations as described in Acts 17. I do not believe this argument places all other religions on the same footing as the OT. I once heard a missionary whose work had been in a Buddhist context suggest that the teachings of Buddha could in fact replace the OT functionally for Buddhists. This is not an uncommon suggestion in some non-evangelical missiological traditions. I am not making that argument here. I do agree that Paul uses the pagan culture and religion of the Athenians in the same way he uses the OT among Jews and Gentile God-fearers, but that is not the same thing as suggesting a replacement for the OT.

14   Exegesis of each passage would be needed to determine when "empty" would best fit the author's intention and when "demonic" would best fit. Both are taught in Scripture.

A Look Back Before Moving On

Our first main question addressed the "movement issue." In that section we attempted to show biblical precedents for believers in the true God remaining within the cultural (and even religious) forms in their context.

My point here is to attempt to outline a framework for a biblical understanding of how a movement to Jesus could claim to be in some sense a fulfillment of the religion (or aspects of the religion) inside of which it remains.

At this stage it might be helpful to summarize what I think the implications of Acts 17 are for insider movements. I will focus on just three.

Implication 1. Paul does not claim that all of paganism is a preparation for Jesus. He challenges the thinking of the Athenians and argues from inside of their worldview framework in order to change that framework.

Therefore an insider approach to Islam or any other religion will need to address the areas that must be transformed by biblical truth. The six keys from Acts outlined earlier are thus of critical importance in this regard. Those keys serve to keep an insider movement rooted in the canonical Scriptures. The fourth "self-" (self-theologizing) is also largely dedicated to this end.

Implication 2. Paul assumes that altars and poets and other such things will be found that agree with biblical truth, and he uses them freely, without trying to show that he is only using them because they show the Bible to be true. His theology sees God as the designer who has placed each nation in its era and area in order to find him. Also, he is not afraid of being misunderstood and taken for a pagan simply because he uses pagan altars and poets to prove his point.

Therefore an insider approach can freely use religious and secular aspects of the culture to communicate biblical truth. This includes the texts and ceremonies of the religion one is seeking to reach. Missionaries should not fear that doing so might cause others to confuse them as being "Muslim" or "Hindu." The Athenians, frankly, were still not sure what category to place Paul in, and he did not seem to worry about that issue. This is not a lack of integrity on Paul's part.[15] I believe Paul was attempting to elicit among the Athenians what I would call a "hermeneutic of curiosity."

Implication 3. Paul's teaching indicates that he believed God had actually designed the locations and times and indeed cultures in which people lived so that they could seek God and find him. There was an intentional design on God's part. This design, in Paul's view, accounts for why the Athenians would have an altar to an unknown god. In the context of the scene in Athens, we should conclude that God's own hand was involved in the Athenians making that altar, and that he did so in order that they would seek and question and someday find him. This is in contrast to the idea that the altar was a convenient accident that Paul used. Paul's theology of culture as articulated in Athens shows us that the altar was no accident.

Therefore missionaries among peoples of other religions can and should approach their work with the same expectations Paul had. I should expect, in my work among Muslims, that I will find in the

---

15 This is a frequent accusation leveled against those who promote insider movements. Sometimes the accusation is aimed at cross-cultural workers who adopt the term "Muslim" for themselves, for example, or allow themselves to be thought of as Muslim. Sometimes the accusation is aimed at "insiders" who do not extract themselves from, say, Islam. The question of integrity and religious labels is worthy of a paper all its own.

Qur'an, the Hadith, worship in the mosque, and indeed in the hajj itself the Islamic equivalents of "altars to an unknown god" and "poets" whom I can quote to proclaim biblical truth. This is true of Islam generally, but each of the widely varying cultural expressions of Islam would have additional "altars" and "poets." These things are not accidents; they are there by God's design. They are, we might say, the fingerprints of God within the religions of the world.

One Final Question

Before concluding this section, we need to address one final question about insider movements. At the beginning of this section we raised the question of the relationship between insider movements and the religious context in which they emerge. So far we have focused our attention on developing a biblical perspective for understanding culture and religion and how a movement to Jesus might relate to them or indeed be "inside" of them.

It is also important to ask whether it matters how nonbelieving members of the religion view the movement. For example, there will be Muslims who do not follow Jesus and are not part of the "insider movement." If they do not accept the insider's interpretation of the Qur'an, or if they reject the so-called "altars" and "poets" the movement claims are fulfilled by the truth of the gospel, does this mean the insider movement's claims are invalid? In other words, whose criteria—indeed, whose hermeneutic—will determine the validity of the interpretation of the Qur'an or Hadith offered by a Muslim insider movement?

The simplest answer would be to ask another question. Whose application of the Old Testament determined the validity of the Jewish insider movement to Jesus in Acts? Jesus and the apostles shared much in common with the way of reading the Old Testament of their contemporary Jews. The main difference is found in their application of various Old Testament passages to Jesus specifically. It is clear that in this specific point, the apostles and Jesus himself had a different "hermeneutic" than the prevailing religious establishment when they read and taught the Old Testament.

Although they used the same interpretive assumptions in reading the Old Testament, the apostles were applying a "key" to the Old Testament: Jesus himself. In the same way, Paul used a different "key" in speaking of the altar he discovered in Athens and of the poets he quoted.

Before Paul's sermon, who would have guessed that the altar to the unknown god was really an altar to the God of the Old Testament? And yet in both examples one can see the logic and the "fulfillment" after the fact once one accepts the hermeneutic.

Clearly not all of the Athenians who heard Paul did in fact accept this hermeneutic. But that did not cause Paul to question his interpretation of the altar in Athens. Neither Jesus nor the apostles assumed that their hermeneutic of the Old Testament was invalid because the other Jewish leaders did not accept it.

Similarly, the fact that not all Muslims will accept my reading of the Qur'an in the light of Jesus does not mean that my reading is wrong or invalid. I have a different starting point and a different hermeneutic, shaped by a worldview that has Christ at the center. Reading the Qur'an with Christ as my starting point and with the assumptions of Acts 17 shaping my expectations, there will be many discoveries of "altars" and "poets." This will be true for other Islamic writings, rites, and practices. This will be true in other religious contexts as well.

Summary: Part 2

In this paper I began with a working definition of insider movements. I linked such movements to the wider conversation about people movements, but added the religious factor to the mix of what it means to be "inside" a culture.

I have attempted to wrestle with the insider movement issue from two major perspectives, each with its own questions. I will restate those perspectives and questions here:

1. "Insider movements" in the Bible: what are the models and dynamics of a healthy, vital movement to Jesus? This question forces us to articulate and address valid concerns about how movements to Jesus develop on a biblically grounded foundation.

2. Can a "movement to Jesus" be an "insider movement"? What is the relationship of the emerging Jesus movement (and its biblical worldview and discipleship) to the worldview, religious life, and cultural context inside of which the movement is "moving"? This question forces us to articulate and address valid concerns about how movements to Jesus develop within the cultural and religious framework of their particular context. A major factor in this question will be the issue of developing a biblical theology of culture and God's involvement in it.

In both parts of this chapter I have focused my attention on the fundamental issue of whether insider movements can be called biblical. In part 1, this involved us in a discussion of Acts to uncover the biblical dynamics of movements generally. We examined six keys in Acts based on Luke's use of the word "devoted." In that section we also took a slight detour to discuss the issue of biblical precedents for religious insiders. We focused on both Namaan and the Samaritan woman as models for this phenomenon.

In part 2 we sought to discuss the relationship of insider movements to their religious context. We examined Acts 17 and uncovered a theology of culture and religion that further supports the idea that a movement to Jesus can be an insider movement. This includes crucial assumptions based on Paul's teaching in Athens—that such a movement will find areas to correct in the religion and culture, but also areas of fulfillment in the religion and culture. The latter become visible when we read a culture and religion through a new Jesus-centered hermeneutic for interpreting the texts and practices of the religion and culture.

If space permitted, the next logical step would be to outline some examples of such altars and poets from Islamic, Hindu, Buddhist, or other contexts. In a future paper I would like to develop an exegesis of the Qur'an, for example, based upon a new "Jesus hermeneutic," and address the areas of correction and fulfillment that such a hermeneutic would surface in the text.

A new "Jesus" reading of the Qur'an is, of course, just one piece of what an insider movement would develop in its life and practice. There are many facets of culture and religion that are not a part of the official texts or forms of Islam. The same is true for Hindus and Buddhists.[16] These too would need to be addressed by the movement.

Conclusion

In my introduction I said that I believe the issue of insider movements is as important a question as the rediscovery of certain aspects of biblical truth in the Protestant reformations. Let me conclude by explaining that a bit.

---

16 And Christians!

I believe that the Lord is enabling his people to rediscover gems of biblical truth that have always been in front of us but which we have not seen fully or applied consistently. The reformations of the sixteenth century were fueled by a rediscovery of the biblical texts (and especially the biblical truth of justification by faith), then shaped by a consistent application of that biblical truth to church practice, polity, worship, and even Scripture translation. In the same way, I believe we're on the brink of a similar wave of reformations[17] that will be fueled by the rediscovery of a thoroughly biblical theology of culture and religion, one shaped by a consistent application of that biblical truth to mission practice and the movements that emerge among Muslims and Hindus and Buddhists as a result of that reformation.

If I am right, then the mission movement will need to not only keep looking for better ways to recruit and train and send missionaries, but also acknowledge the need for a paradigm shift. The harvest is indeed vast, and the laborers too few. But we don't just need more laborers; we also need a new paradigm of what we're sending them into the harvest to do.

It is my hope that this paper has articulated some of the biblical bases for that paradigm shift and thus in a small way helped to enable us, with God's help, to catalyze new "Six Devoted" insider movements to Jesus.

Bibliography

Hesselgrave, David J. "People Movements." In *Evangelical Dictionary of World Missions,* edited by A. Scott Moreau, 743–44. Grand Rapids, MI: Baker, 2000.

Lewis, Rebecca. "Promoting Movements to Christ within Natural Communities." *International Journal of Frontier Missiology* 24, no. 2 (2007): 75–76.

Shenk, Wilbert R. "Rufus Anderson and Henry Venn: A Special Relationship?" *International Bulletin of Missionary Research* 5, no. 4 (1981): 168–72.

---

17 While my focus in this paper is on the Muslim, Hindu, and Buddhist contexts, the same recovery of biblical truth is seeding new thinking about church planting among "postmoderns," among others. Hence I refer to "reformations" in the plural.

CHAPTER 26

The Incarnational Model of Jesus, Paul, and the Jerusalem Council[*]

J. Dudley Woodberry

The Incarnational Models of Jesus and Paul

With Jesus we see the divine model for incarnating the gospel among people whose worldview was similar to that of most Muslims, and with Paul we see how that model was lived out in different religiocultural contexts.

The Model of Jesus

His incarnation is announced as, "And the Word became flesh and lived among us, and we have seen his glory, the glory as of a father's only son, full of grace and truth" (John 1:14).[1] He in turn gave us that same glory: "The glory that you have given me I have given them" (17:22). And he gave us a similar mission: "As the Father has sent me, so I send you" (20:21).

Further, God sent his Son to be incarnated under the same law that guided the people whom he sought to redeem: "God sent his Son . . . , born under the law, in order to redeem those who were under the law" (Gal 4:4,5). Therefore, as we follow Jesus we might go under a similar law—or remain under that law—for the redemption of those under that law.

A number of observations appear relevant to our topic. First, Jesus observed the Mosaic law, but rejected any traditions of the elders that conflicted with the teachings of Scripture (Matt 15:1–9). And he internalized and deepened its meaning in the Sermon on the Mount. Therefore, his incarnational model includes following and internalizing the Mosaic law. Second, qur'anic and Islamic law in general draw heavily on Jewish law with its roots in Mosaic law.[2] The Qur'an even includes all of the Ten Commandments, although keeping the Sabbath is associated particularly with the Jews (20:8; 22:30; 7:180,163; 17:23; 6:151; 24:2; 5:38; 4:112,32). And Islamic law did not develop the priestly and sacrificial functions and ritual in the same way as Judaism did. Therefore, although there are some differences, much of Islamic law is similar to Mosaic law and can be internalized and interpreted as fulfilled in Christ.

---

[*]   Excerpt from J. Dudley Woodberry, "To the Muslim I Became a Muslim?," *IJFM* 24, no. 1 (2007): 23–28, with minor revisions. Reprinted by permission.

[1]   Scripture quotations in this chapter are taken from the New Revised Standard Version (NRSV) unless otherwise stated.

[2]   See Robert Roberts, *The Social Laws of the Quran* (London: William and Norgate, 1925); Jacob Neusner, Tamara Sonn, and Jonathan Brockopp, *Judaism and Islam in Practice: A Sourcebook* (New York: Routledge, 2000); Neusner and Sonn, *Comparing Religions through Law: Judaism and Islam* (New York: Routledge, 1999); Woodberry in *UIM*, chap. 45; and Charles Cutler Torrey, *The Jewish Foundation of Islam* (New York: Jewish Institute of Religion, 1933).

Thirdly, the leaders of the temple and synagogues had corrupted Judaic worship and rejected Jesus, but he and his first followers continued to identify with Judaism and to participate in temple and synagogue worship. Therefore a case may be made for Muslims who follow Jesus to continue to identify with their Muslim community and participate, to the extent their consciences allow, in its religious observance.

The Model of Paul

Paul wrote to the church in Corinth, where the local religion even promoted immorality:

> To the Jews I became as a Jew, in order to win Jews. To those under the law I became as one under the law . . . so that I might win those under the law. To those outside the law I became as one outside the law (though I am not free from God's law but am under Christ's law) so that I might win those outside the law. . . . I have become all things to all people, that I might by all means save some. (1 Cor 9:20–22)

After showing the outworking of this in specific situations, he passes the model on to us: "Be imitators of me, as I am of Christ" (1 Cor 11:1). The same Paul who argued in the epistles to the Romans and Galatians against bondage to the Law also had Timothy circumcised when he was going to minister among Jews (Acts 16:3) and took converts with him into the temple to be purified (Acts 21:26). As we have noted, Islamic law is based on the law of Judaism. Even if it were not, however, Paul teaches adaptability even to a pagan culture like Corinth as long as one is guided by conscience and by the desire to glorify God and see people be saved (1 Cor 10:23–33).

The Incarnational Model of the Jerusalem Council

In Acts 15 we see how the early church leaders dealt with a missiological problem that resulted from the gospel crossing a cultural barrier—though it was from those who followed the Law to those who did not, rather than the reverse, as in our present considerations. Nevertheless we can identify and apply the criteria they used.

1. How God Is Working

Paul and Barnabas "reported the conversion of the Gentiles . . . and . . . all that God had done with them" (vv. 3,4), how "God, who knows the human heart, testified to them by giving them the Holy Spirit, just as he did to us; and in cleansing their hearts by faith he has made no distinction between them and us" (vv. 8,9). And they told the "signs and wonders that God had done through them among the Gentiles" (v. 12). Then Simeon told "how God first looked favorably on the Gentiles" (v. 14).

There are now case studies of insider movements in a number of regions in Asia and Africa that demonstrate how God is working, with phenomenal growth in one South Asian country that we in the School of Intercultural Studies at Fuller Theological Seminary have been studying, with repeated visits, for years. This movement and others with which we are in contact give clear evidence that God is working in them. One Protestant denomination now directs most of its ministries among Muslims to equipping members of these movements. In the spring of 2003 I was privileged to hear firsthand reports of those from each of their regions, and again it was clear that God was at work in these people.

There are significant movements to Christ from Islam in North Africa and Central Asia that are not insider movements nor very contextualized to Islamic culture. The contexts are different. Whether or not there was a previous national church and, if so, how much rapport it had with the Muslims are significant. My assignment, however, is to evaluate the insider movements.

2. The Call of God

At the Jerusalem Council Peter rose and said, "My brothers, you know that in the early days God made a choice among you, that I should be the one through whom the Gentiles would hear the message of the good news and become believers" (v. 7). And God through a vision showed him that, for the sake of the kingdom, he should break traditional dietary rules that kept Jews and Gentile apart (Acts 10).

In the case studies that we are following today, followers of Christ have likewise believed themselves called to break the traditional barriers between communities to incarnate the gospel in the Muslim community. In many cases God has confirmed the call by transforming lives through Christ.

3. Reason

Peter in the council in Jerusalem asks, "Why are you putting God to the test by placing on the neck of the disciples a yoke that neither our ancestors nor we have been able to bear?" (Acts 15:10). The apostles and elders, with the consent of the whole church, then sent a letter to the disciples in Antioch presenting their decision with the words, "It has seemed good to the Holy Spirit and to us . . ." (vv. 22,23,28). Thus they used their own reasoning along with the guidance of God's Spirit.

When we apply reason to the present discussion we see reasons for and reasons against insider movements of disciples of Christ within the Muslim community. In most Muslim people groups, the determinants of peoplehood are drawn from a wide range of social domains, including religion, language, culture, politics, nationality, ethnicity, and family. Apostasy, then, may be viewed by the community as a renunciation of all these determinants of their peoplehood and worth. Add to this the fact that in these communities the word "Christian" is conventionally used to describe Western society, with connotations of aggression and immorality, or to designate some local ethnic group that has different (and often distasteful) customs.

The question then arises as to whether Muslims may accept Jesus as Savior and Lord while remaining socially and legally Muslim. In the Qur'an itself the word *islam* just means "to submit" to God (2:112), and Jesus' disciples bear witness that "we are Muslims" (literally, "those who submit") (3:52; 5:111). The Qur'an also speaks of certain individuals who received the book before the Qur'an who said, "We were Muslims before it" (28:52,53). Muslim qur'anic commentators say that some or all of those individuals were Christians.[3] Thus there is at least some textual rationale for disciples of Christ from Muslim contexts to continue to include "Muslim" in their identity. However, because the word has developed in modern usage a more restrictive meaning, it would seem more transparent to use a designation such as "I submit to God (*aslamtu* in Arabic) through Isa al-Masih (the qur'anic title meaning 'Jesus the Messiah')."

This approach could be seen as following the historical pattern of designating groups within the Muslim community by their founder, such as the Hanbalites (after Ahmad b. Hanbal) or the Ahmadiyya

---

3   Jane Dammen McAuliffe, *Qur'anic Christians: An Analysis of Classical and Modern Exegesis* (Cambridge: Cambridge University Press, 1991), 240–46.

(after Ghulam Ahmad), though, as in the latter example, some Muslims may reject the group as heretical or non-Muslim.

Other disciples of Jesus from Muslim contexts have adopted the designation Hanif, which in the Qur'an referred to the religion of Abraham that pre-Islamic monotheists like Waraqa b. Nawfal sought. He was a cousin of Muhammad's first wife, Khadija, and became a Christian.[4] The Qur'an says that Abraham was not a Jew or a Christian, but a *hanif,* a *muslim* (3:67), and described him as one who submitted (*aslama*) to God (4:125). 'Umar, the second Muslim caliph, even used the term *hanif* to describe himself when he met with a Christian leader.[5] Its value is that it is generally an acceptable term that has been used to refer to people like Ibn Nawfal, who became a Christian. Even the Apostle Paul calls those who belong to Christ "Abraham's offspring" (Gal 3:29).

An advantage of insider movements is that they can provide an opportunity for the gospel to be incarnated into a Muslim culture with a minimum of dislocation of those elements of Muslim societies that are compatible with or adaptable to the gospel. And, although they have aroused intense opposition, sometimes instigated by members of traditional churches, they have frequently allowed more opportunity and time for ordinary Muslims to hear and see the gospel lived out than when the new disciples of Christ are expelled upon conversion or join a traditional church with a different ethnic and cultural constituency that has little rapport with the Muslim majority. Likewise, insider movements allow faith and spiritual maturity to develop in a context relevant to the new disciples' background and probable ministry.

On the other hand, there can be drawbacks. There is not a clear break initially with nonbiblical teachings of Islam. Discipling raises greater challenges, as does building bridges with traditional churches, if there are any.

4. Theology

Peter, before the Jerusalem Council, raised the theological argument that God "in cleansing their [the Gentiles'] hearts by faith . . . made no distinction between them and us" (Acts 15:9) and went on: "We believe that we will be saved through the grace of the Lord Jesus, just as they will" (v. 11). That is the decisive element, not whether they follow the Law or not. Theological themes that are relevant to insider movements include that of the faithful remnant, which refers to those with a genuine relationship of faith with God (Amos 5:15). Although it originally applied to the faithful remnant of God's people Israel (Isa 46:3), it includes those from other nations (Isa 45:20; 66:18). Additional themes include the kingdom (or kingly rule) of God, which like yeast will quietly transform individuals and groups from within (Matt 13:33), and salt, which likewise influences its surroundings (Matt 5:13).

The people of the kingdom who form the local churches and the universal church are, of course, especially relevant. Even the believers who meet in houses are called churches (Rom 16:51; 1 Cor 16:19), and these would correspond to the groups that meet regularly in houses for worship and Bible study that are at the core of the insider movements with which I am familiar. Expressing the universal church becomes the great challenge for them, because it is the body of Christ incarnated in the world today (1 Cor 12:12–27).

---

4   Alfred Guillaume, *The Life of Muhammad: A Translation of Ibn Hisham's Recension of Ibn Ishaq's Sirat Rasul Allah* (London: Oxford University Press, 1995), 83, 99, 103.

5   Uri Rubin, "Hanif" in *Encyclopedia of the Qur'an,* vol. 2, ed. Jane Dammen McAuliffe (Leiden: Brill, 2002), 403.

5. Scripture

James before the council then shows how the inclusion of the Gentiles also agreed with Scripture (Acts 15:15–17). When we look for Scripture that is relevant to insider movements, we see that in the Old Testament God sometimes worked outside the channels of his chosen people—through Melchizedek, for example. We even observe the prophet Elisha apparently condoning Naaman going into a pagan temple with the king he served and bowing with him before an idol (2 Kgs 5:17–19).

In the New Testament, Jesus in the Sermon on the Mount internalized and deepened the Law (which, as we have noted, was similar in many ways to Islamic law). At the same time, he did not let it hinder his relating with those he came to save (Luke 7:36–50). Paul, while arguing against the necessity of following the Law, nevertheless observed the Law in order to advance his ministry with the Jews, as in his circumcising of Timothy (Acts 16:3), having his own hair cut when under a vow (Acts 18:18), and performing the purification rites in Jerusalem when James and the elders there encouraged him to do so because of the Jews (Acts 21:26).

On the other hand, the epistle to the Hebrews gives some warnings to some believers who have remained under the umbrella of their original faith. The epistle was apparently written to Jewish followers of Christ who were under persecution and were conducting themselves as a form of Judaism (perhaps because Judaism was then a recognized religion by Rome, but Christianity was not). They are warned of the peril of falling away (6:1–8) and are called to persevere (10:19–39).[6]

6. Guidance of the Holy Spirit

At the Jerusalem Council, Peter noted that God testified to the inclusion of the Gentiles in the church by giving them the Holy Spirit (Acts 15:8), and, in the joint communiqué to the church in Antioch, the apostles and elders said that "it has seemed good to the Holy Spirit and to us" not to impose any further burden on the Gentiles than some essentials (v. 28). Jesus had promised, "When the Spirit of truth comes, he will guide you into all the truth" (John 16:13). Many of those whom I have met in insider movements have manifested the indwelling of the Spirit of God by their spiritual fruit, wisdom, and devotion. Because of the limitation of formal training opportunities for believers in insider movements, they are highly dependent on the Bible as interpreted and applied by the Holy Spirit to them. But my questioning of numbers of them and the reports of others that I trust lead me to conclude that, although they are different from traditional Christians, they certainly evidence the guidance of the Bible and the Spirit.

7. The Essentials

When the apostles and elders in Jerusalem stated that circumcision was not necessary, they were dealing with salvation. When they added some "essentials" (Acts 15:28,29), they were dealing with fellowship and morality. The prohibition of fornication (vv. 20,29) obviously had to do with the low Greco-Roman morality out of which the Gentiles came. As for food offered to idols, although Christians were free to eat it, the act might cause others to stumble (1 Cor 8:1–13). Therefore believers should not exercise that freedom (Acts 15:20,29). The same was true of blood and meat that contained blood. Since the law of

---

6   Denis Green, "Guidelines from Hebrews for Contextualization," in *Muslims and Christians on the Emmaus Road: Crucial Issues in Witness among Muslims*, ed. J. Dudley Woodberry (Monrovia, CA: MARC, 1989), 233–50.

Moses, which forbade the eating of blood, had been so widely preached (v. 21), eating it might hinder table fellowship with many Jews.

How does all this apply to disciples of Christ within the Muslim community? First, there is freedom to observe the Law or not to do so, since salvation does not come through the Law. But because relationships and fellowship are so important, the disciples of Christ should not use their freedom in a way that might unnecessarily hinder their relationships with Muslims or traditional Christians.

Acts 15 ends with Paul and Barnabas separating in their missionary work because they could not agree on whether to take John Mark (vv. 36–41). Here we see that when we cannot agree, we can nevertheless carry on God's work in separate spheres until we can reach agreement.

Some Critical Issues

There are a number of critical issues, some of which have been treated above.

Use of the Term "Muslim"

A case has been made above for the use of the term "Muslim" by followers of Christ, but it is often best to qualify it, in some way indicating that our submission is through Isa al-Masih (Jesus the Messiah). In any event we are not to deny Jesus Christ. Further, although disciples of Christ from Muslim backgrounds may legitimately retain their Muslim legal and cultural heritage, it is far more problematic for a Christian-background person to attempt this. The outsider might be helpful in suggesting biblical guidelines, but those from a Muslim background are in a better position to understand the meaning of labels and identity in their contexts, hence to answer these questions.

Attending the Mosque and Using the Qur'an

Again, insiders understand better what attending the mosque or using the Qur'an means in each context, so they are in a better position to decide what is best. One factor to consider is the motive. Our research shows that many were first attracted to Christ through the Qur'an. One North African, who had led a number of his family members to Christ, said that no one would listen to him if he did not continue to use the Qur'an along with the Bible and attend the mosque. We do know that the early Jewish Christians, like many Messianic Jews today, continued to attend the synagogue, and the Judaic establishment at the time was hostile to Christians (Acts 9:1,2; 23:2), even as many Muslims are today. If people continue in the mosque, however, they must not say or do anything against their conscience (Rom 14:14). In studying Muslim followers of Christ over a number of years, I have found that, as they study the Bible and meet with other disciples of Jesus, these two resources become increasingly important in their spiritual growth.

Reciting the Confession of Faith

I have enquired of those in insider movements what they do with the *shahadah,* the confession "There is no god but God, and Muhammad is the Apostle of God." One answered that some say that in his polytheistic context, Muhammad was like an Old Testament prophet. This reflects the ambiguity of the Nestorian patriarch Timothy (d. 823), who responded to the Caliph al-Mahdi's question concerning what he thought of Muhammad with the words, "He walked in the path of the prophets."[7] Most of

---

7   Jean-Marie Gaudeul, *Encounters and Clashes: Islam and Christianity in History,* vol. 1 (Rome: Pontificio Istituto di Studi Arabi e Islamici, 1990), 34–46.

those I asked, however, said that they kept quiet when the part about Muhammad was recited or they quietly substituted something that was both biblically and qur'anically correct, like "Jesus is the Word of God."

The Unity of the Church

In the early church, as we have seen, James, Cephas, and John were chosen to go to the Jews, and Paul and Barnabas to the Gentiles (Gal 2:9). Each evangelistic thrust was relatively homogeneous. The Jews and Gentiles could keep much of their own identity and follow Christ. But to express the universal church, they needed to have fellowship, which was expressed by eating together. This required some additional adjustments. So with the insider movements, there is much freedom for them to retain their identity, but over time some adjustments will need to be made for the sake of fellowship in the broader church. The same Paul who argued for the freedom of the Jewish and Gentile churches to retain their own identity also argued that Christ had broken down the wall between Jew and Gentile so they might be one body, the body of Christ (1 Cor 12:12–27). In like manner traditional Christian and Muslim Christ-centered communities should have the same freedom to retain their own identity, but must express the unity of the body of Christ by their love one for another. This is how Christ is and will continue to be incarnated in the world today.

Bibliography

Gaudeul, Jean-Marie. *Encounters and Clashes: Islam and Christianity in History*, vol. 1. Rome: Pontificio Istituto di Studi Arabi e Islamici, 1990.

Green, Denis. "Guidelines from Hebrews for Contextualization." In *Muslims and Christians on the Emmaus Road: Crucial Issues in Witness among Muslims*, edited by J. Dudley Woodberry, 233–50. Monrovia, CA: MARC, 1989.

Guillaume, Alfred. *The Life of Muhammad: A Translation of Ibn Hisham's Recension of Ibn Ishaq's Sirat Rasul Allah*. London: Oxford University Press, 1995.

McAuliffe, Jane Dammen. *Qur'anic Christians: An Analysis of Classical and Modern Exegesis*. Cambridge: Cambridge University Press, 1991.

Neusner, Jacob, and Tamara Sonn. *Comparing Religions through Law: Judaism and Islam*. New York: Routledge, 1999.

Neusner, Jacob, Tamara Sonn, and Jonathan Brockopp. *Judaism and Islam in Practice: A Sourcebook*. New York: Routledge, 2000.

Roberts, Robert. *The Social Laws of the Qoran*. London: William and Norgate, 1925.

Rubin, Uri. "Hanif." In *Encyclopedia of the Qur'an*, vol. 2, edited by Jane Dammen McAuliffe, 402–3. Leiden: Brill, 2002.

Torrey, Charles Cutler. *The Jewish Foundation of Islam*. New York: Jewish Institute of Religion, 1933.

CHAPTER 27

Acts 15

*An Inside Look**

Harley Talman

The Holy Spirit is doing the unexpected: multiplying disciples of Jesus within non-Christian religious traditions, in movements often designated "insider movements" (IMs). Are there solid biblical and theological foundations that support IMs? The present volume provides significant scriptural perspectives and theological foundations on this question. This chapter will focus solely on the contribution of Acts chapter 15 to this issue. In the first half I will argue that the author of Acts 15 provides God's people with a model of a theological process and principles that can guide us in addressing missiological controversies such as IMs, particularly among Muslims. In the second half I will address specific concerns raised by an author who is critical of IMs.

Acts and Paradigms for Cultural Diversity

A highly regarded study by NT scholar Dean Flemming maintains that Luke wrote Acts not just to promote mission to the Gentiles, but to provide paradigms of how the Spirit-guided believers are to deal with cultural diversity: Palestinian Jews, Hellenistic Jews, Samaritans, Gentiles, and a eunuch. The crescendo builds as God demolishes these sociological and religious barriers and climaxes in Acts 15. The rest of Acts fleshes out the implications of the Jerusalem Council's decision.[1] Brian Rosner avers, "The book of Acts without chapter 15 would be like a wedding ceremony without the crucial pronouncement."[2] Flemming regards Acts 15 as "a decisive moment in the encounter between faith in Christ and culture within the life of the early church, which helps to give the task of incarnating the gospel a historical and theological basis." The crisis precipitating the council concerned entrance requirements to the messianic community: must Gentiles who believe in Jesus conform to the social identity and religious traditions of the Jewish believers, following the example of Jesus and his disciples?[3]

---

* Excerpt from Jeffrey Morton and Harley Talman, "Does the Jerusalem Council of Acts 15 Support Insider Movement Practices?," *Evangelical Review of Theology* 37, no. 4 (2013): 308–20, with minor revisions. Reprinted by permission. This chapter contains the Talman portion of the discussion. The final section, "Where We Agree and Differ," and substantial material in the notes did not appear in the original publication due to space constraints.

1 Dean Flemming, *Contextualization in the New Testament: Patterns for Theology and Mission* (Downers Grove, IL: IVP Academic, 2005), 43.

2 Brian Rosner, "The Progress of the Word," in *Witness to the Gospel: The Theology of Acts*, ed. I. Howard Marshall and D. Peterson (Grand Rapids, MI: Eerdmans, 1998), 227, cited in Flemming, *Contextualization in the New Testament*, 43.

3 Flemming, *Contextualization in the New Testament*, 43–44. While Flemming does not directly address insider movements, I find his study offers tacit support.

The council's proceedings are relevant to IMs, because the key concerns in both are the same: Is justification solely through faith in Christ and purification by the Spirit, or is proselytism required? Can communities of believers multiply and grow to maturity as disciples of Christ Jesus within a Gentile (or Muslim) society, or do they need to abandon their native society to become proselytes in a traditionally Jewish (or Christian) church and subculture? (For that is the choice they have.) Jews recognized two types of proselyte: (1) "proselytes of the gate" (*ger toshav*) were resident aliens who followed some of the Jewish customs, but not circumcision and Torah observance;[4] (2) "proselytes of righteousness" (*ger tzedek*) were full-fledged Jews who adhered to all Jewish doctrines and religious requirements, including circumcision and ritual immersion.[5] The latter was demanded by the Pharisee party.

The Pharisees based their theological position both on Scripture (e.g., Gen 17:9–14) and ancient tradition. For them, Flemming explains, "circumcision was not simply an optional cultural form; it was a matter of religious life and death—the indispensable symbol of the covenant relationship. If Jewish . . . law observance and the Jewish way of life . . . were divinely sanctioned, how could they possibly be negotiable?"[6] Had they prevailed, the progress of mission to non-Jewish peoples would have been greatly hindered. "Theologically it would declare that God's grace and the gift of the Spirit were not fully sufficient for salvation."[7]

James cites Amos 9:12 because it validates Peter's witness to God's activity of including Gentiles in his messianic kingdom, not as proselytes but as "Gentiles who are called by my name" (Acts 15:17 ESV). "Sharply put," says Flemming, "God's present activity among the Gentiles becomes the hermeneutical key for understanding the biblical text. . . . Amos, rightly interpreted, gives Scripture's grounding for the theological principle of salvation for the Gentiles by faith apart from circumcision" and adherence to the Mosaic law.[8] The gospel renders proselyte conversion unnecessary, because it gives all peoples and cultures equal standing before God.[9] Kevin Higgins observes,

> While the Pharisee believers have already argued their case from the Torah, James, in effect, is looking at the whole canon. . . . The inclusion of the Gentiles was akin to the Holy Spirit's action in forming Israel itself. . . . James does not say that God was adding the Gentiles to his people Israel, but that he was forming a people for himself from among the Gentiles.[10]

---

4   James' recommendation may imply that he saw the new believers as falling under this category and the "Holiness Code" in Lev 17–18, which applied to "the aliens that sojourn among them." Less probable is the view that proselytes of the gate were bound only to conform to the seven commands given to Noah.

5   Josephus describes the latter as those who adopt the Jewish customs and adhere to Jewish laws and ways of worshiping God—i.e., those who have become Jews. See *Antiquities* 14.7.2.

6   Flemming, *Contextualization in the New Testament*, 45.

7   Ibid.

8   Ibid., 46. Bock observes, "Even a committed Jewish believer such as James can affirm that Gentiles can be included among believers directly without having to become Jews. This is an innovation of the new era that Jesus and the distribution of the Spirit on Gentiles have brought." Darrell L. Bock, *Acts*, Baker Exegetical Commentary on the New Testament, ed. Robert W. Yarbrough and Robert H. Stein (Grand Rapids, MI: Baker Academic, 2007), 502.

9   Flemming, *Contextualization in the New Testament*, 49.

10   Kevin Higgins, "Acts 15 and Insider Movements among Muslims: Questions, Process, and Conclusions," *IJFM* 24, no. 1 (2007): 29–40.

David Peterson concurs: "They constitute a new people of God and not simply a large addition to the existing people known as Israel. The critical question is therefore how these two peoples relate to each other"[11] in expressing their belonging to the one body of Christ.

The council's decree allowed Jews to fellowship with Gentile believers without incurring a perceived defilement that could hinder their outreach to fellow Jews who heard Moses read every Sabbath (Acts 15:21).[12] Although these prohibitions had scriptural precedent, they seem to have been a contextual compromise[13] to provide a *modus vivendi* for Gentile believers living among Jewish believers.[14]

Acts 15 and the Intercultural Context

How is Acts 15 relevant to IMs? Flemming understands Luke as presenting a "paradigmatic narrative" of "God's people articulating their faith within an intercultural context, which carries implications for the church in any generation." Luke's concern is not merely the council's theological conclusions, but its theological process, which can guide us in addressing missiological questions that emerge when the gospel crosses cultural barriers. Two important criteria appear: (1) the testimony of field workers that Gentiles have received the Holy Spirit apart from circumcision (which seemed to conflict with the theological understanding of many Jewish believers), and (2) a fresh look at Scripture to see if the observed phenomenon harmonizes with it.[15]

Dudley Woodberry delineates seven criteria that were utilized to resolve the crisis that resulted from Gentiles coming to faith in Christ: (1) how God is working, (2) the call of God, (3) reason, (4) theology, (5) Scripture, (6) the guidance of the Spirit, and (7) essentials for fellowship.[16] If we apply these criteria to IMs, we get the following results:

- Case studies reveal astounding growth of movements of Muslims who believe fully in Christ Jesus while remaining inside their Muslim communities.
- As God called Peter to give the gospel to Gentiles (Cornelius' household), so many Muslim disciples feel led to remove historic barriers by incarnating the gospel within the Muslim community, and the Spirit confirms this by their transformed lives.

---

11   David G. Peterson, *The Acts of the Apostles*, Pillar New Testament Commentary (Grand Rapids, MI: Eerdmans, 2009), 432.

12   Flemming, *Contextualization in the New Testament*, 47. Becky Lewis observes: "The apostles and elders agreed that the Scriptures had predicted that God's salvation was for all peoples, not just Jews and proselytes. They also agreed that God had shown His acceptance of the Gentile believers by giving them His Holy Spirit. So, using these two criteria to justify their decision, they decided 'not to make it difficult for the Gentiles turning to God' (Acts 15:19) by adding on to their faith in Christ a requirement of conversion to the Jewish religious forms. In order to promote a peaceful coexistence between Jewish and Greek believers, the council asked the Gentiles to follow a few laws given in Leviticus to outsiders residing among the Jews: no eating of blood, strangled meat, or food polluted by idols, nor any practice of sexual immorality. However, all of these laws, except the last one, were removed before the end of the New Testament by Paul, who reduced them to a matter of conscience (Rom 14)." Lewis, "The Integrity of the Gospel and Insider Movements," *IJFM* 27, no. 1 (2010): 44 (*UIM*, chap. 28).

13   Flemming, *Contextualization in the New Testament*, 50. With Gentiles living in pagan contexts, Paul permits believers to eat food offered to idols in certain situations (1 Cor 8–10).

14   Joseph A. Fitzmyer, *Acts of the Apostles*, Anchor Bible Commentary (New York: Doubleday, 1998), 557.

15   Flemming, *Contextualization in the New Testament*, 48. He describes these two criteria as "the appeal to the church's experience of God's activity" and "the work of the Spirit in the community as the context for creative theologizing."

16   See Woodberry in *UIM*, chap. 26. Higgins' aforementioned article builds upon Woodberry.

- Salvation is by grace through faith in Christ, not by proselyte conversion to a new religion. (Muslim disciples remain in their communities but meet in homes for Bible study and worship.)
- The inclusion of Gentiles into the people of God in a nontraditional way was in accord with Scripture (Acts 15:15–17)—so also with insider movements.
- Just as the work of the Spirit was evident among the Gentiles, so too Muslim insiders manifest spiritual fruit, wisdom, and devotion. Due to limited formal training options, they rely more heavily on the Holy Spirit to teach and guide.
- Peter thought it unreasonable to burden Gentile disciples with a yoke of law (v. 10). Similarly, adopting Christianity (as a culture, civilization, and religion) puts an unnecessary burden of cultural baggage and misunderstanding upon Muslims, who can express their discipleship to Christ in different, but biblical, ways.
- The council added some "essentials" (vv. 28,29) to facilitate fellowship and ethics.[17] Likewise, for Muslim believers

  > there is freedom to observe the Law or not to do so, since salvation does not come through the Law. But because relationships and fellowship are so important, these disciples of Christ should not use their freedom in a way that might unnecessarily hinder their relationships with Muslims or traditional Christians.[18]

- Both groups retained their distinct identities, but adjustments were required to facilitate fellowship as a demonstration that Christ had demolished the barrier between Jew and Gentile (1 Cor 12:12–27), as Woodberry affirms:

  > So with the insider movements, there is much freedom for them to retain their identity, but over time some adjustments will need to be made for the sake of fellowship in the broader church. . . . In like manner traditional Christian and Muslim Christ-centered communities should have the same freedom to retain their own identity, but must express the unity of the body of Christ by their love one for another.[19]

---

17 Woodberry says, "The prohibition of fornication (vv. 20,29) obviously had to do with the low Greco-Roman morality out of which the Gentiles came. As for food offered to idols, although Christians are free to eat it, the act might cause others to stumble (1 Cor 8:1–13). Therefore, believers should not exercise that freedom (Acts 15:20,29). The same is true of blood and meat that contains blood. Since the law of Moses, which forbids the eating of blood, had been so widely preached (v. 21), eating it might hinder table fellowship with many Jews." *UIM*, chap. 26.

18 Ibid. Fitzmyer connects the four prohibitions to Leviticus 17–18, which regulated conduct for the aliens sojourning among Israel; see Fitzmyer, *Acts of the Apostles*, 557. Peterson objects that this ignores "the argument that God has taken for himself a new and distinctive people from among the nations." Peterson, *The Acts of the Apostles*, 435. Bock sees the prohibition of blood and strangled animals as referring to Leviticus 17:10–14 and 18:6–30, but the warning against sexual immorality as associated with pagan temple worship—though he admits Fitzmyer's view of intrafamilial relationships in Leviticus 17–18 is possible. Table fellowship is one concern, but the list exudes an "ethos" of respect, cultural sensitivity, and concern for mission. See Bock, *Acts*, 505–7.

19 Woodberry, chap. 26.

Thus we see the relevance of the Jerusalem Council's deliberations and decision with regard to how we reflect on insider movements. The essence of its significance is expressed by Flemming:

> Acts 15 describes a church on a journey to a deeper understanding of its identity as the one people of God comprised of two distinct cultural groups who believe in Jesus. Neither group must surrender its cultural identity, and Jews may continue to observe their ancestral traditions.[20] . . . The resolution of the Council allows for theological diversity regarding the way of life and approach to missionary outreach of the two cultural groups. By the same token, not even the original, divinely sanctioned culture of God's elect nation has the right to universalize its particular expression [of faith in Christ].[21]

Because of Acts 15, Jewish Christ followers accept Western Christians whose manner of discipleship has departed from the divinely mandated practices of the OT (followed by Jesus and his disciples) so they could remain insiders to the Western cultural tradition, in spite of its pagan roots.[22] Mark Kinzer has called for a bilateral ecclesiology between Jews and Gentiles in the one body of Messiah.[23]

But this is still too limiting, because the Gentiles are nations. As Gavriel Gefen argues, "There is no one monolithic Gentile ecclesia. As Jews, it is easy for us to see everyone else as lumped into the one category of Gentile. . . . The one body we speak of is meant to consist of a multilateral ecclesia."[24] He believes that it was largely Hellenized Jews in Antioch who worked with Paul to develop the first "Greco-Roman expression beyond Judaism," but rightly asserts, "To consider their locally appropriate adaptations of following Jesus as being 'the' expression of new covenant faith for every kind of Gentile, at all times and in all places, would serve to distort the Gospel for so many peoples."[25]

Acts 15 required that Jewish believers recognize the freedom of Gentile believers "to live a life that is determined by Christ and his Spirit."[26] Christians must give that same liberty to believers from non-Christian religious traditions.

---

20   Peterson thinks that the mention of the Apostolic Decree in Acts 21:25 indicates that the shoe was now on the other foot. Outnumbered by Gentiles, Jews were being pressured to adopt the Gentile way of life. Luke is showing how the church was taking steps to allow them to continue to practice Torah. See Peterson, *The Acts of the Apostles*, 436.

21   Flemming, *Contextualization in the New Testament*, 52. Bock concurs, "As long as the gospel is not compromised, then diversity of expression can be tolerated." Bock, *Acts*, 508.

22   See George Barna and Frank Viola, *Pagan Christianity? Exploring the Roots of our Church Practices* (Carol Stream, IL: BarnaBooks, 2012). In contrast to early house churches and city congregations of the NT that had no specifically Christian buildings, clergy, liturgy, or religious calendar, Western Christianity adopted practices such as sacred places, steeples, pews, pulpits, order of worship, Sunday morning worship, the sermon, the processional, the priest, one pastor, clergy, ordination, clerical robes, choir, choir robes, dressing up for church, and a truncated Lord's Supper instead of a meal, etc.

23   Mark Kinzer, *Postmissionary Messianic Judaism: Redefining Christian Engagement with the Jewish People* (Grand Rapids, MI: Brazos Press, 2005).

24   Gavriel Gefen, email to author, April 17, 2013.

25   Email to author, April 18, 2013.

26   Peterson, *The Acts of the Apostles*, 433.

Responding to Concerns

[Talman here responds to Jeffrey Morton's critique of his essay.]

Jeff, I appreciate your summary of Acts 15. The clear statement of your concerns gives us opportunity to clear up major misconceptions. Your assertions (in italics) are followed by my response under four categories: church, Scripture, identity, and religion and discipleship.

Church

"Most proponents of IM believe a follower of Jesus may remain in his socio-cultural-religious context . . . with little to no connection with the church that is not of the believer's context."[27] Since we are talking about IMs as movements of the gospel inside social structures and networks, these believers' primary connection is naturally with other believers inside their own social network. Moreover, are you asking more of insider churches than you do of traditional ones? How much contact does the average American evangelical church have with the church that is not of its context? Do Baptist churches have close connections with Pentecostal churches in the same city?

Building of relationships with the broader body of Christ often occurs when a church engages in mission and is forced to think beyond its local context. One of the most encouraging aspects of the growing IMs is the way that they move across ethnic and national boundaries into new contexts. Connections between believers from other cultural, linguistic, ethnic, and religious backgrounds more commonly occur at the leadership level. Leaders of these movements also interact with the Western Christians and Christ followers from other religious traditions. If they were not interacting in these ways, we would know very little about what is happening.

Scripture

I agree with much of what you write about Scripture, but I will relegate differences over secondary issues to the footnotes.[28] My chief objection is your assertion that IM proponents impose preordained conclusions on Scripture.

---

27   Quotations of Jeffrey Morton are from Morton and Talman, "The Jerusalem Council of Acts 15," 308–311, 316–318.

28   Morton's statements on these other issues (in quotation marks and italics) are followed by Talman's responses:

"Every historical event is unique and non-reproducible; the story from Acts 15 is sui generis.*"* While this view was not uncommon in times past, it does not reflect current scholarly thinking about Luke-Acts.

"While the reader may develop principles from such a recorded event, it is vital not to make the text mean more than it does." Every IM theologian would agree with you.

"The two of us disagree on most issues IM comprises." You only delineate a few of these, but I would presume that you share many other convictions with IM proponents, such as (1) that salvation is found in Christ alone; (2) that every believer if at all possible needs to be involved with a local church; (3) that the Holy Spirit transforms a new believer so that the light of Christ will now shine through this new believer to his or her community; (4) that God is at work among Muslims, drawing them to saving faith in Jesus; (5) that the Great Commission passage commands us to make disciples of all nations, and thus we have a large body of missionaries trying by the grace of God to bring the wonderful message of Jesus and his kingdom to the lost Islamic world; (6) that we can thank God for all who are laboring among Muslims regardless of the various doctrines, attitudes, and philosophies of ministry they represent, rejoicing that Christ is proclaimed (Phil 1:15–18); etc. These things are at the heart of IM proponents' convictions.

Unfortunately, you seem not to grasp the way that Acts 15 is used by most proponents of IMs. We maintain that Luke is concerned not just with the council's theological conclusions, but its theological process—which assists us in addressing missiological questions that result from the gospel crossing cultural barriers. One of these is how to determine if a phenomenon outside our normal Christian experience (like IMs) is a work of the Spirit or not. Two criteria are clearly present: (1) reports from field workers that the Gentiles have received the Holy Spirit apart from circumcision (in apparent conflict with the testimony of the OT), and (2) reflection on Scripture to see whether it is in harmony. Since we follow the same process that the Jerusalem Council followed, do you disapprove of how they approached Scripture?

Identity

"Acts 15 presents a theological question, not one about cultural identity." Is this not the theological question: "Is salvation available to both Jew and Gentile apart from circumcision?" If so, then the theological question is about identity, for cultural identity is a part of who a Gentile and a Jew were (circumcised = Jew, uncircumcised = Gentile). Bock and other scholars recognize this.[29] These two issues are inseparable. The story emphasizes that salvation is by faith in Jesus alone, and therefore it allows a Gentile to remain a Gentile who follows Jesus, without becoming a Jew marked by circumcision.

Furthermore, even if we were to grant that the identity issue for the Gentiles is not primary, the explicit point of conflict in Acts 15 is this: "Must Gentiles be circumcised and keep the law of Moses to be saved?" The point of controversy in our context is, "Must Muslims repudiate their birth identity as Muslims to grow to maturity in Christ?" While these may be different questions, the criteria for evaluating the answer are a primary contribution of Acts 15.

"Gentile is an ethnic, linguistic identity whereas Muslim is a socioreligious identity." Such a distinction cannot be maintained, for circumcision was a religious, social, and ethnic marker; therefore it too encompassed socioreligious identity. Circumcision of a Gentile would often cut off his social and religious relation-

---

"The nature of historical narrative demands caution: care when creating analogies from the story to the present, and prudence when developing principles." I agree, and of course this applies equally to your reading of the narrative.

"The book of Acts is historical narrative rather than gospel or apocalyptic." You offer no documentation for this statement, so it is not clear what you mean by "gospel" or "historical narrative." I would have thought that the Gospels are historical narratives. And since Luke introduces the book of Acts as a continuation of the Gospel of Luke ("the former account . . . of all that Jesus both began to do and teach" [1:1]), it is difficult to accept your assertion that the two accounts are of different literary genres.

"The burden of making the case of biblical foundations for IM is upon its proponents since IM offers a new understanding and application of certain passages." There is nothing new under the sun. Reading church history, one sees that others who have gone before us have had similar understandings and applications, like Hudson Taylor, who also was often criticized. But the fruit of his work has stood the test of time, and his name still brings a certain sense of respect when mentioned among Chinese believers.

"God rose to the challenge, creating a people (laos) for himself (v. 14c) that included the Gentiles—transforming them from ethnos, *the LXX term for Gentiles—to* laos, *the term for the Jews."* You are not implying that God was transforming the Gentiles into Jews, are you? Actually, *laos* is a broad term for the people of God. It is used in the NT to include the Gentiles, and was not exclusively used in reference to the Jews. See John J. Kilgallen, "Acts 13.38–39: Culmination of Paul's Speech in Pisidia," *Biblica* 69, no. 4 (1988): 482.

29 Bock observes, "Even a committed Jewish believer such as James can see and affirm that Gentiles can be included among believers directly without having to become Jews. This is an innovation of the new era that Jesus and the distribution of the Spirit on Gentiles have brought. Bruce (1990, 339) notes that these Gentiles are sheep not of this fold (John 10:16)." Bock, *Acts,* 502.

ships, and could even result in death (see "The Costs of Circumcision for Gentiles").[30] Consequently, circumcision was at the heart of both groups' identity.

"The text is silent on the matter of Gentiles/Muslims changing their identity." This may not be explicit, but it was certainly involved in the decision not to make it difficult for the Gentiles who were turning to Jesus, and for the sake of unity asking them to do these minimum things, abstaining from practices that were deeply offensive to Jews. The text respects each group's identity, recognizes the differences, and seeks to promote their unity in Christ.

Religion and Discipleship

"Some proponents of IM suggest the text teaches that a change of religion is not necessary for salvation." Is changing religion really necessary for salvation? Is the gospel a religion? Many evangelicals reject this and insist it is about a relationship with God through Christ. Our differing perspectives depend on what you mean by "a change of religion." Is "religion" defined in an essentialist or a nonessentialist manner?[31] If the former, then a change of religion is needed. However, the essentialist concept of religions has been widely discredited by the academy—there is simply no monolithic set of beliefs and practices held by all who hold any "religious" identity.[32] The same was true of first-century Judaism.[33]

If Islam is defined in a cultural or sociological manner, then there is no need for a change, because what we are talking about is *not a religion, but a socioreligious community.* Having a nonessentialist perspective enables us to see how Muslims, Hindus, Buddhists, Jews, or others outside of traditional "Christianity" may still be regarded as members of their socioreligious communities, even though they do not adhere to certain tenets found in textbook definitions of religion. Even atheists can frequently remain part of such a socioreligious community.[34]

"Most critics of IM . . . advocate biblical discipleship and the necessary inclusion into local congregations where possible or at least Muslim convert congregations. The body of Christ is essential to every believer."

---

30 This sidebar lists the tremendous social, cultural, and religious implications of circumcision for Gentiles. We are indebted to Richard Jameson for his heretofore unpublished synthesis of this topic.

31 See Talman, chap. 37; Richardson, chap. 39; Richard, chap. 40; and the glossary.

32 Dietrich Jung highlights the problem of an essentialist view of Islam: "How is the persistence of this specific image of Islam to be explained against all empirical evidence? Having worked and lived in various Muslim countries in the Middle East and beyond, I have been confronted with so many different Islams. No scholarly erudition is required to see the enormous variety. . . . Why, so the mind-boggling question, do then so many Muslims and non-Muslims nevertheless retain this essentialist image of 'true Islam' in their minds?" Jung, *Orientalists, Islamists and the Global Public Sphere: A Genealogy of the Essentialist Image of Islam* (Sheffield, UK: Equinox Publishing, 2011), 1. See also Ronald Lukens-Bull, "Between Text and Practice: Considerations in the Anthropological Study of Islam," *Marburg Journal of Religion* 4, no. 2 (1999): 1–10.

33 J. Andrew Overman states, "So varied was Jewish society in the land of Israel during this period, and so varied were the Jewish groups, that scholars no longer speak of Judaism in the singular when discussing this formative and fertile period in Jewish history. Instead we speak about Judaisms. In this time and place there existed a number of competing, even rival Judaisms" (e.g., Jewish followers of Messiah, Pharisees, Sadducees, Essenes, and zealots, who varied widely in their beliefs and practices). See Overman, *Church and Community in Crisis: The Gospel according to Matthew,* New Testament in Context (Valley Forge, PA: Trinity Press International, 1996), 9, cited in Charles H. Talbert, *Reading the Sermon on the Mount: Character Formation and Ethical Decision Making in Matthew 5–7* (Grand Rapids, MI: Baker Academic, 2006), 5.

34 In Israel today, the majority of Jews are either atheist or agnostic, yet they remain part of Judaism. The same phenomenon can be observed with secular Muslims.

The Costs of Circumcision for Gentiles

The tremendous social, cultural, and religious implications of circumcision for Gentiles included: **(1) Religious Blasphemy.** Greek gods were created in the image of man. To modify the "born" appearance of the body was to blaspheme the gods. The Greeks believed that a human being was born complete and perfect. This is why they glorified the body (e.g., naked statues and athletic events). "Nature out of her abundance ornaments all the members, especially in man. In many parts there is manifest ornamentation, though at times this is obscured by the brilliance of their usefulness. The ears show obvious ornamentation, and so does the skin called the foreskin [*posthē*] at the end of the penis and the flesh of the buttocks."* **(2) Immodesty.** A man was not considered indecently exposed unless the tip of his penis was showing. Athletes, who competed in the nude, would pull the foreskin over the tip of the penis and fasten it with a *kynodesme*. **(3) Social and Economic Harm.** Enjoying oneself in a Greek gymnasium or Roman bath, where nudity was de rigueur, was a popular and stylish pastime. Here politics was discussed and business deals concluded. Athletic contests and exhibitions were also conducted in the nude. Participation in athletics was often a prerequisite for social advancement. Thus a circumcised male would have been greatly disadvantaged in business and shamed in social circles. **(4) Immorality.** To the Greeks and Romans, both mutilations were illegal and therefore would have been the ultimate in mindless, barbaric irreverence, excess, and depravity. **(5) Criminal Punishment.** "Jews are permitted to circumcise only their sons on the authority of a rescript of the Divine Pius; if anyone shall commit it on one who is not of the same religion, he shall suffer the punishment of a castrator."† **(6) Denial of Citizenship in Some Greek Cities.** In Alexandria and perhaps in other cities formed on the Greek model, citizenship and the important privileges that went with it were granted only to *ephebes,* those trained for citizenship in the *ephebaion.* Since local law forbade Jews becoming citizens and since *ephebes* regularly exercised naked in the gymnasium, a Jew who appeared naked with a circumcised penis was unable to circumvent the law. **(7) Exile and Confiscation of Property.** "Roman citizens, who suffer that they themselves or their slaves be circumcised in accordance with the Jewish custom, are exiled perpetually to an island and their property confiscated; the doctors suffer capital punishment. If Jews shall circumcise purchased slaves of another nation, they shall be banished or suffer capital punishment."‡ **(8) Possible Death Penalty.** "Thus Flavius Clemens, a nephew of the emperors Titus and Domitian, when with his wife Domitilla he embraced the Jewish faith, underwent circumcision, for which he suffered the . . . penalty of death."§

—*Richard Jameson*

---

* Galen, *De usu partium corporis humani* 11.13, translation from *Galen: On the Usefulness of the Parts of the Body,* ed. and trans. Margaret Tallmadge May, vol. 2 (Ithaca, NY: Cornell University Press, 1968), 529.

† *Digesta* 48:8:11; translation from Amnon Linder, ed., *The Jews in Roman Imperial Legislation* (Detroit: Wayne State University Press, 1987), 100.

‡ Paulus, *Sententiae* 5:22:3–4, in Linder, *Jews in Roman Imperial Legislation* (n. 64), 117–20.

§ *The Jewish Encyclopedia: A Descriptive Record of the History, Religion, Literature, and Customs of the Jewish People from the Earliest Times to the Present Day,* vol. 4, s.v. "circumcision," 95.

You imply that we differ, yet IM proponents likewise advocate biblical discipleship and the importance of every believer being part of a congregation of Spirit-led, Bible-obeying Christ followers. Muslim insiders who trust Jesus as Lord and Savior typically congregate in homes. If, however, you mean that Muslims must reject their community and become proselytes to a religion called "Christianity" or change their legal, political, or socioreligious status to become like those who are born into a socioreligious community of "Christians," then we must disagree. They are free to do this or not to do this, as the Lord leads—but the gospel does not require people to become proselytes.

"Gentiles who followed Jesus by faith did give up their former religions—whatever idol-based or animistic religion that was." We agree. New Muslim Christ followers do turn away from folk Islamic, idol-based, and animistic practices in order to serve the one true God. They trust Christ for forgiveness of sins and are delivered from their fears and bondage to fortune tellers, shamans, and healers. Gentiles were expected to turn from idolatry and from idolatrous practices, but they were not expected to turn from being Gentiles to Judaism.

Believers of all cultures are free to retain any and all elements, values, beliefs, and practices of their culture (which includes their religious culture and traditions) that are compatible with the Bible. Those that are not must either be rejected or else reinterpreted (just as we have done with Christmas trees and Easter eggs). In your footnote, you equate Islam with idolatry, overlooking the Qur'an's explicit, repeated, and vehement condemnation of idolatry. In fact, Muslims often have an even greater concern about it than do "Christians." The parallel you attempt to make is inaccurate. Finally, you have not defined Islam. What is it? It appears that you have an essentialist definition of Islam, which is the basis for your objections to IMs. I have already pointed out the problems associated with an essentialist approach to defining Islam. IM proponents do not suggest that believers may continue to hold unbiblical beliefs and practices of "religion" (as you define it), but rather that believers may remain within their socioreligious community as obedient disciples of Jesus.

"Trusting Jesus for forgiveness of sin entails turning from one's former religion, a religion that did not trust Jesus." It is rather ironic that you accuse IM proponents of eisegesis while at the same time you anachronistically impose your notion of "religion" onto the passage. Where in the text of Acts 15 is this statement made or even implied? The New Testament speaks loudly concerning turning from idolatry and shifting one's total allegiance to Jesus, etc., but religion as a conceptual category is not in view in the text.

Conclusion: Where We Agree and Differ

We can agree on a number of points. You correctly observe that IM proponents are taking an *a posteriori* approach. But there is nothing wrong with such an approach as long as it does not unduly impact exegesis. The Jerusalem Council heard what was happening and wondered if it was indeed of God. Renewed reflection on Scripture led them to conclude that it was. Likewise, the fact of IMs surfaced the same question and the search for an answer from the Scriptures. If our *a posteriori* approach is invalid, then you must also reject the Jerusalem Council's as defective (which I know you would not do).

You also correctly see that the theological issue of salvation was at stake in Acts 15. However, you seem to miss the point of circumcision for the early church. Salvation was dependent upon being a member of the covenant community, and circumcision was one of the rituals required to enter this community. As Flemming maintains, "Circumcision was not simply an optional cultural form; it was a matter of religious life and death—the indispensable symbol of the covenant relationship. If Jewish . . . law observance and the Jewish way of life were divinely sanctioned, how could they possibly be negotiable?"[35] The theological issue was, "Is circumcision a requirement for salvation or not?" In the face of a great weight of biblical evidence that supported the necessity of circumcision, James said no, based on passages in the Prophets and the testimony to what the Spirit had done.

But the Jerusalem Council dealt with a second issue beyond justification (v. 1)—that of sanctification (v. 5). Flemming states, "James is apparently drawing out the pragmatic social implications of the soteriological decision of the church" regarding "the conditions of their [Gentiles'] membership in the Messianic community."[36] Pharisee believers thought that it was necessary "to command them to observe the law of Moses." The chief concern of Acts 15 is, "Can or should a Gentile be a disciple of Christ without adopting Messianic Jewish identity or conforming to Messianic Jewish religious practices?" You have missed or minimized this.

Similarly, the membership conditions for the community of Christ is our issue today. Must one adopt a culturally "Christian" religious identity? Must one adopt the religious traditions of one of the Christian denominations to be an acceptable member of the body of Christ? Does God require conformity to a "Christian" religious tradition? Did God dictate the features of those traditions? He did dictate the religious practices of the Old Testament. Flemming therefore posits, "If Jewish cultural distinctives, including law observance and the Jewish way of life, were divinely sanctioned, how could they possibly be negotiable?"[37] If the council could say they were not required, then how much more are our diverse church traditions not required?

Furthermore, it is particularly significant that the letter sent to the churches says nothing about faith, justification, or righteousness, and it treats conformity to Jewish-Christian practices as an unnecessary "burden." Your limiting the issue to justification does not take into account this concern for the tremendous cost to a Gentile proselyte in undergoing circumcision.[38] It would have indeed been a great trouble or burden.[39]

It is important to answer the question, why did the Jewish believers continue to observe the Law? Was it simply obedience to God, or did they believe it was essential for their continued life and witness in the community? If it was for conformity to their birth culture, then these Torah-observant Jewish followers of Jesus are a precedent for IMs, as are the Gentile believers. If it was to be more righteous, then why did they not require the Gentiles to observe the same practices? Although the objectors in 15:1 and 15:5 mention circumcision, none of the discussion mentions it, nor does the letter. Thus the council's deliberations about observing the OT laws, of which circumcision is one, are concerned more with the second issue, discipleship, than they are with salvation.

We also agree that there is not an *exact* parallel between Gentiles and Muslims, just as there is not between Jews and Muslims.[40] But exact correspondence is not necessary for there to be relevance—

---

35 Flemming, *Contextualization in the New Testament*, 45.

36 Ibid., 44, 47.

37 Ibid., 45.

38 Nicolaus, a convert to Judaism from Antioch, did move to Jerusalem and fully integrate into the Greek-speaking Jewish community. This could well have been due to the immense cultural cost of taking on circumcision, which became the norm for many Jewish converts.

39 The letter does enjoin conformity to four rules of behavior. Many commentators see this as facilitating table fellowship. Ben Witherington III understands them as all being associated with pagan temple worship; see Witherington, *The Acts of the Apostles: A Socio-rhetorical Commentary* (Grand Rapids, MI: Eerdmans, 1998), 459–67.

40 Gavriel Gefen, a Torah-observant Jewish follower of Christ, regards Gentile believers as insiders to their cultural communities. See Gefen in *UIM*, chap. 7.

if significant parallels do exist[41] or if we can derive or apply principles. The principle that underlies IMs is involved with both groups.

I am unable to agree with your assertion: "The Muslim way of life is influenced by the religious practices of Islam, but there is no such flavour to *Gentile*. . . . Gentiles share no identifiably common trait known as *Gentilism* derived from their religious practices or worldviews."[42] In fact there are significant parallels: (1) like Muslims, Gentiles represented many different ethnic groups and languages, but were unified by a metalanguage/culture (Greek vs. Arabic); (2) despite the diversity of their pagan religious expressions, they were socioreligiously united ("Caesar is Lord"); and (3) the way of life of the Gentiles was heavily influenced by their religious beliefs. If nothing else, you must at least agree that they had religious lives and that Acts 15 makes it clear that, to follow Jesus, they did not need to adopt the Jewish religion of Jesus' first followers. The requirement for Gentiles was simply faith in Jesus. Obviously, Gentiles were to turn from their evil practices—some of which were religious in nature. Accordingly, IM advocates insist that any practices contrary to the gospel are to change, but the rest may be retained or reinterpreted.[43] A case in point: Acts 15 tells Gentiles not to eat food offered to idols, but later Paul says that they may, unless it causes another to stumble or involves idolatry (1 Cor 8–10). Otherwise food offered to idols (a religious aspect of the culture that the Corinthians well understood, hence their worries about it) may be eaten without qualms.

Your assertion that Islam is "a religion that is the antithesis of biblical Christianity" reflects assumptions that are rooted in your essentialist view of Islam. This is unfortunate, because essentialism has been essentially abandoned as a valid paradigm among scholars of religion. Yet it drives your analysis and conclusions and seems to blind you to the diversity that actually exists among Muslims. It is this diversity that can allow insider believers to be faithful disciples of Christ while remaining part of their socioreligious community.[44]

One parallel that you may agree with is this: as the Jewish community believed that membership in the covenant community was essential for salvation, so Muslims often believe salvation is only found in the *ummah*. A crucial discipleship issue for IMs is helping new believers realize that their salvation comes only through the person and work of Jesus—not through their good standing in the *ummah*. However, following Jesus does not require that they abandon their community—any more than the Jews were required to abandon theirs. IM advocates share many of your concerns. But our answer is

---

41   See Richard Jameson and Nick Scalevich, "First-century Jews and Twentieth-century Muslims," *IJFM* 17, no. 1 (2000): 33–38.

42   Similarly, how can you separate being culturally Jewish and religiously Jewish in Acts 15? Do you really believe that first-century Jews thought in those categories? Is this not eisegesis?

43   For explanation of their retaining Muslim social identity, but rejecting or reinterpreting unbiblical beliefs and practices, see John Travis, "Messianic Muslim Followers of Isa: A Closer Look at C5 Believers and Congregations," *IJFM* 17, no. 1 (2000): 53–59; and Travis and Woodberry in *UIM*, chap. 4.

44   For example, you claim, "The characterization of Jesus as the 'Word of God' being quranically correct is misguided at best. Jesus as *kalimatullah* means that Jesus is a message from Allah. He is a word *from* Allah, not the word *of* Allah (cf. Qur'an 3:45). This is hardly the meaning of *logos* in the New Testament." But the highly respected classical Muslim commentator Ibn Abbas declared that Jesus was created by the word of God and is that Word. This *is* the same meaning as the *logos* in the NT. So was Ibn Abbas not a Muslim? It should also be noted that whereas 3:45 states that Jesus is *kalimatun minuh*, "a word from God," elsewhere the Qur'an declares that he is *Kalimatuhu*, "his Word" (4:171). This construct in Arabic grammar clearly says that Jesus is "*the* Word of God" (even if most Muslims try to make it mean "*a* word"). These two statements taken together justify the position of Ibn Abbas, which the essentialist view of Islam as a fixed set of beliefs cannot accommodate.

not to require new believers to abandon their birth community, but rather to address the specific issues through intense, obedience-based discipleship.

To sum up, Acts 15 teaches that faith in Jesus is available to all peoples everywhere. We must not make it difficult for those who are turning to Christ and must allow and even encourage them to shine in their natural cultural settings. We should seek to respect one another and build bridges that appropriately enhance the unity of Christ's church, just as the council of Jerusalem did. It is appropriate for IM proponents to utilize the process portrayed in Acts 15 as their paradigm for assessing issues such as insider movements. Biblical discipleship and participation in a functioning *ekklesia* within their own context is normative for insider movements, and they do have connections with the body of Christ from outside their context. The issue of identity cannot be excised from what transpired in Acts 15. Last of all, holding to a nonessentialist view of religion allows us to accept insider movements as valid expressions of biblical discipleship for those from non-Christian religious traditions.

Bibliography

Bock, Darrell L. *Acts*. Baker Exegetical Commentary on the New Testament. Edited by Robert W. Yarbrough and Robert H. Stein. Grand Rapids, MI: Baker Academic, 2007.

Fitzmyer, Joseph A. *The Acts of the Apostles*. Anchor Bible Commentary. New York: Doubleday, 1998.

Flemming, Dean. *Contextualization in the New Testament: Patterns for Theology and Mission*. Downers Grove, IL: IVP Academic, 2005.

Higgins, Kevin. "Acts 15 and Insider Movements among Muslims: Questions, Process, and Conclusions." *International Journal of Frontier Missiology* 24, no. 1 (2007): 29–40.

Jung, Dietrich. *Orientalists, Islamists and the Global Public Sphere: A Genealogy of the Essentialist Image of Islam*. Sheffield, UK: Equinox, 2011.

Kilgallen, John J. "Acts 13.38–39: Culmination of Paul's Speech in Pisidia." *Biblica* 69, no. 4 (1988): 480–506.

Kinzer, Mark. *Postmissionary Messianic Judaism: Redefining Christian Engagement with the Jewish People*. Grand Rapids, MI: Brazos Press, 2005.

Lukens-Bull, Ronald. "Between Text and Practice: Considerations in the Anthropological Study of Islam." *Marburg Journal of Religion* 4, no. 2 (1999): 1–10.

Morton, Jeffrey, and Harley Talman, "Does the Jerusalem Council of Acts 15 Support Insider Movement Practices?" *Evangelical Review of Theology* 37, no. 4 (2013): 308–18.

Overman, J. Andrew. *Church and Community in Crisis: The Gospel according to Matthew*. New Testament in Context. Valley Forge, PA: Trinity Press, 1996.

Peterson, David G. *The Acts of the Apostles*. Pillar New Testament Commentary. Grand Rapids, MI: Eerdmans, 2009.

Rosner, Brian. "The Progress of the Word." In *Witness to the Gospel: The Theology of Acts*, edited by I. Howard Marshall and D. Peterson, 215–33. Grand Rapids, MI: Eerdmans, 1998.

Travis, John. "Messianic Muslim Followers of Isa: A Closer Look at C5 Believers and Congregations." *International Journal of Frontier Missions* 17, no. 1 (2000): 53–59.

Viola, Frank, and George Barna. *Pagan Christianity? Exploring the Roots of Our Church Practices*. Carol Stream, IL: BarnaBooks, 2008.

Witherington, Ben. *The Acts of the Apostles: A Socio-rhetorical Commentary*. Grand Rapids, MI: Eerdmans, 1998.

CHAPTER 28

The Integrity of the Gospel and Insider Movements[*]

Rebecca Lewis

Concerns have arisen over the emergence of "insider movements" across the non-Christian world. For many of us, it seems that the very nature and integrity of the gospel is at stake in this discussion.

We have been led into this debate by the need to respond to developments on the field. Individuals, families, and communities are claiming to know and submit to Jesus as their Lord and Savior, but refusing to identify themselves as "Christians" in the common sense of the word. Some of these people are Muslims who claim to have found that Jesus himself is the "straight path" that they have pleaded with God to show them five times each day. Others are Hindus or Buddhists seeking a personal relationship with Jesus in the midst of cultures similar to the idolatrous pantheon of the Greco-Roman world or the Stoic philosophers of the first century. Though most people in these insider movements believe in the supreme authority of the Bible and the absolute lordship of Jesus Christ, they are remaining members of their communities, including most aspects of their religious culture. If these were just a few people, they could be overlooked. However, when movements to faith in Christ of this nature develop, with followers numbering in the hundreds or thousands, some assessment is necessary.

Are these movements to Christ from God or not? Do they advance his kingdom on earth or do they hinder it? Will they bring the power of the gospel into these cultures like yeast in the dough? Or will the gospel be diluted or contaminated to the point of ineffectiveness, overwhelmed by religious and cultural syncretism? Should we pray for, protect, and emulate these fledgling movements? Or should we warn, correct, and if necessary, disown them?

I believe there is ultimately only one thing that matters at the heart of this debate, and it is not contextualization. The core issue is this: is the very nature and integrity of the gospel being revealed and upheld, or is "a different gospel" being preached and believed, as Paul warns?

To answer this question, we must turn to the Bible as the authority for our faith and practice, especially to the book of Acts and the epistles of Paul.

What Do I Mean by "the Integrity of the Gospel"?

As Paul sought to fulfill his calling, we see two important facets in his defense of the gospel for the Gentiles. I believe that both facets are required for the integrity of the gospel to be maintained.[1]

First, Paul emphasized the unchanging content of the gospel message. Through Christ's death and resurrection, the living God was reconciling the world to himself. Adam and Eve brought upon

---

[*]   Originally published in a slightly different form in *IJFM* 27, no. 1 (2010): 41–48. Reprinted by permission.

1   Let me explicitly state that salvation is through the Lord Jesus Christ alone, the sole authority for our faith is the canonized Bible, and the body of Christ consists of all who put their faith in Jesus Christ as Lord and Savior.

all mankind the curse of sin and death by rejecting God's command out of desire to become like gods. Jesus, the second Adam, turned this upside down, and though "being in very nature God, did not consider equality with God something to be used to his own advantage" (Phil 2:6). Instead he walked Adam's path without sin, yet paying the price of sin, thereby establishing by grace a means for us to know and enjoy the living God forever. This is the unchanging message we proclaim in all contexts.

Christians who are supportive of insider movements are concerned that this message not be altered by adding additional requirements such as adherence to Christian religious traditions, thereby clouding or encumbering the gospel. Others, however, are concerned that without requiring adherence to traditional practices and theological formulations, this central truth cannot be preserved. Both sides are concerned that the gospel message is getting lost.

The second facet of the gospel that Paul emphasized is the unchanging scope of God's plan—the power of the gospel itself to penetrate and transform families within all cultures. Today we believe that God will fulfill his plan to "bless all the families of the earth." But like the first-century believers, we are not in agreement about how this is going to happen. Again, the integrity of the gospel is at stake.

Maintaining the Integrity of the Gospel When It Moved from the Jewish to the Greek World

From the time God first proclaimed the gospel to Abraham, he made it clear that his plan was to bless all the families of the earth through Abraham's descendants (Acts 3:25; Gal 3:8). But what did this mean? Did this mean that they were to go out and make proselytes, cultural and religious converts, of all peoples? Did it mean that "God-fearing Jews from every nation under heaven" would hear and believe the good news, then take it back home with them, as happened at Pentecost (Acts 2:5)?

In the book of Acts we read that the apostles began proclaiming the gospel with the assumption that it was only for the Jews. Evidently they thought that by doing so they were maintaining the integrity of the gospel. Since circumcision was the sign of the covenant God had made with Abraham, and Pentecost was the celebration of the giving of the Law on stone tablets to Moses, the gospel as a new covenant and the coming of the Holy Spirit at Pentecost were the fulfillment, not the abrogation, of all God's promises in the Hebrew Scriptures. So it would have made sense to the disciples that those coming into the kingdom of God would be Jews, saved by faith in Christ and discipled through the God-given Jewish religious framework within which all the disciples lived.

Therefore the disciples began to confidently spread the message of Christ inside the Jewish religious community. They preached in the temple and synagogues—even though their own religious leaders repudiated Jesus as the Messiah, actively persecuted them and other followers of "the Way," and forbade them to preach. They believed their religious tradition to be the right one, and the only one acceptable to God. The result, as Acts 6 reveals, was that Hebraic Jews, Hellenized Jews, converts to Judaism, and "a large number of priests" of the Jews were coming to faith, but no Gentiles. These Jewish believers remained in their Jewish communities, or fled to other Jewish communities when persecuted, taking their faith with them.[2]

---

2   At the very end of Acts (28:17–29), Paul is in Rome talking to nonbelieving Jews who still view faith in Jesus as the Messiah to be a sect of Judaism.

But What Happened When Non-Jews Started to Come to Faith?

The first non-Jews to turn to Christ in large numbers were the Samaritans. Jesus had given Samaritan believers the freedom to worship "in the Spirit and in truth" without requiring them to become prose- lytes or to come to the Jewish temple or synagogues (John 4), where Jewish believers were congregating. Jesus affirms this non-Jewish version of faith in himself as "the kind of worshipers the Father seeks" (v. 23). The Samaritans themselves grasped both key aspects of the gospel, exclaiming, "We know that this man really is the Savior of the world!" (v. 42).

Jesus revealed both the power and the scope of the gospel by saving the Samaritan villagers, with- out requiring Samaritan believers to enter the Jewish religious framework. The disciples seemed to accept this inclusion of the Samaritans into God's kingdom, even though the Samaritans followed a "heretical" version of the Jewish religion. When Philip won many Samaritans to faith in Christ, Peter and John came to pray that they would receive the Holy Spirit. Then Peter and John preached the gospel in many Samaritan villages on their way back to Jerusalem (see Acts 8:25). These Samaritan believ- ers remained in their Samaritan villages, as they would not have been welcomed into Jewish villages, but they were accepted as fellow believers by the Jewish believers and the apostles who visited them. Perhaps it was easy for the Jewish believers to accept these Samaritan believers following Jesus apart from becoming Jewish proselytes, because the Samaritans were circumcised, tried to follow the God of Abraham in the Torah, and had similar religious laws.

Can the Gospel Transform Pagans without the Framework of the Jewish Laws?

Unlike the easy acceptance of Samaritan believers, a heated theological debate arose over the very na- ture of the gospel itself when pagan Romans and Greeks began to come to faith in Christ. The message of the gospel was not in question, but the scope of its application was a matter of contention. Did the gospel message bring grace only to those who joined the family of faith as it was then construed (the circumcised believers who kept Mosaic law), or could the gospel bring salvation to all, regardless of their social and religious context? Two events brought this question to a head.

First, God showed Peter the power of his gospel to save the Gentiles, apart from adopting Jewish identity, by introducing Peter to the Roman centurion Cornelius and his household. Before Peter could even finish his presentation of the gospel, God's Holy Spirit came on all of them, much to Peter's shock. Though other Jewish believers criticized Peter for associating with Romans, upon hearing that the Holy Spirit had come upon Cornelius and his family, they exclaimed, "So then, even to Gentiles God has granted repentance that leads to life!" (Acts 11:18). They were beginning to understand that there are two necessary facets of the gospel, both the message and its ability to save people in all cultures and contexts. Until then, their understanding of the gospel had been incomplete.

Second, Greeks were coming to faith as well. In Antioch the Greek believers were called "Chris- tians" (Acts 11:26).[3] Although these Greek believers did not convert to the Jewish form of faith in

---

3   Craig S. Keener, writing on this verse, notes that the term "Christian" was used not in a religious sense but in a political one: "'Christians' occurs in the New Testament only here, as a nickname given by outsiders, and in 1 Peter 4:16, as something like a legal charge. The title is formed on the analogy of adherents to a political party: the 'Caesarians,' the 'Herodians,' the 'Pompeians' and so forth." Keener, *The IVP Bible Background Commentary: New Testament*, 2nd ed. (Downers Grove, IL: IVP Academic, 2014), 354.

Christ, they nevertheless felt a sense of unity with the Jewish believers and sent a benevolent donation for needy Jewish believers to the elders in Jerusalem through Barnabas and Saul. The Jewish believers seem to have tolerated a few pagans who had become believers in Christ without accepting their religious framework, but they were alarmed when it became a movement.[4]

The Greek believers must have seemed pagan and syncretistic to the Jewish believers, whose religious traditions had been practiced by Jesus and the apostles and had their roots in over a thousand years of Scripture and tradition. So some Jewish believers argued that the Greek believers must adopt circumcision, which was the distinctive mark of the covenant between God and his people, as well as the religious traditions given through Moses, which were followed by the Jewish believers.

How Did the Jerusalem Council Maintain the Integrity of the Gospel?

By Acts 15, a sharp dispute had broken out between Paul and Barnabas and some Jewish believers from Judea who came to Antioch and began teaching the Greek believers (the "Christians") that their salvation was not yet complete. Paul and Barnabas traveled to Jerusalem to resolve the matter under debate: is conversion to the identity and religious traditions of the Jewish believers necessary for salvation for those coming out of Greek pagan background? At this juncture, it was not the content, or message, of the gospel that was under debate.[5] What was under debate was the scope and nature of the gospel: did the message of Jesus Christ only have the power to save those who also accepted the religious framework in which Christ himself was incarnated, or could the gospel save those in an alien context as well?

By defending the power of the gospel to save believers who retained their Gentile culture and identity, Peter sought to preserve the integrity of the gospel. He made a plea to the apostles and elders in Jerusalem on behalf of the Gentiles, saying,

> God, who knows the heart, showed that he accepted them [the Gentiles] by giving the Holy Spirit to them, just as he did to us. He did not discriminate between us and them, for he purified their hearts by faith. Now then, why do you try to test God by putting on the necks of Gentiles a yoke that neither we nor our ancestors have been able to bear? No! We believe it is through the grace of our Lord Jesus that we are saved, just as they are. (Acts 15:8–11)

The apostles and elders agreed that the Scriptures had predicted that God's salvation was for all peoples, not just Jews and proselytes. They also agreed that God had shown his acceptance of the Gentile believers by giving them his Holy Spirit. So, using these two criteria to justify their decision, they decided to "not make it difficult for the Gentiles who are turning to God" (Acts 15:19) by adding on

---

4   The term "Christians" was not a widespread term for Greek/Roman followers of Christ in the early centuries, with Roman historians often referring to believers as "atheists" because they did not believe in the Greek gods or the emperor as a god. There is no indication that the term "Christians" was applied to the Jewish believers during the first century.

5   Paul may have seen that the content of the gospel of grace could not be preserved apart from the scope being preserved. In his letter to the Romans, Paul speaks of the "weak in faith" as those who trust in God plus dietary and festival laws, or who lean on observance of particular customs and not on God alone (Rom 14). In other words, those who demanded Jewish customs and identity from non-Jewish followers of Christ were making Jewish religious rites and traditions a condition of God's acceptance, thus "nullifying the grace of God" (Gal 2:21; see also 3:17).

to their faith in Christ a requirement of conversion to the Jewish religious forms. In order to promote a peaceful coexistence between Jewish and Greek believers, the council asked the Gentiles to follow a few laws given in Leviticus[6] to outsiders residing among the Jews: no eating of blood, strangled meat, or food polluted by idols, nor any practice of sexual immorality. However, all of these laws, except the last one, were removed before the end of the New Testament by Paul,[7] who reduced them to a matter of conscience (Rom 14).

Paul Persisted in Fighting for the Integrity of the Gospel

Paul's battle for the gospel seemed over, but it was not. The apostles had made a pivotal decision: the movement to Christ among the Greeks was from God, and the Greek "Christians" should not be required to adopt the religious traditions of the church in Jerusalem. However, the written pronouncement from the Jerusalem apostles was clearly not the end of the issue. In his subsequent letters, Paul had to argue repeatedly that the gospel must move into the Gentile people groups unhindered by external religious expectations. The integrity of the gospel was at stake.

Paul was not ashamed of the gospel message, precisely because he had seen its power to save, apart from religious traditions, not just the Jew but also the Gentile (Rom 1:16,17). As a result, Paul could confidently proclaim that the gospel has revealed a righteousness that is by faith alone. So he hammered this point in through several chapters of Romans, a letter written to believers in Rome, where faith in Christ was still seen as a sect of Judaism (Acts 28:22): "God does not show favoritism" (Rom 2:11). "A person is not a Jew who is one only outwardly, nor is circumcision merely outward and physical. No, a person is a Jew who is one inwardly; and circumcision is circumcision of the heart, by the Spirit, not by the written code" (2:28,29). "Jews and Gentiles alike are all under the power of sin" (3:9). Before circumcision and before the giving of the Law, Abraham was made righteous by faith alone, so "he is the father of all who believe but have not been circumcised" (4:11).

Paul had changed the mark of the covenant from an external mark (circumcision, Gen 17:13) to an internal mark ("circumcision of the heart, by the Spirit, not by the written code," Rom 2:29). What a shock this teaching must have been to Jewish believers! What? Abraham is the father of uncircumcised believers (Rom 4:11)? Abraham is the father of Gentiles refusing to adopt the Abrahamic sign of the covenant and the laws given through Moses? Paul had declared that the mark of belonging to God's people was not external but internal—a changed heart.

Paul explained that God had demonstrated that all those who have Abraham's faith are Abraham's children, apart from any outward religious requirements. God had revealed this truth by calling

---

6   Fitzmyer in his commentary on Acts notes that the rules James proposed "seek only a *modus vivendi* of Gentile among Jewish Christians and imply no salvific purpose in them. The four things that James would impose are derived from part of the Holiness Code in Leviticus 17–18, which proscribed certain things not only for 'anyone of the house of Israel,' but also for 'the aliens that sojourn among them.'" Joseph A. Fitzmyer, *The Acts of the Apostles*, Anchor Bible Commentary (New York: Doubleday, 1998), 557. These four laws were required in the OT law for those foreigners living among the sons of Israel. It seems that James believed that only a few Gentiles would join the community of faith, and would be subsumed under and live among the Jewish community.

7   Rom 14; 1 Cor 8; 10:23–11:1. The rules concerning kosher food were necessary if Greek believers wanted to eat with Jewish believers; however, they would likewise hinder Greek believers from eating with their nonbelieving relatives, so Paul made it a matter of doing what least offends the conscience of the person you are eating with, noting that idols are nothing and therefore meat offered to them is not significant either. It seems clear that Paul did not consider it "syncretistic" to adapt in this way.

Abraham "father of many nations" and by crediting to Abraham righteousness on the basis of his faith alone (Rom 4:16–18).

This message of inclusion in God's family on the basis of faith alone was good news to the Gentiles, but it was disturbing to many Jewish believers, who felt Paul was dismantling their religious traditions. These Jewish believers did not understand why God would want Gentile believers to set aside the religious framework he had established for the Jews.

Likewise, it is disturbing today for Christians who value their religious traditions to see believers arising in other cultural contexts set these aside as optional or inappropriate for their context. The message of inclusion is good news to us also as long as we are the Gentiles getting included. It starts to get more difficult to accept when we recognize that we are now in the position of those Jewish believers, with two thousand years of our own valuable teachings and traditions that we want everyone to build on. We doubt that God would bypass the collective wisdom of our religious writings and traditions, building his church afresh in new cultures as he did among the first-century Greeks.

Are the foundations of the Bible and the Holy Spirit sufficient for God to build his church without going through traditional Christianity as we know it? Could it be that God is once again starting movements of true faith in Jesus Christ, making new people groups into "children of Abraham," by faith in the gospel alone?

These are questions we would rather not ask. Why would God bypass traditional Christianity? Perhaps because it would astonish the world, revealing the true power of the gospel. Perhaps because the integrity of the gospel itself is at stake.

Will a Simple Gospel Result in Immature Disciples?

A valid concern about insider movements today is that a simple faith like Abraham's, a faith in Christ and the Bible without a religious framework drawn from historical Christianity, will not give these new groups of believers enough guidance for mature discipleship. Paul spoke to this concern himself. Having shown that the gospel is powerful enough to save anyone, regardless of their religious context, Paul went on to prove that Gentile believers would be transformed even if they did not have the benefit of the Mosaic law and the existing discipleship system of the Jews.

First, Paul showed that the religious traditions of Jewish believers had not delivered them from their sinful nature (Eph 2:3), nor from bondage to demonic forces (Gal 4:3). Therefore, neither would these traditions deliver the Gentiles from sin, and they could merely lead to a new type of bondage (4:9). Second, Paul delineated in Romans chapters 6–15 that it is the gospel that is the transformative power in the life of a believer. The believer's "old self was crucified with him [Christ]" (6:6), so he "has been set free from sin" (6:7), and now he is "alive to God in Christ Jesus" (6:11). The benefit reaped "leads to holiness, and the result is eternal life" (6:22), so that "those who are led by the Spirit of God are the children of God" (8:14). Third, Paul summarized the result, or fruit, of having the Holy Spirit in one's life in Galatians 5:22,23: love, joy, peace, patience, kindness, goodness, faithfulness, gentleness, and self-control. These characteristics are signs of the Holy Spirit's work in a believer's life in any culture or context.[8]

---

8   Jonathan Edwards argued that all religions demonstrate characteristics like mystical experiences, miracles, speaking in tongues, rules for pious behavior, etc. He pointed out that the fruit of the Spirit, in particular the ability to love your enemy, is the only religious experience that Christ alone can produce; see his works *Treatise*

Paul concluded that it is the Holy Spirit that delivers believers from their sinful nature so that the moral law of God is fulfilled—holiness without legalism. Paul was teaching that the Holy Spirit will accomplish in the life of a believer something no religious tradition or institution can ever accomplish.

What Does the "Mystery of the Gospel" Mean for Today?

In his letter to the Romans, Paul systematically demonstrated that it is the gospel itself, apart from all the God-given traditions of the Jews, that brings the transformation of obedient faith into the life of believers from any background. He recognized that God was doing something significantly different in his day, calling it a "mystery, which for ages past was kept hidden in God, who created all things" (Eph 3:9).

When moving the gospel into the Greek world, God did not overturn his word, but he did overturn the religious traditions his people had built upon it. The mystery he revealed to Paul was that the Greeks did not have to adopt the religious form of the Jewish believers to become joint heirs and "children of the promise" with them. Paul said, "This mystery is that through the gospel the Gentiles are heirs together with Israel, members together of one body, and sharers together in the promise in Christ Jesus" (Eph 3:6). Some take this to mean that the Greek believers and the Jewish believers had homogenized or fused together into a new "Christian" culture. They assume that the first-century believers had neither the Torah-abiding forms of the Jewish apostles nor the cultural forms of the Greek believers so prominent in later Christianity (statues, mosaics, and endless discussions of philosophical/theological nuances).

It is more accurate to recognize that in the first century there were in existence at least two radically different religions based on Jesus Christ. There was the Jewish version, breathing life into the laws of Moses and Jewish ritual holy days, and there was the Greco-Roman version, turning their philosophy-loving hearts into theology-loving hearts that explored the nuances of the Trinity and the Incarnation. Today people of many different cultures are becoming followers of the Lord Jesus Christ. And they are claiming their biblical right to live out their faith in diverse ways that are nevertheless grounded on the supreme authority of the Bible. Are we ready to accept them as joint heirs with us if they belong to Muslim or Hindu cultures and do not adopt the religious forms and traditions we have constructed over time, and do not even take on a "Christian" identity?

Paul affirmed that in spite of their different cultural and religious practices, these Jewish and Greek believers were all made one, joint heirs in Christ. The gospel had destroyed the "dividing wall of hostility"; that is, their prejudice and enmity toward one another (Eph 2:14,16). It did not destroy their respective cultures. Having recognized that they were received by God equally, without merit, they had no right to boast over one another or to consider their own religious expression of faith in Christ to be more salvific than the other. Therefore we can likewise expect today that allowing radically different expressions of faith in Christ will break down walls of hostility while preserving distinct cultural identities. This humility and freedom of expression of faith is integral to maintaining the integrity of the gospel, so that the power of salvation is always clearly by faith and not by outward works.

---

on Religious Affections and *The Nature of True Virtue*. Neither "right doctrine" nor "right practice," apart from the rebirth through the Holy Spirit, is transformative.

Why Does Paul Forbid Them to Change Religious Expressions of Their Faith?

It is difficult to understand Paul's teaching on these issues. It is easy to accept that he was trying to gain a freedom for the gospel to move unhindered into new cultures. That seems compassionate. But why would he get upset if some of the new Greek believers wanted to become Jewish proselyte believers? That seems harsh. After all, conversion to Judaism had been going on for centuries. What would it matter if the Greek believers wanted to take the full step into joining the Jewish apostles in their version of faith in Christ?

Again, Paul's main concern was clearly for the integrity of the gospel. He did not want it to appear that there was more merit with God to be a believer within the religious stream of Israel than to be a believer within any other context. Therefore Paul emphasized the importance of the gospel not being linked to changing cultures, even religious cultures. He said, "For in Christ Jesus neither circumcision nor uncircumcision has any value. The only thing that counts is faith expressing itself through love" (Gal 5:6).

> Nevertheless, each person should live as a believer in whatever situation the Lord has assigned to them, just as God has called them. This is the rule I lay down in all the churches. Was a man already circumcised when he was called [already a Jew or a convert to Judaism]? He should not become uncircumcised [throw off the Jewish law and culture]. Was a man uncircumcised when he was called [a non-Jew]? He should not be circumcised [he should not convert to the Jewish religion as part of his faith in Christ]. Circumcision is nothing and uncircumcision is nothing. Keeping God's commands is what counts. Each person should remain in the situation they were in when God called them. (1 Cor 7:17–20)

At first it appears that Paul was saying that the Lord has assigned to each of us the family and people group we are born into,[9] and when he calls us to himself, he also calls us to reach out to those around us in that community and not remove ourselves from that situation.[10] However, the crux of Paul's argument is actually that no one should consider one religious form of faith in Christ to be superior to another. "The only thing that counts," Paul emphasized, "is faith expressing itself through love," "keeping God's commands," and becoming a "new creation" (1 Cor 7:19; Gal 5:6; 6:15). As believers we need

---

9   Does this mean people born into bad situations must remain there? No, because Paul makes clear that a slave should take the opportunity to become free. Today people group barriers are breaking down, and some people have lived in multiple cultures and are descended from many people groups, so the rule to remain in one's situation must be viewed in that context.

10   There are exceptions, Paul himself taking on the missionary call to incarnate in another culture. Missionaries adapt to the language and culture they are entering so that those they are witnessing to can understand without knowing the missionary's language or culture. Paul became like the Greeks culturally in order to reach them. He did not spend his time denouncing the goddess Artemis (Diana) in Ephesus, the center for worship of her. Instead he lifted up Christ. Paul did not ask the Greek believers to take on any of his religious forms or culture. He knew that the power for salvation lay in the gospel message itself. The transformed life came from the power of the Holy Spirit in one's life, which was dependent on hearing and believing the truth (Rom 15:17–21). Everything else was a distraction at best, "a different gospel" at worst.

to be able to look past differences in religious culture and see the Holy Spirit working in the lives of our fellow citizens of the kingdom.

Paul considered this point so crucial to the integrity of the gospel that he laid it down as a rule for all the churches (1 Cor 7:17). He said it even more forcefully in Galatians:

> Those who want to impress people by means of the flesh are trying to compel you to be circumcised [i.e., convert to the Jewish form of faith in Christ]. The only reason they do this is to avoid being persecuted for the cross of Christ.[11] Not even those who are circumcised obey the law, yet they want you to be circumcised that they may boast about your circumcision in the flesh.[12] May I never boast except in the cross of our Lord Jesus Christ. . . . Neither circumcision nor uncircumcision means anything; what counts is the new creation. Peace and mercy to all who follow this rule—to the Israel of God. (Gal 6:12–16)

Paul considered this rule so important that he gave his signature to it, saying, "See what large letters I use as I write to you with my own hand!" (Gal 6:11).

Paul stood at a very crucial juncture in history—a critical point when the gospel could have easily become locked within the Jewish community. So Paul spoke very forcefully to ensure that the gospel was not limited to Jews and their proselytes. He called any "gospel" that denies the power of Christ to save those from every people group, without proselytism, "a different gospel—which is really no gospel at all." He warned that those trying to add to faith in Christ a conversion to specific religious forms were "throwing you into confusion and are trying to pervert the gospel" (Gal 1:6,7). In Galatians 5:2–4 Paul became even more vehement: "Mark my words! I, Paul, tell you that if you let yourselves be circumcised, Christ will be of no value to you at all. . . . You who are trying to be justified by the law [outward religious expressions] have been alienated from Christ; you have fallen away from grace." Wow! Why was Paul so upset and so insistent that the very integrity of the gospel was at stake? Because the Judaizers[13] were not preaching a gospel of salvation by grace through faith in Jesus Christ alone. Instead they were adding the requirement of religious conversion (change of outward forms and religious identity) to the inner transformation, implying that the work of the Holy Spirit was not sufficient by itself.

---

11 Non-Jewish Christians were being more heavily persecuted in the Roman Empire than Jewish believers, who had an imperial exemption from emperor worship. Also, Jewish believers experienced less persecution from fellow nonbelieving Jews if their sect was leading Gentiles to convert to Judaism.

12 The Judaizers wanted to be able to boast about conversions to their version of faith in Christ, as if it were better, though they were not even practicing their own rules very well. Longenecker notes regarding this verse, "Probably, therefore, what Paul means here in 6:13 is that despite the loftiness of their assertions and their rigid theology, the Judaizers, at least in Paul's eyes, fell short of keeping all the law scrupulously themselves." Richard N. Longenecker, *Galatians*, Word Biblical Commentary 41 (Dallas: Word, 1998), Logos Bible Software e-book, S. 293.

13 The term "Judaizers" was used only to refer to Jewish believers who added on to the gospel that conversion to Jewish religious forms and a Jewish religious identity was a requirement for salvation. Some today similarly teach that a conversion to Christ also requires a conversion to "Christian" religious forms and identity for salvation.

Is This Discussion about Missiology or the Integrity of the Gospel?

When people start turning to Christ in large numbers but refusing to identify with traditional Christianity, we should be cautious. It is important to analyze these Jesus movements just as carefully as the apostles and elders in Jerusalem analyzed the Greek movement to Christ.

We should not trivialize this discussion as a new radical contextualization[14] or a new missiological strategy designed to make it easy for Muslims to come to Christ.[15] Something much more profound is at stake: the integrity of the gospel itself.

Can we apply Paul's insights from God about Gentile believers to today's insider movements? God revealed to Paul that his promise of salvation by faith in Christ alone extends to all people. Grasping this "mystery," Paul advocated for a Greek movement to God through Christ, spreading inside Greek culture, just as the Jewish movement to Christ was spreading inside the Jewish networks. He saw that the marvel of the gospel is that it has the power to save and transform people within any socioreligious context. That power brings far more glory to God than would be the case if God could only transform believers within a single religious construct.

Rather than simply presenting a missiological strategy, Paul was setting a template for how the gospel penetrates radically different cultures. Today we have the opportunity to reaffirm the power of the gospel to move into other cultures and other religious frameworks and transform them from the inside out. But if we demand that all believers adopt our own religious traditions and identity,[16] then we are actually undermining the integrity of the gospel. We are subtly communicating that Jesus Christ cannot save people and gather them into his kingdom without using other religious traditions and institutions of godly men who have gone before. We are saying that the gospel alone is not powerful enough to save "to the uttermost" (Heb 7:24,25 KJV).

---

14 The existing Jewish believers were focused on contextualization issues, while Paul was trying to uphold the integrity of the gospel. The Jewish believers found it hard to accept it as a gospel issue. They wanted to add things on, like becoming kosher or getting circumcised, to ensure that the Greeks had become true believers in their Messiah. It was hard for them to see how being better believers would undermine the gospel. They wanted to make sure that when the gospel went into the Greek culture, it did not become syncretistic. They did not understand how that concern showed a lack of faith that the gospel by itself, through faith alone, was sufficient to not just save but transform those who believed it—to circumcise their hearts. Paul spends far more time warning believers about syncretism with their own perceived ideas of what "righteousness" looks like, a righteousness from any source other than faith in Jesus alone, than he spends warning about syncretism with pagan practices or beliefs. Why? Perhaps because it is this kind of ethnocentric syncretism that makes us unable to recognize and to receive as brothers those who are believing in Jesus but staying significantly distinct from us.

15 This is exactly the charge Paul faced in Galatia. Longenecker notes, "Evidently the Judaizers were claiming that Paul only presented half a gospel in his evangelistic mission in Galatia, purposely trimming his message so as to gain a more favorable response." *Galatians*, S. 18.

16 All through history the church has tended to slip into the mode of thinking that new people groups coming to Christ need to end up joining our form of the faith and looking like us. The Reformation broke the gospel loose from the Catholic stranglehold on the religious form of faith in Christ, much to their shock. Now we Protestants run the risk of being equally convinced that all new believers must follow Jesus the way we do, be "Christians" like us. Paul essentially said to the Jewish believers, "Let's be honest, we are not even that good at our own version of the faith." Let's be humble and acknowledge that even our own evangelical Protestant forms of Christianity are not free from syncretism with our cultural values. And yet Christ is able to save us in the midst of it through our faith in him.

Today God is granting faith in Jesus Christ to Muslims, Hindus, and Buddhists in increasing numbers. They are believing in his death and resurrection on their behalf, receiving him as their Lord and Savior, accepting the supreme authority of the Bible, and being transformed by the Holy Spirit. But they are not becoming "Christians" in name or adopting traditional Christian religious forms or identity. Could the gospel, stripped of two thousand years of godly writings and traditions, really be that powerful?

I hope we can make the same decision that the apostles did in Acts 15. They welcomed Greek pagans as followers of Christ without requiring the Greek believers to adopt their own religious expression of that faith, opening the way of faith for all non-Jewish people groups. Let us boldly affirm that apostolic decision and say, "God, who knows the heart, shows that he accepts Muslim and Hindu believers by giving the Holy Spirit to them, just as he did to us. He did not discriminate between us and them, for he purified their hearts by faith. . . . We believe that it is by the grace of our Lord Jesus that we are saved, just as they are. . . . Therefore we should not make it difficult for people in other religious cultures who are turning to Christ."

Bibliography

Edwards, Jonathan. *The Nature of True Virtue*. Ann Arbor: University of Michigan Press, 1991 [1765].

———. *A Treatise Concerning Religious Affections*. Whitefish, MT: Kessinger, 2010 [1746].

Fitzmyer, Joseph A. *The Acts of the Apostles*. Anchor Bible Commentary. New York: Doubleday, 1998.

Keener, Craig S. *The IVP Bible Background Commentary: New Testament*. 2nd ed. Downers Grove, IL: IVP Academic, 2014.

Longenecker, Richard N. *Galatians*. Word Biblical Commentary 41. Dallas: Word, 1998. Logos Bible Software e-book.

CHAPTER 29

The Supremacy of Scripture

The Transcultural and Timeless Authority for Local Theology in Global Conversation

Harley Talman

Sola scriptura is the foundational principle of the Protestant Reformation; it insists that the Bible alone is God's inspired and authoritative word and thus the Bible should be the sole standard for Christian doctrine and practice. The Reformers also held to the perspicuity of Scripture, the doctrine that its primary teaching is clear and accessible to the ordinary person who comes to it in humble faith. Accordingly, the Bible does not demand an official interpreter outside of itself. This view was contrary to teachings of the historic churches of that time (the Orthodox and Catholic traditions), which placed interpretation in the hands of church authorities and sacred tradition. However, among many Protestant churches and missions, *sola scriptura* is only a slogan that has given way in practice to the canonization of creeds and confessions (*plus* the distinctive beliefs and practices of each particular association or denomination).[1]

Is not the Bible enough? Are not Jesus and his kingdom enough? Or must believers in non-Christian contexts adhere to one of the traditions of Christian doctrine, ritual, and practice? And if so, which one? Orthodox? Catholic? Reformed? Baptist? Assemblies of God? Adventist? The Bible is indeed the only supracultural authority for defining the faith "once for all delivered to the saints" of all ages and cultures. In contrast, the great creeds and confessions of church history, while they attempt to express important biblical truths, are nevertheless not transcultural. This last point is widely recognized, even among conservative evangelical Protestant scholars. Harvie Conn declares, "Creeds, as an expression of the confessional character of all theologizing, are 'historically situational.' They are human acts of confession of God's unchanging good news, addressed to specific human cultural settings."[2] The same is true of theology. Richard Muller maintains, "All expressions of Christian doctrine are rooted in history and are, therefore, historically and culturally conditioned."[3]

In consequence of this contextual conditioning, the creeds as written cannot adequately address the needs of believers in diverse cultural settings, times, and places. Bruce Nicholls observes,

> The failure of missionary communicators to recognize the degree
> of cultural conditioning of their own theology has been devastating
> to many Third World churches, creating a kind of Western theo-

---

1 Donald McGavran, "The Biblical Base from Which Adjustments Are Made," in *Christopaganism or Indigenous Christianity?*, ed. Tetsunao Yamamori and Charles R. Taber (Pasadena, CA: William Carey Library, 1975), 36–37.

2 Harvie M. Conn, *Eternal Word and Changing Worlds: Theology, Anthropology, and Mission in Trialogue* (Phillipsburg, NJ: Presbyterian & Reformed, 1984), 242.

3 Richard Muller, "The Role of Church History in the Study of Systematic Theology," in *Doing Theology in Today's World: Essays in Honor of Kenneth S. Kantzer*, ed. John D. Woodbridge and Thomas Edward McComisky (Grand Rapids, MI: Eerdmans, 1991), 91.

logical imperialism and stifling the efforts of national Christians to theologize within their own culture.[4]

Asian theologian Melba Maggay laments, "The domination of Western theological formulations has led to a situation where in order to speak to their people, Christians in Asia and Africa are taught to answer questions raised by Greek sophists in the fourth century A.D."[5]

While it is quite natural for Western trained workers to teach the theological formulations of their own religious traditions, non-Western followers of Christ need to see these truths in the Scriptures themselves and express them in terms appropriate to their own language and culture. If the gospel message is to become fully integrated into the life of a new cultural context, an indigenous expression of theology must arise. This occurs when the Bible is translated into the vernacular and believers led by the Spirit of God study the Scriptures together, self-theologize, and express biblical truths in ways that are meaningful to their own language and cultural setting. In non-Western cultures, we should expect contextually appropriate creeds to follow a narrative format; address critical issues of worldview, doctrine, and heresy in each culture; arise from actual contextual conflicts, crises, or felt needs (not from outside expectation or imposition); and be expressed in culturally relevant language, concepts, categories, genre, and forms.[6]

New churches learn to do theology best by addressing relevant and pressing questions in their own context rather than memorizing formulaic responses to disputes of the ancient past.

Authentic and effective theologizing begins with reflection on the Scriptures in light of the immediate context (worldview, culture, and mission history) and personal experience of the local believers. Interaction with the theological reflection of the outside church in the early stages can easily abort the birth of a vital, indigenous, biblical theology.[7] However, Western (or Western-trained) "alongsiders" can enhance the process of local theologizing by acquainting these believers first with biblical creeds. This could later be followed with the functions, benefits, and dangers of extrabiblical, historical, and local creeds. But exposing local teachers and leaders to the historic creeds of Christianity should be done at an appropriate time, when the issues addressed in the creeds become real or pressing theological questions in their local context. This could be when they start asking the same questions that the creeds sought to answer, when problems arise, when false teaching emerges, or when through globalization they become engaged in theological discussions at a global level.

Furthermore, any study of these creeds should be concerned with two important issues: their terminology and their meaning. The less people understand their meaning, the more they cling to their terms and sentences. (This applies to Western Christians as well.) The creeds were expressed in the lan-

---

4   Bruce J. Nicholls, *Contextualization: A Theology of Gospel and Culture* (Downers Grove, IL: InterVarsity Press, 1979), 25.

5   Melba P. Maggay, "Theology, Context, and the Filipino Church," in *Communicating Cross-culturally: Towards a New Context for Missions in the Philippines*, ed. Melba P. Maggay (Quezon City: New Day, 1989), 55–57. Quoted in Miriam Adeney, "Mission Theology from Alternate Centers," in *The Good News of the Kingdom: Mission Theology for the Third Millennium*, ed. Charles Van Engen, Dean S. Gilliland, and Paul Pierson (Eugene, OR: Wipf & Stock, 1998), 183.

6   See Larry Dinkins, "Toward Contextualized Creeds: A Perspective from Buddhist Thailand," *IJFM* 27, no. 1 (2010): 5–9, for more detailed considerations.

7   For the domains and development of appropriate theology see Mark A. Harlan, *A Model for Theologizing in Arab Muslim Contexts*, EMS Dissertation Series (Pasadena, CA: WCIU Press, 2012), 30–36.

guage and categories of the conceptual system of the time. Since they were contextualized to an ancient Greek context, they must be recontextualized to modern and other contexts if they are to be accurately understood. Secondly, there is a need for background information on the creeds. Because each creed affirms one viewpoint out of the many that were in dispute at the time, one cannot understand their intent without understanding what they were affirming and rejecting. Thus the propositional content of the creeds needs to be made available in forms that are comprehensible and appropriate to the audience's language and context.[8] Then those believers can search the Scriptures and come to a reasoned position of their own on these issues, and decide if and how to express them in the terms and categories of their own language.

While we in the West would hope that insiders will arrive at positions that are similar in meaning to those of the historic church (and be closer to them than are most modern Protestants), we should respect their right to come to their own Bible-based conclusions. At the same time, believers from Christian traditions in the West need to remember that centuries transpired before various creeds addressed particular christological and Trinitarian issues. This will hopefully allow us to extend grace in allowing believers from non-Western, non-Christian backgrounds at least a few decades, if needed, to examine and process such issues.

With regard to an internally driven felt need for creeds, we observe how the church fathers did not seek to scrutinize the inscrutable but were content to cite the terms as they appeared in Scripture with very little elaboration.[9] The fathers would have preferred to leave it at that—and just affirm their faith in God, Christ, and the Holy Spirit—because the Scriptures do not explain their inner relations, and their natures are beyond human understanding.[10] (This is just what we find in the Apostles' Creed, the most widely used creed of all time. Sticking to biblical terminology and affirmations might also be the most natural and appropriate policy as the gospel makes its entry into new frontiers.) The church fathers said it was only because heretics taught ideas about Christ and the Trinity that conflicted with Scripture and apostolic tradition that it was necessary for them to formulate creeds (using concepts and terms of their time) that rejected these views.

Nonetheless, these ancient creeds could be very relevant to contemporary believers from Muslim, Hindu, Jewish, and other non-Christian backgrounds who struggle to understand who Jesus is. Theologians and teachers among them could benefit from understanding the divergent views they hear from different Christian groups, such as adoptionism from many liberals, modalism from Jesus-only Pentecostals, social Trinitarianism from many evangelicals, and the Nicene understanding from others.

Intercultural theologizing should take place as conversation occurs between believers from churches and theological traditions of other cultures, as well as individuals of differing educational and social strata, both past and present.[11] Such theological dialogue is important, since the body of Christ is one body whose differing members equip each another. As David Bosch declares, "All theologies, including

---

8   The creeds also need to be recontextualized to modern Western readers if they are to overcome their ignorance or misunderstandings about them.

9   Louis Berkhof, *The History of Christian Doctrines* (Grand Rapids, MI: Baker, 1937), 38.

10   Theologians often talk of the "economic Trinity" when referring to the roles and acts of the three Persons in revelatory history and of the "ontological Trinity" in regard to their inner relations from before Creation.

11   Steve Strauss, "The Role of Context in Shaping Theology," in *Contextualization and Syncretism: Navigating Cultural Currents,* ed. Gailyn Van Rheenen (Pasadena, CA: William Carey Library, 2006), 119–20. I am indebted to Strauss for some of the other sources quoted in this paper.

those in the West, need one another: they influence, challenge, enrich, and invigorate each other."[12] They can also correct each other and protect against syncretism. Conn's exhortation is fitting: "Every church must learn to be both learner and teacher in theologizing."[13] Westerners also have theological blind spots that non-Westerners may see and provide correction to, even enriching Western theological understandings.[14]

Unfortunately, Christians in the West are too often paternalistic and regard theologizing as a one-way street. Because their theological formulations seek to convey truths from the Bible (which is absolute truth), Westerners often mistakenly regard these formulations as objective, supracultural truth. Then they naturally expect non-Western theologians to receive them "as is" or with no more than fine tuning.[15]

Although all theologies are historically and culturally conditioned, nevertheless they are an attempt at expressing universal truths of the Scripture to those contexts. Hence confessions and creeds of past or other contexts are significant. But as Strauss advises, "The church must neither ignore them nor unthinkingly parrot them. . . . Simply to repeat confessions is decidedly not to understand them or be faithful to them"[16]—if for no other reason than that

> the forms of creeds and confessions will rarely (if ever) be equal
> to the truth they are expressing. In certain cultures and situations
> a different form might be the only way to express the same con-
> fessional truth. And in all cases, the source for theologizing must
> be the Scriptures themselves, not the theological forms of another
> context.[17]

But our theological traditions become the exegetical lens by which we interpret the Bible, its terms, and its texts. Consequently Thiselton warns,

> Mere interpretations of texts can themselves take on the status of
> controlling paradigms in our lives, which, when they become both
> all-powerfully directive and unchallengeably "for-ever fixed" begin
> to assume a quasi-idolatrous role, as securities in which we place
> *absolute* trust.[18]

This may help to explain why insider movements have come under severe scrutiny and criticism in some conservative evangelical denominations. A leader from one Christian organization that has some workers assisting such movements told me that they were criticized for being "weak" in teaching the creeds. One of the most theologically sophisticated and orthodox Bible scholars I know has been falsely accused of heretical Christology, largely because he supports translation of biblical terms based on ex-

12   David J. Bosch, *Transforming Mission: Paradigm Shifts in Theology of Mission* (Maryknoll, NY: Orbis, 1991), 456.

13   Conn, *Eternal Word*, 252.

14   Strauss, "The Role of Context," 121.

15   Ibid., 120.

16   Ibid., 123.

17   Ibid., 118.

18   Anthony C. Thiselton, *New Horizons in Hermeneutics: The Theory and Practice of Transforming Biblical Reading* (Grand Rapids, MI: Zondervan, 1992), 124; emphasis in the original.

egesis rather than on the basis of their theological meaning in the creeds. As Strauss observes, "When theology controls exegesis, the priority of the biblical text is lost."[19]

Conclusion

The Scriptures alone should be the standard for evaluating and expressing theological truth, but each cultural context requires local theologians to express biblical truth indigenously so it can be meaningful and transforming. Nonetheless, self-theologizing should include dialogue with the global and historic body of Christ. The creeds, confessions, and theology of Western Christianity are significant, but they are not the supracultural litmus test of biblical truth; they are culturally conditioned formulations that should be neither ignored nor aped. At the same time, Western theologians need to listen to and learn from non-Western believers, including those from non-Christian religious contexts. May all act in accord with an affirmation of the supremacy of Scripture as the transcultural and timeless authority for local theology done in global conversation.

Bibliography

Berkhof, Louis. *The History of Christian Doctrines*. Grand Rapids, MI: Baker, 1937.

Bosch, David J. *Transforming Mission: Paradigm Shifts in Theology of Mission*. Maryknoll, NY: Orbis, 1991.

Conn, Harvie M. *Eternal Word and Changing Worlds: Theology, Anthropology, and Mission in Trialogue*. Phillipsburg, NJ: Presbyterian & Reformed, 1984.

Dinkins, Larry. "Toward Contextualized Creeds: A Perspective from Buddhist Thailand." *International Journal of Frontier Missiology* 27, no. 1 (2010): 5–9.

Harlan, Mark A. *A Model for Theologizing in Arab Muslim Contexts*. EMS Dissertation Series. Pasadena, CA: WCIU Press, 2012.

Maggay, Melba P. "Theology, Context and the Filipino Church." Postscript to *Communicating Cross-culturally: Towards a New Context for Missions in the Philippines*, edited by Melba P. Maggay. Quezon City: New Day, 1989.

McGavran, Donald. "The Biblical Base from Which Adjustments Are Made." In *Christopaganism or Indigenous Christianity?*, edited by Tetsunao Yamamori and Charles R. Taber, 35–55. Pasadena, CA: William Carey Library, 1975.

Muller, Richard. "The Role of Church History in the Study of Systematic Theology." In *Doing Theology in Today's World: Essays in Honor of Kenneth S. Kantzer*, edited by John D. Woodbridge and Thomas Edward McComisky, 77–98. Grand Rapids, MI: Eerdmans, 1991.

Nicholls, Bruce J. *Contextualization: A Theology of Gospel and Culture*. Downers Grove, IL: InterVarsity Press, 1979.

Strauss, Steve. "The Role of Context in Shaping Theology." In *Contextualization and Syncretism: Navigating Cultural Currents*, edited by Gailyn Van Rheenen, 99–128. Pasadena, CA: William Carey Library, 2006.

Thiselton, Anthony C. *New Horizons in Hermeneutics: The Theory and Practice of Transforming Biblical Reading*. Grand Rapids, MI: Zondervan, 1992.

---

19 Strauss, "The Role of Context," 26.

CHAPTER 30

Church in Context[*]

Herbert Hoefer

Introduction

I did the original research for the book *Churchless Christianity* twenty-five years ago in South India. At that time, there was very little organized theological reflection among the hundreds of thousands of (what I then termed) "non-baptized believers in Christ" (NBBCs). We rejoice that now theological reflection is taking place, both among the caste Hindu believers in Christ and among the missionaries working with them around the country.

One of the blessed signs of this development is that these NBBCs now have defined themselves. They call themselves "Jesu *bhaktas*." A *bhakta* is a devotee, derived from *bhakti,* which is devotion. There are numerous *bhakti* (devotional) schools of Hinduism that affirm that a pious Hindu can relate to God through the deity that makes the most sense to him. These believers in Christ are defining themselves in terms that make sense to them and to their communities.

Another significant development is the one I want to focus on in this paper. Jesu bhaktas have come to take issue with the very title of my original book. They say, "We are neither 'churchless' nor 'Christian.'" Their rejection of the term "Christian" is well understood in missiological circles. It is a term that is problematic in most areas of the world where mission work was carried out during colonial times. The term is understood as accepting Western culture and rejecting national culture. Thus many ancient peoples around the world use the term "Christian" disparagingly, and many culturally rooted converts feel uncomfortable using the term for themselves.

More problematic in missiological circles, however, has been the rejection of the term "church." Recently Tim Tennent has traced the history of this debate in a fine article, and he concludes that membership in the church is essential for authentic practice of the Christian faith.[1] Significantly, the emerging Jesu bhakta theology would agree with Dr. Tennent to a great degree. They see themselves as part of the church, not as "churchless." However, their understanding and practice of church is different from the traditional Western model. Sometimes the term they now use is "faith community," a vague enough term that it can encompass a great variety of cultural expressions, as we will see.

In this article, I will attempt to develop the broad theological framework in which we must develop our ecclesiology. I feel a major reason that we have imposed a Western pattern of church upon other cultures is because we have failed to develop our doctrine and practice in concert with the full biblical

* Originally published in a slightly different form in *EMQ* 43, no. 2 (2007): 200–208. Reprinted by permission.

1 Timothy C. Tennent, "The Challenge of Churchless Christianity: An Evangelical Assessment," *IBMR* 29, no. 4 (2005): 171–77.

revelation. Any doctrine and practice of church must embrace all other elements of God's revelation and command. Since the formulating and implementing of these biblical principles will differ from culture to culture, so will our doctrine and practice of the church.

Theological Principles

As we work this issue through theologically and practically, we need to set our ecclesiology within the larger context of other relevant doctrines and principles. I would like to discuss some of these principles and propose possible implications for our understanding of the church in missiological contexts.

Dr. Tennent discusses Luther's formative perspectives on ecclesiology, particularly the concept of the "invisible church," known only to God through faith, and the "visible church," known to us by profession of faith or church membership (cf. Matt 7:21–23; Mark 7:6; 1 Cor 1:2; 2 Tim 2:19). Thus not everyone who is on church rolls (the visible church) is actually in the body of Christ through faith (the invisible church, known only to God). Likewise, there are people who are totally unknown to us in the visible church but known to God as his own. Sometimes this distinction is made by speaking of the capital-*C* Church and the small-*c* church.

To this discussion of Reformation principles I would like to add four more.

Reformation Principles

One is the *adiaphora* principle. This Reformation principle was that any church practice or policy that does not compromise the gospel of salvation by grace through faith is a matter of *adiaphora*, a matter of indifference and freedom. Therefore Luther could accept much of the traditional liturgy, church structures, sacramental practices, etc., and leave them intact. His was a conservative Reformation, attempting to provide stability in people's lives wherever proper.

The second Reformation principle is derived from the *adiaphora* principle. It was expressed as *bene esse* versus *esse*. There are matters that are beneficial (*bene esse*) but not essential (*esse*). The common topic to which this principle is applied is that of the episcopacy. The episcopal church order was considered of the *bene esse* by the Lutheran Reformers, not of the *esse* of the church. In traditional Roman Catholicism, the episcopal structure of the church was considered essential to its validity, but among these Protestants it was considered beneficial but not essential. How the church structured and organized itself was a matter of freedom. It did not affect the heart of the gospel.

The third relevant principle is one that is used primarily in Lutheran circles. It is the distinction between the "left hand" and the "right hand" of God (or the Kingdom of the Left and the Kingdom of the Right). This distinction states that God has two ways that he battles the forces of Satan on earth. One is with his "right hand," the church. The other is with his "left hand," the government and other social agencies. With his left hand, God controls evil; and with his right hand, he cures it. In the church, one lives by faith, and Holy Scripture is the authority for life and doctrine. In the society, one lives by human reason, and sociopolitical structures are normative.

Obviously, there is a tension in this matter for the Christian, who lives in both at the same time. She must apply human reason in the discussions of the Kingdom of the Left, and she must use Scripture as the sole norm in the Kingdom of the Right. There will be times when she must stand against issues in the Kingdom of the Left because of scriptural instruction, but she recognizes that scriptural arguments will not be authoritative for many in the Kingdom of the Left.

The fourth Reformation principle is *sola fide*, "faith alone." In the historical context, the phrase was used to object to the requirement of works to gain God's favor and his mercy in the final judgment. Instead, the Reformers insisted that God gives us salvation as a pure gift because of Christ. We need only receive that gift in faith. "For it is by grace you have been saved, through faith—and this is not from yourselves, it is the gift of God—not by works" (Eph 2:8,9). "Whoever does not believe will be condemned" (Mark 16:16).

In our present discussion, then, we would never insist on church membership as a necessity for salvation. From the thief on the cross to the Ethiopian eunuch to the jailor in Philippi, we are confident they were saved through faith alone, whether they could join a church or not. They are filled with the Holy Spirit by God's gift of grace through faith, for "no one can say, 'Jesus is Lord,' except by the Holy Spirit" (1 Cor 12:3).

Additional Theological Principles

There are three additional theological principles that we must apply in working out our ecclesiology in mission contexts. One is the traditional doctrine of the "orders of creation." This doctrine is that God has instituted some basic structures for the maintenance of society's stability: marriage, family, government, courts, social mores. These structures are common to all societies, though taking many different forms. Especially in view of the power of sin in our fallen world, these structures must be guarded and secured, or sin will run rampant and the world will self-destruct.

A second general doctrine that must be considered in this discussion is the doctrine of Creation. This doctrine is traditionally identified with the work of God the Father, the Creator of the world. The understanding is that God has made all things, including the *ethne* (cultures, people groups) of the world. The peoples of the world in the vast variety of cultural expression are his valued possession, from the scattering after the Tower of Babel to the Great Commission in Matthew 28 to the ingathering at the end of time "from every nation, tribe, people and language" (Rev 7:9). Culture is not God's enemy, but his valued creation—corrupted and sin-ridden as it is in our fallen world.

Finally, there is the biblical concept of the "kingdom of God." The rule of God extends to more than the church. God's love and concern and will are extended to all people, whether they acknowledge and serve him or not. "God so loved the world" (John 3:16). God's prophets spoke not only to his people, but to the nations. He raises up a pagan ruler to serve his divine purpose as his "shepherd" and "anointed" (Is 44:28; 45:1). His kingdom comes wherever and whenever his will is done, as he has us express in the prayer Jesus taught us.

Practical Implications

What are the implications of these theological, biblical concepts for our doctrine of the church in a mission context?

1. The "visible community" that Dr. Tennent advocates certainly is of the *bene esse* of the gospel. Some form of fellowship is highly helpful for sanctification. The form that this faith community takes may well differ from culture to culture, as we see developing now in India.

Furthermore, even the most conservative advocates of *extra ecclesiam nulla salus*[2] acknowledge that there are exceptional situations. Ultimately, church membership is an *adiaphoron*.[3] It is not essential for salvation. The ancient dictum about baptism would apply also here: "It is not the lack of baptism that condemns, but the despising of baptism." Or another: "Baptism is necessary, but not absolutely necessary."

In my original research in the late 1970s for *Churchless Christianity*, I found several instances where Jesu bhakta women were gathering regularly for worship, sometimes under Christian church leadership and sometimes independently. Subsequently, I have also found new forms of faith communities evolving.

The Jesu bhaktas do not despise fellowship with fellow believers—they desire it and are developing various ways to achieve it, usually separate from the established church bodies: pilgrimages; Christian *sanyassis*; mass rallies; Christian friends; standing outside the church on Sundays; joining in Christian worship—even Holy Communion—though without formally joining the church through baptism; Bible correspondence courses; Christian *ashrams*; Internet discussions; etc. These are forms of spiritual fellowship and accountability that are familiar and comfortable to them from their Hindu cultural background.

2. The issue among the Jesu bhaktas is not participation in fellowship with Christians, but membership in a church. In Indian law, baptism into a Christian congregation changes their legal status in the country. They are considered legally to have left their previous community and joined a different community, now governed by a different civil law (marriage, inheritance, divorce, family, etc.). Most Jesu bhaktas welcome Christian pastors and Bible women into their home for prayer and study, but they may hesitate to go to the church.

These Jesu bhaktas value their culture and their family, as they should—and as God does. They want to do everything to keep these orders of creation intact in their life and be an effective servant of God within these structures. Missiologically, they are an ongoing presence of God's call within walls where a church person could rarely enter. They are servants and witnesses of the kingdom, outside the structures of the church. In fact, if they joined the church, they would lose their place and opportunity in this kingdom work.

3. The church is not an order of creation. It is not a "community" in the sociological, theological sense. Believers are not expected to find their family life or their financial support or their civil law within the church. That is provided by our Lord in the Kingdom of the Left, in the structures of the orders of creation.

God has made us social beings, people who need other people in all aspects of life: psychologically, socially, economically, politically, etc. His kingdom of love extends over all these structures of our life. We are called to respect his rule in all these venues and to serve his rule in our various roles.

Ideally, therefore, we do not extricate people from their God-given community when they come to the Lord. We also do not expect the church to become their community. The early church assumed many aspects of community, as we have it recorded in Acts 2–6, but we know it did not last long, and it was fraught with many problems, mixing church and state. What God has ordained to provide his creatures through the orders of creation, we should keep intact if at all possible. Where God has placed

---

2   "Outside the church there is no salvation."—Ed.

3   I.e., a matter of conscience.—Ed.

people in their order of creation, we should expect them to serve faithfully as his new creation, his leaven and salt and light and ambassador.

4. We do not set up a "new law." We do not make church membership into a good work required to secure salvation. The certainty of our salvation is not because of our church membership but because of the faith that God has worked in our hearts by the Holy Spirit, receiving his gracious gift. People's faith is to be in God's promise, not in their church membership.

Likewise, we do not bring unnecessary stumbling blocks to those who are new and weak in faith. Church people can be like the Pharisees whom Jesus castigated, who "tie up heavy, cumbersome loads and put them on other people's shoulders, but they themselves are not willing to lift a finger to move them" (Matt 23:4). In certain mission contexts, through church membership we extricate people from their God-ordained support system of family and community. Then often we are unable—and unwilling—to do all it takes to bring them into the orders of creation we live in.

By our insistence on church membership we may cause them to stumble in their beginning walk of faith with the Lord. "And if anyone causes one of these little ones—those who believe in me—to stumble, it would be better for them if . . . they were thrown into the sea" (Mark 9:42). We don't expect our weakest brothers in the faith to be our greatest heroes, sacrificing all for the Lord, often far beyond anything most of us have ever done in our faith walk.

Therefore, as we work out our ecclesiology in a mission context, we take into consideration all of these biblical principles. The integrity and role of the church is a prime theological concern, but not at the sacrifice of any of these other biblical principles. Our theological and practical goal is to integrate and implement all of these seven theological precepts as we work out our doctrine and practice of the church.

Clearly, the issues are much more complex and fuzzy in the flux of mission work. Often the rules and traditions that govern our established church life cannot be applied easily in mission situations. This organizational aspect of the church's life is in the Kingdom of the Left and thus a matter of adiaphora. Rather, the church is to focus everything toward its primary commission of the Kingdom of the Right, to "go and make disciples of all nations" (Matt 28:19). Therefore we intently heed Jesus' caution against "setting aside the commands of God in order to observe your own traditions" (Mark 7:9).

Likewise, the forms and practices of church that evolved in one culture over hundreds of years cannot automatically be taken as normative in new, evolving mission situations. It will take time, under the guidance of the Holy Spirit, for these new forms to develop. A dominant church culture does not want to impose worship or ecclesiastical forms that they are comfortable with. We could end up "frustrating" the Spirit (see Gal 2:21 KJV) in his movements to enable new believers to develop their own faith traditions rooted in their own cultures and history. In their own forms, these believers can grow in faith and can spread the faith more readily. The established church is a partner along this path, being readily available but also duly cautious not to interfere in the growing process of this new form of church.

Practical Example

Obviously, these are issues that arise in mission contexts all over the world, especially in highly developed societies. Let me give an example of how it may typically play out among the hundreds of thousands of high-caste Jesu bhaktas of India.

A man named Radhakrishnan goes to a mass rally at the invitation of a Christian coworker. There he hears the gospel preached and the challenge to go to Jesus with his life burdens. Radhakrishnan has not found peace or direction when he has laid his troubles before his Hindu gods. He believes that there are many gods and goddesses, so it is no violation of conscience for him to appeal to Jesus. He prays, and he does experience a new sense of peace.

As he continues to pray, Mr. Radhakrishnan finds more and more of his problems getting resolved in unexpected ways. He asks a local pastor to come visit in his home, to learn more about this Jesus and to have Jesus' representative pray with him. Soon Mr. Radhakrishnan is convinced that Jesus is the real God. He prays only to him, and he shares his new experience of God with his family and community. He stops going to the temple, but he does not prevent his wife from carrying on her traditional home rituals or from going to their family temple.

Mr. Radhakrishnan begins listening to Christian radio programs and enrolls in a Bible correspondence course. He becomes more and more convinced that Jesus is the only true God. As his knowledge of the faith grows, so does his boldness in witness. He goes to occasional mass rallies and discusses Jesus with a few Christian friends at work.

One of these coworkers asks Mr. Radhakrishnan if he is ready for baptism. Mr. Radhakrishnan understands that this rite will make clear to himself and to his community that he is now a Jesu bhakta, a devotee of Jesus alone. He has no difficulty with that, for he has already made it clear to everyone. When he shares his intention with his family, however, they point out to him that this is not a simple profession of allegiance to Jesus. It is not just a spiritual matter. It is a rite that will change his legal status in the country as a Hindu if it is administered by the church.

He would now come under Christian civil law in the country and be considered a member of the "Christian" community rather than his traditional community. Members of his community, then, will see him as one who has rejected their cultural traditions and social ties. They will not give sons and daughters in marriage outside of their community. He will be unable to fulfill his solemn obligation as a father to arrange his children's marriages, for the Christians also will mostly likely not provide matches outside of their caste.

The pastor who visits him in his home for prayer and study is from a Protestant church. But Mr. Radhakrishnan has never gone to worship there. They are all from the outcaste background, and they would be as uncomfortable to have him there as he would be to be there. When he goes to church, he goes to the Roman Catholic church, for there he can melt into the large crowd quite anonymously, like he does at the mass rallies. He also likes the roadside shrine with the statue of Jesus outside the Roman Catholic church, for he can easily stop at that shrine anytime he passes by, just as he used to do with the shrine of the Hindu god he had worshiped. Mr. Radhakrishnan has even gone forward for Holy Communion when it is offered with that large crowd, though he has little idea of the deeper meaning of the rite. For him, it is another way to present himself to his Lord and to receive his blessing.

How should the Protestant pastor advise Mr. Radhakrishnan? Should he baptize him privately and not list him on the church roster? That would be against church rules. In addition, Mr. Radhakrishnan has been very open about his faith, and he sees no point in doing something so sacred and important secretly. He would like to be baptized, but he doesn't see it as essential. He is confident of the love and commitment of Christ to him.

Mr. Radhakrishnan enjoys his visits with the pastor, his visits to the Roman Catholic church, and other contacts with the church's ministry such as rallies and radio programs. What more should the pastor encourage him to do? Will joining his congregation and getting to know all the struggle and confusion there make him stronger in the faith or weaker? If Mr. Radhakrishnan actually takes church baptism and joins, how will he be received, and how will he carry on in life without his ancestral community?

Now Mr. Radhakrishnan is introducing the pastor to other members of his community. If he joins the church, all those relationships will at least be strained, if not totally broken. People in his community have admired the new sense of peace and integrity that they see in Mr. Radhakrishnan. They have always respected him, and they listen intently to his words about his new Lord, Jesus. His people will look at him and at the pastor very differently if they see that Mr. Radhakrishnan's faith in Jesus has caused him to break with his community life and responsibilities.

Right now, this pastor is Mr. Radhakrishnan's best contact with the nurture and guidance of the church. However, when the pastor gets transferred to another parish, who knows what the attitude of the new pastor will be? Mr. Radhakrishnan may be left very alone, or even judged and rejected. He knows it may well be hard to stand in the tension between the established church and his community and culture. However, he knows from experience that Jesus will not let him down.

Can we leave Mr. Radhakrishnan in this tenuous position? Will joining a church make things better or worse for his walk with the Lord? What is the church's responsibility to him in their service to the wider kingdom work of our Lord?

Conclusion

These are some of the broad questions and considerations about church in the mission context of Jesu bhaktas in India. It's not simple, and it's not clear. It is something that must be worked out on an individual basis, determining what will strengthen and guide the faith and witness of each Jesu bhakta in her or his context. It's something in which the established church can be a great help or a great detriment, a tool of God enabling faith and witness or a tool of Satan destroying faith and witness.

We pray fervently for wisdom and courage, both for ourselves in the "visible church" and for his Jesu bhaktas in the "invisible church." By our common faith and our common life in the Holy Spirit, we are jointly members of Christ's body called to embrace each other, so that "speaking the truth in love, we will grow to become in every respect the mature body of him who is the head, that is, Christ. From him the whole body, joined and held together by every supporting ligament, grows and builds itself up in love, as each part does its work" (Eph 4:15,16).

Bibliography

Tennent, Timothy C. "The Challenge of Churchless Christianity: An Evangelical Assessment." *International Bulletin of Missionary Research* 29, no. 4 (2005): 171–77.

CHAPTER 31

All Things Are Yours[*]

H. L. Richard

In a classic text on cross-cultural ministry, Paul stated his policy of becoming all things to all men so that by all means he might save some (1 Cor 9:22). This is sometimes treated as a specialist approach for experts in cross-cultural encounter, but the Bible presents it as a model for all ministry. It is exemplified in the incarnational pattern of Jesus, who, due to the Father's great love for the world, was sent as a true human being into a specific historical and cultural context to announce and effectuate salvation for the world.

Paul's readiness to live like a Jew among Jews and like a Gentile among Gentiles (1 Cor 9:20,21) was also rooted in a fundamental principle spelled out earlier in his first letter to the Corinthians. There had been factionalism among the Corinthian believers; some sided with Paul, some with Apollos, some with Peter. Paul rebuked this in various ways in a discussion covering the first three chapters of 1 Corinthians, coming to a climax at the end of chapter three. There he completely turned the tables and said that, rather than the apostles owning factions of the believers, the entire body of Christ owned all of the apostles.

In a typically Pauline flight to the highest elevations and deepest recesses of theological thought, Paul then jumped from the Corinthian ownership of the apostles to the stunning affirmation that "all things are yours" (1 Cor 3:21). That sounds hyperbolic, but Paul spelled it out so it could not be dismissed as a mere rhetorical flourish: the world is yours, life and death are yours, the present and the future are yours, so yes, indeed, I really mean that "all are yours" (v. 22). This, of course, is through Christ the Lord (v. 23).

The commentarial tradition of the church has not applied this Pauline emphasis on the possession of all things to cross-cultural situations, but it clearly is an underlying principle that allowed Paul in practice to become all things to all men. What many commentaries do point out is that in affirming this possession of all things by the disciples of Christ, Paul was adapting a truism of some of the philosophical schools of the time, which had particular relevance to the Corinthian context, where wisdom was a hot topic of discussion. The wise man among the Stoic philosophers was one who rose above all situations and problems by remaining in control of his thoughts and actions rather than being driven by external events.[1] Paul brought this Stoic concept into submission to Christ, where it was transformed

---

[*] Originally published in a slightly different form in *MF,* May–June 2011. Reprinted by permission.

[1] See the documentation referred to by Conzelmann in support of his summary that according to the Stoic principle, "All things belong to the wise man," i.e., he is lord over all that comes to him from without. Hans Conzelmann, *1 Corinthians: A Commentary on the First Epistle to the Corinthians,* trans. James W. Leitch (Philadelphia: Fortress Press, 1975), 80.

into a larger and more profound theological truth that he affirmed to weak and immature Corinthian believers, who were failing in some very basic aspects of spiritual life.

The possession of all things by the disciples of Christ was spelled out as a fundamental missiological concept by the Dutch missiologist Johan Herman Bavinck. He did not tie his exposition to Paul's teaching in 1 Corinthians 3:31, but the relation of the two is unmistakable. Bavinck was concerned about syncretistic tendencies in the Roman Catholic theology and practice of "accommodation," wherein non-Christian practices are adopted by the church. He wrote,

> Here note that the term "accommodation" is really not appropriate as a description of what actually ought to take place. It points to an adaptation to customs and practices essentially foreign to the gospel. Such an adaptation can scarcely lead to anything other than a syncretistic entity, a conglomeration of customs that can never form an essential unity. . . . We would, therefore, prefer to use the term *possessio,* to take in possession. The Christian life does not accommodate or adapt itself to heathen forms of life, but it takes the latter in possession and thereby makes them new. . . . Within the framework of the non-Christian life, customs and practices serve idolatrous tendencies and drive a person away from God. The Christian life takes them in hand and turns them in an entirely different direction; they acquire an entirely different content. Even though in external form there is much that resembles past practices, in reality everything has become new. The old has in essence passed away and the new has come. Christ takes the life of a people in his hands, he renews and re-establishes the distorted and deteriorated; he fills each thing, each word, and each practice with a new meaning and gives it a new direction. Such is neither "adaptation," nor accommodation; it is in essence the legitimate taking possession of something by him to whom all power is given in heaven and on earth.[2]

The profound implications of Paul's teaching and of Bavinck's concept of *possessio* need to be at the center of biblical discussions of cross-cultural ministry, especially with regard to other religious traditions. These insights point to a positive approach to other religious traditions rather than a blanket renunciation or repudiation of them. Rather than renouncing the Buddhist heritage, a Buddhist who comes to Christ needs to be oriented towards taking possession of that heritage. Clearly there is a necessary discerning and sifting process in taking possession of truths and practices from other faith traditions; Paul, after all, was rebuking false wisdom in the Corinthians, and Bavinck clearly calls for a reorientation towards Christ.

---

2   Bavinck, *An Introduction to the Science of Missions* (Philadelphia: Presbyterian & Reformed, 1960), 178–79. Bavinck's use of "Christian" and "non-Christian" in this paragraph indicates that he wrote in the mid-twentieth century. In the current clash-of-civilizations era, these terms carry many misleading connotations, and most people do not like to be identified by what they are not (non-Christians). It is preferable to refer to "disciples of Christ" (or "*bhaktas* [devotees] of Christ" in Hindu contexts) rather than "Christians," since spiritual commitment is not necessarily perceived in the term "Christian" but is definitely indicated in the alternate terms.

Careful nuancing of this truth is essential in a number of directions. First, the missionary movement is still emerging from the shadow of colonialism, and nothing stirs anti-Christian emotions quite as much as a triumphalistic or domineering attitude. Can a Christian disciple of Jesus take possession of another faith tradition without straying into this offensive mindset? It is a delicate procedure to be undertaken with deep humility, yet Paul did not shirk from stating this truth into a complex situation in Corinth. Cross-cultural workers will rarely have the insight, sensitivity, or humility to successfully negotiate this terrain, even with guidance from local believers, yet they must not draw back from the implications of Paul's teaching. Bavinck recognized the inadequacy of the cross-cultural worker as well: "The newly formed church is usually a better judge in such matters than we [missionaries] are."[3]

It is not possible for every part of the body of Christ to take possession of every aspect of life; rather, some parts of the body will more particularly be related to different aspects of God's profoundly diverse world. It is particularly those who come to faith from Buddhist families who must wrestle with the meaning of *possessio* in Buddhist contexts, while people from Hindu and Muslim and postmodern contexts seek to apply this insight in their particular worlds. Cross-cultural workers will, of course, join as servants in the engagement of these issues in the various contexts.

It must be affirmed again that there can be no facile embracing of anything and everything taught or practiced in other religious traditions. All is brought under Christ, and a sifting and filtering is necessary. Yet teaching new disciples of Jesus in other faith traditions that "all things are yours" and that it is their responsibility in Christ to take possession of their religiocultural heritage challenges some assumed paradigms. Primarily challenged is the necessity of "conversion to Christianity." If Buddhists who turn to Christ are taught that Buddha is theirs, are they really called to renounce Buddhism? Obviously they are called to discern and sift much that is unbiblical among the many traditions that are currently called Buddhism, but if they take possession of that heritage, how or why can or should they also renounce it? The same applies to the other major faith traditions, all of which are as much about culture as they are about theology, and all of which are multicultural as well as multitheological.

The problem of neo-imperialist triumphalism is trumped by a missiology that rejects "conversion to Christianity" as an essential aspect of the gospel. The new disciple of Jesus is under a mandate from Christ and the New Testament to live within (take possession of) his or her birth community and religiocultural heritage. This kind of surrender to the lordship of Christ, leading to *possessio* of one's heritage in conformity to Christ, can be viewed from another angle as well: to the birth community of the new disciple, be it Buddhist, Hindu, Muslim, or other, it is not a rejection of the old or transfer to the new, but rather citizens of the original community taking possession of the truth of the gospel. Thus hegemonic religious imperialism is avoided, and the interpenetration of the gospel among all civilizations and faiths is accomplished.

It is surely obvious, but will be stated here in closing, that this is not a simple process. Bavinck recognized this as well: "It is naturally much easier to speak theoretically of taking possession, than it is to give practical advice. The question of possession leads to the greatest problems throughout the entire world."[4] Redefining the problems and complexities of cross-cultural encounter and contextualization in terms of *possessio* rather than of conversion and repudiation seems a helpful first step towards affirming in a fresh way the multicultural nature of the gospel and of its call for all peoples to surrender to Christ within their own heritage.

---

3   Ibid., 177.

4   Ibid., 179.

"The city does not need the sun or the moon to shine on it, for the glory of God gives it light, and the Lamb is its lamp. The nations will walk by its light, and the kings of the earth will bring their splendor into it" (Rev 21:23,24).

Bibliography

Bavinck, Johan Herman. *An Introduction to the Science of Missions*. Philadelphia: Presbyterian & Reformed, 1960.

Conzelmann, Hans. *1 Corinthians: A Commentary on the First Epistle to the Corinthians*. Translated by James W. Leitch. Philadelphia: Fortress Press, 1975.

1. What does Taylor's "kingdom paradigm" (chap. 20) mean for those with strong Christian denominational backgrounds? Do you agree with him that "religious traditions and institutions are instruments of God's mission rather than the goal of God's mission"? Discuss the implications for discipleship in cultures with strong religious traditions and institutions.

2. What surprises you in Talman's study of the Old Testament's view of other religions (chap. 21)? How would you compare or contrast it with the New Testament's perspective? What are the most significant implications of this study for you?

3. Explain the distinctions between the Greek words *proselytos*, *epistrophe* (and related words *strepho/epistrepho*), and *aparche* in their NT usage (Roberts and Jameson, chap. 22). Is conversion to Christianity necessary to be a true follower of Jesus? Be sure to define what you mean by "Christianity."

4. What are tangible ways we can lead believers to "influence their own families and relatives and friends and work colleagues in their own communities" (Ridgway, chap. 23)?

5. What does "kingdom sowing" (Higgins, chap. 24) look like in your context?

6. Discuss Rebecca Lewis' definition of an "insider movement" (quoted in Higgins, chap. 25). Does this clarify any important things for you?

7. Do you consider the Jerusalem Council's process in Acts 15 to be a valid approach for assessing insider movements? Explain your reasoning. Does Talman (chap. 27) adequately address concerns about church, Scripture, identity, religion, and discipleship?

8. Lewis (chap. 28) presents Paul's template for how the gospel is to move through diverse cultural and religious frameworks. How can this be applied to other cultures you have come across?

9. What does *sola scriptura* mean for an indigenous faith community (Talman, chap. 29)? Are creeds necessary in every context where people already have the Scriptures? What are some potential problems with outsiders trying to contextualize creeds that have already been contextualized to their own or other contexts?

10. What theological and/or practical principles from the Hindu Jesu bhakta movement described by Hoefer (chap. 30) are also applicable to your own congregation or Christ-centered community?

11. How should Richard's explanation of 1 Corinthians 3:21 and Bavinck's concept of *possessio* (chap. 31) impact insider movements and our cross-cultural mission?

CONTEXTUALIZATION, RELIGION, AND SYNCRETISM

Part 4 consists of two sections, the first on contextualization and the second on religion and syncretism.

Our journey of exploring contextualization begins in Lebanon, where, in chapter 32, Greek Melkite Archbishop Gregoire Haddad issues a stunning call for "Liberating Christ from Christians, Christianity, and the Church." Haddad ardently insists that if all humanity is to access the absolute Christ, he must be freed from the real but relative expressions of him found in institutional Christianity.

Chapter 33 is Andrew Walls' classic essay "The Gospel as Prisoner and Liberator of Culture." Walls imagines an interplanetary scholar making periodic visits to study the earth religion of Christianity in different centuries and places. The lack of recognizable similarity in the characteristics and concerns of these samples challenges the existence of what modern evangelicals think of as "historic Christianity." An underlying cause of the current IM controversy may be uncovered in Walls' observation about the historic tension between what he terms the gospel's "indigenization principle" and its "pilgrim principle."

In chapter 34, Mark Young, president of Denver Seminary, addresses theologians wary of contextualization. He explores the nature of theology, theological confession, and Scripture, arguing that theology must not be viewed as "a static, transcultural set of propositions, but rather as dynamic and contextual confessions of belief" centered on "the person and purpose of the one true God as revealed in the Bible." Some criticism and concern over insider movements is rooted in a failure to recognize the validity of the kinds of contextual expressions Young endorses.

In chapter 35, looking through the spectacles of a historian of missions, the late Ralph D. Winter, we are challenged to view insider and other movements as neither "unofficial Christianity" nor "radical contextualization," but portents of a "Third Reformation." This begins our transition to serious reflection on the concept of "religion."

In chapter 36, Charles Kraft contends that Jesus must be the model for the communication and expression of our faith. We must begin with incarnational communication of the gospel; then those who believe must live out and express their faith in insider ways. Kraft clarifies the important distinction between the message of Scripture, the gospel, and faith on one hand, and religion on the other. In explaining these differences, he frees us to view insider movements as an example of appropriate contextualization.

Section 1 raises questions concerning the relationship between the gospel as the biblical message and Christianity as both a religion and a cultural movement; section 2 expounds upon the theme of religion and shows the relevance it has to our attitude toward and understanding of insider movements. It is important that we explore our concept of Christianity in greater depth by focusing on the nature of "religion." The matter of religion is integral to how we perceive and respond to insider movements. This will also transition us into the sensitive subject of syncretism.

In chapter 37, Harley Talman introduces us to the complexity and confusion inherent in defining or understanding what a religion is and does.

Chapter 38, Kyle Holton's thoughtfully provocative "(De)Franchising Missions," challenges Westerners obsessed with abstract categories of classification to rethink our understandings of religion, church, institutions, and missions. In so doing, we may create conceptual space for insider movements in our thinking.

In chapter 39, theologian and religious studies scholar Kurt Anders Richardson answers the question, "What does the word 'religion' really mean?" Richardson illuminates the comprehensive nature and complex role of religion as cultural system and way of life. His definition and exposition enable us to see through much of the fog that our notions of "religion" have cast over insider movements.

We then delve into the challenging issue of syncretism. In chapter 40, H. L. Richard describes the holistic nature of religion in most of the world, arguing that modernity's conception of "religion" is itself a syncretistic concept.

David Taylor in chapter 41 illuminates the difference between biblical contextualization and syncretism and explains how demonic influences in a culture are overcome.

We conclude this part with chapter 42, the testimony of Taweeporn Sarun, a "loving, devoted follower of Christ" who has chosen to live out her faith while remaining "within Buddhism." Read how she trusts Christ to guide her in the small details of life in order to avoid potentially harmful spiritual syncretism.

SECTION 1

Contextualization

CHAPTER 32

Liberating Christ from Christians, Christianity, and the Church*

Archbishop Gregoire Haddad

The most terrible thing that has happened to Christ in history, in particular after Christianity became the state religion during the time of the emperor Constantine in the fourth century, was that Christ became subordinate to the Christian religion and the institutional church. He became so stuck to them and so deeply entangled in them that it is almost impossible to distinguish him from Christianity—not only for the believers who live on the inside, but especially for everyone else looking from outside. They consequently condemn Christ when they condemn the church.

This deep entanglement between Christ, who is the absolute value, and the Christian religion and institutional church, which are the relative expression of the incarnation of Christ and his extension in history, has kept those who look to him from being able to discover him as he really is. For though Christ is the absolute value for all people—all people need him more than anything else—this historical enmeshing prevents them from reaching him. This entanglement must be broken, however difficult it is and whatever the grave consequences.

Liberating Christ from the Christians

First of all, it is necessary to liberate Christ from the Christians. Everyone agrees with this in principle, because he is relevant not only to Christianity but to all religions, faiths, and creeds, whether spiritual or temporal. Christ said to his disciples, "The teachers of the law and the Pharisees sit in Moses' seat. So you must be careful to do everything they tell you. But do not do what they do, for they do not practice what they preach" (Matt 23:2,3).

So now, disciples of Christ (both leaders and ordinary believers) should answer those who criticize Christianity and Christ because of the lives of Christians (and especially their leaders): Listen to their words, "but do not do what they do."

Liberating Christ from the Institutional Church

But distinguishing must go even further—to distinguishing between Christ and the church, which should present him to the world and testify to him as its core message. In other words, the church must go beyond distinguishing between him and people (who, admittedly, are simply unable to incarnate Christ) to the distinction between him and the institutions themselves, which go beyond the people and are usually summarized in the phrase "institutional church."

---

* Excerpt from Gregoire Haddad, "Relative Christianity, the Absolute Christ, and the Choices of Christians," published in the Arabic-language journal *Afaq* 21 (1998). Translated and reprinted by permission.

This institutional church, whatever it may be—Catholic, Orthodox, or Protestant; Eastern or Western; international, national, or local—has always considered itself the only institution that owns Christ. In other words,

- it has the right to him, even rights over him;
- it represents him officially;
- it speaks in his name;
- it infallibly interprets his teachings;
- it distributes his blessings, treasures, and sacraments to people;
- in his name, it guarantees eternal salvation to people, or gives them "eternal life insurance."

Thus it acts like any corporate monopoly.

Thus the institutional church has monopolized Christ, just as any capitalist corporation monopolizes a certain product, or as a publishing house keeps its copyright for one of its publications.

Christ has become a captive of the churches, like a hostage they have locked up, and no one can get to him except through them. As churches are being rejected more and more in today's world by those outside, and even by those inside, Christ is getting rejected along with them.

Since the churches are secondary and relative in importance to people, while Christ is the absolute value that they need, "the way and the truth and the life," it is essential, indeed an urgent priority, to liberate Christ from the churches and from every institutional church. It is the duty of those who still have faith within the churches to share in this battle to liberate Christ.

When some commodity, like bread, is vital for human life, monopolizing it is a crime. So it is the greatest duty to break the power of the monopoly, even if this leads to changing many societal structures. Here the second absolute standard—man—must give priority to this vital issue.

Since it is true that "man does not live by bread alone, but by every word that comes from the mouth of God" (Matt 4:4 NET), and since Christ is the Word that man lives by, and since some church structures are monopolizing Christ and keeping people from him, then one of the most important duties is to break this power of monopoly and to remove these structures that lock up Christ from those who need him.

If there were some economic commodities vital for all citizens in a certain nation, and they were under the control of some capitalists, and consequently only benefitted a very few people, it would be a duty of the state itself, whether it was socialist or capitalist, to nationalize these goods and make them available to everyone in the nation, not just the lucky few.

Since the church considers that Christ is a fundamental "vital commodity," an absolute necessity for every person, it is the most elementary deduction of logic that this church must remove the hand of the spiritual capitalists, who enjoy Christ with no concern for others who have a right to him.

If the church structure itself prevents Christ from reaching everyone in the nation, this church structure must disappear. The institutional church must die so that Christ may live and become the life of everyone—the life of those who are now in the institutional church structure as well as those outside of it. Christ said, and the church repeats on every special holiday, "Unless a kernel of wheat falls to the ground and dies, it remains only a single seed. But if it dies, it produces many seeds" (John 12:24). These words do not apply only to humans as individuals, but also to communities, and first of all to the church community.

Liberating Christ from Christianity

It is not enough to liberate Christ from Christians as individuals, and from the institutional church—that is to say, social institutions—that he may become the value that is absolute, liberated, and evident to all people. For there are barriers and restrictions besides individuals and institutions that prevent his being liberated, or indeed, his being completely nationalized. It is Christianity itself. Christianity, in addition to being individuals and institutions, is a group of theological and ritualistic expressions which throughout history have incarnated the presence of Christ and served as a witness to him. It is Christian civilization or civilizations—Eastern, Western, or some other. It is Christian culture, and all thinking influenced by Christ and the New Testament. It is Christian art, architecture, sculpture, painting, music, and poetry, which has accompanied Christians throughout the ages.

It is language itself, the manner of thought and expression, not just in mere words (such as Greek, Latin, and Syriac words) but ways of expressing and thinking. Civilization, culture, art, and language have had a deep influence on the lives of believers in Christ through the ages. They are expressions of the absolute value of Christ, his relationship to man, and man's relationship to him. They are relative expressions, but necessary, inevitable expressions. Every expression is relative, and necessarily relative, and thus transitory.

In the world today, new necessities have emerged concerning relative expressions. On the one hand, they seem absolute: that this particular expression from this civilization, this philosophy, this culture, this art, and this ideological structure is indispensable to communicate the values that Christ brought, and to communicate Christ, the absolute value. As a result, other civilizations, cultures, philosophies, arts, and languages seem like strangers to him and his values. Christianity becomes a decrepit regional phenomenon. And Christ becomes a prisoner of historical, relative Christianity.

Since all civilizations and cultures, regional or global, must serve humanity; since historical Christianity, with its relative expressions, is suspected or rejected by these civilizations and cultures without consideration of the values that it presents to humanity; and since Christ, in the view of Christianity, is necessary to each person—the focus and the absolute value—it is a priority to liberate Christ from Christianity itself, from all its embodiments and historical expressions.

It is essential to free Christ from the clutches of Christianity so that Christ can be available to everyone in every civilization, culture, language, and nation, whether religious, atheistic, or agnostic. Then Christ can speak well to everyone, without a mediator, and without any cultural foreignness. At that point, some of the biggest obstacles that keep people from meeting Christ and keep the true face of Christ from being revealed to people will have been removed for all people.

CHAPTER 33

The Gospel as Prisoner and Liberator of Culture[*]

Andrew Walls

Is There a "Historic Christian Faith"?

Let us imagine a long-living, scholarly space visitor—a professor of comparative interplanetary religions perhaps—who is able to get periodic space grants which enable him to visit earth for field study every few centuries. Let us further assume that he wishes to pursue the study of the earth-religion Christianity on principles of Baconian induction, observing the practices, habits, and concerns of a representative sample of Christians, and that he exploits the advantage he has over any earthbound scholar by taking his sample across the centuries.

Let us assume his first visit to be to a group of the original Jerusalem Christians, about 37 CE. He notes that they are all Jews; indeed, they are meeting in the temple, where only Jews can enter. They offer animal sacrifices. They keep the seventh day punctiliously free from work. They circumcise their male children. They carefully follow a succession of rituals, and delight in the reading of old law books. They appear, in fact, to be one of several "denominations" of Judaism. What distinguishes them from the others is simply that they identify the figures of Messiah, Son of Man, and Suffering Servant (figures all described in those law books) with the recent prophet-teacher Jesus of Nazareth, whom they believe to have inaugurated the last days. They live normal family lives, with a penchant for large, close families; and they have a tightly knit social organization, with many common meals taken in each other's houses. Law and joyful observance strike our spaceman observer as keynotes of the religion of these early Christians.

His next visit to earth is made about 325 CE. He attends a great meeting of church leaders—perhaps even the Council of Nicaea. The company come from all over the Mediterranean world and beyond it, but hardly one of them is Jewish; indeed, on the whole, they are rather hostile to Jews. They are horrified at the thought of animal sacrifices; when they talk about offering sacrifices they mean bread and wine used rather as it was in the house meals our observer noticed in Jerusalem. They do not have children themselves, since church leaders are not expected to marry, and indeed, most of them regard marriage as an inferior, morally compromised state; but they would regard a parent who circumcised his children as having betrayed his faith. They treat the seventh day as an ordinary working day: they have special religious observances on the first day, but do not necessarily abstain from work or other activities. They use the law books that the Jerusalem Christians used, in translation, and thus

---

[*] Published as chap. 1 in Andrew F. Walls, *The Missionary Movement in Christian History: Studies in the Transmission of Faith* (Maryknoll, NY: Orbis, 1996). Reprinted by permission. This article was first published in *Faith and Thought* 108, nos. 1 and 2 (1982): 39–52. A slightly revised form appeared in *Missionalia* 10, no. 3 (1982).

know the titles Messiah, Son of Man, and Suffering Servant; but "Messiah" has now become almost the surname of Jesus, and the other titles are hardly used at all. They give equal value to another set of writings, not even composed when the Jerusalem Christians met, and tend to use other titles—"Son of God," "Lord"—to designate Jesus.

Their present preoccupation, however, is with the application of another set of words to Jesus— words not to be found in either set of writings. The debate (and they believe it of absolutely fundamental importance) is over whether the Son is *homo-ousios* with the Father, or only *homoi-ousios* with him.[1]

The dominant factors which the outsider notices as characteristic of these Christians are the concern with metaphysics and theology, an intense intellectual scrutiny, and an attempt to find precise significance for precise terms. He thinks of the Jewish Christians in the temple nearly three centuries back, and wonders.

The best cure for his wonderment is the still greater wonder of a journey to Ireland some three centuries later still.

A number of monks are gathered on a rocky coastline. Several are standing in ice-cold water up to their necks, reciting the Psalms. Some are standing immobile, praying—with their arms outstretched in the form of a cross. One is receiving six strokes of the lash because he did not answer "Amen" when the grace was said at the last meal of brown bread and dulse. Others are going off in a small boat in doubtful weather, with a box of beautiful manuscripts and not much else, to distribute themselves on islands in the Firth of Clyde, calling the astonished inhabitants to give up their worship of nature divinities and seek for joy in a future heavenly kingdom. Others are sitting quite alone in dark caves by the seashore, seeking no intercourse with men.

He ascertains from these curious beings that their beautiful manuscripts include versions of the same holy writings that the Greek fathers used. He notices that the Irish use the same formula that he heard being hammered out in Nicaea in 325 CE; somewhat to his surprise, because they do not in general seem very interested in theology or very good at metaphysics. They attach great importance to the date on which they celebrate their main festival, Easter; an outsider is most likely to notice their desire for holiness and their heroic austerity in quest of it.

Our spaceman delays his next visit until the 1840s, when he comes to London and finds in Exeter Hall a large and visibly excited assembly hearing speeches about the desirability of promoting Christianity, commerce, and civilization in Africa. They are proposing that missionaries armed with Bibles and cotton seeds be sent a distance of four thousand miles to effect the process. They are also proposing a deputation to the British government about the necessity of putting down the slave trade, raising a subscription to promote the education of Black mechanics, agreeing that letters be written, pamphlets and articles published. The meeting has begun with a reading from the same book (in English translation) that the other Christians used, and there have been many other quotations from the book; indeed, a large number of people in the meeting seem to be carrying it. On enquiry, the observer finds that most also accept without question the creed of Nicaea. Like the Irish, they also use the word "holy" quite a lot; but they are aghast at the suggestion that holiness could be connected with standing in cold water, and utterly opposed to the idea of spending life praying in an isolated cave. Whereas the Irish monks were seeking to live on as little as possible, most of this group look remarkably well fed. What impresses the outsider is their activism and the involvement of their religion in all processes of life and society.

---

1   *Homo-ousios*, "of the same essence"; *homoi-ousios*, "of similar essence."—Ed.

In 1980 he comes to earth again, this time to Lagos, Nigeria. A white-robed group is dancing and chanting through the streets on their way to their church. They are informing the world at large that they are Cherubim and Seraphim; they are inviting people to come and experience the power of God in their services. They claim that God has messages for particular individuals and that his power can be demonstrated in healing. They carry and quote from the same book as the Exeter Hall gentlemen. They say (on being shown the document in a prayer book) that they accept the creed of Nicaea, but they display little interest in it: they appear somewhat vague about the relationship of the Divine Son and the Holy Spirit. They are not politically active, and the way of life pursued by the Exeter Hall gentlemen is quite foreign to them; they fast like the Irish, but only on fixed occasions and for fixed purposes. The characteristic which springs most readily to the spaceman's mind is their concern with power, as revealed in preaching, healing, and personal vision.

Back in his planetary home, how does our scholar correlate the phenomena he has observed? It is not simply that these five groups of humans, all claiming to be Christians, appear to be concerned about different things; the concerns of one group appear suspect or even repellent to another.

Now in no case has he chosen freakish examples of Christians. He has gone to groups which may, as far as such statements can be permissible at all, be said to reflect representative concerns of Christians of those times and places, and in each case the place is in the Christian heartlands of that period. In 37 CE most Christians were Jews. Not only was Jerusalem the Christian center; Jerusalem Christians laid down the norms and standards for other people. By 325 CE few Christians were Jews, the main Christian centers lay in the eastern Mediterranean, and the key language for Christians was Greek. By 600 CE, the balance had shifted westward, and the growing edge of Christianity was among the northern and western tribal and semitribal peoples, and Ireland was a power center. In the 1840s Great Britain would certainly be among the outstanding Christian nations, and certainly the one most notably associated with the expansion of the Christian faith. By 1980 the balance had shifted again, southwards; Africa is now the continent most notable for those that profess and call themselves Christians.[2]

So will our visitor conclude that there is no coherence? That the use of the name Christian by such diverse groups is fortuitous, or at least misleading? Or does he catch among the spheres some trace of Gilbert Murray's remark that representative Christians of the third, thirteenth, and twentieth centuries would have less in common than would a Catholic, Methodist, and freethinker, or even (glancing round the College Common Room and noting the presence of Sir Sarvepalli Radhakrishnan) "a well-educated Buddhist or Brahmin at the present day?"[3] Is shared religion in the end simply a function of shared culture?

Our spaceman may, however, note that between the five groups he has visited there is a historical connection. It was Christians scattered from Jerusalem who first preached to Greeks and founded that vast Greek edifice he observed in 325; it is in Eastern Christianity that we must seek some of the important features and some of the power of Celtic Christian religion. That Celtic religion played a vital part in the gradual emergence of the religion of Exeter Hall. And the Cherubim and Seraphim now in Lagos are ultimately a result of the very sort of operations which were under discussion at the Exeter Hall meeting.

---

2   See David B. Barrett, "AD 2000: 350 Million Christians in Africa," *International Review of Mission* 59, no. 233 (1970): 39–54; A. F. Walls, "Towards Understanding Africa's Place in Christian History," in *Religion in a Pluralistic Society: Essays Presented to Professor C. G. Baëta*, ed. J. S. Pobee (Leiden: Brill, 1976), 180–89.

3   Gilbert Murray, *Five Stages of Greek Religion* (Whitefish, MT: Kessinger, 2003 [1935]), 167.

But besides this historical connection, closer examination reveals that there are other definite signs of continuity. There is, in all the wild profusion of the varying statements of these differing groups, one theme which is as unvarying as the language which expresses it is various; that the person of Jesus, called the Christ, has ultimate significance. In the institutional sphere, too, all use the same sacred writings, and all use bread and wine and water in a special way. Still more remarkable is the continuity of consciousness. Each group thinks of itself as having some community with the others, so different in time and place, and despite being so obviously out of sympathy with many of their principal concerns. Still more remarkable, each thinks of itself as in some respect continuous with ancient Israel, even though only the first have any conceivable ethnic reason to do so, and even though some of the groups must have found it extremely hard to form any concept of ancient Israel or any clear idea of what a Jew might be or look like.

Our observer is therefore led to recognize an essential continuity in Christianity: continuity of thought about the final significance of Jesus; continuity of a certain consciousness about history; continuity in the use of the Scriptures, of bread and wine, of water. But he recognizes that these continuities are cloaked with such heavy veils belonging to their environment that Christians of different times and places must often be unrecognizable to others, or indeed even to themselves, as manifestations of a single phenomenon.

The "Indigenizing" Principle

Church history has always been a battleground for two opposing tendencies, and the reason is that each of the tendencies has its origin in the gospel itself. On the one hand, it is of the essence of the gospel that God accepts us as we are, on the ground of Christ's work alone, not on the ground of what we have become or are trying to become. But if he accepts us "as we are," that implies he does not take us as isolated, self-governing units, because we are not. We are conditioned by a particular time and place, by our family and group and society, by "culture" in fact. In Christ God accepts us together with our group relations, with that cultural conditioning that makes us feel at home in one part of human society and less at home in another. But if he takes us with our group relations, then surely it follows that he takes us with our "dis-relations" also; those predispositions, prejudices, suspicions, and hostilities, whether justified or not, which mark the group to which we belong. He does not wait to tidy up our ideas any more than he waits to tidy up our behavior before he accepts us sinners into his family.

The impossibility of separating an individual from his social relationships and thus from his society leads to one unvarying feature in Christian history: the desire to "indigenize," to live as a Christian and yet as a member of one's own society, to make the church (to use the memorable title of a book written in 1967 by F. B. Welbourn and B. A. Ogot about Independent churches in Africa) *A Place to Feel at Home*.

This fact has led to more than one crisis in Christian history, including the first and most important of all. When the elders at Jerusalem in the council of Acts 15 came to their decision that Gentiles could enter Israel without becoming Jews, had they any idea how close the time would be when most Christians would be Gentiles? And would they have been so happy with their decision had they realized it? Throughout the early years, the Jerusalem church was in a position to set the standards and to make the decisions, because of its direct connection with the Savior and its incomparably greater knowledge of the Scriptures. And when its historic decision opened the door wide for Gentile believers in the Jewish Messiah, there must have been many who assumed that, nevertheless, Gentile Christians as they matured would come to look as much like Jerusalem Christians as was possible for such benighted heathen. At least Acts 21:20 suggests that, while being decently glad of the "mission field" conversions recounted by Paul, they continued to think of Jerusalem as the regulative center of God's saving word. What were the thoughts of those who fled from Jerusalem as the Roman armies moved in to cast down the temple? Did they realize that the future of Messiah's proclamation now lay with people who were uncircumcised, defective in their knowledge of Law and Prophets, still confused by hangovers from paganism, and able to eat pork without turning a hair? Yet this—and the fact that there were still many left to speak of Jesus as Messiah—was the direct result of the decision of the Jerusalem Council to allow Gentle converts "a place to feel at home." So also was the acceptance of Paul's emphatic teaching that since God accepts the heathen as they are, circumcision, food avoidances, and ritual washings are not for them. Christ has so made himself at home in Corinthian society that a pagan is consecrated through his or her Christian marriage partner (1 Cor 7:14). No group of Christians has therefore any right to impose in the name of Christ upon another group of Christians a set of assumptions about life determined by another time and place.

The fact, then, that "if any man is in Christ he is a new creation" does not mean that he starts or continues his life in a vacuum, or that his mind is a blank table. It has been formed by his own culture and history, and since God has accepted him as he is, his Christian mind will continue to be influenced by what was in it before. And this is as true for groups as for persons. All churches are culture churches—including our own.

The "Pilgrim" Principle

But throughout church history there has been another force in tension with this indigenizing principle, and this also is equally of the gospel. Not only does God in Christ take people as they are: he takes them in order to transform them into what he wants them to be. Along with the indigenizing principle, which makes his faith a place to feel at home, the Christian inherits the pilgrim principle, which whispers to him that he has no abiding city and warns him that to be faithful to Christ will put him out of step with his society; for that society never existed, in East or West, ancient time or modern, which could absorb the word of Christ painlessly into its system. Jesus within Jewish culture, Paul within Hellenistic culture—take it for granted that there will be rubs and frictions, not from the adoption of a new culture but from the transformation of the mind towards that of Christ.

Just as the indigenizing principle, itself rooted in the gospel, associates Christians with the particulars of their culture and group, the pilgrim principle, in tension with the indigenizing and equally of the gospel, by associating them with things and people outside the culture and group, is in some respects a universalizing factor. The Christian has all the relationships in which he was brought up, and has them sanctified by Christ, who is living in them. But he has also an entirely new set of relationships, with other members of the family of faith into which he has come, and whom he must accept, with all their group relations (and "dis-relations") on them, just as God has accepted him with his. Every Christian has dual nationality, and has a loyalty to the faith family that links him to those in interest groups opposed to that to which he belongs by nature.

In addition—as we observed to be the case in all the spaceman's varied groups of representative Christians—the Christian is given an adoptive past. He is linked to the people of God in all generations (like him, members of the faith family), and most strangely of all, to the whole history of Israel, the curious continuity of the race of the faithful from Abraham. By this means, the history of Israel is part of church history,[4] and all Christians of whatever nationality are landed by adoption with several millennia of someone else's history, with a whole set of ideas, concepts, and assumptions which do not necessarily square with the rest of their cultural inheritance; and the church in every land, of whatever race and type of society, has this same adoptive past by which it needs to interpret the fundamentals of the faith. The adoption into Israel becomes a "universalizing" factor, bringing Christians of all cultures and ages together through a common inheritance—lest any of us make the Christian faith such a place to feel at home that no one else can live there—and bringing into everyone's society some sort of outside reference.

The Future of Christian Theology and Its Cultural Conditioning

In the remainder of this paper I would like to suggest something of the relevance of the tension between the indigenizing and the pilgrim principles for the future of Christian theology.

First, let us recall that within the last century there has been a massive southward shift of the center of gravity of the Christian world, so that the representative Christian lands now appear to be in Latin America, Sub-Saharan Africa, and other parts of the southern continents. This means that Third World theology is now likely to be the representative Christian theology. On present trends (and I recognize that these may not be permanent) the theology of European Christians, while important for them and their continued existence, may become a matter of specialist interest to historians (rather as the theology of the Syriac Edessene Church is specialist matter for early church historians of today, not a topic for the ordinary student and general reader, whose eyes are turned to the Greco-Roman world when he studies the history of doctrine). The future general reader of church history is more likely to be concerned with Latin American and African, and perhaps some Asian, theology. It is perhaps significant that in the last few years we have seen for the first time works of theology composed in the Third World (the works of Latin American theologians of liberation, such as Gutiérrez, Segundo, and Miguez Bonino) becoming regular reading in the West—not just for missiologists, but for the general theological reader. The fact that particular Third World works of theology appear on the Western market is not, however, a necessary measure of their intrinsic importance. It simply means that publishers think them sufficiently relevant to the West to sell there. Theology is addressed to the setting in which it is produced.

This is perhaps the first important point to remember about theology: that since it springs out of practical situations, it is therefore occasional and local in character. Since we have mentioned Gutiérrez, some words of his may be quoted here. Theology, he says, arises spontaneously and inevitably in the believer, in all who have accepted the gift of the word of God. There is therefore in every believer, and every community of believers, at least a rough outline of a theology. This conviction leads to another: whatever else theology is, it is what Gutiérrez calls "critical reflection on Christian praxis in the light of the word."[5] That is, theology is about testing your actions by Scripture.

In this, of course, we are hearing the typical modern Latin American theologian, who is stung by the fact that it has taken Marxists to point out things that Amos and Isaiah said long ago, while Christians have found good theological reasons to justify the position of Jeroboam, Manasseh, and

---

4   "The first fact of the Church [is] that we are Gentiles who worship the God of the Jews"—with *their* psalms, in Gentile languages but their concepts. See Paul van Buren, "The Mystery and Salvation and Prayer," in *Ecumenical Institute for Advanced Theological Studies Yearbook* (Jerusalem, 1977–78), 37–52.

5   Gustavo Gutiérrez, *A Theology of Liberation: History, Politics, and Salvation,* 15th Anniversary ed., with new introd. (Maryknoll, NY: Orbis, 1988), xxix.

Dives, and is nagged by the remark of Bemanos that "God does not choose the same men to keep his word as to fulfil it." But it is likely to be the way of things also in Africa. The domestic tasks of Third World theology are going to be so basic, so vital, that there will be little time for the barren, sterile, time-wasting bypaths into which so much Western theology and theological research has gone in recent years. Theology in the Third World will be, as theology at all creative times has always been, about doing things, about things that deeply affect the lives of numbers of people. We see something of this already in South African Black theology, which is literally about life and death matters (as one South African Black theologian put it to me, "Black theology is about how to stay Christian when you're a Black in South Africa, and you're hanging on by the skin of your teeth"). There is no need to go back to wars of religion when men shed blood for their theologies, but at least there is something to be said for having a theology about things which are worth shedding blood for. And that, Third World theology is likely to be.

Because of this relation of theology to action, theology arises out of situations that actually happen, not from broad general principles. Even the Greek church, with centuries of intellectual and rhetorical tradition, took almost two hundred years to produce a book of theology written for its own sake, Origen's *De Principiis*. In those two centuries innumerable theological books were written, but not for the sake of producing theologies. The theology was for a purpose: to explain the faith to outsiders, or to point out where the writer thought someone else had misrepresented what Christians meant.

It is therefore important, when thinking of African theology, to remember that it will act on an African agenda. It is useless for us to determine what we think an African theology ought to be doing: it will concern itself with questions that worry Africans, and will leave blandly alone all sorts of questions which we think absolutely vital. We all do the same. How many Christians belonging to churches that accept the Chalcedonian Definition of the Faith could explain with any conviction to an intelligent non-Christian why it is important not to be a Nestorian or a Monophysite? Yet once men not only excommunicated each other but shed their own and others' blood to get the right answer on that question. The things which we think are vital points of principle will seem as far away and negligible to African theologians as those theological prize fights among the Egyptian monks now seem to us. Conversely, the things that concern African theologians may seem to us at best peripheral. Remembering the emergence of theology at a popular level, it is noteworthy how African Independent churches sometimes seem to pick on a point that strikes us by its oddity or irrelevance, like rules about worship during the menstrual period. But this is usually because the topic, or the sort of topic, is a major one for certain African Christians, just as it apparently was for the old Hebrews, and it needs an answer, and an answer related to Christ. There often turns out to be a sort of coherence in the way in which these churches deal with it, linking Scripture, old traditions, and the church as the new Levitical community—and giving an answer to something that had been worrying people. In short, it is safe for a European to make only one prediction about the valid, authentic African biblical theology we all talk about: that it is likely either to puzzle us or to disturb us.

But is not the sourcebook of all valid theology the canonical Scriptures? Yes, and in that, as the spaceman found, lies the continuity of the Christian faith. But as he also found, the Scriptures are read with different eyes by people in different times and places; and in practice, each age and community makes its own selection of the Scriptures, giving prominence to those which seem to speak most clearly to the community's time and place and leaving aside others which do not appear to yield up their gold so readily. How many of us, while firm as a rock as to its canonicity, seriously look to the book of Leviticus for sustenance? Yet many an African Independent church has found it abundantly relevant. (Interestingly, Samuel Ajayi Crowther, the great nineteenth-century Yoruba missionary bishop, thought it should be among the first books of the Bible to be translated.)

The indigenizing principle ensures that each community recognizes in Scripture that God is speaking to its own situation. But it also means that we all approach Scripture wearing cultural blinders, with assumptions determined by our time and place. It astonishes us when we read second-century Christian writers who all venerated Paul, and to whom we owe the preservation of his writings, that they never seem to understand what we are sure he means by justification by faith. It is perhaps only in our own day, when we do not read Plato so much, that Western Christians have begun to believe that the resurrection of the body is not the immortality of the soul, or to recognize the solidly material content of biblical salvation. Africans will have their cultural blinders, too, which will prevent or at least render it difficult for them to see some things. But they will doubtless be different things from those hidden in our own blind spots, so they should be able to see some things much better than we do.

That wise old owl Henry Venn of the Church Missionary Society, reflecting on the Great Commission in 1868, argued that the fullness of the church would only come with the fullness of the national manifestations of different national churches:

> Inasmuch as all native churches grow up into the fullness of the
> stature of Christ, distinctions and defects will vanish. . . . But it
> may be doubted whether, to the last, the Church of Christ will
> not exhibit marked national characteristics which, in the overruling
> grace of God, will tend to its perfection and glory.[6]

Perhaps it is not only that different ages and nations see different things in Scripture—it is that they need to see different things.

The major theological debate in Independent Africa[7] just now—item 1 on the African theological agenda—would appear to be the nature of the African past. Almost every major work by an African scholar in the field of religions—Harry Sawyerr,[8] Bolaji Idowu,[9] J. S. Mbiti,[10] Vincent Mulago[11]—is in some way dealing with it. Now each of the authors named was trained in theology on a Western model, but each has moved into an area for which no Western syllabus prepared him, for each has been forced to study and lecture on African traditional religion—and each has found himself writing on it. It seems

---

6 "Instructions of the Committee of the Church Missionary Society to Departing Missionaries," June 30, 1868, in W. Knight, *Memoir of the Rev. H. Venn: The Missionary Secretariat of Henry Venn; Prebendary of St. Paul's, and Honorary Secretary of the Church Missionary Society* (London: Longman, 1880), 284.

7 Independent Africa is here distinguished from South Africa, where different conditions have produced different priorities and a different debate.

8 See Harry Sawyerr, *God: Ancestor or Creator? Aspects of Traditional Belief in Ghana, Nigeria and Sierra Leone* (London: Longman, 1970).

9 See Bolaji Idowu, *Olódùmarè: God in Yoruba Belief* (London: Longman, 1962); and Idowu, *African Traditional Religion: A Definition* (Maryknoll, NY: Orbis, 1973).

10 See John S. Mbiti, *New Testament Eschatology in an African Background: A Study of the Encounter between New Testament Theology and African Traditional Concepts* (London: Oxford University Press, 1971); Mbiti, *African Religions and Philosophy* (London: Heinemann, 1969); and Mbiti, *Concepts of God in Africa* (New York: Praeger, 1970).

11 See Vincent Mulago, "Christianisme et culture africaine," in *Christianity in Tropical Africa*, ed. C. G. Baëta (London: Oxford University Press, 1968), 308–28.

to me, however, that they all approach this topic not as historians of religions do, nor as anthropologists do. They are still, in fact, Christian theologians. All are wrestling with a theological question, the prime one on the African Christian's intellectual agenda: Who am I? What is my relation as an African Christian to Africa's past?

Thus, when Idowu concludes with such passion that the *oriicis* are only manifestations of Olódùmare, and that it is a Western misrepresentation to call Yoruba religion polytheistic, the urgency in his voice arises from the fact that he is not making a clinical observation of the sort one might make about Babylonian religion; he is handling dynamite, his own past, his people's present. One can see why a non-Christian African writer like Okot p'Bitek, who glories in pre-Christian Africa, accuses John Mbiti and others so bitterly of continuing the Western missionary misrepresentation of the past. It is as though he were saying, "They are taking from us our own decent paganism, and plastering it over with interpretations from alien sources." Here speaks the authentic voice of Celsus.

The mention of Celsus reminds us perhaps that African Christians are not the first people to have a religious identity crisis. Gentile Christians had precisely the same issue to face—an issue that never faced the Jewish missionaries, Paul, Peter, Barnabas. They knew who they were ("circumcised on the eighth day . . . of the tribe of Benjamin . . ."; Phil 3:5), just as Western missionaries for more than 150 confident years knew who they were. It is our past that tells us who we are; without our past we are lost. The man with amnesia is lost, unsure of relationships, incapable of crucial decisions, precisely because all the time he has amnesia he is without his past. Only when his memory returns, when he is sure of his past, is he able to relate confidently to his wife, his parents, or know his place in a society.

Early Gentile Christianity went through a period of amnesia. It was not so critical for first-generation converts; they responded to a clear choice, turned from idols to serve the living God, accepted the assurance that they had been grafted into Israel. It was the second and third generations of Christians who felt the strain more. What was their relation to the Greek past? Some of them (some indeed in the first generation, as the New Testament indicates) solved the problem by pretending their Greek past did not exist, by pretending they were Jews, adopting Jewish customs, even to circumcision. Paul saw this coming and roundly condemned it. You are not Jews, he argues in Romans 9–11; you are of Israel, but grafted into it. And defying all the realities of horticulture, he talks about a wild plant being grafted into a cultivated one. But one thing he is saying is that Gentile Christianity is part of the wild olive. It is different in character from the plant into which it is grafted. Such is the necessity of the indigenizing principle.

Later Gentile Christians, by then the majority in the church and in no danger of confusing themselves with Jews, had a major problem. Yes, they were grafted into Israel. The sacred history of Israel was part of their history. Yes, the idolatry and immorality of their own society, past and present, must have nothing to do with them. But what was God doing in the Greek world all those centuries while he was revealing himself in judgment and mercy to Israel? Not all the Greek past was graven images and temple prostitution. What of those who testified for righteousness—and even died for it? Had God nothing to do with their righteousness? What of those who taught things that are true—that are according to reason, *logos*, opposed to the great lies taught and practiced by others? Had their logos nothing to do with The Logos, the light that lighteth every man coming into the world? Is there any truth which is not God's truth? Was God not active in the Greek past, not just the Jewish? So Justin Martyr and Clement of Alexandria came up with their own solutions, that there were Christians before Christ, that philosophy was—and is—the schoolmaster to bring the Greeks to Christ, just as was the Law for Jews.

This is no place to renew the old debate about continuity or discontinuity of Christianity with pre-Christian religion, nor to discuss the theology of Justin and Clement, nor to consider the correctness of Idowu and Mbiti. My point is simply that the two latter are wrestling with essentially the same problem as the two former, and that it seems to be the most urgent problem facing African Christians today, on their agenda. Until it is thought through, amnesia could make African Christianity tentative and unsure of its relationships, and unable to recognize important tasks. More than one answer may emerge; the early centuries, after all, saw the answer of Tertullian as well as of Clement. And there may be little that outsiders can do to assist. Once again Paul saw what was coming. "Is He not," he asks his Jewish interlocutor, and on the most thoroughly Jewish grounds, "the God of the Gentiles also?" (Rom 3:29,30 GNT).

The debate will certainly reflect the continuing tension between the indigenizing and the pilgrim principles of the gospel. Paul, Justin, and Clement all knew people who followed one without the other. Just as there were "pilgrims" who sought to follow, or to impose upon others the modes of thought and life, concerns and preconceptions which belonged to someone else, so there were Greek-educated "indigenizers" who sought to eliminate what they considered "barbarian" elements from Christianity such as the Resurrection and the Last Judgment. But these things were part of a framework that ultimately derived from the Christian faith, and thus they played down, or ignored, or explicitly rejected, the Old Testament, the Christian adoptive past. Perhaps the most important thing to remember about the opponents of these Gnostics is that they were just as Greek as the Gnostics themselves, with many of the same instincts and difficulties, but they knew instinctively that they must hold to their adoptive past, and in doing so they saved the Scriptures for the church. Perhaps the real test of theological authenticity is the capacity to incorporate the history of Israel and God's people and to treat it as one's own.

When the Scriptures are read in some enclosed Zulu Zion, the hearers may catch the voice of God speaking out of a different Zion, and speaking to the whole world. When a comfortable bourgeois congregation meets in some Western suburbia, they, almost alone of all the comfortable bourgeois of the suburbs, are regularly exposed to the reading of a nonbourgeois book questioning fundamental assumptions of their society. But since none of us can read the Scriptures without cultural blinders of some sort, the great advantage, the crowning excitement which our own era of church history has over all others, is the possibility that we may be able to read them together. Never before has the church looked so much like the great multitude whom no man can number out of every nation and tribe and people and tongue. Never before, therefore, has there been so much potentiality for mutual enrichment and self-criticism, as God causes yet more light and truth to break forth from his word.[12]

---

12 I have quoted here sentences from my paper "Africa and Christian Identity," which first appeared in the Mennonite journal *Mission Focus* 6, no. 7 (1978), and was later reprinted in *Mission Focus: Current Issues,* ed. W. R. Shenk (Scottdale, PA: Herald Press, 1980), 212–21.

Bibliography

Barrett, David B. "AD 2000: 350 Million Christians in Africa." *International Review of Mission* 59, no. 233 (1970): 39–54.

Gutiérrez, Gustavo. *A Theology of Liberation: History, Politics, and Salvation.* 15th Anniversary edition, with a new introduction. Maryknoll, NY: Orbis, 1988.

Idowu, Bolaji. *African Traditional Religion: A Definition.* Maryknoll, NY: Orbis, 1973.

———. *Olódùmare: God in Yoruba Belief.* London: Longman, 1962.

Mbiti, John S. *African Religions and Philosophy.* London: Heinemann, 1969.

———. *Concepts of God in Africa.* New York: Praeger, 1970.

———. *New Testament Eschatology in an African Background: A Study of the Encounter between New Testament Theology and African Traditional Concepts.* London: Oxford University Press, 1971.

Mulago, Vincent. "Christianisme et culture africaine." In *Christianity in Tropical Africa,* edited by C. G. Baèta, 308–28. London: Oxford University Press, 1968.

Murray, Gilbert. *Five Stages of Greek Religion.* Whitefish, MT: Kessinger, 2003 [1935].

Sawyerr, Harry. *God: Ancestor or Creator? Aspects of Traditional Belief in Ghana, Nigeria and Sierra Leone.* London: Longman, 1970.

van Buren, Paul. "The Mystery and Salvation and Prayer." In *Ecumenical Institute for Advanced Theological Studies Yearbook,* 37–52. Jerusalem, 1977–78.

Walls, Andrew F. "Towards Understanding Africa's Place in Christian History." In *Religion in a Pluralistic Society: Essays Presented to Professor C. G. Baèta,* edited by J. S. Pobee, 180–89. Leiden: Brill, 1976.

———. "Africa and Christian Identity." In *Mission Focus: Current Issues,* edited by W. R. Shenk, 212–21. Scottdale, PA: Herald Press, 1980.

Venn, Henry. "Instructions of the Committee of the Church Missionary Society to Departing Missionaries," June 30, 1868. In W. Knight, *Memoir of the Rev. H. Venn: The Missionary Secretariat of Henry Venn; Prebendary of St. Paul's, and Honorary Secretary of the Church Missionary Society* (London: Longman, 1880), 284.

CHAPTER 34

A Necessarily Wary Enterprise?

North American Evangelicals and Contextualization*

Mark Young

Picking up a porcupine is a necessarily wary enterprise. No matter how desirable or important it may seem to pick up a porcupine, our instincts warn us that those razor sharp quills warrant caution.

From the very beginning, conservative evangelicals in North America reacted cautiously to contextualization.[1] In part their concern was due to the term's formal introduction in the 1970s through the World Council of Churches (WCC), an organization that many evangelicals had grown to distrust.[2] Furthermore, since some of the most persistent voices for contextualization in those early days were associated with liberation theology in the Latin American context, some evangelicals in North America became even more concerned that the term did not reflect the social and cultural values of the conservative wing of the movement. Viewing liberation theology through the lens of the Cold War, many saw it as a threat to their theology and an assault on the American values of democracy and capitalism. Guilt by association sullied the image of contextualization among these conservative evangelicals. In some cases the concept was rejected outright; others saw the need to explore the concept and simply chose different terminology to describe the same process and goal. In my own theological training in the late 1970s, the term "contextualization" was treated with caution if not outright suspicion.

Even though we can identify sociocultural and geopolitical realities in the 1970s as reasons for caution on the part of evangelicals in North America, we should not dismiss evangelical wariness toward contextualization as solely based on issues of that historical and cultural context. Caution has framed evangelical consideration of contextualization throughout the four decades that we've used the term in mission circles because it seems to challenge deeply held theological values and commitments that have shaped the movement's existence and identity. In particular, conservative evangelicals view contextualization warily because they suspect that it threatens belief in absolute, transcultural truth as revealed in the Bible. That's why evangelicals tend to resonate with a cautious definition of contextualization like that penned by B. J. Nicholls: "The translation of *the unchanging content of the Gospel* of the Kingdom into verbal form meaningful to the peoples in their separate cultures and within their particular existential situation."[3]

---

* Originally published in a slightly different form as chap. 5 in *Global Mission: Reflections and Case Studies in Contextualization for the Whole Church,* ed. Rose Dowsett (Pasadena, CA: William Carey Library, 2011). Reprinted by permission.

1 See Charles H. Kraft, ed., *Appropriate Christianity* (Pasadena, CA: William Carey Library, 2005), 22–26.

2 S. Coe, "In Search of Renewal in Theological Education," *Theological Education* 9 (1976): 233–43.

3 Bruce J. Nicholls, "Theological Education and Evangelization," in *Let the Earth Hear His Voice,* ed. J. D. Douglas (Minneapolis: World Wide Publications, 1975), 675; emphasis added. For further development of this

Because evangelicalism does not have a historic ecclesial identity but exists transdenominationally, consistency and continuity in the movement's identity are based on common creedal commitments. Nicholls' language, "the unchanging content of the Gospel," is bedrock dogma for conservative evangelicals.[4] It expresses evangelical belief that absolute truth, valid for all cultural contexts, is revealed by God in the Bible. Furthermore, conservative evangelicals believe that "the unchanging content of the Gospel" is propositional. They seek not just common belief in the gospel but also common language to confess that belief. This commitment is a highly valued legacy built upon the development of creedal formulations dating back to the early church.

If a commitment to the idea of unchanging truth in Scripture and a commitment to common confessional language in expressing that truth fuel the wariness of conservative evangelicals in contextualization theory and practice, perhaps ongoing reconsideration of the nature of theology, theological confession, and Scripture may be needed before conservative evangelicals can more willingly embrace contextualization. Are there ways to discuss these fundamental theological commitments that may energize evangelicals to embrace contextualization more naturally? Yes. Are conservative evangelicals in North America willing to have this discussion? Maybe.

Unfortunately, many conservative evangelicals fear critical thinking and dialogue about these foundational issues. For some, such conversation threatens their personal sense of security built upon an uncritical certainty of belief. For others, the risk to their own professional identity and security is too great. In many ecclesiastical and mission relationships, common confession acts as social power. When membership in a faith community depends upon the assessment of any member's adherence to common confessional language (e.g., signing an organization's doctrinal statement to join or remain in it), vigorous theological conversation is muted, because members fear expulsion by those who hold social power over them; yet it is exactly this kind of theological conversation that contextualization demands.

Contextualization requires the freedom to explore and risk intellectually without the fear of dire social and financial consequences.[5]

Contextualization and the Nature of Theology

How could we reconsider the nature of theology and theological confession in order to stimulate more meaningful contextualization? Perhaps Paul Hiebert's application of set theory to a theological consideration of Christian conversion provides a starting point. In a landmark article,[6] Hiebert discussed how four different concepts of a mathematical set affect the way we understand the term "Christian." He postulates four kinds of sets based on the following two variables: (1) the basis for being included in a set, and (2) the nature of the boundaries that define the set. For our purposes in this chapter, two

concept of contextualization, see Stephen B. Bevans, *Models of Contextual Theology* (Maryknoll, NY: Orbis, 2002), 37–53.

4   In the early years of the debate conservative evangelicals preferred the term "indigenization" to "contextualization" because of this commitment. See Charles R. Taber, *The World Is Too Much with Us: "Culture" in Modern Protestant Missions* (Macon, GA: Mercer University Press, 1991).

5   Social and economic power influences the development of contextualized theologies and ministries worldwide far more than we care to admit. Exclusion from institutions, agencies, and denominations acts as a powerful restraint on creative thinking and ministry, especially when such exclusion means loss of financial support.

6   See Hiebert, "The Category 'Christian' in the Mission Task," in *Anthropological Reflections on Missiological Issues* (Grand Rapids, MI: Baker, 1994).

of Hiebert's concepts of sets—bounded sets and centered sets—may be helpful for reconsidering the nature of theology and theological confessions.

According to Hiebert, bounded sets are formed on the basis of common intrinsic characteristics. Taxonomies, so typical in Western scientific thought, exemplify bounded sets well. Bounded sets have clear lines of demarcation (boundaries) for inclusion and exclusion depending upon the possession of those intrinsic characteristics that define the set. Something either has those characteristics or it doesn't. Bounded sets clearly demarcate what's outside the set from what's inside it. Therefore the boundaries of the set define it and become the focal point of attention for those creating and maintaining it.

Whereas bounded sets are defined by the possession of shared characteristics, centered sets develop on the basis of a member's relationship to the center point of the set. In a centered set, boundaries do not determine membership in the set; rather, boundaries emerge and change as members relate to the center of the set. No matter where a member may be spatially in relation to the center, as long as there is a positive relationship to the center, it is a member. A positive relationship is illustrated by a member moving toward the center rather than away from it. The concepts of movement and orientation for set membership imply that affective criteria influence inclusion in the set. Whereas bounded sets are static, centered sets develop dynamically.

Using Hiebert's categories to reflect on the nature of theology and theological confession, one could argue that conservative evangelicals tend to view both as a bounded set of propositions. Diverse theological and ecclesiastical traditions within evangelicalism select various intrinsic characteristics of the propositions that make up their own bounded set. Common intrinsic characteristics may come from broad theological traditions (e.g., Calvinism and Arminianism) and historic creeds. Ecclesiastical hierarchies, academic guilds, denominational and mission leaders, and local religious power brokers—those who believe they possess the set and are responsible to maintain it—arbitrate the inclusion and exclusion of discrete propositions and those who hold them. What these groups all have in common is not just shared confession, but a shared commitment to the value of control. Set boundaries create security and identity for those who control them. When theology and theological confession are viewed as a bounded set, they function as static boundaries of intellectual and social control.

Although theology and theological confession are often assumed to be simply conceptual, in reality they are intensely social and cultural. In reality, evangelical theology as a bounded set of propositions is formed, possessed, and controlled by a confessing community along conceptual, social, and cultural lines. Conservative evangelicals tend to diminish the reality of contextual influences on theology, insisting rather that theological truth is transcultural and theological confession must be as well. Many believe, therefore, that adoption of a bounded set of propositions in diverse cultural settings requires use of common language regardless of context. When conservative evangelicals downplay the personal, social, and cultural dimensions of theological belief and confession, the language of absoluteness and objectivity rules theological discourse, and the boundaries of belief are drawn with uncritical certainty. In this approach to theology, contextualization cannot and must not occur.

As noted before, when theology is viewed as a bounded set of propositions, the confessional community (church, mission, denomination, etc.) possesses the set, and focuses primarily on its boundaries in order to determine whether any given proposition is inside or outside the set. Boundary maintenance is considered essential to maintaining the integrity of the set and the identity of the confessional community. Those who propose changing a bounded set risk exclusion from the confessional community that possesses it. In this approach to theology, theological understanding must remain bounded by

the propositions of a community's common confessional language as embodied, for example, in a doctrinal statement or creedal confession. The goal of theological discourse, therefore, is to reinforce the
boundaries and strengthen allegiance to the community guarding them. In this regard confessional
statements serve a magisterial function that often inhibits the development of new understandings.

Historic creeds and confessions of Christian truth create both a sense of unity and continuity for
evangelicals. Their role must never be underestimated. However, we must admit that creeds are historic
documents expressed through the linguistic forms deemed to best express common understanding and
belief at the time and place of their composition. Creeds arose as confessing communities sought to
reshape or reinforce conceptual boundaries and group solidarity. Exclusion from the community, and in
some cases even more severe penalties, befell those whose beliefs were deemed outside the boundaries
of the set.

Because the truth of Scripture is seen as unchanging, many conservative evangelicals view theological confession as immutable also. For these evangelicals, the boundaries of theological confession have
been fixed historically and must remain as they are. The beliefs and the language of belief are therefore
static and must be fiercely defended. Unfortunately, a bounded-set view of theology does not invigorate
contextualization. In fact, insistence on the perpetuation in diverse contexts of theological language
that was crafted in one historic context may inhibit a confessing community's ability to understand the
truth embodied by that language originally.

On the other hand, contextualization may demand rearticulation of creedal language in order to
preserve common belief across cultures and times. Steve Strauss notes,

> Forms established by churches of one culture and period of his-
> tory should not be considered the exclusive way that Christians in
> another time and culture can express the same theological truth.
> Creeds and confessions are expressions of biblical truth for specific
> times and places. As such, they unite the universal church around
> a common history and serve as examples of theology that was both
> biblical and relevant in the past. But the forms of creeds and con-
> fessions will rarely (if ever) be equal to the truth they are expressing.
> In certain cultures and situations a different form might be the only
> way to express the same confessional truth.[7]

For conservative evangelicals to more freely embrace contextualization, theology cannot be viewed as
a static, transcultural set of propositions, but rather as dynamic and contextual confessions of belief.
The goal of contextualization is to help create understanding of the meaning of the great confessional statements of historic Christianity as a basis for belief. It is the perpetuation of ancient Christian
belief—more than the repetition of theological propositions—that drives contextualization. Belief
grounds and exceeds confession. Thomas Oden writes,

> To say credo (I believe) genuinely is to speak of oneself from the
> heart, to reveal who one is by confessing one's essential belief, the
> faith that makes life worth living. One who says credo without

---

7   Steve Strauss, "The Role of Context in Shaping Theology," in *Contextualization and Syncretism: Navigating
Cultural Currents, ed. Gailyn Van Rheenen (Pasadena, CA: William Carey Library, 2006), 118.

willingness to suffer, and if necessary to die for the faith, has not genuinely said credo.[8]

Belief is the source and goal of contextualized theological confession.

Theology as a Centered Set

In order to encourage contextualization among evangelicals, theology needs to be viewed more as a centered set of beliefs than a bounded set of propositions. Membership in a centered set, according to Hiebert, is defined by orientation and movement toward the center of the set. When applied to the nature of theology and theological confession, a centered-set perspective illustrates the importance of valuing the center of the set and maintaining allegiance to it. A centered-set view humanizes theology and theological confession by expressing the affective dimension of human belief. Membership in the set requires common belief—common valuing and allegiance to the center of the set—not just agreement on common language.

This perspective on theology allows evangelicals to retain the sense of personal security and identity based in belief in unchanging truth revealed in Scripture, while at the same time admitting to the contextual limitations of all theological creeds and confessions. Furthermore, by emphasizing the affective dimension of theological development and belief, a centered-set metaphor captures the personal, social, and contextual character of theology. Theological propositions are not disembodied truth statements that are included in the set just on the basis of logical consistency and historic confessional language. In a centered-set view, theological propositions are personal (communal) statements of belief in, the value of, and allegiance to the center of the set.

Identifying the center of the set—the focal point of belief and allegiance—becomes the primary task of the confessing community in a centered-set approach to theology. Unfortunately, agreement on the center of the set has proven to be more elusive for evangelicals than one would think or hope. For example, many conservative evangelicals in North America have viewed the inerrancy of the Bible as the very center of the set. The Evangelical Theological Society (ETS) made affirmation of belief in the inerrancy of the Bible the sole criterion for membership at its founding in 1949.[9] Conservative evangelicals in North America continue to use statements on inerrancy in this way. However, the elevation of inerrancy as the watershed issue for evangelical identity is inadequate to describe the theological center of the complex and dynamic global evangelical movement today.

Although "core convictions" like biblicism, conservative piety, and evangelism are widely used to identify evangelicalism in North America and Europe, these common characteristics "have never by themselves yielded cohesive, institutionally compact or clearly demarcated groups of Christians."[10] Diverse social, institutional, cultural, theological, and personal alliances splinter evangelicals into sometimes more, sometimes less, cooperative identities and entities. Is there a center to evangelical theology? Can we hope to express it? Yes.

---

8   Thomas Oden, *The Living God: Systematic Theology*, vol. 1 (Peabody, MA: Hendrickson, 2006), 11.

9   According to the ETS website, the original intent of the society's founders was to form a doctrinal basis for ETS rather than a doctrinal statement or confession of faith. The statement was amended to include Trinitarian language. See http://www.etsjets.org/?q=website_constitution_amendment_announcement.

10   Mark A. Noll, *The Rise of Evangelicalism: The Age of Edwards, Whitefield, and the Wesleys* (Downers Grove, IL: InterVarsity Press, 2003), 19. See also David W. Bebbington, *Evangelicalism in Modern Britain: A History from the 1730s to the 1980s* (London: Unwin Hyman, 1989), 1–17.

At the center of evangelical theology must be belief in the one true God as revealed in the Bible, who acts to redeem humanity so that all may worship him alone. Belief in, allegiance to,[11] and the worship of the God of the Bible, the one true God—Father, Son, and Spirit—reside at the center of evangelical theology. Although various propositional statements about the person and work of our God reveal divergent articulations of that belief, allegiance, and worship, the center of evangelical theology must remain the person and purpose of the one true God as revealed in the Bible. He is the point of reference and orientation for evangelical theology, and thus the point of reference and orientation for all contextualization.

When we affirm that the center of evangelical theology is belief in, allegiance to, and the worship of the one true God as revealed in the Bible, we aver that we may not simply make up what we want to believe about the one true God and his work in the world. We believe in and worship the one true God, who has revealed himself in human history and mercifully given us the written record of it in the Bible. Therefore, our belief in, allegiance to, and worship of the one true God develops around what Don Carson calls "the turning points of redemptive history" as recounted to us in the Bible. He writes, "However loyal one judges oneself to be to Jesus, it is difficult to see how such loyalty is a mark of Christian thought if the Jesus so invoked is so domesticated and selectively constructed that he bears little relation to the Bible."[12] These "turning points of redemptive history" as described in the biblical record fill out our vision of God as

- the one who has created, sustains, and rules over the universe and all that is in it;
- the one who has redeemed sinful humanity from its hopeless and hapless estate through the death of the Son and his resurrection from the dead;
- the one who has privileged and empowered his people by the Spirit to testify of him throughout all the earth; and
- the one who will consummate human history and restore all creation according to his eternal plan.

Whatever else evangelical theologies may include, they must be believed in the light of this essential image of the one true God as revealed in the Bible.

Theology as Partial Overlapping Centered Sets

Human depravity and finitude limit the scope of all theological knowledge. A centered-set approach to theology assumes that all theologies are partial because they are developed by finite and fallen humans in distinct cultural and historical contexts. No single theology encompasses all that can be known about the one true God because no human has exhaustive knowledge of God.[13] Each faith community's theology develops around whatever is deemed necessary to express its belief in, allegiance to, and worship of the one true God. Affirmations and propositions included in one community's set may not be a part of other communities' sets.

If all evangelical theologies are partial and contextual, yet centered on the belief in, allegiance to, and worship of the one true God, overlapping sets of affirmations and propositions in diverse evan-

---

11 Allegiance to the one true God implies commitment, loyalty, esteem, and love.

12 D. A. Carson, *Christ and Culture Revisited* (Grand Rapids, MI: Eerdmans, 2008), 44.

13 In my classes I draw a large circle on the marker board and ask students, "If this circle represents all that can be known about Christ as revealed in Scripture, how much of this circle does your theological tradition encompass?" Most have never considered that their theological system does not contain all that can be known about God as revealed in Scripture.

gelical communities emerge. Common belief is not necessarily expressed in common propositions, yet some theologies will share common language. The articulation of common belief must involve the development of contextually appropriate theological affirmations and propositions for each confessional community.[14] In order to pursue theological contextualization, evangelicals will have to admit that common belief in, allegiance to, and worship of the one true God may not always share common theological language, even though such should be sought in order to enhance unity of belief and identity. Common beliefs center evangelical theologies, but the trajectories of development in both content and language for each theological set are shaped by the peculiar cultural contours of each context.

Contextualization and Bibliology

Because bibliology is the watershed issue for many conservative evangelicals in North America, some of whom seem to value agreement on matters of inspiration and inerrancy as highly as the common belief in the deity of Christ and the efficacy of the gospel, a reconsideration of what evangelicals believe about the Bible may be necessary for greater freedom and facility in contextualization. It is not coincidental that initial evangelical wariness toward contextualization occurred during the same decade that conservative evangelicals had publicly reignited the "battle for the Bible" in North America.[15] That battle hasn't stopped, and issues of bibliology continue to play a major role in evangelical wariness toward contextualization.

It may be tempting to see contextualization as solely an issue of the interpretation and application of the Bible, but that view may be too limited. Evangelical caution toward contextualization is first influenced by how we view the Bible, then by the question of how we interpret and apply it.

When the term "evangelical" is used in a global sense, it almost always connotes those who make the Bible their "final rule for faith and practice."[16] Evangelicals affirm this identity through the practice of distilling propositions of truth and principles for life from Scripture just about every time we read it. Evangelicals see the Bible as the source of universally true propositions about God and universally valid principles for godly living.

This view of Scripture spurs evangelicals to identify some propositions and principles as "biblical" and others as "not biblical." When propositions and principles are deemed "biblical" in a particular evangelical confessional community, it is assumed that these are universally binding for all who view Scripture as the final rule for faith and practice. Even though we use the term freely, it seems that evangelicals frequently do not clearly articulate what it means when we say that a proposition or a principle for godly living is biblical. What does it mean to say that there are biblical principles for marriage, for child rearing, for money management, and for dozens of other dimensions of human experience? In many cases "biblical" simply means that a statement, value, or behavior in a given contemporary context resembles selected statements, values, and behaviors found in a text of Scripture. For example, based on Moses' example of delegated judicial authority to selected leaders in Exodus 18:17–23, many evangelicals affirm that such delegation of authority is a biblical principle for leadership. Once we describe a principle as biblical, it is typically considered to be universally valid in all contexts.

---

14 Steve Strauss, "The Role of Context," 18.

15 Harold Lindsell, *The Battle for the Bible* (Grand Rapids, MI: Zondervan, 1976).

16 Evangelical Steering Committee, "An Evangelical Manifesto: A Declaration of Evangelical Identity and Public Commitment" (paper, Washington, DC, May 7, 2008), http://www.anevangelicalmanifesto.com/docs /Evangelical_Manifesto.pdf.

Unfortunately, this approach to the Bible often leads to an ethnocentric elevation of the interpreter's values and behaviors as "biblical" based on a selection of those passages in Scripture that more closely mirror already acceptable behaviors in the interpreter's culture. On the other hand, passages that describe behaviors that do not fit the interpreter's own cultural setting are simply ignored. These passages, and the behaviors they describe or prescribe, are frequently dubbed "cultural," and are not treated as authoritative for the interpreter's context and faith community. This approach to the Bible arbitrarily elevates some passages to a position of authority for contemporary faith and practice while relegating others to a role that is not. For example, whereas the delegation of responsibility by a leader can be considered "biblical" in those cultures where it fits the interpreter's cultural norms, it may be routinely overlooked as simply "cultural" by those in settings where such delegation does not naturally fit the profile of authority and leadership. In North America we would gladly assert that delegation of responsibility is "biblical," but quickly disavow other behaviors found in biblical texts that offend our own cultural values. For example, few in North America would argue that a father should give his raped daughter, a virgin, to her rapist in exchange for money, even though such behavior is prescribed in Deuteronomy 22:28–29. Deuteronomy 22:28–29, we must conclude, is "cultural" and therefore does not create a "biblical" principle for godly living today. The rather arbitrary designation of some behaviors found in the text of Scripture as "biblical" and others as "cultural" is difficult to defend hermeneutically, yet widely practiced.

Once a behavioral principle is deemed "biblical" by one faith community, it is assumed by that community to be universally applicable in every setting, even if it may communicate in a given cultural setting values and beliefs that are inconsistent with belief in, allegiance to, and worship of the one true God. This egregious practice is seen throughout the church globally, particularly in the areas of marriage, finances, gender roles, and leadership. When we inconsistently apply the moniker "biblical" to some behaviors and not to others, the task of contextualization suffers and those with social power in mission relationships stifle contextualization.

This understanding and use of the term "biblical" is based on a rather limited view of the nature of the biblical text and seemingly does not engage the whole of Scripture. Perhaps it would be helpful to see the Bible as more than a book of propositions about God and principles for godly living. It is, after all, first and foremost a story, coherent and meaningful when read as a whole. The Bible is not just a story, however. Evangelicals believe that it is the story of human history and existence in a world of competing stories. "The Bible is universal history: it sets forth a story of the whole world from its beginning to its end. It is the true story of the world, and all other stories are at best partial narratives, which must be understood within the context of the biblical story."[17]

Chaturvedi Badrinath, a Hindu scholar of world religions, challenged the church in India to go beyond a view of Scripture that limits it to a book of religious propositions and principles:

> I can't understand why you missionaries present the Bible to us in
> India as a book of religion. It is not a book of religion—and anyway
> we have plenty of books of religion in India. We don't need any
> more! I find in your Bible a unique interpretation of universal histo-
> ry, the history of the whole of creation and the history of the human
> race. And therefore a unique interpretation of the human person as

---

17   Craig G. Bartholomew and Michael W. Goheen, "Story and Biblical Theology," in *Out of Egypt: Biblical Theology and Biblical Interpretation*, ed. Craig Bartholomew et al. (Grand Rapids, MI: Zondervan, 2004), 151.

> a responsible actor in history. That is unique. There is nothing else
> in the whole religious literature of the world to put alongside it.[18]

When viewing the Bible as the only true story of human history and existence, evangelicals see that its purpose is to reveal, in the radically pluralistic contexts of its origin, the person of the one true God and his purpose for humanity. Every passage, when read within the whole story of Scripture, reveals something of the one true God and how he accomplished his eternal purpose. Each passage can be evaluated in the light of the character and purpose of the whole story, as the revelation of the person and purpose of God so that all may believe. Two questions dominate the interpretive task: "What do these behaviors, values, and teachings reveal about the one true God in that context?" and "How do these behaviors, values, and teachings contribute (both positively and negatively) to the accomplishment of God's eternal purpose?" The answers to those questions create a foundation for interpreters to formulate principles for godly living based upon serious linguistic, literary, theological, and sociocultural examination of the passages in their original settings. In this way, the entire Bible is viewed as authoritative. Indeed, the biblical text speaks authoritatively to every dimension of human experience. It contains hundreds of characters, stories, and teachings that describe how the one true God was revealed in human history and how he prosecuted his purpose through his people.

On the basis of careful, culturally sensitive exegesis, evangelicals in every context have the privilege and responsibility to develop propositions about the character of the one true God and principles for godly living that contribute to the prosecution of his universal redemptive purpose in their own context. The faith community's task is to confess and to live in such a way that the character and purpose of the one true God is clearly communicated in their context. When they shape their behavior to reveal God and to accomplish his purpose, they can confidently speak of being biblical in their own setting. In this regard, evangelicals face the possibility that some behavior or value that is determined to be biblical in one contemporary setting may not be so in another setting. In other words, we must admit the possibility that discrete behaviors and values that reveal the person and purpose of the one true God in one setting may communicate something very different in another setting. It is the privilege and responsibility of each faith community under the leadership of the Holy Spirit to diligently study the text of Scripture to understand how the person and purpose of God were revealed in the biblical setting and then diligently study their own context in order to bring their own behaviors, values, and teachings under the authority of Scripture.

When read this way, the Bible becomes intensely missional, and the faith community's motivation for creating a true vision of the one true God for their own culture through their beliefs, values, and practices drives the hermeneutical task. "Biblical" then takes on a more expansive meaning that gives each faith community a sense of their privileged role in the grand purpose of God and a dose of humility toward their own cultural limitations in interpretation and application. That gives urgency and rationale to every faith community in the task of contextualization.

Wary but Not Fearful

Embracing contextualization with restraint will likely continue as the modus operandi for evangelicals from North America. And that's good. Contextualization should be a necessarily wary enterprise for

---

18   Lesslie Newbigin, *A Walk through the Bible* (Vancouver, BC: Regent College Publishing, 2005), 4, quoted in Bartholomew and Goheen, "Story and Biblical Theology," 151.

evangelicals. Our fundamental understanding of the nature of theology and the Bible demands caution when formulating beliefs, values, and behaviors for the purpose of prosecuting God's universal redemptive purpose. But we need not be fearful of contextualization; it is our privilege and responsibility in every context to create a testimony of the gospel that shouts the truth about God and his purpose to a lost world. For us, contextualization is not the end, but a means to the end that all evangelicals must share—the worship of the one true God by all peoples.

Bibliography

Bartholomew, Craig G., and Michael W. Goheen. "Story and Biblical Theology." In *Out of Egypt: Biblical Theology and Biblical Interpretation,* edited by Craig Bartholomew, Mary Healy, Karl Möller, and Robin Parry, 144–71. Grand Rapids, MI: Zondervan, 2004.

Bebbington, David W. *Evangelicalism in Modern Britain: A History from the 1730s to the 1980s.* London: Unwin Hyman, 1989.

Bevans, Stephen B. *Models of Contextual Theology.* Maryknoll, NY: Orbis, 2002.

Carson, D. A. *Christ and Culture Revisited.* Grand Rapids, MI: Eerdmans, 2008.

Coe, S. "In Search of Renewal in Theological Education." *Theological Education* 9 (1976): 233–43.

Evangelical Steering Committee. "An Evangelical Manifesto: A Declaration of Evangelical Identity and Public Commitment." Paper, Washington, DC, May 7, 2008. http://www.anevangelicalmanifesto.com/docs/Evangelical_Manifesto.pdf.

Hiebert, Paul. "The Category 'Christian' in the Mission Task." In *Anthropological Reflections on Missiological Issues.* Grand Rapids, MI: Baker, 1994.

Kraft, Charles H., ed. *Appropriate Christianity.* Pasadena, CA: William Carey Library, 2005.

Lindsell, Harold. *The Battle for the Bible.* Grand Rapids, MI: Zondervan, 1976.

Nicholls, Bruce J. "Theological Education and Evangelization." In *Let the Earth Hear His Voice,* edited by J. D. Douglas. Minneapolis: World Wide Publications, 1975.

Noll, Mark A. *The Rise of Evangelicalism: The Age of Edwards, Whitefield, and the Wesleys.* Downers Grove, IL: InterVarsity Press, 2003.

Oden, Thomas. *The Living God.* Vol. 1 of *Systematic Theology.* Peabody, MA: Hendrickson, 2006.

Strauss, Steve. "The Role of Context in Shaping Theology." In *Contextualization and Syncretism: Navigating Cultural Currents,* edited by Gailyn Van Rheenen, 99–128. Pasadena, CA: William Carey Library, 2006.

Taber, Charles R. *The World Is Too Much with Us: "Culture" in Modern Protestant Missions.* Macon, GA: Mercer University Press, 1991.

CHAPTER 35

A Third Reformation?
Movements of the Holy Spirit beyond Christendom[*]
Ralph D. Winter

Insider movements: this idea as a mission strategy was so shockingly new in Paul's day that almost no one (either then or now) gets the point. First of all, be warned: many mission donors and prayer warriors, and even some missionaries, heartily disagree with the idea.

One outstanding missionary found that even his mission board director could not agree. He was finally asked to find another mission agency to work under. Why? His director was a fine former pastor who had never lived among a totally strange people. After a couple of years of increasingly serious correspondence between the director and the missionary family, the relationship had to come to an end.

Okay, so this is serious business. Why is "insider movements" such a troubling concept? Well, everywhere Paul went, "Judaizers" followed him and tried to destroy the insider movement he had established. Some of those Judaizers were earnest followers of Christ who simply could not imagine how a Greek—still a Greek in dress, language, and culture—could become a believer in Jesus Christ without casting off a huge amount of his Greek culture, getting circumcised, following the kosher dietary rules and the "new moons and Sabbaths," etc.

The flagrant language of Paul's letter to the Galatians is one result. The very serious text of his letter to the Romans is another. Years ago the scales fell off my eyes when I read that "the people of Israel, who pursued the law as the way of righteousness, have not attained their goal. Why not? Because they pursued it not by faith but as if it were by works" (Rom 9:31,32).

Paul was not saying that the Jewish religious culture was defective or that the Greek culture was superior. He was emphasizing that heart faith is the key element in any culture—that forms were not the key thing, but the faith. Greeks who yielded in heart faith to the gospel did not need to become Jews culturally and follow Jewish forms.

Paul said, in effect, "I am very, very proud of a gospel that is the power of God to save people who obey God in faith, no matter whether they follow Jewish or Greek customs" (cf. Rom 1:16). But the real trick is not simply for people of faith in every culture to stay and stagnate in their own cultural cul-de-sac, but both to retain their own culture and at the same time recognize the validity of versions of the faith within other cultures and the universality of the body of Christ.

Different sources of European Christianity flowed over into the United States, producing some two hundred different "flavors" of Christianity—some born here (Mormons, Jehovah's Witnesses), some quite biblical, some not so biblical, some very strange. The same thing happens on the mission

---

[*] Originally published in a slightly different form in *MF*, September–October 2005. Reprinted by permission.

field: a lot of different movements emerge. The ideal is for the gospel to become effectively expressed within the language and culture of a people and not just be a transplant from the missionary's culture.

H. Richard Niebuhr's famous book *Social Sources of Denominationalism* is known for pointing out that different denominations did not just have doctrinal differences (often very minor) but usually reflected, at least for a time, social differences that were the real difference. Note, however, that the Christian faith was in many cases an "insider movement" and was expressed within different social streams, taking on characteristics of those different streams.

But back to missions. The Jewish/Greek thing is far more and far "worse" than the differences between Methodists, who pray that their trespasses be forgiven, and Presbyterians, who pray that their debts be forgiven!

No, in Paul's day circumcision was undoubtedly a major barrier to adult Greek men becoming culturally Jewish followers of Christ. Another sensitive point was the question of eating meat that had been offered to idols, and so on.

Later in history, the Jewish/Greek tension was paralleled by a Latin/German tension. This time we see a profound difference in attitudes toward clerical marriage versus celibacy and the use of Latin in church services. For centuries Latin was the language of Europe, enabling ministers, attorneys, medical doctors, and public officials to read the books of their trade in a single language. That lasted a long time! For centuries a unifying reading language did a lot of good. But the Bible did not come into its own until it was translated into the heart languages of Europe. The deep rumbling that modernized Europe was the unleashed Bible.

It is an exciting and maybe disturbing thing—the idea that biblical faith can be clothed in any language and culture. Witness the awesome reality in the so-called mission lands today. Whether Africa, India, or China, it may well be that the largest number of genuine believers in Jesus Christ do not show up in what we usually call Christian churches!

Can you believe it? They may still consider themselves Muslims or Hindus (in a cultural sense).

Alas, today Christianity itself is identified with the cultural vehicle of the civilization of the West. People in mission lands who do not wish to be "Westernized" feel they need to stay clear of the Christian church, which in their own country is often a church highly Western in its culture, theology, interpretation of the Bible, etc.

For example, in Japan there are "churches" that are so Western that in the last forty years they have not grown by a single member. Many astute observers have concluded that there is not yet "a Japanese form of Christianity." When one emerges, it may not want to associate with the Western Christian tradition except in a fraternal way.

In India we now know that there are actually millions of Hindus who have chosen to follow Christ, reading the Bible daily and worshiping at the household level, but not often frequenting the West-related Christian churches of that land.

In some places thousands of people who consider themselves Muslims are nevertheless heart-and-soul followers of Jesus Christ who carry the New Testament with them into the mosques.

In Africa there are more than 50 million believers (of a sort) within a vast sphere called "the African Initiated Churches." The people in the more formal "Christian church" may not regard these others as Christians at all. Indeed, some of them are a whole lot further from pure biblical faith than Mormons. But if they revere and study the Bible, we need to let the Bible do its work. These groups range from the wildly heretical to the seriously biblical within over ten thousand "denominations," which are not related to any overt Christian body.

Thus not all "insider" movements are ideal. Our own Christianity is not very successfully "inside" our culture, since many "Christians" are Christian in name only. Even mission "church planting" activities may or may not be "insider" at all, and even if they are, they may not be ideal.

Around the world some of these movements do not baptize. In other cases they do. I have been asked, "Are you promoting the idea of non-baptized believers?" No; in reporting the existence of these millions of people, we are reporting on the incredible power of the Bible. We are not promoting all the ideas they reflect or the practices they follow. The Bible is like an underground fire burning out of control! In one sense we can be very happy.

How Should We Respond?

What will be, what should be, the mission response to this major new factor? Shall we call it "unofficial Christianity" and just live with it? Shall we drop the term "Christianity" altogether and start counting not Christians but Bible believers?

We need to pause and think clearly. "Christianity" is not a biblical term. Even the word "Christian," which is in the Bible only three times, is apparently a "sneer" word employed by outsiders and not a word the New Testament believers called themselves. That is, NT believers were in some cases, by others, called "Christians," but apparently no one in the NT ever called himself a Christian. When Agrippa asked Paul if he were trying to make him into a Christian, Paul did not make any use of the word (Acts 26:28,29).

My personal perspective is that we recognize again that our mission is simply the biblical faith. We preach Christ, not Christianity. In this regard I see a parallel to the New Testament biblical faith escaping the Jewish cultural tradition and being born from within the Greek culture. I see this phenomenon in the book of Acts not as a unique *event* but as a major example of a *process* that must happen over and over again as missionaries cross into new cultures.

We see in the NT the consternation of Jewish followers of Christ viewing the Greek followers of Christ as somehow inferior. And the Greek believers apparently also looked down on Jewish believers—or Paul would not have defended them in Romans 14.

Not only do we see the Greek believers scoffing at the Jewish wrappings. We see earnest Jewish followers of Christ, the "Judaizers," insistently seeking to make the Greek followers more Jewish. Do we today sometimes think like the Judaizers? Do we seek to make Muslim and Hindu followers of Christ more "Christian" by urging them to call themselves "Christian," or by following certain Western Christian customs?

Is This Radical Contextualization?

What we are talking about goes beyond ordinary "contextualization." Some have called it "radical contextualization." What we call this phenomenon is not the point. It is really not a new phenomenon. Christianity itself is the result of *radical contextualization.*

When the gospel moved beyond the Jewish cradle in which it was born, it not only took on Greek clothing; it carried within it the same biblical demands of heart faith. When later it was taken up by Latin-speaking people, it outwardly changed again, so much that eventually the Greek church and the Latin church movements went separate ways. Still later as biblical faith penetrated the Teutonic forests of Middle Europe, it divested itself of a good deal of the Latin tradition and now reappeared as a German, Lutheran tradition. At about the same time, it broke away as an English phenomenon. These new traditions were much more than a change of language.

The biblical faith became at an early point a Celtic phenomenon, and there was antagonism for a long time between Roman and Celtic forms of faith. A bit later than the Celtic but before the Lutheran, we see the biblical faith emerge within the Arabic tradition in the form of Islam, which is only partially biblical.

Many ancient observers felt that Islam was simply an Arabic form of Christianity. But the Christianity to which Muhammad was exposed was very weak and defective.[1] It possessed only parts of the Bible, and in particular it had a defective understanding of the doctrine of the Trinity. Muhammad was apparently able to evaluate *the defective trinity* of the Christians he knew, and rejected it, just as we today reject such a misunderstanding.

Meanwhile Christianity for many centuries was tied in with local governments that could not allow social diversity, and so Christians of one sort even tried to exterminate Christians of another sort, and certainly opposed the followers of Islam. Instead of sharing the Bible and studying it together, they simply tried to remove the cultural diversity through persecution and even genocide. In general, Christians have actually been more intolerant than Muslims. This is the view of Dr. Dudley Woodberry at Fuller Seminary.

What Can We Do?

One thing we can try to do. We can go humbly to these groups and try to help them understand the Bible more clearly *without assuming they will accept our form of Christianity when they read the Bible*. Furthermore, we can rejoice that there are millions outside the formal Christian tradition who are hungering and thirsting after righteousness and who have in their hands the Bible. Isn't that better than to add more millions who may call themselves Christians but who do not pay much attention to the Bible and who can hardly be described as "hungering and thirsting after righteousness"?

Thus the idea of "radical contextualization" is an incredibly new frontier. It's not just how many minority peoples are left. It's how many large blocs are still untouched or unchosen. It's how many peoples that are supposedly already "reached" are not really reached.

Well, is it possible that within these large blocs of humanity we have achieved (with trumpets blaring) only a *form* of Christianity that ranges from sturdy and valid but foreign, to maybe superficial or phony? Something that from the point of view of these large blocs has been acceptable only to a minority and is not going anyplace? Can't we recognize that it's not important, nor helpful—not merely impossible—to make very many Muslims identify with the cultural stream called "Christianity"? If someone is a born-again believer, isn't that enough?

In other words, is it our mission to insist on a change of name and a change of clothing? Isn't the Bible, isn't Jesus, God's Son, more important to them than what they call themselves or how they wor-

---

1   A number of scholars believe that Muhammad encountered various kinds of Arab Christians, both heterodox and orthodox. See Abdiyah Akbar Abdul-Haqq, *Sharing Your Faith with a Muslim* (Minneapolis: Bethany House, 1980), 16–17; J. M. Ritchie, "Christianity in the Qur'an," *Encounter* 81 (1982): 11. For the Qur'an criticizing tri-theism and other heresies, see C. Jonn Block, *Expanding the Qur'anic Bridge: Historical and Modern Interpretations of the Qur'an in Christian-Muslim Dialogue, with Special Attention Paid to Ecumenical Trends* (Minneapolis: Routledge, 2013), 290.—Ed.

ship? In this regard are we afraid that our supporters, our donors, are forcing us to report on how many "Christians" or "Baptists" we have created, or how many church buildings we have brought into being that look like our own church buildings?

Take for example the nineteenth-century Protestants in this country. As the Catholics streamed into this country after 1870, the Protestant churches spent something like $500 million to win Catholics, and yet after fifty years of sincere home mission work had only won a handful of families. That is, we can't realistically set out to win over people to a new faith if we intermix the requirement that they identify with a different community in a substantially different culture. Thus we can't make Catholics into Protestants in large numbers. And apart from those who want to be Westernized, we can't readily make Muslims or Hindus over into our cultural form of Christianity.

This gives rise to the idea of a "Third Reformation." The first reformation was the shift from Jewish clothing to Greek and Latin clothing. A second happened when our faith went from Latin Christianity to German Christianity. This "second" reformation is *the* Reformation that everyone talks about, of course.

But now Western Christianity, if it really wants to give away its faith, is poised to recognize (and to become sensibly involved with) something already happening under our noses—a Third Reformation. Sorry to say that, as before (both in the time of Paul and in the Reformation), this rising phenomenon probably will involve astonishment and antagonisms. The Bible itself describes vividly the profound antagonisms between Jewish and Greek forms of the faith. History records vividly the same thing between Latin and German forms of the faith. In each case the burning question has been, "Just how biblical are these various forms?"

Should We Go beyond Contextualization?

We may need to go beyond mere radical contextualization. The biblical faith has gone beyond Judaism. The NT has shown us how that can and must be done for the sake of the Gentiles. We have now also long seen how our biblical faith has been able to go beyond Roman Catholicism. To go beyond Judaism did not invalidate the faith of those believing Jews who remained Jews. To go beyond Roman Catholicism does not invalidate the faith of those believing Catholics who have stayed behind. Is it time to allow for the possibility that some people around the world will choose to go *beyond Christianity* as we know it?

This has already begun to happen. We have already noted the existence of millions of Africans who are eagerly following Christ and the Bible but not identifying with any form of traditional Christianity. The Lutheran-Missouri Synod study[2] describes millions of devout followers of Jesus and the Bible in the one city of Chennai (Madras) alone who have not chosen to call themselves Christians, nor to identify with the socioecclesiastical tradition of Christianity, and who still consider themselves Hindu. That report indicates that there are many more of this kind of devout believer than all the devout believers in that place who do identify with the social tradition of Christianity. Or take China. What about all those millions in the house churches? When the Bamboo Curtain rises, how certain can we be that they will wish to be identified with formal Christianity—in China or anyplace else?

---

2   Herbert Hoefer, *Churchless Christianity* (Pasadena, CA: William Carey Library, 2000).

The NT Judaizer had only one solution: make people of any background into Jews. The Roman Catholics have for the most part had only one solution: make everyone into a Catholic. Have evangelicals done the same? For the most part, yes.

We have seen our gospel work fairly well—to draw people into evangelicalism, a Westernized evangelical movement. But by and large this has happened only if they belonged to a minority or an oppressed group—like tribal peoples, or Koreans under the Japanese, people who had more to gain by giving up much of their cultural identity. In all such cases worldwide, people have seen the value of identifying with a foreign import that would befriend them and take their side. But by now we have lapped up most of these minorities and oppressed peoples. The future is correspondingly bleak for the further extension of our faith into the vast blocs of Chinese, Hindus, Muslims, and Buddhists *unless we are willing to allow our faith to leave behind the cultural clothing of the Christian movement itself.* Do we preach Christ or Christianity?

Apparently our real challenge is no longer to extend the boundaries of Christianity but to acknowledge that biblical Christian faith has already extensively flowed *beyond Christianity* as a cultural movement, just as it has historically flowed beyond Judaism and Roman Catholicism. Our task may well be to allow and encourage Muslims and Hindus and Chinese to follow Christ without identifying themselves with a foreign religion. The Third Reformation is here!

Bibliography

Abdul-Haqq, Abdiyah Akbar. *Sharing Your Faith with a Muslim.* Minneapolis: Bethany House, 1980.

Block, C. Jonn. *Expanding the Qur'anic Bridge: Historical and Modern Interpretations of the Qur'an in Christian-Muslim Dialogue, with Special Attention Paid to Ecumenical Trends.* Minneapolis: Routledge, 2013.

Hoefer, Herbert. *Churchless Christianity.* Pasadena, CA: William Carey Library, 2000.

Ritchie, J. M. "Christianity in the Qur'an." *Encounter* 81 (1982): 1–13.

CHAPTER 36

The Incarnation, Communication, and Insider Movements*

Charles H. Kraft

We lose a lot when we reduce the gospel to words. The usual translation of John 1:1, "In the beginning was the Word . . . ," misleads us into a kind of static, word-oriented concept of God's communication. How much better does J. B. Phillips' translation get across the truth of the dynamic character of our faith when he translates "At the beginning, God expressed Himself." We then recognize the fact that God wrapped that message in a person, a real live human being who himself is the message from God. Jesus showed us both the message and the method. *The message is a person; the method is incarnation.*

What is called today "the incarnational approach" is a focus on the communicator becoming a part of the culture of the people he or she seeks to win. *Incarnation is by definition, then, an insider approach to getting God's messages across.*

Our Message Is a Person

Jesus not only came—he *became*. He spent thirty-three years among us, communicating that when God gets close, it's good news rather than bad news. This is the insider approach.

Jesus gave himself to us and for us; his whole ministry was couched in a close relationship with the twelve and many more (e.g., the women, the family of Lazarus). His message was a *life message*, not simply a word message. He said, "I came to bring life, abundant life" (John 10:10), and "I am the way, the truth and the life" (John 14:6). And life is communicated through *life rubbing against life to produce life.*

The message, the gospel, is not simply *about* Jesus. Jesus *is* the message, the gospel we seek to contextualize, and we are the personal representatives of that message today. *We are Jesus to others today.* So, to contextualize Jesus, we must contextualize ourselves. And this involves both *being* (who we are) and *doing* (what we do). Our being is to be like Jesus. Our doing is to demonstrate God in the midst of human life. The Apostle Paul articulated this message when he said, "Imitate me just as I imitate Christ" (1 Cor 11:1).

Relationship, then, is the key—from God's early relationship with Adam to his relationship with Noah, with Abraham, with Joseph, with Moses, with David, with everyone in Scripture and beyond Scripture, and most perfectly with his Son, Jesus. In the same way Jesus says to stay in relationship with him, to abide in him and bear fruit (John 15)—fruit that *demonstrates* God's love, his compassion, his mercy, his healing, his grace, his righteousness, his very character. It was carried in the person of Jesus and is today carried in our persons.

---

*   To be published in a slightly different form as chap. 1 in Charles H. Kraft, *Issues in Contextualization* (Pasadena, CA: William Carey Library, forthcoming). Printed here by permission. Unless otherwise noted, Scripture quotations in this chapter are the author's paraphrase.

Communication specialists tell us that *people are themselves the major part of any message they bring.* Person communication, and to some extent written communication, depends on the relationship between communicator and receptor(s). Messages, then, involve content plus relationship. The content of any message is wrapped in the relationship between the communicator and his or her audience. The relational part of the communication interpenetrates every part of what is said and done, influencing powerfully every aspect of the way the event is interpreted by the receptors.

The scary thing here is that each of us *is* our message, and how we relate to those who receive messages from us is a crucial part of the message we seek to put across. How sad it is when we hear of cross-cultural workers who define their ministries in terms of words or tasks. They have been influenced by our society to "wordify" the message. Much of our theological training is word, proposition, and information oriented.

These wordsmiths often carry our society's baggage when they see themselves as specialists rather than as persons. We can weep when we hear of Bible translators or development workers or teachers, or even pastors and evangelists, who carry out their specialties with precious little focus on how they are relating to the people around them. This is an outsider approach, and their relationships—or lack of them—send a very loud message. Their behavior, as opposed to their words, says, "Our faith stands for a distant God, an uninvolved God, a God who speaks about or specializes in what he thinks is important but pays little attention to what his actions communicate."

The first name given to Jesus was Emmanuel, "God is with us." So to communicate him we have to be genuinely *with* those we seek to win and disciple. Contextualization, then, is the process by which Jesus in us is expressed in such a way that people *feel* his incarnation, his life being lived among them. All else that we talk about in contextualization studies is derivative of this "presence communication." *To contextualize the gospel is to bring Jesus' presence into the lives of a people.*

Faith, Not Religion

Insider movements focus on the essence of what it means to follow Jesus. They are fundamentally about faith in Jesus, not religion. The underlying fact here is that the term "religion" often refers to cultural phenomena. It connotes a system made up of such things as belief in God or spirits, rituals used to express an allegiance to that God or spirit, doctrines, often a holy book or books, holidays, plus numerous other cultural items and beliefs.

Religions, because they are cultural in nature, can be *adapted* to new cultures. Adaptation is external, resulting in smaller or larger changes in the forms (including rituals) of the religion. *A religion cannot be contextualized. It can only be adapted by making changes in external features.*

Biblical faith, however, can be *contextualized*, a process in which appropriate meanings may be carried by quite different forms in various cultures. The reason it can be contextualized is the fact that none of the cultural forms or terms through which the gospel is expressed are required. Most cultural forms employed in one culture can be substituted for in another culture, because the essence of the message is a faith, not a religion.

A faith, though it lies beneath the cultural structuring of a religion, is quite different from a religion. A religion involves one in activities of various kinds. The essence of faith, though, is the commitment to something or someone. When talking about a faith, it is the commitment or allegiance that is in focus, not the cultural structuring in terms of which that commitment is expressed. Most faiths can be expressed through a variety of cultural structures.

The gospel requires no particular cultural forms. Because the gospel has historically been "captured" by the West, it is often considered Western, even though its origin is not Western. Discipleship to Jesus *is an allegiance, a relationship, from which flows a series of meanings that are intended to be expressed through the cultural forms of any culture.* These forms are intended, then, to be inside, chosen for their appropriateness to convey proper biblical meanings in the receptors' contexts.

Jesus spoke of our faith as a seed, not a tree. We have often taken our full-grown trees to other peoples, trees that were at home in our soil but are out of place in the new context. One of the things Jesus meant by picturing our faith as a seed is that the tree or bush that springs from that seed does not look like it came from another place. It flourishes inside, nourished by the new soil and water, and looks like it belongs.

As faith grows in the new soil, it is intended to be dynamic as it was in New Testament days. When it is alive, people are growing, changing, creative. When revival hits, we can count on movement and creativity, even heresy.

Most people and groups that come to Christ start out with at least some sub-ideal beliefs and practices. Much of the criticism of approaches to contextualization that advocate insider movements seems to be based on the fear that if people start one way, there is little hope of them ever maturing into something better. The assumption seems to be that if people start with sub-ideal customs, they will continue in those customs forever.

Such an attitude, though, demonstrates our unwillingness to trust both the Holy Spirit and the people who turn to Christ. Our tendency is to treat both people and God as if they can't handle the faith without our control. But biblical faith and discipleship are to be dynamic, starting inside, perhaps with help from alongsiders, and continuing to change and grow.

To summarize the differences between a religion and a faith, I offer the following chart.

Religion	Faith
Structural, Cultural/Worldview	Personal/Family/Group/Social
Rituals, Rules	Relationship
Beliefs	Commitment/Allegiance
Perform	Obey
Adapt	Contextualize
Borrow/Accept/Imitate (e.g., worship forms)	Create/Grow (e.g., new cultural forms)
"One size fits all"	Cultural varieties of expression
Like a tree that must be transplanted	Like a seed that gets planted
Like a loaf of bread that gets passed on	Like yeast that gets put in raw dough
An Institution	A Fellowship

Insider Movements Are Appropriate Movements

An insider movement is a movement that is by definition a culturally appropriate expression of a faith commitment. It is "inside," appropriate to the culture in which it exists rather than to some outside culture. The judgment as to whether a movement is appropriate or not is to be made by insiders. So such a movement is to be expressed in terms that are understandable to insiders who have not become bicultural—that is, the message is for typical insiders of that group who have no exposure to foreign culture.

In Japan (and many other places) it is easy to identify Christian church buildings. They look like they have been imported from eighteenth-century America. They don't look Japanese. Nor do they look like places of spiritual power. That a place that purports to serve a religious function look like a place of power is a requirement in a Japanese context. If in that context the buildings are to be interpreted as representing the High God and understood as power places, they will need to be built in Japanese style with something that looks to Japanese people like a shrine (a spiritual power source) on the premises.

People regularly adopt new customs. One or two or a few customs can easily be borrowed from another culture without upsetting things. But if people need to adopt a hundred poorly understood foreign customs to practice a new faith, the situation is quite different. Then the faith feels foreign to insiders. It's as if they were learning to follow a foreign Christ and to speak their language with a foreign accent.

Many who follow Christ in our day have not only expressed allegiance to Jesus but have converted to Western Christianity as well, the religion of the visiting carriers of the gospel. A savvy missiologist of yesteryear looking at this problem said something like: If Africans poured their full-fledged African-ness into their faith expression, would the rest of the world even recognize it as biblical faith? Perhaps not. There are some African movements to Christ that present just such a challenge to Westerners.

Expressions of Christ-centered faith should be as different from culture to culture as are most other cultural practices. When this is not the case, I believe we are insulting both the God who was in Jesus (2 Cor 5:19)

Not Syncretism, but Assimilation*

"Eclecticisms pick and choose; syncretisms combine; but only life assimilates."

[As Gandhi advised,] "Study the non-Christian religions more sympathetically to find the good that is within them in order to have a more sympathetic approach to the people." This hits home. For undoubtedly we Christians have approached the non-Christian religions not always with sympathetic insight to see the good, but with critical attitudes to find the bad. The mentality behind that was, if we found something good, then that was one reason why we should not come with the gospel. But that older mentality was in large measure replaced with one of appreciation, for we saw that Jesus "came not to destroy but to fulfill," so that every truth found anywhere was a truth that pointed to him who is the Truth. We could therefore rejoice in finding truth anywhere, knowing that it was God-implanted and would be God-fulfilled in Christ. We knew that Jesus was not the enemy of any truth, found anywhere, but would lovingly gather it up in himself and fulfill it. But the end would not be a patchwork of truths; it would be a new product. This would not be eclecticism or syncretism. "Eclecticisms pick and choose; syncretisms combine; but only life assimilates." The gospel is life, so like a plant it reaches down into the soil of every culture and takes out things which have an affinity to its own life and takes them up into its purposes and makes a new product out of them according to the laws of its own being. The end is neither eclecticism nor syncretism, but life assimilating. We can be sympathetic to truth found anywhere and be true to our own gospel. We would be untrue if we took unsympathetic attitudes.

—*E. Stanley Jones*

---

* Excerpt from E. Stanley Jones, *Mahatma Gandhi: An Interpretation* (Nashville: Abingdon-Cokesbury Press, 1948), 53–54.

and the man Jesus (1 Tim 2:5), who lived as an insider to reach others who would then accept the faith and express it in insider terms and practices.

Faith Is Accompanied by Power Demonstrations

Most of the peoples of the world are acutely aware that *everything in human experience has ramifications in both the human and spiritual realms.* Though these two realms function together in the world, often we who bring the message have not seen what is going on at the spirit level. This means that receptors are often more aware of the spirit world than are we who initially bring the message. A lack of awareness of the spiritual dimension puts us in a poor position to see our message accompanied by demonstrations of spiritual power. We must bring a powerful, relevant insider faith message rather than the powerless, secularized religion practiced by most churches in the West.

Insider movements will give an important place to demonstration of spiritual power in Jesus' name for healing, transformation, and miraculous protection. Insider followers of Jesus will also engage in spiritual warfare—warfare against spiritual powers that have oppressed them and their people. Our Master paid a lot of attention to the devil and what he was doing. He spent a lot of time freeing people from this enemy—he came to destroy his works (1 John 5:8). Insider movements will spend a lot of time and energy confronting what the devil has been doing, and demonstrating the power of God through Christ over him.

Conclusion

Jesus, in the incarnation, became an insider, using his culture and way of life to serve God. He did not start anything too complicated for his followers to continue. He did not import foreign customs signaling that what he established would forever be labeled "foreign." He fought against rules, regulations, and practices that had been instituted by and for earlier generations, and against the arrogance of those who imposed them, considering them sacred. By contrast, we who work cross-culturally have often proclaimed a message that says, "Become like us culturally and God will accept you." We have assumed, as one of my colleagues put it, "we have had two thousand years of experience with the gospel; we know how things ought to be run." My response was that we need to find out how God wants to work with a particular people and communicate the message accordingly.

An incarnational approach is an insider approach, focused on faith, not religion, seed sowing rather than tree planting, dealing with the receptors' needs in ways that they understand as representing an insider Jesus. Like Jesus' message, it is accompanied by power demonstrations exhibiting the love of God and his desire to free captives from the grip of Satan. Like Jesus, we who bring the message leave this live message in the receptors' hands, to grow and multiply inside the families and communities of their birth. An insider movement starts with incarnational communication and continues inside a society as an insider activity expressed in insider ways to honor Jesus.

SECTION 2

Religion and Syncretism

CHAPTER 37

Reflections on Religion
Harley Talman

Assumptions about the meaning and nature of "religion" are a major contributor to confusion about insider movements. However, most people are oblivious to this fact, because we all "know" what religion is.[1] Yet specialists in the field of religious studies are at the point of despair in attempting to achieve a common understanding of what a religion is. Seth Kunin concludes,

> Although the word "religion" is used throughout the full range of discourse (popular and academic) in Western society, both about itself and about other societies, the exact definition of the term has provided an ongoing challenge to scholars—with seemingly as many definitions as there are scholars of the subject. . . . Whether religion exists and whether it can be adequately defined are the central issues for religious studies and in fact are questions that go to the very heart of the existence of religious studies as an academic discipline.[2]

Karen Armstrong concurs with this lack of consensus and contrasts the peculiar notion held by moderns in the West with that of other faith traditions:

> In the West we see "religion" as a coherent system of obligatory beliefs, institutions, and rituals, centering on a supernatural God, whose practice is essentially private and hermetically sealed off from all "secular" activities. But words in other languages that we translate as "religion" almost invariably refer to something larger, vaguer, and more encompassing. The Arabic *din* signifies an entire way of life. The Sanskrit *dharma* is also "a 'total' concept, untranslatable, which covers law, justice, morals, and social life." *The Oxford Classical Dictionary* firmly states: "No word in either Greek or Latin corresponds to the English 'religion' or 'religious.'" The idea of religion as an essentially personal and systematic pursuit was entirely absent from classical Greece, Japan, Egypt, Mesopotamia, Iran, China, and India. Nor does the Hebrew Bible have any abstract

---

1   See H. L. Richard's sidebar in chap. 39.

2   Seth D. Kunin, ed., *Theories of Religion: A Reader*, with Jonathan Miles-Watson (New Brunswick, NJ: Rutgers University Press, 2006), 1.

> concept of religion; and the Talmudic rabbis would have found it impossible to express what they meant by faith in a single word or even in a formula, since the Talmud was expressly designed to bring the whole of human life into the ambit of the sacred.[3]

Armstrong observes, "The only faith tradition that does fit the modern Western notion of religion as something codified and private is Protestant Christianity, which, like religion in this sense of the word, is also a product of the early modern period."

The eminent Jewish Talmud scholar Daniel Boyarin makes plain how our modern categories of "Jewish" and "Christian" are anachronistic. At the time of Christ, he says,

> There was no Judaism at all, nor was there Christianity. In fact, the idea of "a religion," that is, one of a number of religions to which one might or might not belong, had not come on the scene yet and wouldn't for centuries. By the third century (or even earlier) Christianity became a name for what Christians called themselves, but Jews were not to have a name for their religion in one of their own languages until sometime in the modern period. . . . Until then terms meaning Judaism as a religion of the Jews were used only by non-Jews.
>
> So then, what are we talking about? We are not talking about a separate institution, a separate sphere of "religion," still less of a "faith" of the Jews. We are talking about the complex of rituals and practices, beliefs and values, history and political loyalties that constituted allegiance to the People of Israel, not a religion called Judaism.[4]

Boyarin challenges the prevailing notion of religions as "fixed sets of convictions with well-defined boundaries." Such an idea makes it impossible for a person to belong to more than one of the major religious traditions. The "checklist" approach to religions defines them according to specific beliefs and practices—like the Trinity and the incarnation, or keeping the Sabbath and dietary laws. But this does not correspond with present realities on the ground—and it certainly was not true of Judaism during the early centuries of Christianity, where there were conflicting religious ideas among Jewish groups. For example, some Jews believed in a human messiah and thought Jesus was he; others anticipated a divine messiah, but could not imagine him to be the Nazarene carpenter; some saw the "Son of Man" as a second, divine being; others understood this figure to represent faithful Israelites; and so on.[5]

We moderns define members of religions by using "checklists." But there are significant problems with this approach. First, which group or individual gets to decide what particular beliefs or practices are essential?[6] I have several times given a group of highly committed evangelical Christians a list of

---

3   Karen Armstrong, *Fields of Blood: Religion and the History of Violence* (New York: Alfred A. Knopf, 2014), 4–5. As evangelicals we reject Armstrong's theological liberalism, but her understanding of "religion" is not controversial.

4   Daniel Boyarin, *The Jewish Gospels: The Story of the Jewish Christ* (New York: The New Press, 2012), 2.

5   Ibid., 7–9; see also Boyarin's chaps. 1 and 2.

6   Ibid., 9.

ten doctrinal beliefs, asking them to identify which ones are necessary for salvation; their answers have ranged from one to ten, reflecting nothing like a consensus. Another big problem for the checklist approach is what to do with those who represent a combination of the lists.[7] This, of course, is a key feature of insider movements.

In attempting to eliminate disunity and dissension in the Roman Empire, political and ecclesial authorities employed a checklist approach to draw the borders around Christianity, separating it from non-Christianity and Judaism. Ecumenical councils of the church defined orthodoxy—not just in terms of ontological Christology, but also in mandating the date for Easter observance. At Nicaea, Boyarin declares,

> Easter was severed once and for all within orthodox churches from its calendrical and thematic connections with Passover. In the end what was accomplished by Nicaea and Constantinople was the establishment of a Christianity that was completely separated from Judaism. . . . Between Nicaea and Constantinople, many folks who considered themselves Christians were written right out of Christianity. Christians who practiced Judaism, even only by holding Easter at Passover (which included practically the entire church of Asia Minor for a few centuries), especially were declared heretics. . . . Options for ways of believing or being Christians were cut off through this process of selection, especially the option to be both Christian and Jew at the same time. One could not believe in Jesus and go to the synagogue on Sabbath: we won't let you.[8]

Checklists invariably become instruments of power. After Christianity became the official religion of the Roman Empire, iconic figures in Christian history delineated the borders of religion and enforced them; the rabbis did the same.[9] Jerome, for example, wrote to Augustine about those who affirmed the Nicene Creed but prayed at the synagogue and observed the Sabbath and food laws, "While they desire to be both Jews and Christians, they are neither the one nor the other."[10] He refers to them as *minei* (sectarians) and "Nazarenes"; the rabbis' prayer of curses, also of Jerome's era, uses the same terms.[11] Boyarin continues, "According to Jerome's report, even this is not a Jewish condemnation of Christians in general but rather applies to those poor folks who couldn't tell the difference properly and thought they were both."[12] Furthermore,

> These seemingly innocuous checklists are really tools of power, not simply description. If, thunders Jerome, you believe in the Nicene Creed, get out of the synagogue, and you will be a Christian. If you stay in the synagogue and drop your belief in Christian doctrine,

---

7   Ibid., 9–10.

8   Ibid., 13–15.

9   Ibid., 12. Boyarin and recent scholarship regard the Council of Jamnia, supposedly convened in Yavneh around 90 CE, as a Talmudic invention patterned after the Christian councils at Nicaea and Constantinople.

10   Ibid., 16.

11   This is attested in the fifth century, but earlier forms appear in the third, according to Boyarin; ibid., 18.

12   Ibid., 19.

> then the Pharisees will agree to call you a Jew. Fill in the boxes
> correctly on the checklist, or you are neither a Christian nor a Jew.[13]

Boyarin advances an alternative approach: "Instead of a checklist for who is a Jew, which inevitably, as we have seen, leads to arbitrary exclusions, we could use the idea of family resemblances in order to recapture the period of religious fluidity that followed Jesus' death."[14] Family members do not all share any particular set of characteristics, but enough similarities are apparent for them to be recognized as belonging to the family.[15] This pliable perspective on religions more accurately reflects what we observe in most societies, or at least in segments of them. Where this perspective is operative, the society can recognize the "family resemblances" of Hindu devotees of Jesus, "new Buddhists," or Muslim followers of Christ. This gives them the social space and freedom to grow into insider movements.

But paradigm shifts are difficult, and why change what we have "always" done? Unfortunately, more than sixteen centuries of checklist tradition have blocked from our memory those first centuries of blended belonging. So with checklists in hand, Christian sentinels vigilantly guarded the border with Judaism; but then in the twentieth century Jews embracing Yeshua as Messiah stormed past the carefully guarded border of Christendom and into the kingdom of God. Disciples of Christ in other religious traditions are likewise taking the kingdom by force, but Christians who scrutinize their checklists are oblivious to the family resemblances of their insider brethren.

Bibliography

Armstrong, Karen. *Fields of Blood: Religion and the History of Violence*. New York: Alfred A. Knopf, 2014.

Boyarin, Daniel. *The Jewish Gospels: The Story of the Jewish Christ*. New York: The New Press, 2012.

Kunin, Seth D. *Theories of Religion: A Reader*. With Jonathan Miles-Watson. New Brunswick, NJ: Rutgers University Press, 2006.

---

13 Ibid., 20.
14 Ibid.
15 Ibid., 20–21.

CHAPTER 38

(De)Franchising Missions[*]
Kyle Holton

The Western Obsession with Religious Classification

Years ago, I sat with a few Muslim friends who spoke a language called Chiyao. Dressed in whatever garments resembled prayer robes, many of the men wore lacy Victoria's Secret negligees purchased at the local market—a last stop for used clothing from the West. At the time, we were sharing a meal after a Friday prayer service. My language teacher, a respected imam, had preached and then requested for me to say a few words. After the liturgy, we had retired to a member's home for food and conversation. Since my discussion had referenced the prophet Isa, the discussion evolved into a comparison of Christianity and Islam as understood by my friends. They discussed scriptural references, and one imam remembered a text found in the New Testament that discussed how God was one. From the vaguely remembered Scripture, the man suggested that since God held the world together, surely the two sacred scriptures represented paths that approached the great mystery of God. This was no relativistic gesture to all religious forms but an admission to a perceived overlap among the two texts of Qur'an and *Injil* (Gospel).

These same imams who orally sift the rationality of textual theology also live in a world that is deeply bioregionally biased. The fears and hopes of their neighbors further define the context of their religiosity. Many Yao imams push the limits of orthodox Islam and use Arabic scripts as objects imbued with spiritual power. I've seen Arabic texts soaked in water and drunk as a tea to ward off insanity. I've been offered textual firebreaks, in which Arabic prayers of protection inscribed on paper are put in a perimeter around residential spaces.

The comical scene of discussing the relationship between Islam and Christianity with men dressed in Victoria's Secret gowns is made more strange for Westerners when the narrative turns away from talk of religious doctrine and is directed to the daily ministerial needs of people. The situation is conceptually ineffable to Western taxonomic systems. What religion is this? What are the central beliefs? For many missiologists, these situations are labeled syncretistic or folk. This missiological label has always been a dumping ground for people who do not fit within traditional religious groups.[1]

---

[*] Originally published in a slightly different form in *Missio Dei: A Journal of Missional Theology and Praxis* 4, no. 2 (2013), http://missiodeijournal.com/article.php?issue=md-4-2&author=md-4-2-holton. Reprinted by permission.

[1] Though a report from the Pew Research Center suggests that only 5.9 percent of the world are folk religionists, it is a subjective assessment to decide when an adherent has effectively blended beliefs to be defined as a folk religionist. Furthermore, folk religionists often belong to other religions, such as Islam or Christianity. Consequently, such a low percentage underestimates vast populations within the world's religions. Even Pew Research

My initial dialogue and relationship with the mosque was not without consequence. Many people discussed my religious identity. I distinctly remember one day when I sat with a good neighbor who introduced me to a family member as "one of us, a Muslim." The statement took me by surprise. It is always an interesting experience to be introduced. What will people say? How do they view me? Is the description accurate? What did my neighbor actually mean by labeling me as a Muslim? How would you have responded?

Recent dialogue concerning these issues of religious identity has circulated throughout evangelical magazines.[2] However, a framework for classifying the situation has been developed and refined within evangelical mission organizations. John Travis, a missionary among Muslims, wrote an article for the *Evangelical Missions Quarterly* that has continued to frame the discussion about contextualization and so-called insider movements to this day.[3] Travis suggested six different categories to organize the response believers have to the gospel and the way the church is structured as the movement grows. Coming from a strictly Islamic context, Travis's framework is rooted in regions where Muslims live within a society that is saturated with not only the religion of Islam but the culture of Islam as well.[4] Travis labels his categories from C1 to C6, in which the *C* denotes "Christ-centered communities."[5]

Negatively stated, the current debate among missiologists about insider movements reveals a Western obsession with taxonomy that categorizes disputable concepts such as religion, Christology, and ecclesiology. Undergirding all discussion among evangelicals concerning insider movements, the discussion is based on an assumption that the world can be carved into religions, that assent to ontological

---

admits to the difficulty: "Folk religions are challenging to measure. Less institutionalized and more diffuse than many other faiths, folk religions often are omitted as a category in surveys even in countries where they are widely practiced." Pew Research Center, "Folk Religionists," in *The Global Religious Landscape* (December 18, 2012), http://pewforum.org/global-religious-landscape-folk.aspx.

2   See, for instance, Timothy C. Tennent, "The Hidden History of Insider Movements," *CT*, January–February 2013; and other articles in the same issue.

3   John Travis, "The C1 to C6 Spectrum: A Practical Tool for Defining Six Types of 'Christ-centered Communities' ('C') Found in the Muslim Context," *EMQ* 34, no. 4 (1998): 407–8.

4   In contrast, descriptive anthropologists, such as Clifford Geertz, and post-liberal theologians, such as George Lindbeck, argue that all religions function as cultures. See Geertz, *The Interpretation of Cultures* (New York: Basic Books, 1973); and Lindbeck, *The Nature of Doctrine: Religion and Theology in a Postliberal Age* (Louisville: Westminster John Knox, 1984).

5   Many critics and proponents of insider movements who use the C1–C6 taxonomy tend not to give proper consideration to folk religionists, who make up a large portion of all the world religions. Further, even many Muslim authorities would scoff at the leaders and followers of Islam in northern Mozambique. Adherents of the world's religions, such as Christianity and Islam, tend to marginalize the syncretist and snub the overt mixture of religious systems, the lack of doctrinal knowledge, and the general illiterate, magical consciousness found in folk religion. From my perspective, many have taken the "Christ-centered communities" that follow "Jesus as the risen Lord and Savior and the Bible as God's word" and assumed an evangelical soteriology or Christology. In my recent interactions with the Travis family, I have learned that this was not the intent behind the Spectrum, given the folk religious context in which the Travises worked. As noted by Travis, the C-spectrum considers the sociocultural identity. Folk religionists may exhibit unorthodox beliefs or practices but often maintain a strong identity with world religions such as Islam. Nevertheless, identity often fissures between stated orthodoxy and local variations. For my purposes, I do not want to suggest that the C-spectrum isn't flexible enough for the folk religionist; rather, I want to highlight the importance for identification with Jesus, specifically in the C5 context, of following an indigenous soteriology and Christology and not a prefabricated theological paradigm, which may remain resident within the assumptions of Western organizations working within C5 contexts.

doctrinal statements about Jesus—found in documents such as the Nicene Creed—are a sign of salvation, and that an ecclesiology is understood in mainly institutional form.

Positively stated, the indigenizing process in which Jesus is adapted into new contexts, such as insider movements, represents a deconstruction of religious institutionalization, offering the West a chance to witness a Christology that is not obsessed with ontological pronouncements of being, but a Christology that is postured to an oral, phenomenological way of being. The nomenclature of *insider* provides a helpful lens to review the nature of God's kingdom, thereby flattening institutional religion and cultivating a people who *do* Christology in the way of faith instead of mimicking ontological belief statements shaped in the tradition of Western Christology.

Religion Is Not Real

Ultimately, all heuristic devices such as the one devised by Travis contain an inherent bias; they explain or emphasize some things but not others. Certainly the C-spectrum is limited in that it only looks at language, culture, religious forms, and religious identity; it does not encompass other aspects like the degree of folk practice or the theology of the group.[6] It may be assumed by critics of C5 communities that Christianity is a kind of institutional religion that can be divided into a separate sphere away from other religious ideas. From such a perspective, Jesus is the founder of religion. For this reason they may oppose the idea of C5 communities, since they assume insider adherents blend two religions.

Fundamentally, insider movements raise an important basic question: what is the relationship of Jesus to religion? Insiders and their supporters do not believe Jesus came to found a religion at all, but rather to form a redemptive Way. Therefore, discipleship does not demand adoption of a new religious system; rather, it can be navigated within the religious community of one's birth. It is no longer Christianity versus other religions, but Christ *among* the religions. Insiders bring Jesus with them if they pray in the mosque.

Religion is neither a useful concept nor a practical reality; Christianity as a religion is a modern construction that confuses the role of Jesus as the Messiah. Many historians suggest that Jesus was merely a revolutionary and Paul was the builder of the religion. We are so comfortable with the idea of religion, we assume that the natural result of Jesus' ministry was a new religion. However, recent scholarship has questioned not only the legitimacy of our modern concept of religion but also the absence of a religious framework in Paul's theology.

William Cavanaugh persuasively reveals the historic roots of religion as a concept that originated during the wars of the late Medieval era.[7] By blaming war on "religion," the political state managed to overthrow the power of the Roman Church and create a secular space. Cavanaugh suggests,

> What is at issue behind these wars is the creation of "religion" as a
> set of beliefs which is defined as personal conviction and which can
> exist separately from one's public loyalty to the State. The creation

---

6   Though I find the phenomenological description of insider adherents to be worthy of reflection, more critical assessment of classification models such as the C1–C6 framework must develop, as Travis himself acknowledges; see chap. 51.

7   William T. Cavanaugh, "'A Fire Strong Enough to Consume the House': The Wars of Religion and the Rise of the State," *Modern Theology* 11, no. 4 (1995): 397–420.

of religion, and thus the privatization of the Church, is correlative
to the rise of the State.[8]

Consequently, the concept of religion was created by the state to disenfranchise the authority of Christendom. Before the sixteenth and seventeenth centuries, "religion" only referred to the practices of monastic orders. Cavanaugh cites Thomas Aquinas's view that as a virtue, "*religio* is a habit, knowledge embodied in the disciplined actions of the Christian."[9]

Religion as a modern concept was given a twofold meaning. First, by universalizing historical manifestations of *religio*, religion became a specific interior posture. Second, *religio*, as an interiorized disposition, could be categorized as a system of beliefs. With the rise of the secular state, the evolution of religion was defined as an interior assent to a system of beliefs that must be sufficiently benign not to challenge state authority. Religion was privatized.[10]

The Church Is Not an Institution

With the advent of Christendom via the great councils, the seeds of modern religion germinated long before the medieval period. Though a secular state was not created until the seventeenth century, the church was infected with worldly, institutional power during the great ecumenical councils of Nicaea and Chalcedon, which in turn cultivated a demand for the secular. Since these councils, the Christian tradition has maintained a dominant thread of religious institutionalization. The advent of timeless creedal formulations was authorized by a Christological ontology.

Mary Douglas defines institutions as conventions that categorize the world by an ontological legitimation.[11] First, conventions are groups that agree to rules for consistent coordination. Conventions offer the gears for momentum in production and social structure by creating stable boundaries and laws. As a form of differentiation, conventions require boundaries for regulation and outsider identification. Second, conventions are institutionalized by ontological legitimation. Ultimately, conventions become institutions by rationalizing a framework through abstraction to the ontic; the institutional culture is universalized. Practically speaking, the institution grounds its beliefs, values, and behaviors (i.e., conventions) into an explanation of the way the world is at bottom. Moreover, the authority of the institution is unified with this ontological essence and is universalized for all cultures and perspectives.

For centuries, the church has functioned as an institution. In fact, many may wonder why this is an issue to discuss. The church-as-institution runs counter to a kingdom ethic performed and announced

---

8   Ibid., 403.

9   Ibid., 404.

10   If religion exists, then we can divide the world into religious and secular values, religious traditions and cultural practices. For example, only with religion can we differentiate C4 and C5 communities. Due to this bifurcation between the religious and the secular, or religion and culture, some Western missionaries only give lip service to the self-theologizing principle. As a religion, the recipe (system of beliefs) used in the franchised kitchen of evangelical Christianity must be maintained and protected. It is upsetting to me that the doctrinal recipe maintained is like a fast food menu devoid of nutrition. Like a McDonald's hamburger that tastes the same in New York City or Moscow, so formulaic doctrinal religion cultivates a global network of homogeny. Upholding the ontological Christology of Jesus as the cornerstone element of a system of beliefs, Western Christianity can remain without performative content and works to serve a way of life that is private—subservient to existing institutions of worldly power. In others words, we allow the way of Jesus to function as a privatized religion.

11   Mary Douglas, *How Institutions Think*, Frank W. Abrams Lectures (Syracuse: Syracuse University Press, 1986), 46.

by the wisdom of Jesus. However, in the current stage of the argument, the issue is how institutions—such as the church—classify the world around them. Institutions classify the world and funnel thought into specific categories. Again citing Mary Douglas, the institution squeezes "ideas into a common shape so that we can prove rightness by sheer numbers of independent assent" and "systematically direct individual memory and channel our perceptions into forms compatible with the relations they authorize."[12] The act of classifying is akin to brand creation within the world of marketing. By dividing the world into ontologically grounded labels,[13] institutions hide their dominating presence. Citing Ian Hacking, Douglas describes how the process of classification runs "from people making institutions to institutions making classifications, to classifications entailing actions, to actions calling for names, and to people and other living creatures responding to the naming."[14] Consequently, institutions create a universe through taxonomy.

> The instituted community blocks personal curiosity, organizes public memory, and heroically imposes certainty on uncertainty. In marking its own boundaries it affects all lower level thinking, so that persons realize their own identities and classify each other through community affiliation.[15]

Many missiologists think we have overcome the institutional injustice of colonialism, which had more to do with state power than the gospel. However, when believers are organized into a classification system without providing space for self-theologizing—even though the C-spectrum was not intended for this purpose (see Travis, chap. 51)—the colonial institution is hidden behind the taxonomy. By relying on false categories such as "secular" and "religious," these categories rely on an institutional framework that pushes the way of Jesus into the private world by calling it religion. Furthermore, missiologists who support the institution of evangelicalism promulgate a type of taxonomy that reifies a system of adherent quantification and levels all fields of theological diversity. Adherents must be defined as ontological types and not according to the local, bioregional systems already existing. In this sense, employing a classification framework may introduce a nonindigenous church institution. The framework does not accept the inherent bioregional diversity of people, but forces a world of quantification based upon a grid of evangelical theology. Similarly, the C5 category is nervously debated, not because the adherents' theology is wrong, but because the American missiological institution funded by evangelicalism finds difficulty in quantifying hidden believers.[16] My concern is that the C-spectrum is often used to classify various missiological communities without also accepting the indigenous theology that often flowers in C5 communities. In so doing, modern evangelical missions resembles a franchising process in which the theological recipe is universalized, consistency of organization and taste is maintained, and choices are limited to marginal decisions that create an impression of freedom. By allowing clients to choose

---

12 Ibid., 91–92.

13 Ontological labels attempt to move beyond the task of Adam and the act of naming—a fundamentally linguistic act. Ontological labels classify the world into essences that cannot be translated. Ontological categories are as far down as possible, since the description ultimately hits the wall of being. Consequently, when institutions label the world, they calcify a rigid system of essences.

14 Douglas, *How Institutions Think,* 101–2.

15 Ibid., 102.

16 In this context, believers who do not fit within acceptable categories cannot be counted.

which type of condiment they want with their Christian Big Mac, the institution is reified and maintains authority.

A Constructive Response

I wish to affirm aspects of the insider movement paradigm that will lead to a way of Jesus that cuts across institutional religion. These comments are meant to be a proposal for further reflection. Put succinctly, insider movements represent creative spaces for reimagining our traditional ways of following Christ, not as a religion but as people shaped by performative Christology and centered on the celebration of the kingdom of God uniquely symbolized in the act of hospitality.

Not a Religion but a People

Many theologians in the postliberal camp have suggested that a proper understanding of missions should be centered not on religion but on the formation of a people.[17] For my purposes, I merely want to allude to Douglas Harink's work in *Paul among the Postliberals*.[18] Harink develops two key issues for our discussion. First, the Reformation doctrine of "faith in Jesus" needs to be, ironically, reformed. Gathering current scholarship, Harink suggests a better translation of *pistis Christou* as the "faith of Christ," which makes sense of Paul's larger theological paradigm.[19] In this light, Jesus' faith or loyalty to a way of life, to the bitter end, has soteriological significance. Said differently, the way of Jesus—his parabolic words of wisdom and shape of life—is justified via resurrection by his loyalty to the kingdom's impossibility. Jesus' loyalty revealed a Way of Life. Consequently, the modern soteriology of confessional assent to a rigid doctrinal statement is skewed; an anthropological reading of "faith in Christ" cultivates a human-centered focus on the person of Jesus and the human's ability to "accept" him. Rather, soteriology must be reformatted away from a non-localized, abstract confession to a life pattern that is analogous to the way of Christ.

Second, Harink suggests Paul's own mission of converting the Roman world did not include an understanding of religion. In other words, Paul did not see his work as converting people from one religion to another new one. Rather, Paul's task was to form a people out of the local context. The cultivated people bears witness to Jesus by the "shape of its life." Harink suggests that the shape of this life is a culture formed, "in which social order and material goods are redescribed by being reinscribed within another, scriptural narrative and another cruciform, social practice."[20] In contrast, "faith in Jesus" (the traditional paradigm) works as synecdoche for a whole religious system of beliefs that effectively cognitivize the way of Jesus and maintain a religion instead of a skill-based discipline that forms people in the local context.

Not a Human Institution but the Kingdom Of God

Is the above description still a kind of institution? During institutional periods of transformation, translation, and growth, authorities often attempt to disseminate a body of material that identifies the

---

17 For a popular description focusing on the missional nature of the church, see Rodney Clapp, *A Peculiar People: The Church as Culture in a Post-Christian Society* (Downers Grove, IL: InterVarsity Press, 1997).

18 Douglas Harink, *Paul among the Postliberals: Pauline Theology beyond Christendom and Modernity* (Grand Rapids, MI: Brazos Press, 2003).

19 Ibid., 25–30.

20 Ibid., 213.

institution. For example, franchising a restaurant is ultimately concerned with strict adherence to the sacred recipes guarded in the ancestral center located and replicated through structures of authority. Likewise, religious institutions such as churches, mosques, and temples work to promulgate a consistent cosmos across diverse regions. From a human institutional perspective, insider movements represent two possible functions. First, such movements use guerrilla tactics for conversion and competition by disrupting another religious institution from the inside. This perspective hopes a fresh Christian movement will disrupt and destabilize the mosque or temple. Though there may be room for marginal contextualization, adherents assume the insider movement is a step towards proper ecclesial being[21] and organization. Accordingly, the insider movement is risky. Members must maintain a strict, orthodox dogma with a veneer of foreign religiosity, giving time for the movement to gain momentum. Nevertheless, there is the fear that unorthodox ideas and practices will infect the emerging movement and slow the momentum towards outward ecclesial being. The second perspective assumes the borders of the institution are interior to the believer. As long as a rigid confessional faith is maintained, then the borders remain within the heart. The adherent can still be counted as a type of Christian as long as orthodoxy is given assent.

Both of these institutional views of insider movements are based on maintaining proper religious boundaries. However, a people shaped by the way of Jesus have a kind of anti-institutional ethic that runs within them. Beyond this essay there are rich resources for deinstitutionalizing Jesus, though for now I refer to my favorite source for uncovering a deconstructive ethic in Jesus. John Caputo asks, "Does the kingdom of God have borders or a border patrol?"[22] Indeed, the parabolic word of Jesus upturns or turns inside out the institutional borders we create. Caputo suggests the hospitality of Jesus' parable in Luke 14:12 exemplifies the genus of parables in which the "borders of the kingdom become porous, wavering in a kind of 'holy undecidability'" by dissolving our categories such as Christian, Jew, and Muslim.[23] The hospitality of the kingdom is like what I experienced among my Yao friends as we ate together; invitation of outsiders as insiders upturns our sense of institutional membership. In fact, membership to the anti-institutional framework of the kingdom requires a performance of hospitality that moves beyond cultural and religious boundaries.

In this light, insider movements reveal the possibility of kingdom upheaval. Religious taxonomists endanger the movement by classifying it and trying to control it. Much like a dead animal that is lifelike in the hands of a taxidermist, adherents are endangered by the taxonomist, who forces a classification on them that will suck out their lifeblood, leaving only a lifeless form to quantify and nail onto the wall of the Western missiological hunting lodge. Christianity has much to learn from Islam. If we allow insider movements to self-germinate without the overshadowing theological dogma that is couched in abstract, religious language, then we may perhaps hear the kingdom of God come out of the mosque and rebuke our insider hubris.

---

21 I use the term "ecclesial being" as a way to refer to both the external organization of Christian religion as well as the assumed internal structure of faith.

22 John D. Caputo, *The Weakness of God: A Theology of the Event*, Indiana Series in the Philosophy of Religion (Bloomington, IN: Indiana University Press, 2006).

23 Ibid., 268. The host rejects the insiders and drags the outsider into the feast.

Not Ontological Christology but Performative Christology

The last ingredient I would suggest is rooted in orality. I would like to briefly sketch key areas for missiological reflection in scholarship on the divergent worldviews of orality versus literacy, and on how the oral universe of many folk religionists may approach Christology. Though global, literate society is quickly overtaking oral culture, I still believe a majority of folk religionists operate in a nontextual worldview that literate society can learn.

Syncretism and Muslim Disciples of Jesus

[The following excerpt is from an interview with "Abu Jaz," who is involved in a contextualized movement of Muslims to Jesus in Africa.]

First, we cannot rule out syncretism at the beginning of a new believer's life. The purpose of discipleship is to separate their old beliefs from their new beliefs. So when they put their faith in Jesus, they may have at the same time Muhammad in their heart. But when they start to pray in the name of Isa for their own need, they experience joy, assurance, and peace. And when they pray in the name of Jesus and find people healed and demons cast out, they completely stop thinking about Muhammad. It is a process of the Holy Spirit.

[We should] categorize people in how they relate to Jesus: where are these people, and where is Jesus in their life? We should ask, "Does this person accept Isa as Lord of their life?"

Before [they believe in Isa], Muslims acknowledge Muhammad as the final prophet of God. Then we tell them about Isa al-Masih. They already know that Isa al-Masih was a prophet that raised people from the dead. They know that Isa al-Masih did miracles and that he will come as the sign of the day of judgment.

Even though they know all this, they are not intentionally thinking about Isa; they are thinking about Muhammad. But when we tell them the gospel, they begin to think about Isa intentionally as the one who will save them from the day of judgment, from Satan, from antichrist, from death.

At that point, they mix Muhammad with Isa al-Masih. Before, Isa was not the issue. Muhammad was the issue. But when they hear about Isa, they start to bring Isa up to the level of Muhammad. Before, Muhammad was the one who controlled their life. But when they hear the good news of the kingdom of God, they start to think about Isa. Now syncretism has started; before there was no syncretism.

If missionaries don't ever want problems with syncretism, then just leave them with Muhammad [grins].

But syncretism did not start with us. It started even in Paul's time. That was the reason Paul wrote the epistle to the Galatians. It is not [an] issue because we are Muslims; syncretism starts because people normally start with their own religious background. When people start to think about Isa intentionally, the Holy Spirit has room to lead them into all truth, even if they first mix Isa and Muhammad. The Holy Spirit through time will glorify Isa al-Masih in their lives.

---

* Excerpt from Gene Daniels, "Worshiping Jesus in the Mosque," *Christianity Today*, January–February 2013, with minor revisions.

First, the work of Walter Ong is well known and wide in scope. The characteristics of oral people provided in *Orality and Literacy* are helpful to gauge and uncover the cognitive difference between oral and literate people.[24] Two aspects of orality interest me here. First, people who depend on the spoken word, and do not depend on the written word, live much closer to the "human lifeworld"[25] and show a more situational, less abstract perspective.[26] Powers of rationality are directed towards the concrete problems of life without the need for abstract classification systems. Without abstract analytical categories, knowledge is maintained via apprenticeship and not stripped from its locality. Further, knowledge professed is rooted in experience. Oral people are great phenomenologists.

Second, oral people have a more participatory framework, and this is exemplified in communication that is agonistically toned.[27] As I write this essay, I am afforded a peace with my own thoughts. Able to work out my argument free from attack, I must only occasionally direct my writing towards counterarguments that I am consciously aware of. In the oral universe, communication is strongly participatory. Consequently, proverbs, sayings, and parables operate as counterstatements to a message that has already been pronounced. My own communication in the mosque was most readily celebrated and accepted when I structured riddles and arguments into my oration. In effect, people would spill out of the mosque still debating the words spoken. There are clear connections here to Jesus' way of communication in which he spoke to goad people into participation instead of preaching for audience assent.

These two aspects of orality are integrated in Ong's basic premise—spoken words are sounds that "are not things, but events."[28] For a literate mind, this is most unusual. We are used to viewing our words as they are typed on a screen. We have so thoroughly ingrained chirography into our logic, we often visualize our thoughts as written words. Moreover, when we view our words as things, we can objectify them. From this one move, a process of objectification occurs and induces an ontologizing bias of ideas. For the oral mind, words are an event of participation. The event opens up a nonrepetitive moment when thoughts collide and the world becomes. As sounds, words fade off the echoing cliffs of our ears. Words happen in time, not space. In this light, orality fosters a phenomenology of becoming, while literacy is one of being; words perform while texts exist as objects. It does not take much of a conceptual leap to see how a Christology of text focuses on the being of Jesus, while a Christology of sound performs Jesus. If the Word marked the beginning of the world, then the Word is first a spoken word, not a written word. We cannot objectify the Word by inscribing the sound and gazing at the naked scratches we have created on paper.[29] In my mind, a concrete place to reimagine missiology is to develop a Christology that is centered on performance instead of abstract objectification of the written

---

24   Walter J. Ong, with John Hartley, *Orality and Literacy: The Technologizing of the World*, 30th Anniversary ed. (New York: Routledge, 2002).

25   Ibid., 42.

26   Ibid., 49ff.

27   Ibid., 43ff.

28   Walter J. Ong, "Before Textuality: Orality and Interpretation," *Oral Tradition* 3, no. 3 (1988): 265.

29   Taking cues from Ong, Werner Kelber suggests that the tension of orality and literacy is present in our earliest Gospel—Mark. Kelber hypothesizes that the various christological heresies of the fourth century represent communities that adapted the oral wisdom sayings of Jesus. See Werner H. Kelber, *The Oral and the Written Gospel: The Hermeneutics of Speaking and Writing in the Synoptic Tradition, Mark, Paul, and Q*, Voices in Performance and Text (Bloomington, IN: Indiana University Press, 1983). There is the tantalizing idea that Christian heresy originated out of the oral-literate division. Regardless, my sense is that the Word-as-event helps Western Christianity move beyond certain dualisms such as object/subject and pre-Easter Jesus / post-Easter Christ.

word. The oral folk religionists of the globe who do not fit into Western taxonomies are surely capable of helping us with such a task as they perform the Way within their own landscapes.

Conclusion

The way of Jesus not only deconstructs the ideological fences, doctrinal barbed wire, and institutional cattle guards of franchised Christianity—like the toppled temple of the first century—but also rebuilds a technique of living that cuts through Western classifications by turning them inside out. Those who take the parabolic Word of hospitality (Luke 14:12) into the mosque are practicing Christology by opening up Jesus' wisdom, which cuts across the human institution. If the word of God is a spoken word, then it is an event—not a doctrine or an abstract thesis of the divine. Analogically, those who speak the word of God in the mosque, temple, or church will invite the narrative of Jesus into their experience. Consequently, the C5 community is not a static state of being, but a becoming. The Word as event shows the inability to institutionalize, grab, ground, or inherit the kingdom. Does Jesus not show a Christology instead of defining one? Does Jesus not embody the kingdom of God that refuses to maintain the boundaries of our limited religious imaginations?

In reflection on my own experience, I wonder: can I accept the label "Muslim" given to me? Perhaps I am one of those disciples of Jesus who went to the mission field and lost my faith in institutional Christianity but deepened my loyalty to the way of Jesus. Named "Muslim" in Yao, I discovered a place where a people could be formed and inscribed with the sacred event of hospitality. All attempts to classify the event of the kingdom of God are crumbling towers of Babel. Perhaps now we may begin to postulate an insider movement within institutional Christianity.

Bibliography

Abram, David. *Spell of the Sensuous: Perception and Language in a More-Than-Human World*. New York: Vintage, 1996.

Caputo, John D. *The Weakness of God: A Theology of the Event*. Indiana Series in the Philosophy of Religion. Bloomington: Indiana University Press, 2006.

Cavanaugh, William T. "'A Fire Strong Enough to Consume the House': The Wars of Religion and the Rise of the State." *Modern Theology* 11, no. 4 (October 1995): 397–420.

Clapp, Rodney. *A Peculiar People: The Church as Culture in a Post-Christian Society*. Downers Grove: InterVarsity Press, 1997.

Corwin, Gary. "A Humble Appeal to C5/Insider Movement Muslim Ministry Advocates to Consider Ten Questions." *International Journal of Frontier Missiology* 24, no. 1 (Spring 2007): 5–20.

Daniels, Gene. "Worshiping Jesus in the Mosque." *Christianity Today,* January–February 2013.

Douglas, Mary. *How Institutions Think*. Frank W. Abrams Lectures. Syracuse, NY: Syracuse University Press, 1986.

Geertz, Clifford. *The Interpretation of Cultures*. New York: Basic Books, 1973.

Harink, Douglas. *Paul among the Postliberals: Pauline Theology beyond Christendom and Modernity*. Grand Rapids, MI: Brazos Press, 2003.

Higgins, Kevin. "The Key to Insider Movements: The 'Devoted's' of Acts." *International Journal of Frontier Missions* 21, no. 4 (Winter 2004): 155–65.

Kelber, Werner H. *The Oral and the Written Gospel: The Hermeneutics of Speaking and Writing in the Synoptic Tradition, Mark, Paul, and Q*. Bloomington: Indiana University Press, 1983.

Lindbeck, George. *The Nature of Doctrine: Religion and Theology in a Postliberal Age.* Louisville, KY: Westminster John Knox, 1984.

Ong, Walter J. "Before Textuality: Orality and Interpretation." *Oral Tradition* 3, no. 3 (October 1988): 259–69.

———. *Orality and Literacy: The Technologizing of the World.* With John Hartley. 30th Anniversary edition. New York: Routledge, 2002.

Pew Research Center. "Folk Religionists." In *The Global Religious Landscape* (December 18, 2012). Demographic Study. Publications. Religion. http://pewforum.org/global-religious-landscape-folk.aspx.

Tennent, Timothy. "The Hidden History of Insider Movements." *Christianity Today,* January–February 2013.

Travis, John. "The C1 to C6 Spectrum: A Practical Tool for Defining Six Types of 'Christ-centered Communities' ('C') Found in the Muslim Context." *Evangelical Missions Quarterly* 34, no. 4 (October 1998): 407–8.

———. "Messianic Muslim Followers of Isa: A Closer Look at C5 Believers and Congregations." *International Journal of Frontier Missions* 17, no. 1 (Spring 2000): 53–59.

———. "Why Evangelicals Should Be Thankful for Muslim Insiders." *Christianity Today,* January–February 2013.

CHAPTER 39

Considering Religion(s)
What Does the Word Really Mean?
Kurt Anders Richardson

Hindu, Muslim, Buddhist, Jewish, and other insider followers of Jesus assert that they feel the liberty to remain within their socioreligious communities and retain their socioreligious, communal identity without compromising their submissive relationship with Jesus Christ, their Lord. Some (outsiders) take the stance that remaining within one's socioreligious community is not possible because allegiance to Jesus requires that one distance oneself from one's non-Christian religion. At the core of this disagreement is what constitutes religion. For example, Islam is defined as a religion. Yet what is meant by "religion"? Is it a set of core beliefs? Is Christianity also a religion? It is vital that we define the word "religion" so we understand what we are talking about. That is the aim of this article.

Religion as a Cultural System

Those who study "religion" as a discipline state that it is a term closely connected with "worldview." One of the most instructive definitions of religion is provided by Clifford Geertz. He defines it as a "cultural system" or "worldview."[1] This definition has endured the test of half a century of critique and modification. Religion as a cultural system is not a dream state, disconnected from reality. A religion is meant to represent or model reality to its adherents in a coherent manner.

Geertz states that religions are models of the conditions of life where life is lived.[2] Religions provide meaning and guidance for everyday life with prescriptions for action, whether at birth, death, events of loss or of abundance. For Christian theologians, what is valuable in this approach is that religions are intelligible based upon their social structures as well as psychological motivations. Any particular religion authoritatively binds its adherents to a way of life and also authorizes their actions in the name of that religion. Religions exert unrivalled authority to incorporate beliefs into everyday life as they guide large populations through a wide range of commitments and habits of behavior. Religions provide meaning that is embodied, social and public. Religions do this through liturgies and rituals.

Thus religions bind together beliefs and practices that powerfully motivate action and social order. Religions offer a unified vision of reality through the cultural systems' sacred writings, narratives,

---

1   Clifford Geertz, "Religion as a Cultural System," chap. 4 in *The Interpretation of Cultures* (New York: Basic Books, 1993), 87–125; cf. Daniel L. Pals, *Seven Theories of Religion* (New York: Oxford University Press, 1996); Fred Inglis, *Clifford Geertz: Culture, Custom and Ethics* (Cambridge, UK: Polity Press, 2000); Kevin Schilbrack, "Ritual Metaphysics," in *Thinking through Rituals: Philosophical Perspectives*, ed. Kevin Schilbrack (London: Routledge, 2004), 128–47.

2   Geertz, *The Interpretation of Cultures*, 129.

"consecrated behaviour,"[3] laws, public defense, economics, technology, art, and family life. Religions also create an environment where the adherents develop positive feelings when they live in accordance with the way their religion sees and interprets the world. In this way, religion as a construct is much more than a set of a core of beliefs. It has many more dimensions to it.

One dimension of religion is that since it is a worldview that is shared by a community, it also has a political dimension to it. Being political, religions have played a significant role in the ways civilizations have developed. As states formed over the centuries, local tribes and their religions were absorbed or even eliminated depending upon the dominant religion. Since ancient times, dominant polytheistic religions often absorbed tribal religions. Monotheistic religions tended to eliminate or at least convert tribal religions to monotheism.[4] With the exception of Judaism, the monotheist religions and empires of Christianity and Islam have exclusively pursued elimination and conversion (i.e., whatever was not eliminated was converted). Multiple gods have been "converted" into angels or saints by the monotheist religions. Well into the modern world of the last five centuries, the monotheistic religions have maintained incomparable loyalty to their worldviews, even in the face of secularism and genocide.

Religions play a major role in our world. In addition to the points made above, "religion" is a legal and political term for over one billion people in the world of democratic constitutions.[5] Religions as the worldview of communities of tribes or of nations have historic, traditional status in many laws and constitutions. These religions teach great narratives of origin and of destiny to their members, and being a member of the religion is often equated with citizenship. Thus religions also function as national myths (stories). A national myth, or narrative, provides the basis for the creation of rituals, which in turn function to sustain any given society, especially in times of conflict and crisis.

The Character of Monotheistic Religion

Biblical monotheism, with its prophetic revelations and consequent Scriptures, coinciding with other features of early science and technology, is regarded by many as appearing within human affairs in a window of time frequently called the "axial age."[6] Biblical monotheism also provided the groundwork for the development of other monotheisms. By the end of the twentieth century, biblical monotheism played a dominant role in shaping people's perception of the world and shaping their devotion. Indeed, the monotheistic and even messianic features of biblical monotheism have also impacted other major religions of the world. Many representatives of the Hindu religions would claim a monotheism that stands ultimately behind all the particularities of the other monotheisms. The notion of the messianic appears in many forms of Buddhism, etc.

Monotheism has been studied and critiqued in the field of comparative religious studies. Monotheisms have come under particular scrutiny because of their attachments to empire. Due to their connections to empire, in particular the Christian and Islamic monotheism, there has been a significant

---

3   Ibid., 112.

4   See one of the most significant texts on monotheism, Jan Assmann, *The Price of Monotheism*, trans. Robert Savage (Stanford: Stanford University Press, 2009).

5   See Ran Hirschl, *Constitutional Theocracy* (Cambridge, MA: Harvard University Press, 2010).

6   A term presented by the philosopher Karl Jaspers for the period of world history 800–200 BCE, used currently in the popular writing on religion—see, for instance, Karen Armstrong, *The Great Transformation: The Beginnings of our Religious Traditions* (New York: Knopf, 2006).

level of violence caused by the binary categories of truth and error, right and wrong, and triumph and defeat. If "winners write history," monotheists have written a lot of it.

The political and military influence that monotheist religions have exerted in the world has been a source of criticism. One of the leading questions in the critical study of religion is whether monotheisms are inherently more violent than other religions.[7] It is without question that non-monotheistic religions are also not free from criticism in this manner. Human beings do not need religion to be violent, but religions certainly can be utilized to justify violence. Human beings possess the capacity for defensive reaction and attack.

In contrast to the violence, the biblical monotheistic tradition has demonstrated that humans also have profound capacities for sensitivity and moral awareness, which provide the basis for communal responsibility and the pursuit of reconciled relations.

In the globalized world two phenomena intersect: (1) principles of human rights, which carry with them religious liberty, and (2) interreligious encounter. Christian and Islamic monotheism are to varying degrees missional. However, many contemporary Christians are critical of the Christian religion's attachment to empire and view this as completely antithetical to biblical faith and mission. For these Christians, interreligious encounter continues to be missional, evangelistic, and ever hopeful of people acknowledging Jesus Christ as the one and only Savior.

"Religionless" Christianity

Sensitive to the cultural excesses of monotheistic movements, in the late twentieth and now twenty-first centuries, movements have begun where Christians have been searching for a "religionless Christianity,"[8] separating not only the true Christian faith from the "Christian religion" but also freeing the Christian faith from any authority other than Jesus Christ.

The one New Testament appearance of the term "religion" in the epistle of James stands in contrast to this definition of religion. James writes, "Religion that is pure and undefiled before God, the Father, is this: to care for orphans and widows in their distress, and to keep oneself unstained by the world" (1:27 NRSV). This is not the place to explore this text on its own terms; suffice it to say that it does not play to the politics of religion with a true/false distinction. Instead, religion "that is pure and undefiled" is about imitating God in his compassion and holiness. It is also about allegiance to divine rule rather than to human rule, whatever the political consequences.

Therefore, for at least two centuries a number of teachers of the gospel of Jesus Christ have objected to a systematization of the faith that juxtaposes "faith" in Jesus with the "religion" of Christianity. Since this juxtaposing has happened in a number of contexts, postcolonial thinkers regard the term "Christianity" as hegemonic or politically aggressive—a Western religiopolitical construct imposing "true and

---

7   See Regina M. Schwartz, *The Curse of Cain: The Violent Legacy of Monotheism* (Chicago: University of Chicago Press, 1997); but also Jonathan Kirsch, *God against the Gods: The History of the War between Monotheism and Polytheism* (New York: Viking Compass, 2004); Jon Levenson, "Judaism, Christianity, and Islam in Their Contemporary Encounters: Judaism Addresses Christianity," in *Religious Foundations of Western Civilization: Judaism, Christianity, and Islam,* ed. Jacob Neusner (Nashville: Abingdon, 2006), 581–608; Bruce Lincoln, *Religion, Empire, and Torture: The Case of Achaemenian Persia, with a Postscript on Abu Ghraib* (Chicago: University of Chicago Press, 2007).

8   Dietrich Bonhoeffer, *Letters and Papers from Prison,* ed. Eberhard Bethge (New York: Touchstone, 1997), 280, 282. Bonhoeffer acknowledges that Karl Barth, his teacher, was the first to radically critique religion and its Christian embodiment (285–87).

Insider Movements: Disputes over the Meaning of Religion[*]

The core issue in debates about insider movements relates to religion and what religion means. I have been in discussions with supporters of insider movement phenomena where there is manifest frustration over how to appropriately speak of these things; are these movements socioreligious or sociocultural or religiocultural or what? The problem is that insider movements (at least at their best) are holistic and refuse the modern compartmentalized understanding of religion.

Whatever happened to holistic mission?

The core question here becomes exactly how a holistic gospel should face a holistic Islam (or Hinduism, etc.). Should there be a total supplanting, including changes of name and dress? If the change is holistic but more subtle and nuanced, surely a change of religious label and community identity misrepresents the true change and amounts to a syncretistic association with traditional Western definitions of religion. Harvie Conn maintains that

> the fruits of this are displayed in a Christian community where Kingdom lifestyle is narrowed to the confines of an ecclesiasticized subculture and there is little interest in the larger questions of culture and society. Turning to Christ is not always seen as also a turning to culture, where the believer rediscovers his human origins and identity, and a turning to the world in acceptance of the mission on which Christ sends the believer in eschatological pilgrimage. In this process conversion does not remake, it unmakes. The results of this are tragic for Muslim listeners.[†]

Insider movements are all about changing this established pattern. Compartmentalized views of religion are rejected. Holistic transformation of individual, family, and social life is sought. Being holistic, no reason is seen for changing the religio-politico-socio-cultural-historical label that in modern times became a compartmentalized religious label. This is what the insider movement debate is all about, but this has not been recognized far enough to become the central point under discussion.

—*H. L. Richard*

---

[*] Excerpt from H. L. Richard, "New Paradigms for Religion, Multiple Religious Belonging and Insider Movements," *Missiology: An International Review* (forthcoming). Printed here by permission.

[†] Harvie M. Conn, "The Muslim Convert and His Culture," in *The Gospel and Islam: A 1978 Compendium*, ed. Don M. McCurry (Monrovia: MARC, 1978), 105.

---

false"[9] ways of relating to God upon the entire world, as one religion imposing itself over and against all others.

Though there is a biblical basis for such movements in the Christian faith, such movements for reform are not usually well received. Religious power brokers (religious teachers, priests, shamans, mullahs, etc.) look for ways to justify and promulgate their religions because their worldviews provide the means for people to relate to and interpret their experiences of this world in "appropriate and beneficial" ways. Undermining these worldviews is seen as destabilizing the community.

---

9   One of the most enduring slogans in the history of Christian theology: "true and false religion."

Conclusion

To summarize, a religion is far more than a set of beliefs and practices regarding ultimate questions of life and death. A religion is a cultural system of teaching, ritual, and moral practice that connects human beings to the whole of their existence, all the while allowing varying degrees of diversity and nonconformity within its borders. It is a way of life woven from the strands of a people's narratives, sacred writings, beliefs, rituals, liturgies, myths, laws, customs, technology, art, family life, politics, economics, and social structures. It serves to preserve social order, often including ethnic, legal, political, and national identity and even citizenship.

Religions encounter one another and discover themselves to be rival interpretations of reality. Islam recognized this in its encounter with Judaism and Christianity.[10] The other major religions of the world recognized this as well and have reacted not merely because of a different cosmology, but because of the imperial designs of "Christian empire" that once wedded missionary and military activity. This connection is still being made due to people's experience of the West's military presence throughout the world.

The religions of the world may have aspects of them that are repugnant, but as we have seen, the religion of Christianity is not exempt from this problem. Since religion is defined as a cultural system, a religion can experience change in certain areas as long as its broader context and the community are not threatened or destabilized.

Current movements in the world demonstrate that faith in Christ can be differentiated from one's religion. Faith in Christ as differentiated from and yet existing within particular religions or religious contexts is actually a subtext and minority report running through the biblical narratives. Abraham, Joseph, Naaman, Daniel, and Paul exemplify those who lived as minorities in dominant religious contexts, adapting to their contexts without compromising their faith.[11] Since these men are narrative exemplars of faith in varied religious contexts, they provide models of interreligious encounter for biblical believers.

The Holy Spirit continues to convince many Christ followers about a "nonreligious" existence in the world and for the world. For them to live a "nonreligious" life for the glory of the Lord can probably happen more effectively within their own cultures than it can within the religion of Christianity. Even though the religions of the world will undergo massive changes at the level of individual human beings, these religions remain cultural systems in the world. The world of cultural systems is the world that Jesus had in mind when he prayed for his disciples to be "in but not of" (John 17:14–16). The differentiation of faith in Jesus and in Jesus-based communities can be experienced and advanced not only through translation of the gospel into other languages, but also as it is lived out inside the world's cultural systems/religions.

---

10 See Qur'an 2:148; 5:48; 23:62.

11 For example, Daniel bore the name of a foreign god, faithfully served a polytheistic king, and was counted as one of the empire's shamans or power people. Nebuchadnezzar placed Daniel in charge of all the "wise men" (2:48), i.e., the "magicians, enchanters, astrologers, and diviners" (4:6–9). Yet Daniel was always faithful to the God of the Bible in this milieu.

Bibliography

Armstrong, Karen. *The Great Transformation: The Beginnings of our Religious Traditions*. New York: Knopf, 2006.

Assmann, Jan. *The Price of Monotheism*. Translated by Robert Savage. Stanford: Stanford University Press, 2009.

Bonhoeffer, Dietrich. *Letters and Papers from Prison*. Edited by Eberhard Bethge. New York: Touchstone, 1997.

Geertz, Clifford. *The Interpretation of Cultures*. New York: Basic Books, 1973. See esp. chap. 4, "Religion as a Cultural System."

Hirschl, Ran. *Constitutional Theocracy*. Cambridge, MA: Harvard University Press, 2010.

Inglis, Fred. *Clifford Geertz: Culture, Custom and Ethics*. Cambridge, UK: Polity Press, 2000.

Kirsch, Jonathan. *God against the Gods: The History of the War between Monotheism and Polytheism*. New York: Viking Compass, 2004.

Levenson, Jon. "Judaism, Christianity, and Islam in Their Contemporary Encounters: Judaism Addresses Christianity." In *Religious Foundations of Western Civilization: Judaism, Christianity, and Islam*, edited by Jacob Neusner, 581–608. Nashville: Abingdon, 2006.

Lincoln, Bruce. *Religion, Empire, and Torture: The Case of Achaemenian Persia, with a Postscript on Abu Ghraib*. Chicago: University of Chicago Press, 2007.

Pals, Daniel L. *Seven Theories of Religion*. New York: Oxford University Press, 1996.

Schilbrack, Kevin. "Ritual Metaphysics." In *Thinking through Rituals: Philosophical Perspectives*, edited by Kevin Schilbrack, 128–47. London: Routledge, 2004.

Schwartz, Regina M. *The Curse of Cain: The Violent Legacy of Monotheism*. Chicago: University of Chicago Press, 1997.

CHAPTER 40

Religious Syncretism as a Syncretistic Concept
The Inadequacy of the "World Religions" Paradigm in Cross-cultural Encounter*
H. L. Richard

This chapter focuses on syncretism in Western Christianity as seen in the paradigm of "world religions" that is assumed in both popular thought and in missiological scholarship. Syncretism is a complex topic with various usages and nuances, yet in Christian circles the term is most often used as a pejorative against developments in non-Western churches that do not neatly align with Western Christianity. But, alternatively, this Christianity of the West is itself syncretistic, and never more so than when employing the distinctly Western construct of "religion."

My intention is to survey different definitions of syncretism in order to provoke discussion of the meaning of "religion" and of the concept of "world religions." I will then introduce current scholarship that demonstrates the Enlightenment origins of this established perspective on "religion," calling for a fundamental shift in intellectual paradigm. Traditional Christian thought is indicted as syncretistic due to the infusion of this Enlightenment worldview, yet this analysis also opens stimulating perspectives on issues of crucial concern for missiology. I will conclude with some practical suggestions for beginning to move beyond the syncretistic "world religions" paradigm.

Thinking about Syncretism

Perusing standard reference works on religion and missions reveals definitions of syncretism with subtle differences in meaning. Mark Mullins in the *Dictionary of Asian Christianity* points out a difference between standard usages in the social sciences and in missiology.

> Syncretism is usually understood as a combination of elements from two or more religious traditions, ideologies, or value systems. In the social sciences, this is a neutral and objective term that is used to describe the mixing of religions as a result of culture contact. In theological and missiological circles, however, it is generally used as a pejorative term to designate movements that are regarded as heretical or sub-Christian. . . . The legitimate cultural reshaping of Christianity is referred to as the "inculturation" or "contextualization" of the Gospel, though most social scientists would also include these cultural adaptations as examples of syncretism.[1]

* Originally published in a slightly different form in *IJFM* 31, no. 4 (2015): 209–15. Reprinted by permission.

1 Mark R. Mullins, "Syncretistic Movements," in *Dictionary of Asian Christianity*, ed. Scott Sunquist (Grand Rapids, MI: Eerdmans, 2001), 809.

S. R. Imbach in the *Evangelical Dictionary of Theology* is clearly in accord with this, but note the centrality of the concept of "religion" in this definition.

> Syncretism. The process by which elements of one religion are assimilated into another religion resulting in a change in the fundamental tenets or nature of those religions. It is the union of two or more opposite beliefs, so that the synthesized form is a new thing. It is not always a total fusion, but may be a combination of separate segments that remain identifiable compartments.[2]

It is tempting to base this entire chapter on this definition, as the assumptions about "religions" and their "fundamental tenets or nature" go to the very heart of what this chapter is addressing. It is certainly ironic that some Western Christian definitions of syncretism are demonstrably syncretistic in their use of the category "religion."[3] Before laying out the case for this observation, some further comments on syncretism will be noted.

In a major work on syncretism and dialogue, Andre Droogers laid out a basic definition that is, again, rooted in assumptions about religion and that brings together elements of the two previously cited definitions.

> Syncretism is a tricky term. Its main difficulty is that it is used with both an objective and a subjective meaning. The basic objective meaning refers neutrally and descriptively to the mixing of religions. The subjective meaning includes an evaluation of such intermingling from the point of view of one of the religions involved. As a rule, the mixing of religions is condemned in this evaluation as violating the essence of the belief system. Yet, as will be shown, a positive subjective definition also belongs to the possibilities.[4]

The "trickiness" of syncretism needs to be kept constantly in mind. This chapter is dealing with a very slippery concept that is "generally used as a pejorative term" (Mullins above), and seeks to turn the pejorative back on the Western churches that all too often casually see a sawdust speck of syncretism in the non-Western churches while missing the plank that is in their own eye.

D. A. Hughes in InterVarsity's *New Dictionary of Theology* points out a major problem with the broad use of syncretism as including a positive sense of borrowing from other religious traditions.

> [Syncretism] is also used in a broader sense to describe the process of borrowing elements by one religion from another in such a way as not to change the basic character of the receiving religion. It is

---

2   S. R. Imbach, "Syncretism," in *Evangelical Dictionary of Theology*, ed. Walter A. Elwell (Grand Rapids, MI: Baker, 1984), 1062.

3   Larry Posten, in an appeal for contextualization without syncretism, is more deeply implicated in syncretism by his strong emphasis on the centrality of religion. "First, we must *determine to the best of our ability what are the actual religious practices and religious objects of a particular culture that are purely religious in nature.*" Posten, "'You Must Not Worship in Their Way': When Contextualization Becomes Syncretism," in *Contextualization and Syncretism: Navigating Cultural Currents*, ed. Gailyn Van Rheenen (Pasadena, CA: William Carey Library, 2006), 252; emphasis in the original.

4   Andre Droogers, "Syncretism: The Problem of Definition, the Definition of the Problem," in *Dialogue and Syncretism: An Interdisciplinary Approach*, ed. Jerald D. Gort et al. (Grand Rapids, MI: Eerdmans, 1989), 7.

> questionable, however, whether such a broad definition is helpful,
> since it makes every religion syncretistic to some extent.[5]

The positive sense of syncretism certainly "makes every religion syncretistic to some extent," but one could also argue that every religion is syncretistic even in the negative sense. The issue, of course, is what one means by "religion." The lack of discussion of that term in these various definitions is troubling at best and perhaps empties their points of any clear meaning. Scrutiny of paradigms for religion and world religions is the focal point of this chapter.

Finally, for this initial discussion of syncretism, Scott Moreau has presented a carefully nuanced definition in the *Evangelical Dictionary of World Missions*. Moreau avoids "religion" talk, referring rather to "idea, practice, or attitude."

> Syncretism. Blending of one idea, practice, or attitude with another.
> Traditionally among Christians it has been used of the replacement
> or dilution of the essential truths of the gospel through the incor-
> poration of non-Christian elements. . . . Syncretism of some form
> has been seen everywhere the church has existed. We are naïve to
> think that eliminating the negatives of syncretism is easily accom-
> plished.[6]

Moreau, by avoiding talk related to essences of "religions," was able to acknowledge both positive and negative syncretism in every church, and his further discussion of those points in the article referenced is highly recommended.

The Concept of "World Religions"

Numerous books and academic courses introduce the major religions of the world with varying levels of sophistication.[7] In missiological circles it is also common to speak about the "world religions" as if that were a meaningful term, even though world religions textbooks often challenge this traditional language.[8] This alone is a massive problem that needs to be addressed, but as the roots of this imprecision or distortion are traced out below, it will be seen that what is at play here is syncretism.

---

5   D. A. Hughes, "Syncretism," in *New Dictionary of Theology*, ed. Sinclair B. Ferguson and David F. Wright (Downers Grove, IL: InterVarsity Press, 1988), 670.

6   Scott Moreau, "Syncretism," in *Evangelical Dictionary of World Missions*, ed. A. Scott Moreau (Grand Rapids, MI: Baker, 2000), 924.

7   Some books and courses, in line with the approach of this chapter, now present what John Stratton Hawley calls "guerilla warfare" against their own basic structure. "One clear-headed approach is to wage a steady program of guerilla warfare against the hapless [world religions] textbook—perhaps even against the stated subject matter of the course itself." See Hawley, "Comparative Religion for Undergraduates: What's Next?" in *Comparing Religions: Possibilities and Perils?*, ed. Thomas A. Idinopulos, Brian C. Wilson, and James Constantine Hanges (Leiden: Brill, 2006), 118.

8   Note Friedhelm Hardy's comment in *The World's Religions* as an example of this: "The conventional labels of 'Buddhism,' 'Jainism' or 'Sikhism' neither exhaust the (very large) range of the traditions we can identify outside the most unhelpful title of 'Hinduism,' nor do they, for the most part, even define proper 'religious systems.'" Hardy, "The Classical Religions of India," in *The World's Religions*, ed. Peter Clarke et al. (London: Routledge, 1988), 573–74.

Current academic work has challenged the commonly understood sense of "religion," although without the development of an acceptable alternate paradigm. Richard King traces the concept of religion to the Greco-Roman world, where the meaning focused on "tradition," with a recognition of the plurality of traditions.[9] With the rise of Christianity the term was redefined as "a matter of adherence to particular doctrines or beliefs rather than allegiance to ancient ritual practices."[10] This meaning was then exported and underlies the present concept of "world religions," but this interpretation involves a "Christian" reading of different sets of data that really do not fit the paradigm. Frits Staal powerfully makes this point.

> The inapplicability of Western notions of religion to the traditions of Asia has not only led to piecemeal errors of labeling, identification and classification, to conceptual confusion and to some name-calling. It is also responsible for something more extraordinary: the creation of so-called religions.[11]

In light of these realities King suggests that

> it is important to realize that the "world religions" as they are usually portrayed are idealized and largely theoretical constructs that bear some relationship to, but are by no means identical with, the actual religious expression of humankind, especially in the premodern era. One should also note that such "universal" faiths are simultaneously the homogenizing and imperialistic ideologies of a religious world. In effect by focusing upon the brahmanical strands of Indian religion, the theological treatises of Catholicism, or the scholarly Qu'ranic commentaries of Islam, one inevitably marginalizes a significant proportion of human religious experience and expression.[12]

The Enlightenment Roots of the Concept of "World Religions"

In 1962 Wilfred Cantwell Smith wrote *The Meaning and End of Religion*, a seminal work critiquing the very concept of religion. He traced the roots of the modern usage of the term to the Enlightenment, where the centrality of the intellect indicated that truth and doctrine were most important in religion.

> This is the view of the Enlightenment, evinced not only in the religious realm but as a comprehensive world outlook which stressed an intellectualist and impersonalist schematization of things. In pamphlet after pamphlet, treatise after treatise, decade after decade the notion was driven home that a religion is something that one believes or does not believe, something whose propositions are true

---

9   Richard King, *Orientalism and Religion: Postcolonial Theory, India and "The Mystic East"* (New Delhi: Oxford University Press, 1999), 35ff.

10   Ibid., 37.

11   Frits Staal, *Rules without Meaning: Rituals, Mantras and the Human Sciences* (New York: Peter Lang, 1989), 393, quoted in ibid., 144.

12   King, *Orientalism and Religion*, 67–68.

or are not true, something whose locus is in the realm of the intelligible, is up for inspection before the speculative mind.[13]

Smith adamantly objected to the intellectualizing and reification of religion, seeing personal faith as the vital reality that was obscured by this idealistic construct. "There is nothing in heaven or on earth that can legitimately be called *the* Christian faith," he asserted. "There have been and are the faiths of individual Christians."[14] This certainly seems to be an overreaction, as there are clearly confessional communities and not merely individual faith expressions; but Smith's critique of religion as an inadequate (or erroneous) Enlightenment construct was reaffirmed by later scholarship.

This intellectualizing of religion also began the compartmentalizing and trivializing of it. Jonathan Z. Smith pointed out that "religion was domesticated. . . . The Enlightenment impulse was one of tolerance and, as a necessary concomitant, one which refused to leave any human datum, including religion, beyond the pale of understanding, beyond the realm of reason."[15]

W. C. Smith returned to his theme of Enlightenment distortions thirty years later and had an even harsher conclusion.

> When I wrote *The Meaning and End* I knew that "religion" was a Western and a modern notion. I had not yet seen, but now do see clearly, that "religion" in its modern form is a secular idea. Secularism is an ideology, and "religion" is one of its basic categories. . . . It sees the universe, and human nature, as essentially secular, and sees "the religions" as addenda that human beings have tacked on here and there in various shapes and for various interesting, powerful or fatuous reasons. It sees law, economics, philosophy (things we got from Greece and Rome) as distinct from religion.[16]

More recently this point has been powerfully outlined by Timothy Fitzgerald, who traces in detail the transition from a medieval focus on religion as Christian Truth that covered all of life to the modern sense of dichotomized and compartmentalized religion that stands in contrast with the secular.

> One thing which has presumably always been clear, even to scholars in religious studies who tend to attribute to every culture "a religion," or even several: the English-language category religion has for almost all its history been inseparable from the Christian incarnation and Christian theology, and required a process of abstraction and modern fetishism and animism before it was ready to incarnate in different manifestations in different cultural con-

---

13 Wilfred Cantwell Smith, *The Meaning and End of Religion: A New Approach to the Religious Traditions of Mankind* (New York: Macmillan, 1962), 40.

14 Ibid., 191; emphasis in the original.

15 Jonathan Z. Smith, *Imagining Religion: From Babylon to Jonestown*, Chicago Studies in the History of Judaism (Chicago: University of Chicago Press, 1982), 104.

16 W. C. Smith, "Retrospective Thoughts on *The Meaning and End of Religion*," in *Religion in History: The Word, the Idea, the Reality,* ed. Michel Despland and Gérard Vallée (Waterloo, ON: Corporation Canadienne des Sciences Religieuses / Wilfrid Laurier University Press, 1992), 16. This focus on the Enlightenment's contribution to a reductionist understanding of "religion" is not meant to suggest that there were no positive results from the Enlightenment, even in the area of "religion"—particularly religious tolerance.

texts. But when this contested term is projected onto other peoples, who think in entirely different languages, there is always ambiguity about whether the projector is imagining "religion" to encompass all institutions on analogy with medieval and early modern ideas, therefore seeing it as indistinguishable from holistic culture; or whether "religion" is imagined in the Calvinistic mode as radically separated from the profane world; or whether "religion" is more simply a projection of the Western religion-secular dichotomy whereby religious practices are assumed to be different in kind from political, economic and technical/instrumental ones.[17]

Thomas Idinopulos likewise documents the compartmentalization and trivialization of religion when secularism became dominant.

The word, religion, acquired its own distinct meaning when the forces of secularization became so dominant in western culture that religious belief and practice became distinctly human acts. For once secularity became fully evident in society it was possible to speak by contrast of the religious way of life.[18]

Idinopulos objects to this development, suggesting that in both "archaic" peoples and in modern life there is evidence of "the interweaving of religion with everything else in life."[19]

Richard King provides a good summary statement for this discussion.

As a number of scholars have pointed out, both our *modern* understanding of "religion" as a "system of beliefs and practices" and the academic field of religious studies are a product of the European Enlightenment. . . . As such its [the term "religion's"] continued unreflective use cross-culturally, while opening up interesting debates and interactions over the past few centuries (and creating things called "interfaith dialogue" and "the world religions"), has also closed down avenues of exploration and other potential cultural and intellectual interactions.[20]

This line of analysis leads to King's conclusion that "the continued unreflective use of the category of 'religion' . . . does not carry us forward in our attempt to understand better the diverse cultures and civilizations of the world."[21]

This is not a conclusion that can be merely observed by a missiological world that purports to wrestle with understanding and communicating into the diverse cultures and civilizations of the world.

---

17   Timothy Fitzgerald, *Discourse on Civility and Barbarity: A Critical History of Religion and Related Categories* (Oxford: Oxford University Press, 2007), 104–5.

18   Thomas A. Idinopulos, "The Strengths and Weaknesses of Durkheim's Methodology for the Study and Teaching of Religion," in *Reappraising Durkheim for the Study and Teaching of Religion Today,* ed. Thomas A. Idinopulos and Brian C. Wilson (Leiden: Brill, 2002), 10.

19   Ibid.

20   King, *Orientalism and Religion,* 39; emphasis in the original.

21   Ibid., 43.

If King is right, radical change of missiological paradigms and terminologies is required. Since King speaks for a considerable consensus in the academic world, then if he is wrong the missiological world must enter the fray and, at the very least, defend whatever it is that it might think to be the true understanding of "world religions."

Missiology, the Enlightenment, and World Religions

I have attempted a brief summary of the case that a "world religions" paradigm developed out of the Enlightenment compartmentalization of religion within a dominantly secular world. It is a perspective at odds with the holism of biblical faith, yet Western Christians, many of whom boast of a biblical worldview, seem to have embraced terms and ideas from this alien worldview.

It is not as if missiology has completely failed to notice the significance of these discussions. Over thirty years ago Harvie Conn objected to the dichotomization of religion and culture, calling for a biblical missiology that puts all of life under the lordship of Christ, not merely "religious" life.

> Cultural anthropology has increasingly refuted the bifurcation of religious from cultural life, of the sacred from the secular in the world's ethne. But the Pietist mythologization of individualism into a theological construct has hindered the church from incorporating that insight into missionary methodology.[22]

The example of this Western syncretism with Enlightenment thought on religion is by no means singular. Andrew Walls has implicated the entire nineteenth century missionary movement as fundamentally syncretistic, although he does not use that pejorative label: "Nineteenth century missions were part of an Enlightenment project, stamped by Enlightenment ideals; the evangelical Christianity that underlay them had made its peace with the European Enlightenment and operated in its categories."[23] In a lecture Walls later applied this perspective to current Western missiological thought. "One of the things we have to get beyond in the next stage of Christianity is the Enlightenment. We can't give it up ourselves because it is part of our identity. But we have to realize it is not part of everyone's background."[24]

The supposition of syncretism among Western Christians is not new.[25] The process of rooting out Enlightenment-related syncretism will be so complex that it may never be fully achievable, as Walls notes. But as Western missionaries call other peoples to battle against syncretism, they must engage battle with their own hearts and minds regarding their own homegrown varieties of syncretism.

This chapter barely introduces the complex issue of "world religions" as an example of Enlightenment-rooted syncretism in missiological and popular thought.[26] A thorough analysis of "Hinduism"

---

22   Harvie Conn, "Conversion and Culture: A Theological Perspective with Reference to Korea," in *Gospel and Culture*, ed. John Stott and Robert T. Coote (Pasadena, CA: William Carey Library, 1979), 214.

23   Andrew Walls, *The Cross-cultural Process in Christian History* (Maryknoll, NY: Orbis, 2002), 244.

24   Walls, "Turning Points in World Church History" (unpublished lectures, William Carey International University, Pasadena, CA, April 14–16, 2011).

25   For example, see David J. Hesselgrave, "Syncretism: Missionary Induced?" in Van Rheenen, *Contextualization and Syncretism*, 79ff.; Nelson Jennings, "Suburban Evangelical Individualism: Syncretism or Contextualization?" in Van Rheenen, *Contextualization and Syncretism*, 159–78; and other studies in the same anthology.

26   David Bosch painted a devastating picture of Enlightenment influences on Christian missions, but did not focus on the "world religions" paradigm; see Bosch, *Transforming Mission: Paradigm Shifts in Theology of Mission*

and "Buddhism" and "Christianity" as empty reifications should be presented here, but space and time forbid.[27] But be forewarned that many practitioners of these traditions will likely object to this deconstruction of their reified paradigms. The resistance experienced in interreligious encounter often forces mission practitioners to grip even tighter their own syncretistic paradigm. Thus, the vital question, who speaks for any of these traditions? Who has the right to speak for Hinduism, or for Christianity? Which of the many Hinduisms is the truly valid expression? Which type of Christianity is the legitimate one, when each seems to claim that for itself?

Missiology all too easily employs the binary language of "religion" and "culture" without any recognition of the problems involved, let alone a serious grappling with numerous profound implications. When syncretism is discussed and defined in terms of religions and their intermixing, particularly when "cultural" elements are considered acceptable for adaptation but "religious" elements are viewed as tainted, this is itself an expression of the syncretism within Enlightenment constructs.

Paradigms or terminologies that suggest that there is an essence of Hinduism or Islam are likewise syncretistic, reflecting the Enlightenment reification of masses of disparate and even contradictory ideas and practices into the neat package of "world religions." Paradigms or terminologies that define syncretism based on religious concerns, without recognition of the presuppositions involved in Western use of religious phraseology, are also syncretistic. These lines of thought can lead one towards despair, because Westerners are deeply, even subconsciously, implicated in Enlightenment thought, as pointed out by Andrew Walls.

A Way Forward?

Is there a way forward for missiology and missiologists, not to mention popular parlance and lay Christians? Scott Moreau is certainly right that "we are naïve to think that eliminating the negatives of syncretism is easily accomplished," and this is most definitely true in relation to our own syncretisms.

Three steps can be taken to begin extricating our understanding of Christian faith from syncretistic bonding to Enlightenment-rooted paradigms and terminologies related to religion. These steps are just a beginning towards long-term solutions that might root out the depths of this syncretism based on deep reflection and interaction with ongoing discussions of these matters in the secular academy.[28]

One first step towards transcending the inadequate paradigm of "world religions" as it is expressed in both academic and popular discourse would be *to insist on always speaking in the plural and never in the singular.* "Buddhism" gives a false impression of unity; speaking of "Buddhist traditions" avoids the suggestion of unity and takes a significant step away from the false reification of the "world religions"

(Maryknoll, NY: Orbis, 1991), 262–345; cf. 477–83. This chapter could be considered a further application of Bosch's principles to an area not yet clearly seen when he wrote.

27 The power that these reified categories manifest is a point not overlooked in scholarly analysis, and qualifies the "emptiness" of the reifications. See, for an example in cross-cultural contexts, Arvind-Pal Mandair's reference to "someone for whom the concept of religion may not have existed in their language(s) prior to their accession to the dominant symbolic order imposed by the colonizer/hegemon, but for whom this now exists as if it had been an indigenous concept all along . . . [necessitating] distancing oneself from the concept of religion while fully acknowledging that the vestiges of 'religion' continue to haunt their very existence and the possibilities of cultural formation." Mandair, *Religion and the Specter of the West: Sikhism, India, Postcoloniality, and the Politics of Translation* (New York: Columbia University Press, 2009), 434.

28 Is there sufficient representation from the missiological field in the discipline of religious studies? Is there even adequate interaction with ideas generated from within that discipline?

paradigm. Similarly, "Christianity" should not be referred to in the singular; there is too much diversity present for the usage in the singular to carry any substantial meaning.

Second, rather than being content with the lazy use of these broadly general terms (even in plural forms), it is decidedly preferable that *contextually specific terms be employed*. "Hinduism" does not consider the world to be an illusion, and it would be simply erroneous to affirm this about "Hindu traditions." The Advaita Vedanta tradition, one school among the Hindu traditions, has often suggested that the world is an illusion, with contested understandings of not only that term but also of how truly representative it is of Advaitic thought. Similarly, one can speak quite *meaningfully* about even such a broad category as American evangelical Christianity, although more *meaningfully* about American evangelical Anglicans/Presbyterians/Baptists, etc. Each of the major "religious" traditions has "confessional" groupings that can be *meaningfully* spoken about (many of these claim to be the true spokespersons for their "world religion"). Careful thought is needed to speak *meaningfully* in terms of these subgroupings, avoiding the broad—and usually demonstrably false—generalizations often used for world religions in the singular.

Third, *the "change of religion" terminology needs to be abandoned as a meaningful way to speak of someone becoming a disciple of Jesus*. This seems to be increasingly the trend, since the meaning of "Christian" is deeply distorted even in the "Christian" world, let alone among Muslims or Hindus. This represents a significant departure in missiological parlance, as referring to "converts" from Hinduism or Buddhism to Christianity is just the normal way to think and speak about many people historically and in the present. Yet this traditional terminology has been questioned by many outside the Western world, with an increasing exploration and embracing of "multiple religious belonging" and of "insider movements" that reject the "change of religion" paradigm.[29]

A recent statement from leaders of Roman Catholic, Protestant, and evangelical thought on witness and dialogue illustrates the assumption that Christians expect people of other faiths to "change religion," without reflecting on the roots or implications of this terminology.

> Christians are to acknowledge that *changing one's religion* is a decisive step that must be accompanied by sufficient time for adequate reflection and preparation, through a process ensuring full personal freedom.[30]

The intent of this impressive interconfessional statement is clearly to reduce interreligious tensions and to call Christians to high ethical standards. Yet by yoking itself to the "change of religion" terminology,

---

29 On multiple religious belonging, see Catherine Cornille, ed., *Many Mansions? Multiple Religious Belonging and Christian Identity*, Faith Meets Faith (Maryknoll, NY: Orbis, 2002); Kang-San Tan, "Dual Belonging: A Missiological Critique and Appreciation from an Asian Evangelical Perspective," *Mission Studies* 27, no. 1 (2010): 24–38; and Tan, "The Inter-religious Frontier: A 'Christian-Buddhist' Contribution," *IJFM* 29, no. 1 (2012): 23–32. See my paper "New Paradigms for Religion, Multiple Religious Belonging and Insider Movements," *Missiology: An International Review* (forthcoming), which further explores these matters.

30 World Council of Churches, Pontifical Council for Interreligious Dialogue, and World Evangelical Alliance, "Christian Witness in a Multi-Religious World: Recommendations for Conduct," June 28, 2011, 5; emphasis added. Available at https://www.oikoumene.org/en/resources/documents/wcc-programmes/ interreligious-dialogue-and-cooperation/christian-identity-in-pluralistic-societies/christian-witness-in-a-multi-religious-world. The language of religious freedom, development, and universal human rights is rooted in Enlightenment constructs; see Fred Dallmayr, *Alternative Visions: Paths in the Global Village* (Lanham, MD: Rowman and Littlefield, 1998), 247ff.

Christian bondage to Enlightenment categories is perpetuated. If the argument of this chapter is valid, this entire "change of religion" paradigm also represents a syncretistic (albeit subconscious) concession to an Enlightenment worldview. Certainly great respect needs to be shown to individuals who, under the current paradigm, want to change religions and religious labels, whether into or out of Christianity, but this should no longer be seen as normative when the basic paradigm in play has been exposed as syncretistic.

The challenge of "religion" and of transcending the Enlightenment worldview that dominates the Western world—and that increasingly influences all the world through modernization and globalization—is a complex matter that defies easy solution. The discipline of missiology should be at the forefront of confessional Christian efforts to grapple with these constructs. Yet it hardly seems to be on the agenda, as Enlightenment-speak about "world religions" and "changing religions" is ubiquitous, suggesting that missiology as a discipline has not yet adequately engaged discussions and controversies in the field of religious studies.

May those who interact with this chapter embrace the three suggested steps and contribute to deeper and abler developments towards better paradigms and terminologies for the future.

Bibliography

Bosch, David J. *Transforming Mission: Paradigm Shifts in Theology of Mission.* Maryknoll, NY: Orbis, 1991.

Conn, Harvie. "Conversion and Culture: A Theological Perspective with Reference to Korea." In *Gospel and Culture,* edited by John Stott and Robert T. Coote, 195–239. Pasadena, CA: William Carey Library, 1979.

Cornille, Catherine, ed. *Many Mansions? Multiple Religious Belonging and Christian Identity.* Faith Meets Faith. Maryknoll, NY: Orbis, 2002.

Dallmayr, Fred. *Alternative Visions: Paths in the Global Village.* Lanham, MD: Rowman and Littlefield, 1998.

Droogers, Andre. "Syncretism: The Problem of Definition, the Definition of the Problem." In *Dialogue and Syncretism: An Interdisciplinary Approach,* edited by Jerald D. Gort, Hendrik M. Vroom, Rein Fernhout, and Anton Wessels, 7–25. Grand Rapids, MI: Eerdmans, 1989.

Fitzgerald, Timothy. *Discourse on Civility and Barbarity: A Critical History of Religion and Related Categories.* Oxford: Oxford University Press, 2007.

Hardy, Friedhelm. "The Classical Religions of India." In *The World's Religions,* edited by Peter Clarke, Friedhelm Hardy, Leslie Houlden, and Stewart Sutherland, 569–659. London: Routledge, 1988.

Hawley, John Stratton. "Comparative Religion for Undergraduates: What's Next?" In *Comparing Religions: Possibilities and Perils?,* edited by Thomas A. Idinopulos, Brian C. Wilson, and James Constantine Hanges, 115–42. Leiden: Brill, 2006.

Hesselgrave, David J. "Syncretism: Missionary Induced?" In Van Rheenen, *Contextualization and Syncretism,* 71–98.

Hughes, D. A. "Syncretism." In *New Dictionary of Theology,* edited by Sinclair B. Ferguson and David F. Wright. Downers Grove, IL: InterVarsity Press, 1988.

Idinopulos, Thomas A. "The Strengths and Weaknesses of Durkheim's Methodology for the Study and Teaching of Religion." In *Reappraising Durkheim for the Study and Teaching of Religion Today,* edited by Thomas A. Idinopulos and Brian C. Wilson, 1–14. Leiden: Brill, 2002.

Imbach, S. R. "Syncretism." In *Evangelical Dictionary of Theology,* edited by Walter A. Elwell. Grand Rapids, MI: Baker, 1984.

Jennings, Nelson. "Suburban Evangelical Individualism: Syncretism or Contextualization?" In Van Rheenen, *Contextualization and Syncretism,* 159–78.

King, Richard. *Orientalism and Religion: Postcolonial Theory, India and "The Mystic East."* New Delhi: Oxford University Press, 1999.

Mandair, Arvind-Pal. *Religion and the Specter of the West: Sikhism, India, Postcoloniality, and the Politics of Translation.* New York: Columbia University Press, 2009.

Moreau, A. Scott. "Syncretism." In *Evangelical Dictionary of World Missions,* edited by A. Scott Moreau. Grand Rapids, MI: Baker, 2000.

Mullins, Mark R. "Syncretistic Movements." In *Dictionary of Asian Christianity,* edited by Scott Sunquist. Grand Rapids, MI: Eerdmans, 2001.

Posten, Larry. "'You Must Not Worship in Their Way': When Contextualization Becomes Syncretism." In Van Rheenen, *Contextualization and Syncretism,* 243–63.

Smith, Jonathan Z. *Imagining Religion: From Babylon to Jonestown.* Chicago Studies in the History of Judaism. Chicago: University of Chicago Press, 1982.

Smith, Wilfred Cantwell. *The Meaning and End of Religion: A New Approach to the Religious Traditions of Mankind.* New York: Macmillan, 1962.

———. "Retrospective Thoughts on *The Meaning and End of Religion.*" In *Religion in History: The Word, the Idea, the Reality,* edited by Michel Despland and Gérard Vallée, 13–21. Waterloo, ON: Corporation Canadienne des Sciences Religieuses / Wilfrid Laurier University Press, 1992.

Staal, Fritz. *Rules without Meaning: Rituals, Mantras and the Human Sciences.* Toronto Studies in Religion 4. New York: Peter Lang, 1989.

Walls, Andrew. *The Cross-cultural Process in Christian History.* Maryknoll, NY: Orbis, 2002.

———. "Turning Points in World Church History." Unpublished lectures, William Carey International University, Pasadena, CA, April 14–16, 2011.

Tan, Kang-San. "Dual Belonging: A Missiological Critique and Appreciation from an Asian Evangelical Perspective." *Mission Studies* 27, no. 1 (2010): 24–38.

———. "The Inter-Religious Frontier: A 'Christian-Buddhist' Contribution." *International Journal of Frontier Missiology* 29, no. 1 (2012): 23–32.

Van Rheenen, Gailyn, ed. *Contextualization and Syncretism: Navigating Cultural Currents.* Evangelical Missiological Society 13. Pasadena, CA: William Carey Library, 2006.

World Council of Churches, Pontifical Council for Interreligious Dialogue, and World Evangelical Alliance. "Christian Witness in a Multi-Religious World: Recommendations for Conduct." June 28, 2011. Available at https://www.oikoumene.org/en/resources/documents/wcc-programmes/interreligious-dialogue-and-cooperation/christian-identity-in-pluralistic-societies/christian-witness-in-a-multi-religious-world.

CHAPTER 41

Contextualization, Syncretism, and the Demonic in Indigenous Movements

David Taylor

Introduction

One of the most difficult issues missionaries have had to wrestle with through the centuries is what to do with aspects of culture that are tied to the demonic. This is not a new issue for missions or God's redemptive work in the world, but it is one that we are beginning to explore anew in the aftermath of colonial mission practice, which tied Christianization with Westernization. Missions commonly displaced traditional art forms, such as instruments and dances, because they were tied to pre-Christian religious forms. In their place Westerners imported their own worship forms. In doing so, Western missionaries unfortunately projected a false paradigm of culture and God's redemptive work within it. This practice has handicapped generations of believers in former mission fields. It is therefore imperative that we explore this issue in greater depth, not only for the new fields that are yet to be pioneered, but also for old ones that have not yet experienced the fullness of their freedom in Christ.

Three Responses

Generally speaking, believing communities have responded in three ways to religious cultures (see fig. 41.1 below). They can be roughly defined as *isolation, accommodation,* and *transformation*. On the isolation end of the spectrum are groups such as the Quakers. Historically, Quakers have called Wednesday "the fourth day" rather than use a pagan name associated with a pagan god. Such groups maintain as rigid a separation as possible from the surrounding culture and thus, over time, become more and more of a subculture.[1] On the other end are groups that respond with accommodation; they are syncretists who bring their culture into the gospel. In the middle are those seeking transformation, who are bringing the gospel into culture.

Accommodation results in a compromised gospel, and the root cause of it is *fear*. This fear comes largely from a sense of hopelessness in the face of social intimidation or the powers of darkness. The result is appeasement. In contrast, the root cause of isolationism is *doubt* in God's desire and willingness to transform culture. The result is a legalistic system that lives by rules designed to ensure no contamination occurs. Between these two we find the biblical ideal to which thoughtful contextualizers aspire. It does not happen overnight, nor is it achievable without much spiritual contending from one generation to the next. That is because the root cause of transformation is *faith* and an understanding of

---

1   In a mission field context, this is often the result of foreign forms being imported, which causes a kind of hidden or occult syncretism. Here, underlying worldviews remain unchanged while outward observance to foreign religious traditions gives the appearance of Christian adherence.

Christ's supremacy over all things, leading to the freedom of the believer to live by the Spirit. It is not governed by rules but by principles. It is defined more by where the heart is than by external behaviors.

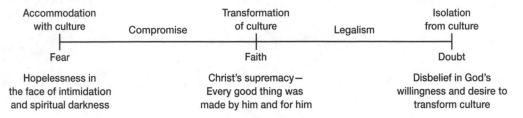

Fig. 41.1 The church and culture: finding our freedom in Christ

While it is clear what isolationism is, it may not be so clear where the line between accommodation and transformation is. In fact, the two may look very similar to each other externally. Different communities may be practicing similar rituals, for example. But what they mean by them is vastly different. Thus the issue is not so much what they are doing, but why they are doing it. As we will see, this issue of motive is crucial when dealing with demonic influence.

In this regard, in every indigenous movement, it is important that believers approach the issue of the demonic as led by the Spirit and the word of God. As outsiders it is not our place to dictate the application of scriptural principles within another culture; our task is to make sure that those scriptural principles are understood. It is therefore the purpose of this chapter to outline in broad strokes what those scriptural principles are for engaging with the demonic and to recommend a process for working through this issue in any culture.

Biblical Foundations

It is important for every believer to understand four basic principles concerning the transforming power of God in our world and his mission of redemption through Christ.

First, *there needs to be a clear recognition of the value of every culture from God's perspective.* Any theology of culture must rest on the foundation that all humanity is made in the image of God. As such, our human creativity is an expression of our God-given capacity to bring glory to our Creator. Whatever is good within a culture is an expression of God's goodness. The task given to humans to "fill the earth and subdue it" (Gen 1:28), often called the Cultural Mandate, ensured that the world would be full of diverse peoples and languages. When humanity attempted to create uniformity at the Tower of Babel, God intervened to enforce the Cultural Mandate (Gen 11:1–9). Paul told the Athenians, "From one man he made every nation of men, that they should inhabit the whole earth; and he determined the times set for them and the exact places where they should live" (Acts 17:26). This truth reminds us that God is sovereign over culture. He desires diversity and is the author of it. He created and designed the unique circumstances by which this diversity would be manifested throughout the nations of the earth. This diversity will continue throughout eternity (Rev 5:9; 21:24).

Second, *every people must be taught that Satan is at work to steal, kill, and destroy what belongs to God. He is a usurper of God's power, glory, and dominion.* Every evil thing in the world is a corruption of some good thing. In that sense, there is no such thing as "pure" evil, which is more of a dualistic concept than a biblical one. All evil is the perversion of goodness, the interception of pure intentions, and the distortion of God-ordained purposes. Seen in this light, every indigenous movement is a kind of refor-mation—an initiative by the Spirit of God through the word of God to reclaim what belongs to God. As a usurper of God's authority, Satan seeks to capture what belongs to God and make it his own. The *missio Dei* is the exact opposite. The Scripture says, "The reason the Son of God appeared was to destroy the devil's work" (1 John 3:8). The mission of the enemy is to "steal, kill and destroy" (John 10:10). Put succinctly, the mission of God is the reclamation of everything in this world that was designed to reflect his glory.

Third, *we need to know that Christ has overcome all the powers of darkness and that his Spirit is pres-ent to redeem everything that belongs to him.* Unlike the Gnostics, who could not believe that something so pure could come into a world so evil, the Scriptures present a completely different perspective of Christ's mission: it is because God *loves* the world that he sent his Son to reclaim it for his own. Daniel foresaw his kingdom as a small rock that would grow into a mountain that would fill the whole earth (Dan 2:35). Put another way, the mission of Christ is not an evacuation plan but an occupation plan. "For he must reign until he has put all his enemies under his feet" (1 Cor 15:25). Only then will the end come, once he has "destroyed all dominion, authority and power" (1 Cor 15:24). The reason this is so is because "all things were created by him and for him. He is before all things, and in him all things hold together" (Col 1:16,17). The world doesn't belong to the evil one; it belongs to our God. He doesn't fear the darkness. His light overcomes and dispels it. He embraces the leper, eats with sinners, and defends the condemned. He entered into our world and became one with those he was sent to redeem. And he said, "As the Father has sent me, I am sending you" (John 20:21).

Finally, *as followers of Jesus we must understand who we are—that we carry his authority and dominion into this world as agents of reconciliation. Because he has overcome, we too shall overcome.* As representatives of the authority of Jesus on this earth, we are called to be in the world but not of it. We are salt, light, and yeast. We are the wheat among the tares. Our mission is to work *within*, because that is what Jesus did. The gates of hell must yield to our advance and allow us entrance. We have been granted authority to demolish every stronghold that sets itself up against God and to be the ambassadors of Christ's mis-sion to "reconcile to himself all things, whether things on earth or things in heaven" (Col 1:20).

Ultimately, this is what it comes down to for followers of Jesus. Do we understand who we are in Christ—that we are seated in the heavenly realms with the Son of God? Scripture says that at his name every knee will bow and every tongue confess that he is Lord (Phil 2:9–11). As bearers of Christ in this world, we possess all the required authority to "trample on snakes and scorpions and to overcome all the power of the enemy" (Luke 10:19). We are not overcome by evil, but we overcome evil with good (Rom 12:21). Whatever we bind on earth shall be bound in heaven (Matt 18:18). If two of us agree on anything in his name, it will be given to us—more than we can possibly ask or imagine (Matt 18:19; Eph 3:20).

These are the truths that every believer must understand when engaging the forces of darkness in this world. Every time we celebrate December 25 as the birthday of Christ rather than worshiping Saturn, we should remember this reality: Christ is Lord over all! Every time we refer to Jesus as the Son of *God*, we are saying, in part, that he is the son of a Nordic deity (originally called *Godan* by the Lom-bards, from which our English word "God" derives)—a deity with a very colorful mythology, to say the least. Over a thousand years ago Jesus became the son of *their* god! He entered into their cosmology and became Lord over all. And that is what he is.

The very reason the Bible does not command us to use a single word for God, as the Jehovah's Witnesses would like us to do, is because our God is a contextualizer. He established this at Pentecost when the disciples began to declare the praises of God in multiple languages from around the world. But there is more to it than just language. God did this for the very purpose of connecting his story with every people's story in the world. This, in part, is what it means to reconcile *all* things back to God. Every culture, including the "religious" dimensions of every culture, belongs to God. He is the one who decides what to keep, what to discard, and what to reinterpret. And he chooses to do this through us, his church (Eph 3:10,11).

Three Crucial Questions

Having established that Christ is Lord over all, that all things were created by him and for him, it now comes down to a matter of faith and application. This is what Paul wanted believers who were married to nonbelievers to understand. He explained that the nonbeliever is sanctified *because* of the believer (1 Cor 7:14)! In other words, no contamination of the believer occurs in this environment, even though the nonbeliever is under the control of the evil one. In fact the reverse is true—contamination, in a good way, is happening in the opposite direction! The same held true with the issue of meat sold in the marketplace that had been sacrificed to idols (1 Cor 10). Paul explains that even though the meat was sacrificed to demons (v. 20), the supremacy of Christ holds fast, "for the earth is the Lord's and everything in it" (v. 26). Therefore he commands, "Eat anything sold in the market" (v. 25). And why? Because "whether you eat or drink or whatever you do, do it all for the glory of God" (v. 31). In other words, it's a matter of where your heart is. Satan has no power over the pure in heart, because "to the pure all things are pure" (Titus 1:15).

In deciding what to keep, discard, reinterpret, or redeem within any culture, believers need to work toward a process for addressing these issues as a community. Although this will differ within each culture, three areas Paul identifies in writing to Greek churches may be useful as a general reference point or point of departure. These three areas can be explored with three questions regarding a particular traditional practice: (1) Is it beneficial to the common good? (2) How does it affect the unity of believers? (3) How does it affect witness among nonbelievers?

With regard to the first question, in addressing a controversy among the Thessalonican church, Paul writes, "They forbid people to marry and order them to abstain from certain foods, which God created to be received with thanksgiving by those who believe and who know the truth. For everything God created is good, and nothing is to be rejected if it is received with thanksgiving, because it is consecrated by the word of God and prayer" (1 Tim 4:3,5). What Paul is saying is that if something is useful and can be redeemed through God's word and prayer, it is made holy and should not be rejected. So the overall benefit of a particular practice or tradition must be weighed. In the case of Thessalonica, there seems to have been an extreme reaction to the problems of immorality and food sacrificed to idols, the two major issues confronting the Greek church. The response of some was complete abstinence, but as the expression goes, this was tossing out the baby with the bathwater.

The eyes of faith will see the good in almost everything, and it is this goodness that should be preserved and defended. For example, in the case of meat sacrificed to idols in the Greek context, the benefit here was obvious: good food! Some of the best food in the Roman Empire was prepared by chefs affiliated with temples, which were basically the restaurants of the time. Paul explicitly speaks of a person whose faith and freedom in Christ enables them to eat in an idol's temple (1 Cor 8:10).

He cautions, however, that exercising this freedom may cause others to stumble, which brings us to the second consideration.

In applying the freedom of the believer to receive all things with thanksgiving, Paul also gives helpful instructions about accepting "him whose faith is weak" (Rom 14:1). Paul says that if eating meat causes his brother to stumble, he will never eat meat again (1 Cor 8:13). At the same time, he cautions, do not let what is good be spoken of as evil (Rom 14:16). So Paul is not saying that the community should resort to the least common denominator of acceptability as a legalistic rule. What he is urging is that harmony and unity take priority over all things. If a particular matter is not essential for living or for practicing the faith, there may be times when, as a believer, I should avoid doing something in the presence of someone who might be offended by this. An example in Western culture might be the issue of drinking alcohol. For some people this is the "devil's brew," and drinking it opens a person to demonization. For others it is something made by God that should be received with thanksgiving and used responsibly.[2]

Finally, whatever the issue under discussion may be, it is necessary to examine how the practice might affect witness among nonbelievers. For example, Paul talks about a situation in which a believer is invited to eat with a nonbeliever:

> If some unbeliever invites you to a meal and you want to go, eat whatever is put before you without raising questions of conscience. But if anyone says to you, "This has been offered in sacrifice," then do not eat it, both for the sake of the man who told you and for conscience' sake—the other man's conscience, I mean, not yours. For why should my freedom be judged by another's conscience? If I take part in the meal with thankfulness, why am I denounced because of something I thank God for? (1 Cor 10:28–30)

So the issue here is not whether the believer has the right to eat food sacrificed to idols or whether the meat will cause some kind of defilement to the believer. The problem is that the nonbeliever is eating the meat *because* it has been sacrificed to idols and is inviting you to do the same. In such a case, Paul says to decline, and this may open up an opportunity for further discussion. Here, ironically, Paul is modifying or clarifying the instruction of Jesus to "eat whatever is set before you" (Luke 10:7). This command itself is subject to the freedom we have in Christ!

How this area of concern for witness may be applied will obviously differ from case to case and from culture to culture. The point is that this is an area where believers should be mindful of how to maintain the purity of their witness, while continuing to engage meaningfully with the nonbelieving world. As a general rule, we should err on the side of engagement in order to maximize witness, while being sensitive to possible exceptions to this rule from time to time as the context may require.

---

2 Note, however, that Paul is not talking about harmony with outsiders like the Judaizers who are trying to influence insiders to abandon their culture. Of such people Paul warns the Corinthian church, "Do not be unequally yoked" (2 Cor 6:14). This is purely a matter of internal harmony with believers in a particular community who are at varying levels in their maturity and faith. So far from suggesting that the Corinthians placate those trying to limit their freedom in Christ, Paul is simply advocating the wise use of this freedom within a community context.

Avoiding Syncretism

As indigenous believers are exercising their freedom in Christ, the question of maintaining the purity of the gospel will, and must, always persist. At the same time, the paralyzing fear of syncretism is probably the greatest hindrance to effective transformation within cultures. To be sure, the risk of syncretism is ever present; and yet, though the fear may be well founded, the failure to contextualize does not ensure that syncretism will not occur. The aversion to developing contextualized alternatives to rituals in many traditional mission fields has not ensured that believers will be free from demonic influence. It actually ensures the opposite, as local Christians continue to resort to pre-Christian practices to deal with the spiritual realities that their secularized Western Christianity does not address.

Even today in Christian sub-Saharan Africa, tribal chieftains are still installed using the pagan rituals from pre-Christian times. Many of these tribal chieftains lose their Christian faith in the process. Could it be that one of the reasons sub-Saharan Africa has suffered as much as it has is because these covenants with demons have never been renounced, and continue to be reinforced from one generation to the next by those with the covenantal authority over the land? Why is it that after one hundred and fifty years of evangelical Christianity in sub-Saharan Africa, there is no alternative to these pagan rituals for the installation of chiefs in thousands of Christian tribes? Is it because the gospel was presented as merely a gateway to another world rather than the power of God for transforming culture and society in the here and now? For such people, the gospel becomes merely an add-on—useful for one dimension of life but not for others.

Clearly a reductionist gospel impedes transformation and guarantees that syncretism will persist even after decades of missionary efforts. But how do we know which direction we are heading in? Where is the dividing line between syncretism and contextualization? In simple terms, the difference can be defined by whether or not the biblical message has been preserved in all its fullness when being transmitted from one culture to another. With contextualization, indigenous forms are given biblical meaning. With syncretism, foreign forms are imported and the meaning is lost. To achieve effective cross-cultural transmission of the gospel, we must first "decontextualize" our faith tradition from centuries of sacred orthopraxy. This process can be uncomfortable and even disturbing for some. When bringing Jesus to another culture, for example, is it necessary to tell them that he was born on December 25, or could it be that this is completely irrelevant? (Easterners know it was actually January 6, if folks are really interested.) Must we teach people to pray as we learned in Sunday school—"Bow your heads, fold your hands, and close your eyes"? Never mind that people did the exact opposite in the Bible (e.g., John 17:1; 1 Tim 2:8). It is even more disturbing when we discover that some indigenous forms are better than our own and closer to biblical examples!

But still we are afraid—if we use indigenous forms, won't people be confused? How can we tell if syncretism is taking place? Another way to put this question is, How do we know if biblical meaning is being preserved? While there is no perfect way to test for this, three areas in particular are important to examine: salvation, allegiance, and transformation. As the process of contextualization is occurring in an indigenous movement, these three areas can provide clues as to which direction the movement is headed. These areas can be addressed with three questions: (1) Is salvation in something other than or in addition to Jesus? (2) Is allegiance to Christ alone? (3) Is the gospel transforming lives and society?

The all-sufficiency and supremacy of Jesus to save, restore, and redeem is the hallmark of every authentic gospel movement. The same issues that the early church had to wrestle with to keep the gospel pure and Jesus the main thing are present everywhere in the world. Jesus plus religion is the devil's playground. While religious traditions are not a bad thing in and of themselves, when they become substitutes for the real thing they stand as a hindrance to instead of a reinforcement of the truth. This is the greatest syncretism to be guarded against. It has nothing to do with what people are doing, in terms of religious practices and forms, but rather with what they are *thinking* about what they are doing. Syncretism at the worldview level is the most subtle and the most dangerous form, because it is hardest

Fear of Syncretism[*]

A major hindrance to many, especially those who have received theological instruction, is the fear that they might open the door to an aberrant form of Christianity. They see Latin American "christo-paganism" and shy away from what is called Christian but is not really. Fearing that if they deviate from the Western Christianity they have received, they are in danger of people carrying things too far, they fall back on the familiar and do nothing to change it, no matter how much misunderstanding there might be in the community of unbelievers concerning the real meanings of Christianity.

There are, however, at least two roads to syncretism: an approach that is too nativistic and an approach that is too dominated by foreignness. With respect to the latter, it is easy to miss the fact that Western Christianity is quite syncretistic when it is very intellectualized, organized according to foreign patterns, weak on the Holy Spirit and spiritual power, strong on Western forms of communication (e.g., preaching) and Western worship patterns, and imposed on non-Western peoples as if it were scriptural. It is often easier to conclude that a form of Christian expression is syncretistic when it looks too much like the receiving culture than when it looks "normal"—that is, Western.

But Western patterns are often farther from the Bible than non-Western patterns. And the amount of miscommunication of what the gospel really is can be great when people get the impression that ours is a religion rather than a faith and that, therefore, foreign forms are a requirement. To give that impression is surely syncretistic and heretical. I call this "communicational heresy."

But what about the concept of syncretism? Is this something that can be avoided, or is it a factor of human limitations and sinfulness? I vote for the latter and suggest that there is no way to avoid it. Wherever there are imperfect understandings made by imperfect people, there will be syncretism. That syncretism exists in all churches is not the problem. Helping people to move from where they are to more ideal expressions of Christian faith is what we need to address.

As long as we fear something that is inevitable, however, we are in bondage. I remember the words of one field missionary who was studying with us: "Until I stopped worrying about syncretism, I could not properly think about contextualization." Our advice to national leaders (and to missionaries), then, is to stop fearing syncretism. Deal with it in its various forms as a starting point, whether it has come from the receiving society or from the source society, and help people to move toward more ideal expressions of their faith.

—*Charles H. Kraft*

---

* Excerpt from Charles H. Kraft, "Why Isn't Contextualization Implemented?" in *Appropriate Christianity*, ed. Charles H. Kraft (Pasadena, CA: William Carey Library, 2005), 67–79. Reprinted by permission.

to detect and can persist for generations. This happens most often when foreign religious traditions and forms are imported and presented as the only way to follow Jesus. The attempt to Judaize believers in the Greek context forced Paul to write some of his strongest admonitions:

> Mark my words! I, Paul, tell you that if you let yourselves be circumcised, Christ will be of no value to you at all. (Gal 5:2)

> I am afraid that just as Eve was deceived by the serpent's cunning, your minds may somehow be led astray from your sincere and pure devotion to Christ. (2 Cor 11:3)

> But now that you know God—or rather are known by God—how is it that you are turning back to those weak and miserable principles? Do you wish to be enslaved by them all over again? You are observing special days and months and seasons and years! (Gal 4:9,10)

Again, the issue here is not the forms themselves but the importation of these forms. Paul continued to call himself a Pharisee after he became a believer; he went to the temple to make an offering, and even had Timothy circumcised (see Acts 23:6; 21:26; 16:3). The issue is how to bring Christ within culture and let him transform it from the inside out, rather than bringing Christ along with foreign religious traditions into a new context and expecting transformation to occur. Paul remained a Pharisee because he was a Pharisee—a Pharisee who followed Jesus. He never stopped being a Jew, but what he learned by the Spirit was that Greeks could follow Jesus as Greeks, have their own unique identity, and develop their own traditions—which would become quite distinct from the Jewish traditions.

Concluding Thoughts: The Role of Outsiders

In spite of the risks and inherent problems outsiders can create inside foreign cultures, apostolic workers can nonetheless make a very positive contribution, especially in the early years of an indigenous movement. This positive apostolic function often takes two principal forms. The first is in the role of the consultant who acts as a sounding board for difficult issues, especially as they relate to contextualization and cultural transformation. There may be blind spots, for example, that insiders are unable to see, or matters of biblical interpretation that the apostolic outsider has helpful background knowledge about. The second role is that of the defender, especially when external influences seek to take believers away from their "sincere and pure devotion to Christ" (2 Cor 11:3). We see both activities in the ministry of the Apostle Paul.

With regard to the first, we frequently find Paul giving Greek believers valuable perspective on how to respond to the decision of the Jerusalem Council in Acts 15. The Council exhorted them to "abstain from food sacrificed to idols" (v. 29). But Paul acts as a filter for this decision, helping Greeks understand how to apply it within the context of their freedom in Christ. He explains that the issue is not whether the food is contaminated—the issue is whether one's conscience is free and pure. So it is a motive issue, not a defiled meat issue.

With regard to the second role, in some instances Paul is quite forceful in his exhortation. He urges the Corinthian church to separate themselves from the Judaizers (2 Cor 6:17).[3] He commands them

---

3   This passage introduces a long discourse on false brethren seeking to infiltrate the community of believers and take away their freedom in Christ. These men are identified with the Judaizers in 2 Cor 11:22. The passage in 2 Cor 6 is therefore not talking about separating from the world, marrying nonbelievers, or whether to engage in

to not be yoked together with them. In some cases an outsider might be more aware of the dangers, especially when the outsider is an "insider" to the culture that is seeking to impose itself on others. In this case, Paul was very familiar with the intent and methods of the Judaizers, and he understood what was at stake for the gospel and the indigenous church. So he warned every Greek church: have nothing to do with these people—they are false brethren masquerading as followers of Christ (2 Cor 11:13).

Helping insiders navigate these difficult relational issues is one of the most valuable roles an outsider can play. There are relationships within the community, where varying levels of faith exist together; there are relationships with local believers involved in Western-related traditions; and there are the anti-contextualizers, who label insiders syncretists in order to compel them to accept a foreign religious tradition. Paul's forceful response to the Judaizers and his gracious response to insiders struggling with faith issues will prove a helpful guide to apostolic workers serving as consultants and liaisons for indigenous movements. Almost two thousand years later, we are still confronted with many of the same issues in missiology. Fortunately, we have an incredible guide in the form of the Scriptures to direct us in moving forward.

---

business with nonbelievers (though commonly applied to these issues as a proof text), but about separating from false brethren who are masquerading as believers.

CHAPTER 42

Avoiding Syncretism

The Testimony of a Jesus-following Buddhist*

Taweeporn Sarun

On Saturday, Dow and I were working to translate Bible study materials from English to Thai. We hit the word "syncretism" and had to work hard to find and to understand the meaning. The best we came up with was "a bird with two heads."[1]

If a new believer has clearly understood the gospel, and is free to remain in his or her old religious context, and attends all the religious activities, and appears to be involved in all the traditions and practices of that religion, isn't there a great danger that he or she will slip into syncretism, resulting in the worship of two or more gods? The answer is yes.

This is true of every context. A Western believer in Christ is in danger of loving God and also money (Matt 6:24). Or, as was present in Judaism and is maybe present in the church today, there was the syncretistic behavior of "neglecting the commandment of God" and "hold[ing] to the tradition of men." Jesus was also saying to them, "You are experts at setting aside the commandment of God in order to keep your tradition. For Moses said, 'Honor your father and your mother'" (Mark 7:8–10 NASB).

Here in Thailand, one of the greatest detriments of Christianity is the negative effect it has on the extended family who are Buddhists. So I have chosen to continue to live within Buddhism even though I am a loving, devoted follower of Christ.

Am I in danger of syncretism? Yes. Wednesday, before seeing Dow, I was with friends at a temple. I went into the temple and engaged in an activity called *tamboon*. Translated, it means "to make merit." You carry two *joss* sticks and a lotus flower and verbalize your desires. It might be thought of as a form of prayer, though you are not praying to someone, but hoping to change or improve your karma, good luck. I entered the area of tamboon with the joss sticks and flower and asked the God of heaven to bless my family and specifically to help my sister-in-law financially. She is struggling to keep her daughter in school. Because the economy is bad, her sales are down.

Friday was Macha Bucha day, a very important Buddhist holy day. I was walking a long distance to the market to buy some food. It was very hot. As I walked, many cars passed me by. The people who own these cars are not wealthy; they are just regular middle-class Thai people. I asked myself, "Why don't we have a car?" Then I thought, "When I get to the market I will do tamboon at the Chinese temple there. It is a very highly regarded temple, and tamboon there would be very good." Then I heard a clear voice in my heart say, "You do not need to go anywhere or do anything; your Father in heaven will take care of all your needs." This made me very excited for a moment. But then I thought that it

---

* Originally published in a slightly different form as "Syncretism," *MF*, May–June 2011. Reprinted by permission.

1 From *syn*, "with," and *kres*, "group, party," thus "merging two parties."

might just be wishful thinking. Maybe I did not really hear God speak. So I went to the market and went to the very entrance of the temple, and I heard the voice again. I chose to believe God and did not seek the "good luck" of tamboon.

After talking with Dow I recognized that both these events were very similar on the outside but very different on the inside. On the outside they both look to the observer's eye as possibly syncretistic. But on the inside, where it matters, only the second event was syncretistic. I trusted something other than God my Father for my well-being.

On Saturday evening, my sister-in-law called and told me that a man had entered her shop, bought all of the product in the shop, and also bought all the inventory in her warehouse. She was very excited that God heard and answered my prayers.

1. Haddad's article (chap. 32) poses huge challenges for Christians and the church. Are his conclusions realistic? What are some steps Christians can take to "liberate" Christ for other cultural and religious forms?

2. Pretend you are the "long-living, scholarly space visitor" in Walls' story (chap. 33). What stood out or surprised you as you visited each group of Christians from various contexts between 37 and 1980 CE? Has the expression or articulation of the gospel changed over time?

3. Mark Young (chap. 34) writes that "conservative evangelicals view contextualization warily because they suspect that it threatens belief in absolute, transcultural truth as revealed in the Bible," and that bounded-set theology is a form of social control. Do you agree with this assessment? What do you think constitutes "absolute, transcultural truth"?

4. How might centered-set theology create greater unity and understanding among Christians around the world? How might it create greater disunity and misunderstanding?

5. Living cross-culturally often shows us, perhaps for the first time (and painfully!), that we are selective in which parts of Scripture we regard as authoritative and which as cultural. How is this tendency different from responsible contextualization? How can we become better listeners to what God is revealing to people in this new context through his word?

6. In chapter 35, Ralph D. Winter states, "Everywhere Paul went, 'Judaizers' followed him and tried to destroy the insider movement he had established." Do you agree with this statement? Why or why not?

7. Do you believe a "Third Reformation" is here? Why or why not? What evidence might you use to support your view?

8. How would you define a religion? How does your definition contrast with others' conceptions? Does the Bible speak of faith in Jesus this way? In what sense, if any, can forms from two religious traditions be integrated and not violate Scripture?

9. What instances of syncretism do you see in Western contexts? How does one determine what is syncretistic or not? Give some examples of cultural accommodation that is not theologically syncretistic.

10. When people first accept Christ as Lord, it is possible to completely avoid syncretism? How can we challenge syncretism while allowing the Holy Spirit to work among new communities of believers? Are you open to people challenging syncretism in your own life?

APPROACHES IN WITNESS

INTRODUCTION TO PART 5

> How far should one go in identifying with another people? . . . Just
> as far as our conscience will allow us to go.
>
> —WILBUR STONE[*]

Our study now shifts to the strategies, aims, methods, and approaches of ministry related to insider movements.

Chapter 43 features a report by Henry H. Riggs, who addressed the 1938 Near East Christian Council's inquiry into the endemic failure of evangelism and church planting among Muslims. "Shall We Try Unbeaten Paths in Working for Moslems?" outlined the contours of what we now refer to as the IM paradigm.

In 1969 Southern Baptist missionary Virginia Cobb prepared a position paper on missionary methods for the Tehran Conference; we have included it here as chapter 44 and entitled it "An Approach to Witness." Cobb's call resonates with the aims and approach of those involved in insider movements.

In chapter 45, a classic work of scholarship on contextualization, J. Dudley Woodberry documents the Jewish and Christian origins of the five pillars of Islamic religious practice. Given those origins, he argues for the appropriateness of their reuse by Muslim disciples of Jesus.

In chapter 46, Martin Accad explores Christian approaches toward Islam and Muslims. Employing a scale of syncretistic, polemical, existential, and apologetic approaches, he proposes a more evenhanded, suprareligious, "kerygmatic" position.

Chapter 47, a contribution by John and Anna Travis, outlines seven key roles that have been played by "alongsiders" in laying groundwork for, facilitating, or supporting insider movements.

Chapter 48, a major revision of Harley Talman's article "Become Like, Remain Like," presents the Apostle Paul's two-pronged incarnational mission strategy.

In chapter 49, Alex Smith argues for a return to the original approach of "evangelizing whole families," an approach that was changed after the Protestant Reformation. What Smith advocates is also characteristic of insider movements, which occur as the gospel moves along natural relational networks.

Finally, in chapter 50, Tim and Rebecca Lewis illustrate the effectiveness of a family approach to church planting among Muslims, which contrasts with contemporary Western models.

---

[*] "Islamic Studies—The Insider's Approach" (unpublished paper), 7. A version of this paper was later published as chap. 24 in *World Mission in the Wesleyan Spirit*, ed. Darrell L. Whiteman and Gerald H. Anderson (Franklin, TN: Providence House, 2009).

Shall We Try Unbeaten Paths in Working for Moslems?*

Henry H. Riggs

During the years 1936 to 1938 the Near East Christian Council conducted an Inquiry into the causes of the "relative sterility" of efforts for the conversion of Moslems. Questionnaires were sent out and the replies received were tabulated and sent out again for comment and criticism. This Inquiry was prompted by a deep concern over the fact that, with certain conspicuous exceptions, work has gone on among Moslems decade after decade without the creation of a true indigenous church, or any considerable number of converts out of which such a church might conceivably be formed.

The Inquiry started with the conviction that if, first, the causes for failure could be studied and courageously brought out into the open, then, secondly, that might open the way for discovering new methods or lines of approach which might overcome or avoid those obstacles, so as to lead to a more fruitful effort in this field.

With regard to the first question, the results of the Inquiry were very gratifying. From replies which came from Christian workers of many ways of thinking, there emerges a fairly clear and united statement of what those causes of failure are. The Report of the Inquiry says, on this subject:

The replies received have had a cumulative effect in focusing attention upon two *special* hindrances, which appear adequate to explain the lack of success pointed out:

1. *Christian teaching does not mean the same to the Moslem that it does to the Christian.* The Moslem mind has been conditioned by definite teaching against a distorted conception of Christianity; so that some of the most essential elements of the Christian message mean to the Moslem things that are repulsive to him, and would be equally inacceptable to the Christian if he saw them in the same way. What is divine truth in the mind of the Christian worker, as it reaches the mind of the Moslem listener is a falsehood which he rightly rejects. Illustrations:

a. The Christian believes that Jesus is the Son of God, and this is frequently regarded as the crucial test of the acceptance of Christ. To the Christian this means something about Jesus. He is that kind of a being. His character, his power, his peerless teaching proclaim a being who, in that peculiar sense "came forth from God." The Moslem thinks of none of these things. His mind turns to the question "Can God beget children?" For him to say yes means degrading God. He insists that God is not carnal but spiritual and absolute.

b. Christian faith centers around the belief that Christ is divine. The more intimately we come to know Christ, the more vivid is "Our conviction that he is 'God made flesh.'" But the Moslem, when he hears of the deity of Christ, is immediately driven away from a consideration of his wonderful person,

---

* Originally published in a slightly different form in *The Moslem World* 31, no. 2 (April 1941): 116–26. Public domain. Archaic spellings (e.g., "Moslem") and usages reflect the era in which the report was written.

because his mind is filled with the thoughts, "God is one, not two or three." And to even think of any other as divine is the horrible sin of *shirk*. Similarly and for the same reason, the blessed and mighty work of the Holy Spirit can mean to the Moslem nothing of what it means to the Christian, as a part of the doctrine of the Trinity.

c. The terrible pollution of sin, power to overcome sin, and the forgiveness of sin through Christ; these things are tremendously real to the Christian. But the Moslem is not impressed by our message about sin; first because of the different words used by Moslem and Christian and also because, to him, sin is a matter in an entirely different sphere; to be forgiven, to be freed, means to him merely a relaxation of the strict requirements of the Absolute Sovereign.

d. Similarly the Moslem who hears of the Atonement cannot think of "God in Christ reconciling the world unto himself." He has been taught to deny the death of Christ on the ground that it would be wrong for God to permit a sinless person to suffer for others.

2. In the thought of the Moslem, a change of religion is primarily a change of group connection and group loyalty. "Every convert to Christianity is a dead loss to the community." "The Moslem Community is a noble and sacred thing, a social-political-religious fellowship for which the believer is willing to give his life." "The greatest handicap against which the Christian Missionary has to strive is the power of Moslem solidarity." "There are thousands of men and women who believe in Christ and are trying to follow him, but they cannot bring themselves to face the break with their own community."

The great fact pointed out in these statements is very evident. But is this unwillingness to break with their own community due only to lack of courage or conviction? Not always. Many cases have been reported of true believers in Christ who have refused to break with the Moslem community because they wish to live among their own people to make Christ known to them!

But even where the deterrent is fear or unwillingness to take the consequences, it is still true that this bond of Brotherhood is one of the strongest bulwarks of Islam; and so long as the Christian missionary undertaking appears to be a frontal attack against this great and (to the Moslem) precious fellowship, so long that powerful instrument will effectively oppose the progress of the gospel.

We cannot forget that the sad history of the conflict between Islam and Christendom, past and present, makes it inevitable that the Moslem should see in our missionary zeal, merely a part of the imperialistic arrogance to which he has become accustomed; and with his mental equipment we cannot expect him to distinguish between the political and the spiritual elements of imperialism. It is a very sobering thought for all of us to reflect that possibly, if we could see our own spirit as it actually is, we might find that the Moslem is not altogether wrong in sensing a spiritual arrogance in our effort to bring him to leave his own group and join ours.

✣

The replies to the second question were far less conclusive and united. They revealed very deep differences of opinion, not so much on the primary question, "What methods or lines of approach offer hopes of better success?" as on the secondary aspect of the question, which might be stated as, "Is it wise and right for us to try some of the new methods suggested?" Discussion which has followed the publication of this report has served to accentuate rather than to bridge those differences of opinion; and also to divert attention from the main results of the inquiry.

In the Conference on Moslem work held in Delhi in early December, 1938, and in the Moslem Lands Group at the Tambaram Conference immediately following it, the Report was brought up for discussion. In both Conferences discussion was almost entirely devoted to a few of the suggestions, mainly regarding unbaptized believers. Objections to the encouragement of such believers were so urgent as to crowd out almost entirely any real consideration of the underlying principles quoted above. These facts are here stated in order to call attention to the fact, later pointed out by The Near East Christian Council itself, that the following suggestions do not represent accepted plans, but only the opinions of individuals so expressed.

In answer to the second question, "What methods or lines of approach offer hope of better success?" suggestions have been mainly along two lines.

The first is, "The way to overcome these hindrances is more devotion, more effort, more prayer, more faith, and above all, more love." Many and moving expressions of this conviction have come in, and point to the fact that we who would win others to Christ must look first of all to our own faithfulness and consistency as witnesses for Christ.

But other suggestions have come in along quite another line. "We must try to find a way around these obstacles," so that we shall not be in the position of attacking Islam frontally, and at its strongest points. These suggestions involve very serious changes in our approach, and should be studied with particular care, keeping in mind, of course, that differing conditions due to political situations and cultural background in different parts of the Near East make the answer found in one area perhaps inapplicable in another.

These suggestions are based upon the belief that it is possible and it is necessary to recast our message and approach to Moslems so that, without relaxing our effort as messengers of Christ, we may win them to him without overcoming the special obstacles described. Our aim is one—to bring men into direct and personal relationship with Jesus Christ, as Teacher, Saviour and Lord. If this is accomplished, all else can be left to the guidance of the indwelling Christ, whose Spirit works such "diversity of manifestation."

The following proposals are put forward for study, prayer and experiment, as possible ways to attain the goal.

1. *To avoid the obstacle of the Moslem antagonism to the main Christian doctrines;*

a. A sympathetic understanding of the mind and heart of Moslems is a prime necessity for anyone who would bring to them the message of Jesus Christ. Anyone who unthinkingly presents the gospel only from the point of view of the Christian, without understanding what it will mean to the Moslem, becomes responsible for results which in many cases have proved to be absolutely the opposite of what was intended.

b. Our one effort must be to make Jesus Christ effectively known to the Moslem. Islam has already provided imperfect knowledge of Jesus, and a certain reverence for him. But we must start with that very imperfect knowledge and proceed to enrich it from the gospel story and from the experience of the Christian life, till they can see him as he is. We must guard carefully against the premature introduction of thoughts which will divert the attention of the inquirer from Christ himself. His reverence will grow to adoration as he becomes acquainted with Christ, and with his power in the life of those who surrender to him.

c. In view of the almost certain misunderstandings resulting from the discussion of doctrines, doctrinal questions need to be handled with extreme care, remembering that Christ's method left his own disciples to formulate the deepest truths for themselves under God's guidance, and he himself said, "Upon this rock will I build my church." Public proclamation of our most cherished beliefs to those unprepared to understand them too often leads to an indignant rejection which closes the heart to the appeal of Christ himself.

d. Get the inquirer to study the New Testament, and especially the Gospels, as the adequate and original source and authority for the understanding of Jesus. Do not urge him to accept our interpretations.

2. *To avoid the obstacles which result from the ancient jealousy between the Christian and the Moslem group-organizations;*

a. Remembering that deep suspicion separates these two groups, we need to overcome that suspicion by a frankness and absolute honesty in which acts and words conform to what we profess to hold as our purpose. At all costs we must avoid anything which the inquirer or his neighbors may interpret as clandestine efforts to alienate him from his own people. In this matter the circulation of literature other than the Scripture should be done with understanding watchfulness.

b. It is the conviction of a large number of workers among Moslems that the ultimate hope of bringing Christ to the Moslems is to be attained by the development of groups of followers of Jesus who are active in making him known to others while remaining loyally a part of the social and political groups to which they belong in Islam. The ideal is that there should thus come into being a church whose only head is Christ, and which does not carry the stigma of being an alien institution, drawing men away from their natural social and political connections. In spite of the stupendous difficulties in the way of such an outcome, many workers are convinced that only as the spiritual significance of Christ is thus separated from external and unhappy connections in past and present can the way be opened for the power of Christ to do its work in the Moslem world.

c. To such followers of Jesus the term "secret believer" has been applied, sometimes with a degree of deprecation. To clarify our attitude towards such believers it might be stated that we lovingly encourage secret believers to go forward in the Christian life without publicly professing themselves as Christians in the sense of separation from the fellowship of their own people. But the purpose of such a course is to make possible a more effective witness, in life, in words, and in the reading of the Gospels, to the power of Christ in their own lives, among their own people. Experience has shown that unless such effective witness develops into a group of such believers, a solitary believer seldom survives. The essential function of the church can never be ignored. The aspiration here expressed is that the church of Christ might take root within the social-political body called Islam, and not as an alien body encroaching from without.

d. If such a line of effort is to be followed, certain very practical questions must be met. The first is that the name Christian, in the Near East, has almost exclusively a racial, political and social group-connotation, and does not suggest either a new way of life or a spiritual rebirth within. If a group of believers is to grow up as indigenous and not alien, they cannot take on themselves that particular name. Some other terminology must be developed.

e. Similarly, baptism is almost universally recognized as the sign of the definite transfer to a new group-connection, and is thus the inevitable signal for casting out the convert from the fellowship of his own people. It does not mean, to the Moslem, as it does to the Christian, repentance, a new birth, and total surrender to our Lord. There are some who believe that some spiritual equivalent of baptism, free from the false significance which has grown up in the thought of the Moslem, can and must be devised.

f. The Moslem community life includes such matters as marriage and divorce, inheritance, etc. Unless a convert is officially transferred to the Christian registry, he is confronted with serious problems in reconciling his new life with such non-Christian relationships. Faith and great patience, with God's guidance, must solve these and many other problems of personal status.

g. But the greatest unsolved problem in this connection is that of providing spiritual fellowship and nurture for believers who thus remain a part of their Moslem social-political group. Without such fellowship and nurture the new believers seem doomed to lapse into the old way of life and thought. The hope for such a solution seems to lie along two lines: (i) That indigenous Christians develop such a loving and sympathetic relationship with their neighbors that such spiritual fellowship might grow up without raising the question of propaganda and the transfer of group-loyalties. (ii) That young missionaries, in the spirit of self-emptying which brought our Lord into this world, might overcome the barrier between Christian foreigner and Moslem native by "growing up" among Moslem people. Remember the words of the almost-persuaded non-Christian to the missionary, "If I could feel that you love me as much as you care for my soul, it might have been different."

✤

The two quotations given above cover the Findings of this Inquiry. The rest of the Report was made up of an explanatory introduction and extended quotations from comments received in the course of the study.

The reason for repeating this material at this time is the conviction that the results of this inquiry deserve more calm and purposeful consideration than they have thus far received. Much earnest thought and prayer and labor on the part of many busy Christian workers went into this effort. It would be a sad waste if the controversial nature of some of the issues raised should be permitted to prevent adequate consideration of the main issue. Every Christian working among Moslems should face honestly the facts pointed out concerning the two main obstacles noted. Is our present activity actually drawing men to Christ, or repelling them from him? If the latter, wherein are we responsible, by using the wrong methods, for bringing about the defeat of our purposes, and the purposes of our Master?

To facilitate this further study, I would venture to restate the practical suggestions on which there has been the most vigorous difference of opinion:

1. That in view of the inescapable distortion of ideas about the formal statement of Christian doctrine, all discussion of doctrinal matters should be avoided so far as possible, and that our message should be concerned with Christ's way of living, and the power of Christ himself to enable us to live such lives.

2. That because the name "Christian" is universally understood to refer to racial, political and social group-connections, those who would accept Christ should not be urged to take that name upon themselves.

3. That because the rite of baptism has, in the minds of most people in the Near East, no relation to the beginning of a new life, but is solely the mark of transfer to the Christian community, the use of that rite for the Moslem convert be discontinued.

With regard to points 2 and 3 it has been agreed by all that active witness for Christ, and some form of fellowship among believers, are essential for the Christian life. If these external forms are to be relinquished, these essentials of witness and fellowship must be assured within the Moslem environment—admittedly a most difficult problem to be worked out.

So much for the Moslem Inquiry conducted by the Near East Christian Council, with the word of caution that the Report is emphatically not a pronouncement of the Council, but a collection of personal opinions and suggestions. Along the same line I wish now to add some suggestions of my own, quite unconnected with what has gone before. First, I wish to plead that we, as followers of Christ, should cease to think of Islam as an adversary to be overcome, and recognize it as an ally in the spiritual world-crisis of today. As never before, the issue is being drawn between God and no-god, between life guided by moral Realities and life controlled by selfishness unrestrained. In this struggle Islam and Christianity stand shoulder to shoulder. Some of us have been shamed to find that the Moslem has been the first to realize this: as when, more than once, a brokenhearted Moslem has appealed to me, a Christian missionary, for sympathy and advice in the presence of growing atheism and moral break-down among his own people.

Something analogous to this has come to pass in our relationship to the Oriental Churches. Some of us can remember when we, as Protestant missionaries, felt that it was our task to pluck individuals out of those churches, as brands from the burning; and we felt a secret uneasiness at anything which strengthened those churches so as to make the plucking more difficult. That day has happily passed, and we now greatly rejoice at the daily growing strength of those same churches, and are thankful if we can help them, both personally and in the training of their leaders, always in loyalty to the old Churches, to which we look as the greatest hope for the coming of the kingdom among their people.

The two cases are not parallel, let us admit; but they are certainly analogous. "Islam" is a noble name for the faith which Moslems and Christians alike inherit from the earliest Monotheism, and which, down the ages, has stood like a rock against the way of life which knows no higher law than self. Most of us have thought in terms of drawing men away from Islam, of gradually undermining and ultimately overthrowing this great structure. Is there not a better way? Can we not rid ourselves of our instinctive feeling of antagonism to Islam as an organism, and think in terms of its regeneration from within? Can we not sincerely give ourselves to the effort to strengthen those forces that tend toward such regeneration?

It is indeed a staggering question to ask how we can aim to strengthen Islam and still be loyal to Jesus our Master. Light on this subject seems to come from a fact noted by one of the speakers at the Hartford Conference[1] who pointed out that Islam has shown a marvellous power to assimilate alien elements into its own life. In various ages it has assimilated philosophy and science and morality from other systems, and has been strengthened thereby. It is not unreasonable to expect that Islam will yet assimilate other and better elements; in fact, that process is going on apace, at several points, which might be mentioned.

There is no essential reason why Islam might not, for its own strengthening, assimilate Jesus Christ.

In direct contradiction to that statement seems to stand the fact of Mohammed. I do not think that it falls to me, or to any other Christian, to discuss that problem. It belongs to those whose loyalty to Mohammed or to Christ is to be made real in their lives. But this can be said: for the Moslem, Mohammed is not a living leader, but a dead hero. They do not call themselves "Mohammedans," and great as is their reverence for him as their prophet, their conception of him is more or less idealized, according to the light which individuals have found on the meaning of his life.

On the other hand, written into the Koran is the acceptance of Jesus as a messenger from God, and of the Gospel as his message. Why should it be thought inconceivable that it might some day become a vital part of the teaching of Islam that the Jesus-way of living is the hope of the world, and that the

---

1   Dr. J. E. Merrill, "The Christian Witness to Moslems." [This is the extent of the documentation provided in Riggs' report. The reference is presumably to Rev. John E. Merrill, a Congregational minister with the American Board of Commissioners for Foreign Missionaries who served in Turkey and Syria.—Ed.]

still-living Jesus is the vital power to make that way of life a reality? These are, after all, the essential messages of our faith. It seems an impossible dream, but it is impossible only with men, that some day the mollah in his mosque may be preaching his most powerful sermons on "The Prophet Jesus, on him be peace!" Some day Moslem scholars may unite in a serious and honest effort to discover the original Gospel, which tradition says has been lost. From documents written centuries before Mohammed's day they will try to reconstruct the "Gospel" which Mohammed so revered. This reconstruction may not exactly correspond to our New Testament canon; but it would surely put into the hands of Moslems, as a part of their own literature, an adequate picture, from authentic sources, of Jesus and his teaching.

But after all, our purpose is not to look at beautiful dreams; what are we *doing* to make them come true? Already, in many scattered places, there are points where this assimilation of Jesus Christ is taking place. Individuals whom many of us know, and countless others known only to God, have found new life in Christ, but are still a part of their own community. Some, it is true, have not dared to come out; but others, very courageously, have dared to remain among their own, with the definite purpose of working for this assimilation within that great fellowship. Thus far we have given them scant encouragement. We have stood guard, with our creeds and our shibboleths and labels, and, as many a missionary can testify from heartbreaking experience, one by one these flickering flames have been snuffed out, for the lack of a word of courage and understanding sympathy! May God forgive us!

There is much that we can do, when we sincerely turn to the ministry of helpfulness. The heart-hungry Moslem who talks with a Christian friend might go away, not feeling that he has been, bluntly or subtly, enticed away from his faith, but inspired with a new hope of what that faith may mean to him and to his people. What would it mean if every student who goes out from a Christian school with a new vision of life and service could somehow be sent forth with an enthusiasm to build his best into his own community, and that best could include all that he has seen and sensed during his school days of what Jesus really does to the lives and spirits of people! And so with all our contacts with Moslems. Now there is always the disturbing undercurrent of mutual suspicion that our friendliness is but a veil over an ulterior purpose; or a doubt that that ulterior purpose ought to be pursued, if it is not. If Moslem and Christian could in perfect frankness and sincerity work together, understanding that what we have to offer is sincerely offered without any demand for a return, then we could truly help. Not tentatively and with reservations, but with all that zeal and self-sacrifice with which our fathers labored along other lines, we could then work for the coming of God's reign among his worshipers, the Moslems.

After all, this situation is not new. John, like many of us, forbade the unknown wonder-worker "because he followeth not us." Jesus said, "Forbid him not." The crux of the matter was that through that stranger, whatever his name or allegiance, the power of Christ was working miracles. Wherever, today, that same power is working its miracles in a transformed life, God grant us the breadth of heart that our Master showed, so that we may be able to forget that "he followeth not us," and not only "forbid him not," but lovingly strengthen, inspire and guide those who would follow Jesus within the great fellowship of Islam.

CHAPTER 44

An Approach to Witness[*]

Virginia Cobb

In advance of the Tehran Conference of June 1969, fellow missionaries in Lebanon asked missionary Virginia Cobb to prepare their position paper on missionary methods for work among Muslims.

Detained in Beirut, Lebanon, by illness, Miss Cobb did not reach Tehran in time to present her paper to the conference. It was read for her by missionary J. W. (Bill) Trimble and by conference consensus was named "the" paper of the meeting. The hope was expressed by all present that Miss Cobb's paper could be given wide circulation among Baptists and other Christians.

This paper might well be called a part of the legacy of the late Miss Cobb. Its message is by no means limited to missionaries among Muslims, or just to missionaries, for that matter. Its advice is so scripturally basic that it can apply to Christian witness anywhere. At the same time, because it seeks to avoid traditions in order to major on the Person of the gospel, it may be adversely criticized or even rejected by some.

⁘

Often where we have no answer we can have an attitude that will lead us as we search for the answers. This is the view of Dr. Kenneth Cragg, a missionary teacher and writer.

What should be our attitude as Christians toward Muslims?

Attitude

We are not warring with Islam. If we were, we couldn't afford to give any quarter, to let anything go unchallenged, to admit any good or truth. We would be happy to damage it as much as possible, to show every weakness or inconsistency. But this is contrary to the spirit of Christ. And a major error in any struggle is to pursue the wrong enemy. Our enemy is evil, God's enemy. Islam teaches love of God, supreme loyalty to him, great reverence, and high principles of character.

One strong criticism of Christian missions has been that they have destroyed men's faith in Islam without winning those men to Christ, leaving them much worse off. It cannot be God's will that we leave men in worse condition than we found them! And it should not be necessary. A sincere Muslim is nearer to God and to Christ than a man with no faith. Christianity, like Islam, has produced wars, persecutions, bigotry, and empty forms; we do not, therefore, war against it, but seek a truer understanding of it.

---

[*] Originally published in a slightly different form in *The Commission* 32, no. 9 (September 1970): 5–9. Used by permission from the International Mission Board. The introduction (italicized) appeared with the original magazine article.

We are not debating with Islam to prove that our views are correct and theirs incorrect. Were we, we might rely on polemics, logical proofs, etc. But no one is won by this method or convinced against his will. This approach makes the basic mistake of acting as if Christian faith were credence rather than commitment to a Person, an act of the intellect rather than of the whole person. It ignores the fact that our doctrines came about as an attempt to explain in comprehensible terms our experience; i.e., they follow, rather than precede, experience.

We are not trying to change anyone's religion. Religion consists of affiliation with a group, cult, ethic, dogma, and structure of authority—clergy, book, orthodoxy. The New Testament is quite clear that none of these saves. It is possible to change all of them without knowing God. If we stress these we may give the impression that these things *are* the Christian faith.

Our attitude should be one of *love and acceptance.* God accepts and loves them as they are. He is already reconciled to them, "not counting their trespasses against them" (2 Cor 5:19 RSV). If we, the

Digging Wells or Building Fences[*]

A visitor to an Australian outback cattle ranch was intrigued by the seemingly endless miles of farming country with no sign of any fences. He asked a local rancher how he kept track of his cattle. The rancher replied, "Oh, that's no problem. Out here we dig wells instead of building fences."

The implication, I hope, is obvious. There is no need to fence cattle in when they are highly motivated to stay within range of water, their most important source of life.

. . . It is much more realistic and helpful to think of Christianity as a centred set, a set defined by movement towards the centre, the person of Jesus. Now, conversion is the point at which a person turns towards the centre and begins the journey. That new, fragile follower of Jesus (about whom he or she may know very little) is as much part of the centred set as is the missionary who told him the gospel story. The fact that the missionary has a degree in theology is irrelevant to defining the set. The fact that they are both moving towards the central goal is what matters.

Bounded sets are static. Once within the set, no further attention to definition or development is needed. A Granny Smith apple is a Granny Smith apple whether it is ripe or unripe, rotten or shriveled up. Those factors may be very significant to the consumer of the apple—but they have no bearing on its designation as a member of the set.

What I am suggesting is that it is both more biblical and more risky to entertain a centred-set approach to Christian faith. Centred-set Christianity is defined by active, dynamic relationship to Jesus. There is no place in centred-set Christianity for us to shelter behind the fence of theological orthodoxy, denominational superiority, or a verbal assent to gospel values which bears no resemblance to lifestyle.

Jesus clearly does not undervalue doctrine or the study of scripture or verbal commitment. But what he does is to indicate that they cannot be used as "fences" to define disciples. The emphasis throughout the gospels is never primarily on what theological understanding people had but on whether they were willing to follow Jesus.

—Sheila Pritchard

---

* Excerpt from Sheila Pritchard, "Wells or Fences? A Paradigm for Spiritual Growth," *Concentric Circles* (blog), July 11, 2011, http://sheilapritchard.blogspot.com/2011_07_01_archive.html.

ministers of his reconciliation, are "reconciled" to them, we will accept them as persons as able as ourselves and as deserving of respect and a hearing for their views. We will not go to straighten them out or tell them all the answers. If we are reconciled to them, we will be able to appreciate all that is true, good, commendable, and worthy in their lives as individuals and in their culture and religion.

We need stronger *faith in the power of the truth.* It is in no danger from the fullest, best possible expression of contrary views, from the teaching of the Qur'an, or from comparison, scrutiny, or the honest admission of the failures of historic Christianity or of Christian people. Nor is it in danger if we forego the temptation to defend the nonessential, secondary parts of our beliefs and practices in order to keep the door open for discussion and emphasis on the (very few) essentials. Our insecurity and defensive attitude only hinder.

We need stronger faith in the reality of the living Christ. Everything does not depend on us. We do not have to present and gain assent to a complete system of theology and ethic. Some early disciples were content to say, "Come and see." If we introduce them to a living Person, he will draw them, reveal himself to them, and teach them directly.

Contact

Identification

Christ in his incarnation came to dwell in the midst of those he came to save, and became like them in everything but sin. This meant a full entering into the life of the people. It meant speaking their language, using terms and concepts they understood, dealing with problems they faced and values they held.

This principle cannot be applied by setting up a meeting place and inviting people to come. It cannot be applied by living in relative isolation from them, in a separate quarter, or with little day-to-day contact. It cannot be applied by using the terminology Christians have grown accustomed to and others do not know (Holy Spirit, rebirth, etc.).

It means close association, sharing in everything possible, and an awareness of their concerns, problems, hopes, value system. Speaking their language means not just grammar and syntax but studying their culture and religion to learn the terms and values they comprehend.

Love

Christ's love was a genuine concern for the total welfare of those he came to save. It was demonstrated, not spoken. It was not limited to salvation from judgment but included healing, moral teaching, crossing of social barriers, comforting, calming, freeing, touching the untouchables, and befriending sinners. He did these things not merely as bait, but in many instances where no mention is made of "evangelism."

To love as he did means seeking the good of others in every sphere, actively and without reciprocation, without even appreciation, without conversions. It means accepting the inconvenience or hurt they may cause us without lessening our positive efforts on their behalf. Perhaps the only way we can prove—to ourselves or others—that we love in this way is to be really concerned about the "this-worldly" welfare of some who reject the message, to feel real friendship for some outside the circle of believers, to keep on serving those we feel will not be won.

How can we expect a Muslim to accept a bare statement of a belief so different, against which he is already conditioned, with no demonstration of its power or meaning? What would be required to make *you* give serious consideration to another religion? God won us by coming to us and outloving our enmity. We can only present his gospel by going to them and outloving their suspicion, enmity, and rejection.

Therefore, there must be *some concrete demonstration of love.* It can be personal, in the relationship between friends, or institutional—schools, hospitals, English classes, reading rooms, community centers (manned by the right people), radio programs, and publications that are directed to real human needs. We have seen in two different types of Muslim neighborhoods in Beirut that community service projects will draw overwhelming numbers, open to friendship and understanding, willing to listen to whatever is said tactfully. The services rendered must be a sincere expression of concern, *with no other motive.* Active, unselfish service in the name of Christ is more likely to win converts than zealous "preaching for results," which often turns persons away.

Law of Reciprocity

Jesus clearly taught that we are in some measure able to control, and therefore responsible for, the type of response we elicit (Luke 6:37,38). If we give genuine friendship, openness to all that is good, respect and sensitivity for all that is dear to others, we may expect the same. If we go with closed minds, rejection of their ideas, suspicion, fear, or superiority, we may expect the same. If we refuse to listen in the truest sense, can we expect them to listen? The example of our attitude toward Islam may set the pattern for their attitude toward Christianity.

Rapport

Here *attitude is all-important.* For if we make contact or have Muslims in our institutions or services, and then show an attitude of superiority or condemnation or enmity, or show disrespect to what is sacred to them, we not only lose them but create further animosity. Our relationship with them should be such as to inspire confidence in our sincere desire to serve them, our fair-mindedness, sensitivity, and appreciation of all that is good. We should emphasize every point of agreement, encourage every true direction, praise all that is praiseworthy, put the best possible interpretation on every teaching or practice.

Our message is a Person we've experienced, not a doctrine, system, religion, book, church, ethic. Christ is extremely attractive to Muslims. They have the highest respect for him and yearn to know more about him. We can present the person Jesus and his teachings as our supreme and only emphasis, the only thing we have to add to the foundation of reverence for God and moral emphasis already found

Bounded Sets vs. Centered Sets[*]

In the bounded set, it is clear who is in and who is out, based on a well-defined ideological-cultural boundary—usually moral and cultural codes as well as creedal definitions . . . but it doesn't have much of a core definition beyond these boundaries. It is hard at the edges, soft at the center. [The centered set] is like the Outback ranch with the wellspring at its center. It has very strong ideology at the center but no boundaries. It is hard at the center, soft at the edges. We suggest that in the centered set lies a real clue to the structuring of missional communities in the emerging global culture and corresponding missional church.

—*Michael Frost and Alan Hirsch*

---

[*]   Michael Frost and Alan Hirsch, *The Shaping of Things To Come: Innovation and Mission for the 21st Century Church* (Peabody, MA: Hendrickson, 2003), 206–8.

in Islam. Our faith in him is that once we lead a person to him, he will, in direct contact with that person, transform and guide in all else.

What of doctrines related to Christ himself? Jesus didn't insist on a certain view of himself as prerequisite to discipleship. He called men to follow him unconditionally, and after two years of living with them asked what their conclusion was. He used the same method of induction with John the Baptist. It is safe to leave people to draw their own conclusions after sincerely seeking to know Christ and experience him.

"Seek ye first the kingdom" means that all else can be and must be sacrificed for the highest goal. We have many valued truths and emphases that may have to be left out of our efforts with others until long after they have come to know Christ for themselves, laying upon them "no greater burden than these necessary things" (Acts 15:28 RSV). Many of our institutional forms as well as the details of doctrine hinder more than they help people coming from a different way of life, while Christ and his teachings attract with power. We must lay aside the weight of nonessentials for the sake of the essential.

Decision

Christ presented the truth, the call, but never persuaded. He let men come to decision in personal freedom, and even discouraged some who misunderstood what was involved. We teach the competence and responsibility of every individual and, therefore, must urge each person to do only and exactly what he is convinced in his own heart he must do. We can only emphasize his responsibility before God to obey his best light. If he feels he should be a more faithful Muslim, we should encourage him to do so to the best of his ability, and to try to understand what that means in the fullest sense. If he feels he should try to follow Christ's teachings, we should encourage that, and wait until he feels the need for something more.[1] When he feels he should commit himself to Christ regardless of the cost, we should encourage that and stand by him in facing the dangers that may follow.

The convert and the seeker need real fellowship. They have severe "culture shock" and need dependable, understanding friends. Since the national churches at present are very slow to provide this, and the Muslim often remains a relative outsider even if baptized, there may need to be other arrangements for fellowship—small groups or personal contacts.

Some converts may feel they can do more good by remaining within their own community, although in informal contact and fellowship with Christians. Jesus called no one to leave Judaism, and the first Christians remained in synagogue and temple for some time. Our responsibility is to maintain the ties of fellowship and personal support.

Who? The national believers are now showing a little more interest in reaching non-Christians. However, their attitude is usually more likely to alienate than win. Therefore we must take the lead in the approach described here, even in opposition to national Christian opinion.

However, a secondary aim and effect of our ministry to Muslims will be helping national believers to overcome prejudice by personal acquaintance with others. When they really know some Muslims, many are wise enough and kind enough to change those things in their approach and attitude that offend. They will then develop their own methods of presenting Christ to Muslims.

---

1   I.e., ". . . and wait until he feels the need for something more" should characterize our attitude of respect and expectant hope.—Ed.

Results

The effectiveness of the truth and the drawing power of Christ are sufficient to guarantee that some will be won in these ways. However, we have centuries of Christian enmity and harshness and rejection of Islam to atone for and undo; we have walls of prejudice built up through the centuries to break down; we have deeply ingrained attitudes in both Christians and Muslims to change. Many years of friendship, love, service, with reciprocation and without much fruit, may be required before there exists a better atmosphere for the open sharing of views and open commitment to Christ. We must be willing to pay this price also.

Summary

We must have an attitude of love and acceptance, and strong faith in the power of the truth.

We must get into the midst of people, identify with them, and love them in deed, not word, in some concrete ways.

We must emphasize Christ as a living person, and leave all else in a secondary position.

We must talk openly, freely, and respectfully of religious matters, whether in regard to our religion or theirs, and emphasize the responsibility of the individual to God, to act according to his own best light.

We must do these things patiently for many years, regardless of the immediate results.

CHAPTER 45

Contextualization among Muslims
*Reusing Common Pillars**
J. Dudley Woodberry

As I stood recently in the great mosque in Qairawan in present-day Tunisia, I looked at the collection of pillars from various sources that had been organized together into one harmonious whole. The early Muslim builders had freely incorporated pillars from previous Christian churches, as was also done elsewhere in the empire.[1] The columns were modified and whitewashed so that they would blend into their new home.

These pillars illustrate what also took place in early Muslim religious observance, for what have come to be known as the "pillars" of Islam are all adaptations of previous Jewish and Christian forms. If this fact were better understood, some of the current Muslim and Christian reaction to contextualization should be alleviated, for it would not seem artificial.

The present study looks first at some current plans or blueprints that have been drawn up for using these pillars of faith and the reaction that they have elicited from Muslims and Christians. Then an attempt will be made to add to this material in two ways. First, we shall look more closely at the previous use of these pillars by Jews and Christians to see the extent to which we can reutilize what was originally our own. Secondly, we shall evaluate a contemporary people movement to Christ among Muslims where the believers are adapting the pillars of their previous faith to bear the weight of their new faith in Christ.

Present Plans for the Pillars

Present formulations of Christian worship that utilize forms that are familiar to Muslims have arisen as Muslim converts have felt uncomfortable in existing churches and as evangelists have increasingly seen the variety of forms in which allegiance to Christ can be expressed.

The Need for Contextualization

This year I received a letter from a West African country that described some converts who objected to attending the local church for the following reasons:

> Their customs are too different from ours. They keep their shoes on,
> sit on benches (and close to women at that), and they beat drums in

---

* Originally published in a slightly different form in *The Word among Us: Contextualizing Theology for Mission Today,* ed. Dean S. Gilliland (Waco, TX: Wipf & Stock, 1989), 282–312. Reprinted by permission.

1 J. Pedersen, "Masdjid," *Shorter Encyclopaedia of Islam* (Leiden: Brill, 1961), 339B–340A.

church. We are used to worshiping God by taking our shoes off, sitting and kneeling on mats, and chanting prayers in the Arabic and
_____ languages. Also we teach our women at home. If we go to the
_____ church, we will feel very uncomfortable. What's more, our
other Muslim friends will not join us. If we worship God the way
we are used to, other Muslims will be interested. But we will pray
in the name of Jesus and teach from the Arabic and _____ Bible.[2]

Not only have the worship forms been irrelevant or offensive to the person of Muslim background, but the Bibles used have often shrouded the gospel in foreign terms. The traditional Urdu and Bengali Bibles, for example, often used Hindu rather than Muslim vocabulary.

Even the most commonly used Arabic translation of the Bible by Eli Smith and Cornelius Van Dyck (first published in 1865) adopted some Syriac religious and ecclesiastical terms not seen in Muslim Arabic. Likewise it utilized some Syriac names of Bible characters that are different from those adopted by the Qur'an—for example, Yuhanna rather than Yahya for John and Yasu' rather than Isa for Jesus. The translators consciously avoided using the wording and style of the Qur'an.[3]

An Omani sheikh lamented: "I have the Gospel, too. One of your missionaries gave me a copy twenty years ago. I frequently get it down and try to read it, but its Arabic is so strange that I understand nothing."[4]

Such problems led to the recent attempts to develop contextualized materials.

Current Studies on Contextualization

Attention focused on contextualization in the Muslim world when the School of World Mission at Fuller Theological Seminary devoted a year to Islam. One of the early results was an article in 1977 by John Wilder of Pakistan entitled "Some Reflections on Possibilities for People Movements among Muslims," in which he advocated that the model of Messianic Judaism be used in Muslim evangelism. Followers of Jesus from Islam could use their traditional forms of worship even as "completed Jews" used theirs.[5]

In 1978 the North American Conference for Muslim Evangelization was held in Glen Eyrie, Colorado. A number of the foundation papers were devoted to contextualization and were included in the compendium *The Gospel and Islam*.[6] These included "The Gospel and Culture," where Paul Hiebert distinguished between the gospel and culture, showing how culture is the vehicle that carries the message of the gospel and how the gospel in turn judges a culture.[7]

Donald N. Larson in "The Cross-cultural Communication of the Gospel to Muslims" developed the concept of "bi-passing," in which Muslims and nominal Christians of different cultural backgrounds can move directly into a "new humanity" (Eph 2:15) without either having to "pass" into the other's culture and become culturally like them as a precondition of becoming a Christian.[8] Bashir Abdol Massih in

---

2   Letter dated March 1, 1987.

3   For a broader discussion of the anti-qur'anic bias of Arabic Bible translation, see Samuel P. Schlorff, "The Missionary Use of the Qur'an: An Historical and Theological Study of the Contextualization of the Gospel" (unpublished ThM thesis, Philadelphia: Westminster Theological Seminary, 1984), 61–71.

4   Paul W. Harrison, "The Arabs of Oman," *The Moslem World* 24 (1934), 269.

5   *Missiology: An International Review* 5, no. 3 (1977), 301–20.

6   Don M. McCurry, ed., *The Gospel and Islam: A 1978 Compendium* (Monrovia, CA: MARC, 1979).

7   Ibid., 58–70.

8   Ibid., 71–84.

"The Incarnational Witness to the Muslim Heart" illustrates the effectiveness of such a ministry by a case study of a priest from an ancient Eastern church.[9]

Harvie M. Conn in "The Muslim Convert and His Culture" argues that the sociological barriers to conversion by Muslims are greater than the theological and then deals with barriers to their conversion. He sees these as misunderstanding conversion as a one-step decision rather than as a progress to Christ, as an individual decision rather than a multipersonal decision in many cultures, and as a purely "spiritual" decision rather than involving all of life.[10] Charles Kraft introduced a linguistic model in his "Dynamic Equivalence Churches in Muslim Society." He argues that our goal should be to foster groups of God's people in "Muslim" cultures that function in their own culture in ways equivalent in their dynamics to biblically recommended examples.[11]

Finally, Charles R. Tabor shows how the term "contextualization" goes beyond "indigenization" in "Contextualization: Indigenization and/or Transformation." Unlike "indigenization," "contextualization" does not focus exclusively on the cultural dimension but also on social, political, and economic questions. It does not treat culture as static but recognizes that cultures are in the process of change. It recognizes that all cultures, including the missionary's, have elements of the demonic as well as the divine. Thus Christian missions must take into account these dimensions of the Muslim contexts.[12]

Since there was understandable overlapping of ideas in these articles, it was helpful for Phil Parshall to come out with a more comprehensive study in 1980, *New Paths in Muslim Evangelism: Evangelical Approaches to Contextualization*.[13] Here he dealt with the principles and application of contextualization and gave two case studies.

One of the questions that arises for converts is the extent to which they may continue in the Muslim community. Phil Parshall addressed this five years later in *Beyond the Mosque: Christians in Muslim Community*.[14] He concludes that converts should remain in their society but, following a transitional period, will ultimately need to leave mosque worship because of theological incompatibility.[15]

Questions of contextualization were again raised at an international conference of the Muslim Track of the Lausanne Committee for World Evangelization in Zeist, Holland, in 1987. Most of the papers, other than area studies, are collected in *Muslims and Christians on the Emmaus Road*.[16] Considerable suspicion of contextualization was found to exist among Christians in various parts of the Muslim world, and Phil Parshall in his assigned paper on "Lessons Learned in Contextualization"[17] was not able to show much progress from case studies since the publication of *The Gospel and Islam* in 1979 and his own *New Paths in Muslim Evangelism* in 1980. Hence this present study will seek to evaluate a contemporary case situation.

Rafique Uddin, a Muslim convert, reported in "Contextualized Witness and Worship" on Muslim forms that he and other converts were finding meaningful in expressing their new allegiance to God

---

9   Ibid., 85–96.

10   Ibid., 97–113.

11   Ibid., 114–28.

12   Ibid., 129–54.

13   Grand Rapids, MI: Baker.

14   Grand Rapids, MI: Baker, 1985.

15   Ibid., 183.

16   J. Dudley Woodberry, ed., *Muslims and Christians on the Emmaus Road: Crucial Issues in Witness among Muslims* (Monrovia, CA: MARC, 1989).

17   Ibid., 277–92.

in Christ.[18] Florence Antablin in "Islamic and Christian Architecture" showed another area of mutual borrowing where similar styles have been able to express and frame the worship of both communities.[19]

Denis Green in "Guidelines from Hebrews for Contextualization" did raise some cautions. The recipients of the epistle appear to have been a group of Christians who retained their old Hebrew worship forms like a sect of Judaism. They were in danger of remaining in an ossified contextualization without moving on to maturity. The parallel dangers are obvious for Muslim converts who continue to use Muslim forms in Muslim society.[20]

Space does not permit the discussion of monographs on specific topics—for example, bridging concepts like divine blessing[21] and honor,[22] explanations of the doctrines of God and Christ in a Muslim context,[23] the use of the Qur'an in Christian witness,[24] and the use of Islamic theological terminology in Bible translation.[25]

Contextualized materials have been available for some time. A book for Sufi mystics, *The Way of the Sevenfold Secret*, has been published in Arabic, English, Persian, and French since it appeared in 1926.[26] It focuses on seven biblical themes that are of concern to Sufis, such as illumination and abiding in God. Wide evangelistic use has been made of Fouad Accad's *Seven Muslim Christian Principles*, which follows steps leading to salvation by quoting from the books that Muslims recognize—the *Tawrat* (Torah), *Zabur* (Psalms), *Injil* (Gospel), and Qur'an.[27]

Scripture portions have been attractively presented in Muslim dress; for example, *The Pillars of Religion in the Light of the Tawrat Zabur and Injil*.[28] Bible correspondence courses have also been put into contextualized form. Sobhi W. Malek's Allah-u Akbar Bible Lessons, for example, use Muslim terms and forms of expression wherever possible.[29] Of special note is an Arabic life of Christ (Sirat al-Masih), based on a harmony of the Synoptic Gospels but using qur'anic idiom and style.[30] For the most part, it has been well received by Muslims.

---

18 Ibid., 293–98.

19 Ibid., 299–314.

20 Ibid., 255–76.

21 Larry G. Lenning, *Blessing in Mosque and Mission* (Pasadena, CA: William Carey Library, 1980).

22 Evertt W. Huffard, *"Thematic Dissonance in the Muslim-Christian Encounter: A Contextualized Theology of Honor"* (PhD diss., Fuller Theological Seminary, 1985); and Huffard, "Culturally Relevant Themes about Christ," in *Woodberry, Emmaus Road*, 177–92.

23 Michael Nazir-Ali, *Frontiers in Muslim-Christian Encounter* (Oxford, UK: Regnum, 1987), 15–37.

24 Schlorff, "The Missionary Use of the Quran."

25 Fritz Goerling, "The Use of Islamic Theological Terminology in Bible Translation and Evangelism among the Jula in Cote d'Ivoire" (ThM thesis, Fuller Theological Seminary, 1989).

26 Lilias Trotter, *The Way of the Sevenfold Secret* (Cairo: Nile Mission Press, 1926).

27 Subsequently included in Fouad Elias Accad, *Building Bridges: Christianity and Islam* (Colorado Springs, CO: NavPress, 1997).

28 Robert G. Bratcher (Beirut: The Bible Society, 1984).

29 For their rationale, see Sobhi W. Malek, "Allah-u Akbar Bible Lessons: Aspects of Their Effectiveness in Evangelizing Muslims" (DMiss diss., Fuller Theological Seminary, 1986).

30 *Sirat al-Masih bi-Lisan Arabi Fasih* (Larnaca, Cyprus: Izdihar, 1987). For a comparison of this style with existing Arabic Bible translations, see David Owen, "A Classification System for Styles of Arabic Bible Translations," *Seedbed* 3, no. 1 (1988): 8–10. For reactions to it, see Schlorff, "Feedback on Project Sunrise (Sira): A Look at 'Dynamic Equivalence' in an Islamic Context," *Seedbed* 3, no. 2 (1988): 22–32.

Reactions of Christians and Muslims

Despite the need for contextualization that has been seen, Christian communities in the Muslim world have often opposed it. The opposition echoes a comparable tension in the early church between the Hebrew Christians, who used Jewish forms, and the new Gentile Christians, who felt free to use other forms. Gabriel Habib, the Greek Orthodox director of the Middle East Christian Council, in a letter to many evangelical leaders in North America, asserted,

> Unfortunately, we have all too frequently attempted to "contextual-ize" our sharing of the gospel—at the risk of diminishing the value of the churches' spiritual heritage. The loss of such a precious spiri-tual heritage in our efforts to communicate the message of Christ diminishes the real potential of accumulated spiritual experience.[31]

In a questionnaire for Arab Christians in Jordan and Bahrain, Bruce Heckman asked, "How do you feel about Muslim believers using Islamic styles of worship when they meet together?" The negative answers included, "The use of Islamic styles of worship is wrong. We cannot accept expressions of worship that relate to idolatry or strange rituals." Another affirmed, "I personally believe Islamic worship is devised by the devil. The worship structure of Muslim believers should therefore be different and not attached to the past."[32]

Bruce Heckman then asked, "What could be the effects of using Islamic styles of worship?" The negative answers included, "Those using Islamic style of worship would deviate from true Christianity." Another believed, "Using old forms of worship would take them back to the life from which they were delivered." Still another affirmed, "Continuity with the past will tie the Muslim believer to darkness."[33]

Not only resident Christians but Muslims too have objected to Christian contextualization. In Arabia, *Islamic World Review* (July 1987) charged:

> Christian missionaries are now adopting a new, underhanded style in their outreach to Muslims. Known as the Contextualized Ap-proach, it means they now speak in the context of the people and the culture of the country where they are operating, and are less honest in their dealings with simple, often illiterate, peasants. They no longer call themselves openly Christians in a Muslim area, but "followers of Isa." The church is no longer a "church," but a "*Masjid Isa*." Missionaries avoid calling Jesus the "Son of God" to Muslims, who no matter how ignorant will be alarmed by the term. He is called to them "*Ruhullah*" (the Spirit of God).[34]

The Malaysian *New Straits Times* (March 24, 1988) reported on a government white paper on Chris-tian attempts at contextualization in which the church "would emulate the Muslim practice of reading the Qur'an when reading the Bible, sitting on the floor, using the rehal (wooden stand) to prop up the

---

31 Dated July 3, 1987.

32 Bruce Heckman, "Arab Christian Reaction to Contextualization in the Middle East" (MA thesis, Fuller Theological Seminary, 1988), 73–75.

33 Ibid., 80–81.

34 "Islam and Missions: Mohammad or Christ?" 1.

Bible," and wearing clothing traditionally worn by Muslims. Such practices are seen as deceptive, confusing, and causing "suspicion between Malays and Christians."

Considerable debate was caused in Malaysia when *The Star* (April 5, 1988) reported on a bill passed by the Selangor state government forbidding non-Islamic religions to use the following words: *Allah* (God), *Rasul* (Apostle), *Fatwa* (legal opinion), *Wahyu* (from *Wahy*—revelation), *Iman* (faith), *Imam* (leader of mosque prayer for the Muslim community), *Ulama* (religious scholars), *Dakwah* (from *dawa/Da'wa*—lit., "call, mission"), *Nabi* (prophet), *Hadith* (Prophetic tradition), *Syariah* (from *shari'a*—religious law), *Injil* (Gospel), *Ibadah* (religious duties such as prayer), *Qiblat* (direction of prayer), *Salat* (ritual prayer), *Kaabah* (cubical building in Meccan Mosque), *Haj* (from *Hajj*—pilgrimage), *Kadi* (religious judge), and *Mufti* (giver of legal opinions; today sometimes the religious leader).

To these prohibited words were added such exclamations as *Subhanallah* (Praise be to God!), *Alhamdulillah* (Praise be to God!), *Lailahaillallah* (There is no god but God!), and *Allahu Akbar* (God is greater!). A similar bill was passed in Malacca[35] as had previously been done in Kelantan, Trengganu, Negri, Sembilan, and Penang.[36]

Whatever the final outcome, it is significant that the Muslim community felt these words and exclamations were exclusively their own. Their opposition to such contextualization as well as the similar opposition of many Christians might be alleviated if it were shown how many of the religious terms and worship forms are the common heritage of both communities.

Previous Use of the Pillars by Jews and Christians

Islam may be viewed as originally a contextualization for the Arabs of the monotheism inherited directly[37] from Jews[38] and Christians[39] or indirectly through Arab monotheists.[40] This interpretation of the earlier preaching would be supported by references to the Qur'an as an Arabic Book confirming

---

35 *The Star*, April 7, 1988.

36 *Berita NECF: A Bimonthly Publication of the National Evangelical Christian Fellowship of Malaysia* 1, no. 1 (April–May 1988): 5.

37 Suggested by surah 16:103/105.

38 See, e.g., Abraham Geiger, *Judaism and Islam*, trans. F. M. Young (New York: KTAV, 1970); Charles Torrey, *The Jewish Foundation of Islam* (New York: Jewish Institute of Religion Press, 1933); Alfred Guillaume, "The Influence of Judaism on Islam," in *The Legacy of Israel*, ed. Edwyn R. Bevan and Charles Singer (Oxford, UK: Clarendon Press, 1928), 129–71; W. Montgomery Watt, *Muhammad at Medina* (Oxford, UK: Clarendon Press, 1956), 192–220. On the possible influence of unorthodox variants affected by Christian monastic piety, see S. D. Goitein, *Jews and Arabs: Their Contact through the Ages*, 3rd rev. ed. (New York: Schocken Books, 1974), 57–58. On the possible influence of a late offshoot of the Qumran community, see Chaim Rabin, *Qumran Studies* (London: Oxford University Press, 1957), 112–30.

39 See, e.g., Tor Andrae, *Les origines de l'Islam et le Christianisme*, trans. Jules Roch (Paris: Adrien-Maisonneuve, 1955); Richard Bell, *The Origin of Islam in its Christian Environment* (London: Macmillan, 1926); J. Spencer Trimingham, *Christianity among the Arabs in Pre-Islamic Times* (London: Longman, 1979); Watt, *Muhammad at Medina*, 315–20.

40 See, e.g., Hamilton A. R. Gibb, "Pre-Islamic Monotheism in Arabia," *Harvard Theological Review* 60 (1962), 269–80; J. Fueck, "The Originality of the Arabian Prophet," in *Studies on Islam*, ed. and trans. Merlin Swartz (New York: Oxford University Press, 1981), 86–98; Watt, *Muhammad at Mecca* (Oxford, UK: Clarendon Press, 1960), 158–61.

the earlier revelation (e.g., surah 46:12 Egyptian ed./11 Fluegel ed.).[41] Later, of course, Islam was given a more universal mission. All that is necessary for our purposes, however, is to show that the pillars of faith along with their vocabulary were largely the previous possessions of Jews and Christians. Any reusing of them, then, is but the repossession of what originally belonged to these communities.

The earliest Muslim exegetes showed no hesitation to recognize the Jewish and Christian origin of many religious terms in the Qur'an, even though later the orthodox doctrine was elaborated that the Qur'an was a unique production of the Arabic language.[42] Arthur Jeffery argued that Syriac was the major source of borrowed vocabulary.[43] This borrowing is of special interest, because a number of the words banned to non-Muslims in parts of Malaysia can be shown to have been used by Jews or Christians before the advent of Muhammad (570–732). They are treated here because of the relevance of a number of them to the "pillars" of Muslim faith and practice.

Allah, for example, is of Christian Syriac origin and was in use long before Muhammad's time.[44]

Wahy (revelation) is at least etymologically related to Jewish-Aramaic and Christian Ethiopic words and is used by the pre-Islamic poets.[45]

Nabi (prophet) is probably from Jewish Aramaic rather than Syriac and was apparently known to the Arabs long before Muhammad.[46]

Injil (Gospel) obviously is based on the Greek *euangelion* and probably came through the Ethiopic of Christian Abyssinia.[47]

The *Qiblat* (direction of prayer) obviously predates Muhammad. We find allusion to it in 1 Kings 8:44 and clear reference to it in Daniel 6:10. Syriac Christians faced the east, and Jews faced Jerusalem—the direction from which it was changed in surah 2:142/136–152/147. One tradition, reported by Tabari, even ascribes the change to remarks by Jews concerning Muhammad's dependence on Judaism.[48]

Salat (ritual prayer) may be from Jewish Aramaic but is more probably from Syriac and was familiar in pre-Islamic times.[49]

Haj (pilgrimage) is from the Hebrew *hag*, meaning "festival," in Exodus 23:18 and Psalm 81:4 (v. 3 in the English).

Similar Jewish or Christian pre-Islamic usage can be found for banned exclamations as well—for example, *Subhanallah* (Praise be to God!). *Allah* has already been traced to the Syriac before Muhammad, and *subhan* can be as well.[50] Likewise, the Semitic scholar E. Mittwoch finds *Allahu Akbar* (God is greater!) similar to the benedictions of the Jewish prayers performed three times a day. There were, of course,

---

41 Cf. Watt's view, based partly on surah 19:16–33/34, that Muhammad originally thought that the monotheism he preached was identical to that of the Jews and Christians (*Medina*, 315 and 315n).

42 Arthur Jeffery, *The Foreign Vocabulary of the Quran* (Baroda: Oriental Institute, 1938), vii–viii.

43 Ibid., 19.

44 Ibid., 66; and Bell, *Origin of Islam*, 54.

45 A. J. Wensinck, "Wahy," *Shorter Encyclopaedia of Islam*, ed. H. A. R. Gibb and J. H. Kramers (Leiden: Brill, 1961), 622A.

46 Jeffery, *Foreign Vocabulary*, 276.

47 Ibid., 71–72.

48 A. J. Wensinck, "Kibla," in *Encyclopaedia of Islam*, 2nd ed., vol. 5, ed. H. A. R. Gibb et al. (Leiden: Brill, 1986), 82; Mahmoud M. Ayoub, *The Qur'an and Its Interpreters*, vol. 1 (Albany, NY: State University of New York Press, 1984), 167–75; Abu-l 'Abbas al-Baladhuri, *Kitab futuh al-buldan*, trans. Philip K. Hitti as *The Origins of the Islamic State*, vol. 1 (New York: Columbia University, 1916), 15.

49 Jeffery, *Foreign Vocabulary*, 198–99; A. J. Wensinck, "Salat," in *Shorter Encyclopaedia of Islam*, 491B.

50 Jeffery, *Foreign Vocabulary*, 161–62.

alterations of meaning as words and practices moved from Jewish and Christian systems of thought to a Muslim one; but, as will be seen, the systems were similar enough that the core meanings remained.

Pillar 1: Confession of Faith (*Shahadah*)

The first part of the Muslim confession of faith (*shahadah*—"I bear witness that there is no god but God") is based on verses like surah 37:35/34 ("There is no god but God") and 112:1,2 ("Say, He [is] God, One [*ahad*]. God the Alone."). The wording, as Hartwig Herschfeld[51] indicates, is apparently based on the *Shema* in Deuteronomy 6:4 ("Hear O Israel, the Lord our God is One [*ahad*] Lord"). Both emphasize the same word, *ahad*. The Talmud of Jerusalem cites certain rabbis as counseling the faithful to put emphasis on this word.[52]

Not only is the form of the shahadah similar to the Shema and apparently based on it, but the functions of the two are the same. They not only introduce every formal service of worship but are the basic confessions for both faiths. It was those confessions that separated the Hebrews and the Muslims from the surrounding polytheists. Both also linked the affirmation of who God is with the obligations due him. The Shema, especially in its longer form in Numbers 15:37–41, introduces commandments. The relationship is pointed out in Mishna Berakhoth 2:213, where it says that one takes on "the yoke of the kingdom of heaven" by reciting the first sentence and "the yoke of the commandments" by reciting the subsequent part.[53] Furthermore, that which is affirmed in the first sentence of the Shema—the unity of God—forms the basis for the first commandment of the Decalogue: "Thou shalt have no other gods before me" (Ex 20:3 KJV). The same relationship between confession and obligation is seen in the shahadah, for this first pillar affirming what God is, is followed by four pillars concerning obligations to him. The same linkage is found in the Qur'an 20:14: "In truth, I am God. There is no god but I; therefore serve Me, and perform the prayer of My remembrance."

That which has been said about the Shema in the Old Testament can also be said about it in the New, for Jesus gives it as the most important commandment in Mark 12:29,30.

In looking for the meaning of these confessions to the devotees, we must note their simplicity and clarity. Further, both shahadah and Shema require more than intellectual assent. The shahadah is prefaced by "I bear witness," and the Shema is introduced by "Hear O Israel": both require confession. This is more than James speaks of in 2:19: "You believe that God is one; you do well. Even the demons believe—and shudder" (RSV).

As it involves rejection of polytheism, it also involves the rejection of intermediaries and associates with God in popular beliefs. In Sufi mysticism it involves the rejection of all earthly gods, like wealth. It means seeing his signs in all things. "Wherever you turn, there is the face of God" (surah 2:115/109).[54]

---

51   Hirschfeld, *New Researches into the Composition and Exegesis of the Qoran* (London: Royal Asiatic Society, 1902), 35.

52   Mose Schwab, trans., *The Talmud of Jerusalem*, bk. 1 (London: Williams and Norgate, 1886), chap. 2, no. 3 (34–35); D. Masson, *Le Coran et la revelation Judeo-Chretienne*, vol. 1 (Paris: Adrien-Maisonneuve, 1958), 32.

53   Torrey, *The Jewish Foundation of Islam*, 133–34. On the *Shema* as a confession of faith, see Mishna *Berakoth* 2:2 in *The Mishna*, trans. Herbert Danby (London: Oxford University Press, 1949), 3; George Foot Moore, *Judaism in the First Centuries of the Christian Era*, vol. 1 (Cambridge, MA: Harvard University Press, 1950), 465; Vernon H. Neufeld, *The Earliest Christian Confessions* (Grand Rapids, MI: Eerdmans, 1963), 34–41.

54   For the meaning of the *shahadah* see Wensinck, *The Muslim Creed: Its Genesis and Historical Development* (Cambridge: Cambridge University Press, 1932), 17–35; Wilfred Cantwell Smith, *The Faith of Other Men* (New York: Harper and Row, 1963), 51–62. For the meaning of God's unity to a Sufi mystic, see Seyyed Hossein Nasr, ed., *Islamic Spirituality: Foundations* (New York: Crossroad, 1987), 312–15.

Many traditions mention only the uniqueness or unity of God as the essential article of belief.[55] The traditional confession goes on, however, to declare, "Muhammad is the Apostle of God," based on qur'anic passages like surah 4:134/135. We shall not deal with this part extensively here, because it is obviously an addition to Jewish and Christian faith. We must, however, consider it, because it is one of the questions that converts are having to deal with in the case study we shall be considering.

The confession first says something about Muhammad's function—a revealer of God's will. Thus it declares that God has something to say to humans, who must now respond. Since what is said is understood to be declared in the Qur'an, we must form an attitude toward the Qur'an—which contains much that is affirmed by the Bible along with some statements contrary to the Bible. To what extent may the Qur'an be used in Christian witness to Muslims?[56] Although the Bible does not have a parallel use of non-Judaic materials for evangelistic purposes, biblical writers under the guidance of the Spirit of God did feel free to incorporate materials from their neighbors.[57] Jesus adapted materials of the rabbis in his teaching.[58] Paul quoted from non-Christian sources.[59] Likewise, many, like Fouad Accad and converts in the case study that will be evaluated, have found the Qur'an to be a useful bridge for interpretation, even when they do not ascribe personal authority to it.

The Isawa of Nigeria became followers of Jesus from reading about him in the Qur'an. Another West African, who taught Islam in a Muslim college, started a pilgrimage that led to faith in Christ about a year ago when he read the accounts of Jesus in the Qur'an.

The second part of the confession also says something about Muhammad's status—that is, that he is a prophet like the biblical ones and is in fact the final one, their seal. This raises the question of the Christian's attitude toward Muhammad.[60] Viewed in his context of a polytheism that was similar to that among Israel's Old Testament neighbors, his message had a similar prophetic tone—"Turn to the one Creator God." He might be viewed as an apostle to the Arabs of polytheistic Arabia. Unfortunately, however, he comes chronologically after Christ but denies such basic Christian affirmations as the Incarnation. Therefore the Christian cannot affirm that he is "the Apostle of God."

When Christians look for a substitute affirmation, it is noteworthy that Islam's most celebrated theologian, Abu Hamid al-Ghazali (d. 1111), twice gives the confession in a form that both Muslims and Christians can accept—the shahadah with the name of Jesus substituted for Muhammad: "There is no god but God and Jesus is the Apostle of God."[61] The Christian might substitute one of the early Christian confessions reflected in the New Testament, such as "Jesus is Lord" (Rom 10:9).[62]

---

55 See Wensinck, *A Handbook of Early Muhammadan Tradition* (Leiden: Brill, 1960), s.v. "unity."

56 For an extensive discussion, see Schlorff, "The Missionary Use of the Quran."

57 E.g., Ps 104 reflects the hymn of praise of Akhnaton to the sun.

58 E.g., the parable of the judge and the widow (Luke 18:2–5) adapts Ben Sirach 35:15–19.

59 Paul in Acts 26:14 quotes Euripides, *Bacchae,* line 795. These and other illustrations are found in an unpublished report by Georges Houssney of a Beirut Study Group involving Emmett Barnes, Kenneth Bailey, and Colin Chapman.

60 For an extensive discussion, see Kenneth Cragg, *Muhammad and the Christian: A Question of Response* (London: Darton, Longman and Todd, 1984).

61 Ghazali, *Al-Qustas al-Mustaqim,* ed. V. Chelhot, 68, cited in Chelhot, "La Balance Juste," *Bulletin d'Etudes Orientales* 15 (1958): 62; Ghazali, *al-Munqidh min al-dalal (The Deliverer from Error),* 3rd ed., ed. Jamil Saliba and Kamal 'Ayyad (Damascus: Matba'at al-Jami'a al-Suriya, 1939), 101, in W. Montgomery Watt, *The Faith and Practice of al-Ghazali* (London: Allen and Unwin, 1953), 39.

62 Other early biblical confessions are: "Jesus is the Son of God" (John 4:15); "You are the Christ, the Son of the Living God" (Matt 16:15); and longer formulations in Phil 2:6–11; 1 Cor 15:3–7; Rom 1:1–4; 1 Tim 3:16. On the earliest Christian confessions see Paul Feine, *Gestalt des apostolischen Glaubensbekenntnisses in der Zeit des*

Pillar 2: Ritual Prayer (*Salat*)

In the Asian case study we shall be analyzing below, Muslims watched Christian relief workers come and selflessly serve them. They said that they should be called angels because they were so good, kind, and honest, "but they do not say their prayers." It was not until they were seen praying publicly that they were finally accepted as godly.

One of the first definitions of a Muslim was one who "pronounces the name of the Lord and prays" (surah 87:15). Yet the term chosen (verb *salla*—"to bow"; noun *salat*) had long been used for institutionalized prayer in synagogues and churches. *'Aqama 'l-salat* (to perform the prayer) was apparently borrowed from the Syrian church while Muhammad was still in Mecca, but the roots of the prayer service are also seen in Judaism, as will be shown in the terminology, postures, and content.[63]

Although the Old Testament mentions morning and evening prayer (Ex 29:39; Num 28:4), Judaism developed three prayers a day on the pattern of Psalm 55:17 (cf. Dan 6:11) as is seen in the Talmud of Jerusalem.[64]

Christian monks prayed seven times a day on the pattern of Psalm 119:164. The Qur'an does not mention the five prayers but gives a variety of prayer times (surah 2:238/239; 17:78/80; 20:130; 24:58/57). The Traditions, however, clearly list five;[65] so Islam took a middle position.[66] Of significance for Muslim converts is the fact that the early Jewish Christians maintained their former institutionalized prayer times and places (Acts 3:1; 10:9; 16:13).

The removal of sandals in places of prayer (surah 20:12) follows the Hebrew pattern (Ex 3:5) also practiced by many Eastern churches.

Preparations

The ablutions also reflect the earlier faiths. The minor ritual ablution (*wudu'*) is used to get rid of "minor" ritual impurity (*hadath*). The Jewish influence here is evident by the latter part of Muhammad's life: "You, who believe, when you prepare for the prayer, wash your faces and your hands up to the elbows and rub your heads and your feet up to the ankles" (surah 5:6/8; cf. 4:43/46). The Old Testament tabernacle had a basin for washing the hands and feet of the priests before they entered the presence of the Lord (Ex 30:17–21; 40:30–32), and others too were to consecrate themselves when coming into his presence (1 Sam 16:5). Muslims follow the same order in their ablutions as the Jews do—the face, then the hands, then the feet. The name of God is pronounced, and the right side is done before the left. Each part is washed three times.[67]

Neuen Testament (Leipzig: Verlag Doerffling & Franke, 1925); Vernon H. Neufeld, *The Earliest Christian Confessions* (Grand Rapids, MI: Eerdmans, 1963); Oscar Cullmann, *The Earliest Christian Confessions*, trans. J. K. S. Reid (London: Lutterworth Press, 1949); J. N. D. Kelley, *Early Christian Creeds*, 2nd ed. (London: Longman, 1960); O. Sydney Barr, *From the Apostles' Faith to the Apostles' Creed* (New York: Oxford University Press, 1964).

63 See the classic study by E. Mittwoch, *Zur Entstebungsgeschichte des islamischen Gebets und Kultus* in *Abhandlungen der preussen Akademie der Wissenschaften* (Berlin, 1913) philosophy-history Kl., no. 2.

64 *Berakhot* 4:1.

65 Imam al-Bukhari, *Sahih al-Bukhari* (Arabic-English), trans. M. Muhsin Khan, vol. 1 (Beirut: Dar al-Arabia, n.d.), bk. 8 (*Salat*), chap. 1, 213–14.

66 For the argument that Islam chose a middle position as noted in a slightly different context in surah 2:143/137, see S. D. Goitein, *Studies in Islamic History and Institutions* (Leiden: Brill, 1968), 84–85.

67 Guillaume, "The Influence of Judaism on Islam," 162–63.

"Major" ritual impurity (*janaba* or major *hadath*) requires washing of the total body (*ghusl*) before prayer. This is necessitated by such occurrences as seminal discharge or menstruation.[68] It is also common practice before Friday noon prayers and the two major annual feast days of *Id al-Fitr* and *Id al-Adha*. The qur'anic distinction is based on surah 5:6/8–9, which adds to a prior description of the minor ablutions (*wudu'*), "if you are in a state of pollution, purify yourself."

Again similar details are found in Judaism, where occurrences such as seminal discharge and menstruation require bathing the body (Lev 12:1–5; 14:8; 15; 17:15; Num 19:19). The Friday bath in Islam corresponds with the Sabbath bath in Judaism. Likewise, the bathing of the convert to Islam corresponds with proselyte immersion in Judaism, which, of course, was the precursor of Christian baptism.[69] In the light of the fact that both Christian baptism and Muslim proselyte ghusl are reinterpretations of Jewish proselyte immersion, it might be possible to perform Christian baptism as proselyte ghusl without causing the furor that arose earlier from the suggestion of a possible alternate initiation rite for baptism.[70]

Another parallel is rubbing the hands and face with sand (*tayammum*) if water cannot be found, which is permitted by both the Qur'an (surah 4:43/46; 5:6–9/9–12) and the Talmud.[71] Christian baptism too has been performed in the desert with sand.[72]

The function of the ablutions is purity from defilement (4:43/46; 5:6/8–9; 87:14,15), and water from heaven is also "to put away . . . the defilement of Satan" (8:11). The intention is inward purity, which is seen as both an act of God (5:6/9; 24:21) and of the worshipers themselves (9:108/109) resulting in Paradise (20:76/78). Therefore the purification obviously involves the forgiveness of sin.

The Bible likewise associated ablutions with purity of heart (Ps 24:3,4; Isa 1:16–18; Ezek 36:25,26; John 3:4,5; Heb 10:22). Jesus went further in shifting the emphasis from the ablutions to purity of heart (Matt 15:1–20; Mark 7:1–23; Luke 37:44). The writer of the epistle to the Hebrews makes ablutions merely a foreshadowing of inner purity provided through Christ (Heb 6:1,2; 9:10–14). Church fathers like Tertullian and Chrysostom emphasized that such rituals were deprived of value unless accompanied by purity of heart.[73]

Christ and the church, however, made the ablution of proselyte baptism more prominent than the other two faiths and emphasized the symbolism of being dead to sin and buried with Christ and being resurrected with him to newness of life. The other two faiths, as has been seen, practiced a proselyte baptism, *mikveh* and *ghusl* respectively; but circumcision has been a more central confession of faith for Judaism, as has the shahadah for Islam.

Along with ablutions, another preliminary essential in Muslim prayer is the proper orientation (*qibla*). It comes from *'aqbala 'ala* (direction toward a point) and, as has been noted, has ancient roots. The garden of Eden was toward the east (Gen 2:8). The door of the tabernacle was toward the east (Ex 27:13), as was that of the temple in Ezekiel's vision (47:1), the direction from which the glory of God came (48:2).

---

68 *Sahih al-Bukhari*, vol. 1, bk. 5 (*Ghusl*), 156–176; G. H. Bousquet, "Ghusl," in *Encyclopaedia of Islam*, 2nd ed.

69 Guillaume, 162.

70 On the controversy, see Parshall, "Lessons Learned in Contextualization," 279.

71 Jacob Neusner, trans., *The Talmud of Babylonia*, bk. 1, *Tractate Berakhot* (Chico, CA: Scholars Press, 1984), fol. 15A (chap. 2, sec. 22, 116); A. J. Wensinck, "Tayammum," in *Shorter Encyclopaedia of Islam*, 589A.

72 Cedrenus, *Annales*, ed. Hylander (Basle, 1566), 206, in ibid.

73 Masson, *Le Coran*, 470.

Zechariah compared Christ to the rising sun (Luke 1:78), thereby associating him with Malachi's prophecy of the sun of righteousness that would come with healing (4:2). Thus Christians in the early centuries prayed toward the east,[74] even though Jesus had made plain to the woman of Samaria that places and orientation were not important in the worship of God (John 4:19–24).

The Jews prayed toward Jerusalem (1 Kgs 8:33; Dan 6:10), a practice regulated in the Talmud.[75] Muslims for a time prayed toward Jerusalem (sixteen or seventeen months according to al-Bukhari).[76] It remained a center of devotion because of the temple area (now the Dome of the Rock and the Aqsa Mosque), where Muhammad is reported to have gone in his night journey (surah 17). The direction of prayer, however, was changed to Mecca in surah 2:142/136–152/147. As Jerusalem had been the center of the world for Jews (Ezek 5:5), Mecca became the center of the world for Muslims.[77] Mosques came to include a *mihrab* (niche indicating the direction of Mecca) as some synagogues had a *mizrah* (indicating the east, the direction from which salvation comes).[78]

In noting the prescribed direction of prayer, the Qur'an (surah 2:115/109), like the Talmud, recognized that God was everywhere.[79] The Qur'an, however, notes that true piety does not consist in the direction you face but is to believe in God, the Last Day, the angels, the Book, and the Prophets, to give of one's substance to the needy, to perform the prayer and pay alms, to fulfill one's covenant, and endure adversity (2:177/172).

The worshipers also must pronounce their intention (*niya*) to perform the salat, specifying the length. Although the term does not appear in the Qur'an, it probably developed under Jewish influence to become analogous to the Hebrew *kavana* and the Latin Christian *intentio*. The value of any religious duty depends on the intention of the devotee.[80] As thus developed, the meaning approaches that of Jesus in the Sermon on the Mount, where he moves the focus from the external act to the heart condition (Matt 5:17–28).

Praying

The Muslim postures of prayers also replicate those of Jews and Christians. First, there is the posture of standing (*qiyam*, surah 22:26/27). In the Old and New Testaments, worshipers stood to pray (1 Kgs 8:14,22; Neh 9:2; Mark 11:25). Jewish daily prayers (*tefilla*) include a portion called the *'amida* (standing), indicating the posture when they were performed.[81] The second posture is bowing (*ruku*, surah 22:26/27,77/76), which is the equivalent of the Jewish *keri'a*[82] and communicates the sense of humble servitude that the genuflection does in the Roman Catholic mass.

---

74 Ibid., 531.

75 *The Talmud of Jerusalem*, trans. Schwab, bk. 1 (Berakhoth), chap. 4, nos. 6–7, 91–93.

76 *Sahih al-Bukhari*, vol. 4, bk. 60, chap. 20, 18.

77 Masson, *Le Coran*, 507–8.

78 Ibid., 511. [Jews in North Africa, Central and Southern Europe, and North America all pray toward Jerusalem and thus toward the east by default. Synagogues elsewhere in the world facing north, south, or west toward Jerusalem will often also have a marker on the wall denoting the direction of east.—Ed.]

79 *Baba Bathra*, fol. 25A, in *The Babylonian Talmud: Seder Nezikin*, ed. I. Epstein, trans. Maurice Simon and Israel A. Slotki (London: The Soncino Press, 1935), 124–25.

80 Abu Hamid al-Ghazali, *Ihya Ulum-id-Din*, trans. Fazal-ul-Karim (Lahore: Islamic Book Foundation, 1981), bk. 4, chap. 7, 389–407; Guillaume, "Influence of Judaism," 156; Wensinck, "Niya," in *Shorter Encyclopaedia of Islam*.

81 Mittwoch, *Zur Entstebungsgeschichte*, 16; Wensinck, "Salat," 493B.

82 Mittwoch, *Zur Entstebungsgeschichte*, 17; Wensinck, "Salat," 493B.

The third posture is prostration with the forehead on the ground (*sujud*, surah 22:26/27,77/76). Again, this form is found in both the Old and New Testaments (Gen 22:5; Num 16:22; 1 Sam 24:9; Neh 8:6; Matt 26:39). The sujud is the equivalent of the Jewish *hishtahavaya* and a similar Eastern Christian form.[83] On Yom Kippur rabbis and cantors still prostrate themselves in this way, and I have observed Coptic Orthodox monks and worshipers do this in worship. Prostration with the body fully extended is practiced in Roman Catholic ordination and consecration and on Good Friday and Saturday.

The fourth posture is half kneeling and half sitting (*julus*). Kneeling is a biblical form (1 Kgs 8:54; 2 Chr 6:13; Ps 95:6; Acts 20:36; 21:5). Sometimes the hands are lifted up as in biblical times (Ps 28:2; 134:2; 1 Tim 2:8).

The content of the prayers also has stylistic agreement with Jewish and Christian prayers.[84] The repetition of "God is greater" (*Allahu Akbar*) corresponds with benedictions like "God is blessed" in the Jewish *tefilla*.[85] The recitation of the *Fatiha*, the first chapter of the Qur'an, includes materials that would be common in Jewish and Christian prayers. In fact, the missionary statesman Samuel Zwemer recited it in a public gathering in Calcutta in 1928 and then concluded with the words "in Jesus' name, Amen." "Praise be to God" (*al-hamdu li-llah*) at the beginning of the Fatiha holds a similar position in chapters and passages of the Qur'an and corresponds to a similar blessing in Syriac literature.[86]

After blessings upon Muhammad, which, of course, would be an addition to Jewish and Christian worship, the prayer concludes with the worshiper turning to the left and the right and saying, "Peace be upon you." This form also concludes the main Jewish prayer, the *'amida*,[87] and the "passing of the peace" is often included in the celebration of the Christian Eucharist.

The Friday prayer is mentioned in surah 62:9, where the day is called "the day of Assembly" (*yawm juma al-Jum'a*), the same meaning as the Hebrew name *yom ha-kenisa* for the Sabbath.[88] The development of these prayers during the Umayyad Period (AD 661–750) may have been under Christian influence.[89] The choice of a day each week was a result of Jewish and Christian contacts, according to a Tradition: "The Jews have every seventh day a day when they get together [for prayer], and so do the Christians; therefore, let us do the same."[90]

Goitein argues that Friday was chosen because it was a market day in Medina, when people could more readily come to prayer.[91] Unlike the Jewish Sabbath and the Christian Sunday, it was not a day of rest. Surah 62:9 suggests they leave their trafficking to come to prayers. Unlike the biblical account of Creation, where God rested the seventh day and the children of Israel were to do likewise (Gen 2:2–3;

83 Mittwoch, *Zur Entstehungsgeschichte,* 17; Wensinck, *Mohammed en de Joden te Medina,* 2nd ed. (Leiden: Brill, 1928), 104, cited in Wensinck, "Salat," 494A.

84 For Christian parallels, see A. Baumstark, "Juedischer und Christlicher Gebetstypus im Koran," *Der Islam* 16 (1927): 229.

85 Mittwoch, *Zur Entstehungsgeschichte,* 16; Guillaume, "Influence of Judaism," 156.

86 Goitein, *Studies,* 75, 75n.

87 *Yoma,* 53B, in *The Babylonian Talmud: Seder moed Mo'ed,* v. 2/5, ed. I. Epstein, trans. Leo Jung (London: The Soncino Press, 1938), 250.

88 Goitein, *Studies,* 117–18.

89 C. H. Becker, "Zur Geschichte des Islamischen Kultus," *Der Islam* 3 (1912): 374–419; Hava Lazarus-Yafeh, *Some Religious Aspects of Islam* (Leiden: Brill, 1981), 40.

90 Al-Qastallani II, 176, cited in Goitein, *Studies,* 112.

91 Goitein, *Studies,* 113–14.

Ex 20:8), the Qur'an makes a point of noting that God was not tired after the six days of Creation (surah 50:38/37)—a topic also raised by Jewish scholars.[92]

The supererogatory night vigil (*salat al-lail*; *tahajjud*, meaning "waking," in 17:79/81) reflects the Syriac Christian ascetic practice of keeping awake (*shahra*).[93] Its function included merit (especially during Ramadan, the month of fasting, and before the two major annual festivals),[94] and it loosens one of the knots that Satan ties in the hair of a sleeper.[95]

The imam who leads the prayers corresponds to the *sheliah tsibbur* of Jewish worship. Both can be done by any qualified person in the community.[96]

Meaning and Function

When we turn to the meaning and function of prayer in Islam to see how adaptable aspects of it are for Christian worship, we encounter formidable misunderstandings between the two communities. Constance E. Padwick, who has done so much to lead us into the heart of Muslim prayer,[97] said of several excellent books on Christian prayer in Arabic,

> When put into the hands of Moslems (unless those educated in Christian schools) these books have proved to be nearly unintelligible. Not only are the fundamental thoughts of Moslem readers about God and about prayer very different from those of the Christian writers, but through the centuries the church has developed her own Arabic Christian vocabulary, and even when she uses the same word as the Moslem, she may read into it a Christian meaning of which he knows nothing. The first and most obvious example of this is the very word "salat," which for the Moslem means the prescribed prayers of the five hours, and for the Christian is full of many rich and delicate meanings.[98]

We have, however, seen sufficient overlapping of forms and shall see an overlapping of meanings and functions; so there can be understanding and adaptation of prayers between the two communities.

First it is necessary to make the distinction between corporate liturgical worship (*salat*) and personal invocation (*du'a*)[99]—a distinction found in both traditions (e.g., surah 14:40/42; Matt 6:6–13; Acts 4:24–31). Islam and liturgical Christians focus on the former, and nonliturgical Protestants emphasize the latter. Here we shall direct our attention to orthodox/orthoprax meanings and functions rather than those of the mystical Sufis and folk Muslims.[100]

---

92 See the second-century AD Midrash Haggadah entitled *Mekhilta* on Ex 20:11 in Lazarus-Yafeh, *Some Religious Aspects*, 143n8.

93 Bell, *Origin of Islam*, 143; Wensinck, "Salat," 495A.

94 Ibn Maja, *Siyam*, bab. 68, cited in Wensinck, "Tahadjdjud," in *Shorter Encyclopaedia of Islam*, 559.

95 Abu Da'ud, *Tatawwu*,' bab. 18, in Wensinck, "Tahadjdjud," 559.

96 Mittwoch, *Zur Entstebungsgeschichte*, 22; Becker, "Islamischen Kultus," 386; Wensinck, "Salat," 496A.

97 Padwick, *Muslim Devotions: A Study of Prayer Manuals in Common Use* (London: SPCK, 1961); and Padwick, "The Language of Muslim Devotion," *The Muslim World* 47 (1957): 5–21, 98–110, 194–209.

98 Quoted in Samuel M. Zwemer, *Studies in Popular Islam* (London: Sheldon Press, 1939), 15.

99 See Louis Gardet, "Du'a," in *Encyclopaedia of Islam*, 2nd ed., 617–18.

100 For these see, e.g., Nasr, 111–18; Louis Massignon, *Essai sur les origines du lexique technique de la mystique musulmane* (Paris: Vrin, 1968), 259; Wensinck, "Salat," 498B–499A; Bill Musk, "Popular Islam: The Hunger of

The concept of acquiring merit through prayer is strong in Islamic thought—both in the Traditions[101] and in contemporary practice. Recently a nine-month-pregnant Syrian woman explained, "In my condition the merit is multiplied 70 times."[102]

Judaism developed a strong legalism (e.g., Tobit 12:9),[103] as did the postapostolic church, which led to Alexander of Hales (d. 1245) advancing the doctrine of the treasury of merit. Protestants, however, although seeing the rewards of prayer (Matt 6:5,6) and that good can lead to life and divine acceptance (Acts 10:35; Rom 2:6,7), do not see it as merit but as the fruit of faith. Salvation is not seen as a result of merit (Tit 3:5); therefore Protestants would want to eliminate this function of prayer.

Muslims have viewed the salat as a duty,[104] yet it is more. Muhammad is reported to have said, "The salat is the comfort of my eyes."[105] Likewise he is quoted as saying, "If one of you performs the salat, he is in confidential conversation with God."[106] It functions to intensify belief: "Between man and polytheism and unbelief lies the neglect of salat."[107]

The prayer has been described as providing cleansing: "The salat is like a stream of sweet water which flows past the door of each one of you; into it he plunges five times a day; do you think that anything remains of his uncleanness after that?"[108] Likewise we read, "An obligatory salat is a cleansing for the sins which are committed between it and the following one."[109] Since the salat proper does not include penitence, the anticipated forgiveness is apparently based on human merit and divine mercy. However, it is common practice to insert before the final pronouncement of peace, "O God, forgive me my former and my latter [sins], my open and my secret [sins] and my extravagances and what Thou dost know."[110] Furthermore, as has been seen, the ablutions include a sense of inner cleansing.

The ritual prayer includes many themes that Christians share:

1. Witness ("I bear witness that there is no god but God" in the call to prayer—which, however, also witnesses to Muhammad's apostleship; cf. Deut 6:4)
2. God's mercy ("In the name of God, the Compassionate, the Merciful" in the Fatiha; cf. Ps 86:5 and pre-Islamic use of these introductory words in south and central Arabia and in early Arabic manuscripts of the Bible after Muhammad)[111]

---

the Heart," in McCurry, *The Gospel and Islam*, 218.

101 E.g., prayer in the mosque is considered twenty-five times more meritorious than elsewhere; see *Sahih al-Bukhari*, vol. 1, bk. 8 (*Salat*), chap. 87, 277.

102 Yvonne Haddad, "The Impact of the Islamic Revolution in Iran on the Syrian Muslims of Montreal," in *The Muslim Community of North America*, ed. Earle H. Waugh, Baha Abu-Laban, and Regula B. Qureshi (Edmonton, Alberta: University of Alberta Press, 1983), 175–76.

103 "Good is almsgiving, which delivers from death and purges away all sin." *The Book of Tobit*, trans. and ed. Frank Zimmerman (New York: Harper, 1958), 111.

104 *Sahih al-Bukhari*, vol. 1, bk. 8 (*Salat*), chap. 1, 211.

105 Ahmad b. Hanbal, vol. 3, 128, 285, cited in Wensinck, "Salat," 498A.

106 *Sahih al-Bukhari*, vol. 1, bk. 8 *(Salat)*, chap. 38, 244.

107 Muslim, *Sahih Muslim*, trans. Abdul Hamid Saddiqi (Lahore: Ashraf, n.d.), vol. 1 (*Iman*), trad. 146, 48.

108 Malek, *Qasr al-salat fi 'l-safar*, trad. 91, cited in Wensinck, "Salat," 498A.

109 Malek, *Qasr*, vol. 2, 229, cited in Wensinck, "Salat," 498A.

110 Tradition from Muslim, *Adhkaru 'n-Nawawi*, 33, cited in Padwick, *Muslim Devotions*, 173.

111 Regis Blachere, *Introduction au Coran*, 2nd ed. (Paris: C-Gt.-P. Maisonneuve, 1959), 142–44; Y. Moubarac, "Les etudes d'epigraphie sud-semitique et la naissance de l'Islam," *Revue des Etudes Islamique* (1957): 58–61; B. Carra de Vaux and L. Gardet, "Basmala," in *Encyclopaedia of Islam*, 2nd ed., 1084–85; *Mt. Sinai Arabic Codex 151*, 2 vols., ed. Harvey Staal (Leuven, Belgium: Peepers, 1985).

3. Praise to God ("Praise be to God" in the Fatiha; cf. Heb *Halelou Yah* and Latin Christian "Alleluia")

4. God's sovereignty ("Lord of the worlds" in the Fatiha; cf. Talmudic *Melek ha 'olam*—king of the universe)

5. Judgment ("King of the Day of Reckoning" in the Fatiha; cf. Matt 25:34; John 5:22; Rom 2:2,3; 1 Cor 15:24)

6. Worship ("Thee do we worship" in the Fatiha; cf. Ex 24:1; the Hebrew *shaha* and Greek *proskyneo* indicate prostration)

7. Refuge ("To Thee we cry for help" in the Fatiha; cf. Ps 46:1)

8. Guidance ("Guide us in the right path" in the Fatiha; cf. Ps 31:3; 119:1)

9. God's glory ("Glory to my Lord" in the *ruku*; the nominal form of *sabbaha* is used, borrowed from the Hebrew and Aramaic *shabeah* of Jewish worship)

10. God's greatness ("the Great" in the *ruku*; cf. Ps 48:1)

11. God's exaltation ("the Most High" in the *sujud*; cf. Ps 83:18)

12. Petition and intercession (possible in the *du'a*; cf. 1 Tim 2:1)

Obviously there is considerable overlapping of the themes of Muslim and Christian prayer.[112] Christian prayer can include most of Muslim prayer except the emphasis on Muhammad and, for Protestants, prayer for the dead. This has been evident in the study of the salat with its inclusion of the Fatiha.[113]

Muslim prayer cannot include quite as much of Christian prayer because of the references to God as Father, Jesus as Lord, the Trinity, and the crucifixion of Christ. Although Muslims may misunderstand parts of the Lord's Prayer, its themes resonate in Muslim devotion,[114] and a Tradition even says that Muhammad proposed a prayer that is obviously a free rendering of the Lord's Prayer without the initial words "Our Father."[115]

The Mosque

Some Muslim followers of Christ stay for at least a time in the mosque as the early Jewish followers of Christ remained in the temple and synagogue. Where whole villages have turned to Christ, they have reutilized the mosque for a church. Others have continued mosque-like worship. To evaluate the appropriateness of these approaches, we shall seek to determine the extent to which the mosque has been influenced by synagogues and churches and what its meanings and functions are.

The word for a mosque, *masjid*, is from the Aramaic and has the root meaning "to worship or prostrate oneself," found also in the Ethiopic *mesgad*, used of a temple or church.[116] In the Qur'an it is a

---

112 See, e.g., Padwick, *Muslim Devotions,* 173n97; Kenneth Cragg, ed., *Alive unto God: Muslim and Christian Prayer* (London: Oxford University Press, 1970); Marston Speight, "Muslim and Christian Prayer," *Newsletter of the Task Force on Muslim Christian Relations* (Hartford, CT: National Council of Churches and Duncan Black Macdonald Center), no. 12 (March 1980): 1–3.

113 See Cragg, "A Study in the Fatiha," in *Operation Reach* ([Beirut and Jerusalem]: Near East Christian Council, September–October, 1957), 9–18.

114 Masson, *Le Coran,* 521–24. For comparisons of the Lord's Prayer and the Fatiha, see Cragg, *Alive unto God,* 18–19; and Colin Chapman, "Biblical Foundations of Praying for Muslims," in Woodberry, *Emmaus Road,* 334–42.

115 Ignaz Goldziher, *Muhammedanische Studien* (Halle, Germany: Max Niemeyer, 1889–1990), 2:386 (*Muslim Studies,* trans. S. M. Stern [London: Allen & Unwin, 1971], 350).

116 Jeffery, *Foreign Vocabulary,* 263–64; Pedersen, "Masdjid," 330A.

general word that is used not only of Muslim sanctuaries but also of the Christian sanctuary associated with the Seven Sleepers of Ephesus (surah 18:21/20) and the Jewish temple in Jerusalem (if we adopt the traditional interpretation of surah 17:1). Ibn Khaldun (d. 1406) still used the word in a general sense to include the temple of Solomon.[117] The underlying meaning of "synagogue" and "church" (*ekklesia*) was "gathering," as it was for *jami'*, a word that increasingly came to be used for mosques.

Muhammad certainly knew about synagogues and churches or chapels, for they are mentioned in the Qur'an (surah 20:40/41). As Islam spread, various arrangements with Christian and Jewish sanctuaries developed. In Damascus, tradition says that the Church of St. John was divided, half for Muslims and half for Christians. In any event, the two centers of worship were beside each other until the mosque incorporated the church.

In Hims in Syria and Dabil in Armenia, Muslims and Christians shared the same buildings. Umar, the second caliph, built a mosque on the site of the temple in Jerusalem, where later the Dome of the Rock was built.

Many churches and synagogues were transformed into mosques. Muslims were told, "Perform your salat in them [churches and synagogues]; it will not harm you." The transfer of buildings was further facilitated whenever they were associated with biblical people who were also recognized by Islam. On the other hand, Umar is reported to have declined to perform the salat in the Church of the Holy Sepulcher to guard against its being made into a mosque.[118]

The mosque performed many functions. It was primarily for worship but also was a place for public political assembly, or even for strangers who needed a place to sleep and eat. Worship included not only prayer but might include the repetition of the names and praises of God, a practice cultivated by the Sufis.[119]

Mosque worship also included the recitation of the Qur'an. Here the influence of the previous monotheistic faiths is evident. *Qur'an* is from the Syriac *qeryana*, used to denote the "reading" or "reciting" of the Scripture lesson by Christians,[120] as the Muslim *qira'a* ("the recitation" itself) is the equivalent of the *Qeri'a* of the synagogue.[121] Sermons too were included, especially at Friday noon. Evidence of Jewish and Christian influence would seem to include the requirement of two sermons, with the preacher standing but pausing to sit down in between. This would correspond with the practice of the rabbi sitting in between the reading of the Torah and the Prophets while the Law was rolled up.[122]

The earliest mosques were open spaces with an arbor or booths (*zulla*), but they soon developed under Christian influence. Pillars and other materials were taken from churches, and the booths replaced with pillared halls. The caliph Abd al-Malik (646–705) had Byzantine builders erect the Dome of the Rock in Jerusalem, consciously copying the dome of the Church of the Holy Sepulcher. His son, al-Waled (d. 715), not only had Byzantine architects transform the basilica of St. John the Baptist

---

117 Frank Rosenthal, trans., *The Muqaddimah*, 3 vols. (New York: Pantheon, 1958), 2:249.

118 Pedersen, "Masdjid," 330–37.

119 Gardet, "Dhikr," in *Encyclopaedia of Islam*, 2nd ed.

120 J. Horovitz, "Quran," *Der Islam* 13 (1923): 66–69.

121 Guillaume, "Influence of Judaism," 156; Theodor Noeldeke, *Geschichte des Qorans*, 2nd ed. (Leipzig, 1909), 3:116–248; R. Paret, "Kira'a," in *Encyclopaedia of Islam*, 2nd ed.

122 Mittwoch, *Zur Entstebungsgeschichte*, no. 2; Becker, "Islamischen Kultus," 374–419; Becker, "Die Kanzel im Kultus des alten Islam," in *Orientalische Studien Theodor Noeldeke zum siebzigsten Geburtstag*, ed. Carl Bezold, 2 vols. (Giessen, 1906), 331ff.; *Sahih al-Bukhari*, vol. 2 (*Jum'a*), chap. 28, 24; Wensinck, "Khutba," in *Encyclopaedia of Islam*, 2nd ed.

in Damascus into the Umayyad Mosque, but used Christian architects to direct the building of the mosques of Mecca and Medina. When he was inspecting the work in Medina, an old man said, "We used to build in the style of mosques; you build in the style of churches."[123]

The minaret may have been influenced in a number of ways. It was not part of the earliest mosques, but was included when churches such as the basilica of St. John in Damascus became mosques. It had a watchtower—the meaning of *manara*, its common name. It may also have been influenced by the dwelling towers of Christian ascetics in North Africa, where it had the name *sawma'a* (saint's cell) and was used as such in Egypt and Syria.

The *mihrab* ("niche" indicating the direction of prayer) was not in the earliest mosques. In churches it was a principal niche that might contain the bishop's throne or an image or picture of a saint. Muslim literature attests that it was taken over from churches. It was even opposed because it was inherited from churches and was compared with altars as the holiest place. It is the place where the imam stands.[124] Churches that became mosques, such as the Sophia in Istanbul, often had to alter the inside to indicate the *mihrab*. A Roman Catholic orphanage in Kabul, Afghanistan, supervised by the Islamicist S. de Beaurecueil, had two orientations so that Christians and Muslims could worship in the same room.

The *minbar* is probably a loan word from Ethiopic and means "seat, chair."[125] Traditions indicate that the original maker was a Byzantine or Coptic Christian. 'Amr, the companion of Muhammad who conquered Egypt, had one made in his mosque, and it was said to be of Christian origin. Obviously it was analogous to a Christian pulpit.

A platform (*dakka*) from which the *mu'adhdhin* gives the call to prayer is found in larger mosques. There is also a *kursi* (wooden stand with a seat and a desk to hold a Qur'an). The seat is for the reader (*qari, qass*). Water for ablutions is often provided in a basin (*fisqiya* or *piscina*, which in the Mishna and Syriac is *piskin*). Unlike in churches, pictures and images are banned. The use of carpets is traced back to Muhammad, who used a mat woven of palm leaves.[126]

Of interest here is that Rabbi Abraham, who inherited the position of "leader of the Jews" upon the death of his father Maimonides in 1237, demanded that pillows be removed from synagogues and carpets and prayer mats be used. He believed that Islam (and especially the Sufis) had preserved many practices of the former Jewish sages, such as the use of these along with prostration and kneeling, ritual immersions, and nightly prayers.[127]

Since Islam expresses a total way of life and traditionally "religion" and "politics" were not separated, the functions of the mosque were, and to a lesser extent still are, broader than those of most churches today. Originally the caliph was appointed the leader of the salat and the preacher (*khatib*) for the community and was installed on the *minbar*. In the provinces, governors served a similarly broad function, administering "justice among the people" and the salat. The mosque also served as a court of justice. Some early *qadis* (judges) sat in judgment beside the *minbar* or in the square beside the mosque—practices that were also associated with churches.[128]

---

123 F. Wuestenfeld, *Geschichte der Stadt Medina* (Goettingen, 1860), 74, cited in Pedersen, "Masdjid," 339B–340A.

124 Pedersen, "Masdjid," 340–43.

125 Ibid., 343.

126 Ibid., 343–46; *Sahih al-Bukhari*, vol. 1, bk. 8 (*Salat*), chaps. 20–21 and 54, 231–32, 254–55.

127 Lazarus-Yafeh, *Some Religious Aspects*, 88–89.

128 *Sahih al-Bukhari*, vol. 9, bk. 89 (*Ahkan*), chaps. 18–19, 209–211; Pedersen, "Masdjid," 347–48; Adam Mez, *The Renaissance of Islam*, trans. S. Khuda Bakhsh and D. S. Margoliouth (London: Luzac, 1937), 233.

To determine the extent to which Muslim followers of Christ may still worship in a mosque or mosque-like context, we need to determine the function of both mosques and churches. Contemporary mosques are more like Christian chapels (where people only worship) than local churches (where people are also members), although many mosques in the United States have also assumed the latter function. The early Christian community applied themselves to teaching, fellowship, breaking of bread, prayer, performing signs and miracles, sharing, and praising God. They continued to go regularly to the temple but broke bread in their homes (Acts 2:42–47). Here we at least have a precedent for continuing the incomplete worship even as the new believers remembered Christ's death (the completion of the worship) in their homes. Paul continued to go to the synagogue and temple until put out (e.g., Acts 19:8,9; 21:26–29). James too still worshiped in the synagogue or a place called a synagogue (Jas 2:2).

Pillar 3: Almsgiving (*Zakat*)

Zakat is obligatory almsgiving of a prescribed percentage of different kinds of property (2.5 percent for most), which is distributed to the needy. The Qur'an specifies the recipients of various kinds of alms as parents, relatives, orphans, the poor, the needy, travelers, those who work on [collecting] them, those whose hearts are to be conciliated, slaves, debtors, and for God's purposes (surah 2:115/211; 9:60).

It is an Aramaic loan word that originally was a general term for virtue but came to be used by the rabbis for charitable gifts, an understandable shift when almsgiving was considered as particularly virtuous. The same shift in meaning can also be traced in the Qur'an from virtue in general (87:14; 92:18) to almsgiving (7:156/155; 21:73).[129]

Sadaqa is another qur'anic word for almsgiving. It too is a loan word from the Hebrew *tsedaqa* or *tsedeq*, meaning "honesty" or "righteousness," but was used by the rabbis of almsgiving. The relationship between upright actions (*tsedeq*) and caring for the poor is already seen in Daniel 4:24–27. The word *sadaqa* is used in two ways in the Qur'an and the Traditions. First, it is a synonym of *zakat* (obligatory alms) in the Qur'an (surah 9:58–60,103/104–104/105) and the Traditions (where al-Bukhari talks about *sadaqa* in sections on *zakat*). Secondly, *sadaqa* is used of voluntary almsgiving (e.g., surah 2:263/265–264/266), sometimes called *sadaqat al-tatawwu'* (alms of spontaneity).[130]

'Ushr is a tithe on produce levied for public assistance. It was similar to the tithes on the land of the Mosaic law (Lev 27:30–33; Num 18:21–26). In places half went to the poor and half went to the ruler.[131]

Almsgiving had great importance in all three monotheistic faiths. The Qur'an makes a clear distinction between believers, who give alms (surah 8:2–4; 23:1–4), and disbelievers, who do not (41:7/6). There is considerable concern that alms be given to the poor (9:60), as there is in the Old Testament (Deut 15:11; Prov 19:17) and the New Testament (Matt 6:1–4; 25:35–46).

There are a number of parallels between the Qur'an and the Bible. One has to do with not giving to be seen by people. The Qur'an indicates that God does not love those who dispense their goods ostensibly to be seen by people (surah 4:38/42), in a context that suggests almsgiving. Likewise Jesus said, "When you give alms, sound no trumpet before you, as the hypocrites do . . . that they may be praised by men" (Matt 6:1–4 RSV). In the Qur'an, however, public giving is all right: "Say to my servants who believe, that they . . . expend of that. We have provided them, secretly and in public" (surah 14:31/36).

---

129 Jeffery, *Foreign Vocabulary*, 153; J. Schacht, "Zakat," in *Shorter Encyclopaedia of Islam*, 654.

130 *Sahih al-Bukhari*, vol. 2, bk. 24 (*Zakat*), chap. 41, 310; T. H. Weir, "Sadaka," in *Shorter Encyclopaedia of Islam*.

131 A. Grohmann, "Ushr," in *Shorter Encyclopaedia of Islam*.

It says, "If you publish your freewill offering, it is good; but, if you conceal them and give to the poor, that is better" (2:271/273). Al-Ghazali (d. 1111) even argued in his major work, the *Ihya*, that much can be said for both open and secret alms, depending on the circumstances and the motive.[132]

Another parallel between the Qur'an and the Bible has to do with the attitude and conduct that accompanies almsgiving. Surah 2:262/263 says, "Those who expend their wealth in the way of God then follow not up what they have expended with reproach and injury, their wage is with their Lord." Paul speaks of the importance of attitude in 2 Corinthians 9:7: "Each of you should give . . . not reluctantly or under compulsion, for God loves a cheerful giver."

Still another parallel between the two Scriptures has to do with God's recompense. Although the Qur'an warns not to give in order to gain more (surah 74:6), rewards are promised: "What you give in alms desiring God's face—those they receive recompense manifold" (30:39/38). The reward is compared to the multiplication of corn when it is planted (2:261/263).

Proverbs 19:17 likewise promises, "He who is kind to the poor lends to the Lord, and he will repay him for his deed" (RSV). Jesus also said, "Give, and it will be given to you" (Luke 6:38). The rich young ruler, whose focus on wealth kept him from following Jesus, was told, "Go, sell your possessions and give to the poor, and you will have treasure in heaven. Then come, follow me" (Matt 19:21). Jesus knew that "where your treasure is, there your heart will be also" (Matt 6:21).

There is an area in which alms accomplish a function with which Protestants would take issue. The Qur'an affirms:

> Whosoever forgoes it [legal retribution] as a freewill offering (*sadaqa*), that shall be to him an expiation (*kaffara*) [for his own sins]. . . . The expiation [for breaking oaths] is to feed ten poor persons . . . or to clothe them, or to set free a slave. . . . Expiation [for slaying game during pilgrimage is] food for poor persons. (Surah 5:45/49,89/91,95/96)

The Roman Catholic canon in the Apocrypha has a similar teaching: "Almsgiving atones for sin" (Ecclus 3:30), and "Almsgiving delivers from death and saves people from passing down to darkness" (Tobit 4:7).

Some of the church fathers also associated almsgiving with the forgiveness of sins. The second epistle attributed to Clement of Rome claims, "Almsgiving is excellent as penitence for sin; fasting is better than prayer, but almsgiving is better than either. . . . Almsgiving alleviates sin" (16:4). Cyprian, Athanasius, Jerome, and Augustine also associated almsgiving with the forgiveness of sins.[133]

Much more could be said on the function of *zakat* in contemporary Muslim economics.[134] But, from a Christian perspective, we need to note that Jesus expected it to be a regular part of the believer's practice (Matt 6:3), and James classified attention to orphans and widows in their affliction to be part of religion that is pure and undefiled before God (Jas 1:27). Yet underlying all Christian giving should be the response of gratitude for God's "inexpressible gift" (2 Cor 9:11–15 RSV).

---

132 Ghazali, *Ihya Ulum-id-Din,* vol. 1, chap. 5, sect. 4, 219–21.

133 Masson, *Le Coran,* 608, 608n3.

134 See, e.g., John Thomas Cummings, Hossein Askari, and Ahmad Mustafa, "Islam and Modern Economic Change," in *Islam and Development: Religion and Sociopolitical Change,* ed. John L. Esposito (Syracuse: Syracuse University Press, 1980), 25–47.

Pillar 4: Fasting (*Sawm*)

Fasting is listed as a characteristic of those who submit to God—that is, true Muslims (surah 33:35). Many Christians, however, believe it is wrong, or at least unwise, to keep the fast of Ramadan.[135] To evaluate this, as with the other pillars, we need to look at the roots, meaning, and function of Muslim and Christian fasting.

The words that Muslims use, *sawm* and *siyam*, originally had a different meaning in Arabic, "to be at rest." In Judeo-Aramaic usage, however, they already meant "fasting," which suggests this was the source of Muslim usage. This connection is supported by the Qur'an, which makes the prescription to fast a continuation of the prescription to those before them (2:183/179). The Traditions are even more specific:

> The Prophet came to Medina and saw the Jews fasting on the day of *'Ashura*. He asked them, "What is this?" They told him, "This . . . is the day on which God rescued the children of Israel from their enemy. So Moses fasted this day." The Prophet said, "We have more claim to Moses than you." So the Prophet fasted on that day and ordered Muslims to fast on it.[136]

The first year in Medina, the fast was "a few days," apparently the ten days of penance leading up to the Jewish Day of Atonement—*'Ashura* (the "tenth" in Hebrew-Aramaic), the word Muslims use. It was also a time of seclusion for the pious in the place of worship—a practice that later was incorporated by Muslims into the last ten days of Ramadan and called *i'tikaf* when that month was made the required fast.

Other practices are also similar to those of Judaism. Abstaining from eating and drinking in the day but not at night was Jewish.[137] Even in biblical times this was sometimes practiced (Judg 20:26; 2 Sam 1:12; 3:35). Likewise the Qur'an says, "Eat and drink until the white thread becomes distinct to you from the black thread at dawn" (surah 2:187/183). The source is the Jewish Mishnah.[138]

Fasting has played a significant role in Judaism and Christianity—including fasts of extended periods, like the month of Ramadan. Moses, Elijah, and Jesus all fasted forty days and nights (Deut 9:9,18; 1 Kgs 19:8; Luke 4:1–2). Jesus expected people to fast (Matt 6:16–18), and Paul fasted frequently (Acts 13:2; 2 Cor 6:5; 11:27). Fasting was emphasized by the church fathers, and the forty-day fast or self-denial of Lent is even mentioned at the Council of Nicaea in 325.[139]

When we look at the meanings and functions of Muslim and Christian fasting, we see many parallels and some differences. Firstly, for the Muslim, fasting is above all an act of obedience, for it is prescribed for them (surah 2:183/179). Secondly, it is an act of commemoration of the "descent" of the first verses of the Qur'an on the twenty-seventh of Ramadan (44:1–5/4). Thirdly, in the Traditions it has developed the meaning of contrition and forgiveness that is more prominent in the Judeo-Christian tradition. One says, "All sins are forgiven to one who keeps Ramadan out of sincere faith and hoping

---

135 Donald R. Richards, "A Great Missiological Error of Our Time: Keeping the Fast of Ramadan—Why We Shouldn't," *Seedbed* 3 (1988): 38–45.

136 *Sahih al-Bukhari*, vol. 3, bk. 31 (*Sawm*), chap. 70, 124.

137 W. O. E. Oesterly and G. H. Box, *The Religion and Worship of the Synagogue* (London: Pitman and Sons, 1907), 326, 404.

138 *The Talmud of Jerusalem*, bk. 1 (Berakhoth), chap. 1, paragraph 5, 15.

139 See Masson, *Le Coran*, 573–74.

for a reward from God." Another affirms, "When the month of Ramadan starts, the gates of heaven are open and the gates of hell closed." The reference to the gates of heaven being open seems to be based on the old Jewish practice of praying when the temple gates were open since that was a propitious time.[140] This same sense of pardon is found in the fasts for expiation (surah 2:196/192; 15:89/90,95/96).

The concept is very prominent in the biblical examples (Ex 32:30; Deut 9:25–29; Neh 1:4–6; 9:1–2; Matt 12:41), as it is in the Torah.[141] Likewise the Roman Catholic Church has used the fast as penitence and preparation before the Mass and leading into Holy Week.

The nights of Ramadan are times of joy and celebration, and decorations are often put in the streets during the month. Although fasting was used to express sorrow in biblical times (e.g., 2 Sam 1:11,12), it can also be a time of joy (Zech 8:19).

Christians are given warnings against the misuse of fasting (Matt 6:16–18; Luke 18:10,12), but Jesus expected his disciples to fast (Mark 2:18–20). It is interesting that Paul includes his going hungry as one of the deprivations he endured so that he would "put no obstacle in any one's way" (2 Cor 6:3 RSV). Lack of fasting is seen by Muslims as being irreligious. God asked the Israelites, "Was it really for me that you fasted?" (Zech 7:5). We need to ask ourselves the same question.

Pillar 5: Pilgrimage (*Hajj*)

Not too much attention will be given to the pilgrimage, since it was an adoption and reinterpretation of pagan rituals. The Traditions make this clear. Muhammad's wife Aisha, for example, told how the pagans used to enter a consecrated state (*ihram*) in the name of the idol Manat. Out of honor for that idol, they did not perform the pilgrimage ritual between the hills of al-Safa and al-Marwa at the Kaaba until the Qur'an explained that they were now symbols of God (surah 2:158/153).[142]

Despite its pagan origin, many of its elements were those that God adopted for use in the schoolhouse of his children Israel. The word *hajj* is the Hebrew *hag* used in Psalm 81:4 (v. 3 in English) for a sacrifice when the Israelites were gathered in Jerusalem. Likewise the word *qurban*, frequently used to describe the Festival of Sacrifice during the pilgrimage, is used for "offering" or "consecrated" in Leviticus and Numbers.

Muslims are required to perform the pilgrimage once in their lifetime, if possible, as the Israelites were to go to Jerusalem three times a year. One of these, the Feast of Tabernacles, has a number of similarities to the hajj—for example, going seven times around the sanctuary (Ps 26:6) as Muslims do around the Kaaba and standing before God as an act of worship.

The concept of the Mosque of Mecca being *haram* (a sacred place restricted to Muslims—surah 9:28) has its counterpart in the Court of the Gentiles, who could not enter the temple. Mecca is seen as the place of the Last Judgment, as Jerusalem is in Judaism. Abraham is associated with the Kaaba, as Jews associate him with Mt. Moriah (Gen 22:2) under the temple area. The Kaaba has a covering (*kiswa*) replaced every year like that of the tabernacle. The direction of prayer for Muslims and Jews has been toward their respective sanctuaries. As the temple had a place for ablutions, the Meccan mosque has *zam zam* water, later supplemented. As Muslim pilgrims put on white clothing when in a consecrated state, so the high priest put on holy garments (Lev 16:4). Likewise the hair is not cut when one is in a consecrated state, as was the case with the biblical Nazarite vow (Num 6:5).

---

140 *Sahih al-Bukhari*, vol. 3, bk. 3 (*Sawm*), chaps. 5–6, 69–70; Goitein, *Studies*, 100.

141 *The Torah: A New Translation of the Holy Scriptures* (Philadelphia: Jewish Publication Society, 1902), 212.

142 *Sahih al-Bukhari*, vol. 6, bk. 60 (*Tafsir*), chap. 284, 362–63.

If all these elements were used by God in his schoolhouse for his people, can they not serve again for lessons as he gathers a new people for himself? The lessons will no longer be in Mecca. As Jesus told the woman of Samaria, worship will not be restricted to specific locations (John 4:20–24). God, however, used pilgrimages to teach the people lessons including his holiness and their unity as a people. We shall need to find ways to do the same.

Current Reusing of the Pillars

The case study we are considering is in a Muslim country that has had missionaries and churches for many years but had seen very few conversions from the Muslim community. Almost all the Christians were from another religious group.

Five years ago the church responded to a natural catastrophe by sending twenty Christian couples to serve, only one from a Muslim background. Their work was appreciated, but their Muslim neighbors would not eat the food they gave them. It was assumed that the Christians were "unclean" when they prepared it because they did not bathe (ghusl) in the morning when they may have had sexual relations the night before. When they changed their bathing habits, their Muslim neighbors ate their food. The Christians were called angels because of their service but were still considered "irreligious" because they did not perform ritual prayers (salat). Even when God answered their prayers miraculously, their neighbors did not follow Christ until the Christians were seen to perform ritual prayers.

Less than three years ago a more contextual approach was adopted with help from some who had studied with Fuller School of World Mission personnel. Only Muslim converts were employed in the villages, and many thousands have since responded. God has used a number of factors along with the contextualization. The New Testament had been translated using Muslim vocabulary rather than words from the other religion, and copies had been sold throughout the villages. Natural catastrophes had occurred that were interpreted as divine judgment, and the Christian couples had responded with a holistic ministry. These Christians had prayed for the sick, the natural catastrophes, and personal relationships, and God had answered with amazing power. Muslims who opposed the conversions were even stricken with ailments.

An important factor was that some of the Christian leaders knew the Qur'an well. The Muslims believed that Muhammad would be an intercessor on the Last Day.[143] The Christians challenged this, for Muhammad, they said, is not mentioned by name in the Qur'an as an intercessor. They pointed out that only one whom God approves may intercede (surah 19:87/90; 20:109/108; 53:26/27). The *Injil* (Gospel), which the Qur'an affirms, says that God approved of Jesus (Matt 3:17; Mark 1:11; Luke 3:22) and states that he is the only mediator between God and humanity (1 Tim 2:5). This would fit in with the common interpretation of surah 43:61 as designating that the return of Jesus will be a sign of the Last Hour.

Decisions are normally made in groups. The chairman announced that another meeting would be held the following month. If the *'ulama* won, the followers of Jesus should return to Islam. On the other hand, if they lost, he and his relatives would follow Jesus.

In another situation a Sufi mystic leader learned in a Good Friday message that the veil of the holy of holies was torn from top to bottom. He cried, "Why should I bother with the Law any more if Jesus

---

143 This could be based on 20:109/108; 34:23/22; and 43:86, but Muhammad is not mentioned by name.

has opened up the holy of holies?" He is leading his disciples to follow Jesus. Attempts are made to keep social units together by only baptizing people if the head of the family is also being baptized.

Conversions are following the web pattern along family, friendship, and occupation lines. When whole villages come, the mosque remains the center of worship. Teachers of their new faith are supported locally in the pattern of the imams of the mosque.

Muslim convert couples developed a prayer ritual that follows the Muslim pattern but expresses their new allegiance to God through Jesus. Morning prayer starts with the normal "intention" (*niya*) to pray but adds "in the name of my Lord and Savior Jesus Christ" before the traditional exclamation "God is greater" (*Allahu Akbar*). In the first *rak'a* (the basic ritual that is repeated), Psalm 23 or any other biblical passage is recited. The rest of the rak'a follows the traditional postures and praises to God, although "All praise to Jesus Christ" may be substituted for the first.

The Lord's Prayer is recited in the second rak'a, plus another passage if desired. After two rak'as, the worshiper adds to the thanksgiving, "Please give me favor to worship you this way until your [Christ's] second coming." Then the regular greeting and blessing are given to the ones on the right and left of the worshiper. A time for *du'a* (spontaneous prayer) is suggested for intercession and petition. The *iqama* is altered to:

> God is love. God is love.
> And praises belong to God.
> Present. Present before God.
> Present. Present in the name of Jesus Christ.

The remaining four daily prayers plus any additional rak'as at these times follow the same pattern with different Scripture passages indicated for each.[144] After the night prayer, a special prayer of three rak'as is suggested. In the first, John 1:12 is recited with the prayer: "O Almighty God, the experience that you have given me to be your child through placing my faith in Jesus Christ and accepting him as my personal savior, give the same experience to the lives of the _ million Muslims of _."

In the second rak'a, John 3:16 is recited with the prayer: "O God, the experience that you have given to me to have eternal life through your gift of grace in the Lord Jesus Christ, I claim the same experience in the name of Jesus Christ for the lives of _ million Muslims of _. Please acknowledge this."

Psalm 117:1–2 is recited in the final rak'a. At the conclusion, time is spent in intercession for the country, government officials, believers and their leaders, neighbors, relatives, and oneself.

We have seen that the so-called "pillars of Islam" had for the most part been used before by Jews and Christians, and with some adjustments are being used again. Their forms, meanings, and functions have been sufficiently similar to allow this to happen. Yet there are many factors that could weaken or topple them and what they support. One is the problem of training leadership for such a creative and rapidly growing movement. A second is how to build bridges to other segments of the church without inhibiting growth. The demise of the Nestorian Church gives mute witness to the results of being isolated.

A third problem is how to reuse Muslim forms without retaining Muslim meanings such as merit. A fourth is how to avoid an ossified contextualization that inhibits maturity—an apparent problem of

---

144 Ps 24:1–6; 25:1–7,8–14,15–22; 26:1–8; 34:1–8; 91:1–7; 92:1–8; 134:1–3; 136:1–9; 139:1–6; 141:1–5; 145:1–5; Isa 61:1–3; Matt 5:3–12; John 1:1–5; 2 Cor 5:18,19; Gal 3:26–29; Eph 1:3–8,11–14; Phil 2:5–11; Col 1:15–20; Titus 2:11–14; Heb 2:1–4,10–12; 2 Pet 1:5–9; Rev 5:9,10,12,13.

the Jewish believers to whom the epistle to the Hebrews was written. Despite the dangers, we are seeing God blessing the refurbishing of these pillars in our day as they bear the weight of new allegiances to God in Christ.

What is happening can be visualized in the Hagia Sophia, a fourth-century church that was close to its Jewish and Eastern foundations. Its pillars held up a dome on which was painted the face of Christ. Muslims made the church into a mosque—altering the direction of prayer, adding the names of Muslim heroes, and painting over some of the Christian mosaics. Over the face of Christ in the dome they painted the qur'anic words "God is the Light of the heavens and earth" (surah 24:35). The same pillars continued to hold up this witness. Should the artisans painstakingly remove its paint as they have from some of the other Christian pictures, they could once again see "the light of the knowledge of the glory of God in the face of Christ" (2 Cor 4:6 RSV). And the same pillars would continue to hold it up.

Bibliography

Accad, Fouad. *Building Bridges: Christianity and Islam.* Colorado Springs, CO: NavPress, 1997.

———. *Seven Muslim Christian Principles.* Limassol, Cyprus: Ar-Rabitah, n.d.

Andrae, Tor. *Les Origines de l'Islam et le Christianisme.* Translated by Jules Roch. Paris: Adrien-Maisonneuve, 1955.

Ayoub, Mahmoud M. *The Qur'an and Its Interpreters.* Albany, NY: State University of New York Press, 1984.

Baladhuri, Abu-l 'Abbas, al-. *Kitab Futuh al-Buldan.* Translated by Philip K. Hitti as *The Origins of the Islamic State.* New York: Columbia University, 1916.

Barr, O. Sydney. *From the Apostles' Faith to the Apostles' Creed.* New York: Oxford University Press, 1964.

Baumstark, A. "Juedischer und Christlicher Gebetstypus im Koran." *Der Islam* 16 (1927): 229.

Becker, C. H. "Die Kanzel im Kultus des alten Islam." In *Orientalische Studien Theodor Noeldeke zum siebzigsten Geburtstag,* edited by Carl Bezold. 2 vols. Giessen, 1906.

———. "Zur Geschichte des Islamischen Kultus." *Der Islam* 3 (1912): 374–419.

Bell, Richard. *The Origin of Islam in Its Christian Environment.* London: Macmillan, 1926.

Blachere, Regis. *Introduction au Coran.* 2nd ed. Paris: C-Gt.-P. Maisonneuve, 1959.

Bousquet. G. H. "Ghusl." In *Encyclopaedia of Islam,* 2nd ed., edited by P. J. Bearman, Th. Bianquis, C. E. Bosworth, E. van Donzel, and W. P. Heinrichs. Leiden: Brill, 1960–2005.

Bratcher, Robert G. *The Pillars of Religion in the Light of the Tawrat Zabur & Injil.* Beirut: The Bible Society, 1984.

Bukhari, Imam, al-. *Sahih al-Bukhari* (Arabic-English). Translated by M. Muhsin Khan. 9 vols. Beirut: Dar al-Arabia, n.d.

Carra de Vaux, B., and L. Gardet. "Basmala." In *Encyclopaedia of Islam,* 2nd ed., edited by H. A. R. Gibb et al. Leiden: Brill, 1986.

Cedrenus. *Annales.* Edited by Hylander. Basel, 1566. Cited in A. J. Wensinck, "Tayammum," in *Shorter Encyclopaedia of Islam,* edited by Hamilton A. R. Gibb and J. H. Kramers. Leiden: Brill, 1997.

Chapman, Colin. "Biblical Foundations of Praying for Muslims." In Woodberry, *Muslims and Christians,* 334–42.

Cragg, Kenneth, ed. *Alive unto God: Muslim and Christian Prayer.* London: Oxford University Press, 1970.

———. *Muhammad and the Christian: A Question of Response.* London: Darton, Longman and Todd, 1984.

———. "A Study in the Fatiha." *Operation Reach.* Beirut and Jerusalem: Near East Christian Council (September–October 1957): 9–18.

Cullmann, Oscar. *The Earliest Christian Confessions.* Translated by J. K. S. Reid. London: Lutterworth Press, 1949.

Cummings, John Thomas, Hossein Askari, and Ahmad Mustafa. "Islam and Modern Economic Change." In *Islam and Development: Religion and Sociopolitical Change*, edited by John L. Esposito, 25–47. Syracuse: Syracuse University Press, 1980.

Danby, Herbert, trans. *The Mishna.* London: Oxford University Press, 1949.

Epstein, Isidore, ed. *The Babylonian Talmud.* Translated by Maurice Simon and Israel A. Slotki. London: Soncino Press, 1935.

Feine, Paul. *Gestalt des apostolischen Glaubensbekenntnisses in der Zeit des Neuen Testament.* Leipzig: Verlag Doerffling & Franke, 1925.

Fueck, J. "The Originality of the Arabian Prophet." In *Studies on Islam*, translated and edited by Merlin Swartz, 86–98. New York: Oxford University Press, 1981.

Gardet, Louis. "Dhikr." In *Encyclopaedia of Islam*, 2nd ed., edited by H. A. R. Gibb et al. Leiden: Brill, 1986.

———. "Du'a." In *Encyclopaedia of Islam*, 2nd ed., edited by H. A. R. Gibb et al. Leiden: Brill, 1986.

Geiger, Abraham. *Judaism and Islam*, translated by F. M. Young. New York: KTAV, 1970. Originally published as *Was hat Mohammed aus dem Judentum aufgenommen?*, 1898.

Ghazali, Abu Hamid, al-. *Ihya Ulum-id-Din.* Translated by Fazal-ul-Karim. Lahore: Islamic Book Foundation, 1981.

———. *Al-Munqidh min al-dalal (The Deliverer from Error).* 3rd ed. Edited by Jamil Saliba and Kamal 'Ayyad. Damascus: Matba'at al-Jami'a al-Suriya, 1939.

———. *Al-Qustas al-Mustaqim.* Edited by V. Chelhot. Cited in V. Chelhot, "La Balance Juste," *Bulletin d'Etudes Orientales* 15 (1958): 62.

Gibb, Hamilton A. R. "Pre-Islamic Monotheism in Arabia." *Harvard Theological Review* 60 (1962): 269–80.

Goerling, Fritz. "The Use of Islamic Theological Terminology in Bible Translation and Evangelism among the Jula in Cote d'Ivoire." ThM thesis, Fuller Theological Seminary, 1989.

Goitein, S. D. *Jews and Arabs: Their Contact through the Ages.* 3rd rev. ed. New York: Schocken Books, 1974.

———. *Studies in Islamic History and Institutions.* Leiden: Brill, 1968.

Goldziher, Ignaz. *Muhammedanische Studien.* 2 vols. Halle, Germany: Max Niemeyer, 1889–90.

Grohmann, A. "Ushr." In *Shorter Encyclopaedia of Islam*, edited by Hamilton A. R. Gibb and J. H. Kramers. Leiden: Brill, 1997.

Guillaume, Alfred. "The Influence of Judaism on Islam." In *The Legacy of Israel*, edited by Edwyn R. Bevan and Charles Singer, 129–71. Oxford: Clarendon Press, 1928.

Haddad, Yvonne. "The Impact of the Islamic Revolution in Iran on the Syrian Muslims of Montreal." In *The Muslim Community of North America*, edited by Earle Waugh, Baha Abu-Laban and Regula Qureshi, 165–81. Edmonton, Alberta: University of Alberta Press, 1983.

Harrison, Paul W. "The Arabs of Oman." *The Moslem World* 24, no. 3 (1934): 262–69.

Heckman, Bruce. "Arab Christian Reaction to Contextualization in the Middle East." MA thesis, Fuller Theological Seminary, 1988.

Hirschfeld, Hartwig. *New Researches into the Composition and Exegesis of the Qoran.* London: Royal Asiatic Society, 1902.

Horovitz, J. "Quran." *Der Islam* 13 (1923): 66–69.

Huffard, Evertt W. "Thematic Dissonance in the Muslim-Christian Encounter: A Contextualized Theology of Honor." PhD dissertation, Fuller Theological Seminary, 1985.

———. "Culturally Relevant Themes about Christ." In Woodberry, *Muslims and Christians,* 177–92.

Jeffery, Arthur. *The Foreign Vocabulary of the Quran.* Baroda: Oriental Institute, 1938.

Kelley, J. N. D. *Early Christian Creeds.* 2nd ed. London: Longman, 1960.

Lazarus-Yafeh, Hava. *Some Religious Aspects of Islam.* Leiden: Brill, 1981.

Lenning, Larry G. *Blessing in Mosque and Mission.* Pasadena, CA: William Carey Library, 1980.

Malek, Sobhi W. "Allah-u Akbar Bible Lessons: Aspects of Their Effectiveness in Evangelizing Muslims." DMiss dissertation, Fuller Theological Seminary, 1986.

Massignon, Louis. *Essai sur les origines du lexique technique de la mystique musulmane.* Paris: Vrin, 1968.

Masson, Denise. *Le Coran et la revelation judeo-chretienne.* Paris: Adrien-Maisonneuve, 1958.

McCurry, Don M., ed. *The Gospel and Islam: A 1978 Compendium.* Monrovia, CA: MARC, 1979.

Mez, Adam. *The Renaissance of Islam.* Translated by S. Khuda Bakhsh and D. S. Margoliouth. London: Luzac, 1937.

Mittwoch, E. *Zur Entstebungsgeschichte des islamischen Gebets und Kultus.* In *Abhandlungen der preussen Akademie der Wissenschaften,* vol. 2. Berlin, 1913.

Moore, George Foot. *Judaism in the First Centuries of the Christian Era.* Cambridge, MA: Harvard University Press, 1950.

Moubarac, Y. "Les etudes d'epigraphie sud-semitique et la naissance de l'Islam." *Revue des Etudes Islamique* (1957): 58–61.

Mt. Sinai Arabic Codex 151. 2 vols. Edited by Harvey Staal. Leuven: Peepers, 1985.

Muslim. *Sahih Muslim.* Translated by Abdul Hamid Saddiqi. Lahore: Ashraf, n.d.

Nasr, Seyyed Hossein, ed. *Islamic Spirituality: Foundations.* New York: Crossroad, 1987.

Nazir-Ali, Michael. *Frontiers in Muslim-Christian Encounter.* Oxford, UK: Regnum, 1987.

Neufeld, Vernon H. *The Earliest Christian Confessions.* Grand Rapids, MI: Eerdmans, 1963.

Noeldeke, Theodor. *Geschichte des Qorans.* 2nd ed. Leipzig, 1909.

Oesterly, W. O. E., and G. H. Box. *The Religion and Worship of the Synagogue.* London: Pitman and Sons, 1907.

Owen, David. "A Classification System for Styles of Arabic Bible Translations." *Seedbed* 3, no. 1 (1988): 8–10.

Padwick, Constance E. "The Language of Muslim Devotion." *The Muslim World* 47 (1957): 5–21, 98–110, 194–209.

———. *Muslim Devotions: A Study of Prayer Manuals in Common Use.* London: SPCK, 1961.

Paret, R. "Kira'a." In *Encyclopaedia of Islam,* 2nd ed., edited by H. A. R. Gibb et al. Leiden: Brill, 1986.

Parshall, Phil. *Beyond the Mosque: Christians in Muslim Community.* Grand Rapids, MI: Baker, 1985.

———. "Lessons Learned in Contextualization." In Woodberry, *Muslims and Christians,* 251–65.

———. *New Paths in Muslim Evangelism: Evangelical Approaches to Contextualization.* Grand Rapids, MI: Baker, 1980.

Pedersen, J. "Masdjid." In *Shorter Encyclopaedia of Islam,* edited by Hamilton A. R. Gibb and J. H. Kramers. Leiden: Brill, 1961.

Rabin, Chaim. *Qumran Studies.* London: Oxford University Press, 1957.

Richards, Donald R. "A Great Missiological Error of Our Time: Keeping the Fast of Ramadan—Why We Shouldn't." *Seedbed* 3 (1988): 38–45.

Rosenthal, Frank, trans. *The Muqaddimah.* 3 vols. New York: Pantheon, 1958.

Schacht, J. "Zakat." In *Shorter Encyclopaedia of Islam,* edited by Hamilton A. R. Gibb and J. H. Kramers. Leiden: Brill, 1997.

Schlorff, Samuel P. "Feedback on Project Sunrise (Sira): A Look at 'Dynamic Equivalence' in an Islamic Context." *Seedbed* 3, no. 2 (1988): 22–32.

———. "The Missionary Use of the Quran: An Historical and Theological Study of the Contextualization of the Gospel." ThM thesis, Westminster Theological Seminary, 1984.

Schwab, Mose, trans. *The Talmud of Jerusalem.* Bk. 1. London: Williams and Norgate, 1886.

Sirat al-Masih bi-Lisan Arabi Fasih. Larnaca, Cyprus: Izdihar Ltd., 1987.

Smith, Wilfred Cantwell. *The Faith of Other Men.* New York: Harper & Row, 1963.

Stern, S. M., trans. *Muslim Studies.* London: Allen & Unwin, 1971.

The Talmud of Babylonia. Translated by Jacob Neusner. Chico, CA: Scholars Press, 1984.

The Talmud of Jerusalem. Translated by Moses Schwab. London: Williams and Norgate, 1886.

The Torah: A New Translation of the Holy Scriptures. Philadelphia: Jewish Publication Society, 1902.

Torrey, Charles. *The Jewish Foundation of Islam.* New York: Jewish Institute of Religion Press, 1933.

Trimingham, J. Spencer. *Christianity among the Arabs in Pre-Islamic Times.* London: Longman, 1979.

Trotter, Lilias. *The Way of the Sevenfold Secret.* Cairo: Nile Mission Press, 1926.

Watt, W. Montgomery. *The Faith and Practice of al-Ghazali.* London: Allen & Unwin, 1953.

———. *Muhammad at Mecca.* Oxford: Clarendon Press, 1960.

———. *Muhammad at Medina.* Oxford: Oxford University Press, 1956.

Weir, T. H. "Sadaka." In *Shorter Encyclopaedia of Islam,* edited by Hamilton A. R. Gibb and J. H. Kramers. Leiden: Brill, 1997.

Wensinck, A. J. *A Handbook of Early Muhammadan Tradition.* Leiden: Brill, 1960.

———. "Khutba." In *Encyclopaedia of Islam,* 2nd ed., edited by H. A. R. Gibb et al. Leiden: Brill, 1986.

———. "Kibla." In *Encyclopaedia of Islam,* 2nd ed., edited by H. A. R. Gibb et al. Leiden: Brill, 1986.

———. *Mohammed en de Joden te Medina.* 2nd ed. Leiden: Brill, 1928.

———. *The Muslim Creed.* Cambridge: Cambridge University Press, 1932.

———. "Niya." In *Shorter Encyclopaedia of Islam,* edited by Hamilton A. R. Gibb and J. H. Kramers. Leiden: Brill, 1997.

———. "Tahadjdjud." In *Shorter Encyclopaedia of Islam,* edited by Hamilton A. R. Gibb and J. H. Kramers. Leiden: Brill, 1997.

———. "Tayammum." In *Shorter Encyclopaedia of Islam,* edited by Hamilton A. R. Gibb and J. H. Kramers. Leiden: Brill, 1997.

———. "Wahy." In *Shorter Encyclopaedia of Islam,* edited by H. A. R. Gibb and J. H. Kramers, 622A. Leiden: Brill, 1961.

Wilder, John. "Some Reflections on Possibilities for People Movements among Muslims." *Missiology: An International Review* 5, no. 3 (1977): 301–20.

Woodberry, J. Dudley, ed. *Muslims and Christians on the Emmaus Road: Crucial Issues in Witness among Muslims.* Monrovia, CA: MARC, 1989.

Wuestenfeld, F. *Geschichte der Stadt Medina.* Goettingen, 1860.

Zimmerman, Frank, ed. and trans. *The Book of Tobit.* New York: Harper & Bros., 1958.

Zwemer, Samuel M. *Studies in Popular Islam.* London: Sheldon Press, 1939.

CHAPTER 46

Christian Attitudes toward Islam and Muslims
*A Kerygmatic Approach**
Martin Accad

With widespread mutual misunderstandings and misrepresentations that inform contemporary thinking between Christianity and Islam, East and West, there reigns an atmosphere of fear in many circles with regard to Christian-Muslim dialogue. "Dialogue" has often become a dirty word that insinuates either syncretism or polemics. But between these two extremes, are there any other viable positions on a spectrum of Christian-Muslim interaction? The purpose of this chapter is to propose a balanced, suprareligious approach to Christian-Muslim interaction, which will be called "kerygmatic interaction."

Fear of Dialogue Today

The word "dialogue" today is often misunderstood, whether it is used in so-called conservative or more liberal or secular milieus. The conservative will view it as inevitably leading to syncretism, whereas the liberal will fear that it will be used as a vehicle for polemics. The religious will fear to engage in dialogue lest it force them to compromise, whereas the secular will shun it as a platform for the assertion of exclusion. The relativist will use dialogue to flatten out differences, whereas the absolutist will use it to demonstrate the superiority of their own views.

I would like to suggest, however, that these two opposite positions stand in fact at the ends of a spectrum of potential positions and attitudes. Christian interaction with Islam need not be limited to a position of either syncretism or polemics. In fact, these two extremes hardly qualify as dialogue, since the first abolishes the distinction between two legitimate dialogical partners, and the second is too engaged in self-affirmation to be able to practice any form of listening. As such, both of these extreme positions belong to the category of monologue, since no dialogical partner is ever seriously engaged. Since these two positions do exist on the spectrum, I am calling the continuum a Spectrum of Christian-Muslim Interaction rather than Christian-Muslim Dialogue, in order to preserve the neutrality of the engagement. In this chapter I will describe the various positions on the spectrum, giving particular focus to the middle position, the kerygmatic interaction, in an attempt to help the reader develop a balanced attitude to the Islamic realities that are becoming more and more part of our global world, East and West.

Interaction between Christians and Muslims should no longer be viewed as one option among many. In the midst of religious and political conflicts that are continually and increasingly challenging

---

* Originally published in a slightly different form in *Toward Respectful Understanding and Witness among Muslims: Essays in Honor of J. Dudley Woodberry*, ed. Evelyne A. Reisacher (Pasadena, CA: William Carey Library, 2012), 29–47. Reprinted by permission.

the world we live in, the question should no longer be whether dialogue is necessary but rather what kind of dialogue needs to be carried out between the peoples of the world.[1]

The Urgency to Witness and the Challenges We Both Face

Given the sociopolitical importance of Christian-Muslim engagement, a topic in itself, the urgency of dialogue lies particularly in the fact that both religions are in essence mission-minded. Christians and Muslims cannot properly be called Christian and Muslim if they do not engage in witness to the world, including to each other. The Qur'an defines Muhammad's message as a universal message addressed to all of creation: "Verily this is no less than a Message to (all) the Worlds: (With profit) to whoever among you wills to go straight" (at-Takwir [81]:27,28 Yusuf Ali).

Qur'anic verses like the one above contain a clear summons to the Islamic *ummah* (community) to spread the message of Islam to the entire world. Likewise, the Gospels are clear on this point as well, particularly in the famous passage known as the Great Commission. The message of Jesus also is to be proclaimed throughout the world:

> Then Jesus came to them and said, "All authority in heaven and on earth has been given to me. Therefore go and make disciples of all nations, baptizing them in the name of the Father and of the Son and of the Holy Spirit, and teaching them to obey everything I have commanded you. And surely I am with you always, to the very end of the age." (Matt 28:18–20)

Both Christians and Muslims need legitimately to be able to proclaim and testify to the message that they have received with neither aggressiveness nor fear of reprisal, but rather in an atmosphere of mutual respect, love, and humility. It is no secret, however, that a Muslim who would turn away from Islam and adopt Christianity as his or her religion is going to face, in most cases, some severe reprisals. Even though the Qur'an is not explicit about this, all the major legal schools of Islam down through history have been unanimous on the fate of the so-called apostate. They must technically face the death penalty. Although such a penalty has seldom been implemented, it must be pointed out that the legal prescription is clearly challenged by Article 18 of the United Nations Universal Declaration of Human Rights, which states,

> Everyone has the right to freedom of thought, conscience and re-ligion; *this right includes freedom to change his religion or belief*, and freedom either alone or in community with others and in public or private, to manifest his religion or belief in teaching, practice, wor-ship and observance.[2]

Christians are also met with a serious challenge today when attempting to witness in a Muslim context. The message that the media and leadership—political and religious—set forth is one that either demonizes or idealizes Islam. In the Christian church context, the attitude is more often one of de-monization. Christians have always advocated that we are to love sinners but hate sin. This is a moral

---

1   Before reading any further, I recommend taking the "Test of Attitude to Islam and Muslims" (TAIM), which is found as Exhibit 1 (with its key as Exhibit 2) at the end of this chapter. The remainder of the chapter builds on the test results.

2   Emphasis added. See http://www.un.org/Overview/rights.html.

distinction that is fairly easy to maintain, as it is accompanied by the notion that we are all sinners outside the grace of God. However, there is today a parallel notion, which is spreading alarmingly fast, that we are to love Muslims but hate Islam. This notion is disturbing, for it is a very short step from the demonization of Islam and Muslims altogether. In reality, one observes that most people are unable to maintain such a theoretical separation between an ideology and its adherents.

The premise of the present chapter is the following: Your *view* of Islam will affect your *attitude* to Muslims. Your *attitude* will, in turn, influence your *approach* to Christian-Muslim interaction, and that *approach* will affect the ultimate *outcome* of your presence as a witness among Muslims.

How then do we develop a *view*, an understanding, of Islam that will foster in us the right attitude and approach in order for our relationships to be fruitful? It is in the context of reflecting over this question that I have developed what I now call the SEKAP Spectrum of Christian-Muslim Interaction (see fig. 46.1 below). SEKAP is an acronym that abbreviates the five dialogical positions (D1–D5) identified along the spectrum: Syncretistic, Existential, Kerygmatic, Apologetic, and Polemical. The five positions were further defined by asking ten questions: (1) What is my view of religions generally? (2) What is my understanding of Islam? (3) How do I view Muhammad? (4) What is my perception of the Qur'an? (5) How do I view Muslims? (6) What is my opinion about their eternal destiny? (7) Why do I relate to Muslims at all? (8) What approaches do I adopt? (9) What outcomes may I expect? (10) How much knowledge of Islam does this require on my part? The "Test of Attitude to Islam and Muslims" (TAIM) was developed based on these ten questions.

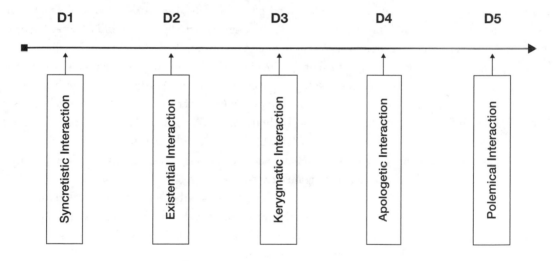

Fig. 46.1 The SEKAP Spectrum of Christian–Muslim Interaction

The Syncretistic Approach to Christian-Muslim Interaction
All Roads Lead to Mecca

In his conclusion to a chapter on Christianity and other religions, theologian John Hick cites from the Hindu Bhagavad Gita: "Let me then end with a quotation from one of the great revelatory scriptures of the world: 'Howsoever man may approach me, even so do I accept them; for, on all sides, whatever path they may choose is mine.'"[3]

The fact that Hick has to resort to a citation from outside the Christian Scripture to summarize his pluralist view begs the question as to how Christian his position actually is. Syncretism differs from pluralism. Pluralism is a category with primary concern for the question of salvation, whereas syncretism is an approach to religions that more comprehensively treats their various aspects, in addition to salvation, with a desire to reconcile their differences.[4] Syncretism relativizes differences between religions, whereas pluralism emphasizes the cultural particularity of each religious system while affirming their objective equality. As a general, all-inclusive attitude toward other religions—and here particularly regarding the attitude of Christians and Christianity toward Muslims and Islam—I have therefore chosen to call the approach to Christian-Muslim interaction at the D1 end of the spectrum syncretism rather than pluralism.

Whereas the syncretistic approach to Islam would consider all religions on an equal footing, it would also be somewhat suspicious of all religions, viewing them as a potential obstacle to peace between individuals, communities, and eventually between nations. At the same time, this position would consider that the positive contribution of religions lies mainly in the moral standards that they can instill in individuals within their societies. In that view, Islam is primarily seen as a sociopolitical phenomenon like any other successful religious movement of human history. Muhammad is considered to have been a sociopolitical leader who knew how to use his contemporary economic and historical realities to the advantage of his community and personal ends. The Qur'an is viewed as a literary achievement of Muhammad himself or some of his entourage, which the prophet of Islam used in order to impress a society that was strongly attracted to poetic literature. And in that light, Muslims would be simply considered to be adherents of a religious ideology in the same way as other religious peoples.

Syncretistic interaction is carried out with the purpose of inviting Muslims to be a positive part of a multicultural and multireligious universal humanity in all of its rich plurality. This is done by relativizing religious differences by dialoguing primarily about social, economic, and political topics, without necessarily requiring any deep knowledge of Islam. Due to the secular nature of this dialogue, it will generally take place among lay or secular scholars who may belong to various religious communities. This type of dialogue is likely to alienate religious leaders on either side.

Although this type of dialogue may offer some helpful scholarly perspectives on religion, chiefly adopting a history-of-religions approach, no deep impact into the day-to-day relationships of communities at the grass roots will be achieved. For it is generally the religious leaders who are most influential at the popular level of a culture that is religious to the core.

The Polemical Approach to Christian-Muslim Interaction: Seek and Destroy

Polemical interaction between Christianity and Islam stands at the other end of the spectrum. The word "polemical" comes from the Greek word *polemos*, which simply means "war." The polemical approach to Christian-Muslim interaction is precisely that approach that adopts warlike strategies in

---

3   John Hick and Brian Hebblethwaite, eds., *Christianity and Other Religions: Selected Readings* (Philadelphia: Fortress Press, 1980), 190.

4   The clear focus and concern for salvation inherently present in these different views is evident, for example, in the very title of Dennis L. Okholm and Timothy R. Phillips, eds., *Four Views on Salvation in a Pluralistic World* (Grand Rapids, MI: Zondervan, 1996).

Examine Your Attitude[*]

Those involved in efforts to communicate Christ among Muslims should examine or perhaps re-examine their personal attitudes towards both Islam and towards Muslim peoples. . . . The attitude we take toward another people and their religious faith will greatly impact (enhance or impede) our efforts to build meaningful personal relationships with them through which we might then share Christ. If we view their religious faith and religious practices as mere superstition—or worse, as demonic or satanic—then we typically approach the followers of such faiths in a condescending, confrontational, even combative, way.

On the other hand, if we embrace their religious efforts as being an authentic attempt to encounter the divine, we can then work to build upon points of contact within Islam to demonstrate how Christ is the ultimate fulfillment of their religious quest. Perhaps like the Apostle Peter, we need to learn that God is aware of and respects every person who is genuinely seeking to relate to him (Acts 10:34,35). Do we really respect their religious pursuits? Such attitudes and approaches tend to reduce the potential for conflict and enhance one's efforts at building personal relationships, thus facilitating attempts to share the gospel message.

—*Wilbur Stone*

---

* Excerpt from Wilbur Stone, "Islamic Studies—The Insider's Approach" (unpublished paper), 2. A version of this paper was later published as chap. 24 in *World Mission in the Wesleyan Spirit*, ed. Darrell L. Whiteman and Gerald H. Anderson (Franklin, TN: Providence House, 2009).

relating to the other religion, where one seeks to destroy and uproot the tenets of another in order to replace them with one's own. Many examples of this approach are found in the history of interaction between Christianity and Islam. One of the most ancient and classical ones is the treatment of Islam by John of Damascus, a Greco-Arab Eastern church father of the eighth century (675–753), whose father was a medical doctor at the court of the Umayyad caliph. John of Damascus dealt with Islam at the end of his treatise *Against Heresies*, calling it the "heresy of the Ishmaelites."

The polemical approach will generally hold a triumphalist view of Christianity in total exclusion of other religions. The ideology promoted is often a highly institutionalized form of Christianity, the religious substitute to Islam. All other worldviews are seen as simply wrong and as having nothing good to offer to Christians through dialogue. In this view, Islam is viewed as an evil and a thorn in the flesh of Christianity. Early such approaches gave rise to an apocalyptic genre of literature that considered that God had allowed the emergence of Islam as a punishment for the complacency of Christians. As bearer of that religion, Muhammad is viewed as having been possessed by demons, an antichrist whose mission was to deceive all people. The Qur'an was consequently inspired by the devil and is full of lies and deceit, to the point that merely reading it renders a person unclean. As a result, Muslims are the deceived followers of a religion that will lead them to hell.[5]

The chief reason why a Christian holding that view would seek to engage Islam is often to demonstrate to Muslims that Islam is false and deceitful. The message is communicated by accentuating

---

5 Two striking examples of this kind of approach are the ninth-century Byzantine writers Nicetas of Byzantium and George Hamartolos. The first begins by calling the Qur'an "abominable" and "barbarous," and Muhammad "perverse," "bestial," and possessing the "perversity of Satan." See J. P. Migne, ed., *Patrologia graeca*, vol. 105. The second ends up referring to Muslims as "men whose slimy souls would befit pigs." Ibid., vol. 110.

religious differences and proclaiming that Muslims will go to hell if they do not reject Islam. A variant to this aggressive proclamation is often a loss of interest in evangelism altogether, with the consideration that Muslims are not even worthy to hear the gospel.

The most likely outcome of such a discourse is aggressive reaction. At the same time, promoters of this approach will often justify it by pointing out that many Muslims are being won to Christianity. That does seem to be the case through such TV programs as those of Coptic priest Zakaria Botros.[6] Yet the cost in terms of intercommunal conflict is high, and the converts either have to remain secret Christians or have to be extracted out of their societies to avoid being harmed, leading to the accentuation of the chasm between religious communities. Those engaged in such an approach will often be quite convincing to the listener or reader, since they will have acquired a very thorough knowledge of all the weaknesses and problems in Islam. Though the negative outcomes of this approach will probably mark religious communities in the Muslim world for decades, it can nevertheless not be dismissed altogether. The nagging reality is that numerous Muslim converts to Christianity are staunch supporters of Father Zakaria, for he undoubtedly gives a voice to their repressed frustration that has resulted, quite frankly, from numerous experiences of oppression and persecution by their families, communities, and governments. As we consider this approach as evangelical Christians driven by God's call to mission, however, we also have to keep in mind the very serious consideration that no one openly using the polemical approach will be able to maintain a transparent presence in the Muslim world.

The Existential Approach to Christian-Muslim Interaction: Fostering Societies of Diversity

At the D2 point on the spectrum of attitudes regarding dialogue, one would find the existential approach to interaction. I use the term "existential" here in a nontechnical and nonphilosophical sense, as it pertains to human existence. At the same time, existentialism as a philosophy, whether theistic or atheistic, arose in skeptical reaction to the affirmation of the primacy of reason.[7] In that sense, the use of the term in the present context is appropriate, since this approach to Christian-Muslim interaction has as its primary focus sociological rather than theological concerns. The concerns are existential rather than rational. The questions asked by this approach are, How can adherents of both Christianity and Islam live better side by side? How can they acquire the level of tolerance that will promote peace rather than conflict among them? How can we build a better society for the future, one that respects pluralism and diversity?

In this type of Christian-Muslim interaction, religions are distinctively defined and differentiated, but Christ may be seen as not the only way to God and salvation. For those who engage in existential interaction, goodness and morality are the essence of all religions. This position will allow for a more significant divine role in the emergence of religions. In this view, Islam is a religion that originated from God, but like all religions, it underwent many human influences as well. If Muhammad did receive to some degree a divine calling to be God's prophet to the Arabs, then the Qur'an contains substantial elements of the divine truth and is to be respected as Scripture. Therefore, in the end, those Muslims who have been faithful Muslims will be saved.

---

6   See http://www.fatherzakaria.net/.

7   For existentialism as a philosophy, see, for example, John Macquarrie, "Existentialism," in *The Encyclopedia of Religion*, ed. Mircea Eliade (New York: Macmillan, 1987).

Christians who engage in this type of interaction will do so in order to encourage mutual social and religious understanding and tolerance between Christian and Muslim communities. In order to achieve this end, they will interact at social, economic, and political levels, affirming common ground and avoiding divisive issues. It can be expected that some positive transformation of mutual perceptions and relationships will ensue from this dialogue, as well as greater tolerance and appreciation between religious communities. At least some knowledge of the broad lines of Islam is necessary at that level. An excellent example of this approach can be seen in the Second Vatican Council, where the view of other religions was primarily expounded by the Catholic theologian Karl Rahner. In its 1965 Declaration on the Relation of the Church to Non-Christian Religions, the council declared,

> If in the course of the centuries there has arisen not infrequent dissension and hostility between Christian and Muslim, this sacred Council now urges everyone to forget the past, to make sincere efforts at mutual understanding and to work together in protecting and promoting for the benefit of all men, social justice, good morals as well as peace and freedom.[8]

The conciliatory tone of this statement is evident. It results from the recognition of a long history of conflict between Christianity and Islam. With its focus on the promotion of social justice and good morals, peace and freedom, it typically represents this level of existential interaction.

The Apologetic Approach to Christian-Muslim Interaction: Drawing from the Wealth of History

There is much in the New Testament to justify adopting a fourth type of interaction, which I have called apologetic interaction (D4). The Apostle Paul uses that approach numerous times in his epistles as a tool for the confirmation of the gospel, and Peter makes the famous exhortation to "always be prepared to give an answer (*apologia*) to everyone who asks you to give the reason for the hope that you have." Significantly, he adds in the same breath, "But do this with gentleness and respect" (1 Pet 3:15). That approach, then, should not so much be defensive, with the negative undertones of the English usage of the term. But rather it should be used as a tool to clarify and clear out misconceptions regarding the Christian faith. In the Gospels, the only place where a Greek form of the term is used is in Jesus' two sending discourses in Luke 12:11 and 21:14. Jesus exhorts his disciples not to linger on what defense (*apologia*) they will present to those who arrest them, for God will give them in time the words of wisdom that they need.

The main problem of this approach is the way that it has been used historically, locking up the discourse of both Christians and Muslims in generally sterile arguments that were passed along over the centuries. By the eleventh century, as I have demonstrated elsewhere,[9] what we keep coming across is a relentless repetition of the same arguments on both sides, often reflecting even a literary borrowing

---

8   Hick and Hebblethwaite, *Christianity and Other Religions*, 82–83.

9   Martin Accad, "Corruption and/or Misinterpretation of the Bible: The Story of the Islamic Usage of *Tahrīf*," *The Near East School of Theology Theological Review* 24, no. 2 (2003): 67–97; M. Accad, "The Gospels in the Muslim Discourse of the Ninth to the Fourteenth Century: An Exegetical Inventorial Table (Parts I–IV)," *Islam and Christian-Muslim Relations* 14, no. 1 (2003): 67–81, 205–20, 337–52, 459–79; and M. Accad, "The Interpretation of John 20:17 in Muslim-Christian Dialogue (8th–14th Centuries): The Ultimate Proof-Text," in *Christians at the Heart of Islamic Rule*, ed. David Thomas (Leiden: Brill, 2003), 199–214.

of age-old arguments. As I have shown, by that time the conversation based on Christian and Muslim Scriptures had been taken out of any original interpretive endeavor. This led to extreme eisegesis rather than proper exegesis, to the point where the discourse emerges at best as two separate monologues.

Essentially, this position holds that there is one ultimate truth: God. Judaism and Christianity are the only divinely established religions, and Christ, who is at the center of Christianity, is the only way to salvation. Islam is viewed as a human phenomenon whose understanding of God is misleading due to the fact that Muhammad himself was misled. The phenomenon of Qur'anic revelation perhaps reflects that Muhammad had some psychological problems that led him to believe that he had received a prophetic calling. Hence the Qur'an is a plagiarism of the Bible and contains many mistakes and inaccuracies. Within that framework, Muslims are being misled by a worldly religion that drives them away from the worship of the true God.

In this type of interaction, Christians will engage with Muslims solely for the purpose of evangelism, seeking to demonstrate to them the truth of Christianity and to refute the validity of Islam. Primary methods used are public debates that make heavy use of apologetic arguments, as well as a reliance on apologetics and polemics in private attempts to convert Muslims to Christianity. Although some Muslims will be convinced to become Christians under the influence of heavy apologetic demonstrations of the truth of Christianity, circular argumentation should be expected due to the long history of learned arguments and counterarguments on both sides. Both Christians and Muslims at that level will often study and memorize standard answers to age-old questions.

The Kerygmatic Approach to Christian-Muslim Interaction: The Gospel as God Proclaimed It

Finally, we come to the kerygmatic level of interaction (D3), which, I believe, has the potential of being most fruitful for Christ's gospel as good news and most conducive to peace in our age of great conflicts. Without dismissing the other four approaches altogether, I believe that it is through this kerygmatic approach that we will be able to think in the most Christlike way about Islam and Muslims. "Kerygmatic" comes from the Greek word *kerygma* and the verb *kerysso*, more often found in the Gospels in the form of the present participle *kerysson* (proclaiming). The *kerygma* in the New Testament is both the act of proclaiming and the proclamation itself. It is connected with the proclamation of God's good news concerning repentance, the kingdom, and Jesus—first by John the Baptist (Matt 3:1; Mark 1:4; Luke 3:3), then by Jesus himself (Matt 4:23; 9:35; Mark 1:14,39; Luke 4:4; 8:1), and later by the disciples in the book of Acts (20:25; 28:31). One significant characteristic of the *kerygma* in the Apostle Paul's usage of the term is that it is not designed to be enticing through the use of wise human words, but rather relies entirely on the power of God's Spirit (1 Cor 2:4). This is why Paul entreats Timothy to proclaim (*keryxon*) the message in season and out of season (2 Tim 4:2). And when he finds himself before the tribunal in Rome, even though the session is officially supposed to be his first defense (*en te prote mou apologia*) (2 Tim 4:16), he considers it an opportunity for the proclamation (*kerygma*) to be heard fully by all the Gentiles (2 Tim: 4:17).[10]

I want to retain from this Pauline usage the difference between the *kerygma* and the *apologia*, the difference in attitude between an apologetic defense of one's beliefs on the one hand, and a positive

---

10 On the various meanings of the concept, both inside and outside of the biblical text, see Gerhard Kittel and Gerhard Friedrich, eds., *Theological Dictionary of the New Testament*, trans. Geoffrey W. Bromiley (Grand Rapids, MI: Eerdmans, 1966), s.v. "Kerygma."

proclamation of it on the other. The kerygmatic approach to Christian-Muslim interaction is thus devoid of polemical aggressiveness, apologetic defensiveness, existential adaptiveness, or syncretistic elusiveness; not because any of these other four approaches is necessarily wrong, but because that is the nature of the *kerygma*: God's gracious and positive invitation of humanity into relationship with himself through Jesus. It needs essentially no militant enforcers, no fanatical defenders, no smart adapters, and no crafty revisers.

For the kerygmatic Christ follower, religions are recognized to be an essential part of the human psychological and sociological needs. At the same time, God is seen to be above any religious system. Although God is the absolute truth, no single religious system is infallible or completely satisfactory. I would contend that the Gospels indicate that Jesus himself, who is never seen as denying his Jewishness, had this attitude. He was at peace with his religious identity as a Jew, practiced the requirements of the Law from childhood, entered the Jewish places of worship, and was trained in Jewish theology and methods. At the same time, whenever Jesus expressed frustration in the Gospels, it was generally either toward some stratified religious institutional form such as the Sabbath, or toward stubborn institutional religious leaders. His message cut through the safety of the legalistic boundaries of righteousness, and his invitation to relate to God was extended to the marginalized and outcast of his society. Further, through carefully crafted parables, Jesus proclaimed himself to be the inaugurator of God's kingdom in fulfillment of God's promise to the nations, and he established himself as the final criterion of admission into that kingdom as the way to the Father.

Therefore, in recognition that social organization is a natural human phenomenon toward which we are all inclined, the kerygmatic position and attitude does not consist in rejecting one's religious heritage, for it would soon be replaced by another form of ideology. In the kerygmatic approach it is Christ himself who is at the center of salvation rather than any religious system. The *kerygma* is never a message of condemnation, but it brings condemnation to those who are stuck within religious boundaries. The principal difference between this position and the other positions on the dialogical spectrum is that the conversation is removed entirely from the realm of institutionalized religious talk. One theologian who captured this worldview was Karl Barth. In a chapter he titled "The Revelation of God as the Abolition of Religion," he said, "We begin by stating that religion is unbelief. It is a concern, indeed, we must say that it is the one great concern, of godless man."[11]

The kerygmatic approach that we are here advocating is therefore the equivalent of this Barthian revelation of God. The *kerygma* upheld by this approach is nothing less than God's own revelation in Christ. How then does a kerygmatic, suprareligious approach to the way of Christ develop a meaningful view and expression of the Islamic phenomenon? To this we now turn.

View of the Islamic Phenomenon

Whereas the kerygmatic position adopts a suprareligious approach to understanding and relating to God in Christ, it views Islam as an institutionalized religious phenomenon par excellence. It can adequately be said that Islamic law, *shari'a*, is the most authentic manifestation of Islam. In a very real sense, this places it in the category of a sociopolitical phenomenon dressed up in religious clothing. This does not make the religious manifestation of Islam less real or genuine, at least from the perspective of its adherents. One could say that Islam was particularly successful because of its strong religious ideological component.

---

11 Hick and Hebblethwaite, *Christianity and Other Religions*, 35.

Based on a reading of the Qur'an itself, the kerygmatic approach considers that Islam preserved many important and positive elements from the Judeo-Christian tradition. As such, Islam contains much truth about God and his revelation. On the other hand, because the kerygmatic perspective seeks to be supremely Christ-centered, it also considers that Islam lacks many of the essential truths of God's good news as revealed and proclaimed in and by Jesus Christ in the Gospels.

Islam's Prophet in the Kerygmatic Approach

The kerygmatic approach would maintain that Muhammad, Islam's messenger, believed that he received a genuine divine calling to be God's prophet to the Arabs. Muhammad's personality is complex and cannot be defined entirely through one single period of his life. He was a charismatic, prophetic leader in Mecca and in the early Medinan period, but then became much more of a political, military, economic, and social leader, particularly in the later Medinan period. Qur'anic evidence seems to indicate that he saw himself very much in continuation of the Judeo-Christian prophetic line, his mission being to turn his people away from idolatry and to the worship of the one God.

From a purely human perspective, and laying aside a theological understanding of revelation and inspiration, Muhammad's personality is not unlike that of some of the Old Testament prophets and men of God. Helpful insight regarding this question can be found in an ancient dialogue between Timothy I, the patriarch of the Church of the East, and the 'Abbasid Caliph Al-Mahdi, a conversation that took place near the end of the eighth century. Having been asked by the caliph about his opinion concerning the prophet of Islam, Timothy draws a parallel between him and some of the Old Testament prophets. Like them, "he taught the doctrine of the unity of God," "drove his people away from bad works, and brought them nearer to the good ones," "separated his people from idolatry and polytheism, and attached them to the cult and the knowledge of one God," and "taught about God, His Word and His Spirit." Timothy compares Muhammad to Moses, as he "not only fought for God in words, but showed also his zeal for Him in the sword." Further, Timothy adds, like Abraham, Muhammad "turned his face from idols and their worshippers, whether those idols were those of his own kinsmen or of strangers, and he honoured and worshipped only one God." Timothy ends his treatment of this subject by stating, "Who will not praise, O our victorious King, the one whom God has praised, and will not weave a crown of glory and majesty to the one whom God has glorified and exalted? These and similar things I and all God-lovers utter about Muhammad, O my sovereign."[12]

This perspective offered by Timothy I, patriarch of the Church of the East, is helpful in our attempt to make sense of Islam's messenger. A kerygmatic approach believes in the finality of Jesus Christ, in whom the fullness of God's good news was revealed. But this need not prevent us from admitting the greatness of Muhammad, and perceiving him, if not as a prophet, nonetheless as a *messenger*, a *rasul*, who carried an important divine message to his people, leading them away from polytheism and drawing them to the worship of the one God.

Islam's Holy Book, the Qur'an, as Viewed in the Kerygmatic Approach

"By the Book that makes things clear, We have made it a Qur'an in Arabic, that ye may be able to understand [and learn wisdom]" (az-Zukhruf [43]:2,3 Yusuf Ali).

---

12 Alphonse Mingana, ed., *1. Timothy's Apology for Christianity. 2. The Lament of the Virgin. 3. The Martyrdom of Pilate*, Woodbrooke Studies 2 (Cambridge, UK: W. Hefer & Sons, 1928), 61–62. Available at http://darkwing .uoregon.edu/~sshoemak/102/texts/timothy.html.

"So have We made the [Qur'an] easy in thine own tongue, that with it thou mayest give Glad Tidings to the righteous, and warnings to people given to contention" (Maryam [19]:97 Yusuf Ali).

"Verily, We have made this [Qur'an] easy, in thy tongue, in order that they may give heed" (ad-Dukhan [44]:58 Yusuf Ali).

"And We have indeed made the Qur'an easy to understand and remember: then is there any that will receive admonition?" (al-Qamar [54]:17 Yusuf Ali).

Numerous verses in the Qur'an seem to indicate that Muhammad's message was his genuine attempt to provide what he believed to be the essential elements of the Judeo-Christian Scriptures to his Arab people in a language that they could understand; namely, Arabic. Some scholars have advanced that the very word *Qur'an* is actually a borrowing from Syriac *qeryana*, which means simply "lectionary."[13] In that view, the Qur'an was originally largely an Arabic lectionary of the Bible, not entirely unlike a Jewish Targum.

In the first verse cited above, the wish of the Qur'an is, literally, that those who receive this Arabic book would perhaps come to a proper understanding (*la 'allakum ta 'qilun*) of matters about God. The next three verses are God's assertion to Muhammad that he has provided him with the Qur'an in Arabic in order to make it easy for him (*yassarnahu*, lit., "we have made it easy") as he proclaims the message.

There are several verses in the Qur'an that seem to support the view that in the initial Meccan and early Medinan period, Muhammad perceived his message to be a continuation of the Judeo-Christian tradition. God encourages his messenger by telling him that if his own tribe, Quraysh, does not receive his message, they should ask the People of the Book (Christians and Jews), who will confirm to them that the message is authentic. There is an assumption at that stage that Christians and Jews will naturally receive his message since it does not stand in contradiction with their own Scriptures.

"And before thee also the messengers We sent were but men, to whom We granted inspiration: if ye realise this not, ask of those who possess the Message" (an-Nahl [16]:43 Yusuf Ali).

"And thus [it is] that We have sent down the Book to thee. So the People of the Book believe therein, as also do some of these [pagan Arabs] and none but Unbelievers reject our signs" (al-'Ankabut [29]:47 Yusuf Ali).

Both of these passages, according to Muslim commentators, were revealed in Mecca. A third verse, cited below, is less optimistic in outlook. It is a Medinan verse that reflects Muhammad's disappointment with the way that Jews and Christians have rejected his message, as though it contained some elements that were foreign to their own Scriptures.

"And when there came to them a messenger from Allah, confirming what was with them, a party of the People of the Book threw away the Book of Allah behind their backs, as if [it had been something] they did not know!" (al-Baqara [2]:101 Yusuf Ali).

From that point onward, namely, the later Medinan period, Muhammad begins to dissociate himself from the Judeo-Christian tradition. One of the most striking manifestations of this is the change in the direction of prayer (*qibla*), which is introduced in Surat al-Baqara [2]:143–145. Initially the community of Muhammad had prayed in the direction of Jerusalem, as did the Jews and the Oriental Christians. Al-Wahidi's treatise on *Asbab an-Nuzul* (The Occasions of the Revelations) mentions with regard to verse 144 that Muhammad received this new instruction sixteen months after his arrival in

---

13　For this view in recent scholarship, see Christoph Luxenberg, *The Syro-Aramaic Reading of the Koran: A Contribution to the Decoding of the Language of the Koran* (Berlin: Hans Schiler, 2007).

Medina. This was roughly the time period when Muhammad's relationship with the Jews of Medina especially had seriously deteriorated.[14]

Muslims Seen through the Kerygmatic Perspective

If we believe the traditional Islamic account of the development of Muhammad's early community, we may conclude that Arabs who received the initial Meccan message essentially found themselves at a similar place as the kinsmen of the biblical patriarch Abraham, with a clear invitation to abandon polytheism and take up the worship of the one God. During the early Medinan period, however, the community surrounding Muhammad found itself in conflict with those with whom it had sought continuity, particularly the Jews of Medina. Furthermore, not unlike the Jews of Jesus' time, they had to reckon with a picture of Jesus that conflicted in many aspects with the one that was developing within Muhammad's message. Due to growing economic, social, and political conflict with the Medinan Jews, the result was a rejection of that picture and a growing distance from the Judeo-Christian tradition.

Today, a kerygmatic perception of Muslims would say that even though Muslims have as their foremost concern to please God, they lack the ability to enjoy that deep and personal relationship with God that, according to the Gospels, is only possible for those who respond to Christ's invitation to approach God as Father through a brotherly sonship with himself. It is this view of the Islamic phenomenon as I have developed it here, including the understanding of where Muslims are in their search and journey toward God, that motivates a follower of Christ to be a witness, to share this divine *kerygma* with Muslims. We now turn briefly to the purpose, methods, and outcomes of this endeavor.

Purpose of Relationship with Islam and Muslims

Against the background of the position developed above, those Christ followers who hold a kerygmatic understanding of Islam will engage with Muslims on two solid foundations: respect and trust. On the one hand, neither the syncretistic attitude to religions that plays down the uniqueness of a person's spiritual experience, nor the polemical attitude that seeks to emphasize the negative aspects of another person's worldview, will foster mutual respect between two people. On the other hand, both existential and apologetic approaches will shy away from true engagement, the first seeking to stay away from God talk, and the latter (in its extreme form) raising a defensive wall without ever engaging creatively and positively. These are of course somewhat generalizations, but they are helpful to identify further the middle way. Kerygmatic persons do not shy away from engagement. And because they do so based on a thoughtfully developed framework and understanding of Islam, they can do so respectfully, with a genuine desire to learn through a mutual exchange of perceptions about God and faith. Engagement with Islam at a kerygmatic level will almost always be enriching for all involved.

In the context of this mutually enriching relationship of respect, trust will develop, to the point where meaningful conversation can take place. Meaningful, life-transforming conversation can hardly take place outside such respect and trust. And the kerygmatic person knows that any meaningful conversation about Christ should be life-transforming, as the uniqueness that Christ brings to our human relationship with God is shared. But it is important to emphasize that this engagement does not go merely in one direction. The relationship of trust and respect that is developed through the kerygmatic approach should precisely be mutual. Kerygmatic engagement creates an opportunity to listen to what

---

14 An English translation of this work can be found at http://www.altafsir.com. See especially http://www.altafsir.com/AsbabAlnuzol.asp?SoraName=2&Ayah=144&search=yes&img=A.

Muslims have to say about religious issues as well, the opportunity to learn and stand corrected rather than stick to our own perceptions of what they believe, so that misunderstandings and misperceptions may be dissipated.

Methods Used in the Kerygmatic Approach to Islam and Muslims

The practice of the kerygmatic approach in Christian-Muslim interaction knows few boundaries. Every occasion is suitable to bear witness respectfully to Christ's good news. A Christ follower using that approach will happily make use of the Qur'an and other elements of the Islamic tradition as appropriate and acceptable bridges of communication.

This approach will not shy away from discussion forums on theological, doctrinal, social, cultural, and other issues. No topic is taboo, since a respectful exchange is prepared and assumed. At the kerygmatic level, dialogue takes place between religious and scholarly leaders who have a deeply rooted faith and are willing to share uncompromisingly with genuine people. As a result, the outcome of such exchange is deep and reaches the grass roots.

My emphasis on a middle way, the kerygmatic approach, does not negate the legitimacy of using other types of interaction found on the D1–D5 spectrum. In my experience, different settings and audiences may require different styles and approaches. I personally would in most cases avoid D1 and D5, save in some exceptional circumstances where the depth of a friendship may allow and call for the tackling of a hot and problematic issue at a D5 level. In general, I would favor a combination of D2 and D3 in a public setting, where the tackling of social issues (D2) is crucial and more likely to be fruitful. In private settings, I would favor a combination of D3 and D4, the apologetic approach often serving to clarify certain deep-rooted misunderstandings that Muslims have about Christ and the Bible. Whereas tackling such issues in public is often futile, it can be quite appropriate in conversation with a nondefensive Muslim friend who is genuinely seeking to understand. Finally, I find myself leaning toward D2 in conversation with Muslim religious leaders, and more toward D4 in conversation with less prominent Muslims.

From a missional perspective, the nonaggressive and suprareligious nature of the kerygmatic attitude and discourse has the potential to avoid the immediate alienation of a Muslim who wishes to explore the implications of God's good news in Christ by other members of that person's community. This means that extraction of such a person from his or her community—whether induced or self-imposed—can be avoided, so that the community as a whole may benefit from Christ's transforming power.

Exhibit 1: Test of Attitude to Islam and Muslims (TAIM)

For each issue, circle *one* letter that best reflects your position. The key can be found in Exhibit 2 at the end of this chapter.

1. My view of religions is that:
   a. All roads lead to Rome.
   b. Goodness and morality are the essence of religions.
   c. They are an essential part of the human psychological and sociological need. Although God is the absolute truth, no single religious system is infallible or completely satisfactory.
   d. There is only one ultimate truth, and that is God.
   e. There is only one religion that is truly from God: Christianity.

2. Islam was:
   a. A religion that originated from God, but like all religions, it has undergone many human influences as well.
   b. A sociopolitical phenomenon, successful because of its strong religious ideological element, which was carried over essentially from the Judeo-Christian tradition.
   c. A human phenomenon whose understanding of God is misleading.
   d. A scheme developed and carried out by the devil.
   e. A sociopolitical phenomenon like any other successful religious movement of human history.

3. Muhammad was:
   a. A charismatic prophetic and political leader who genuinely believed he had received a divine prophetic calling for his people.
   b. Misled and may have had some psychological problems that led him to believe that he had received a prophetic calling.
   c. Possessed by demons, an antichrist whose mission was to deceive all people.
   d. A shrewd sociopolitical leader who knew how to use his contemporary economic and historical realities to the advantage of his community and personal ends.
   e. To some degree the recipient of a divine calling to be God's prophet to the Arabs.

4. The Qur'an:
   a. Was a plagiarism of the Bible and contains many mistakes and inaccuracies.
   b. Was inspired by the devil and is full of lies and deceit. Merely reading it renders a person unclean.
   c. Was a literary achievement of Muhammad himself or some of his entourage, which Muhammad used in order to impress a society that was strongly attracted to poetic literature.
   d. Contains substantial elements of the divine truth and is to be respected as Scripture.
   e. Was Muhammad's genuine attempt to provide what he believed to be the essential elements of the Judeo-Christian Scriptures in the Arabic language.

5. Practicing Muslims are:
   a. The deceived followers of a religion that has nothing good to offer the world.
   b. Adherents of a religious ideology that offers a viable code of ethics and makes them into good citizens.
   c. Viewed positively by God when they faithfully strive to be pious and devout.
   d. Primarily concerned to please God, but they lack the ability to enjoy a deep personal relationship with him through Christ.
   e. Being misled by a worldly religion that drives them away from the worship of the true God.

6. In the end:
   a. Muslims will all go to hell, because they have fallen to deception.
   b. Muslims will not be saved, because they did not come to the knowledge of Christ.
   c. Muslims who are genuine seekers may come to a knowledge of Christ even based on the Qur'an.
   d. Muslims will be saved if they are faithful to the religion of Islam.
   e. Muslims, like all other people, will be saved by the unlimited benevolence of God.
7. My purpose in relating to Muslims is:
   a. To evangelize them by demonstrating to them the truth of Christianity and refuting the validity of Islam.
   b. To have an opportunity to witness about the unique elements that Christ brings to enrich human beings' relationship with God.
   c. To encourage mutual social and religious understanding and tolerance between Christian and Muslim communities.
   d. To invite Muslims to be a positive part of a multicultural and multireligious universal humanity in all of its rich plurality.
   e. To demonstrate to Muslims the falsity and deceitfulness of Islam and save as many of them as possible from perdition.
8. In interacting with Muslims, the best methods are:
   a. The use of the Qur'an, the Bible, and other elements of both traditions as a foundation for discussing theological, doctrinal, social, and cultural issues.
   b. The affirmation of common ground and avoidance of divisive issues.
   c. To dialogue on social, economic, and political issues.
   d. To accentuate religious differences and use polemics to discredit Islam, or not to relate to Muslims at all.
   e. Public debates that make heavy use of apologetic arguments.
9. I believe that my interaction with Muslims should lead:
   a. To positive transformation of mutual perceptions and relationships.
   b. To greater tolerance and appreciation between communities.
   c. To the accentuation of differences between religious communities and to the prevailing of Christianity.
   d. Muslims to convert to Christianity by being convinced of the prevailing truth of Christianity above all other religions.
   e. To deep impact into Muslim societies without creating immediate enmity between members of the community, avoiding "extraction" for those who might take up Christ.
10. In order to interact effectively with Muslims, I believe that:
    a. I need to comprehend Islam as a political reality.
    b. I need to learn all the weaknesses and problems in Islam.
    c. I need to acquire a thorough knowledge of the answers to Islamic questions and challenges.
    d. I need to acquire a thorough insider's knowledge of Islam.
    e. I need to comprehend the broad lines of Islam as a religion.

Exhibit 2: Key to the TAIM

Assign yourself the numerical value that corresponds with your answer to each question, and then calculate your total.

1. **My view of religions:** a=1, b=2, c=3, d=4, e=5
2. **Islam:** a=2, b=3, c=4, d=5, e=1
3. **Muhammad:** a=3, b=4, c=5, d=1, e=2
4. **The Qur'an:** a=4, b=5, c=1, d=2, e=3
5. **Practicing Muslims:** a=5, b=1, c=2, d=3, e=4
6. **In the end:** a=5, b=4, c=3, d=2, e=1
7. **Purpose:** a=4, b=3, c=2, d=1, e=5
8. **Best methods:** a=3, b=2, c=1, d=5, e=4
9. **Outcome:** a=2, b=1, c=5, d=4, e=3
10. **Extent of knowledge of Islam:** a=1, b=5, c=4, d=3, e=2

Total: _____

Interpretation of TAIM Results:
10–12: Syncretistic *Attitude to Islam and Muslims*
13–22: Existential *Attitude to Islam and Muslims*
23–32: Kerygmatic *Attitude to Islam and Muslims*
33–42: Apologetic *Attitude to Islam and Muslims*
43–50: Polemical *Attitude to Islam and Muslims*

Bibliography

Accad, Martin. "Corruption and/or Misinterpretation of the Bible: The Story of the Islamic Usage of *Taḥrīf.*" *The Near East School of Theology Theological Review* 24, no. 2: (2003): 67–97.

———. "The Gospels in the Muslim Discourse of the Ninth to the Fourteenth Century: An Exegetical Inventorial Table (Parts I–IV)." *Islam and Christian-Muslim Relations* 14, no. 1 (2003): 67–81, 205–20, 337–52, 459–79.

———. "The Interpretation of John 20:17 in Muslim-Christian Dialogue (8th–14th Centuries): The Ultimate Proof-Text." In *Christians at the Heart of Islamic Rule*, edited by David Thomas, 199–214. Leiden: Brill, 2003.

Hick, John, and Brian Hebblethwaite, eds. *Christianity and Other Religions: Selected Readings.* Philadelphia: Fortress Press, 1980.

Kittel, Gerhard, and Gerhard Friedrich, eds. *Theological Dictionary of the New Testament.* Translated by Geoffrey W. Bromiley. Grand Rapids, MI: Eerdmans, 1966.

Luxenberg, Christoph. *The Syro-Aramaic Reading of the Koran: A Contribution to the Decoding of the Language of the Koran.* Berlin: Hans Schiler, 2007.

Macquarrie, John. "Existentialism." In *The Encyclopedia of Religion*, edited by Mircea Eliade. New York: Macmillan, 1987.

Mingana, Alphonse, ed. *1. Timothy's Apology for Christianity. 2. The Lament of the Virgin. 3. The Martyrdom of Pilate.* Woodbrooke Studies 2. Cambridge, UK: W. Hefer & Sons, 1928. Available at http://darkwing.uoregon.edu/~sshoemak/102/texts/timothy.html.

Okholm, Dennis L., and Timothy R. Phillips, eds. *Four Views on Salvation in a Pluralistic World.* Grand Rapids, MI: Zondervan, 1996.

CHAPTER 47

Roles of "Alongsiders" in Insider Movements
Contemporary Examples and Biblical Reflections
John and Anna Travis

Do insider movements occur spontaneously as sovereign moves of the Spirit, or do they involve the activity of God's people from outside the community as well?

Both history and Scripture suggest that all Jesus movements involve both human and divine actions. In what would at first appear to be a spontaneous movement in the book of Acts—the pouring out of the Holy Spirit followed by three thousand decisions to follow Jesus—divine and human activity is apparent, both during and preceding this movement.[1] In insider movements with which we are familiar, both the hand of God and the labors of Jesus followers are clearly seen.

The present study focuses on roles that certain outsiders, whom we refer to as "alongsiders," can play in advancing insider movements. We share examples from the lives of alongsiders we know as well as relevant passages from Scripture. We hope this writing will give fresh input and encouragement to those called to alongsider ministries.

"Alongsider" Defined and Described

The term "alongsider" refers to an outsider (Jesus follower from another culture or area) whom God has prepared to walk alongside insiders in their journey of faith in Jesus. Alongsiders we know devote themselves to understanding the language, culture, and hearts[2] of the people God calls them to serve. They have learned to view the "other," regardless of religion or culture, as a fellow creation of God who, like themselves, needs the salvation and transformation that is offered through Jesus. Alongsiders may be young or old, male or female, and from any number of educational and cultural backgrounds, yet they all seem to share two traits.

First, through their study of Scripture and field experience, alongsiders have acquired a *kingdom-centered* rather than *religion-centered* ministry focus. In working with Muslims, Hindus, Buddhists, and

---

1   This movement, recorded in Acts 2, was preceded by the translation of the OT into Greek (before 200 BC); the ministry of John the Baptist, calling the people to repentance; the miraculous birth of Jesus; the development of the Twelve; the sending out of the seventy-two and the women who accompanied them; the miracles and preaching of Jesus and his band; Jesus' death, resurrection, appearances for forty days, and ascension; and the 120 obediently praying and waiting as we see described in Acts 1.

2   Numerous passages illustrate that Jesus is more concerned with the inside (heart) than outward appearances. He sees through the life circumstances of those he encounters, and he understands and speaks to the heart. Some examples of this are in his interactions with Zacchaeus, the woman at the well, and the Pharisees, and in his parable of the two men who came to pray at the temple (Luke 18:9–14).

Jews, their focus is on seeing the kingdom come near and transform these various socioreligious groups from the inside out, rather than on encouraging separation and change of religious affiliation.[3]

The second trait is a willingness to minister in obscurity. For security reasons, alongsiders generally cannot announce to the outside world what God is doing in the movements they have seen. Alongsiders also realize that serving a movement is not about *them* or building up *their* ministry, or even the ministry of their group. Rather it is about seeing fellowships of Jesus followers blossom in situations where often the alongsider's name and labors will be known only to God and to a handful of insiders.

Particular Challenges of Alongsider Ministry

We have the privilege of knowing a number of alongsiders, seeing firsthand how God has used them to advance insider movements. Listening to their stories, we have identified seven ministry roles they assume.[4] Most of these roles are similar to the ministries of Jesus followers in other types of movements as well. The main difference with alongsider ministry in insider movements is in how they face and overcome the following challenges.

The first challenge is how to find and develop the first few believers, or "people of peace,"[5] without the alongsider assuming some form of leadership role, possibly inhibiting an insider-led movement. Alongsiders often come to the field with years of ministry experience and training, and strong, literate Bible study skills. This expertise can unintentionally overwhelm or undermine emerging insider leaders. Alongsiders involved with the first few believers in a movement must therefore introduce the good news in ways that empower, impart, encourage, facilitate, catalyze, and enable reproducible ways of engaging Scripture without controlling or directing an emerging movement.

The second challenge, related to the first, is how to share biblical truth in ways that do not undermine or separate insiders from their own people, thus inhibiting their ability to influence their family and community. Christians have often viewed other faiths or cultures primarily in terms of what in them is wrong or unbiblical. There will be times in which alongsiders are involved with insiders in examining various beliefs and worldviews (see below), but the first step is always to affirm what is already biblically good and praiseworthy. Too often well-intentioned outsiders have spoken ill of another's culture, causing new believers to reject their family and culture.

The third challenge—the other side of the second challenge—is how to help new followers of Jesus think biblically and critically about their culture and religion, allowing Scripture, illumined by the Spirit (not necessarily the interpretation of the alongsider or Christian tradition), to be the final measure of what is good and right. In all insider movements with which we are familiar, we see that as insiders study Scripture, they are choosing to *retain* key aspects of their culture and religious community, *reinterpret* others, and *reappraise* or *reject* still others. Trusted alongsiders have often helped insiders with this sensitive, crucial process.

---

3   Some insiders in time may wish to change religions, something they have every right to do. The point is that the decision was not encouraged or forced upon them by alongsiders or other outside Christians; it must be a choice the insiders have prayerfully and carefully made on their own.

4   We are also privileged to have personally experienced service in each of these roles at one time or another over the last twenty-five years.

5   The term "person of peace" refers to those individuals who first welcome the good news of the kingdom and open the door for others to hear and believe as well (e.g., in the village ministry of the seventy in Luke 10:1–9 and the twelve in Matt 10:11–14, or Cornelius and his *oikos* in Acts 10:24).

Related to the third challenge is the fourth—how to help insiders *self-theologize*, expressing the message of Jesus in ways understandable and meaningful to family and friends. Ideally this should happen whenever the gospel crosses any cultural or religious barrier; however, it is especially crucial in insider movements, where the communities may already be predisposed against the gospel. Self-theologizing helps integrate the old (the existing community) with the new (following Jesus), finding vocabulary, thought forms, subject matter, and communication styles that are culturally appropriate. Failure to develop a local theology can cause the gospel to seem foreign.[6] Conversely, self-theologizing helps a people see that Jesus is truly on their side and for them.

The fifth challenge is how to encourage Jesus-centered body life among the insiders when the alongsider cannot model or participate in such fellowships. Since the insiders are not joining local, preexisting traditional churches, where they might find encouraging worship, teaching, literature, fellowship, Bible study, and corporate prayer (not to mention safe places to meet), they must find alternative ways to gather that are both biblical and viable. Small insider home groups, often meeting in obscurity, must rely heavily upon inductive group Bible study, the direct guidance of the Holy Spirit, and the use of spiritual gifts (e.g., teaching, healing, discernment, helps; see Rom 12:3–8; 1 Cor 12:4–31; Eph 4:7–13).

The sixth challenge is one of identity and lack of role models for the alongsiders. Having no official role or status in an insider movement, yet assisting in some ways, can place alongsiders in awkward positions. Home churches may sometimes not understand, and very few mentors or role models exist for alongsiders. Most alongsiders, like the insiders themselves, are pioneers, learning as they go. Some love these kinds of challenges and ambiguities; others are frustrated and cannot sustain them long term.

Having looked briefly at these challenges, we now turn to the ministry roles of alongsiders and Scriptures related to them. Alongsiders may be involved in one or all of these roles at various points. Most are needed before movements begin, or in the early days of a movement; some are needed as movements mature.

Seven Roles and Related Scriptures

The following seven roles are presented with two caveats. First, the number of roles we identify, seven, is somewhat arbitrary. Someone else may combine several of these roles together, reducing their number; others may expand them, seeing more than seven distinct roles. Second, these roles are based on our observations as well as our personal involvement as alongsiders in a particular insider movement.[7] As such, due to this subjectivity, there may be some roles we have missed.

---

6   See Charles R. Taber, "Is There More Than One Way to Do Theology? Anthropological Comments on the Doing of Theology," *Gospel in Context* 1, no. 1 (January 1978): 4–10, 22–40. Here Taber asks, "What is to prevent Africans, Asians, and others from using their culturally conditioned methodologies in the interpretation of the biblical texts, just as we do? If we want to insist that our approach is universal, we must justify the claim: what is it that might give our particular style transcultural validity? Why should we be in a privileged position? . . . What is needed now is for Africans and Asians to start afresh, beginning with the direct interaction of their cultures with the Scriptures rather than tagging along at the tail end of the long history of western embroidery."

7   The movement in which we were involved as alongsiders is described in *UIM*, chap. 16.

1. Intercessors

We place the role of *intercessors* first because of the centrality of prayer in any type of movement to Jesus.[8] Most alongsiders would say that it was after intercession that breakthroughs were attained and through intercession that insider movements are sustained. Intercession paves the way for a movement by asking God to cause signs and wonders to take place (Acts 4:29,30), move on human hearts, hold back demonic strongholds, call workers, and bring about maturity in new believers.[9] In addition, God speaks to intercessors and gives them love for those they are called to serve.

Example: We know groups of alongsiders who set aside seasons of intercession and fasting for their adopted people, such as five hours per day for extended periods of time, all night once a week, one entire month, or one full day a week over a period of many years. We were part of a four-year season of intercession on our field that involved many hours per week. This was preceded by utter desperation for God to move, and thankfully was followed by the beginning of a Jesus movement within the religious community of our adopted people. This small movement continues to this day and has slowly spread to several neighboring towns and villages.

Biblical reflections: Regarding intercessory prayer, we look to the life of our Lord. At every key juncture in his life, we find Jesus off alone, interceding before the Father. Prayer was central in his ministry.[10] Intercession was demonstrated as well by Old Testament prophets and leaders as they repented for the sins of those who had gone before them.[11] Intercession was integral in the ministry of the apostles in the earliest Jesus movements (see, for example, Acts 6:3,4). The temple was to be a house of prayer for all nations (Mark 11:17), and intercessors continue this work, joining Jesus in his intercession at the right hand of God (Heb 7:25).

2. Learners

Alongsiders are *learners*. They have a message to share, but they first seek to understand before insisting on being understood. In pursuit of this, alongsiders have often lived with local families who do not yet

---

8   The late church historian Dr. J. Edwin Orr spent a lifetime studying what factors led to the world's great revivals. He concluded that the only trait he saw in common in all the different revivals was intentional corporate intercessory prayer preceding all of these movements. See Orr, "The Role of Prayer in Spiritual Awakening by J. Edwin Orr," YouTube video, 25:50, from a speech recorded at the National Prayer Congress in October 1976, posted by Calvary Chapel of Philadelphia, August 24, 2014, https://www.youtube.com/watch?v=KxGDPCEVW60.

9   Epaphras' work as an intercessor is mentioned in Col 4:12. Paul's role as an intercessor is apparent throughout the Epistles, e.g., in 2 Tim 1:3.

10   The NT records Jesus praying at his baptism (Luke 3:21); early in the morning (Mark 1:35); in the wilderness (Luke 5:16); all night before a big decision (Luke 6:12); with thankfulness (Matt 11:25; Luke 10:12); when facing bad news (Matt 14:13); before saying or doing anything (John 5:19; 12:49; 14:10); before raising the dead (John 11:41); after taxing ministry (Matt 14:22; Mark 6:47; John 6:15); before challenging his followers (Luke 9:18); at his transfiguration (Matt 17:8; Mark 9:8; Luke 9:28); when teaching his followers how to pray (Matt 6:9; Luke 11:1); for children (Matt 19:3); for his disciple Peter, who was facing temptation (Luke 22:32); for his followers to be indwelt by the Spirit (John 14:16,17); for all his future followers (John 17); before facing the Cross (Matt 26; Mark 14; Luke 22; John 12); for God to forgive his enemies (Luke 23:34); in his pain (Matt 27:46; Mark 15:34); with tears (Heb 5:7); and as he died (Luke 23:46).

11   Moses (Ex 32; 34), Hezekiah (2 Chr 29), Jeremiah (Jer 14; 31), Daniel (Dan 9), Nehemiah (Neh 1), Ezra (Ezra 9; 10), Solomon (1 Kgs 8).

follow Jesus, going through the process the Brewsters have called *bonding*.[12] Most alongsiders engage in extended times of formal or informal ethnographic interviewing, trying to gain insight into the religious heritage and worldview of those they are called to reach. While cross-cultural field workers in other types of ministry often do the same, this learning aspect is particularly crucial for alongsiders, as they will need to understand in depth how God is already at work in the religion and culture of those they serve; failure to do this would make it hard for them to see what is already biblical and praiseworthy in the religion or culture in question, or what is truly wrong, even demonic. Those who intimately understand the hearts and minds of the people are in a much better position to understand these dynamics.

Example: As learners, many alongsiders have gone through the bonding process, some for a month, but others up to a year or longer. One team of alongsiders we know are not able to live in the homes of local families but have rented attached rooms or structures close to them in the very center of Muslim neighborhoods in order to learn and bond. We lived with two families, one month in a village setting, followed by two months with an urban family. All our teammates, both nationals and expatriates, also lived for a minimum of one month with a family. Living with a family not only created bonds of friendship; it also allowed us to enter into a web of relationships through extended families that involved participation in weddings, holidays, funerals, and other key life-cycle events. Several alongsiders we know, who have eventually seen Jesus movements within the religious community around them, have first studied with their local friends the holy book(s) viewed as authoritative in those contexts before going on to study the Bible with those same friends.

Biblical reflections: Scripture abounds with examples of godly people who, either through the circumstances of life or by design, became cross-cultural learners, powerfully used by God. We see Daniel learning the language, culture, sciences, and religion of the Babylonians, eventually becoming a change agent for God's purposes in that polytheistic culture.[13] Moses was raised biculturally, knowing firsthand the ways and language of the Egyptians. Joseph lived in Potiphar's household (Gen 39:1,2), and God used this to prepare him for a work far beyond what Joseph imagined. And in the New Testament we see Jesus sending out the seventy two-by-two to the villages where he would later go, having them stay with local families, eating and drinking what was offered them, not traveling from house to house, thus allowing them to see those of peace who would receive the message of the kingdom. Upon their return, we find them "debriefing" this field time with Jesus, the one who had sent them out to learn and grow spiritually (Luke 10:17-20).

3. Friends

We use the word "friend" here in two ways. First, alongsiders become friends with those who do not yet follow Jesus. As these cross-cultural relationships form, the subtle "us" versus "them" mentality begins to disappear. Our Muslim, Hindu, or Buddhist neighbors become dear friends and sometimes the

---

12 Thomas and Betty Sue Brewster in their seminal *Bonding and the Missionary Task: Establishing a Sense of Belonging* (Pasadena, CA: Lingua House, 1982) advocate cross-cultural workers living with local families when first arriving on the field as a way to acquire language and culture and understand the hearts and lives of the people they will serve. They refer to this process as *bonding*, likening it to the bonding that occurs between a mother and child as the newborn first enters the world.

13 We see in Dan 1:4,17 and 4:8 that Daniel studied the Chaldeans' literature, wisdom, and language, and was even named after one of their gods.

adopted uncles and aunties of our children. From this level of affection[14] and intimacy, heart-to-heart discussion can happen, and it becomes more natural to speak of Jesus and how someone can know him.

Example: One such alongsider friend we know is a man I will call "Alan." Alan has shared that his best friend, next to his own family members, is the leader of a mosque near his home. Alan began his relationship with this man by volunteering to teach English to the children in the mosque. What amazes me about Alan is that when he spends his free time hanging out at his friend's house watching TV or drinking coffee, this is not a "ministry strategy" but rather something he does because he loves to share life with this mosque leader.

A second type of friend describes those who have deep, long-term relationships with key leaders of insider movements, friendships often spanning decades. Many insider leaders are greatly strengthened by having such an alongsider friend, someone from outside their group who can be a confidant and counselor, especially in shame-based cultures where gossip is rampant. These insider leaders are pioneers who face many kinds of dilemmas, especially in cultures where leaders are expected to play large roles in the lives of those in their group.

Example: Two long-term alongsider friends I have known have stood by their insider friends through thick and thin—illnesses, imprisonments, depression, slander, marriage difficulties—as well as through the joys of children getting married, grandchildren being born, and seeing many new people put their faith in Jesus. These friends, often in other countries much of the year, keep in touch regularly through texting, phone calls, Skype, and email. They meet face-to-face as often as they can. Both insider and alongsider sense that God put them together, and both benefit by this unique cross-cultural friendship.

Biblical reflections: In Scripture we see that Paul not only counted on the friendship of his coworkers,[15] but his work was marked by friendship with those he served.[16] Jesus, too, longed for the friendship of his disciples, especially in one of his darkest hours.[17]

4. Workers of Miracles

We use the term *workers of miracles* for alongsiders whom God has anointed and uses regularly in physical healing, inner healing, and deliverance from the demonic, as well as interpreting dreams, prophecy, and other miracles, both with Jesus followers and those who do not yet follow him. An alongsider can assume the role of a worker of miracles without negatively impacting a movement by becoming its "leader." Workers of miracles can serve at strategic moments when deep-set spiritual problems arise. While all believers should pray for miracles, those we call alongsider workers of miracles are recognized by trusted insiders as being especially gifted and experienced, likely having what the Bible refers to as gifts of healing, discernment of spirits, and/or prophecy (1 Cor 12:10,28,30; see also Rom 12:6).[18]

Examples: We have known a number of alongsiders who have had a ministry of inner healing and deliverance that was a great blessing to a movement. We have also had the privilege of being involved

---

14 Paul expressed deep affection for those he served among (2 Cor 2:4; 12:15; Phil 4:1).

15 Paul's friends treated him with kindness and cared for him (Acts 27:3). Philemon was both a coworker and friend for Paul (Phlm 1:1).

16 Paul and his coworkers shared their very selves as well as the good news (1 Thess 2:8). Paul took risks by opening his heart and expressing deep affection for those he served (2 Cor 6:11–13).

17 Jesus asked for friendship and prayer support when facing his darkest hour (Matt 26:37,38).

18 Many who were taught that such gifts ceased after the NT era have modified their views after witnessing the Spirit work in miraculous ways through people he has gifted in the ways described here.

in this kind of alongsider ministry. Especially in places where folk practices are common, those coming to faith often need freedom through renouncing magical practices, getting rid of charms and amulets, and breaking ties with shamans and power practitioners.

While folk practices can create barriers to the gospel that must be removed, on the other hand, their presence in a society indicates the people's awareness of the spiritual realm. In such contexts, miracles in Jesus' name can open the way for many to hear the gospel. We have known alongsiders whom God used to work miracles of healing, which then opened the way for the good news to be proclaimed.

In addition, prayer for healing of past traumas and emotional wounds can help Jesus followers learn to forgive others and be free from troubling issues of the past. In cases of demonization, alongsiders can lead Jesus followers in prayers of deliverance. Having this kind of alongsider available to assist the movement through training and personal prayer is a great asset.

One alongsider we know prayed for Muslim women in her neighborhood for a variety of ailments—physical, emotional, and spiritual—and then invited them to her home for a study related to health and stress. This group of women, with the help and encouragement of this alongsider, embraced Jesus and became a "covenant community" where they studied the Bible, shared their lives, and prayed for each other, their families, and their neighbors. They became familiar with healing prayer and spiritual warfare. Within a number of years, this original group experienced growth and multiplication, meeting in many homes and branching out to a neighboring town as well. This movement today involves entire families and brings the blessings of the kingdom of God through Isa to their neighborhoods. The alongsider and her prayers were powerfully used of God to see this small insider movement begin.

Biblical reflections: Scripture overflows with accounts of anointed workers of miracles (see 1 Cor 12:10) whom God used in early Jesus movements, showing the beginning of the fulfillment of Jesus' words to his followers: "Very truly I tell you, whoever believes in me will do the works I have been doing, and they will do even greater things than these, because I am going to the Father" (John 14:12).

We are inspired to read how the Lord worked miracles through the disciples (Mark 16:20; Acts 2:43; 5:12), Peter and John (Acts 3:1–16; 5:15), Stephen (Acts 6:8), Philip (Acts 8:6,13), Ananias (Acts 9:10–18), Paul (Acts 19:11,12; Rom 15:18,19), Paul's friends (Acts 14:20), Barnabas (Acts 14:3; 15:12), Agabus (Acts 11:27–30), and the recipients of the letter to the Hebrews (Heb 2:3,4). Paul shared how much patience was required in his ministry of miracles (2 Cor 12:12). James urged that elders should pray with people and believers should confess sins and pray with each other, saying that God would make them workers of miracles (Jas 5:13–16). As miracle workers take risks to see God work, they may need patience, like Paul, remembering that even Jesus met with resistance to miracles at times (Mark 6:1–6). Many miracles may be required before the fruit of allegiance to Jesus results, as we see when the ten lepers are healed by Jesus and only one comes back to pledge his allegiance to the Master (Luke 17:12–19).

5. Proclaimers

For the good news to enter a new area, either a person or some form of media must cross a religious and social barrier; the gospel does not come out of thin air. In every insider movement we have seen, the growth of the movement can be traced back to one or two insiders who first received the gospel and then persuaded their family and friends to embrace it as well. Although some of these movements began with a dream or a vision, the Lord often directed the first insiders to an alongsider who could proclaim the full message of the gospel to him or her.

What makes alongsider *proclaimers* unique is that they are not linking the gospel to the concept of "changing religions" to follow Isa. In addition, they are constantly looking for potential people of peace (Luke 10:5,6; Matt 10:11–13) whom God will use to help lead groups of their coreligionists in following Jesus.

Example: While all Jesus followers are called to share the good news, those we are calling proclaimers very likely have what Scripture calls the gift of evangelism (Eph 4:11). One alongsider proclaimer we know is the type of person who, with just twenty-four hours in a particular city, grabs a taxi to the biggest mosque (sharing Jesus with the taxi driver on the way) and then, upon arrival at the mosque, meets the imam and begins to tell him how Isa the Messiah came for Muslims, Christians, and all people, and that this very day he could accept Isa. This particular proclaimer was used by God to help lead to Jesus some of the first Muslims in what later became a small insider movement across a number of villages. For years he mentored five men who were the leaders of this still-growing movement, even though the alongsider has now moved to another country. Alongsider proclaimers will always be needed to both catalyze new works and work alongside Jesus movements, as so many millions have yet to hear the good news of Jesus.

Biblical reflections: Scripture records the creative work of proclaimers in diverse religious contexts. We see Jesus, the disciples, Peter and John, and Paul and Silas with Jews (Matt 4:23,24; 10:5–8; Acts 4:1,2; 17:1–3); Ananias with Saul the Pharisee (Acts 9:10–20; 22:12–16); Jesus with a Samaritan woman and townspeople (John 4:7–41); Philip with a Samaritan sorcerer (Acts 8:5–24); and Peter and John in Samaritan towns (Acts 8:25). We see the man whom Jesus had healed and delivered with Gentiles (Mark 5:18–20); Peter with a God-fearer who was a Roman (Acts 10:1–48); people of Cyprus and Cyrene with Hellenists (Acts 11:20); Paul with Athenian philosophers (Acts 17:18–34); and many other instances.

6. Equippers

Whereas proclaimers are often first to bring the good news to a particular group of people, *equippers* are alongsiders whom God uses to help mature or assist certain key insider leaders and/or movements.[19] They see emerging leaders and movements with eyes of faith, and are close enough to understand the issues they face. As fellow members of God's kingdom and workers uniquely prepared by God, equippers are able to suggest certain activities that could put a movement ahead without undermining its insider leadership.

Equippers may offer spiritual mentoring, marriage counseling, a methodology of inductive Bible study, approaches for multiplication, tools for Bible translation, skills in development of businesses or curricula, or other assistance. They may help insiders think through issues of transformation of traditions.[20] They may wisely connect insider leaders to others with specific expertise, offering assistance in what may be very difficult for insiders to do alone. This generally calls for a high level of language skill, cultural understanding, and relational wisdom.

Examples: One equipper we know spent many months with a seasoned leader of an insider movement, working on a two-year leadership development curriculum based on Luke and Acts for newer

---

19　Some alongsider equippers may be active before movements begin, trusting that their service will equip future leaders and movements.

20　Which can be retained? Which need to be confronted by the gospel or rejected, reinterpreted, or reassessed?

movement leaders. This equipper, trained in seminary, could have attempted the creation of a curriculum on his own. But that would have resulted in a less indigenous training experience and, more importantly, would have bypassed a key leader God raised up for this movement. Instead, they carefully worked through Luke and Acts inductively, discovering key principles together under the guidance of the Spirit. Insider leaders then introduced the Luke- Acts curriculum to eight fellow insider leaders. In less than ten years, 150 home group leaders in the movement were engaged in this two-year leadership training centered on inductively studying Luke and Acts.

In another country, a network or team of alongsiders was formed to serve a number of developing insider movements across several different language groups. They were involved in Bible translations, offering technical support related to Greek and Hebrew terms, checking translation, and training translators. One of these translations has had an enormous impact as movements begin and mature across this country. The impetus for this translation came from insiders who realized they needed a more culturally relevant translation to reach their own people, combined with the experience of alongsiders who had been in grassroots ministry and were likewise thoroughly convinced of the need for this type of translation.

Like Barnabas and James in the life of Paul, these alongsider equippers are learning to walk the fine line of offering some counsel but not too much, of leading in some ways but not overleading. Equippers empower insider leaders to fulfill the role God has for them in insider movements.

Biblical reflections: In the earliest Jesus movements, we see God preparing certain people to equip others, who then turn to empower yet others (2 Tim 2:2). Philip was assisted in his ministry among Samaritans by Peter and John, who were used by God to pray for the believers to be filled with the Holy Spirit. Peter and John must have been positively impacted by the experience, because before returning to Jerusalem, they entered several other Samaritan towns to bring the good news (Acts 8:14–17,25).

An important aspect of equipping is making the right connections at the right time. It is interesting to note Paul's explanation of his interactions with Jewish leaders in Jerusalem, especially regarding the timing involved. After his miraculous encounter with the Lord, and the receiving of his calling to the Gentiles, he did not immediately connect with leaders already in place. Did this give time for God's radical call on Paul's life to be developed, away from the strict, long-standing religious boundaries observed by those godly leaders like James (Gal 1:18–24)? Yet the time did come for those connections to be made.

God used Ananias (Acts 9:10–20), Barnabas (Acts 4:36,37; 9:26,27; 11:21–26), Peter (Acts 15:7–11), and James (Acts 15:13–21; 21:17–26; Gal 2:9) in the life of Paul. Ananias gave Saul his earliest spiritual input in the way of Jesus. He obeyed the Lord's voice (though it went against everything he knew and had heard), found Saul, prayed for his healing, and spoke prophetically to him concerning his calling. Barnabas saw Saul with eyes of faith, believing God was calling him, though he was certainly a diamond in the rough when Barnabas first started encouraging him. Peter assisted Saul (by this point called Paul) when Jewish followers of Jesus heard that Gentile followers of Jesus were remaining uncircumcised. He verified the legitimacy of Paul's calling with the testimony of his own experience with Cornelius. James listened well when Paul shared with the Jerusalem leaders how the good news was breaking out of the known Jewish religious structures. James gave his spiritual input, backed by Scripture, and kept the door open for Paul's radical ministry among Gentiles. Years later, Paul sought out those leaders in response to a revelation from God, and even dared to take an uncircumcised Gentile Jesus follower (Titus) with him. He was greatly relieved when the Jewish leaders did not pressure

Titus to change religions—that is, to be circumcised (Gal 2:1–10). James welcomed Paul, giving him wise counsel, though the contrast between the callings on each of their lives had only increased. While these relationships were not without some conflict,[21] Paul greatly benefited by input from those God sent to equip him.

Paul then poured into many other lives, like those of Priscilla and Aquila (Acts 18:2,3,18), Timothy (Acts 16:3; 1 Tim 1:18; 2 Tim 3:10), and Onesimus (Col 4:9; Phlm 1:10). Priscilla and Aquila went on to mentor Apollos (Acts 18:24–26), who then became a blessing to many. Timothy equipped many believers in the Gentile movements, and Onesimus was of great value in the work as well. In the later years of his ministry, Paul could say that nearly all those he equipped were non-Jewish leaders in the Gentile Jesus movements (Col 4:11).

Another aspect of equipping is depicted clearly in the New Testament: Paul and others helped support growing Jesus movements through the writing of letters to individuals, groups, and networks.[22]

7. Interfacers

Similar to the way God used Paul, Barnabas, and Peter in Jerusalem to explain Gentile ministry to fellow Jewish believers, advocating for the right of Gentiles to follow Jesus without being circumcised (that is, without taking on a Jewish religious identity),[23] the Lord will also call some who have seen insider movements firsthand to explain to Christians what God is doing behind the scenes, inside other socioreligious communities. We call this alongsider role that of the *interfacer*.

Example: We know numbers of interfacers who have met with national Bible society leaders, mission leaders, pastors, interested Christians, and heads of Christian denominations in certain Muslim countries. A particular seasoned alongsider couple serves in an interfacer role in Asia, helping national church leaders in their denomination understand and advocate for insider movements that their own church members have been involved in starting. Their work as interfacers has resulted in the development of many effective national alongsiders.

Another veteran alongsider, and the insider leaders with whom he works, invited several national pastors who might typically be hesitant about insider movements to meet together. The pastors saw the grace of God in the lives of the insiders and spontaneously decided to wash their feet. Everyone was moved to tears. A year later in another location, some alongsiders, insider believers, and national Christians gathered for a few days. This time insider leaders washed the feet of the Christians, saying, "Please forgive us! When you sent people to bring us the gospel years ago, we killed many of them." Once again, there were many tears. This kind of strategic interface, where one group does not dominate the other, and where each comes to learn, can be a beautiful example of the body of Christ in action.[24] Another positive outcome of this type of meeting and of the work that interfacers can do is to help insiders see ways that they can relate to the wider body of Christ.

Biblical reflections: When looking at only the outward forms used in certain Jesus movements within Muslim, Jewish, or Hindu communities, the outside Christian world may assume that these believers

---

21 Paul had conflict with Peter (Gal 2:11), friends of James (Gal 2:12), and Barnabas (Acts 15:39).

22 Paul, Peter, and others were inspired by the Spirit and expended great effort to write letters (Col 4:16; 1 Pet 5:12).

23 Acts 15 records the Jerusalem gathering, where leaders deliberated the question, Can uncircumcised non-Jews be fully recognized as the people of God through Jesus?

24 The insiders we know personally all see themselves as part of the body of Christ.

are not being true to God—or that they are not even part of God's kingdom. We see a similar situation in the Old Testament in Joshua's day (Josh 22:10–34). When those who had settled to the west of the Jordan observed from afar a large altar built by the two and a half tribes who had settled east of the Jordan, they jumped to the conclusion that their brothers to the east had fallen into idolatry, treachery, and rebellion. The western tribes feared judgment from God not only upon those tribes to the east but on themselves as well. So they prepared to make war against their fellow Israelites from the two and a half tribes to the east. Thankfully, the leaders met first. When the accusation from the western tribes was presented to the eastern leaders, they were shocked. The eastern leaders explained that they did not build the altar for idolatrous sacrifice, as was assumed. Instead they intended it as a witness to coming generations that, though their tribes settled on the east side of the Jordan, it would forever be known that they were fully part of God's people, one with the tribes of the west, and that their God was the same God, the one true God. This satisfied the western leaders, who brought back the good news to their tribes, and there was never again talk of making war on the eastern tribes.

In the New Testament, Jesus had to rebuke his own followers for incorrectly judging the deliverance ministry of someone who "was not following us" and for trying to stop his ministry. (This took place not long after their own failed attempt to cast out the demon oppressing a boy who couldn't speak.) They mentioned this to Jesus, who told them, "Do not stop him; for no one who does a deed of power in my name will be able soon afterward to speak evil of me. Whoever is not against us is for us" (Mark 9:38–40 NRSV; see also Luke 9:49,50). Although Jesus affirmed this person's ministry in his name, the sons of Sceva, who were trying deliverance in Jesus' name in a different situation, ran into severe difficulties. The problem with Sceva's sons, apparently, was that they did not know the Lord Jesus; therefore they did not have authority in his name (Acts 19:13–17).

In Acts 15 we see Jewish followers of Jesus reacting to news of Gentiles becoming part of the people of God by following Jesus, but without the follow-up of religious change via circumcision. They gave the scriptural argument that these Gentiles were not saved unless and until they were circumcised. Thankfully, after testimonies, deliberation, and a deeper look at Scripture, it was decided that these uncircumcised Gentile followers of Jesus were indeed saved and part of the people of God.

In each of these events recorded in Scripture, God used interfacers to explain, testify, and interpret for God's people what was actually happening in other groups. The leaders of the tribe to the east of the Jordan explained to leaders from the other tribes the intent behind their altar. Jesus explained to his disciples that the person doing deliverance in his name was actually on their side. Peter, Barnabas, Paul, and finally James advocated before the other leaders in Jerusalem on behalf of the Gentile Jesus followers, showing their legitimate place within the people of God, equal to the Jewish followers of Jesus.

Conclusion

Alongsiders are in a process that often begins with intercession for a particular people group. Many then live among the people for whom they have prayed, often with local families. In time, true bonds of friendship are forged. When alongsiders serve as proclaimers, their time as learners and friends helps them know how to share the good news in ways that make sense. Some alongsiders serve as workers of miracles, or as equippers as movements develop. Some alongsiders attempt to explain what they have seen and experienced to those who are eager to know what God is doing inside other religious communities, interfacing between insider believers and Christians outside the situation.

In any given insider movement, alongsiders may be involved in only some of the roles mentioned in this chapter. Most of these roles are most commonly needed before movements begin or soon after; some are needed at later stages. May these recent examples be only the beginning of how God will prepare more insiders and alongsiders to work with him in seeing Jesus movements advance inside the many and diverse religious communities of our world.

Bibliography

Brewster, Thomas, and Betty Sue Brewster. *Bonding and the Missionary Task: Establishing a Sense of Belonging.* Pasadena, CA: Lingua House, 1982.

Orr, J. Edwin. "The Role of Prayer in Spiritual Awakening by J. Edwin Orr." Filmed October 1976. YouTube video, 25:50. Posted by Calvary Chapel of Philadelphia, August 24, 2014. https://www.youtube.com/watch?v=KxGDPCEVW60.

Taber, Charles R. "Is There More Than One Way to Do Theology? Anthropological Comments on the Doing of Theology," *Gospel in Context* 1, no. 1 (January 1978): 4–10, 22–40.

CHAPTER 48

Become Like, Remain Like (Take Two)*
Harley Talman

Before I had ever met a Muslim, I took a course on Islam. I was shocked to learn what Muslims believe about Christianity, appalled by their misconceptions about Christian theology. Later I learned from mission scholars that cultural, social, and communal barriers also prevented Muslims from following Christ and were probably even more powerful than any of their theological objections.

"Become Like"

When I moved to a Muslim country years ago, I chose to "become like" the local Muslims and adopt their culture, imitating the Apostle Paul's practice as expressed in 1 Corinthians 9:19–22 (emphasis added):

> Though I am free and belong to no one, I have made myself a slave to everyone, to win as many as possible. To the Jews I became like a Jew, to win the Jews. To those under the law I became like one under the law . . . so as to win those under the law. To those not having the law I became like one not having the law . . . so as to win those not having the law. To the weak I became weak, to win the weak. *I have become all things to all people* so that by all possible means I might save some.

Paul's practice of adapting to specific cultures seemed logical. He became like the people he sought to win: the Jews, whose religion had biblical origins; pagan Gentiles, who were "free from the Mosaic law"; and even the "weak," whose religious scruples kept them from enjoying the benefits of freedom in Christ.

With this in mind, I dressed like the local people, wore a full beard like the religious Muslims, and immersed myself in their culture and studied their religion. Consequently I was often asked, "Are you a Muslim?" "Not as you understand," I would reply, "but according to the true meaning of the word— one who is submitted. I've submitted myself to God (Arabic *muslim*) through following *al-Masih Isa, salamuh 'alayna* (Christ Jesus, his peace be upon us). This is the true meaning of the word, according to the Qur'an, for it says that the disciples of Jesus were 'muslims' (surah 3:52)." This opened up abundant natural opportunities to tell stories from the *Injil* (Gospel) about his life, miracles, and teaching. Over time, I was able to share key biblical truths and correct misunderstandings and objections to the

---

* Originally published in a significantly different form as "Become Like, Remain Like," in *Perspectives on the World Christian Movement*: *A Reader,* 4th ed., ed. Ralph D. Winter and Steven C. Hawthorne (Pasadena, CA: William Carey Library, 2009), 146–48. Reprinted by permission.

gospel using Arab proverbs, Islamic concepts, and the many qur'anic verses that speak highly of Jesus and affirm the Bible's veracity. Admittedly, implementing an incarnational lifestyle and ministry can be uncomfortable and complicated—and even misunderstood (cf. Acts 21:21ff.)! But I found that the more I "became like" my Muslim friends, the more likely they were to comprehend biblical truth and come closer to Christ.

"Remain Like"

But what happens to Muslims *after* they come to faith in Christ? Muslims who embrace the gospel are often encouraged, or even compelled, to "become like" the national Christians in their community (or like the foreign missionaries). They become "converts" not only in matters of faith, but also in lifestyle, lingo, culture, and communal identity. Moreover, "becoming a Christian" is perceived by their Muslim family and neighbors as joining one of the large, mostly nominal, ancient "Christian" communities (Orthodox, Catholic, Nestorian, etc.) or else turning into an immoral, decadent Westerner. The resulting persecution and expulsion from the Muslim community is not necessarily for following Christ but for bringing shame upon their family, rejecting their culture, and betraying their community. This pattern has not only been unfortunate, but often unnecessary and even unscriptural, running counter to at least two important gospel principles in 1 Corinthians 7.

An astounding theological truth in this chapter is that *the unholy does not defile the holy.* A stunning reversal of the Mosaic law is effected by the coming of Christ. Jesus was not defiled by contact with the unclean, such as lepers, the hemorrhaging woman, or the dead daughter of Jairus (Mark 5:21–43). Instead, the opposite occurred, and the unclean were made clean by contact with the holy Jesus. Thus the Apostle Paul declares that a believer can remain with an unbelieving spouse and not be defiled. In fact, the presence of the believer sanctifies, makes holy, the unbelieving mate (1 Cor 7:14). Gordon Fee links the word in this text to Romans 11:16: "If the part of the dough offered as first fruits is holy, so the whole batch is holy; and if the root is holy, so are the branches." Paul considers the Jewish disciples of Jesus to be the "first fruits" that sanctify (set apart) the "whole batch" (unconverted Israel) for God's salvific purposes.[1] Because the believing parent has made the unbelieving parent "holy," even the yet-to-believe children are made holy—in a parallel to unbelieving Israel. For Paul, in Fee's view, "as long as the marriage is maintained the potential for their realizing salvation remains. To that degree they are sanctified in the believing spouse."[2] This reflects Paul's "high view of the grace of God at work through the believer towards members of his/her own household (cf. 1 Pet 3:1), and for him that constitutes grounds enough for maintaining the marriage."[3] Thus in the cases of both spouse and children, unbelievers are made holy, consecrated to God.

A second significant principle is in verse 17, where the Apostle Paul instructs believers to "remain" in their calling, "as the Lord has assigned to each one." This emphasizes that the situation in which a believer was called is his God-given station for living out his divine calling (cf. Acts 17:26). With extensive experience in the Middle East and as a NT scholar, Kenneth Bailey observes,

> There is no special cultural identity required for discipleship in the
> kingdom of God. The Jew does not have to become a pig-eating
> Gentile. The Gentile does not have to be circumcised and join the

---

1   Gordon D. Fee, *The First Epistle to the Corinthians* (Grand Rapids, MI: Eerdmans, 1987), 300–301.

2   Ibid., 300. Quotation of Rom 11:16 is from the NIV as adapted by Fee.

3   Ibid., 300, 302.

Jewish-Christian branch of the church. There is no sacred culture and no sacred language. Paul is writing in Greek, not in Hebrew. He tells his readers that regardless of their ethnic origins (Jewish or Greek) there is an "assignment," a "calling" from the Lord tailored to who they are that does not require becoming someone else. From the time of Constantine onward, the times and places where this vision of Paul has not been honored are legion.[4]

Overzealous separatists overlook this important truth. Paul's association policy in 1 Corinthians has nothing to do with unbelievers—for then we would have to leave this world; instead, we are not to associate with immoral believers (5:9–13). This principle has religious, social, and cultural implications. If someone came to faith as a Jew (circumcised), he should not seek to "pull over the foreskin" (through surgical procedure, as Hellenistic Jews sometimes did due to social embarrassment—7:18).[5] Likewise, Gentiles should not seek to be circumcised and adhere to the Mosaic law and Jewish way of life (presumably because they believed such was necessary for salvation or perhaps for sanctification). The apostle makes clear that there is no one particular expression of faith that a believer must adopt—because "circumcision is nothing and uncircumcision is nothing. Keeping God's commands is what counts" (7:19).

In application of these principles, we see that a Muslim follower of Christ can remain in the Muslim community. First, his association with unbelieving Muslims does not defile him. Rather, like a believer who "sanctifies" an unbelieving spouse, his presence sets apart the community to experience (potentially) God's purpose of salvation. Second, God assigned him to that community as the context for living out his calling.

"Become Like . . . Remain Like"

Understanding both of these truths is essential to creating movements of Christ followers. Many missionaries have realized that they must "become like" the community they are trying to reach, motivated by a desire to win the most people to Christ. But actually, to see the greatest followings of Christ emerge and flourish, outsiders need to help those who believe to remain in their divinely assigned context—sin (1 Cor 5–6) and idolatry (1 Cor 8–10) excepted. By so remaining, the gospel of salvation can move through the believer's entire network of relationships, making possible a movement to Christ.

I like the way David Anthony explains it: We "become like" them so they can "remain like" their people (but as new creations). Like a chameleon whose skin color changes to adapt to its environment, so we adjust to our new cultural environment (as governed by the "law of Christ"—1 Cor 9:21), but our inner character and identity in Christ remains the same. In contrast, the skin of the local believers does not change, although their hearts are transformed, producing an aura that gives light to their whole *oikos*.[6] This sounds good, but what might it actually look like?

My team engaged in a contextualized ministry to Muslims in Africa. We adapted to the local customs and religious culture and sought to express God's love through holistic humanitarian work, de-

---

4   Kenneth E. Bailey, *Paul through Mediterranean Eyes* (Downers Grove, IL: InterVarsity Press, 2011), 217.

5   *NET Bible* (Biblical Studies Press, 2005), 1 Cor 7:18n15.

6   David Anthony, email to author, August 20, 2012, citing illustration of R. Deal, "Accountability in Contextualization" (paper presented at Asian Practical Theology Conference, city not stated for security, 2009).

spite political instability and physical danger. We trained various groups of sheikhs and village leaders in community health and development. This opened doors for us to teach them about spiritual health and the message of the gospel. We made it clear that we were not asking them to convert, to change their identity and become "Christians." Rather, they should enter the kingdom of God by giving their allegiance to the Savior-King, Jesus the Messiah, and obeying his teaching, which includes living by "every word that comes from the mouth of God" (Matt 4:4)—that is, the entire Bible.

In keeping with traditional decision-making processes, sheikhs interacted with our new teaching to reach a consensus. As a result, well over one hundred sheikhs trusted in Jesus as the Messiah who has authority to forgive their sins. They could continue with religious practices like *salat* (ritual prayer) and fasting, but now according to Jesus' instructions (see Matt 6). Most importantly, they were in a position to lead the thousands of people in their villages to become like them in their allegiance to Christ and the authority of the Bible while remaining Muslim in identity and culture. It's that simple: *we become like so they remain like.*

Bibliography

Bailey, Kenneth E. *Paul through Mediterranean Eyes: Cultural Studies in 1 Corinthians.* Downers Grove, IL: InterVarsity Press, 2011.

Fee, Gordon D. *The First Epistle to the Corinthians.* Grand Rapids, MI: Eerdmans, 1987.

Talman, Harley. "Become Like, Remain Like." In *Perspectives on the World Christian Movement: A Reader,* 4th ed., edited by Ralph D. Winter and Steven C. Hawthorne, 146–48. Pasadena, CA: William Carey Library, 2009.

CHAPTER 49

Evangelizing Whole Families[*]

Alex G. Smith

Reaching Whole Families and the Rediscovery of This Approach Following the Reformation

Prior to the Reformation, much pioneer church growth occurred, mostly from ingatherings of whole families, clans, tribes, and peoples. Historians like Kenneth Scott Latourette and Stephen Neill, as well as missiologists such as Bishop J. Waskom Pickett and Donald McGavran, have affirmed that from the earliest centuries of the church, family, group, and people movements were foundational to the extension of the church.[1]

Stephen Neill's chapter "Conquest of the Roman World, A.D. 100–500" in *A History of Christian Missions* indicates that the key to the extension of the church was the movement of the gospel from people to people and country to country until the whole of the Roman Empire was reached. Writing about Asia Minor to Emperor Trajan around the year 112, Younger Pliny "was dismayed by the rapid spread of the Christian faith in the rather remote and mainly rural province of Bithynia in northwest Asia Minor." Pliny made note of "many in every period of life, on every level of society, of both sexes . . . in towns and villages and scattered throughout the countryside." The "evidence of Pliny is unimpeachable; we seem to encounter here one of the first mass movements in Christian history."[2] Here was an obvious major family movement. Near the end of the fourth century, in the time of John Chrysostom, the population of Antioch was not less than a half a million, and "half the inhabitants at that time were Christian."[3] Neill writes that "the church of North Africa was a church of bishops. Every town, almost every village, had its bishop," in contrast to the rest of Christendom, where "bishops were located only in the cities" and were few in number.[4]

Armenia became another Christian kingdom, reached through witness from Cappadocia. Tradition says that when Gregory the evangelist and wonder worker became Bishop of Cappadocia "there were only seventeen Christians in the city, but when he died thirty years later there were only seventeen

---

[*]   Originally published in a slightly different form in *MF*, March–April 2012. Reprinted by permission.

1   See Latourette, *A History of Christianity,* vol. 1 (New York: Harper & Row, 1953), 100; Neill, *A History of Christian Missions* (Harmondsworth, Middlesex, UK: Penguin, 1964), 31–77; Pickett, *Christian Mass Movements in India* (Lucknow: Lucknow Publishing, 1933), 37–38; and McGavran, *Understanding Church Growth* (Grand Rapids, MI: Eerdmans, 1970), 173–74, 296–97.

2   Neill, *A History of Christian Missions*, 31.

3   Ibid., 32.

4   Ibid., 38.

pagans."[5] Armenia became the first known case in which the conversion of the king was the first step in the conversion of the whole country. King Tiridates accepted Christianity as the religion of his state. The families of aristocracy and common people followed en masse. A second factor was the association of the church with the language and thought of the people, for Gregory preached in Armenian. The third element came as the New Testament was translated into that language in 410.[6]

Another case occurred through Patrick, who returned to Ireland in 432, staying until his death in 461. At the time of his return, "Ireland was almost wholly, if not entirely, a heathen country." By "the time of his death, Ireland was largely a Christian country."[7] In 493 Clovis, king of the Franks, married a Christian princess of Burgundy. She did her best to convert him. Later, in a crisis, "Clovis swore that, if victory was his, he would become the servant of the God of the Christians. He kept his vow; on Christmas day 496, he was baptized with three thousand of his warriors."[8] In 596 Pope Gregory the Great sent Augustine to Canterbury, England. King Ethelbert of Kent had married Bertha, a Christian princess from Gaul. Augustine's preaching converted the king, and by the end of the year Augustine had baptized ten thousand Saxons.[9] Among the Franks and other Europeans, Boniface had a particular practice or habit: "When a group, often under the influence of a chieftain or ruler, had decided to become Christian, it was customary to baptize" them "without any long delay."[10] Thus for more than a thousand years the church expanded across nations through massive family movements.

The Reformation of the 1500s faced a different situation than the early pioneer settings, which were mostly among unevangelized people groups. Primarily, the Reformers were dealing with largely nominal, already churched communities. Throughout the Dark Ages, moral corruption and unbiblical practices had saturated the church, resulting in spiritual weakness and large-scale nominalism. Under these conditions the primary focus of the Reformation was within the churched communities across Europe. In these Christianized populations the call for renewal of personal faith and individual salvation was rightly warranted. In that context a change of emphasis to the individual was correct. The Reformation thereby brought renewal and revitalization to the existing church. Faced with the consequent Roman Catholic Counter-Reformation, much of the Reformers' energy, at least until 1648, was spent in "fighting for their lives."[11]

As Ralph Winter pointed out, the Reformers did not organize new mission structures comparable to the former missionary training monasteries. In fact, they discarded the monastic system.[12] It was likely that Christian meditation, frequently nurtured in the monasteries, also ceased to be practiced around that period. This was one weakness of the new movement. Thus the Reformation did not spawn major missions across cultures to new unevangelized populations for more than another two hundred

---

5   Ibid., 53–54.

6   Ibid., 54.

7   Ibid., 56.

8   Ibid., 58.

9   Ibid., 67–68.

10   Ibid., 77.

11   Ibid., 220.

12   Ralph D. Winter, "The Two Structures of God's Redemptive Mission," in *Perspectives on the World Christian Movement: A Reader*, 3rd ed., ed. Ralph D. Winter and Stephen C. Hawthorne (Pasadena, CA: William Carey Library, 1999), 226–27.

years.[13] There was little thought of missions.[14] (During the seventeenth century, a few exceptions arose in Europe—notably the Moravian mission movement, which started in 1732.) Consequently, when William Carey and others launched the modern Protestant mission era in the late 1700s, the Reformers' pattern of converting "individual by individual" was carried over as a dominant evangelistic and mission strategy. Unfortunately, this renewed pioneer outreach to frontier unreached peoples did not generally return to the earlier biblical model and historical pattern of evangelizing whole families, tribes, and *ethne*. At the restarting of the major mission enterprise, a definite change in methodology seems to have occurred.

In his 1970 article "The History of Mission Strategy," R. Pierce Beaver succinctly notes this changed emphasis of mission strategy following the Reformation. The aim of seventeenth-century Protestant missions of the Dutch, British, and Americans was that peoples like the East Indians and Native Americans "would be converted, individually receive salvation, and be gathered into churches." In reaching the Native Americans at Martha's Vineyard, Thomas Mayhew followed "a slow, individual, personal approach." Beaver summarized nineteenth-century missionary strategy of the Protestants as being "aimed at individual conversions, church planting, and social transformation" through actions of "evangelism, education and medicine."[15]

When did the family approach change to an individual one? At the point when Reformation mission to unevangelized nations was restarted—almost three hundred years later. The Reformers' theology and practice in reaching out to new unreached peoples did not return to the earlier biblical family approach. Instead, individual evangelism, individual salvation, and calling to individual personal holiness were emphasized—a theological shift. The move from biblical theology to systematic theology helped advocate this ignoring of family evangelistic approaches too. Calvin's *Institutes*, as well as synthesized or summarized creeds, or shortened theological tenets like the Westminster Catechism, tended to focus on the individual growth and not on evangelizing and discipling whole families and their entire extended families.

Nevertheless, God's Spirit often overruled in his harvest and spontaneously gathered whole family networks, tribes, and people groups into the church, especially in the non-Western world. One wonders how much greater the ingathering might have been and how much more speedily evangelization accomplished had family and group evangelistic approaches been the intentional method of modern missions, particularly among Hindus, Buddhists, and Muslims.

Modern illustrations of family and people movements include the Mizo, Naga, Karens, Toba Bataks, Karo Batak, and many others who transferred their allegiance to Christ as family after family came into the church fold, until a large majority had become Christians.

The Family Group Approach: Myths and Objections

Myths and ignorance concerning individual evangelism or conversion abound. Some sound quite plausible, but deeper scrutiny often explodes the myths. The first objection is, "Salvation is only an individual thing, not a family thing." Individuals can and do convert but, among resistant populations, usually will lack the solidarity of the group's backing, often essential for survival and added growth. Individual converts can soon become social misfits or fringe people in society. Where a movement of

---

13 Paul Pierson, "A History of Transformation," in Winter and Hawthorne, *Perspectives*, 263.

14 Neill, *A History of Christian Missions*, 220–26.

15 R. Pierce Beaver, "The History of Mission Strategy," in Winter and Hawthorne, *Perspectives*, 244, 249.

families or multi-individual, mutually interdependent decisions of small or large unified groups occur, stability is more likely than for several scattered individuals. Strong individuals sometimes can be innovators and catalysts to reach their own family networks if motivated to do so.

A second retort says, "Students are so receptive; we should go for them now and not worry about their families." Asian youth in universities have some freedom to choose. But what about after they graduate? Who chooses their wives, work, and jobs? Mostly the parents and elders come back into force after graduation. Even student churches do not remain student-oriented forever.

Thirdly, "Youth work and children's ministry are superior, because they build for the future generation. The old generation is 'dyed in the wool,' of the old way, and can't change." Again, in Asia the family structure and its control indicate that most children have no power of decision or control of action until adulthood. So while we should not neglect the youth, we are wiser to reach them along with their families.

Fourth, some advocate, "Children and youth are more important because they are easier to reach and mold. Save a child and you save a life. Save a broken adult or family and you have no end of troubles to solve." Generally, conversion and growth in family groups provides the best stability, normality, and strength for youth. They should be cherished and reached, but this is best done in the context of the whole family. Taking deliberate steps to reach out to the families of interested scholars and children is a vital strategy. The worst sin of evangelism is to reach a child but neglect his or her family, which is their nurturing ground and controlling entity.

Fifth, some say, "It is better to have a few individuals who are genuine Christians than whole families that need so much work that you never are sure that they will become strong." There is no guarantee that "our" isolated individual believers are holier, stronger, or more stable than those in family groups.

Sixth, "Separating individual believers from their unsaved families is biblical, better, and builds them stronger in the face of opposition." They are to "come out from among them and be separate." This misinterprets the Word. History proves that these views are wrong, on all counts. Codependent "rice" Christians usually turn out not to be the strongest disciples.

A seventh objection is, "Only individuals can have a relationship with Christ, not so for the diverse family." This is true for "personal" salvation generally, but here we are talking about the best strategy for producing long-term stability against often fierce opposition, particularly among resistant peoples. The family comprised of a majority of new believers becomes its own nurturing force, closing ranks on the outside powers of opposition. Families throughout Scripture have been kept by the grace covering of God.

Eighth, "Group and family movements are shallow, weak, and unstable." This can be true if post-decision nurture and teaching are absent. Family movements require suitable postconversion evaluation with sustained teaching, training, discipleship, and consolidation. But in the end the strength and solidarity of the Christian family stands tall. The strong Christian family can be a powerful model and tool for extending the gospel throughout the extended family and local community. History proves this.

Ninth is a sad commentary: "Winning one by one individually is always the way we did it back home in our churches, so let's do it in missions too." The thinking advocate of indigenous methods will question whether this is a theologically good mission strategy. It has the seeds of proud ethnocentrism and ignorance of social and family structure across cultures.

Tenth, "Massive numbers of families coming into the church dilute it and produce nominalism." Not necessarily so, depending on the prompt nurture and training given. Individual converts can be weak and nominal and can just as easily dilute the church. Often they may not have the strength to stand alone against the opposition of the family or village.

An eleventh view suggests, "Doing God's work with a few individuals is better than distributing our energies among the multitudes or multiple families." This mentality can produce the small, insular ghetto church and favors a fortress mentality instead of the vision for reaching out to the whole community or people group in self-sacrificing service.

Twelfth, some feel, "If we do not accept the individual when opportunity to believe arises, they usually miss the salvation boat." While not advocating the rejecting of individuals, the group approach is one of faith in God and hope for the family by exercising love to the whole interrelated group. Often the "one by one against the tide approach" only shuts the family off to the gospel.

Lastly, "Individual salvation through 'one on one' is the proven, successful method of some major evangelistic agencies. This form of evangelism is taught in churches, seminaries, and Bible colleges." Unfortunately, it is also passed on to new and old native converts of foreign missions as the best or only way to do real evangelism. Maybe changing this approach to "one on a whole family" would be an even better method, with stronger and more extensive effect. It would be more culturally appropriate too.

Concluding Practical Applications and Suggestions

Modern societies face growing dilemmas of enormous moral declension and ethical challenges. These complexities demand that the church return to stress the family in its involvement with local communities, rather than remaining apart in insular isolation. The more the church is involved locally with the families of its surrounding society, the more effective and valued it will become. This conclusion primarily offers advice to Christians; it suggests some vital principles to apply to reaching families; and finally, it recommends a key simple model to win families.

First of all, the church must accept responsibility in regard to family groups. Christians might well repent for failures to serve families in their immediate communities. Often the church's ambassadors have unwittingly contributed to family breakdowns and domestic divisiveness, not only through neglect but also by their policies and practices in service and evangelism. Their tactics have frequently isolated individual converts from their families instead of integrating loving ministry to their whole families through the church.

Church workers and missionaries should study and understand the sociological and cultural dynamics of families, the familial structures, and their decision-making patterns. Making decisions in Asian families is often not an individual thing but a family affair. So the church needs to take the whole family into account when anticipating increased and lasting conversion.

Notice that Christ's Great Commission commands us to "make disciples" (plural), not "disciple" (singular).[16] Neither did Jesus instruct us to do that individually, "one by one." The emphasis is more likely "*ethnos* by *ethnos*," or family group by family group, tribe by tribe, and people by people (Matt 28:18–20). The apostles obviously understood Jesus' command, as from the beginning they won and incorporated whole families into the church. Few isolated, individual converts are highlighted in the New Testament. The apostles then extended the family movements out to reach Romans, Greeks, Gentiles, Goths, and so forth. "Family by family" was the primary approach and the usual mode of response for more than a millennium and a half.

---

16   Matt 28:19,20 in the Greek says *matheteusate panta ta ethne* (lit., "disciple all nations"), which captures the group or corporate emphasis the author speaks of.—Ed.

Second, the following are some vital principles and practical tactics for reaching whole families:

- Change the way we pray, from patterns of just individuals to lifting up whole families, their extended families, and their family webs and networks before God.
- Focus outreach ministry and service objectives on specific families as the clear goal or reason for evangelism. This intentional strategy may produce quite surprising results.
- Experiment with creative ways to reach whole families. Test models, methods, and strategies to do this. Research the effects of the process and its results. Recycle the best lessons learned.
- Foster friendly relationships with whole families over time. Effort taken to invest in gaining connections with families does take energy, but it is well spent.
- Develop family-friendly tools and approaches to families rather than just to individuals. Mass media has tended to major on resources focused on individuals, with little on families.
- Teach and encourage new, interested seekers to begin sharing the good news with their families and their relatives, even before they themselves become committed believers.
- Allow time for the dissemination of the good news to penetrate and permeate whole family networks, before calling families to commit prematurely. Diffusion helps here.
- Practice patience, persistence, and perseverance in order to see whole families reached, penetrated, won, and discipled. Pressure to show results back home, pushing for speedy decisions, and commando approaches are to be resisted rigorously. As Rome was not built in a day, neither are genuine converts or family conversions produced instantly.
- Incorporate family accessions into house churches from the start. Most of the cutting-edge extension of the church and its multiplication in Asia is found in tiny fellowships—usually less than fifteen or twenty members, sometimes only five to eight.
- Evaluate results in terms of families won, not just individual converts. Statistics should reflect both categories. The more vital is the number of new families brought into the kingdom.

Not only can heads of households start family movements, but sometimes they are started just from one relative's Christian witness to the family also. From there the movement is purposely spread throughout the extended family networks, across natural bridges of relatives and friends. It takes discipline to keep the group in mind.

Normally, time for diffusion of the gospel and its permeation to all members of the family network is required. Clear understanding and acceptance of the gospel may take even up to two and sometimes more years. By not withdrawing from normal relationships, interaction, and customary events of the family and the local community, Christians' witness can portray genuine faith and commendable ethical living to the society at large.

As family movements occur, it is essential to nurture the movements so that each member of the family affirms personal faith and relationship with Christ. Nurture adds spiritual depth to the members of believing families. Usually family house church fellowships are easily initiated. Unpaid local family leaders can be trained to function in them and to mobilize relatives for more extension into other family networks.

Bibliography

Beaver, R. Pierce. "The History of Mission Strategy." In Winter and Hawthorne, *Perspectives*, 241–52.

Latourette, Kenneth Scott. *A History of Christianity*. 2 vols. New York: Harper & Row, 1953.

McGavran, Donald A. *Understanding Church Growth*. Grand Rapids, MI: Eerdmans, 1970.

Neill, Stephen. *A History of Christian Missions.* Harmondsworth, Middlesex, UK: Penguin, 1964.

Pickett, J. Waskom. *Christian Mass Movements in India.* Lucknow: Lucknow Publishing, 1933.

Pierson, Paul. "A History of Transformation." In Winter and Hawthorne, *Perspectives,* 262–68.

Winter, Ralph D., and Steven C. Hawthorne, eds. *Perspectives on the World Christian Movement: A Reader.* 3rd ed. Pasadena, CA: William Carey Library, 1999.

Winter, Ralph D. "The Two Structures of God's Redemptive Mission." In Winter and Hawthorne, *Perspectives,* 220–30.

CHAPTER 50

Planting Churches
*Learning the Hard Way**
Tim and Rebecca Lewis

"Church planting is easy!" we thought. Within a few months of landing in a North African city, we already had a group of men and women meeting in our home. Joining that fellowship were some Muslim-background believers who had previously come to faith in the Lord through the testimony of others. We lined our living room with couches, in the local style, served sweet mint tea, and wore *djellabas*. We hoped a contextualized fellowship could grow into a solid church. T, a seminary graduate, functioned as the pastor, but rotated leadership. We sang and studied the Bible in English, Arabic, and French. The participants came from Berber, Arab, French, Spanish, Scottish, and American backgrounds. We even collected an offering for the poor. We thought we had planted a truly multicultural New Testament house church.

However, before the year was out, this church was already collapsing. The believers came from all over the city and had little in common. We wanted them to become like a family, but they were not interested. If T was gone on a trip, no one came.

Gathering a contextualized group of believers was our attempt to plant a church that would last by applying insights from the past. For at least sixty years, missionaries had been winning individuals to Christ in this country. But they had been returning to Islam to regain the families and communities they had lost. So, in the last twenty years, missionaries began gathering them together in hopes of creating community, but the churches thus planted did not last. Thinking the churches were too foreign, which made the families and government oppose them, we were now trying to contextualize the fellowships, but they too were falling apart.

We gave up and started over. Perhaps we were gathering people from too many different backgrounds together. This time we determined to gather only believers from one people group—the one we were focusing on. So when the opportunity arose, we introduced the only two known believers from that tribe. We expected them to embrace with joy. Instead they backed away with suspicion. Later, each one reprimanded T for introducing them. Each feared the other would expose him as a Christian to his hometown or to the government.

Now we thought, *"Church planting is so hard!"* Our contextualized, multicultural fellowship had failed. Our contextualized, monocultural group had also failed. How were we ever going to get believers to trust each other enough to plant a church?

---

* Originally published in a slightly different form in *Perspectives on the World Christian Movement: A Reader*, 4th ed., ed. Ralph D. Winter and Stephen C. Hawthorne (Pasadena, CA: William Carey Library, 2009), 690–93. Reprinted by permission.

As it turned out, we needed to reevaluate our assumptions about what the church is and how one is started. First, God unexpectedly showed us a completely different way to plant churches. Then, we noticed how Jesus planted a church cross-culturally and how he instructed the disciples to start a church.

God Showed Us a Different Way

God overhauled our concept of church by planting a church himself within our people group. To be accurate, he didn't really plant a church; he planted the gospel into a community that already existed.

Struggling with our failure to plant a church, we received an entirely unexpected letter. The hand-carried letter notified us that two brothers from our people group had finished a Bible correspondence course. They now wanted to meet a believer. We promptly sent off our best Arabic speaker to their distant town. When he arrived at their house, it was packed. Our team member wondered if he had stumbled onto a wedding, so he hesitantly asked for Hassan, who had written the letter.

Hassan and his brother rushed forward to welcome him into their household. They had gathered all their relatives and close friends to hear their honored guest explain what they had learned in their course. They eagerly received the gospel and pledged as a group to follow Jesus. Our teammate was thrilled. When he returned home, we shared his amazement.

This new church, consisting of an extended family and friends, continues strong to this day. Decades later, they are still spreading the gospel from town to town through their natural networks. They study the Word together, pray, baptize, and fellowship in ways they have determined best fit their community. No outsiders have ever tried to contextualize what has taken place. They have never had a leader or funding from outside their relational network. They do not feel any need for them.

"Is this church planting?" we asked. It was so different than what we had been doing. For decades, faithful workers had been forming churches, only to have them collapse in one to ten years. When we arrived, there was only one fellowship left, struggling along in the largest city. We ourselves had witnessed the genesis and demise of several more groups. Was there another way?

We compared the two ways of church planting. Our way consisted of forming a church by gathering together believers we knew. Their faith preceded their commitments to each other. We were the connecting center of the relationships, whether the church was contextualized or not, multicultural or monocultural. Of course, we hoped to turn leadership over to the believers as their commitments to each other grew. Instead, the churches collapsed. The way we were building community was a pattern common within our own culture but not theirs.

But a church developed in a different way when the gospel was planted into Hassan's family. The believers encouraged each other *within* their natural community. Their commitments to each other preceded their faith. Members could no more easily leave the church than they could leave their family. We provided occasional biblical input, such as translated Scriptures, but little else. We were truly outsiders.

Could faith growing *within* a family or network be a more effective way of establishing churches within communal societies? If so, how could we do this as outsiders? As we looked at the Scriptures, we noticed two things for the first time: Jesus had planted a church cross-culturally *within* a Samaritan village, and he had given his disciples instructions on how to plant the gospel *within* communities.

Jesus Taught Us a Different Way

"How do we plant a church this other way?" we wondered. We began by looking at the way Jesus planted a church in a Samaritan community (John 4). The Samaritans, like Muslims today, worshiped the God

of Abraham. Like the Samaritans, the Muslims "worship what they do not know." Because of their emphasis on purity, the Jews considered the Samaritans defiled and excluded them from the temple and all regular worship of God.

So the Samaritan woman was shocked when Jesus asked her for a cup of water, because of the long-standing enmity between their people groups. And when Jesus offered her eternal life, she turned it down, because she knew her people could never join the Jewish religion. "Interesting," we thought. Our Muslim friends often turned down salvation in Jesus because they could not imagine joining the Christian religion.

But Jesus removed that barrier. When the Samaritan woman pointed out that Jews worshiped in the temple, but Samaritans on the mountain, Jesus clarified that changing religious forms was not the issue. Instead, he said, "A time is coming and has now come when the true worshipers will worship the Father in the Spirit and in truth, for they are the kind of worshipers the Father seeks" (v. 23). The woman was so overjoyed that they too could become true worshipers that she ran back and told her whole village.

As a result, the Samaritans invited Jesus to come *into* their community for two days. Jesus persuaded them that he "really is the Savior of the world" (v. 42), not just the Savior of the Jews. Many believed, and Jesus left behind a church inside that community, like the one in Hassan's family. Jesus did not try to get them to come out of their community to join with Jewish or Samaritan believers from elsewhere. We had never noticed this part of the story before!

This story was not a parable; Jesus faced the same barriers we were facing! All the Muslims we knew had been taught that to worship God through Christ they would have to leave their family and join the Christian group, who had been their enemies for fourteen hundred years. But somehow Hassan and his family had seen things the way Jesus did: they could become true worshipers without leaving their community.

Then we saw, for the first time, that Jesus had also taught the disciples how to plant a church *within* a community. In Luke 10, he told seventy disciples to look for a "man of peace"—someone who would invite them *into* his own household. They were to remain in that household, sharing the gospel with all who came into that home, and not go from house to house. If no one in a particular village invited them *into* their household, they were told to leave and go on to another village. Amazingly clear!

We had never thought of looking for people who would invite us *into* their family or community to talk about Jesus! But Jesus and the disciples had planted churches this way.

"We can copy what Jesus did!" we realized. We can begin by telling our Muslim friends that worshiping God in spirit and truth does not require them to change religious systems. If some receive this news with joy and invite us back to tell their whole family, we can go *into* their community. As happened in Hassan's family, those who decide to follow Jesus can grow in faith together. Instead of trying to get believers from different communities to form a lasting new group, we could, like Jesus, establish a church *inside* their natural community.

Conclusion

After fifteen years, we had learned the hard way that—in communal cultures—we couldn't plant a lasting church by gathering random believers into new groups. It didn't matter if they were contextualized or not, multicultural or monocultural; after a few months or years, these groups would fall apart.

Instead we needed to find a person of peace who would invite us into their own community to share the gospel. Jesus was welcomed *into* the Samaritan village. The seventy disciples were welcomed *into* a home. In the same way, Peter was welcomed *into* Cornelius' household, and Paul was welcomed by Lydia *into* her household.

In each case, they were welcomed *into* a cohesive community, so the gospel was shared with the whole group. As a result, people *already committed to each other* came to faith together. A church was born *within* a natural community, without creating a *new* group just for fellowship. It reminded us of something Ralph Winter had said: "The 'church' (i.e., committed community) is already there, they just don't know Jesus yet!"

1. Henry Riggs' 1938 report (chap. 43) on the findings of the Near East Christian Council's Inquiry appears to be the first description of what we now call the insider paradigm. Riggs' report touches on many issues, both practical and theoretical, that are being discussed today. Which of Riggs' ideas or suggestions most stand out to you as you read this seminal article?

2. A common focus in Western missions today is "results," or numbers of new believers. Insider movements challenge this, because they cannot always be quantitatively defined. How does Cobb's exhortation (chap. 44) to focus on an attitude of love, genuine friendship, honesty about mistakes, and the power of the truth of the gospel help to dispel the drive for quick results?

3. What similarities and differences between the Bible and the Qur'an do you notice from reading Woodberry's article (chap. 45)? Which values or beliefs are the same, and which are different? To what extent does the Qur'an promote affirmation of and belief in the Bible? How, if at all, may the Qur'an be used in gospel witness to Muslims?

4. How does Accad's SEKAP Spectrum (chap. 46) relate to your own practice of dialogue? What have you found to be effective or beneficial in your witness for Christ?

5. Do you identify as an "alongsider"? If so, where do your strengths lie? Can you add other challenges or roles of alongsiders to the Travises' list (chap. 47)?

6. Do you agree with Talman's theological argument (chap. 48), drawn from 1 Corinthians 7, that "the unholy does not defile the holy"? How does this affect your view of insider movements?

7. How does Smith's article (chap. 49) inform your broader understanding of insider movements? How can whole families be invited to become followers of Jesus, as happened in the case of Cornelius' household? What role does culture play in this?

8. How does the Lewises' experience with church planting (chap. 50) challenge or reinforce your own model for church planting? Why did the attempt to create a new community, by putting former strangers together, consistently fail? What are the strengths of introducing the "yeast of the gospel" into preexisting community structures like extended families?

PART 6
CONCERNS AND MISUNDERSTANDINGS

INTRODUCTION TO PART 6

> One of the most unfortunate dynamics in today's world is that spiritual issues are largely understood in terms of competing religions. If I were the devil, I would try to limit Jesus' message of the kingdom to a diluted notion of adherence to a certain religion, rather than a message of falling in love with the risen Messiah.
>
> —FRANK DECKER[*]

Thus far we have observed unusual ways of God working, unimagined paths of discipleship, deeper understandings of Scripture, complex issues of faith and culture, and alternative approaches to ministry. Not surprisingly, this has resulted in some confusion. This sixth division of our study will delineate some of the major misconceptions and concerns that have been expressed in regard to these Jesus movements among non-Christian religious communities.

A little over fifteen years ago John Jay Travis' publication of the C1–C6 Spectrum occasioned strong criticism of C5 movements. In chapter 51, he explains the intended use of the C-spectrum, some of its limitations, and the need for other models.

In chapter 52, Brother Yusuf, the leader of a large Muslim insider movement, responds to some tough questions raised by a critic.

One of the most contentious questions in movements among Muslims is whether or not a Christ follower can continue affirming Muhammad as a "messenger" of God in any sense of the word. In chapter 53, Harley Talman presents surprising and insightful examples of the wide range of Muslim and Christian positions on this issue. He also notes findings from contemporary scholarship that will challenge most readers' assumptions and perspectives on this issue.

Because they think "Allah" is a pagan deity, some Christians oppose the idea of Muslim disciples of Christ remaining within the Muslim community. In chapter 54, Jesse Wheeler offers a concise consideration of reasons for regarding Allah as the God that Jews and Christians worship, albeit with some different theological understandings.

---

[*] "Fog Alert," The Mission Society, accessed May 31, 2015, http://www.themissionsociety.org/learn/multimedia/unfinished/mag-templ/article/48067.

Many who are sensitive to the spiritual forces at work in different religions of the world might expect believers to separate themselves from everything associated with those religions. In chapter 55, Anna Travis, with her extensive experience in deliverance and healing ministry among Muslims, tackles this issue head-on.

In chapter 56, Rebecca Lewis points out some potential pitfalls of these movements, along with prescriptions for avoiding these dangers.

This part concludes with chapter 57, in which Michael Roberts clarifies essential issues in our controversy by succinctly listing areas of agreement and potential disagreement between advocates and opponents.

CHAPTER 51

The C1–C6 Spectrum after Fifteen Years

Misunderstandings, Limitations, and Recommendations[*]

John Jay Travis

Friends recently asked my wife and me how we became involved in outreach among Muslims and about the origins of the C1–C6 Spectrum.[1] We shared with them our personal journeys.

I explained that in the 1970s I had the privilege of living with a Muslim family in Asia as a university student. I was a nominal Christian at the time. Some years later, when I was a committed follower of Jesus, my wife and I moved to that same Muslim country, spending a month with the family with whom I had previously lived. We ended up living for more than twenty years in that country and raising our own family there—all the while sharing the good news of Jesus with Muslim neighbors and friends.

Regarding the C1–C6 Spectrum, I explained that it was my attempt to describe six types of fellowships that I had seen people born Muslim either form or join after they began to follow Jesus. Each type of fellowship I referred to as a different form of *Christ-centered community* (hence the letter *C* in the Spectrum). I had not initially planned to publish the Spectrum,[2] and only did so when some who knew of it were objecting to certain types of fellowships it describes.[3]

I explained that the Spectrum was primarily *descriptive*. I had hoped it would increase awareness among cross-cultural workers of various ways God was moving among Muslims. I had also hoped it would bring greater unity and mutual respect among workers who were using different ministry approaches but who had the same goal of seeing God's kingdom grow. I mentioned to our friends some of the limitations I saw in the Spectrum as well.

After hearing our story, our friends felt that the Spectrum had often been misunderstood or misused and that it would be good to write an article explaining its intended use and limitations. This chapter is my response to their suggestion.

---

[*] This article will appear in the October 2015 issue of *EMQ*.

1 See John Travis, "The C1 to C6 Spectrum: A Practical Tool for Defining Six Types of 'Christ-centered Communities' ('C') Found in the Muslim Context," *EMQ* 34, no. 4 (1998): 407–8. See also *UIM*, chap. 4, fig. 4.1, for an illustration of the Spectrum.

2 In this chapter, I will often refer to the C1–C6 Spectrum as simply the C-spectrum or the Spectrum. Elsewhere it has also been referred to as the C1–C6 Continuum or the C-scale.

3 See Phil Parshall, "Danger! New Directions in Contextualization," *EMQ* 34, no. 4 (1998): 404–10; and a response by John Travis, "Must All Muslims Leave 'Islam' to Follow Jesus?" *EMQ* 34, no. 4 (1998): 411–15.

Use and Description of the C-spectrum

The C-spectrum has been used widely in mission circles and literature over the past fifteen years to differentiate various types of Christ-centered communities (biblical *ekklesiae*) found in the Muslim world. It has been adapted for use in other socioreligious contexts as well.[4]

The Spectrum is framed around two central issues: (1) the socioreligious identity[5] of fellowships of Jesus followers who were born Muslim and (2) the linguistic, cultural, and religious forms they use.[6] It is assumed that each of these types of Christ-centered communities follows Jesus as the risen Lord and Savior and the Bible as God's word. Any group along the Spectrum could, however, become sub-biblical if adherence to Scripture becomes weak. The following is a brief description of the six basic types of Christ-centered communities (see also chap. 4, fig. 4.1).

The first type of Christ-centered community, which I called C1, refers to churches in the Muslim world that use distinctly non-Muslim, "Christian" forms (music, liturgy, architecture, prayer posture, etc.) and hold their worship services in languages other than the mother tongue of the surrounding Muslim population. Thousands of these churches exist in the Middle East, Asia, and Africa, some of them predating Islam (e.g., Eastern Orthodox and Armenian churches).

C2 refers to churches similar to C1, except that the worship is conducted in the mother tongue of the surrounding Muslim population.[7] In terms of socioreligious identity, the central issue of the C-spectrum, members of C1 and C2 fellowships refer to themselves as Christians or by the name of their denomination/church (e.g., Orthodox, Catholic, or Coptic). Muslim-background believers are found in various C2 congregations or in specialized subgroups associated with them.[8]

C3 refers to fellowships that incorporate local or indigenous ethnic and cultural forms such as music, dress, and artwork rather than distinctively Western or Christian ones. C3 groups thus aim to develop indigenous expressions of congregational life while avoiding forms that appear "Islamic."[9] As with C1 and C2 communities, C3 groups refer to themselves as Christian.

The fourth type, C4, differs from C3 in that, instead of avoiding Islamic forms (religious terminology, holidays, personal names, diet, dress, prayer posture, etc.), these groups retain them, filling them where necessary with new biblical meaning. In general they avoid the label "Christian" due to the un-

---

4   Scales or spectrums to describe both Hindu- and Buddhist-background fellowships have been developed. Michael Frost and Alan Hirsch have alluded to the Spectrum's application in the postmodern West as well; see Frost and Hirsch, *The Shaping of Things to Come: Innovation and Mission for the 21st-Century Church* (Peabody, MA: Hendrickson, 2003), 117–21.

5   For an explanation of the term "socioreligious," see chap. 1.

6   C1 through C4 groups are identified by socioreligious identity, language, culture, and forms, whereas C5 and C6 are distinguished by socioreligious identity alone.

7   Though they use the daily language of the local Muslim population in worship, they seldom use the same religious terms as local Muslims—such as *Isa* for Jesus, *Yahya* for John the Baptist, or *Zabur* for Psalms.

8   A local seminary student carried out a demographic study of C1 and C2 churches in the part of the Muslim world where I lived. In that context, C1 churches consist of mostly non-Muslim-background believers. They use the national language, which is understood by local Muslims but is not their mother tongue. However, the researcher concluded that in nearly every C1 church there were at least a small number of Muslim-background believers.

9   An underlying assumption of C3 groups, therefore, is that "cultural" and "Islamic" forms can be separated in Muslim societies. C3 groups would typically avoid using Muslim terminology.

fortunate cultural baggage it carries.[10] C4 groups tend to refer to themselves as "followers of Isa" or in other, similar terms that focus on Jesus and allegiance to him.

The fifth type of Christ-centered community, C5, consists of groups of Muslims who follow Jesus as Lord and Savior and the Bible as God's word without taking the step of leaving the religious community of their birth. Some C5 groups relate with Christian-background believers for friendship and spiritual interaction, but they form and lead their own groups (*ekklesiae*) for prayer, fellowship, and Bible study. By remaining part of the Muslim community, they are a source of salt and light for family and friends. The Spectrum does not attempt to describe C5 in terms of linguistic, cultural, and religious forms, as there is too much variance worldwide to discern a common pattern.[11]

Finally, C6 refers to the many small and scattered groups of Jesus followers who are underground, isolated, or restricted in their ability to meet. Their context limits their ability to gather openly (e.g., in certain strict Islamic states) and makes public witness difficult, yet many find creative ways to connect with other Jesus followers and share the good news discreetly as God's Spirit leads. Similar to C5, these Jesus followers retain their Muslim identity as they follow Jesus as Lord and Savior. As with C5, the Spectrum does not attempt to describe them in terms of linguistic, cultural, or religious forms.[12]

Seven Common Misunderstandings and Misuses

Much has been written about these six general types of Jesus-centered communities since the Spectrum was first published in 1998. Some literature has been for or against various points along the Spectrum, with most of the discussion focused on C5.[13] Other literature does not critique the types of fellowships per se, but rather discusses the strength or weakness of the model itself.[14]

Some critiques have dealt squarely with what I have written and intended. Others, however, have been based on misunderstandings or misuses of the Spectrum. Below I address common misunder-

---

10 Among Muslims, the terms "Christian" and "Christianity" often denote ethnic or political realities associated with Western peoples and cultures, including immoral Hollywood films, immodest dress, alcohol misuse, anti-Islamic sentiments, and certain political agendas. These terms are not generally used by Muslims to refer to someone who truly believes in Jesus and follows him any more than Christians use the term "Muslim" to mean "someone submitted to God."

11 Elsewhere I have described particular C5 groups with which I am familiar; see chaps. 4 and 16. As a general category of the C-spectrum, what makes a C5 type of group distinct is maintaining a Muslim socioreligious identity. In other words, they integrate the practice of their biblical faith in Jesus into their everyday life in the religious community of their birth. A "C5 movement" would therefore be synonymous with an insider movement. I know of C5 group members who refer to themselves with various descriptions such as "Holy Spirit Muslims," "Muslim believers," "Muslim followers of Jesus," or simply "Muslims."

12 Little can be said about the language and ways in which these groups worship because they are underground.

13 For a series of articles advocating the validity of C5, see *IJFM* 17, no. 1 (2000). For critiques of C5, see Parshall, "Danger! New Directions"; and Timothy Tennent, "Followers of Jesus (Isa) in Islamic Mosques: A Closer Examination of C5 'High Spectrum' Contextualization," *IJFM* 23, no. 3 (2006): 101–15. For a view of both sides of the issue, see Joseph Cumming, "Muslim Followers of Jesus?" *CT*, November 2009 (*UIM*, chap. 3); and the series of cover story articles with Gene Daniels entitled "Worshiping Jesus in the Mosque," *CT*, January–February 2013.

14 See Barnett in *UIM*, chap. 62, and the sidebar by Green, chap. 58. See also their chapters in *Longing for Community: Church, Ummah, or Somewhere in Between?*, ed. David Greenlee (Pasadena, CA: William Carey Library, 2013), 19–66.

standings and misuses, followed by my own critique of the Spectrum, where I point out some of its limitations and make suggestions for the future.

The first common misunderstanding has to do with what the letter *C* represents. It does not stand for "contextualization," "cross-cultural church-planting spectrums," or "Christian"—all terms that have been mistakenly used. It stands for "Christ-centered communities"; in other words, fellowships or groups of Jesus followers—biblical *ekklesiae*.

Second, the Spectrum is meant to show how groups of Jesus followers who were *born Muslim* express their faith, *not* how cross-cultural workers among Muslims express theirs. Unfortunately the first article critiquing the Spectrum[15] focused much of its attention on a few foreign field workers who had assumed a Muslim identity to reach Muslims. This actually has nothing whatsoever to do with the Spectrum, yet the idea of cross-cultural workers "becoming C5" keeps resurfacing in Spectrum discussions.

Third, no point along the Spectrum is intended to be better or more biblical than any other. Any expression of faith in Jesus along the Spectrum could be appropriate for a particular culture or group (see chap. 63).[16] I was shocked recently to learn that, in one country, many cross-cultural workers had understood C6 to be the ideal because it was the highest number on the Spectrum![17] The reason for portraying these different types of fellowships along a flat, linear spectrum was to communicate that in God's eyes all members of God's kingdom are of equal value before him, regardless of their cultural or socioreligious labels.

Fourth, the Spectrum is not intended to be exhaustive. It highlights six types of fellowships, but other expressions or variations are entirely possible. When I used the word "spectrum" I had in mind a range of colors placed side by side, with theoretically infinite shades between them. Many have understood this, often describing a particular fellowship as being between or similar to some point on the Spectrum (e.g., "between C2 and C3" or "like C4 but . . ."). For some, however, there has been misunderstanding when they could not find a direct correlation between a type of fellowship they knew of and one of the six basic Spectrum descriptions.

Fifth, points along the Spectrum are not to be seen as static or unchangeable, as some have assumed. Over time a fellowship could change, taking on a different socioreligious identity from what it held previously. Spectrum descriptions are only snapshots of the moment and do not reflect change or direction.

Sixth, the Spectrum was designed to describe groups, not individual Jesus followers. This is an easy mistake to make (I have done it myself), since fellowships are made up of individuals who presumably reflect the characteristics of the group. It is therefore quite natural to refer to someone as a C4 believer, meaning that person displays the characteristics and socioreligious identity associated with a C4 group. However, this has caused some to misunderstand the model since individual Muslim-background be-

---

15 See Parshall, "Danger! New Directions."

16 As stated earlier, any group along the Spectrum could become sub-biblical if adherence to the Bible becomes weak. Some would argue that C1 or C2 types are more biblical or less prone to error than, say, C4 or C5. The reality of the situation does not bear this out. Some of the most nominal and sub-biblical groups fall into C1 or C2 categories.

17 Interestingly, another misunderstanding they had was that C5 groups are secretive about their faith and reluctant to witness, which is not the case at all.

lievers they know do not fit perfectly into any particular point along the Spectrum.[18] Individuals, in fact, may have more than one socioreligious identity. For example, an MBB group may be linked to a C2 church, clearly C2 in its identity and forms. Yet in certain situations, individual members may still identify with the Muslim community, even at times feeling culturally or socially Muslim themselves. Additional, more detailed models are needed to bring out nuances such as dual or multiple identities.[19]

The seventh and greatest misuse of the Spectrum is the way some have added to or redefined the meaning of C5 to include Islamic practices and beliefs that they *assume* Jesus-following Muslims must be retaining. This has created a straw man that critics can then attack.[20]

The reality on the ground is that, as C5 groups engage the Bible under the guidance of the Spirit of God, they come to their own convictions about Muslim beliefs and practices. Some are rejected, some are reinterpreted, and those not in conflict with the Bible are generally continued. As serious disciples, they are learning how to navigate their new faith in Jesus in the midst of being part of the religious community of their birth. Because particulars of how this happens vary from group to group, the original description of C5 focused only on their allegiance to Jesus as Lord and Savior and the Bible as God's word, and not on what they reject or retain from Islam.[21]

Limitations of the C-spectrum

All models have limitations and can only approximate reality. I see two limitations in particular with the C-spectrum.

The first is in what it does *not* describe. It addresses language, culture, religious forms, and group identity, but does not describe intangibles such as the motivations, life experiences, or aspirations of those in the groups. Why do some groups of Jesus followers form or join C1 or C2 churches while others join or form C4 or C5 fellowships? Or what political, cultural, and legal factors and pressures might influence certain groups toward a C3 expression of faith but others toward C6—the latter becoming what some have described as "catacomb believers"?[22] I am sure many of the criticisms people have for one or another expression of faith along the Spectrum would be greatly reduced if they could walk for a while in the shoes of others, understanding their hearts and life stories.[23]

---

18   In practice, many have noted that individual Jesus followers have two or three different types of identity used in different social contexts. It is my opinion that groups, on the other hand, are more likely to have a single identity as they negotiate who they are collectively with the larger community. It may be possible, however, that groups also have more than one identity, which would show a limitation in the use of the Spectrum.

19   See Adams, chap. 61; Barnett, chap. 62; and the sidebar by Green, chap. 58.

20   The following are examples I have heard of altered descriptions or additions to C5 that clearly depart from my original definition: viewing Muhammad as on par with Jesus, viewing the Qur'an as having higher authority than the Bible, using only the Muslim holy book for discipleship, and forcing frequent mosque attendance. No C5 group I am acquainted with holds to any of the above beliefs or practices.

21   See the empirical research by Naja, chap. 15.

22   Father Jean-Marie Gaudeul coined the phrase "catacomb believers" to refer to Muslims who follow Jesus privately or underground, even as many early Christ followers did, meeting in the catacombs of ancient Rome. See Gaudeul, *Called From Islam to Christ: Why Muslims Become Christians* (East Sussex, UK: Monarch, 1999), 264–65, 288.

23   In chap. 63 I share some social, cultural, and historical factors that may influence new followers of Jesus toward certain choices of religious identity in terms of the C-spectrum.

A second limitation is that this flat, linear model,[24] while helpful in showing variety, can also be limiting if understood as portraying six distinct categories positioned side by side, without overlapping, sharing, or blending of characteristics. As many have noted when trying to use the one-dimensional Spectrum as a means of classification, some fellowships defy description and contain elements from a number of points along the Spectrum.

Four Recommendations in Using the C-spectrum

In spite of its limitations, the C-spectrum is commonly used worldwide. I offer four recommendations for those who use it.

1. It is best used among colleagues who have a clear and common understanding of what descriptions within the Spectrum mean. It can serve as a convenient nomenclature and starting point for discussion. To use it *between* different ministries and organizations, however, is risky due to the variety of ways in which one group or another understands it.

2. Because it can be misunderstood or misapplied, it is often more helpful, as long as appropriate security measures are set in place,[25] to employ narrative and story when discussing ministry in Muslim contexts. Narratives, case studies, and longer descriptions, given by those actually on site and involved, help unpack some of the complexities of context (legal, political, and social) and can bring out the motivations, hopes, and life experiences of Jesus followers. In addition, by avoiding C-spectrum labels, the emotional baggage those terms carry for some can be eliminated so that parties can hear and not talk past each other.

3. Better graphics could avoid the appearance of rigidity and static categories that a one-dimensional graphic might communicate. (The original article on the Spectrum did not show any graphic—it only presented in a list the six basic types of fellowships.)

4. The effectiveness of the C-spectrum would be greatly enhanced if augmented by other models and tools now being developed. Tim Green's model, discussed by Eric Adams in chapter 61, and Jens Barnett's model in chapter 62 are great steps forward in this direction.

Conclusion

The C-spectrum has been commonly used as a heuristic tool to describe certain types of Christ-centered fellowships found in Muslim contexts. It focuses on the outward forms of some of these fellowships as well as their socioreligious identity. While helpful in some ways, the Spectrum has also been misunderstood or misused. The present chapter has dealt with common misunderstandings and misuses, limitations of the model, and recommendations for its future use.

Hopefully, future use of the C-spectrum can be augmented by other models and descriptive tools, some of which are mentioned throughout *UIM*. Narratives and case studies, with appropriate anonymity and safeguards, can bring out nuances and complexities that a spectrum or scale cannot.

---

24 Barnett (chap. 62) uses the term "one-dimensional" rather than "linear."

25 Extreme caution is necessary when field workers obtain and communicate data for such stories and narratives; they must assess the potential risks to people and institutions. Research concerning Muslims open to Jesus involves great risk and could bring harm on those being interviewed, as well as on the field workers associated with them. Concealment of names, locations, and other identifying factors is necessary in order to carry out a safe and ethical study. Narratives and case studies in *UIM* employ this level of caution and anonymity.

In the spirit of the original intent of the C-spectrum, let us acknowledge the wide variety of expressions of life in the kingdom that groups of Jesus followers choose. Since God's wisdom and the creativity of his people will certainly yield still more variety in the years ahead, we would do well to rejoice in all that God does in the lives and families of Muslims, whom he loves.

Bibliography

Barnett, Jens. "Refusing to Choose: Multiple Belonging among Arab Followers of Christ." In Greenlee, *Longing for Community,* 19–28.

———. "Living a Pun: Cultural Hybridity among Arab Followers of Christ." In Greenlee, *Longing for Community,* 29–40.

Frost, Michael, and Alan Hirsch. *The Shaping of Things to Come: Innovation and Mission for the 21st-Century Church.* Peabody, MA: Hendrickson, 2003.

Gaudeul, Jean-Marie. *Called From Islam to Christ: Why Muslims Become Christians.* East Sussex, UK: Monarch, 1999.

Green, Tim. "Conversion in the Light of Identity Theories." In Greenlee, *Longing for Community,* 41–52.

———. "Identity Choices at the Border Zone." In Greenlee, *Longing for Community,* 53–66.

Greenlee, David, ed. *Longing for Community: Church,* Ummah, *or Somewhere in Between?* Pasadena, CA: William Carey Library, 2013.

Parshall, Phil. "Danger! New Directions in Contextualization." *EMQ* 34, no. 4 (1998): 404–10.

Tennent, Timothy. "Followers of Jesus (Isa) in Islamic Mosques: A Closer Examination of C5 'High Spectrum' Contextualization." *IJFM* 23, no. 3 (2006): 101–15.

Travis, John. "The C1 to C6 Spectrum: A Practical Tool for Defining Six Types of 'Christ-centered Communities' ('C') Found in the Muslim Context." *EMQ* 34, no. 4 (1998): 407–8.

———. "Must All Muslims Leave 'Islam' to Follow Jesus?" *EMQ* 34, no. 4 (1998): 411–15.

CHAPTER 52

Responding to Christian Concerns[*]

Interview with Brother Yusuf

Gary Corwin: *Have you fully considered the enormous gulf that exists between Messianic Jewish churches and what you are advocating as Messianic Islam?*

Brother Yusuf: There is no Messianic Islam. This is not even possible. I do not know of any Messianic mosques, and I do not agree with the concept. A mosque is simply a house of worship. It is not wrong for the disciples of Jesus to pray in a house of worship. It is a quiet and reverent place. This also gives them an opportunity to talk to others, especially in the late afternoon, when the heads of families sit around and talk. Reaching the heads of families is a key to reaching the community.

I don't really like the term "Messianic Muslim," because it is not a term that insiders can use with members of their own community. The word for "Messianic" in my language is the same as the word for "Christian." People would think we were saying we were "Christian Muslims," but the word "Christian" refers to people in a different ethnic community. It would be nonsense. In fact, we do not need any labels at all. When we visit a mosque, we just talk and behave like insiders to the culture, which we are, and people accept us. After a few visits, when we have gotten to know some people, we begin to talk to them about the Messiah.

We have *jamats* (house churches), where people meet for prayer, worship, Bible study, and discussion. People participate frequently, sometimes every day. Holy Communion is celebrated every month or two. Believers are baptized. These practices are based on the Bible. As for the participants, their identity is primarily that of disciples of the Lord Jesus Christ, and secondarily as members of the Muslim community.

Contrary to what some people might advocate or imagine, we do not teach the brethren that they should go to the mosque or that they should refrain from going, and there is no expectation that either will be a permanent state. Some go because this has been their custom and they like to spend time praying in a house of prayer. Others go because it gives them an opportunity to speak to their friends there about the Lord Jesus.

---

[*]   Excerpt from Gary Corwin, "A Humble Appeal to C5/Insider Movement Muslim Ministry Advocates to Consider Ten Questions," with responses from Brother Yusuf, Rick Brown, Kevin Higgins, Rebecca Lewis, and John Travis, *IJFM* 24, no. 1 (2007): 5–20. Reprinted by permission. Corwin's questions have been truncated and the other respondents' answers omitted due to space considerations and a desire to give prominence to the insider believer's perspective. See the article online at www.ijfm.org for the full context of the discussion.

Gary Corwin: *Have you considered that the Jerusalem Council of Acts 15, far from supporting both cultural and religious contextualization, settles on a strong affirmation of the former combined with a strong stand against the latter?*

Brother Yusuf: In Acts 15 it was decided that the Gentile believers did not need to follow the Jewish forms of life and worship. They were not required to visit the temple or synagogue, attend the feasts, make the various sacrifices, or even be circumcised. So the Gentiles worshiped God in their own fashion. That sounds like some kind of religious contextualization. One has to wonder how the apostles could set aside the law of Moses like that. The answer, of course, is Jesus. It is because of the work of the Lord Jesus that the Jewish Christians could accept as their brothers anyone whom Jesus accepted, even if he was not circumcised and did not worship as they did. Similarly we teach the brethren that they should love and accept everyone who truly believes in Jesus, whether they are associated with C5, C4, or C3 churches. We wish others would do the same.

The Jerusalem Council said the Gentiles should not eat meat sacrificed to idols. I presume that this was because it would be a form of idol worship. Similarly we teach people to serve God and worship him alone. We teach them to be faithful disciples of the Lord Jesus Christ.

Gary Corwin: *Whether one is saying the Lord's Prayer while going through the motions of the* salat, *or rationalizing the many meanings of the term "prophet" while one is declaring Muhammad is Allah's prophet in the* shahadah, *the message communicated by the very action to all those around is a declaration of adherence to the doctrines of Islam. Complex explanations based on the multiple meanings of words, or theological gymnastics that point out that only Allah knows man's heart, may at times win the day in defending oneself before unfriendly government tribunals. It is hard to imagine, however, that they will not ultimately be viewed as deceit. In light of the centuries-old accusation by Muslims that Christians are deceivers, at best it has to be considered a highly questionable strategy.*

Brother Yusuf: Some people in our movement say the shahadah and some do not. This is an individual choice. What we have found in actuality is that saying the shahadah does not harm the believer's witness to Jesus. On the contrary, it gives him a hearing. It can also be a starting point to discuss our Savior: Muhammad did a great thing in destroying the idols in Arabia. John the Baptist was a great prophet because he pointed people to the Lamb of God, in whom alone we can find salvation.

What one believes about Muhammad is of little consequence. Affirming Muhammad does not in fact affirm a body of doctrine. There are four main schools of Sunni Islam, in addition to various Shi'ite sects, and they have different sets of tradition and doctrine. Affirming Muhammad does not affirm any one of these. One can say the shahadah without affirming any of them, as is the case with most cultural Muslims.

Gary Corwin: *Have you considered the incongruity of asserting and/or leaving the impression that C5 approaches are the only hope to reaching Muslims in any significant numbers (a common occurrence), and also arguing that we cannot know the extent of such insider movements because they are difficult to distinguish from unconverted Muslims?*

Brother Yusuf: John Travis developed the C1–C5 scale, not to describe a range of strategies, but to describe a range of expressions of Christ-centered community. We do not promote C5 as the only strategy or even insist on conformity to it. We seek only to follow the Lord's leading. Some people in our movement say the shahadah and some do not; some of them pray in mosques and some do not (and

following Qur'anists maintain that Muhammad's message should be interpreted in harmony with the Scriptures instead of relying on later traditions that contradict them.[6]

4. *Muhammad of the revisionist historians.* Applying higher critical methods to the study of Islam, revisionist scholars may reject almost anything attributed to or about Muhammad, including the Qur'an, unless it is corroborated by non-Islamic sources. Thus one revisionist will only grant that Muhammad "as a prophet of the Arabs who taught a vaguely defined monotheism . . . may have existed."[7] While many theories of the most radical revisionists are not widely accepted, their research convincingly discredits the traditional and popular narratives at a number of points.

Where one lands on the spectrum between traditional Islamic and radical revisionist views of history will greatly impact one's perspective on Muhammad's identity. Was he the legendary Prophet of popular Islamic piety? Was he the founder of a new religion that was antagonistic toward Jews and Christians? Was he the founder of a reform movement of monotheists that included numbers of Jews and Christians for some decades?[8] Was he a prophet of the Arabs about whom we know virtually nothing with any confidence? Or was he something else?

Muslim Followers of Jesus and Various Views of Muhammad

Just as diverse views and convictions are held by Christians on many important matters, such as eschatology and the use of spiritual gifts, we also find varied views and practices among Muslim followers of Jesus. Some say the shahadah, some do not, some say only the first part, and others reinterpret, alter, or expand it. The following examples illustrate this variety.

Saying the Confession with Simplicity and Sincerity

Brother Noah explains his view of Muhammad:

> What makes a person a prophet? How do we accept a person as
> a prophet? A prophet is one who calls people to God, who calls

---

6   C. Jonn Block seems to be representative of this; see Block, *Expanding the Qur'anic Bridge: Historical and Modern Interpretations of the Qur'an in Christian-Muslim Dialogue with Special Attention Paid to Ecumenical Trends* (New York: Routledge, 2014).

7   Spencer asserts that Muhammad's "life story is lost in the mists of legend, like those of Robin Hood and Macbeth"; see Spencer, *Did Muhammad Exist?*, 214. Spencer summarizes the findings of the revisionists, whose theories and findings are worthy of careful consideration. However, dismissing out of hand all Islamic sources that lack outside corroboration would seem to many to be an excessively radical approach.

8   This controversial proposal of a leading historian, Fred Donner, steers something of a middle course between radical revisionist and traditional histories. Donner believes Muhammad began an ecumenical movement of monotheist "Believers" that respected and incorporated Jews and Christians for two to three generations after his death. Its focus was on devotion (especially prayer and almsgiving) and the practice of righteousness and good deeds in preparation for the day of judgment. See Donner, *Muhammad and the Believers*, 39–89. Donner asserts that this "confessionally open" ecumenical movement was "in no way antithetical to the beliefs and practices of some Christians and Jews—unlike the situation that developed a century later." They could belong not only because of their religious identities but because they were "inclined to righteousness" (69–70). Donner's proposal is generally consistent with the extant but limited material evidence. For critical reviews of Donner, see Gerald Hawting, *Journal of Religion* 91, no. 2 (April 2011): 284–85; Jack Tannous, *Expositions* 5, no. 2 (2011): 126–41; Robert Hoyland, *International Journal of Middle East Studies* 44, no. 3 (August 2012): 573–76; and Patricia Crone, "Among the Believers," *Tablet Magazine*, August 10, 2010, http://tabletmag.com/jewish-news-and-politics/42023/among-the-believers.

people to repentance, who calls his people to turn away from sin to God. John the Baptist came and called all the people to repent and turn to God. He proclaimed the coming of the Messiah. In one Gospel John the Baptist introduced the Messiah to the people. We see the result of his call. People came and were baptized by him as preparation to receive the Messiah.

Muhammad was born in Arabia, where people used to worship 360 gods and goddesses. They were idol worshippers. They were a nation who lived side by side with the people of God, who worshipped the God of Abraham. This Arab nation knew that they were also children of Abraham, but they did not know the God of Abraham. Muhammad in his time called his people to the God of Abraham.[9] He told them that these 360 gods are not the true God, that they have no power, and that we need to worship the true God, the God of our ancestors Abraham and Ishmael. He introduced Isa Al-Masih to his people. Muhammad told his people that Isa is the Messiah, He is the Word of God, He is the Spirit of God and He is a miracle and sign to the world. We see the result of his call even today.

John the Baptist proclaimed the coming of the Messiah to his people; and Muhammad introduced the Messiah to his people. John the Baptist called his people to repent and turn away from sin and turn to God; Muhammad called his people to repent and turn away from sin and turn to the true God, the God of Abraham. He also said there is only one true God, the God of Abraham. Who can call the nations to the true God and be successful if he is not instructed by God?

Saying that Muhammad is a prophet does not mean that Jesus is not the Messiah and the Lord. It also does not mean that Muhammad is Messiah or Lord. Muhammad never claimed either of those titles. So someone can say the *shahadah* and at the same time can believe in Jesus as his Savior and Lord.[10]

---

9 Brother Noah's understanding reflects the traditional Islamic view of the Arabs in Muhammad's context. But a growing number of scholars hold that numerous Arab Christians (heterodox and orthodox) and Arab Jews were present, and perhaps Zoroastrians as well. Entire Arab tribes were Christian and Jewish; the polytheistic tribes knew of the God of Abraham, Allah, but worshipped him along with Jesus and Mary, and a multitude of idols in the Kaaba. Also, the Qur'an's repeated condemnation of idolatry does not require the audience to be primarily pagan, as the traditional Islamic narrative proposes for the first period of Muhammad's preaching. We recall that the Old Testament prophets frequently spoke to the Israelites, the people of YHWH, about their idolatry.

10 In Rick Brown, "Biblical Muslims," *IJFM* 24, no. 2 (2007): 73.

Saying the Confession with Nontraditional Meaning

A Muslim who preached the gospel of Christ was charged with apostasy. At his trial, he gave testimony that he was a follower of Jesus and that he shared the gospel with other Muslims. Ordered by the judge to say the Confession, he complied. The judge then asked him to explain exactly what he meant when he affirmed Muhammad as God's messenger. The defendant replied that before they were a nation, the Arab tribes were idolaters who raided and attacked each other. However, God sent Muhammad to turn them from their idolatry to worship the one true God and unite them into one nation. The judge deemed this to be an acceptable confession and acquitted him. It may be noted that this confession cites historical facts that few would deny, and the hand of God in them can be acknowledged by those who believe in God's sovereignty.[11]

Another example comes from a strongly Muslim country during a time of suppression of Christian influences. A pastor of Muslim background was interrogated publicly by the religious authorities and asked if he regarded Muhammad as a prophet. In all sincerity he said, "Yes, he is the prophet of Islam." Although their intentions were to find a way to convict him of apostasy, they accepted this response and released him.

Saying a More Inclusive Confession

A Jesus movement in Asia was viewed with favor by most of the local Muslim community, but in one village meeting some radicals confronted Abdo, a Jesus Muslim, and his partner Daoud. The encounter became increasingly heated. Daoud interceded silently for Abdo to know what would be the wise and courageous thing to say. The radicals questioned whether Abdo was truly part of their society or was an imposter. They demanded that he say the Confession.

As the situation became extremely threatening, Abdo replied that the Confession is something a member of the Islamic community declares when performing the ritual prayer (*salat*). Abdo wondered why he was being forced to state the Confession when he was not performing salat. The radicals were not satisfied with this response and pressed him to pronounce the Confession. So Abdo paused for a few seconds and then stated the Confession. He paused again, and then, led by the Holy Spirit, boldly declared, "Isa al-Masih is the Word of God, Isa al-Masih is the Spirit of God." The group exploded with anger and was on the verge of killing them when the authorities intervened and arrested Abdo and Daoud.

A high-ranking official and two religious scholars came to the prison and confronted Abdo. In the presence of about twenty prisoners, the following transpired:

> *Official:* Why did you say that [Isa al-Masih is the Word and Spirit of God]?
>
> *Abdo:* Because the Qur'an says it.
>
> *Official:* Yes, I know that, but when you put it that way, it makes me begin to think that if Isa al-Masih is the Word of God, and Muhammad is the messenger of God, then Muhammad must at most be the servant of the Word!
>
> *Abdo:* . . . [Grins]

---

11   Rick Brown, "Contextualization without Syncretism," *IJFM* 23 no. 3 (2006): 132.

In court there was a great deal of questioning about Abdo's confession—especially his allusion to the words of the Qur'an about Jesus. In the end his confession was determined to be true to the Qur'an, but his act of honoring Jesus "excessively" was judged to have violated a statute against upsetting the adherents of a major faith in that country. He was sentenced to two and a half years in prison. After serving two years, including several months in utterly wretched conditions, Abdo was released on probation. He remains very enthusiastic in reaching people with the gospel.

Abdo verified to me that his stating of the Confession was a mark of "civilizational identification": "Hey, guys, I'm not a Westernized defector from our culture who has gone and burned all of his bridges to our rich heritage—I'm one of you . . . but you need to hear from me about Isa al-Masih!"

Others have observed Abdo and some of his colleagues telling Muslims that Muhammad and the Qur'an are like a one-way sign on the highway pointing back to Isa al-Masih and the *Injil*: "If you can see this, you just passed your exit to the straight way." In this sense they seem to ascribe to Muhammad a prophetic function as God's messenger to the Arabs.

Saying the Confession with Dubious Sincerity

In a place where the law requires every citizen to say the shahadah, the police arrested a house-church leader and demanded that he make the confession of faith or die. He did so, but was quick to point out that according to Islamic law the Confession is only valid if uttered with sincere intention (*niya*), and that only God knows if a person is sincere. The police understood that he was indicating that his shahadah was not sincere, but they could not execute him, because he had complied with the law by saying it—so they beat him up and then released him. The pastor was then able to continue his ministry in the Muslim community.[12]

Scholars Who Are Reassessing Muhammad and His Movement

The fact that *some* Muslim followers of Jesus will say the Confession evokes a strong reaction from many Christians, who see it and Muhammad's message as absolutely unbiblical and syncretistic. And because of this, they may also oppose all insider movements.

Yet many committed Christian scholars of Islam are reassessing Muhammad and the movement he founded in light of the findings of revisionist historians. While critical scholars are not agreed on what transpired, they do agree that external evidence from archaeology significantly contradicts the traditional Islamic narrative of the emergence of the movement that Muhammad founded. For example, a coin found in Palestine dated to the 640s or 650s is inscribed with the name "Muhammad" and an image of a man holding a cross.[13] Similar coins were minted by Muslim caliphs for up to a century. However, the Christian symbols were removed during the Umayyad era.[14] Significantly, all inscriptions, coins, and papyri featuring the shahadah until AD 685 contain only the phrase "There

---

12 Ibid.

13 Spencer, *Did Muhammad Exist?*, xiv.

14 Reynolds, *Emergence of Islam*, 160; see also Spencer, *Did Muhammad Exist?*, xiv, and chap. 2, "Jesus, the Muhammad." This may have begun as early as the 660s. The Syriac *Maronite Chronicle* states that Mu'āwiya issued "gold and silver coins that broke from the widely used Byzantine coin type, no longer including the traditional depiction of the cross." But this may be an "anachronism based on the author's knowledge of 'Abd al-Malik's famous coin reform in the 690s." See Michael Philip Penn, *When Christians First Met Muslims: A Sourcebook of the Earliest Syriac Writings on Islam* (Oakland, CA: University of California Press, 2015), 55–56.

is no god but God," with no mention of Muhammad. This would not have hindered Jews, Christians, or other monotheists from participation in the movement.[15] The absence of archaeological evidence of widespread violence and destruction of churches and towns in Syria-Palestine indicates that the original movement was not hostile to Christianity.[16]

Many non-Muslim historical documents in the formative period also contradict the traditional Islamic version of history.[17] The Armenian chronicle of Sebeos records an early (seventh century) non-Muslim perception of Muhammad[18] and his mission among the sons of Ishmael.[19] Sebeos writes of Muhammad as being in alliance with the Jews and notes that the movement's first governor of Jerusalem was a Jew.[20] In Egypt during the early period of Islam, the Arabic papyri make no mention of "Muslims," but instead we only find the terms "believers" (*mu'minûn*) and "emigrants" (*muhajirûn*).[21] Syrian Christians saw the movement as being linked to descendants of Abraham and Hagar through Ishmael, who confessed one God. A document written by Syrian Christians in 644, a little more than

15 Donner, *Muhammad and the Believers*, 112. Sometimes the anti-polytheism denunciation "who has no associate" also appeared, but this was not an obstacle for true monotheists.

16 Ibid., 114.

17 Apparent evidence to the contrary is the brief, negative mention of an Arab prophet by a Christian in the earliest extant document, *Doctrina Jacobi nuper baptizati*. But this is, in Block's judgment, "little more than an opportunistic dismissal of the prophet of the Saracens in order to bolster the position of Jesus in a tract designed to convert the Jews to Christianity." Block, *Expanding the Qur'anic Bridge*, 123. The tract's author has minimal or no experience with the Arab prophet, but seeks to extinguish any Jewish speculations about his possible messiahship (based on rumors of the Arab prophet's military victories) and contributes little or nothing to our understanding of actual Muslim-Christian relations in the period (ibid., 124).

18 Sebeos writes, "[Muhammad] as if by God's command appeared to them as a preacher [and] the path of truth. He taught them to recognize the God of Abraham, especially because he was learnt and informed in the history of Moses. Now because the command was from on high, at a single order they all came together in unity of religion. Abandoning their vain cults, they turned to the living God who had appeared to their father Abraham. . . . He said: 'With an oath God promised this land to Abraham and his seed after him forever. . . . But now you are the sons of Abraham and God is accomplishing his promise to Abraham and his seed for you. Love sincerely only the God of Abraham, and go and seize the land which God gave to your father Abraham.'" R. W. Thomson, trans., *The Armenian History Attributed To Sebeos*, with James Howard-Johnson and Tim Greenwood (Liverpool: Liverpool University Press, 1999), 95–96.

19 See Jonathan Culver, "The Ishmaelite Promise and Contextualization among Muslims," *IJFM* 17, no. 1 (2000): 62–69; Culver, "The Ishmael Promises in the Light of God's Mission: Christian and Muslim Reflections" (PhD diss., Fuller Theological Seminary, 2001); Mark Harlan, "Identity: True Sons of Ishmael," chap. 12 in *A Model for Theologizing in Arab Muslim Contexts*, EMS Dissertation Series (Pasadena, CA: WCIU Press, 2012); and Tony Maalouf, *Arabs in the Shadow of Israel: The Unfolding of God's Prophetic Plan for Ishmael's Line* (Grand Rapids, MI: Kregel, 2003). Block argues that Sebeos affirmed the Ishmaelites' covenantal right to the land but denounced the way that they claimed it, portraying them as the fourth beast of Dan 7. See Block, *Expanding the Qur'anic Bridge*, 148.

20 Donner cautions us regarding the complete historicity of the account, since Christian polemicists of the time loved to discredit opponents with guilt by association with the Jews; see Donner, *Muhammad and the Believers*, 114. Spencer rejects the historical accuracy due to outside corroboration, but notes the lack of hostility to Jews; see Spencer, *Did Muhammad Exist?*, 33.

21 Reference to the work of Petra Sijpesteijn of Leiden University is made by Anton Wessels, *The Torah, the Gospel, and the Qur'an: Three Books, Two Cities, One Tale* (Grand Rapids, MI: Eerdmans, 2013), 106. Their self-identity as "emigrants" indicates a mentality of *hijra* with its notions of entering a devout community, striving (even militantly) in the path of God, and adopting a non-nomadic lifestyle. See Donner, *Muhammad and the Believers*, 39–89, 134.

a decade after the traditional date of Muhammad's death, describes a religious discussion between the emir of the "immigrants"[22] (the Arab conquerors) and the Syrian patriarch. John of Sedreh noted that the immigrants accepted the Torah, like Jews and Samaritans, and described how Jewish scholars with the emir examined the Christians' quotations from the Scriptures. Much of their discussion was about the Scriptures; yet there was no reference to the Qur'an (perhaps indicating that it was not yet in circulation) and no mention of a new religion. The term *Islam* was never used.[23] In fact, the archaeological record provides no evidence of the words *Islam* and *Muslim* as designating a distinct religion until 691.[24]

Syriac Christian sources viewed the conquest as an ethnic Arab one more than a sectarian religious one.[25] John of Phenek (d. 690s), a Nestorian Christian, observed, "Among them [the Arabs] there are many Christians, some of whom are from the heretics, others from us." Syriac writers referred to their leaders in primarily secular and political terms, not by religious titles. Muhammad was called "the first king of the immigrants," and occasionally called "the Guide," "Teacher," "Leader," or "Great Ruler."[26] A letter (c. 647) from Isho'yahb III, the Nestorian patriarch in Iraq, states that the Arabs "not only do not fight Christianity, they even commend our religion, show honor to the priests and monasteries and saints of our Lord, and make gifts to the monasteries and churches."[27]

Some surmise that after the Second Civil War (680–92), 'Abd al-Malik sought to restore Umayyad political rule by appealing to religious authority and designating himself as Muhammad's successor. (The first attested documentary use of *khalifa* [caliph] occurs in this period.)[28] Stephen Shoemaker concludes, "There is considerable evidence to suggest that primitive Islam transformed rapidly from a non-confessional monotheistic faith with an extremely short eschatological timeline into an imperial religion grounded in a distinctively Arabian and Arab identity."[29]

In subsequent centuries, imperial Islam grew increasingly negative toward Christianity.[30] During the Crusades and the reconquest of Spain, mutual hostility increased markedly, as seen, for instance, in

---

22 The contrasting words reflect different perspectives. "Emigrants" was these believers' self-identity in Egypt, while "immigrants" was Syrian Christians' perception of their occupying conquerors.

23 Abdul-Massih Saadi, "Nascent Islam in the Seventh Century Syriac Sources," in *The Qur'an in Its Historical Context*, ed. Gabriel Said Reynolds (New York: Routledge, 2008), 217–19. Syriac Christian sources are judged to be more objective than those of the Byzantines, who were more polemical due to their direct political and territorial losses to the Arabs.

24 J. Little, "The Revisionist History of Islam's Origins," *Researching Islam* (blog), January 31, 2014, http://research-islam.blogspot.com/2014/01/the-revisionist-history-of-islams.html.

25 "Arab" was a linguistic or cultural identity, not a political one. It would be erroneous and anachronistic to suppose that an Arab nationalistic political identity existed. Donner states, "There is almost no evidence for the existence of a collective 'Arab' political identity before the Believers created their empire." *Muhammad and the Believers*, 218.

26 Saadi, "Nascent Islam," 217–18.

27 Donner, *Muhammad and the Believers*, 114.

28 Ibid., 211.

29 Stephen J. Shoemaker, *The Death of a Prophet: The End of Muhammad's Life and the Beginnings of Islam* (Philadelphia: University of Pennsylvania Press, 2012), 20.

30 Block provides historical evidence that for up to a century, Christians generally viewed Muhammad's doctrines similarly to how they did other branches of Christianity that had alternative christological views. See Block, *Expanding the Qur'anic Bridge*, 126. Of course each group regarded all other views as heretical. Reynolds rejects the traditional view of Islam's origins and its sacred text, as does Spencer. Many scholars view "orthodox" Islam as likely representing something that existed two or three centuries after Muhammad.

the change from Muslims understanding *tahrif* (corruption) as Jewish and Christian distortion of the *meaning* of the Scriptures to corruption of the actual *text* of the Scriptures.[31]

Yet even apart from a revisionist version of Islam's history, a growing number of committed Christian scholars of Islam have rendered a more generous appraisal of Muhammad and his message, especially in the early years. They are able to recognize Muhammad as an important religious leader whose message contains much that the Bible affirms, even if Islam did later become antagonistic to Christianity.[32] They point out that the Qur'an exalts Jesus far above all other persons.[33] It repeatedly affirms "the previous scriptures," and even commands Muhammad in cases of doubt about the meaning of the Qur'an to consult those who read the Bible.[34] Dozens of verses in the Qur'an make a compelling case for interpreting it in ways that confirm or harmonize with the Bible rather than contradict it. Some leading contemporary scholars of the Qur'an have demonstrated that many of its passages make much better sense when interpreted in light of the Bible rather than according to Islamic tradition (which is highly suspect).[35] A number of Christian scholars of Islam believe that key qur'anic verses that allegedly contradict fundamental Christian doctrines are actually combating Christian heresies; substantial textual and historical evidence supports this understanding.[36]

Dispassionate assessments of Muhammad might mitigate the record of his polygamy and actions against his enemies in light of their being largely for the sake of strengthening Islam's position. While some of Muhammad's actions are offensive to modern standards and sensibilities, the focus of his contemporaries' criticisms was not his violations of *morality*. Rather, Muhammad's stance against idolatry and departure from tribal traditions stirred fear over the consequences of violating taboos and forsak-

---

31 See Martin Accad, "Corruption and/or Misinterpretation of the Bible: The Story of the Islamic Usage of *Tāhrif*," *Near East School of Theology Theological Review* 24 (2003): 67–97; Abdullah Saeed, "The Charge of Distortion of Jewish and Christian Scriptures," *The Muslim World* 92 (Fall 2002): 419–36.

32 As a result of this more negative stance toward Christianity, many Christians lay the blame for the bad fruit of the Islamic system upon the root, Muhammad. However, following this logic, the responsibility and blame for the religious system that developed under the Pharisees, who shut the door to Jews who sought to enter kingdom of heaven (Matt 23:13), should be placed upon the shoulders of Moses. This is certainly not justifiable. Similarly, we would have to blame Peter and Paul (and even Jesus) for what Christianity became in medieval Roman Catholicism.

33 See Geoffrey Parrinder, *Jesus in the Qur'an* (London: Oneworld, 1995).

34 See surah 10:94. A multitude of verses affirm and command belief in the Law, Psalms, and the Gospel. See also Samy Tanagho, *Glad News! God Loves You My Muslim Friend* (Colorado Springs, CO: Biblica, 2003), 7–24; Fouad Elias Accad, "The Qur'an as a Bridge to the Bible," chap. 2 in *Building Bridges: Christianity and Islam* (Colorado Springs, CO: NavPress, 1997).

35 Reynolds persuasively argues that many stories of Muhammad were generated much later by Muslims far removed from the original context in order to explain the meaning of baffling qur'anic phrases. See Reynolds, *The Qur'an and Its Biblical Subtext*; cf. Reynolds, "The Qur'an," pt. 2 in *Emergence of Islam*; as well as Basetti-Sani, *The Koran in the Light of Christ*.

36 Block, *Expanding the Qur'anic Bridge*, 290. Block makes use of historical evidence to argue that (1) surahs 4:171 and 5:73 are not a rejection of the Trinity but actual tri-theism as promoted by John Philoponus (ibid., 44–52); (2) surah 19:35 corrects the adoptionism of the Nestorians; (3) surah 5:116 condemns Mariolatry; (4) the rejection of Jesus as "son of God" in surah 9:30 pertains to Christian corruption of an apocryphal 4 Ezra text; and (5) Muhammad defended the Christianity of his in-law, Waraqa ibn Nawful (ibid., 290). Cf. Basetti-Sani, *The Koran in the Light of Christ*, passim.

ing tribal deities and practices.[37] Moreover, in evaluating Muhammad's character, we should not forget that even biblical prophets were guilty of serious ethical breaches. The Bible shows David's sins to include pride/presumption (in numbering the people), adultery, and murder. Solomon had "seven hundred wives of royal birth and three hundred concubines" and "loved many foreign women." Solomon also participated in idolatry in his later years (1 Kgs 11:1–6), as did Gideon (Judg 8:27). Whatever his sins and moral deficiencies, Muhammad worshipped the God of Abraham alone, and did not engage in outright idolatry.

Additionally, his use of force and political means for the sake of religion was not foreign to the Semitic mentality. Gideon and David combined military, political, and spiritual leadership. Nehemiah used violence to enforce God's law and preserve communal purity, beating and pulling out the hair of those who had married or given sons in marriage to foreign women (Neh 13:25).

This more positive attitude toward Muhammad by some contemporary Christians is not a radical innovation, but rather a return to what was often seen among Eastern Christians in the first centuries of Christian-Muslim encounter. Martin Accad explains why attitudes in the West toward Islam went south, so to speak:

> Within the Byzantine Empire, on the other hand, where direct contact with Muslims was minimal besides the relationship of political and military enemies, Byzantine Christians such as Nicetas of Byzantium (c. 842–912) or George Hamartolos (9th century) developed an extremely harsh and exclusivist polemical discourse on Islam rather than any real "theology." And it is this very harsh Byzantine view that has generally had a significant impact on medieval Europe and hence on the development of the Western view. Alternatively, the Eastern attempts at theologizing, which were possible up until the end of the first millennium, became far more difficult to sustain after Islam became the unchallenged ruler in the region, and after the demographics also turned decidedly in its favor.[38]

Unfortunately, after a millennium of spiteful scholarship, most Christians today assume that their forebears always regarded Muhammad in abjectly negative terms.[39] But that was not the case then, nor is it now. In the final section of this article, we shall look at an early Eastern affirmer of Muhammad and his message, Timothy I, and several respected Christian thinkers in the modern era who follow the patriarch's example.

---

37 W. Montgomery Watt, *Islam and Christianity Today: A Contribution to Dialogue* (London: Routledge, 1983), 60–61. I agree with Watt in this regard, as well with his conclusion that Muhammad is not an exemplar for humanity when judged by modern standards—only the incomparable Christ sets a moral standard that challenges all humans in all times and places.

38 Martin Accad, "Towards a Theology of Islam: A Response to Harley Talman's 'Is Muhammad Also among the Prophets?'" *IJFM* 31, no. 4 (2014): 192.

39 Block, *Expanding the Qur'anic Bridge*, 281. Block traces the change to a polemical attitude toward Muhammad to John of Damascus in the eighth century and details the history of deliberate malice in scholarship.

Christian Scholars Who Are Reassessing Muhammad and His Message

The famous patriarch of the Church of the East Timothy I, in his debate with Caliph al-Mahdi (781), declared that Muhammad "walked in the path of the prophets and trod in the track of the lovers of God," and that "all believers rejoice in the good that he did," teaching the unity of God and driving people away from idolatry, polytheism, and bad works, and toward good works. "Muhammad taught about God, His Word and His Spirit, and since all prophets had prophesied about God, His Word and His Spirit, Muhammad walked, therefore, in the path of all the prophets."[40] While some view the final phrase as mere diplomacy and not as conceding any kind of prophethood, Timothy's position on the issue is not clear.[41] However, near the end of the debate, Timothy argues for the Trinity based on the affirmations of Christ as the Word of God and Spirit of God in surah 4:171. In apparent reference to the words of this qur'anic passage, he calls them "divinely inspired," inferring that God, at least in this instance, was speaking through Muhammad and the Qur'an.[42]

A contemporary Arab Christian scholar of Islam, Martin Accad, has attempted, as Timothy I did, to focus largely on the good he sees in Mohammad's vocation. He advocates authentic engagement with Islam that mediates between the traditional apologetic/polemic and liberal syncretistic/existential positions. While emphasizing the proclamation of God's full and final revelation in Christ apart from institutional religion, Accad also states, "This need not prevent us from admitting the greatness of Muhammad, and perceiving him, if not as a prophet, nonetheless as a *messenger*, a *rasūl*, who carried an important divine message to his people, leading them away from polytheism and drawing them to the worship of the one God."[43]

Bishop Bill Musk, another evangelical Islamicist, also affirms key aspects of Muhammad's prophetic message:

> If "truth" as conveyed by the Bible is primarily about relationship between God and humanity, rather than a collection of propositions to be acknowledged, then surely all statements from Muhammad that reflect the reality of God's self-revelation are prophetic. I do not want to undermine the importance of propositional

---

40 Timothy I, "Timothy's Apology for Christianity," trans. Alphonse Mingana, in *Encounters and Clashes: Islam and Christianity in History*, vol. 2, ed. Jean-Marie Gaudeul (Rome: Pontifical Institute for Arabic and Islamic Studies, 1984), 242, cited in Block, *Expanding the Qur'anic Bridge*, 126.

41 Block notes that Timothy had a strong, positive relationship with the caliph and interprets Timothy as willing to concede prophethood to Muhammad—if granted an interpretation of the Qur'an that would allow for the Trinity and the crucifixion. See Block, *Expanding the Qur'anic Bridge*, 132. He interacts with Samir's nine arguments against this (ibid., 131n488).

42 Timothy declares, "If Christ is the Word of God and Spirit of God as the Qur'an testifies, He is not a servant, but a Lord, because the Word and Spirit of God are Lords. It is by this method, O our God-loving King, based on the law of nature and on divinely inspired words and not on pure human argumentation, word and thought, that I both in the present and in the first conversation have demonstrated the Lordship and Sonship of Christ and the divine trinity." N. A. Newman, ed., *The Early Christian-Muslim Dialogue: A Collection of Documents from the First Three Islamic Centuries (632–900 A.D.): Translations with Commentary* (Hatfield, PA: Interdisciplinary Biblical Research Institute, 1993), 239, cited in Block, *Expanding the Qur'anic Bridge*, 93.

43 Martin Accad, "Christian Attitudes toward Islam and Muslims: A Kerygmatic Approach," chap. 1 in *Toward Respectful Understanding and Witness among Muslims: Essays in Honor of J. Dudley Woodberry*, ed. Evelyne A. Reisacher (Pasadena, CA: William Carey Library, 2012), 40.

statements derived from biblical text. But I do want to suggest that those are secondary. After all . . . the Bible is not an end in itself; it bears witness to Another. Nor did God simply bellow into humans' ears a handful of propositions. "Truth," in its Christian sense, is more subtle, more nuanced, than that. It finds its essence in a Person. Where the Prophet Muhammad gained insight into who that Person is—for example in his conviction, against a polytheistic background, of the oneness of God—his utterances to that effect are truly in the lineage of the biblical prophets. Whether and to what extent Muhammad himself lived by such insights will be evaluated by the One who will evaluate all of us.[44]

An opinion that cannot be easily dismissed is that of the renowned Reformed theologian Herman Bavinck:

In the past the study of religions was pursued in the interest of dogmatics and apologetics. The founders of (non-Christian) religions, like Mohammed, were simply considered imposters, enemies of God, and accomplices of the devil. But ever since those religions have become more precisely known, this interpretation has proved untenable; it clashed both with history and psychology. Also among pagans, says Scripture, there is a revelation of God, an illumination of the Logos, a working of God's Spirit (Gen. 6:17; 7:15; Ps. 33:6; 104:30; Job 32:8; Eccles. 3:19; Prov. 8:22f; Mal. 1:11,14; John 1:9; Rom. 2:14; Gal. 4:1–3; Acts 14:16,17; 17:22–30).[45]

Lastly, Timothy Tennent, president of Asbury Theological Seminary and professor of world Christianity, is another prominent evangelical who ascribes a type of prophetic function to Muhammad. Tennent embraces Charles Ledit's designation of two kinds of prophecy: "theological" and "directive." The former pointed to, and ceased at, the coming of Christ. Taking a cue from Aquinas, Ledit labeled as "directive prophecy" those instances where God sovereignly enlists persons outside the covenant to accomplish his purposes, such as giving guidance to people or even correcting the covenant people. In this vein, Muhammad united the Arabs and turned them from paganism and idolatry to monotheism

44 Bill Musk, *Kissing Cousins? Christians and Muslims Face to Face* (Grand Rapids, MI: Kregel, 2005), 82.

45 Bavinck, *Reformed Dogmatics*, vol. 1, *Prolegomena* (Grand Rapids, MI: Baker Academic, 2003), 318. Others in line with Bavinck cite biblical support for Spirit-induced prophecy outside the biblical canon that is not necessarily infallible. The NT gift of prophecy (unlike NT apostleship) was not necessarily infallible; for 1 Cor 14:29–31 and 1 Thess 5:19–21 require that the pronouncements of prophets be sifted, not necessarily accepted or rejected *in toto*. See D. A. Carson, *Showing the Spirit: A Theological Exposition of 1 Corinthians 12–14* (Grand Rapids, MI: Baker, 1987), 94–98; Wayne Grudem, "Gifts of the Holy Spirit (2): Specific Gifts," chap. 53 in *Systematic Theology: An Introduction to Biblical Doctrine* (Grand Rapids, MI: Zondervan, 1994). Parallels can be seen in church and mission history. In West Africa the charismatic prophet William Harris claimed to have been called by God to be a prophet through a vision. Western missionaries testified to the spectacular impact of his ministry and considered it to be of God, but some of his prophetic pronouncements missed the mark. See Harley Talman, "Is Muhammad Also among the Prophets?," *IJFM* 31, no. 4 (2014): 177–78.

and an ordered society, also preparing a potential bridge to the gospel of Christ.[46] Despite the hostilities that later transpired with Jews and Christians, Tennent avers, "We should not let the whole history of Islam cloud our assessment of Muhammad. If it can be said that God spoke 'directive prophecy' through Cyrus, who announced the end of exile (2 Chron. 36:22; Ezra 1:8), then why could God not have spoken a directive word through Muhammad?"[47]

The above examples are sufficient to show that some prominent Christian scholars have recognized or affirmed Muhammad as a messenger or prophet in some capacity. These scholars' positions are not driven by an agenda of contextualization or insider movements. Rather, other issues, varied and complex, are causing them to reassess their stance on Muhammad.

One such issue that for many conservative evangelicals has precluded any possibility of reconsidering a constructive prophetic function for Muhammad is the theological view that restricts prophethood to narrow binary categories. Thus if Muhammad's message was not inspired and infallible, as was the revelation given to the prophets in the biblical canon, he must be a false prophet. Or if true prophecy ended with the writing of the last New Testament book or with the close of the canon, then any subsequent prophet is necessarily a false prophet. But this view of prophecy has been challenged by many evangelical Christians. Elsewhere I address this issue in detail, offering biblical and historical justification for expanding traditional theological categories of prophethood.[48]

As noted in the preceding section, an important factor behind this reassessment is that the reliability of Islamic historical sources concerning Muhammad and Islam is undergoing critical scrutiny. Non-Muslim historical documents and archaeological evidence do not support the Islamic narrative. Theories about the origins of the Qur'an and Islam, as well as the Islamic doctrine of abrogation, are being challenged. Textual criticism of the Qur'an, previously a taboo, even in academia, is opening possibilities for harmonizing verses that were previously considered irreconcilable. This comprehensive project is still in its infancy, and it will likely take many years before these questions are adequately answered. The results of this scholarly activity will eventually substantiate or weaken the case for consideration of Muhammad as prophet in some capacity. But at present, as well as in the past, there are respected Christian leaders and scholars who recognize Muhammad as having a prophetic message or function in some sense.

Conclusion

As was stated at the outset, what a follower of Christ may say and think about Muhammad is a controversial and complex question! It is just one more issue over which followers of Christ hold strong feelings about their differing theological convictions. Throughout history Christians have held diverse and contrary opinions about Muhammad. But given that some notable Christian scholars, both ancient and modern, can see Muhammad as having had a prophetic message or function of some sort, it should be less controversial that some Muslim followers of Christ do as well. Doing so does not preclude their

---

46 Timothy C. Tennent, *Theology in the Context of World Christianity: How the Global Church Is Influencing the Way We Think About and Discuss Theology* (Grand Rapids, MI: Zondervan, 2009), 43–44.

47 Ibid., 44. Tennent insists that such an affirmation does not require Christians to accept Islamic ideas of Muhammad's infallibility or his being the final prophet. Moreover, it does not obviate Muslims' need for the gospel of Christ for salvation.

48 See Talman, "Is Muhammad Also among the Prophets?," 169–90.

holding a biblical theology and worldview when the preeminence and significance of Christ is not jeopardized.

We must, however, recognize that what a person says about Muhammad is of great consequence in the Muslim community. Thus when teaching in Eurasia I encouraged participants to affirm, when asked by Muslims for their opinion of Muhammad, the many good things he did (preaching belief in the God of Abraham, denouncing idolatry and injustice, uniting the Arab tribes, etc.). At the end of the training a Muslim-background evangelist told me,

> Once a Muslim asked me my opinion of Muhammad. I replied, "He's a false prophet." The Muslim punched me in the mouth and knocked out a tooth. I wish I had heard this earlier, for then I would still have my tooth!
>
> My current roommate is a Muslim, and my many conversations with him about the gospel had been fruitless. But I did as you said and told him how I appreciated all of the good things that you told us that Muhammad did. The following morning, when I awoke, I found him reading the Bible for the first time.

Muslims believe that God has sent out many "messengers" in addition to Muhammad, most notably Abraham, Moses, David, and Jesus. For a Muslim to refuse to say the Confession is taken as completely disavowing any divine purpose for Muhammad. While Muslim followers of Jesus are willing to die before they would deny Jesus as Lord, they may not feel obliged to die for denying that God had a mission for Muhammad. By the same token, let us not forget that in Muslim countries, Christian nationals and missionaries carefully avoid publicly denying Muhammad. So it would seem hypocritical for them to insist that Muslim disciples of Christ should do so.[49]

Widely divergent views of Muhammad are held by both Muslim disciples of Jesus and non-Muslim disciples of Jesus, even though they share the same commitment to the Bible. As long as Jesus and the Bible are the ultimate and governing authority in the life of a Muslim follower of Jesus, saying the Confession in ways similar to those cited above does not inherently preclude biblical faithfulness.[50] The Apostle Paul's admonition may provide us with the wisest course of action: "Do not have disputes over differing opinions" (Rom 14:1 NET). Individual conscience should be determinative: the "strong" (who feel they can say it) should not look down on or condemn the "weak" (who do not feel they can say it), and vice versa, for "who are you to pass judgment on another's servant?" (14:2–4 NET). May we accept the brother whose convictions differ from our own, and leave it to the believer's conscience in light of those convictions and the Spirit's leading as to how each one comes to assess and express the role of Muhammad, the prophet of Islam.

---

49   Brown, "Contextualization without Syncretism," 132.

50   Certainly, there are situations or contexts where saying the Confession would be wrong—for example, where the Confession is used in animistic or occult practices of folk Islam. Or if saying the Confession communicates that Muhammad is Master, Lord, Savior, or Mediator instead of Christ, then a believer should not say it. However, some say that since this is the underlying meaning in the mind of most Muslims, the hearers will assume that a Christ follower who says the Confession believes just as they do. But if a Jesus Muslim who utters the Confession is preaching Jesus, then it is clear to the hearers that he or she does not share this view of Muhammad. We need to appreciate that the contextual meaning and significance of the Confession is best understood by the person within that context, not by outsiders.

Bibliography

Accad, Fouad Elias. *Building Bridges: Christianity and Islam*. Colorado Springs, CO: NavPress, 1997.

Accad, Martin. "Christian Attitudes toward Islam and Muslims: A Kerygmatic Approach." Chap. 1 in *Toward Respectful Understanding and Witness among Muslims: Essays in Honor of J. Dudley Woodberry*, edited by Evelyne A. Reisacher. Pasadena, CA: William Carey Library, 2012.

———. "Corruption and/or Misinterpretation of the Bible: The Story of the Islamic Usage of *Taḥrīf*." *Near East School of Theology Theological Review* 24 (2003): 67–97.

———. "Towards a Theology of Islam: A Response to Harley Talman's 'Is Muhammad Also among the Prophets?'" *International Journal of Frontier Missiology* 31, no. 4 (2014): 191–93.

Basetti-Sani, Giulio. *The Koran in the Light of Christ*. Chicago: Franciscan Herald Press, 1977.

Bavinck, Herman. *Prolegomena*. Vol. 1 of *Reformed Dogmatics*. Grand Rapids, MI: Baker Academic, 2003.

Block, C. Jonn. *Expanding the Qur'anic Bridge: Historical and Modern Interpretations of the Qur'an in Christian-Muslim Dialogue with Special Attention Paid to Ecumenical Trends*. New York: Routledge, 2013.

Brown, Rick. "Biblical Muslims." *International Journal of Frontier Missiology* 24, no. 2 (2007): 65–74.

———. "Contextualization without Syncretism." *International Journal of Frontier Missions* 23, no. 3 (2006): 127–33.

Carson, D. A. *Showing the Spirit: A Theological Exposition of 1 Corinthians 12–14*. Grand Rapids, MI: Baker, 1987.

Culver, Jonathan. "The Ishmaelite Promise and Contextualization among Muslims." *International Journal of Frontier Missions* 17, no. 1 (2000): 62–69.

———. "The Ishmaelite Promises in the Light of God's Mission: Christian and Muslim Reflections." PhD dissertation, Fuller Theological Seminary, 2001.

Donner, Fred M. *Muhammad and the Believers: The Origins of Islam*. Cambridge, MA: Belknap Press of Harvard University Press, 2010.

———. "The Qur'an in Recent Scholarship: Challenges and Desiderata." In *The Qur'an in Its Historical Context*, edited by Gabriel Said Reynolds, 29–50. New York: Routledge, 2008.

Grudem, Wayne. "Gifts of the Holy Spirit (2): Specific Gifts." Chap. 53 in *Systematic Theology: An Introduction to Biblical Doctrine*. Grand Rapids, MI: Zondervan, 1994.

Harlan, Mark. "Identity: True Sons of Ishmael." Chap. 12 in *A Model for Theologizing in Arab Muslim Contexts*. EMS Dissertation Series. Pasadena, CA: WCIU Press, 2012.

Maalouf, Tony. *Arabs in the Shadow of Israel: the Unfolding of God's Prophetic Plan for Ishmael's Line*. Grand Rapids, MI: Kregel, 2003.

Musk, Bill. *Kissing Cousins? Christians and Muslims Face to Face*. Grand Rapids, MI: Kregel, 2005.

Newman, N. A., ed. *The Early Christian-Muslim Dialogue: A Collection of Documents from the First Three Islamic Centuries, (632–900 A.D.): Translations with Commentary*. Hatfield, PA: Interdisciplinary Biblical Research Institute, 1993.

Parrinder, Geoffrey. *Jesus in the Qur'an*. London: Oneworld, 1995.

Penn, Michael Philip. *When Christians First Met Muslims: A Sourcebook of the Earliest Syriac Writings on Islam*. Oakland, CA: University of California Press, 2015.

Reynolds, Gabriel Said. *The Emergence of Islam: Classical Traditions in Contemporary Perspective*. Minneapolis: Fortress Press, 2012.

———. *The Qur'an and Its Biblical Subtext*. New York: Routledge, 2010.

Rippin, Andrew. *Muslims: Their Religious Beliefs and Practices*. Vol. 1, *The Formative Years*. New York: Routledge, 1990.

Saadi, Abdul-Massih. "Nascent Islam in the Seventh Century Syriac Sources." In *The Qur'an in Its Historical Context*, edited by Gabriel Said Reynolds, 217–22. New York: Routledge, 2008.

Saeed, Abdullah. "The Charge of Distortion of Jewish and Christian Scriptures." *The Muslim World* 92 (Fall 2002): 419–36.

Shoemaker, Stephen J. *The Death of a Prophet: The End of Muhammad's Life and the Beginnings of Islam*. Philadelphia: University of Pennsylvania Press, 2012.

Spencer, Robert. *Did Muhammad Exist? An Inquiry into Islam's Obscure Origins*. Wilmington, DE: Intercollegiate Studies Institute, 2012.

Talman, Harley. "Is Muhammad Also among the Prophets?" *International Journal of Frontier Missiology* 31, no. 4 (2014), 169–90.

Tanagho, Samy. *Glad News! God Loves You My Muslim Friend*. Colorado Springs, CO: Biblica, 2003.

Tennent, Timothy C. *Theology in the Context of World Christianity: How the Global Church Is Influencing the Way We Think About and Discuss Theology*. Grand Rapids, MI: Zondervan, 2009.

Thomson, R. W. *The Armenian History Attributed to Sebeos*. With James Howard-Johnson and Tim Greenwood. Liverpool: Liverpool University Press, 1999.

Timothy I. "Timothy's Apology for Christianity." Translated by A. Mingana. In *Encounters and Clashes: Islam and Christianity in History*, vol. 2, edited by Jean-Marie Gaudeul. Rome: Pontifical Institute for Arabic and Islamic Studies, 1984.

Watt, W. Montgomery. *Islam and Christianity Today: A Contribution to Dialogue*. London: Routledge, 1983.

CHAPTER 54

"Is Allah God?"

Five Reasons I Am Convinced*

Jesse S. Wheeler

A number of years ago, upon learning of my intention to pursue the academic study of Islam, a dearly beloved relative of mine felt compelled to ask, "Is Allah God?"

This question took me by surprise, for I felt as though I was being put to the test, as if my evangelical credentials were being put on trial.

However, I have come to understand that this question comes from a place of legitimate concern about moral relativism, compromise, and a desire to be faithful. I, however, have also come to understand that, as a result of who my Lord and Savior is, the closer we grow in faithfulness and commitment to him, the closer we in fact find ourselves in the midst of those "not like us," with arms outstretched in love, hearts full of grace, and minds ready to listen.

Therefore, as a committed follower of Christ, five reasons I am convinced Allah is in fact God are:

1. *"Allah" is the Arabic word for God.* Simple as that. At its most basic, Allah is God for no other reason than the simple fact that "Allah" has been the Arabic word for God for centuries. Millions of Arabic-speaking monotheists living throughout the Middle East, Africa, Eurasia, and the Americas worship Allah. And they have worshiped him for centuries. Muslim. Christian. Jew. To denigrate Allah is to denigrate the object of faith for millions, including millions of our own Christian brothers and sisters in faith. To illustrate, I offer the closing plea of one Middle Eastern evangelical Christian to his brothers and sisters in the West, from his article "Allah and the Christian Arab": "PLEASE never never [speak] against the glorious name of Allah, a name that has been loved and revered by millions of God's children down through the centuries."[1]

2. *"Allah" is the "pre-Islamic, Aramaic-derived" Arabic word for God.* It is often claimed that "Allah" originated within pre-Islamic Arabian paganism, was exported throughout the Middle East and North Africa via the Arab conquests, and was subsequently adopted by Arabic-speaking Christians and Jews. However, historical and etymological evidence rather compellingly point us in the opposite direction. Historically, Judaism and Christianity were both widespread and well known within pre-Islamic

---

* Originally published in a slightly different form on the blog of the Institute of Middle East Studies (Arab Baptist Theological Seminary), April 25, 2013, http://imeslebanon.wordpress.com. Printed here by permission of the author.

1 Rafique, "Allah and the Christian Arab," *Seedbed* 13, no. 1 (1998): 7, quoted in Rick Brown, "Who Was 'Allah' before Islam? Evidence that the Term 'Allah' Originated with Jewish and Christian Arabs," in *Toward Respectful Understanding and Witness Among Muslims: Essays in Honor of J. Dudley Woodberry* (Pasadena, CA: William Carey Library, 2012), 178.

Arabia, and they shared a common name for God.[2] That name was Allah. Furthermore, *Allah* is in all etymological likelihood derived (via Syriac) from Aramaic, the third most common language of the Bible and *the language Jesus Christ himself spoke*. Any guess as to the Aramaic word for God used by Jesus? *Alâh-â.*[3]

3. *Muslims themselves maintain that they worship the same God as Christians and Jews, the God of Abraham, Moses, Jesus, etc.* As followers of Christ, it is imperative for us to listen to people on their own terms and in their own words, "not via the distorted and defensive lenses" of historical animosity. When the Qur'an, Muhammad, and the early Muslim community therefore speak of the "one true God," they intentionally speak of Allah, the *one* God already known to Christians and Jews. Islam self-consciously views itself as both a continuation of and corrective to that which came prior. Islam recognizes the prophets and apostles of Judaism and Christianity; holds a special, if incomplete, view of Jesus Christ; and in principle honors, despite allegations of corruption by some, our respective holy books. Islam clearly recognizes a common affinity with both Judaism and Christianity and deliberately worships the God of both Christians and Jews: Allah.

4. *Although vital differences remain, Christian and Muslim beliefs about God are significantly more similar than some might initially suppose.* To paraphrase Miroslav Volf in *Allah: A Christian Response*, the similarities between Christian and Muslim conceptions of God in their description of God's being, character, and ethical expectations allow us to conclude with confidence that Muslims and Christians do, in fact, worship the same God. Volf asserts that "normative" Christians and Muslims "agree on the following six claims about God":

1. There is only *one* God, the one and only divine being.
2. God created everything that is not God.
3. God is radically different from everything that is not God.
4. God is good.
5. God commands that we love God with our whole being.
6. God commands that we love our neighbor as ourselves.[4]

Volf is therefore led to affirm that (1) "*to the extent that* Christians and Muslims embrace the normative teachings of Christianity and Islam about God, they believe in a common God," such that "the God of whom the Christian holy books and great religious teachers speak is the same God of whom the holy book and the great religious teachers of Muslims speak"; and that (2) "*to the extent* that Christians and Muslims strive to love God and love neighbor, they *worship* that same true God," such that "God requires Muslims and Christians to obey strikingly similar commands as an expression of their worship."[5]

History, etymology, and (very important) questions of salvation aside, when Christians and Muslims begin to unearth the theological substance of their respective traditions, a remarkable amount of common ground emerges.

---

2   This is attested to by scholars as diverse as Rick Brown ("Who Was 'Allah,'" 147–78); Imad N. Shehadeh ("The Predicament of Islamic Monotheism," *Bibliotheca Sacra* 161 [April–June 2004]: 142–62); and Fouad Elias Accad (*Building Bridges: Christianity and Islam* [Colorado Springs, CO: NavPress, 1997], 22).

3   However, the final *â* is often dropped. And in Syriac this becomes *Alâhâ*. Furthermore, the Aramaic *Alâh/ Alâhâ* is cognate to the Hebrew word *Elôh*.

4   Miroslav Volf, *Allah: A Christian Response* (New York: HarperCollins, 2011), 110.

5   Ibid., 123–24.

5. *I think Jesus would want me to.* In his encounter with the Samaritan woman at the well (John 4), Jesus reveals something quite remarkable in regard to the manner in which we should understand and interact with those of different social and religious backgrounds. It is a well-known biblical fact that Jews and Samaritans, who shared a "significantly similar, albeit vitally different" faith in the *one* true God, hated each other with a passion. So, when the Samaritan woman inquires as to the differences in faith and practice between Jews and Samaritans, Jesus, rather than condemn her "inaccurate ritual practices," offers instead the "most important teaching on worship in the entire New Testament"[6] and a life-altering encounter with himself. In this encounter, Jesus affirms the truth of previous revelation. But he also builds upon rather than condemns the elements of truth already present within Samaritan religion.[7] In doing so, Jesus simultaneously

- honors and respects the preexisting worship of *both* Jews *and* Samaritans of the one true God, whether fully understood or not;
- challenges the exclusivity of *both* Jewish *and* Samaritan religious and social practice; and
- reveals the centrality and uniqueness of his own mission as the fulfillment of *both* Jewish *and* Samaritan hopes for the salvation of the world.

So, as the contemporary relationship between Christianity and Islam has often been likened to that between the ancient Judeans and Samaritans,[8] I feel fully justified in

- respecting the worship of *both* Christians *and* Muslims of the one true God, whilst also
- challenging the exclusivity of *both* Christian *and* Muslim religious and social practice, and
- proudly affirming the centrality and uniqueness of Jesus Christ as the full revelation of God and the fulfillment of *both* Christian *and* Muslim hopes for the salvation of the world.

Bibliography

Accad, Fouad Elias. *Building Bridges: Christianity and Islam.* Colorado Springs, CO: NavPress, 1997.

Bailey, Kenneth E. *Jesus through Middle Eastern Eyes: Cultural Studies in the Gospels.* Downers Grove, IL: IVP Academic, 2008.

Brown, Rick. "Who Was 'Allah' Before Islam? Evidence that the Term 'Allah' Originated with Jewish and Christian Arabs." In *Toward Respectful Understanding and Witness among Muslims: Essays in Honor of J. Dudley Woodberry*, edited by Evelyne A. Reisacher, 147–78. Pasadena, CA: William Carey Library, 2012.

Chapman, Colin. "Examining Our Attitudes." Chap. 3 in *Cross and Crescent: Responding to the Challenge of Islam.* Downers Grove, IL: Intervarsity Press, 2007. Kindle edition.

Shehadeh, Imad N. "The Predicament of Islamic Monotheism." *Bibliotheca Sacra* 161 (April–June 2004): 142–62.

Volf, Miroslav. *Allah: A Christian Response.* New York: HarperCollins, 2011.

---

6   Kenneth E. Bailey, *Jesus through Middle Eastern Eyes: Cultural Studies in the Gospels* (Downers Grove, IL: IVP Academic, 2008), 210.

7   Christian theologian Wolfhart Pannenberg describes this as "the incurable religiosity of all humankind." As there is only one God and each of us is created in his image, all humans have a natural desire for God—hence religion. Through Christ alone that desire is satisfied.

8   See, for example, Colin Chapman, "Examining Our Attitudes," chap. 3 in *Cross and Crescent: Responding to the Challenge of Islam* (Downers Grove, IL: InterVarsity Press, 2007), Kindle ed.

CHAPTER 55

In the World but Not of It

Insider Movements and Freedom from the Demonic

Anna Travis

In *Understanding Insider Movements*, most of the Jesus followers described are part of Hindu and Muslim communities, although Buddhist, Jewish, and Sikh insiders are also mentioned. Supernatural beings and powers are understood differently among these groups, but the prevailing spiritual worldview is similar to the one into which Jesus was born. This worldview takes dark, unseen forces seriously and develops strategies to combat them.[1] *Power people* (shamans, diviners, healers), *power objects* (amulets, charms), *power rituals* (incantations, exorcisms), *power times* (auspicious or ominous hours, days, and seasons), *power places* (shrines, altars) and *power beings* (deities, angels, demons) are part of everyday life in contemporary traditional societies where most insider movements take place, in much the same way as they were in Jesus' day.

Teachings and practices contrary to the gospel, including reincarnation, rejection of the New Testament as Scripture, worship of a pantheon of gods, or reliance on loyalty to certain institutions for salvation, surround new Jesus followers. A keen awareness of the supernatural and some level of involvement with folk religious or related practices[2] is also common. These beg the question, Is it helpful, even necessary, for new Jesus followers to leave their religious community[3] and enter a branch of Christianity in order to become free from demonic forces? Or should we ask this question: *How can insider followers of Jesus become free and stay free from demonic oppression even while remaining part of the religious community of their people?*

Spiritual warfare and the ministry of deliverance from demons are topics with many available resources.[4] To date, however, little has been written on how followers of Jesus in insider movements deal with the spiritual forces around them. I share my insights on this topic out of firsthand field experience

---

1   See Clinton E. Arnold, *Powers of Darkness: Principalities and Powers in Paul's Letters* (Downers Grove, IL: InterVarsity Press, 1992), for an excellent discussion of the spiritual dynamics of ancient Palestine and the surrounding areas.

2   Not all folk practices are harmful, such as the use of traditional herbal medicines. Harmful folk practices would be those that invoke evil spirits and/or are aimed at harming others (curses, voodoo, witchcraft, spells, etc.). For an excellent discussion of folk religious practices worldwide, see Paul G. Hiebert, R. Daniel Shaw, and Tite Tienou, *Understanding Folk Religion: A Christian Response to Popular Beliefs and Practices* (Grand Rapids, MI: Baker Academic, 1997).

3   See Talman, chap. 37; Richardson, chap. 39; and Richard, chap. 40, for important discussions of the meaning and significance of "religion." For perspectives on the biblical response toward other religions, see Talman, chap. 21.

4   See, for instance, James K. Beilby and Paul Rhodes Eddy, *Understanding Spiritual Warfare: Four Views* (Grand Rapids, MI: Baker Academic, 2012); Edward F. Murphy, *The Handbook for Spiritual Warfare* (Nashville:

with deliverance ministry and intercessory prayer.[5] I offer this chapter as a discussion starter in a widening conversation, not an exhaustive treatment of the subject.

Let us clarify working definitions and assumptions for this study before turning to the biblical framework and narrative examples of these principles.

Working Definitions and Assumptions

In this study, the term "demonic" refers to any spiritual bondage or oppression caused by demons in any area of a person's life.[6] The term "spiritually free" describes the condition of living in freedom from demonic oppression and bondage.

Our first assumption is that *dark powers and principalities are active throughout the world* and are not restricted to any one culture or religion. We often quickly spot what we assume are demonic elements in other socioreligious communities, all the while being unaware of the demonic elements in our own environment.[7] We remind ourselves that as we all struggle against the cosmic powers of this present darkness, we all must take up the whole armor of God in order to stand firm (Eph 6:10–18).

The second assumption is that *power confrontations were normative* in the work of Jesus and the early church. These have continued in one form or another both in church life and in mission over the ensuing centuries. In the New Testament, deliverance in Jesus' name took place among Jews and also cross-culturally with Samaritans and pagan Gentiles (e.g., worshipers of Artemis). During the first two centuries of church history as Gentiles came to faith, they routinely went through deliverance as preparation for baptism.[8] Throughout church history, deliverance ministry has been seen as a sign of the kingdom, an act of mercy and healing for the tormented, and part of the process of spiritual transformation.

The third assumption is that *intercessory prayer is required* for any advancement of the kingdom of God where spiritual powers of darkness are confronted. In discussing how Jesus followers in insider movements deal with the demonic, an even more pressing question is how insider movements can begin in the first place in environments where demonic forces have long kept the gospel from taking hold.

Dutch Sheets provides an example of intercession for such people groups in his book *Intercessory Prayer:*

> I am [before the throne of God] asking the Father to extend mercy
> and bring salvation to the people of [country X]. The Father could

---

Thomas Nelson, 1996); and C. Peter Wagner and F. Douglas Pennoyer, eds., *Wrestling with Dark Angels: Toward a Deeper Understanding of the Supernatural Forces in Spiritual Warfare* (Ventura, CA: Regal, 1990).

5   I would like to express my thanks to my husband and field coworker, John Travis, coeditor of *UIM*, and to David Taylor, associate editor of *UIM*, for their assistance in thinking through and writing this chapter. For this reason I will most often use "we" and "us" in this chapter.

6   For a broader study on this topic, see Beilby and Eddy, *Understanding Spiritual Warfare,* which presents the writings of four authors who hold differing views on spiritual warfare and the demonic. Each takes a different approach to the topic: (1) standing against the demonic found in evil institutions and systems; (2) standing against the demonic by living holy lives in right relationship with God; (3) direct confrontation with demons in deliverance ministry, reminiscent of biblical accounts of Jesus and the early church; and (4) authoritative intercessory prayer against demonic beings over territories and peoples, what some call "territorial spirits."

7   Jesus' teaching on the speck in our brother's eye and the log in our own (Matt 7:3–5) is important to keep in mind in this discussion.

8   Clinton E. Arnold, *3 Crucial Questions about Spiritual Warfare* (Grand Rapids, MI: Baker, 1997), 107.

reply, "How can I do this? They are sinners. They worship false gods, which is really worshiping Satan. And besides, they don't even want me to do this. They themselves have never asked." I answer, "Because Jesus interceded or mediated for them. . . . So, as he taught me, I'm asking for your Kingdom to come and your will to be done in [country X]. . . . I am asking you to do it based entirely on the redemptive work he has already done."[9]

Until God's people take these peoples before his throne, the evil one will keep them in bondage, and what is recorded in Lamentations will be true of them: "Their fathers sinned and are no more, and they bear their punishment" (5:7). For this reason God calls us to pray as in Psalm 79—prayers that cannot be prayed by those still in darkness: "O God, do not hold against [them] the sins of past generations; may your mercy come quickly to meet [them], for [they] are in desperate need. Help [them], O God our Savior, for the glory of your name; deliver [them] and forgive [their] sins for your name's sake" (vv. 8,9).

This Psalm 79 prayer was set to music by a colleague of ours in the local language and recorded. As the mixed group of musicians (Jesus followers and pre-followers of Jesus[10]) recorded the song, electrical equipment shut on and off, static came through the speakers, and lights flickered. Not one person in the group passed it off as a coincidence. They knew there was a reaction in the spiritual realm to the words of this prayer. It took the group many attempts until the song was finally successfully recorded. And it took many years of this kind of intercessory prayer before dark forces were forced to retreat enough for a few new Jesus movements among this people group to begin.

Toward a Biblical Framework for Spiritual Transformation Addressing Culture, Religion, and the Demonic

Followers of Jesus have always confronted the demonic in their surrounding communities as part of spiritual transformation. Scripture teaches that Jesus followers are no longer "of the world" yet are still in it (John 17:15–18). Followers of Jesus who remain inside their socioreligious communities are no different—except that the world they are "in but not of" includes the world religion of their birth.

Five themes will be covered in this framework: (1) the peoples and cultures of the world, (2) the evil one in the world, (3) Jesus overcoming the world, (4) Jesus followers being in the world but protected from the evil one, and (5) Jesus followers giving no place to the evil one.

The Peoples and Cultures of the World

God created humanity in his image, gave them the mandate to "fill the earth and subdue it" (Gen 1:28), and has stayed involved in the process ever since. Paul told the Athenians, "From one man he made every nation of men, that they should inhabit the whole earth; and he determined the times set for them and the exact places where they should live" (Acts 17:26). God is sovereign over peoples and their

---

9   Dutch Sheets, *Intercessory Prayer: How God Can Use Your Prayers to Move Heaven and Earth* (Ventura, CA: Regal, 1996), 42.

10   We have taken up the practice (in hope and faith) of referring to those who have not yet embraced the gospel as "pre-followers of Jesus" instead of using the more common term, "unbelievers," especially given that the word for "unbeliever" in Muslim contexts also means "infidel" (*kafir*). We who follow Jesus do not like being called infidels by radical Islamists, so we have chosen to refrain from using this term.

diverse cultures; this diversity will continue throughout eternity (Rev 5:9; 21:24). Whatever is good within a culture points to God's goodness and glory.

The Evil One in the World

The evil one seeks to capture what belongs to God—to steal, kill, and destroy (John 10:10). Satan is "the god of this world" (2 Cor 4:4), and the whole world lies under his power (1 John 5:19). He has rulers, authorities, powers, and spiritual forces of evil that war against God and his kingdom (Eph 6:12). His influence or attack is felt to some extent throughout the entire world—in every government, every institution, every religion, every culture, and every person (Rom 3:23; 1 John 3:8). Every culture is therefore in need of transformation; every person is in need of freedom and protection from the evil one. For this very reason Jesus came: to destroy the devil's work (1 John 3:8).

Jesus Overcoming the World

It is because God loves the world that he sent Jesus to reclaim it as his own. His light shone into the darkness, and the darkness could not overcome it (John 1:5). When he touched contagious lepers he was not infected; instead they were healed. He was not contaminated by sinners; instead they were forgiven. He did not succumb to the devil's temptation to avoid the Cross; instead Jesus made a public spectacle of Satan through it (Col 2:15), being raised from death to life in victory (Rom 1:4) and exalted far above his enemies at the right hand of God (1 Pet 3:22).

The overcoming victory of Jesus is extended in the world through the kingdom of God. Daniel foresaw this kingdom as a small rock that would grow into a mountain filling the whole earth (Dan 2:35). Jesus described it as yeast that works all through the batch of dough and a tiny mustard seed that rises to become greater than everything around it (Matt 13:33; Mark 4:31,32). He said to his followers, "As the Father has sent me I am sending you" (John 20:21); "In this world you will have trouble. But take heart! I have overcome the world" (16:33).

In the World but Protected from the Evil One

Praying for his followers, Jesus said, "I am not asking you to take them out of the world, but I ask you to protect them from the evil one" (John 17:15). In the parable of the wheat and tares, Jesus describes the people of the evil one and the people of the kingdom as mixed together in the world; God's plan in this age is not to separate the two, since it could harm the people of the kingdom to do so (Matt 13:24–30,37–43).[11] Paul expects that Jesus followers will continue to relate with people in the world (1 Cor 5:9,10). John tells us that the whole world lies under the power of the evil one, but that Jesus protects those who are born of God (1 John 5:18,19).

Giving No Place to the Evil One

Jesus said, "There is nothing that enters a person from outside that is able to defile him. Rather the things that come out of a person are the things that defile him" (Mark 7:15). As followers of Jesus, we are protected and not defiled so long as we give no place inside our hearts to the evil one. Instead of taking his followers out of demonic places, Jesus takes places that have been given to demons out of his followers' hearts as they obey him. Jesus is the ultimate example of one who has given no place inside

---

11 For misapplication of biblical teaching on separation, see *UIM*, chap. 5, under the section titled "Misunderstandings of Scripture and Theology Related to Insider Movements."

himself to the evil one. Just before going to the Cross, he said, "The ruler of the world is coming, and he has nothing in Me" (John 14:30 NASB)—no claim or power over him.[12]

The transforming power of the gospel conforms us more and more to the image of Christ (2 Cor 3:18), so this becomes increasingly true of us as well: *the evil one has no place—no claim or power over us.* We must renounce and get rid of whatever the evil one has in us[13] in order to live in victory over him in this world—in this evil age where he is still the ruler.

As we consider followers of Jesus in insider movements, we may immediately jump to their need to renounce what we consider idolatrous practices associated with the religious community of their people. Certainly people anywhere are at severe risk of demonic oppression unless idolatry is eliminated from their lives. However, we can quickly become reductionistic in our view of idolatry. Scripture likens idolatry to arrogance in the OT (1 Sam 15:23), and in the NT equates it with greed, stating that an "immoral, impure or greedy person . . . is an idolater" (Eph 5:5; cf. Col 3:5). 1 John 5:21 in the NIV reads, "Dear children, keep yourselves from idols"; the NLT reads, "Dear children, keep away from anything that might take God's place in your hearts."[14] These present idolatry (arrogance, greed, immorality, impurity—indeed, anything that might take God's place in our hearts) as a pervasive problem of the human heart, not just what members of world religions do when they bow down in front of statues, repeat certain phrases, or burn incense.

When the new Gentile Jesus followers in Corinth asked Paul about eating food sacrificed to idols in the temple (1 Cor 8:1), Paul's response was twofold. First, believers must know that there was only one God and only one Lord, Jesus Christ, in the midst of many so-called gods. Second, believers must know that the idol was nothing. Even though others eating such food acknowledged other gods (in reality, demons—1 Cor 10:20), believers could eat without being defiled, protected from demonic influence as long as they gave no place inside themselves to the idol (1 Cor 8:7). The outward religious custom of eating food sacrificed to idols became a non-issue for Jesus followers—they were no worse if they did not eat, and no better if they did (1 Cor 8:8); idolatry was a matter of the heart.[15]

Paul explained that Gentile followers of Jesus could still eat meat, even though as a sacrifice to idols it was sacrificed to demons (1 Cor 10:20). Believers could eat it and be protected, "for the earth is the Lord's and everything in it" (1 Cor 10:26; cf. Ps 24:1), and "to the pure all things are pure" (Titus

---

12 In the NKJV, John 14:30 reads, "The ruler of this world is coming, and he has nothing in Me." The ESV reads ". . . he has no claim on me," and the NLT reads ". . . he has no power over me." *The Pulpit Commentary* explains that there is nothing in Jesus "on which evil can fasten." See H. D. M. Spence, ed., *The Pulpit Commentary*, vol. 17, *John* (Grand Rapids, MI: Eerdmans, 1950).

13 The New Testament provides plentiful admonitions to Jesus followers to get rid of and renounce what does not please God (e.g., John 8:43–51; Rom 13:12; 2 Cor 4:2; Eph 4:22–32; Col 3:8; Titus 2:11–13; Jas 1:21; 1 Pet 2:1). As followers of Jesus in insider movements read or hear these passages, they must seek God's wisdom and leading as to how they will obey these commands in their particular family, community, and situation. 1 John 5:21 (NLT) reads, "Dear children, keep away from anything that might take God's place in your hearts."

14 Other passages of Scripture place idolatry in the context of long lists of attitudes and practices such as disputes, strife, stubbornness, and impurity (Gal 5:19–21; 1 Pet 4:3). In today's parlance, the list might sound like this: materialism, not getting along with people, doing it our own way, being too intimate before marriage, visiting questionable websites.

15 Another important but separate aspect of food sacrificed to idols is the stumbling of others. Paul instructed believers to be mindful of people with a weak conscience—that is, new believers who still did not fully understand that there was only one God and one Lord and that the idol truly was nothing. In other words, believers are to be cautious in the presence of new believers who do not yet fully understand their authority in Christ over demons.

1:15). However, if believers were eating meat and giving a place in their thinking to the idol, those people were defiled (1 Cor 8:7). In this way Paul was showing that idolatry is a matter of what is inside a person.[16]

In order to experience spiritual freedom, Jesus followers must not only be transformed in the area of idolatry but also in other heart issues, such as unresolved anger, which is often an indication of unforgiveness. Even letting the sun go down on our anger gives a place inside us to the devil (Eph 4:26,27).

We now turn to some examples of insider followers of Jesus becoming spiritually free.

Becoming Free

The following accounts include both victories and failures in seeing insider followers of Jesus become free of demonic influence.[17] Thankfully, by understanding the failures, we and they are seeing an increase in the victories. These testimonies are followed by a model that summarizes scriptural teaching on becoming free that has been useful to insiders.

Nelam's Story

Nelam, a Muslim mother, came to faith in Jesus in her forties, and several members of her extended family soon joined her. For many generations this family had practiced folk Muslim arts,[18] with at least one family member working full-time as an occult practitioner. The family first received the gospel with joy, but as the topic of renouncing involvement with magic came up, it was clear that they were putting their hope for freedom from poverty in occult rituals and objects. Fellow Jesus followers made visits week after week, reading Bible passages and giving testimonies of renouncing occult involvement. Finally several family members admitted that they would not relinquish their magic arts, with the income and hope it generated, in order to follow Jesus. Several years later, they still struggle with poverty, and their friends who follow Jesus continue to pray for them. Nelam and her family members' refusal to renounce occult involvement gives a place to the evil one such that they do not experience the victory of Jesus over the darkness in their environment and in their lives.

Waji's Story

Waji, on the other hand, was willing to renounce his involvement with folk practices. Waji, an Asian Muslim father and grandfather, came to faith after hearing the good news from our friend Ghazi. Waji regularly gathered with other Jesus followers to read the New Testament and pray.

One evening Ghazi called us for help in praying for Waji, who was being heavily oppressed by demons. My husband, John, joined Ghazi in praying for deliverance.

Waji, like many Muslims, added folk practices to his usual religious observances. One benefit Waji enjoyed as a result of occult involvement was supernatural strength for lifting objects and doing physical labor. Many demons had gained entrance into his life over the years, and now they were actively throwing him against the walls of his house and using his vocal chords to speak.

---

16 We will not discuss here another important but separate aspect of eating meat sacrificed to idols: the stumbling of others. Here we are looking only at the personal demonic effect on the follower of Jesus.

17 Names have been changed to protect the identity of those mentioned in these accounts.

18 They had served as shamans, relied on amulets for protection, performed certain rituals to obtain occult power, calculated favorable times using numerology, visited ancient graves for healing, and called on evil spirits to increase their wealth.

Over several hours, dozens of evil spirits were cast out as Ghazi commanded each spirit to leave in Jesus' name. Waji directed John and Ghazi to collect the many occult power objects he owned—amulets, scrolls, a knife—and together they destroyed them.[19] A once overly muscular man was now collapsed on the floor, happily repeating, "I'm free! I'm free!" Waji continued to grow in his faith, and his testimony resulted in several family members and neighbors coming to faith in Jesus over the next few years.

One day, though, we got word that Waji was refusing to talk to a certain neighbor. He had been paid less for a repair job than what was agreed on, and he became so angry that eventually he would not open the door to anyone, including Ghazi. To our knowledge, this situation has never been resolved, and Waji is still spiritually oppressed.

After the incident with Waji, other members in that same group of Jesus followers began having disputes with each other. I visited some of the women, hoping to do peacemaking. Each conversation would end up with a recounting of hurt feelings starting in childhood, and a comment like ". . . And when she said that to me last week, it reminded me of the way my mother used to talk to me!" My encouragement to forgive those who had sinned against them fell on hearts hardened by pain and resentment. The devil got his way and the group disbanded. Some moved away; thankfully, others joined other groups and are still walking in the obedience of faith. These experiences caused us to seek God for more effective ways to help Jesus followers become free of demonic influence. One answer came in learning to pray not only for renouncement of idolatry and occult involvement but also for healing of hurting hearts.

Daud's Story

Some time after we began regularly praying with Jesus followers for healing of their hearts, we were sharing at a small outreach training gathering in Asia. We had the privilege of praying for Daud, a new believer (not from Muslim background). During group prayer, Daud suddenly lunged out of his seat. We watched in amazement as he assumed the position of a four-legged creature and slid slowly across the floor, barely using his own limbs. As we commanded the demonic force to be shut down in Jesus' name, he quickly became calm, but started grasping one of his ears. John and one or two others took him aside and asked about his ear. He explained that prior to coming to faith, he had been very active in a martial arts group known as the Flying Tigers. One of the group's rituals involved piercing the ear and wearing a particular amulet in the form an earring. Though he had removed this amulet after coming to faith, the demon associated with it was still able to overtake him, cause his body to take the shape of a flying tiger, and move him across the floor.

In prayer Daud repented for occult involvement, renounced all allegiance to demons, and reaffirmed his allegiance to the Lord Jesus. However, the demon refused to leave. The group continued to pray and ask God if there was any place inside him given to the evil one. Childhood memories of his

---

19 In this case, Waji was the person in authority in his household and had the ability to decide to destroy the objects that he had relied on. In other cases, new believers find themselves in families that continue to rely on such objects, but the believers are not in the position of family authority to destroy them. It is all the more important for them to learn their authority in Christ over demons. They can claim this authority over themselves, forbidding any demon associated with such objects to harm them (Luke 10:19: "I have given you authority to trample on snakes and scorpions and to overcome all the power of the enemy; nothing will harm you"). Because of their place in Christ, insider followers of Jesus can survive and thrive even in demonic environments, since they are giving no place to the evil one in their hearts and exercising their authority in Christ over the evil one.

mother came to his mind. Daud poured out his heart to God, telling him how terrible he felt when she was involved with several different men and how bitter he still was toward her. Then he waited for the healing touch that only God could give him, and as he sensed that God was near him in the midst of even the worst times in childhood, his deep pain began to lift. He found himself asking forgiveness for hating his mother and telling God that he forgave her from his heart. Then the demon quickly left in Jesus' name, and he was filled with peace. Daud went on to share the good news with Muslims, including the story of his own deliverance in Jesus' name. As a result of this experience and many others like it, we saw how people are set free from demonic influence as they renounce idolatrous practices *and* forgive those who have hurt them.

Anisa's Story

Anisa, a Muslim follower of Jesus, became free from demonic influence after she sought prayer for the healing of her heart. Anisa was being discipled by our friend Jasmine (a Muslim-background follower of Jesus), and asked her for help when she realized she was unable to forgive people who hurt her, including her own parents. As Jasmine and Anisa prayed about this, Anisa remembered that when she was little she would ask her parents for snack money, and because they were so poor at the time they would decline her request, but with anger. Anisa began to cry, feeling the familiar sense of worthlessness.

Jasmine asked her to read Matthew 18:21–35, the parable of the unmerciful servant and the need to forgive seventy-seven times, and then prayed, "Lord, show Anisa what you think of unforgiveness." Anisa said that she felt God was sad; she felt cold and guilty. Jasmine prayed that God would help her to forgive by healing her heart, and then Anisa felt like her body was being "enveloped in a white light." She was more aware of how wrong her unforgiveness was, and finally she forgave her parents and others. She believed for the first time that God really loved her personally. Anisa was then reminded of a visit she had made to an occult practitioner before she came to faith. She confessed this sin and felt a heaviness leave her. Within a week after this time of prayer, a physical ailment that had bothered her all her life suddenly left her.[20]

Now, as Anisa continues meeting with a handful of other believers, she is experiencing freedom in Jesus. If ever she has the thought, *I am worthless,* she can counter with assurance, "No, I am worthy because God loves me!" She is more at peace, is less "hypersensitive," and can much more readily forgive others. Friends have commented to Anisa that they can see the difference in her life. She has had the privilege of leading at least two of her family members to faith and continues to follow Jesus as a Muslim within her Muslim family and community.

We have seen and heard many similar accounts of the work of the Spirit in the lives of Jesus followers to free them from demonic oppression and protect them from evil as they continue to live out their faith in Jesus within their families, communities, and yes, even their world religions.

The Two Hands Model

These insiders, like many others, are part of communities where awareness of spiritual forces is great and interest in becoming free and protected from evil spirits is widespread. Therefore the ministry of healing and deliverance is high priority for many of them. In response to the request of a handful of in-

---

20 Did this healing happen because she repented for visiting an occult practitioner? Or because she forgave people who hurt her? Or did God just decide to bless her? We do not know for certain, but any of these are possibilities.

siders, I distilled into a simple model some principles that came out of our studies with Charles Kraft,[21] as well as our own experience in healing and deliverance ministry. It includes ten prayer steps, one for each finger, on two hands uplifted in prayer.[22]

The left hand (the "unclean" hand in Muslim culture) represents areas of bondage that need to be renounced: generational bondage, curses and words that cause bondage, occult involvement, unhealthy relationships with other people, and secrets. As these areas are dealt with in prayer, the Jesus follower gets hands-on experience in using the authority over the evil one that Jesus received from God and passes on to his followers (Matt 28:18; Luke 9:1,2; 10:19).

The right hand (the "good" hand in Muslim culture) represents five steps of prayer for healing of the heart: asking God to cause us to remember what he wants to heal,[23] pouring out our hearts to God, waiting for God's presence in the pain, repenting and forgiving, and finally, casting out evil spirits. Descriptions, Bible studies, and example prayers are included for each of the ten areas.[24]

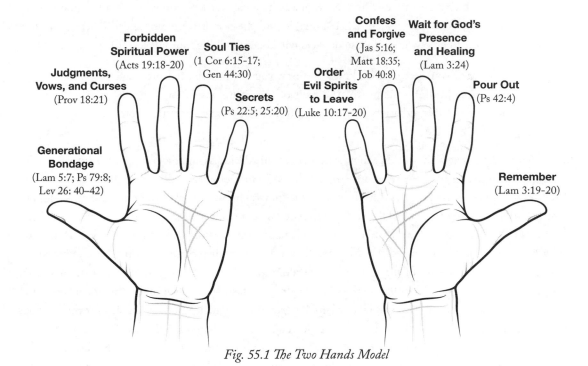

Fig. 55.1 The Two Hands Model

21   In Dr. Kraft's classes at Fuller Seminary, he invited students to observe as he prayed for various volunteers. Although I gained much from class lectures and reading Kraft's books, I was most impacted by watching ministry sessions. Not only did I end up having the privilege of praying for people from many backgrounds over the following years, but I became aware of my own need for healing and freedom and experienced a new depth of personal spiritual transformation.

22   Muslims pray with hands uplifted.

23   Since heart wounds often begin in childhood, God often brings childhood situations to the mind of the person receiving prayer.

24   John and Anna Travis, "Deep-level Healing Prayer in Cross-cultural Ministry: Models, Examples, and Lessons," in *Paradigms Shifts in Christian Witness: Insights from Anthropology, Communication, and Spiritual Power*, ed. Charles E. Van Engen, Darrell Whiteman, and J. Dudley Woodberry (Maryknoll, NY: Orbis, 2008), 106–15.

We have used this model with Jesus followers in insider movements among various people groups in at least five different countries. It was designed with the hope that others would adapt and use it in other contexts, and we are happy to see that this is taking place.

Staying Spiritually Free

The preceding section has discussed how Jesus followers find spiritual freedom through renouncing sin and bondage, seeking heart healing, forgiving those who have hurt them, and commanding demons to leave. Once spiritually free, the crucial issue is how to stay free.[25]

This freedom from the evil one comes about by walking in holiness and obedience to God's word, allowing him to transform individuals and families. This transformation involves retaining what is already good, redeeming or reinterpreting other aspects of culture and religious life, and finally, rejecting those things that Jesus followers sense is unredeemable. Ephesians 5:8–17 is a fitting backdrop for this process. Ephesus, like many places where movements happen, was a region where many came to faith (Acts 19:18,26), miracles occurred (19:11,12), magic and the occult were renounced (19:19), and folk religion was shown to be powerless in the debacle with Sceva and his sons (19:13–16).

> For you were once darkness, but now you are light in the Lord. Live as children of light (for the fruit of the light consists in all goodness, righteousness and truth) and find out what pleases the Lord. (Eph 5:8–10)

Jesus followers we know realize that they were in demonic darkness and have now come into the light. As the light shines in their hearts and they read the word of God, especially in small groups, they can discern what pleases the Lord. As children of light, they retain whatever in their culture and religious community is pleasing to God while working to redeem or transform what is not.

In the Muslim area where we lived for more than twenty years, Jesus followers loved Ramadan. They kept the month-long fast as they always had: no food or drink from sunup to sundown, and a huge celebration at the end of the month. As we spoke with Jesus followers, however, it became clear that one thing had changed—their reason for keeping the fast. Where we lived, the general Muslim understanding of Ramadan was that if they kept it perfectly the entire month, their sins for the previous eleven months would be forgiven. The Jesus followers, however, had an entirely different motivation. They knew their sins were forgiven through the sacrifice of Jesus and not by keeping the fast. I remember hearing my friend frequently exclaim during fasting month, *"Alhamdulillah* (praise be to God), I now have a Savior!" For Jesus followers the fast was kept to draw nearer to God, intercede for family and friends, and show solidarity with their community.

One Ramadan, the insiders put on a fast-breaking dinner, to which we were invited. Sixty or so people were in attendance. About half were Jesus-following Muslims, while the others were pre-followers. Two leaders shared passages from the *Injil* (New Testament), cross-referencing them with passages from the Qur'an. We marveled, knowing those in attendance would most likely never darken the door of a Chris-

---

25 It is important to note that in the case of insider followers of Jesus, just as with any of us who follow Jesus, they may experience spiritual freedom at a certain time but later realize they need further freedom. Often this is not because the earlier healing, deliverance, or transformation didn't "stick," but because the awareness of the need for transformation increases as followers of Jesus mature. Therefore we have seen and expect to see insiders grow in both becoming free and staying free throughout their spiritual journey (2 Cor 3:18).

tian church—but here among their own people, in their own neighborhood, in the middle of Ramadan, they were hearing the good news of Jesus and his kingdom from one of their own. These Jesus followers were reinterpreting and redeeming a practice inside their religious community. Instead of coming under demonic oppression during the Muslim fasting month, they were experiencing spiritual freedom.

In another place, Muslims often visit shrines to seek help or healing from shamans.[26] We have met Jesus followers who, now free from demonic oppression connected with such shrines, regularly make themselves available to pray in the name of Jesus at shrines such as these.[27] Unlike many believers from Western cultures, these insider Jesus followers do not exclude that middle zone of spiritual power spoken of by Hiebert.[28] We are moved by the compassion and boldness of these redeemed, Jesus-following "holy men"!

> Have nothing to do with the fruitless deeds of darkness, but rather
> expose them. It is shameful even to mention what the disobedient
> do in secret. But everything exposed by the light becomes visible—
> and everything that is illuminated becomes a light. This is why it is
> said: "Wake up, sleeper, rise from the dead, and Christ will shine
> on you." (Eph 5:11–14)

In the process of retaining what is good and transforming or redeeming what is not, it may become apparent to insider Jesus followers that some deeds are utterly fruitless and completely dark. Insiders immersed in the Bible and led by the Spirit of God will have discernment over which aspects of their culture and religion are redeemable and which are truly demonic and must be eliminated. We have seen them in obedience to Jesus get rid of those objects or rituals of power they felt were displeasing to God.

A friend of mine (who later came to faith) explained in detail how to curse a person who deserved disaster by reciting verses from her holy book. She had always felt a little guilty about cursing people and wondered if God was really behind such behavior. After knowing Jesus, she was sure that God did not allow cursing of others, and this was confirmed as she continued to read the New Testament with her group. She and fellow Jesus followers rejected and renounced this demonic behavior.

> Be very careful, then, how you live—not as unwise but as wise,
> making the most of every opportunity, because the days are evil.
> Therefore do not be foolish, but understand what the Lord's will is.
> (Eph 5:15–17)

Recognizing that the days are evil, insiders we know correct one another in their small home groups when someone is not living wisely or by the word of God. They diligently study the Scriptures to know

---

26 Shrines often contain the gravesites of well-known Muslim holy men.

27 See Charles H. Kraft, "Appropriate Contextualization of Spiritual Power," in *Appropriate Christianity*, ed. Charles H. Kraft (Pasadena, CA: William Carey Library, 2005), 375–95. In this thought-provoking article, Kraft asks in what ways Christ-centered spiritual power can be contextualized for greater effectiveness in cross-cultural ministry.

28 Paul Hiebert observes that Westerners who serve in traditional societies, while emphasizing ultimate spiritual truth as well as practical solutions in the empirical world (medical care, etc.), often exclude the "middle zone" of spiritual power. Hiebert notes, "When tribal people spoke of fear of evil spirits, they [Western field workers] denied the existence of the spirits rather than claim the power of Christ over them." See Hiebert, "The Flaw of the Excluded Middle," *Missiology: An International Review* 10 (January 1982): 44.

what God's will is[29] and help one another stay spiritually free as they remain in their community. As with the above examples of Ramadan (originally viewed as a means of salvation) or the shrine (usually a place of dark power), these Jesus followers use old forms and practices, but with new biblical meaning and godly power.[30] In order to see what this may look like in other contexts, it might be helpful to briefly note the extent to which Western Christianity centuries ago took pagan forms and filled them with new meanings and power.

Western Christians are immersed in the remnants of their pagan religious heritage. This is reflected in some of the traditions surrounding the two most sacred Christian holidays, Christmas and Easter, the use of church bells and choirs,[31] and even the names of the days of the week. Yet today these originally demonic forms have taken on new meanings. For example, no one today continues to view Monday as the day to honor the pagan moon goddess, or Wednesday as the day to worship Woden, chief god of the Teutonic pantheon, who required human sacrifice for victory in battle.[32] Throughout mission history, Bible translations have often used the name of the local or tribal high god when referring to God. In this way the accounts and teachings of Scripture alter the meaning of familiar terms and fill them with truth. In these cases the problem is not with the forms per se but with the meaning ascribed to them by those who use them. Taking old forms and giving them new meaning is a normal phenomenon as the gospel grows in new areas, and we should not be concerned when insider followers of Jesus take elements that their religion and culture offer and fill them with new meaning.

We close this part of the study with a message from Kandaswami Chetti, a Hindu follower of Jesus who believed that spiritual transformation and spiritual freedom are attainable in non-Christian environments if Jesus followers rely upon the power of the Spirit of Christ. He penned the following words a century ago in response to the prevailing expectation of local Christians that he would leave the religion of his birth due to its inherent sinfulness and become a member of the Christian community. His response draws upon the story *The Pilgrim's Progress*.

> There is nothing essentially sinful in Hindu society any more than
> there is anything essentially pure in Christian society . . . such that
> one should hasten from the one to the other like the Pilgrim from
> the City of Destruction to the Heavenly City. The City of Destruc-
> tion is unfortunately so overspread as to include within its borders
> tracts belonging to both civilizations, while the Heavenly City

---

29 See Rom 12:9–21; Gal 5:16–6:10; Eph 4:17–6:18; Col 3:1–4:6.

30 Field workers also report their experience that some forms, though they may still be used by new followers of Jesus, are not given new spiritual meaning but instead take on a nonspiritual, strictly cultural meaning.

31 Choirs were part of pagan Greek temple life. "Some have tried to argue that the Christians borrowed choirs and chanting from the Jewish synagogue. But this is highly unlikely as the third- and fourth-century Christians borrowed little to nothing from the Jews. Instead they drew heavily from the surrounding Greco-Roman culture." Frank Viola and George Barna, *Pagan Christianity? Exploring the Roots of Our Church Practices* (Carol Stream, IL: BarnaBooks, 2008), 159.

32 The Old English names for the days of the week (Sunnendaeg, Monandaeg, Tiwesdaeg, Wodensdaeg, Thuresdaeg, Frigedaeg, Saeternesdaeg) were derived from the names of European pagan deities who were worshiped on those days. See E. G. Richards, *Mapping Time: The Calendar and Its History* (New York: Oxford University Press, 1998), 280, 391.

requires for its realization *the working of the Spirit of Christ* in one society as well as in the other.[33]

Chetti saw that the key for escape from the evil one's destruction did not lie in leaving the Hindu socioreligious community of his birth to enter the Christian religion, but instead in the working of the Spirit of Christ. Chetti believed that both Hindu and Christian "societies" needed the transforming work of Christ's Spirit. From what he states above, he clearly believed those positive elements of Hindu society and culture could be safely retained by the follower of Jesus without being a spiritual deterrent.

Helping Others Become Free

As insiders come to faith, become free from demons, stay free, and take leadership in insider movements, they need to be involved in helping others become free; indeed, a central feature of insider movements is that they are led by insiders.[34] Although alongsiders[35] may be available to help with some of the ministry of deliverance, the insiders themselves will carry the lion's share of this responsibility. Jesus said to his disciples, "As you go, proclaim this message: 'The Kingdom of heaven has come near.' Heal the sick . . . , drive out demons. Freely you have received; freely give" (Matt 10:7,8). Even as this chapter is being written, we are encouraged to see the beginnings of a multiplying ministry of driving out demons among some insiders, and we hope to see this greatly increase.

Not many years ago I had the privilege of praying for issues of the heart with a dear friend who is a leader in an insider movement. God healed her of pain from being unjustly accused of stealing something when she was a child. As she spoke out forgiveness to those who had wronged her, she sighed heavily, shed a few tears, and said, *"Alhamdulilah*, that tormenting, accusing evil spirit is gone!" The next day she shared what God had done for her with a group of new followers of Jesus in an insider Bible study group. One of the women heard the story and started to have a strong demonic reaction. The group assumed that God would set her free, just like in the testimony they had just heard, and in keeping with several Bible passages they had read together over the last few months. They led her in prayer to renounce occult involvement and forgive people who had hurt her. God healed her heart of various painful situations in childhood, which gave her more grace to forgive people who had hurt her both in childhood and as an adult. The group ordered the evil spirit(s) oppressing her to leave in Jesus' name, and they were gone.

We know of colleagues, both insiders and alongsiders, who are developing and using similar approaches to the Two Hands Model described earlier. One example is a model developed by our friend Imran, a mature insider who has personally experienced powerful healing and deliverance in his walk with Jesus. Imran created a pocket-sized black booklet called "Casting Demons Out." He begins the sixteen-page booklet with a discussion of how the Qur'an affirms the authenticity of the Bible—the *Taurat* (Torah), *Zabur* (Psalms), and *Injil* (New Testament or Gospels)—and how the Bible should be read and believed by Muslims.[36] He then proceeds to ask and discuss answers to three central questions:

---

33 Chetti's full statement appears in *UIM* as chap. 10.

34 Refer to the definition of "insider movement" in chap. 1.

35 See chap. 47 on the roles of alongsiders.

36 Since he is writing as a Muslim to Muslims, he must first establish the legitimacy of the Bible as God's word so that he can be free to quote and base the deliverance model on the Bible.

Q: How do evil spirits get in?

A: Through personal sin, occult involvement, sins of ancestors, and trauma.

Q: How can evil spirits be cast out?

A: Through repentance and healing in Jesus' name by the power of the Spirit.

Q: How can a person remain protected?

A: Stay away from what God forbids.

Imran concludes with several example prayers based on the Bible, such as asking to be filled with the Spirit of God.

Badi, a Muslim follower of Jesus and father of two, came to faith after he was delivered from an oppressing demon in Jesus' name. Several years later, his teenage daughter started experiencing demonic attacks. At least one time, the attack on her began when a whole group of her schoolmates had demonic reactions simultaneously—a known phenomenon in this society. Imran heard about Badi's daughter's dilemma and gave him a copy of his black booklet. Badi, in faith, prayed the example prayers with his daughter and added some of his own words. She was beautifully delivered from demons in Jesus' name and has not experienced any attacks since then. Our hope is that these and other models can be tried and adjusted for various socioreligious contexts.

In the same way that God has called many of us to intercede for peoples who do not yet have the gospel, using divine weapons in prayer, we are seeing the first signs of God doing the same for certain insiders, who are interceding on behalf of others. I was delighted to hear this account from an insider leader:

> Sometimes when we meet together, someone says that he or she cannot stop thinking about a particular friend or relative. Day after day, God brings to mind the person and the area where that person lives. We conclude that God wants the gospel to be brought to that group. But we know we can't just casually enter a new area, since there is a spiritual battle to be fought. We sense that God wants us to recruit at least forty of us who follow Jesus to agree that the area mentioned will be cleared of opposition and open to the good news. Usually, not all forty of us can gather in one place, but we are in communication with each other, agreeing in prayer. When we sense God has opened the way, a group of us begin visiting people we know in that area. We have seen several new groups of Jesus followers started in this way.

My hope is that wherever God has placed his people to begin wrestling in prayer for peoples who do not yet have the gospel, God will also call insiders in the movements that begin there to carry on the work of intercession until the full harvest comes in.

Summary and Concluding Thoughts

At this crucial point in history, as the gospel begins to grow in a variety of socioreligious communities for the first time, followers of Jesus would do well to pray for one another that we all will walk in victory over the evil one. In this way insiders will not be alone in contending against the evil one, both for their own lives and for those who have not yet embraced the good news of Jesus.

May our insider brothers and sisters continue to shine like stars in the world religions of their people, blameless and innocent in the midst of a crooked and perverse generation as they work out their salvation with fear and trembling, knowing it is God who is at work in them, just as he is in us (Phil 2:12–15; Acts 15:8).

Bibliography

Arnold, Clinton E. *3 Crucial Questions about Spiritual Warfare*. Grand Rapids, MI: Baker, 1997.

———. *Powers of Darkness: Principalities and Powers in Paul's Letters*. Downers Grove, IL: InterVarsity Press, 1992.

Beilby, James K., and Paul Rhodes Eddy. *Understanding Spiritual Warfare: Four Views*. Grand Rapids, MI: Baker Academic, 2012.

Hiebert, Paul G. "The Flaw of the Excluded Middle." *Missiology: An International Review* 10 (January 1982): 35–47.

———, R. Daniel Shaw, and Tite Tienou. *Understanding Folk Religion: A Christian Response to Popular Beliefs and Practices*. Grand Rapids, MI: Baker Academic, 1997.

Kraft, Charles H. "Appropriate Contextualization of Spiritual Power." In *Appropriate Christianity*, edited by Charles H. Kraft, 375–95. Pasadena, CA: William Carey Library, 2005.

Murphy, Edward F. *The Handbook for Spiritual Warfare*. Nashville: Thomas Nelson, 1996.

Richards, E. G. *Mapping Time: The Calendar and Its History*. New York: Oxford University Press, 1998.

Sheets, Dutch. *Intercessory Prayer: How God Can Use Your Prayers to Move Heaven and Earth*. Ventura, CA: Regal, 1996.

Travis, John, and Anna Travis. "Deep-level Healing Prayer in Cross-cultural Ministry: Models, Examples, and Lessons." In *Paradigms Shifts in Christian Witness: Insights from Anthropology, Communication, and Spiritual Power*, edited by Charles E. Van Engen, Darrell Whiteman, and J. Dudley Woodberry, 106–15. Maryknoll, NY: Orbis, 2008.

Viola, Frank, and George Barna. *Pagan Christianity? Exploring the Roots of Our Church Practices*. Carol Stream, IL: BarnaBooks, 2008.

Wagner, C. Peter, and F. Douglas Pennoyer, eds. *Wrestling with Dark Angels: Toward a Deeper Understanding of the Supernatural Forces in Spiritual Warfare*. Ventura, CA: Regal, 1990.

CHAPTER 56

Possible Pitfalls of Jesus Movements
*Lessons from History**

Rebecca Lewis

The Jesus movements that are springing up these days in non-Christian religious contexts seem radically different from anything we have seen before. The questions many are asking are, "Will these movements result in syncretistic or heretical faiths? Will they connect people to God through Christ, or will they keep people from eternal life?"

One way to foresee possible pitfalls in these movements is to look at similar movements in history. The first movements to Christ began inside well-developed religious contexts before the emergence of Christianity as a distinct religious system. The Jewish Jesus movement, called "the Way" (Acts 9:2; 19:9,23; 22:4; 24:22), grew inside the Jewish religious structure, and these believers continued to follow the extensive religious behavioral and dietary laws of their religious culture. The Greco-Roman Jesus movement, whose followers were called "Christians" (from the Greek word for the Messiah, "Christ"), spread within a religious context with a highly defined pantheon of gods (not unlike Hinduism) and respected tradition of philosophical literature.

Some believe the Apostle Thomas started a Jesus movement in India where the believers were called Nazraani Margam (*Nazraani* meant "Nazarenes" in Syriac, and *Margam* means "the Way" in Malayalam), which developed into what is called the Mar Thoma church today.

In the fourth century, the emperor Constantine's sponsorship accelerated the development of the Greco-Roman Jesus movement into a religious institution, complete with Greek and Roman cultural, religious, and political forms, such as icons, solar/lunar holy days, and the diocese structure. Other contemporary Jesus movements were either isolated from this process or chose to reject the political, ecclesiastical, theological, and creedal control of the developing papal Christianity.

These and many later movements show us the potential pitfalls associated with movements to Jesus that either are isolated from, or refuse to be associated with, the main forms of Christianity during their times.

Potential Pitfall #1: Inadequate discipleship or insufficient
access to Scripture can lead to syncretism.

Examples from history: The Greek movement to Jesus had the Old Testament in Greek, the Septuagint, and many believers were literate in the Greek language, a huge advantage when discipling with written text. However, the Greek believers, for many reasons, did not enter into the Jewish believers' religious stream or take advantage of well-developed Jewish training and synagogue structures. Paul's letters reveal the problems that faced the Greek believers as they tried to live out their faith in an entrenched

---

* Originally published in a slightly different form in *MF*, May–June 2011. Reprinted by permission.

pagan religious context. The New Testament books became the foundational discipling documents of the rapidly multiplying fellowships of the second century, and itinerant multiethnic apostolic teams helped to spread the message while empowering local elders and local believers whom the Lord was gifting as pastors, teachers, administrators, and so on.

Did this model prevent syncretism and heresy from happening? No. Some groups in the Greek Jesus movement were syncretistic, combining their faith with Greek philosophies that elevated asceticism and celibacy on the one hand or hedonism and promiscuity on the other. Other groups rejected all things Jewish, even the Old Testament. Yet other groups combined their faith with occult or mystery religions or Gnosticism. Even those groups that became the orthodox mainstream adopted Greek religious practices, such as the use of icons and philosophical disputation, elements that were not present in the simultaneous Jewish Jesus movement. As heresies arose in this movement, they were fought off by well-discipled Greek believers from inside the Jesus movement, not by Jewish believers, who were busy with other problems in their own movement. In this way, they maintained the integrity of the central message for three centuries in an environment with entrenched religious beliefs and hostile political forces.

What lessons can we learn from this? It is highly unlikely that movements can completely avoid syncretism, but correction can come when local apostles, leaders, and apologists extensively study the Word in their heart language.

But what about movements to Jesus in other religious contexts—those that had no effective and accurate Bible translation into their language, those that were illiterate, or those making their own translations without adequate linguistic, theological, and exegetical understanding? Such movements often came up with new or variant understandings, in some cases touching on important theological issues.

Examples from history: As the gospel expanded beyond the Greek-speaking world, having the Bible only in Greek became inadequate. Early translations into other languages were the Syriac/Aramaic translation of the Bible (Old Syriac and the Peshitta), Latin (Old Latin and the Vulgate), Armenian, Georgian, Nubian, Ethiopian, and Egyptian Coptic translations. These early translations were done by people fluent in the local language and culture, as well as Greek language and culture.

Because these cultures were significantly different from the contexts that the Greek New Testament was revealed in, theological differences arose almost immediately. Most problematic was different understandings from the Greek view concerning the nature of Christ, with the Armenian, Ethiopian, and Coptic believers concluding that Jesus had only a divine nature (the Monophysite position); and the Syrian-Nestorian believers concluding he had two natures, one human/noneternal and one divine/ eternal. This latter perspective led the Nestorians to conclude that Mary could not be the "mother of God" as the Greek councils insisted, but only the "mother of Christ," a position that led to them being dubbed heretics by the Roman church.

History shows that translating the Scripture into various languages inevitably ignites theological debates, no matter how carefully it is done, because words frequently do not have exact equivalents in other languages. So when a word or phrase, such as "Son of God," is translated in a word-for-word fashion, it can have significantly different connotations or meanings in different languages. Some translators try to add footnotes to words or insert phrases that help maintain the original meaning.

Some may conclude that it is safer not to translate Scripture and simply rely on the Greek or on existing translations. This choice can be even more problematic. When Islam arose, the communities that had the Bible in their own languages proved largely immune to its advance, and many of them continue to exist to this day. However, when the Nestorians had evangelized distant lands, they took the Syriac Bible with them, translating only bits and pieces, plus some liturgy and hymns, into local languages. By the time Islamic, Turkic, and Mongol invasions cut off communications with the Syrian churches, believers in these Persian, Turkish, or Mongol people groups were still worshiping in Syriac, which most did not understand. Likewise, native North African communities that only had the Bible in Greek or Latin, but no local translations, had a faith that was not deeply rooted and indigenous. During the Islamic conquests, people groups without the Bible in their own language eventually converted.

What lessons can we learn from this? It is crucial that all Jesus movements have an effective and accurate translation in their local language, which is ideally done by bilingual, bicultural people.

Potential Pitfall #2: Attachment to community customs and identity can
lead to syncretism and/or conflict with community leaders.

Believers in Jesus movements maintain their community identity and often continue to follow the same customs as their family. They are not like "secret believers," who have told neither friends nor family of their faith. Such secrecy does not lead to movements. Nevertheless, by continuing local customs, many of which are religious to some extent, these Jesus movement believers might revert to relying on legalistic or occult religious practices or local gods to help them, rather than maintaining trust in Jesus alone. In addition, it is possible that leaders in the community could object to these believers reinterpreting or partially fulfilling local customs, and eventually initiate persecution of them.

Examples from history: In any culture, believers are subject to syncretism to the extent that they continue to live by the worldview, not merely the religious practices, of those around them. However, throughout history, believers have managed to continue to participate in the celebrations or even religious practices of their culture while transforming their meanings.

For example, the believers in the early Jewish Jesus movement continued to follow the Jewish religious rites (Acts 21:20–24), to attend synagogues, and to meet in the temple, even though most of their fellow Jews were rejecting their message, which they were actively sharing in these contexts. They continued the practices while denying their sufficiency for salvation. The Greek believers, freed by the apostles from becoming Jews to follow Christ, did not defame the local Greek gods (Acts 19:37) and ate the local meat, some of which had been sacrificed to idols (Rom 14; 1 Cor 8; 10:25–33), maintaining relationships with their nonbelieving, pagan family and friends, while denying the power of idols to save. Both of these Jesus movements experienced periods of persecution but continued to grow for centuries, each reaching millions of believers.[1]

Neither Jesus movement celebrated Jesus' birthday. Christian writers in the early centuries (such as Origen and Arnobius) considered the celebration of the birthdays of famous people or gods a pagan practice. It was only when large numbers of pagans entered the newly official church in the fourth century that the annual pagan winter solstice festival, around December 25, was officially deemed a special day to commemorate Christ's birth (Christ Mass). John Chrysostom (c. 400) wrote that it was appropriate that Jesus' birth would be celebrated on the day of the Sun's rebirth, since he is the light of the world. It is likely that confusion existed for some time between the pagan religious meaning of the festival and the newly instituted celebration of the birth of Christ, because initially the majority of the

---

1   See Rodney Stark, *The Rise of Christianity: How the Obscure, Marginal Jesus Movement Became the Dominant Religious Force in the Western World in a Few Centuries* (Princeton, NJ: Princeton University Press, 1997).

population was still pagan. But paganism was eclipsed by the Christian faith, and Christmas was eventually stripped of its pagan meaning, even though the debauchery and gluttony of the pagan celebration have never been fully eradicated and the holiday has picked up other pagan elements from Germanic cultures. As a result, many Christian reform movements have banned Christmas for various lengths of time. Nevertheless, few today would argue that genuine believers cannot appropriately celebrate this Christian religious holiday that has no biblical basis. There are many other historical examples of the church continuing local religious and other practices while infusing new meaning into them, with the old meanings eventually disappearing.

It is important to understand that early Jesus movements were not adhering to and transforming their local traditions to avoid persecution but to continue in relationship with the lost of their communities. For example, if Jewish believers had started eating nonkosher foods, they would have had to leave their families and communities. Greek believers had to be able to eat meat sacrificed to idols to eat with nonbelieving family and friends. Nevertheless, these Jesus movements did suffer persecution from their own communities in spite of keeping most local customs. Many Jewish believers, like Stephen and James, were martyred by fellow Jews in spite of keeping the Law and other Jewish customs. Once proof of worship was instituted, Gentile followers of Jesus also faced persecution for refusing to worship the emperor. Jewish believers in Jesus, like other Jews, were exempt from this requirement. The Romans accepted Judaism as the religion of a distinct ethnic group, encompassing all Jewish sects. But followers of Jesus who were not ethnically Jewish or officially converts did not enjoy the Jewish exemption. So Paul notes in Galatians 6:12 that some Greek believers were being persuaded to convert to being Jewish believers in Christ to avoid persecution. Today, Jesus movements that stay inside their socioreligious contexts similarly experience waves of persecution, because their distinctive faith in Christ is undeniable. So believers may be tempted to leave their communities, and even move to other countries, to avoid persecution. But remaining in relationship with their communities can eventually lead to the kinds of movements we see in the early church.

What lessons can we learn from this? When believers use local cultural practices, even religious ones, but infuse them with new meanings, they are largely successful in continuing to spread the gospel in their communities, eventually bringing faith transformation to many. However, these believers are frequently persecuted by others from their local communities for the changes they are introducing.

Potential Pitfall #3: Believers can be pressured to act against their conscience.

When believers from different areas end up with different practices, they can find it difficult to accept each other. Furthermore, in today's world, with significant diasporas and easy travel, people from the same people group can come to Christ in different ways and develop a variety of expressions of their faith. John Travis tried to express some of this complexity in his C1–C6 scale describing the varieties of practice and identity that exist in Christ-centered communities from Muslim contexts.

The biggest problems arise when those expressing their faith in one form try to force or pressure other believers from similar backgrounds to conform to their own version of the faith. This pressure goes both ways: Sometimes those who have rejected all religious forms of their birth culture insist that all believers must do the same. On the other hand, we sometimes find that believers who express their faith through many of their birth religious forms, and maintain their birth identity, try to force all believers to do the same.

Examples from history: When Jesus movements in different areas maintain local practices, and these movements come into contact with believers from other backgrounds, their practices (such as forms of prayer and special holidays and feasts) can be unacceptable to each other. The historical record shows that each group tends to condemn the other group or try to get them to conform to their own practices. For example, in the third century, after the Greek movement to Christ had gained a large following, it began to condemn those who were in the Jewish movement to Christ, even though the original disciples had, like them, remained fully practicing Jews. In the seventh century, after two hundred years of isolation, the spreading, independent Celtic movement to Christ started by St. Patrick was forced by the Roman church to change the way they did their Masses, celebrated Easter, and cut their hair in order to be acceptable. Once the Latin Vulgate (common Latin) Bible gained favor over the original Greek in Rome, the pope tried to force all the Greek-speaking churches to switch to Latin services, eventually leading to a total break between the Roman Latin and Greek Orthodox churches. Likewise, the Mar Thoma believers in India survived many centuries using the Aramaic/Syriac hand-copied Scriptures, only to be condemned by the Portuguese Catholics arriving in 1500 because they refused to accept Romanization, which included switching to Latin, celibacy of priests, transubstantiation, prayer to Mary and to saints, use of icons, and other things the Mar Thoma church had never practiced. Thankfully, the idea that all believers must agree on external rites, language of worship, and holidays has been put to rest; however, believers still have the tendency to judge which religious forms are acceptable based on their own cultural expectations rather than the Bible.

Paul faced a situation where some Jewish followers of Jesus were putting intense pressure on Greek believers to leave their pagan socioreligious communities and join the kosher, circumcised, Law-keeping community of Jewish believers. Paul strongly condemned this practice.

But Paul also dealt with Greek believers who were continuing to eat meat in idol temples (1 Cor 7:10) and who were in conflict with other Greek believers who refused to eat meat that might even possibly have been sacrificed to an idol. This situation was a conflict between believers coming from the same religious and ethnic background. In 1 Corinthians 7 Paul defends both positions as valid, but makes clear that each believer should be careful to follow his or her own conscience, while taking into consideration the conscience of other believers. Paul says a believer should not force other believers to act against their conscience, nor behave in their presence in ways that wound their conscience.

What lessons can we learn from this? Believers should not force other believers to act contrary to the dictates of conscience, whether those believers are from other socioreligious contexts or whether they are from the same context. The New Testament makes clear what kind of moral and theological issues are not merely matters of conscience and individual conviction.

Potential Pitfall #4: Christian leaders can undermine Jesus movements, even unintentionally.

There are two main ways that leaders of institutional Christianity have historically undermined Jesus movements happening in other socioreligious contexts. The most common way is that they have become alarmed by what is happening, causing such an uproar that the governments in those areas ban the movements and any Scriptures they may have translated. The second way happens unintentionally, when movements to Jesus spring up in countries with significant antipathy toward self-identified "Christian" nations. If leaders in these Christian nations put pressure on rival governments to treat followers of Jesus in their territories kindly, implying "they belong to us" even when the Jesus movements are insisting they do not, persecution or massacres may follow.

Examples from history: There were mass movements to Jesus in northern Europe during the time of Constantine. However, their Arian theology was heretical, as they took the term "Son of God" so literally that they believed that Jesus Christ was a distinct god who was "begotten" or created by God before the creation of the world. Unfortunately, Christian leaders did not respond to these movements with concern, praying for northern Europeans, sending orthodox missionaries, and working to see that they had Scriptures they could read. Instead, under Contantine and later emperors, they convened church councils that condemned them and backed harsh measures, even military violence, against them. This pattern continued for hundreds of years in Europe, where those coming to Christ in mass movements (including many we would not consider heretical, such as Protestant groups) were lined up against certain church criteria and blacklisted or killed if they fell short.

This tragic pattern spread outside of Europe as well. Unfortunately, Christian leaders persuaded even nonbelieving rulers to stamp out Jesus movements. In Japan in the sixteenth century, hundreds of thousands of Japanese came to faith through the ministry of Francis Xavier and the Jesuits, who used the Japanese name for the Most High God in their outreach. When Dutch Protestants arrived, they protested so vehemently against such practices that the Japanese emperor banned all Jesus movements, and thousands were killed, dispossessed, or subjected to government torture until they recanted. The survivors of the movement, who became known as *Kakure Kirishitan*, "hidden Christians," chose to practice their faith secretly, using only Buddhist forms and having only oral Latin Scriptures. Over time they added their martyred saints to their objects of worship. To this day the Japanese are very wary of foreigners bringing the gospel. In China a similar Chinese movement to Christ emerged, which the pope opposed after a "Chinese Rites" controversy in the early eighteenth century, in which critics labeled their use of Chinese religious rites syncretistic. After the Papal Bull was issued, the Chinese emperor in turn sent out edicts banning the Christian faith in China. The spread of the gospel in China was stopped for over one hundred years. The Catholic Church reversed their decision on this in 1939 after a full investigation!

The second way of undermining movements was first modeled by the emperor Constantine, infamous for getting a Jesus movement massacred because he approved of it. Though Rome and Persia had been enemies for centuries, when Constantine decided to favor the followers of Christ who had been formerly persecuted by his government, he sent a polite letter to the rulers of Persia encouraging them to do the same. The Persian authorities feared that believers in Jesus would now become a "fifth column" favorable to Rome, especially if they came under the developing papal structure. So they began a massacre of Jesus followers in which over fifty thousand believers ultimately perished.

What is the lesson to be learned from this? Attempts to judge and control Jesus movements by Christian leaders residing in other cultures have, almost without exception, been ill informed and had disastrous consequences. This has often been the case whether leaders decided to condemn the movements or to express their approval and support. Conversely, independent Jesus movements that had the Bible in a language they could read and were left relatively alone by other church traditions (like the Ethiopian, Armenian, Mar Thoma, Celtic, etc.) fared much better and moved toward orthodox doctrine.[2]

---

2   The Armenian Apostolic movement gained momentum in AD 301, when the king of Armenia became a believer. These believers distanced themselves from the Greco-Roman church in 373, inventing their own alphabet and translating their own Bible within fifty years. By the fifth century other movements to Christ had arisen on the periphery of the Roman world: an Ethiopian movement was well established by 330, with its own translation

In Summary

The history of Jesus movements in various socioreligious contexts shows that syncretism and persecution are inevitable. Nonetheless, there are wise and foolish ways of responding. High-profile foreign leaders can bring harsh reprisals on believers in Jesus movements either by expressing condemnation of them or by expressing approval, thereby implying authority over or ownership of them. Those of us from other nations seeking to see these movements flourish can best assist them by making sure that locally effective translations of the Scripture are readily available and by praying for them. It is also important to avoid pressuring those coming to Christ to express their faith in ways acceptable to us, by forcing certain religious practices on them or forcing them either to stay in or to leave their communities against their conscience. There are many examples of large Jesus movements with Scripture in their heart language that have stayed on track with very little outside assistance.

Bibliography

Haddan, A. W., and W. Stubbs, eds. Vol. 1 of *Councils and Ecclesiastical Documents Relating to Great Britain and Ireland*. Oxford, UK: Clarendon, 1869. Available at https://archive.org/details/councilsecclesia01hadd.

Stark, Rodney. *The Rise of Christianity: How the Obscure, Marginal Jesus Movement Became the Dominant Religious Force in the Western World in a Few Centuries*. Princeton, NJ: Princeton University Press, 1996.

---

of the Bible by 500; the Persian church broke off from the West in 425, and by 430 the Nestorian church was moving into Arabia and Persia, reaching China by 635; a huge movement to Christ in northern European tribes was sparked by Arius (and condemned at the council of Nicaea for its inadequate Christology); the Celtic movement arose in isolation in Britain and Ireland, and it was written of them in the seventh century, "Britons are contrary to the whole world, enemies of Roman customs, not only in the Mass but also in regard to the tonsure [the haircuts of their monks, said to reflect Druid priestly haircuts]." See A. W. Haddan and W. Stubbs, eds., *Councils and Ecclesiastical Documents Relating to Great Britain and Ireland* (Oxford, UK: Clarendon, 1869), 1:112. Available at https://archive.org/details/councilsecclesia01hadd.

CHAPTER 57

Where We Agree . . . and Don't?*
Michael Roberts

Key Characteristics of Insider Movements

Believers within insider movements have a primary identity as followers of Christ, and a secondary identity with their birth culture.

Believers within insider movements remain within their birth culture, society, and community, but reject its spiritual aspects that are not consistent with the Bible.

Insider movements have the Bible as their final authority, not the Bible plus Christian traditions, creeds, councils, confessions, and doctrinal statements.

Believers in insider movements generally do not see the need for "conversion" from one religious system to another.[1]

Believers in insider movements are generally bold witnesses for Christ. This could go without saying, as movements do not result from "secret" believers.

In insider movements, those spreading the gospel are "inside" or "within" the context in which they are proclaiming Christ. For example, the Jewish followers of Christ were Jewish and thus were insiders in the Jewish culture. The phrase "insider movements" does not imply that there is another movement outside of it.

Areas of Agreement

Insider proponents and opponents generally agree on the following points:

The gospel involves transformation, change, dying to self, being born again by the Spirit, surrendering all to Christ, trusting him as Lord and Savior, repentance, acknowledging sin and rebellion, turning from idols and sin to holiness and God, putting off the old nature and its practices, and putting on the new nature in a new creation. If there is no transformation, there is no saving faith. Whatever else "remaining" means in 1 Corinthians 7, it does imply a spiritual and moral change.

Faith in Christ is the only way of salvation.

There must be a transfer of allegiance to Christ from everything else.

Anything that is demonic or clearly against the Bible must be renounced and rejected. For Muslims, this would include any views of Muhammad as a savior, mediator, or intercessor, view of the Qur'an as a final authority, and anything that is in contradiction to the Bible.

---

* Paper presented at the Bridging the Divide conference, Houghton College, Houghton, NY, June 20–24, 2011. Printed here by permission of the author.

1 See *UIM,* chap. 22.

Muslim followers of Christ should not be secretive in their faith, but rather identify with Christ and confess Christ as Lord. Persecution for the sake of Christ should not be avoided.

New believers from Muslim background should not go to the mosque for their fellowship or spiritual growth.

Christian-background workers among Muslims should not become Muslims.

Translation should be done from the original languages, not from another translation, such as English. Any changing of the meaning of the Greek/Hebrew/Aramaic words and phrases in translation is wrong, whatever the motivation.

The Islamic and qur'anic view of Christ, salvation, and redemption is sub-biblical and not salvific. Muslims who trust Christ as Lord and Savior must develop a biblical worldview in core beliefs and values.

Unity with the body of Christ is important for new believers from all backgrounds.

Areas of Disagreement

Proponents of insider movements generally also believe the following, some of which is disputed by opponents:

Christian traditions can make God's word void, just as Jewish traditions made the Old Testament void.[2]

Not everything in Islam is demonic, and "formal Islam" does not equal idolatry. When an issue is not directly addressed in the Bible, a believer is free to act according to his own conscience on the matter. He may follow his culture to the extent that it is compatible with the Bible.[3]

Islam is not the enemy, but rather Satan is the enemy.[4]

There are many different manifestations of Islam in different areas. Islam is not monolithic, and one localized view of Islam may not apply elsewhere. Furthermore, what is viewed as "formal Islam" may be irrelevant to local contexts.

1 Corinthians 7:17–24 is relevant to the Islamic context. First, 1 Corinthians is the only Epistle that has two different audiences: the Corinthian church, and everyone everywhere who calls on Jesus Christ as Lord.[5] Second, Paul's exhortation to remain in the state in which believers are called is repeated three times for three different aspects of life (sociodemographic, religious/cultural/communal, and

---

2   Mark 7:5–13. For a list of Christian traditions that are not based on the Bible, see Frank Viola and George Barna, *Pagan Christianity? Exploring the Roots of Our Church Practices* (Carol Stream, IL: BarnaBooks, 2008). Among the aspects of modern Christianity from non-Scriptural sources they mention in their book are church buildings, sacred places, steeples, pews, pulpits, and balconies; order of worship, Sunday morning worship, altar calls, individual salvation, the sinner's prayer, pre-tribulation theology, the sermon, and the processional; the priest, one pastor, clergy, and ordination; clerical robes, choir, choir robes, and dressing up for church; minister of music or worship team; tithing and clerical salaries; baptismal issues, "personal Savior," and a truncated Lord's Supper instead of a meal; Christian education, theologies, seminaries, ordination, Bible college, Sunday school, and youth pastors.

3   See Rom 14; 1 Cor 10.

4   See Eph 6:12.

5   1 Cor 1:2 .

socioeconomic).[6] This is in a context of more than twenty references to or implications of remaining.[7] And Paul further universalizes this when he states that this is his rule for all the churches.[8]

"Taking off the old"[9] does not mean that Muslims who trust Christ should cease to be part of their families, communities, cultures, and societies, but rather that their changed new life in Christ and their words should be a witness to their families, communities, cultures, and societies.

Jesus' statement that families will be divided over him[10] is not a command or a goal, but rather a prophecy about what happens in some families when only some of them put their trust in Jesus. The primary goal of a Muslim follower of Christ toward his family, society, community, and culture is to be a witness to it, not to leave it.

Not all persecution a believer receives is because of Christ. Some persecution is for dishonoring parents or culture, or for insensitivity.

The Holy Spirit in the heart of an "insider believer" in Christ as Savior and Lord, in interaction with the "insider believer's" conscience, is fully able to guide him in how he should relate to his culture/society/community/religion—what to keep and what to change or renounce,[11] and outsiders do not need to encourage him to change or leave communities. Indeed, outsiders have an imperfect view of the insider culture and should not make those decisions for them.

We believe that Christianity as it exists today is very different from what Jesus intended his church to be, and that imposing the name "Christian" and the "joining of Christianity" on Muslims who trust Christ are not New Testament mandates.[12] Adding those requirements to the gospel changes it to a different gospel.[13] The gospel is Jesus plus nothing—not plus circumcision, not plus denominations, not plus the title "Christian," not plus joining "Christianity," and not plus adopting Western theological formulations, creeds, confessions, catechisms, or doctrinal statements.

There is a difference between being ashamed of Christ and not using the title "Christian" to self-describe.

The gospel does not necessarily imply socioreligiocultural change.

"Insider believers" who have trusted in Christ and are following him as Lord and Savior are already part of the body of Christ, whether or not they retain their religious birth identity. Christian religious forms, traditions, and identity are not required for salvation.

There is a difference between (1) the church, the body and bride of Christ, consisting of all true believers in Christ in all times and locations, and (2) local institutional churches, most of which are mixed between regenerate believers and unregenerate unbelievers. Thus unity with the body of Christ does not necessarily mean unity with all institutions that call themselves "churches."

---

6   1 Cor 7:17,20,24.

7   1 Cor 7:8,10,11,12,13,17,18,18,20,21,23,24,26,27,27,32,34,37,38,39,40.

8   1 Cor 7:17.

9   Eph 4:22.

10   Matt 10:34–39.

11   John 14:26.

12   The expressions "Christianity" and "becoming a Christian" are not in the Bible, and the word "Christian" is only one of over two thousand phrases that the New Testament uses or implies to describe putting one's faith in Christ.

13   The book of Galatians, especially 1:6–10; 3:1–5,10; 5:1–12.

Any time there are two or more believers in Christ sharing the word of God, enlightened by the Spirit of God, there is church.[14]

The Bible is the final authority, not the Bible as interpreted by the various traditions, church history, confessions, catechisms, doctrinal statements, etc.

One can be a follower of Christ while living in a non-Christian socioreligious environment, just as one can live in a Christian socioreligious environment and not be a follower of Christ.

One can enter the kingdom of God without going through Christianity.

Insider movements are something God is doing in his sovereignty.

Jesus did not come to found a religion,[15] but a movement that would transcend all religions and cultures.

God in his sovereignty has allowed "redemptive analogies" in every culture, which he uses to prepare people for the gospel;[16] for example, a longing for the Messiah in Judaism, or stories about Jesus in the Qur'an.

The focus of the New Testament is "going to" the nations, not "being a light to" the nations.[17]

Bibliography

Bosch, David J. *Transforming Mission: Paradigm Shifts in Theology of Mission*. Maryknoll, NY: Orbis, 1991.

Petersen, Jim. *Church without Walls: Moving beyond Traditional Boundaries*. Colorado Springs, CO: NavPress, 1992.

Richardson, Don. *Peace Child*. Ventura, CA: Gospel Light, 1974.

Viola, Frank, and George Barna. *Pagan Christianity? Exploring the Roots of Our Church Practices*. Carol Stream, IL: BarnaBooks, 2008.

---

14 See Matt 18:20. See also Jim Petersen, *Church without Walls: Moving beyond Traditional Boundaries* (Colorado Springs, CO: NavPress, 1992).

15 David J. Bosch, *Transforming Mission: Paradigm Shifts in Theology of Mission* (Maryknoll, NY: Orbis, 1991), 50.

16 Acts 17:25–28. See Don Richardson, *Peace Child* (Ventura, CA: Gospel Light, 1974). Over two hundred "redemptive analogies" have been identified in the Qur'an.

17 Matt 28:19–20; Isa 49:6.

1. Based on John Travis' clarifications about the C1–C6 Spectrum (chap. 51), how have you seen it misunderstood or misapplied?

2. What strikes you from Brother Yusuf's account (chap. 52)? How are his insights into or view and definition of C5 helpful? What is your reaction to the way Brother Yusuf contrasts Muslim believers' "commitment to God" with many missionaries'/church people's "commitment to their institutions"?

3. How does Talman's chapter (53) challenge your understanding of prophethood? Which of the four identities of Muhammad do you consider most accurate and why? Is it possible for insiders to affirm Muhammad as some sort of prophet and still be fully faithful to Jesus? Why or why not?

4. Do you agree with Wheeler's conclusions about "Allah" (chap. 54)? Why or why not? What questions or concerns does he raise that you might want to explore further?

5. Compare issues of spiritual power and the demonic faced by believers in non-Christian religious communities with those faced by believers in culturally Christian contexts. Which of Anna Travis' ideas (chap. 55) best demonstrate that believers can live free, spiritually victorious lives inside a non-Christian religious context?

6. According to Lewis (chap. 56), what potential pitfalls do Jesus movements face? Learning from history, what preventative or prescriptive measures can be taken to avoid them? As you reflect on the shaping of the early Christ followers, how might Buddhists, Hindus, or Muslims who want to follow Christ take a similar path?

7. What new insights into the characteristics of insider movements does Michael Roberts (chap. 57) provide? What are your thoughts on the statement "Jesus did not come to found a religion, but a movement"?

PART 7
IDENTITY

Believing in God means accepting that something exists beyond knowl-edge. If you don't share this belief, why do you insist on calling yourself a Muslim?

Believing in God can also mean being at odds with him. I don't pray regularly, and I don't fast during Ramadan. In that sense, I'm not religious. But I perceive myself as a Muslim. It's my cultural community. For me, Islam is also my homeland and my language, and my Arabic can't be separated from all of that. You can distance yourself from Islam but remain within the heart of Islam.

—HAMED ABDEL-SAMAD, INTERVIEW WITH *DER SPIEGEL*[*]

The issue of identity is central to any discussion of insider or Jesus movements. Many questions arise—for instance, how do Jesus-following Muslims, Hindus, Jews, or others who have never left the religious community of their birth identify themselves? Do they have an internal spiritual identity and a different socioreligious or cultural identity? Can people truly believe that Jesus is Lord and Savior, and still see themselves as being part of their own Jewish, Hindu, or Muslim community? These and other, related questions are explored in the following chapters.

In chapter 58, Rebecca Lewis sees insider movements as expressions of God's covenant with Abraham. Their distinctive features—preexisting communities becoming the church, and membership being retained in their socioreligious community—are biblical. She points out that neither Jesus nor the early church required joining a new religion in order to enter the kingdom of God.

In chapter 59, Kevin Higgins defends the idea that a Jesus-following Muslim can maintain Muslim identity along with his or her identity as a "fully biblical disciple of Jesus." Furthermore, he shows how a biblical understanding of "church" opens the way for us to see members of insider movements as part of both the body of Christ and the local Muslim community.

In chapter 60, South Asian scholar Joshua Iyadurai views insider movements as indigenous expressions of the gospel without the accoutrements of Western Christianity. He identifies the

---

[*] "Political Scientist Hamed Abdel-Samad: 'Islam Is Like a Drug,'" *Spiegel Online*, September 17, 2010, http://www.spiegel.de/international/germany/political-scientist-hamed-abdel-samad-islam-is-like-a-drug-a-717589.html.

Enlightenment's influence on Western worldview and differences in cultural patterns as underlying causes of disagreement over IMs.

In chapter 61, Eric Adams describes how transformation of identity in insider movements occurs, using the three-tiered model of identity developed by Tim Green and Kathryn Kraft.

Jens Barnett researched how Muslim followers of Christ negotiate the various aspects of their identity. In chapter 62, he explains how past paradigms have blinded us to what is actually happening in the identity crisis of new believers. As a result, he calls for the development of new models.

In chapter 63, John and Anna Travis present factors in the Muslim world that may influence Muslim-background believers, their families, or their communities toward various identities found along the C-spectrum, such as "Christian," "follower of Isa," "Muslim follower of Jesus," or underground believer.

In chapter 64, Richard Jameson observes some cultural factors that contribute to contrasting positions and dispositions in the IM controversy; he then exhorts us to recognize the role of divine creativity in bringing Muslims to Christ in diverse ways. This applies equally to those from other faith communities.

CHAPTER 58

Insider Movements

*Honoring God-given Identity and Community**

Rebecca Lewis

All movements to Christ are amazing works of God! But not all movements are the same. How is an "insider movement" different from other movements to Christ?

Three distinct types of movements to Christ among unreached peoples have been described in the last century: "insider movements," "people movements," and "church-planting movements." None of these types of movements began as a "new creative missiology" or outreach technique. Many movements to Christ have happened throughout history. However, recently three types of movements were analyzed and described by those watching them happen and wondering if they were biblical. The most controversial of these types of Jesus movements has been recently called "insider movements."

Insider movements can be defined as movements to obedient faith in Christ that remain integrated with or inside their natural community. In any insider movement there are two distinct elements: (1) The gospel takes root within preexisting communities or social networks, which become the main expression of "church" in that context. Believers are not gathered from diverse social networks to create a "church." New parallel social structures are not invented or introduced. (2) Believers retain their identity as members of their socioreligious community while living under the lordship of Jesus Christ and the authority of the Bible.[1]

In contrast, people movements—identified by J. Waskom Pickett, then analyzed by Donald Mc-Gavran[2]—are mass movements in which whole communities decide as a group to leave their former religious affiliation in order to become Christians. People movements, like insider movements, keep the community intact, but unlike insider movements, the community's religious affiliation and identity are changed.

Believers in the third type of movements, church-planting movements (CPMs), as described by David Garrison, also "make a clean break with their former religion and redefine themselves with a distinctly Christian identity."[3] CPMs promote movements by simplifying church structure and empowering local leaders, but they do not require either of the two key elements of insider movements.[4]

---

* Originally published in a slightly different form in *IJFM* 26, no. 1 (2009): 16–19. Reprinted by permission.

1 See Rebecca Lewis, "Promoting Movements to Christ within Natural Communities," *IJFM* 24, no. 2 (2007): 75.

2 See Pickett, *Christian Mass Movements in India: A Study with Recommendations* (New York: Abingdon, 1933); and McGavran, *The Bridges of God* (New York: Friendship Press, 1955).

3 Garrison, "Church Planting Movements vs. Insider Movements: Missiological Realities vs. Mythological Speculations," *IJFM* 21, no. 4 (2004): 154.

4 Garrison points out that using family networks to spread the gospel is a *common*, but not *universal*, factor in CPMs. See Garrison, *Church Planting Movements* (Richmond, VA: Office of Overseas Operations, International Mission Board of the Southern Baptist Convention, 2000), 37–38. Note, however, that in CPMs, the formation of *new structures* is assumed.

Usually CPMs consist of newly created fellowships with a clear Christian identity, which tends to associate them with Western Christianity.

In all three types of movements, those coming to Christ share a new spiritual identity as members of the kingdom of God and disciples of Jesus Christ. But in the case of insider movements alone, this new spiritual identity is not being combined with a change of sociopolitical-religious identity. But is it legitimate biblically for people to come to genuine faith in Christ, gaining a new spiritual identity, yet retain their birth identity and community?

God's Covenant with the Peoples of the Earth

God made an irrevocable covenant with Abraham that is the golden thread of the gospel that runs through Scripture. "He said to Abraham, 'Through your offspring all peoples on earth will be blessed'" (Acts 3:25). As they come to faith, the believers among the peoples of the earth become joint heirs with us of this covenant (Gal 3:5–14): "He [Christ] redeemed us in order that the blessing given to Abraham might come to the Gentiles [non-Jewish people groups] through Christ Jesus, so that by faith we might receive the promise of the Spirit" (v. 14). No one can change or set aside this covenant, which promised, "If you belong to Christ, then you are Abraham's seed, and heirs according to the promise" (Gal 3:29). The book of Revelation confirms that every tribe, tongue, and people will be represented in the kingdom of God.

The Scripture seems to indicate that God determined in advance which tribe, people, or community, and therefore birth identity, a person is born into, and where those communities will live in time and location. For example, Paul declares to the Athenians that God "made all the nations . . . and marked out their appointed times in history and the boundaries of their lands" (Acts 17:26). Paul is not proclaiming that God therefore endorses how these nations are living or what they are believing. The Greek culture was full of infanticide, slavery, idolatry, and sexual immorality. Paul is merely stating the fact that God has established these families, and has already planned to fulfill his purposes in all people groups everywhere. Paul goes on to say, "God did this so that they would seek him and perhaps reach out for him and find him, though he is not far from any one of us. 'For in him we live and move and have our being.' As some of your own poets have said, 'We are his offspring'" (vv. 27,28).

The point Paul is making to the Athenians in this passage is that he is not preaching about some foreign god who belongs to a different place and people group—a common understanding at that time. Instead Paul affirms that the god of which he speaks is the God who has created and established them as a people group, and has helped them before, and now is seeking to reach out to them. He is saying, in essence, "The creator God of the whole world has always been your God, here with you. You have in fact been worshiping him without knowing him" (cf. v. 23). Paul was not trying to single out individual Greeks to pull into a community of Jewish believers, so he did not want them to conclude he was merely talking about a Jewish god. Paul was seeking to give them a vision of what God's plan was for all of them, their whole people group. It seems that Paul believed that God had sent him to Athens to announce his plan of salvation for the Greek people, just as when he preached the gospel to the Jews he announced the fulfillment of God's plan of salvation for the Jews.

Like Paul, we can encourage those becoming believers to catch God's vision and plan for their whole people group. If indeed God has a plan for them and their people, like the Jewish believers, the Samaritan believers, and the Greek believers, then they can remain in their families and networks and retain their birth identities, honoring the relationships in which God has put them. Staying inside their communities is not honoring or condoning their culture or religious practices, but honoring God's plan to bring his blessing and transforming power to their extended families and people group as he promised, like yeast in the dough.

Let us examine more closely the two distinctive elements that can be seen in insider movements, as well as their biblical basis.

Preexisting Communities Become the Church

How can the gospel take root within preexisting communities in such a way that the community or network becomes the main expression of "church" in that context? To understand how "the church" is often being expressed in insider movements, in various socioreligious communities, let's contrast "planting" a church with "implanting" a church.[5]

Typically, when people seek to "plant a church," they try to create a new social group. Individual believers, often strangers to one another, are gathered together into new fellowship groups. Church planters try to help these individual believers become like a family or a community. This pattern of "aggregate church" planting (also termed the "attractional model")[6] works in individualistic Western societies. However, in societies with tight-knit communities, the community is undermined when believers are taken out of their families into new authority structures. The affected families frequently perceive the new group as having "stolen" their relatives, and the spread of the gospel is understandably opposed. Even if the new fellowship group is very contextualized to the culture, the community feels threatened and the believers feel torn between their family and the group.[7]

By contrast, a church is "implanted" when the gospel takes root within a preexisting community and, like yeast, spreads within that community. No longer does a new group try to become like a family; instead the God-given family or social group, having come to faith in Christ, becomes the family-based church in that local situation. The strong relational bonds already exist; what is new is their commitment to Jesus Christ. Believers within the preexisting family or community network learn how to study the Word and to provide spiritual fellowship for each other, and testimonies and praise arise within their everyday gatherings and interactions (as in Deut 6:6–9).

This type of church (also termed the "transformational model")[8] was birthed in many households in Acts, such as those of Cornelius, Lydia, and the Philippian jailer. The redemption of preexisting communities is a valid fulfillment of God's covenant with Abraham that all the families of the earth would be blessed (Gen 12:3; 28:14). When the gospel is implanted in this manner, the families and clans that God created are redeemed and transformed instead of broken apart. The larger community and society are also blessed in significant ways as believers mature spiritually while remaining within their relational networks. The gospel is less likely to be seen as a threat to the community, and often the gospel flows into neighboring relational networks.

---

5   In both cases, the assumption is being made that "a church" is not a building, institution, or meeting, but a functional local community of mutually supportive believers under the lordship of Jesus Christ.

6   See Andrea Gray and Leith Gray, "Paradigms and Praxis: Part I: Social Networks and Fruitfulness in Church Planting," *IJFM* 26, no. 1 (2009): 20.

7   Some people equate C5 churches with insider movements. However, not all C5 communities result in insider movements. For an insider movement to occur, C5 believers must remain genuine members of their family and community networks, not creating odd or competing religious institutions or events.

8   See Gray and Gray, "Paradigms and Praxis," 20.

Insider movements may arise if the believers maintain a bold witness to their faith within their community, but often persecution arises as well, clearly seen in both the Jewish and Roman contexts in the New Testament. Believers in insider movements, just like those that leave their families or communities to join aggregate churches, are part of the global church, the body of Christ, through their spiritual rebirth. However, because insider believers remain in their families and networks, honoring

"Identity Studies," a Complex Minefield*

Making sense of identity is notoriously difficult, as *different disciplines define identity in different ways.* While psychologists typically use such terms as "the inner self," anthropologists (along with some sociologists) treat identity as a collective label marking out different groups. Social psychologists bridge these opposed notions by analyzing "identity negotiation" between individuals and groups. In the vast literature on identity there is no universally agreed-upon definition, even before taking theological perspectives into account!

A second cause of complexity is that *identities are shifting and fragmenting* under the impact of globalization. As "waves of social transformation crash across virtually the whole of the earth's surface,"[†] old certainties disintegrate. Travel and the internet expose people to new worldviews; migration and intermarriage create new hybrid identities; pluralizing societies challenge assumed alliances of faith, ethnicity, and nationality. Minarets which once dominated the skylines of Muslim cities now compete with forests of TV aerials and satellite dishes. "The days of closed, homogeneous, unchanging societies are rapidly going and they will not come back," comments Jean-Marie Gaudeul.[‡]

As identities themselves evolve, *understandings of identity follow suit*—a third cause of complexity. In Western thought, the "Enlightenment definition" of identity was followed by the "sociological definition" and now the "postmodern definition," which delights in "a bewildering, fleeting multiplicity of possible identities."[§] Meanwhile, collectivist understandings of identity ("We are, therefore I am") remain important, especially in non-Western societies.

For the above reasons and others, the field of "identity studies" resembles a minefield. Should we, daunted, simply forgo the attempt to pick our way through it? Should we erect a warning sign: "Abandon Hope All Ye Who Enter Here"? I believe not, for this minefield is also a goldmine to those who persevere, yielding treasures of insight on identity issues facing Christ's followers from Muslim background.

—Tim Green

---

[*] Excerpt from Tim Green, "Conversion in the Light of Identity Theories," in *Longing for Community: Church, Ummah, or Somewhere in Between?*, ed. David Greenlee (Pasadena, CA: William Carey Library, 2013), 41–51, with minor revisions. Reprinted by permission.

[†] Anthony Giddens, *The Consequences of Modernity* (Stanford: Stanford University Press, 1990), 5–6, quoted in Stuart Hall, "The Question of Cultural Identity," in *Modernity and Its Futures*, ed. Stuart Hall, David Held, and Tony McGrew (Cambridge, UK: Polity Press, 1992), 275–316.

[‡] *Called from Islam to Christ: Why Muslims Become Christians* (Crowborough, UK: Monarch, 1999), 225–26.

[§] Stuart Hall, "The Question of Cultural Identity," in Hall, *Modernity and Its Futures*, 275–316. Michel Foucault has strongly influenced postmodern notions of identity.

God-given community, the gospel has now spread the promised blessing of God to yet another family, tribe, or people group.

Believers Retain Their Socioreligious Identity

In many countries today, it is almost impossible for a new follower of Christ to remain in vital relationship with their community without also retaining their socioreligious identity. In these places, the term "Christian" does not mean "a sincere believer in Jesus Christ." In India, for example, "Christian" has become a socioreligious-political category (like Muslim, Hindu, Tribal, etc.) written on one's identity card at birth. Though the categories may vary, similar practices exist in other countries as well. Changing one's identity from "Muslim" or "Hindu" to "Christian" is often illegal or is viewed as betrayal by one's family and friends. However, the gospel can still spread freely in such places when insider believers gain a new spiritual identity, living under the lordship of Jesus Christ and the authority of the Bible, but retain their socioreligious identity.

Retaining Identity: Is It Biblical?

Does one have to go through Christianity to enter God's family? The New Testament addresses a nearly identical question: "Do all believers in Jesus Christ have to go through Judaism in order to enter God's family?" It is important to realize that, for both questions, the nature of the gospel itself is at stake.

The woman at the well in John 4 at first refused Jesus' offer of eternal life because, as a Samaritan, she followed an Abrahamic religion that the Jews reviled as corrupt. As a result, she could not go to the temple or become a Jew. But Jesus distinguished true faith from religious affiliation, saying God was seeking "true worshipers [who] worship the Father in the Spirit and in truth" (vv. 19–24). Realizing that Jesus was "the Savior of the world" (v. 42), not just of the Jews, many Samaritans in her town believed. Later in Acts we see that Samaritan believers remained in their own communities and retained their Samaritan identity (Acts 8:14–17). But at first the disciples did not understand that, just as they could remain Jews and follow Jesus, the Samaritans could also remain Samaritan.

Then the Holy Spirit revealed to the apostles that even the Gentile believers from pagan backgrounds did not have to go through Judaism in order to enter God's family (Acts 15). In Antioch, Jewish believers were telling Gentile believers they must become Jews to be fully acceptable to God. Paul disagreed and brought the issue to the lead apostles in Jerusalem. The issue was hotly debated, because the Jews had believed for centuries that conversion to the Jewish religion was required to become part of the people of God. But the Holy Spirit showed the Jewish apostles that they should not "burden" Gentile followers of Christ with their religious traditions and forms (Acts 15:19,28).

Two Criteria

To make this decision, the apostles used two criteria: the giving of the Holy Spirit to the Gentiles coming to Christ, and the guidance of Scripture (Acts 15:5–19). First, they heard that the Holy Spirit had descended on believers from a pagan background who were not practicing the Jewish religion. Second, they realized the Scriptures had predicted that this would happen. These two criteria were sufficient for the apostles to conclude that God was behind this new movement of believers who were remaining Gentile. Therefore they did not oppose it or add on demands for religious conversion. If we use the same two criteria today, insider movements affirm that people do not even have to go through the religion of Christianity, but only through Jesus Christ, to enter God's family.

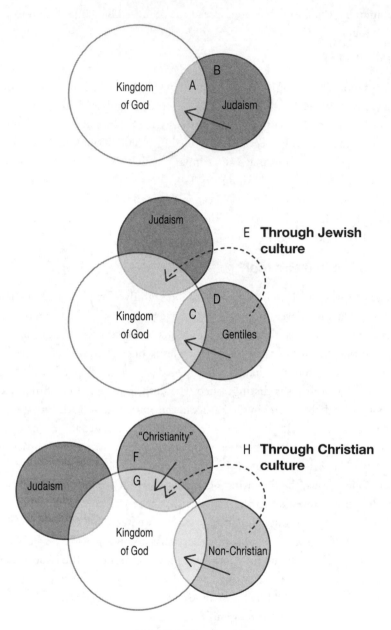

Fig. 58.1 Kingdom circles

Paul wanted people to understand that this truth had been part of the gospel from the beginning. He pointed out that God promised Abraham that all people groups would receive the Spirit through faith in Jesus Christ alone (Gal 3:8–26). As a result, Paul publicly rebuked Peter and Barnabas for "not act-ing in line with the truth of the gospel" when they "force[d] Gentiles to follow Jewish customs" (Gal 2:11–21). Paul warned that to add religious conversion to following Christ would nullify the gospel. He also affirmed that not through any religion but "through the gospel the Gentiles are heirs together . . . in the promise in Christ Jesus" (Eph 3:6).

Thus the gospel reveals that a person can gain a new spiritual identity without leaving his or her birth identity, and without taking on a new socioreligious label or going through the religion of either Judaism or Christianity. The "kingdom circles" (see fig. 58.1) illustrate this issue. Because believers retain their birth identity, insider movements honor God-given identity.

A New Creation in an Old Environment

Paul saw the faults of both the Greek and the Jewish social systems (Rom 1–3), yet he admonished both groups to remain in their own cultures, emphasizing that God had the power, and had planned, to save through Jesus Christ, in both contexts. There is no doubt that some cultures and religions are more blindly evil than others, whether we speak of cannibalistic tribes, state-sponsored terrorism, or Americans globally marketing tobacco and pornography, as well as promoting the violent killing of infants in their mother's womb. It is difficult to be identified with birth communities perpetrating evil and simultaneously have a primary spiritual identity in Christ, but we all are identified with both believing as well as nonbelieving communities, whether we like it or not. All believers everywhere must continually oppose the evil in their own personal life, as well as in their family, culture, religion, and state.

History has shown that all movements to Christ are equally prone to syncretism, whether they remain inside their own culture or adopt a foreign culture. Believers determined to study God's word and obey it eventually become less syncretistic. No culture or religion is good enough to save anyone without Christ's atonement and the work of the Holy Spirit; conversely, no culture or religion is so evil that God cannot work in the hearts of many who continue to identify with and live among their people group. As Paul said, "What counts is the new creation" (Gal 6:15).

So what do we do when working in unreached people groups with strong community structures? Perhaps it would help to recognize that the Muslims are like our Samaritans, with their Abrahamic religion, and the Hindus are like our Gentiles, with their idols and temples. Yet, like the Samaritans and the Gentiles, through the gospel alone they can be made heirs together with us in the promise of Christ Jesus. So how can we encourage the gospel to take root within their God-given communities, redeeming and transforming them? Here are some suggestions:

1. When entering a community, ask God to lead you to a person seeking God or desiring to learn God's word who wants to invite you into their family or community to talk about Jesus. Invest in those people as a group. "Do not move around from house to house" (Luke 10:7).[9]

2. When witnessing, always make clear that God has both planned and promised blessing for their family and people group from the beginning of time—the blessing of forgiveness, freedom from sin, and a restored relationship with himself.

3. Many have been taught that Jesus is only the Savior of the "Christians" instead of the Savior of the world. Help them understand that this idea is not true, like Jesus did in John 4:23. You may need to explicitly explain to some people that they do not have to join a "Christian people group" in order to be saved, pointing them to a relationship with God through Christ.

4. If well-meaning Christians tell seekers that they must come to God not just through Christ but also through joining institutional Christianity, help the Christians understand this requirement is

---

9   Frequently in insider movements, an individual will believe first and then invite the "outsider" witness into their community, as happened in John 4. Sometimes, however, the insider believer will spread the gospel through their networks by themselves, and the outsider will never enter their communities.

"not . . . in line with the truth of the gospel" (Acts 10; 15; 1 Cor 7:17–19; Gal 2:14–21; 3:6–9,14; 5:6; 6:12–16; Eph 3:6; Col 2:16–23).

5. When discipling, encourage believers to remain within their God-given communities, loving and honoring their families, even if they face persecution as a result. Show them that Jesus said they will be like "yeast in the dough" or "a light that illumines the whole household." Help them win their family and friends so they can fellowship with others within their own preexisting communities instead of isolating themselves by joining a group outside their community for fellowship. Avoiding extracting people from their birth communities is not merely a matter of expediency, but a matter of faithfully planting the gospel like yeast into the dough of a nonbelieving community, so the covenantal blessing of Abraham can be passed on to another people group.

6. Encourage believers to study the Word together within their communities and to seek guidance from the Holy Spirit (John 16:14; Acts 20:32). Trust the Holy Spirit, as the apostles did, to guide the new believers and to redeem their pagan or heretical religious practices as he chooses, which may vary from one insider movement to another.

Let the nations be glad that they too have direct access to God through Jesus Christ! This is the power of the gospel!

Bibliography

Garrison, David. *Church Planting Movements*. Richmond, VA: Office of Overseas Operations, International Mission Board of the Southern Baptist Convention, 2000.

———. "Church Planting Movements vs. Insider Movements." *International Journal of Frontier Missions* 21, no. 4 (2004): 151–54.

Gray, Andrea, and Leith Gray. "Paradigms and Praxis: Part I: Social Networks and Fruitfulness in Church Planting." *International Journal of Frontier Missiology* 26, no. 1 (2009): 19–28.

Lewis, Rebecca. "Promoting Movements to Christ within Natural Communities." *International Journal of Frontier Missiology* 24, no. 2 (2007): 75–76.

McGavran, Donald. *The Bridges of God*. New York: Friendship Press, 1955.

Pickett, J. Waskom. *Christian Mass Movements in India: A Study with Recommendations*. New York: Abingdon, 1933.

CHAPTER 59

Dual Identity and the Church in the Book of Acts[*]

Kevin Higgins

I am privileged to have been involved in a number of discussions with colleagues who are concerned about insider movements. One issue is the question of having a new identity as a follower of Jesus and the relationship of this new identity to the "church." Below we will see that one can maintain a dual identity and be a fully biblical disciple of Jesus; being a member of the church does not require a denial of one's other identities but is actually lived out within them.

We see in Acts that "the church" emerged very early within the religious expressions of the people of Israel, and that the members of "the church" continued to attend temple and synagogue, as well as meeting in homes and in public places such as the temple courts for gatherings designed apparently for believers in Jesus.[1] In fact, many denominational traditions look back to Pentecost as the "birthday" of the church.

Also, the separation of Jewish followers of the Messiah (the Way) from the temple and synagogue was not simply a decision based on the awareness that the rest of the Jewish population was not accepting the Messiah. The rise of active persecution, excommunication, and the introduction into the synagogue liturgy of curses apparently aimed at followers of Jesus were the precipitating factors.[2]

Up to that point, it can be argued from the New Testament that the church was a movement within the social and religious life of the Jewish people. This movement took structural or formal expression as it met in separate homes or public gatherings and as its members continued in the temple and synagogue. They did not cease to be the church in the temple worship, and they did not cease to be Jewish in the home meeting. There was a dual identity.[3]

I would like to clarify here that I do not intend to suggest that this dual identity was anything like what some people might mean when they accuse another person of living a double life. I do not mean to

---

[*] Excerpt from Kevin Higgins, "Identity, Integrity and Insider Movements: A Brief Paper Inspired by Timothy C. Tennent's Critique of C-5 Thinking," *IJFM* 23, no. 3 (2006):117–23. Reprinted by permission.

1   See Acts 3:1 and also 9:2, where Paul clearly expects that in Damascus he will find followers of "the Way" in the synagogues. This is why he seeks letters to recommend him to the synagogue leaders. Later (in Acts 21:17–24), Jewish leaders (who follow Jesus as Messiah) express their concerns about the large numbers of Jewish believers who have heard that Paul no longer keeps the Law. So they urge Paul to make a public expression of his Jewishness.

2   See the discussion of this development in Rodney A. Whitacre, *John, IVP New Testament Commentary* (Downers Grove, IL: IVP Academic, 1999), 244. Whitacre concludes that the separation from the synagogues took place in the second half of the first century—that is, about one generation following many of the events of Acts.

3   Returning for a moment to Acts 21, it is worth noting that James clearly is aware of and affirms the fact that there are two Jesus movements. One was a Jewish identity Jesus movement and one was a Gentile identity Jesus movement. Using my terminology, both movements maintained a dual identity.

communicate the idea that these two identities (Jewish and follower of Jesus) were somehow unrelated or did not overlap. The two identities are more like two circles that overlap to a great degree (though not fully).

One simple example may be helpful. Shortly after Pentecost, Peter himself is said to have gone to the temple at the hour of prayer (Acts 3). The temple leadership was part of the machinery that had crucified Peter's Messiah and Lord. There were severe theological differences between Peter and the temple leadership. However, the early Jesus movement maintained a dual identity even in the face of those theological differences.[4]

I am suggesting here that the biblical definition of "church" does not necessarily refer to a "bounded" or "closed" set social grouping that prevents a member of his body, the church, from also being a "member" of another social or even religious structure or expression. However, a clarification is needed lest I be misunderstood. On one side, I do see church as a closed set, for only those who are born from above and incorporated by the Spirit into his body are members of the church! But as such, they are not thereby excluded from living in and among other social and religious structures as yeast in the dough.

Let me offer a brief outline of my understanding of church. I will highlight points I see as pertinent to the question of insider movements.

1. *The church is the body of Christ and the assembly of believers who have been saved by grace through faith.* The church is therefore a creation of God in Christ through the Holy Spirit. It is not a human organization or institution, although clearly forms and structures do factor in as tangible ways in which this community expresses itself visibly. No human being can "make" a church or join the church except by being born again by the Spirit. Every believer is a member of the church and, as such, is called to live out his or her membership in the body of Christ, the church, as a full-time lifestyle in every venue of life.

Key Point: Being a member of the church is not simply a question of leaving one social structure and joining another. Not attending mosque and attending a gathering of believers does not equate with being a disciple. And on the other side, one's identity as a born-again member of the body can and does overlap with one's identity in other spheres of life, including one's religious life.

2. *Every local church body is an expression of the universal church body. And every time believers meet together, they are an expression of the body.* Of course, not every gathering of believers contains all of the elements of all that the Scriptures teach regarding "church." The primary marks of a mature expression of the church include these functions from Acts 2:42–47: the church exists where there is apostolic teaching, fellowship, breaking bread (both as real meals, and the Lord's Supper), prayer/worship, the miraculous work of the Holy Spirit, radical generosity in community life, intentional gathering together (publicly in the "temple," and as believers house to house), and the ongoing addition of new believers.[5]

---

4   The point of this line of argument is, I hope, clear. I fully agree that Judaism is a different case in many ways than Islam. However, the fact is that at a very practical level, the early Jewish followers of Jesus faced much the same situation as do Muslim followers of Jesus today. Some who object to IMs do so in part on the basis of the fact that new believers will not receive true teaching if they attend the mosque, and will in fact hear things in direct opposition to the gospel. This is certainly true, but it was also true in the temple and the synagogues of the first century AD, and yet the early movement did not stop attending solely for that reason.

5   It may be worth noting here that the "church growth movement" has helped to contribute to a particular misunderstanding of the references to meeting in the temple courts, especially in Acts 2. This may cause us to miss some of the importance of this passage for our discussion here. The tendency in church growth–related works has been to see Acts 2:42–47 as a model of the cell and celebration (small group and large worship gathering) gather-

The Necessity of Dual Belonging*

When I became a Christian at the age of seventeen, I had to stop reading my past religious texts. . . . However, after years of studying and teaching Buddhism, and further reflection on my own conversion to Christ, I have come to realize that one cannot completely suppress past identities and belief systems. Instead, one stage of wholesome growth in Christian discipleship requires a return, retrieval and reintegration of those appropriate elements from one's socioreligious past. I suggest that this fresh reintegration provides both deep-level transformation and a more holistic development of what usually has been a very compartmentalized faith. . . . For authentic Asian Christian theology to fully mature, dual belonging is not an option, but rather a necessary evangelical imperative for those from Asian religious traditions.

—Kang-San Tan

* Excerpt from Kang-San Tan, "Dual Belonging: A Missiological Critique and Appreciation from an Asian Evangelical Perspective," in *Mission Studies* 27 no. 1 (2010): 23–25.

Key Point: Saying "yes" to insider movements does not require a "no" to church, although IM proponents have been portrayed as saying so.[6] Some form of community of believers will need to take shape in an insider movement. However, the forms and degrees of maturity of such a church will vary. Acts 2 portrays the early members of the church being church in separate gatherings for believers, and in the religious life of the temple (where the official leadership was opposed to the gospel). I would call this a dual identity.

3. *We can see in Acts 14:21–28 that a mature church is also marked by having elders in each local congregation, duly selected and appointed by recognized apostolic leadership.* Further, in 1 Corinthians 11–14 we see that a mature church is marked by regular celebration of the Lord's Supper and the use of all the gifts of the Holy Spirit, exercised under the leadership of the Holy Spirit for the edification of the body. Some specific churches are farther along or not as far along in the process of fully expressing the nature of the church.

Key Point: The functions in my third point clearly require some form of gathering and a process of developing leadership. While Scripture gives examples of how and when churches gathered, it also reveals a variety of forms, times, places, and models (polities) of leadership. None of this precludes an

---

ings in a church. A case can be made for that position, but it misses the fact that the temple was more than a public gathering place for the believers. It was that, but it is also significant that they met as believers in the courts of this specifically religious place, even though the "religion" as practiced and believed then was not in agreement with or even friendly to the gospel as taught and believed by the apostles.

6 Tennent suggests that IM thinking would lead one to assume that it is possible to say yes to Jesus but no to the church. See Timothy C. Tennent, "Followers of Jesus (Isa) in Islamic Mosques: A Closer Examination of C-5 'High Spectrum' Contextualization," *IJFM* 23, no. 3 (2006): 101–15. Many disagree with Tennent's assumptions. Travis in his seminal piece clearly states that C1 through C6 describes varying expressions of *ekklesia*, church, or in his preferred term, "Christ-centered communities." See Travis, "The C1 to C6 Spectrum: A Practical Tool for Defining Six Types of 'Christ-centered Communities' ('C') Found in the Muslim Context," *EMQ* 34, no. 4 (1998): 407–8; see also his restatement of this in "Contextualization among Muslims, Hindus and Buddhists: A Focus on 'Insider Movements,'" *MF*, September–October 2005, 12. I have also argued for a definition of insider movements that clearly includes intentional Jesus-centered community among believers; see *UIM*, chap. 25. The crux of this discussion concerns one's understanding and usage of the word "church."

ongoing social identity as a Muslim (or Hindu, Buddhist, Jew, etc.). There are movements in Islam today, for instance, that function outside of the official structures and develop their own forms of leadership and membership, whose members have a dual identity.

4. *The church's ultimate purpose is to participate in, and be the first fruits of, the transformation of the universe under the headship of Jesus Christ.* The church's primary "strategy" to fulfill its purpose is to multiply itself through functions such as those listed in Acts 14:21–28: evangelizing the lost, discipling those who believe, strengthening/encouraging the disciples, selecting and training and appointing elders in every church, and connecting with and participating with other churches in the ongoing expansion of the gospel.

Key Point: I have intentionally left traditional language in place, but those same biblical functions can take place as an insider movement, albeit with altered forms and vocabulary.

What I have advocated here is movements to Jesus in which disciples are added to the church by the Holy Spirit as they are born again, living out that membership in forms of life that are fully biblical but culturally shaped, and doing so without denying their identity as Muslims (or Hindus, Buddhists, Jews, etc.) within their society.

Bibliography

Tennent, Timothy C. "Followers of Jesus (Isa) in Islamic Mosques: A Closer Examination of C-5 'High Spectrum' Contextualization." *International Journal of Frontier Missions* 23, no. 3 (2006): 101–15.

Travis, "The C1 to C6 Spectrum: A Practical Tool for Defining Six Types of 'Christ-centered Communities' ('C') Found in the Muslim Context." *EMQ* 34, no. 4 (1998): 407–8.

———. "Contextualization among Muslims, Hindus and Buddhists: A Focus on 'Insider Movements.'" *Mission Frontiers,* September–October 2005.

Whitacre, Rodney A. *John.* IVP New Testament Commentary. Downers Grove, IL: IVP Academic, 1999.

CHAPTER 60

Consuming Peanuts in the USA and India

*Reflecting on the Controversy over Insider Movements**

Joshua Iyadurai

Recently I traveled from Minneapolis to Los Angeles on my way back from a conference dealing with insider movements. The hostess offered me a choice of snacks: cookies or peanuts. I chose peanuts that were packaged in an attractive red wrapper that stated, "Lightly Salted Peanuts." The other side contained the following details of ingredients and nutrition facts:

	Amount/Serving	%DV*	Amount/Serving	%DV*
Serving Size 1 Pack (12g)	Total Fat 6g	10%	Total Carb. 2g	1%
Servings 1	Sat. Fat 1g	5%	Dietary Fiber 1g	5%
Calories 70	Trans Fat 0g		Sugar 1g	
Calories from fat 60	Cholest. 0g	0%	Protein 3g	
	Sodium 40mg	2%		
	Vitamin A 0% Vitamin C 0% Calcium 0% Iron 2%			

Percent Daily Values (DV) are based on a 2,000 calorie diet
Ingredients: Peanuts roasted in peanut and/or canola oil, salt

I enjoyed the peanuts, but there were so few that they didn't seem significant enough to have all the information mentioned above.

This triggered my thoughts back to India, where peanuts are sold not only in attractive packets, but also on roadsides wrapped in newspapers. In some places, the peanuts are fried in front of us and served in a piece of paper.

Peanuts sold in the USA and in India have the same nutritional values, but how they are sold and consumed is different. In the USA, buyers need to know everything about the product before buying. Companies must provide all the details before it comes to retail. But in India, the information about the product is not required when sold on the roadside, in buses, or on trains. The similarity is that in both places people eat peanuts while traveling!

But the consumer culture is different in these two countries. In the USA, although many people might not look at the ingredients and nutrition facts, the producer is careful to provide all the information for legal reasons. In India, most people are not bothered about the details of peanuts. Some might be comfortable buying from any shop on the roadside; some might buy from a grocery store; some prefer to buy only from supermarkets. It depends upon their taste and family practices.

---

*   Originally published in a slightly different form in *EMQ* 49, no. 4 (2013): 454–59. Reprinted by permission.

The essence of consuming peanuts lies in the nutrition and the pleasure one derives by eating them. How it is wrapped is immaterial for people in India, but it is important for people in North America.

Similarly, the essence of the gospel lies in its effects on the person and the community that receives the gospel. How the gospel is wrapped is a matter of choice in a cultural context. I see IMs as indigenous expressions which do not require all the paraphernalia attached to Western Christianity.

Western Consumer Mission Paradigm

When someone from the USA visits India and sees how peanuts are sold and consumed, there are two types of response. One is to join the locals and enjoy the fun. The other is to be disgusted and complain. It is legitimate for a visitor to say, "It is unclean, unhygienic, and unhealthy; the wrapper does not contain any information about the content," etc. But people in India are accustomed to these practices. It is not a matter of what is right or wrong. Instead, we must ask, "What is suitable for an individual? What is suitable in a culture?"

When the gospel is presented in the Muslim world, converts[1] appropriate it in a way suitable in their context. They adopt a particular way of following Jesus and have experienced Jesus personally, which has enabled them to see their lives and world differently. The essence of the gospel is the personal experience of Jesus, and the effect of the gospel is the transformation of individuals and communities.

To some extent, Western mission efforts are conditioned by Western consumer culture, which would like to market the gospel in the same way products are sold. The gospel can come with a brand: Baptist, Presbyterian, Methodist, Episcopal, Pentecostal, etc. Each brand has its own emphasis on a certain aspect of the gospel, similar to the ingredients in a product. Baptists are concerned about what kind of baptism those in IMs are given. Episcopalians may ask, "Did they take baptism?" Methodists might be keen to know whether those in IMs follow Holiness tradition. Pentecostals might be interested in knowing whether they speak in tongues. Others might ask, "Are they Trinitarian? Do they see Jesus as the Son of God? What do they call God?"

These factors are important for converts in following Jesus; however, the Western consumer mission paradigm would like to see everything made clear on the wrapper when it is presented. This paradigm likes to offload our systematic theology in the name of gospel presentation.

This paradigm perceives the gospel as a product to be sold in the religious market. Hence labels, brand names, sales techniques, etc., take center stage. But the gospel is not a product; it is a person—Jesus. When we introduce one person to another, we do not read out his or her resume or hand over a bio; instead, we share the person's name and a few other things about him or her. We expect the two individuals to interact, and in the process they come to know each other.

Converts in IMs are introduced to Jesus and begin a journey of knowing him. But the Western consumer mission paradigm would like to see the converts describe everything about Jesus instantly. This is similar to asking me to state clearly and accurately everything recorded on the peanut wrapper. I was interested in eating the peanuts, not memorizing the nutrients. It is also irrelevant to ask converts about the nuances of theological terms. The mission is not about presenting theological terms, categories, and terminologies accurately, but introducing the person of Jesus.

---

1   Dr. Iyadurai uses the term "convert" throughout this chapter in the sense of one who spiritually turns to Christ, not necessarily with a formal change of religion.—Ed.

Modern Western Paradigm of Mission

The West is greatly conditioned by the European Enlightenment paradigm of reality. Although we claim to live in a postmodern world, I find many evangelicals holding the fort for modernity. Some exalt reason and consider any emotional experience related to Christianity anathema.

Reason vs. Experience

Modernity projected that reason was supreme and knowledge was possible only through reason. By this it shut the door on revelation and experiential knowledge. However, there are other ways of knowing truth—through emotion and intuition. The world is historical, relational, and personal. It does not exist independently, "out there," to be explored by an individual objectively. The individual is not independent of the knowable; there is no autonomy of the knower. Knowledge is historically and culturally conditioned. Knowledge is a product of culture. This is very much in line with the biblical understanding of "knowing": it is more of an experiential knowledge than an objective discovery.

The modern Western paradigm of mission is concerned with presenting the gospel rationally, which would appeal to the intellect. This paradigm is more concerned about how we accurately, logically, and convincingly argue the gospel. But the gospel is not a set of abstract concepts; it is not systematic theology. The gospel is the person Jesus Christ. Knowledge of God is primarily derived from the personal experience of Jesus and revelation in Scripture. Therefore the mission is to invite people to experience Jesus Christ.

Jesus invited people to follow him—not to simply adopt his teachings, but to walk with him. It was an invitation to experience him. When Andrew and another disciple were curious to know about Jesus, Jesus invited them to "come and see." Jesus' conversation with Nicodemus was again an invitation to experience the new birth, which cannot be rationally understood. The mistake of Nicodemus was that he was trying to rationalize what Jesus was talking about.

Mission is not about building a great enterprise of Christianity; it is about inviting people to experience Jesus. Experiential knowledge of Jesus is the starting point, which includes a rational dimension. Experiential knowledge is a lifelong process. Converts begin their journey of faith when they accept Jesus as Lord and Savior. It's a long road on which the Spirit of God, not the missionary, is the constant companion.

Fixed Identity vs. Multiple Identities

Modernity elevated the self to the ideal and talked of the autonomous self as capable of being good and as an independent and sovereign entity. Individualism was the product of modernity, and the individual was elevated above the community. It held the view that individuals were capable of discovering the truth objectively, by their own efforts, through rational investigation.

The modern Western mission paradigm is being carried away by individualism in some aspects and is focused on reaching individuals with a rational gospel. Great emphasis is laid on individuals making a rational choice of accepting the gospel. This paradigm presents the gospel as valid beliefs, while portraying the beliefs and practices of Islam as irrational. The outcome of this emphasis is discontinuity; it burns bridges with communities, cultural practices, and social identities.

In line with postmodernity, indigenous communities regard the self as a creation of cultural, social, political, and historical realities. The self has no existence without these realities. The self itself is plural, it is relational, and one changes according to the situation or the external realities.

If individuals are products of a community, then when they receive the gospel, we need to be sensitive to their roots in the community. The focus of mission is to be the community rather than uprooting the individual. Therefore the emphasis should not be on discontinuity, but on the spiritual identity of the individual. While they are excited about their spiritual identity as followers of Jesus, converts from other religions prefer to keep their social/religious identity as Hindus or Muslims.

Let me share an example. Janaki was the wife of a businessman and was not allowed to attend church or any other Christian activities for nearly thirty years. Externally, she fulfilled all the Hindu religious requirements as a wife, while internally she followed Jesus. Eventually the whole family received the gospel, and she felt vindicated in her stand of retaining her social/religious identity as a Hindu for such a long period. This is true of many other converts from Hinduism and Islam in India.

When we look at how Jesus went about doing the mission of God, it is clear that he did not want the Samaritan woman to become a follower of Judaism in order to follow him. He did not expect the centurion to become a follower of Judaism to heal his servant. Jesus did not expect the Canaanite woman to become a follower of Judaism to heal her daughter; rather, he exalted her as a model of faith to the Jews. In the book of Acts, Cornelius was not asked to become a follower of Judaism, but Peter was asked to have a paradigm shift with regard to his understanding of purity and pollution.

Mission in and to Islamic Societies

Mission in and to Islamic societies needs a paradigm shift in order to let the people define their spiritual identity based upon their experience of Jesus within their own communities. It is the mission of God, in which God is at work above what we could imagine. Instead of holding on to the Enlightenment paradigm of mission, the church needs to move hand in hand with God, who is active in communities.

Identity is an issue in this context. Some might ask how converts could call themselves Muslims and Christians, since it is a deception. Here again, modernity sees reality in categories—for example, the First World, Second World, and Third World. In line with this, the modern Western paradigm of mission would like to fix *people* into categories. We understand from social scientists that identity, whether personal or social, is not fixed. Personal identity changes in different life situations, and social identity changes in different social contexts.

Better integration of multiple identities leads to well-being and smooth sailing in social functions. Integrated identities draw elements even from conflicting social groups to present a multifaceted self to negotiate conflicting contexts. If this is how individuals determine social behaviors based upon their multiple identities in different social contexts, then we find converts do the same in their social contexts.

Social psychologists claim that people creatively adapt traditional identities to new situations. This is true in the case of converts in India. Although the boundaries between Christianity, Hinduism, and Islam are clearly marked, converts redraw the boundaries so that they can cross them by creating multiple identities. Converts articulate that they continue the religious practices of Hinduism/Islam for social reasons, not for spiritual purposes. They offer new meanings to the same practices they have been following.

When the boundaries are loosely marked, it is easier to move from one identity to another. Maintaining uniformity and cohesiveness is very important for membership in a social group. When the family invites them to go to temple or mosque, the convert goes with them and activates the identity of Hindu or Muslim. However, converts try to maintain their new identity as followers of Jesus by injecting new meaning into the practice—they go there and pray to Jesus.

Converts adopt another strategy to redraw the boundaries of religions by differentiating between religious and spiritual identity. They see their conversion experience as a religious experience of Jesus, and Christianity as the institutional form of religion. In this way, they deploy their religious identity as Hindus or Muslims while claiming to have a spiritual identity as followers of Jesus by virtue of their personal experience of Jesus.

The converts' management of multiple identities is not a deception, but a display of humanness. We all manage our multiple identities according to different contexts. Even Jesus managed his multiple identities. Being the Son of God, did he ever declare that he was the Son of God? Rather, we find that he intentionally hid his identity. In a hostile social context, his aim was to embrace the Cross at the right time rather than exposing his identity and being stoned to death prematurely.

If those in IMs are accused of deception, then on the same scale Jesus is to be accused of deception. The modern Western mission paradigm likes to see everything in fixed categories. For modernity, reality is either/or; for indigenous paradigms, reality is a spectrum.

In the end, the contentious issue here is not theological, but instead is a conflict of paradigms between Western consumer/modern paradigms and indigenous cultural paradigms. May we let the indigenous societies enjoy the peanuts in the way they relish them.

CHAPTER 61

Heart Allegiance and Negotiated Identity*

Eric Adams

Abdullah decided to follow Jesus as Lord. His wife, father, mother, neighbors, and friends were angry with him and treated him as an apostate, threatening to kill him if he continued in this way. Under extreme pressure he fled to a European country to find freedom to live as a Christian.

We've all heard similar stories. And for the average Western Christian, the ending to this one represents a reasonable solution to a tense situation. What's more, we value what we view as the bottom line: a believer has been given freedom to worship Jesus. Yet associated with this sequence of events are some tragic, often overlooked, consequences:

- The new believer is now perceived as a traitor, having betrayed his faith and people.
- He has been ripped out of his network of family and friends, essentially committing cultural and social suicide in order to follow Jesus.
- The best, most culturally informed witness to Jesus has been removed from that Muslim community.
- The wrong messages are being reinforced—namely, that becoming a Christian means joining a foreign culture (government) or that foreigners are luring the community's loved ones from the true *ummah* (Muslim community of faith).
- Sadder still, while the foreign church receiving this believer is delighted to have a "Muslim convert" (and will perhaps even give him the opportunity to share his testimony repeatedly), the "convert" will rarely find wholehearted acceptance in that church. More likely, he will experience the same suspicion and mistrust on the part of the Christian community as Paul did after his conversion on the Damascus road.

Many believers go through this *extraction experience* for the sake of their new faith. A few make a successful transition and establish a new life in a new culture with a new identity. Unfortunately, many more suffer the loss of family, cultural identity, and community, an experience that sometimes leaves deep psychological wounds.

Is extraction the only option for new believers from a Muslim culture? Are there ways for new believers to integrate their identity in Christ within their cultural and family identities, even in Muslim societies?

---

* Originally published in a slightly different form in *IFJM* 30, no. 1 (2013): 21–25. Reprinted by permission.

A Three-tier Model of Identity

There are models that convince me that extraction does not have to be the only option, and is even unnecessary in many cases. I have seen believers from Muslim backgrounds remain within their communities and retain their cultural identities while giving vibrant testimony to their newfound faith in Jesus to those around them.

I recently came across a framework that defines the issues that Muslims struggle with as they come to faith in Christ. This three-tier model of identity is based on the parallel research of Tim Green and Kathryn Kraft.[1] I will give a synopsis of this model and describe some ways that I have observed it being lived out.

According to Green and Kraft, each person's identity can be viewed on three levels: core, social, and collective.

Core Identity: This includes a person's heart-level beliefs, values, and worldview, all of which give meaning and direction to life. Put another way, it encompasses a person's "heart allegiances," where she seeks her worth, where she puts her trust, where she spends her time and resources. These can include family, career, status, or wealth; or on a darker side, addictions or other "idols" she serves.

Social Identity: This includes the many roles lived out within the various social circles to which a person belongs. He is a husband, a son, an uncle; he is a soldier, accountant, teacher, carpenter, pilot, student, etc. Each person also fills or is known by informal roles in his community: elder, gossip, good neighbor, confidant, volunteer, delinquent, etc.

Collective Identity: This encompasses the labels given by groups with whom the person is associated. Commonly the person does not have an option not to bear the label. For example, one might be Asian, White, British, Muslim, Pashtun, or from a certain class or segment of society, etc. One can be born into such labels, or receive them at different stages in life, but once received they do not usually change quickly over the course of a lifetime. For example, a Korean born in America who maintains strong ties to a Korean community, or prefers a Korean lifestyle, can be perceived and labelled as Korean all their life despite their American citizenship.

What insights does this model give us for understanding the choices Muslims have when they choose to follow Jesus as Lord?

I recently attended an event that featured a diverse, multinational panel of people who were all born into a Muslim family and had chosen to follow Jesus. To a person, all of them had shifted their core identity to that of someone who follows Jesus as Lord. They shared how the change in heart allegiance compelled them to seek changes in their social and collective identities. Their stories differed greatly. Some had made tragic choices, while others had successfully negotiated these transitions.

It has become increasingly common for Muslims to be drawn to the Jesus of the Bible, often through a combination of power encounters, truth encounters,[2] and knowing a Christian who lives out the teachings of Jesus in a compelling way.[3] These experiences often precipitate a crisis of convic-

---

1   See Tim Green, "Conversion in the Light of Identity Theories," in *Longing for Community: Church,* Ummah, *or Something in Between?,* ed. David Greenlee (Pasadena, CA: William Carey Library, 2013), 41–51; and Kathryn Kraft, presentation at the Bridging the Divide conference, Houghton College, Houghton, NY, June 17–19, 2012.

2   See Charles H. Kraft, "Contextualization in Three Crucial Dimensions," chap. 7 in *Appropriate Christianity* (Pasadena, CA: William Carey Library, 2005).

3   J. Dudley Woodberry, Russell G. Shubin, and G. Marks, "Why Muslims Follow Jesus: The Results of a Recent Survey of Converts from Islam," *CT,* October 2007.

tion through which such Muslims shift their core allegiance to Jesus and begin to follow him as Lord. Sometimes this is a quick process; other times it takes years to develop the courage and resolve to act on this deep core identity shift.

New believers commonly change their convictions at a core identity level to be consistent with their faith in Jesus, while their social and collective identities remain the same. As a result, they experience great psychological and relational dissonance. This dissonance pushes them to search for resolution.

One option is to hide their new allegiance from friends, family, and community. However, failure to acknowledge this shift in core identity usually causes deep internal crisis. This inner turmoil can lead some to deny Jesus and turn away from him, choosing instead to "become Muslim" again.

Another option for those seeking resolution is to reject their social and collective identities. When they remain at home this rejection may manifest itself in various ways. They may call themselves a "Christian," indicating that their allegiance is with a community other than that of their family or close friends. They may stop taking part in community activities (religious or cultural) or start new behaviors (how they worship or dress or eat). Naturally, their family and friends will be confused or concerned for them. Regarded as "infidels," they will suffer social ostracism and persecution.

Others who reject their social and collective identities may choose to flee to a community that allows them to maintain their new core identity. This results in the extraction profile illustrated in the story at the beginning of this article. While such a choice can result in deep psychological scarring due to the losses involved, some are able to make a home in this new identity and culture. As noted above, many find this choice too traumatic and decide to return to their former culture, renounce their faith, and become Muslim again. A few are even able to mature in their new faith in a foreign culture, gain a vision to reach their own people, and then return to their home country to attempt to rebuild bridges to family and friends, while continuing in their faith and identity in Jesus.

Today there is a renewed interest in exploring options for new believers to integrate a core identity of allegiance to Jesus within their existing social and collective identities. What follow are just a few illustrative case studies of how individuals have successfully communicated their new conviction of faith within their existing relational networks.

Negotiating Identity: Some Examples

Let us consider a few true stories (with names changed due to security concerns) of some difficult but ultimately more satisfying journeys.

A Common Pilgrimage

Foreign Christians living in a Muslim community meet Muslims who want to know more about Jesus. Rather than work with these seekers individually, in isolation from their natural networks of family and friendships, the foreigners ask them to draw in their family and friends who might also be interested in knowing about Jesus so they can explore who Jesus is together. Gospel truths are discussed and processed within these natural relational networks, and they begin to transform this subset of the community. As the members of this network decide to submit to Jesus and enter the kingdom of God together, they maintain their preexisting trust relationships. Even as they have been on their journey toward faith in Jesus, they have already begun to function as a community and to develop a new sense of identity on several levels.[4]

---

4   Leith Gray and Andrea Gray, "Paradigms and Praxis: Part I: Social Networks and Fruitfulness in Church Planting," *IJFM* 26, no. 1 (2013): 19–28.

In this example, seekers share their exploratory journey towards Jesus together and process their reactions to the claims and person of Jesus as a community. When, as a group, they decide to shift allegiance to Jesus, their relationships and community are retained, but their social identity with each other changes. With trust relationships intact, they follow Jesus together and function, in essence, as an *oikos*, or house church. Many nonbelieving friends and family eventually accept them as "followers of Jesus" (largely because of the witness of their lives) and do not reject them as infidels. From the strength of community and demonstration of redeemed relationships among themselves, they attract others from the surrounding Muslim society to also follow Jesus.

When a new believer is encouraged to live out his changed heart within his network of family and friends, the transformation process, while it may seem slow, can be long lasting and its impact profound, as in the next account.

Salt and Light

Rauf, after learning about Jesus and developing a desire to follow him, became friends with several belonging to an Isai Jamaat (fellowship of Jesus' people). The new friends asked him to not seek to leave town, but to return to his family and be "salt and light" to them in order to demonstrate his transformed heart and win them too to faith in Jesus. This he did faithfully. By God's grace, after a few years, first his brother, then his sister, and then his parents also embraced Jesus. They chose to all be baptized at one time, and would meet with other believing families and friendship groups nearby. This community of networked families is able to withstand persecution and even thrive in the midst of it. In fact, their perseverance has become a significant witness to the surrounding Muslim community.[5]

In this example (in which foreigners played no part), the new believer was encouraged to communicate with family his new allegiance to Jesus through serving them, not through aggressive apologetics. Although he was tempted to flee his situation, he continued within his relational networks and found many opportunities to demonstrate Christ-like living through forgiving, serving, and becoming a better husband/son/brother. By serving them he both gained a hearing and negotiated a new social identity. Over time networked families and friendship groups of Jesus followers become more and more visible in a culture. The surrounding society recognizes the distinctives of this subgroup and often labels them as something different from a "normal" Muslim (e.g., those "Isa [Jesus] followers," as in Acts 11:26). Even with this label they are often allowed to coexist within the larger Muslim community because they have retained a local cultural identity, are known and accepted, and often are even respected as moral and godly people.

Faith in the Fire

Often severe persecution acts as a pressure cooker, forcing the believer to come to terms with identity issues, as in the following account.

Aisha told her family of her growing interest in and subsequent trust in Jesus. Her sister also wanted to believe, but her teenage son, during a bout of rebelliousness, reported his own mother to the authorities. Although he thought they would just scold and release her, she was thrown into prison, tortured, beaten, and pressured over many months to recant her faith. She later reported, "God was right beside me, giving me comfort and strength, even when I thought I might die from how they were treating me." She emerged with her faith deepened, conscious that she had not been alone in the midst of the suffering. Back at home, she now receives grudging

---

5   This case study is from personal communication.

respect from her neighbors, who know that she still believes despite the government's claim that the region remains "100 percent Muslim." With this small margin of tolerance, she and her now-believing husband continue to grow spiritually, experiencing God's continuing help despite the lack of fellowship. They delight in explaining their faith to their neighbors and friends using passages from both the Qur'an and the Bible.[6]

In this example the believer had to endure intense persecution, yet God's presence and help in the midst of that suffering validated her faith. This resiliency to harassment and torment that came from the experience of God being with her through her ordeal was a profound witness to her husband and others. The respect she earned not only allowed her to gain a new level of social acceptance within society, but also to continue her witness to draw others into the kingdom.

Defending the Hope Within

A few years ago Hassan, a middle-aged leader in his Asian community, was imprisoned for apostasy after a jealous co-worker (eager to disrupt a development project for personal gain) reported him to police as being a follower of Jesus. After months of imprisonment he was brought before a panel of Islamic leaders. He defended his allegiance to Jesus using verses from the Qur'an and the Bible in a way that demonstrated that he still valued his community—and that true Muslims should follow Jesus. At the end of his defense, the leaders concluded, "If you follow Jesus in this way, it is acceptable." They asked him to write up his defense to pass around to other Muslim leaders.[7]

In this example the new believer, following months in prison, defended his new faith with apologetic reasoning. Through his defense the religious leaders could understand that he had not rejected his cultural identity by following Jesus. They saw that he was no longer just a Muslim culturally, but even exhibited characteristics of godliness to which they aspired. They recognized his choice to follow Jesus as permissible within the bounds of their interpretation of religion. Their acceptance of his decision in turn allowed him the space to negotiate an acceptable social identity within his family and community, thus paving the way for others to believe in the same way.

Collective Identity

In these examples and many others that could be cited, the collective identity ("Muslim" label) remains in place by default. In societies where being "Muslim" is defined more by one's identification with a cultural way of life (by virtue of being a citizen of that society) than by a strict and narrow theological (e.g., Islamist) narrative, many committed new followers of Jesus have established a new social identity acceptable to their local Muslim community and remain vibrant witnesses of their newfound allegiance to Jesus. Judgment is often suspended as to whether they are still "Muslim" (in the sense of still belonging to the society), while their transformed lives earn them a hearing.

Many believers who find themselves in this position greatly prefer this sequence of events. They believe that if they are given the label "Christian," usually perceived as a negative, even political, label in Muslim societies, they will forfeit the freedom to share widely the hope within them, and their testimony will be marginalized or rejected outright.[8]

---

6   Based on description by Mohit Gupta, "Servants in the Crucible: Findings from a Global Study on Persecution and the Implications for Sending Agencies and Sending Churches" (unpublished manuscript, 2013).

7   A case study from personal experience.

8   This case study is from personal communication.

However, because the identity of these groups is distinctive—their allegiance to Jesus forces a divergence away from a traditional Muslim identity, just as Paul's allegiance to Jesus caused him to increasingly move away from a traditional Jewish identity—over time they are often given new labels by the Muslim community, such as "followers of Jesus."

Within the "pale of Islam" exists a mystical group, the Sufis, who practice an Islam of a very different kind. While many strict orthodox Muslims regard them as heretics, most Muslims accept Sufis as members of the Muslim community because of this group's values and deeply held spiritual beliefs. Jesus followers who continue to retain a collective "Muslim" identity of some kind may, like the Sufis, one day be able to maintain a cultural position within the pale of Islam, even as their new *collective identity* is tied to the person of Jesus.

Developing a Stable Collective Identity

Research based on surveys, discussions, and interviews from a 2007 consultation on fruitful practices for work among Muslims has discerned an interesting pattern.[9] has discerned an interesting pattern. In places where hostility to the gospel and persecution of believers is most intense, believers choose to gather as small house churches of four to thirty members. Even as they establish a social identity with like-minded followers of Jesus, they stay small in number to avoid much of the attention of those who would persecute them.

However, as these small house groups begin to multiply and network together, they gain both strength in numbers and a more pronounced identity as a community. Once they reach a critical mass where they are too large to ignore or intimidate by persecution, they take on a more visible corporate presence, negotiating a new collective identity within society.

This collective identity is forged in part by their efforts to be salt and light at the community level, doing good in the society around them and demonstrating that they are exemplary citizens, fathers, mothers, children, and families. They use community events such as weddings, festivals, and funerals as opportunities for witness. They challenge unjust laws in the courts and press for the rights of the oppressed. In several countries new believers have sparked debates as to whether their traditional cultural identity requires that a citizen be Muslim.

In short, these emerging faith communities are negotiating new labels as necessary for their collective identity within their societies, resulting in increasing acceptance and roles of influence within these societies.

A Biblical Pattern

We can observe a similar pattern in the New Testament book of Acts. The early church was small, caught between the Jewish and Roman cultures. Because they were fully committed to Jesus as Lord they found that they could no longer fully identify with either culture. A small group of Jesus' followers and disciples saw the power of this wholehearted allegiance to draw family, friends, and eventually many thousands into their community. As these diverse communities banded together, they began to be recognized as a distinct group, and were labelled "the Way" or derided as "little Christs," or *Christians*. These fellowships of faith became established in the Roman Empire, and, through their obedience of

---

9   See Travis and Woodberry in *UIM*, chap. 4; Eric and Laura Adams, "The Gathering of Reproducing Fellowships," in *From Seed to Fruit: Global Trends, Fruitful Practices, and Emerging Issues among Muslims*, 2nd ed., ed. J. Dudley Woodberry (Pasadena, CA: William Carey Library, 2011), 115–28.

faith, God used them to take the gospel to other cultures, repeating this pattern over and over again throughout redemptive history until this day.

After his conversion on the Damascus road, the Apostle Paul, former zealous persecutor of the followers of Jesus in his day, was shunned and mistrusted by the small community of Christians; in fact, we lose sight of Paul for fourteen years. While Paul was living in Tarsus, Barnabas was used by the Holy Spirit to seek him out and draw him into active work—taking the gospel to the Gentiles. Because of Barnabas (the "son of encouragement"), the world was changed.

Similarly, we need to be like Barnabas in behalf of those in the Muslim world whose heart allegiance belongs to Jesus. We need to understand how to help these believers negotiate their new allegiance within their social and collective identities in healthy, effective ways. If we can learn to support them to do this successfully—not prescribing or directing how they should do this, but empowering them through the Word and by our trust that God can reveal the wise path to them—God can work through them to transform their cultures and societies, and the world will again be changed.

Bibliography

Adams, Eric, and Laura Adams. "The Gathering of Reproducing Fellowships." In *From Seed to Fruit: Global Trends, Fruitful Practices, and Emerging Issues among Muslims*, 2nd ed., edited by J. Dudley Woodberry (Pasadena, CA: William Carey Library, 2011), 115–28.

Gray, Leith, and Andrea Gray. "Paradigms and Praxis: Part I: Social Networks and Fruitfulness in Church Planting." *International Journal of Frontier Missiology* 26, no. 1 (2013): 19–28.

Green, Tim. "Conversion in the Light of Identity Theories." In *Longing for Community: Church, Ummah, or Somewhere in Between?*, edited by David Greenlee (Pasadena, CA: William Carey Library, 2013), 41–51.

Gupta, Mohit. "Servants in the Crucible: Findings from a Global Study on Persecution and the Implications for Sending Agencies and Sending Churches." Unpublished manuscript, 2013.

Kraft, Charles H. "Contextualization in Three Crucial Dimensions." Chap. 7 in *Appropriate Christianity*. Pasadena, CA: William Carey Library, 2005.

Woodberry, J. Dudley, Russell G. Shubin, and G. Marks. "Why Muslims Follow Jesus: The Results of a Recent Survey of Converts from Islam." *Christianity Today*, October 2007.

CHAPTER 62

Searching for Models of Individual Identity

Jens Barnett

As John Travis has reemphasized in this volume,[1] the C-spectrum was developed to help describe different types of Christ-centered *community* found in Muslim societies. That is, it was originally intended to model *group identity*—the socioreligious "label" and cultural symbols claimed by a *group* of believers as they attempt to negotiate space for themselves within society.[2] Another aspect of group identity, also commonly depicted using the C-spectrum, is how a Christ-centered community is perceived by the society surrounding it—"from the outside in," so to speak.[3]

Although the C-spectrum was intended to model group identity, this has not stopped people (including myself!) from wrongly attempting to apply it to individuals at times. In fact, it is quite common to read articles in which the writer applies the C-spectrum to all three of these aspects above, blurring the concepts by appearing to treat them as one and the same thing.[4]

The issue here is that identity is multidimensional, or "layered." Of course, these layers *are* intimately related to each other, and so it is natural—perhaps even helpful at times—to observe an individual believer's behavior and draw conclusions as to where they might "fit" on the C-spectrum. The problem is, though, that Travis' model was never intended to be applied to more than the "group" dimension. Attempting to apply a one-dimensional continuum to multiple aspects of identity can blur our thinking, and perhaps even blind us to more complex phenomena taking place within individual believers' lives.[5]

How many dimensions does religious identity have then? Timothy Tennent tells us, "There are, of course, two sides to the question of identity. There is how *others* (in this case, Muslims) identify you and then there is your own *self*-identity."[6] I would like to suggest, however, that there are several more

---

1   See chap. 51.

2   See Travis' original article, "The C1 to C6 Spectrum: A Practical Tool for Defining Six Types of 'Christ-centered Communities' ('C') Found in the Muslim Context," *EMQ* (October 1998): 407–8.

3   Joshua Massey's chart helpfully depicts both these aspects; see Massey, "God's Amazing Diversity in Drawing Muslims to Christ," *IJFM* 17, no. 1 (2000): 7.

4   See, for example, Phil Parshall, "Lifting the Fatwa," *EMQ* 40, no. 3 (2004): 288–93, where he applies C-spectrum terminology to individual identity—"So, do we have C1, C2, C3, C4, C5 or an amalgam of all five?" (289–90); group identity—"A highly respected evangelical Islamist checked out a large C5 movement" (293); and even missionaries—"I practice C5" (288)!

5   Using a one-dimensional spectrum to plot both a group's claimed and perceived identities can be problematic even, since these two dimensions may not always coincide with each other. The Ahmadiyya sect in Pakistan is a good example of this: they claim to be Muslims and yet are perceived to be infidels. As insider movements take on prophetic roles within society, or grow large enough to affect power balances, claimed and perceived identity may need to be plotted separately.

6   Timothy C. Tennent, "Followers of Jesus (Isa) in Islamic Mosques: A Closer Examination of C-5 'High Spectrum' Contextualization," *IJFM* 23, no. 3 (2006): 101–15.

aspects to identity than that. Consider, for example, the following layers of socioreligious identity, ranging from most private to most public:

1. An individual's ego-level identity (both their faith in Christ and their inner sense of socioreligious identity)
2. An individual's claim to have a certain group identity (confession of faith)
3. A group's collective recognition/acknowledgement of an individual's identity (belonging or membership within the faith community)[7]
4. A group's public claim concerning its socioreligious group identity (through use of cultural symbols, witness, lifestyle, etc.)
5. Society's perception of a group's identity (recognition/categorization as good, weird, infidel, etc.)

Moreover, we also need to avoid the temptation to treat "socioreligious identity" as if it can be neatly separated from ethnicity, nationality, tribe, class, political identity, etc., or to assume that people only have one of each type. In today's globalized world, these different "threads" of identity are rapidly splitting and unraveling into a tangled mess![8]

Whatever our views are on insider movements, if we want to continue to move forward in meaningful discussion with others, we need to develop models of identity that are nuanced enough to deal with the complex, tangled, and layered nature of identity today. My own impression is that the debate has become somewhat bogged down and polarized in recent years, and that part of the problem has been a blurring of the issues due to an overly simplistic discussion of identity. I am hoping that Travis' clarification of the C-spectrum and the new models for identity introduced in this volume will help inspire some fresh thinking and conversation.

While the C-spectrum was specifically developed to describe layers 5 and 4 from the list above, and Tim Green proposes a three-layer model of identity touching on aspects of all five,[9] my particular area of interest has been the individual (layers 1–3). This is due to having lived for eighteen years with my family in the Arab Middle East, and spending much of this time involved in discipleship of believers with a Muslim religiocultural background. Towards the end of this period I completed an MA thesis that used grounded theory principles to study identity issues among around twenty of my Christ-following friends. The end result was a model of identity that helped shed light on several issues that were coming up in their lives.

Before describing the model that was developed and introducing some of these friends,[10] I would like to share some of the journey leading up to it. My purpose in this is to encourage us to think about identity in fresh ways. Although you will certainly find flaws in some of the diagrams that follow,

---

7   Belonging is found in "the dialogical interaction between a sincere confession and a collective recognition." See Raimundo Panikkar, "On Christian Identity: Who Is a Christian?," chap. 10 in *Many Mansions? Multiple Religious Belonging and Christian Identity*, ed. Catherine Cornille (Maryknoll, NY: Orbis, 2002), 136.

8   See Enoch J. Kim's discussion of "urban multi-identifications," for example, in Kim, "'Us' or 'Me'? Modernization and Social Networks among China's Urban Hui," in *Longing for Community: Church,* Ummah, *or Somewhere in Between?*, ed. David Greenlee (Pasadena, CA: William Carey Library, 2013), 89–96.

9   See Tim Green, "Conversion in the Light of Identity Theories," in *Longing for Community: Church,* Ummah, *or Somewhere in Between?*, ed. David Greenlee (Pasadena, CA: William Carey Library: 2013), 41–52. See also his sidebar in *UIM*, chap. 58.

10   I use the term "friends" since they are my friends, and also due to the clumsiness, inadequacy, or inappropriateness of other commonly used expressions or acronyms to describe this group. The narratives in this chapter are extracted from my thesis; see Jens Barnett, "Conversion's Consequences: Identity, Belonging, and Hybridity

I hope they will inspire you to start your own process of rethinking the identity issues in the context you are in. Perhaps this goal is more important than trying to convince you to like the model I finally came up with myself!

Adding More Dimensions

My voyage of discovery began out of a sense of frustration with the C-spectrum. I had (wrongly!) been trying to apply it to my friends as individuals, and they just did not "fit"! As I started to look more closely at how others were using the C-spectrum, I found that many of those using the spectrum constructively needed to add extra dimensions. Figures 62.3 to 62.6 below show my initial efforts to depict some of these ideas graphically in the context of the original C-spectrum.

Rebecca Lewis (fig. 62.1), for example, starts with the C-spectrum, but she corrects a common mistake by pointing out that you cannot sensibly plot contextualization and syncretism on the same axis.[11] Instead she adds syncretism as a second dimension, citing "folk Catholicism" as an example of syncretism, where pagan beliefs can become mixed with foreign "Christian" forms.[12]

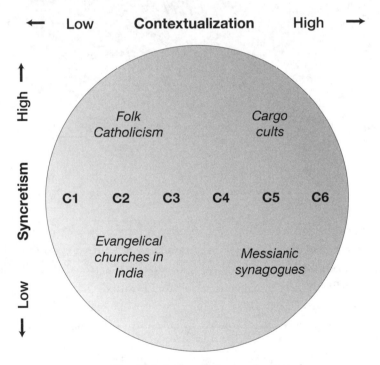

Fig. 62.1 A two-dimensional approach

---

amongst Muslim Followers of Christ" (MA thesis, Redcliffe College, 2008). Pseudonyms are used and some irrelevant details changed to protect the privacy of these individuals.

11 See John Travis et al., "Responses: Four Responses to Tennent," *IJFM* 23, no. 3 (2006): 126. Parshall and Tennent make this mistake—rather like "mixing apples and oranges." See Parshall, "Danger! New Directions in Contextualization," *EMQ* 34, no. 4 (1998): 404–10; and Tennent, "Followers of Jesus (Isa)."

12 Travis et al., "Four Responses," 126.

Rick Love (fig. 62.2) has an interesting two-dimensional take on the C-spectrum categories.[13] He suggests that there are both emotional and practical dimensions to the Muslim religious identity. For example, "Gulf Arabs" have high levels of both emotional identification and faithful practice, and so he believes they "may require a C5 level of contextualization." However, since Kazakhs are low identity and low practice, he thinks they may be "good candidates for a C3 approach."[14]

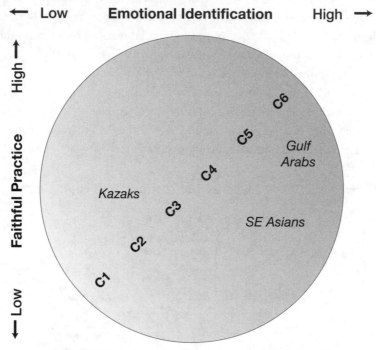

Fig. 62.2 Emotional and practical aspects of religious identity

John Ridgway's writing helped me realize that identity is *layered* by making a distinction between *external culture* and *inner faith* (fig. 62.3).[15] This is reminiscent of Wilfred C. Smith's idea that religion involves a dialectic process between "cumulative tradition" and "personal faith."[16] Ridgway suggests that when a nominal Muslim is born again, her "spiritual identity" enters the kingdom of God, just as any nominal Christian's would. At the same time, however, she may still feel some natural sense of belonging towards the community she was physically born into. This is her "physical identity."

---

13 Rick Love, *Muslims, Magic and the Kingdom of God: Church Planting among Folk Muslims* (Pasadena, CA: William Carey Library, 2000), 193–4.

14 Although I find Love's approach very helpful, he unfortunately repeats several common mistakes in his use of the C-spectrum, including using prescriptive language, restating the idea that there are "degrees" of contextualization, and overgeneralizing (e.g., which "Gulf Arabs" is he talking about?). Travis mentions some of these and others in *UIM,* chap. 51.

15 John Ridgway, "Insider Movements in the Gospels and Acts," *IJFM* 24, no. 2 (2007): 85.

16 Wilfred C. Smith, *The Meaning and End of Religion* (Minneapolis: Fortress Press, 1991), 156.

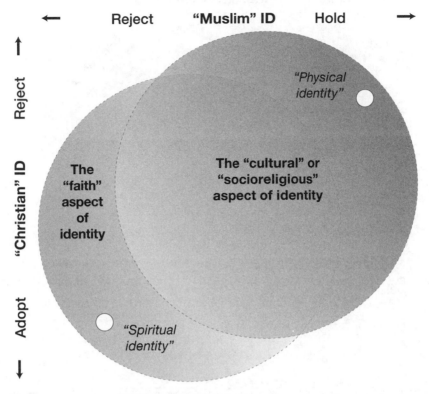

Fig. 62.3 Religious identity as layered aspects

Experimenting with Berry's Acculturation Model

Creating these graphs reminded me of an acculturation model widely used in immigration studies. John Berry's two-dimensional model[17] seeks to capture the sense of dual belonging that immigrants can feel as they adapt to a new culture while still relating to their old. Berry suggests that *assimilation, separation, integration,* and *marginalization* are four typical strategies immigrants choose as they respond to this challenge.

I decided to see if overlaying the C-spectrum onto Berry's model might be helpful (fig. 62.4 below). The four strategies listed above would correspond to the four possible combinations of either "rejecting" or "holding" one's Muslim cultural identity while at the same time "rejecting" or "adopting" a new Christian cultural identity. Thus, in my context, an extreme "insider strategy" could tend towards isolation due to *separation* from local ethnic[18] Christian communities, while extreme cases of extraction would tend towards the total rejection of one's "Muslim" cultural identity through *assimilation.*

---

17 John W. Berry et al., *Cross-cultural Psychology: Research and Applications* (Cambridge: Cambridge University Press, 2002), 353.

18 The evangelical churches in the country in which my research was based tend to be ethnically homogenous; that is, almost all members have "Christian" written on their birth certificates. Since this label is inherited, it primarily denotes a person's tribal or ethnic heritage. Many local "Christians" bolster this sense of ethnic identity by claiming to be pure descendants of the land's indigenous inhabitants prior to Islamic colonization from the Arabian Peninsula.

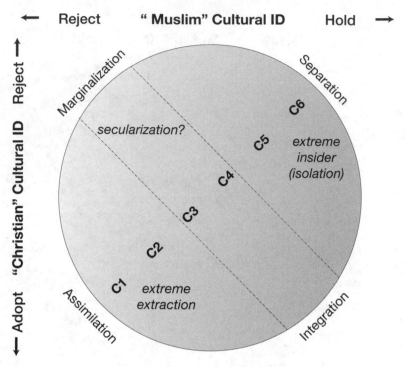

Fig. 62.4 Acculturation model

According to figure 62.4, it looked possible that C3–C4 believers could be found anywhere in the zone between *marginalization* and *integration*. What might that look like in practice? Also, the C3 rejection of both Christian and Muslim religious symbols[19] implies a kind of secularization to me. I wonder if Western evangelicalism unintentionally promotes this cultural value from the Enlightenment sometimes. Furthermore, in most discussions of Berry's acculturation model, "preferences for integration are expressed over the other three strategies, with marginalization being the least preferred,"[20] and yet in a missions setting would not this sort of integration be considered syncretism? What would it mean to both "hold" and "adopt" in practice?

I am not suggesting we use the Berry model here. Two dimensions are certainly twice as good as one, but his model is still criticized for being ridiculously simplistic.[21] My purpose in relating my journey here is rather to encourage us to think a little more "outside the box." In reality, there are many more than two cultural systems influencing our friends' lives. Once we begin adding extra dimensions, the possibilities seem endless. How can a simple model take all these into account?

What Is Actually Happening?

One question I was asking in my master's paper was, "What is happening?" Although the polarized nature of the insider movement debate sometimes makes it seem there are only two possible identity

---

19 The definition of C3 is that members use "religiously neutral" cultural forms (Travis, "The C1 to C6 Spectrum," 407), implying that it is possible to discern some sort of secular divide between religious and non-religious cultural forms. This is a cultural idea based on the West's "scientific" worldview.

20 Berry et al., *Cross-cultural Psychology*, 356.

21 See Floyd W. Rudmin, "Critical History of the Acculturation Psychology of Assimilation, Separation, Integration, and Marginalization," *Review of General Psychology* 7, no. 1 (2003): 3–37.

options, I found that none of my friends fit very well into either of these boxes. For example, all of my "insider" friends were regularly interacting with ethnic Christians through books, media, and friendships. On the other hand, a group of my most brazenly converted "Christian" friends would often get upset if an ethnic Christian made insensitive comments about Islam or Muslims, which to me indicated some lingering sense of belonging. Actually, there appeared to be a long-term drift away from both poles towards something more complex. This was especially the case for nonexiles, who were perhaps less able to avoid situations similar to these two examples above, and so were confronted more often with a sense of dual belonging.

I began to realize that something else was happening, a process I had first noticed in my own home. We now live in Scandinavia, but my children were born and grew up in the Middle East. What I have noticed is that my children are sometimes refusing—or perhaps unable—to choose between these two cultural identities. They are holding on to both 100 percent, which pulls them down towards "integration" on Berry's chart.

Hybridity

Although Berry's "integration" category seems to imply *mixing*, simultaneously holding 100 percent and adopting 100 percent adds up to 200 percent, which cannot actually be plotted in two dimensions. Instead the graph bulges out, opening up into a "third space" that is not even on Berry's chart (fig. 62.5). It forces something new to happen, something Homi Bhabha calls "third space hybridity."[22]

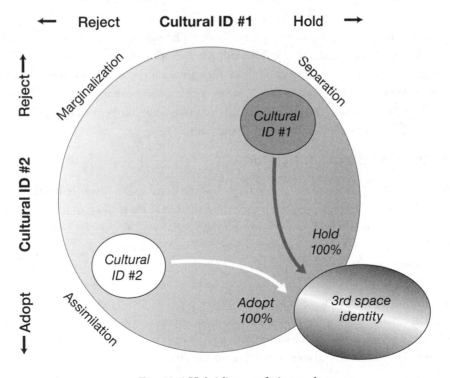

Fig. 62.5 Hybridity—refusing to choose

---

22 Homi K. Bhabha, *The Location of Culture* (London: Routledge, 2004), 312.

The best way I have found to describe hybridity is to use the metaphor of a fault line. Cultures are like tectonic plates, fossilized crusts that resist change. When two cultural plates come together, something

more than just "mixing" takes place. All of that mass needs to go somewhere, whether up or down. The fault line itself can be highly unstable too, with molten culture just waiting to break free and spurt out through cracks in the crust. This makes an intercultural border zone very interesting, since it is here new features of cultural geography are born.

Several years ago, I realized my children were "third culture kids" (TCKs).[23] Many of the symptoms were plain to see. For example, my then sixteen-year-old daughter had "desert-moose" as her email address and even made a "desert moose" tee shirt. As you can see from the tee shirt design, she was not just mixing Scandinavian and Middle Eastern symbols; she had created something else, something entirely new!

We often see this hybridity in our children outwardly as "mixing and matching." For example, my daughter went through a stage of wearing a Scandinavian jersey with an Arab scarf. It goes deeper too, though, as she juggles Scandinavian values with her Middle Eastern modesty.

How should I respond when my son exclaims to his sister, "You are such a tease!" Did I just hear him pronounce *tease* using the "heavy" Arabic letter *T*? My daughter is sure he did, and complains loudly, since that word in Arabic is rather rude. Yet my son has perfectly rendered the pronunciation to be ambiguous. He has a twinkle in his eye, but I cannot be sure what he intended to say. I wonder if he meant both, or perhaps, even more complicated, whether for him the same sound somehow carries both meanings. Hybridity makes life complicated, filling it with the ambiguity of intercultural puns.

When I first showed the "desert moose" picture at a missions conference, several were moved to tears. Why? Because many of us know what cultural hybridity feels like personally or have children who struggle being TCKs. Hybridity can be a lonely and painful struggle.

Modeling the Complexity of Hybridity

It was only after learning about hybridity from my children that I began to notice hybridity was at work in my "friends" as well. Again, all the symptoms were there, but I was blind to it until I had learned a new paradigm through which to view and interpret their behavior. I am concerned that if we do not develop new models through which to understand identity, we will find it hard to move on in the current debate. Even worse, we can be blinded to what is happening in our friends' lives and therefore unable to support them.

For this reason, I want to suggest that a dialogical model can be a helpful addition to our analytical toolkits. Firstly, it has space for the multiple aspects and layers of individual identity that we are now beginning to see discussed. Also, since hybridity is a product of dialogical processes, it seems some kind of dialogical model is necessary to comprehend or address it.

---

23   A term to label cultural hybridity in expatriate children, first coined by Ruth Hill Useem, "Third Culture Kids: Focus of Major Study," *Newslinks* (newspaper of the International School Services) 12, no. 3 (1993).

One such model is Hubert Hermans' "dialogical model of the self."[24] Although he mainly uses his model within the field of clinical psychology, Hermans claims it is needed to understand the increasingly widespread issue of multiple-group belonging in today's globalized world.[25] In his model the self is "decentered" and consists of

> a dynamic multiplicity of relatively autonomous *I*-positions. In this conception, the *I* has the possibility to move from one spatial position to another in accordance with changes in situation and time. The *I* fluctuates among different and even opposed positions, and has the capacity imaginatively to endow each position with a voice so that dialogical relations between positions can be established. The voices function like interacting characters in a story, involved in a process of question and answer, agreement and disagreement. . . . As different voices, these characters exchange information about their respective *Me*'s, resulting in a complex, narratively structured self.[26]

A Dialogical Model of the Self

Inspired by Hermans, figure 62.6 is an attempt to depict a dialogical model.

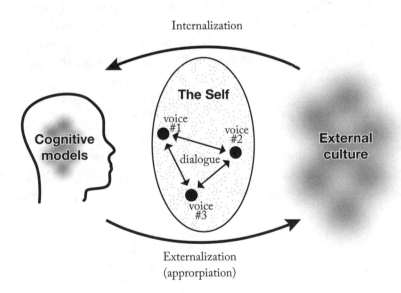

Fig. 62.6 A dialogical model of the self

External culture represents the cultural context my friend lives in. His context is not at all uniform or singular. Arab, secular, Islamic, and other cultural traditions are all present and interacting with

---

24 See Hubert J. M. Hermans, "The Dialogical Self: Toward a Theory of Personal and Cultural Positioning," *Culture and Psychology* 7, no. 3 (2001): 243–81.

25 See Hubert J. M. Hermans and Giancarlo Dimaggio, "Self, Identity, and Globalization in Times of Uncertainty: A Dialogical Analysis," *Review of General Psychology* 11, no. 1 (2007): 31–61.

26 Hermans, "The Dialogical Self," 248.

each other to varying degrees. Moreover, since my friend is a believer, the context of his daily life also involves relationships with ethnic Christians and immersing himself in the biblical narratives. The "fuzzy" spots are an attempt to depict this complex interaction between the different cultural systems that make up his context.

The two large arrows represent two fundamental cultural processes.[27] The first is the *internalization* of *external culture*, through which my friend constructs in his mind a collection of *cognitive models* that represent the world outside.

These *cognitive models* can be envisaged as filing cabinets in the mind, full of detailed maps, scripts, narratives, and roles that describe the world and how to live in it.[28] As can be seen, the fuzzy complexity of the "external culture" is also internalized, becoming multiple interacting *worldviews*.[29] Each worldview overlays and interprets reality, in much the same manner as a memorized bus route, street map, and metro network can overlay and "interpret" the same physical space in a city.

Perhaps an example would be helpful at this point. My friend Thani once complained to me that he can't worship when the church sings, "Send your fire, Lord!" The problem was that he has internalized two meanings for the word "fire." The "Muslim" one is very negative, signifying flaming judgment, while the "Christian" one is positive, signifying the Holy Spirit. However, since he has both of these interpretations in his head—one screaming, "Run!" and the other saying, "Stay!"—he cannot help but laugh to himself at the irony of his situation. Yet the moment he does this, he becomes an objective observer of himself and so "drops out" of the corporate worship experience. This sense of *ambivalence* (i.e., having simultaneous, conflicting feelings) over cultural symbols is a classic symptom of hybridity.

The second large arrow in figure 62.6 represents the process of *externalization*, where the believer draws on his cognitive models in order to take part in society. Doing so, he joins the conversation that in turn shapes external culture for the next generation.

For example, because he belongs to an Arab tribe, my friend Awal is exposed to the tribal narratives, scripts, and symbols that make up his tribe's cultural system. This is just one of the multiple influences that make up his external culture. As he internalizes these, Awal constructs a cognitive model of what "father" means within his tribal context. He can then *appropriate* this model by taking up a father's role and acting it out in his community. In doing this, Awal's words and actions become part of the external culture experienced by his children.

The Self as a "Stage"

Through envisaging himself (i.e., his "self") as "father," Awal perceives situations from a father's perspective. Another way to say this is that Awal experiences the father's perspective as a *voice* speaking

---

27   I take a constructionist approach to culture. See Peter Berger and Thomas Luckmann, *The Social Construction of Reality: A Treatise in the Sociology of Knowledge* (London: Penguin, 1991).

28   Bradd Shore, *Culture in Mind: Cognition, Culture, and the Problem of Meaning* (New York: Oxford University Press, 1996), 42.

29   One problem with modernistic models of identity is that they often presuppose a single "worldview" inside a very Western and individualistic Freudian "ego" at the very core of the self. This in turn creates all kinds of problems in trying to define a person's "primary" identity, or place different aspects of their identity into some kind of hierarchy with "religious" on top. The problems multiply when one tries to use this individualistic model in collectivist cultures. I use "worldview" differently here, as a source of cultural information external to the self.

within him.[30] Moreover, voices from other roles, such as "husband" and "employee," can also be present at the same time, and enter into dialogue with each other. Naturally, there will sometimes be a clash of perspectives or priorities that Awal needs to resolve creatively.[31] If one thinks about it, much of the incessant "self-talk" going on in our own minds as we make decisions is between different roles or senses of belonging.

To depict this conversation, I have drawn a *stage*, representing Awal's self, in between—but separate from—the externalization and internalization processes. On the stage there are three voices, with smaller arrows representing a dialogue with each other. Each of these roles or voices has been first learned from external culture and then brought onto the stage from the store of cognitive models held in the mind.

This model has been a useful tool to help me understand my friends' actions at times. Take, for example, the situation I mentioned earlier where a group of my friends would become upset if ethnic Christians made insensitive comments about Islam. Paradoxically, this same group of bold Christian converts would happily sit together exchanging sharp criticisms of Islam amongst themselves. Once, during a discipleship course we were running, their sensitivity became so problematic that we had to caution visiting lecturers that Islam was this group's "homeland." We explained that, although someone may emigrate and take on a new nationality, they might still be sensitive to remarks about their homeland—especially comments made by nonnatives. This imagery proved successful in lowering tensions—but why?

The apparent inconsistency of my friends' responses cannot be easily understood using a one-dimensional scale. To see these responses as resulting from an inner dialogue between two "voices" on the stage of self is perhaps more helpful. One voice is the C2 "Christian" identity they strongly claim to have, and the other, fainter voice is the voice of their Muslim "homeland."[32] The homeland imagery had legitimized the sense of dual belonging my friends felt in a way that even ethnic Christians could empathize with. Recognizing that there can be a conversation taking place inside our friends is not automatically a scary issue of "compromise" or "syncretism." We ourselves are all continually evaluating between personal roles, desires, and responsibilities. Some voices can be very faint or even saying something that is clearly wrong. Yet I believe allowing the dialogue to take place and seeking to find and follow Christ in the midst of that process leads to a deeper, more comprehensive discipleship. It is surely healthier than pretending the voices do not exist at all, especially since the collapse of internal

---

30 Hermans, "The Construction of a Personal Position Repertoire: Method and Practice," *Culture and Psychology* 7, no. 3 (2001): 329.

31 Hermans believes dialogical processes are foundational to the self's creativity: "Contrasts, conflicts, disagreements, and contradictions between components of the self, are seen as intrinsic to a well-functioning self in general and to its innovation in particular." Hermans, "The Dialogical Self: One Person, Different Stories," in *Self and Identity: Personal, Social, and Symbolic,* ed. Yoshihisa Kashima, Margaret Foddy, and Michael Platow (Mahwah, NJ: Lawrence Erlbaum Associates, 2002), 95.

32 In this model, a sense of belonging to a group is also a "voice" on the stage of self. In contrast to the West's traditionally individualistic models of self, Hermans argues that "collective voices, as represented by groups . . . or by significant others . . . are constituent parts of the self and organize the self to a significant degree." Hermans, "Construction of a Personal Position Repertoire," 360. The dialogical model is thus also applicable to non-Western collectivist societies.

dialogue caused by suppressing voices appears to "result in behavior or self-experience that parallels schizophrenia."[33]

Awal's Inner Dialogue

The inner conflict and ambivalence felt by Thani, who mapped two definitions for "fire" to one symbol, is a relatively simple example of hybridity. What happens with more complex culture-laden symbols such as "father"? Since each cultural system comprising Awal's context includes its own definition of "father," it is quite possible for *several* distinct "father" voices to be internalized and come into dialogue with each other on the stage. Listening to Awal, I often had the strange sensation I was eavesdropping on a private conversation. The flow was often disjointed, swinging to and fro, contradicting, justifying, and modifying itself. In the excerpt from my interview with Awal that follows, one can get a sense of this relentless internal dialogue. For example, rehearsing to me his reasons for returning home after emigrating to the West, Awal appears to contrast Christianity, the West, and freedom with Islam, home, tribal honor, and morality. Using the dialogical model, one can perhaps picture a "tribal father" and "Muslim father" standing in close proximity, debating with a stereotypical "Western Christian father" on the other side of the stage:

> A while ago my daughter asked me, "Dad, what am I *really*? Am I a Muslim or a Christian?"
>
> I said, "You're a Muslim that follows Christ. Our Muslim identity is written on our identity [cards], it's our extended family, our heritage, our people—but we follow Christ as a family. Although it has made life difficult for us, I will never regret my decision to follow Christ . . ."
>
> But that is so hard for them. My daughter—who is now a teenager, you know—asked me, "Dad, what is going to happen to me? Will I ever get married?" It's a very difficult time. They need to find their own way. . . .
>
> We are not Christians. . . . We are Muslims. It is among Muslims we find acceptance and belonging. . . . We have experienced so much love from Muslim society and so much rejection from Christians. Our children have felt this and it is hard for them to understand. . . .
>
> I no longer care what Christians think. I care what Muslims think. However, even if our president asked me, "What is Christ to you?" I would tell him my faith. I will not compromise Christ, ever—but I am not a Christian. . . .
>
> We had emigrated . . . but we have moved back to . . . our home. . . . It is better here. . . . To be honest, if I am—God forbid—going to lose them, I would rather have my children grow up to be Muslims, than to grow up to be gay, drug users, or promiscuous. At least they would be honorable, and have morals and values. . . .

---

33   Paul Henry Lysaker and John Timothy Lysaker, "Narrative Structure in Psychosis: Schizophrenia and Disruptions in the Dialogical Self," *Theory and Psychology* 12, no. 2 (2002): 211–12.

Awal's emigration and return graphically illustrate the force of this dialogue and the instability it can create in believers' lives.[34] The continual pressure to surrender total allegiance to one "primary" cultural identity is matched by the refusal to choose between them. I am reminded of the closing lines in Salman Rushdie's semi-autobiographical story "The Courter," in which the narrator says,

> I, too, have ropes around my neck. I have them to this day, pulling me this way and that, East and West, the nooses tightening, commanding, *choose, choose.* I buck, I snort, I whinny, I rear, I kick. Ropes, I do not choose between you. Lassoes, lariats, I choose neither of you, and both. Do you hear? I refuse to choose.[35]

Hybridity and Cultural Change

How does hybridity relate to witness within the community and cultural transformation? First of all, it is important to distinguish hybridity from syncretism. Whereas syncretism is traditionally understood as meaning "mixing,"[36] hybridity carries with it a sense of newness and innovation. Syncretism is synthesis, the fruit of Hegel's thesis-antithesis *dialectic* process. Hybridity, however, is the fruit of *dialogical* processes. As with synergy or brainstorming, the results can be quite creative and far more than a simple synthesis of the parts. Bhabha calls hybridity "where newness enters the world" and "the location of culture,"[37] since entirely new cultural forms are born on the boundaries between the old. Sadly, the insider movement debate has often been framed in a dichotomistic way recently, and that seems to leave very little room for—or expectation of—new cultural expressions of Christ following to arise.

By refusing to choose, my friends have —to different degrees—taken up *liminal*[38] identities in the borderlands between traditional cultural categories. For this reason they can take up roles as *prophetic insiders*. I believe this is an important insight for the insider movement conversation. No believer, in any community, can be an entirely "typical" specimen from their culture. Following Christ will always pit us against the *status quo*, making us very strange "specimens" indeed. However, being very *different* is not the same as becoming an *outsider*. An outsider has lost the right, and perhaps even the cultural ability, to speak meaningfully into their community, and so they are cut off from any chance for effective witness. For me, *prophetic insider* captures the dual aspects of both radically challenging culture and culturally relevant communication. The prophetic insider "crying in the wilderness" takes a stance similar to a hybrid immigrant, who "is empowered to intervene *actively* in the transmission of

---

34 Some may see the above quote as a damning indictment of IM missiology; however, throughout the more than twenty years I have known him, Awal has boldly and consistently identified himself as a Christian to his family, tribe, state, and local church, and he still does. Rather, this quote shows that even well-respected C2 converts and their families are grappling with identity issues that cannot be understood using simplistic one-dimensional thinking.

35 Salman Rushdie, "The Courter," chap. 9 in *East, West: Stories* (New York: Pantheon, 1994), 211.

36 "Syncretism. Blending of one idea, practice, or attitude with another. Traditionally among Christians it has been used of the replacement or dilution of the essential truths of the gospel through the incorporation of non-Christian elements." A. Scott Moreau, "Syncretism," in *Evangelical Dictionary of World Missions*, ed. A. Scott Moreau, Harold Netland, and Charles Van Engen (Grand Rapids, MI: Baker, 2000), 924–25.

37 See Bhabha, *The Location of Culture.*

38 Liminality is an ambiguous threshold state between incommensurable social identities such as child and adult or single and married. This idea is developed by Victor Turner, *The Ritual Process: Structure and Anti-Structure* (New York: Aldine de Gruyter, 1995), 95, and applied to hybridity by Homi Bhabha, *The Location of Culture*, 199.

cultural inheritance . . . rather than *passively* accept its venerable customs and pedagogical wisdom. He or she can question, refashion or mobilize received ideas . . . [and] is empowered to act as an agent of change."[39] By having a liminal identity that occupies two worlds, prophetic insiders maintain the right to speak as insiders, and can therefore act as a "bridge" over which outside sources of truth may enter into their community.[40] Mazhar Mallouhi, a well-known Syrian believer, expresses his calling using similar terms, saying, "When one follows Christ, one's own culture and identity should be enriched. Light should be brought into that culture. That is why it is so important for me to stay and live within my Muslim cultural community."[41]

The dialogical paradigm gives insight into how actively engaging with culture can bring about change. Mikhail Bakhtin, father of the dialogical paradigm, describes this process in relation to language below:

> There are no "neutral" words and forms . . . that can belong to "no one," language has been completely taken over, shot through with intentions and accents. . . . Each word tastes of the . . . contexts in which it has lived its socially charged life. . . . The word in language is half someone else's. It becomes "one's own" only when the speaker populates it with his own intention, his own accent. . . . Prior to this moment of appropriation, the word does not exist in a neutral and impersonal language (it is not, after all, out of a dictionary that the speaker gets his words!), but rather it exists in other people's mouths, in other people's contexts, serving other people's intentions: it is from there that one must take the word, and make it one's own.[42]

What Bakhtin describes here is a raging semiotic battle over who gets to define the meaning of cultural symbols. A prophetic insider has the right and the capability to take part in this battle by appropriating words and roles they have learned and using them for new purposes out in their community. In this way, they imitate Paul's passion to "take captive every thought to make it obedient to Christ" (2 Cor 10:5).

Mazhar Mallouhi appears to be doing just this when he boldly claims to be a "Muslim," while at the same time openly rejecting two pillars that are normally included in any standard "textbook" definition of Islam:

> *Interviewer:* Are there any aspects of the practice of Islam that you feel you must leave behind?
>
> *Mallouhi:* Really only two things: the *shahada* (the Islamic creed— "There is no God but God and Muhammad is his prophet") and the

---

39   John McLeod, *Beginning Postcolonialism* (Manchester: Manchester University Press, 2000), 218–19.

40   And vice versa. The global church desperately needs to hear the prophetic voices of believers from Muslim backgrounds too.

41   Paul-Gordon Chandler, *Pilgrims of Christ on the Muslim Road: Exploring a New Path between Two Faiths* (Lanham, MD: Cowley, 2007), 196.

42   Mikhail M. Bakhtin, "Discourse in the Novel," in *The Dialogic Imagination: Four Essays,* ed. Michael Holquist, trans. Caryl Emerson and Michael Holquist (Austin: University of Texas Press, 1981), 293–94.

pilgrimage to Mecca. Often I encourage Muslim followers of Jesus to write their own *shahada*.[43]

Syncretism?

Mallouhi's definition for "Muslim" is highly unorthodox, yet he is loved and accepted as a member of the Muslim *ummah* (community) by Muslims around the world—including high-profile leaders. Some of us may find this rather irritating. Surely rejecting the standard *shahadah* proves that Mallouhi is not a "real" Muslim! If one believes "Muslim" has a fixed "textbook" definition, Mallouhi's claim can come across as syncretism or compromise—even dishonest. However, words do *not* have fixed meanings. Dictionary definitions are dependent on a word's *usage*, which drifts and changes with successive cycles of internalization and externalization. Therefore, Mallouhi's claim to be a "Muslim" can also be understood as contesting the very meaning of the symbol itself. Is this syncretism? From a dialogical point of view, I think it is too soon to say. If Mallouhi and others succeed in broadening the meaning of this and other symbols within their culture, then it is not. If they fail, then maybe it was. Before I explain what I mean by this, we need to remind ourselves that, according to *The Evangelical Dictionary of World Missions*,

> many scholars today challenge the need to define syncretism in its negative traditional sense. The meaning of the term has broadened to a more neutral concept of interpenetration of two or more paradigms. In this sense, since all churches are culture-based, every church is syncretistic.[44]

We can clearly see this in European Christianity, where much of the symbolism around our Christmas and Easter celebrations was once pagan before it was successfully "made obedient to Christ." It is important to realize, however, that the association of new biblical meanings to these forms cannot have occurred across the whole of Europe overnight. A dialogical approach recognizes that cultural change in a community is not instantaneous, nor is it uniform. Since transformation of a culture will *always* involve the contesting of cultural symbols, pockets of confusion in the initial stages seem, to me, unavoidable. If we define syncretism semiotically, as the association of a nonbiblical meaning to a symbol or form, then some degree of syncretistic confusion may well be a normal stage on the way to good contextualization. Occasionally, therefore, it may only be in hindsight that one can pronounce something as syncretistic in the negative sense, when appropriation of a symbol has failed.

Conclusion

In the past, ethnicity, geography, religion, and empire have often coincided to form singular, sharply defined identities. However, as globalization, pluralism, and migration continue to unravel these strands of identity, more nuanced tools are needed to capture the dynamics we are today witnessing on the mission field. In this chapter I have shared some of my journey in trying to understand and support my friends as they seek to follow Jesus—some of whom I have now known for over twenty years. The dialogical paradigm has helped me to discern and respond to discipleship situations I would have missed had I attempted to wrongly apply the C-spectrum group-identity model to them as individuals,

---

43 Chandler, *Pilgrims of Christ*, 187.
44 Moreau, "Syncretism," 924.

or use some creative two-dimensional variant. Just as some of my missions colleagues were moved to empathy by my daughter's "desert moose" picture, I hope this chapter can help us recognize hybridity and respond with greater empathy and understanding.

It is not my goal in this chapter to enthusiastically "advocate" multiple belonging, hybridity, liminality, or syncretism. These phenomena are not always the colorful cosmopolitan fun that some postmodern writers make them out to be. In fact, there is often much pain and heartbreak involved. Rather, my goal is to show that these things *already exist* in the lives of our friends and that we need tools to help us grapple with the issues they raise. Even if we disagree with some of the hybrid expressions we are seeing today, we need better models in order to appropriately understand and challenge those aspects we feel are in error. Some degree of ambiguity should be expected as new identities arise, and there should be space available for this to happen.

Finally, I am praying for many more models of identity to be developed, and that this will help us move forward in the current insider movement debate, enabling us to serve our friends—and each other—with empathy, trust, and respect.

Bibliography

Bakhtin, Mikhail M. "Discourse in the Novel." In *The Dialogic Imagination: Four Essays,* edited by Michael Holquist, translated by Caryl Emerson and Michael Holquist, 259–422. Austin: University of Texas Press, 1981.

Barnett, Jens. "Conversion's Consequences: Identity, Belonging, and Hybridity amongst Muslim Followers of Christ." MA thesis, Redcliffe College, 2008.

Berger, Peter, and Thomas Luckmann. *The Social Construction of Reality: A Treatise in the Sociology of Knowledge.* London: Penguin, 1991.

Berry, John W., Ype H. Poortinga, Seger M. Breugelmans, Athanasios Chasiotis, David L. Sam. *Cross-cultural Psychology: Research and Applications.* Cambridge: Cambridge University Press, 2002.

Bhabha, Homi K. *The Location of Culture.* London: Routledge, 2004.

Chandler, Paul-Gordon. *Pilgrims of Christ on the Muslim Road: Exploring a New Path between Two Faiths.* Lanham, MD: Cowley, 2007.

Hermans, Hubert J. M. "The Construction of a Personal Position Repertoire: Method and Practice." *Culture and Psychology* 7, no. 3 (2001): 323–66.

———. "The Dialogical Self: One Person, Different Stories." In *Self and Identity: Personal, Social, and Symbolic,* edited by Yoshihisa Kashima, Margaret Foddy, and Michael Platow, 71–99. Mahwah, NJ: Lawrence Erlbaum Associates, 2002.

———. "The Dialogical Self: Toward a Theory of Personal and Cultural Positioning." *Culture and Psychology* 7, no. 3 (2001): 243–81.

———, and Giancarlo Dimaggio. "Self, Identity, and Globalization in Times of Uncertainty: A Dialogical Analysis." *Review of General Psychology* 11, no. 1 (2007): 31–61.

Kim, Enoch J. "'Us' or 'Me'? Modernization and Social Networks among China's Urban Hui." In *Longing for Community: Church,* Ummah, *or Somewhere in Between?,* edited by David Greenlee, 89–96. Pasadena, CA: William Carey Library, 2013.

Love, Rick. *Muslims, Magic and the Kingdom of God: Church Planting among Folk Muslims.* Pasadena, CA: William Carey Library, 2000.

Lysaker, Paul Henry, and John Timothy Lysaker. "Narrative Structure in Psychosis: Schizophrenia and Disruptions in the Dialogical Self." *Theory and Psychology* 12, no. 2 (2002): 207–20.

Massey, Joshua. "God's Amazing Diversity in Drawing Muslims to Christ." *International Journal of Frontier Missions* 17, no. 1 (2000): 5–14.

McLeod, John. *Beginning Postcolonialism.* Manchester: Manchester University Press, 2000.

Moreau, A. Scott. "Syncretism." In *Evangelical Dictionary of World Missions*, edited by A. Scott Moreau, Harold Netland, and Charles Van Engen. Grand Rapids, MI: Baker, 2000.

Panikkar, Raimundo. "On Christian Identity: Who Is a Christian?" Chap. 10 in *Many Mansions? Multiple Religious Belonging and Christian Identity.* Edited by Catherine Cornille. Maryknoll, NY: Orbis, 2002.

Parshall, Phil. "Danger! New Directions in Contextualization." *Evangelical Missions Quarterly* 34, no. 4 (1998): 404–10.

———. "Lifting the Fatwa." *Evangelical Missions Quarterly* 40, no. 3 (2004): 288–93.

Ridgway, John. "Insider Movements in the Gospels and Acts." *International Journal of Frontier Missiology* 24, no. 2 (2007): 77–85.

Rudmin, Floyd W. "Critical History of the Acculturation Psychology of Assimilation, Separation, Integration, and Marginalization." *Review of General Psychology* 7, no. 1 (2003): 3–37.

Rushdie, Salman. "The Courter." Chap. 9 in *East, West: Stories.* New York: Pantheon, 1994.

Shore, Bradd. *Culture in Mind: Cognition, Culture, and the Problem of Meaning.* New York: Oxford University Press, 1996.

Smith, Wilfred C. *The Meaning and End of Religion.* Minneapolis: Fortress Press, 1991.

Tennent, Timothy C. "Followers of Jesus (Isa) in Islamic Mosques: A Closer Examination of C-5 'High Spectrum' Contextualization." *International Journal of Frontier Missions* 23, no. 3 (2006): 101–15.

Travis, John. "The C1 to C6 Spectrum: A Practical Tool for Defining Six Types of 'Christ-centered Communities' ('C') Found in the Muslim Context." *Evangelical Missions Quarterly* (October 1998): 407–8.

———, Phil Parshall, Herbert Hoefer, and Rebecca Lewis. "Responses: Four Responses to Tennent." *International Journal of Frontier Missions* 23, no. 3 (2006): 124–26.

Turner, Victor. *The Ritual Process: Structure and Anti-Structure.* New York: Aldine de Gruyter, 1995.

Useem, Ruth Hill. "Third Culture Kids: Focus of Major Study." *Newslinks* (newspaper of the International School Services) 12, no. 3 (1993).

CHAPTER 63

Societal Factors Impacting Socioreligious Identities of Muslims Who Follow Jesus[*]

John and Anna Travis

Scripture declares that every human being is created and known by God, lovingly and uniquely shaped in his or her mother's womb (Ps 139:13–15). When considering the world's nearly 1.7 billion Muslims, we can easily lose sight of the uniqueness of each one. Likewise, each of the approximately fifty Muslim-majority countries of the world and the many Muslim-minority countries, and the hundreds of cultures and languages they represent, is also in some way unique.

The last few decades are the first time in history that large numbers of Muslims from some of these countries and cultures have accepted Jesus as Lord and Savior. This has resulted in the formation of numerous Muslim-background Christ-centered fellowships, which, like the peoples and cultures they represent, encompass great diversity.[1]

The C1–C6 Spectrum is a model that attempts to illustrate this diversity. The Spectrum describes six types of Christ-centered fellowships that Muslim-background believers (MBBs)[2] either join or form as they follow Jesus.[3]

The premise of this chapter is that a variety of societal factors (e.g., historical, cultural, religious, and political) impact the various ways MBBs express their faith in Jesus in different contexts, though they are still led by the same Holy Spirit. Awareness of these factors can give us a greater appreciation for how God is at work in different ways throughout the Muslim world, meeting Muslims in the midst of their real-life circumstances. Why is this important? Taking the time to ask why MBBs might be following Jesus in a certain way takes us a step closer to seeing them as unique sons and daughters God has created.

This study will examine data from the 2007 Global Trends and Fruitful Practices (GTFP) Consultation along with some factors impacting contemporary Muslim societies, suggesting how those factors

---

[*] Originally published in a slightly different form in *From Seed to Fruit: Global Trends, Fruitful Practices, and Emerging Issues among Muslims*, 2nd ed., ed. J. Dudley Woodberry (Pasadena, CA: William Carey Library, 2011), 193–205. Reprinted by permission.

1 Two recently published books show the amazing increase in people born Muslim now following Jesus, largely since the year 2000. See Jerry Trousdale, *Miraculous Movements: How Hundreds of Thousands of Muslims Are Falling in Love with Jesus* (Nashville: Thomas Nelson, 2012); and David Garrison, *A Wind in the House of Islam: How God Is Drawing Muslims around the World to Faith in Jesus Christ* (Monument, CO: WIGTake, 2013).

2 The expression "Muslim-background believer" (MBB) refers to a person born Muslim who follows Jesus. I will use the same term for all such persons, not making the distinction that some do in using "MBB" for those who do not retain Muslim identity and "MB" (Muslim believer) for those who do.

3 See *UIM*, chap. 4, fig. 4.1, for a visual representation of the C-spectrum; and chap. 51 for a description of the tool, common misunderstandings, and recommendations for future use.

might impact the types of fellowships and socioreligious identities chosen by Muslims who are following Jesus. We will look first at the GTFP data and several caveats to this present study.

The 2007 GTFP Consultation Data

In 2007, scholars, mission leaders, and 280 field workers gathered for a four-day consultation aimed at bringing greater clarity to how the good news of Jesus is taking root in Muslim contexts.[4] The field workers, from thirty-seven nationalities and fifty-six different ministries, had served on teams that helped to plant 738 fellowships throughout the Muslim world.[5] The field workers sat at tables sharing their experiences and analyzing compiled data from more than 5,800 surveys filled out by other workers in the Muslim world. The following is a summary of the types of fellowships identified by this research along with the relative percentage of each type in terms of C-spectrum categories:

    C1 fellowships—1 percent of the total number of fellowships reported

    C2 fellowships—5 percent of the total number of fellowships reported

    C3 fellowships—28 percent of the total number of fellowships reported

    C4 fellowships—37 percent of the total number of fellowships reported

    C5 fellowships—21 percent of the total number of fellowships reported

    C6 fellowships—8 percent of the total number of fellowships reported

What this data clearly indicates is that great diversity exists in the types of fellowships being planted in the Muslim world. The research, however was not designed to answer the central question of this chapter—namely, *why* different groups of Muslim-background believers gravitate toward different types of fellowships or toward the socioreligious identities[6] associated with them.[7]

Caveats to This Study

Before looking at various factors that impact these newly planted fellowships, there are several important caveats.

The first regards the impact that cross-cultural gospel messengers and church planters have on choices MBBs make, irrespective of any societal factors. Whether gospel messengers are citizens of that country or foreigners, they are likely to promote the planting of fellowships in line with their own

---

    4   The story of this consultation is told in Woodberry, *Seed to Fruit*, passim.

    5   Ibid., xviii.

    6   Religious labels or identities—Christian, Hindu, Jew, Muslim—refer to more than one's spiritual beliefs; they also refer to a myriad of cultural and social practices embraced by people born and raised in those religious communities. Viewed in this way, many with minimal or unclear spiritual beliefs could still identify in a social or belonging sense as Jewish, Catholic, Muslim, etc. The term "socioreligious" refers to the community or group, whether nominal or observant, that would refer to itself by that religious label. See *UIM*, chap. 1, for a discussion of socioreligious identity.

    7   The C1–C6 Spectrum presents four different socioreligious identities among Muslim-background believers. C1, C2, and C3 fellowships, although differing in forms, all have clearly stated "Christian" religious identities, with some C1 and C2 churches in the Middle East even predating Islam. C4 groups refer to themselves as "Isa followers," "followers of God through Isa," or with some other such label to avoid the often negative stereotypes associated with the term "Christian" in Muslim contexts. C5 fellowships are known as groups of Muslims who follow Jesus as the risen Savior. C6 refers to individuals or very small groups of Muslims who follow Jesus underground, often in very hostile environments, and would be known simply as Muslims in the eyes of the surrounding population.

methodology or church background.[8] Not knowing of more than one type of fellowship that they could join or form, the new Jesus followers are often inclined, therefore, to simply follow the lead of the one who first shared Christ with them.

The second caveat relates to the first: How many different types of fellowships already exist in a given area? If in a particular region, for instance, only one type of fellowship exists—for example, only C2 or only C5—the message understood by new followers of Christ may be that this is the best or only legitimate way to follow Jesus. If, however, many different types of fellowships in terms of C-spectrum categories exist in a given area (as they did where we worked for many years), the new believers are more inclined to consider a variety of options.

A final caveat involves the particular societal factors this study addresses. The choice of factors is based on our own experiences in the Muslim world. Though these experiences have been informed by numerous interactions with MBBs, field workers, other individual researchers,[9] and some recent Pew Research Center reports,[10] they do not represent the results of a comprehensive field-based research project. We may have inadvertently overlooked some important factors, and we do not intend for the ideas presented here to be seen as a new model of ministry. Other chapters in this book shed more light on the highly complex nature of personal faith and group religious identity.[11] We do hope that this study, however, will generate further discussion.

Societal Factors Impacting the Contexts of MBBs

From an idealized Islamic perspective, religion, culture, and politics form a united, integrated whole within Muslim societies. As Martin Goldsmith states,

> Islam is within the whole warp and woof of society—in the family, in politics, in social relationships. To leave the Muslim faith is to break with one's society. Many a modern, educated Muslim is not all that religiously minded; but he must, nevertheless, remain a Muslim for social reasons, and also because it is the basis for his political belief. This makes it almost unthinkable for most

---

8   We recently spoke with a well-known Muslim author who is a follower of Jesus. We asked him what factor(s) he thought influenced the socioreligious identities of Muslims who follow Jesus. (He thoroughly understood the question, as it was an issue he has struggled with himself.) Without batting an eye he said, "The missionaries."

9   We are indebted to J. Dudley Woodberry, who has described five conditions that are creating openness to the gospel on the part of Muslims. Some of these conditions overlap with the societal factors we discuss in this study. The five circumstances are (1) political factors (especially resurgent Islam), (2) natural catastrophes coupled with the loving response given by Christians, (3) migrations of Muslim populations to new areas, (4) the desire for blessing or power that is met when healing prayer is offered in Jesus' name, and finally, (5) ethnic and cultural resurgence on the part of some Muslim minorities. See Woodberry, "A Global Perspective on Muslims Coming to Faith in Christ," in *From the Straight Path to the Narrow Way: Journeys of Faith*, ed. David Greenlee (Waynesboro, GA: Authentic, 2006), 11–13.

10   From 2008 to 2012 the Pew Research Center conducted an in-depth public opinion survey involving 38,000 face-to-face interviews with Muslims in 39 countries, using 80 locally spoken languages. The results of this research have been published in stages, available on the Center's website (http://www.pewglobal.org/). I will mention several of these reports and related findings throughout the chapter.

11   See John and Anna Travis, chap. 47; Talman, chap. 48; Adams, chap. 61; Barnett, chap. 62; and Green in the sidebar in chap. 58 for limitations of the C-spectrum and other models of identity.

Muslims even to consider the possibility of becoming a follower of some other religion.[12]

In spite of this idealized communal unity, numerous conflicting political, social, cultural, ethnic, regional, religious, and historical factors impact specific Muslim contexts,[13] which in turn can influence ways in which MBBs follow Jesus.

Political factors are multifaceted. Some Muslim societies have secular democratic governments with relative religious freedom. Some are kingdoms under autocratic rule. Some Islamic countries are under *shari'a* law, where, although seldom enforced, the penalty for conversion to another religion is death. This causes those who follow God through Jesus to instinctively consider C-spectrum-type options in light of their political realities.

A variety of communal factors come into play at the grassroots, or neighborhood, level in terms of following Jesus. In some contexts, it is not governmental policies but rather family and peer pressure that have the greatest impact on the life of an MBB. In some parts of Africa, as well as certain parts of Indonesia, Muslims and Christians live side by side, and in some cases one family will have both Christian and Muslim members.[14] In other settings, however, leaving Islam is tantamount to social suicide, resulting in divorce; loss of one's children; loss of income, status, and inheritance; physical violence; or even honor killing within families in extreme cases.

Religious, demographic, and cultural factors also impact C-spectrum choices. For instance, how long ago did the society embrace Islam, and how intertwined or fused is Islam with the local culture now? In any given Islamic milieu, is there a local Christian population? If so, how long ago was the gospel introduced to that population? Are those Christians welcoming and open to receiving Muslim-background believers as equal members, and eventually leaders, in their fellowships? Or are they defensive and suspicious of them, thus making existing Christian-background fellowships less-than-ideal vehicles for enfolding Muslim-background believers? Are these Christians largely nominal, or do they have a vibrant faith in Christ? Are current Christian-Muslim interactions friendly, distant, or hostile? Is ethnicity or religious identity the stronger tie that binds? Is there room in a given context for one to be, for example, an authentic Turk, Kazakh, Tunisian, or Saudi, and not be a Muslim? In some Islamic milieus, limited pluralism exists; in other places it is rare or entirely missing.

Closely linked to this are the aspirations of Muslims of a particular ethnic group and the future directions in which they are headed. Are they in a time of innovation, or even trying to break free of

---

12 Goldsmith, "Community and Controversy: Key Causes of Muslim Resistance," *Missiology: An International Review* 4, no. 3 (1976): 318.

13 The Pew Research Center recently published two reports that help us understand many of the social and religious dynamics shaping the Muslim world. The first explores Muslim views of *shari'a* law, civil legal systems, women's rights, morality, democracy, and Western culture; see Pew Research Center, "The World's Muslims: Religion, Politics and Society," April 30, 2013, http://www.pewforum.org/2013/04/30/the-worlds-muslims-religion-politics-society-overview/. The second deals more with sectarian and religious issues; see Pew Research Center, "The World's Muslims: Unity in Diversity," August 9, 2012, http://www.pewforum.org/2012/08/09/the-worlds-muslims-unity-and-diversity-executive-summary/.

14 While most of North Africa is Muslim, some parts of West Africa at the village level have this type of diversity and pluralism, especially in areas where both Islam and Christianity have only recently been introduced. While Indonesian ethnic groups tend to embrace exclusively one religion or another, some ethnic groups (e.g., the Javanese of central Java), have more tolerance for an individual to be Muslim or Christian and still be accepted by the community.

a past that, in part, involved Islam?[15] How much has globalization, Westernization, or postmodern thought influenced the society? Globalization causes some Muslims to search for spiritual options different from Islam, while others feel compelled to deepen their commitment to Islam, longing to maintain what feels familiar and stable.

Ethnic realities also play a part. Some Muslim nations are multiethnic; others are relatively mono-cultural. Where several distinct Muslim ethnic groups live side by side, does one group tend to be politically, economically, or socially oppressed by other Muslim groups? This trend is seen today, for example, with some Berbers in North Africa, some Sub-Saharan African Muslims, and some Kurds in the Middle East. These groups have all felt mistreated by fellow Muslims.

The degree of Muslim socioreligious variance in any given area is also a contributing factor. For example, is there tolerance for unorthodox or folk expressions of Islam? Or are there local Sufi groups, many of which have a longstanding history of regarding Isa as the model for life and godliness?[16] Not only may the presence of folk or Sufi expressions of Muslim piety open the way for the gospel; they may also increase the possibility for new expressions of faith in Jesus to emerge from within the Muslim community. An example of this could be groups of Muslims who study and obey the other three, generally neglected Muslim holy books, the *Tawrat*, *Zabur*, and *Injil*.[17]

Another crucial factor is the historical interaction Muslims have had with those known as Christians in the past.[18] Were the only "Christians" they have ever known colonial European soldiers and administrators?[19] Has there ever been an authentic, loving, relevant messenger of the gospel living in their midst?[20] Is there a Bible in the local language, and does it use the terminology and literary forms of the Muslims? Have gospel messengers, past or present, communicated a simple, loving message focusing on the good news of the life, death, and resurrection of Jesus for all peoples, or have Muslims heard messages on the cultural superiority of the Christian religion and their need to change religions to be saved?[21]

---

15   This seems to have been the case with numbers of Muslims who were formerly under Communist rule in some areas of Eastern Europe, such as Albania and parts of Central Asia.

16   How Muslims view Muslim Sufi orders depends largely on the region. The Pew Research report "The World's Muslims: Unity in Diversity" indicates, for example, that 77 percent of South Asian Muslims consider Sufis to be fellow Muslims, in contrast to only 50 percent in the Middle East and North Africa and 24 percent in Southeast Asia.

17   In Islam, *Tawrat*, or the book of Moses, refers to either the Torah or the entire Hebrew Scriptures; *Zabur*, or the book of David, is the Psalms; and *Injil*, or the book of Jesus, is the Gospels or the entire New Testament. Muslims acknowledge the validity of these three books, although they are seldom studied or followed.

18   One of the Pew Research Center reports on Muslims' attitudes found that Muslim views of Christians varied significantly from country to country. See "Chapter 3. Views of Religious Groups," in "Mixed Views of Hamas and Hezbollah in Largely Muslim Nations," February 4, 2010, http://www.pewglobal.org/2010/02/04/chapter-3-views-of-religious-groups/. Of the ten Muslim-majority countries surveyed, Turkey (which is in some ways the most Westernized of the countries surveyed) had the most negative view of Christianity—68 percent viewed Christians negatively, followed by Pakistan with 61 percent. A look at Turkey's history shows, however, that their historical enemies (Greeks, Armenians, and Eastern European nations) have been viewed as "Christian" kingdoms with, from the Muslim perspective, "Christian" armies.

19   Most of today's Muslim world has been under European colonial domination at some point in history.

20   A recent survey indicated that the lifestyle and witness of Christian(s) whom MBBs had personally known ranked highest as a factor in their decision to follow Jesus. See J. Dudley Woodberry, Russell G. Shubin, and G. Marks, "Why Muslims Follow Jesus," *CT*, October 2007.

21   While the issue of religious identification will eventually come up when talking to Muslims about Jesus, messengers of the gospel must emphasize the biblical truth that we are saved by grace through faith in Jesus, not

This question is highly relevant, because gospel communicators, whether nationals or expatriates, regardless of the context of a given people, can heavily influence the type of faith that emerges in terms of the C-spectrum.[22]

Increased education and the Internet are impacting the Muslim world in many ways. Until recently, advanced educational opportunities were often quite limited, and freedom to consider other religious or spiritual beliefs was nonexistent for most. Many Muslims today, however, study abroad or in large metropolitan areas in their own country, where they are exposed to new philosophical and spiritual ideas. Education for women is also becoming more widely embraced in the Muslim world, according to recent research.[23] Even for those who do not have the option of advanced education, Internet cafes have made the world accessible, and many Muslims have been spiritually impacted by what they have discovered reading or interacting online.

Finally, on the individual level, what has been a person's experience with Islam? Does he or she feel that Islam meets life's deepest spiritual needs? Or is he or she tired of Islam, possibly no longer believing it is the only true path to God? Has he or she experienced kindness and concern or harshness and hypocrisy on the part of coreligionists? These factors can shape the ways individual Muslims see faith and religious identity and how they express their faith in Christ. Some may have come to disdain Islam, wanting a clean break with the past. Others may see Islam as the culture they are part of and choose to follow Jesus while remaining inside that community. We now look more specifically at how these factors could impact C-spectrum choices.

Societal Factors and C-spectrum Choices

This discussion begins with C6, because many, perhaps most, Muslims begin their journey with Jesus as secret or underground believers. The social climates that most strongly influence MBBs toward C6 are those in which Islamic governments declare changing religions illegal, even punishable by imprisonment or worse. These small groups of secret or underground believers, called "catacomb" Christ followers by Father Jean-Marie Gaudeul,[24] might also be found where not only governmental but strong familial and social pressure militate against changing religions. The GTFP data indicated that 8 percent of the more than seven hundred MBB fellowships the research identified were C6.

---

by joining a particular religion.

22 A case in point is the story of our friend, whom we call "Achmad." Some national Christians lovingly and tirelessly shared the gospel with him. After a supernatural encounter with God, he accepted Christ and became a member of their traditional C1 church at their warm invitation. He knew of no other option for fellowship. Years later he encountered believers in a C4 group and learned much from them. He later sensed God's call to join a C5 group, as he deemed that type of fellowship the one most apt to reach his family members and friends who did not yet follow Jesus. Other members of his family, however, had already come to faith and joined a traditional C1 church. This illustrates that personal preference may vary from individual to individual even in the same family, that gospel messengers can impact the C-spectrum choices MBBs make, and that MBBs may make C-spectrum changes over time.

23 One Pew Research report indicates widespread Muslim support for equal education between male and female youths: 96 percent in Lebanon supported equal education, 93 percent in Indonesia, 89 percent in Turkey, and 87 percent in Pakistan. See Pew Research Center, "Chapter 1. Muslim Views on Extremist Groups and Conflict," in "Mixed Views of Hamas and Hezbollah."

24 *Called from Islam to Christ: Why Muslims Become Christians* (Crowborough, East Sussex, UK: Monarch, 1999), 264–65, 288.

The GTFP data found that 21 percent of the fellowships were of the C5 type. These C5 expressions of faith have often emerged in situations where Muslim identity and cultural identity are deeply intertwined, and yet the sociopolitical environment is fluid enough for Muslims to discreetly meet in homes to study the Bible and fellowship with other Muslim followers of Jesus. Although both C5 and C6 believers hold many beliefs that are different from those of other Muslims, culturally and socially they remain part of the surrounding Muslim community, participating in its life in ways that do not violate their consciences or Scripture. Believers we know in C5 fellowships long to stay a part of their families and communities, remaining as witnesses to the new life they have experienced through Jesus. The existence of C5 expressions of faith depends largely on the ability of MBBs to show solidarity with the community, while expressing biblical truth in ways that do not shame or attack their Muslim family and friends and do not compete with existing leadership in the religious community.

C4 fellowships are found in contexts where MBBs have distanced themselves from a Muslim religious identity but are not comfortable with a Christian identity either. This is usually due to negative cultural and historical associations Muslims have with Christendom and the West. Those in C4 fellowships still resonate strongly with Islamic forms. Like C5, they wish to live with the dress, terminology, diet, and other cultural forms they have always known, and retain most Muslim forms (reinterpreting them when appropriate) rather than embracing outside "Christian" or Western socioreligious forms. Not calling themselves either Muslim or Christian, they find some other way of describing who they are spiritually (e.g., "followers of Isa," "believers," etc.). The GTFP data indicated that more than a third (37 percent) of the fellowships identified in the research were C4, in spite of the fact that, at times, being seen as neither Christian nor Muslim raises some of its own unique challenges.[25]

Though C4, C5, and C6 fellowships have differing socioreligious identities, all incorporate Muslim forms to varying degrees. For some this means continuing to use cultural and religious forms that are familiar, while for others it involves deliberate effort to maintain continuity with their heritage and community.[26]

In contexts where Muslims apply strong social and political pressure in their communities at the expense of social and religious liberties, it has caused some Muslims to want nothing to do with Islam again. This has launched many on a search for new spiritual options, and some form or join a C1, C2, or C3 fellowship, where Islamic forms and identity are rejected altogether.

C3 fellowships, though they reject Muslim identity and forms, are characterized by efforts to incorporate non-Islamic aspects of the surrounding culture, such as folk music, artwork, and traditional ethnic dress.[27] Such groups often develop in places where new believers desire to have a Christian identity yet maintain their natural ethnic and cultural identity, allowing themselves to be known as

---

25 Some have found the Muslim reaction to the term "follower of Isa," as opposed to more familiar categories such as "Muslim," "Sunni," "Christian," etc., to be problematic. In some contexts an unrecognized term can be perceived as threatening or subversive. In other places this term is well received and opens up discussions on what it means to follow and who Isa really is.

26 Something we have frequently heard from those in C5 fellowships is that as they begin to tell other Muslims about Jesus, even if they are relating as Muslims to fellow Muslims, they are accused of having changed religions. A process begins whereby they struggle to find ways to show their loyalty and solidarity with the community while not denying Jesus. Some are able to carve out space for themselves and their fellow Jesus followers inside the Muslim community; others face persecution and are eventually shunned or expelled by the community.

27 This raises the question, to what extent can religious and cultural forms be separated in a holistic Muslim society? Many of the cultural forms used by C3 groups are based on pre-Islamic forms and practices.

"Turkish Christians" or "Tunisian Christians." The GTFP research indicated that 28 percent of fellowships identified were C3.

C1 and C2 fellowships are usually planted by and affiliated with national or international Christian denominations. Some of these denominations in the Muslim world, such as the Coptic Church of Egypt and numerous Orthodox churches in other parts of the Middle East and Asia, predate Islam. In some parts of the Muslim world, MBBs are drawn to C1 and C2 groups due to their institutional strength and recognized legitimacy. The GTFP data indicated that 5 percent of the fellowships identified were C2 and only 1 percent C1.

A final word should be said about C-spectrum categories and religious persecution. All six types of fellowships can and often do suffer persecution for the name of Jesus, and C-spectrum choices do not seem to be related to the avoidance of persecution.[28]

Summary and Closing Thoughts

The GTFP data indicates diversity in the forms of fellowships and socioreligious identities of Muslims who follow Jesus. This study identified several societal factors that seem to influence these choices, without suggesting a predictive model of ministry.

An important caveat highlighted by this study is that the personal preferences and methodologies of gospel messengers, irrespective of particular societal factors, significantly contribute to the choices MBBs make. This raises several crucial points.

Firstly, messengers of the gospel, as servants of both God and those they are called to serve (1 Cor 9:19), must be willing to adjust their methods for the sake of those who do not yet understand the good news of Jesus (1 Cor 9:20–23). Thus, when considering C-spectrum options, the primary considerations should be how God is leading and what is best for new Jesus followers, regardless of the personal preferences or background of the gospel messenger.[29]

Secondly, due to either the influence of gospel messengers or some of the societal factors mentioned above, when the gospel first enters a people group, it tends to be embraced by early adopters and limited segments of the society.[30] This often results in only one type of fellowship being planted initially in any given area. These first-fruits fellowships may not be representative of the people group or the nation as a whole. In time, as the gospel goes deeper and wider, into other segments of the society, additional approaches will be taken and different C-spectrum expressions may arise. In time we will likely see multiple socioreligious identities among MBBs in the same people group or area.

Finally, there is no one ideal type of Muslim-background fellowship or socioreligious identity. God may lead Muslims in one area to follow Jesus in particular ways, yet lead Muslims in other areas in different ways. May all of us whom God has called to work among Muslims remain pliable in our

---

28 The field research of Ben Naja (chap. 15) found that although 92 percent of the Jesus followers in a particular movement had some form of Muslim social identity, a full 47 percent of them reported undergoing various forms of persecution for their faith in Christ.

29 On philosophical, strategic, or theological grounds, some MBBs and cross-cultural workers are opposed to certain positions on the C-scale. We are not suggesting that one violate his or her conscience or calling. Within those parameters, however, a worker should be as flexible in approach as possible for the sake of those who have not yet embraced the good news, just as churches and parachurch organizations in many parts of the world today offer a wide range of spiritual expressions depending upon the context of the community.

30 This pattern is reported repeatedly. Students, the poor, intellectuals, mystical groups, or a particular ethnic group may be the earliest responders to the gospel in any given context.

Master's hands, willing to adjust our methods and to bless the multitude of ways God is at work among Muslims in our day.

Bibliography

Garrison, David. *A Wind in the House of Islam: How God Is Drawing Muslims around the World to Faith in Jesus Christ.* Monument, CO: WIGTake, 2013.

Gaudeul, Jean-Marie. *Called from Islam to Christ: Why Muslims Become Christians.* Crowborough, East Sussex, UK: Monarch, 1999.

Goldsmith, Martin. "Community and Controversy: Key Causes of Muslim Resistance." *Missiology: An International Review* 4, no. 3 (1976): 317–23.

Trousdale, Jerry. *Miraculous Movements: How Hundreds of Thousands of Muslims Are Falling in Love with Jesus.* Nashville: Thomas Nelson, 2012.

Woodberry, J. Dudley. "A Global Perspective on Muslims Coming to Faith in Christ." In *From the Straight Path to the Narrow Way: Journeys of Faith*, edited by David Greenlee, 11–22. Waynesboro, GA: Authentic, 2006.

———, ed. *From Seed to Fruit: Global Trends, Fruitful Practices, and Emerging Issues among Muslims.* Pasadena, CA: William Carey Library, 2007.

———, Russell G. Shubin, and G. Marks. "Why Muslims Follow Jesus." *Christianity Today*, October 2007.

CHAPTER 64

God's Creativity in Drawing Muslims to Jesus

Richard Jameson

In the early chapters of Acts we find two types of Gentile Christ followers from Antioch. The first type is represented by Nicolas (the seventh deacon chosen to oversee the problem raised by the Greek-speaking Jews in Acts 6:1). Acts 6:5 describes him as a convert (*proselytos*) to Judaism. In Acts 11 we find a second type of Antiochian believer—those who did not convert to Judaism. Rather they forged a new identity for themselves without importing what would have been viewed as a foreign religious community. Their communities did not know what to call these believers. They weren't Jews. Yet they constantly gave witness as followers of one called "the Christ." Thus they were labeled *Christianoi*, which can be translated "Christ followers."[1]

For more than twenty years I have been working in the Muslim world, and I am observing a phenomenon similar to what happened in the early church. Two very distinct communities of believers from Muslim background (BMBs) are emerging: those who are converts to Christianity and those who are forging a new identity for themselves from within their sociocultural community.

Converts to Christianity

Although Gentiles from both communities were "converts" to Christ, until the first Gentile church was birthed in Antioch, the only Gentiles in the church were also converts to Judaism (Acts 2:5; 6:5). Similarly, the majority of BMBs in today's world have been converts to the Christian religion. In general, these BMB converts have followed a common path to Christ. This journey starts with a growing apathy tending to antipathy towards Islam. This hostility towards the religion of their birth springs from at least four causes.

Muslim-on-Muslim Violence

Wherever Muslims have been killing Muslims, a segment of the Muslim population has grown discontented with Islam. Muslims have bombed mosques in Iraq. Muslims have attacked Muslim funeral services in Pakistan. As a result, a portion of the population has begun to think, "If this is Islam, I don't want to have anything to do with it."

---

1   "By its whole formation it is a word which defines the one to whom it is applied as belonging to the party of a certain *Christos*, very much as *Hērōdianos* is a technical term for the followers of Herod (Mark 3:6; 12:13; Matt 22:16)." K. H. Rengstorf, "Χριστιανός [*Christianos*]," in *New International Dictionary of New Testament Theology*, vol. 2, ed. L. Coenen, E. Beyreuther, and H. Bietenhard (Grand Rapids, MI: Zondervan, 1986), 343.

Arab Oppression of Ethnic Minorities

A specialized form of Muslim-on-Muslim violence has been seen in ethnic oppression by Muslim-majority governments. On March 16, 1988, Saddam Hussein ordered his military to attack the Kurdish town of Halabja with poison gas. Perhaps as many as five thousand people died immediately, and thousands more died subsequently of their injuries. The Kurdish people have been oppressed by Muslim governments in surrounding countries as well. Iran, Turkey, Iraq, and Syria have all oppressed their Kurdish minority populations. Among a segment of the population, this has resulted in hatred towards Islam and openness to the gospel. Oppression of ethnic minorities in North Africa has resulted in similar openness to the gospel.

Fundamentalist Resurgence in a Secularized Muslim Society

When Islamic fundamentalism was imposed on people who had grown accustomed to the liberal secular policies of the Shah of Iran, a significant segment of the population became disenchanted with Islam. This has provided an opportunity for the gospel. Perhaps as many as two thousand Iranians per day are becoming followers of Christ.

Personal Issues

Rashid was raised in a very conservative Islamic home. As a boy he would often ask his imam questions about aspects of Islamic theology that troubled him. He was consistently told not to ask those kinds of questions. This resulted in a frustration with Islam, which led him to become a secular Muslim.

Rahmat was naturally left-handed. As a small child, his parents would tie his left hand behind his back so that he would not use his "unclean" hand in inappropriate ways. This left Rahmat feeling that his religion made him a second-class citizen.

Another major factor for both men and women, but especially women, is relationships. The intolerance of the Muslim community when a loved one converts or if a Muslim has the misfortune to fall in love with a Christian can lead to a growing dissatisfaction with one's religion of birth.

At a time when the discontentment of marginalized Muslims is in full bloom, they encounter Jesus. Sometimes it is through dreams, visions, or some miraculous event. Other times it is through the Scriptures and friendship with true followers of Christ. Tens of thousands of these marginalized and discontented Muslims, throughout the Muslim world, have converted to Christianity in the last thirty years.

In virtually every Muslim society one finds the aforementioned marginalized Muslims. This could be pictured as the darker outer fringe of the circle in figure 64.1. Muslim peoples are different one from another. Among some peoples this fringe area seems to be quite wide. Among other groups it seems to be razor thin. Over the last fourteen hundred years most Muslims who have come to Christ have come from this outer fringe area.

In every Muslim society, a significant percentage of the population is quite content. Islam for them is much more than a religious system. It is their family, their culture, their customs, and their language. Leaving this community is not entertained as an option. This is represented by the lighter core of the diagram.

Fig. 64.1 A typical Muslim community

In recent years we have begun to see Muslims come to Christ from the core of these communities. These emerging communities are unique.

"In Christ" Muslims

This community of followers of Christ[2] has followed a very different path to Jesus. Sometimes through their own reading of the Qur'an, sometimes through the testimonies of other followers of Christ, these Muslims have discovered the testimony about Jesus within the Qur'an. The message they have received through Muhammad[3] has directed them to read and study the New Testament (*Injil*). This in turn has led these Muslims to a personal encounter with the living Jesus.

This growing community of faith in Christ has retained their Muslim identity. Rather than converting to Christianity, these believers consider themselves to be Muslim followers of Christ. Their Muslim neighbors and friends recognize them to be a different kind of Muslim. Yet, because of the way they dress, the way they talk, and their continued respect for the pillars of Islam and the school of Islamic jurisprudence common in their part of the world, they have retained their Muslim identity within their communities.

The emergence of these communities of "in Christ Muslims" has given rise to significant controversy in missiological circles. Both these emerging communities and those walking alongside these movements, encouraging them in their growing obedience to the Scriptures without demanding that they abandon their religious community of birth, are facing growing criticism in the Western Christian press.

A missiologist who has spent his entire missionary career in the Arab world, in reaction to what has been described as "insider movements," wrote a list of nine crucial questions and his answers. The answers to these questions are designed to present a sharp contrast between those who would identify themselves as Christians and the surrounding Muslim community.[4]

1. "Is Allah, as identified by Muslims, the same God as YHWH, identified by Jews and Christians from their Scriptures?"

    "No! The ascribed attributes of Allah and YHWH depart at the level of his covenantal nature and are illuminated in the 'names of God' that further manifest his character."

---

2   It is hard to know how to refer to these believers. Do we emphasize the core or the collective identity? I sometimes refer to them as "in Christ" Muslims, emphasizing their core identity. In other places I emphasize their collective identity and refer to them as Muslim followers of Christ. The two terms are somewhat interchangeable in that they emphasize different aspects of the same group of growing disciples.

3   The source of the Qur'an and the subsequent development of Islamic theology is often raised in this context. Most opposed to the "in Christ" Muslim phenomenon believe that Islam is inspired by demons. I have come to the conclusion that one of the ways that the Lord is bringing glory to himself is by taking what appeared to be a great satanic victory and accomplishing his purposes through it. This truth is graphically illustrated in the life of David. David's great moral failure (Satan's apparent victory) was with Bathsheba. David's adultery, murder, and deceit ultimately resulted in the divided kingdom and rampant idolatry throughout the nation. Yet both Jesus' legal and biological genealogies go back to David through children born to Bathsheba. Our heavenly Father could have used one of David's other wives. However, he chose to take Satan's great victory in David's life and ultimately use it for his greatest glory in the Incarnation. Our heavenly Father seems to delight in doing this. The Cross is another example of this truth.

4   J. Raymond Tallman, "The Role of the Academy in Missiological Formation" (academic convocation address, Golden Gate Baptist Theological Seminary, March 11, 2010).

2. "Is Mohammad a Prophet?"

   "No! My response to any other person claiming to be such since the time frame of the Apostolic era, with the Canon of Scripture established soon thereafter, would be the same. 'Prophets' are those who received revelation from God, and their message remains trans-cultural and is not time limited."

3. "Is the Qur'an a book to be considered as part of 'Holy Scripture' which includes both the Old and New Testaments?"

   "No! It cannot be considered as delivered from heaven directly from God. The progress of divine written revelation as defined by Scripture is fully complete with the Old and New Testament canons established."

4. "Is the Isa of the Qur'an the same as the Jesus of the Injil (Gospel) acknowledged by Muslims as a 'holy book'?"

   "No! Some, but certainly not all, references to Jesus in the Qur'an are accurate. 'The final—book closed—identification of Jesus' in Islam falls far short of identifying either who he is or what he accomplished."

5. "Is Ishmael equally a recipient of 'the divine promise' so clearly given to Isaac from Abraham?"

   "No! Scripture remains clear concerning the unique role of Isaac as related to the Messiah and the future kingdom of God. Ishmael is honored as an elder son of Abraham by a cultural promise of great significance."

6. "Is the kingdom of God, as spoken of in Scripture, able to expand its boundaries to include Muslims seeking God and acknowledging Jesus as a Prophet?"

   "No. Kingdom citizenship comes by 'spiritual birth.' Spiritual birth comes by arriving at the conclusion that the Jesus of the Bible is the one to be received as both Lord and Savior."

7. "Do 'mosques' (*jamaat*) qualify as 'church' in New Testament terms?"

   "No! As a place of worship both the forms of worship and their meaning are not adequate. As a place of 'fellowship' they only satisfy the generic meaning of the word and do not rise to 'body life' concepts associated with biblical community definition. They certainly do not fit the universal concept of 'Church' as the 'body of Christ.'"

8. "Can baptism be relegated to non-essential for true Muslim followers of Jesus?"

   "No! Baptism is a clear cultural marker not to be ignored. It identifies the follower of Jesus with his death, burial and resurrection and it identifies the follower with the universal 'body of Christ.' It is a declaration of one's cultural allegiance to Jesus as Lord and Savior and the kingdom of God as our primary citizenship."

9. "Can Messianic Fellowships of Jewish believers be equated with Jesus Muslim fellowships?"

   "No, the experience of the Jew who accepts the Old Testament as we have is entirely different than the Muslim seeker who considers the Old and New Testaments as corrupted."

Those walking alongside communities of "in Christ Muslims" might address the same issues with a different set of questions and answers:

1. Is there enough truth about Allah as identified by Muslims to use this as a starting point in leading a Muslim to a full knowledge of the God of the Bible?

    Yes! All of the ninety-nine beautiful names of Allah, at least conceptually, are found in the Old and New Testaments. Although the understanding of the meaning of these names may be different, this at least provides us with enough commonality to begin.

2. Can a growing disciple of Christ have a positive and respectful attitude towards Muhammad?

    Yes! We have seen many Muslims come into the kingdom who have lowered Muhammad from his exalted position within their religion of birth but kept a positive, respectful attitude towards him.

3. Can a growing disciple of Christ maintain a positive and respectful attitude towards the Qur'an?

    Yes! Many have come to Christ following the road signs found within the Qur'an. These signs have pointed people to the Bible and to Jesus as revealed in the Scriptures. When coming to Christ through this route, disciples maintain a high respect for the truth found in the Qur'an.

4. Is there enough truth about Isa in the Qur'an to use this as a starting point to lead Muslims to the fuller knowledge of Jesus as revealed in the written Scriptures?

    Yes! The Qur'an contains an amazing amount of true information about Jesus. This has proven to be a wonderful starting point in reaching Muslims with the gospel.

5. Are the descendants of Ishmael recipients of some unique promises from God?

    Yes! Apart from the promise of covenantal blessing for all peoples, which is only through Jesus, all the promises to Isaac are echoed to Ishmael. Isaiah 60 (and other Scripture) makes clear that these promises have ongoing validity to Ishmael's descendants.

6. Is the kingdom of God, as spoken of in Scripture, able to expand its boundaries to include Muslims who through repentance put their faith in Jesus as their crucified and resurrected Lord?

    Yes! Our heavenly Father accepts people from every tribe, nation, people, language, and religion who put their faith in Jesus, who died for their sins.

7. Can a true follower of Christ worship God anywhere as long as his heart is right?

    Yes! As Jesus said to the Samaritan woman, it is not the place of worship that matters. Worshiping in the Spirit and truth is what matters. Worship and fellowship are not dependent upon the building in which they occur; rather worship and fellowship are dependent solely upon the hearts of those gathering in the name of Jesus as members of his body.

8. Should those from Muslim background be given the freedom to baptize in a way that does not communicate becoming a traitor to one's own people?

    Yes! If given the opportunity, those from Muslim background are very creative in developing baptismal forms that communicate the biblical meaning of baptism without unnecessarily insulting their families or their cultures.

9. Are there striking parallels between Muslim and Jewish communities that have given rise to similar expressions of faith from within both communities?

Yes! Uncompromising monotheism, holistic integration of religion into every aspect of life, salvation by works, rejection of atonement through Christ, and rejection of Christian interpretation of their "book" are just a few of the parallels.

Commonalities between the Two BMB Communities

As men and women have come to Jesus along these two divergent paths, I have observed a number of similarities among them. Believers from both groups are wholeheartedly committed to Jesus Christ as Lord and Savior of their lives. Both groups are committed to the Scriptures and use the New Testament as their primary book for discipleship. Both groups evidence the fruit of the Spirit in their daily lives. In both groups, the Holy Spirit is confirming their radical message about Jesus through signs and wonders. Both communities of faith show evidence of being full of the Spirit and wisdom. Both groups are committed to seeing their people freed from the spiritual bondage experienced in Satan's kingdom. Many from both groups would identify themselves as being culturally Muslim. And both groups have a primary identification with all true followers of Christ from all nations and all languages of the world.

Differences between the Two BMB Communities

Despite these similarities, there are some marked differences between the two communities. For the most part, Muslim-background converts to Christianity have come to Christ in spite of or in reaction against Islam. "In Christ" Muslims have come to Christ through what they perceive to be the testimony of the Qur'an. Some of the differences these two disparate routes to Christ have produced are as follows.[5]

Religious Identification. Muslim-background converts tend to identify with the broader community of people who call themselves "Christian" and would readily think of themselves by this name. On the other hand, "in Christ" Muslims retain the worldwide Islamic community as their broader religious community, not Christendom. They would identify themselves as Muslims. Many don't like the term "Muslim-background" since to them it seems to imply that they quit being Muslims when they became followers of Christ. Within their communities they seem to be viewed as a new sect of Islam.

Interpretation of the Qur'an. Converts to Christianity believe that the traditional Islamic interpretation of qur'anic verses concerning the person and work of Christ is the only appropriate interpretation. This interpretation consistently contradicts the message of the New Testament. Thus converts tend to see minimal common ground between the Qur'an and the New Testament. On the other hand, "in Christ" Muslims believe that Yunus (10):94[6] teaches that the books that came before the Qur'an should provide the primary interpretive basis for the Qur'an. When the Bible becomes the lens through which the Qur'an is evaluated and interpreted, a radically different understanding of its teaching emerges.

---

5   In order to illustrate the differences between these two groups I run the risk of stereotyping individuals. I am presenting general profiles of the two groups, and any given individual may not fit the profile for his or her group on one or more of these items.

6   "So if you are in doubt, [O Muhammad], about that which We have revealed to you, then ask those who have been reading the Scripture before you. The truth has certainly come to you from your Lord, so never be among the doubters."

Thus "in Christ" Muslims find considerable common ground between the New Testament and the Qur'an.

Deception or Signposts. Converts to Christianity feel deceived by Islam. The entire religion is thought to be deceptive and controlled by the father of lies.[7] They want to rescue their people from this deception. Islam is thought to be like a burning building. People need to be rescued from the fire before they perish. In contrast, Muslim followers of Christ are grieved that their people can't see the signposts pointing to Jesus and the Gospels in the Qur'an. They recognize that Islamic traditions have masked these signposts. But they are committed to helping other Muslims discover and follow these signposts to Jesus.

Humor or Honor. Converts to Christianity may be offended when non-Muslims criticize Islam. However, among themselves they are free to joke about Muhammad, the Qur'an, and other aspects of their former faith. For them, the Islamic confession of faith is blasphemous and could never be said by a true follower of Christ. In contrast, Muslim followers of Christ maintain a respect for Muhammad and the Qur'an. They came to Christ through what they understood to be the testimony of the Qur'an. In actual practice Muhammad fades to insignificance as Jesus assumes his rightful place in their lives as King of kings and Lord of lords.

Method of Evangelism. Both converts to Christianity and Muslim followers of Christ are committed to evangelizing their own people. For both, the transforming work of the Holy Spirit in the lives of believers and signs and wonders play a significant role in leading others into a personal relationship with Jesus. However, converts tend to prefer a polemical approach to evangelism. Before they came to Christ, they grew indifferent to or sometimes opposed to Islam. Thus for converts, initial evangelism is often geared towards revealing all that is bad within their former religion. Once a person agrees that Islam is bad or inadequate, then there is openness to the gospel. Muslim followers of Christ use the Qur'an in conjunction with prayer, meeting social needs, and personal testimony as their primary tools for evangelism. For them the Bible has become the standard for interpretation and the filter through which they determine what is from God and what is not. As a result they have come to a new understanding of what the Qur'an and Islamic traditions teach about Jesus. The common ground that they find between the Bible and the Qur'an provides the bridge for their outreach to their communities. One Muslim follower of Christ shares his testimony as follows:

> Before I knew Jesus, I was in a dark cave. All I had for light was
> one flickering candle. Since it was the only light I had, I thought
> it was quite bright and I was quite proud of my candle. For many
> years, when I would meet Christians, I felt as though they were
> trying to blow out my candle. This made me angry and defensive.
> Then a dear friend came and used my candle to guide me out of the
> cave into the bright sunlight of Jesus Christ. Once I came into the
> light of Christ, I looked down at my candle and realized that it was
> feeble and weak. But I didn't throw it in the mud and stomp on it.
> Rather I thought of all my friends and relatives who were still in the

---

7   The following qur'anic verse is often quoted: "But they [the Jews] were deceptive, and Allah was deceptive, for Allah is the best of deceivers [*Wamakaroo wamakara Allahu waAllahu khayru al-makireena*]!" (surah 3:54). To be fair, I've never seen a Muslim translate this verse in this way. Yusuf Ali translates the same verse thus: "And (the unbelievers) plotted and planned, and Allah too planned, and the best of planners is Allah."

darkness of the cave of Islam with only their meager candles. So I
took my candle and went back into the cave in order to lead others
into the light of Christ.

Religious Vocabulary. Converts to Christianity tend to prefer Christian vocabulary. They have embraced
the standard translations of the Scriptures used by the Christian communities in their regions. Often
they oppose the idea of having more than one translation of the Scriptures in their language. This community is often the most vocal in speaking against Muslim-idiom translations. In speaking of Jesus,
some do not want to use *Isa*, the name found in the Qur'an. In a few cases converts take a "Christian"
name to replace their "Muslim" name when they are baptized. In contrast, Muslim followers of Christ
continue to use exclusively Islamic religious vocabulary and names. They are strong advocates for some
of the newer translations of the Scripture that preserve the vocabulary from their Islamic background
and attempt to interpret for the reader difficult theological concepts such as "Son of God."[8]

Pillars of Islam. Converts to Christianity find the forms of Islam to be a slavery from which they
have been set free. One friend of mine related that after twenty years as a Christian he was invited to
join some Muslim followers of Christ in their prayers at the mosque. Immediately he felt an oppressive
heaviness as the weight of legalism again came crushing down on his shoulders. In contrast, some Muslim followers of Christ find the prayers and fasting within Islam to be a joyous response to the love of
God, which has been poured out for their sake through Christ. For some, these religious forms provide
a way for them to continue to identify with their communities and a platform from which they can share
the good news about Jesus. For others who rarely practiced the pillars of Muslim faith before coming to
Christ or come from communities where they are rarely practiced, their ethnicity and ongoing engagement with the community is enough for them to retain a "Muslim" social identity and maintain the
natural relationships along which the gospel flows.

Attitudes towards One Another. Finally, converts to Christianity have often paid a very high price to
follow Christ. Their decision to convert to Christianity has often meant interrogations, torture, social
ostracism, imprisonment, loss of family, and sometimes loss of country. For many converts, only fear
would motivate one to maintain one's identity within Islam. These converts feel that Muslim followers
of Christ are compromising their faith and "pretending" to be Muslims in order to avoid persecution.
On the other hand, Muslim followers of Christ find converts to Christianity very difficult to understand. They ask, "Why would one turn one's back on one's culture, people, and religion to become a
Christian?" For them, converts to Christianity have burned their bridges and lost their most natural
means for reaching their own people with the gospel.

The following chart summarizes the differences between these two kinds of BMB communities.

---

8 "In Christ" Muslims are coming to their theological consultants and saying, "The way this is currently literally translated, it means to us in our language that the Father God engaged in sex with a mother god and produced
a child god. Is that what is intended?" When the theological consultant says no, the local believers ask, "So what
does it mean?" They then plead for a meaning-based paraphrase instead of a literal translation of this phrase. See
the footnote in "Read This First!" that explains briefly why translation issues are not treated in *UIM*.

Converts to Christianity	"In Christ" Muslims
Call self "Christian"	Call self "Muslim"
Hold traditional Muslim interpretation of Qur'an	Interpret Qur'an based on the Bible
Raise children as Christians	Raise children as Muslim "followers of the Messiah"
View Islam as a deceptive religion	View Islam as a candle leading to Jesus
Hold Muhammad and Qur'an in low esteem	Hold Muhammad and Qur'an in high esteem
See attacks on Islamic traditions as integral to evangelism	See Qur'an and Islamic traditions as stepping-stones leading to Jesus
Prefer religious terms borrowed from Christian cultures	Prefer native religious terms common to the Muslim culture
See pillars of Islam as bondage	See pillars of Islam as ways to express faith in God in Christ

Conclusion

Divergent contexts have given birth to very different types of Christ followers from Muslim background. How should we respond in the West? Should we choose sides? Should we line up behind one community or the other? Should we defend those with whom we most agree and attack those with whom we tend to disagree? Or can we come together as the body of Christ, rejoicing in all that the Lord is doing to draw Muslims to himself? Can we recognize that our God is amazingly creative in the ways that he calls Muslims to saving faith in Christ? Can we walk alongside these brothers and sisters from Muslim background from across the contextual spectrum, encouraging them in their faith and calling them to greater faithfulness and obedience as we ourselves work towards the same in our own lives?

Bibliography

Rengstorf, K. H. Χριστιανός [Christianos]. In *New International Dictionary of New Testament Theology*, vol. 2, edited by L. Coenen, E. Beyreuther, and H. Bietenhard, 343. Grand Rapids, MI: Zondervan, 1986.

Tallman, J. Raymond. "The Role of the Academy in Missiological Formation." Academic convocation address, Golden Gate Baptist Theological Seminary, March 11, 2010.

1. Who determines whether or not particular cultural, religious, or ethnic elements should be altered or eliminated, and how is this determined? Is this a personal decision or a group decision? Who "owns" this process? Consider the book of Acts and Paul's letter to the Galatians: by focusing on certain practices, how did the "Judaizers" distract people from the gospel and lead them into syncretism from their own religious culture?

2. What parts of Scripture would you use to explain why people should or should not shift aspects of their identity to reach out to people of other faiths? Have you ever taken on a new identity in some way to talk to someone very different from you about Jesus? If given the opportunity again, would you do something different?

3. What "identity markers" are inclusive of all the people of God? What identity markers do you hold that might prevent you from seeing others as fellow members of the kingdom of God?

4. In what ways might the values and worldviews of modern Westerners and traditional non-Westerners contribute to different attitudes toward fixed versus multiple identities and insider movements (Iyadurai, chap. 60)?

5. Explain the distinction between core, social, and collective identities (Adams, chap. 61). How would you describe these with reference to yourself?

6. In what ways does (or should) one's identity change after making the decision to submit to the lordship of Christ and the authority of the Bible? In what ways does a group's identity take new shape? What elements are "retained" versus "changed" altogether, and how should this process take place?

7. What are some challenges faced by Muslim-background believers (MBBs) with hybrid identities (Barnett, chap. 62)? What are the strengths of such identities? How does hybridity differ from syncretism? Illustrate how new cultural forms might emerge from hybridity in identity. What could this mean for the second generation of MBBs in a given context—in terms of community, marriage, job, burial, etc.?

8. To what extent do political, social, cultural, religious, and historical factors affect identity, both individually and communally (John and Anna Travis, chap. 63)? How do these factors affect your own identity when you are in a different context than the one in which you were raised?

9. Discuss the factors that may contribute to a follower of Christ choosing to be either a convert to Christianity or an "in Christ" Muslim (Jameson, chap. 64).

10. Look at the nine practical and theological questions posed in the section entitled "'In Christ' Muslims" in chapter 64. Which questions and answers fall more in line with your theology: those of the Christian missiologist or those of the "in Christ" Muslims? Or are your questions somewhere in the middle?

Where do we go from here? We conclude this anthology with a hopeful glimpse of what could be and a resolution to better understand, bless, and come alongside God's work among the peoples of the world in their diverse religious communities. Included here are the reflections of two experienced practitioners who express their desire to approach the IM discussion with love, gentleness, and discernment.

We offer a short excerpt from respected missiologist Phil Parshall's article "Lifting the Fatwa." In 1980 Parshall blazed a trail for contextualization in *New Paths in Muslim Evangelism*. As others went down somewhat different paths than he had foreseen, Parshall publicly voiced his concerns in 1998. He was then surprised to learn that a mission leader was praying that "Phil will lift his fatwa against our ministry among the followers of Ishmael." Some six years later Parshall again took stock of the situation and published an assessment. While still very concerned over a number of issues, his response below marks a way forward in humility and wisdom.

This is followed by thoughts from missions statesman Paul McKaughan. In more than four decades in mission, McKaughan served as a field worker, headed Mission to the World (the mission arm of the Presbyterian Church in America), directed the 1989 Lausanne Congress in Manila, and led the Evangelical Fellowship of Mission Agencies for fifteen years.[1] His sage reflections on the IM controversy clearly reflect "wisdom from above" as we look to the future.

Finally, the editors close this volume by synthesizing key points in our understanding of insider movements and drawing some conclusions from our study.

Lifting the Fatwa[2]

Phil Parshall

Adherents to some or all of the C5 position are growing. The country where C5 was birthed now lays claim to tens of thousands of MBBs of the C5 variety. Thousands of C4 MBBs are found there as well. Scores of missionaries and several evangelical mission boards are practicing and promoting C5 in a significant number of Muslim countries.

I personally have known many of these missionaries, some for twenty years. There is no doubt that they are sincere and long with all their hearts to see Muslims come to Christ. In one instance, a highly

---

1 The EFMA represented more than 100 organizations and 20,000 foreign missionaries. It later became The Mission Exchange; a subsequent merger was named Missio Nexus.

2 Excerpt from Phil Parshall, "Lifting the Fatwa," *EMQ* 40, no. 3 (2004): 288–93. Reprinted by permission. *Fatwa*: An edict of a religious nature pronounced by an Islamic authority.

respected evangelical Islamist checked out a large C5 movement and declared it to be a wonderful work of God. Armstrong comments:

> Those that will be involved in encouraging a movement for Jesus in Islam cannot be heresy-hunters or suspicious types, always ready to pounce on every manifestation of Christ that does not immediately match what they have been used to before. They cannot be the kind of people that can only see "black and white," for the world they will be laboring in will be full of shades of gray.[3]

Armstrong continues, "If we are, regrettably, the mission that plants a heresy, are those that adhere to it any worse off than before?" It is his view that such a "heresy" could be a future stepping stone for those Muslims to come to full-blown faith in Christ.

I struggle to form a personal position on such an important issue. The Lord has been speaking to me as I have been seeking to process the macro picture. Scripturally, I have been meditating on these verses:

- Romans 14:10: "Why do you judge your brother or sister? Or why do you treat them with contempt?"
- Romans 14:13: "Let us stop passing judgment on one another."
- Romans 15:2: "Each of us should please our neighbors for their good."
- Romans 15:7: "Accept one another, then, just as Christ accepted you."

I am quite aware of other New Testament scriptures that call theological aberrants "dogs," call down a curse on them, and designate them as antichrists. In church history we find the same theme in the Inquisition. Even the Reformers had heavy words for those who dared disagree with their interpretation of Scripture.

And so, where do we end up? Consider the *fatwa*—which was never decreed!—lifted. I do not want to end my life (now sixty-five years into it) known as a heresy hunter. Yes, I will continue (with greater sensitivity, I trust) to voice my concerns. But if I am to err toward imbalance, I want it to be on the side of love, affirmation, and lifting up my colleagues as better than myself. Even at this late stage in life, I am not prepared to profess personal infallibility. As for who is right or wrong, and to what degree, let us lean heavily on the ultimate Judge of our hearts' intents.

A Few Thoughts and Proposals on "Insider Movements"[4]

Paul McKaughan

Systems Thinking and Sin

Many years ago, as I was introduced to the discipline of "systems thinking," I was told that "my personal system" was the circle I drew around the things I could influence or control. The inference for a dispersive person like I am was that one shouldn't waste time and energy worrying about the things outside that circle but carefully manage the things in your personal and corporate system.

As I have gotten older, I have recognized that I don't draw that significant line that defines the system in which I function; I rather recognize and accept it. It is the Holy Spirit who, through God's

---

3   Brian Armstrong, in a personal communication.

4   This is the entire edition of *McKaughan Musing* (blog), September 20, 2011. Printed here by permission.

word, brothers and sisters in Christ, and even circumstances, creates the boundaries that define the contours of the system he entrusts to my stewardship.

When I ignore those boundaries and get involved outside my system with things that I feel necessitate my urgent intervention, or items that I am sure absolutely require my astounding and unique gifts, disaster is not far behind. I have come to recognize that my presumptuous boundary jumping really comes from my dual sins of pride and unbelief.

My prideful nature tells me that God speaks more clearly to me or, at the very least, I understand him more clearly than my brother or sister. My sin of unbelief is shown in that I have real doubts that the Almighty can get his point across to those who may lack my dedication, intellect, or training, even though he has called them to be a part of his family and his Spirit resides within them.

Rather than limit myself to the system in which God has placed me and trust him and his people to take care of theirs, pride and unbelief seem to exercise a strong magnetic attraction that draws my attention away from my own system and calling. Often my presumptuous intervention also messes up what he desires to do within the "system" I illicitly invaded.

Good Theology and Obedience Are Contextual

My second reflection is that the best theology comes out of the interaction of the Scripture with a specific context. Missions are always on the cutting edge of doing theology. Because of God's quest for worshipers among all peoples, we are always searching the Scriptures for the point at which the grace of God's word impacts the sense of need he has placed within people in that new culture, identity, and worldview.

Throughout church history and across diverse cultures, the Holy Spirit seems to have applied specific facets of his comprehensive revelation about God, man, and redemption. Obedience to God's word rather than mere knowledge is what counts with the Creator. Obedience to that revelation is always specific and quite concrete. What the lordship of Christ means across church history and diverse cultures is often quite distinctive.

Recognizing My Limitations

My third thought comes from my father, who is now with the Lord. Dad was a wonderfully wise and godly minister of the gospel. When I left home to prepare for the ministry, he took me aside and gave me some awesome advice. He said, "Son, when you see great and godly men arrayed on opposite sides of any major biblical truth, don't think you are going to resolve that issue." He was saying, "Paul, you should study and come to your biblical theological positions, but leave those outside your system (the metaphor I started with) to the Holy Spirit." My father knew that being a world-class theologian was not in my future. I have found that my father's admonition was good advice; still, pride and unbelief tend to lead me to dogmatic conclusions that I feel compelled to apply to those outside my system. I am often unwilling to grant to others the grace that our Father seems to extend to me.

The Existential Reality

In these days our evangelical community across the world is debating, as we should, the limits and connections between cultural identity and faith in Christ. This is especially intense in those cultures where religion plays a dominant role in framing one's identity. In almost every mission focused on unreached people, I have found a healthy and intense dialogue going on concerning what it means to be a follower of Jesus within these cultures. In these religious/cultural communities the Holy Spirit is drawing people to himself in historically unprecedented numbers. New communities of those who follow Christ and honor God's word are adopting many new forms. All of us seem to feel a compelling need to define what obedience looks like for others who accept the lordship of Jesus.

As evangelical missionaries, we once insisted that to follow Christ one had to completely break with one's culture because it was steeped in a "heathen" religious system that was unredeemable. We saw nothing good in it. In some places it was even required that followers of Jesus take new, Westernized biblical names to mark their new identity. At the same time, we seemed unaware of the degree to which our own culture and biblical understanding were comprised of a multitude of extrabiblical accretions. As a result, around the world many Christian churches we helped bring into being are seen as foreign. Many consider these Christian churches the very embodiment of foreign and Western culture. In the view of the populace, Christianity is an expression of a corrupt Western "modernity" that actively seeks to subvert what they see as morally superior in their own national/religious identity. This perception obscures the truths of God's grace. The churches that have taken root in many places seem out of step with the needs and God-shaped aspirations of the people who surround them.

Today, many are questioning the necessity of leaving the dominant culture, and even its religious expression, to follow Christ. Must one leave behind the culture/religion in which he or she was born to take up an identity that seems foreign and Western to those around them? This is especially difficult where calling oneself a Christian means taking on an identity that stands for many negative characteristics that are in conflict with the truths of Jesus and the good news of the gospel. In these ongoing discussions the debate is often heated and the tensions quite fierce.

The Challenge

People involved on both sides of the issues (both missionaries and nationals) are appealing to those of us outside their reality for theological legitimization. In the West we seem quite ready, even anxious, to invade their system and context to settle an ongoing dispute that is not really ours. Rather than bringing peace, we are stoking the flames of strife and division in their world.

My Personal Conclusions and Proposed Steps of Obedience

As I travel, people are constantly asking me what my theological position is on the "insider movements" or the use of "dynamic equivalents" in Bible translation. These issues have the potential to cause major theological fissures in the evangelical mission movement here in the US. This greatly concerns me. Personally, the three or four reflections I started out with have led me to hold lightly my personal positions on these issues. I fully realize many of you may consider my position and proposals a good old-fashioned cop-out. You may be right, but here they are.

I have never worked or lived in a Muslim, Buddhist, or Hindu culture. There are sincere, knowledgeable, and biblically obedient brothers and sisters on each side, and at various points on the continuum concerning these issues. They are sincerely attempting to follow the Scriptures and the Holy Spirit's leading in these matters. They all seek to extend Christ's reign in their cultures and countries. I must trust the Holy Spirit to guide them. God has not placed these issues within my system. I feel I must be a peacemaker rather than a partisan in this conflict.

It took hundreds of years for the early followers of Christ to develop the theological formulations we now accept as normative. It has taken generations for us in the West to discover the weaknesses of our former mission patterns, so years, even generations, may pass before we see the full fruit of these various efforts to follow Christ more contextually and completely. I must exercise patience and not make precipitous value judgments as to the right or wrong conclusions of my brothers and sisters. Such patience is definitely not natural for me. I come from a rather egocentric culture and generation that tends to believe that history really starts with us.

The world of the Islamic, Hindu, or Buddhist follower of Christ is outside my system, experience, and calling. I have never lived or worked in those regions of the world, nor have I faced the tensions and pressures my new brothers and sisters in Christ face every day. I feel called to practice five disciplines amid the tensions I have alluded to. I will state them as succinctly as possible.

1. I will hold my own positions on these important issues tentatively and share them carefully and in a spirit of love.

2. I will leave the judgment as to who the true followers of Christ are to him. It is he alone who calls and imparts life according to his will and purpose.

3. I will grant my brothers and sisters time for their views to mature and their practices to be further shaped by the Holy Spirit's leading as they pursue a growing understanding of biblical truth and obedience in their context.

4. I will actively seek to promote peace among followers of Christ as they seek to be faithful followers of Jesus as Lord and his word as authoritative. My brothers and sisters may practice this obedience in very different ways.

5. I will oppose those here or in the field who seek to promote strife and division within his family.

One last thought: In my pilgrimage the Holy Spirit has made me much more aware of my own theological compromises with my culture. I have once again become aware of how often I fail to see the degree to which I have allowed my own culture's worldview to shape my understanding of what it means to follow Jesus. I deeply desire to be more obedient as I follow Christ and obey God's word in my own culture and as I interact with those who have experienced his grace in very different cultural/religious settings.

From the Editors
Harley Talman and John Jay Travis

Nothing is more powerful than an idea whose time has come.[5]

Over the last two centuries, the kingdom of God has expanded to virtually every country of the world, and its community of members, the body of Christ, has grown exponentially. Yet most of the new followers of Jesus have been from what are often called the minor religious traditions—the world's many animists and worshipers of tribal or ethnic deities—as well as people whose religious identity was quite nominal, as in the formerly Communist countries. Precious few have come to Jesus from societies in which major non-Christian religious traditions are deeply embedded in the culture and identity. This includes people groups that self-identify as Muslim, Hindu, Buddhist, Jewish, Shinto, Sikh, Jain, and others.

In recent years, however, this is changing. Today increasing numbers of Muslims, Hindus, Jews, and others of the world's major religious groups are coming to saving faith in Jesus. In following Jesus,

---

5   An oft-quoted, free rendering of a statement by Victor Hugo: "One withstands the invasion of armies; one does not withstand the invasion of ideas" (*History of a Crime*, 1877).

some of them join an existing denomination or church if one exists. Others form or join more informal fellowships of Jesus followers, gathering frequently for prayer, Bible study, and worship, usually meeting in homes. In some places these fellowships grow and multiply along family lines and social networks, turning into movements. Some of these are insider movements, the central topic of this book.

The phrase "insider paradigm" is used in chapter 2. This refers to the idea that people from non-Christian religious communities can enter the kingdom of God through accepting Jesus as Lord and Savior, without leaving their own community to join an existing church or assume a Christian social identity (Catholic, Protestant, Orthodox, or other). While a number of seminal articles, some stretching back to the late 1800s, point to the essence of the insider paradigm, this present volume is the first attempt to present the phenomenon of insider movements in a comprehensive way. To this end the sixty-four chapters of *UIM* contain seminal writings, case studies and testimonies, biblical and theological perspectives, mission theory and strategy, identity studies, and responses to common misunderstandings. We can draw a number of conclusions from these chapters.

1. *Insider movements are real.* Numerous case studies and testimonies presented throughout *UIM* come from the firsthand accounts of field workers and insiders themselves. It is striking that this insider expression of faith is not confined to certain geographical locations or religious communities. Most of the literature focuses on Muslims, but *UIM* presents Hindu, Jewish, Buddhist, and Sikh examples as well. When talking about the reality of these movements, it is important to bear in mind that those being described are real people—men, women, and children—in real-life situations. They are not statistics or abstract concepts. Jesus is graciously showing each of these individuals and communities that he is *for* them, saving, healing, and transforming them. The facts *UIM* discusses show that just as Jesus touched and loved Jews, Gentiles, and Samaritans during his earthly life, so today in insider movements Jesus is found to be close, immediate, and relevant by those who otherwise might have little chance of knowing him.

Many ask about the numbers of people in these movements. Estimates are hard to come by, and any form of research must be approached with the greatest care. Reports of ministry taking place among unreached people groups, in particular among Muslims and Hindus, could place field workers and new followers of Jesus in harm's way, making it crucial not to publicly mention names, people groups, or actual locations.

2. *Insider expressions of faith vary greatly from movement to movement.* While some general statements can be made about how insider movements tend to start, multiply, and grow spiritually, it is impossible to determine universal principles or formulas. Movements, by definition, *move* and are in flux. Insiders are reading the Bible, often inductively, and are listening for the voice of the Spirit of God. They are learning day by day what it means to follow Jesus while remaining part of their families and communities. However, the actual expressions and forms they use vary greatly, even within the same country or people group.

3. *Insider movements challenge the typical Western view of religion.* Religions have typically been viewed as prescribed sets of doctrinal beliefs. This doctrinally based approach has been called by some the "essentialist view of religion(s)." Recent scholarship and numerous chapters in *UIM*, however, indicate that the cultural view of religion may offer a more accurate explanation, or at least an important additional perspective on what holds people together in religious communities. This perspective suggests that many, perhaps most, members of religious communities are not there by deliberate choice, but rather are within the community by default due to social factors such as birth, family, culture, and

ethnicity. It follows that even when members of that religious community no longer adhere to all the typical doctrines of the religion, many still remain for social and cultural reasons, participating in holidays and other celebrations and activities. This dynamic is observed in the lives of many of the world's Catholics, Protestants, Jews, Muslims, Hindus, and others. The fact that many, for a variety of reasons, want to remain part of their historical religious communities even when they hold some significantly different beliefs from most of their coreligionists is a driving force behind the phenomenon of insider movements.

4. *Insider movements call attention away from religion and back to the kingdom of God.* There is an important distinction between the many religions of the world, which includes all branches of Christianity, and the kingdom of God. The New Testament refers to the kingdom of God (or kingdom of heaven) over one hundred times. Jesus taught that he was the way that any person could enter this kingdom, whether Jew, Gentile, or Samaritan. In *Transforming Mission*, David Bosch points out that Jesus proclaimed the kingdom and, by making disciples, established a kingdom-centered community. Jesus' focus, however, was not on "founding a new religion."[6] The Acts of the Apostles, the story of how the kingdom spread and communities formed, opens with a summary of what Jesus did just prior to his ascension—"appearing to them over forty days and speaking about the kingdom of God" (1:3)—and closes with a summary of Paul's ministry in Rome, where he is seen "proclaiming the kingdom of God and teaching about the Lord Jesus Christ" (28:31).

What this means in terms of insider movements is that although insiders do not "change religions" when they follow Jesus, they do enter the kingdom of God; God has delivered them from the kingdom of darkness and transferred them to the kingdom of his beloved Son (Col 1:13). This understanding, called the "kingdom of God paradigm" in chapter 20 calls our attention away from religion and back to the kingdom, giving us eyes to see insiders not as "coreligionists" but rather, through Jesus, as fellow members of God's kingdom.

5. *Insider movements expand our view of the body of Christ to include all whom Jesus has saved and called his own.* There is a distinction between membership in a branch or denomination of the Christian religion (Christianity) and membership in the body of Christ. Since the time Gentile Christianity eclipsed the Jewish Jesus movement, many have viewed the body of Christ as synonymous with either the Christian religion or a particular branch or denomination of it. It would follow, then, that one becomes a part of the body of Christ by joining a branch of Christianity. The phenomenon *UIM* presents, however, makes it clear that this is not the case, that being part of the true body of Christ is not granted by calling oneself a Christian or belonging to a particular denomination—Catholic, Orthodox, Protestant, or other. Rather, one becomes a part of Christ's body by the grace of God when one chooses by faith to follow Jesus as Lord and Savior. Though individual church organizations or denominations may have membership requirements and even different definitions of "church," becoming a part of the worldwide body of Christ is not something conferred by any religion or human institution; it depends solely on a divine interaction between Jesus and those who put their faith in him. It is therefore Jesus who makes those who follow him a part of both God's kingdom and his body. The tragedy is that members of non-Christian religious cultures have almost universally assumed that they could not have access to Christ as Lord and Savior unless they changed religions and joined some branch of Christianity.

The Bible teaches that God so loved the world that he gave his only Son, so that everyone who believes in him might be saved. Jesus and the early church received all who believed in him, regardless

---

6   David J. Bosch, *Transforming Mission: Paradigm Shifts in Theology of Mission* (Maryknoll, NY: Orbis, 1991), 51.

of their tribe, religion, or station in life, as evidenced by the inclusion of Jews and Pharisees (John 8:31; 11:45; Acts 14:1; 15:5,21), Samaritan villagers (John 4), and God-fearing Gentiles (Acts 10).

6. *Jesus-centered discipleship and spiritual transformation are happening through insider movements.* Because insider followers of Jesus want to obey all that Christ commanded them to do and believe, they are rejecting, revising, or reinterpreting any customs or beliefs from their traditional religious heritage that are incompatible with what is taught in the Bible. For example, some Orthodox Jews follow Jesus as Messiah while remaining part of their Jewish religious community and family, even though Judaism officially denies that Jesus is the Messiah. Some Muslims follow Jesus and trust in his death and resurrection for their salvation while remaining part of their Muslim community and family, even though Islam traditionally denies that Jesus died for our salvation. Parts 2 and 7 of this book demonstrate that while the issue is complex, many have encountered God through Jesus, often via dreams and other miracles, and are faithfully following him while remaining part of the religious community of their birth.

In terms of spiritual transformation, insider believers, like all followers of Christ, must face challenges in dealing with unbiblical and demonic aspects of their culture. What do Jesus-following Hindus do with the thousands of gods and goddesses their religious community embraces? How do Jesus-following Muslims participate in the Ramadan fast when the rest of the community sees it as a means of forgiveness of sins? And in cultures where one's family appeases the spirits daily, how do followers of Jesus respectfully decline their family's expectations? *UIM* describes at least three ways insiders are dealing with these and similar issues. First, when insiders meet to pray and study Scripture together, they invite the Spirit of God to guide them, to show them which aspects of their customs and beliefs are already in line with Scripture and which need revising or rejecting. Second, when they realize that certain practices (e.g., the use of charms, black magic, spells, shamans, curses, or certain rituals) might open the door to the demonic, they reject these practices and turn to God through Jesus to meet their needs for healing, deliverance, answers to prayer, and closeness to God. Third, if they discern the actual presence of demons, they take action to close any doors that would allow evil spirits access to their lives, commanding the spirits to depart in Jesus' name (see chap. 55).

7. *Alongsiders can have roles in insider movements.* God calls some Jesus followers from outside the community, whether nationals or expatriates, to walk alongside insiders in their faith journey with Jesus. Numerous chapters in *UIM* allude to the work of these men and women, whom we call "alongsiders," and their roles are described specifically in chapter 47 as those of intercessors, learners, friends, workers of miracles, proclaimers, equippers, and interfacers. Insiders view themselves as part of the body of Christ, and most insiders welcome alongsider friends who accept them as brothers and sisters in Christ even though they do not belong to the same socioreligious institutions.

8. *Open discussion has increased understanding and addressed certain concerns and misconceptions about insider movements.* J. Dudley Woodberry addresses this issue in the foreword. We repeat his words here:

> God is working across the spectrum of Jesus followers as never before. If we from different perspectives can sit around a table as a group of us did recently, we can seek to understand each other, change our perspectives if needed, and cooperate where we can. If we do, that table can be a foretaste of the table that Jesus is preparing for all his followers in his kingdom (Mark 14:25).

Examples of such meetings are those held by the Overseas Ministries Study Center in 2006, the one facilitated by the International Society for Frontier Missiology in 2007, and a series of yearly meetings of Bridging the Divide beginning in 2011. As a result of such gatherings, channels of communication have been opened. Many misconceptions and erroneous assumptions have been voiced, openly discussed, and corrected. People of different opinions on insider movements have mutually benefited by the interaction. In some unique settings where there was not seen to be a detriment or risk to movements, insider believers have met face to face with Christian believers. The Christians came to recognize the insider believers as brothers and sisters, even if they still disagreed on some issues. This is as it should be, for throughout history the global body of Christ, in spite of its diversity, has accepted as fellow believers all who follow Jesus as Lord and Savior as revealed in the Bible. It is clear that insider followers of Jesus hold these same beliefs and risk their lives for them.

However, as valuable as these meetings have been, they are few and far between and benefit a relatively small number of people. Our hope is that this book will help dispel many misconceptions and contribute to an improved understanding so that meaningful dialogue can take place. Although a book cannot provide personal acquaintance with insider believers, we trust that their testimonies will enable readers to connect with them on a heart level. It has been our prayer that in addressing IMs from numerous perspectives, the hope of most readers for a more complete understanding will be realized.

Insider Movements and Us

The senior pastor of my (John's) home church invited my wife and me for lunch to talk about insider movements. The main question he had was whether the Muslims (and Hindus, Jews, and others) who "follow" Jesus actually *know* him as Lord and Savior or if they merely respect him as a great teacher or prophet, so we told stories of the faith and transformed lives of the many insiders we know. Two days later we left for a month overseas.

When we came back, our pastor described what had happened to him a few days after our lunch discussion. At the conclusion of the Sunday service a group of men were waiting in the lobby for him. With heavy accents, they introduced themselves as Muslims from the Middle East. They went on to explain that they had all encountered Jesus and were loving and following him as Muslims. Our pastor's mind was reeling as he heard these words, remembering our lunch meeting the week before.

These Muslims said to him, "Pastor, we just heard your sermon and we agree with it. Our question to you is this: will you accept us as your brothers in Christ?" Our pastor relates,

> I think I only asked one clarifying question, i.e., "If something in your culture called you to do one thing and Jesus asked you to do another, what would you do?" They could hardly understand why I would ask such a question. Without pausing or flinching, they said, "We would obey Jesus. Jesus is Lord!" I learned a lot from them that day about the person of Jesus, and that our submission to his lordship is the key issue. This is what led to the tears—both in them and in me.

These men hugged and shed tears of joy in our church lobby. Our pastor called it a divine appointment.

As we look back on this book, what does it all mean for us? Are we looking at an anomaly, or could we be seeing a fundamental shift in mission and cross-cultural witness? How should we respond? We close with three recommendations:

1. We encourage mission agencies to familiarize their personnel with the basic concepts of this book. How tragic it would be if, due only to a lack of exposure, cross-cultural workers inadvertently

shut down something God was doing in the lives of those who were ready to follow Jesus but who saw no reason to change religions in order to do so.

2. We encourage church leaders to familiarize their congregations with the basic concepts of this book. Consider starting a book discussion group or making insiders a regular prayer focus of your church. The possibility of encounters such as the one that happened with our pastor is only increasing.

3. We encourage those who have friends from other religious communities—Hindu, Muslim, Buddhist, or other—to carefully consider what has been said in this book. How tragic if, due to tradition alone, we felt we must call our friends to change religions in order to be right with God, when in fact these friends could become the first fruits of a new Jesus movement inside their families and communities!

Questions for Reflection

1. In what ways do you relate to the perspectives of Parshall and McKaughan on attitude and relationships? If the guidelines they suggest were implemented, what might be some positive outcomes in discussions over different types of ministries and expressions of faith?

2. Which of Travis and Talman's conclusions and suggestions most significantly affect your response to the issue of insider movements? Which of these conclusions do you want to explore and understand more fully?

3. What attitudes, ideas, or strategies do you view as critical for constructive discussion of the topic of insider movements? What guidelines should critics and proponents of insider movements follow in their public discourse? (See also the recommendations under "Actions" in appendix 2.)

The Samaritan Religion

Samuel Livingway

I recently visited the Samaritan village on the top of Mt. Gerizim in the West Bank of the Palestinian territories. I spoke with a man who considers himself to be the next in line for the high priesthood of the Samaritans. This gentleman brought out an unbroken genealogy from Adam to modern times and showed us that there were 163 generations between himself and Adam. He spoke of the ancient traditions of the Samaritan religion, as the oldest religion, with "the oldest language, the oldest history, and the oldest Bible." Scholars debate many of these claims, but the Samaritans believe that they adhere to the original Abrahamic tradition.

Research about Samaritans reveals that they truly do represent a separate religion from Judaism. John MacDonald in *The Theology of the Samaritans* writes, "Samaritanism is not a form of Judaism; it is no heterodox religion. It is a development of one religion with the aid of the ideology of another."[1]

Samaritans: A People with Their Own Religion

Samaria is located between Jerusalem and Galilee. A small Samaritan community still exists today, but in Jesus' day the Samaritans were a large ethnic group. However, being a Samaritan was much more than simply a matter of ethnic identity or place of birth. In theological dictionaries and the field of Samaritan studies, Samaritanism is consistently referred to as its own religion.[2] The *Dictionary of New Testament Theology*, for instance, states, "The context shows *Samar(e)ites* to be a geographical, and thus indirectly an ethnological term, but at the same time to be a religious group designation."[3] Samaritans had (and still have today) their own ethnoreligious identity.[4]

---

1 MacDonald, *The Theology of the Samaritans,* The New Testament Library (London: SCM, 1964), 419.

2 See Joachim Jeremias, "Σαμάρεια, Σαμαρίτης, Σαμαρῖτις," in *The Theological Dictionary of the New Testament, Abridged in One Volume,* ed. Gerhard Kittel (Grand Rapids, MI: Eerdmans, 1985), 7:88–94. See also Ida Glaser, "Facing Samaritan Religion," chap. 11 in *The Bible and Other Faiths: What Does the Lord Require of Us?* (Carlisle, UK: Langham Global Library, 2014); and John Bowman, *The Samaritan Problem: Studies in the Relationships of Samaritanism, Judaism, and Early Christianity* (Eugene, OR: Pickwick, 1975), 29–56.

3 Klaus Haacker, "Samaritan," in *Dictionary of New Testament Theology,* vol. 3, ed. Colin Brown (Grand Rapids, MI: Zondervan, 1971).

4 Samaritan as a distinct ethnoreligious identity is an established sociological and anthropological category. See Reinhard Pummer, *The Samaritans* (Leiden: Brill, 1987). Pummer opens his introduction with this comment: "Today the Samaritans are the smallest *religio-ethnical* group in existence. There are only a little more than 500 individuals in all" (ibid., 1; emphasis added). At the end of the introduction he states, "The Samaritans are also interesting to sociologists and anthropologists as an extremely small group that has succeeded in maintaining its identity over 2000 years" (25).

Samaritans were residents of Samaria, yet they highlighted the religious element in their self-identification: "They preferred to refer to themselves as *samerim*, 'keepers' (of Torah), and to distinguish themselves from *someronim*, 'inhabitants of Samaria.'"[5] It is also suggested that the name of the place came secondarily because the people there first identified as *samerim*. As "keepers" of their religion, and by emphasizing the religious nature of their identity, Samaritans sought to distinguish themselves from the Jewish religion. This is certainly part of the reason that the Jewish leaders had the Samaritan temple destroyed in 128 BC. Ferguson states, "The earliest references to a rival religious community based on Mt. Gerizim near Shechem are from the second century B.C. (Sirach 50:25–26; 2 Macc. 5–6; cf. Testament of Levi 5–7; Jubilees 30)."[6]

Samaritans had their own priesthood, their own place of worship (temple), their own scripture (an altered version of the Pentateuch),[7] their own sacrificial system,[8] and their own Wisdom literature/religious writings. (Except for the temple, they have retained most of these elements down to modern times.) Clearly they had their own religion.

Samaritans also had an aberrant theology. The *Malef*, a textbook for young Samaritans, speaks of "the light which was the Holy Spirit, which he manifested in the form of our Lord Moses in the invisible and visible world." Bowman says, "This light, i.e., the Holy Spirit, is considered by the Samaritans to be the pre-existent Moses."[9] Moses was also called "the apostle of God, the sun and light of the world, the faithful one of God's house, the crown and diadem of the world."[10] Moses preexisted, according to Samaritans, and was the incarnate Spirit of God.

So we can see that Samaritans were considered a *rival religious community with aberrant religious beliefs*. They were people who had a distinct theology, unique religious practices, and their own history. But most importantly, they had their own religious identity.

Samaritans: Biblical Data

Jesus' interaction with the Samaritans serves as the best example of how we can relate to others from another religion. Jesus, by his silence, denies that there is any relationship between being a Samaritan and being demon-possessed in John 8:48. He rebukes his disciples for wanting to punish or destroy the Samaritans in Luke 9:51–56. In the parable of the Good Samaritan, it is the one from the enemy religion who is lauded by Jesus as the faithful one. This is in contradistinction to others who are clearly associated with the Jewish religion—the priest and the Levite. However, the best extended example of how Jesus relates to Samaritans comes from John 4 in his interaction with the Samaritan woman and her village.

When Jesus encountered this woman, he didn't come with polemics but instead came and started a conversation. Soon it developed into a spiritual conversation. He came bringing truth and revelation

---

5   Everett Ferguson, *Backgrounds of Early Christianity*, 2nd ed. (Grand Rapids, MI: Eerdmans, 1993), 499.

6   Most Samaritan scholars agree that the references to Samaritans in 2 Kgs 17 do not relate to the religious group around the time of the New Testament. See Everett, *Backgrounds of Early Christianity*, 499.

7   Samaritans consider their Pentateuch to be the only authoritative scripture. It has significant changes in the Ten Commandments and identifies the location of the temple as Mt. Gerizim. There are also nearly six thousand variations from the Masoretic text, although most of these are simply scribal and grammatical variants.

8   I have attended the annual Passover sacrifice in which many sheep are still slaughtered and blood is wiped on the foreheads of the Samaritans.

9   Bowman, *The Samaritan Problem*, 63.

10   MacDonald, *Theology of the Samaritans*, 147.

regarding her personal life. He got to the heart level quickly. It seems he began to reveal himself in a contextual way by referring to "living water," a term used in Samaritan Wisdom literature in numerous places.[11]

Regarding religion, Jesus also told this Samaritan woman that it's not about religious form or practice, whether you worship on this mountain or that one, but about worship in Spirit and truth. He did mention that the Samaritans worshiped what they didn't know,[12] and that Jews worshiped what they did know, "for salvation is from the Jews. But"—and it's a major adversative—"an hour is coming and *now* is" (John 4:22; emphasis added). Salvation was from the Jews, but Jesus made it clear four verses later where that salvation lay when he said, "I who speak to you am he." Jesus was revealing himself. Salvation was through the Messiah—the woman didn't have to convert to Judaism.

This was the same message the Apostle Paul would later deliver to the Gentiles. The message was simple: it was Jesus plus nothing! It wasn't about religion or religious identity; it was about relationship to the living God through Christ. Paul also seems to have felt the freedom to use or not use his religious identity as he saw fit. In Philippians 3:4–7 he declares that his ethnic, tribal, and religious identities are of the flesh, that they are even rubbish, compared with knowing Christ. But in Romans 11:1 he claims these identities (as an Israelite, a descendant of Abraham, of the tribe of Benjamin) because he is passionate about reaching his "brothers, kinsmen according to the flesh, who are Israelites" (Rom 9:3–4). It is also interesting to note that when Paul claimed his Roman identity prior to his scourging in Acts 22:25, the next night the Lord said to him, "As you have solemnly witnessed to My cause at Jerusalem, so you must witness at Rome also" (Acts 23:11). Paul's principle of becoming all things to all people, so as by all means to win some, holds true even with identities that carry religious meaning (1 Cor 9:19–23). Earthly identifiers, whether they have religious meaning or not, have no efficacy for salvation. Compared to knowing Christ, they are nothing. Jesus said to the Samaritan woman, "I who speak to you am He." There is salvation in no one else. And because we are so transformed by his presence, to the point that there is neither Jew nor Greek, slave nor free, male nor female, then we are free to use those same identities, or be identified by them, in his service, always submitting ourselves to his lordship.

Returning to Samaria, we see that Jesus moved beyond forms of worship and sacred sites in Jerusalem or Gerizim; he moved beyond Judaism and Samaritanism, religious identities. He taught the woman about worship in Spirit and truth through himself. In the end, the Samaritans received this truth when they said, "We have heard for ourselves and know that this One is indeed the Savior of the world" (John 4:42). "Many Samaritans from that city believed in Him" (John 4:39). In John's Gospel, to believe is to be given the right to be a child of God (1:12).

The new believers in Sychar were still identified as Samaritans! What were the implications of being called a Samaritan as a follower of Jesus? What would change, and what would they retain? What would be transformed and informed? Would they still go to the Samaritan religious gatherings and do washings and pray with their hands open? The New Testament is silent about the particulars, but we do know that these new believers were still being called Samaritans. Samaria is also prioritized in Acts when Jesus commissions the apostles to go to Jerusalem, Judea, Samaria, and the ends of the earth (1:8).[13]

---

11 See Higgins, chap. 24.

12 I believe that Jesus said these words with compassion and sadness, while also quickly offering himself as the solution.

13 In Acts 8, when the apostles go to the Samaritans, I take it to be a different city than Sychar in John 4. Here there are clear practices that need to be rejected (e.g., Simon the magician). In IMs there are always practices and

Samaritans: Similarities with Muslims in Belief and Practice

Consider the following similarities between Samaritans and Muslims:

1. An uncompromising belief in and worship of the one God
2. Avoidance of images
3. Practice of circumcision
4. Observance of festivals
5. A sense of being the chosen people, with attachment to the land given to the fathers (associated in the Samaritans' case with Joseph/the northern tribes)
6. Expectations of a glorious destiny[14]

Consider as well the fact that Samaritan prayer services are preceded by a ceremonial washing, or ablution, during which the Samaritan recites the appropriate prayers. The order of the washing is (1) hands, (2) mouth, (3) nose, (4) face, (5) ears, (6) right leg, and (7) left leg. This corresponds to Muslim ablution (*wudu'*). To the reader who understands Islamic practices, the following parallels will also be evident. The hands are held in a "reading" position during prayer. Worshipers bless themselves by wiping with the right hand over their face. The Samaritans even use Islamic terms such as *qibla* for the direction of prayer.[15]

Whereas Samaritans are a distinct people group and share an *ethno*religious identity, Muslims do not belong to any one ethnic bloc but rather share a *socio*religious identity, connected by both a transcultural religious identification and a local national or social affiliation. Being a Muslim is being a part of both a religion and a culture/society. One is considered a Muslim for many reasons that go beyond theology. Islam is not a monolith; there are many shades and contours, even different beliefs and practices, under the umbrella of Islam.[16] There is likely much more variance among Muslims than ever existed among Samaritans. However, both groups have another feature in common: just as there were Samaritans within the first-century Samaritan community who believed that Jesus was the Savior of the world and continued to be identified as Samaritans, so today there is evidence of Muslims who are in Christ and are still identified as Muslims.[17]

Bibliography

Bowman, John. *The Samaritan Problem: Studies in the Relationships of Samaritanism, Judaism, and Early Christianity.* Eugene, OR: Pickwick, 1975.

Ferguson, Everett. *Backgrounds of Early Christianity.* 2nd ed. Grand Rapids, MI: Eerdmans, 1993.

Glaser, Ida. "Facing Samaritan Religion." Chap. 11 in *The Bible and Other Faiths: What Does the Lord Require of Us?* Carlisle, UK: Langham Global Library, 2014.

---

beliefs that are rejected, reformed, or retained. But in Acts 8 there is no indication of anyone changing his or her identity as a Samaritan.

14 See Ferguson, *Backgrounds of Early Christianity*, 534–36.

15 Bowman points out that this term was probably not borrowed from Islam but was rather from a common pre-Islamic linguistic source; see Bowman, *The Samaritan Problem*, 15.

16 For further reflections on the diversity of Islam, see Ingvar Svanberg and David Westerlund, eds., *Islam outside the Arab World* (Abingdon, Oxfordshire, UK: Routledge, 1999); and Tamara Sonn, *Islam: A Brief History*, 2nd ed. (Chichester, West Sussex, UK: Wiley-Blackwell, 2009).

17 See David Garrison, *A Wind in the House of Islam: How God Is Drawing Muslims around the World to Faith in Jesus Christ* (Monument, CO: WIGTake, 2014).

Haacker, Klaus. "Samaritan." In *Dictionary of New Testament Theology,* vol. 3. Edited by Colin Brown. Grand Rapids, MI: Zondervan, 1971.

Jeremias, Joachim. "Σαμάρεια, Σαμαρίτης, Σαμαρῖτις." In *The Theological Dictionary of the New Testament, Abridged in One Volume,* vol. 7, edited by Gerhard Kittel, 88–94. Grand Rapids, MI: Eerdmans, 1985.

MacDonald, John. *The Theology of the Samaritans.* The New Testament Library. London: SCM, 1964.

Pummer, Reinhard. *The Samaritans.* Leiden: Brill, 1987.

Sonn, Tamara. *Islam: A Brief History.* 2nd ed. Chichester, West Sussex, UK: Wiley-Blackwell, 2009.

Svanberg, Ingvar, and David Westerlund, eds. *Islam outside the Arab World.* Abingdon, Oxfordshire, UK: Routledge, 1999.

World Evangelical Alliance (WEA) Evangelical Relationships Commitment[*]

The Evangelical Relationships Commitment is a modern rewording of the eight Practical Resolutions originally agreed at the 1846 Assembly that launched the Evangelical Alliance. They were written to guide members in their relationships with other Christians. We hope they will help you as you build good, positive working relationships in all areas of your Christian life.

Affirmations

We welcome as Christian brothers and sisters all who experience the grace of new birth, bringing them to that fear and knowledge of God which is expressed in a life of obedience to His word.

We recognise our Christian duty of trust and mutual encouragement to all who serve Christ as Lord, not least to those who conscientiously prefer not to be identified with the same churches, alliances, or councils as ourselves.

We respect the diversity of culture, experience, and doctrinal understanding that God grants to His people, and acknowledge that some differences over issues not essential to salvation may well remain until the end of time.

Actions

We urge all Christians to pray as Christ prayed, that we may be one in the Father and the Son, and so by the Spirit promote personal relationships of love, peace, and fellowship within the Body of Christ, His universal Church.

We encourage all Christians earnestly to contend for biblical truth, since only as we are open to learn from others and yield fuller obedience to the truth will we be drawn closer to Christ and to each other.

We call on each other, when speaking or writing of those issues of faith or practice that divide us, to acknowledge our own failings and the possibility that we ourselves may be mistaken, avoiding personal hostility and abuse, and speaking the truth in love and gentleness.

We owe it to each other, in making public comment on the alleged statements of our fellow Christians, first to confer directly with them and to establish what was actually intended; then to commend what we can, to weigh the proportional significance of what we perceive to be in error, and to put a charitable construction on what is doubtful, expressing all with courtesy, humility, and graciousness.

We rejoice in the spread of the Gospel across the world and urge all Christians to commit themselves to this task, avoiding unnecessary competition and cooperating, wherever possible, in the

[*]   See http://www.eauk.org/connect/about-us/basis-of-faith.cfm#erc.

completion of Christ's kingdom of peace, justice, and holiness, to the glory of the one God—Father, Son, and Holy Spirit.

"Practical Resolutions of the Evangelical Alliance" is an update of the original eight general resolutions crafted when the Evangelical Alliance was formed in 1846.

Endorsed by Evangelical Alliance Council and the Evangelical Leaders Forum (a diverse group jointly facilitated by the Evangelical Alliance and the British Evangelical Council), the new document is now being commended to wider evangelicalism as a guide to our relationships as we work out our evangelical witness in the world.

Review of *A Theological Analysis of the Insider Movement Paradigm from Four Perspectives* by Doug Coleman[*]

Bradford Greer

The title of this dissertation led me to assume that Dr. Doug Coleman was going to provide a theological analysis of insider movements. Many missiologists are eagerly awaiting studies of this nature. However, what Dr. Coleman actually does is to analyze articles written by what appear to be primarily Western authors who have written in favor of insider movements.[1] Due to this, the dissertation could have been more appropriately entitled "A Theological Analysis of Articles Written in Defense of the Insider Movement Paradigm." This clarification in the title would have helped me properly align my expectations and would have spared me from my initial disappointment.

Nonetheless, Dr. Coleman demonstrates clearly within this dissertation that he is, first and foremost, a Christian scholar. His analysis of these writings is irenic and generously fair. Even though he may disagree with authors over specific issues, he refers to these authors with respect and grace. In this way he continues to keep the bar high for Christian scholarship.

Dr. Coleman was transparent about his research methodology and the assumptions behind it. However, I was disappointed to find one dimension in his research methodology lacking. Being that missiology is an interdisciplinary academic field that primarily researches the dynamics that happen when the church, Scripture, and any given culture intersect, I generally expect that a missiological dissertation will engage with a specific culture or a select number of cultures rather than a selection of articles. This fieldwork grounds the research and safeguards it from becoming ethereal. Dr. Coleman was transparent about the absence of this engagement in his introduction.[2] However, the lack of field research (describing how a particular group or groups of followers of Christ from other religions are engaging with the Scripture in their context) appears to have negatively impacted his ensuing methodology and analysis. I saw this impact in three fundamental assumptions that shape Dr. Coleman's methodology, assumptions that appear to have gone unnoticed by Coleman. These assumptions surface as one works through the dissertation. Field research likely would have revealed to Dr. Coleman at least two of these assumptions and enabled him to make appropriate adjustments.[3]

---

[*]   Originally published a slightly different form in *IJFM* 28, no. 4 (2011): 206–11. Reprinted by permission. The editors include this appendix as a model of respectful scholarly dialogue over the IM issue. Responding to Doug Coleman's doctoral dissertation, which had rendered a negative judgment of these movements, Bradford Greer gently exposes erroneous assumptions and methodological weaknesses.

[1]   See Doug Coleman, *A Theological Analysis of the Insider Movement Paradigm from Four Perspectives: Theology of Religions, Revelation, Soteriology and Ecclesiology*, EMS Dissertation Series (Pasadena, CA: WCIU Press, 2011), 22.

[2]   Ibid.

[3]   Dr. Coleman, in his response to this review ("Doug Coleman Responds to Bradford Greer's Critique," *IJFM* 29, no. 1 [2012]: 47–53), seems to feel that his field experience was an adequate substitute for field research.

The first assumption that Dr. Coleman makes is to view Islam through an essentialist lens. Essentialism defines faith in very limited terms. Islam, for instance, is often described in terms of a particular set of classical interpretations of Islamic sacred and legal literature.[4] However, when one watches faith in practice, one notices the incredible diversity in what is actually believed. This is why defining a world religion like Islam in an essentialist manner is problematic. Coleman's essentialist view of Islam causes him to conceptualize and define Islam in a monolithic manner and disregard the significance of the actual diversity in faith and practice that exists within and across Islamic communities.[5]

The second assumption that Dr. Coleman makes is to conceptualize culture in a monodimensional manner. Thus he appears to assume that a culture can be divided into independent categories rather than viewing it as a multidimensional mosaic of interconnected parts. Thus Dr. Coleman is able to speak about Islam as a religion as if it can be isolated from Islamic cultures.

The third unnoticed assumption is a bit surprising for a dissertation that claims to be substantially theological in nature. It appears that Dr. Coleman disregards the impact of hermeneutics on exegesis and the interpretation of Scripture and assumes that holding to a high view of Scripture either nullifies or minimizes the impact of personal story and theological/church tradition(s) upon one's understanding of Scripture.

Now, we evangelicals do not have a magisterium upon which to rely for authorization of our interpretation of Scripture. It is customary in evangelical academic theological discourse for analysts to follow certain procedures as they approach the Scriptures. Scholars are expected to reflect upon and articulate the assumptions that they bring to the text—in other words, describe their hermeneutical lens. One's hermeneutical lens is often shaped by one's theological and church tradition(s) as well as one's personal journey. After this honest and transparent reflection, if the methodology behind the exegesis is acceptable and the analysis consistent, then the conclusions can be considered viable. A fellow academic may not agree with the fundamental assumptions that comprise an analyst's hermeneutical lens, but the analysis and conclusions are generally to be considered viable. This process is important because evangelicalism embraces a wide range of potentially conflicting theological traditions (such as Presbyterianism, Methodism, Pentecostalism, etc.). This transparency in methodology facilitates us as academics to stand united in Christ even though we may disagree on particular theological points.

However, in his "Key Assumptions" section, Coleman downplays the significance of one's hermeneutical lens on the interpretive process. He states, "The role of experience and worldview and their impact on hermeneutics is worth debating, but the basic starting point for methodology should be the text of the Bible."[6] He proceeds to state that he views Scripture as inerrant and coherent. Thus it appears that Coleman assumes that holding to a high view of Scripture either nullifies or minimizes the impact of personal story and theological/church tradition(s) upon how one reads the text.

However, this is questionable. Field research, if done according to academic standards, provides necessary data that expose and verify or challenge the assumptions one carries into one's analysis. This is why field research at the doctoral level in missiology is valued. Since all theological analysis is shaped by one's context, without data from field research expanding Coleman's context, Coleman's analysis can be viewed as circular or motivated reasoning—that is, crafting an argument to support a viewpoint to which he had a prior commitment.

4   See Dietrich Jung, *Orientalists, Islamists and the Global Public Sphere: A Genealogy of the Essentialist Image of Islam* (Sheffield, UK: Equinox, 2011), 5.

5   For an example of this, see Coleman, *A Theological Analysis*, 176–77.

6   Ibid., 20.

This compels me to conclude that a naive realist epistemology shapes his hermeneutical lens.[7] The downside of naive realism is that it tends to narrow analysts' ability to observe data and discern nuances that do not align with or that contradict their assumptions or analysis. It also can cause analysts to be overconfident about their conclusions. The impact of naive realism can be subtle, and it can be pervasive. Does this naive realist epistemology render Dr. Coleman unaware of his essentialist and monolithic view of Islam and his monodimensional view of culture? These appear to be interrelated.

At least, with regard to his theological traditions, Dr. Coleman acknowledges that he holds to a Baptist ecclesiology. However, the reader is left to fill in the details of his hermeneutical lens.

As I read through Dr. Coleman's work, I saw these three assumptions emerge and shape his analysis and his conclusions as he interacted with the articles.

Dr. Coleman begins his analysis by looking at the insider movement paradigm and theology of religions. Coleman adopts a soteriological conceptual paradigm for analyzing religions and the statements about religions by insider movement paradigm (IMP) proponents, viewing them as either exclusivistic, inclusivistic, or pluralistic.[8]

Dr. Coleman is generously fair as he presents the IMP proponents' view that God is at work in some ways in other religions, and that members of these religions can come under the lordship of Christ and enter the kingdom of God without aligning themselves with "Christianity" (that is, primarily Western cultural expressions of the Christian faith), and remain within their "socioreligious" communities. He credits the IMP proponents with being exclusivistic, noting that "their writings indicate that they affirm the necessity of hearing and believing in the gospel of Jesus Christ in order to be saved."[9]

In this section Coleman focuses in on the writings of one proponent in particular, Kevin Higgins, because Higgins has written the most about the theology of religions. Reflecting on these writings with the aforementioned soteriological paradigm, Coleman recognizes that

> Higgins both affirms and rejects elements of all three traditional categories. In a technical sense, he appears to affirm an exclusivist position regarding soteriology. Higgins finds some agreement with inclusivists regarding ways in which God may be at work in the religions and the positive value they may hold. Other than the admission that it perhaps provides the best explanation for the Melchizedek event, Higgins seems to find little agreement with pluralism.[10]

---

7   This perception of his naive realism is reinforced by Coleman's later statement that "missiology should be driven and governed by biblical and theological teaching and parameters" (22). The statement is true. However, it neglects to acknowledge the significant impact of cultural context on the person doing the biblical exegesis and interpretation.

8   Ibid., 26–28. Coleman defines these terms in this manner: "Exclusivism holds that Jesus is the only Savior and that explicit knowledge of and belief in God's special revelation, particularly the gospel of Christ, is essential for salvation. At the other end of the spectrum, pluralism views all paths or religions as valid, leading to God, and potentially salvific. Inclusivists, however, consider Jesus to be the only Savior, but do not believe explicit knowledge of the gospel is necessary for salvation."

9   Ibid., 28.

10   Ibid., 37–38.

Yet Coleman acknowledges that he has difficulty incorporating the assertion that "it is permissible to remain in one's pre-salvation non-Christian religion while redefining or reinterpreting aspects of it."[11] Coleman earlier describes how Higgins conceptualizes this "remaining." He writes,

> Dividing religion into three dimensions, Higgins suggests that the "remaining" may look different in each. For example, Naaman modified some of his beliefs and behavior, but at the level of belonging appears to have continued just as before. . . . Finally, Higgins asserts that a biblical understanding of conversion does not require an institutional transfer of religion, but ". . . the reorientation of the heart and mind (e.g., Rom 12:1ff.)."[12]

Yet even with this recognition that there is a change in beliefs and in behavior, it appears impossible for Coleman to accept that a follower of Christ can remain in his or her "religion."

This is where Coleman's unmentioned assumptions impact his analysis. In Coleman's monodimensional view of culture, a community is comprised of aggregate parts. Thus one can divide and isolate aspects of the culture (in this case, religion) rather than seeing all these aspects as inextricably interrelated.[13] In addition, since he essentialistically and monolithically defines "religion" (in particular, Islam), then it is obvious how remaining within it would be seen as impossible. This exemplifies how Dr. Coleman's assumptions limit his analysis and conclusions.

Reading this chapter reminded me of Stephen's speech in Acts 7. In his book *The New Testament and the People of God*, N. T. Wright points out that the land and the temple were key identity markers for the people of Israel.[14] Stephen's speech undermined these identity markers. Stephen pointed out how God had been with Abraham, Moses, and Joseph outside the land. Solomon, who had built the temple, recognized that the temple could not contain God. For Stephen, the presence of God and the responsive obedience of his people to his presence were the vital identity markers for the people of God. Is not this what Kevin Higgins' quote articulates—that one's true identity as a follower of Jesus is fundamentally comprised of one's allegiance and obedience to Jesus and his word and the manifestation of Jesus' presence among his people by their change of behavior? All other identity markers are inconsequential.

Coleman proceeds to look at the Christian doctrine of revelation and the insider movement paradigm. As the discussion begins, one is confronted with a limitation as to Dr. Coleman's development of the Christian understanding of revelation. Coleman appears to regard general revelation as if it were a static enterprise by God—that is, something that God has done previously in space and time. Coleman states,

> At the most basic level, Scripture indicates that creation confronts man with the existence of God and informs him to some extent of

---

11 Ibid., 38.

12 Ibid., 35.

13 This monodimensional view of culture as being comprised of aggregate parts is reflected in this quote by Coleman: "[Rebecca] Lewis also points out that conversion to a certain cultural form of Christianity is not necessary for membership in the kingdom, and may even prove to be a hindrance. This, too, is a helpful distinction, although her application of it leads to a false dichotomy. She fails to mention the possibility of a new form of biblical faith appropriate to the local culture yet distinct from other religious communities and identities." *A Theological Analysis*, 74.

14 Wright, *The New Testament and the People of God* (Minneapolis, MN: Fortress Press, 1992), 224-227, 232.

God's attributes, specifically his eternal power and divine nature
(Rom 1:20). Furthermore, God has placed awareness of moral responsibility within man's conscience (Rom 2:14,15).[15]

Though this perception of God's putting information about himself in the creation and in human
conscience as a static event may be a classic perception in theology, it does not adequately reflect the
biblical testimony. As evangelicals, we make a distinction between natural theology (that which man
can discern about God through this "static" information) and general revelation (God actively revealing
himself to people through what he has made and through an active involvement in people's consciences). Coleman appears to overlook this dimension in general revelation as the active, ongoing act of God
in revealing himself to people. Does a naive realist approach to the doctrine of revelation cause him to
overlook this significant distinction in his analysis?

This subtle distinction reshapes Dr. Coleman's analysis of direct and special revelation. It removes
the discussion from being a strictly rational, analytical process and intentionally appreciates how God is
personally engaged in each step of the revelatory process with each person and with communities across
space and time. The personal testimony of many Muslims that they have come to faith in Christ through
visions, dreams, or a healing demonstrates God's personal involvement in this self-revelatory process.

How did and does this ongoing, active working of God impact the way the Qur'an was composed
or impact the way the Qur'an is read by Muslims? As Coleman acknowledges, this is difficult to determine. Nonetheless, what he acknowledges is that God has used the Qur'an to lead people to faith
in Christ. Coleman quotes Dean Gilliland, whose research found that 30 percent of Nigerian Fulbe
believers indicated that qur'anic references to Jesus led them to seek more information about Jesus.[16]

While Coleman acknowledges that IMP proponents do not affirm "the Qur'an as the 'Word of
God' or inspired scripture," he feels that "the Christian understanding of revelation and the sufficiency
of the Bible raise significant questions regarding such an approach, especially in light of the Muslim
view of the Qur'an and Muhammad."[17] He states,

> The Bible's teaching on these matters sets it at odds with the tra-
> ditional Muslim interpretation of the Qur'an. Christians cannot
> accept the Muslim view that ". . . the message revealed through
> Muhammad—the Qur'an—must be regarded as the culmination
> and the end of all prophetic revelation."[18]

Though this traditional understanding of the Qur'an may be the understanding of many Muslims
across the globe, it is not the only understanding. There are those who identify themselves as Muslims
and believe that the Qur'an is only a collection of stories. How should this acknowledgment of the
actual diversity in belief that exists within Islamic communities impact Coleman's analysis? This is
another example of how Coleman's essentialism limits him.

It appears that Coleman joins the ranks of those who feel that if the Qur'an is used, insider believers may ascribe an undue authoritative status to all the content in the Qur'an. This, from an outside
standpoint, appears to be a valid concern. This leads Coleman to conclude,

---

15   Coleman, *A Theological Analysis*, 83.

16   Ibid., 107.

17   Ibid., 81.

18   Ibid., 99.

Regarding Islam, the IMP, and the doctrine of revelation, this chapter suggested that the Qur'an contains both general and special revelation, the latter via oral tradition. It was also noted that traditional Muslim interpretations of the Qur'an conflict with God's revelation in the Bible. Nevertheless, some missiologists advocate reading Christian meaning into the Qur'an without providing warrant for their hermeneutic, other than pointing to Paul's approach in Acts 17.[19]

What Dr. Coleman fails to realize is that the reason IMP proponents have defended the practice of reading the Qur'an through a Christ-centered lens is because this is what insider believing communities have done. Though I may agree or disagree with Coleman's analysis of Acts 17 and the implications of what Paul's use of the altar to the unknown god and his use of local folklore indicate, a bigger issue arises here. The issue is this: What authority do outsiders actually have as they assess and evaluate what insider believing communities do? Where do outsider theological concerns cross the line and actually exemplify a form of theological imperialism—a theolonialism (that is, an ethnocentric imposition of one's religious subculture and traditions)?

What Dr. Coleman (and those he quotes who concur with his conclusions) does not appear to understand (and therefore cannot appreciate) is that the Qur'an is an integral part of the narrative world of most, if not all, Muslims. Even for Muslims who do not accept the Qur'an as a sacred text and acknowledge that it exerts no influence in shaping their lives or values, it still can be an integral part of their world.[20] This reminds me of a discussion a few believing friends from Muslim backgrounds were having years ago. They were discussing how they used the Qur'an to present their faith. I asked them if I could use the Qur'an in these ways. They unanimously and without hesitation said, "No. It is our book, not yours." Even though they were followers of Christ, they unanimously owned the Qur'an as an integral part of their world.

Therefore, are not insider believing communities duly authorized by the Lord to determine how they use their Islamic texts, how much "authority" they ascribe to them, and how they ultimately interpret them? As long as they hold the Scriptures as the ultimate and final authority in their lives, is there a problem with believing communities determining how they use something that is so integrally a part of their narrative world?

This question of who holds the authority arises again in Coleman's ensuing discussion of soteriology. With regard to soteriology and the IMP, Dr. Coleman's assumptions shape his analysis. He states, "The most basic claim of the Insider Movement paradigm is that biblical faith in Jesus does not require a change of religious affiliation, identity, or belonging."[21] Coleman defines what he means by religious affiliation when he writes, "[IMP proponents argue that] salvation does not require a change of religious affiliation and, therefore, a faithful follower of Jesus Christ can remain within the socioreligious community of Islam."[22] I appreciate that Dr. Coleman describes religious affiliation as remaining

---

19 Ibid., 133.

20 For an example of this in the life of one Muslim scholar, see how Hamed Abdel-Samad speaks about the Qur'an in "Political Scientist Hamed Abdel-Samad: 'Islam Is Like a Drug,'" *Spiegel Online*, September 17, 2010, http://www.spiegel.de/international/germany/political-scientist-hamed-abdel-samad-islam-is-like-a-drug-a-717589.html.

21 Coleman, *A Theological Analysis*, 135.

22 Ibid., 135.

within one's socioreligious community, making this distinct from one's allegiance to Christ. This is an important distinction. Nonetheless, to Coleman, for a follower of Christ to remain in his or her Islamic socioreligious community is incongruous. Since Coleman views culture as a composite of aggregate parts, he assumes that religion and culture are separable. IMP proponents assert that in many contexts they are not separable. Thus IMP proponents differentiate between one's allegiance to Christ, which can never be compromised, and one's affiliation with one's socioreligious community, which can be retained if the insider so chooses.

Reflecting on this, Coleman provides an extensive analysis of two texts the IMP proponents have used to justify this "remaining": Acts 15 and 1 Corinthians 8–10. Dr. Coleman does especially well in revealing the nuances behind the discussion and the decision of the Jerusalem Council in Acts 15.

Regarding IMP claims about Acts 15, Coleman states that

> advocates are correct in understanding this passage as fundamen-
> tally a debate about salvation, and whether Gentiles were required
> to follow the Law in order to be saved. Acts 15:1 makes it clear that
> teachers from Judea saw circumcision as essential for salvation, or
> at least a necessary evidence of true faith. Furthermore, some of
> the believers from among the Pharisees also added that Gentiles
> should "observe the Law of Moses" (Acts 15:5). These constituted
> the two demands related to Gentile salvation (v. 21). The issue in
> Acts 15 is ". . . not merely post-conversion behaviour but what con-
> stitutes true conversion in the first place."[23]

This, however, as Dr. Coleman points out so well, is not an adequate description of the issue. For the Council came up with certain prohibitions in their letter. These prohibitions indicate that the Council was concerned that Gentile Christians completely disassociate themselves from idolatry and idolatrous practices[24] and even "refrain from activities that even resembled pagan worship, thereby avoiding even the appearance of evil."[25]

Coleman concludes his analysis of soteriology by saying,

> Not only does union with Christ represent the central truth of
> salvation and the core of Paul's experience and thought, it also
> functions as the reason for his prohibition of both sexual immoral-
> ity and idolatry. Theologically, to be united with Christ in salvation
> is incompatible with both of these.[26]

I think all IMP proponents would agree with his statement. Where the disagreement arises is in Dr. Coleman's application of this truth. He appears to make the error of "direct transferability,"[27] equating first-century idolatrous worship with attendance at Muslim religious ceremonies. He states,

---

23 Ibid., 139–40.

24 Ibid., 145.

25 Ibid., 146.

26 Ibid., 193.

27 For a description of direct transferability, see Roy E. Ciampa, "Ideological Challenges for Bible Translators," *IJFM* 28, no. 3 (2011): 139–48.

> The point here is not whether Insider believers must avoid mosque premises entirely, or even whether faith in Jesus requires them to adopt the term "Christian" or refuse labels such as "Muslim," "full Muslim," or "Isahi Muslim" (that is, a "Jesus Following Muslim"). In view here is continued participation in the Muslim religious community. If remaining in one's religious community is an essential part of Insider Movements, and if participating in mosque worship or other clearly religious events is required for maintaining one's status as a "Muslim" religious insider, the approach is contrary to Paul's teaching in 1 Corinthians 8–10.[28]

What Dr. Coleman fails to recognize is that so many differences exist between first-century Mediterranean–world idol worship (along with dining at temples in Corinth) and Muslim religious ceremonies in the twenty-first century that these should not be equated.

This error of direct transferability and his assumed essentialism compel Dr. Coleman to construct a single image of Islam as well as what an insider believer's appropriate response to it should be. However, at least one insider believer, Brother Yusuf, does not necessarily agree with Coleman's image or response.[29] The question arises: Who then is authorized to construct the authoritative image of Islam (as if there is only one) and the appropriate response to that image? Is it Coleman or the insider believer? According to Coleman, he—the outsider—is authorized.[30]

It appears that Dr. Coleman oversteps the boundaries here and exhibits a form of theolonialism. His essentialist definition of Islam limits his range of movement in this area. He does not realize that Islam is actually defined by Islamic communities and that these communities define it in different ways. This is why Islam looks different across and within Islamic communities.[31]

---

28 Coleman, *A Theological Analysis*, 176–77.

29 Ibid., 178.

30 Ibid., 175–76.

31 In his response to my review, Coleman asserts that over his ten years on the field he noticed the diversity among Muslims with regard to beliefs and practices and the meaning of those practices. See "Coleman Responds," 47. However, it appears that he failed to recognize the significance of this diversity. It appears that this is where essentialism limited his perspective, his theologizing, and his range of movement. In the West, South, and East, we also see a remarkable diversity in beliefs and practices and the meaning of these practices among those who identify themselves as Christian. If believers in Jesus can remain as yeast within traditionally non-evangelical socioreligious communities, such as Roman Catholic or liberal Protestant, then why can they not remain as yeast within their Muslim socioreligious communities as followers of Jesus? If they do remain within their socioreligious communities, how do they remain? In what religious practices do insiders actually participate? What do they believe about these practices? How do they view these practices in the light of Scripture? These questions are left unanswered, because Coleman's analysis is based upon articles and not upon the actual beliefs and practices of a community of insiders. Therefore, when Dr. Coleman suggests that if insiders pray in a mosque they are likely praying to another "god" and this is prohibited in 1 Cor 8–10 ("Coleman Responds," 48), this is because an essentialist view of Islam is defining to whom they are praying and pre-ascribing meaning to their praying. Is Dr. Coleman right in his perception? He may be. Yet, can Muslims and insider communities have a different understanding of God than an essentialist understanding would ascribe to them? The IMP articles indicate that this is the case. We simply cannot know the answer to this without data collected from actual insider communities. This is why field research is an integral component of missiological analysis.

Coleman concludes his analysis by focusing on the ecclesiology that appears in the writings of the IMP proponents. Coleman graciously acknowledges that the IMP proponents have not been anti-church. He notes that in their writings IMP proponents have stated that though insider believers may continue some form of mosque attendance or visitation, they also participate in separate gatherings of those who are followers of Jesus. What is troubling for Coleman is that he finds the ecclesiology of the IMP proponents deficient.

Coleman is transparent about the fact that his hermeneutic for his ecclesiology is Baptist; that is, it is based upon the principle of regenerate church membership. Coleman admits that his ecclesiological perspective, though based upon Scripture, is somewhat idealistic. He writes, "The ideal of regenerate church membership does not mean it is always perfectly executed in any local body of believers; only God ultimately knows with certainty the spiritual state of any individual who professes faith."[32] What also shapes Coleman's ecclesiology is that his approach to church is "separatist." It is not without warrant that Coleman is neither a Presbyterian nor an Anglican. Had he been, would he have been so inclined to begin his analysis with the epistle to the Hebrews?

Dr. Coleman points out how IMP proponents have compared insider believers with early Jewish believers. IMP proponents have stated in their writings that since early Jewish believers remained fully within Judaism for many decades, this justifies insider believers remaining as active members within their socioreligious communities. However, Dr. Coleman points out that

> as the temple of God and the New Testament people of God, the church possesses a unique continuity with Israel and Judaism. . . . In spite of this continuity, [the letter to the] Hebrews argues that the old covenant has been fulfilled in Christ and, therefore, the church is to sever ties with Judaism. Remaining in or returning to Judaism, a divinely inspired system, constituted a serious spiritual danger for the early Jewish believers.[33]

I think that Peter O'Brien nuances the problem these believers were facing a bit better than Coleman. It appears that the problem was that they were in danger of abandoning their identity in Christ and corporate fellowship and returning to "a 'reliance on the cultic structures of the old covenant' in order to avoid persecution."[34] To abandon Christ and rely once again upon these structures was a serious danger. In the light of this, Dr. Coleman raises an important concern. For insiders to abandon their identity in Christ and corporate fellowship with other insider believers in order to avoid persecution would be wrong. I think an appropriate way to value Coleman's concern would be to help insider believers understand the historical context of the letter to the Hebrews and its historical application. This would facilitate their ability to discern what the Spirit would say to them in their context in the light of what is written.

---

32 Ibid., 227.

33 Ibid., 244.

34 O'Brien further describes this danger: "But whatever the precise reasons, it is the outcome of such a turning away that is of great concern to the author. 'Christ, his sacrifice, and his priestly work are so relativised that they are effectively denied, and apostasy is only a whisker away. It is to prevent just such a calamity that the author writes this epistle.'" Peter T. O'Brien, *The Letter to the Hebrews,* Pillar New Testament Commentary (Grand Rapids, MI: Eerdmans, 2010), 13.

A significant weakness arises in Coleman's analysis when he begins to look at how IMP proponents describe how church is practiced. His ecclesiological presuppositions, combined with a lack of field research, make him appear somewhat unable to cope with the on-the-ground realities that exist in various Islamic contexts.

This becomes evident when Coleman cannot appreciate Rebecca Lewis' assertion that insider believers "do not attempt to form neo-communities of 'believers-only' that compete with the family network (no matter how contextualized)"; instead, "insider movements" consist of believers remaining in and transforming their own preexisting family networks, minimally disrupting their families and communities.[35] Dr. Coleman views this as an "apparent rejection of regenerate church membership."[36] He somehow assumes that nonrelated individual believers can be brought together and form a separate "neo-community" of "believers-only." It appears to me that his presuppositions, combined with a lack of field research, impact how he interprets what Lewis actually describes.

Coleman posits that forming churches with redeemed believers who are not necessarily related would be much more biblical. Bringing together individuals who are truly converted would create a more formalized church structure. Membership would be established clearly through baptism, not based upon relational ties. A formal membership would heighten the value of the celebration of the Lord's Supper and would in turn facilitate church discipline.[37] In his view, the benefit of this formalization is forfeited when extended family units are the foundation for the church.

In the area where I have worked for over twenty-five years, grouping of unrelated "believers" often does not result in the formation of meaningful "churches." These groups are comprised usually of men, and these believers tend to bond with the foreigner(s) connected to the group rather than to one another. These "believing" individuals form little relational trust or relational accountability among themselves. The foreigner usually has no access to their communities or their families to discover how these "believers" actually live out their lives. Therefore, since there is no knowledge of how these individuals actually live, there is no possibility of church discipline. What has also happened in these contexts is that if any "believers" discover the misdeeds of another, these believers often have no relational capacity to address the issue. If they try to address the misbehaving believer, that believer can cause immense problems for those confronting him. As a result, little if any church discipline takes place.

In contrast, relational trust usually exists within extended family groups and among close friends. When extended family members and close friends come together and form a believing community, then these people know how the others in their community are living. Those who are the leaders within the group can discipline those who are not living appropriately, or these leaders can appeal to outside help if necessary. Thus Dr. Coleman's concerns appear to have arisen from his lack of engagement with

---

35 Coleman, *A Theological Analysis*, 226.

36 Ibid., 226.

37 Ibid., 229–31. Coleman writes, "The above discussion of ordinances, church membership, and church discipline inevitably leads to the conclusion that in order to be faithful to biblical teaching and fulfill its responsibilities, a church must strive for clarity in several matters. First, since membership and the ordinances are for believers, a church must determine as much as is humanly possible the spiritual state of those who are candidates for baptism and membership. It must also refrain from indiscriminately offering the Lord's Supper to anyone in attendance, with no effort to define and explain the proper recipients. In the exercise of its covenant responsibilities, including church discipline, the church must also understand who constitutes its membership" (ibid., 231–32). I did not see these concerns justified in the quotes by Lewis that he provided.

church planters. This is why field research is invaluable in missiology. It roots one's analysis in what actually occurs in given cultural contexts.

In conclusion, Dr. Coleman's dissertation provides a valuable service in that it provides a scholarly lens through which to evaluate the writings of proponents of the insider movement paradigm. Dr. Coleman is irenic and thorough in his treatment of the subject matter. However, his methodology and his analysis are naturally impacted by his assumptions. What is problematic in his research is that he appears to hold to three questionable assumptions of which he is incognizant. First, he repeatedly views Islam through an essentialist lens and speaks of it in a monolithic manner. He does not seem to recognize the actual diversity in belief and practice that can exist within Islamic contexts. Second, he also views culture monodimensionally; therefore it is assumed that religion is something that can be separated from culture. He does not realize how integrated Islam is with the cultures in question. This essentialism and monodimensional view of culture appear to make it difficult for him to see how followers of Christ can remain within their socioreligious communities. The third assumption he makes is that a high view of Scripture negates or minimizes the impact of culture and worldview on exegesis and interpretation of Scripture. This indicates that he holds to a naive realist epistemology. Does this naive realist epistemology, along with the other two assumptions, limit his conceptual categories and his range of movement in his theologizing? It does appear so. Finally, since Dr. Coleman's research is primarily textual, it lacks the benefit of field research. Conducting field research would have exposed Dr. Coleman to the weaknesses embedded in his assumptions and positively impacted his analysis and conclusions.

Bibliography

Abdel-Samad, Hamed. "Political Scientist Hamed Abdel-Samad: 'Islam Is Like a Drug.'" *Spiegel Online,* September 17, 2010. http://www.spiegel.de/international/germany/political-scientist-hamed-abdel-samad-islam-is-like-a-drug-a-717589.html.

Ciampa, Roy E. "Ideological Challenges for Bible Translators." *International Journal of Frontier Missiology* 28, no. 3 (2011): 139–48.

Coleman, Doug. *A Theological Analysis of the Insider Movement Paradigm from Four Perspectives: Theology of Religions, Revelation, Soteriology and Ecclesiology.* EMS Dissertation Series. Pasadena, CA: WCIU Press, 2011.

———. "Doug Coleman Responds to Bradford Greer's Critique." *International Journal of Frontier Missiology* 29, no. 1 (2012): 47–53.

Jung, Dietrich. *Orientalists, Islamists and the Global Public Sphere: A Genealogy of the Modern Essentialist Image of Islam.* Sheffield, UK: Equinox, 2011.

O'Brien, Peter T. *The Letter to the Hebrews.* Pillar New Testament Commentary. Grand Rapids, MI: Eerdmans, 2010.

Wright, N. T. *The New Testament and the People of God.* Minneapolis, MN: Fortress Press, 1992.

GLOSSARY

The following key terms appear often throughout this book and in wider discussions of insider movements. For specific religious, theological, or missiological terminology not defined here, the reader is encouraged to consult a reference work.

alongsider. An outsider (Jesus follower from another culture or area) whom God has prepared to walk alongside and assist insiders in their journey of faith in Jesus.

attractional model. Paradigm of ministry in which the gospel attracts believers from different backgrounds or social groups and gathers them into new congregations. Compare *transformational model*.

C1–C6 Spectrum. A missiological tool developed by John Travis to describe a range of Christ-centered communities (*C*) found in Muslim contexts in terms of socioreligious identity and the forms through which they express their faith. Also called the C-spectrum; sometimes called the C-continuum or the C-scale.

contextualization. In missiology, how the gospel is expressed and responded to appropriately in a given cultural context.

ekklesia. Greek; plural *ekklesiae*. The assembly of believers in the New Testament, usually translated "church." Used here more often than "church" because of the traditional connotations of the latter.

essentialist view of religion(s). An approach to religions that regards each religious system as basically monolithic, defined by an "essence" of core ideas, beliefs, and values shared by all its adherents.

incarnational. Patterned after the incarnation of Christ. This model of contextual ministry emphasizes identification with the host culture.

insider. A follower of Jesus who remains within his or her own socioreligious context, seeking to maintain as much presence and participation in the culture as is biblically possible.

insider movement (IM). A group or network of people from a non-Christian religious tradition who have embraced the life and teaching of Jesus Christ as described in the Bible while remaining relationally, culturally, and socially part of the religious community of their birth.

non-baptized believer in Christ (NBBC). A term coined by Herbert Hoefer to describe a Hindu follower of Christ who has not changed his or her legal and social status in the Hindu community by being baptized in a traditional Christian church.

socioreligious. A term used to describe the integrated social-religious group identity and practices found in many cultures. For many of the world's peoples, religion and culture are widely overlapping, even inseparable, categories. In some models of identity, one's socioreligious identity is distinguished from one's spiritual, ego, or core identity.

syncretism. In missiology, the combination of unscriptural values, beliefs, and practices with scriptural ones, resulting in a sub-biblical faith and a compromised message. This often occurs when indigenous pagan meaning is attached to "Christian" forms introduced from a foreign culture.

transformational model. Paradigm of ministry in which the gospel is implanted into and transforms a preexisting social network. Compare *attractional model*.

Abdul-Haqq, Abdiyah Akbar. *Sharing Your Faith with a Muslim*. Minneapolis: Bethany House, 1980.

Abu-Lughod, Lila. *Veiled Sentiments: Honor and Poetry in a Bedouin Society*. Berkeley, CA: University of California Press, 1986.

———. *Writing Women's Worlds: Bedouin Stories*. Berkeley, CA: University of California Press, 1993.

Accad, Fouad Elias. *Building Bridges: Christianity and Islam*. Colorado Springs, CO: NavPress, 1997.

———. *Seven Muslim Christian Principles*. Limassol, Cyprus: Ar-Rabitah, n.d.

Accad, Martin. "Corruption and/or Misinterpretation of the Bible: The Story of the Islamic Usage of *Tahrīf*." *Near East School of Theology Theological Review* 24, no. 2 (2003): 67–97.

———. "The Gospels in the Muslim Discourse of the Ninth to the Fourteenth Century: An Exegetical Inventorial Table (Parts I–IV)." *Islam and Christian-Muslim Relations* 14, no. 1 (2003): 67–81, 205–20, 337–52, 459–79.

———. "The Interpretation of John 20:17 in Muslim-Christian Dialogue (8th–14th Centuries): The Ultimate Proof-Text." In *Christians at the Heart of Islamic Rule*, edited by David Thomas, 199–214. Leiden: Brill, 2003.

Allen, Roland. *Missionary Methods: St. Paul's or Ours?* Grand Rapids, MI: Eerdmans, 1962 [1912].

———. *The Spontaneous Expansion of the Church: And the Causes Which Hinder It*. Eugene, OR: Wipf & Stock, 1997 [1927].

Ammerman, Nancy T. "Religious Identities and Religious Institutions." In *Handbook of the Sociology of Religion*, edited by Michele Dillon, 207–27. New York: Cambridge University Press, 2003.

Anderson, John D. C. "The Missionary Approach to Islam: Christian or 'Cultic.'" *Missiology: An International Review* 4, no. 3 (1976): 258–99.

Andrae, Tor. *Les origines de l'Islam et le Christianisme*. Translated by Jules Roch. Paris: Adrien-Maisonneuve, 1955.

Arai, Jin. "Religious Education in Christ-with-Culture from a Japanese Perspective." *Religious Education* 91, no. 2 (1996): 222–23.

Archer, Margaret Scotford. *Structure, Agency, and the Internal Conversation*. New York: Cambridge University Press, 2003.

Armstrong, Karen. *Fields of Blood: Religions and the History of Violence*. New York: Alfred A. Knopf, 2014.

———. *The Great Transformation: The Beginnings of our Religious Traditions*. New York: Knopf, 2006.

Assmann, Jan. *The Price of Monotheism*. Translated by Robert Savage. Stanford: Stanford University Press, 2009.

Ayoub, Mahmoud M. *The Qur'an and Its Interpreters*. Albany, NY: State University of New York Press, 1984.

Baeq, Daniel Shinjong. "Contextualizing Religious Form and Meaning: A Missiological Interpretation of Naaman's Petitions (2 Kings 5:15–19)." *International Journal of Frontier Missiology* 27, no. 4 (2010): 197–207.

Bailey, Kenneth E. *Jesus through Middle Eastern Eyes: Cultural Studies in the Gospels*. Downers Grove, IL: IVP Academic, 2008.

———. *Paul through Mediterranean Eyes: Cultural Studies in 1 Corinthians*. Downers Grove, IL: IVP Academic, 2011.

Baladhuri, Abu-l 'Abbas, al-. *Kitab Futuh al-Buldan*. Translated by Philip K. Hitti as *The Origins of the Islamic State*. New York: Columbia University, 1916.

Banks, Marcus. *Ethnicity: Anthropological Constructions*. New York: Routledge, 1996.

Barnett, Jens. "Conversion's Consequences: Identity, Belonging, and Hybridity amongst Muslim Followers of Christ." MA thesis, Redcliffe College, August 2008.

———. "Living a Pun: Cultural Hybridity among Arab Followers of Christ." In Greenlee, *Longing for Community*, 29–40.

———. "Refusing to Choose: Multiple Belonging among Arab Followers of Christ." In Greenlee, *Longing for Community*, 19–28.

Barr, O. Sydney. *From the Apostles' Faith to the Apostles' Creed*. New York: Oxford University Press, 1964.

Barrett, David B. "AD. 2000: 350 Million Christians in Africa." *International Review of Mission* 59, no. 233 (1970): 39–54.

Bartholomew, Craig G., and Michael W. Goheen. "Story and Biblical Theology." In *Out of Egypt: Biblical Theology and Biblical Interpretation*, edited by Craig Bartholemew, Mary Healy, Karl Möller, and Robin Parry, 144–71. Grand Rapids, MI: Zondervan, 2004.

Bartlotti, Leonard N. "Negotiating Pakhto: Proverbs, Islam and the Construction of Identity among Pashtuns." PhD thesis, Oxford Centre for Mission Studies / University of Wales, UK, 2000.

Basetti-Sani, Giulio. *The Koran in the Light of Christ*. Chicago: Franciscan Herald Press, 1977.

Baumstark, A. "Juedischer und Christlicher Gebetstypus im Koran." *Der Islam* 16 (1927): 229.

Bavinck, Herman. *Reformed Dogmatics*. 4 vols. Grand Rapids, MI: Baker Academic, 2008.

Bavinck, Johan Herman. *An Introduction to the Science of Missions*. Philadelphia: Presbyterian & Reformed, 1960.

Bearman, P. J., Th. Bianquis, Clifford Edmund Bosworth, E. Van Donzel, and W. P. Heinrichs, eds. *The Encyclopedia of Islam*. New ed. Leiden: Brill, 2005.

Beaver, R. Pierce. "The History of Mission Strategy." In *Perspectives on the World Christian Movement: A Reader*, 3rd ed., edited by Ralph D. Winter and Steven C. Hawthorne, 241–52. Pasadena, CA: William Carey Library, 1999.

Bebbington, David W. *Evangelicalism in Modern Britain: A History from the 1730s to the 1980s*. London: Unwin Hyman, 1989.

Becker, C. H. "Die Kanzel im Kultus des alten Islam." In *Orientalische Studien Theodor Noeldeke zum siebzigsten Geburtstag*, edited by Carl Bezold. 2 vols. Giessen, 1906.

———. "Zur Geschichte des Islamischen Kultus." *Der Islam* 3 (1912): 374–419.

Bell, Richard. *The Origin of Islam in Its Christian Environment*. London: Macmillan, 1926.

Berger, Peter, and Thomas Luckmann. *The Social Construction of Reality: A Treatise in the Sociology of Knowledge.* London: Penguin, 1991.

Berkhof, Louis. *The History of Christian Doctrines.* Grand Rapids, MI: Baker, 1937.

Berry, John W., Ype H. Poortinga, Seger M. Breugelmans, Athanasios Chasiotis, David L. Sam. *Cross-cultural Psychology: Research and Applications.* Cambridge: Cambridge University Press, 2002.

Bevans, Stephen B. *Models of Contextual Theology.* Maryknoll, NY: Orbis, 2002.

Bhabha, Homi K. *The Location of Culture.* London: Routledge, 2004.

Blachere, Regis. *Introduction au Coran.* 2nd ed. Paris: C-Gt.-P. Maisonneuve, 1959.

Block, C. Jonn. *Expanding the Qur'anic Bridge: Historical and Modern Interpretations of the Qur'an in Christian-Muslim Dialogue with Special Attention Paid to Ecumenical Trends.* Minneapolis: Routledge, 2013.

Bock, Darrell L. *Acts.* Baker Exegetical Commentary on the New Testament. Edited by Robert W. Yarbrough and Robert H. Stein. Grand Rapids, MI: Baker Academic, 2007.

Bosch, David J. *Transforming Mission: Paradigm Shifts in Theology of Mission.* Maryknoll, NY: Orbis, 1996.

Bowman, John. *The Samaritan Problem: Studies in the Relationships of Samaritanism, Judaism, and Early Christianity.* Eugene, OR: Pickwick, 1975.

Boyd, Robin H. *India and the Latin Captivity of the Church.* London: Cambridge University Press, 1974.

Bratcher, Robert C. *The Pillars of Religion in the Light of the Tawrat Zabur & Injil.* Beirut: The Bible Society, 1984.

Brewster, Thomas, and Betty Sue Brewster. *Bonding and the Missionary Task: Establishing a Sense of Belonging.* Pasadena, CA: Lingua House, 1982.

Brown, Colin, ed. *New International Dictionary of New Testament Theology.* 4 vols. Grand Rapids, MI: Zondervan, 1971.

Brown, Rick. "Biblical Muslims." *International Journal of Frontier Missiology* 24, no. 2 (2007): 65–74.

———. "Brother Jacob and Master Isaac: How One Insider Movement Began." *International Journal of Frontier Missiology* 24, no. 1 (2007): 41–42.

———. "Contextualization without Syncretism." *International Journal of Frontier Missions* 23, no. 3 (2006): 127–33.

———. "The Kingdom of God and the Mission of God: Part 1." *International Journal of Frontier Missiology* 28, no. 1 (2011): 5–12.

———. "The Kingdom of God and the Mission of God: Part 2." *International Journal of Frontier Missiology* 28, no. 2 (2011): 49–59.

———. "Who was 'Allah' Before Islam? Evidence that the Term 'Allah' Originated with Jewish and Christian Arabs." In *Toward Respectful Understanding and Witness among Muslims: Essays in Honor of J. Dudley Woodberry,* edited by Evelyne A. Reisacher, 147–78. Pasadena, CA: William Carey Library, 2012.

———, and Christopher Samuel. "The Meanings of κυριος 'Lord' in the New Testament." SIL Publications, 2002.

Buckser, Andrew, and Stephen D. Glazier. *The Anthropology of Religious Conversion.* Lanham, MD: Rowman and Littlefield, 2003.

Bukhari, Imam, al-. *Sahih al-Bukhari* (Arabic-English). Translated by M. Muhsin Khan. 9 vols. Beirut: Dar al-Arabia, n.d.

Carson, D. A. *Christ and Culture Revisited*. Grand Rapids, MI: Eerdmans, 2008.

———. *Showing the Spirit: A Theological Exposition of 1 Corinthians 12–14*. Grand Rapids, MI: Baker, 1987.

———, and Douglas J. Moo. *An Introduction to the New Testament*. 2nd ed. Grand Rapids, MI: Zondervan, 2005.

Caton, Steven C. *Peaks of Yemen I Summon: Poetry as Cultural Practice in a North Yemeni Tribe*. Berkeley, CA: University of California Press, 1990.

Cavanaugh, William T. "'A Fire Strong Enough to Consume the House': The Wars of Religion and the Rise of the State." *Modern Theology* 11, no. 4 (1995): 397–420.

Chandler, Paul-Gordon. *Pilgrims of Christ on the Muslim Road: Exploring a New Path between Two Faiths*. Lanham, MD: Cowley, 2007.

Chapman, Colin. "Biblical Foundations of Praying for Muslims." In *Muslims and Christians on the Emmaus Road: Crucial Issues in Witness among Muslims*, edited by J. Dudley Woodberry, 334–42. Monrovia, CA: MARC, 1989.

———. *Cross and Crescent: Responding to the Challenge of Islam*. Downers Grove, IL: InterVarsity Press, 2007.

Ciampa, Roy E. "Ideological Challenges for Bible Translators." *International Journal of Frontier Missiology* 28, no. 3 (2011): 139–48.

Coe, S. "In Search of Renewal in Theological Education." *Theological Education* 9 (1976): 233–43.

Coleman, Doug. "Doug Coleman Responds to Bradford Greer's Critique." *International Journal of Frontier Missiology* 29, no 1 (2012): 47–53.

———. *A Theological Analysis of the Insider Movement Paradigm from Four Perspectives: Theology of Religions, Revelation, Soteriology and Ecclesiology*. EMS Dissertation Series. Pasadena, CA: WCIU Press, 2011.

Conn, Harvie M. "Conversion and Culture: A Theological Perspective with Reference to Korea." In *Gospel and Culture*, edited by John Stott and Robert T. Coote, 195–239. Pasadena, CA: William Carey Library, 1979.

———. *Eternal Word and Changing Worlds: Theology, Anthropology, and Mission in Trialogue*. Phillipsburg, NJ: Presbyterian & Reformed, 1984.

———. "The Muslim Convert and His Culture." In *The Gospel and Islam: A 1978 Compendium*, edited by Don M. McCurry, 97–113. MARC: Monrovia, 1979.

Constantineanu, Corneliu. *The Social Significance of Reconciliation in Paul's Theology: Narrative Readings in Romans*. New York: Continuum, 2010.

Conzelmann, Hans. *1 Corinthians: A Commentary on the First Epistle to the Corinthians*. Translated by James W. Leitch. Philadelphia: Fortress Press, 1975.

Cook, David. "Why Did Muhammad Attack the Byzantines?" In *Political Islam from Muhammad to Ahmadinejad: Defenders, Detractors, Definitions*, edited by Joseph Morrison Skelly, 27–34. Santa Barbara, CA: Praeger Security, 2010.

Corwin, Gary. "A Humble Appeal to C5/Insider Movement Muslim Ministry Advocates to Consider Ten Questions." *International Journal of Frontier Missions* 24, no. 1 (2007): 5–20.

Cragg, Kenneth, ed. *Alive unto God: Muslim and Christian Prayer*. London: Oxford University Press, 1970.

———. *Muhammad and the Christian: A Question of Response.* London: Darton, Longman and Todd, 1984.

———. "A Study in the Fatiha." *Operation Reach.* Beirut and Jerusalem: Near East Christian Council (September–October 1957): 9–18.

Crump, David. *Knocking on Heaven's Door: A New Testament Theology of Petitionary Prayer.* Grand Rapids, MI: Baker Academic, 2006.

Cullmann, Oscar. *The Earliest Christian Confessions.* Translated by J. K. S. Reid. London: Lutterworth Press, 1949.

Cumming, Joseph. "Did Jesus Die on the Cross? Reflections in Muslim Commentaries." In *Muslim and Christian Reflections on Peace: Divine and Human Dimensions,* edited by J. D. Woodberry, O. Zumrut, and M. Koylu, 32–50. Lanham, MD: University Press of America, 2005.

Cummings, John Thomas, Hossein Askari, and Ahmad Mustafa. "Islam and Modern Economic Change." In *Islam and Development: Religion and Sociopolitical Change,* edited by John L. Esposito, 25–47. Syracuse: Syracuse University Press, 1980.

Dallmayr, Fred. *Alternative Visions: Paths in the Global Village.* Lanham, MD: Rowman and Littlefield, 1998.

Daniels, Gene. "Worshiping Jesus in the Mosque." *Christianity Today,* January 2013.

Decker, Rodney J. "Some Notes on Semantics, Illustrated with *ekklesia.*" *NT Resources* (blog). Accessed May 23, 2013. http://ntresources.com/blog/documents/ekklhsia3G.pdf.

Dickson, Kwesi A. *Uncompleted Mission: Christianity and Exclusivism.* Maryknoll, NY: Orbis, 1991.

Dinkins, Larry. "Toward Contextualized Creeds: A Perspective from Buddhist Thailand." *International Journal of Frontier Missiology* 27, no. 1 (2010): 5–9.

Donner, Fred M. *Muhammad and the Believers: the Origins of Islam.* Cambridge, MA: Belknap Press of Harvard University Press, 2010.

———. "The Qur'an in Recent Scholarship: Challenges and Desiderata." In *The Qur'an in Its Historical Context,* edited by Gabriel Said Reynolds, 29–50. New York: Routledge, 2008.

Driscoll, Mark. *Doctrine: What Christians Should Believe.* Wheaton, IL: Crossway, 2010.

Droogers, Andre. "Syncretism: The Problem of Definition, the Definition of the Problem." In *Dialogue and Syncretism: An Interdisciplinary Approach,* edited by Jerald D. Gort, Hendrik M. Vroom, Rein Fernhout, and Anton Wessels, 7–25. Grand Rapids, MI: Eerdmans, 1989.

Dunn, James D. G. *Baptism in the Holy Spirit: A Re-examination of the New Testament Teaching on the Gift of the Spirit in Relation to Pentecostalism Today.* Philadelphia: Westminster Press, 1970.

Dyrness, William. *Poetic Theology: God and the Poetics of Everyday Life.* Grand Rapids, MI: Eerdmans, 2011.

Edersheim, Alfred. *The Life and Times of Jesus the Messiah.* Grand Rapids, MI: Eerdmans, 1971.

Edwards, Jonathan. *The Nature of True Virtue.* Ann Harbor: University of Michigan Press, 1991 [1765].

———. *A Treatise Concerning Religious Affections.* Whitefish, MT: Kessinger, 2010 [1746].

Eickelman, Dale F. *The Middle East and Central Asia: An Anthropological Approach.* 3rd ed. Englewood Cliffs, NJ: Prentice-Hall, 1998.

———. "Popular Religion in the Middle East and North Africa." In *The Oxford Encyclopedia of the Modern Islamic World,* edited by John L. Esposito, 339–43. Oxford: Oxford University Press, 1995.

———. "The Study of Islam in Local Contexts." *Contributions to Asian Studies* 17 (1982): 1–16.

Esposito, John L. *What Everyone Needs to Know about Islam.* Oxford: Oxford University Press, 1995.

Farhadian, Charles E. *Introducing World Religions: A Christian Engagement*. Grand Rapids, MI: Baker Academic, 2015.

Farquhar, J. N. *The Crown of Hinduism*. London: H. Milford, 1913.

Fee, Gordon D. *The First Epistle to the Corinthians*. Grand Rapids, MI: Eerdmans, 1987.

Feine, Paul. *Gestalt des apostolischen Glaubensbekenntnisses in der Zeit des Neuen Testament*. Leipzig: Verlag Doerffling & Franke, 1925.

Ferguson, Everett. *Backgrounds of Early Christianity*. 3rd ed. Grand Rapids, MI: Eerdmans, 2003.

Fitzgerald, Timothy. *Discourse on Civility and Barbarity: A Critical History of Religion and Related Categories*. Oxford: Oxford University Press, 2007.

Fitzmyer, Joseph A. *Acts of the Apostles*. Anchor Bible Commentary. New York: Doubleday, 1998.

Flemming, Dean. *Contextualization in the New Testament: Patterns for Theology and Mission*. Downers Grove, IL: IVP Academic, 2005.

Froystad, Kathinka, ed. *Blended Boundaries: Caste, Class, and Shifting Faces of "Hinduness" in a North Indian City*. New Delhi: Oxford University Press, 2005.

Fueck, J. "The Originality of the Arabian Prophet." In *Studies on Islam*, translated and edited by Merlin Swartz, 86–98. New York: Oxford University Press, 1981.

Garrison, David. *Church Planting Movements*. Richmond, VA: Office of Overseas Operations, International Mission Board of the Southern Baptist Convention, 2000.

———. *Church Planting Movements: How God Is Redeeming a Lost World*. Monument, CO: WIGTake, 2004.

———. "Church Planting Movements vs. Insider Movements." *International Journal of Frontier Missions* 21, no. 4 (2004): 151–54.

———. *A Wind in the House of Islam: How God Is Drawing Muslims around the World to Faith in Jesus Christ*. Monument, CO: WIGTake, 2013.

Gaudeul, Jean-Marie. *Called from Islam to Christ: Why Muslims Become Christians*. Crowborough: East Sussex, UK: Monarch, 1999.

———. *Encounters and Clashes: Islam and Christianity in History*, vol. 1. Rome: Pontificio Istituto di Studi Arabi e Islamici, 1990.

Geertz, Clifford. *The Interpretation of Cultures*. New York: Basic Books, 1973.

Geiger, Abraham. *Judaism and Islam*. Translated by F. M. Young. New York: KTAV, 1970.

Ghazali, Abu Hamid, al-. *Ihya Ulum-id-Din*. Translated by Fazal-ul-Karim. Lahore: Islamic Book Foundation, 1981.

———. *Al-Munqidh min al-dalal (The Deliverer from Error)*. Edited by Jamil Saliba and Kamal 'Ayyad. 3rd ed. Damascus: Matba'at al-Jami'a al-Suriya, 1939.

———. *Al-Qustas al-Mustaqim*. Edited by V. Chelhot. Cited in V. Chelhot, "La Balance Juste," *Bulletin d'Etudes Orientales* 15 (1958).

Gibb, Hamilton A. R. "Pre-Islamic Monotheism in Arabia." *Harvard Theological Review* 60 (1962): 269–80.

Glaser, Ida. *The Bible and Other Faiths: Christian Responsibility in a World of Religions*. Downers Grove, IL: IVP Academic, 2005.

Goerling, Fritz. "The Use of Islamic Theological Terminology in Bible Translation and Evangelism among the Jula in Cote d'Ivoire." ThM thesis, Fuller Theological Seminary, 1989.

Goitein, S. D. *Jews and Arabs: Their Contact through the Ages*. 3rd rev. ed. New York: Schocken Books, 1974.

———. *Studies in Islamic History and Institutions*. Leiden: Brill, 1968.

Goldingay, John, and Christopher J. H. Wright. "'Yahweh Our God Yahweh One': The Old Testament and Religious Pluralism." In *One God, One Lord: Christianity in a World of Religious Pluralism*, 2nd ed., edited by Andrew D. Clarke and Bruce W. Winter, 43–62. Grand Rapids, MI: Baker, 1992.

Goldsmith, Martin. "Community and Controversy: Key Causes of Muslim Resistance." *Missiology: An International Review* 4, no. 3 (1976): 317–23.

Goldziher, Ignaz. *Muhammedanische Studien*. 2 vols. Halle, Germany: Max Niemeyer, 1889–90.

Gottschalk, Peter. *Beyond Hindu and Muslim: Multiple Identity in Narratives from Village India*. New York: Oxford University Press, 2000.

Gray, Andrea, and Leith Gray. "Paradigms and Praxis: Part I: Social Networks and Fruitfulness in Church Planting." *International Journal of Frontier Missiology* 26, no. 1 (2009): 19–28.

Green, Denis. "Guidelines from Hebrews for Contextualization." In *Muslims and Christians on the Emmaus Road: Crucial Issues in Witness among Muslims*, edited by J. Dudley Woodberry, 233–50. Monrovia, CA: MARC, 1989.

Green, Tim. "Conversion in the Light of Identity Theories." In Greenlee, *Longing for Community*, 41–51.

———. "Identity Choices at the Border Zone." In Greenlee, *Longing for Community*, 53–66.

Greenlee, David. *Longing for Community: Church, Ummah, or Somewhere in Between?* Pasadena, CA: William Carey Library, 2013.

Grudem, Wayne. *Systematic Theology*. Grand Rapids, MI: Zondervan, 1994.

Guillaume, Alfred. "The Influence of Judaism on Islam." In *The Legacy of Israel*, edited by Edwyn R. Bevan and Charles Singer, 129–71. Oxford: Clarendon Press, 1928.

———. *The Life of Muhammad: A Translation of Ibn Hisham's Recension of Ibn Ishaq's Sirat Rasul Allah*. London: Oxford University Press, 1995.

Haddad, Yvonne. "The Impact of the Islamic Period in Iran on the Syrian Muslims of Montreal." In *The Muslim Community of North America*, edited by Earle Waugh, Baha Abu-Laban, and Regula B. Qureshi, 165–81. Edmonton, Alberta: University of Alberta Press, 1983.

Haight, Roger. *Christian Community in History: Comparative Ecclesiology*. 3 vols. New York: Continuum, 2005.

Hammond, Phillip E. "Religion and the Persistence of Identity." *Journal for the Scientific Study of Religion* 27, no. 1 (1988): 1–11.

Hardy, Friedhelm. "The Classical Religions of India." In *The World's Religions*, edited by Peter Clarke, Friedhelm Hardy, Leslie Houlden, and Stewart Sutherland, 569–659. London: Routledge, 1988.

Harlan, Mark A. *A Model for Theologizing in Arab Muslim Contexts*. EMS Dissertation Series. Pasadena, CA: WCIU Press, 2012.

Harrison, Paul W. "The Arabs of Oman." *The Moslem World* 24, no. 3 (1934): 262–69.

Hawley, John Stratton. "Comparative Religion for Undergraduates: What's Next?" In *Comparing Religions: Possibilities and Perils?*, edited by Thomas A. Idinopulos, Brian C. Wilson, and James Constantine Hanges, 115–42. Leiden: Brill, 2006.

———. "The Music in Faith and Morality." *Journal of the American Academy of Religion* 52, no. 2 (1984): 243–62.

Heckman, Bruce. "Arab Christian Reaction to Contextualization in the Middle East." MA thesis, Fuller Theological Seminary, 1988.

Hermans, Hubert J. M. "The Construction of a Personal Position Repertoire: Method and Practice." *Culture and Psychology* 7, no. 3 (2001): 323–66.

———. "The Dialogical Self: One Person, Different Stories." In *Self and Identity: Personal, Social, and Symbolic,* edited by Yoshihisa Kashima, Margaret Foddy, and Michael Platow, 71–99. Mahwah, NJ: Lawrence Erlbaum Associates, 2002.

———. "The Dialogical Self: Toward a Theory of Personal and Cultural Positioning." *Culture and Psychology* 7, no. 3 (2001): 243–81.

———, and Giancarlo Dimaggio. "Self, Identity, and Globalization in Times of Uncertainty: A Dialogical Analysis." *Review of General Psychology* 11, no. 1 (2007): 31–61.

Hick, John, and Brian Hebblethwaite, eds. *Christianity and Other Religions: Selected Readings.* Philadelphia: Fortress Press, 1980.

Hiebert, Paul G. *Anthropological Reflections on Missiological Issues.* Grand Rapids, MI: Baker, 1994.

———. "The Flaw of the Excluded Middle." *Missiology: An International Review* 10 (January 1982): 35–47.

———, R. Daniel Shaw, and Tite Tienou. *Understanding Folk Religion: A Christian Response to Popular Beliefs and Practices.* Grand Rapids, MI: Baker Academic, 1997.

Higgins, Kevin. "Acts 15 and Insider Movements among Muslims: Questions, Process, and Conclusions." *International Journal of Frontier Missiology* 24, no. 1 (2007): 29–40.

Hirschfeld, H. *New Researches into the Composition and Exegesis of the Quran.* London: Royal Asiatic Society, 1902.

Hirschl, Ran. *Constitutional Theocracy.* Cambridge, MA: Harvard University Press, 2010.

Hirst, Jacqueline Suthren, and John Zavos. "Riding a Tiger? South Asia and the Problem of 'Religion.'" *Contemporary South Asia* 14, no. 1 (2005): 3–20.

Hitti, P. K. *History of the Arabs.* 6th ed. London: Macmillan, 1956.

Hoefer, Herbert. *Churchless Christianity.* Pasadena, CA: William Carey Library, 2001.

Horovitz, J. "Quran." *Der Islam* 13 (1923): 66–69.

Huffard, Evertt W. "Culturally Relevant Themes about Christ." In *Muslims and Christians on the Emmaus Road,* edited by J. Dudley Woodberry, 177–92. Monrovia, CA: MARC, 1989.

———. "Thematic Dissonance in the Muslim-Christian Encounter: A Contextualized Theology of Honor." PhD dissertation, Fuller Theological Seminary, 1985.

Ibbetson, Denzil. *Report on the Census of the Panjáb Taken on the 17th of February 1881.* Calcutta: Superintendent of Government Printing, 1883.

Idowu, Bolaji. *African Traditional Religion: A Definition.* Maryknoll, NY: Orbis, 1973.

———. *Olódùmare: God in Yoruba Belief.* London: Longman, 1962.

Inglis, Fred. *Clifford Geertz: Culture, Custom and Ethics.* Cambridge, UK: Polity Press, 2000.

Jeffery, Arthur. *The Foreign Vocabulary of the Quran.* Baroda: Oriental Institute, 1938.

Jones, E. Stanley. *The Christ of the Indian Road.* New York: Abingdon Press, 1925.

———. *Mahatma Gandhi: An Interpretation.* Nashville: Abingdon-Cokesbury Press, 1948.

———. *The Unshakable Kingdom and the Unchanging Person.* Nashville, TN: Abingdon Press, 1972.

Jung, Dietrich. *Orientalists, Islamists and the Global Public Sphere: A Genealogy of the Essentialist Image of Islam*. Sheffield, UK: Equinox, 2011.

Kärkkäinen, Veli-Matti. *An Introduction to the Theology of Religions: Biblical, Historical and Contemporary Perspectives*. Downers Grove, IL: InterVarsity Press, 2003.

Keener, Craig S. *The IVP Bible Background Commentary: New Testament*. 2nd ed. Downers Grove, IL: IVP Academic, 2014.

Kelley, J. N. D. *Early Christian Creeds*. 2nd ed. London: Longman, 1960.

Khan, Dominique-Sila. *Crossing the Threshold: Understanding Religious Identities in South Asia*. London: I.B. Tauris, 2004.

Kilgallen, John J. "Acts 13.38–39: Culmination of Paul's Speech in Pisidia." *Biblica* 69, no. 4 (1988): 480–506.

Kim, Enoch J. "'Us' or 'Me'? Modernization and Social Networks among China's Urban Hui." In *Longing for Community: Church, Ummah, or Somewhere in Between?*, 89–96.

King, Richard. *Orientalism and Religion: Postcolonial Theory, India and "The Mystic East."* New Delhi: Oxford University Press, 1999.

Kinzer, Mark. *Postmissionary Messianic Judaism: Redefining Christian Engagement with the Jewish People*. Grand Rapids, MI: Brazos Press, 2005.

Kirsch, Jonathan. *God against the Gods: The History of the War between Monotheism and Polytheism*. New York: Viking Compass, 2004.

Kittel, Gerhard, and Gerhard Friedrich, eds. *Theological Dictionary of the New Testament*. Translated by Geoffrey W. Bromiley. Grand Rapids, MI: Eerdmans, 1966.

Kraemer, Hendrik. *The Christian Message in a Non-Christian World*. Kregel / International Missionary Council, 1947.

Kraft, Charles H., ed. *Appropriate Christianity*. Pasadena, CA: William Carey Library, 2005.

———. "Dynamic Equivalence Churches in Muslim Society." In *The Gospel and Islam: A 1978 Compendium*, edited by Don M. McCurry, 114–24. Monrovia, CA: MARC, 1979.

———. "What Kind of Encounters Do We Need in Our Christian Witness?" *Evangelical Missions Quarterly* 27, no. 3 (1991): 258–65.

Kraft, Kathryn A. *Searching for Heaven in the Real World: A Sociological Discussion of Conversion in the Arab World*. Eugene, OR: Wipf & Stock, 2013.

Kunin, Seth D. *Theories of Religion: A Reader*. With Jonathan Miles-Watson. New Brunswick, NJ: Rutgers University Press, 2006.

Lane, Jan-Erik, and Svante O. Errson. *Culture and Politics: A Comparative Approach*. Burlington, VT: Ashgate, 2005.

Latourette, Kenneth Scott. *A History of Christianity*. 2 vols. New York: Harper & Row, 1953.

Lazarus-Yafeh, Hava. *Some Religious Aspects of Islam*. Leiden: Brill, 1981.

Lenning, Larry G. *Blessing in Mosque and Mission*. Pasadena, CA: William Carey Library, 1980.

Levenson, Jon. "Judaism, Christianity, and Islam in Their Contemporary Encounters: Judaism Addresses Christianity." In *Religious Foundations of Western Civilization: Judaism, Christianity, and Islam*, edited by Jacob Neusner, 581–608. Nashville: Abingdon, 2006.

Lewis, Rebecca. "Promoting Movements to Christ within Natural Communities." *International Journal of Frontier Missiology* 24, no. 2 (2007): 75–76.

Lincoln, Bruce. *Religion, Empire, and Torture: The Case of Achaemenian Persia, with a Postscript on Abu Ghraib.* Chicago: University of Chicago Press, 2007.

Lipner, Julius J. *Brahmabandhab Upadhyay: The Life and Thought of a Revolutionary.* New Delhi: Oxford University Press, 1999.

Littell, Franklin H. *The Origins of Sectarian Protestantism: A Study of the Anabaptist View of the Church.* New York: Macmillan, 1964.

Love, Rick. *Muslims, Magic and the Kingdom of God: Church Planting among Folk Muslims.* Pasadena, CA: William Carey Library, 2000.

Lukens-Bull, Ronald. "Between Text and Practice: Considerations in the Anthropological Study of Islam." *Marburg Journal of Religion* 4, no. 2 (1999): 1–10.

Luxenberg, Christoph. *The Syro-Aramaic Reading of the Koran: A Contribution to the Decoding of the Language of the Koran.* Berlin: Hans Schiler, 2007.

Lysaker, Paul Henry, and John Timothy Lysaker. "Narrative Structure in Psychosis: Schizophrenia and Disruptions in the Dialogical Self." *Theory and Psychology* 12, no. 2 (2002): 207–20.

MacDonald, John. *The Theology of the Samaritans.* The New Testament Library. London: SCM, 1964.

Macquarrie, John. "Existentialism." In *The Encyclopedia of Religion.* Edited by Mircea Eliade. New York: Macmillan, 1987.

Maggay, Melba P., ed. "Theology, Context and the Filipino Church." Postscript to *Communicating Cross-culturally: Towards a New Context for Missions in the Philippines,* edited by Melba P. Maggay. Quezon City: New Day, 1989.

Malek, Sobhi W. "Allah-u Akbar Bible Lessons: Aspects of Their Effectiveness in Evangelizing Muslims." DMiss dissertation, Fuller Theological Seminary, 1986.

Mallampalli, Chandra. *Christians and Public Life in Colonial South India, 1863–1937: Contending with Marginality.* New York and London: RoutledgeCurzon, 2004.

Mandair, Arvind-Pal. *Religion and the Specter of the West: Sikhism, India, Postcoloniality, and the Politics of Translation.* New York: Columbia University Press, 2009.

Marranci, Gabriele. *The Anthropology of Islam.* Oxford, UK: Berg, 2008.

Massey, Joshua. "God's Amazing Diversity in Drawing Muslims to Christ." *International Journal of Frontier Missions* 17, no. 1 (2000): 5–14.

Massignon, Louis. *Essai sur les origines du lexique technique de la mystique musulmane.* Paris: Vrin, 1968.

Masson, D. *Le Coran et la revelation judeo-chretienne.* Paris: Adrien-Maisonneuve, 1958.

Mbiti, John S. *African Religions and Philosophy.* London: Heinemann, 1969.

———. *Concepts of God in Africa.* New York: Praeger, 1970.

———. *New Testament Eschatology in an African Background: A Study of the Encounter between New Testament Theology and African Traditional Concepts.* London: Oxford University Press, 1971.

McAuliffe, Jane Dammen. *Qur'anic Christians: An Analysis of Classical and Modern Exegesis.* Cambridge: Cambridge University Press, 1991.

McCurry, Don M., ed. *The Gospel and Islam: A 1978 Compendium.* Monrovia, CA: MARC, 1979.

McDermott, Gerald. "What If Paul Had Been from China? Reflections on the Possibility of Revelation in Non-Christian Religions." In *No Other Gods before Me: Evangelicals and the Challenge of World Religions,* edited by John G. Stackhouse, 17–35. Grand Rapids, MI: Baker, 2001.

McGavran, Donald A. "The Biblical Base from Which Adjustments Are Made." In *Christopaganism or Indigenous Christianity?*, edited by Tetsunao Yamamori and Charles R. Taber, 35–56. Pasadena, CA: William Carey Library, 1975.

———. *The Bridges of God: A Study in the Strategy of Missions.* Eugene, OR: Wipf & Stock, 2005 [1955].

———. *Understanding Church Growth.* Grand Rapids, MI: Eerdmans, 1970.

McLeod, John. *Beginning Postcolonialism.* Manchester: Manchester University Press, 2000.

McPartlan, Paul. *Sacrament of Salvation: An Introduction to Eucharistic Ecclesiology.* Edinburgh: T&T Clark, 1995.

Medearis, Carl. *Speaking of Jesus: The Art of Not-Evangelism.* Colorado Springs, CO: David C. Cook, 2011.

Mez, Adam. *The Renaissance of Islam.* Translated by S. Khuda Bakhsh and D. S. Margoliouth. London: Luzac, 1937.

Mingana, Alphonse. "Syriac Influence on the Style of the Koran." *Bulletin of the John Rylands Library* 11 (1927): 84.

———, ed. *1. Timothy's Apology for Christianity. 2. The Lament of the Virgin. 3. The Martyrdom of Pilate*, Woodbrooke Studies 2. Cambridge, UK: W. Hefer & Sons, 1928. Available at http://darkwing .uoregon.edu/~sshoemak/102/texts/timothy.html.

Mittwoch, E. *Zur Entstebungsgeschichte des islamischen Gebets und Kultus.* In *Abhandlungen der preussen Akademie der Wissenschaften*, vol. 2. Berlin, 1913.

Moore, George Foot. *Judaism in the First Centuries of the Christian Era.* Cambridge, MA: Harvard University Press, 1950.

Moreau, A. Scott. "Syncretism." In *Evangelical Dictionary of World Missions*, edited by A. Scott Moreau, Harold Netland, and Charles Van Engen. Grand Rapids, MI: Baker, 2000.

Morrison, S. A. "Thoughts on Moslem Evangelism." *The Moslem World* 32 (1944): 203–6.

Moubarac, Y. "Les etudes d'epigraphie sud-semitique et la naissance de l'Islam." *Revue des Etudes Islamique* (1957): 58–61.

Mt. Sinai Arabic Codex 151. 2 vols. Edited by Harvey Staal. Leuven: Peepers, 1985.

Muck, Terry C., Harold A. Netland, and Gerald R. McDermott, eds. *Handbook of Religion: A Christian Engagement with Traditions, Teachings, and Practices.* Grand Rapids, MI: Baker Academic, 2014.

Mulago, Vincent. "Christianisme et culture africaine." In *Christianity in Tropical Africa*, edited by C. G. Baèta, 308–28. 1968.

Muller, Richard. "The Role of Church History in the Study of Systematic Theology." In *Doing Theology in Today's World: Essays in Honor of Kenneth S. Kantzer*, edited by John D. Woodbridge and Thomas Edward McComisky, 77–98. Grand Rapids, MI: Eerdmans, 1991.

Murray, Gilbert. *Five Stages of Greek Religion.* Whitefish, MT: Kessinger, 2003 [1935].

Musk, Bill. *Kissing Cousins? Christians and Muslims Face to Face.* Grand Rapids, MI: Kregel, 2005.

———. "Popular Islam: The Hunger of the Heart." In *The Gospel and Islam: A 1978 Compendium*, ed. Don M. McCurry, 208–21. Monrovia, CA: MARC, 1979.

Muslim. *Sahih Muslim.* Translated by Abdul Hamid Saddiqi. Lahore: Ashraf, n.d.

Nasr, Seyyed Hossein, ed. *Islamic Spirituality: Foundations.* New York: Crossroad, 1987.

Nazir-Ali, Michael. *Frontiers in Muslim-Christian Encounter.* Oxford: Regnum, 1987.

Neill, Stephen. *A History of Christian Missions.* Harmondsworth, Middlesex, UK: Penguin, 1964.

Netland, Harold. *Encountering Religious Pluralism: The Challenge to Christian Faith and Mission*. Downers Grove, IL: InterVarsity Press, 2001.

Neufeld, Vernon H. *The Earliest Christian Confessions*. Grand Rapids, MI: Eerdmans, 1963.

Neusner, Jacob, and Tamara Sonn. *Comparing Religions through Law: Judaism and Islam*. New York: Routledge, 1999.

Neusner, Jacob, Tamara Sonn, and Jonathan Brockopp. *Judaism and Islam in Practice: A Sourcebook*. New York: Routledge, 2000.

Nicholls, Bruce J. *Contextualization: A Theology of Gospel and Culture*. Downers Grove, IL: InterVarsity Press, 1979.

———. "Theological Education and Evangelization." In *Let the Earth Hear His Voice*, edited by J. D. Douglas. Minneapolis: World Wide Publications, 1975.

Niebuhr, H. Richard. *Christ and Culture*. New York: Harper & Row, 1956.

Noeldeke, Theodor. *Geschichte des Qorans*. 2nd ed. Leipzig, 1909.

Noll, Mark A. *The Rise of Evangelicalism: The Age of Edwards, Whitefield, and the Wesleys*. Downers Grove, IL: InterVarsity Press, 2003.

O'Brien, Peter T. *The Letter to the Hebrews*. Pillar New Testament Commentary. Grand Rapids, MI: Eerdmans, 2010.

Oberoi, Harjot, ed. *The Construction of Religious Boundaries: Culture, Identity, and Diversity in the Sikh Tradition*. Delhi: Oxford University Press, 1994.

Oden, Thomas. *The Living God*. Vol. 1 of *Systematic Theology*. Peabody, MA: Hendrickson, 2006.

Oesterly, W. O. E., and G. H. Box. *The Religion and Worship of the Synagogue*. London: Pitman and Sons, 1907.

Okholm, Dennis L., and Timothy R. Phillips, eds. *Four Views on Salvation in a Pluralistic World*. Grand Rapids, MI: Zondervan, 1996.

Ott, Craig, and Harold A. Netland. *Globalizing Theology: Belief and Practice in an Era of World Christianity*. Grand Rapids, MI: Baker Academic, 2006.

Overman, J. Andrew. *Church and Community in Crisis: The Gospel according to Matthew*. New Testament in Context. Valley Forge, PA: Trinity Press, 1996.

Owen, David. "A Classification System for Styles of Arabic Bible Translations." *Seedbed* 3, no. 1 (1988): 8–10.

Padwick, Constance E. "The Language of Muslim Devotion." *The Muslim World* 47 (1957): 5–21, 98–110, 194–209.

———. *Muslim Devotions: A Study of Prayer Manuals in Common Use*. London: SPCK, 1961.

Paige, Terence. "Early Gentile Christianity, Conversion, and Culture-shift in the New Testament." Paper presented at the Bridging the Divide conference, Houghton College, Houghton, NY, June 20–24, 2011.

Pals, Daniel L. *Seven Theories of Religion*. New York: Oxford University Press, 1996.

Panikkar, Raimundo. "On Christian Identity: Who Is a Christian?" In *Many Mansions? Multiple Religious Belonging and Christian Identity*. Edited by Catherine Cornille. Maryknoll, NY: Orbis, 2002.

Parrinder, Geoffrey. *Jesus in the Qur'an*. London: Oneworld, 1995.

Parshall, Phil. *Beyond the Mosque: Christians in Muslim Community*. Grand Rapids, MI: Baker, 1985.

——. "Danger! New Directions in Contextualization." *Evangelical Missions Quarterly* 34, no. 4 (1998): 404–10.

——. "Lessons Learned in Contextualization." In *Muslims and Christians on the Emmaus Road: Crucial Issues in Witness among Muslims,* edited by J. Dudley Woodberry, 251–65. Monrovia, CA: MARC, 1989.

——. "Lifting the Fatwa." *Evangelical Missions Quarterly* 40, no. 3 (2004): 288–93.

——. *New Paths in Muslim Evangelism: Evangelical Approaches to Contextualization.* Grand Rapids, MI: Baker, 1980.

Peek, Lori. "Becoming Muslim: The Development of a Religious Identity." *Sociology of Religion* 66, no. 3 (2005): 215–42.

Pernau, Margrit. "Multiple Identities and Communities: Re-Contextualizing Religion." In *Religious Pluralism in South Asia and Europe*, edited by Jamal Malik and Helmut Reifeld, 147–69. New Delhi: Oxford University Press, 2005.

Petersen, Jim. *Church without Walls: Moving beyond Traditional Boundaries.* Colorado Springs, CO: NavPress, 1992.

Peterson, David G. *The Acts of the Apostles.* Pillar New Testament Commentary. Grand Rapids, MI: Eerdmans, 2009.

Pickett, J. Waskom. *Christian Mass Movements in India: A Study with Recommendations.* New York: Abingdon, 1933.

Pierson, Paul. "A History of Transformation." In *Perspectives on the World Christian Movement: A Reader,* 3rd ed., edited by Ralph D. Winter and Steven C. Hawthorne, 262–68. Pasadena, CA: William Carey Library, 1999.

Pinnock, Clark H. *A Wideness in God's Mercy: The Finality of Jesus Christ in a World of Religions.* Grand Rapids, MI: Zondervan, 1992.

Pummer, Reinhard. *The Samaritans.* Leiden: Brill, 1987.

Rabin, Chaim. *Qumran Studies.* London: Oxford University Press, 1957.

Reisacher, Evelyne A., ed. *Toward Respectful Understanding and Witness among Muslims: Essays in Honor of J. Dudley Woodberry.* Pasadena, CA: William Carey Library, 2012.

Reynolds, Gabriel Said. *The Emergence of Islam: Classical Traditions in Contemporary Perspective.* Minneapolis: Fortress Press, 2012.

——. *The Qur'an and Its Biblical Subtext.* New York: Routledge, 2010.

Richard, H. L. *Following Jesus in the Hindu Context.* Pasadena, CA: William Carey Library, 1998.

——. "Is Extraction Evangelism Still the Way to Go?" *Evangelical Missions Quarterly* 30, no. 2 (1994): 170–74.

——, ed. *Rethinking Hindu Ministry: Papers from the Rethinking Forum.* Pasadena, CA: William Carey Library, 2011.

Richards, Donald R. "A Great Missiological Error of Our Time: Keeping the Fast of Ramadan—Why We Shouldn't." *Seedbed* 3 (1988): 38–45.

Richardson, Don. *Peace Child.* Ventura, CA: Gospel Light, 1974.

Ridgway, John. "Insider Movements in the Gospels and Acts." *International Journal of Frontier Missiology* 24, no. 2 (2007): 77–85.

Ritchie, J. M. "Christianity in the Qur'an." *Encounter* 81 (1982):1–13.

Roberts, Robert. *The Social Laws of the Qoran.* London: William and Norgate, 1925.

Rosenthal, Frank, trans. *The Muqaddimah*. 3 vols. New York: Pantheon, 1958.

Rosner, Brian. "The Progress of the Word." In *Witness to the Gospel: The Theology of Acts*, edited by I. Howard Marshall and D. Peterson, 215–33. Grand Rapids, MI: Eerdmans, 1998.

Rudmin, Floyd W. "Critical History of the Acculturation Psychology of Assimilation, Separation, Integration, and Marginalization." *Review of General Psychology* 7, no. 1 (2003): 3–37.

Saadi, Abdul-Massih. "Nascent Islam in the Seventh Century Syriac Sources." In *The Qur'an in Its Historical Context*, edited by Gabriel Said Reynolds, 217–22. New York: Routledge, 2008.

Saeed, Abdullah. "The Charge of Distortion of the Jewish and Christian Scriptures." *The Moslem World* 92 (2002): 419–36.

Saldanha, Julian. *Conversion and Indian Civil Law*. Bangalore: Theological Publications in India, 1981.

Sanneh, Lamin. *Translating the Message: The Missionary Impact on Culture*. 2nd ed. Maryknoll, NY: Orbis, 2009.

———. *Whose Religion is Christianity? The Gospel beyond the West*. Grand Rapids, MI: Eerdmans, 2003.

Sawyerr, Harry. *God: Ancestor or Creator? Aspects of Traditional Belief in Ghana, Nigeria and Sierra Leone*. London: Longman, 1970.

Schilbrack, Kevin. "Ritual Metaphysics." In *Thinking through Rituals: Philosophical Perspectives*, edited by Kevin Schilbrack, 128–47. London: Routledge, 2004.

Schlorff, Samuel P. "Contextualization in Islamic Society: Issues and Positions." *Seedbed* 3, no. 1 (1988): 3–4.

———. "Feedback on Project Sunrise (Sira): A Look at 'Dynamic Equivalence' in an Islamic Context." *Seedbed* 3, no. 2 (1988): 22–32.

———. "The Missionary Use of the Quran: An Historical and Theological Study of the Contextualization of the Gospel." ThM thesis, Westminster Theological Seminary, 1984.

Schreiter, Robert J. *Constructing Local Theologies*. Maryknoll, NY: Orbis, 1985.

Schürer, Emil. *The History of the Jewish People in the Age of Jesus Christ*. 4 vols. Edinburgh: T&T Clark, 1986.

Schwartz, Regina M. *The Curse of Cain: The Violent Legacy of Monotheism*. Chicago: University of Chicago Press, 1997.

Senior, Donald, and Carroll Stuhlmueller. *The Biblical Foundations for Mission*. Maryknoll, NY: Orbis, 1983.

Shehadeh, Imad N. "The Predicament of Islamic Monotheism." *Bibliotheca Sacra* 161 (April–June 2004): 142–62.

Shenk, Wilbert R. "Rufus Anderson and Henry Venn: A Special Relationship?" *International Bulletin of Missionary Research* 5, no. 4 (1981): 168–72.

Shore, Bradd. *Culture in Mind: Cognition, Culture, and the Problem of Meaning*. New York: Oxford University Press, 1996.

Sinclair, Daniel. *A Vision of the Possible: Pioneer Church Planting in Teams*. Waynesboro, GA: Authentic, 2006.

Singh, David Emmanuel. "Hundred Years of Christian-Muslim Relations." *Transformation: An International Journal of Holistic Mission Studies* 27 (2010): 225–38.

———. "Sunder Singh and N. V. Tilak: Lessons for Missiology from 20th Century India." Papers presented at the Seoul Consultation, March 22–24, 2009. Available at http://www.edinburgh2010

.org/en/study-themes/9-mission-spirituality-and-authentic-discipleship/seoul-consultation.html.

Sirat al-Masih bi-Lisan Arabi Fasih. Larnaca, Cyprus: Izdihar Ltd., 1987.

Smart, Ninian. *The World's Religions.* Cambridge: Cambridge University Press, 1998.

Smith, Jonathan Z. *Imagining Religion: From Babylon to Jonestown.* Chicago Studies in the History of Judaism. Chicago: University of Chicago Press, 1982.

Smith, Wilfred Cantwell. *The Faith of Other Men.* New York: Harper & Row, 1963.

———. *The Meaning and End of Religion: A New Approach to the Religious Traditions of Mankind.* New York: Macmillan, 1962.

Spencer, Robert. *Did Muhammad Exist? An Inquiry into Islam's Obscure Origins.* Wilmington, DE: Intercollegiate Studies Institute, 2012.

Spina, Frank Anthony. *The Faith of the Outsider: Exclusion and Inclusion in the Biblical Story.* Grand Rapids, MI: Eerdmans, 2005.

Staal, Fritz. *Rules without Meaning: Rituals, Mantras and the Human Sciences.* Toronto Studies in Religion 4. New York: Peter Lang, 1989.

Staffner, Hans. *Jesus Christ and the Hindu Community: Is a Synthesis between Hinduism and Christianity Possible?* Anand, Gujarat, India: Gujarat Sahitya Prakash, 1988.

Stern, S. M., trans. *Muslim Studies.* London: Allen & Unwin, 1971.

Stevenson, A. R. "Whoever Shall Confess Me before Men . . ." *The Moslem World* 37, no. 2 (1947): 99–106.

Stietencron, Heinrich Von. *Hindu Myth, Hindu History: Religion, Art and Politics.* Delhi: Permanent Black, 2005.

Strauss, Steve. "The Role of Context in Shaping Theology." In *Contextualization and Syncretism: Navigating Cultural Currents,* edited by Gailyn Van Rheenen, 99–128. Pasadena, CA: William Carey Library, 2006.

Strong, David K., and Cynthia A. Strong. "The Globalizing Hermeneutic of the Jerusalem Council." In *Globalizing Theology: Belief and Practice in an Era of World Christianity,* edited by Craig Ott and Harold A. Netland, 127–39.

Swidler, Ann. "Culture in Action: Symbols and Strategies." *American Sociological Review* 51 (April 1986): 273–86.

———. *Talk of Love: How Culture Matters.* Chicago: University of Chicago Press, 2001.

Syrjänen, Seppo. *In Search of Meaning and Identity: Conversion to Christianity in Pakistani Muslim Culture.* Helsinki: Finnish Society for Missiology and Ecumenics, 1984.

Taber, Charles R. "Is There More Than One Way to Do Theology? Anthropological Comments on the Doing of Theology." *Gospel in Context* 1, no. 1 (January 1978): 4–10, 22–40.

———. *The World Is Too Much with Us: "Culture" in Modern Protestant Missions.* Macon, GA: Mercer University Press, 1991.

Talman, Harley. "Is Muhammad Also Among the Prophets?" *International Journal of Frontier Missiology* 31, no. 4 (2014): 169–90.

Tan, Jonathan Y. "Rethinking the Relationship between Christianity and World Religions, and Exploring Its Implications for Doing Christian Mission in Asia." *Missiology: An International Review* 39, no. 4 (2011): 497–509.

Tan, Kang-San. "Dual Belonging: A Missiological Critique and Appreciation from an Asian Evangelical Perspective." *Mission Studies* 27, no. 1 (2010): 24–38.

———. "The Inter-religious Frontier: A 'Christian-Buddhist' Contribution." *International Journal of Frontier Missiology* 29, no. 1 (2012): 23–32.

Tanagho, Samy. *Glad News! God Loves You My Muslim Friend.* Colorado Springs, CO: Biblica, 2003.

Tennent, Timothy C. "The Challenge of Churchless Christianity: An Evangelical Assessment." *International Bulletin of Missionary Research* 29, no. 4 (2005): 171–77.

———. "Followers of Jesus (Isa) in Islamic Mosques: A Closer Examination of C-5 'High Spectrum' Contextualization." *International Journal of Frontier Missions* 23, no. 3 (2006): 101–15.

———. "The Hidden History of Insider Movements." *Christianity Today*, January–February 2013.

———. *Invitation to World Missions: A Trinitarian Missiology for the Twenty-first Century.* Grand Rapids, MI: Kregel, 2010.

———. *Theology in the Context of World Christianity: How the Global Church Is Influencing the Way We Think About and Discuss Theology.* Grand Rapids, MI: Zondervan, 2007.

Thiselton, Anthony C. *New Horizons in Hermeneutics: The Theory and Practice of Transforming Biblical Reading.* Grand Rapids, MI: Zondervan, 1992.

Thomas, Kenneth J. "Allah in Translations of the Bible." *The Bible Translator: Technical Papers* 52, no. 3 (2001): 301–5.

Timothy I. "Timothy's Apology for Christianity." Translated by A. Mingana. In *Encounters and Clashes: Islam and Christianity in History*, vol. 2, edited by Jean-Marie Gaudeul. Rome: Pontifical Institute for Arabic and Islamic Studies, 1984.

Torrey, Charles Cutler. *The Jewish Foundation of Islam.* New York: Jewish Institute of Religion, 1933.

Travis, John. "The C1 to C6 Spectrum: A Practical Tool for Defining Six Types of 'Christ Centered Communities' ('C') Found in the Muslim Context." *Evangelical Missions Quarterly* 34, no. 4 (1998): 407–8.

———. "Contextualization among Muslims, Hindus and Buddhists: A Focus on 'Insider Movements.'" *Mission Frontiers*, September–October 2005.

———. "Messianic Muslim Followers of Isa: A Closer Look at C5 Believers and Congregations." *International Journal of Frontier Missions* 17, no. 1 (2000): 53–59.

———. "Must All Muslims Leave 'Islam' to Follow Jesus?" *Evangelical Missions Quarterly* 34, no. 4 (1998): 411–15.

———. "Producing and Using Meaningful Translations of the Taurat, Zabur and Injil." *International Journal Frontier Missions* 23, no. 2 (2006): 73–77.

———, Phil Parshall, Herbert Hoefer, and Rebecca Lewis. "Responses: Four Responses to Tennent." *International Journal of Frontier Missions* 23, no. 3 (2006): 124–26.

———, and Anna Travis. "Deep-level Healing Prayer in Cross-cultural Ministry: Models, Examples, and Lessons." In *Paradigm Shifts in Christian Witness: Insights from Anthropology, Communication, and Spiritual Power*, edited by Charles Van Engen, Darrell Whiteman, and J. Dudley Woodberry, 106–15. Maryknoll, NY: Orbis, 2008.

Trimingham, J. Spencer. *Christianity among the Arabs in Pre-Islamic Times.* London: Longman, 1979.

Trotter, Lilias. *The Way of the Sevenfold Secret.* Cairo: Nile Mission Press, 1927.

Trousdale, Jerry. *Miraculous Movements: How Hundreds of Thousands of Muslims Are Falling in Love with Jesus.* Nashville: Thomas Nelson, 2012.

Turner, Max. "The Spirit and Salvation in Luke-Acts." In *The Holy Spirit and Christian Origins: Essays in Honor of James D. G. Dunn*, edited by Graham N. Stanton, Bruce W. Longnecker, and Stephen C. Barton, 103–16. Grand Rapids, MI: Eerdmans, 2004.

Turner, Victor. *The Ritual Process: Structure and Anti-Structure*. New York: Aldine de Gruyter, 1995.

Vander Werff, Lyle L. *Christian Mission to Muslims: The Record*. Pasadena, CA: William Carey Library, 1977.

Van Engen, Charles. *God's Missionary People: Rethinking the Purpose of the Local Church*. Grand Rapids, MI: Baker, 1991.

Vanhoozer, Kevin J. "'One Rule to Rule Them All?' Theological Method in an Era of World Christianity." In *Globalizing Theology: Belief and Practice in an Era of World Christianity*, edited by Craig Ott and Harold A. Netland, 85–126. Grand Rapids, MI: Baker Academic, 2006.

Vawter, Bruce. *On Genesis: A New Reading*. New York: Doubleday, 1977.

Viola, Frank, and George Barna. *Pagan Christianity? Exploring the Roots of Our Church Practices*. Carol Stream, IL: BarnaBooks, 2008.

Volf, Miroslav. *Allah: A Christian Response*. New York: HarperCollins, 2011.

Walls, Andrew F. "Africa and Christian Identity." In *Mission Focus: Current Issues*, edited by W. R. Shenk, 212–21. Scottdale, PA: Herald Press, 1980.

———. *The Missionary Movement in Christian History: Studies in the Transmission of Faith*. Maryknoll, NY: Orbis, 1996.

———. "Towards Understanding Africa's Place in Christian History." In *Religion in a Pluralistic Society: Essays Presented to Professor C. G. Baëta*, edited by J. S. Pobee, 180–89. Leiden: Brill, 1976.

Warner, R. Stephen. "Work in Progress toward a New Paradigm for the Sociological Study of Religion in the United States." *American Journal of Sociology* 98, no. 5 (1993): 1044–93.

Watt, W. Montgomery. *The Faith and Practice of al-Ghazali*. London: Allen & Unwin, 1953.

———. *Islam and Christianity Today: A Contribution to Dialogue*. London: Routledge, 1983.

———. *Muhammad at Mecca*. Oxford: Clarendon Press, 1960.

———. *Muhammad at Medina*. Oxford: Oxford University Press, 1956.

Wensinck, A. J. *A Handbook of Early Muhammadan Tradition*. Leiden: Brill, 1960.

———. *Mohammed en de Joden te Medina*. 2nd ed. Leiden: Brill, 1928.

———. *The Muslim Creed*. Cambridge: Cambridge University Press, 1932.

Whitacre, Rodney A. *John*. IVP New Testament Commentary. Downers Grove, IL: IVP Academic, 2007.

Wilder, John W. "Some Reflections on Possibilities for People Movements among Muslims." *Missiology: An International Review* 5, no. 3 (1977): 302–20.

Wilson, J. Christy. "Public Confession and the Church." *The Moslem World* 31, no. 2 (1941): 127–39.

Winter, Ralph. "The Kingdom Strikes Back: Ten Epochs of Redemptive History." In *Perspectives on the World Christian Movement: A Reader*, 4th ed., edited by Ralph D. Winter and Steven C. Hawthorne, 209–27.

Witherington, Ben. *The Acts of the Apostles: A Socio-rhetorical Commentary*. Grand Rapids, MI: Eerdmans, 1998.

Woodberry, J. Dudley. "Do Christians and Muslims Worship the Same God?" *Christian Century*, May 18, 2004.

————, ed. *From Seed to Fruit: Global Trends, Fruitful Practices, and Emerging Issues among Muslims.* 2nd ed. Pasadena, CA: William Carey Library, 2011.

————. "A Global Perspective on Muslims Coming to Faith in Christ." In *From the Straight Path to the Narrow Way: Journeys of Faith*, edited by David Greenlee, 11–22. Waynesboro, GA: Authentic, 2006.

————, ed. *Muslims and Christians on the Emmaus Road: Crucial Issues in Witness among Muslims.* Monrovia, CA: MARC, 1989.

————. "The Relevance of Power Ministries for Folk Muslims." In *Wrestling with Dark Angels*, edited by C. Peter Wagner and F. Douglas Pennoyer, 313–31. Ventura, CA: Regal, 1990.

————, Russell G. Shubin, and G. Marks. "Why Muslims Follow Jesus: The Results of a Recent Survey of Converts from Islam." *Christianity Today,* October 2007.

Wright, Christopher J. H. *The Mission of God: Unlocking the Bible's Grand Narrative.* Downers Grove, IL: IVP Academic, 2006.

————. "Theology of Religions." In *Evangelical Dictionary of World Missions,* edited by A. Scott Moreau, 951–53. Grand Rapids, MI: Baker, 2000.

Wright, N. T. *The New Testament and the People of God.* Minneapolis, MN: Fortress Press, 1992.

————. *Simply Jesus: A New Testament Vision of Who He Was, What He Did, and Why He Matters.* HarperCollins, 2011.

Wuestenfeld, F. *Geschichte der Stadt Medina.* Goettingen, 1860.

X. "A Letter from the Near East." *The Moslem World* 32 (1942): 76.

Zwemer, Samuel M. *Studies in Popular Islam.* London: Sheldon Press, 1939.

————. "The Dynamic of Evangelism." *The Moslem World* 31, no. 2 (1941): 109–15.